REFERENCE

WITHDRAWN

Poetry Criticism

Guide to Gale Literary Criticism Series

For criticism on	Consult these Gale series
Authors now living or who died after December 31, 1999	*CONTEMPORARY LITERARY CRITICISM (CLC)*
Authors who died between 1900 and 1999	*TWENTIETH-CENTURY LITERARY CRITICISM (TCLC)*
Authors who died between 1800 and 1899	*NINETEENTH-CENTURY LITERATURE CRITICISM (NCLC)*
Authors who died between 1400 and 1799	*LITERATURE CRITICISM FROM 1400 TO 1800 (LC)* *SHAKESPEAREAN CRITICISM (SC)*
Authors who died before 1400	*CLASSICAL AND MEDIEVAL LITERATURE CRITICISM (CMLC)*
Authors of books for children and young adults	*CHILDREN'S LITERATURE REVIEW (CLR)*
Dramatists	*DRAMA CRITICISM (DC)*
Poets	*POETRY CRITICISM (PC)*
Short story writers	*SHORT STORY CRITICISM (SSC)*
Literary topics and movements	*HARLEM RENAISSANCE: A GALE CRITICAL COMPANION (HR)* *THE BEAT GENERATION: A GALE CRITICAL COMPANION (BG)* *FEMINISM IN LITERATURE: A GALE CRITICAL COMPANION (FL)* *GOTHIC LITERATURE: A GALE CRITICAL COMPANION (GL)*
Asian American writers of the last two hundred years	*ASIAN AMERICAN LITERATURE (AAL)*
Black writers of the past two hundred years	*BLACK LITERATURE CRITICISM (BLC)* *BLACK LITERATURE CRITICISM SUPPLEMENT (BLCS)*
Hispanic writers of the late nineteenth and twentieth centuries	*HISPANIC LITERATURE CRITICISM (HLC)* *HISPANIC LITERATURE CRITICISM SUPPLEMENT (HLCS)*
Native North American writers and orators of the eighteenth, nineteenth, and twentieth centuries	*NATIVE NORTH AMERICAN LITERATURE (NNAL)*
Major authors from the Renaissance to the present	*WORLD LITERATURE CRITICISM, 1500 TO THE PRESENT (WLC)* *WORLD LITERATURE CRITICISM SUPPLEMENT (WLCS)*

ISSN 1052-4851

Poetry Criticism

*Excerpts from Criticism of the Works
of the Most Significant and Widely
Studied Poets of World Literature*

Volume 93

Michelle Lee
Project Editor

PN
1010
P499
v.93

GALE
CENGAGE Learning

Detroit • New York • San Francisco • New Haven, Conn • Waterville, Maine • London

Poetry Criticism, Vol. 93

Project Editor: Michelle Lee

Editorial: Dana Barnes, Kathy D. Darrow, Kristen Dorsch, Jeffrey W. Hunter, Jelena O. Krstović, Thomas J. Schoenberg, Lawrence J. Trudeau

Data Capture: Frances Monroe, Gwen Tucker

Indexing Services: Factiva, Inc.

Rights and Acquisitions: Margaret Abendroth, Scott Bragg, and Jacqueline Key

Composition and Electronic Capture: Gary Leach

Manufacturing: Rhonda Dover

Associate Product Manager: Marc Cormier

For product information and technology assistance, contact us at **Gale Customer Support, 1-800-877-4253.**
For permission to use material from this text or product, submit all requests online at **www.cengage.com/permissions.**
Further permissions questions can be emailed to **permissionrequest@cengage.com**

While every effort has been made to ensure the reliability of the information presented in this publication, Gale, a part of Cengage Learning, does not guarantee the accuracy of the data contained herein. Gale accepts no payment for listing; and inclusion in the publication of any organization, agency, institution, publication, service, or individual does not imply endorsement of the editors or publisher. Errors brought to the attention of the publisher and verified to the satisfaction of the publisher will be corrected in future editions.

Gale
27500 Drake Rd.
Farmington Hills, MI, 48331-3535

LIBRARY OF CONGRESS CATALOG CARD NUMBER 81-640179

ISBN-13: 978-0-7876-9890-4
ISBN-10: 0-7876-9890-3

ISSN 1052-4851

Printed in the United States of America
1 2 3 4 5 6 7 13 12 11 10 09

REFERENCE

Contents

Preface vii

Acknowledgments ix

Literary Criticism Series Advisory Board xi

D. J. Enright 1920-2002 1
English poet, novelist, essayist, critic, and memoirist

Thomas Hood 1799-1845 39
English novelist, poet, short story writer, playwright, essayist, and autobiographer

X. J. Kennedy 1929- 126
American poet, editor, translator, and anthologist

John Greenleaf Whittier 1807-1892 163
American poet, essayist, editor, critic, journalist, novelist, and short story writer

Literary Criticism Series Cumulative Author Index 367

PC Cumulative Nationality Index 481

PC-93 Title Index 485

Preface

*P*oetry Criticism (PC) presents significant criticism of the world's greatest poets and provides supplementary biographical and bibliographical material to guide the interested reader to a greater understanding of the genre and its creators. Although major poets and literary movements are covered in such Gale Literary Criticism series as *Contemporary Literary Criticism (CLC), Twentieth-Century Literary Criticism (TCLC), Nineteenth-Century Literature Criticism (NCLC), Literature Criticism from 1400 to 1800 (LC),* and *Classical and Medieval Literature Criticism (CMLC),* PC offers more focused attention on poetry than is possible in the broader, survey-oriented entries on writers in these Gale series. Students, teachers, librarians, and researchers will find that the generous excerpts and supplementary material provided by PC supply them with the vital information needed to write a term paper on poetic technique, to examine a poet's most prominent themes, or to lead a poetry discussion group.

Scope of the Series

PC is designed to serve as an introduction to major poets of all eras and nationalities. Since these authors have inspired a great deal of relevant critical material, PC is necessarily selective, and the editors have chosen the most important published criticism to aid readers and students in their research. Each author entry presents a historical survey of the critical response to that author's work. The length of an entry is intended to reflect the amount of critical attention the author has received from critics writing in English and from foreign critics in translation. Every attempt has been made to identify and include the most significant essays on each author's work. In order to provide these important critical pieces, the editors sometimes reprint essays that have appeared elsewhere in Gale's Literary Criticism Series. Such duplication, however, never exceeds twenty percent of a PC volume.

Organization of the Book

Each PC entry consists of the following elements:

- The **Author Heading** cites the name under which the author most commonly wrote, followed by birth and death dates. Also located here are any name variations under which an author wrote, including transliterated forms for authors whose native languages use nonroman alphabets. If the author wrote consistently under a pseudonym, the pseudonym will be listed in the author heading and the author's actual name given in parenthesis on the first line of the biographical and critical introduction. Uncertain birth or death dates are indicated by question marks. Single-work entries are preceded by the title of the work and its date of publication.

- The **Introduction** contains background information that introduces the reader to the author and the critical debates surrounding his or her work.

- The list of **Principal Works** is ordered chronologically by date of first publication and lists the most important works by the author. The first section comprises poetry collections and book-length poems. The second section gives information on other major works by the author. For foreign authors, the editors have provided original foreign-language publication information and have selected what are considered the best and most complete English-language editions of their works.

- Reprinted **Criticism** is arranged chronologically in each entry to provide a useful perspective on changes in critical evaluation over time. All individual titles of poems and poetry collections by the author featured in the entry are printed in boldface type. The critic's name and the date of composition or publication of the critical work are given at the beginning of each piece of criticism. Unsigned criticism is preceded by the title of the source in which it appeared. Footnotes are reprinted at the end of each essay or excerpt. In the case of excerpted criticism, only those footnotes that pertain to the excerpted texts are included.

- Critical essays are prefaced by brief **Annotations** explicating each piece.

- A complete **Bibliographical Citation** of the original essay or book precedes each piece of criticism.

- An annotated bibliography of **Further Reading** appears at the end of each entry and suggests resources for additional study. In some cases, significant essays for which the editors could not obtain reprint rights are included here. Boxed material following the further reading list provides references to other biographical and critical sources on the author in series published by Gale.

Cumulative Indexes

A **Cumulative Author Index** lists all of the authors that appear in a wide variety of reference sources published by Gale, including *PC*. A complete list of these sources is found facing the first page of the Author Index. The index also includes birth and death dates and cross references between pseudonyms and actual names.

A **Cumulative Nationality Index** lists all authors featured in *PC* by nationality, followed by the number of the *PC* volume in which their entry appears.

A **Cumulative Title Index** lists in alphabetical order all individual poems, book-length poems, and collection titles contained in the *PC* series. Titles of poetry collections and separately published poems are printed in italics, while titles of individual poems are printed in roman type with quotation marks. Each title is followed by the author's last name and corresponding volume and page numbers where commentary on the work is located. English-language translations of original foreign-language titles are cross-referenced to the foreign titles so that all references to discussion of a work are combined in one listing.

Citing *Poetry Criticism*

When citing criticism reprinted in the Literary Criticism Series, students should provide complete bibliographic information so that the cited essay can be located in the original print or electronic source. Students who quote directly from reprinted criticism may use any accepted bibliographic format, such as University of Chicago Press style or Modern Language Association (MLA) style. Both the MLA and the University of Chicago formats are acceptable and recognized as being the current standards for citations. It is important, however, to choose one format for all citations; do not mix the two formats within a list of citations.

The examples below follow recommendations for preparing a bibliography set forth in *The Chicago Manual of Style*, 14th ed. (Chicago: The University of Chicago Press, 1993); the first example pertains to material drawn from periodicals, the second to material reprinted from books:

Linkin, Harriet Kramer. "The Language of Speakers in *Songs of Innocence and of Experience*." *Romanticism Past and Present* 10, no. 2 (summer 1986): 5-24. Reprinted in *Poetry Criticism*. Vol. 63, edited by Michelle Lee, 79-88. Detroit: Thomson Gale, 2005.

Glen, Heather. "Blake's Criticism of Moral Thinking in *Songs of Innocence and of Experience*." In *Interpreting Blake*, edited by Michael Phillips, 32-69. Cambridge: Cambridge University Press, 1978. Reprinted in *Poetry Criticism*. Vol. 63, edited by Michelle Lee, 34-51. Detroit: Thomson Gale, 2005.

Suggestions are Welcome

Readers who wish to suggest new features, topics, or authors to appear in future volumes, or who have other suggestions or comments are cordially invited to call, write, or fax the Associate Product Manager:

Associate Product Manager, Literary Criticism Series
Gale
27500 Drake Road
Farmington Hills, MI 48331-3535
1-800-347-4253 (GALE)
Fax: 248-699-8054

Acknowledgments

The editors wish to thank the copyright holders of the criticism included in this volume and the permissions managers of many book and magazine publishing companies for assisting us in securing reproduction rights. Following is a list of the copyright holders who have granted us permission to reproduce material in this volume of *PC*. Every effort has been made to trace copyright, but if omissions have been made, please let us know.

COPYRIGHTED MATERIAL IN *PC*, VOLUME 93, WAS REPRODUCED FROM THE FOLLOWING PERIODICALS:

American Journal of Semiotics, v. 12, summer, 1995. Copyright © by the Semiotic Society of America, 1995. Reproduced by permission.—*American Literature,* v. 28, May, 1956. Copyright © 1956 by Duke University Press. Copyright renewed. All rights reserved. Used by permission of the publisher.—*American Periodicals,* v. 17, 2007. Copyright © 2007 by the Ohio State University. Reproduced by permission.—*Christian Science Monitor,* April 18, 2006 for "A Poet Who Celebrates the Joy of Verse" by Elizabeth Lund. Reproduced by permission of the author.—*Contemporary Literature,* v. 9, winter, 1968. Copyright © 1968 by the Board of Regents of the University of Wisconsin System. Reproduced by permission.—*Criticism,* v. XXXVIII, fall, 1996. Copyright © 1996 by Wayne State University Press. Reproduced with permission of the Wayne State University Press.—*English,* v. VI, spring, 1946. Copyright © by the English Association, 1946. Reproduced by permission.—*Essays in Literature,* v. 1, spring, 1974. Copyright © 1974 by Western Illinois University. Reproduced by permission.—*Explicator,* v. 64, fall, 2005. Copyright © 2005 by Helen Dwight Reid Educational Foundation. Reproduced with permission of the Helen Dwight Reid Educational Foundation, published by Heldref Publications, 1319 18th Street, NW, Washington, DC 20036-1802.—*Keats-Shelley Journal,* v. XIII, winter, 1964. Copyright © by the Keats-Shelley Association of America, Inc., 1964. Reproduced by permission.—*Language Arts,* v. 78, January, 2001. Copyright © 2001 by the National Council of Teachers of English. Reproduced by permission of the publisher.—*Modern Age,* v. 47, spring, 2005. Reproduced by permission.—*Notes and Queries,* v. 53, September, 2006 for "'Tenderly' and 'With Care': Thomas Hood's 'The Bridge of Sighs' and the Suicide of Harriet Shelley" by Bryan Rivers. Copyright © 2006 by Bryan Rivers. Reproduced by permission of Oxford University Press, as conveyed through Copyright Clearance Center, Inc., and the author.—*Parnassus,* v. 4, fall/winter, 1975 for "Across the Irish Sea" by Michael Wood. Copyright © 1975 by the Poetry in Review Foundation, NY. Reproduced by permission of the publisher and the author.—*PN Review,* v. 25, 1998. Reproduced by permission of Carcanet Press Limited.—*Resources for American Literary Study,* v. 26, 2000. Copyright © 2000 by the Pennsylvania State University. Reproduced by permission of the publisher.—*Sewanee Review,* vol. LXXIX, January-March, 1971. Copyright © 1971 by Robert Penn Warren. Reproduced by permission of William Morris Agency, Inc. on behalf of the Literary Estate of Robert Penn Warren.—*Studies in the American Renaissance,* 1993. Copyright © 1993 by Joel Myerson. All rights reserved. Reproduced by permission.—*World Literature Today,* v. 61, winter, 1987; v. 68, autumn, 1994. Copyright © 1987, 1994 by *World Literature Today.* Both reproduced by permission of the publisher.

COPYRIGHTED MATERIAL IN *PC*, VOLUME 93, WAS REPRODUCED FROM THE FOLLOWING BOOKS:

Byatt, A. S. From "A Sense of Religion: Enright's God," in *Life by Other Means: Essays on D. J. Enright.* Edited by Jacqueline Simms. Oxford University Press, 1990. Copyright © 1990 by A. S. Byatt. Reproduced by permission of Oxford University Press.—Clubbe, John. From *Victorian Forerunner: The Later Career of Thomas Hood.* Duke University Press, 1968. Copyright © 1968 by Duke University Press. All rights reserved. Used by permission of the publisher.—Dunn, Douglas. From "'The Thunder of Humanity': D. J. Enright's Liberal Imagination," in *Life by Other Means: Essays on D. J. Enright.* Edited by Jacqueline Simms. Oxford University Press, 1990. Copyright © 1990 by Douglas Dunn. All rights reserved. Reproduced by permission of Oxford University Press.—Flint, Joy. From *Thomas Hood: Selected Poems.* Fyfield Books, 1992. Selection, introduction and notes copyright © 1992 by Joy Flint. All rights reserved. Reproduced by permission of Carcanet Press Limited.—Keller, Karl. From "John Greenleaf Whittier: Criticism," in *Fifteen American Authors Before 1900: Bibliographic Essays on Research and Criticism.* Edited by Robert A. Rees and Earl N. Harbert. The University of Wisconsin Press, 1971. Copyright © 1971 by the Regents of the University of Wisconsin. All rights reserved. Reproduced by permission.—Leary, Lewis. From *John Greenleaf Whittier.* Twayne, 1961. Copyright © 1961 by Twayne

Gale Literature Product Advisory Board

The members of the Gale Literature Product Advisory Board—reference librarians from public and academic library systems—represent a cross-section of our customer base and offer a variety of informed perspectives on both the presentation and content of our literature products. Advisory board members assess and define such quality issues as the relevance, currency, and usefulness of the author coverage, critical content, and literary topics included in our series; evaluate the layout, presentation, and general quality of our printed volumes; provide feedback on the criteria used for selecting authors and topics covered in our series; provide suggestions for potential enhancements to our series; identify any gaps in our coverage of authors or literary topics, recommending authors or topics for inclusion; analyze the appropriateness of our content and presentation for various user audiences, such as high school students, undergraduates, graduate students, librarians, and educators; and offer feedback on any proposed changes/enhancements to our series. We wish to thank the following advisors for their advice throughout the year.

D. J. Enright
1920-2002

(Full name Dennis Joseph Enright.) English poet, novelist, essayist, critic, and memoirist.

INTRODUCTION

A prolific writer of both poetry and prose, Enright is best remembered for his talents as an observer of the many cultures he encountered in his international academic career, and for his sympathetic rendering of the experiences of the working class and the underclass.

BIOGRAPHICAL INFORMATION

Enright was born March 11, 1920, in Warwickshire, England, to George and Grace Cleaver Enright. His Irish father was a postman and a lapsed Catholic, while his mother was an occasionally church-going Methodist. Enright's working class upbringing is the subject of *The Terrible Shears: Scenes from a Twenties Childhood* (1973), one of his most well-known works of poetry. After distinguishing himself at the local Leamington College, Enright won a scholarship to Downing College, Cambridge, where he earned a bachelor's degree (with honors) in English in 1944 and a Master's degree in 1946. In 1949 he earned a D. Litt. degree from the University of Alexandria, Egypt. That same year Enright married Madeleine Harders, a French literature teacher at the university; the couple had one daughter. For the next twenty years, Enright held teaching positions at a number of European and Asian Universities, including Birmingham University; Konan University, Kobe, Japan; Free University of Berlin; Chulalongkorn University, Bangkok, Thailand; the University of Singapore; and the University of Leeds, Yorkshire, England. From 1975-80 he served as honorary professor of English at the University of Warwick, Coventry, England. Enright was a successful and popular teacher, esteemed by students and colleagues alike. In addition to his teaching, he held editorial positions at *Encounter* magazine in London from 1970-72 and Chatto and Windus, publishers, from 1971-73; he then served as a member of the board of directors at Chatto and Windus until 1982.

Enright's many years as an expatriate clearly influenced the thematics of his poetry and prose. Many of his experiences abroad are reported in *Memoirs of a Mendicant Professor* (1969). These experiences included a number of unfortunate encounters with local officialdom, some of them the result of misunderstandings. Enright perhaps contributed to the misunderstandings by publicly discussing his occasional opium use. The most serious of these incidents was the result of his remarks on government attempts to influence the direction of cultural development, given during his inaugural address—entitled *Robert Graves and the Decline of Modernism*—at the University of Singapore in 1961. Enright was publicly chastised by an official of the Singaporean government, defended by advocates for free speech as well as his students, and encouraged by many colleagues to resign his position in protest. However, he accepted a compromise involving a written statement to the effect that he had no intention of interfering in Singaporean politics—a statement that was published alongside a conciliatory reply from a second governmental official.

Enright's awards include the Cholmondeley Award (1974), the Society of Authors traveling scholarship (1981), and a Queen's Gold Medal for Poetry (1981). He received honorary doctorates from the University of Warwick in 1982 and the University of Surrey in 1985, and was named a Fellow of the Royal Society of Literature in 1961 and an Officer of the Order of the British Empire in 1991. Enright spent the last twenty years of his life writing, publishing a number of volumes of poetry and prose until his death on December 31, 2002, of cancer; he was 82.

MAJOR WORKS

Enright began writing during his college years, regularly contributing essays—mostly on German literature—to *Scrutiny,* the journal founded by his Downing tutor. F. R. Leavis. His first poetry collection, *Season Ticket,* appeared in 1948 and was followed five years later by *The Laughing Hyena and Other Poems,* considered his first major collection. Many of its poems, such as "The Egyptian Cat," "Arab Music," and "University Examinations in Egypt," involve his experiences in Alexandria from 1947 to 1950. It also includes the poem "The Chicken's Foot," praised for its remarkably realistic detail and sometimes compared to the later works of T. S. Eliot. Many of the poems written during Enright's tenure in Japan are contained in the collections *Bread Rather than Blossoms* (1956) and *Some Men Are Broth-*

ers (1960). These poems, many of which examine the lives of the poor, are considered Enright's finest work. The first volume contains two of his most famous individual poems, "Akiko San" and "The Short Life of Kazuo Yamamoto." The second volume, also inspired by his experiences in Berlin and Bangkok, includes "Apocalypse," "Entrance Visa," and "The Noodle-Vendor's Flute."

The autobiographical volume, *The Terrible Shears* (1973), was written after Enright returned to England, abandoned teaching, and began working as an editor and director of a publishing house. The poems contained in the volume attempt to recreate his childhood experiences in a working class environment in the 1920s. His representations of his Midlands childhood are realistic and unsentimental, but have been considered rather flat by some critics. *Paradise Illustrated* (1978) and *A Faust Book* (1979) are satirical interpretations—at the linguistic level—of *Paradise Lost* and *Faust*.

In 1981, Enright published *Collected Poems,* which he followed with *Collected Poems 1987, Selected Poems 1990* and *Collected Poems 1949-1998*. In addition to his poetry, Enright also authored four novels: *Academic Year* (1955), *Heaven Knows Where* (1957), *Insufficient Poppy* (1960), and *Figures of Speech* (1965). He also produced several essay collections, a journal, and a memoir, *Injury Time: A Memoir* (2003).

CRITICAL RECEPTION

One of the most defining characteristics of Enright's poetry is his humanism, evident in the typical subject matter of his poems—described by Philip Gardner as "the inescapable involvement of the man of conscience with the lives and sufferings of his fellows." Douglas Dunn contends that "more than any other poet of his generation, he has been consistent in confronting social and political subjects with passionate intelligence and abundant feeling." Janet Montefiore finds that Enright "seeks the common ground of shared humanity without denying difference," difference here taken to encompass not only race and culture, but also economics.

Children often figure as central players in Enright's poems; Walsh reports that for Enright, "the child . . . faithfully represents the common run of men . . . because he is, like them, and more than most of them— the victim of power." The poem "The Short Life of Kazuo Yamamoto" was inspired by a newspaper report of the suicide of a 13-year-old shoeshine-boy. Enright ironically contrasts the "headaches" of the "great ones" with the headache experienced by the unfortunate child, who ended his suffering with rat poison rather than aspirin. The poem is considered one of Enright's finest, and in general, his representations of children have

been well received. However, critics have been less favorably impressed by Enright's portrayal of his own childhood. Michael Wood, in his review of *The Terrible Shears: Scenes from a Twenties Childhood,* admires Enright's "scrupulously unaccented version of his past," but believes that "it rapidly becomes clear that Enright's virtues as a tough-minded rememberer don't really help his poetry much, indeed, tend to do it in." Dunn also criticizes *The Terrible Shears,* claiming that Enright's "attempt to write about social class is largely unconvincing."

Besides children, other powerless individuals are the typical characters inhabiting Enright's world; according to Walsh, these characters include "the noodle-vendor, the trishaw driver, the one-eyed boy, the aged woman." Montefiore cites Enright's poems about Asian beggars as well as one of his most famous poems about a prostitute, "Akiko San." She also notes his concern for the common laborer, evident in "Processional," which relates the story of construction workers killed in an accident caused by a contractor's refusal to adhere to safety regulations in the interest of speed.

Critics often comment on Enright's keen powers of observation covering a wide variety of subject matter, his commitment to realism and avoidance of romanticism or sentimentality. For Dunn, Enright's early poems "are quite self-consciously about facing up to reality and achieving a viable angle of approach to recent history and topical, observable scenes and people." This almost clinical commitment to realism, however, does not preclude the passing of judgment. Dunn contends that Enright's "acceptance of life is plain, ordinary, and critical in its recognition of human suffering; his detachment is an enabling artifice that creates a sympathetic angle of observation, a literary lens that makes it possible for him to record the scene while leaving room for comment." Similarly, while noting Enright's "sense for the reality residing in, defined by, the exact and lucid detail," Walsh notes that "the observation of the poet is not, of course, the neutrality of the mirror. It depends on a particular attitude and carries a special tone. In Enright's case . . . the attitude is pitying, the tone ironic."

Many critics contend that Enright's best poetry was written during his years in Japan. According to Philip Gardner, the Japan poems—dealing with "overpopulation, poverty, landslides, suicides, streetwalkers rather than Geisha,"—best exhibit Enright's talent "for X-raying through the public 'face' of a country to the bones beneath." Gardner reports that Enright typically avoids references to stereotypical representations of the country involving temples, tea ceremonies and cherry blossoms. Dunn maintains that "stating that Enright's Eastern poems are his best is not enough. They stand among the best poems of their time."

PRINCIPAL WORKS

Poetry

Season Ticket 1948
The Laughing Hyena and Other Poems 1953
Bread Rather than Blossoms 1956
The Year of the Monkey 1956
Some Men Are Brothers 1960
Addictions 1962
The Old Adam 1965
Unlawful Assembly 1968
Selected Poems 1969
In the Basilica of the Annunciation 1971
The Typewriter Revolution and Other Poems 1971
Daughters of Earth 1972
Foreign Devils 1972
The Terrible Shears: Scenes from a Twenties Childhood 1973
Rhyme Times Rhyme 1974
Sad Ires and Others 1974
Paradise Illustrated 1978
A Faust Book 1979
Walking in the Harz Mountains, Faust Senses the Presence of God 1979
Collected Poems 1981
Instant Chronicles 1985
Collected Poems 1987 1987
Selected Poems 1990 1990
Under the Circumstances 1991
Old Men and Comets 1993
Collected Poems 1949-1998 1998

Other Major Works

Commentary on Goethe's "Faust" (criticism) 1949
Academic Year (novel) 1955
Literature for Man's Sake: Critical Essays (essays) 1955
The World of Dew: Aspects of Living Japan (essays) 1955
The Apothecary's Shop: Essays on Literature (essays) 1957
Heaven Knows Where (novel) 1957
Insufficient Poppy (novel) 1960
Robert Graves and the Decline of Modernism (address) 1961
Figures of Speech (novel) 1965
Memoirs of a Mendicant Professor (essays) 1969
Fields of Vision: Essays on Literature, Language, and Television (essays) 1988
Interplay: A Kind of Commonplace Book (prose) 1995
Play Resumed: A Journal (journal) 1999
Signs and Wonders: Selected Essays (essays) 2002
Injury Time: A Memoir (memoir) 2003

CRITICISM

Philip Gardner (essay date winter 1968)

SOURCE: Gardner, Philip. "D. J. Enright Under the Cherry Tree." *Contemporary Literature* 9, no. 1 (winter 1968): 100-11.

[*In the following essay, Gardner discusses Enright's humanism with particular attention to the poems written while Enright was living and teaching in Japan.*]

In a wry little poem, **"The Fairies,"** D. J. Enright neatly sums up his response to the foreign countries in which he has worked:

> Hard up at the time, the fairies gave me
>   what they could: the gift
> Of laying the right hand on the wrong door-knob . . .
> As I muse on the goodliness of my hosts,
>   the capital food and wine and
> The right-minded discourse, that hand goes out
> And takes hold of the knob and turns it gently
>   and the closet door swings eagerly open
> And out falls a skeleton with a frightful crash.[1]

Enright's inaugural lecture at the University of Singapore, on which this poem presumably comments, aroused governmental hostility by criticizing the banning of jukeboxes. Such a skeleton appears to an outsider comparatively small; it is his poems about Japan that display to the full his talent for dropping bricks, for X-raying through the public "face" of a country to the bones beneath.

The "humanism," the concern for individuals rather than governments, that conditions this response first made its appearance in *Academic Year,* a novel based on Enright's experience as a lecturer at the University of Alexandria. This description of the novel's most significant character, Bacon, the "unofficial kind of man" who has taught in Egypt for twenty years, clearly suggests the practicality of Enright's response to human problems:

> His life was comfortable, reasonably full, and—the few who knew him well suspected—might turn out to be valuable. He thought so too: a urinal here, fresh milk there, one or two human beings temporarily freed from debt.

The personal effort is humble, within the limits of the possible, and so not to be shirked, despite the largeness of the issue itself, which Bacon expresses more abstractly: "the idea of the individual would have to be salvaged from the mud, and soon—before it sank entirely out of sight." Enright reiterates this problem in his preface to *Poets of the 1950's,*[2] and says that "the poet's task . . . is to get beneath the mud"—a task which requires "a fairly tough intelligence and an unwillingness to be deceived."

These qualities are admirably in evidence in the Japan poems which make up his volume **Bread Rather than Blossoms** (1956) and comprise the largest "ethnic group" in **Some Men Are Brothers** (1960). The tensions of a Japan in transition, in the years 1953 to 1956 when Enright was a visiting lecturer at Kōnan University near Kōbe, seem to have bred an equivalent tension in the poems which makes them a significant microcosm of his verse: certainly the fact that they far outnumber his poems about any of the five other countries in which he has taught indicates how deeply Japan got under his skin, and the pointed observations of his prose commentary *The World of Dew*[3] confirm this diagnosis.

One looks in vain among these poems for testimonials to the Japan of the tourist brochures, the Japan of cherry-blossom, Mount Fuji, Kyōto temples, Nōh, Tea Ceremony, Flower Arrangement, and Zen. All these aspects appear, but as a background against which Enright asserts the human beings and the human values which, for him, they negate. James Kirkup, who came later to Japan and taught at Tōhoku University in Sendai, is more soothing, more pictorial, imitating *haiku* in English;[4] for Enright the tiny *haiku* is **"Art for the sake of Something Very Misty Indeed."** He prefers the less honored *senryu*, which "at least . . . manages to contend with vulgar and undignified situations"; or, I should suspect, a more idiosyncratic *haiku* like this one by Issa:

> Three ha'pence worth
> Of fog I saw
> Through the telescope.[5]

Here is the kind of authentic response which Enright misses in so much Japanese art: the thing described as it is, not as officialdom or a "thin mystique" would like it to be. Enright's approach to Japan is in the same spirit; he is unwilling (and, as we have seen from **"The Fairies,"** unable) to follow the face-saving injunction of **"Amplifier"**: "For honorable hearts can abstain from remarking / What honorable eyes may happen to see." What he remarks, and remarks on, is a Japan of overpopulation, poverty, landslides, suicides, streetwalkers rather than geisha, and

> Concentration campuses, throbbing with ragged
>   uniforms
> And consumptive faces, in a land where the literacy
> Rate is over 100%, and the magazines
> Read each other in the crowded subways.[6]

For Enright, the enigma of the mysterious and inscrutable East is so much obscurantism manufactured by a national vanity to distract attention from inadequacies that, if pointed out, could perhaps be dealt with:

> The only enigma that I saw
> Was the plump sayings of the politicians
> Against the thin faces of the poor.[7]

This sharp contrast, in various guises, recurs throughout the Japan poems, so that, in the words of William Walsh, they lack "the unflurried simplicity of a single, total experience" and are "harassed by disagreement and protest."[8] But this comment is intended as description rather than denigration, and Enright himself obviously finds such tension poetically necessary: "Poetry is written on a battlefield," he says; and again: "No man at peace makes poetry." In *The World of Dew* he describes Japan as "the testing ground of humanism. An excess of man and an insufficiency of man's means: if your faith in man survives this test, it is impregnable." This "faith in man" is the positive pole which prevents Enright's poems from seeming to bite the hand that fed him, however much they may have embarrassed his Japanese hosts; and it is apparent that it emerged not too damaged: "If the Japanese can finally liberate themselves from the past and survive the present, they should do great things. There is an unused fund of virtue in them."

Slightly condescending as those final sentences of *The World of Dew* sound, they still convey the tenderness, the sense of human likeness, which underlies Enright's frequent criticisms of Japan; the condescension is perhaps a naturally irritated reaction to the "smug conviction [of 'certain Japanese'] that they and their country are so peculiarly unique and so unfathomably deep that no foreigner can hope to write successfully about them." For Enright "nothing is exotic if you understand," and his poetry attempts to correct the overbalance of interest in *Japonaiserie* by stressing that the Japanese are not "human dolls" but "real people, real people, real people." In **"Purchas His Pilgrimes"** he emphasizes the fact that the closed windows of Tokugawa Japan were once and for all shattered by the atomic bomb, whose effects were not entirely destructive: the lesson has emerged that "children of the gods" and "sons of men" are basically the same:

> We peer into that dust, speechless and undressed,
>   to glimpse the final proof
> That none of us are gods, thank God, that all
>   of us are human, at the best.

This humanity, this "fund of virtue" Enright finds preeminently in the ordinary Japanese people, rather than in the upper classes with their constricting code of decorum and "expected" behavior; certainly one feels that the twisted hypersensitivity of the kind of people depicted in Yasunari Kawabata's novel *Thousand Cranes* is markedly different from the friendliness—despite the language difficulty—displayed towards the foreigner by taxi-drivers, small shopkeepers, and country people on local trains in remote parts of Japan.

Enright's poem **"Happy New Year"** pictures the money-worries of the traditionalist banker which debar him from the simple pleasures accessible to those with no worries of *that* sort:

> He showed his ancient incense burners, precious
>   treasures, cold and void.
> His family too he showed, drawn up in columns,
>   and his fluttering spouse.
> We bowed and wept together over the grim new year.

The characteristic pun, "drawn up in columns," emphasizes the tongue-in-cheek politeness of the poet's sympathy; his admiration is for the eternal resilience of the poor and their ability to enjoy themselves:

> The poor are always with us. Only they
>   can find a value in the new.
> They are the masters of their fourpenny kites
> That soar in the open market of the sky.
> Whatever wrongs await, they still preserve some rites.

The pun here, one feels, is not merely a device which Enright frequently cannot resist, but a neat shorthand for conveying his sense of the essential rightness of the human claim on enjoyment, a quality all too often subordinated to the cold correctness of "proper" behavior.

The "wrongs" which await include earthquakes, landslides, and typhoons. **"House Down"** employs a pattern of sound-repetitions which vividly conveys the flurry of activity into which every year many Japanese are thrown by natural disasters:

> eyes are dry and open, quick to spy out every
>   able-bodied splinter,
> Splint the lintel with a fractured table, match
> Up ancient patches, prop the falling with the fallen,
>   and with sad and sure dispatch
> Place the displaced within an altered jigsaw.

An "insufficiency of man's means" indeed! Yet even in the face of this the ordinary virtues of common humanity and its will to survive still show through:

> Only the back, common or garden,
> Can bear a lifetime of this ever-breaking burden.
> Only the unprized eyes could face those winds
>   unflinching.
> Only the heart, so inexpensive, so well-wearing,
> Would run to pluck from utter ruin
>   a fresh, familiar poverty.

Sometimes, though, the burden is too much, particularly for a child, and in one of his finest and most economical poems, **"The Short Life of Kazuo Yamamoto,"** Enright's admiration for Japanese resilience turns to pity for one who no longer found himself able to "bear the unbearable." The newspaper report[9] on the thirteen-year-old orphaned shoeshine-boy who "wanted to die because of a headache" needs no more underlining than the first two verses provide to emphasize the horror of his suicide and the baffled inadequacy of his reason. But in the last verse Enright tightens the screws and with controlled but scathing irony lays this one of many unnecessary deaths at the doors of politicians who are trying to run before they can walk:

> Elsewhere the great ones have their headaches, too,
> As they grapple with those notable tongue-twisters
> Such as Liberation and Oppression.
>   But they were not talking about you,
> Kazuo, who found rat-poison cheaper than aspirin.

The poem's allusive title makes us aware of the omitted word: "happy," the adjective missing from Kazuo Yamamoto's life. And though the poem may seem politically naive in a world where only "international incidents" cut any ice,[10] it is a naiveté which the poet has a license, and a duty, to assert: underneath the political complexities, we feel the acuteness, the poetic truth of Enright's juxtaposition. For him the only meaningful abstraction is one without capital letters:

> Only a silly shamefaced poem dare propose
> That happiness is all that really counts—
>   least abstract of abstractions.[11]

Politics is one ivory tower which seems to Enright to be blind to the fate of individuals; the other is Japanese tradition and Japanese art, with their stylization and precise rules which are for him a denial of the merely human and an attempt to pretend that the real physical world and its inconveniences are only an illusion of the unpurified mind. In **"A Kyōto Garden"** Enright describes the neatly-planned miniature world of Japanese landscape-gardening where everything is designed to purify the viewer and bring him the peace of an aesthetic contemplation in which "the eye need never be averted, nor the nose." This viewer, however, refuses to be so purified, and asks, as usual, the awkward question: "What feeds this corpulent moss, whose emptied blood, / what demon mouths await?" Peace of mind, where so many are debarred from it, is too conscience-pricking a privilege, and the only aspect of the garden which brings Enright any satisfaction is the one which connects it to the disorganized world outside and to the common man:

> but then you notice that the pines wear crutches—
>   typhoons show no respect for art or craft;
> you sigh with happiness, the garden comes alive:
>   like us, these princelings feel the draught.

It is no surprise, therefore, to find that he scornfully dismisses the detached ritual of the Tea Ceremony and the Zen mystique of unworldliness which surrounds it:

> This garden is not a garden, it is an
>   expression of Zen;

The trees are not rooted in earth, then,
    they are rooted in Zen.
And this tea has nothing to do with thirst:
    it says the unsayable.

Typhoons, we have seen, give short shrift to this view; and even if they did not, the existence of so many more pressing demands on human time and effort should be enough to reduce the cult of Tea to a selfish luxury: "Beyond the bamboo fence are life-size people, / Rooted in precious little, without benefit of philosophy."

Like the Tea Ceremony, the aloof, aristocratic Nōh drama, with its extreme stylization of gesture and austere use of stage properties, is an art-form for which Enright has only a frigid regard: "it is art-cum-religion, a mixture which always fills me with misgivings." But even Kabuki, which he clearly enjoys, feeling that it has "that right kind of stylization which has not lost touch with its human origins," does not always succeed in reinterpreting for its audiences the life to which they return when they leave the theatre; their pity is reserved for the daughter they have seen on the stage "sold into a brothel with a modest groan," and is quickly forgotten in the flurried scramble for a taxi home:

> Art's not so long, it seems, that its drawn tears
> extend across the footlights to the same distresses:
> here in small rooms while actors doff their robes,
> there in small rooms the daughters doff their dresses.[12]

It seems to Enright that, in Japan, value is attached not to how closely art approximates to life, but to how near man comes to being himself a "work of conscious art." Just as the government declares certain historic temples or gardens to be "National Treasures," and therefore subject to special protection, so, when a man has refined himself into a consummate artist, will it extend the same dubious honor to him. **"Psalm 72: Man Declared a Treasure"** broadly satirizes this strange tendency. Bunraku—the Puppet Play—is now a dying art; the puppets used in its performances are highly prized. Mr. Yamashiro-no-Shōjō, as a result of his prowess of voice as a reciter-accompanist of Bunraku plays, has, though a mere human, attained the same treatment—a treatment which, because they do not possess his artistic skill, the mass of "junior workers round the cloaca" do not receive:

> Let Mr. Yamashiro-no-Shōjō be heard in the lanes of
>   Tophet,
> Let Mr. Yamashiro-no-Shōjō be honored as a prophet.
> Clap hands, all you who suffer from the buffets
> Of fate. For one of your fellows is prized as highly
>   as one of his puppets.

But life can sometimes have its revenges on art: it is an ironic comment on this topsy-turvydom that, a few years ago, a junior puppeteer of the same Ōsaka theater destroyed a number of puppets, perhaps envious of their privileged position.

Although Enright's humanism was already present in his Egyptian novel, Japan, by providing the contrasting friction of a traditional formalism, sharpened and defined it in his poetry; it is in ***Bread Rather than Blossoms*** that we first truly find his characteristic subject-matter: the inescapable involvement of the man of conscience with the lives and sufferings of his fellows. His dissatisfaction with Japanese poetry springs from its apparent lack of this kind of concern: "in no western literature of any period has the gap between art and ordinary life been so wide."

But whether this gap becomes either too wide or too narrow depends on the poet's vigilantly maintaining within himself the precarious equilibrium of man and poet. This double loyalty is not easy: just as the Japanese poet errs in the direction of art for its own sake, so "a sharp reaction" against this orientation in favor of truth to life "can throw one into a narrow preoccupation with the more obvious hardships and miseries of contemporary Japan and so lead to an inordinate amount of moralizing."[13] A warning, "intended for myself," against undue moralizing is conveyed in the poem **"Busy Body under a Cherry Tree."** In one sense the cherry tree may stand for much in Japan that is shallowly pictorial, "a tree / Whose fruit is eaten only by the eyes";[14] but it is undeniably beautiful, and in another sense symbolizes the enviable perfection which only that kind of art which is free of propaganda may attain:

> the cherry's body all year round is busy
> Against one week of showered gifts without advice,
> For it is silent, for its deeds suffice.

Yet even while he indulges his nostalgia Enright betrays, in the ambiguity of the last phrase, the complexity of his commitment. What, for a poet, are his "deeds"? Do they, in fact, "suffice"? If the deeds are literal ones, the kind which for Bacon seemed within the limits of the possible, are they ever enough to abolish the misery of others more than "temporarily"? Obviously not—which does not remove the need to do them. But in the poem **"Where Charity Begins"** Enright, by juxtaposing two separate confrontations with beggars, suggests that in the twisted context of world politics kindness may be so risky that the first response of "a little money" may become calloused into the highly vicarious sympathy of the roving cameraman:

> Charity. Oh yes, all this we'd seen was charity.
>   Make a picture of where your heart once bled,
> Move the world's conscience, or provoke an inci-
>   dent—
>   All simpler than to fill an empty mouth with
> bread.

Yet though poetry may be a poor substitute for money, it is better than nothing at all. Yet, again, because the poet is a man, the "deeds" which metaphorically are his poems clearly do not suffice either, especially if they draw too much attention to themselves and away from the occasions which provoke them. So the poet-man is continually trying to compensate for the inadequacy of one kind of "deed" with the inadequacy of the other kind. The cherry-blossom suffices because the cherry is only a tree, not a man.

Asked, in 1962, "Do you see this as a good or bad period for writing poetry?" Enright replied that "in a scientific and technological age, many writers are bound to feel doubts about the usefulness of [their] writing."[15] One can see that the humanist poet, with his particularly strong sense of the real, objective existence of human problems—and his feeling that, while as a poet he may be called upon only to describe them, as a man he is partially responsible for helping in their solution—would begin to have misgivings about his art qua art. Certainly Enright's Japan poems show that his occasional hankerings for poetic purity are outweighed by his doubts about poetry itself: for him, literature is subordinate to life. In **"The Poet in Retirement"** he says:

> The poet has prepared himself for when he will
> No longer write.
> 　　In that new darkness, what new light?
> After words, people: that's how all art should end.
> 　　For art is short, but life is long.

It is no hypocrisy that, despite his inversion of the old adage, Enright has continued to produce volumes of verse: the artistic impulse does exist. But the attitude expressed here has important repercussions in the kind of poetry Enright's is: it explains his lack of emphasis on "style." Not that his poems, particularly those of his Japan period, have no style; but it certainly consists far less in quotable passages of fine writing than in an habitual ironic stance and a system of careful and often punning cross-references which heightens by repetition the significance of key phrases. For Enright too much "appliqué" style is felt to be a betrayal of subject-matter, as this mention of the opposite view, in *Academic Year,* makes clear. Bacon and Packet are discussing a dilettante volume of poems completely insulated from the grittiness of Egyptian everyday life:

> "What *does* he write about then?" Packet had asked. "He doesn't write *about*. Sensibility, refinement, and money: when one has all that, one does not write *about*—one just writes. Subject matter, El Hamama would say, is the betrayal of style: it should be left to journalists, who need it to conceal their lack of style."

Enright is no mere journalist; but he does feel that poetry should be "*about* something" and that the something should be "people, preferably other people."

This being so, the humanist poet has a special duty not to "tart up" experience but render it straightforwardly so that the reader's response will be less one of admira-

tion for poetic skill than one of sympathy for the person or situation described. Even "humanism," in the wrong hands, can become a mere gimmick; the Japanese poet whom Enright advises, in **"Changing the Subject,"** to deal with human themes instead of "the moon, and flowers, and birds and temples, / and the bare hills of the once holy city" dresses up his portrayal of "those who sleep in the subway" with so much rhetoric that the real becomes the artificial:

> "Are they miners from Kyushu?" Neither he nor I will
> 　　ever dare to ask them.
> For we know they are not really human, are as apt
> 　　themes
> 　　　　for verse as the moon and the bare hills.

Enright fully realizes the dangers: the reproof is for himself too. When William Walsh says:

> the poet-observer has the privilege of not enduring what those he watches suffer. And isn't there a touch of pretension, a degree of conceit, in translating human suffering so directly into art?

Enright has anticipated him, in a poem about a human derelict, called **"Written Off"**: "The shame would be to write of such a thing."

Despite, however, Enright's scruples about the possible pitfalls of humanist poetry, one's final judgment is decidedly not that he falls into them. Rather one admires the unending effort to balance the respective claims of life and art, realizing that the emphasis placed on the former demands of the poet considerable artistic self-denial without bringing the man the compensating sense of having solved the problems of the world in which he lives. As Enright has ruefully put it in **"To an Alexandrian Poet"**:

> And so it seems I'm poorer, in the end, than you—
> Have lost what you have found, and nothing gained
> 　　beside
> (The beggar fidgets in his rags and eyes me sullenly)
> 　　　　　　　—neither a cure for beggars'
> 　　legs,
> Nor your large graceful house and manners.[16]

If this last line is true, the limitation it describes is, in the circumstances, an honorable one. As for the "cure for beggars' legs," that will take a long time to discover. All the poet can do is to point to the facts, recommend such humble attempts as are within the grasp of any one human individual, and, like "the poet in retirement," hope

> that those who close one of his books
> 　　will pause, before beginning on the next.

Notes

1. *Addictions* (London, 1962), p. 61. All poems quoted are to be found in *Bread Rather than Blos-*

soms (London, 1956) or *Some Men Are Brothers* (London, 1960), except where otherwise indicated.

2. Tokyo, 1955, p. 12.

3. London, 1954. All quotations are from the First Japan Edition, Tokyo, 1956.

4. *Refusal to Conform* (London, 1963), pp. 84-89.

5. Translation by Geoffrey Bownas and Anthony Thwaite, *Penguin Book of Japanese Verse* (Harmondsworth, 1964), p. 124.

6. "In Memoriam," *Addictions*, p. 11.

7. "Oriental Politics."

8. *A Human Idiom* (London, 1964), p. 167.

9. *The World of Dew*, pp. 207-208.

10. "News," *Addictions*, p. 29.

11. "Tourist Map."

12. "The Popular Theatre."

13. *Poets of the 1950's*, p. 103.

14. "Samisen Music."

15. *The London Magazine*, February 1962, p. 38.

16. *The Laughing Hyena* (London, 1953), p. 30.

William Walsh (essay date 1974)

SOURCE: Walsh, William. "Poetry I: 1953-60." In *D. J. Enright: Poet of Humanism*, pp. 21-39. London: Cambridge University Press, 1974.

[*In the following excerpt, Walsh discusses the philosophical and ethical concerns that motivate much of Enright's early poetry.*]

Becoming a poet in the 1950s must have been one of the severest disciplines anyone could put himself to. That difficult, dangerous period when a talent is forming had to be passed in a time governed more than most by fictions of status, affluence, acceptance. A sensibility had to be constructed not in a society whose system ran with and supported a current of genuine life but in a marshmallow world with convictions hardly robust enough either to accept or reject. But if it was hard, it wasn't unpopular. There was a clutch of poets who began to arrive in the 1950s. They called themselves *The Movement*. But I am inclined to think that what they had in common wasn't motion—they had no agreed point of departure and certainly no concerted destination—but rather a posture, a negative stance.

> After so many (in so many places) words,
> It came to this one, No.

Epochs of parakeets, of peacocks, of paradisiac birds -
Then one bald owl croaked, No.

> ('Saying no')[1]

These young poets who depended above all on a freshness of contact with actuality, but who lived in a world infatuated with illusion, developed, had to develop, a cool evasive skill and an aptness in the tactics of disengagement. This was part of the success many of them had in devising a sensibility in keeping with the times, together with the voice through which it could be projected. The sensibility was agile and fluent, the voice casual and intelligently modulated. There was nothing stark or grand in the one, nothing inflatedly poetic in the other. A detached and modest manner, a dry decency of feeling, an utterance, in which, at its best, the contours of the verse are fitted exactly to the curves of contemporary speech—these are the marks of a poetry which strikes the reader as being authentically and altogether naturally modern.

There are, of course, traces in these poets of strain and youth and earlier manners—the jagged and impeded line, the blatantly cerebral energy, the laborious construction. But in all of them at their best, and especially in the one who seems to me one of the most individual in character and most representative of the times, the poetical movement is light and gliding and unreluctant. Here are some lines from **'The Laughing Hyena by Hokusai'**[2] which show the skilful manoeuvring of a liquid, lively rhythm:

> For him it seems everything was molten. Court-ladies
>   flow in gentle streams,
> Or, gathering lotus, strain sideways from the curving
>   boat,
> A donkey prances, or a kite dances in the sky, or soars
>   like sacrificial smoke.
> All is flux; waters fall and leap, and bridges leap and
>   fall.
> Even his Tortoise undulates, and his Spring Hat is
>   lively as a pool of fish.

The events of the poet's life play an important part in a poetry which has a solidly objective character. On the whole the poets of the 1950s do not look on a sequence of poems as a variety of poses best calculated to display aspects of the fascinating ego. Enright himself, as I have explained, has spent most of his career since Cambridge abroad, and this international experience seems to have a peculiar relevance to modern life. To be so closely in touch with the intelligent young of several countries gives access to a sensitive part of the modern world: as a teacher of a self-conscious generation he is in direct touch with people's intimately human concerns; as a post-imperial Englishman his human shape is unmuffled by the toga, his relationships undistorted by the hypocrisies of power or obedience. He writes in **'Entrance Visa'**:[3]

We were the Descendancy. Hurt but not surprised.
Atoning for our predecessors' every oath and sneer,
We paid in poverty the rich men's debt.

With no pretensions but to be human (both a modest and a gigantic ambition), the poet is qualified to join a dozen communities in as many lands. To say that he joins is perhaps too strong a way to describe his relation to the community. He is aware of the sense in which each place is for him only 'a change of homelessness'; and he has to preserve that measure of detachment necessary for the attentive and adequate observer. On the other hand, wearing no more than the nakedness, the anonymity, of humanity and being also 'a perpetual refugee' may well be the essential entrance visas into many countries, as well as the most difficult to secure. So much of the poetry of the 1950s is like this, the poetry of the observant wanderer who, wherever he is, always cunningly sites himself to catch some eloquent notation of the human scene. A mere list of subjects from one of Enright's books, ***Some Men Are Brothers,*** will suggest something of the variety of the world seen by this sharp contemporary eye and something of the agility with which the observer-poet gets into position: sitting in a German park, meeting an Egyptian at a cocktail party, Berlin dustbins and funeral facilities, a noodle-vendor's flute, Mr Yamashiro-no-Shōjō who is declared a Human National Treasure, a barge full of rice, a kite flight, a Japanese story (1687) called *The Conspectus of Sodomites,* the last male quagga left alive.

The poet's glance, we can tell from his treatment of these subjects, wry and original as it is, is bent upon reality. The existence of these 'sad and naughty persons', their odd and slippery jobs, their ambiguous yet appealing relationships, is fully and firmly established—and with the minimum of descriptive reference. (These poems are quite unpadded, and rest elegantly on nothing more than their own bones.) Disciplined observation, we realise, can be a remarkably productive poetic instrument; it is, indeed, an important and neglected human power.

The flame-tree shames us, one and all:
    for what fit audience, though few, do we afford?

('A Day in an Undisciplined Garden')[4]

And to notice a thing with the poet's fine, unblurred particularity is to rescue it from falling into the refuse of life.

If we do not observe, who will?
Will anything observe or mourn for us?

('Insects')[5]

The observation of the poet is not, of course, the neutrality of the mirror. It depends upon a particular at-

titude and carries a special tone. In Enright's case as with most of these poets the attitude is pitying, the tone ironic.

Only one subject to write about: pity.
Self-pity: the only subject to avoid.
How difficult to observe both conditions!

('How right they were, the Chinese poets')[6]

The pity is without the least taint of *de haut en bas*; it is a level, unfussy feeling, of which the impulse is seeing in another's plight an extension of one's own and recognising his nature within one's own self. It is an acknowledgement of the common thing in men: 'And being common / Therefore something rare indeed.' 'Men are brothers', murmurs this voice, lucidly, lovingly, a simplicity which is immediately corrected to a more astringent, complicated comment, 'Some men are brothers.' The peculiar flavour of these poems comes from combining the mild (a favourite word of this poet), the mild taste of charity with the acrid one of 'real cities, real houses, real time'.

Enright's poetry, I am convinced, is deeply serious. I am aware in it, for all its spry and modern matter, of a traditional—not a conventional—wholesomeness of feeling, and for all its mobility of manner, of a steadiness of moral centre. But I hope I have not suggested that it is in any way solemn. It also shows, like much modern writing, the disillusioned urchin grimacing behind a respectable back or the dead-pan peasant pulling the Unesco Fellow's leg. This poet, it is clear from his poetry—quite apart from his other writings—is a man of considerable learning, even *gravitas*; he is also, equally clearly, an outrageously mischievous comic: Johnson and Boswell curiously sharing a single skin. This is a blend of temperaments which is very much of the present and decidedly attractive. Perhaps the best figure for this sensibility is the subject of one of his own poems, **'The Noodle-Vendor's Flute'**,[7] an ingenious device, 'merely a rubber-bulb and metal horn', made like this to keep the lips from being frozen by the night winds. In itself it is a kind of snook cocked at a more literary flute. It cries the vendor's wares as he cycles from spot to spot on the look-out for manholes and late drunks, and it is the accompaniment, like most poetry in the 1950s, to the difficult and rather comic business of making a living.

The puffing vendor, surer than a trumpet,
Tells us we are not alone.
Each night that same frail midnight tune
Squeezed from a bogus flute,
Under the noise of war, after war's noise,
It mourns the fallen, every night,
It celebrates survival—
In real cities, real houses, real time.

An accompaniment to the difficult and rather comic business of making a living—yes. But also an accompaniment to the difficult, comic business of living itself. For it is living which interests this poet, not life; not the portentous abstraction but its multiple definitions. 'To live is compulsory'; one isn't free to take up an attitude or to have large assumptions about that. And what is compulsory *in* living is this and that, the particular event, the specific action, the peculiar disappointment. The history which presses on the poet is not the history of historians but simply his own; he feels griefs not grief; he meets men not man. Living is not a cloudy gesture but a precise act. It is a kind of collision with reality. Part of the equipment of any poet is a sense of human reality better developed than in the rest of us. In Enright this is a sense for the reality residing in, defined by, the exact and lucid detail. We can see this sense operating in a remarkable early poem, **'The Chicken's Foot'**,[8] of which this is the second part:

> At the end of this little street, unnamed, unfamed, a street
> that one might take
> Unseeingly, to cheat the wind or to avoid one's friends,
> A street like others, unduly ravaged by the tempest's tail,
> Vulnerable to nature's riots though inured to man's—
> At the bottom of this fluttered street, flat in the choked gutter,
> I saw the neat claws, the precise foot, of a chicken—
> Bright yellow leggings, precious lucid nails, washed by the waters,
> Victim of our bellies, memorable sermon, oh murdered singing throat,
> Confronting the battered traveller, fingers spread in admonition.
>
> The wind howled louder in derision: oh literary pedestrian,
> Small bankrupt moralist, oh scavenger of the obvious symbol!
> But entering the huge house, where the wind's scattered voices,
> Hot with insidious history, chill with foreboding, surged through my body,
> The chicken's foot, naked and thin, still held my mind between its claws—
> The cleanest thing, most innocent, most living, of that morning.

The run of this verse, combining an unimpeded movement with a balanced disposition of phrase, recalls the manner of the later Eliot. Eliot has clearly been a formative influence on Enright's poetry, not an influence on imagery, tone or theme, but a rhythmical one—the most intimate kind of influence one poet can have on another. Eliot's presence, however, is usually more absorbed, less distinct, than it is here. There is, I am sure, a reason for the insistence with which the poet calls attention to it in this poem. **'The Chicken's Foot'** is a markedly 'literary' poem. In one sense the chicken's foot lies 'flat in the choked gutter' at the end of a little street. But it is also somewhere else. The formal literary manner, the

traditional regularity of alliteration, the memory of Eliot, the reference to Chaucer, all set up an elaborate literary background wholly at odds with the humble bit of rubbish—a tessellated pavement on which the shocking, severed thing is flung. It is this, gleaming brilliantly against a pile of abstractions, which is 'The cleanest thing, most innocent, most living, of that morning' and this which holds not only the poet's but the reader's mind between its claws. And how vividly the reader heeds these ridiculously but impressively admonitory fingers. 'Heeding' is a very heightened form of observation. It takes a poet's power to tighten our slack vision into this intense activity, a poet's perceptiveness to turn the chicken's foot (or any object) from what it customarily is, a dim centre surrounded by 'a foggy sphere of influence', into

> . . . the neat claws, the precise foot, of a chicken—
> Bright yellow leggings, precious lucid nails . . .

By the end of the poem the chicken's foot has been invested with a clear Chaucerian pathos, unmuddied by sentimentality in a context which invites it. One check on sentimentality—often a fault of muzziness and incomplete realisation—is the firm definition of the object, the cleanliness of its outline. It is given an existence and a dignity of its own. A second check is the mockery aimed at the poet himself for finding so much significance in so commonplace a thing. One sees how the derisory phrases, 'literary pedestrian', 'bankrupt moralist', 'scavenger of the obvious symbol', while they deflate the poet, also suggest something about morals and symbols. Perhaps they too are rubbishy and defeated, victims of our souls instead of our bellies.

The effectiveness of **'The Chicken's Foot'** depends, as with many of Enright's poems, on the exact defining of the central symbol. It is this which the poet, recognising its importance in his art, calls in another poem: 'The point of repose in the picture, the point of movement in us.' Enright's method, designed to fix this point accurately, is a discipline of clarity. It is a discipline which is averse to the attractions—the warm attractions—of the irrational. Enright wants his verse to move in a lucid, sensible air, not because he is in any way ignorant of hidden depths and subterranean disasters, but because he chooses to inhabit a clearer, Chaucerian universe. With such a care for clarity, so personal a bias towards light and intelligibility, the poet is bound to be troubled not only by 'the darkness of words', 'sinister symbols under ruin's shadow',[9] but by their ordinary duplicities. There is always in words a reluctance to be persuaded into coherence, and every poet has to struggle with this recalcitrance. Words are stubborn. They are today, even more than before, blandly evasive, ambiguous and sly. A contemporary poet has also to contend with something like a moral degeneracy in the words he uses. And yet it is from these elements, refractory, devious and dishonest, that the poet has to compose a structure of genuine feelings. No wonder that the poet recommends in **'A Desert Cure'**[10] a regime of austerity for words.

> Now is the time to take and know them—words—go
>   with them
> All the way, till the gasping tram sinks to its knees
> In the open desert, devoid of palm-tree, or mirage, for
>   refuge—
> Only the dry donkey to receive you, and the stinging
>   dust.
>
> Or trap them in the stony customs shed: rap their
>   dishonest hands
> That slide towards false papers, or proffer folded notes
>   in coveted
>   currencies.
> Do not spare: for elsewhere they would tear you:
> Barbs in an enemy's watching mouth, claws on a
>   friend's blind tongue,
> The morning snake that creeps beneath the door.
>
> Why is truth naked? Look at the long robes, sacred
> Caftan and gallabieh, English suiting, committee-man
>   in ties and devil's
>   tails.
> Lies dress the best. Leave them to die there—words—
> On the verge of meaning, or purge in the open desert:
> Shaken by the silent wind, shattered by the speechless
>   sand.

One can see how the poet repelled by the dishonesty of words might want in the end to leave them there, to bleach in the open desert 'on the verge of meaning'. But he might instead turn back to the beginning, to words which are also on the verge of meaning—in the mouths of children. During those few years when a child has come to feel at ease with words but is not yet expert in the hypocrisy of cliché, he uses language with an awkward and unprompted honesty, as something original and alive. In a world where language moves between the poles of the committee and the advertisement, this gives an attentive listener, like this poet, the opportunity, as rewarding as it is rare, to hear language stirring into life. He can attend, as in a miniature play, to language performing the strange unpredictable motions of assuming new life. He can see, illustrated outside himself, the actions that words go through in his own mind. There are a number of poems, for example, **'Blue Umbrellas'**, **'First Death'**, **'End of a Hot Day'**, in which Enright makes the wayward, disconcertingly apt comment of a child the centre of a poem, disposing the poem round it or allowing it to grow from the child's words with skilled and gentle restraint. **'Blue Umbrellas'**[11] takes off from one of those childish remarks which are, as it were, sideways to reality yet in some odd way also faithful to it:

> 'The thing that makes a blue umbrella with its tail—
> How do you call it?' you ask. Poorly and pale
> Comes my answer. For all I can call it is peacock.

> Now that you go to school, you will learn how we
>   call all sorts of things;
> How we mar great works by our mean recital.
> You will learn, for instance, that Head Monster is not
>   the gentleman's
>   accepted title;
> The blue-tailed eccentrics will be merely peacocks;
>   the dead bird will no longer doze
> Off till tomorrow's lark, for the letter has killed him.
> The dictionary is opening, the gay umbrellas close.

These words convey—with a fine economy and with regret that is also an unsentimental acceptance of the inevitable—a sense of that passage in a child's life from the time when his words are still marked by the bite of particularity to the time when they present the smooth undifferentiated surface of adult formulae. This passage isn't simply to be identified with the movement from language which is wholly concrete to language which is completely abstract. The smallest child, using the simplest words, is performing a remarkably abstract and theoretic act, and the conventional adult using the most fatigued language still keeps some faint contact with the concrete. But the young child uses language in an active, discovering way, and not, as he will later, as an instrument with which to attach general labels to passive experiences. With the young child—as with the poet—there is a bracing of energy between word and thought, a tension between word and thing. Even his oddest failures, his queerest gaffes, although as description they may be formally irrelevant, still contain a fundamental relevance to life. The Head Monsters and the blue umbrellas, although they may fail to raise the common image, surprise us by communicating the primary attribute of Headmasters and peacocks—their peculiar, living identity. The child's terms, although they may lack the symmetry of convention, display the proportions of life.

What makes the child's use of language distinctive, and what makes it so attractive to the contemporary poet, is that children are among the few in a more and more highly conditioned society capable of giving an unlicensed comment or an unpredictable reply. This capacity of the child is, of course, to be attributed to lack of experience, and not acuity of insight. But its result, the things said and offered, exhibits characteristics of freshness and vitality almost wholly bleached out of the current language. For a short time the child's sayings, unworn by routine, not yet smoothed down into a featureless response, present a human awkwardness and spontaneity rare enough to deserve a poet's attention. The child's words simply do not fit in; and in our world that is as good as a high degree of originality.

Dealing with a child's experience raises at once for the writer a technical problem, the one indeed that engaged Henry James's interests in *What Maisie Knew*. The problem is clearly more pressing in fiction but it cannot be avoided even in poetry. James saw that one cannot leave the child's consciousness alone, confused and obscure as it must be, to register the theme. The writer must piece out the child's partial, discontinuous understanding with an adult commentary. He can do this explicitly by making adult elucidation an answer to, or a commentary upon, the child's experience and the whole is turned into a pattern of stimulus and response, or he can do it implicitly by remaining within the universe of the child and by using adult understanding to clarify and order all that is obscurely contained in the child's faintly glimmering comprehension. In **'End of a Hot Day'** Enright uses the first method, in **'First Death'** the second.

> At last we can look at the melted moon:
> The grass is cool like olives: the cicadas
> Are almost tender. 'Here at least is peace,'
> We are trusting, 'after the day's hot murders'—
> When the cat slinks by, a bird in his mouth
>   betrayed by the evening's truce.
>
>   The child runs for a box,
> The small remains are buried under the oily light.
> She is happy: 'He will sleep in the box all night,
> And tomorrow push his head through, like the
>   daffodil.'
>   We swallow her bitter pill.
>
> Tomorrow will be hot again; she will forget
> To wait for the stone to roll away, the green feather
>   to sprout, the twisted beak to twitter.
> Every age has its advantages, and every weather.
> Shall I beat the cat who ate the bird who ate
>   the worm who might have eaten me?
>
> **('End of a Hot Day')**[12]

The crisp language and the muted imagery of taste recall by contrast the day's brutal heat, and make the treachery of the cat, like death itself, both natural and shocking. The child's remark, so pretty and fantastic, points up the savagery and hopelessness of the hot day. And yet her charmingly irrelevant words are an element in the situation—one of the advantages of her age and this weather—and deserve, as much as the bird's death, to be acknowledged, if the experience is to be fully rendered. Accepting the complexity of the concrete is what the poet is doing here and what he is justifying in the whip of the nursery-rhyme conclusion:

> Shall I beat the cat who ate the bird who ate
>   the worm who might have eaten me?

I should not want to suggest that this poem was of more than minor interest, or that it was, even within its limits, completely successful. There is, for example, a slight loss of focus, and of propriety, in the phrase, 'she will forget / To wait for the stone to roll away'. No qualification of this sort, however, can be urged against **'First Death'**,[13] a brilliant evocation of the fundamental experience in a child's life, its first shattering meeting with human death:

> It is terrible and wonderful: we wake in the strange
>   night
> And there is one bed empty and one room full: tears
>   fall,
> The children comfort each other, hugging their knees,
>   for what will the future be now, poor things?
>
> And next day there is no school, and meals are
>   disorderly,
> Things bought from shops, not the old familiar dishes.
> New uncles come from far away, soft-voiced strangers
> Drinking extraordinary wines. A kind of abstract
>   kindliness
> Fills the house, and a smell of flowers. Impossible to
>   be bad—
>
> Other nights pass, under conceded night-lights and a
>   cloud
> Of questions: shall we ever go back to school? Ever
>   again
> Go to the pictures? Are we too poor for new shoes?
>   Must we move
> To a council house? Will any of our friends remember
>   us?
> Will it always be kind and quiet and sad, like this?
>
> Uncles depart. We go for a week to a country aunt,
> Then take a lodger. New shoes are bought—Oh, so
>   this is the future!
> How long will it last, this time? Never feel safe now.

One cannot but be impressed by the delicate rightness of tone in a poem where it would be only too easy to slide into the portentous and sentimental. It is a success, it seems to me, which depends on a set of exact, supple and beautifully maintained balances. For example, there is the nice equilibrium between general reflection and tight defining detail, between 'It is terrible and wonderful' and 'hugging their knees', or between 'A kind of abstract kindliness' and 'a smell of flowers'. Then there is the proportion between the new, impersonal atmosphere and the nagging questions which worry the children: on the one hand new uncles, soft-voiced strangers, extraordinary wines, on the other

> . . . shall we ever go back to school? Ever again
> Go to the pictures? Are we too poor for new shoes?
>   Must we move
> To a council house? Will any of our friends remember
>   us?
> Will it always be kind and quiet and sad, like this?

If the tone does not sag, if the feeling does not loosen, that is because of the buoyancy and lightness of the rhythm which carries them, and which is itself a balance of phrases contrasted in weight and length, at one point unfolding slowly and easily, at another shutting down with abrupt finality. One can see too how the structure of the whole poem (which is pretty well repeated in the structure of each stanza) balances two distinct elements of the experience one against the other, the tremors of the children's disturbed present against premonitions about the future. The total effect of the poem is to bring home to the reader the children's suspicions—and then their terrified realisation—that the future is no simple flowering of a fragrant present, but the intrusion into their lives of a dangerous, treacherous force. Against its unpredictable and brutal workings they can offer only the sense of their powerlessness. 'Never feel safe now.'

So that the child in Enright's poetry is doubly significant. His capacity for the unrehearsed reply in a merely echoing world makes him significant *because* he is unrepresentative. But the child in another way faithfully represents the common run of men—those to whom Enright is most intimately drawn—because he is, like them, and more than most of them—the victim of power. It is the ultimate powerlessness which is communicated so directly in **'First Death'**, a sense not just of the inevitability of death, whether another's or one's own, but of the shattering of certainties and stabilities so that one must from now on hold oneself and one's beliefs tentatively and flinchingly. And it is powerlessness of this kind—bitterly acknowledged but also shruggingly accepted—which marks the figures thronging Enright's poetic world—the noodle-vendor, the trishaw driver, the one-eyed boy, the aged woman, 'the pimpled students in their costive dress', the girl in the bush:

> Perfect for the part, perfect,
>   Except for the dropsy
> Which comes from polished rice.

('A Polished Performance')[14]

or Kazuo Yamamoto who found rat poison cheaper than aspirin, and Akiko San, the dumpy-legged, worried prostitute.

From the many sketches of these people—quick scrawls flicked down on any available paper—the reader gradually gets a view of the humanity that the poet sees. It is a view which is Oriental in its setting but Western in its sardonic precision—and I am not sure that it isn't universal in its truth. At its centre lies the recognition of the powerlessness of men. But perhaps, it seems to be suggested too, powerlessness isn't simply deprivation. It may also be the state of having not only necessities but illusions scraped away, and above all the illusion of power. The concomitant of powerlessness is a bitter sense of reality. The poor, the poet notes, wake up quickly. The poor, the appalling Eastern poor, are men reduced absolutely to their elements, men stripped of everything but a residual human nature. All they own is a human identity but that is positive and incorruptible. In their indifference and passivity they have the look of statues, of statues hardly carved at all and barely to be recognised as human by an eye accustomed to more

opulent outlines. But they also have the continuing resistance of stone. In **'Rice Coming Into Town'**[15] it is this human nature which is deeply implicit in the details, this mere odour of humanity which is contrasted with sophisticated man:

> The barge lies low along the river,
> Deep in rice.
> Silent statues at its prow and stern
> (Dreaming old ballads of blood and gold?)
> Watch their images dissolve
>   into that foreign life.
> Those whom power has not yet
>   tended to corrupt
> (Beyond the common power
> To grow a crop or mildly cheat a neighbour).
>
> They watch their silent images
>   melt into the water:
> As they melt—so it seems—
> Into a gorging town, a coup d'état,
> A street of ministries, of restaurants,
> A smell of jasmine, opium, petrol,
> A brace of schools, a pack of characteristics,
> A voice heard in the councils of the world.
>
> Statues, too tired to talk?
>   Too wise? Too ignorant?
> (Dreaming new thoughts of blood and gold?)
> Will power ever manage to corrupt
>   (even tend to)
> All of these?
>   How much power is there in this world?

Upon such scenes as these, and on their merely human occupants, the poet turns a gaze which is accurate, tender and sceptical—a characteristic blend of qualities. The accuracy is in the notation, the tenderness is for the object, the scepticism is for himself. After all the poet-observer has the privilege of not enduring what those he watches suffer. And isn't there a pretension, a degree of conceit, in translating human suffering so directly into art, as he hints in an untitled poem in *Some Men Are Brothers*?

> Simply, he was human, did no harm, and suffered for
>   it.
> His name?—We might be tempted by its liquid vowel
>   sounds,
>   the richness of its rhythms—
>
> I've said too much already.
>   Writers of epitaphs, in your conceit, remember:
> There may be relatives still living.

Scepticism may be too hard, too intellectual a word for the wry, deflationary attitude which we feel to be so distinctly a modern mood. (Not that in Enright's writing we are ever unaware of the movement of an athletic intelligence.) Scepticism as it appears here is a preference for the bone of actuality and a distaste for the obesity of cliché, whether moral or intellectual. And it isn't with Enright simply negative or just tediously clever. It takes its stand—I mustn't be diffident about using such terms of a writer who is fundamentally serious—on a metaphysic, a view of man, and a morality, the morality of a common human nature. The view of man which stresses his uniqueness, and the morality which insists on his unity, show themselves in a nice balance in the tiny poem, 'Man':[16]

> We should treasure this cobra
> Were it the only one.
> Can't Nature take the human hint,
> Must we help her on?
>
> Soul, then morals, tried and failed.
> If this fails too, there's only tooth and claw.
> Yet brothers are exhausting, row on row:
> Give me a friend—he murmured—three or four,
>
> Who know all men are brothers, even though
> They may not like their brothers saying so.

The metaphysic gets its urgency from a prevailing sense of the special precariousness of modern existence—life lived along a precipice; the morality gets its strength from the poet's exact, accurate understanding of his own feelings. There is nothing gusty or Whitmanesque in his 'all men are brothers' since he doesn't attempt to hide that 'brothers are exhausting, row on row'. What is so characteristic of Enright, as of today, is that serious views are held so flippantly. To Enright it is quite natural (though on occasion, perhaps, only irresistible) for the poet as clown to see life as a farce. And few of us I fancy—and certainly not the young—will find the conditions of modern life such as to make this notion of its absurdity inexplicable. To Enright there is little difference between practising an art and acting the monkey or between honouring the muse and taking the mickey—at the expense of himself as well as of others.

> Once again the Year of the Monkey is here.
> I was born in the Year of the Monkey—
> Surely a fellow can talk about himself a bit,
>   in his own year?
>
> Monkeys are like poets—more than human.
> Which is why they do not take us very seriously.
> Not to be taken seriously is rather painful.
>   To a corner of my cage I retired, mysteriously,
> And had sad thoughts. (They may have been deep.)
> Big eyes damp with a semi-permanent tear, my thin
>   hands
>   held my heavy head from tumbling into sleep.
>
>   (**'Monkey'**)[17]

There is a sharp discrepancy, of which the poet is well aware, between this comedian's manner and the subjects which a poet with so distinctly contemporary a sensibility is bound to treat—which itself may be part of what makes him so much of the moment. **'Stop that clowning at once if not sooner'**[18] is a poem which makes this contrast explicit:

> Giggling on the edge of a precipice—
> Shameful! They'll think you haven't noticed it.
> Or worse, that you're the sort of person
>   for whom abysses don't exist,
> Being one coarse-grained vacant space yourself . . .
>
> For the time needs—
>   stop giggling on the brink of precipices
> While I'm talking to you!—
>   heavyweight intellects, sober serious men.
>
>   'Unfortunately it gets them,'
> Giggling on the verge of nothing.
> 'Here's a profound hole, yet no deeper than a coffin.'
> Hoping that not too many (even that he may not)
>   fall into it,
> Wagging his arms and legs, and hoping . . .

Hope—smaller and greyer than optimism—is one of the homely clutch of qualities (a modest decency, a mild charity, an unemphatic tolerance) celebrated in this verse. These unpretentious, appealing virtues, as human as a hiccup and as common, preserve the human idiom in a context full of violence and terror. And that after all is what good poems like good acts (which, the poet points out, *are* achieved though seldom by oneself) try to do—to make audible the inflections of a human voice in conditions in which it may be suffocated by mechanisation in a long twilight or annihilated by politics in a flash. It is this voice, mostly offhand, occasionally intense, at other times sly, glum, comic, irritable but always real, which is the true subject as well as the natural medium of a poetry trying above all to construct and preserve a human idiom, and to defend and praise the validity of private experience. In **'The Monuments of Hiroshima'**[19] the poet makes the point by exposing the contrast which exists between even the diminished vitality of common, silly obituary phrases and the ghastly language and results of State action:

> The roughly estimated ones, who do not sort well
>   with our common phrases,
> Who are by no means eating roots of dandelion,
>   or pushing up the daisies.
>
> The more or less anonymous, to whom no human
>   idiom
>   can apply,
> Who neither passed away, or on,
>   nor went before, nor vanished on a sigh.
>
> Little of peace for them to rest in, less of them
>   to rest in peace:
> Dust to dust a swift transition, ashes to ash
>   with awful ease.
>
> Their only monument will be of others' casting—
> A Tower of Peace, a Hall of Peace, a Bridge of Peace
>   —who might have wished for something lasting,
> Like a wooden box.

Poetic intentions of this kind are natural to one who believes that 'civilisation consists in the diminution of human tears' and who prefers the paddy-fields where the ancient woman spoons its ration of hot harsh food to each rice plant, or a tram-ride through the ancient capital to 'the cafés where the cultured pique and pine' or 'the largish whitish newish building . . . devoted to the study of the Liberal Arts and Humanities'. Enright, clearly, feels more at home with the humble tom-fool than with 'polished Monsieur Angst'. Many—more as he develops—of his poems appear to be written in opposition. Very few express the unflurried simplicity of a single, total experience. In this sense these poems are impure. They tend more and more to be harassed by disagreement and protest. Even in a poem called **'The Peaceful Island'**,[20] which is about a day spent away from the city, its vices and charlatan voices, in a place where

> The islanders' speech is soft and slow:
> No aids to their dialect have yet been printed;
> It sounds like the surge of the sea on powdery sands;
> It is empty of oaths . . .

we find the poet, dizzy with lack of sleep, passing the time by throwing stones at bottles, which represent a procurer, a flinty industrialist, a well-known poet and an expert in traditions. On occasion even, the poet-observer becomes the poet-demonstrator and the poem a cross gesticulation or a yelp of anger. But more often his antagonism is cool and directed. It is turned, as you would expect from one who is above all on the side of what is real, however sleazy its form, against frauds and cryptos, the conmen of the intellect: against the superior person ('the gentleman of spiritual truths'), 'grave intellectuals doing their strip-tease', politicians—

> The only enigma that I saw
> Was the plump sayings of the politicians
> Against the thin faces of the poor . . .
>
> ('**Oriental Politics'**)[21]

against critics, who dig for the profound, and scholars (choosing a glittering fragment of Zen, or the cracked semblance of an Emblem . . .).

If I have been using terms like hostility, conflict, protest, antagonism, this has been in an effort to acknowledge a characteristic quality of Enright's poetry—that it is so honestly, so acutely personal. In these poems the poetry is of the person and the person is in the poetry. Which poses the question: what portrait—or since Enright works with light fleeting touches—what sketch of this person begins at length to appear? It seems to be that of someone who sees himself as small, unsuccessful and shabby, a half-deserving, half-predestined victim, the opposite of the big, booming canary in the cage who is:

> —Florid, complacent, rent-free and over-fed,
> Feather-bedded, pensioned, free from wear and tear.
>
> ('**Displaced Person Looks at a Cage-Bird'**)[22]

Not, it is clear, the central man, who presumably belongs to and unites both wings, but the wretched man in the middle like the lowest member of the great tribe of Wang:

> As the evening dies, their thoughts incline towards
>   both,
> neither quite present, neither quite absent.
> Would you call this exile? It seems like what life is.
>
> ('**Exile?'**)[23]

The model of this person is not 'the noble poet with his noble theme, *contemporain de jours prodigieux*', but the Egyptian student in Birmingham or the Japanese dancing girl or the workman grumbling mildly over his wage—people who don't know it all, who in a world tending to abolish it keep alive the old human habit of *naïveté*.

> Take solace where you find it. In your gardener, say—
> For bed and board, he chops the jungle from your
>   square of lawn.
> Perhaps he'll keep the queer old habit just alive . . .
>
> ('**Words Without Songs'**)[24]

Or perhaps he won't. Perhaps the jungle will choke the lawn.

Such is the *persona* of the observer in these poems of observation; and since there is in human nature an irresistible tendency to assimilate the seen to the seer (a tendency which becomes in the tension of art what Coleridge called a coincidence of subject and object), we find that for Enright the central, the establishing figure in life, is someone like this too. His representative character is the private man, the cheerful, stricken occupant of the middle air. He is the one with a hankering for health, physical and moral, who is just the same riddled by ordinary diseases and common faults. He suffers the usual sufferings in the usual way: he complains and puts up with them. He is neither innocent nor knowing. His standards have slipped a bit, but on the other hand he has broadened his acquaintance with the style of human beings. This is someone I can recognise—and not merely from looking outwards. His outline, his wrinkles and voice are all familiar and cherished. His existence, which these poems movingly evoke and confirm, is proof, a demonstration in today's words, of the survival, patient and resolute, of a common human being.

> Was Freud entirely right? We rise to chase those inner
>   phantoms,
> Who often end by chasing us. The sleeping dogs
> Start up from every corner: they have not read the
>   textbooks
> That bid us pat their heads. The only bone they want
>   is us . . .

Was Goethe wholly wrong? It is by onward striding
We lay our ghosts, he said. Seeking neither to avoid
  nor meet.
No tree stays small through fear of meeting lightning:
The strawberry finds its ripeness in the straw.
                  They grow,
  or rest,
In light or darkness. Doing what they have to do,
And suffering what, and only what, they must.

             ('Baie des Anges, Nice')[25]

Notes

1. *Some Men Are Brothers.*

2. *The Laughing Hyena.*

3. *Some Men Are Brothers.*

4. *Ibid.*

5. *Ibid.*

6. *Bread rather than Blossoms.*

7. *Some Men Are Brothers.*

8. *The Laughing Hyena.*

9. *'Life and Letters', in The Laughing Hyena.*

10. *The Laughing Hyena.*

11. *Bread rather than Blossoms.*

12. *Ibid.*

13. *The Laughing Hyena.*

14. *Some Men Are Brothers.*

15. *Ibid.*

16. *Ibid.*

17. *Ibid.*

18. *Ibid.*

19. *Bread rather than Blossoms.*

20. *Some Men Are Brothers.*

21. *Bread rather than Blossoms.*

22. *Some Men Are Brothers.*

23. *Ibid.*

24. *Ibid.*

25. *The Laughing Hyena.*

Michael Wood (essay date fall/winter 1975)

SOURCE: Wood, Michael. "Across the Irish Sea (Austin Clarke, Enright, Larkin)." *Parnassus* 4, no. 1 (fall/winter 1975): 41-49.

[*In the following excerpt, Wood gives a mixed review of Enright's* The Terrible Shears, *drawing a link between Enright's desire to present his past utterly without adornment and the flatness of some of the book's verse.*]

The subtitle of Enright's *The Terrible Shears* is "Scenes from a twenties childhood," but the scenes are really brief glimpses, thoughts, memories, moments the poet seems slightly surprised to have still in his possession: school, Christmas, books, knives, Cambridge, Grandma, Grandpa, Uncle Jack, the father's death, the death of a baby sister, the mother making do by keeping house for aging bachelors. There are all the ingredients here for a grim socialist novel, all humility and grueling hard work, or even for a working-class idyll, for that matter, all cheery pluck and heroic endurance, but what Enright gives us is the coolest of backward glances, a scrupulously unaccented version of his past. At times he seems to have shut himself out of these poems by sheer discretion, but in general the project of remembering without fuss a set of places and people and earlier selves that all now seem, even to Enright, quaint and scarcely believable, comes off extremely well. There are nice touches of wit—

    I don't remember learning about sex
    In the school lavatories;
    Though I remember the lavatories . . .

    Sickness too was different in those days,
    People tended to die of it . . .

—and there are poems that crackle along with a wonderful dry energy:

    A woman thrust her way into the house,
    Desirous to save the soul of a schoolboy.

    An obliging schoolboy, would do anything
    For peace, excepting kneel in public.
    But no, she would not go, she would not go,
    Till crack on their knees they fell together.
    His soul was lost forever . . .

    When Granpa wasn't pushing old ladies
    Through the streets of the Spa
    He would cut the grass on selected graves.
    Sometimes we went with him. Dogs
    Had done their business on the hummocks.
    The water smelt bad in the rusty vases.
    The terrible shears went clack clack . . .

But these alert rhythms are the exception in the book, and it rapidly becomes clear that Enright's virtues as a tough-minded rememberer don't really help his poetry much, indeed tend to do it in. Enright's signature in this volume is a flat, final line which occurs again and again, in all kinds of forms:

    But in the end I had to call my mother . . .

    Someone will pay for this . . .

    The Bath chair went back to the owners . . .

    It seemed hardly worth continuing with school . . .

Some years later he died without issue . . .

Perhaps there is nothing to remember . . .

"Putting up with things / Was a speciality of the age," Enright says, and "How docile the lower orders were / In those days." But the deadness, the glum *prose* of those closing lines, intended to thwart temptations to poetic uplift, comes out as another renowned English speciality: refusing to make a scene in a public. A poet who refuses so resolutely to make public scenes ends up not making poetry at all. I admire Enright's sentiments and intelligence a great deal, but ultimately *The Terrible Shears,* for all its scruples, seems a willful, almost an arty book, because it dresses up as strangled poetry what might have been a set of very attractive prose notes, and one wonders what prejudice drove Enright to a verse line he didn't need and couldn't make work often enough.

Douglas Dunn (essay date 1990)

SOURCE: Dunn, Douglas. "'The Thunder of Humanity': D. J. Enright's Liberal Imagination." In *Life by Other Means: Essays on D. J. Enright,* edited by Jacqueline Simms, pp. 74-87. Oxford: Oxford University Press, 1990.

[*In the following essay, Dunn discusses the connection between Enright's morality and his poetic style and concludes that the poetry written in Egypt and Japan counts as Enright's best.*]

You could tell that a state of mind was on its way out when it became fashionable to stick 'wishy-washy' in front of 'liberal'. It had begun to suffer from worthiness. A mentality that included a wide variety of practitioners, it looked as if it represented the *absence* of definition, whether politically, culturally, or intellectually; it looked too good to be true. Its political demise was more visible than any other. Ethical seriousness, intelligence, and humour had to be shown to the door by a re-energized Conservative Party whose 'liberals' did not survive for very long—they were called 'wets', an epithet rather similar to 'wishy-washy'. Militants on the Left went in for name-calling of the same pejorative order, and if something like a liberal mentality on the defensive suppressed stridency and rancour within the Labour Party, it has always looked more like an electoral strategy. One can always believe otherwise, of course.

To many, poetry seems ill at ease with the liberal intellect. Eccentricities, extremes, and the unpredictable fit poetry better, or so it is alleged, than the discriminatory and the reasonable. 'Ratiocination drives Poetry away', wrote Goethe, 'but she is a friend of what is reasonable.'

However, ratiocination is not the issue. Feeling and intelligence are at stake here, the friendship between Poetry and the reasonable. Their affinity might be elective as much as natural, for, like many states of virtuous concord, an affable relationship with one might mean that you don't see as much as you'd like of another, whose friends will accuse you of having made the wrong alliance. In D. J. Enright's poetry, for example, founded as it is on a liberal mentality, imagination plays a different role than in poetry where reasonable feelings take second place in deciding what is said and how.

As it develops through his first two or three books, Enright's style seeks to identify itself as on the side of clarity and plainness. It tends to the laconic and relishes brevity and the aphoristic. Increasingly, fat stanzas favoured for their intricate regularity, opulent figurativeness, ornamental diction, and anything associated with the prolix, will come to feel as if banished from his repertoire or never to have crossed his mind as possibilities. 'One represents an obscure and well-known poet', he says in **'The Peaceful Island'** where he throws stones at a row of empty bottles. Other targets for his good-natured vandalism include a pimp, a 'flinty industrialist', and someone 'expert in traditions and hopes for war'.

Attention paid to lives beyond his own feels like the compelling reason for the attitudes and stylistic formations of his poetry. In these earlier books the poems are quite self-consciously about facing up to reality and achieving a viable angle of approach to recent history and topical, observable scenes and people. In **'Life and Letters'** he withdraws from the temptation to exploit compassion for the victims of history. 'And history—my own—oh nothing more portentous—/ Pressed me both ways', is followed by a gesture in imagery that tries to invalidate Romantic grandiloquence: 'The near stars smelt of jasmine, and the moon—that huge fallafel—faintly of garlic.' Wittily, slyly, Enright has it both ways; as an antithesis, the line holds a lyrical perception and its wilfully demotic counterpart. 'For history—in the smallest sense—had fallen about me', continues his fastidious qualifications, stressing an attempted reasonableness that does not gainsay a lyric impulse—a sensible lyricism—and prepares for the poem's final lines:

> Which is why I try to write lucidly, that even I
> Can understand it—and mildly, being loath to
>   face the fashionable terrors,
> Or venture among sinister symbols, under ruin's
>   shadow.
> Once having known, at an utter loss, that utter
>   incomprehension
> —Unseen, unsmelt, the bold bat, the cloud of jasmine,
> Truly out of one's senses—it is unthinkable
> To drink horror from ink, to sink into the darkness of
>   words,

> Words one has chosen oneself. Poems, at least,
> Ought not to be phantoms.

>> (*CP* [*Collected Poems 1987*], 14)

Post-War disillusionment, together with the mercy of small pleasures, seem obvious sources of the feeling in **'Life and Letters'**. In a more general sense, what the poem rejects can be suggested by quoting four lines from Heine's 'Believe Me!' if only to point out that Enright's quarrel with poetic irresponsibility is a recurrent one:

> But songs and stars and flowers by the ton,
> Or eyes and moons and springtime sun,
> No matter how much you like such stuff,
> To make a world they're just not enough.[1]

Doubtless, Enright's strategy accorded to a considerable extent with how the literary times were tending in the shape of the Movement. Working abroad, however, as Enright chose or was fated to do for much of his life—Egypt, Japan, Germany, Thailand, and Singapore—detached him from at least the more crucial of those characteristically English restraints that fudge the point where poetry, society, and politics meet. History 'in the smallest sense' or history as 'portentous' fits in comfortably with English attitudes to ambition—'We were the Descendancy', he writes in **'Entrance Visa'**, 'Hurt but not surprised.' More than any other poet of his generation, he has been consistent in confronting social and political subjects with passionate intelligence and abundant feeling. Indeed, his work feels awkward in the context of the Movement, even if it shares in common with Larkin's poetry (for instance) a few general principles of style and attitude. Larkin's world, however, is astoundingly narrow when compared to Enright's international reach of Englishness. It would be unjust to say that he is more generous than Larkin; he is more generous than just about everybody.

Experience of Japan would leave Enright certain that 'Poems, at least, ought not to be phantoms', but any lingering trace of history as portentous or embarrassingly massive was to be modified by the need to reply to what he witnessed. His Japanese poems are populated by underdogs, beggars, typhoon victims, Hiroshima's casualties, bar-girls, and a suicidal shoeshine boy. It is a country in receipt of **'Edible Aid'**, with a strong presence of poverty and 'the monstrous life' that the seventeen syllables of *haiku* cannot express through its redundant preciosity. Sad, sorrowful poems that they are, they have touches of lightness, of a liberal sanity, or sometimes a sturdy metre, that enliven them in such a way as to place them on the side of conscience and responsibility, but at the same time they are complicated by Enright's temperamental hedonism. As much as anything else it might be a matter of tone:

> Only one subject to write about: pity.
> Self-pity: the only subject to avoid.
> How difficult to observe both conditions!
>
> . . . . .
>
> But make no mistake. Suffering exists, and most of it
>> is not yours.
> Good acts are achieved, as good poems are. Most of
> them
>> not by you.

> (**'How right they were, the Chinese poets'**, *CP,* 22)

Some of them even have a grumbling, grim humour—**'Displaced Person Looks at a Cage-Bird'**, or **'The Pied Piper of Akashi'**. A poem like **'Broken Fingernails'** remarks on its own methods while pictorializing a scene:

> A shabby old man is mixing water with clay.
> If that shabby old man had given up hope
> (He is probably tired: he has worked all day)
> The flimsy house would never have been built.
>
> If the flimsy house had never been built
> Six people would shiver in the autumn breath.
> If thousands of old men were sorry as you
> Millions of people would cough themselves to death.
>
> (In the town the pin-ball parlours sing like cicadas
> Do not take refuge in some far-off foreign allusion
> (In the country the cicadas sing like pin-ball parlours)
> Simply remark the clay, the water, the straw,
>> and a useful person.

>> (*CP,* 22)

Of a shoeshine boy who wanted to die because he had a headache:

> The policeman took it down, adding that
>> you were quite
> Alone and had no personal belongings, other than a
> headache.

'Elsewhere the great ones have their headaches, too', he continues,

> As they grapple with those notable tongue-twisters
> Such as Sovereignty and Subjection.
>> But they were not talking
>> about you,
> Kazuo, who found rat poison cheaper than aspirin.

> (**'The Short Life of Kazuo Yamamoto'**, *CP,* 17-18)

His idiom is undeceived; it conspires with what he observes to show that he is neither reconciled to bruising topicality nor Parnassianly detached. His acceptance of life is plain, ordinary, and critical in its recognition of human suffering; his detachment is an enabling artifice that creates a sympathetic angle of observation, a literary lens that makes it possible for him to record the scene while leaving room for comment. 'The poor are always with us. Only they can find a value in the new', for example, is pretty insolent in its implications as well as bald and laconic. **'Happy New Year'**, however, shows Enright close to his best, supple, almost funny in his depiction of a New Year encounter with a banker who bewails '"A hard year for Japan"'.

> He clapped me by the hand, he led me to his bright
>   new house.
> He showed his ancient incense burners, precious
>   treasures, cold and void.
> His family too he showed, drawn up in columns,
>   and his fluttering spouse.
> We bowed and wept together over the grim new year.
>
> I walked away, my head was full of yen, of falling
>   yen.
> I saw the others with their empty pockets,
> Merry on the old year's dregs, their mouths
>   distilled a warm amen!
>
> The poor are always with us. Only they can find
>   a value in the new.
> They are the masters of their fourpenny kites
> That soar in the open market of the sky.
> Whatever wrongs await, they still preserve some rites.
>
> *(CP, 19-20)*

Anachronistic or traditional Japan is contrasted with 'the new', and 'the others with their empty pockets' with the banker whose 'saké-smelling tear suffused his reddened eye'. It is remarkably simple, but also subtle, casual-seeming, though pruned to the bare bones of a narrative. 'And yet and yet' in the first stanza probably echoes the celebrated *haiku* by Issa written on the death of his only son, which acknowledges the limitations of Buddhist acceptance, and perhaps also of art and poetry:

> The world of dew
> Is a world of dew and yet,
> And yet.

That risky pun—'some rites'—is a long way from the manners of Japanese poetry. Its ruefulness feels peculiarly English; it is characteristic of Enright's injurious flippancy, the way in which he can rearrange the reader's expectation by guiding a dispiriting subject into humorous moments. Perhaps it is largely a matter of temperament that he can do this convincingly. In any case his writing depends on a personality more interesting than that of a man intent on telling stories of misfortune and poking you in the eye with pictures of deprivation.

His idiom becomes more grimly waggish in **'The Monuments of Hiroshima'**. Here his ruefulness makes him seem a *farceur* of apocalypse, but speaking on behalf of atomized victims. 'Little of peace for them to rest in', he says, 'less of them to rest in peace.' The skin creeps, not just at the fact, but the bleak joke of it, just as in the first two lines the English clichés of death feel as if they are being admonished at the same time as their demotic humour is savoured.

> The roughly estimated ones, who do not sort well
>   with our common phrases,
> Who are by no means eating roots of dandelion,
>   or pushing up the daisies.

The next verse works with something like a a dignified, negative lyricism, winking, perhaps, at graveyard poetry in the process, raising the tone:

> The more or less anonymous, to whom no human
>   idiom
>   can apply,
> Who neither passed away, or on,
>   nor went before, nor vanished on a sigh.
>
> *(CP, 19)*

Worthy gestures, big constructions, are diminished in proportion to how the dignity of the dead could be restored were there anything of them left to fit the average expectations of a coffin. Or not restored. Irony, after all, is irony—the creating of mental space within which a considerable degree of doubt is possible.

The oppositional sentiments of Enright's Japanese poems were probably too local for their force to be felt by some English readers of the time. In *Memoirs of a Mendicant Professor,* Enright stated that 'The blank unbridgeable chasm between an exquisite sensitivity towards the arts and a stolid insensitivity towards human suffering was just a little more than a Western softie like myself could accommodate.'[2] But if the immediate subjects of these poems are Japanese that does not suggest that we should fail to attend to the uninsular Englishness of a poetry already benefiting from an affection for Brecht and Cavafy as well as an expertly idiosyncratic interpretation of recent poets such as Lawrence, Auden, and MacNeice, perhaps even Kipling (those long lines, for example). There is something indigenously English about Enright's wit. His clownish, ironic sorrowfulness, his melancholy and his distrust of it, would seem to me to have a touch of Warwickshire about them. I can't help but quote a remark of Ford Madox Ford's from his *A History of Our Own Times*: 'a man must have a certain insularity if he is to live. Given that your glass is reasonably large it is out of your own glass that you had better drink.' What you put into your glass, of course, is entirely up to you.

Enright's hedonism is inseparable from his compassion. In *Memoirs of a Mendicant Professor* he wrote of Japanese bar-girls that 'These girls seemed to me instances of the most arrant, most heart-breaking wastage of human goodness which I had encountered outside books'. In **'Tea Ceremony'**, after dismissing Zen otherness, he takes sides with 'life-size people, / Rooted in precious little, without benefit of philosophy'. (Like MacNeice, he reloads clichés: 'Beyond the bamboo fence . . .'; 'precious little'; 'without benefit of . . .'.)

> So pour the small beer, Sumichan. And girls,
>   permit yourselves a hiccup, the thunder

Of humanity. The helpless alley is held by
   sleeping beggars under
Their stirring beards, and the raw fish curls
At the end of the day, and the hot streets cry
   for the careless scavengers.

                       (*CP*, 20-1)

These are exhilarating lines. Their rhetoric directs them into unusual literary territory—a mixture of a toast, an insult to ceremonial, advocacy, and the evocation of the circumstances of somewhere else—this latter element is not 'exotic', it is just interesting. **'Akiko San'** elegizes a bar-girl and is as affirmative as that passage from **'Tea Ceremony'**. However, the invention of 'a modest Jerusalem', and later 'Jerusalem' itself, indicate an affectionate defensiveness that rubs close to the sentimental. It is possible to agree with this poem and at the same time regret that it has stepped outside the lucid moral circumference of Enright's other Japanese poems. In **'Akiko San'** he is all wish and feeling. Its notes are sweet, but the more acidic tenderness, the stringency and ironic hygiene of the poems surrounding it, isolate **'Akiko San'** as a different kind of poem, leaving the impression that its whole-heartedness does not suit him, and that a different kind of equally whole-hearted commitment does.

Enright's Japanese poems have preoccupied me because they are so good. They are close to the thing itself as the fright of the world was in the 1950s. They show a 'liberal imagination' at full cry and dedicated to the reality of the moment:

And I, like other listeners,
See my stupid sadness as a common thing.
And being common,
Therefore something rare indeed.
The puffing vendor, surer than a trumpet,
Tells us we are not alone.
Each night that same frail midnight tune
Squeezed from a bogus flute,
Under the noise of war, after war's noise,
It mourns the fallen, every night,
It celebrates survival—
In real cities, real houses, real time.

     ('The Noodle-Vendor's Flute', *CP*, 32-3)

That an Englishman should have written about such feelings in the 1950s is not just exceptional, but, I believe, unique, given their particularity, and, that being the case, their universal extension. How impertinent of a poet, and an Englishman too, to put his finger on the pulse of a decade! And the vulgarity of it, the temerity, to write as if the world and its societies mattered more than poetry!—Why, that's what we expect of *foreigners*, like Camus, or Brecht! What insulting presumptuousness, to speak of 'real cities, real houses, real time', and yet he's talking about Japan! Talk about selling the pass? This man sells it *repeatedly*!

Discussions of recent English poetry have been prone to what Lionel Trilling described as 'irritable mental gestures which seek to resemble ideas'. Enright's absence from an intimate literary scene was therefore fortunate, an enabling circumstance, even if—especially in Singapore—survival at times depended on 'silence, exile, cunning, hysterics, sloth, "low posture" (as the sociologists call it) and simple-mindedness . . .' In any case, England, 'that nest of stinging birds', has always distrusted poetry when it touches on politics, a proximity which liberalism in literature takes for granted—or, in Trilling's words, 'the inevitable intimate, if not always obvious connexion between literature and politics'. And yet if there was an emotional topically in Larkin's poetry of the same period, supported by the realism of his urban imagery, that seems to be about as far as average taste was prepared to go. A less selfish, more damaging, more critical present-dayness always seems to court the suspicion of the English reader.

But like most writers of a liberal tendency Enright has been apolitical, a purveyor of benevolent anarchy. 'Political scientists, the morticians of our age', he says in *Memoirs of a Mendicant Professor*. It is not the remark of someone who takes politics seriously; or, rather, it is the opinion of a man who takes the consequences of politics very seriously indeed. Unlike most English poets he has elicited official wrath. His chastening experience in Singapore, and being beaten up by policemen in Bangkok (which left him sensitive to the 'faint but still perceptible odour of rubber truncheons') can be supposed to have stiffened his highly agreeable gift for speaking back, polishing, indeed, the brass of his neck. His writing certainly takes on a more hazardous immediacy. 'It's not the easy life you think, this sanity', he says, beginning **'Doctor Doctor'**, a tart but also funny portrayal of an expatriate predicament:

Look—
The streets fall down, and blame you
In cracked voices for expatriate indifference.
   . . . . .

Extending your feet to a baby bootblack
You perceive your shoes have been abducted.
Bar-girls will relieve you of the exact amount.
Do not argue. It is the exact amount.
   . . . . .

(You think it is easy, all this sanity?
Try it. It will send you mad.)
   . . . . .

On the walls, eastern godlings spew into pewter pots.
You have knocked everybody's drink over:
Everybody is drinking double brandy.

                       (*CP*, 75-6)

A freer verse with more room for impish humour forms an important element in the diffrence between the idiom of his poems of the Sixties onwards and the metrical style of his Japanese poems. Brecht and Cavafy seem to have been sources of guidance here, but influences explain less than we tend to believe in the determination of how and why a poet modifies his style. 'Why?' is in any case a more interesting question to put and the answer seems to be a simple need to reply to a climate of opinion which placed Enright in a position of alleged notoriety. Yet it is noticeable in the poem that the particularity of its subject coincides with an ability to universalize it. **'Doctor Doctor'** continues:

> Do not complain.
> In this world you have no alibi.
> You disagreed with history, now history disagrees
>   with you.
> 'Guilty'—plead this—'guilty but sane.'

Although still undeceived, Enright's poetry now becomes disenchanted; its purpose is to disenchant, but its scepticism and wit keep hopelessness at bay.

> Nothing human is alien to me.
> Except knives, and maybe the speeches
> Of politicians in flower.

> **('Political Meeting'**, *CP*, 68)

> In this vale of teargas

> Should one enter a caveat,
> Or a monastery?

> **('Unlawful Assembly'**, *CP*, 88-9)

> You need defeat's sour
> Fuel for poetry.
> Its motive power
> Is powerlessness.

> **('Cultural Freedom'**, *CP*, 92)

> The more rational you are
> (What you have paid for
> You will expect to obtain
> Without further payment)
> The less your chances of remission.

('How Many Devils Can Dance on the Point . . .', *CP*, 111-12)

With **'Prime Minister'**, **'Meeting the Minister for Culture'**, **'What became of What-was-his-name?'**, and **'Come to Sunny S'** Enright can be seen sailing close to the wind. He has described the first of these poems as 'harmless', and 'a not unsympathetic general study'—but we should not be taken in—'applicable to almost any Prime Minister of any newly independent country who finds himself under the necessity of issuing orders for the arrest of the young men so recently his comrades in the struggle against the imperialist power'. Although pirated by dissidents operating outside Singapore the poem did not land Enright in trouble. It is still uncompromising in its treatment of the psychol-

ogy of political ruthlessness. Psychological insight is also the strength of **'What became of What-was-his-name?'**

> Funny,
> After three years
> A new generation hangs around the place,
> Hardly one of them has heard of M—.
> It makes you feel your age.

> (*CP*, 80-2)

But as Enright says, the argument of his poem about a political prisoner backfired. 'All I had managed to do, it seemed, was to encourage a man to stay in prison.' M—, Enright thought, wasn't the sort to accept prison as a 'favourite freedom', which is sometimes the choice of professional martyrs.

> He seemed to me a food and drink man.
> But he must have done something very bad.
> The papers said nothing about it.

Actual circumstances and the cast of the poem are reminiscent of Brecht in poems like **'The Burning of the Books'**. Increasingly, Enright devoted his imagination to parable-making or the invention of witty narratives or poems of plain speaking. Liberalism, however, is seen as having backfired too. M—'s fate, Enright says, serves as 'an epitome of the liberal in the world as it is'. M—chose to go to jail, and stay there, rather than recant, even when imprisonment condemned him to total ineffectiveness.

> . . . the liberal, the man who believes in truth and justice, or in fairness and decency, he cannot be trusted. He is the enemy of all doctrine—it was his sort of person who said 'there is no general doctrine which is not capable of eating out our morality if unchecked by the deep-seated habit of direct fellow-feeling with individual fellow-men'—and every politician's hand will be against him. His politics were shifty to begin with and they will continue to be so. He sees good in practically everything, he sees bad in practically everything; he grants you your point, and then expects you to grant him a point in return. He cannot be relied on, he is undisciplined, unrealistic, ungrateful, and he pampers his little private conscience. Prison is his proper place.[3]

Enright is describing his own convictions in that marvellously nimble passage of simmering irony. Has any other contemporary British poet been so articulate in defence of the humanity which we all claim to believe in? I doubt it. Yet his sociable, garrulous, inventive, often funny poetry disdains the sombre garments of 'commitment' as that notion has been re-processed and over-exposed until it now lies down in a state of exhaustion. His commitment is diffuse; it is the weather of his poetry, and there is a satisfying amount of it. He is a poet who welcomes 'little mercies, / A something to be going on with'; he is also the poet of **'Dreaming in the Shanghai Restaurant'**—'I would like to be that elderly Chinese gentleman',

He is interested in people, without wanting to
      convert them or pervert them.
He eats with gusto, but not with lust;
And he drinks, but is not drunk.
He is content with his age, which has always suited
      him.
When he discusses a dish with the pretty waitress,
It is the dish he discusses, not the waitress.

. . . . .

I guess that for him it is peace in his time.
It would be agreeable to be this Chinese gentleman.

(*CP,* 59-60)

He is also the poet of *The Terrible Shears* and *Instant Chronicles,* an autobiographical poet who explains his life, recollects, sifts his memory for stories, and the poet of *Paradise Illustrated* and *A Faust Book,* a learned poet, a literary poet, but one who wears his erudition with playful lightness.

Personally, I believe Enright's poems written in Egypt and the Far East to be his best. What he lived and felt in Japan, Thailand, and Singapore, matters of daily witness, offered him a grimmer, more dramatic range of subjects than England afforded, and with them a more testing challenge to his tough-mindedness. Some sort of literary and personal release might also have been triggered off by being 'far from the home where the Beowulf roams'. Circumstances in the Far East made it natural that his poetry should reflect political realities. In *The Terrible Shears,* his attempt to write about social class is largely unconvincing. His poems set in the Far East are simply more ambitious, more sustained, more passionate than the snippets of *The Terrible Shears.*

To end by stating that Enright's Eastern poems are his best is not enough. They stand among the best poems of their time. Their gestures are exemplary. He faces the affronts of the world and does more than stay sane, but increases in sanity; and he perfects a style that is equal to dramatizing the emotional and intellectual experiences of witnessed poverty, hardship, authoritarian governments, unprincipled manœuvres of one kind or another, and the dismal fates which people are prone to have imposed upon them. All this, too, is conducted by a personality that is attracted to life's enjoyments. Perhaps his poetry is best read as testimony on how to stay sane in the world as it was, and as it is. 'Things aren't what they were, of course: they never were.'

Notes

1. Trans. Hal Draper, *The Complete Poems of Heinrich Heine* (OUP, 1982).

2. *Memoirs of a Mendicant Professor,* 38. That was in Japan. Enright then proceeds to indulge in a spot of tetchiness: 'But in England things were very different of course, it was not people who

suffered there, it was the arts and the intellect. So my mutterings seemed strangely incongruous, an outburst of Kulturbolschevismus which left Apeneck Amis looking like a museum curator. When I pleaded my case with Donald Davie (who had reviewed my Japanese poems) he remarked that it was queer and not right that disagreement about a body of poems should resolve itself into conflicting diagnoses about what was wrong with English or Japanese society, since that was the kind of thing which should concern us as intellectuals but not as poets. Yes, it was queer. I should have written the poems in Japanese, or else written them about England. Or better still, written aboutlessly.'

(See Donald Davie's essay, p. 150, later in this book, where he returns to the question. Ed.)

3. DJE, *Memoirs of a Mendicant Professor,* 174-5.

Select Bibliography

References in the book are to the page numbers of the paperback *Collected Poems 1987*

POETRY

Season Ticket, Aux Editions du Scarabée, Alexandria, 1948.

The Laughing Hyena and Other Poems, Routledge and Kegan Paul, 1953.

Bread Rather than Blossoms, Secker and Warburg, 1956.

Some Men Are Brothers, Chatto & Windus, 1960.

Addictions, Chatto & Windus, 1962.

The Old Adam, Chatto & Windus, 1965.

Selected Poems, Chatto & Windus, 1968.

The Typewriter Revolution and Other Poems, Library Press, New York, 1971.

Unlawful Assembly, Chatto & Windus, 1968.

Daughters of Earth, Chatto & Windus, 1972.

Foreign Devils, Covent Garden Press, 1972.

The Terrible Shears: Scenes from a Twenties Childhood, Chatto & Windus, 1973; Wesleyan University Press, 1974.

Rhyme Times Rhyme (juvenile), Chatto & Windus, 1974.

Sad Ires, Chatto & Windus, 1975.

Penguin Modern Poets, 26: Dannie Abse, D. J. Enright, Michael Longley, Penguin, 1975.

Paradise Illustrated, Chatto & Windus, 1978.

A Faust Book, OUP, Oxford and New York, 1979.

Collected Poems, OUP, 1981 (with new poems).

Instant Chronicles, A Life, OUP, 1985.

Collected Poems 1987 (enlarged edition), OUP, 1987 (including *Instant Chronicles,* additional poems, and new poems); paperback (Oxford Poets).

Selected Poems 1990 [from *Collected Poems 1987*], OUP, 1990, paperback (Oxford Poets).

NOVELS

Academic Year, Secker & Warburg, 1955; repr. Buchan & Enright, 1984; OUP (Twentieth-Century Classics) 1985.

Heaven Knows Where, Secker & Warburg, 1957.

Insufficient Poppy, Chatto & Windus, 1960.

Figures of Speech, Heinemann, 1965.

The Joke Shop (juvenile), Chatto & Windus, 1976; David McKay Co., New York.

Wild Ghost Chase (juvenile), Chatto & Windus, 1978.

Beyond Land's End (juvenile), Chatto & Windus, 1979.

ESSAYS

Literature for Man's Sake, Kenkyusha, Tokyo, 1955; repr. Richard West, 1976.

The Apothecary's Shop: Essays on Literature, Secker & Warburg, 1957; Dufour, 1959; repr. Greenwood Press, 1975.

Conspirators and Poets, Chatto & Windus, 1966; Dufour, 1966.

Man Is an Onion: Reviews and Essays, Chatto & Windus, 1972; Library Press, 1973.

A Mania for Sentences, Chatto & Windus, 1983; Godine, 1985.

The Alluring Problem, An Essay on Irony, OUP, 1986.

Fields of Vision, Essays on Literature, Language, and Television, OUP, 1988.

WRITINGS

A Commentary on Goethe's 'Faust', New Directions, 1949.

The World of Dew: Aspects of Living Japan, Secker & Warburg, 1955.

Robert Graves and the Decline of Modernism, lecture, Craftsman Press, Singapore, 1960. (Repr. in *Conspirators and Poets,* see above.)

Memoirs of a Mendicant Professor (autobiography), Chatto & Windus, 1969; repr. Carcanet Press, 1990.

Shakespeare and the Students, Chatto & Windus, 1970; Schocken, 1971.

EDITIONS AND ANTHOLOGIES

Poetry of the 1950's: An Anthology of New English Verse, Kenkyusha, Tokyo, 1955.

The Poetry of Living Japan (with Takamichi Ninomiya), John Murray, Grove, 1957.

English Critical Texts. 16th Century to 20th Century (with Ernst de Chickera). OUP, 1962.

John Milton, *A Choice of Milton's Verse,* introduced and selected, Faber, 1975.

Samuel Johnson, *The History of Rasselas, Prince of Abissinia,* with introduction, Penguin, 1976.

Oxford Book of Contemporary Verse, 1945-1980 (with introduction), OUP, 1980.

Oxford Book of Death (with introduction), OUP, 1983.

Fair of Speech, The Uses of Euphemism, ed. and contributor, OUP, 1985.

Faber Book of Fevers and Frets, Faber, 1989.

A. S. Byatt (essay date 1990)

SOURCE: Byatt, A. S. "A Sense of Religion: Enright's God." In *Life by Other Means: Essays on D. J. Enright,* edited by Jacqueline Simms, pp. 158-74. Oxford: Oxford University Press, 1990.

[*In the essay below, Byatt discusses the themes of faith and religion as they recur throughout Enright's writings, describing the poet's relation to religion as fundamentally ironic and often ambiguous.*]

'Strange that a sense of religion should / Somehow survive all this grim buffoonery!', reflects D. J. Enright, recalling his childhood Sundays in ***The Terrible Shears.*** That 'sense' did survive and indeed is pervasive, in his poetry. In the more recent ***Instant Chronicles,*** the 'short thoughts' include:

> Quite often heard to call on God—
> Though not expecting an answer.
>
> For who else could he call on—
> On some temporal lord and master?
>
> Angry with the one for being there;
> With the other for not, still angrier.
>
> (*CP* [*Collected Poems 1987*], 317)

Anger with God for being absent is one form of the Enright religion. Sometimes it appears that God was once there, and good, as in the poem **'High-mindedness of an English Poet'** which takes on the advocate of Job-like patience in modern politics.

Job is the case he cites
Whose readiness to sing
Under the frequent scourge
Was a fine and sacred thing—
But God was living then,

And you and I, my dear,
Seeing the bad go free
The good go by default
Know more than one sole state
Where this sweet bard would be
Appointed laureate.

(*CP* [*Collected Poems 1987*], 117)

This sense of the past existence of a good God is, however, comparatively rare. (Christ is different; we come to Him later.) Anthropos, feeling his age, also feels the death of God, but more as a loss of a sense of profundity in things. He has fewer things to hide from we are told. Religions are not supposed to burn him:

. . . Once there were torrents to cross,
Forests to explore, and the nature of God.
The objects that squat on his desk
Afford him no refuge.

(*CP*, 205-6)

The demonologizing of the desk-things is akin to much of the peculiar, not quite malign energy of modern non-mysterious objects in the most recent poems, such as **'Psalm for Supersunday'**.

The nature and origin of Enright's argument with God can be discerned, directly and obliquely, in ***The Terrible Shears***. There is a kind of sociological picture of accepted religion, its tedium and its fears and puzzles that most of us who are old enough will remember, working-class or not. The God of this world is a Sunday God, and the Sundays on which the child goes to Sunday School and the Church are seen, ironically, as at best, God's time off.

It was a far cry from that brisk person
Who created the heaven and the earth in
Six days and then took Sunday off.

(*CP*, 133-4)

The tone of the description of the Sunday School is childish mockery and adult pity and indignation mixed:

In Sunday school a sickly adult
Taught the teachings of a sickly lamb
To a gathering of sickly children.

Nevertheless it is at the end of this poem that Enright remarks on the strange persistence of a 'sense of religion', and concludes 'Perhaps that brisk old person does exist / And we are living through his Sunday.' Connected to this sense of Sunday emptiness, as opposed to fullness, is the child's inability to respond to

the masses of flowers in the town's gardens, admission free on Sundays. They 'were emblematic / Of something, I couldn't make out what'. They press round him, muttering 'too softly for me to hear':

I never learnt their true names.
If I looked at them now,
I would only see the sound of Sunday church bells.

(*CP*, 127)

The effect here of Sunday is, as so often in these poems, both muffling and deadening, and obscurely enlivening at the same time. The flowers never come to life in terms of the Pathetic Fallacy, but their Sundayness has its vitality.

The accounts of people are both comic and terrible, often both at once, depending on how seriously we take religion at all. The poet's mother is Protestant and has a Protestant mistrust of the religion of his father, a 'lapsed Catholic'.

My mother's strongest religious feeling
Was that Catholics were a sinister lot;
She would hardly trust even a lapsed one.
My father was a lapsed Catholic.

(*CP*, 133)

Here the word 'lapsed' carries also the weight of Enright's sense, wholly informing the language and the shape of the poems, of man's fallen nature. (Remember the Voice of the Bard, in the *Songs of Experience*, 'Calling the lapsed soul'.) Various short poems in this sequence enact the Fall, obliquely, ironically. Consider **'The Soul of a Schoolboy'**:

A woman thrust her way into the house,
Desirous to save the soul of a schoolboy.

An obliging schoolboy, would do anything
For peace, excepting kneel in public.

But no, she would not go, she would not go,
Till crack on their knees they fell together.
His soul was lost forever.

(*CP*, 150)

This is an anecdote, but it somehow makes us both smile and see the riddling weight of the words. 'Anything for peace' is embarrassed or evangelical. 'They fell together' neatly reverses the blundering evangelist's intention, and precisely. They fell *together*. Both sin. And the 'crack' is descriptive, and a Mephistophelean firework.

Equally succinct and full of import is the little poem, **'Two Bad Things in Infant School'**:

Learning bad grammar, then getting blamed for it:
Learning Our Father which art in Heaven.

Bowing our heads to a hurried nurse, and
Hearing the nits rattle down on the paper.

(*CP,* 123)

Here God, as throughout Enright's poems, is associated with language and fallen language. Our Father *which* art in Heaven has something grammatically wrong with it. Juxtaposition involves the blame for the grammar in the saying of the prayer. 'God is a harsh master, who put his creatures in the way of damning themselves and then went on damning them,' said Enright in his Introduction to his selection from *Paradise Lost.*[1] And the bowed head from which the nits fall is a secular bowing which echoes the prayer, comic, yes, but spreading into meaning, because the nits rattle down, they fall, like the sinful. Even the idea of paper connects the prayer to the written language, and the nits to bad words.

And the involvement of religion with language and eventually with poetry, for Enright, is seen in the poems, **'A Sign'** and **'It Is Poetry'**. In **'A Sign'** the young poet retrieves an old broken-backed Bible from the dustbin, describing his scandalized look, and restraint from chiding these 'blasphemers against God's Word'. He makes it quite clear what was sacred to *him*:

At that tender age I couldn't bear
To see printed matter ill treated.
I would have subscribed to the ancient
Oriental taboo against stepping light-
Mindedly over paper inscribed with characters.

(*CP,* 133)

His impressed elders see the episode in terms of religion:

It was read as a sign. The child
Is destined to become Vicar of the Parish Church!
He has rescued Religion from the scrap-heap.

But the poet does not leave us with the contrast between his true respect for print and his supposed respect for religion. Now, he tells us, he could watch unmoved the casting of hundreds of books into dustbins. But would still dive in after Shakespeare and the Bible. And the Bible retains its ambivalent significance.

The poem **'It Is Poetry'** seems at first to sit oddly in this sequence between a poem which begins 'Grandma doddered a bit, / But she was my friend,' and one about the gym teacher. It concerns the damned artist of Thomas Mann's *Doctor Faustus*, Leverkühn, and describes his 'last address / To the cultivated ladies and gentlemen'; these hearers are at first relieved to diagnose what he is saying as 'poetry' and then disturbed to realize they were 'hearing about damnation'.[2] The poem treats damnation and European literature, two preoccupations of the adult Enright, and

is placed where it is *because* it follows the extremely painful, if fiercely understated, description of the dispatch of Grandma to the Workhouse, which she feared. Enright asks,

Perhaps it had to be done,
Did it have to be done like that?

And he goes on to tell us:

It started me writing poems,
Unpleasant and enigmatic,
Which quite rightly no one liked,
But were thought to be 'modern'.

(*CP,* 142)

Here, in the juxtaposition of the local rage against the suffering of the helpless and the innocent, with high modernist art (*Doctor Faustus*) deriving from ancient myth and belief, is a kind of seed or paradigm of Enright's religious poetry.

One steady strand in it is a refusal to understand or accept the pain of the innocent, a refusal local and observed, as in the elegant poem, **'A Polished Performance'** about the large-eyed innocent girl, 'Perfect for the part', of a tourist attraction 'except for the dropsy / Which comes from polished rice'; but also connected to the theological anger of Ivan Karamazov, when Enright's Faust asks Mephistopheles 'Why is it little children suffer, / Guiltless beyond dispute?' and gets the bureaucratic and hellish answer:

'It passes understanding,'
    came the pious answer.
'It may surprise you, but in hell
We need to keep child-murderers and molesters
Segregated from the rest. Feelings run high.'

(*CP,* 220)

Because of his riddling tone of voice, matter of fact, funny and terrible, Enright can make us look at children in war, or depicted in the talons of Hokusai's 'Laughing Hyena, cavalier of evil', who holds

a child's head
Immobile, authentic, torn and bloody—
The point of repose in the picture, the point of movement in us.

(*CP,* 13)

Which says much about the relation of art to life, of what it is to be 'moved', of evil. In a coolly balanced early poem about the Chinese poets, he begins:

Only one subject to write about: pity.
Self-pity: the only subject to avoid.

And ends with a kind of invocation of the absent deity:

One thing is certain. However studious we are, or
   tough,
Thank God we cannot hope to know
The full horror of this world—or whole happiness.

(*CP*, 22)

In an essay in *Fields of Vision*, 'What happened to the
Devil?', Enright is dismissive about modern theology's
lack of interest in Evil. He is reviewing Jeffrey Burton
Russell's *Lucifer,* and endorses Russell's view that 'at a
time when evil threatens to engulf us totally, when evil
has already claimed more victims this century than in
all previous centuries combined', churchmen evince a
lack of interest in the concept.

> Russell opines that some modern theologians have been
> motivated by the thought that the subtraction of Devil /
> Evil from Christianity would 'remove barriers' and 'be
> ecumenical'. Yet it is barely credible that theologians
> could soft-pedal Devil / Evil purely as a tactical,
> popularizing measure: their personal belief in him / it
> would surely need to have waned already. (Otherwise,
> one takes it, they would scarcely leave moral damna-
> tion to Chief Constables.) To get rid of God will remove
> barriers, too, and prove even more ecumenical, for it
> admits convinced atheists to the Church. Why nibble
> away at such marginal matters as the Immaculate
> Conception, the Virgin Birth, the loaves and fishes, the
> Resurrection? As for the Crucifixion, it was all so very
> long ago, as they say, that by the grace of God it may
> not be true.[3]

And again, in this context, he quotes Mann's *Faustus,*
where Leverkühn's 'polymorphous visitor' tells him
that only the Devil now speaks of religion: 'Who else, I
should like to know, is to speak of it today? Surely not
the liberal theologian! After all I am by now its sole
custodian! In whom will you recognize theological
existence if not in me?' It is as though Enright's interest in, if not need for, religion, arises from the certain
existence of the principle of evil, which entails the
desire, if never the certainty, for the existence of
theological good. In his sequences on *Paradise Lost*
and *Faust* he takes on the two most persuasive, elegant,
and verbally inventive literary personifications of evil,
Milton's spirited sly snake and Goethe's (and
Marlowe's) damned and witty Mephistopheles. Both
involve evil in the attractions of language and know
about damnation. The God in both sequences, by
contrast, is a dubious and detached Creator, a kind of
poet who uses poetry to evade humanity and the vigorous human (fallen) users of language. It seems necessary to quote the whole of the following poem, since
editing it distorts it.

> *Walking in the Harz Mountains,*
> *Faust senses the presence of God*
>
> God was a brooding presence.
> Brooding at present over new metres.
> In which his creatures could approach him,

In which they could evade him,
—And he be relieved of their presence,
Through art as Proxy Divine—
Sublimation, as they termed it,
Which could very nearly be sublime—
For which he was truly thankful.

But how active they were, the bad ones!
They brooded rarely.
They talked incessantly,
In poisoned prose from pointed tongues.
How gregarious they were!
They needed friends to wound.

But who had invented tongues?
(One had to be careful when one brooded.)
And even the better ones
(One had to remember)
Were only human . . .
He started to fashion a special measure
For the likes of Gretchen, a still, sad music.

Creation was never finished.

(*CP*, 241)

This God is weary, reluctant to bother his patrician self
(note the use of the reserved 'one', isolating the unique
divinity from even the 'better ones' in plural humanity).
He is a travesty of the romantic God as artist—his art is
a secularized Christ—a 'Proxy Divine'—but its purpose
is to distance the creatures. He invents Wordsworth's
'still, sad music of humanity' for the likes of Gretchen,
the innocent victims, but his concerns are aesthetic. The
last line is splendidly ambiguous. It is God's fatigue
with creation. It is the human sense that there is
something lacking, something indeed not finished about
our raw world. The still, sad music plays, but the devil
has all the best tunes. This God as artist is related to an
earlier Enright God as poet, working at night, attracting
insects to his desk-lamp:

> . . . He gives, He also takes away.
>
> The insects love the light
> And are devoured. They suppose
> I punish them for something,
> My instrument the spring-jawed dragon.
>
> It isn't difficult to be a god.
> You hang your lantern out,
> Sink yourself in your own concerns
> And leave the rest to the faithful.

('**The Faithful**', *CP*, 101)

Both good and evil, and their myths and religious forms,
are for Enright bound up in the nature of poetry and the
imagination. In the essay on the Devil I've already
quoted, he analyses the myth of Frankenstein's Monster
(a kind of unfinished Adam, requiring love and dignity
from his incompetent creator) and that of Dracula (an
embodiment of involuntary, evil destructiveness) as
persisting relics in our culture of 'metaphysical
anxieties':

What this phenomenon, this secret perturbation, has to do with *belief,* to what extent believing is involved, is hard to say. The postulation of a half-way house between belief and disbelief is the best we can manage; that famous 'willing suspension of disbelief for the moment' doesn't fill the bill, nor does the 'hoping' (or fearing) 'it might be so' of Hardy's poem, 'The Oxen'. We can agree with William James that what keeps religion going is 'something else than abstract definitions and systems of concatenated adjectives, and something different from faculties of theology and their professors'. And we shall probably find it easier to assent to Octavio Paz's summing-up: 'Although religions belong to history and perish, in all of them a non-religious seed survives: poetic imagination.' Yet the relationship between imagination and belief remains an indecipherable mystery.[4]

It is in this context that the project of reworking, in ironic, cross-referring fragments, the two great myths of Western salvation and damnation, seems so splendidly ambitious. This essay is about God, not about language, even though God originated the tongues in which we damn ourselves so inventively. The poem in *Sad Ires* on the **'Origin of the Haiku'** is a paradigm in little of the procedures, also in little, but not little, of *Paradise Illustrated* and *A Faust Book.* It opens Miltonically

> The darkness is always visible
> Enough for us to write.

goes on to relate all the 'pain' (pains of hell, pains of composition, strictly incomparable?) of making seventeen syllables, relates how a 'desperate faction' proposed to bring in rhyme, and how they were defeated:

> We are a conventional lot,
> This is a conventional spot,
> And we take some satisfaction
> In writing verse called *free.*

It goes on to appropriate, miniaturize, and yet to enliven and continue, the language of Milton's great myth:

> In between we make up epigrams.
> 'Not to know me argues yourselves unknown',
> Or 'What is else not to be overcome?'
> The mind is sometimes its own place.

—this last a splendidly ironic statement, since its space is two quotations from God and Satan respectively, and its (original) context is lack of freedom.

> Such petty projects—
> Yes, but even an epic,
> Even *Paradise Lost,*
> Would look puny
> In hell, throughout eternity . . .
>
> (*CP,* 157-8)

Space, time, eternity, poetry, heaven and hell, and a technical exercise, all connected. An equal sense of crafted proportion and huge disproportion. Language,

including Milton's, saves. Language does nothing at all about the fact that Enright keeps echoing and half-echoing, 'Why, this is Hell, / And we are in it.' Or 'Y this is L / Nor-my-outfit.'

The Paradise myth, Enright claimed, although it had been criticized for not holding any enduring truth, did, on the contrary,

> engage readers (in diverse Asian countries, for example) who are not Christian either by conviction or, laxly, by environment. For it is the story of our first parents, of the birth of moral consciousness, and preeminently of the perversity in human nature whereby man destroys his happiness even when outward circumstance works in its favour and to his benefit. The Christian myth in some of its elements exerts a greater persisting influence on—or is more actively central to—not only our ethics (increasingly international) but also the darker places of the human psyche than is often supposed, even (or especially) by its conscious adherents.[5]

Enright incarnates this myth, in accounts farcical, grim, joky, of our incorrigible sinfulness. I like particularly, in this context, his picture of himself teaching Hopkins in the Orient (**'More Memories of Underdevelopment'**):

> 'God's most deep decree
> Bitter would have me taste: my taste was me.'

The poet describes himself as a 'lapsed Wesleyan' (lapsed again) who is teaching Father Hopkins to 'these young though ageless Catholics'. He asks

> A lurching humanist,
> Is it for me to instruct you in the fall complete?

He himself is ironically moved by Hopkins's words:

> Yet these words appal me with recognition,
> They grow continuously in terror.

Yet his innocent charges assume that his response is due to his age:

> Oh yes, they tell themselves, the poor old man,
> His taste is certainly him . . .
> And they turn to their nicer thoughts,
> Of salted mangoes, pickled plums, and bamboo shoots,
> And scarlet chillies, and rice as white as snow.
>
> (*CP,* 103)

Their image of themselves is an unfallen paradise, yet it contains a hint of Christian iconography in the last line—though their sins are as scarlet, yet they shall be washed whiter than snow—which is ambiguous, if read one way. Either in this land Christian myths are without force, and scarlet and white tastes are nothing to do with original sin. Or the sin lurks in the innocent taste, as it does in the flowery crown of Marvell's Little T. C., for instance. Either way the contrast between the lapsed humanist with his powerful sense of innate evil and the colourfully wholesome young is piquant.

Such ambiguous resonances have been the stuff of religious poetry through the centuries. I want finally to consider a peculiar kind of Christian presence in Enright's presentation of ordinary language and culture in our demythologized world. In *Paradise Illustrated,* language is the naming of things, pre- and postlapsarian, flowers and creatures before the Fall—'Avalanches, defoliation, earthquakes, eruptions . . . Also perhaps inclemency', as Adam remarks in a fit of 'airy' inventiveness (XIII). In the *Faust Book* language is romantic, as we have seen in the Harz Mountains, or may see in Mephistopheles's argument with the simple primrose. In *Paradise Illustrated* (XIX) Raphael tells Adam that a long book will be written about this very matter, and suggests that the real hero is the Son.

In Section XVIII God and the Son have a dialogue:

> 'My sole complacence,
> Radiant image of My Glory!'
>
> 'What I mean precisely.
> Much further, Father. You must love—
> And love what's hard to love.'
>
> 'Too much talk of love.
> Die man, or someone else must die.'
>
> 'Account me man *pro tem.*
> *Pro tem* account me man.'
>
> Nothing was said about a cross.
> By now the quire was in full swing.
>
>   (*CP,* 187)

I think it is not fanciful to see in the accountant's language, *pro tem,* a version of the Incarnation in the vulgar and mundane—and temporal. In the context of the reduced epic, the language has its Herbertian riddling ambiguity. But in our world, as Enright shows, the myths can be strangely inert, can bristle with oddity and a kind of questionable vampiric life.

There is, again, a childish or innocent version of what I mean in *The Terrible Shears,* in which secular things acquire the moral and emotive power of the sacred ones, even challenge them, as when the poet reflects on the worse fate of women ('**Religious Phase**'):

> He was on secondment. At no time
> Was he ignorant of his state.
>
> His ignorant bewildered mother
> Was another matter.
> In our street the pangs of labour
> Were nearer than those of crucifixion.
> Carpenters were useful, but
> Every family required a mother.
>
>   (*CP,* 149-50)

This draws its strength from its plainness and its relation to what we are told about the poet's mother. More ambivalent in its tone is one of the little poems about Christmas:

> The cracked oilcloth is hidden
> By knife-creased linen.
> On it bottles of Vimto squat,
> A few flakes of browning tinsel
> Settle. It is Christmas—
> Someone will pay for this.
>
>   (*CP,* 123)

'Someone will pay' is the sober truth, and the ironic reference to the atonement that follows the celebration of the birth. Here again the once powerful meanings of the phrases haunt the solid and daily. Something similar is happening in the poem '**Remembrance Sunday**', from *Sad Ires:*

> The autumn leaves that strew the brooks
> Lie thick as legions.
>   Only a dog limps past,
> Lifting a wounded leg.
>   Was it the rocket hurt it?
> Asks a child.
>   And next comes Xmas,
> Reflects the mother in the silence,
> When X was born or hurt or died.
>
>   (*CP,* 173)

This is beautiful and complex, in its contrast of the Miltonic and Dantesque fallen soldiers with the blunt ciphered absence of X, to whom it is all one, whether he was born or hurt or died—he is humanized by the word 'hurt' which carries pain and power. Between Milton and X are a dog (a limp and wounded God?— see the *Faust Book* on dogs and poodles) and a child, concerned with rockets. But this poem too evokes what has gone from our culture, X.

The 'feel' of the presence and absence of Christ is different in a poem like '**The Stations of King's Cross**', which is bizarrely witty, straining for effect, a kind of modern Gongorism. It finds the Passion in ordinary language with fiendish ingenuity.

> At Hammersmith the nails
> At Green Park the tree.
>   . . . . .
>
> He speaks to the maidenforms of Jerusalem
> Blessed are the paps which never gave suck.
>   . . . . .
>
> The first fall, the second fall
> The third fall.
> And more to come.
>
> A sleeve goes, a leg is torn
> A hem is ripped.

This is the parting of garments.

They mock him, offering him vodka.
The effect is shattering.

He is taken down from the strap.
And deposited.

Wilt thou leave him in the loathsome grave?

(*CP*, 156-7)

What sort of poem is this? Why describe the hazards of modern tube-travel in terms of the ancient and once-believed-in journey of the god-man to torture and death? It is not, as we have seen, that Enright takes pleasure in iconoclasm, nor is it any kind of fashionable sick wit. What I think it is is a showing-up of the *vanishing* of what was the centre of our public culture and private myths. Only those of us who know these myths or stories will pick up the system of connections at work. If we do, we will be made uncomfortably aware of the absence from much public life now of any interest in, or ability to make, such connections. Why this is hell nor are we out of it, might indeed be jocularly said of strap-hanging, but this Hell will not be harrowed, and if there is no Man to speak for the strap-hanger, his small concerns will remain small. The language, however, always for those of us who can read it, has acquired a new and savage vitality, almost demonic?

Some of Enright's very recent poems have made me laugh aloud, almost hysterically, partly because they were verbally funny, but partly because they called up obscure emotions I feel, as a resolute anti-Christian, about the vanishing of the whole culture, the whole spread of heaven, hell, and suffering meaning I grew up with. Such poems, or proses, are **'Agape'**, **'Psalm for Supersunday'** and **'Prayer'**.

'Agape' is about the question of whether God struck York Minster because of the consecration of the Bishop of Durham. It rollicks. It is rather naughty, or wicked, in its suggestion that the old God might after all act in a traditional manner and smite those he was displeased with. But its language is couched in a mad debating form that leaves no opening for such a vision:

question: Why did God not strike Durham Cathedral?
 Is it
suggested that His aim is uncertain?

answer: In His mysterious way He reveals that He
 moves in a
mysterious way.

question: Though less mysterious, would it not have
 been
more to the point to strike down Arthur Scargill?

rebuke: The Archbishop of Canterbury does not care
 for talk
of divine intervention unless properly vouched for.

(*CP*, 353)

What is the effect of this? Some people laugh a great deal when I show it to them; some look pained, at bad taste or triviality. I myself believe that the poem *is* a light-hearted but devastating attack on the deadness of modern religion, on the lifelessness acknowledged by Leverkühn's lively visitor. God does not strike any longer. When he appears to, we know it is not him, because we know he is not there (as the Bishop of Durham probably knows also.) What religion we have has no poetic or other vitality. To spell this out is to do the poem a disservice. It works in contrast to the God we all learned about in school, in hours of boredom and flashes of sublimity and vision. It proclaims his absence and ineffectiveness. His mysterious ways are merely a tautology.

'Psalm for Supersunday' is naturalized religion with a vengeance—or not, since it is all safe and sanitized? The supermarket is sanitized, but not Enright's demonic language. This psalm addresses the entropic final vision of the Sunday 'brisk person' of *The Terrible Shears,* and it presents simultaneously the resolutely unheard cry of this person's Proxy Divine, the incarnate, the ruthlessly demythologized and annihilated Christ:

There on the right you shall find bread, white and brown, sliced and unsliced; and on the left new wine in new bottles, made to make men glad. Vinegar is displayed elsewhere and, in Toiletries, sponges.

This was somebody's flesh and blood, they say, speaking metaphorically. The Supermarket, as likewise the lesser clergy, has set its face against metaphors, save in promotional literature. The beef is immaculately presented, not conceived; the lamb will never rise again.

(*CP*, 354)

This is demythologized and desacralized. Bread and wine, vinegar and sponge, are stripped of their associations. The mention of metaphor is peculiarly interesting, because it is detached from any context of meaning. 'They say' this was 'somebody's flesh and blood', where 'they' is vanishing, gossipy, and vague—who say?—and 'someone' is more pallid, amorphous, and ineffective than the X of the earlier poem in which he was born or hurt or died. The vanishing of our contexts and meanings is enacted at us, but because we can still pick up these inert references and remember the power that was in them, they are a form of torment for us. I think the absence of metaphor is more unpleasant than the commercial world of the Sunday Supermarket; to my ear the final secular joke about the cash registers—'Hearken to the sound of bells'—is funnier, perhaps because the joke about money as an alternative God is old, whereas the absence of metaphor and myth is not. Though one remembers, as perhaps was appropriate in the earlier context of the Sunday flowers in which the poet would now 'see' only 'the sound of Sunday church bells', one of George Herbert's lovely, multifarious metaphors for prayer, uniting Heaven and earth, 'Church bells beyond the stars heard'. Enright's absent God at his best and most desired is most often Herbert's God, whose voice, Christ's voice, Enright's Faust hears in parenthesis, signing his demonic contract:

> (Some other words were heard in Faustus' mind.
> *There is in love a sweetnesse readie penn'd:*
> *Copie out onely that, and save expense—*
> But reason could not tell him what they meant.)

Which brings me to a final poem, appropriately entitled 'Prayer'. This again looks like a squib, a verbal *tour de force,* a kind of wicked game with the respectably sacred. But it is not finally that, though it depends upon arbitrary puns (sin / sun / cindy / Sunday) for part of its effect. Much of what I have been looking at in this essay is given a new shape here, at once grisly and gentle, bereft of significance and full of pain, immersed in the world of post-Sunday *pro tem* accountancy. It is awfully funny. Like the world, according to Enright.

> O Cindy
> You who are always well-groomed and cheerful
> As we should be
> Who tie your hair back before going to ballet school
> As we should do
> Who take good care of your costly vestments
> As we should take
> Who is put to bed and made to get up
> Who speak in silent parables
> Concerning charm and deportment and a suitable mar-
>   riage
>   to a tennis star and yachts and a rich social life
> Who grow old like us
> Yet unlike us remain for ever young
> Whose hair is torn out at times
> Whose arms are broken
> Whose legs are forced apart
> Who take away the sin of the world
> To whom a raggedy doll called Barabbas is preferred
> You who are scourged
> And given vinegar to drink from a jar of pickled
>   onions
> Who seem to say, Why have you forsaken me?
> Who like us may rise or may not from the dead
>   in a long white garment
> You after whom the first day of the week is almost
>   named
> Into your hands we commend ourselves.

(CP, 355)

Notes

1. *A Choice of Milton's Verse,* Faber and Faber, 12.

2. This poem is quoted in full by Donald Davie, see p. 156, as is 'A Polished Performance', p. 152.

3. DJE, [D.J. Enright] *Fields of Vision,* 99.

4. *Fields of Vision,* 110.

5. *A Choice of Milton's Verse,* 11.

Select Bibliography

References in the book are to the page numbers of the paperback *Collected Poems 1987*

POETRY

Season Ticket, Aux Editions du Scarabée, Alexandria, 1948.

The Laughing Hyena and Other Poems, Routledge and Kegan Paul, 1953.

Bread Rather than Blossoms, Secker and Warburg, 1956.

Some Men Are Brothers, Chatto & Windus, 1960.

Addictions, Chatto & Windus, 1962.

The Old Adam, Chatto & Windus, 1965.

Selected Poems, Chatto & Windus, 1986.

The Typewriter Revolution and Other Poems, Library Press, New York, 1971.

Unlawful Assembly, Chatto & Windus, 1968.

Daughters of Earth, Chatto & Windus, 1972.

Foreign Devils, Covent Garden Press, 1972.

The Terrible Shears: Scenes from a Twenties Child-hood, Chatto & Windus, 1973; Wesleyan University Press, 1974.

Rhyme Times Rhyme (juvenile), Chatto & Windus, 1974.

Sad Ires, Chatto & Windus, 1975.

Penguin Modern Poets, 26: Dannie Abse, D. J. Enright, Michael Longley, Penguin, 1975.

Paradise Illustrated, Chatto & Windus, 1978.

A Faust Book, OUP, Oxford and New York, 1979.

Collected Poems, OUP, 1981 (with new poems).

Instant Chronicles, A Life, OUP, 1985.

Collected Poems 1987 (enlarged edition), OUP, 1987 (including *Instant Chronicles,* additional poems, and new poems); paperback (Oxford Poets).

Selected Poems 1990 [from *Collected Poems 1987*], OUP, 1990, paperback (Oxford Poets).

NOVELS

Academic Year, Secker & Warburg, 1955; repr. Buchan & Enright, 1984; OUP (Twentieth-Century Classics) 1985.

Heaven Knows Where, Secker & Warburg, 1957.

Insufficient Poppy, Chatto & Windus, 1960.

Figures of Speech, Heinemann, 1965.

The Joke Shop (juvenile), Chatto & Windus, 1976; David McKay Co., New York.

Wild Ghost Chase (juvenile), Chatto & Windus, 1978.

Beyond Land's End (juvenile), Chatto & Windus, 1979.

ESSAYS

Literature for Man's Sake, Kenkyusha, Tokyo, 1955; repr. Richard West, 1976.

The Apothecary's Shop: Essays on Literature, Secker & Warburg, 1957; Dufour, 1959; repr. Greenwood Press, 1975.

Conspirators and Poets, Chatto & Windus, 1966; Dufour, 1966.

Man Is an Onion: Reviews and Essays, Chatto & Windus, 1972; Library Press, 1973.

A Mania for Sentences, Chatto & Windus, 1983; Godine, 1985.

The Alluring Problem, An Essay on Irony, OUP, 1986.

Fields of Vision, Essays on Literature, Language, and Television, OUP, 1988.

WRITINGS

A Commentary on Goethe's 'Faust', New Directions, 1949.

The World of Dew: Aspects of Living Japan, Secker & Warburg, 1955.

Robert Graves and the Decline of Modernism, lecture, Craftsman Press, Singapore, 1960. (Repr. in *Conspirators and Poets,* see above.)

Memoirs of a Mendicant Professor (autobiography), Chatto & Windus, 1969; repr. Carcanet Press, 1990.

Shakespeare and the Students, Chatto & Windus, 1970; Schocken, 1971.

EDITIONS AND ANTHOLOGIES

Poetry of the 1950's: An Anthology of New English Verse, Kenkyusha, Tokyo, 1955.

The Poetry of Living Japan (with Takamichi Ninomiya), John Murray, Grove, 1957.

English Critical Texts. 16th Century to 20th Century (with Ernst de Chickera). OUP, 1962.

John Milton, *A Choice of Milton's Verse,* introduced and selected, Faber, 1975.

Samuel Johnson, *The History of Rasselas, Prince of Abissinia,* with introduction, Penguin, 1976.

Oxford Book of Contemporary Verse, 1945-1980 (with introduction), OUP, 1980.

Oxford Book of Death (with introduction), OUP, 1983.

Fair of Speech, The Uses of Euphemism, ed. and contributor, OUP, 1985.

Faber Book of Fevers and Frets, Faber, 1989.

Peter Firchow (essay date autumn 1994)

SOURCE: Firchow, Peter. Review of *Old Men and Comets* by D. J. Enright. *World Literature Today* 68, no. 4 (autumn 1994): 815.

[*In the following essay, Firchow reviews* Old Men and Comets, *finding this later work as of a piece with Enright's early poetry.*]

Have the angry young men of the fifties turned into the embittered old men of the eighties and nineties? The answer, to judge by D. J. Enright's latest volume of poems, **Old Men and Comets,** must be an ambiguous "yes." Not that Enright and most of his fellow poets of the so-called Movement ever were particularly angry—irritated is perhaps a more accurate word for his sometimes emotional state, though not really a word well suited for publicity purposes (would we still remember a movement of merely "irritated young men"?), so that his seeming disillusion strikes no grand Yeatsian note either. On the whole, it's pretty mild stuff, at least on the surface.

Underneath, to be sure, it can be a little different. Enright's apparently whimsical title, after all, is taken from Swift, who tells us that "old men and comets have been reverenced for the same reason: their long beards and pretences to foretell events." Well, Enright (b. 1920) is now certainly a man old in years, but having remained clean-shaven, it would appear he is meant to be reverenced primarily for his alleged prophetic qualities. Are we then to believe that this poet of cool understatement has now recanted and gone vatic? A comet blazing in the sky, lighting up the darkness, even if only momentarily? A bright star leading us to some new revelation? No, not really, for there's none of Swift's savage indignation in any of this mostly disgruntled augurizing. When Enright peers through a glass darkly, it tends to be filled with beer. Nothing new here; it's the same old ironic brew he's always served.

And that's just how it's intended to be, of course. No grand gestures for those who are now old any more than for those who were once young. No sudden wayside encounters with Crazy Jane's progeny, just an occasional overhearing of a few senile pensioners gossiping in the post office. No beasts slouching off anywhere, just a few, mostly imaginary muggers; no terrible beauties or even not-so-terrible ones, though everything is indeed a little altered, mostly for the worse. There are now more TV cliches, more trivia, more ignorance. Whither is all this leading? More of the same, it looks like. That's the general prediction that runs through this collection, one for which Enright will get precious little reverence—not that he expects any. Our age, we are made to realize, is not one in which "reverence" is an operative concept. It is here perhaps that Enright's vision begins to approach Swift's.

Actually, at least as many of the poems in *Old Men and Comets* look back as look forward, probably more. There's a lot of reminiscing, a lot of invidious comparing past with present, mostly to the detriment of the latter. It's never a whining nostalgia, though; the persona of the poet is always somehow included in the censure, always an attendant lord who will do to swell a scene or two. But even so, there's nothing secondary about these poems. The world they describe may be mediocre and disappointing, but the manner in which they describe it is often memorable and brilliant. "Age is a side-effect of youth," the speaker of **"GP"** tells us, catching just the right note of false euphemism that characterizes late-twentieth-century newspeak. Some of the formal or formless miniatures in the collection (especially the dream fragments) are similarly aphoristic and incisive, though on the whole the mood is one of humor rather than satire. The exception here is the poetry dealing with China and Singapore, toward whose authoritarian social policies Enright displays quite overt displeasure.

These poetic ruminations of the old Enright will, if he is right in his prediction, meet with no reverence, but they should and—I venture to predict—will meet with considerable and deserved admiration. His may not be the biggest or brightest comet in the sky, but it still burns with a steady, reliable, if ironic glow. Let us hope it will come our way again soon.

Janet Montefiore (essay date 1998)

SOURCE: Montefiore, Janet. "A Wise Poet: D. J. Enright." In *Arguments of Heart and Mind: Selected Essays 1977-2000*, pp. 165-76. Manchester: Manchester University Press, 2002.

[*In the following essay, originally published in 1998, Montefiore discusses Enright's evolving poetic voice with examples taken from each stage of his career.*]

D. J. Enright spent most of his working life in Egypt, Germany and the Far East, to whose challenge his poetry responds with wit, humanity, lightly worn learn-ing and an alert, discomposing intelligence standing, as Forster said of Cavafy, 'at a slight angle to the universe'.[1] He is conventionally known as a 'Movement' poet,[2] yet for all their reticence and irony his poems now look closer to Stevie Smith or Brecht than to the crafted formality and English provincialism of Amis or Larkin. Although Enright's voice is so individual, its tones alter considerably through the 505 pages separating the first shocked, enchanted encounter with ancient and modern Egypt in **'Deir El Bahari: Queen Hatsheput's temple'** from the last wry, anecdotal **'Hospital Journal'**, where a deranged fellow-patient shouts from the next bed: 'I want the languages,' he says. / One knows the feeling. / No, he wants the sandwiches.'[3] The distance between this dry, chilling comedy and the early lyricism is suggested in the late poem **'Since Then'**, a two-page list of surrealist new crimes and punishments, ending '"Fair do's," murmured the old Adam, "I am well pleased." / He had come a long way since he named the animals.'[4]

The compassionate ironist with his increasingly dark perception of the human condition has also come a long way since, dazzled by the Alexandrian light, he wrote his loose-knit, long-lined free verse meditations on the transforming powers of art. Entranced with the power of imagination and more inclined towards epiphany than anecdote, these early pieces come surprisingly close, considering the poet's reputation for scrupulous fidelity to human realities, to aestheticising their encounters with the world. Only the autobiographical **'First Death'**, un-selfpitying and obliquely told, points towards the later sparely anecdotal poems. Often the young Enright spells out things which he later prefers to leave powerfully implied, explaining after experiencing a moment of crazy desperation: 'I try to write lucidly, that even I / Can understand it', or subjecting his own vision of 'the neat claws, the precise foot of a chicken' in a rain-drenched gutter to the gale's howled mockery—'O literary pedestrian! / Small bankrupt moralist, O scavenger of the obvious symbol!'[5] Good rhetoric but a touch florid; one can see why he decided to curb that windy, extravagant language. Yet at their best these early poems beautifully enact the swooping energy and grace of the high arts they invoke—not just the anthology-piece **'Laughing Hyena after Hokusai'** but lesser-known poems like **'The Egyptian Cat'** on a mosaic of the sacred animal in Thebes, 'strong and a little malignant . . . tearing a fresh and virgin fish', or the newly reprinted **'Arab Music'** set at night in 'a bare street / Strewn with the refuse of the very poor' whose

>   song soars still, violent and vast: their
> history,
> Daily paper, church, their nuptial bed, their narrow
>   grave
> All held
> Between bare hands, borne on bare midnight voices.[6]

This is no simple tourist romanticism. Intoxication with the 'long versatile rhetorics' does not stop the poet from registering such details as the singers' dirty robes, or in other poems, starved cats, ordure in the gutter, and horribly mutilated beggars. Pity does not become identification: the acknowledgment of difference is as strong as the admiration and sympathy with which the Arab singers are heard and recreated. Many later poems about the poor and oppressed in Eastern countries carry the subtext 'I saw it'; they firmly avoid Whitman's 'I suffered, I was there'. Enright's first-person speaker or impersonal 'you' is always the observing foreign Englishman, not the weary rickshaw driver or the 'shabby old man mixing water with clay'[7] whom he observes. Yet the lyrical response to foreign lands still persists however mutedly and sceptically into his late poetry, as in the elegiac **'Even so'** from *Instant Chronicles* (1985) about a house in Bangkok:

>   Cigarettes
> Like fireflies. Faint gleam of shirt and sarong.
> Silent uproar of the crickets. Unweighty words,
> Mostly unheard. Two silences. One peace.
>
> But these words dim it. Are there things that
> Can't be written, then? Allow a few. Repose.
> It's gone, it's almost gone. And even so,
> A house, a garden, water, silence, cool of dusk.[8]

As often in Enright's poems, simplicity has complex, haunting resonances. The poet mourns a lost moment of peace, yet his echo of Issa's lament for his dead child ('The world of dew is / A world of dew, yet even / So, yet even so . . .')[9] acknowledges that loss is the human condition and that what memory recalls as a painless Eden was not really free of sorrow, its enchantment only a seductive illusion (as several bitter poems from Thailand and the deeply sad novel *Insufficient Poppy* confirm). Yet 'even so' also means 'Yes, this is how it was'. The poet may distrust both memory and elegy— 'these words dim it'—but is still spellbound by the lost paradise conjured in that beautiful just-irregular last line.

Enright's preoccupation with things as opposed to words, his suspicion of the subtle temptations offered by language to falsify or exploit its living referents and his inclination towards story all start to be noticeable in and after the poems he wrote from Japan in the mid-1950s. An unsentimental fellow-feeling for all sorts and conditions of men and women 'in real cities, real houses, real time' manifests itself in the sharp, gentle poems elegising Kazuo Yamamoto, the destitute shoe-shine boy 'who found rat poison cheaper than aspirin', the gentle, polite prostitute Akiko san, or the dying young English teacher of **'In Memoriam'** who married a Japanese orphan and gave her 'a year's happiness, that's all'.[10] Similar qualities appear in the lighter autobiographical poems about teaching English Literature in the East: the ironically anecdotal **'Board of Selection'**, the tongue-in-cheek confession **'I Was a Middle-Aged Corrupter of Youth'**, the rueful comedy of **'To a War Poet'**, on teaching Isaac Rosenberg in Singapore, or the poignant **'R-and-R Centre'** about a lost young American soldier wandering out of the official brothel into a university corridor, who at the poet's offer to show him the library, normally off-limits to GIs, 'trembled / With a furtive pleasure.'[11] This method of sparely telling anecdote later takes on England during the 1920s in Enright's classic autobiographical sequence *The Terrible Shears* (1973), whose understated, haunting short poems of childhood and school days were followed by the cagier epigrams and prose-poems of *Instant Chronicles* (1985).

The poet who holds that 'nothing is exotic, if you understand, if you stick your neck out for an hour or two'[12] seeks the common ground of shared humanity without denying difference. The difficulty of this exercise becomes plain when he writes of people divided from him not just by race or culture but by an economic gulf, as in the poems about beggars in Asia acutely analysed by P. N. Furbank and Shirley Chew,[13] and about poor women with nothing to sell except themselves. The early **'Akiko San'**, about one such woman—'she shall be glorified, if any are'—attempts to imagine a happier (after)life for her:

> She shall smile
> When she wants and be sad if she likes.
> When she suffers from drought
> She shall drink of pure water, not sip watered gin.
> Difference of sex none knows in that land of hot
>   springs
> And there with her likes she shall chatter and laugh
>   in the grace-given memory of different things.

The delicacy with which the poem conveys Akiko's embarrassment as she 'mumbles the harsh foreign name of her wares, with a blush for her wretched pronunciation',[14] does not stop it from becoming a little sentimental; not because, as one English reviewer objected, it 'resurrects the myth of the good-hearted harlot' (to which Enright drily remarked, 'Myth? He should just have said that it was a bad poem'[15]) but because the poet avoids acknowledging the impossibility of his wishes. The later **'J. T. on his Travels'** succeeds much better with harsh realism—'Perhaps you thought she was a child / Perhaps you thought you liked the thought . . . You feel you prefer your own french letter / Hers look second hand'.[16] Better still is the poignant dream of A-Nee, the masseuse of a Bangkok opium house in Enright's fine novel *Insufficient Poppy* (1960). Like Graham Greene's better-known *The Quiet American* (1955), it deals with the casual, unforgivable deaths of 'unimportant' people in a Far East country bedevilled by the Cold War: a friend pointlessly shot in a drunken scuffle, an unpolitical opium addict disappearing into gaol on vague charges of Communism because the police need to show themselves as actively defending the 'Free World', and in the background the half-stated, ever-present possibility of nuclear annihilation in the same empty cause. Aching with sorrow for past and future deaths, the narrator resorts increasingly to opium, and dreams of himself and A-Nee, in a setting of heavenly Jamesian elegance—handsome trees, silver tea-things, a cool sunlit park, a distant crowd of distinguished guests—discussing, of all things, the poetry of Edward Thomas:

> His was a kind of poetry so difficult to do justice to . . . (But A-Nee was doing it.) His matter not sorrow so much as the premonitions of sorrow, as sorrow would be felt when it was too late to feel sorrow; all the more desolating because free from personal disappointment or affront; cosmic because growing out of the earth, from the roots of grass, cavities inside hedgerows, small realities (as small as we). She murmured:
>
> And most I like the winter nests deep-hid
> That leaves and berries fell into:
> Once a dormouse dined there on hazel-nuts
> And grass and goose-grass seeds found soil and grew.
>
> 'He speaks' she continued, 'of what is present. And shows, standing at its side, its ghost. Not ghosts of the past—those plump comforters! but the ghosts of the present. As they will be, when no poet remains to recognize them . . .'
>
> 'But the ghost of a poet remains—could it be—to celebrate those ghostly landscapes—the scorched grass, the atomized nests, the—lost himself, but still mourning the loss of all?'
>
> 'He has prefigured that.' She smiled sadly.
>
> The dim sea glints chill. The white sun is shy,
> And the skeleton weeds and the never-dry
> Rough, long grasses keep white with frost
> At the hilltop by the finger-post . . .
>
> 'It was his own ghost that wrote those words.'[17]

This vision of an illiterate woman 'mildly prognathous, protuberant of eye, wet of lip, in her usual drab *phasin* and creased jacket',[18] dispensing tea and cucumber sandwiches in an elegant English garden while formulating a subtle reading of Thomas as a poet of post-nuclear mourning, is poignantly, absurdly impossible. As in **'Akiko san'** the dreamer gives A-Nee what the real world has denied her, but here the illusion is acknowledged; 'some sharp disregarded little voice, from deep down under those emotions as noble as the waiters, those thoughts as grand as the trees, [spoke] up: "All very nice—but it's not true."' Overwhelmed with grief, the dreamer cries himself awake and finds his tears are real and his pillow wet.[19]

Throughout his work, Enright's quick eye for particular details, wit, anger and sympathy for the powerless make for fine satire and public poetry. True, not all of this

comes off. Several of his later commentaries on life and literature are rather too like unfinished doodles, their throw-away ironies sounding flatly tight-lipped and prosaic. But there are also fine late pieces like **'Carrier Bag'** (1991) sceptically regarding the market-led world of the 1990s, where logo-printed plastic bags wait to take our sins away—'Say, an unwanted baby / She is but two days old / W. H. Smith is her name' (the wry dig at William Blake's 'Infant Joy'[20] creating a characteristically unacademic effect), the needle-sharp **'Psalm for Supersunday'** celebrating the godless world of shopping families 'and their faithful credit cards', or the bitter list of victim-blaming excuses in **'Bad Baby'**: 'The baby cries without reason / This is original sin'.[21] But the best public poems come from Enright's years in the Far East, like the newly reprinted **'Warm Protest'** against an execution in Thailand, which lets nobody off:

> To shoot a man against the National Library wall!
> —The East unsheathes its barbarous finger-nail.
>
> In Europe this was done in railway trucks,
> Cellars underground, and such sequestered nooks.[22]

The slightly later **'To Old Cavafy from a New Country'** (Singapore) is depressingly apt in Britain today. 'They are planning to kill the old Adam / Perhaps at this moment the blade is entering,' ensuring a goody-goody world where, as in the community of industrious citizens planned by New Labour, 'there is no lack of the younger generation / To meet the nation's needs. Skills shall abound. / . . . Only the dead Adam is not transmissive.'[23] Coarser but splendidly hard-hitting are the subversive ironies directed in **'Processional'** at the university's grandees: the Chancellor, Vice-Chancellor and Esquire Bedell, the Acting Head of the School of Education and many more whose titles echo Eliot's *ubi sunt* lament, 'The captains, merchant bankers, eminent men of letters . . . Distinguished civil servants, chairmen of many committees, / Industrial lords and petty contractors, all go into the dark'.[24] Enright, however, is less concerned with mortality in general than with the demise, announced by a clerk, of 'One Science Tower / (Incomplete), and / Two Labourers, Female, Chinese / Aged about 20 and 40 respectively / Who also look rather incomplete'—crushed to death in the rubble of the collapsed tower because

> The scaffolding consisted of old wood left out
> Too long in the monsoon rains, and the women
> Took too much sand with them, because the contractor
> Told them to get a move on, since he
> Was hurrying to finish the job, because . . .
> And they fell through four floors[25]

—because, evidently, that procession of dignitaries who commissioned the contractor wanted their science tower built quick and cheap, with no questions asked about safety regulations. It is a grim little story, all too familiar. Elsewhere, in poems like **'Political Meeting'**, or **'Misgiving at Dusk'** where a 'loudspeaker' produces 'loud political speaking' of which only the menace is comprehensible, the fear, anger and frustration turn into a strange bitter lyricism:

> It is all a vituperative humming.
> Night falls abruptly hereabouts.
> Shaking with lust, the mosquitoes
> Stiffen themselves with bloody possets.
> I have become their stews.
> Mist-encrusted, flowers of jasmine glimmer
> On the grass, stars dismissed from office.[26]

The moment of complex sensation is akin to those Alexandrian poems of imaginative perception, intensified now by economy of language and savage wit. Other poems continue the early fascination with art and imagination, though they are now less concerned with transcendence than limitation, a theme defined in **'How Right They Were, the Chinese Poets'**:

> Only one subject to write about: pity.
> Self-pity: the only subject to avoid.
> How difficult to observe both conditions!

'Difficult' turns out to be an understatement for the moral and aesthetic balancing act demanded in this meditation on the acute, complex tensions between high art and harsh reality. An unfortunate Englishman invited by the Asian poor 'in mimicked American . . . to joyless copulation', trips over their begging children—'Fallen down, you bemoan your trousers and your fall'.[27] This prosaic farce is countered by the elegant chiasmus of the opening couplet whose formal diction recalls Arthur Waley, or Ezra Pound in *Cathay*. Moreover, the poem's title and argument contain an unmistakable dissonant echo of Auden's 'Musée des Beaux Arts'—'About suffering they were never wrong / The Old Masters' (much as the contemporary poem **'Broken Fingernails'** deliberately distances itself from Eliot's fastidious horror of 'the broken fingernails of dirty hands').[28] Whereas Auden praised Breughel's *Icarus* for its unsentimentally inclusive realism, Enright here disowns the European pictorial inheritance of human drama in favour of an Eastern tradition of vividly concentrated visual imagery, admirable for its economy and chastity of execution.

> Death takes us before we become too ridiculous.
> White petals do not despise the bleary eye.
> A river of rice flows out of a stinking midden.

These coolly balanced oppositions end in unsteadiness—not just the Englishman's comic pratfall but rhythmically, the flow of lines being interrupted by a blunt personal admonition:

> But make no mistake. Suffering exists, and most of it
> is not yours.

> Good deeds are accomplished, as good poems are.
> Most of them
> not by you.

The poet who attempts to judge this alien world finds himself judged by it. Although he does not give up his task of seeing and judging, he ends by gratefully acknowledging the impossibility of success. 'Thank God we cannot hope to know / The full horror of this world—or whole happiness.'[29] Why the latter? Presumably because 'whole happiness' would imply indifference to the world's horrors, of which full imaginative knowledge would be humanly intolerable.

This is a wise and salutary poetry which for all its plainness and clarity demands—and rewards—a good deal of work from its reader. The price of that wisdom and health is, as the self-aware poet is much too intelligent not to know, a certain limitation of scope and ambition. That said, one should not underestimate the potential terror and despair of full imaginative knowledge, hinted at in the beautiful, desolating vision of loss in **'Children Killed in War'** and its vain desire to provide 'some simple windless heaven / Of special treats and toys / Like picnic snapshots / Like a magic-lantern show.'[30] (Or like the grieving public who left teddy bears for the massacred schoolchildren at Dunblane.) Even more chilling is the grim meditative poem **'How Many Devils Can Dance on the Point . . .'** which begins with a near-quotation from Marlowe but whose argument and vision are oddly akin to George Herbert. The resemblance lies not of course in form or style, but in an intimate leading of the reader's imagination into a tiny space that, once entered, stretches out to infinity.

> Why, this is hell,
> And we are in it.

Far removed from Herbert's deftly patterned formal beauties and farther still from his tenderness, this poem circles within a devilish logic whereby 'mysterious punishments' lead to crime, crime leads to worse punishments, and even those who apparently escape pain are doomed by a sadistic God to watch helplessly while others suffer:

> Can this be heaven
> Where a thoughtful landlord
> Locates the windows of his many mansions
> To afford you such a view?
> (The chamber, the instruments, the torture.)
> Can it be
> The gratifying knowledge of having pleased
> Someone who derives such pleasure
> From being thus gratified?[31]

As so often, the poem speaks most powerfully in its gaps and silences, the parenthesised words and bare demonstratives—'such a view', 'thus gratified'—carrying a sickeningly powerful charge of implied meaning. A.

S. Byatt has argued in a subtle reading of these mocking 'religious' poems that Enright finds damnation in the leaching of sacred meanings and images out of secular life, as in the harshly comic **'Prayer'**:

> O Cindy
> You who are always well-groomed and cheerful
> As we should be
> Who tie back your hair before going to ballet school
> As we should do
> Who take good care of your costly vestments
> As we should take
> Who is put to bed and made to get up
> Who speak in silent parables
> Concerning charm and deportment and a suitable mar-
>   riage
>   to a tennis star and yachts and a rich social life
> Who grow old like us
> Yet unlike us remain for ever young
> Whose hair is torn out at times
> Whose arms are broken
> Whose legs are forced apart
> Who take away the sin of the world
> To whom a raggedy doll called Barabbas is preferred
> You who are scourged
> And given vinegar to drink from a jar of pickled
>   onions
> Who seem to say, Why have you forsaken me?
> Who like us may rise or may not from the dead
>   in a long white garment
> You after the first day of the week is almost named
> Into your hands we commend ourselves.[32]

Byatt acutely reads this poem as a satiric vision of a 'post-Sunday' world without metaphors, 'bereft of significance and full of pain'.[33] The Mephistophelian mockery is also, I think, a sorrowfully slantways invocation of George Herbert's sonnet 'Prayer' whose listed metaphors, each partial yet all true, amount, as Francis Spufford has written, to a sacred analogy: 'At the back of [Herbert's] poem is the example of Christ's incarnation . . . for the concrete, suffering man Jesus was the most purely truthful representation of the godhead possible, yet did not express all of it'.[34] Not far at the back of Enright's listed invocations of the non-metaphorical uses to which Cindy is put, is a parody of Christ's Incarnation and Passion, the god-man now become a broken doll representing ourselves at our worst and weakest and redeeming nothing. Given a loss so total, the only resource left is to make outrageous jokes about the sorrow felt when, as A-Nee sadly surmised, 'it would be too late to feel sorrow.'[35]

Not, of course, that horror and sadness are anything like the whole story. No discussion of Enright could ignore his playful humour: the unseemly innuendos of **'Metropolitan Water Bawd'**, the enjoyably awful puns of **'An Ew Erra'** ('The trypewiter is cretin / A revultion in poetry'), the computer in **'From Little Acorns'** boasting 'I shall not want for problem-orientated language / The Lord is my backup disc / His rot and his stuff they comfort me', or the prayer for sweet dreams:

> Our Freud which art in heaven
> Give us this night our nightly symbol
> Give us to dream of serpents and cups
> Not of you know what.[36]

The narrative sequences **'Paradise Illustrated'** and **'A Faust Book'** give full rein to the pleasures of parody ('"The subtle snake, the fittest imp of fraud," / So spoke the Fallen Angel, fond of artful sound / So spoke the Fiend, alliteration's friend'), of sharp characterisation (the testy Lord God, the rhetoric-loving Adam, the self-deceived, lecherous Faust) and of the absurdities of language, as when newly-created Adam is commanded to name the animals:

> 'Fido', said Adam, thinking hard
> As the animals went past him one by one,
> 'Bambi', 'Harpy', 'Pooh',
> 'Incitatus', 'Acidosis', 'Apparat',
> 'Krafft-Ebing', 'Indo-China', 'Schnorkel',
> 'Buggins', 'Bollock'—
>
> 'Bullock will do', said the Lord God, 'I like it.
> The others are rubbish. You must try again tomorrow.'

Eve later gets her turn at naming with the plants, much more successfully apart from one unfortunate slip:

> 'Lady's slipper.
> Lady's tresses . . .'
>
> She paused.
> 'Adam's apple.'
>
> 'No', said the Lord,
> 'Strike that out.'
>
> 'Old man's beard, then.'

'A Faust Book' is likewise full of memorable characters, verbal elegance and knockabout comedy; also grim lines like Mephistopheles' no-answer to the problem of evil—'God moves in a mysterious manner / Unlike me. Me you can understand.'[37] The playful wit is the sunny side of Enright's moral imagination, harsh, gentle, sad, always alert to absurdities, its qualities best summed up by his admired Milton—not *Paradise Lost* this time, but 'Comus':

> The leaf was darkish, and had prickles on it,
> But in another Countrey, as he said,
> Bore a bright golden flowre, but not in this soyl:
> Unknown, and like esteem'd, and the dull swayn
> Treads on it daily with his clouted shoon,
> And yet more med'cinal is it than that Moly
> Which Hermes once to wise Ulysses gave.[38]

Attentive readers will find the dark jokes and pointed understatements of Enright's poetry flowering in the mind into tenderness, pity, gaiety and sadness. This is especially true of those poems which grew 'not in this soil' but out of his years in Japan, Thailand and Singapore. And like the Spirit's antidote to Comus' tempting illusions, his sceptical ironies communicate a salutary, disenchanting clarity and wisdom—ordinary-looking, often underestimated 'and yet more medicinal than moly'. Or in his own words,

> a common thing
> And being common,
> Therefore something rare indeed.[39]

Notes

1. E. M. Forster, *Pharos and Pharillon* (London, Hogarth, [1923] 1961), pp. 91, 92.

2. See Blake Morrison, *The Movement: English Poetry and Fiction of the 1950s* (Oxford, Oxford University Press, 1980).

3. D. J. Enright, 'Hospital Journal', *Collected Poems* (Oxford, Oxford University Press, 1998), p. 507.

4. Enright, *Collected Poems*, p. 209.

5. Enright, 'Life and Letters', 'The Chicken's Foot', *Collected Poems*, pp. 10, 12.

6. Enright, 'The Egyptian Cat', 'Arab Music', *Collected Poems*, pp. 4, 7.

7. Enright, 'Broken Fingernails', *Collected Poems*, p. 34.

8. Enright, 'Even so', *Collected Poems*, p. 378.

9. D. J. Enright (ed.), *The Oxford Book of Death* (Oxford, Oxford University Press, 1982): 'Issa', p. 108, tr. Enright.

10. Enright, 'The Noodle-Vendor's Flute', 'The Short Life of Kazuo Yamamoto', 'In Memoriam', *Collected Poems*, pp. 52, 34, 77.

11. Enright, 'Short Life of Kazuo Yamamoto', 'In Memoriam', 'R-and-R Centre', *Collected Poems*, pp. 34, 77, 218.

12. Enright, 'Reflections on Foreign Literatures', *Collected Poems*, p. 78.

13. P. N. Furbank, 'A Humanist Poet', and Shirley Chew, 'Untold Stories', in Jacqueline Simms (ed.), *Life By Other Means: Essays on D. J. Enright* (Oxford, Oxford University Press, 1990), pp. 97-104, 175-187; Helen Vendler, 'Life Itself', *New York Review of Books*, 24 Feb. 2000, p. 29.

14. Enright, 'Akiko San', *Collected Poems*, p. 33.

15. D. J. Enright, *Memoirs of a Mendicant Professor* (London, Chatto & Windus, 1969), p. 37.

16. Enright, 'J. T. on his Travels', *Collected Poems*, p. 149.

17. Enright, *Insufficient Poppy* (London, Chatto & Windus, 1960), p. 179.

18. Enright, *Insufficient Poppy*, p. 180.

19. Enright, *Insufficient Poppy*, p. 182.

20. Enright, 'Carrier Bag', *Collected Poems*, p. 443; William Blake, 'Infant Joy': 'I have no name / I am but three days old . . . I happy am / Joy is my name', *Songs of Innocence* (London, Hart-Davis, [1789] 1967), p. 25.

21. Enright, 'Psalm for Super-Sunday', 'Bad Baby', *Collected Poems*, pp. 428, 492.

22. Enright, 'Warm Protest', *Collected Poems*, p. 84.

23. Enright, 'To Old Cavafy, from a New Country', *Collected Poems*, p. 108.

24. T. S. Eliot, 'East Coker', in *Collected Poems 1909-1962* (London, Faber, 1963), pp. 199-200.

25. Enright, 'Processional', *Collected Poems*, pp. 128-9.

26. Enright, 'Misgiving at Dusk', *Collected Poems*, p. 113.

27. Enright, 'How Right They Were, the Chinese Poets', *Collected Poems*, p. 35.

28. W. H. Auden, 'Musée des Beaux Arts' [1938], *Collected Shorter Poems* (London, Faber, 1967), p. 123; Enright, 'Broken Fingernails', *Collected Poems*, p. 34; Eliot, 'The Waste Land', *Collected Poems*, p. 74.

29. Enright, 'How Right They Were', p. 35.

30. Enright, 'Children Killed in War', *Collected Poems*, p. 145.

31. Enright, 'How Many Devils Can Dance On The Point . . .', *Collected Poems*, p. 163.

32. Enright, 'Prayer', *Collected Poems*, p. 429.

33. A. S. Byatt, 'A Sense of Religion', in Simms (ed.), *Life By Other Means*, p. 174.

34. Francis Spufford, *The Chatto Book of Cabbages and Kings* (London, Chatto & Windus, 1989), p. 13.

35. Enright, *Insufficient Poppy*, p. 178.

36. Enright, 'Metropolitan Water Bawd', 'An Ew Erra', 'From Little Acorns', *Collected Poems*, pp. 165, 166, 446, 271.

37. Enright, 'Paradise Illustrated', 'A Faust Book', *Collected Poems*, pp. 165, 166, 446, 325, 240, 328.

38. John Milton, 'Comus', *Poetical Works vol II*, ed. Helen Darbishire (Oxford, Clarendon, 1955), p. 159.

39. Enright, 'The Noodle-Vendor's Flute', *Collected Poems*, p. 51.

FURTHER READING

Criticism

Dean, Paul. "Writing for Antiquity: The Ironies of D. J. Enright." *The New Criterion* (November 2003): 30-4.

Presents a retrospective on Enright's life while focusing on three later hybrid works: *Interplay: A Kind of Commonplace Book, Play Resumed: A Journal,* and *Injury Time: A Memoir.*

Additional coverage of Enright's life and career is contained in the following sources published by Gale: *Contemporary Authors,* **Vol. 1-4R;** *Contemporary Authors—Obituary,* **Vol. 211;** *Contemporary Authors New Revision Series,* **Vols. 1, 42, 83;** *Contemporary Literary Criticism,* **Vols. 4, 8, 31;** *Contemporary Novelists,* **Eds. 1, 2;** *Contemporary Poets,* **Eds. 1, 2, 3, 4, 5, 6, 7;** *Dictionary of Literary Biography,* **Vol. 27;** *Encyclopedia of World Literature in the 20th Century,* **Ed. 3;** *Literature Resource Center;* *Modern British Literature,* **Ed. 2;** *Something About the Author,* **Vol. 25; and** *Something About the Author—Obituary,* **Vol. 140.**

Thomas Hood
1799-1845

English poet, short story writer, novelist, and editor.

INTRODUCTION

Known for his humorous verse, Hood was considered the master of the pun, although he is best remembered for a serious poem, "The Song of the Shirt" (1843), an attempt to call attention to the plight of underpaid garment workers in London. While his comic poems and stories were popular as light entertainment for the entire family, his attempts at serious poetry—with few exceptions—were generally less well received.

BIOGRAPHICAL INFORMATION

Hood was born on May 23, 1799, in a district of London known as The Poultry. His mother, Elizabeth Sands, belonged to a family who was well known in the engraving business; his father, Thomas Hood, was a Scotsman who was a partner in the bookselling and publishing firm of Vernor and Hood. Hood was one of six children born to the couple, but his only brother and two of his sisters died before reaching adulthood. In 1811, Hood's father died, leaving the family in financial distress and by 1814, Hood's education had to be cut short so that he could help support his mother and sisters. He worked first as a clerk in a counting house, an occupation for which he was ill suited, and then as an apprentice engraver with his uncle, Robert Sands. In 1815, suffering from poor health brought on by overwork, Hood went to live with his paternal relatives in Scotland where he began publishing some of his writing in the *Dundee Advertiser* and *Dundee Magazine*. When he returned to London two years later, he resumed his job as an engraver, and in 1821, took a position as editorial assistant at *London Magazine,* contributing a number of humorous essays and poems. During this same period, Hood met a number of other contributors to the magazine, among them Charles Lamb, William Hazlitt, John Clare, and John Hamilton Reynolds, with whom he later collaborated on a volume of poetry.

Hood married Reynolds's sister Jane in 1824, over the objections of her family, who considered him a poor choice because of his limited financial means and precarious health. The couple's first child was born in

1827, but died soon after her birth, providing the inspiration for Charles Lamb's poem "On an Infant Dying as soon as Born." In 1830, another daughter, Frances Freeling, was born. The couple also had a son, Tom, born in 1835 and immortalized in his father's "A Parental Ode to My Son, Aged 3 Years and 5 Months."

In 1828, Hood became editor of the *Gem,* an annual that contained contributions from Charles Lamb and Hartley Coleridge, as well as Hood's own poetry, including "The Dream of Eugene Aram." For almost ten years, from 1830-1839, Hood produced his own *Comic Annual,* which contained a number of woodcuts, poems, and articles, by Hood and others.

Hood lived in Germany for a period of five years in an attempt to save money and escape his mounting debts, but his health deteriorated further during this self-imposed exile and he returned to London in 1840. The following year he was appointed editor of *New Monthly Magazine,* a position he held until 1844 when he started his own publication, *Hood's Magazine.* By Christmas of that year, however, his health had become so poor that he was completely bedridden. Hood's friends appealed to the government on his behalf, and Prime Minister Robert Peel took up his cause personally and granted Hood a pension. Hood died on May 3, 1845, shortly before his forty-sixth birthday, and was buried in Kensal Green Cemetery.

MAJOR WORKS

Hood's first published volume, *Odes and Addresses to Great People,* written in conjunction with his friend John Hamilton Reynolds, was published anonymously in 1825 and was originally attributed to Charles Lamb by Samuel Taylor Coleridge. Lamb quickly set the record straight and gave credit for ninety percent of the volume to Hood, although exactly which pieces were written by each contributor remains a matter of scholarly debate. According to Hood's notes on a first edition of the text, Reynolds contributed five of the titles, Hood was responsible for eight of the pieces, and the remaining two were a joint effort. Over the next two years, Hood published *Whims and Oddities, First Series* (1826) and *Whims and Oddities, Second Series* (1827). Both contain a combination of prose pieces and light verse, establishing Hood as a master of the pun in such ballads as "Sally Brown," "Nelly Gray," and "Death's

Ramble." A number of other poems in the two collections—"The Last Man," "Jack Hall," and "The Irish Schoolmaster," for example—exhibit Hood's penchant for including grim and rather gruesome elements within his supposedly comic verse.

Hood's first book of serious poetry appeared in 1827, consisting of new poems as well as a number of previously-published pieces, entitled *The Plea of the Midsummer Fairies, Hero and Leander, Lycus the Centaur, and Other Poems.* In 1843, he anonymously published his most famous poem, "The Song of the Shirt," in the Christmas issue of *Punch.* The piece was inspired by a news article about a poor garment worker, struggling to support two children, who was prosecuted for pawning items that belonged to her employer; it was an immediate success. Hood's other well-known serious poem, "The Bridge of Sighs"—also inspired by a newspaper item—recounted the story of the attempted suicide of Mary Furley, sentenced to deportation for killing her infant son in the spring of 1844. The poem was a part of many poetry anthologies in the nineteenth and early twentieth centuries.

CRITICAL RECEPTION

Hood is considered by many scholars and critics to be a master of the pun. Margaret Willy reports that "puns poured from him, with a seemingly effortless exuberance, on every possible occasion, even in the most sober of moods." According to Alfred Ainger, Hood was a pioneer in the use of the pun as "an element in his fancy, his humour, his ethical teaching, even his pathos," and he thus frequently employed puns even in his serious poetry.

Given his personal experience with death and suffering—he lost his brother, mother, and two sisters to consumption—it is not surprising that they were common themes in his poetry. Understandably, his serious poems, among them "The Bridge of Sighs," "The Song of the Shirt," "Haunted House," and "Elm Tree," exhibit the sense of doom that preoccupied the poet, but even his comic poetry often dealt with disasters and catastrophes. Susan J. Wolfson (see Further Reading) contends that "Hood's wit is frequently animated by a sense of the inevitability and the pervasiveness of death," and that even his humorous poetry "is typically sharpened by a vivid imagination of death and a mordant wit about its ghastly events." Willy notes the "sinister dread" expressed in "The Dream of Eugene Aram" as well as the "potent evocation of mystery and evil" and "repulsive images of decay" that pervade "The Haunted House." Laurence Brander (see Further Reading) reports on "the powerful expression of fate and doom, of the crushing inevitability of human suffering" in "The Lady's Dream."

Critics have often maintained that Hood's serious poetry is inferior to his humorous pieces, at least in terms of popular success. Willy suggests that Hood had unfortunately introduced readers first to his comic verse and was then unable to win them over with his serious odes and sonnets; she contends that the reading public is "always reluctant to accord a writer the credit for talents of a very diverse *genre.*" Ainger reports that after the poor reception given *The Plea of the Midsummer Fairies,* Hood realized that he must rely on his humorous verse if he were to earn a living from his writing. Peter Thorogood notes that the commercial failure of the volume prompted the *Monthly Review* to describe Hood as "a comic poet trying to play Hamlet," after which "he was driven back to whimsicality and punning humour, in which, it must be admitted, he had no peer in his own day." Brander, however, contends that Hood's most memorable work consists of the serious "public" poems devoted to social issues, such as "The Song of the Shirt," "The Lay of the Labourer," and "The Bridge of Sighs." In fact, some of the serious poems were tremendously popular with contemporary readers. J. C. Reid reports that "The Song of the Shirt" "ran through the land like a hurricane." It was much admired by Charles Dickens and was reprinted in several British newspapers, translated into a number of other languages, and often recited at public events. John Clubbe notes that Hood's poem "carried his name from one end of England to the other." Roger B. Henkle (see Further Reading) praises Hood's effectiveness "in pleading the case, in comedy and pathos, for the victimized lower classes, the seamstresses, displaced craftsmen, and the impoverished, over whom the fast-rising Victorian economy was running roughshod."

Some critics consider Hood a failed Romantic poet, whose odes and sonnets are far too imitative of the work of John Keats. Alvin Whitley is one such critic; he believes that Hood's serious work was overly influenced by Keats, noting that "the debt to Keats is almost painfully obvious," since in some cases "titles are taken over with little change" and "direct verbal echoes abound." Reid concurs, noting that "several lines" of the title poem of *The Plea of the Midsummer Fairies* "draw upon particular poems by Keats," and in fact, according to Reid, "Hood's whole poetic personality vibrated to that of Keats." Reid to some degree excuses Hood's lack of originality, contending that "it was hardly his fault that he lacked the high vision and dedication and the keen critical intelligence of his predecessor." Similarly, James Reeves (see Further Reading) considers it "inevitable" that Hood's poetry "should not stand up well to a comparison with those of men of extraordinary genius such as the earlier generation of the Romantics." Clubbe (see Further Reading), however, disagrees, contending that "Hood retains our attention today not as a late romantic . . . but as the first Victorian poet—a poet who anticipated many trends in modern poetry. His comic grotesquerie combined with technical virtuosity, his moral humor, his social and humanitarian concern, these—rather than the romantic echoes of an outworn poetic fashion— represent the deeper currents in Hood's literary career."

PRINCIPAL WORKS

Poetry

Odes and Addresses to Great People [with John Hamilton Reynolds] 1825

Whims and Oddities, First Series (poetry and prose) 1826

The Plea of the Midsummer Fairies, Hero and Leander, Lycus the Centaur, and Other Poems 1827

Whims and Oddities, Second Series (poetry and prose) 1827

The Epping Hunt 1829

The Dream of Eugene Aram 1831

Hood's Own; or, Laughter from Year to Year, First Series (poetry and prose) 1839

"The Song of the Shirt" [published in the periodical *Punch*] 1843

Whimsicalities: A Periodic Gathering (poetry and prose) 1844

Poems 2 vols. 1846

Hood's Own; or, Laughter from Year to Year, Second Series (poetry and prose) 1862

The Works of Thomas Hood 7 vols. (poetry, prose, and novels) 1862-63

Miss Kilmansegg and Her Precious Leg: A Golden Legend 1870

Complete Works of Thomas Hood 11 vols. (poetry, prose, and novels) 1882-84

The Haunted House 1896

Other Major Works

National Tales (short stories) 1827

Tylney Hall (novel) 1834

Up the Rhine (novel) 1840

The Letters of Thomas Hood (letters) 1973

CRITICISM

Alfred Ainger (essay date 1893)

SOURCE: Ainger, Alfred. "Preface." In *Humorous Poems*, pp. vii-xxiv. London: Macmillan, 1893.

[*In the following introduction to Hood's humorous poetry, Ainger contends that Hood's comic verse was superior to his serious poetry.*]

Some time in the year 1825 there was published in London a thin duodecimo volume having for title *Odes and Addresses to Great People.* It bore no author's name on the title-page,—only a quotation from the *Citizen of the World,* "Catching all the oddities, the whimsies, the absurdities and the littlenesses of conscious greatness by the way." The little book proved, on examination, to contain some fifteen humorous poems addressed to various public characters of greater or less claim to distinction at that day. There was one to Mr. Graham, the aeronaut; another to M'Adam, the maker of roads; another to Mrs. Fry, the Quaker philanthropist; another to Grimaldi, the clown, and so forth. An acute critic might, even then, I think, have detected not only that these fresh and amusing productions were of unequal merit, but that they were not all by the same hand. But he would, most assuredly, have allowed that wit and ingenuity of a rare kind were to be found among them.

The little volume quickly attracted attention, and was soon in a second edition. Among those into whose hands it fell was Samuel Taylor Coleridge, then residing under Mr. Gillman's roof at Highgate. His delight was great; and in the absence of any information as to the authorship, he at once assumed that such mingled fun and poetry could have emanated from but one living man— and that, the author of *Elia.* Accordingly Coleridge wrote off at once to Charles Lamb:—

> My Dear Charles—This afternoon a little thin mean-looking sort of a foolscap sub-octavo of poems, printed on very dingy outsides, lay on the table, which the cover informed me was circulating in our book-club, so very Grub Streetish in all its appearance, internal as well as external, that I cannot explain by what accident of impulse (assuredly there was no motive in play) I came to look into it. Least of all the title, *Odes and Addresses to Great Men,* which connected itself in my head with Rejected Addresses, and all the Smith and Theodore Hook squad. But, my dear Charles, it was certainly written by you, or under you, or unâ cum you. I know none of your frequent visitors, capacious and assimilative enough of your converse, to have reproduced you so honestly, supposing you had left yourself in pledge in his lock-up house. Gillman, to whom I read the spirited parody on the Introduction to Peter Bell, the Ode to the Great Unknown, and to Mrs. Fry—he speaks doubtfully of Reynolds and Hood. . . .
>
> Thursday night, 10 o'clock—No! Charles, it is you! I have read them over again, and I understand why you have anoned the book. The puns are nine in ten good— many excellent,—the Newgatory, transcendent! And then the exemplum sine exemplo of a volume of personalities and contemporaneities without a single line that could inflict the infinitesimal of an unpleasance on any man in his senses—saving and except, perhaps, in the envy-addled brain of the despiser of your Lays. If not a triumph over him, it is, at least, an Ovation. Then moreover and besides (to speak with becoming modesty), excepting my own self, who is

there but you who could write the musical lines and stanzas that are intermixed?

Lamb writes back on the second of July from Colebrooke Row, Islington, and after telling Coleridge of his own recent illness and the weariness of being without occupation—he had just retired from the India House—he proceeds:—

> The Odes are, four-fifths, done by Hood—a silentish young man you met at Islington one day, an invalid. The rest are Reynolds's, whose sister Hood has lately married. I have not had a broken finger in them. . . . Hood will be gratified, as much as I am, by your mistake.

And Lamb is able to add at the close of his letter: "Hood has just come in; his sick eyes sparkled with health when he read your approbation."

The "silentish young man—an invalid" was then just six-and-twenty years of age. He had been forced to abandon, for health's sake, the engraver's desk to which he had been bound; had become in 1821 sub-editor of the *London Magazine,* and in that service, and at the hospitable table of the publishers, Taylor and Hessey, had both practised his poetic gift and made the most valuable and inspiring friendships of his life,—with Hazlitt, De Quincey, Hartley Coleridge, and, above all, in Hood's affection and admiration, Charles Lamb, then just beginning to contribute his essays to the magazine. One greater genius than any in the list it was not given to Hood to know in the flesh. John Keats had closed his brief life of suffering at Rome in the February of the year in which Hood joined the staff. But it was under the spell of that poetic genius that Hood began his career as poet. Among the friends he owed to the magazine was John Hamilton Reynolds, his future brother-in-law. Reynolds had been one of Keats's closest friends, and himself wrote verse of considerable merit, bearing strong marks of the Keatsian influence. Hood remained sub-editor for two or three years, and contributed many of his longer serious poems, clearly due in subject as well as style to the same influence— his **"Lycus the Centaur," "The Two Peacocks of Bedfont,"** the **"Ode to Autumn,"** and others. But very early in his editorial career he had also printed in the magazine, modestly, among certain imaginary and whimsical "Notices to Correspondents," a short and facetious **"Ode to Dr. Kitchener,"** prelude and model of those which afterwards so captivated Coleridge. But this, with all other of Hood's contributions at this time, was anonymous, and together with the serious poetry, seems to have attracted scant notice. Unsigned poetry, even seventy years ago, was sufficiently abundant, and, for the most part, sufficiently commonplace, for the general reader to pass it by as so much padding. And when the ***Odes and Addresses,*** the joint-production of Hood and Reynolds, appeared anonymously in 1825,

even those who lived in the world of literature were in some doubt as to the authorship.

In 1824 Hood married Jane Reynolds, contrary, it would seem, to the wishes of her family; and indeed, with his health and uncertain prospects, the match may well have been deemed imprudent. In any case the "bread and cheese" question had become urgent. The ***Odes and Addresses*** came out in the year following, to be soon followed by the two series of ***Whims and Oddities***; and in 1827 Hood reprinted his *Serious Poems* from the *London Magazine* with some new matter, including the graceful poem which gave its name to the volume, **"The Plea of the Midsummer Fairies."** This poem was dedicated to Charles Lamb,—the volume, as a whole, to Coleridge, in grateful recognition of the praise he had bestowed on Hood's earlier efforts,—but neither poems nor dedications availed to awaken any interest in the reading public. The volume fell all but dead from the press; and the author, his son and daughter tell us, bought up a large number of the remainder copies, "to save them from the butter-shop."

It now became evident that if Hood was to live by writing, it must be by his humorous, not his serious verse; and though happily his poetic genius was not discouraged, the remaining eighteen years of his life were spent mainly in working that rich and unique vein of which he had given earliest proof in his ***Odes and Addresses.*** He was to show that in the hands of a poet and humorist, the pun—that so-called "verbal wit"—was to take higher rank and subserve quite other purposes than anything of the kind in our literature before. Samuel Johnson once remarked that "little things are not valued, but when they are done by those who can do greater things." But he might have gone further, and said that the little things only become great when they proceed from those who can do greater,—who come to them, that is to say, from a higher ground.

And, with Hood, this higher ground was the poetic heart, and a vividness and rapidity of imagination such as never before had found such an outlet. The same instantaneous perception of the analogies and relations between, apparently, incongruous things that was possessed by Dickens, Hood possessed with regard to words and ideas. The pun, as ordinarily understood, is a play upon the double meanings of words, or on the resemblance of one word to another; and in the hands of one destitute of humour or fancy the pun begins and ends there. It may be purely mechanical, and if so, speedily becomes wearisome and disgusting. To hear of any ordinary man that he makes puns is properly a warning to avoid his society. For with the funny man the verbal coincidence is everything; there is nothing underlying it, or beyond it. In the hands of a Hood the pun becomes an element in his fancy, his humour, his ethical teaching, even his pathos. As ordinarily experienced, the pun is the irreconcilable enemy of these things. It could not dwell with them "in one house." Hood saw, and was the first to show, that the pun might become even their handmaid, and in this confidence dared to use it often in his serious poems, when he was conveying some moral truth, or expressing some profound human emotion. Coleridge, as we have seen, remarking on the excellence of the puns in the *Odes and Addresses,* added, "The Newgatory is transcendent!" Hood was addressing the admirable Mrs. Fry, who, as every one knows, set up a school in Newgate to teach the poor neglected outcasts what they had never heard from Christian lips before. One of the chief points made by Hood is this,—how much better, kinder, wiser, more politic even, it would be to multiply these schools outside, not inside the Prison walls, so that prevention might take the place of cure. "Keep your school out of Newgate" is the burden of Hood's remonstrance:—

> Ah! who can tell how hard it is to teach
> Miss Nancy Dawson on her bed of straw—
> To make Long Sal sew up the endless breach
> She made in manners—to write heaven's own law
> On hearts of granite; nay, how hard to preach,
> In cells, that are not memory's—to draw
> The moral thread thro' the immoral eye
> Of blunt Whitechapel natures, Mrs. Fry!

And then, after a stanza or two, comes the one ending with the play on words that so fascinated Coleridge:—

> I like your chocolate, good Mistress Fry!
> I like your cookery in every way;
> I like your Shrove-tide service and supply;
> I like to hear your sweet Pandeans play;
> I like the pity in your full-brimmed eye;
> I like your carriage, and your silken grey,
> Your dove-like habits, and your silent preaching;
> But I don't like your Newgatory teaching!

The distinctive quality of Hood's puns is exemplified here, but not more notably than in a hundred other instances that crowd upon the memory. The ordinary pun is, for the most part, profoundly depressing, being generally an impertinence; while Hood's at their best exhilarate and fill the reader with a glow of admiration and surprise. The "sudden glory" which Hobbes pronounced to be the secret of the pleasure derived from wit is true of Hood's. There was a pretty drawing-room ballad by his brother-in-law Reynolds, which our grandmothers used to sing to an equally pretty tune, beginning—

> Go where the water glideth gently ever,
>   Glideth by meadows that the greenest be;
> Go, listen to our own belovèd river
>   And think of me!

Hood had a young lady friend who was going to India, and he writes her a playful copy of verses, imitating Reynolds's poem in metre and refrain. Hood noticed that the matrimonial market, already in his day, was somewhat overstocked, and that watchful parents had the comfort of hoping that daughters who lingered in England might yet find husbands in the smaller society of Bombay or Madras, and he adds—

> Go where the maiden on a mariage plan goes,
>   Consigned for wedlock to Calcutta's quay,
> Where woman goes for mart, the same as mangos,
>   And think of me!

The same as man goes! How utter the surprise, and yet how inevitable the simile appears! It is just as if the writer had not foreseen it—as if it had been mere accident—as if he had discovered the coincidence rather than arranged it. This is a special note of Hood's best puns. They fall into their place so obviously, like the rhymes of a consummate lyrist, that it would have seemed pedantic to go out of the way to avoid them. The verses in the present collection supply instances in abundance. Every one remembers Lieutenant Luff's apology for his particular weakness in respect of stimulants—

> If wine's a poison, so is Tea,
>   Though in another shape:
> What matter whether one is kill'd
>   By canister, or grape!

In another poem here given, and less known (suggested by Burns's *Twa Dogs*), the Pointer bitterly complains that his master is such a novice that he never hits a bird, and that now he has taken to a double-barrel the "aggravation" is worse than before:—

> And now, as girls a-walking do,
> His misses go by two and two!

In these last-quoted jests the purpose is, of course, humorous and fantastic, and is little more; but Hood never hesitated to make the pun minister to higher ends, and vindicate its right to a share in quickening men's best sympathies. An apparently little known copy of verses will be found in the present volume, written to support an "Early Closing Movement" of Hood's day, in which his interest was keen as it was in all proposed remedies for suffering and oppression. It seems strange that the verses have never been reprinted in behalf of grievances that still, after fifty years, cry aloud for redress. The poem is **"The Assistant Draper's Petition,"** and the prodigal flow of wit and fancy that marks it, so far from be-littling its purpose, is surely fraught with a rare pathos,—though the point of the jests is chiefly got from the double meanings in well-known trade phrases:—

> Ah! who can tell the miseries of men
>   That serve the very cheapest shops in town?
> Till faint and weary, they leave off at ten,
>   Knock'd up by ladies beating of 'em down!

(Sydney Smith laid it down as a rule that wit and pathos cannot dwell together,—that one must needs kill the other; but he wrote his famous lecture without knowing Thomas Hood.) And then there follows a plea for leisure—leisure to read and to think,—the leisure which noble Institutions like Toynbee Hall are doing so much to foster and improve:

> O come then, gentle ladies, come in time,
> O'erwhelm our counters, and unload our shelves;
> Torment us all until the seventh chime,
> But let us have the remnant to ourselves!
>
> We wish of knowledge to lay in a stock,
> And not remain in ignorance incurable;—
> To study Shakespeare, Milton, Dryden, Locke,
> And other fabrics that have proved so durable.
>
> We long for thoughts of intellectual kind,
> And not to go bewilder'd to our beds;
> With stuff and fustian taking up the mind,
> And pins and needles running in our heads!
>
> For oh! the brain gets very dull and dry,
> Selling from morn till night for cash or credit;
> Or with a vacant face and vacant eye,
> Watching cheap prints that Knight did never edit.
>
> Till sick with toil, and lassitude extreme,
> We often think, when we are dull and vapoury,
> The bliss of Paradise was so supreme,
> Because that Adam did not deal in drapery.

It would be absurd to pretend that Hood's lighter verse is always up to the same level. It was his misfortune to have to write for bread, and to struggle for half a lifetime against poverty and ill-health. Much of his "comic copy" was manufactured, and that too when he was gravely ill, sitting propped up with pillows. The marvel is not that the quality was often so poor, but that he wrote so much that will live. He was only forty-five when he died, and for the last twenty years had dwelt "in company with pain." We probably owe to this circumstance that not only in his serious poetry, his **"Bridge of Sighs," "Song of the Shirt,"** the **"Haunted House,"** and the **"Elm Tree,"** but also in his humorous verse, his fancy turned so habitually to some or other form of death or suffering. A glance at the titles in our index will show how often he found suggestions of humour in "violent ends," in accident and disaster. In the serious poems, indeed, a different origin may be found for this. Hood's own deep compassion and his sense of man's inhumanity was, doubtless, quickened by his own experience of pain and disappointment, and by the shadow of decay and doom that never lifted. But he made no boast of it, or capital out of it; the pessimistic accent is never heard in his verse; he never lost his own cheerful faith in providence, though he early learned that

> There's not a string attuned to mirth,
> But has its chord in Melancholy.

And the treatment of "catastrophe" in his lighter verse is too purely fantastic to be even grim, still less to leave any ill flavour of bad taste. He could never overlook the humorous analogies of things, even when they were his own sufferings. "I am obliged to lead a very sedentary life," he wrote to a correspondent—"in fact, to be very chair-y of myself." And when for his poor wasted frame, his faithful wife was preparing a mustard plaster, he murmured, "Ah! Jane—a great deal of mustard to a very little meat!"

What has been said of Hood's punning faculty applies to the general quality of his humorous verse, namely, that the writer comes to it from a higher ground. Owing to ill-health he had been from childhood an omnivorous reader, but his sympathies were with all that is best in literature. He had trained himself on the best poetic models. Shakespeare and Keats were the inspiration of his earliest verse; and often in the hastiest of comic effusions the eye and practised hand of the poet are discernible. Just as he did not hesitate to let a pun heighten the effect of some poignant reflection, as in the **"Ode to Melancholy,"**—

> Even the bright extremes of joy
> Bring on conclusions of disgust,
> Like the sweet blossoms of the May
> Whose fragrance ends in must,—

so he did not grudge a really noble fancy even to some perfunctory copy for a magazine, where the first aim was to raise a laugh. There is a poem of his about a somnambulist (suggested by a once popular story, Edgar Huntly), the point of which is the contrast of the sleeper's romantic dream with the hard reality of the kitchen stairs down which he falls. The dreamer imagines himself in the rapids above Niagara, and as he nears the brink, he notices the rainbow hovering in the spray below, and feels that the old pledge and covenant of Hope is, in his case, the emblem of despair,—a thought that might have made the fortune of a sonnet or other lyric, had its author reserved it,—but he leaves it there. And this habit makes it difficult to classify his verse, the serious poetry often adopting the humorist's methods and the humorous often containing elements of genuine poetry. The present selection, while excluding the former of these, succeeds, I think, in showing Hood's versatility and ingenuity in the latter. The **"Demon Ship"** exhibits the same hand that depicted the anguish of Eugene Aram: the **"Mermaid of Margate"** is a playful parody of the Romantic legend of Bürger and his English followers; while others, such as **"Sally Brown"** and **"Nelly Gray,"** show the humorous possibilities of the Percy Ballad. The **"Epping Hunt"** is undisguisedly suggested by "John Gilpin," a **"Death's Ramble"** is by the "Devil's Walk" of Coleridge and

Southey—and **"Queen Mab"** shows how well Hood might have written for children, had he chosen to work the vein, in the delightful fashion of Mr. R. L. Stevenson.

True poet and true humorist, Hood doubtless produced too much in both kinds for his fame. Struggling against "two weak evils," poverty and disease, he too often wrote when the fountains of his fancy were dry. But if he diluted his reputation in some ways, he was growing and "making himself" in others more important. He was a learner to the end—widening as well as deepening in his human insight, recognising, as he told Sir Robert Peel in his last pathetic letter, the dangers of a "one-sided humanity, opposite to that Catholic Shakespearian sympathy, which felt with king as well as peasant, and duly estimated the mortal temptations of both stations." Hood's position among our minor poets is peculiar and interesting. He is much loved, but not much written about. Critics will seldom be found analysing and dissecting his "work." The scholar and the artist, the classic and the student of form, have their just and necessary place in our literature, and they will not grudge Hood that certain immortality which he won by paths so different. The large-hearted Landor was certainly not wanting in the qualities which he confessed his despair of attaining in presence of such a writer as this, and yet he clearly felt the difference between his own power, and that which is destined to survive in the "general heart of men," when he wrote—

> Jealous, I own it, I was once,
> That wickedness I here renounce.
> I tried at wit, it would not do;
> At tenderness, that failed me too;
> Before me on each path there stood
> The witty and the tender Hood.

Richard Herne Shepherd (essay date 1906)

SOURCE: Shepherd, Richard Herne. "Memoir of Thomas Hood." In *The Choice Works of Thomas Hood in Prose and Verse*, pp. ix-xv. London: Chatto and Windus, 1906.

[*In the following essay, Shepherd offers a brief overview of Hood's life and writing career.*]

Thomas Hood was born on the 23d May 1799, in the Poultry, at the house of his father, a partner in the firm of Vernor & Hood, booksellers and publishers. His mother was a Miss Sands, sister to the engraver of that name, to whom the subject of our memoir was afterwards articled.

The family consisted of two sons, James and Thomas; and of four daughters, Elizabeth, Anne, Jessie, and Catherine.

Hood's father was a man of cultivated taste and literary inclinations, and was the author of two novels which attained some popularity in their day, although now their very names are forgotten.

Thomas Hood was sent to a school in Tokenhouse Yard in the City, as a day-boarder. The two maiden sisters who kept the school, and with whom Hood took his dinner, bore the odd name of Hogsflesh, and they had a sensitive brother, who was always addressed as Mr H., and who afterwards became the prototype of Charles Lamb's unsuccessful farce.

After the death of his father and his elder brother in 1811, he was apprenticed to his uncle, Mr Robert Sands, the engraver, and plied the burin for some years under his guidance. He thus learnt something of the art which he practised with such pleasant results in after-years in producing grotesque illustrations to his own verses and sketches. This sedentary employment not agreeing with his health, he was sent for change to some relations at Dundee. He remained in Scotland for a considerable time, and made his first appearance in print there in 1814, first in the *Dundee Advertiser,* then edited by Mr Rintoul, and subsequently in the *Dundee Magazine.* These early effusions we have not succeeded in procuring, owing to the difficulty of obtaining access to local periodical publications, or we should have gratified the reader's curiosity by reprinting them.

On his return to London, after practising for a short time as an engraver, and doing some fruitless deskwork in a merchant's office, an opening that offered more congenial employment presented itself at last, when he was about twenty-two years of age. In 1821, Mr John Scott, the editor of the *London Magazine,* was killed in a duel. The magazine passed into the hands of Messrs Taylor & Hessey, who were friends of Hood's, and he was offered and accepted the sub-editorship. His first original paper appeared in the number for July 1821, and he continued to contribute till the summer of 1823.

Hood's connexion with the *London Magazine* was the means of bringing him into contact with many of the chief wits and literati of the time, and more especially with Charles Lamb, whose influence over his style and manner of writing is very clearly traceable. All these literary friendships have been delightfully described in his own "Reminiscences."

One of the contributors to the *London Magazine* was John Hamilton Reynolds, author of an exquisite little volume of verse entitled "The Garden of Florence," whose articles appeared under the pseudonym of "Edward Herbert." The acquaintance thus begun had lasting results. On the 5th May 1824, Hood was married to Reynolds's sister, Jane. In the following year

(1825) he produced conjointly with his brother-in-law his first publication in a separate form, viz., **"Odes and Addresses to Great People."** This little volume rapidly passed through three editions, and made almost as great a stir as the "Rejected Addresses" of James and Horace Smith. A copy of the first edition, marked by Hood himself, and now in the possession of the present publishers, thus apportions the respective authorship of the pieces it contains:—

Ode to Mr Graham	T. H.
Ode to Mr M'Adam	J. H. Reynolds.
Epistle to Mrs Fry	T. H.
Ode to Richard Martin	T. H.
Ode to the Great Unknown	T. H.
To Mr Dymoke	J. H. R.
To Grimaldi	T. H.
To Sylvanus Urban	J. H. R.
To the Steam-Washing Company	T. H.
To Captain Parry	T. H.
To Elliston	J. H. R.
To Maria Darlington	Joint.
To Dr Kitchener	T. H.
To the Dean and Chapter	J. H. R.
To H. Bodkin, Esq.	Joint.

In the present edition we have not thought it necessary or desirable to include those pieces in the above list which are assigned entirely to Reynolds's authorship.

It was in the two series of **"Whims and Oddities,"** (The title of this work was probably suggested by a line in Mr Hookham Frere's poem of "The Monks and the Giants," published some years previously.) however, published in 1826 and 1827, and illustrated by his own pencil, that Hood first hit on the peculiar vein of humour by which he afterwards became most famous. These twin volumes obtained an immediate and decisive success, which is more than can be said of the volume of serious poems, **"Plea of the Midsummer Fairies,"** and of the two volumes of "National Tales," which followed them in rapid succession in 1827. And yet there is an indefinable grace and charm about the graver productions of Hood's muse, and a picturesque and sometimes weird atmosphere of romance and imagination about the prose stories, that have won the suffrages of many later readers, and that made it seem proper to reproduce them here as representative of one important side of Hood's genius, though not the comic or more popular side.

His **"Dream of Eugene Aram,"** first printed in an annual entitled "The Gem," which Hood edited in 1829, is representative of another class of serious poems in which he excelled—"those which consist in the vivid imagination and abrupt lyric representation of ghastly situations in physical nature and in human life."

(Professor Masson in *Macmillan's Magazine,* II. 328 (August 1860), art. *Thomas Hood.*)

In this year Hood left London for Winchmore Hill, where he took a very pretty cottage situated in a pleasant garden. Here the little *jeu d'esprit* of **"The Epping Hunt"** (A companion volume to this, to be entitled "Epsom Races," was announced in characteristic phrase on the back of the cover, but apparently the design was abandoned, as we cannot discover that such a pamphlet ever appeared.) was written and published as a small pamphlet in 1829 (passing into a second edition in 1830), with six illustrations by George Cruikshank.

At Winchmore Hill also his son was born in 1830. In this year Hood commenced his Christmas serial entitled **"The Comic Annual,"** which enjoyed a long run of public favour, and continued to be published every winter, without intermission, until 1839, when it was discontinued; but resumed for one year only in 1842, when the eleventh and last volume appeared. In 1830 Hood also published a series of **"Comic Melodies,"** which consisted of songs written for the entertainments of Mathews and Yates. The motto on the cover of each number was

> A doleful song a doleful look retraces,
> And merry music maketh merry faces."

Over this was a comic illustration of the lines, consisting of some musical notes, the heads of which were filled in with laughing and grimacing countenances.

About this period Hood was on several occasions induced to attempt dramatic composition for the stage. He wrote the libretto for a little English opera, brought out, it is believed, at the Surrey Theatre. Its name is lost now, although it had a good run at the time. Perhaps it may be recognised by some old playgoer by the fact that its *dramatis personæ* were all *bees.* He also assisted his brother-in-law (Reynolds) in the dramatising of "Gil Blas," produced at Drury Lane. For Mr Frederick Yates of the Old Adelphi Theatre he wrote a little entertainment entitled "Harlequin and Mr Jenkins; or, Pantomime in the Parlour," (Printed in Duncombe's edition of "Mathews and Yates at Home.") and for other theatres two farces, entitled "York and Lancaster; or, a School without Scholars," and "Lost and Found." He likewise supplied the text of an entertainment called "The Spring Meeting," for Charles Mathews the elder.

In 1832 Hood left Winchmore Hill, and became the occupier of a house, called Lake House, at Wanstead in Essex. Here he wrote the novel of "Tylney Hall," which was published in the usual three-volume form in 1834.

It should be mentioned that during these years Hood was also a large contributor to the fashionable Annuals of the time, "The Forget Me Not," "The Souvenir," "Friendship's Offering," &c., and to the *Literary Gazette* and the *Athenæum.*

In 1835 the failure of a publishing firm having involved Hood in pecuniary difficulties, he resolved to leave England and live on the Continent. Going over in March of that year, he fixed on Coblenz on the Rhine as the most suitable for his purpose. During about two years that place continued to be the headquarters of the family. In the middle of 1837 he removed to Ostend. From this prolonged exile, which extended on to 1840, arose the volume published in that year and entitled "Up the Rhine," a work written in a series of letters, avowedly after the model of "Humphrey Clinker."

After five years of expatriation, Hood returned to England and took a house at Camberwell. He became a contributor to the *New Monthly Magazine,* then edited by Theodore Hook, upon whose death in the following year (1841), he himself succeeded to the editorship, and continued in that office until 1843, contributing to its pages a number of sketches and verses, which he republished in two volumes in 1844, with illustrations by John Leech, under the title of **"Whimsicalities."** In 1842 he had removed to St John's Wood, where he continued to reside till his death, first in Elm Tree Road, and then in Finchley Road.

In the Christmas number of *Punch* for 1843 appeared the famous **"Song of the Shirt,"** together with a less-known piece, **"The Pauper's Christmas Carol."** There are several other articles, poems, and cuts in the fourth and fifth volumes of *Punch* presumably by Hood.

On New Year's day 1844 was started *Hood's Monthly Magazine and Comic Miscellany,* with a very promising staff of contributors.

Meanwhile Hood's health had been gradually failing. Even during his sojourn on the Continent alarming symptoms had manifested themselves, and since his return to England, matters had gradually grown worse and worse. After some years of suffering and pain, all hope was at last given up. One night in a delirious wandering he was heard to repeat to his wife Jane the lovely words of the Scottish song—

> "I'm fading awa', Jean,
> Like snaw-wreaths in thaw, Jean!
> I'm fading awa', Jean,
>   To the land o' the leal!
> But weep na, my ain Jean,
> The world's care's in vain, Jean,
> We'll meet and aye be fain, Jean,
>   In the land o' the leal!"

An offer of a pension from Government of £100 a year, to be conferred on his wife, as his own life was so precarious, came through Sir Robert Peel in the latter part of 1844, but the grant was to take effect from the previous June. Sir Robert Peel did this welcome and friendly action in the most courteous and generous way,

accompanying it with a letter in which he begged for one return—the opportunity of making Hood's personal acquaintance. The meeting, however, never took place, for Hood grew too ill to allow of its possibility, being only kept alive by frequent instalments of mulled port-wine. He wrote to his benefactor to this effect, and Sir Robert Peel replied in a beautiful and touching letter, earnestly hoping for his recovery. There are few more beautiful traits in the great statesman's character, and few stories more honourable to him, than this of his kindness to poor Hood during the last sad months of supreme suffering. He could die at least with the assurance that those nearest and dearest to him would not be reduced to beggary.

The end grew nearer and nearer. Some weeks ensued of protracted anguish, of almost indescribable suffering, and of convulsive efforts to hold life yet a little longer. At last, on the 3d May 1845, after two days' total unconsciousness, he breathed his last, having scarcely attained the age of forty-six. He was buried in Kensal Green Cemetery, and eighteen months afterwards his faithful and devoted wife was laid by his side.

Walter Jerrold (essay date 1909)

SOURCE: Jerrold, Walter. "Early Comic Writings (1825-1827)" and "The Plea of the Midsummer Fairies, and Other Poems (1827)." In *Thomas Hood: His Life and Times,* pp. 163-201. New York: John Lane, 1909.

[*In the following excerpts, Jerrold discusses the contemporary reception of* Odes and Addresses to Great People, Whims and Oddities, *and* The Plea of the Midsummer Fairies.]

Having followed Hood up to the time of the commencement of his happy married life we may pause to consider the position which he occupied at the time. It has been shown that his talents were early recognised on the *London Magazine,* that he had been honoured with the tribute of a dedication by Barry Cornwall, but to the wider public—the public on whose favour the penman is dependent for his bread and cheese—the name of Hood was but little known until after the publication in February, 1825, of the **"Odes and Addresses to Great People."** The little book was evidently projected by Hood in the autumn of 1824. He had inserted an amusing **"Ode to Dr. Kitchener"** in the *London* as one of his first contributions, and had happily thought of singling out various notabilities and notorieties for a like honour. The subject had evidently been discussed with John Hamilton Reynolds, and his co-operation invited, when Hood wrote the following undated letter from Lower Street, Islington:—

> "My dear Reynolds,—I send you the Ode on Martin, which, with those on Graham and Kitchener, makes three completed.

"These are the names I have thought of to choose from,—Elliston you would make a rich one,—and then there's Pierce Egan or Tom Cribb—ditto—Mr. Bodkin—Mr. McAdam—Mrs. Fry—Hy. Hunt—Sir R. Birnie—Joseph Grimaldi, sen.—The Great Unknown—Mr. Malthus—Mr. Irving—Mr. Wilberforce—Prince Hohenlohe—Capt. Parry—Dr. Combe—Mr. Accum—The Washing Company—Sir W. Congreve—Bish—Cubitt on the Treadmill—Tattersall—Owen of Lanark—Bridgman, on the Iron Coffins—W. Savage Landor, on the use of cork armour and bows and arrows—Fitzgerald on Literature—Dymoke. I think the thing is likely to be a hit—but if *you* do some, I shall expect it to run like wildfire. Let's keep it snug.—Pray, remembrances to Rice—and in the kindliest at Home.—I am, dear Reynolds, yours very truly,

"T. Hood."

Reynolds did co-operate, and the book certainly made a hit, though it cannot but be recognised that it was Hood's work which was the richer in fun, in satire, and in that wonderful play upon words which in this first of his "comic" books he raised to a fine art. Of the fifteen odes and addresses nine were by Hood, five by Reynolds, and one was written in collaboration, and all of the subjects with the exception of three were taken from this list suggested by the former.[1] In the *London Magazine* for January, 1825, there appeared an **"Ode to George Colman the Younger,"** which there can be little doubt was by one of the collaborators, and most probably by Hood. It was it is likely written after the others were already in the publisher's hands, and its appearance in the *London* may have marked the beginning of a temporary renewal of Hood's connection with the magazine. The latest of his acknowledged writings to appear there was the poem **"To a Cold Beauty,"** which had been published in the number for June, 1823. At the beginning of 1825 the *London* started a new series, raising its price from half-a-crown to three shillings and six-pence, and may also have started a new editorial *régime,* for Charles Wentworth Dilke "appears also about this time to have been the editor of the *London Magazine,* in which he wrote, as did at the same time, Lamb, Hood, Reynolds."[2] Hood had probably met Dilke during his own connection with the editorial side of the magazine—indeed their acquaintance is said to have dated from some years earlier—and that he made a reappearance in its pages in the number for February, 1825, is fairly conclusively shown by the twenty-fifth stanza of the **"Ode to Mr. Graham,"** which runs—

"*My* name is Tims.—I am the man
That North's unseen, diminish'd clan
    So scurvily abused!
I am the very P. A. Z.,
The London Lion's small pin's head
    So often hath refused!"

On looking through the magazine for February we find that an article with those unusual initials had been accepted; it was "The Art of Advertising Made Easy,"

giving some examples of the florid advertising of the day, with one or two sly digs at Colburn, the publisher, who was considered a master of the art of puffing, and with whom Hood was later to have business relations. There is something of a modern note about the writer's reference to a periodical almost killed by the art of advertising, and he certainly piques curiosity when he tells us that—

It is pretty well known that a celebrated prose writer of the present day was induced by Bish to try his hand at those little corner delicacies of a newspaper—the Lottery puffs, and that his productions were returned upon his hands as being too modest for use. Poor soul! He thought he could write; and florid Mr. Atkinson, with a pen dipped in his own curling fluid, wrote a flourishing paragraph that put him quite beside himself.

It would be interesting to identify that "celebrated prose writer." Of the **"Ode to George Colman,"** which preceded the volume of **"Odes and Addresses,"** the opening and two closing of its fourteen stanzas may be quoted with some confidence as the work of Hood. Colman, it may be mentioned, had been appointed "Deputy Licenser of Plays" about a year earlier, and had roused the wrath of many playwrights by his excision of any strong expressions from pieces submitted to his ridiculously squeamish attention. The Ode makes continuous fun of this trait.

"Come, Colman! Mrs. Gibbs's chum!
Virtue's protector! Come, George, come,—
    Sit down beside this beech
That flourisheth in Fulham road;
And let me all my heart unload
    Of levity,—and preach!

"Thou'rt alter'd, George, since thy young days
Of wicked verse and heedless plays,
    With double meanings cramm'd;
'White for the harvest' is thine age,
Thou chief curse-cutter for the stage
    And scourger of the damn'd! . . .

"Poor Farce! her mourning now may put on!
And Comedy's as dead as mutton!
    (No sheep must have a *dam*.)
Farewell to Tragedy! her knell
And neck are wrung at once,—farewell
    The Drama!—(dele *dram*) . . .

"Good-bye to Godby[3]! (dele *God!*)
Methinks I see all curtains nod
    To one sad final fall!
Stages must sink from bad to *worser,*—
The sad precursor (dele *cursor*)
    Of ruin frowns on all!

"Who, George—Oh, who that hath of wit
A grain, his fancies will submit
    To nonsense and to Thee?—
What!—come, to be 'run through,' and then

　　Give sovereigns to reward the pen
　　　That cuts us?—

"U. B. D.!"

This foretaste of the work having appeared in the *London* for January, the duodecimo volume **"Odes and Addresses to Great People"** was published by Messrs. Baldwin, Cradock & Joy in the following month. Its reception was immediately gratifying, so much so that before the summer was well advanced a second edition had to be prepared. The *London Magazine* hurriedly produced its meed of praise, devoting more than five pages (largely extracts, it is true) to the work; pointing out that wit, gaiety, good nature, and truth would ensure the work a very extensive popularity, drawing attention to the fact that the satire was a *moral* rather than a personal or political one, and finding that "the vice and a great part of the virtue of the book, both lie in its *puns.*" This instant review may have meant that the authors had still a friend at court, if they were themselves no longer attached to the periodical. Other papers followed suit, and Charles Lamb, ever the kindly, helpful friend, wrote a brief review in the *New Times,* and in doing so happily differentiated the various kinds of pun, showing where, in his view, the pun was a permissible and good thing, and where it was a blot. In the South Kensington Museum is a copy of this review with the following manuscript note on the margin. "The papers are to be sent you daily from us you returning all but those which concern you, *e.g. this,* any containing your writing &c. C. Lamb." That note was evidently addressed to Hood, who, living at Lower Street, Islington, was thus a near neighbour of Lamb's during his tenancy of the house in Colebrook Row.

Though the little book was received with enthusiasm and achieved popularity there were not wanting critics who saw that there was a danger for the author in thus courting public applause by "light verse" when he had shown himself capable of higher things. Wainewright had implored, a couple of years earlier, "let not the shallow induce thee to conceal thy depth." Bryan Waller Procter wrote to a friend shortly after the volume was published to this effect, and showed that the secret of its authorship was known in literary circles.

> Have you read the **"Odes and Addresses to Great People"**?—It is a joint production by that united Beaumont and Fletcher brotherhood—Reynolds and Hood. What a pity it is that Hood should have given up serious poetry for the sake of cracking the shells of jokes which have not always a kernel!

Barry Cornwall was too well circumstanced to remember that a man who has to get his living out of an ink-pot has to devise some means of hitting the popular taste rather than sit down and write only such things as he wishes; has to sacrifice to the Lares and Penates as well as to the Graces. Sir Walter Scott, to whom a copy

of the book was sent, wrote a kindly acknowledgment, wishing "the unknown author good health and good fortune and whatever other good things can best support and encourage his lively vein of inoffensive and humorous satire." A copy sent to Canning did not elicit an acknowledgment.

The success of the volume must have been a source of considerable gratification to Thomas Hood and his wife during their "half-honeymoon" holiday in May, though it was after their return that they received from Charles Lamb the following letter which had been sent him from Samuel Taylor Coleridge. Hood had met Coleridge once at the Lambs' but his silent habit in general company would not have suggested his latent abilities, so that the elder poet was little like to think of him as the author of the arriding book.

> My dear Charles,—This afternoon, a little, thin, mean-looking sort of a foolscap, sub-octavo of poems, printed on very dingy outsides, lay on the table, which the cover informed me was circulating in our book-club, so very Grub Streetish in all its appearance, internal as well as external, that I cannot explain by what accident of impulse (assuredly there was no *motive* in play) I came to look into it. Least of all, the title, *Odes and Addresses to Great Men,* which connected itself in my head with Rejected Addresses, and all the Smith and Theodore Hook squad. But, my dear Charles, it was certainly written by you, or under you, or *una cum* you. I know none of your frequent visitors capacious and assimilative enough of your converse to have reproduced you so honestly, supposing you had left yourself in pledge in his lock-up house. Gillman, to whom I read the spirited parody on the introduction to Peter Bell, the Ode to the Great Unknown, and to Mrs. Fry; he speaks doubtfully of Reynolds and Hood. But here come Irving and Basil Montagu.

> *Thursday night,* 10 *o'clock.*—No! Charles, it is *you.* I have read them over again, and I understand why you have *anon'd* the book. The puns are nine in ten good—many excellent—the *Newgatory* transcendent. And then the *exemplum sine exemplo* of a volume of personalities and contemporaneities, without a single line that could inflict the infinitesimal of an unpleasance on any man in his senses; saving and except perhaps in the envy-addled brain of the despiser of your *Lays.* If not a triumph over him, it is at least an *ovation.* Then, moreover, and besides, to speak with becoming modesty, excepting my own self, who is there but you who could write the musical lines and stanzas that are intermixed?

> Here Gillman, come up to my garret, and driven back by the guardian spirits of four huge flower-holders of omnigenous roses and honeysuckles—(Lord have mercy on his hysterical olfactories! what will he do in Paradise? I must have a pair or two of nostril-plugs, or nose-goggles, laid in his coffin)—stands at the door, reading that to M'Adam, and the washerwoman's letter, and he admits *the facts.* You are found *in the manner,* as the lawyers say! so, Mr. Charles! hang yourself up, and send me a line, by way of token and acknowl-

edgment. My dear love to Mary. God bless you and your Unshamabramizer.

"S. T. Coleridge."

Coleridge's confident ascription of the book to Lamb was soon shown to him to be wrong, for his old friend of many years and Hood's new one of a few replied on July 2—

The Odes are 4-5ths done by Hood, a silentish young man you met at Islington one day, an invalid. The rest are Reynolds's, whose sister H. has recently married. I have not had a broken finger in them.

They are hearty good-natured things,[4] and I would put my name to 'em chearfully, if I could as honestly. I complimented them in a Newspaper, with an abatement for those puns you laud so. They are generally an excess. A Pun is a thing of too much consequence to be thrown in as a make-weight. You shall read one of the addresses over, and miss the puns, and it shall be quite as good and better than when you discover 'em. A Pun is a Noble Thing per se; O never lug it in as an accessory. A Pun is a sole object for reflection (vide *my* aids to that recessment from a savage state)—it is entire, it fills the mind: it is perfect as a sonnet, better. It limps asham'd in the train and retinue of Humour: it knows it should have an establishment of its own. The one, for instance, I made the other day; I forget what it was.

Hood will be gratify'd as much as I am by your mistake. I liked 'Grimaldi' the best; it is true painting of abstract Clownery, and that precious concrete of a Clown; and the rich succession of images and words almost such, in the first half of the Mag. Ignotum.

The last reference is, of course, to the ode to the "Great Unknown," Sir Walter Scott. Despite the views of Lamb and some other critics, it was largely by virtue of the puns and the amazing dexterity both intellectual and verbal at the back of them that these odes and addresses achieved and maintained their popularity. It is sometimes objected at the present day that the poems, being topical, require a large machinery of annotation to make them understandable, but such criticism, while true of parts, is certainly untrue of the whole. It would not be possible to take up any similar body of topical work and find so much of it requiring no such elucidation. The book was hailed at the time of its publication as "one of the wittiest and pleasantest little books since Rejected Addresses," and some later critics have attempted to institute a comparison, but no such comparison is really possible. Each stands *sui generis*: each was something new in literature, and each has had no successor. It is a curious fact that both of these works should have been produced in collaboration. Where Horace and James Smith sought to deal with a single theme as it might have been dealt with by various distinguished writers, and in imitating their various styles added that lightest touch of exaggeration which turned mere imitation into amazingly clever parody, Hood and Reynolds had quite other ends in view. They took the idea of laudatory odes to notable people and converted laudation into satire of a ticklesome and always good humoured character, and in the expression of that satire utilised the pun in a way hitherto unexampled. Samuel Rogers later declared that as a punster Hood was equal to Swift, and fell short of justice in saying so. And on this point Coleridge is surely a truer critic than is Lamb; Coleridge, whom it is difficult to realise appreciating a pun in any other than a spirit of tolerance, than Lamb, who has himself been described as a prince of punsters. To Lamb, however, the pun was a light and airy thing to be used for proper effect in the give and take of familiar talk, and not to be put down in cold type. Hood thought otherwise. To him the pun was a very useful and helpful thing, and certainly its use adds new point to his satire again and again. The **"Odes and Addresses"** are obtainable today in a dozen editions, so that it is not necessary to cite them. In writing prefaces to the second and third editions—which were called for within a year of the book's appearance—the authors dealt whimsically with some of their critics who had objected to the puns, saying firstly—

To the universal objection,—that the Book is over-run with puns,—the Author can only say, he has searched every page without being able to detect a thing of the kind. He can only promise therefore, that if any respectable Reviewer will point the *vermin* out, they shall be carefully trapped and thankfully destroyed.

In the third edition they said no alterations had been made "with the exception of the introduction of a few new commas, which the lovers of punctuation will immediately detect and duly appreciate;—and the omission of the three puns, which, in the opinion of all friends and reviewers were detrimental to the correct humour of the publication."[5] Hood, it has to be recognised, lifted the pun from its position of disrepute to literature. One of the silliest things ever said by a great man was said by Dr. Johnson, when he declared that the man who would make a pun would pick a pocket. The common pun, the mere twisting of the sound of one word so that to the ear it suggests another is of course extremely silly, but the pun in the hands of Hood is quite another matter. The pun, as most of us use it, is merely a mechanical trick; as Hood uses it, it comes as a sort of surprise, as though the double meaning was a mere accident in the saying of an inevitable thing.

If there were not wanting people who for one reason or another disliked the odes, because of the puns or because they recognised Hood's qualities as a serious poet and thought that his flirtation with the comic muse might prove more than temporary, there was cordial congratulation for him on many hands. Another of the old *London* contributors whose letter has been preserved, is Allan Cunningham, who wrote:—

Dear Hood,—Had I behaved honestly to my own heart, this note would have been with you long ago; for much have I laughed over your little book, and often have I silently vowed to compel my sluggish nature to tell you how much I liked it. There was enough of wit visible at first reading to ensure a second, and at the second so many new points appeared that I ventured on a third, and with the fourth I suppose I shall go on discovering and laughing. I was an early admirer of your verses. I admired them for other and higher qualities than what you have displayed in your odes; but I believe a smile carries a higher market price than a sigh, and that a laugh brings more money than deeper emotion. Even on your own terms I am glad to see you publicly. I think you might mingle those higher qualities with your wit, your learning, and your humour, and give us still more pleasing odes than them that you have done. But, 'ilka man wears his ain belt his ain gait.'

Give my respects to Mrs. Hood. I shall have the honour of personally assuring her that I esteem her for her own sake, as well as for that of her facetious husband, when I can make my escape from the bondage of a romance which at present employs all my leisure hours. I remain, dear Hood, your faithful friend,

Allan Cunningham.

The success of the **"Odes and Addresses"** may well have given such promise of future work as to have made Hood's marriage in May possible; it certainly was such as to open up many periodicals to his pen. In the following year (1826) he had a new volume ready, and this he published under the title of **"Whims and Oddities in Prose and Verse."** The volume, which was published by Lupton Relfe, of Cornhill, is notable as being the first illustrated by Hood himself, for it contained forty of those comical cuts with which for many years the author added pictorial point to many of his jests. These comic cuts proved popular, but have at times met with severe criticism, some writers having regarded Hood's pictorial efforts with smiling toleration, hinting that though he was a master of fun he "could not draw." It is therefore interesting to find that an acknowledged critic has spoken most highly of the odd fancies with which the author's pencil varied and newly pointed the work of his pen.

"It sometimes happens that there are great virtues in the work of amateurs which are prevented from receiving due recognition because the amateur is not a master of form. The pen-sketches of Hood, the poet and humourist, were admirably sound in manner, far sounder and better than many laboured attempts by accomplished painters; and yet, as it was evident that Hood's knowledge of form was quite unscientific, it was thought that his sketches had no higher quality than that of making people laugh. Not only was his line very expressive, but his management of the means at his command in lights and darks was always exceedingly judicious. For example, in the scene where four expect-

ant negroes are roasting a white man, he uses positive black on the negroes with the most artistic reserve, it is kept for the two nearest, and only used, even on them, for the deepest shades; the receding distances of the others are expressed by three shades of grey; finally, the white man, who is suspended over the fire, is drawn in very thin outline without any shading whatever, that we may clearly perceive his whiteness. Rembrandt himself could not have arranged the subject better."[6]

The **"Whims and Oddities"** consisted in part of miscellaneous pieces which had been contributed to various periodicals during the preceding four years, and included **"The Ballad of Sally Brown and Ben the Carpenter,"** one of the earliest written and one of the most widely known of Hood's purely comic poems. This had appeared in the "Lion's Head" of the *London Magazine* in March, 1822, and that it had achieved considerable success may be seen from the note with which the author prefaced it on first printing it as his own:

I have never been vainer of any verses than of my part in the following Ballad. Dr. Watts, amongst evangelical muses, has an enviable renown—and Campbell's Ballads enjoy a snug genteel popularity. 'Sally Brown' has been favoured, perhaps, with as wide a patronage as the 'Moral Songs,' though its circle may not have been of so select a class as the friends of 'Hohenlinden.' But I do not desire to see it amongst what are called Elegant Extracts. The lamented Emery, drest as Tom Tug, sang it at his last mortal Benefit at Covent Garden;—and, ever since, it has been a great favourite with the watermen of Thames, who time their oars to it, as the wherrymen of Venice time theirs to the lines of Tasso. With the watermen, it went naturally to Vauxhall:—and, overland, to Sadler's Wells. The Guards, not the mail coach, but the Life Guards,—picked it out from a fluttering hundred of others—all going to one air—against the dead wall at Knightsbridge. Cheap printers of Shoe-lane, and Cow-cross, (all pirates!) disputed about the Copyright, and published their own editions,—and, in the meantime, the Authors, to have made bread of their song, (it was poor old Homer's hard ancient case!) must have sung it about the streets. Such is the lot of Literature! the profits of 'Sally Brown' were divided by the Ballad-Mongers:—it has cost, but has never brought me, a halfpenny.

Hood's reference to his "part" in the verses, and his allusion to "the Authors," suggests that the ballad was not entirely his own, and it is quite possible that it may have been early fruit of collaboration with Reynolds. The success of the earlier topical volume was repeated with the new miscellany, and though in his preface the author made known that he was resolved upon publishing some things of a more serious tone and purpose, yet with this book he may be said to have clinched his reputation, with those whose approval means popularity, as a humorous writer. The next volume to be published was the serious one here hinted at, but it was immediately followed by **"Whims and Oddities: Second Series,"** a volume similar in every way to the first, and, like it, containing some of Hood's most characteristic work in a comic vein, and, in **"The Demon Ship,"** the first of those remarkable poems in which he wrought his readers up to a pitch of excitement only to make them break out in laughter at a ridiculous anti-climax. In the preface, too, he made one of his various whimsical defences of the pun when he said "Let me suggest, however, that a pun is somewhat like a cherry: though there may be a slight outward indication of partition—of duplicity of meaning—yet no gentleman need make two bites at it against his own pleasure."

In these two volumes of the **"Whims and Oddities"** Hood gave the world a number of his most characteristic pieces. Here were the punning ballads of **"Sally Brown," "Nelly Gray," "Tim Turpin," "Mary's Ghost,"** and **"Death's Ramble,"** and those other examples of his playing with the gruesome in **"Jack Hall,"** and **"The Last Man"**; also **"The Irish Schoolmaster."** Most of these pieces and many of the others are reprinted in every selection from Hood's works. They show his peculiar genius as a verbal humorist when it was at its very height, when, like Lamb, he was largely punning for the fun of the thing, and often with a felicity that is simply amazing to the reader. There is nothing of that forced punning which in the later days of H. J. Byron and the pantomime pun reduced the playing with words to contempt. With Hood in these early years of his literary success it seems as though he must have used words with a double meaning almost unconsciously, so easy is it to read his words with their single significance and only by a kind of second sight to see that they bear a further meaning. Stanzas might be taken from any of the pieces mentioned in illustration of this remarkable quality. Here are two from **"Death's Ramble,"** a poem which, as Canon Ainger has said, is ablaze with wit and real imagination:—

> "He met a coachman driving his coach
>   So slow, that his fare grew sick;
> But he let him stray on his tedious way,
>   For Death only wars on the quick. . . .
>
> "Death saw two players playing at cards,
>   But the game wasn't worth a dump,
> For he quickly laid them flat with a spade
>   To wait for the final trump."

Here is another verse, with the same happy use of single words with double meanings, from the **"Mermaid of Margate"**:—

> "And Christians love in the turf to lie
>   Not in watery graves to be;
> Nay, the very fishes would sooner die
>   On the land than in the sea."

Examples might be multiplied to show once more that Hood's puns are not word-twistings of the kind that Oliver Wendell Holmes inveighed against in his remarks on what he happily termed verbicide. It is rare, indeed, that there is any wresting of the form or meaning of a word with Hood; he just allows the word with two meanings to fall pat, so that either meaning may be attached and yet his sentence read logically. And not only do the sentences read logically, but the poems to which they belong are frequently characterised by a richness of fancy and imagination which makes them remarkable quite apart from the verbal wit with which they are marked. At times, indeed, though the manner may be that of the humorist and pun-maker, the matter is essentially that of the poet. In the **"Last Man,"** for example, there is a sense of tragedy and a grimness of humour in combination that remove it quite out of the range of comic verse, and place it by some of his later writings in which these qualities were again blent.

Reference has been made to the impressive story of **"The Demon Ship"** in these volumes. Though it is generally reputed as a self-sufficing narrative, telling how a man in a boat was wrecked in a storm off the Wash and on being picked up by a collier, coming to surrounded by grimy men thought himself in the nether world. In **"Whims and Oddities"** the verse is prefaced by a prose passage. This the author concludes by saying, "The spectre-ship, bound to Deadman's Isle, is almost as awful a craft as the skeleton bark of the Ancient Mariner; but they are both fictions, and have not the advantage of being realities, like the dreary vessel with its dreary crew in the following story, which records an adventure that befell even unto myself." The closing words are sufficiently explicit, but when and where the adventure befell cannot be said, though it may be recalled that Hood was never so pleased when recreating himself as when he had an opportunity of going out in a boat either alone or with some such congenial sailorman as old Tom Woodgate of Hastings.

Though it is chiefly by the verse included in them that the two series of **"Whims and Oddities"** are now remembered, the prose sketches interspersed deserve some mention, for Hood continued such diversifying of his work up to the end. Sometimes these prose sketches are slight stories of a humorous kind, essays, or anecdotes, with accompanying illustrations by the author. Here is the closing portion of a couple of pages on **"The Popular Cupid,"** with a woodcut of an unhealthily chubby little god of love:—

"I can believe in his dwelling alone in the heart—seeing that he must occupy it to repletion;—in his constancy, because he looks sedentary and not apt to roam. That he is given to melt—from his great pinguitude. That he burneth with a flame, for so all fat burneth—and hath languishings—like other bodies of his tonnage. That he sighs—from his size.—I dispute not his kneeling at ladies' feet—since it is the posture of elephants,—nor his promise that the homage shall remain eternal. I doubt not of his dying,—being of a corpulent habit, and a short neck.—But for his lodging in Belinda's blue eye, my whole faith is heretic—*for she hath never a sty in it.*"

Sometimes in these short essays in prose Hood exhibited something of the qualities of his friend Elia, but through most of them ran evidence of his "impertinent custom of punning;" in them, though dealing with varied themes in lightest fashion, there was frequently that vein of serious philosophising usually characteristic of the true humorist. One of these prose bits, entitled "Walton Redivivus: a New River Eclogue," is prefaced by some lines "from a Letter of C. Lamb"—that letter addressed to Hood when at Hastings (see p. 154). Piscator and Viator are engaged in the recreation of the contemplative man in the New River, "near the Sir Hugh Middleton's Head," and here is a scrap of their dialogue:—

"VIA.

What, are there no dace or perch?—

"PIS.

I doubt not but there have been such fish here in former ages. But now-a-days there is nothing of that size. They are gone extinct, like the mammoths.

"VIA.

There was always such a fishing at 'em. Where there was one Angler in former times, there is now a hundred.

"PIS.

A murrain on 'em!—A New-River fish now-a-days, cannot take his common swimming exercise without hitching on a hook.

"VIA.

It is the natural course of things, for man's populousness to terminate other breeds. As the proverb says, 'The more Scotchmen the fewer herrings.' It is curious to consider the family of whales growing thinner according to the propagation of parish lamps.

"PIS.

Aye, and withall, how the race of man, who is a terrestrial animal, should have been in the greatest jeopardy of extinction by the element of water; whereas the whales, living in the ocean, are most liable to be burnt out.

"VIA.

It is a pleasant speculation. But how is this? I thought to have brought my gentles comfortably in an old snuff box and they are all stark dead!

"PIS.

The odour hath killed them. There is nothing more mortal than tobacco, to all kinds of vermin. Wherefore, a new box will be indispendable, though for my own practice, I prefer my waistcoat pockets for their carrying. Pray mark this:—and in the meantime I will lend you some worms."

In *Blackwood's Magazine* the work was hailed in an amusing and appreciative fashion in a sixteen page notice which began with "for three years past have we been pining away for the appearance of a new Cockney." Maga with a flourishing knout ready for use was looking out for a Cockney: "But what a bitter disappointment! Thomas Hood, so far from deserving to be knouted to death, or sent with his stripes into Siberian silence, turns out to be a most admirable fellow—quite of the right kidney—with a warm heart—a sound head—a humour quaint and original—a disposition amiable and facetious—a boon companion, worthy to be carried by proclamation or storm—an honorary member of the Nox-Ambrosial club." There was a passing regret at there being no opportunity of using the knout—"three stripes to a Hunt—four to a Hazlitt! the Cockney is not who could sustain a dozen and live"—and then came a full and appreciative account of the contents of the volume. A writer like Hood, declared the critic, may do some service even to the morality of the rising generation, by his playful muse. One of his prose sketches— the droll "Fancies on a Teacup" is said to be pleasingly reminiscent of Addison, Goldsmith, Elia, and North— "and yet original and Thomas Hoodish." **"The Last Man"** is picked out for special laudation as "worth fifty of Byron's 'darkness' (a mere daub), a hundred and fifty of Campbell's Last Man, and five hundred of Mrs. Shelley's abortion."

The two series of **"Whims and Oddities"** met with considerable success and were reproduced in new editions during the next few years. Their production had, however, a definite effect in establishing the author in the popular regard as a comic writer, and so had an important result in forcing him more or less closely to continue, as he put it, to "breathe his comic vein." Though it is idle to speculate over might-have-beens, it may be believed that could Hood at this moment have taken some editorial appointment which, while ensuring him a living wage, would have left him free to express his genius in his own way, we might have had more of his best and less of that journeyman work which he had to go on producing to earn a livelihood. At the time, however, nothing of this was evident. He had taken his place in the front rank of the funny men of his day, and the audience insisted that he must continue to be funny, and henceforward, with some notable exceptions, it was in the comic way that he had to keep. The success of these three books opened many new channels for his work in magazines and in the annuals which were so prominent a feature of the literature of the time. During the closing years of the third decade of his life his contributions to such miscellanies were many, and met with so cordial a reception as to augur well for the future. Henceforward, too, his writings were often accompanied by his drawings, for though his mastery of the pictorial art may have been small, his little cuts were irresistibly droll and therefore widely appreciated. In prefacing the first of his books which he had thus ornamented he showed that he had no illusions as to his work as comic draughtsman:

> "It will be seen from the illustrations of the present work, that the Inventor is no artist;—in fact he was never 'meant to draw'—any more than the tape-tied curtains mentioned by Mr. Pope. Those who look at his designs, with Ovid's Love of Art, will therefore be disappointed. . . . The designer is quite aware of their defects: but when Raphael has bestowed seven odd legs upon four Apostles, and Fuseli has stuck in a great goggle head without an owner, when Michael Angelo has set on a foot the wrong way, and Hogarth has painted in defiance of all the laws of nature and perspective, he has hope that his own little enormities may be forgiven—that his sketches may look interesting like Lord Byron's Sleeper—'with all their errors.'"

As Thackeray was shortly to be doing, Hood seems ever to have been ready to sketch anything comical that he saw or fancied, and if the work of both of them in this medium sinned against the canons of art, yet it may be said for them that they possessed qualities which make them attractive when the work of many of their more canonical contemporaries has long ceased to interest us. The pencil seems to have been a perpetual source of recreation to Thomas Hood, and as though the verbal possibilities were not sufficient for his ever alert fancy he invented the pictorial pun.

It was apparently after the publication of the second series of **"Whims and Oddities"** that Hood received an appeal for an autograph which is interesting as showing how the persistence of an autograph hunter provided the inspiration for a remarkable piece of verse. The letter evidently tickled the recipient, and was carefully preserved by him, but has not hitherto been printed to throw amusing light on the **"Lines to a Lady on Her Departure for India."** The letter is dated from "22, Hans Place. Thursday, Nov. 8, [1827?]," and runs—

> "Miss Roberts feels quite ashamed of importuning Mr. Hood for favours to which she is aware she possesses no legitimate claim, yet as she is so soon to leave England and perchance forever, she cannot avoid making another appeal to Mr. Hood's generosity, and not a little shocked by the surprising boldness of her former request now only ventures to ask for one of the original drawings from which his last most mirth-exciting **"Whims and Oddities"** were engraved. Mr. Hood may estimate the value which Miss Roberts attaches to such a contribution to her album by the extraordinary, and,

as she fears, unjustifiable exertion she has made to procure it; she is more shocked than she can express at her pertinacity, yet notwithstanding persists in her solicitations, stimulated by the hope of being the sole and fortunate person who on the banks of the Ganges can boast of possessing a souvenir from the gentleman to whom the laughter-loving portion of the community are indebted for so much delight, and in whose works all those who dwell in every civilized quarter of the globe take so lively an interest. In the hope of hearing soon and satisfactorily from Mr. Hood, Miss Roberts takes leave with the sincerest wishes that his health and prosperity may be ever equal to his popularity."[7]

The writer of this persuasive letter was evidently successful in her appeal to Hood. The surmise that the "Lines" referred to above were sent her in response is proved to be accurate by the fact that the manuscript[8] is entitled **"Lines Addressed to Miss Roberts on Her Departure for India."** The verses, which are a parody of a song by John Hamilton Reynolds, "Go where the water glideth gently ever," are in Hood's happiest comic vein, and include a triumphant pun in one of the two stanzas added before the piece was published—

> "Go where the maiden on a marriage plan goes
> Consign'd for wedlock to Calcutta's quay,
> Where woman goes for mart, the same as mangoes,
> And think of me!"

India was then a happy ground for marriageable young ladies, but Miss Roberts, despite the poet's sly hint as to the purpose of her voyage, did not marry. In the facsimile of the original draught of the poem the refrain is "And think of we."

The instant popularity of Hood's early comic writings may be gauged by the way in which his work was imitated and commented upon by rivals and lesser masters of fun. In his "Absurdities" (1827), A. Crowquill addressed the following quatrain "to Thomas Hood, Esq."—

> "Wits may now lay aside their pens,
> Their sallies being no good;
> Till thou art *dead* they cannot hope
> To—*urn a lively Hood.*"

The little book in which that compliment was given was described as "perhaps too direct a copy, and is certainly far off from the merits of the original." In the *Literary Gazette* of March 15, 1827, appeared, over the signature of "Sam Wildfire," "A Free and Friendly Address, to the Author of **'Odes and Addresses, &c.'"** This ran to a dozen stanzas, of which the opening two and the closing one are as follows:—

> "Oh Thomas Hood! Thou soul of fun,
> I know not one in London
> Better than thee to make a pun,
> Or better to be punn'd on!

"Would that I knew thee!—come—reveal!
  Art honest Tom, and good?
Dost thou a pun now never steal
  And turn a Robbin' Hood? . . .

"Oh Tom! how much and oft I've longed
  That then you kindly would
Leave me the mantle that belonged
  To such a funny Hood!"

In the following week's issue the editor inserted a specimen of a reply to the Address, of which these three verses are less than half, signed "Timothy P. Hunter,"—

"O Wildfire! I would not be thee
  For a miser's store of riches;
Though thou in Hood's mantle fain would be
  I would not be in thy b———s!

"For Hood will punish thy bold pun
  That him accused of thieving;
And make thee in future a pun to shun
  By thee in a pun-cheon leaving. . . .

"But do not thou his mantle wear—
  Mind well what thou'rt about;
The prying world will lay thee bare
  And find the false-Hood out."

* * *

"Delightful bard! what praises meet are thine,
  More than my verse can sound to thee belong;
Well hast thou pleaded with a tongue divine,
  In this thy sweet and newly breathed song,
  Where, like the stream, smooth numbers gliding
  throng
Gather'd, methinks I see the elfin race,
  With the *Immortal* standing them among,
Smiling benign with more than courtly grace;
Rescued I see them,—all their gambols trace,
  With their fair queen Titania in her bower,
And all their avocations small embrace,
  Pictur'd by thee with a Shakespearean power—
O when the time shall come thy soul must flee,
Then may some hidden spirit *plead* for thee."

Edward Moxon.

While Thomas Hood was still engaged in practising the art of the engraver, as we have seen, he had written enough verse to justify the contemplation of publishing a volume. We know that with that end in view he submitted his poems to a publisher, but beyond that we know nothing. Whether the manuscript volume was lost, or whether the friendly bookseller was not sufficiently friendly to venture upon publication cannot be said. It is certainly conceivable. Shortly after the episode Hood joined the staff of the *London Magazine,* in the pages of which he published several of his poems, and it may be that some of these were taken from the projected collection. Sub-editorial activities combined with continuous writing—and the pleasant interlude of

courtship—and then the success of the comic books may have caused the postponement of the projected volume. But, be the cause what it may, it remains that though a volume of serious poems was projected in 1821, such was not published until 1827, when Messrs. Longmans, Rees, Orme, Brown & Green issued "'**The Plea of the Midsummer Fairies, Hero and Leander, Lycus the Centaur, and Other Poems,**' by Thomas Hood, Author of '**Whims and Oddities,**' etc., etc." It was pointed out that there was a tactical error on the part of the poet (or his publishers) in accentuating on the title page the fact that he who now came before the public with higher matters was the writer of the popular comicalities. The objection came of recognition of the common idea that the shoemaker must stick to his last: that the man who has been applauded for doing one thing well must not attempt to win applause by doing something other. The story runs that the book was so much of a failure that the author had to buy the edition from the publishers to avoid its being utilised on the counter of the butter-merchant. That a fair number of copies must have passed into circulation is proved by the fact that now—eighty years later—copies of the volume, generally priced at a moderate figure, are by no means rare in second-hand bookdealers' lists.[9] The book certainly cannot have had an extensive sale, and the author's disappointment over its fate may well have led him to the exaggeration as to the buttershop. By the smaller circle—and it is frequently the verdict of the smaller contemporary circle which becomes that of posterity—of poetry lovers, by those friends of Hood's who had recognised his quality from the first, the book was hailed with pleasure for many excellencies.

The chief critical journal of the day, William Jerdan's *Literary Gazette,* in a notice of some length acknowledged that "**Lycus the Centaur**" boasted a number of passages "which would do honour to any poet, age, or country," but by way of general criticism thought Hood showed "too great a leaning, in parts, to those dainty simplicities which are admired in the productions of Lloyd, Lamb, Reynolds, and others of that school; but which we can never consider otherwise than an affectation of imitating the elder bards such as Crashaw, and, in some of his pieces, perhaps, Michael Drayton." Though the reviewer thus found fault with a "school" of writers for going back to our early poets, he was most enthusiastic about Hood's volume as a whole, and likened it to "a lovely summer day, sunny, not scorching; placid, enchanting, its airs balmy and refreshing, its various aspects delicious and even its clouds delightful; so that all minister to enjoyment."

The volume is indeed a remarkable one, and goes far to justify Mary Russell Mitford's claim that Hood was the greatest poet of his age—an age between that of Wordsworth, Shelley, Keats, Byron, and Coleridge (the first and last of these, the only survivors, produced but little poetry after the mid-twenties)—and that of Tennyson and the Brownings. It is worth recalling, perhaps, that Hood's volume appeared in the same year as the Tennysons' "Poems by Two Brothers."

The chief poems of the collection were separately dedicated to Charles Lamb, to S. T. Coleridge, and to J. H. Reynolds,—dedications which are interesting as showing at once the course of the author's friendships and the trend of his literary admiration. The dedicatory letter prefixed to **"The Plea of the Midsummer Fairies"** may be quoted, both as illustration of Hood's friendship with Charles Lamb and as indicating the nature of the poem:—

> My dear Friend,—I thank my literary fortune that I am not reduced, like many better wits, to barter dedications, for the hope or promise of patronage, with some nominally great man; but that where true affection points, and honest respect, I am free to gratify my head and heart by a sincere inscription. An intimacy and dearness, worthy of a much earlier date than our acquaintance can refer to, direct me at once to your name: and with this acknowledgment of your ever kind feeling towards me, I desire to record a respect and admiration for you as a writer, which no one acquainted with our literature, save Elia himself, will think disproportionate or misplaced. If I had not these better reasons to govern me, I should be guided to the same selection by your intense yet critical relish for the works of our great Dramatist, and for that favourite play in particular which has furnished the subject of my verses.
>
> It is my design, in the following Poem, to celebrate, by an allegory, that immortality which Shakespeare has conferred on the Fairy mythology by his Midsummer Night's Dream. But for him, those pretty children of our childhood would leave barely their names to our maturer years; they belong, as the mites upon the plumb, to the bloom of fancy, a thing generally too frail and beautiful to withstand the rude handling of time: but the Poet has made this most perishable part of the mind's creation equal to the most enduring; he has so entwined the Elfins with human sympathies, and linked them by so many delightful associations with the productions of nature, that they are as real to the mind's eye, as their green magical circles to the outer sense.
>
> It would have been a pity for such a race to go extinct, even though they were but as the butterflies that hover about the leaves and blossoms of the visible world. I am, my dear Friend, Yours most truly,
>
> "T. Hood."

Beautifully is the allegory told, rich in such happy phrasings as are characteristic of our older poets of whom Hood was evidently a loving reader. He pictures a gathering of all the powers of fairydom under Queen Titania holding debate with Father Time.

> "And lo! upon my fix'd delighted ken
> Appear'd the loyal Fays.—Some by degrees
> Crept from the primrose buds that open'd then,

> And some from bell-shap'd blossoms like the bees,
> Some from the dewy meads, and rushy leas,
> Flew up like chafers when the rustics pass;
> Some from the rivers, others from tall trees
> Dropp'd, like shed blossoms, silent to the grass,
> Spirits and elfins small, of every class.

> "Peri and Pixy, and quaint Puck the Antic,
> Brought Robin Goodfellow, that merry swain;
> And stealthy Mab, queen of old realms romantic,
> Came too, from distance, in her tiny wain,
> Fresh dripping from a cloud—some bloomy rain,
> Then circling the bright Moon, had washed her car,
> And still bedew'd it with a various stain:
> Lastly came Ariel, shooting from a star,
> Who bears all fairy embassies afar."

The devourer of all things has resolved that the fairies must go the way of the Titan and the Mammoth, and raises his scythe to make away with them when—

> "Just at need a timely apparition
> Steps in between."

The apparition is that of Shakespeare, who, in "The Midsummer Night's Dream," has conferred a time-defying immortality on

> "King Oberon, and all his merry crew
> The darling puppets of romance's view
> Fairies and sprites and goblin elves."

Time fails in his encounter with "that immortal Shade," and Titania bids her elves do all service to the gracious bard to whom they owe their continued existence—

> "Goodly it was to see the elfin brood
> Contend for kisses of his gentle hand,
> That had their mortal enemy withstood,
> And stay'd their lives, fast ebbing with the sand.
> Long while this strife engag'd the pretty band;
> But now bold Chanticleer, from farm to farm,
> Challeng'd the dawn creeping o'er eastern land,
> And well the fairies knew that shrill alarm,
> Which sounds the knell of every elfish charm.

> "And soon the rolling mist, that 'gan arise
> From plashy mead and undiscover'd stream,
> Earth's morning incense to the early skies,
> Crept o'er the failing landscape of my dream.
> Soon faded then the Phantom of my theme—
> A shapeless shade, that fancy disavow'd,
> And shrank to nothing in the mist extreme.
> Then flew Titania,—and her little crowd,
> Like flocking linnets, vanish'd in a cloud."

The whole poem, of upwards of eleven hundred lines, is instinct with beauty and imagination, and in the parleying between the destroyer and those whom he would destroy are some lines of happiest description—such as the closing couplet in the above extract—and of neatest expression, as when, Time boasting that he has destroyed the Titans, a timid fairy retorts—

"Great giants work great wrongs,—but we are small,
For love goes lowly."

The whole poem is a beautiful gem of the imagination fittingly shaped by the poet, a lovely piece of allegory, rich in such happy phrasings as are most frequently found in the writings of our older poets, yet full of a sweet and original freshness. That Lamb appreciated the poem we know. He wrote a brief prose paraphrase which, under the title of "The Defeat of Time; or a Tale of the Fairies," he contributed to Hone's "Table Book," concluding thus:—

> What particular endearments passed between the Fairies and their Poet, passes my pencil to delineate; but if you are curious to be informed, I must refer you, gentle reader, to the **'Plea of the Fairies,'** a most agreeable Poem, lately put forth by my friend, Thomas Hood: of the first half of which the above is nothing but a meagre and a harsh prose-abstract.
>
> *The words of Mercury are harsh after the songs of Apollo.*

In the very choice of his theme for the poem which follows the **"Plea,"** Hood challenged comparison with earlier poets of distinction. But though he took a subject which had already been dealt with in successful fashion he dealt with it himself with a new success. It is a representing of that ancient romance which has proved fascinating to a long succession of generations, the story of Leander—

> Who was nightly wont
> (What maid will not the tale remember?)
> To cross thy stream, broad Hellespont.

Adopting with every appropriateness the six-line stanza of Shakespeare's "Venus and Adonis," Hood began his poem, and at the very outset struck that true Elizabethan note which rings through the whole:—

> Oh Bards of old! what sorrows have ye sung,
> And tragic stories, chronicled in stone,—
> Sad Philomel restor'd her ravish'd tongue,
> And transformed Niobe in dumbness shown;
> Sweet Sappho on her love for ever calls,
> And Hero on the drown'd Leander falls!

In his version of the legend the poet makes a sea-maid enamoured of the spent Leander drag him down to her home beneath the waves, only to find him dead when she reaches it:—

> Down and still downward through the dusky green
> She bore her treasure, with a face too nigh
> To mark how life was alter'd in its mien,
> Or how the light grew torpid in his eye,
> Or how his pearly breath unprison'd there,
> Flew up to join the universal air.

The poem gives a succession of beautiful pictures illustrating the parting of the lovers, the fears of Hero, the struggling of Leander, torn by the necessity of swimming away from her and the desire of staying. Then comes the time when he was enfeebled by his struggling with the waters—

> His face was pallid, but the hectic morn
> Had hung a lying crimson on his cheeks,
> And slanderous sparkles in his eyes forlorn;
> So death lies ambush'd in consumptive streaks;
> But inward grief was writhing o'er its task,
> As heart-sick jesters weep behind the mask.

The closing line of that stanza suggests that the author may already have been rebelling against the call made upon him as jester. To the worn-out swimmer there suddenly appears a sea-maid, painted in words that appropriately suggest without any attempt at definition something elusively beautiful—

> She's all too bright, too argent, and too pale,
> To be a woman;—but a woman's double,
> Reflected on the wave so faint and frail,
> She tops the billows like an air-blown bubble;
> Or dim creation of a morning dream,
> Fair as the wave-bleach'd lily of the stream.

The whole story is beautifully told up to its tragic close, with a delicacy of imagination, a fineness of imagery, a grace of language, that no other poet writing at the time could have bettered.

"Lycus the Centaur" is the tragic story of a man half turned into a horse by a Circean spell. Written as early as 1822, when Hood was worshipping at the shrine of Keats and gradually feeling his way to a more individual way of expressing the poetry that was in him, this poem is perhaps more derivative than those of its companions just noticed. It is however a masterly conception, unequal in treatment, it is true, but containing some magnificent passages descriptive of the emotions of a half brutalised man shunned at once by humanity because he is half brute and by the beasts because he is half man. It starts with the awful experiences of the newly metamorphosed imagined with an impressive grimness of horror:—

> And I gave me to slumber, as if from one dream
> To another—each horrid—and drank of the stream
> Like a first taste of blood, lest as water I quaff'd
> Swift poison, and never should breathe from the
>   draught,—
> Such drink as her own monarch husband drain'd up
> When he pledg'd her, and Fate clos'd his eyes in the
>   cup.
> And I pluck'd of the fruit with held breath, and a fear
> That the branch would start back and scream out in
>   my ear;
> For once, at my suppering, I pluck'd in the dusk
> An apple, juice-gushing and fragrant of musk;
> But by daylight my fingers were crimson'd with gore,
> And the half-eaten fragment was flesh at the core;
> And once—only once—for the love of its blush,
> I broke a bloom bough, but there came such a gush

On my hand, that it fainted away in weak fright,
While the leaf-hidden woodpecker shriek'd at the
    sight;
And oh! such an agony thrill'd in that note,
That my soul, startling up, beat its wings in my throat,
As it long'd to be free of a body whose hand
Was doom'd to work torments a Fury had plann'd;

There I stood without stir, yet how willing to flee,
As if rooted and horror-turned into a tree,—
Oh! for innocent death,—and to suddenly win it,
I drank of the stream, but no poison was in it;
I plung'd in its waters, but ere I could sink,
Some invisible fate pull'd me back to the brink;
I sprang from the rock, from its pinnacle height,
But fell on the grass with a grasshopper's flight;
I ran at my fears—they were fears and no more,
For the bear would not mangle my limbs, nor the boar,
But moan'd,—all their brutalized flesh could not
    smother,
The horrible truth,—we were kin to each other!

Writing to the author a few years later, Hartley Coleridge said, "I am not a graduate in the Academy of Compliment, but I think **'Lycus'** a work absolutely unique in its line, such as no man has written, or could have written, but yourself." John Clare, on the other hand, candidly confessed to the author that he could not understand a word of **"Lycus."**

The volume in which these three poems were published is not a large one, but it contained besides **"The Two Peacocks of Bedfont,"** and seventy pages of "Minor Poems"—the adjective was then used as applicable to length, and had not come to be used in a derogatory sense as implying something less than excellence in quality. Among these shorter pieces was Hood's most exquisite lyrical outpouring in the half-dozen stanzas of **"Fair Ines,"** the poem which made so profound an impression upon Edgar Allan Poe that after reading it he described the author as the most singularly fanciful of modern poets. The critic used "fanciful" of course in the sense of being rich in poetic Fancy, not with its narrower colloquial signification. Like "Kubla Khan," this song might be employed as a standing test of any reader's capacity for appreciating poetry. In it we have musical rhythm, beautiful words, and that rich suggestiveness of a story which lifts it to the realm of pure fancy. Poem after poem might be cited to prove Hood's just title to a place among our truest poets, despite the popular verdict which has ever inclined to throne him supreme among the funny men of our literature. In the handful of pieces at the close of this volume are several of his best-remembered poems—**"A Retrospective Review,"** **"Ruth,"** "I remember, I remember," etc. There can, it may be said, have been little of the autobiographical in the last-named poem, for the description would scarcely apply to the business premises in the Poultry; it is, however, quite likely that the description may have applied to the house at the then fairly countrified Islington Green, whither the Hood family may have

removed while the poet was still in the early and impressionable years of childhood. Of this poem Bernard Barton said, "I would rather be the author of those lines than of almost any modern volume of poetry published during the last ten years. This may seem extravagant, but I know it is written in no complimentary mood."

Among the miscellaneous pieces of this volume are several which show that even in early manhood the poet was, as men of true humour so frequently are, particularly felicitous when dealing with subjects impinging upon the domain of decay and death. There are striking pieces in this vein, showing at once the richness of his fancy and the felicity of his diction. Here, for example, is a magnificent prosopopœia—

> I saw old Autumn in the misty morn
> Stand shadowless like Silence, listening
> To silence, for no lonely bird would sing
> Into his hollow ear from woods forlorn,
> Nor lowly hedge nor solitary thorn;—
> Shaking his languid locks all dewy bright
> With tangled gossamer that fell by night,
>   Pearling his coronet of golden corn.

Another piece, worthy of Coleridge, is an impressive fragment entitled **"The Sea of Death,"** with closing lines which may indeed be described as poetically perfect—

> So lay they garmented in torpid light,
> Under the pall of a transparent night,
> Like solemn apparitions lull'd sublime
> To everlasting rest,—and with them Time
> Slept, as he sleeps upon the silent face
> Of a dark dial in a sunless place.

One more passage may be cited from these "minor poems," showing again how the poet had realised that, as Shelley had put it, "our sweetest songs are those that tell of saddest thought," how humour and sadness are ever more or less closely allied—

> All things are touch'd with Melancholy,
> Born of the secret soul's mistrust,
> To feel her fair ethereal wings
> Weigh'd down with vile degraded dust;
> Even the bright extremes of joy
> Bring on conclusions of disgust
> Like the sweet blossoms of the May,
> Whose fragrance ends in must.
> O give her, then, her tribute just,
> Her sighs and tears, and musings holy!
> There is no music in the life
> That sounds with idiot laughter solely;
> There's not a string attun'd to mirth,
> But has its chord in Melancholy.

Even here it will be seen, as Canon Ainger has pointed out, how extraordinarily felicitous was Hood in utilising the pun. How many readers must have passed over those lines without realising the poignant double meaning which they convey—

> Like the sweet blossoms of the *May,*
> Whose fragrance ends in *must.*

In the same way his lighter pieces are often shot through with threads of deeper thought.

In concluding this notice of this, the only volume by which Hood challenged the verdict of his contemporaries as a serious poet, it may be well to cite a couple of his sonnets further to illustrate the mastery of his materials—

> It is not death that sometime in a sigh
> This eloquent breath shall take its speechless flight;
> That sometime these bright stars, that now reply
> In sunlight to the sun, shall set in night;
> That this warm conscious flesh shall perish quite,
> And all life's ruddy springs forget to flow;
> That thoughts shall cease, and the immortal spright
> Be lapp'd in alien clay and laid below;
> It is not death to know this, but to know
> That pious thoughts, which visit at new graves
> In tender pilgrimage, will cease to go
> So duly and so oft,—and when grass waves
> Over the past-away, there may be then
> No resurrection in the minds of men.

Here we have the thought expressed which, forty years later, George Eliot was to re-render in her better-known verse, "O may I join the choir invisible." The other sonnet, **"To Silence,"** is, perhaps, in the form of its opening lines, a little reminiscent of the stanza in "Childe Harold" beginning "There is a pleasure in the pathless woods"—

> There is a silence where hath been no sound,
>   There is a silence where no sound may be,
>   In the cold grave—under the deep deep sea,
> Or in wide desert where no life is found,
> Which hath been mute, and still must sleep profound;
>   No voice is hush'd—no life treads silently,
>   But clouds and cloudy shadows wander free,
> That never spoke, over the idle ground:
> But in green ruins, in the desolate walls
>   Of antique palaces, where Man hath been,
> Though the dun fox, or wild hyena, calls,
>   And owls, that flit continually between,
> Shriek to the echo, and the low winds moan,
> There the true Silence is, self-conscious and alone.

This is not the place to deal at length with the characteristics of Hood's poetry. Enough has been said perhaps to show that by the publication of this volume in 1827 he had definitely fixed his place among contemporary writers. It is true that **"The Plea of the Midsummer Fairies"** was not a commercial success, but if it was more or less ignored by book-buyers of the day later generations have found in it much of that by which they remember the author, and in a survey of his

life as a whole it is seen to have an important place, indicating by its excellence the quality of his genius as a poet, and showing by its reception how he was more or less strongly compelled to turn his attention to the producing works which in another art would be described as pot-boilers.

Notes

1. Mr. W. A. Longmore has in his possession two copies of the "Odes and Addresses to Great People," one given to himself by Hood, and the other given to a member of the Reynolds family by Reynolds. In the first-mentioned Hood put the author's initials against each piece, while in the other Reynolds initialled those for which he was responsible—and their markings tally in every respect. The allocation of their respective shares is as follows:—

> Ode to Mrs. Graham. T. H.
> Ode to Mr. M'Adam. J. H. R.
> A Friendly Epistle to Mrs. Fry. T. H.
> Ode to Richard Martin. T. H.
> Ode to the Great Unknown. T. H.
> To Mr. Dymoke. J. H. R.
> Ode to Joseph Grimaldi. T. H.
> To Sylvanus Urban. J. H. R.
> An Address to the Steam Washing Co. T. H.
> Ode to Captain Parry. T. H.
> Ode to R. W. Elliston. J. H. R.
> Address to Maria Darlington. Both.
> Ode to W. Kitchener. T. H.
> Address to the Dean and Chapter. J. H. R.
> Ode to Mr. Bodkin. T. H.

2. "Papers of a Critic: selected from the writings of the late Charles Wentworth Dilke: with a Biographical Sketch by his grandson, Sir Charles Wentworth Dilke, Bart.," p. 16. Dilke had been an occasional contributor to the *London* over the signature "Thurma."

3. A celebrated theatrical carpenter.

4. That they were on the whole taken in good part by those be-oded we know from Hood himself, for he has recorded that "the once celebrated Mr. Hunt presented to the authors a bottle of his best 'permanent ink,' and the eccentric Doctor Kitchiner sent an invitation to dinner."

5. Hood's son, in editing his father's works, does not seem to have recognised the humour of the preface, but gravely comments on this: "I have read, and had the two editions read repeatedly, but have failed to detect any of these omissions."

6. P. G. Hamerton's *Graphic Arts,* Chap. X. (1882).

7. The Miss Roberts of this persuasive letter was Emma Roberts (1794?—1840), writer of four books in verse and prose dealing with Indian

subjects, and other volumes. In 1828 she went to India with her sister, who had married a military officer in the East India Company's service.

8. Of which a facsimile is given in *Pen and Pencil*, by Mary Balmanno, 1858.

9. My own copy of the work—the last book to be "snapped up" by me in the old Booksellers' Row—cost me but a single shilling.

Margaret Willy (essay date spring 1946)

SOURCE: Willy, Margaret. "Thomas Hood: The Man and the Poet." *English* 6, no. 31 (spring 1946): 9-13.

[*In the following essay, Willy praises the exuberance of Hood's puns and his mastery of comic verse.*]

The raven croaked, but I persuaded myself it was the nightingale; there was the smell of the mould, but I remembered that it nourished the violets.' Here, in this single sentence, is embodied the whole courageous philosophy of Thomas Hood, friend of Lamb, Coleridge, and John Hamilton Reynolds, who, one hundred years ago last May, was driven by sickness and overwork into a premature grave. Such an utterance might well to-day earn that glib and much-abused title of 'escapism'; but if we look for only a moment into the circumstances of this tragically brief and disappointed life, we find a very different tale from the sentimentalist's refusal to accept sombre realities—and one which is among the most moving in the history of English literature. All his adult years Hood looked steadily in the face of an adversity so relentless that it became one of life's commonplaces, taunting perpetually his highest hopes; his was one of those rare spirits which learn through suffering not only to endure, but to embrace the inevitable with cheerfulness. He was resolved by every means of will and imagination within his power, and however much his body 'might cry craven', to transform 'a serious illness into a comic wellness': the aphorism is characteristic. This philosophical acceptance was, we feel, never the mere passive acquiescence of defeat, but a positive and hard-won virtue: the triumph of never-failing, humorous gaiety over despair.

It was not the disease which has robbed literature, even in the short time since Hood's day, of such figures as Tchekov, D. H. Lawrence, and Katherine Mansfield, which was the sole, nor even perhaps the chief, enemy. Constant poverty and debt, in forcing him—in his own wryly pathetic phrase—to be 'a lively Hood for a livelihood', sapped the creative energy already undermined by illness; and he was left with scant time or reserves of strength for the work where his real aspirations lay. He made the initial error of winning his first

recognition with a book of comic verse; and the public, always reluctant to accord a writer the credit for talents of a very diverse *genre,* would have none of Hood's odes and sonnets in the Keatsian manner which appeared two years later. It is by an ironical though not uncommon fate that only long after his death, when the acclaimed wag of the day is well-nigh forgotten, does this other, more important, facet of the poet engage us: that a genuine artist is seldom appreciated during his lifetime has become a truism. Hood's greatest tragedy lay in being condemned to write constantly beneath his very real gifts, sacrificing his highest potentialities to the struggle for a bare existence. At one period debt drove him to live for ten years abroad, where he wrote a book of travel letters *Up the Rhine* which Dickens confessed to finding 'rather poor'. In 1834 he published a novel called *Tylney Hall*—'a medley', Lamb called it, 'of farce, melodrama, pantomime, comedy, tragedy, punchery, what not?'; and Dickens added his verdict, 'an extraordinary jumble of impossible extravagances'. Most of Hood's time, however, after abandoning a career as an engraver to sub-edit the *London Magazine*—where he met Reynolds, friend of Keats, and subsequently married his sister—was occupied with a succession of periodicals: in 1829 *The Gem,* in which appeared his grimly haunting and haunted narrative poem, *Eugene Aram,* followed by his *Comic Annual,* Colburn's *New Monthly,* and *Hood's Magazine.* The frustration inherent in this enforced sidetracking of his talent from its main stream into the tributaries of ephemeral journalism must have gnawed at him endlessly and it is a lasting tribute to Hood's gallantry of spirit that through all the turmoil he could preserve intact—even if he could not consistently sustain—his gift of a delicate and individual lyricism, and, an even greater achievement, that warm humanity of outlook from embittered moroseness.

In the professional jester, we are told, there dwelt to the end an unassumed, almost school, boyish sense of fun and an inveterate flair for practical joking: an engaging characteristic when so often those compelled to don cap and bells for a living are unsmiling enough behind the scenes. His son relates how Hood gravely persuaded his young wife, while she was still inexperienced in housekeeping, that plaice with red spots were stale and must on no account be bought. His incorrigible penchant for punning, in private as well as public, needs no introduction: this literary fashion—or vice, whichever way we see it—has tended to alienate our sympathy as surely as it enlisted that of his own day. For puns poured from him, with a seemingly effortless exuberance, on every possible occasion, even in the most sober of moods we recall the classic example, which surely only Hood could have carried off so triumphantly, of the swallows in that great reforming poem, **"Song of the Shirt,"** which cling to the eaves and *twit* the poor seamstress with the spring. Even the arch-punster,

Lamb, writing to Coleridge on being suspected of the authorship of Hood's first anonymous volume, felt the puns here to be 'generally in excess. A Pun'—he adds—'is a thing of too much consequence to be thrown in as a makeweight. . . . It is entire . . . a sole object for reflection . . . it fills the mind: it is as perfect as a Sonnet, better.' Yet, for all the overstraining of Hood's comic muse in this sphere, so that many of his jests have for us now an uncomfortably avuncular flavour, he will often achieve a rare felicity of double meaning—a complete coincidence of sense, beyond mere play on sound—in the best of his humorous verse, his recorded sayings, and his letters. The eighty-odd pages of *Miss Kilmansegg and her Precious Leg,* hilariously satirizing the dangers of material riches, abound with such ingenious word-fun: examples wrenched out of their context here would lose their piquancy and precision—the whole rollicking poem must be read to savour them. With what unashamed delight, too, Hood puns throughout *Epping Hunt*:

> Thou art a fool in leaving Cheap
> To go and hunt the deer!
>
> . . . . .
>
> Not chicken-hearted he, altho'
> 'Twas whispered of his eggs!

and so on. We cannot read Hood for long at the top of his punning form without an involuntary chuckle here and there: we are surprised into laughter by the unexpected aptness of some verbal agility, and infected by the gaiety of mood. This incessant flow of inventiveness was, it seemed, an instinctive, almost unconscious, outpouring of an imagination more richly endowed than most with awareness of the flexible possibilities of language; wearied as he was by years of sickness and journeyman labour, Hood punned—Cowden Clarke observes—'languidly, almost as if unable to think in any other way'.

Unlike so many with an acute perception of the ridiculous, either in situation or human foible, Hood seldom sacrificed men's feelings to delight in their failings: his quips were innocent of Pope's polished irony or the sparkling, barbed malice of *Don Juan*—a considerable achievement both in tolerance and self-restraint for an editor of popular periodicals, and one who endured many personal provocations, in that age of literary feuds and slashing invective. Here was a Shandean, Thomas Hood the younger declares, 'who carried out in his life as well as his writings the principles which Sterne confined to the latter'. Suffering and hardship had left their spiritual imprint, tempering the sharp edge of satire and engendering in Hood the gentleness and compassion of a contemporary and fellow-Londoner, Charles Lamb. Indeed, we discern a very Elian quality in this 'silentish young man, an invalid'—as Lamb himself introduced Hood to Col-

eridge—and in the quiet, uncomplaining tenor of a life as outwardly unspectacular and inwardly heroic as that record of patient brotherly devotion for nearly forty years to a sister fitfully deranged. Like Lamb, too, Hood was not a brilliant conversationalist, but, his son records, 'shy and reserved' in society, 'seldom making a joke, or doing it with so grave a face that the witticism seemed an accident, and passed unnoticed'. Compare with this that passage mourning the 'late Elia' in the Preface to the *Last Essays*: 'I have seen him sometimes in what is called good company, but where he has been a stranger, sit silent, and be suspected for an odd fellow; till some unlucky occasion provoking it, he would stutter out some senseless pun . . . which has stamped his character for the evening.' The kinship is unmistakable.

Hood would jest often at the expense of his own melancholy and emaciated appearance—'As happens to prematurely old port wine, I am of a bad colour with very little body', he observed on one occasion; but where the misfortunes of others were involved he was passionately in earnest, his perceptions of cruelty and injustice intensified by bitter personal experience. His picture of the suicide—'young, and so fair!'—in *The Bridge of Sighs* wrings the heart, that deceptive simplicity achieved by the skilled mastery of a difficult and haunting metre.

> Make no deep scrutiny
> Into her mutiny . . .
> Take her up instantly,
> Loving, not loathing—

this is the keynote of Hood's generous, impulsive pity for all humanity 'houseless by night', whether in the body or the spirit. Very often for him, too, in his long struggle there must have been such moments, 'even God's providence Seeming estranged'. Now and again we come upon a line here, torn from the poet by his incredulity at the callous indifference of 'dissolute Man', which surprises by the exquisite, inevitable felicity of its music; both in the vision and the workmanship of this poem we see the true essence of Hood shine clear through the mists of mediocrity and imitation which cloud much of his work, lifting him for a moment right out of the realm of minor poets.

'The rarity Of Christian charity Under the sun' is again the burden of his **"Song of the Shirt,"** published anonymously in *Punch* in 1843. The crusading indignation of Dickens, Kingsley, and all who fought with their pens the nineteenth-century exploitation of the lowly and downtrodden, burns here with a white-hot fire; as surely as *Little Dorrit* pleaded for the reform of debtors' prisons, and *The Water Babies* for the child slaves of the industrial machine, this poem stirred the sluggish imagination and conscience of materialist England.

What Crabbe before him did to expose the sores of rural life, Hood expressed for the victims of his native city's 'cold inhumanity'. 'O God! that bread should be so dear, And flesh and blood so cheap!' is a cry straight from the heart of a humanist who shared and understood the inarticulate misery of humble people. It is significant that these two poems were among Hood's last, when his own bodily suffering increased and the smell of the mould—which he remembered to the last, 'nourished the violets'—was strong in his nostrils.

None of Hood's other serious work ever, perhaps, approached this power and maturity. His long *Plea of the Midsummer Fairies,* inspired by Shakespeare and dedicated to Lamb, is—with *The Two Swans*—full of Spenserian echoes, especially a cloying sweetness of imagery and diction. Very often we detect the influence of the early Keats in that lush extravagance of nature description which was a common failing of the group designated by Lockhart as 'the Cockney School'. *The Poet's Portion* ends in a strikingly Keatsian vein—perhaps the echo is intentional, for its last words, 'a joy for ever', are Keats's own; and the whole of Hood's *Autumn* Ode—particularly the opening of the second verse—might easily and not unworthily have been ascribed to the 'young Endymion':

> Where are the songs of Summer?—With the sun,
> Oping the dusky eyelids of the south,
> Till shade and silence waken up as one,
> And Morning sings with a warm odorous mouth.

and

> O go and sit with her, and be o'ershaded
> Under the languid downfall of her hair. . . .

Not here, but in the respective *Melancholy* Odes do we perceive most clearly the poetic gulf which stretches between Hood and Keats; we have only to read the two poems side by side to discern the difference between the sustained, full-throated song of the nightingale, and the pipings of the chaffinch, tunefully sweet yet slight and short-lived by comparison. Hood's Ode, however, is not without lines which we instantly recognize for authentic poetry, the pathos of

> . . . all the piteous tales that tears
> Have watered since the world was born.

It is perhaps of the mood of gentle, melodious melancholy, enshrined in the lyric of a few stanzas, that Hood is master; and he expresses it in a natural, lilting music reminiscent of the Elizabethans and some seventeenth-century poets—one *Song* ('O lady, leave that silken thread and flowery tapestrie') has Herrick's delicate freshness of sentiment and diction. *The Death Bed* moves us by its restraint and direct, unembellished simplicity, which concentrates in the last verse a world of acceptance of grief and loss:

> For when the morn came dim and sad,
> And chill with early showers,
> Her quiet eyelids closed—she had
> Another morn than ours.

There is, too, a wistful poignancy in Hood's advice *To a Child Embracing his Mother,* in the sad little poem *Autumn* ('The autumn is old, The sere leaves are flying'), and in the *Ballad* with the haunting refrain 'What can an old man do but die?'; all bear out the essential truth that the most moving poetry is often the simplest. We catch glimpses of self-revelation scattered through these shorter lyrics—an occasional, uncharacteristic outburst against the pain of living, and

> . . . cruel care, whose crown of thorns
> Is here for manhood's aching head . . .
> For grief is dark, and care is sharp,
> And life wears on so wearily.

> *(To Hope)*

Here, and in the bitter regrets of his much-anthologized *I Remember, I Remember,* we see for an unaccustomed moment the man who was overwhelmed by 'strife and sorrowing', on whose brow 'Care had set His crooked autograph': it must always seem incredible, one of the everlasting paradoxes of our complex human nature, that these lines sprang from the same pen as the exuberant gusto of *Miss Kilmansegg,* expressing another facet of the same personality. Hood was in some ways very like one of Shakespeare's Fools, with the long mournful countenance and a sharpened awareness of all life's sadness never far beneath the unending stream of fun-making.

There was another, recurring mood in Hood between these extremes of humorous or satirical gaiety and a pensive melancholy. We find this most powerfully expressed in the sinister dread of *The Dream of Eugene Aram,* and in the still more potent evocation of mystery and evil in *The Haunted House,* as direct and unforgettable in its own *genre* as **"Song of the Shirt."** The unknown, unmentionable horror, never stated, is vividly insinuated through a series of repulsive images of decay—the slug on the vacant chair, 'the snail upon the settle', cobwebs hanging 'in mazy tangle', a toad squatting on the hearth, while 'in its winding sheet the maggot slept':

> The air was thick—and in the upper gloom
> The bat—or something in its shape—was winging;
> And on the wall, as chilly as a tomb
> The Death's-Head moth was clinging.

Note the subtlety of that parenthesis—'*or something in its shape*' echoes on fearfully down the corridors of our minds—and the skilful repetition of that one stanza at intervals throughout the poem:

> For over all there hung a cloud of fear
> A sense of mystery the spirit daunted,

And said, as plain as whisper in the ear,
The place is haunted!

Seldom have we met so overwhelming a sense of an intangible evil communicated by means of the concrete and visible world.

A poet can never be entirely separated from his tradition and contemporary background, for his work to be considered in isolation; and the place of Thomas Hood in nineteenth-century poetry, governed strongly as it is by questions of relative stature, is a peculiarly difficult one to estimate. It was perhaps his misfortune to be born into one of the giant ages of world literature; in a lesser one he might well have been acclaimed as a major poet. As it is, overshadowed by Keats—as we have seen—and the other great Romantics, Hood's gifts become dwarfed, and tend even to be neglected to-day: the comparison illustrates all too clearly the difference between talent and genius. Yet on that poetic silence between the death of Byron and the advent of Tennyson, when the tide of Romanticism was on its ebb, the voice of Hood rings with the assurance and purity of a master.

Whether the quality of the best Hood has left could have been sustained at this pitch for longer periods, or even developed further, had precious time and energies not been devoured so remorselessly by journalistic 'pot-boiling'; or whether, on the other hand, he had explored his genius to its limit, are questions which must always remain undecided. All we can affirm with confidence is that Hood's work revealed a high promise fulfilled in at least two memorable poems; and that he never enjoyed that freedom from the fear of want in which alone the creative impulse can achieve its fullest flowering. One other thing, however, is certain: that Thomas Hood's human attainment will endure through the history of literature. There are few tales more poignant than this struggle with poverty, frustration, and sickness for a place in the sun among the poets; few human beings more worthy of our sympathy and admiring esteem than this man whose mature vision enabled him to laugh in the face of adversity and of death itself for a lifetime. Hood wrote his own dry, unself-pitying epitaph: 'Here lies one who spat more blood and made more puns than any man living.' Posterity may well add the postscript from which his innate modesty would have shrunk: 'and one whose indomitable courage is his lasting memorial'.

Alvin Whitley (essay date winter 1956)

SOURCE: Whitley, Alvin. "Keats and Hood." *Keats-Shelley Journal* 5 (winter 1956): 33-47.

[*In the following essay, Whitley explores the strong influence of Keats's poetry on Hood's serious efforts,* *contending that while Hood ignored Keats's major themes, he employed many elements of the Keatsian style in the service of his own preferred themes.*]

I

John Keats and Thomas Hood never met, although they shared many friends—the group, indeed, now known as the Keats circle—and professional contacts. It must have been a perverse accident that they did not meet. John Taylor had worked for Hood's father, a publisher, from 1804 to 1806,[1] and J. A. Hessey had been introduced into the Hood household.[2] After the death of the elder Hood both of them kept a kindly eye on the son of a family of which they had been fond.[3] Their indulgence may even have extended so far as to contemplate publishing, late in 1821, a volume of Hood's early poetry.[4] It is pleasant to imagine, as some have, a meeting between the two poets in the Taylor and Hessey office—Hood's son referred to "the talking over of literary matters between my father and Keats"[5]—but in a recently discovered letter Hood says categorically: "I did not know him personally."[6]

Hood was plunged into the circle, somewhat ironically, a few months after Keats's death. In April, 1821, Taylor and Hessey purchased the *London Magazine,* and in May or June Hood was engaged as "a sort of sub-editor."[7] Aside from his rather vague duties as a reader of manuscripts and proofs, he conducted "The Lion's Head," a monthly column of humorous sallies, and contributed twenty-seven poems and prose sketches.[8] More important, at his job and at a series of monthly dinners which Taylor and Hessey gave for their contributors he met Lamb—and, through Lamb, Wordsworth and Coleridge[9]—De Quincey, T. G. Wainewright ("Janus Weathercock"), B. W. Procter ("Barry Cornwall"), Hazlitt, Talfourd, H. F. Cary, "Poor Clare," Bernard Barton, and Allan Cunningham. Hood's "Literary Reminiscences," written in 1838, contain the fullest account we have of the "Londoners." But the group did not hold together amicably or long. The best writers began to fall away in 1823. Hood's last known contribution was dated June, 1823, although his editorial duties continued into 1824.[10] Taylor and Hessey, good men as they were, nevertheless managed to quarrel with most of their authors. The provocation in Hood's case must have been great, indeed, if he is to be forgiven his bitter words in May, 1825:

> In coming home I killed a viper in our serpentine path, and Mrs. Fernor says I am by that token to overcome an enemy. Is Taylor or Hessey dead? The reptile was dark and dull, his blood being yet sluggish from the cold; howbeit, he tried to bite, till I cut him in two with a stone. I thought of Hessey's long backbone when I did it.[11]

As far as Hood's personal life was concerned, the most important friendship made during the *London* years was with John Hamilton Reynolds, usually considered

Keats's best friend.[12] When Taylor and Hessey assumed the management of the *London,* they invited Reynolds, one of their authors, to contribute. He accepted, beginning in the July or August issue of 1821,[13] and the letters from "Edward Herbert" to his friends in the country constituted one of the most popular features of the journal. Hood and Reynolds must have met, consequently, in the summer of 1821, and Hood was soon introduced into the same ingratiating household that Keats had known. The Reynolds residence was not far from Hood's in Islington, and very rapidly Hood found himself on terms of familiarity with the whole family. Of the slightly older Reynolds, who both as a comic and a serious poet cannot but have made a significant impression on him, Hood could write seventeen years later in a manner which still reflected his youthful admiration.[14]

Hood was fond of all the Reynolds sisters, but with Jane, six years his senior, he soon fell in love. "What do you think of Theodore being in Love?" Hessey asked Taylor, November 5, 1822,[15] employing the nickname which his friends consistently used, and which Charlotte Reynolds seems to have given him.[16] Not long after, the two were engaged,[17] and Hood was soon playing the affectionate part of a prospective son and brother, as is evidenced by his fond letters and poems to Mrs. Reynolds, Charlotte, and Marianne.[18] He took part in important family festivities. For the marriage of Reynolds to Eliza Drewe at Exeter, August 31, 1822, Hood drew up a mock program of the bridal procession to include all the *London*'s famous company.[19] For Marianne's wedding to H. G. Green, he executed a characteristically outrageous water-color sketch.[20] At least once he accompanied his fiancée on a visit to George and Eliza (Reynolds) Longmore at Upwell, Norfolk.[21] On May 5, 1825, Thomas Hood and Jane Reynolds were married at St. Botolph's, Aldersgate. The signing witnesses were George, J. H., and Charlotte Reynolds and James Rice,[22] who, the new Mrs. Hood reported, "was on his best behaviour; but he is generally the terror of all single ladies, though a bit of a favourite with the married ones."[23]

Hood's relationship to Reynolds extended to literature as well. They pooled their resources in comic verse[24] in the anonymous *Odes and Addresses to Great People,* published in February, 1825. The *Odes* consisted of fifteen satiric mock-Pindaric addresses to persons in the public eye, but the "Great Unknown," Sir Walter Scott, is the only one who has remained there. Hood is generally assigned nine of the odes, Reynolds five, and both together one,[25] but in a collaboration of this kind it is impossible to disentangle completely the division of labor. The *Odes* were successful enough to be re-issued twice, and Hood, at least, contemplated a second series,[26] but perhaps the greatest compliment was paid by Coleridge, who was convinced that Lamb was the author.[27]

As Hood turned to literature as a career more and more and Reynolds less and less, there were no further direct collaborations, although Reynolds, still as "Edward Herbert," contributed a poem to Hood's edition of the *Gem* (1829)[28] and a prose sketch and two poems to Hood's first *Comic Annual* (1830),[29] a publication for which he helped design several of the plates. In July, 1827, Hood dedicated **"Lycus, the Centaur"** to Reynolds and in November, 1831, the separate publication of *The Dream of Eugene Aram*—"remembering some partiality you have expressed for the Poem itself;—and, above all, that you stand nearest to me in a stricter form of the brotherhood which the Dream is intended to enforce"[30]— and in his **"Ode to Miss Kelly on Her Opening the Strand Theatre"** in 1833 puffed the *Dramatic Recollections,* which Reynolds had written.[31] Reynolds complimented Hood in print with "A Ryghte Conceytede Verse toe Master Hoode on His Newe Boke of Jestis for 1833"[32] and wrote many of the *Athenaeum*'s laudatory reviews of Hood's books.[33]

The marriage of Hood and Jane Reynolds was a happy though troubled one, and much of the trouble proceeded from the Reynolds family, who, when they were not quarreling with their friends, quarreled with each other. The whole story will probably never be told, for what must have been a large and illuminating correspondence between the Hoods and the Reynoldses has, with a few exceptions,[34] disappeared.

The Hood children, after their parents' death, broke irrevocably with their mother's family.[35] In preparing the *Memorials,* consequently, they were deprived of Hood's letters to Reynolds,[36] and they retaliated by suppressing as many references to the Reynoldses as possible. But enough chance references, in published and unpublished letters to and from common friends, survive to allow us to guess at the course of the families' relationships. They met, quarreled violently, sulked, indulged in mutual recriminations, became reconciled, met, and quarreled again. Hood, for instance, quarreled bitterly with the Greens and Charlotte Reynolds in February, 1835—from the tone of the letter describing it one would assume a final break with the whole family[37]— but in March Jane was staying with her brother's family, to whom Hood sends a friendly invitation.[38] In August, however, Jane Hood speaks righteously of not wanting to nourish anger against her brother.[39] The incident was probably typical. The many unpublished letters I have seen provide a quick succession of kind and angry references.

The difficulties were partly personal, partly financial. The Reynolds sisters were congenitally contentious, and Hood, when his debts forced him abroad from 1835 to 1840, made the mistake which George and Fanny Keats had made of leaving his own incompetently managed affairs in the hands of the even more irresponsible J. H.

Reynolds.[40] Toward the close of Hood's life, it is true, the two families were more distant than usual, but in 1845 Jane refers to being reconciled to her brother at their mother's bedside.[41] The Hood children, as we have seen, made the break complete.

Aside from the Reynoldses, Maria and Charles Wentworth Dilke were the arc of the Keats circle which the Hoods knew best. Hood almost certainly met Dilke through Reynolds and his family probably late in 1822;[42] after Hood's marriage the two families were close for many years—so close indeed that Hood could perpetrate his endless jokes on the grave Dilke with impunity.[43] Mrs. Dilke was godmother to the Hoods' daughter in 1830[44] and Dilke godfather to their son in 1835.[45] The Dilkes visited the Hoods in Germany in September, 1836,[46] and in Belgium in the autumn of 1837.[47] In their infrequent and furtive trips to England the Hoods stayed with the Dilkes.[48] Much of the Dilke-Hood correspondence has survived, and in it are to be found many tantalizing references to other members of the Keats circle, for the Dilkes served as a clearing house of information. Like most of the Keats circle, when he was in trouble Hood went to Dilke for sympathy, advice, and sound judgment on personal and professional matters. Dilke once lamented that "our house is like a Club House" and Mrs. Dilke that "anybody seems to have a right to call upon us,"[49] and they were not far wrong. Evidently, however, Hood presumed on Dilke's Olympian patience once too often. For some unknown reason they quarreled late in 1842 or 1843[50] and never spoke to each other again.

Early in 1830 Dilke, Reynolds, and Hood—along with Allan Cunningham and James Holmes, the printer—had entered into a joint proprietorship of the *Athenaeum*. Dilke gained editorial control in June. In 1831 a managerial crisis occurred. Dilke had determined to lower the price of the magazine from 8*d.* to 4*d.,* and Hood and Reynolds wrote in violent protest. In the end Reynolds considered the course so inadvisable that he withdrew from the proprietorship in June, 1831, Hood presumably acting with him. It was a bad—and a characteristic—miscalculation, for the *Athenaeum* easily became the first literary periodical of the day and a financial success. Both Reynolds and Hood, however, remained on excellent terms with Dilke for some years, and Hood contributed to the *Athenaeum* both humorous and serious verse, letters to the editor (notably a series on "Copyright and Copywrong" in April, 1837), and occasional book reviews (notably of *The Old Curiosity Shop* in 1840 and of *Barnaby Rudge* in 1842[51]). The *Athenaeum,* while conducting a highminded campaign against literary puffery and prejudiced reviewing, gave uniformly good notices to Hood's publications during this same period. Most of them were personally written by Reynolds or Dilke.[52]

II

Though Keats and Hood never met in the flesh, they met in English poetic tradition. Lately it has been one of Hood's major distinctions that he was the first English poet to react significantly to the stimulus of Keats.[53] The tenor of his reaction is of some importance, for it was that of most of the nineteenth-century imitators of Keats. Hood retained, with considerable dilution, the mood, the music, the imagery, the diction, the atmosphere, the settings of Keats's poems; he ignored their principal themes, the intellectual content which we now loosely consider the philosophy of Keats. In two titles, Hood and the Victorians seized on "La Belle Dame sans Merci" and abandoned, to their cost, the "Ode on a Grecian Urn." More particularly, Hood not only exploited the trappings of the Keatsian style; he grafted them on themes conventionally sentimental and moral.

Like many other young men of talent Hood began as an eager imitator. Of his juvenilia there are extant only "The Dundee Guide" (1815)[54]—an imitation of Christopher Anstey's *New Bath Guide,* a sprightly series of satiric letters in the later eighteenth-century conversational style—and "The Bandit" (c. 1817)[55]—a mélange of *The Corsair* and the settings of Scott. As late as 1820 he could not "find time for anything . . . except a few short bagatelles."[56] To a "Social Literary Society" he read poems and prose which were closer to the eighteenth century than the nineteenth. It is little wonder that Taylor and Hessey declined to issue a collection.[57]

In the summer of 1821 Hood met the *London* group, who must still have been lamenting the very recent death of Keats and discussing his genius. He responded instantly. To the *London* for July, 1821, he contributed **"To Hope,"** which began:

> O! take, young Seraph, take thy harp,
>   And play to me so cheerily;
> For grief is dark, and care is sharp,
>   And life wears on so wearily.
>   O! take thy harp!

For the next six years the Keatsian note dominated his serious verse. For all practical purposes, the Keatsian poems were collected in **The Plea of the Midsummer Fairies, Hero and Leander, Lycus the Centaur, and Other Poems** (1827), with the title poems dedicated to Lamb, Coleridge, and Reynolds.[58] Many of them had first appeared in the *London.*

The debt to Keats is almost painfully obvious. Titles are taken over with little change: **"Ode: Autumn," "Ode to Melancholy," "To Fancy," "To Hope," "Lamia."** Direct verbal echoes abound, even—to take the most striking instance—to the point of direct and acknowledged quotation:

And drink of Summer in the cup
Where the Muse hath mix'd it up;
The 'dance, and song, and sun-burnt mirth,'
With the warm nectar of the earth.

("Departure of Summer," 152-155)[59]

Keats's metrics are echoed (though one must remember that Hood was deaf in one ear): **"The Water Lady,"** with additional rhymes, is closely modeled on "La Belle Dame"; **"The Two Swans"** on the Spenserian stanza of "The Eve of St. Agnes"; **"The Two Peacocks of Bedfont"** on the ottava rima of "Isabella"; **"The Departure of Summer," "Ruth," "Autumn,"** and **"Ode to Melancholy"** on the octosyllabic couplets of "The Eve of St. Mark"; **"The Sea of Death"** and **"The Poet's Portion"** on the run-on couplets of *Endymion* and "Lamia." The movement of some of the sonnets, too, is familiar.[60] Hood followed Keats in his choice and use of poetic forms: the lyric, the ode, the sonnet, the narrative. Two Keatsian atmospheres are particularly exploited: the haunting charm of "faery lands forlorn" and the regretful melancholy of "Joy, whose hand is ever at his lips / Bidding adieu."

It is impossible and unnecessary to collate and analyze here all the parallels between Keats and Hood. The discussion of a few representative poems will, I think, reveal the pattern of what was kept, what was changed, and what was lost.

"The Water Lady," suggested, Hood's son noted, by a "little water-colour sketch by Severn (given to my mother by Keats),"[61] is a recasting of "La Belle Dame sans Merci." The form, the diction of Keats remain; his theme does not. Keats's medieval thrall—a strain which was to fascinate the Pre-Raphaelites—is translated into the realm of almost domestic affections. Hood's hero, to be sure, is "made of mortal clay," while "she's divine," but we are not deceived. It is the conventional sentimental mood of wasting regret for a lost love which is attempted: "I know my life will fade away, / I know that I must vainly pine." Keats has been brought to earth, very nearly to the drawing room.

The **"Ode: Autumn"** affords the best possible example. The poem opens with a personification of Autumn—as a male figure—standing shadowless and silent. The poet asks and answers a series of similar questions: where are the songs, the birds, the blooms of summer? They have fled, following the seasons. Some of the creatures of nature are pictured as rejoicing in their hoards; others have flown. Here the Autumn-Melancholy—a female figure—dwells, weeping and reckoning up the dead, while the world looks on sadly. The poem ends with an apostrophe to go and join her; there are enough withered things to make her bower, enough sadness, sorrowing, fear, and despair. Keats, of course, saw and captured the quiet beauty of mellow fruitfulness and fulfilled

ripeness; behind his poem is a pagan acceptance of the natural cycle. Hood gives us a moody description; behind his poem is the vague sentiment: the end of things is always sad, alas and farewell. We are close to "I remember, I remember."

The translation of imagery corresponds to the translation of mood. The essence of Keatsian imagery, I take it, lies in original preciseness and immediacy, usually grounded in sensual perceptions—"With beaded bubbles winking at the brim." Abstractions are either personified or qualified in a strikingly new and exact way—"aching Pleasure," "embalmed darkness." The imagery of "To Autumn" is as precise as the scope of the subject will allow: "barred clouds bloom the soft-dying day," and even a cliché such as "rosy hue" is linked with "touch the stubble-plains."

As Hood was content with the evocation of a general and rather normal mood of sadness and regret, so too—and necessarily—he employed more familiar and generic imagery. His specific references are rather consistently to domestic flora and fauna—squirrels, owls, ants, swallows, roses, elms, and oaks. Descriptive qualifications are equally familiar and general: "golden corn," "merry birds," "inclement skies," "sunny hours," "mournful cypress," "dark yew," "gloomy Winter," "ripe grain," "mossy stone," "flowers faded." The very phrases that attract attention are those lifted bodily from their Keatsian context: "listening / To silence, for no lonely bird would sing / Into his hollow ear from woods forlorn," for example, or "Morning sings with a warm odorous mouth." Across the poem passes a train of spiritless personifications: Silence, Summer, Night, and Beauty. Precision and freshness have been lost. To sigh "tearful spells" is not, among other things, so sensuously exact as to be "Drows'd with the fume of poppies," and to see and hear "gathering swallows twitter in the skies" is not to remark that they "all have wing'd across the main."

Examples of this lyric domestication can easily be multiplied. To mention only the more revealing, **"The Departure of Summer,"** while lamenting just that, reminds us wholesomely that summer will come again, that winter is cozy and jolly, and advises us to read the poets of summer, especially him who sang "The 'dance, and song, and sunburnt mirth.'" **"Ruth"** expands Keats's allusion in the Nightingale ode into a portrait of a patient maiden, not unlike the Solitary Reaper, who is invited to "Share my harvest and my home." The **"Ode to the Moon"** is a remarkable pastiche of *Endymion* and the Psyche and Grecian Urn odes. In a series of conceits the moon is seen as the ideal of the artist, as the divine lover of mortal Endymion, as a pagan goddess whom it is now too late for any but a poet to worship, and as an inspirer of imaginative childhood, now irretrievably lost:

Why should I grieve for this?—O I must yearn,
Whilst Time, conspirator with Memory,
Keeps his cold ashes in an ancient urn,
Richly emboss'd with childhood's revelry,
With leaves and cluster'd fruits, and flowers eterne,—
(Eternal to the world, though not to me,)
Aye there will those brave sports and blossoms be,
The deathless wreath, and undecay'd festoon,
    When I am hears'd within.

                      (61-69)

Hood ends, characteristically, by saluting the moon as a fostering mother and most kindly nurse. Hood's **"Ode to Melancholy,"** which also draws heavily on the Nightingale figure, is not the fine soul's appreciative awareness of the fated death of beauty but rather a moral lament of "Neglectful pride," "cankering scorn," and "honour's dearth" in the world of men and a memento that death knocks at every door, interwoven with distressing episodes of the deaths of mothers and lovers. Religious consolation is provided. **"The Poet's Portion"** celebrates the poet's sensitivity and his ability to render passing things immortal:

                  for, indeed,
Leaves are but wings on which the summer flies,
And each thing, perishable, fades and dies,
Except in thought; but his rich thinkings be
Like overflows of immortality—
So that what there is steeped shall perish never,
But live and bloom, and be a joy for ever!

                      (24-30)

Appropriately enough, Hood's finest Keatsian poem is the complimentary **"Sonnet Written in Keats's 'Endymion.'"**

When Hood attempted, in the mode of Keats, the allegorical narrative or the narrative for its own sake, he tended to flatten symbolic meaning by rendering it merely moral or to introduce a moral to provide a wholesome application. **"Lycus, the Centaur,"** a distraught dramatic monologue, is difficult to follow and interpret. An argument was thoughtfully provided:

Lycus, detained by Circe in her magical dominion, is beloved by a Water Nymph, who desiring to render him immortal, has recourse to the Sorceress. Circe gives her an incantation to pronounce, which should turn Lycus into a horse; but the horrible effect of the charm causing her to break off in the midst, he becomes a Centaur.

The theme was almost certainly suggested by the Glaucus and Scylla episode of Book III of *Endymion,* and Keats is remembered in the descriptions of the personal sensations of Lycus and of the sensuous details of Circe's kingdom, whereof the poem principally consists:

And the snake, not with magical orbs to devise
Strange death, but with woman's attraction of eyes.

                      (56-57)

            I could fancy a thing
Of beauty, but faint as the cloud-mirrors fling
On the gaze of the shepherd that watches the sky,
Half-seen and half-dream'd in the soul of his eye.

                      (154-157)

The grisliness of some parts of **"Isabella"** is expanded into a degree of grotesquerie which Hood may not have intended:

For once, at my suppering, I pluck'd in the dusk
An apple, juice-gushing and fragrant of musk;
But by daylight my fingers were crimson'd with gore,
And the half-eaten fragment was flesh at the core.

                      (25-28)

The moral is more difficult to follow than the narrative line, but it would seem to be that an evil sensualism must give way to selfless love. Lycus, caught between the opposing tugs, without sufficient strength to renounce either, is brutalized and becomes a figure of both pity and disgust.

"The Two Swans: A Fairy Tale" echoes "The Eve of St. Agnes." A swan-maiden with her sad songs fascinates the serpent who guards the prison-tower and so allows the prince to escape. Over the enchanted lake they flee to perpetual happiness. The poem has some of the charm of "faery lands forlorn," and the Keatsian strain is everywhere; but at the very beginning and the very end Hood thrusts home his lesson: true love conquers all evil and malice.

Of **"The Plea of the Midsummer Fairies"** and **"Hero and Leander,"** both a few years later in date, it is not our province to speak except insofar as they show Hood progressing, by way of Keats, to a study of some of Keats's own models—Shakespeare, Spenser, and Marlowe. He hears them, to be sure, through his master's voice, but he is increasing his range and effects. **"The Plea"** celebrates "by an allegory, that immortality which Shakespeare has conferred on the Fairy mythology by his Midsummer Night's Dream." A fairy gathering is interrupted by Saturn, who, as Mutability or all-devouring Time, has come to put an end to a race whose "lives / Are leased upon the fickle faith of men." In long speeches the fairies seek to justify their existence; the scornful Saturn is about to put them to the scythe when a "timely Apparition" steps between, pays tribute to Titania, and puts the destroyer to rout. In the matter of the poem both the Mutability cantos and "Hyperion" have been utilized but sapped of their poetic strength, for, though Hood felt the sadness, he could not feel the awesomeness or the beauty of time and change. In style the Keats-Spenser note is prominent:

And there were crystal pools, peopled with fish,
Argent and gold; and some of Tyrian skin,
Some crimson-barr'd;—and ever at a wish
They rose obsequious till the wave grew thin
As glass upon their backs, and then dived in,
Quenching their ardent scales in watery gloom;
Whilst others with fresh hues row'd forth to win
My changeable regard,—for so we doom
Things born of thought to vanish or to bloom.

(28-36)

But there is also evidence of a reaching for a less intense, more natural middle style:

Then Saturn thus:—'Sweet is the merry lark,
That carols in man's ear so clear and strong;
And youth must love to listen in the dark
That tuneful elegy of Tereus' wrong;
But I have heard that ancient strain too long,
For sweet is sweet but when a little strange,
And I grow weary for some newer song;
For wherefore had I wings, unless to range
Through all things mutable from change to change?'

(289-297)

In **"Hero and Leander,"** which concentrates on Leander's death—he is dragged to the bottom of the sea by a nymph—Keats, except for individual lines and images, is discarded for Marlowe and for the Shakespeare of *Venus and Adonis* and *Lucrece*. Indeed, the poem has been called "probably the most remarkable example in modern verse of almost complete reproduction of the narrative manner of the Elizabethan Ovidians . . . written with the youthful freshness and spontaneity of a contemporary."[62]

It is, perhaps, unfair to criticize Hood's dramatization, "Lamia: A Romance," since he never finished, published, or offered it for production,[63] but it provides a fascinating study in adaptation. The subject matter is from Keats; the style and treatment are not. The dramatic technique is roughly Elizabethan—it is impossible to say whether the play was written for the stage or the closet—the style amorphously theatrical, though with occasional reminders of Hunt's *Rimini*.

Hood employed virtually all of Keats's material. To Lamia, "an Enchantress, by nature a Serpent, but now under the disguise of a beautiful woman," Apollonius, the "greybeard" sophist, and Lycius, however, Hood has added Mercutius, Curio, and Gallo, "young wild gallants of Corinth," Julius, Lycius' brother, and Domus and Picus, Lamia's tippling butler and steward. The plot has also been extended: Apollonius chides and reproves in several scenes; the gallants conspire to torment the two lovers, eventually luring Lycius away with the false news that his father is dying; Julius seeks to rescue his brother from the witch's fascination; Mercutius is "passion-smit" by Lamia and disguises himself

as a servant to be near her. The end, if it is the end, is changed: when Mercutius seizes Lamia and declares his love, she stabs him.

Thematically, Hood has written out the allegory and written in a moral which is similar to and as uncertain as that of **"Lycus."**[64] Lamia is not clearly a supernatural figure. She is "by *nature* a Serpent," one "of Nature's monstrous prodigies,"

witching snakes—Circean birth—
Who, by foul spells and forgeries, can take
The mask and shape of woman—fair externe,
But viperous within. And so they creep
Into young hearts, and falsify the brain
With juggling mockeries.

(IV. 88-94)

When her true nature is discussed, Julius answers the philosopher's blunt "I say she is a snake" with:

You take that literal, which I interpret
But as a parable—a figure feigned
By the elder sages (much inclined to mark
Their subtle meanings in dark allegories)
For those poisonous natures—those bewitching sins—
That armed and guarded with a woman's husk,
But viperous within, seduce young hearts,
And sting where they are cherished.

(VI. 2-9)

In part she is the incarnation of corrupting, sensual evil, luring young innocence to its destruction. Apollonius harps rather violently on the "bond-slaves" of the senses:

What are the senses but our worst arch traitors?
What is a madman but a king betrayed
By the corrupted treason of his senses?

(VI. 67-69)

But what makes her character interesting is that she is, like Lycus, herself ruinously torn between the demands of selfless love and sensual sin. In her last speech her character and her dilemma emerge most clearly. To the absent Lycius she says:

I have been both woman and serpent for thy sake—
Perchance to be scorned in each.

(VII. 100-101)

And of herself:

—but for myself I weep—
The sport of malicious destinies!
Why was I heiress of these mortal gifts
Perishing all whether I love or hate?
alas, I fear
I am here all human, and have that fierce
Thing they call a conscience!

(VII. 107-110, 116-118)

The 1827 volume was a failure. "I had, I remember," Hood wrote, "to bid myself for the waste, for fear of their going to the book-stalls."[65] The reviews either found the volume full of ephemeral nothings or characterized Hood, already known as the author of comic verse and prose, as the comedian who always yearns to play Hamlet.[66] His friends might lament that he "should have given up serious poetry for the sake of cracking the shells of jokes which have not always a kernel,"[67] but Hood had to please to live. He never again published a wholly serious volume nor attempted the Keatsian manner or level.[68] It was only in the last eighteen months of his life that he publicly graduated from the grade of punster. In 1843 he published **"The Song of the Shirt"** and in 1844 **"The Bridge of Sighs."** Both were instantly and fabulously popular. On his deathbed Hood had the satisfaction of being taken seriously.

Notes

1. Edmund Blunden, *Keats's Publisher: A Memoir of John Taylor* (London, 1936), pp. 22-23.

2. Frances Freeling (Hood) Broderip and Thomas Hood (Jr.), *Memorials of Thomas Hood* (Boston, 1860), I, 5-6.

3. Blunden, p. 77.

4. Alexander Elliot, *Hood in Scotland* (Dundee, 1885), pp. 125, 129-130. Hood refers only to "an intelligent book-seller, a friend of mine," but Taylor is almost certainly meant. The volume never materialized.

5. *The Works of Thomas Hood,* ed. Thomas Hood (Jr.) and Frances Freeling (Hood) Broderip (London, 1869-1873), VI, 137 n. But see *Memorials,* I, 10, where Hood's daughter did not think her father was "well acquainted" with Keats, Bailey, or Rice, whom she misnames "Edward."

6. ALS, Hood to one Watson, October 8, 1844, National Library of Scotland.

7. The phrase is Hood's own (*Memorials,* I, 5; *Thomas Hood and Charles Lamb: The Story of a Friendship, Being "The Literary Reminiscences of Thomas Hood,"* ed. Walter Jerrold [London, 1930], p. 99). I suspect the title is pretentious. Hessey kindly told Hood's children in the late 1850's that their father "was engaged to assist the editor in correcting the press, and in looking over papers sent for insertion" (*Memorials,* I, 7). It seems, however, that this was not an independent executive position but rather only that of a slightly glorified proofreader, for Hessey remarked in a letter to Taylor, January 21/22, 1823, that "in fact I can trust nobody but myself" and "if poor Hood had a little more gumption in him he might do,

but I fear he will not have life enough" (*The Keats Circle: Letters and Papers, 1816-1878,* ed. Hyder E. Rollins [Cambridge, Mass., 1948], II, 431-432).

8. The list is on the authority of Hessey: see *Memorials,* I, 9. Hood may occasionally have substituted for Reynolds, the regular but extremely dilatory dramatic critic: see Walter Jerrold, *Thomas Hood: His Life and Times* (London, 1907), pp. 134-135; Frances Freeling (Hood) Broderip and Thomas Hood (Jr.), *Memorials of Thomas Hood,* 2nd ed. (London, 1869), pp. 21-22; *Keats Circle,* II, 459 n.

9. Hood recalled "a discussion on the value of the promissory notes issued by our younger poets, wherein Wordsworth named Shelley, and Lamb took John Keats for choice" (*Hood and Lamb,* p. 107).

10. Blunden, p. 145.

11. Henry C. Shelley, *Literary By-Paths in Old England* (Boston, 1906), p. 340. Taylor and Hessey returned the bitterness: see Blunden, pp. 184-185; Blunden, "New Sidelights on Keats, Lamb, and Others," *London Mercury,* IV (1921), 148. Later in life Hessey could write: "It was always to me a subject of great regret that our acquaintance with him [Hood] and Reynolds ceased, I scarcely know how & why" (*Keats Circle,* II, 475.)

12. For a convenient summary of the relations between the Reynoldses and Keats, see *Keats Circle,* I, cxviii-cxxvi.

13. George L. Marsh, "The Writings of Keats's Friend Reynolds," *SP* [*Studies in Philology*], XXV (1928), 499. There is the speculative possibility that Reynolds contributed as early as 1820: see Marsh, "Newly Identified Writings by John Hamilton Reynolds," *Keats-Shelley Journal,* I (1952), 50-51.

14. *Hood and Lamb,* p. 121.

15. *Keats Circle,* II, 426.

16. See Jerrold, p. 126.

17. Hood's son's assertion, in 1860, that "the match was not entirely approved of by my mother's family" (*Memorials,* I, 17 n.) is probably spite after the fact. The letters of the period indicate the opposite.

18. Letters in Jerrold, ch. VI (pp. 123-162), Shelley, pp. 313-366; poems in *The Complete Poetical Works of Thomas Hood,* ed. Walter Jerrold (London, 1906), pp. 434, 660, 661.

19. Shelley, pp. 325-326; see also Blunden, *London Mercury,* IV, 147.

20. Shelley, p. 349.

21. *Memorials,* 2nd ed., pp. 20-23.

22. *London Magazine,* n.s., II (1825), 317; *NQ [Notes & Queries],* 8th s., V (1894), 397. The officiating minister was Dr. Edward Rice—"our favourite," Jane Hood called him (*Memorials,* 2nd ed., p. 31)—presumably no relation to James: see Hyder E. Rollins, "Louis Arthur Holman and Keats," *Harvard Library Bulletin,* IV (1950), 387.

23. *Memorials,* 2nd ed., p. 31.

24. I have, I think, discounted Hood's official collaboration with Reynolds on the five-act farce, *Gil Blas! At 17, 25, 52* (August, 1822): see my "Thomas Hood as a Dramatist," *The University of Texas Studies in English,* XXX (1951), 187-188.

25. There are in existence several copies of the *Odes* in which one or the other of the authors initialed his contributions. Thus Jerrold (p. 164 n.) and Harry Buxton Forman (*The Letters of John Keats,* 4th ed., ed. M. B. Forman [London, 1952], pp. xxxix-x) assign the Graham, Fry, Martin, Scott, Grimaldi, Steam, Parry, Kitchiner, and Bodkin odes to Hood; the MacAdam, Dymoke, Sylvanus Urban, Elliston, and Ireland to Reynolds; and the Foote to both. One "T. M. T.," who appears to have had some personal knowledge, concurs in this (*NQ,* 2nd s., II [1856], 275). But, unfortunately, George L. Marsh (*John Hamilton Reynolds, Poetry and Prose* [London, 1928], p. 31) records a copy which Reynolds gave to Monckton Milnes and in which he claimed the additional authorship of Graham, Grimaldi, Steam, Parry, and Kitchiner. The Houghton Library at Harvard possesses a copy which, although three odes are unmarked, upsets the Marsh and Buxton Forman lists by assigning Graham, Martin, and Foote to Reynolds, MacAdam and Ireland to Hood. See also *Works,* V, 20, X, 545. Any internal evidence is unconvincing.

26. Alaric A. Watts, *Alaric Watts* (London, 1884), II, 24-25.

27. See *Hood and Lamb,* pp. 124-125, and *The Letters of Charles and Mary Lamb,* ed. E. V. Lucas (London, 1935), III, 7-8. Lamb himself wrote a brief notice of the volume for the *New Times,* April 12, 1825: see *The Works of Charles and Mary Lamb,* ed. E. V. Lucas (London, 1903), I, 285-287.

28. "Sonnet. Copied from the Album of a Wholesale House in the City," p. 24.

29. "The Pillory," pp. 27-32, "Sonnet to Vauxhall," p. 38, "To Fanny," pp. 85-88.

30. *Poetical Works,* pp. 161, 744.

31. *Poetical Works,* pp. 462-463, 757; see also pp. 450-451, 757. Crabb Robinson thought that Hood had helped Reynolds with the script, but see Whitley, *Texas Studies,* XXX, 199.

32. Marsh, *SP,* XXV, 506.

33. Leslie A. Marchand, *The Athenaeum: A Mirror of Victorian Culture* (Chapel Hill, 1941), p. 177. See also *Letters of Thomas Hood: From the Dilke Papers in the British Museum,* ed. Leslie A. Marchand (New Brunswick, 1945), p. 56.

34. Aside from those letters cited in note 18, I know only of one ALS from Jane Hood to Charlotte Reynolds, August 25, 1835, in the possession of Professor Leslie A. Marchand, and one from J. H. Reynolds to Hood, March 13, 1840 (printed in the *Bookman* [London], LXIV [1923], 277-278).

35. Fanny Brawne Lindon refers to the quarrel in a letter to Mrs. Dilke (?), November, 1848: see Hyder E. Rollins, "A Fanny Brawne Letter of 1848," *Harvard Library Bulletin,* V (1951), 373.

36. *Memorials,* I, 10 n.

37. *Letters,* ed. Marchand, pp. 15-28.

38. *Memorials,* I, 53, 58.

39. ALS, Jane Hood to Charlotte Reynolds, August 25, 1835, in the possession of Professor Leslie A. Marchand.

40. Charles MacFarlane, *Reminiscences of a Literary Life* (New York, 1917), p. 107; ALS, Hood to Jane, March 15, 1835, Bristol Central Library.

41. Jerrold, p. 396.

42. Not, of course, as early as 1816, as Dilke's grandson claimed (Sir Charles W. Dilke, *The Papers of a Critic* [London, 1875], I, 2, 54). Mrs. Dilke quarreled with the Reynoldses late in 1821, but there was "every prospect of a reconciliation" in October 1822 (*Letters of Fanny Brawne to Fanny Keats, 1820-1824,* ed. Fred Edgcumbe [New York, 1937], pp. 48-49, 82).

43. A caricature of Dilke, apprehensively perched on a bed too short for him, was used as an illustration in Hood's *Up the Rhine* (1840): see *Works,* III, 230; *Memorials,* II, 26 n.

44. *Letters,* ed. Marchand, p. 82.

45. *Poems Humorous and Pathetic by Thomas Hood the Younger,* ed. (with an introductory memoir) Frances Freeling (Hood) Broderip (London, 1877), p. 4.

46. *Memorials,* I, 175, 177, 180, 185. Fanny Brawne, now Mrs. Lindon, seems to have visited the Hoods sometime in 1835 (*Letters,* ed. Marchand, pp. 28, 76) and again in November, 1836 (ALS, Hood to Jane, November 4, 1836, Bristol Central Library).

47. *Memorials,* I, 266, 271.

48. *Memorials,* II, 1, 36.

49. ALS, Dilkes to Hoods, December 27, 1839, Bristol Central Library.

50. Dilke's grandson says their friendship lasted until 1842 (Dilke, I, 2). The last friendly reference to the Dilkes I can trace is in November, 1842; in 1843 and 1844 Hood refers to the *Athenaeum*'s being closed to him: see my "Hood and Dickens: Some New Letters," *Huntington Library Quarterly,* XIV (1951), 398, 405, 413.

51. Whitley, *Huntington Library Quarterly,* XIV, 385-386, 387.

52. Marchand, pp. 26, 34-37, 69-70, 169-170, 173-178, 210-211, 302-303.

53. The matter has received some treatment in George H. Ford, *Keats and the Victorians* (New Haven, 1944), pp. 7-10; Léonie Villard, *The Influence of Keats on Tennyson and Rossetti* (Paris, 1914), pp. 19-24; Douglas Bush, *Mythology and the Romantic Tradition in English Poetry* (Cambridge, Mass., 1937), pp. 189-192; Federico Olivero, "Hood and Keats," *MLN* [*Modern Language Notes*], XXVIII (1913), 233-235; "Thomas Hood: The Language of Poetry," *TLS* [*Times Literary Supplement*], September 19, 1952, pp. 605-606; John Heath-Stubbs, *The Darkling Plain* (London, 1950), pp. 49-59.

54. *Memorials,* 2nd ed., pp. 9-12.

55. *Poetical Works,* pp. 700-717. A "'Bandit' to match the 'Corsair,'" Hood called it (*Hood and Lamb,* pp. 94-95).

56. Elliot, p. 111.

57. See note 4.

58. *Poetical Works,* pp. 110-196. For the uncollected Keatsian poems, see pp. 399-400, 403, 404-410, 438, 674-699.

59. For a list of direct parallels (I will not record every use of "forlorn"), see Hood's "Ruth," l. 1, Keats's "Ode to a Nightingale," ll. 66-67; "Plea of the Midsummer Fairies," ll. 566-567, "Hyperion," I, 58-59; "Hero and Leander," ll. 269-270, "On a Leander Gem," ll. 12-14; "Hero and Leander," ll. 225-228, "Isabella," ll. 269-272; "Ode: Autumn," l. 17, "Ode to a Nightingale," l. 29; "Ode: Autumn," ll. 41-42, 54-57, "Ode on Melancholy," ll. 5, 21-23; "Two Peacocks of Bedfont," l. 195, "Eve of St. Agnes," l. 263; "Hero and Leander," l. 620, "Lamia," I, 8; "Plea of the Midsummer Fairies," ll. 349-350, "Ode on a Grecian Urn," ll. 33-34; "Plea of the Midsummer Fairies," l. 444,

"Epistle to G. F. Mathew," l. 39; "Ode to Melancholy," ll. 47-61, "Ode on Melancholy," the canceled first stanza ("Though you should build a bark of dead men's bones"); "Ode: Autumn," ll. 1-8, "Hyperion," I, 1-14; "Hero and Leander," ll. 375-376, "Eve of St. Agnes," ll. 289-306; "Hymn to the Sun," "Ode to Psyche," ll. 28-35; "Ode to the Moon," ll. 27-37, "Ode to Psyche," ll. 36-45; "Ode to the Moon," ll. 61-71, contains a clear reference to "Ode on a Grecian Urn," and Ode to Melancholy," ll. 1-34, to "Ode to a Nightingale."

60. Compare, for example, "Sonnet" ("It is not death, that sometime in a sigh") with "When I have fears that I may cease to be."

61. *Works,* V, 154 n.

62. Bush, p. 192. For some parallels with Spenser, Marlowe, and Shakespeare, see pp. 190 n., 191 n.

63. After her husband's death, Jane Hood gave the manuscript to William Jerdan, who published it at the end of the first volume of his *Autobiography* (London, 1852-1853). The date of composition is uncertain. See Whitley, *Texas Studies,* XXX, 185-187.

64. The Lamia image occurs, significantly, in "Lycus," ll. 56-57.

65. *Memorials,* I, 171.

66. *New Monthly,* XXI (1827), 372-373; *Monthly Review,* n.s., VI (1827), 253-261.

67. B. W. Procter; see *The Works of Thomas Lovell Beddoes,* ed. H. W. Donner (London, 1935), p. 597.

68. In his various magazines and miscellanies Hood published for the first, or nearly the first, time important versions of six of Keats's poems: "On a Leander Gem," *Gem,* 1829; "To Mrs. Reynolds's Cat," *Comic Annual,* 1830; "Old Meg," *Hood's Magazine,* June, 1844; "Time's sea hath been five years at its slow ebb," *Hood's,* September, 1844; "Hush, hush! tread softly!" and "High-mindedness, a jealousy for good," *Hood's,* April, 1845. The poems came from the scrapbooks of Jane Hood and Monckton Milnes. Hood may have had something to do with the publication of "In drear nighted December" in the *Gem* for 1830: see my "The Autograph of Keats's 'In Drear Nighted December,'" *Harvard Library Bulletin,* V (1951), 119.

J. C. Reid (essay date 1963)

SOURCE: Reid, J. C. "The Comic and the Serious" and "The Poetry of Conscience." In *Thomas Hood,* pp. 72-95; 200-17. London: Routledge and Kegan Paul, 1963.

[*In the following excerpts, Reid discusses Hood's best known poems, from the early humorous pieces to the serious works on social justice that appeared shortly before his death.*]

During this period of tranquillity, Hood was pursuing his literary endeavours with tireless application; he now had a wife to support as well as sisters. He did some engraving, too, including the large 'The Progress of Cant'. But the success of *Odes and Addresses* encouraged him to attempt something else in a not dissimilar vein, this time independently of Reynolds. He collected several of the pieces he had written earlier for the *London* and other magazines, added some new ones, and, towards the end of 1826, saw them published by Lupton Relfe of Cornhill as his first 'entire book', *Whims and Oddities,* which appeared under the author's name. Among the poems included were '**The Last Man'**, '**The Irish Schoolmaster'** and two of his most celebrated comic ballads, '**Faithless Nelly Gray'** and '**The Ballad of Sally Brown and Ben the Carpenter'**. At least the first verse of the former:

> Ben Battle was a soldier bold
>   And used to war's alarms:
> But a cannon-ball took off his legs
>   So he laid down his arms!

and the last verses of the latter:

> And then he tried to sing 'All's Well',
>   But could not though he tried;
> His head was turned and so he chewed
>   His pigtail till he died.
>
> His death, which happened in his berth,
>   At forty-odd befell:
> They went and told the sexton, and
>   The sexton toll'd the bell.

are among the best-known lines in the language.

It is certain that J. H. Reynolds had a hand in '**Sally Brown'**, although it is impossible to say how much, for it was an early effort of Hood's, appearing in the *London* in March, 1822, when he first knew Reynolds. In the note prefacing the poem in *Whims and Oddities,* Hood wrote: 'I have never been vainer of any verses than of my part in the following Ballad . . . "**Sally Brown**" has been favoured, perhaps, with as wide a patronage as the "**Moral Songs**", though its circle may not have been of so select a class as the friends of "**Hohenlinden**". But I do not desire to see it amongst what are called Elegant Extracts. The lamented Emery, drest as Tom Tug, sang it at his last mortal Benefit at Covent Garden—and, ever since, it has been a great favourite with the watermen of Thames, who time their oars to it, as the wherry-men of Venice time theirs to the lines of Tasso. With the watermen, it went naturally to Vauxhall:—and, overland, to Sadler's Wells. The Guards, not the mail coach, but the Life Guards,—picked it out from a fluttering hundred of others—all going to one

air—against the dead wall at Knightsbridge. Cheap Printers of Shoe Lane, and Cow-cross (all pirates!) disputed about the Copyright, and published their own editions,—and in the meantime, the Authors, to have made bread of their song (it was poor old Homer's hard ancient case!) must have sung it about the streets. Such is the lot of Literature! The profits of "**Sally Brown**" were divided by the Ballad Mongers:—it has cost, but never brought me, a half-penny.'

Hood's references to 'my part' and 'the Authors' implicitly acknowledge Reynolds's share in the poem, but whether John Hamilton contributed more than an idea or a line or two we shall never know. We may safely leave Hood the best lines and the famous verses, for they are typical of his work thereafter, and there is little in Reynolds's own verse to match the aptness of the wit and puns here. In the *Whims and Oddities,* indeed, are present quite clearly the distinctive qualities of Hood's writing—the exuberant punning, the tremendous, but dangerous facility with rhymes, the concern with low life, the bouncing joy in slapstick comedy, the fondness for eighteenth-century descriptive and landscape verse (showing up, for instance, in '**The Irish Schoolmaster**', with its echoes of Shenstone) and the pervasively good-humoured atmosphere throughout.

In much of Hood's early comic verse, there is the tone of the English music-hall in its palmy days—sunny-tempered vulgarity, jokes about food and drunkenness and physical disabilities, and mothers-in-law and marriage, a dislike of pretension and pomposity and a 'looking on the bright side—thumbs up' philosophy. But these pieces also have something special to Hood, not just the vein of sentimental humanitarianism already evident in both some of the 'whims' and in the prose sketches in the 'Elia' manner which are included in the volume, but that individual blend of the grotesque, the comic and the horrible which was to give strength to his later performances in this lighter style.

'**The Last Man'**, for instance, is a remarkable poem that unites the vision of apocalyptic science-fiction with the charnel-house mood of Poe. After a great plague, the hangman-narrator believes himself to be the sole human survivor in the world. But he meets an old beggar, who cheerfully makes the best of things:

> Now a curse (I thought) be on his love,
> And a curse upon his mirth—
> An' it were not for that beggar man
> I'd be the King of the earth,—
> But I promis'd myself an hour should come
> To make him rue his birth.

They walk together through the desolation of a world struck down in the midst of its everyday activities; the horror of the devastation is brought home with sharp economy in lines like these:

For the porters all were stiff and cold
And could not lift their heads;
And when we came where their masters lay,
The rats leapt out of the beds.

But the hangman is angry to see the beggar capering in the king's crown and cloak, and hangs him. As he watches hounds come and rend the body, the thought comes to him:

I know the Devil, when I am dead,
Will send his hounds for me.

And so he is left alone with his conscience.

'The Last Man' is a strangely moving and haunting poem, a horror story that is also a parable. I have no difficulty myself in accepting it exactly as it is—that is, until the last verse where Hood seems to let his readers down from the Gothic terror with an anti-climax, as he does in **'The Demon Ship'** and other poems:

For hanging looks sweet—but, alas! in vain
My desperate fancy begs—
I must turn my cup of sorrows quite up,
And drink it to the dregs,—
For there's not another man alive,
In the world, to pull my legs!

And yet I wonder if he does, whether the grisly pun of the final line is not, in fact, congruous with what has gone before, and does not make quite good sense on two levels, in which the different moods are complementary rather than conflicting. When Hood is at his best, this, indeed, is the effect of his puns, to create an oddly ambivalent atmosphere in which the horror is never quite swallowed up by the farce.

The reviewer in *Blackwood's* for June, 1827, who devoted a long article to a eulogy of *Whims and Oddities* and who found Hood to have 'taste, feeling and genius', quoted the whole of **'The Last Man'**, but saw in it only a clever parody of Thomas Campbell's poem of the same name, and found the very idea of a Last Man more of an absurdity than an atomic age can afford to. Even Hood's wood-cut with which the poem, like several others in the volume, is illustrated, and which the *Blackwood's* reviewer described like this: "**'The Last Man'** is a sort of absurd sailor-like insolent ruffian, sitting with arms a-kimbo, cross-legged and smoking his pipe on the cross-tree of a gallows', has today a disturbing element of 'sick humour' about it that is beyond the reach of the merely farcical. To call it 'Cruikshankish', as *Blackwood's* does, is to imply a good deal more to those who nowadays look at the grotesque, thin-lined, cruelly comic and vaguely sinister illustrations to Dickens than it did to Hood's contemporaries. In a sense, in such poems as **'The Last Man'**, Hood is one of the primary ancestors of 'comédie noire' and, to some degree, of that 'sick humour' with which

the Americans have recently made us familiar. Death, disease, mutilation, physical ills, mental strains, cannibalism are all subjects for his jesting verses, and while the tone, the 'disposition amiable and facetious' of Hood prevents the humour from being either pathological or neurotically unpleasant, the constant preoccupation with illness which his own condition induced, combined with his particular talent for freakish analogies, makes him the innovator of a strain that runs right through Victorian humour, often in forms cruder and in considerably less good taste than his.

Although the success of *Whims and Oddities,* which went into several editions at once, greatly pleased Hood, he felt that those of his friends who believed him to be basically a serious poet may have had the right of it. With a typically humorous inversion of the facts, he announced in the preface to *Whims and Oddities* that 'At a future time, the Press may be troubled with some things of a more serious tone, and purpose—which the Author has resolved upon publishing, in despite of the advice of certain critical friends. His forte, they are pleased to say, is decidedly humorous; but a gentleman cannot be always breathing his comic vein.' The first fruit of such a promise came with the publication in February, 1827, by W. H. Ainsworth of two volumes of stories called *National Tales.* These imitations of the Italian *novella* form, inspired no doubt by Hood's extensive reading, at this time, of Elizabethan literature, were at best tepidly received by the critics, sold only modestly, and were not reprinted. There are no concealed gems or neglected master-pieces here. In the main they are poor stuff, inflated anecdotes set in Arabia, Venice, Persia and England, dull in their formal style, imitative in plot, shallow in characterization and often marked by the anti-Catholic prejudices of Hood whose notions of the Catholic religion were almost wholly derived from Gothic novels and Little England Protestant stereotypes. Some of the stories, it is true, such as 'The Fair Maid of Ludgate', a tale of the Great Plague, have considerable fluency and a certain thin charm. But in general the *National Tales* lack substance and originality and anything of the distinctiveness of *Whims and Oddities.*

Before Hood could undertake another book, calamity over-took his little household. His first child, a girl, was born in April, 1827, but Jane's poor health made the delivery a most difficult one, and the child died immediately after birth. This tragedy deeply affected Thomas and Jane who loved children and longed for infants of their own. After Hood's death, a little lock of golden hair was found wrapped in a piece of paper bearing these touching lines, written in his sorrow:

Little eyes that scarce did see,
Little lips that never smiled;
Alas! my little dear dead child,

> Death is thy father, and not me,
> I but embraced thee, soon as he.

When Thomas wrote to tell Charles Lamb the sad news, his friend replied, 'Your letter elicited a flood of tears from Mary. . . . God bless you and the mother (or should be mother) of your sweet girl that should have been.' A few weeks later he sent to Jane Hood the poem, 'On an Infant Dying as soon as Born', which E. V. Lucas considered in many ways Lamb's most remarkable poem. Lamb identified himself with Hood's sorrow; the lost child became one of the dream children he had never had, and out of this empathy came the gently sincere metaphysical verses that end

> Why should kings and nobles have
> Pictured trophies to their grave;
> And we, churls, to thee deny
> Thy pretty toys with thee to lie,
> A more harmless vanity?

The Hoods treasured this mark of friendship, and later, when Hood was editing *The Gem,* he printed the poem in full in its pages.

The death of their first child was not the only trouble that 1827 brought to the Hoods. During the winter, Thomas suffered a severe recurrence of rheumatic fever, that laid him low for some months. He continued to write furiously during his convalescence, and as soon as he was out of bed, he went to Brighton to seek the strength that seemed always just around the corner. It was virtually the end of his period of reasonable health; from then onwards, he was rarely to be free from physical ills. The immediate cause of his relapse was debilitation brought on by excessive work, since, early in 1827, he had produced, in addition to two volumes of **Whims and Oddities** and the two volumes of *National Tales,* and many contributions to periodicals, his most ambitious collection of serious poems, **The Plea of the Midsummer Fairies and Other Poems.** No matter what the cost in nervous and bodily energy, Thomas Hood was determined to establish himself firmly as a writer, above all as a serious one.

Some of the poems contained in **The Plea of the Midsummer Fairies** had been written in 1821, and even earlier, and belong to the period when Hood was first thinking of issuing a serious volume; he had published thirteen in the *London Magazine* of the 1820's; fifteen only of the thirty-seven poems were new. But the book represented a carefully organized attempt to win a name as a poet of substance. And this despite the fact that when the volume appeared in July, 1827, under the imprint of Messrs. Longmans, Rees, Orme, Brown and Green, the author was described as 'Thomas Hood, Author of **"Whims and Oddities"**, etc., etc.' The longest poems in it were the title-piece, **'Hero and Leander'**, and **'Lycus the Centaur'**, all very much in the current Romantic manner, and showing Hood as a sensitive young writer susceptible to the influences of Coleridge, Wordsworth, Keats, and, behind them, of the Elizabethans.

'The Plea of the Midsummer Fairies' itself was dedicated to Lamb in a prefatory letter, which acknowledges what Hood had learnt from him in love for Shakespeare's plays, and especially for his comedies: 'I desire to record a respect and admiration for you as a writer, which no one acquainted with our literature, save Elia himself, will think disproportionate or misplaced. If I had not these better reasons to govern me, I should be guided to the same selection by your intensive yet critical relish for the works of our great Dramatist, and for that favourite play in particular which has furnished the subject of my verses. It is my design, in the following Poem, to celebrate, by an allegory, that immortality which Shakespeare has conferred on the Fairy mythology by his Midsummer Night's Dream.'

Hood's poem is in many ways an enchanting work, which retains much of its charm for a modern reader. The form is that of the Spenserian stanza with the final alexandrine replaced by a pentameter. In his fancy, the poet views a 'shady and sequester'd scene' in the midst of which is 'Titania and her pretty crew'. The fairy queen is melancholy, for she has dreamt of the passing away of the fairies, whose 'lives are leased upon the fickle faith of men', and of the monstrous figure of Saturn who, representing Time and Change, has come in her dream to destroy the fairy world. No sooner has she described this to her retinue than Saturn himself appears and menaces the little people. Titania pleads with him, and, following her, Puck, Ariel, and other fairies, in long, jewelled speeches, urge their claims to be spared, pointing out that they are the custodians of music, the flowers, love and kindness, the trees, insects, bees and small forest creatures, springs and fountains and nature's sweet sounds, and that they are friends to men and especially to children. Saturn rejects their pleas and has just raised his destroying scythe when

> a timely Apparition
> Steps in between, to bear the awful brunt.

It is Shakespeare himself, to whom Titania makes an eloquent appeal for help. The kind Shade rebukes Saturn, praising the 'kindly ministers of nature', and Mutability, defeated, vanishes, leaving the fairies to pay homage to their preserver.

In this lengthy conceit most of the virtues and defects of Hood's serious verse appear plainly. The poem is far too long—126 stanzas of it—for the slender theme; the detail, often rich and exquisite in a faintly precious way, is excessive; and there is considerable repetition as the stanzas carry the thought along, rather than the thought the stanzas. Yet there is a truly refined sensibility at work here, which, in several places, manages to recapture the atmosphere of Shakespeare's own fairy world, as, for instance, in Puck's words:

> Sometimes we cast our shapes, and in sleek skins
> Delve with the timid mole, that aptly delves
> From our example; so the spider spins,
> And eke the silk-worm, pattern'd by ourselves:
> Sometimes we travail on the summer shelves
> Of early bees, and busy toils commence,
> Watch'd of wise men, that know not we are elves,
> But gaze and marvel at our stretch of sense,
> And praise our human-like intelligence.
>
> Wherefore, by thy delight in that old tale,
> And plaintive dirges the late robins sing,
> What time the leaves are scattered by the gale,
> Mindful of that old forest burying;—
> As thou dost love to watch each tiny thing,
> For whom our craft most curiously contrives,
> If thou hast caught a bee upon the wing,
> To take his honey-bag,—spare us our lives,
> And we will pay the ransom in full hives.

There is also a genuinely Shakespearian ring to stanzas like these:

> Then Saturn with a frown:—'Go forth, and fell
> Oak for your coffins, and thenceforth lay by
> Your axes for the rust and bid farewell
> To all sweet birds, and the blue peeps of sky
> Through tangled branches, for ye shall not spy
> The next green generation of the tree,
> But hence with the dead leaves, whene'er they fly,—
> Which in the bleak air I would rather see
> Than flights of the most tuneful birds that be.'

The weaknesses, which fight against the poem's charm, are its seemingly too calculated slips into deliberate quaintness, and a playfulness that, as in much of the work of the Cockney School, often falls into something close to poetic vulgarity, such as:

> But Puck was seated on a spider's thread,
> That hung between two branches of a briar,
> And 'gan to swing and gambol, heels o'er head,
> Like any Southwark tumbler on a wire,
> For him no present grief could long inspire.

Echoes of earlier writers, even in passages of decided originality, give the reader a feeling of *déjà vu*. Spenser is one obvious model in descriptive stanzas like the ones beginning

> And there were crystal pools, peopled with fish,
> Argent and gold; and some of Tyrian skin,
> Some crimson-barr'd.

Drayton's *Nymphidia,* too, has suggested some of the details of fairy life. But it is above all Keats whose tone is here, especially when Hood delights in the fantastic and sensuous and in the soft golden glow of the scenes:

> 'Twas in that mellow season of the year
> When the hot Sun singes the yellow leaves
> Till they be gold;

in such images as

> others from tall trees
> Dropp'd, like shed blossoms, silent to the grass,
> Spirits and elfins small, of every class;

and in the use of typically Keatsian epithets:

> and deftly strips
> That ruddy skin from a sweet rose's cheek

and

> some bloomy rain
> That, circling the bright Moon, had wash'd her car

and

> . . . in ancient might and hoary majesty.[1]

Several lines unashamedly draw upon particular poems by Keats, e.g. 'like foolish heifers in the holy rite' and 'to some unwasted regions of my brain'. Hood's whole poetic personality vibrated to that of Keats; his poetic instincts were given direction by Keats's example, and during his twenties he felt himself called to carry on the type of imaginative exploration Keats had begun. It was hardly his fault that he lacked the high vision and dedication and the keen critical intelligence of his predecessor.

From the Elizabethans as well, especially Marlowe, Spenser, and Chapman, back to whom he followed Keats, and from Lamb, Hood learned the poetic value of classical myth. This shows most clearly in **'Hero and Leander'**, which may have found its first inspiration in Reynolds's *The Naiad,* but which echoes Marlowe's poem, Shakespeare's 'Venus and Adonis', and 'The Rape of Lucrece' also. Of all the poems in the volume, this is the one that gives most earnest of Hood's poetic power in a traditional vein. Douglas Bush calls it 'probably the most remarkable example in modern verse of almost complete reproduction of the narrative manner of the Elizabethan Ovidians. One cannot quite dismiss as pastiche what is written with the youthful freshness and spontaneity of a contemporary of Shakespeare and Marlowe.'[2] High praise, indeed, but not, I feel, undeserved, for the many felicities of **'Hero and Leander'**, its firm narrative line, its decorative richness and the beauty of its imagery make it an astonishing poem to have come from the pen of a writer usually regarded as primarily a funster and a punster.

Perhaps to avoid comparison with Marlowe, Hood reshaped the classical story. He opens with Leander leaving Hero in the morning to swim back to Abydos; while

The drowsy mist before him chill and dank,
Like a dull lethargy o'erleans the sea.

The description of Leander struggling through the waves contains one of the many intimations of illness that are sown through Hood's poems; here it is a more direct self-revelation than usual, one that expresses both his persistent awareness of physical frailty and a poignant sense of the duality of his own poetic personality:

His face was pallid, but the hectic morn
Had hung a lying crimson on his cheeks,
And slanderous sparkles in his eyes forlorn;
So death lies ambush'd in consumptive streaks;
But inward grief was writhing o'er its task,
As heart-sick jesters weep behind the mask.

In the middle of the journey, Leander encounters a sea-nymph, who falls in love with him:

She's all too bright, too argent, and too pale,
To be a woman;—but a man's double,
Reflected on the wave so faint and frail,
She tops the billows like an air-borne bubble;
Or dim creation of a morning dream,
Fair as the wave-bleach'd lily of the stream.

The nymph drags the exhausted Leander down to her home below the waves, unknowing that this means his death:

She read his mortal stillness for content,
Feeling no fear where only love was meant.

She sings to the corpse, whom she thinks is sleeping, a song of love, full of the verbal exuberance of Elizabethan lyrics, both directly felt and as filtered through Keats:

Look how the sunbeam burns upon their scales,
And shows rich glimpses of their Tyrian skins;
They flash small lightnings from their vigorous tails,
And winking stars are kindled at their fins;
These shall divert thee in thy weariest mood,
And seek thy hand for gamesomeness and food.

At last the nymph realizes that Leander is dead. In an attempt to restore him to life, she brings his body to the surface and lays it on 'the glowing sand'. A group of fishermen bear the corpse away while she is seeking for weeds to make a bed for it. When, in a storm in the night, Hero wanders grief-stricken by the shore, she hears the sea-nymph echo Leander's voice calling 'Hero! Hero!' and, thinking it is her lover, she leaps into the sea; her body is enshrined in a crystal cave by the weeping nymph.

'Hero and Leander' suffers from being loaded with more detail than the story can bear. It is almost as if Hood, city-bred but loving the country, felt obliged to expend his wonder at nature over-generously. Many of the 130 stanzas, in Shakespeare's six-line 'Venus and Adonis' measure, are self-indulgent in their catalogues. Yet this was an Elizabethan fault, too, and it is a measure of Hood's skill in this often enchanting poem that, far from its being merely a clever exercise in pseudo-Elizabethan poetic rhetoric, it has an individual blend of poignancy and colour. The tone of melancholy, especially in the nymph's lament, shades the poem in an attractive way. Echoes there are in abundance, from 'Venus and Adonis' and Marlowe's poem on the same subject. Keats is here, too, in such adjectives as 'hoary' and 'gusty' and phrases like 'golden crevices of morn' and Shelley as well in

Lo! how the lark soars upward and is gone;
Turning a spirit as he nears the sky.
His voice is heard, though body there is none,
And rain-like music scatters from on high;
But Love would follow with a falcon spite,
To pluck the minstrel from his dewy height.

Occasionally Cockney faults of poetic tact mar particular effects, as in the description of Leander's first sight of the nymph:

Like murder's witness swooning in the court,
His sight falls senseless by its own report.

And yet everywhere there is abundance of true talent, especially of a gift for the ringing phrase and a capacity for gnomic lines. The nymph's black hair lies behind her white shoulders

Making her doubly fair, thus darkly set,
As marble lies advantaged upon jet;

when Leander's body is stolen, the nymph goes to her deep home

and there
Weeps in a midnight made of her own hair;

and throughout the poem, the most skilful use of light and colour reflects Hood's training in the pictorial arts:

Poor gilded Grief! the subtle light by this
With mazy gold creeps through her watery mine,
And, diving downward through the green abyss,
Lights up her palace with an amber shine;
There, falling on her arms,—the crystal skin
Reveals the ruby tide that fares within.

However, the most remarkable of the long poems in this volume, although in some ways the most imperfect technically, is **'Lycus the Centaur'**, dedicated to John Hamilton Reynolds, as 'written in the pleasant spring-time of our friendship', that is, in 1822, and described as 'from an unrolled manuscript of Appolonius Curius'. Hood's prefatory note outlines the occasion of the poem, which was suggested to him by the episode of Glaucus, Scylla and Circe in Book III of *Endymion*:

'Lycus, detained by Circe in her magical kingdom, is beloved by a Water Nymph, who, desiring to render him immortal, has recourse to the Sorceress. Circe gives her an incantation to pronounce, which should turn Lycus into a horse; but the horrible effect of the charm causing her to break off in the midst, he becomes a Centaur.' The poem itself is a monologue by Lycus, who tells of his love for the nymph, Aegele, his incurring the jealousy of Circe, the Sorceress's revenge, his greater misery as a centaur than as a man, his rejection by men, and even by children, and his final journey to Thessaly where he meets others of his kind.

'**Lycus the Centaur**' is more characteristically Hood's than is either of the other two long poems. Despite the charm and delicate fancy of '**The Plea of the Midsummer Fairies**', despite the poignancy and rich detail of '**Hero and Leander**' and despite the radiant poetic promise they both display, they are 'literary' pieces; they derive from other men's work in subject and, in part, in treatment; they stand apart from life; for all their delightful natural detail, they smell of books. There is not quite enough personal pressure behind the verses; one never feels that Hood would be capable of high emotional intensity or of the large awe that charges great poetry; in his poems, the tragic becomes the melancholic, and regretfulness, rather than agony, suffuses the lines; gentle pity is more evident here than burning compassion.

'**Lycus the Centaur**' is 'literary', too, in its origins and in its occasional echoes of Keats:

> till one day in the sun,
> In its very noon-blaze, I could fancy a thing
> Of beauty, but faint as the cloud-mirrors fling
> On the gaze of the shepherd that watches the sky;

and in its far from happy echoes of the Cockney poets:

> There were women! there men! but to me a third sex.
> I saw them all dots—yet I loved them as specks.

and

> Where witchery works with her will like a god,
> Works more than the wonders of time at a nod.

The alliterative insistence of the last couplet, typical of the poem as a whole, as well as the bouncing anapaests of the metre, have been praised as fitted to the hysteria of Lycus as he relives the horror of his transformation and the pangs of his rejection. For me, they hamper the poem, and the jolting lines, with their pat rhymes, dilute the seriousness of the theme. Nevertheless, throughout '**Lycus**', we feel something quite special to Hood—a sense of the horrible, of grotesque terror, of thin wires plucked hard, which, if it often assumes a freakish form in his poetry, and in his later work is to be crossed with extravagant humour, was to persist in him as a nightmare vision of life and reality.

In a perceptive discussion of this poem in *The Darkling Plain,* Mr. John Heath-Stubbs writes: 'The poem is a vision of the world as it must have appeared to Hood's imagination, tormented by disease, exposed to the cruel pressure of a hostile world. A sense of pitiful frustration pervades the story'—which seems to me to be a comment more appropriate to the work of Hood's later years rather than to that of a young man still with his disasters before him. Mr. Heath-Stubbs sees in the poem parallels with Dante, as Lycus gazes upon the human form distorted in Circe's victims; and, when Lycus's gesture of affection for a child is rejected by the infant, clearly Hercules, the future destroyer of the race of centaurs, he remarks: 'The Hero, intended as a Saviour-figure for mankind, can only appear as the stern Destroyer for the soul rendered monstrous by sin.' This surely puts more weight on the poem than it can bear, for one of the ways in which Hood's poetry is inferior to that of Keats and of the great Romantics, is in the comparative absence from it of genuine symbolism, innerness and of an interior ethical structure.

At the same time, the mood expressed in '**Lycus the Centaur**' may well be taken as an intuitive response by a sick man to the spiritual enervation and malaise of his time. This comes out especially in those several passages wherein horror and pathos are fused, as in

> For once, at my suppering, I pluck'd in the dusk
> An apple, juice-gushing and fragrant of musk;
> But by daylight my fingers were crimson'd with gore,
> And the half-eaten fragment was flesh at the core;
> And once—only once—for the love of its blush,
> I broke a bloom bough, but there came such a gush
> On my hand, that I fainted away in weak fright,
> While the leaf-hidden woodpecker shriek'd at the sight,
> And oh! such an agony thrill'd in that note,
> That my soul, starting up, beat its wings in my throat;

and, as Lycus strokes the sad men made animals

> So they passively bow'd—save the serpent, that leapt
> To my breast like a sister, and pressingly crept
> In embrace of my neck, and with close kisses blister'd
> My lips in rash love,—then drew backwards, and glister'd
> Her eyes in my face, and loud hissing affright,
> Dropt down, and swift started away from my sight!

The Plea of the Midsummer Fairies also contained another longish piece, '**The Two Peacocks of Bedfont**'. This moral poem about two proud and fashionable ladies transformed into peacocks for their vanity seems better fitted to a comic treatment than to the solemn one Hood gave it, although it has some pleasant touches, such as the words of the preacher, who expresses Hood's own blue-domer religious sentiments:

> Oh go, and gaze—when the low winds of ev'n
> Breathe hymns, and Nature's many forests nod

> Their gold-crown'd heads; and the rich blooms of
> heav'n
> 　　Sun-ripened give their blushes up to God.

The influence of Keats, felt again in this poem, is everywhere apparent in the briefer pieces that make up the volume, in subject, in vocabulary and even in the titles: **'Ode: Autumn'**, **'Ode to Melancholy'**, **'Sonnet: To Fancy'**, and **'Ruth'**, which is inspired by the famous lines in 'Ode to a Nightingale'. Hood's ode on Autumn is especially instructive as showing how, in assimilating Keats, he made something less, but his own, out of the earlier poet. Phrases like 'lustrous eyes' from 'Ode to a Nightingale', 'Where are the blooms of Summer?' after 'Ode to Autumn', and 'Last leaves for a love-rosary' and 'whose doom is Beauty's echoing **'Ode to Melancholy'**, and several similar recollections, show how carefully Hood had read poems known in his day to a comparatively small public. Yet the tones of the two poems on Autumn are radically different. Hood's quite lacks the mellow sensuousness of Keats's, and has nothing of the exuberant fullness of his embrace of the season. Not only has he modified to something approaching blandness the ripeness of the original ode, but he has also tempered its sensuous langour to a dreamy melancholy. Both poems are marked by an underlying reflectiveness, but Hood's outlook is bleaker than that of Keats, both more wan and less convinced of life within the season of fall:

> Oh go and sit with her, and be o'ershaded
> Under the languid downfall of her hair, . . .
> 　　There is enough of sorrowing, and quite
> Enough of bitter fruits the earth doth bear—
> Enough of chilly droppings for her bowl;
> Enough of fear and shadowy despair,
> 　　To frame her cloudy prison for the soul!

Those other poems in this book written wholly or partly under the influence of Keats, Shelley or the Elizabethans show Hood as a very adept imitator. He can weave half-recollections and direct echoes into his poems, write lines similar in feeling and texture to those of his models, and still produce verses that are more than pastiche. The trouble is that his own sensibility and his conception of poetic values are at once less sensitive and less serious than those of Keats, and that he responds to experience in a more ordinary and less intense way. Still, there are times when, on his own level, he manages to express something like Keats's romantic apprehensions of magic and mystery, and his love for the more ambient aspects of the imagination, as in his sonnet, **'To Fancy'**:

> Most delicate Ariel! submissive thing,
> Won by the mind's high magic to its hest,—
> Invisible embassy, or secret guest,—
> Weighing the light air on a lighter wing;—
> Whether into the midnight moon, to bring
> Illuminate visions to the eye of rest,—

> Or rich romances from the florid West,—
> Or to the sea, for mystic whispering,—
> Still by thy charmed allegiance to the will
> The fruitful wishes prosper in the brain,
> As by the fingering of fairy skill,—
> Moonlight, and waters, and soft music's strain,
> Odours, and blooms, and *my* Miranda's smile,
> Making this dull world an enchanted isle.

Some of Hood's sonnets, in fact, deserve to rank high among those written in the nineteenth century, as much for their assurance as for their markedly personal tone. One of his best, **'Silence'**, was imitated by Edgar Allan Poe in his own sonnet of the same name, after he had published Hood's poem in *Burton's Gentleman's Magazine* in 1839, oddly enough over the signature, 'P.'. As has often been remarked, Hood's opening lines recall well-known lines from Byron's 'Childe Harold', beginning 'There is a pleasure in the pathless woods'; and there is perhaps, too, a distant memory here of Shelley's 'Ozymandias', but its muted tone and sombre-hued melancholy are unmistakably Hood's:

> There is a silence where hath been no sound,
> There is a silence where no sound may be,
> In the cold grave,—under the deep, deep sea,
> Or in wide desert where no life is found,
> Which hath been mute, and still must sleep profound:
> No voice is hush'd,—no life treads silently,
> But clouds and cloudy shadows wander free,
> That never spoke, over the idle ground:
> But in green ruins, in the desolate walls
> Of antique palaces, where Man hath been,
> Though the dun fox, or wild hyena, calls,
> And owls, that flit continually between,
> Shriek to the echo, and the low winds moan,
> There the true Silence is, self-conscious and alone.

Whatever reservations we may have about the longer poems of Hood, we must acknowledge his success with the short lyric and song, forms that the Romantics cultivated so capably. Hood went back to the seventeenth century, it would seem, for some of his inspiration, since, at his best, he has a touch of Suckling and Herrick, as in

> It was not in the Winter
> 　　Our loving lot was cast;
> It was the time of Roses,—
> 　　We plucked them as we pass'd;

or

> 　　Spring, it is cheery,
> 　　Winter is dreary,
> Green leaves hang, but the brown must fly;
> 　　When he's forsaken,
> 　　Wither'd and shaken,
> What can an old man do but die?

In these and in poems like **'O lady, leave thy silken thread'**, **'I love thee'**, **'The stars are with the voyager'**, **'Song for music'**, **'Ruth'**, one of the best pieces in the 1827 volume, and **'Fair Ines'**, the lovely poem in which Poe found 'inexpressible charm', Hood establishes his right to be regarded as one of the most gifted writers of the little lyric in English.

The Plea of the Midsummer Fairies introduced this form and, even in later years, when he had largely abandoned wholly serious verse, he continued on occasion to produce such poems. His temperament responded readily to the courtly romanticism of Elizabethan song, and his talent for unpretentious language and languid sentiment, and his taste for the flower and jewel stereotypes of earlier lyrics and for the engaging conceit make his songs successful exercises in an old convention:

> O Lady, leave thy silken thread
>   And flowery tapestrie:
> There's living roses on the bush
>   And blossoms on the tree;
> Stoop where thou wilt, thy careless hand
>   Some random bud will meet;
> Thou canst not tread but thou wilt find
>   The daisy at thy feet.

In the 1827 book, there are, as we have seen, several poems that disclose Hood's preoccupation with death and decay. Further indications of this strain are found in **'I remember, I remember'**, one of his best-known poems and 'A Retrospective Review', both of which, although written by a quite young man, look back upon childhood with nostalgia and a sense of loss more appropriate to a very old one. Although the terms may be in part literary, the mood is obviously perfectly genuine. In the final stanza of **'I remember'**, which, as an expression of the loss of the childhood sense of wonder, has few equals on its own level, he effectively uses the near-pun, that exploitation of the double significance of a word that so often gives an extra strength to his verse, as indeed real puns, used seriously, also do:

> I remember, I remember,
> The fir trees dark and high;
> I used to think their slender tops
> Were close against the sky;
> It was a childish ignorance,
> But now 'tis little joy
> To know I'm farther off from Heav'n
> Than when I was a boy.

'A Retrospective Review', as the punning title indicates, is a less serious approach to the same subject, with some light-hearted puns of this order:

> I'd 'kiss the rod' and be resign'd
>   Beneath the stroke, and even find
>   Some sugar in the cane!

But already the doomed awareness of his life's work, with its endless writing, in pain and sickness, for a scant living, forces its way out in occasional verses of undiluted seriousness:

> No more in noontide sun I bask;
> My authorship's an endless task,
>   My head's ne'er out of school:
> My heart is pain'd with scorn and slight,
> I have too many foes to fight,
>   And friends grown strangely cool!

Since the shadow of Keats lies so heavily on this volume and on almost all the early serious poems Hood wrote, for instance, **'The Poet's Portion'** which ends:

> So that what there is steep'd shall perish never,
> But live and bloom, and be a joy for ever,

this is the appropriate place to mention one work which, although it was not published until many years later, belongs to this period of Keats's influence, and shows his effect on Hood more strongly than anything else the latter wrote. This is **'Lamia'**, a dramatization of Keats's poem. Presumably written in the 1820's, it remained in manuscript until after Hood's death, when Jane sent it to William Jerdan, editor of the *Literary Gazette*. Jerdan had known her husband, and had highly praised *The Plea of the Midsummer Fairies* as like 'a lovely summer day, sunny, not scorching; placid, enchanting, its airs balmy and refreshing'. He gave **'Lamia'** its first publication in his own *Autobiography.*

The theme of the work seems to have fascinated Hood, for he makes more than one reference to it in **'Lycus the Centaur'**, as in

> And the snake, not with magical orbs to devise
> Strange death, but with woman's attraction of eyes.

His closet drama need not detain us long. Even granted that the subject is an unpromising one for a play, Hood completely lacked the theatrical instinct necessary to make it dramatically exciting. He does attempt to give the story dramatic shape, and introduces new characters, but they are thinly conceived, and the dialogue is stuffed with inflated nineteenth-century pseudo-Shakespearean rhetoric:

> Go! desperate man; away!—and fear thy gods,
> Or else the hot indignation in my eyes
> Will blast thee!

The play has none of the inner significance, however vague it be, of Keats's poem, and, although there is some power and insight in the conception of Lamia herself, Hood's attempt can only be called a failure. Perhaps he recognized this himself, since he never published it—an unusual thing for a man who was forced to turn every scrap of writing to profit—and since the huddled ending indicates that it was neither properly finished nor revised. The most interesting thing about **'Lamia'** is that it shows a certain waning of the impact of Keats's style. Despite the many Keatsian touches, of the order of

And gold and silver chafers bobbed about;
And when there came a little gust of wind,
The very flowers took wing and chased the butterflies,

the language is in the main simple and closer to Hood's own in his lyrics.

The 1827 volume, then, was an ambitious assault on the high tors of poetry; it was imitative, yet intelligently and sensitively so; it showed excellent discrimination in its choice of models, most notably Keats, at that time fully appreciated by few; it showed a versatility, a metrical dexterity and a gracious sensibility that gave promise of better things; it contained a number of short poems that succeed completely on their own modest level and others with flashes of pure poetry; all in all, it was one of the most interesting and appealing books of poetry of its decade. Yet the public response was disappointing; the book sold badly, despite the encomiums of friends such as Lamb, who replied to what he described to Hood as 'unworthy to be cared for attacks' with a prose paraphrase of **'The Plea'** in Hone's *Table Book,* and Edward Moxon, who wrote a laudatory notice beginning

> Delightful bard! what praises meet are thine,
>   More than my verse can sound to thee belong;
> Well hast thou pleaded with a tongue divine,
>   In this thy sweet and newly breathèd song.

Tom Hood says in the *Memorials,* 'My father afterwards bought up the remainder of the edition, as he said himself, to save it from the butter shops.' In many journals it was ignored completely; the most common opinion was that it was a pity that Hood had turned from comic and satirical verse for which he had so obviously a flair to write trivialities of this serious kind; the *Monthly Review* went so far as to compare him with the comedian hankering to play Hamlet. Hood's disappointment was profound; his attempt to establish himself as a serious poet had, apparently, lamentably failed. But it is typical of the man's unbounded resilience that he did not waste time lamenting but wrote off *The Plea of the Midsummer Fairies* to experience, and turned at once to writing and compiling another volume of *Whims and Oddities.*

This appeared in October, 1827, and contained the mixture as before—prose pieces, lyrics, comic poems, narrative poems, comic ballads. **'The Demon Ship'** is perhaps the best of those pieces in which Hood leads the reader up the garden path with a horrific description, in this case of a seemingly demonic crew on a black ship, only to let him down with a bump at the end; the ship here proving to be a coal-freighter. **'Bianca's Dream'**, a lightly satirical 'Venetian story' in Byron's manner, has its fair share of verbal tricks and puns:

> Maidens who cursed her looks forgot their own,
>   And beaux were turned to flambeaux where she
> came . . .

> Born only underneath Italian skies,
> Where every fiddle has a Bridge of Sighs,

and so on. **'Death's Ramble'**, an early exercise in the comic-macabre, pours out its grisly puns in stanza-loads:

> He met a dustman ringing a bell,
>   And he gave him a mortal thrust;
> For himself, by law, since Adam's flaw,
>   Is contractor for all our dust.

> He saw a sailor mixing his grog,
>   And he marked him out for slaughter;
> For on water he scarcely had cared for Death,
>   And never on rum-and-water.

> Death saw two players playing at cards,
>   But the game wasn't worth a dump,
> For he quickly laid them flat with a spade,
>   To wait for the final trump!

This volume went into a second edition in 1829, and in 1832 the two series of *Whims and Oddities* were combined and continued to be reprinted up to the 1890's. The reviewers who had ignored his serious verse accepted the new *Whims and Oddities* with joy. Hood was never a man to nurse a wrong, but that his disappointment at the reception of *The Plea* went deeper than his mien at the time indicated is seen from scattered references in his later poems, the lines, for instance **'To a Critic'**, written in a very rough imitation of Chaucer, that begin:

> O cruel one! How littel dost thou knowe
> How manye Poetes with Unhappynesse
> Thou may'st have slaine ere they beganne to blowe
> Like to yonge Buddes in theyre firste sappynesse!

Yet, although he was to write serious verse in the future, never again was he to tempt the critics by issuing a collection of wholly straight verse. The public wanted him to be a funny man; and he would oblige them—for a living.

It has often been claimed that the hostile and indifferent reception given to *The Plea of the Midsummer Fairies* was a disaster for poetry in that it diverted the considerable talents of Hood into second-rate entertainment, and verbal slapstick. It is easy to understand such a point of view when, knowing Hood only as a jester, one comes across the book for the first time. Yet, for all the promise and the real accomplishment of the work, I wonder whether, in fact, Thomas Hood would have been able to do again anything very much better than this had he received support and encouragement. Among his contemporaries of the interregnum, Thomas Moore had written better lyrics, John Clare much more exquisite nature poetry, Thomas Lovell Beddoes was exploring the freakish areas of sensibility with more originality, George Darley, in *Nepenthe* at least, was carrying forward the Keatsian mode, and Alfred Tennyson, whose first volume of poems, written with his two brothers, appeared in the same year as Hood's book, was to develop the post-Keatsian style in directions unglimpsed by Hood.

For all the charm and talent of his early serious poems, I cannot feel that they represent the character of his authentic gifts and individuality, which was for the grotesque, as in **'The Last Man'** and **'Miss Kilmansegg and her Precious Leg'**, the exuberantly comic and pun-crammed piece, the sombre and macabre, as in **'The Dream of Eugene Aram'** and **'The Haunted House'**, the poem of gentle domestic sentiment, as in **'The Death-Bed'**, and **'Farewell Life'**, and such humanitarian verses as **'The Song of the Shirt'** and **'The Bridge of Sighs'**. In these poems is to be found the real Hood the poet, not in the clever, but overly bookish productions that make up the bulk of *The Plea of the Midsummer Fairies*. It was not, however, until Hood had rid himself of his ambition to become another Keats and came to draw his subjects and his emotions more directly from life that he wrote poetry that is remembered. The critics of his first serious book may not have been wholly wrong, then, nor may it have been altogether a bad thing that Hood was diverted into other fields by its failure and so avoided becoming, as well he might, a poet as unreadable and as sterile as Leigh Hunt.

* * *

During 1843, Hood found increasing difficulty in his relations with Henry Colburn, the proprietor of the *New Monthly*. The causes of the disagreement were various. As we have seen, Hood's illnesses, combined with his long-standing distrust of 'publishers and sinners', as he called them, may not have made him easy to deal with, although he carried out his editorial duties conscientiously and enriched the pages of the *New Monthly* with his own excellent contributions; he had also incurred the dislike of the trade by his vigorous support of Talfourd's attempts to reform the Copyright Laws. 'There are plenty of the trade would object to *me*,' he told Dickens in 1843, 'for I have published what I thought of them. Colburn as likely as any, who on the publication of my *last Copyright letter* attempted to call me to account for writing in the Athm. I had all along told him I should write there, and had done so, *till then* without an objection.'

More immediately to the point was Colburn's habit, in common with other publishers of the time, of not drawing a fine enough line between legitimate advertising and reviewing, and 'puffing', that is, sponsoring or commissioning favourable reviews, and using unethical means of pushing forward his own publications. This especially angered Hood, who regarded puffing as a prostitution of the profession of letters. In a letter to Hannah Lawrance marked 'Confidential', he wrote, 'I write in haste a few lines to put you on your guard by telling you of the arrangements for reviewing in the Magazine. I undertook to review all books except Colburn's own with the puffing of which I of course desired to have no concern. They are *done* by the persons of the establishment, Patmore, Williams or Shoberl. If you see the Mag. you will know what wretched things these reviews are.' Peter George Patmore, O. E. Williams, who wrote a life of Sir Thomas Lawrence, and Shoberl were all employed by Colburn as sub-editors, and Hood, who felt that, as editor, he should have complete control of the paper, resented the fact that Colburn's insistence on his printing their puffs degraded his own status and associated him, unwillingly, with a discreditable practice. After his resignation from the *New Monthly,* he told Dickens, on October 19, 1843, 'The result shows that from the beginning the Patmore, Shoberl and Williams trio had resolved on being sub-over-editors—and that if I had not resigned, I should have been resigned.'

One matter that especially rankled with Hood was the affair of *The Tuft-Hunter.* This novel, allegedly the work of Lord William Pitt Lennox, a dandy and writer of trashy fiction, was 'puffed' by Colburn, who published it in 1843, and even submitted it earlier to Hood with a request that he write a preface for it. Hood found it one of the 'grossest cases [of plagiarism] possible', from Scott's *The Antiquary* and *St. Ronan's Well,* and from his own *Tylney Hall*! He suspected Frederick Shoberl of being the real 'author', and applauded Dilke's scathing review in the *Athenaeum* of February 25, 1843. 'Lord L. is a fool,' he wrote to Dilke, 'but the other is a thorough rogue, and double traitor—the *system* deserves denouncing—however, I have thundered a bit at the attempt to connect me with it—and am having my fun out of Colburn.' But the fun, which consisted of the insertion of cryptic gibes in the *New Monthly,* had turned sour before Hood took his holiday in Scotland. He could stand Colburn and his associates no longer, and resigned from the magazine.

Colburn was so angry at Hood's leaving him that, like Queen Victoria on another occasion, he pretended later that the offensive person didn't exist. Three letters addressed to Hood at the office were returned to the senders, marked 'Not Known to Mr. Colburn'; one of these coming into Hood's hands, he sent the following lines to Dilke:

> For a couple of years in the columns of Puff
> I was rated a passable writer enough:
> But, alas! for the favours of Fame!
> Since I quitted her seat in Great Marlborough Street,

In repute my decline is so very complete
That a Colburn don't know of my name!

Now a Colburn I knew in his person so small
That he seemed the half-brother of nothing at all,
Yet in spirit a Dwarf may be big;
But his mind was so narrow, his soul was so dim,
Where's the wonder if all I remember of him
Is—a suit of Boys' clothes and a wig!

Hood was now high and dry again, with his regular source of income cut off, and as soon as he returned from Scotland, he began looking for another editorial post.

He had kept Dickens informed of his position throughout the last difficult weeks on the *New Monthly,* and Dickens, who had himself a good business head, wrote to his friend on September 12, 1843, 'There can be no doubt in the mind of any honourable man that the circumstances under which you signed your agreement are of the most disgraceful kind, in so far as Mr. Colburn is concerned. There can be no doubt that he took a money-lending, bill-broking, Jew-Clothes-bagging, Saturday-night-pawnbroking advantage of your temporary situation.' He also suggested to Hood that he should try to get a position on *Ainsworth's Magazine,* although he was under a false impression that Ainsworth himself was no longer editor. Hood at once wrote to the publishers, Cunningham and Mortimer, offering his services. To his surprise, Ainsworth himself, who was still editor and owner, replied in person, very cordially offering Hood 16 guineas per sheet, 'the highest terms the Magazine can afford', adding, 'Indeed, I may mention confidentially that there will, ere long, be a dissolution of the firm of Cunningham and Mortimer: but this will not effect the Magazine, or its arrangements'. But Hood, who had hoped for a more permanent appointment, declined, salving his embarrassment by telling Ainsworth that the terms were not adequate, and 'besides, to be candid, I do not quite like the unsettled state of the establishment'. He also confided to Dickens that he felt Blanchard, one of Ainsworth's sub-editors, was 'very much in with Colburn, Patmore, and the Marlboro Street gang'.

His next attempt to find a position was a bold one. He had three years before found himself unable to fulfil a commission for the publisher, Richard Bentley; and Bentley had taken Hood's letting him down rather badly. But, hearing that *Bentley's Miscellany* was without an editor, he wrote on October 21 to the publisher offering himself, hoping that, not only would by-gones be by-gones, but that his own prestige would get him the job. Bentley replied with a terse note pointing out that he had a perfectly good editor, Mr. Wilde, and, while feeling obliged by the offer Hood was so good to make, had not 'the remotest idea of making any alteration with regard to the Editorship of that publication'. This left Hood under the awkward obligation of explaining that he had no intention of trying to do Wilde out of his daily bread.

Frustrated on all sides in his attempts to find an editorial chair, Hood was driven once more to rely wholly on his own resources. He would start his own periodical—*Hood's Monthly Magazine and Comic Miscellany*—and be both editor and author as with the *Comic Annual* and *Hood's Own.* His plans were laid in early November, soon after the rebuffs from the other magazines, and he wrote in terms of high excitement to tell Elliot that he had financial backing for it, and that the first issue would appear on January 1. But, before *Hood's Magazine* was launched, he was to write his most famous poem, **'The Song of the Shirt'**, and thus begin his new venture on a wave of publicity and an accession of fame such as he had never experienced before.

He had other things in mind as well. His contributions to the *New Monthly* Colburn had engaged to publish in book form, and the project was duly carried through 'after tedious waitings on Colburn', as he told Elliot. The two volumes of **Whimsicalities,** dated 1844, appeared in December, 1843; they contained his *New Monthly* pieces, with one or two additions, and illustrations by John Leech and Hood himself. Since all the work therein was written before **'The Song of the Shirt'**, they merit a word or two first. The greater number of the pieces are in prose, and amply represent Hood's characteristic manner in his briefer prose works. We can detect four main influences on him—those of Lamb, of Sterne, of Smollett, and of the Gothic novel. The latter form is represented by such 'straight' stories as 'The Tower of Lahneck', crisply told, of two women, one English, one German, who climb to the top of a lofty castle-tower, then, when the stone staircase crumbles behind them, are marooned there; one leaps to her death, the other dies of starvation. Also in the Gothic vein are such less serious pieces as the deliberately and tantalizingly unfinished 'A Tale of Terror'. The relaxed conversational, gently humorous style of pieces like 'The Happiest Man in England' and 'The Omnibus' indicate something of his debt to 'Elia'; the rough-and-tumble incidents and the energetic physical humour of 'Mr. Chubb: A Piscatory Romance' and the comic epistolary method of 'News from China' and 'The Earth-Quakers' show the enduring impression of Smollett on him.

Most of all, it is Sterne who seems to have played the greatest part in shaping Hood's periodical prose. The mixture of sensibility, sentiment and comedy in Sterne accorded with Hood's own temperament, and the informal discursive method of *Tristram Shandy* he found especially suitable for improvised prose pieces written off the top of his head, sometimes while the printer's devil was waiting for copy. So we find *New Monthly* contributions like 'The Grimsby Ghost', 'Mrs. Gardiner', 'The Confessions of a Phoenix' and others, full of irrelevant interpolations, dialogues between the author and imaginary interjectors (in the 'Beachcomber' manner), tiny essays, comic meditations, single sentence chapters, and so on. 'The Longest Hour in My Life', a prolonged account of a fictitious encounter between Hood and a tiger, is spun out cleverly with such devices, and with disquisitions on the nature of Time, which not only recall *Tristram Shandy* and the Lockean theories of Time on which it is based, but specifically refer to it. 'Apropos of Time and his diverse paces,' begins Chapter III, 'he notoriously goes slowly—as Sterne vouches—with a solitary captive.'

References to Sterne and his work, in fact, are commonplace in Hood, who never hesitated to acknowledge his debt. His first prose publication, as we have seen, was 'Sentimental Journey from Islington to Waterloo Bridge', and he later wrote, 'A Friend in Need: An Extravaganza *after* Sterne', while 'English Retrogression' describes a pilgrimage to Calais in search of the hotel room where Sterne had the interview with the Franciscan, and ends with the hotel proprietor exclaiming, 'Sterne?—Diable l'importe!—it is de oder Hotel. Mon Dieu! c'est une drôle de chose—but de English pepels when dey come to Calais, dey always come *Sterne foremost*!'

If any doubts remain as to Hood's devotion to Sterne, such a typical beginning as that to 'The Grimsby Ghost' should dispel them:

'In the town of Grimsby—

'"But stop," says the Courteous and Prudent Reader, "are there any such things as Ghosts?"

'"Any Ghostesses!" cries Superstition, who settled long since in the country, near a church-yard, on a *rising* ground, "any Ghostesses! Ay, man—lots on 'em! bushels on 'em! sights on 'em"', and so on. Hood's prose has not the delicacy, the learning and the intellectual sophistication of Sterne's, nor its sense of high comedy, but it has a virtuosity, a racy tone and good-humoured note which a certain journalistic carelessness mars little.

Among the humorous poems written for the *New Monthly* were such delightful *jeux d'esprit* as **'No!'**:

> No warmth, no cheerfulness, no healthful ease,
>   No comfortable feel in any member—
> No shade, no shine, no butterflies, no bees,
> No fruits, no flow'rs, no leaves, no birds—
>   November!

and serious ones like **'The Elm Tree'**. Hood was particularly fond of this poem, and told Dickens that he intended to issue it as a separate work, with illustrations by William Harvey, whose drawings for **'Eugene Aram'** had helped to establish its popularity. This project remained unrealized. Hood's partiality for **'The Elm Tree'**, which is a rather inflated piece, again betrays his constant awareness of mortality. Sub-titled 'A Dream in the Woods', it is a meditation, suggested by the sighing of a decaying elm, on the dying of the forest, and its felling by a muscular woodman. When the elm is felled, Death takes the place of the woodman, and, gloating over the 'conscious, moving, breathing trunks' he lays low, says that the elm will in the end house all human kind. And the poet ends with an intimation of his own death:

> A secret, vague, prophetic gloom,
>   As though by certain mark
> I knew the fore-appointed Tree
>   Within whose rugged bark
> This warm and living frame shall find
>   Its narrow house and dark.

The **Whimsicalities** were well enough received, but before the collection appeared, Hood had made an indelible mark in a field new to him. *Punch* had been established in 1841, as 'a refuge for destitute wit; an asylum for the thousands of orphan jokes that are now wandering about', as its original advertisement said. Taking some of its character from Hood's *Comic Annual* and his *Magazine*, *Punch* dealt in broad, obvious humour and outrageous puns, but also, and most characteristically, it was a tartly satirical journal. Under its first editor, Mark Lemon, assisted by such gifted wits and commentators as Thackeray, Henry Mayhew and Douglas Jerrold, it mocked the social pretensions of the time, fearlessly lampooned political stupidity, hidebound Toryism and rentier complacency, and stood up courageously as a defender of the poor and the underdog. There was need for such an advocate at this time, when the effects of the industrial revolution were beginning to show themselves in the growth of slums, in starvation, miserable wages and appalling destitution.

Hood's own temperament attracted him to *Punch*. Although his need to earn a living and his health made it impossible for him to play any active part in social reformism, he had long had a keen interest in social conditions. Apart from his articles on copyright, and the prominent role he took in the forming of the Association for the Protection of Literature in 1843, his readiness to respond to appeals for literary work for special distress funds, the consistent tone of humane compassion in his writings, and his several attacks on canting Pecksniffs and Sabbatarians, he had done little more than glancingly refer to social matters in such poems as **'The Assistant Drapers' Petition'** before 1843. The satire of **'Miss Kilmansegg'** is moral and general rather than particular, and, although in its attack on the love of money, it does pinpoint the principal Victorian vice, it is sufficiently broad and grotesque to apply to 'the other fellow'. It was through *Punch* that Hood undertook a new kind of expression, one that was to carry his name to the very ends of Europe—that of humanitarian verse. If we ask why this came as the final phase of his work, there can be many answers—the serious type of utterance was scarcely suited to the pages of his jocular journals, social conditions had worsened in the 1840's to a degree that made it impossible for a man of Hood's sensibility not to be moved by them, and his own life-long suffering had given him the experience essential to the writing of such poetry.

His first contact with *Punch* was not a happy one. Picking up the initial issue, of July 17, 1841, he found a jest using his name, on page 2: 'Mr. T. Hood, Professor of Punmanship, begs to acquaint the dull and witless, that he has established a class for the acquirement of an elegant and ready style of punning.' Hood was upset by this, which he thought a lapse of taste. But a couple of years later, he had become an occasional contributor of jokes and punning riddles to *Punch*'s pages. In the number for November 18, 1843, he essayed a different genre with **'A Drop of Gin'**, the first of his humanitarian poems. Rhetorical and declamatory, it is a warning on the evils of gin, but it does not make the mistake of confusing the symptom with the cause of the disease, as so many temperance reformers did. What other consolation, says Hood, has the 'ragged pauper, misfortune's butt' but the oblivion of gin?

> Then, instead of making too much of a din,
>   Let Anger be mute,
>   And sweet Mercy dilute,
> With a drop of Pity, the Drop of Gin!

The piece goes vigorously along, as so many of Hood's poems do, on a refrain, 'Gin! Gin! a Drop of Gin!', but it fails, largely because he has unsuccessfully married the kind of rhymes and rhythms he used in his comic verse to a serious subject. He did not make the same mistake with **'The Song of the Shirt'**.

This poem was inspired by an article in *Punch* itself, for November 4, 1843, called 'Famine and Fashion', probably written by Douglas Jerrold. A poor woman, named Biddell, with two children to support, was charged with having pawned articles belonging to her employer. In the course of the proceedings, it was disclosed that she received sevenpence a pair for making trousers, and that the most she could make in a week, working fourteen hours a day, was seven shillings. *The Times* had a blistering editorial on the case, and *Punch* vigorously took up the cue. Profoundly stirred by the *Punch* article, Hood wrote **'The Song of the Shirt'** at once, at a single sitting, and sent it to *Punch*. As he posted it off, Jane said to him, 'Now mind, Hood, mark my words; this will tell wonderfully. It is one of the best things you ever did.' She was right.

Although Hood was afraid that the poem would not be quite in *Punch*'s line, Mark Lemon, excited by its power, printed it anonymously in the Christmas (December 16) number, and was rewarded with a trebling of the circulation of his journal.

To say that the success of **'The Song of the Shirt'** was tumultuous would not be to exaggerate. It ran through the land like a hurricane. *The Times* and numerous other papers reprinted it; Mark Lemon dramatized it as *The Sempstress,* first produced at the Theatre Royal, Haymarket, on May 25, 1844; it was translated into German, Italian, French and Russian and in both Russia and Germany did much to inspire native poetry of social consciousness. Dickens and others, who were quick to penetrate the author's anonymity, were loud in their admiration. But, much more importantly, this poem struck down below the levels of professional appreciation to plant itself deep in the hearts of the English people. Printed on broad-sheets and cotton handkerchiefs, sung on street-corners and on the stage, recited at popular gatherings, read from pulpits, and learnt by heart by illiterates, it became one of the genuine songs of the people, an inspired cry from Hood's heart made their own by the sweated and exploited who had no voice to protest against monstrous injustice.

In time, Hood publicly acknowledged the open secret of his authorship. Much touched by the popularity of the poem, he was chiefly moved by hearing that the 'poor creatures', as his son said, 'to whom he had given such eloquent voice, seemed to adopt its words as their own, singing them about the streets to an air of their own adaptation'. By its stirring of the sluggish conscience of the British people, **'The Song of the Shirt'** did more than thousands of newspaper leaders and reams of political propaganda. In the line of Ebenezer Elliott, it was more potent than anything the 'Corn-Law Rhymer' wrote; Gerald Massey, himself in his social poems a disciple of Hood, recognized its power, and James Russell Lowell acknowledged its force in his lines:

> Here lies a poet. Stranger, if to thee
>   His claim to memory be obscure,
> If thou wouldst know how truly great was he,
>   Go, ask it of the poor.

A poem so well known—surely one of the best known in our language—has put itself almost beyond criticism. But we may note that it is characteristically Hood's—in the direct simplicity of its language, such a simplicity as is at the command only of those with a rich and varied vocabulary, in its effective use of repetition and refrain (has any English poet used repetition more skilfully than Hood?), in its concreteness, in its use of the unadorned substantive, in the touches of imaginative richness that light up more than one stanza, driven home by a happy use of internal rhyme:

And a wall so blank, my shadow I thank
    For sometimes falling there.

It is Hood's, too, in the almost inevitable reference to Death, 'the Phantom of Grisly bone', and in the notion of duality, and of that reality that mocks the appearance, which shows itself both imaginatively, in his favourite idea of the 'double':

Sewing at once, with a double thread,
    A shroud as well as a Shirt;

and verbally, with an unexpected and wholly successful pun, placed and used as few other poets would dare; and revealing, perhaps better than anything else in Hood, the poet in the punster;

Work—work—work,
In the dull December light,
    And work—work—work
When the weather is warm and bright—
While underneath the eaves
    The brooding swallows cling,
As if to show me their sunny backs
    And twit me with the spring.

In the same issue of *Punch* which presented **'The Song of the Shirt'**, appeared another poem by Hood in the same vein, **'The Pauper's Christmas Carol'**, with an effective sardonic tone and use of the refrain, 'Christmas comes but once a year':

Full of drink and full of meat
On our Saviour's natal day,
Charity's perennial treat,
Thus I heard a pauper say:—
'Ought I not to dance and sing
Thus supplied with famous cheer!
        Heigho!
        I hardly know—
Christmas comes but once a year.'

But, although its heart is in the right place, this poem lacks the drive and passion of **'The Song of the Shirt'**.

At the end of 1843, the Hoods left their lodgings at Elm Tree Road, and moved to a house of their own again at 28 New Finchley Road, in St. John's Wood. In affectionate memory of the consideration of his patron, the Duke of Devonshire, Hood named the house Devonshire Lodge. It was to be his last home.

The new year began with the first issue of *Hood's Monthly Magazine and Comic Miscellany*. The backing for this came originally from one Edward Flight. Things looked promising. The *Magazine* followed the formula which Hood had already found to be so popular. As his amusing prospectus put it: 'One prominent object . . . will be the supply of harmless "Mirth for the Million" and light thoughts, to a Public sorely oppressed . . . by hard times, heavy taxes, and those "eating cares" which

attend upon the securing of food for the day as well as provision for the future. . . . For the Sedate there will be papers of becoming gravity; and the lovers of Poetry will be supplied with numbers in each Number. As to politics, the Reader of *Hood's Magazine* will vainly search in its pages for a Panacea for Agricultural Distress, or a Grand Catholicon for Irish Agitation.'

The recipe worked again; the first number, which came out on January 1, sold 1,500 copies. For *Hood's Magazine*, the editor had gathered round him some of the most famous names of his time. But almost half the material in this first issue was written by Hood himself. Amongst this was **'The Haunted House'**—'one of the truest poems ever written', said Edgar Allan Poe—'one of the *truest*—one of the most unexceptionable—one of the most thoroughly artistic, both in its theme and in its execution'. It is, in fact, as good a poem as Poe himself ever wrote on the kind of theme he favoured.

Apart from Browning's 'Childe Roland to the Dark Tower Came', I know of no other nineteenth-century poem that so taps the springs of unnamed terror. Hood had never before written with such sustained artistic tact, such allusive assurance, and such a firm control over form. The poem may have been suggested by a fine steel engraving by J. Cousen, after Thomas Creswick, which Hood used as a frontispiece for the number. It is a relentless piling up of the details and images of decay and desolation in an old mansion where some terrible, never explained crime has been committed, a wonderful evocation of the mood of nightmare dread, unmarred by facetiousness or false notes. The total impression is built up with precise strokes and careful selection of detail:

With shatter'd panes the grassy court was starr'd;
The time-worn coping-stone had tumbled after:
And through the ragged roof the sky shone, barr'd
With naked beam and rafter.

O'er all there hung a shadow and a fear;
A sense of mystery the spirit daunted,
And said, as plain as whisper in the ear,
The place is Haunted!

The latter verse, which, with variations, recurs nine times at irregular intervals throughout the poem's 88 stanzas, again shows Hood's mastery of insistent effect, while the cunningly built stanza, with its final emphatic brief line and the echoing double-syllable rhymes, create a curiously portentous impression.

The form of the poem bears a remarkable resemblance to the slow, deliberate movement of a tracking camera in the hands of an Alfred Hitchcock or an Ingmar Bergman. The speaker, as in a nightmare, approaches the deserted mansion through its unhinged gates, past the crumbled pedestals, through the neglected gardens, choked with weeds and over-run with tangled flowers, where birds and rabbits throng undisturbed, through the abandoned orchard where

> on the canker'd tree, in easy reach,
> Rotted the golden apple;

past the shaggy yew and dry fountain to the portal. Then, by stages, through the slowly gaping door, past startled bats, down halls and corridors given over to insects and decay:

> The subtle spider, that from overhead
> Hung like a spy on human guilt and error,
> Suddenly turn'd and up its slender thread
> Ran with a nimble terror.

> The very stains and fractures on the wall
> Assuming features solemn and terrific,
> Hinted some tragedy of that old Hall,
> Lock'd up in Hieroglyphic.

through rooms stifling in mould and must, up the dreary stairs, to more dank rooms where the heraldic symbol of the Bloody Hand keeps its colour where all else has faded, and on the hangings, everything is eroded

> save one ragged part
> Where Cain was slaying Abel,

and where the Death Watch Beetle ticks behind the panelled oak, to the chamber where no life flourishes:

> Across the door no gossamer festoon
> Swung pendulous—no web—no dusty fringes,
> No silk chrysalis or white cocoon
> About its nooks and hinges.

> The spider shunn'd the interdicted room,
> The moth, the beetle, and the fly were banish'd,
> And where the sunbeam fell athwart the gloom,
> The very midge had vanished.

Here, at the end of the quest is the poisonous centre of the whole web of decay, the mysterious and terrible room, where the only traces of the crime that has tained all around it, is a series of fading spots from bed to door.

'**The Haunted House**' is a *tour de force* of the imagination. What gives it its particular atmosphere is the very precision of the details, which, paradoxically, invest the whole thing with the air of nightmare. The opening verses hint that it is a dream; 'in the spirit or the flesh I found | An old deserted Mansion'; yet the first verse says, 'others of our most romantic schemes | Are something more than fiction', suggesting that Hood was aware of a symbolic purpose. The general effect of the poem resembles that of a story by Kafka or a poem by Walter de la Mare, with more of the precise smell of the grave than either has. Little, in fact, is said of the

terror of the place—it is all conjured up by suggestion and impressionistic touches that evoke a mood of mystery and evil.

On one level the poem may be experienced as a capturing of the sense of ghostliness in physical corruption; on another it can be felt as a symbol of Hood himself— the house as the poet crumbling in his illnesses, and its haunting spirit the brooding subconscious from which he could conjure his poems of mystery, darkness, and death. The whole piece is dominated by his ever-present sense of mutability, decay and dissolution. Without a touch of his humour, but with plenty of his grotesque imagination, it evokes the very essence of man's mortality.

'**The Haunted House**' was by far the best of Hood's contributions to the new magazine. But his review of Dickens's *A Christmas Carol* in the same issue shows his continued admiration for the works of his friend. 'If Christmas, with its ancient and hospitable customs, its social and charitable observances, were in danger of decay, this is the book that would give them a new lease,' he said prophetically.

Certain difficulties attended the first number of *Hood's Magazine*. Tired of publishers' ways, Hood had decided to issue the journal from its own offices at 1 Adam Street, the Adelphi. The publishers tried to frustrate this gesture of independence by what Hood called a 'trade combination', presumably some way of blocking or limiting the ordinary means of distribution. But his name, now a household word, and the intrinsic quality of the first number, carried the issue through the obstacles.

It looked as if, at last, Hood was to enjoy a lucrative return from a periodical of his own. But the fate that had dogged his footsteps for years had allowed him only a temporary respite. Trouble struck again in February. It turned out that his proprietor, Flight, was a man of straw, who had, to quote Jane's words, 'engaged in the speculation without sufficient means to carry it on— having been tempted by the goodness of the speculation, and hoping to scramble through it.' Flight was unable or unwilling to pay the printers of the first issue, Bradbury and Evans, and to discharge his debts of some £100 to Hood. Two other printers were tried for the February issue, the second being unable to get it out before February 16. Under such unsatisfactory conditions, Hood managed to get the February issue launched, although rather late; but this fresh anxiety took a heavy toll of his health. Wranglings and negotiations with Flight, and his brother, a silent partner in the proprietorship, resulted in some kind of final settlement, and Flight was replaced as backer, by Andrew Spottiswoode, the Queen's Printer, whom Dickens knew and respected. 'I am certainly a lucky man,' Hood told Dickens on

April 1, 'and an unlucky one, too, for Spottiswoode is far better than the first promise of Flight. By the bye, I have heard one or two persons doubt the reality of Pecksniff—or the possibility—but I have lately met two samples of the breed. Flight is most decidedly Pecksniffian. . . . Conscience—said Flight—Sir, I have lived too long in the world to be a *slave to my conscience!* Was not this capital?'

Harassed by a new multitude of woes, Hood struggled along until May, astonishingly managing to turn out several more poems in his new social vein, including **'The Lady's Dream'**, a variant on the **'Song of the Shirt'** theme, **'The Workhouse Clock'**, an allegory of the torrent of the poor, and **'The Lay of the Labourer'**, a forceful plea for the chance for all to work, with its refrain:

> A spade! a rake! a hoe!
>   A pickaxe or a bill!

Recognizing Hood's extremity, his literary friends rallied round nobly. Monckton Milnes, assiduous in his kindly interest in deserving writers, was tireless in rounding up prominent writers to contribute to the magazine, often without payment. He himself wrote an article on *Coningsby* for the June, 1844, number and one on railways for the March, 1845, one. Dickens, in the midst of his usual hectic activities, promised 'a bit of writing'. 'It has been a cruel business,' Hood told him, 'and I really wanted help in it or I should not have announced it—knowing how much you have to do.' The contribution, duly delivered, was 'Threatening Letter to Thomas Hood from an Ancient Gentleman', in part a satire on the current craze for such midgets as Tom Thumb, which appeared in the *Magazine* for May, 1844. In Hood's need, Frederick Oldfield Ward undertook to conduct the magazine as editor without pay. He it was who, with Milnes, aroused the sympathy of various writers for one who, all now recognized, had only a brief time to live.

The May issue, compiled in the depths of pain and worry, contained, however, astonishingly, Hood's next most celebrated poem, **'The Bridge of Sighs'**. Like **'The Song of the Shirt'**, this was an inspired improvisation, suggested, perhaps, as Alvin Whitley has argued,[3] by *The Times*'s report and the subsequent agitation in March-April, 1844, on the case of Mary Furley, sentenced to be deported for the murder of her infant son and her own attempted suicide. Public clamour brought about a remission of her sentence to seven years' imprisonment. The title seems a fairly obvious one, but it is interesting to note that a popular song of the same name, written by E. Green, about a love triangle in Venice, appeared in the *London Singer's Magazine* for 1838 side by side with several of Hood's own comic poems.

The fame of **'The Bridge of Sighs'** was almost to equal that of **'The Song of the Shirt'**. This, wrote Thackeray, was 'his Corunna, his Heights of Abraham—sickly, weak, wounded, he fell in full blaze and fame of that great victory'. Like the earlier poem, this passionately felt interpretation of the popular heart belongs essentially to the ballad form—Richard Garnett grouped the two poems as 'genuine *Volkslieder* of the nineteenth century'—and in expressing the complete genuineness of Hood's compassion for the lonely, weary and suffering, caught perfectly the instinctive sympathy of the common man. It differs from the willed compassion or ideological logic of the intellectual, and equally from the fabricated sentimentalism of professional viewers-with-alarm; nobody reading the poem could imagine that he was being got at. Above all, it is the pervasive note of genuine Christian charity that ensures the authenticity of the feeling:

> Take her up instantly,
> Loving, not loathing.
> Touch her not scornfully;
> Think of her mournfully,
> Gently and humanly;
> Not of the stains of her,
> All that remains of her
> Now is pure womanly. . . .
>
> Owning her weakness,
> Her evil behaviour,
> And leaving with meekness,
> Her sins to her Saviour!

Few will quarrel with the poem's sentiment, despite a rather pointless attempt to expose the piece as a vulgarization of bits from Goethe's *Faust*.[4] What of its form? Here opinions differ sharply. Oliver Elton described it as 'jarring tuneless dactyls', while W. H. Hudson found that its 'wild effect is marvellously enhanced by the headlong pace and mad jingle of the verses'. Although, to a modern ear, the chime of Hood's feminine rhymes carries an unfortunate echo of Gilbert's patter songs, it seems to me that Hood has instinctively chosen a remarkably apt form for this poem. The metre combines relentlessness with emphasis—as if to say, 'Look at her! Look at her! *You* are to blame!', that element of repetition that underlies nursery rhymes and popular jingles, and, most important of all, the shape and mood of the Litany. Certainly in reading the poem, I cannot myself escape memories of the Litanies of the Virgin and the Sacred Heart. It is highly improbable that anything of this kind was in the mind of the wholly unliturgical and asquiescingly Protestant Hood, but I feel certain that the poem's appeal has been due at least in part to the half-submerged memory of liturgical rhythms, and that the acknowledged religious tone of the poem proceeds largely from this.

It is true that the expression is sometimes clumsy and naïve; and that there are specific lapses, such as

Wipe those poor lips of hers
Oozing so clammily. . . .

Lave in it, drink of it,
Then, if you can . . .

and the rhymes like 'pitiful—city full', 'basement—amazement' which teeter on the edge of absurdity. Taken together with the moving character of the whole poem, these can be accepted as a kind of guarantee of the thing's spontaneous sincerity, as the irregular rhythms of a folk-song are often a guarantee of its authenticity. Yet such an argument, if pressed far enough, would mean that **'The Bridge of Sighs'** is not to be judged by the standards we normally apply to poetry at all.

The danger in this view is that of under-valuing Hood's art and literary tact. He had not only generous human sympathies, an awareness of man's inhumanity to man that enabled him to concentrate in this poem much of what Dickens said of such matters in a whole novel, and that personal experience of suffering that gives especial poignancy to

Even God's Providence
Seeming estranged,

but he had, too, a real flair for the handling of such tricky metres as that of **'The Bridge of Sighs'** and an instinct for the memorable phrase that has made much of the poem part of the familiar currency of the language.

The answer may well lie in recognizing the fact that not only was Hood, inevitably, when we consider the circumstances in which he worked, a very uneven poet, writing good poems, bad poems and poems that are both good and bad, but also that he is one of that rare species, to which Kipling, for instance, belongs, who have the drive, the emotional power, of a popular singer, of a Bessie Smith or a Leadbelly, but at the same time is anything but devoid of art. **'The Bridge of Sighs'** is probably best described by that currently fashionable designation, 'a good-bad poem'; it has glaring faults, even absurdities, it is strained, it is sometimes only a short step away from self-burlesque—yet it compels, it lingers, it moves, it commands attention, it goes deeper into our instinctive responses than the cerebral lines of a poet who has assiduously read his Empson.

Notes

1. For other examples of Keats's influence on Hood, see Federico Olivero: 'Hood and Keats', *Modern Language Notes*, December, 1913, pp. 233-5.

2. *Mythology and the Romantic Tradition in English Poetry*, New York: Pageant Book Co., 1957.

3. 'Thomas Hood and "The Times"', *Times Literary Supplement*, May 17, 1957, p. 309.

4. John Hennig: 'The Literary Relations Between Goethe and Thomas Hood', *Modern Language Quarterly*, Vol. XII, No. 1, March, 1951.

William G. Lane (essay date winter 1964)

SOURCE: Lane, William G. "A Chord in Melancholy: Hood's Last Years." *Keats-Shelley Journal* 13 (winter 1964): 43-60.

[*In the following essay, Lane examines the many personal and professional misfortunes suffered by Hood, which may have accounted for the melancholic tone that pervaded much of his poetry.*]

"There's not a string attuned to mirth
But has its chord in melancholy."

—Hood

A satisfactory life of Thomas Hood has not yet been written; the bulk of his letters has not yet been collected and edited.[1] The first attempt, *Memorials*,[2] by his daughter, Mrs. Frances Freeling Broderip, and his son, Thomas Hood, Jr., has been roundly damned by common reader and scholar alike as "the worst sort of memoir, scrappy, sketchy, ill-informed, sublimely careless of facts and dates . . . nauseating in the pomposity of its dutiful adulation."[3] So bad, indeed, that upon reading the book, Thackeray is said to have exclaimed that there was to be no life ever written about *him*. The second such work, Walter Jerrold's *Thomas Hood: His Life and Times* (1907), is considerably better; but, necessarily based on the *Memorials,* it falls short in many of the same ways, chiefly in scope.[4]

My purpose is to make a synthesis of several disparate pieces of Hood material, hitherto uncollected; to add (by printing the text or describing) eight unpublished letters by Hood and six letters about him and his family; to establish the literary and personal relationship between Hood and Richard Harris Barham,[5] and that between these two writers and the publishers Henry Colburn and Richard Bentley.[6] Five of Hood's letters are addressed to the Royal Literary Fund and Barham's charitable activity in his behalf was chiefly through that institution. I have therefore felt it necessary to give a brief history of that organization up to the time that it was brought to wider public attention by the Case of the Reformers, Dickens, Dilke, and Forster.[7]

I

On 5 May 1825 Thomas Hood, son of a bookseller of the Poultry, married Jane Reynolds, sister of the promising solicitor and friend of Keats, John Hamilton Reynolds[8]—probably with some misgivings on the part of her family. There could be no objection to Hood personally, but professionally there was little as yet to recommend him. He was connected with the *London Magazine* as art editor, but there was no substantial work to establish his name. The obstacles were overcome; the marriage took place as planned; and the couple soon reported their happiness to the family.

The letter[9] Hood wrote to his wife's sisters Mariane and Lot (i.e., Charlotte)[10] during their honeymoon at Hastings is undoubtedly the most charming of all his extant letters. Buoyant in spirit, fanciful and playful in tone,[11] it well attests to the string of mirth upon which, for a time at least, he would play.

Entirely too soon the tone of mirth modulates to the melancholic. In his letter to Charles Ollier,[12] during May, 1827, Hood reveals the twofold ills from which he was seldom again to be free: family woes and publishing worries.

> 2 Robert Street
> Adelphi
> [n.d.]
>
> My dear Sir.
>
> I send you an ode which should have come some days ago—but that I have been knocked up. Mrs Hood has been confined—but our poor little girl was obliged to be sacrificed to the mother's safety.
>
> I wrote to Mr Colburn some time back touching the *Whims & Oddities* accordg to our conversation—but I have not heard from him & am about to give up any expectation of it. I am my dear Sir
>
> Yours very truly
> T. Hood[13]
>
> Let me see you soon.

His subsequent career is succinctly reported by his wife when, shortly before his death, she drew up a holograph memorandum of his life and works. It affords a convenient graph upon which to lay out the events to be recorded in the following pages.

> Mr Hood commenced his Literary career as Sub Editor of the *London Magazine* in 1822.
>
> **The Plea of the Fairies &c** (serious) 1827
>
> 2 series of **Whims & Oddities** each a vol 1826-1827
>
> *National Tales* 2 vols.—1827
>
> *Epping Hunt*—1829
>
> Editor of the *Gem* an Annual in 1829 in which he wrote his serious poem of **Eugene Aram**—afterwards published alone with illustrations by Harvey. 10 Comic Annuals commencing 1830 7 of which were republished as **"Hoods Own"** with additions and Remeniscences [sic] of Life
>
> *Tylney Hall* a novel in 3 vols in 1834

> *Up the Rhine.* 1 vol
>
> Was a contributor at different periods to the *Literary Souvenir—Forget Me Not—Friendships Offering—Athenæum* (in which he published his letters on the Copyright) *Literary Gazette—New Monthly Magazine* in 1840 which articles were republished as another Comic in 1842 when he commenced Editing the *NM.* During his Editorship he wrote the articles which were re-collected as **Whimsicalities—**
>
> As far as I can trace Mr Hood must have made between 8 and 9 hundred designs on the wood—
>
> He went abroad in March 1835 and returned to England in 1840
>
> His money annoyances began about 1833 or 4 caused by the failure of Mr Wright—and his ill health and first attack of hemmorhage [sic] from the lungs was in 1835—
>
> On his return to England his Publishers accounts were so incorrect that he resolved to [take] remove his works elsewhere when Mr Bailey retained them *all* on the plea that he had a quarter share [in the profits] of *one*— the **"Hoods Own"**—instead of a quarter share of the *profits only—*
>
> This was decided by a verdict in Hoods favour a few months back and Judge Tenterdon expressed it as his opinion that a share of the profits did not mean a share of the copyright but being a contract he was compelled to refer it to the Judges in Banco—which will be settled in Sept[r]—But the delay of 3 or 4 years has ruined the property—
>
> I have as far as possible collected in haste all these particulars—
>
> I believe they are tollerably correct—
>
> When I saw Hood on Saturday he desired me on sending to you to enquire for Lady Willoughbys book—will you send it by George if you have it—I shall go to Blackheath I think tomorrow—and will take any letters &c you have for Hood—Please to send him proofs & all information you can about the Mag—as he will else get restless and desire to return home—and its very important that he shall remain at Blackheath during this fine weather he is so much better for the change
>
> Yours very truly
> Jane Hood[14]

II

Richard Bentley was born in London in 1794, the son of Edward Bentley, who with John Nichols, the onetime "Sylvanus Urban" of *The Gentleman's Magazine,* was publisher and part proprietor of the *General Evening Post.* At St. Paul's School, he was a schoolfellow of Barham. Upon leaving there, he went into the printing office of his uncle, John Nichols. In 1819 Bentley joined the printing office of his brother Samuel,[15] who had established his business in Dorset Street, Salisbury Square, and afterward in Shoe Lane. "The Bentley's took high rank among printers and were noted especially for the care with which they printed woodcuts, such as those which illustrate Yarrell's works on natural history."[16]

During the ten-year period after 1819, the firm of Henry Colburn reached major importance. Its competition was not severe, for Constable had fallen with Scott, and Murray was lessening his activity during the panic of 1825-26.[17] Colburn, on the other hand, having made some fortunate monetary and literary speculations, was expanding, and was not seriously curbed by the panic. In September, 1829, he took into partnership his printer Richard Bentley. Colburn shrewdly "tied his balloon to fiction," and established his name as the undisputed champion of the field of fashionable novels.

The new partnership was not a happy one, however, and a quarrel soon developed over the value of copyrights, which Colburn, taking advantage of his partner's inexperience, was inclined to value too highly.[18] Nor did their new publishing ventures, The National Library and the Juvenile Library, succeed. In August, 1832, therefore, they signed an agreement dissolving the partnership. Colburn sold the business to Bentley, but maintained his magazine holdings, which were extensive. In addition a somewhat strange proviso was included in the terms: Colburn was prohibited from setting up in business within twenty miles of London, Edinburgh, or Dublin. Bentley could not expect so easily to eliminate his older and shrewder rival. Sticking to the literal terms, Colburn opened an office at Windsor, twenty-one miles from London. Bentley, who was to show himself quick-tempered in several later affairs, must have been furious. To prevent further duplicity, he accepted payment of a fee to release Colburn from their agreement. The latter lost no time in setting up a new business in Great Marlborough Street. From this time they engaged in bitter rivalry.

Thackeray, keenly aware of all that went on in literary circles and given to drawing on his acquaintances for characters, uses the contention of the two men in *Pendennis,* where Bentley and Colburn become Mr. Bacon and Mr. Bungay, respectively.

> Since they have separated, it is a furious war between the two publishers; and no sooner does one bring out a book of travels, or poems, a magazine or periodical, quarterly, or monthly, or weekly, or annual, but the rival is in the field with something similar. . . . When Bungay engaged your celebrated friend Mr. Wagg [i.e., Hook] to edit the *Londoner,* Bacon straightway rushed off and secured Mr. Grindle [i.e., Dickens] to give his name to the *Westminster Magazine.*[19]

For the two fictional periodicals in Thackeray's account read *New Monthly Magazine* and *Bentley's Miscellany:* the fictionalized version follows closely the actual oc-

currences. Bentley wanted the inimitable Theodore Hook to be editor, but Colburn precluded that possibility by hiring him first. Bentley, perforce, turned elsewhere and his choice attests to his business acumen and foresight. Though Dickens' term as editor proved stormy, his rising fame brought immediate success to Bentley's periodical. Barham, too, in his role of "Thomas Ingoldsby" was an important contributor from the first. Hood, as a reference to Mrs. Hood's Chronology above will show, became an important contributor to Colburn's periodical in 1840, and, after the death of Hook in August, 1841, its editor. The second chapter in the record of these shifting relationships occurred when, in 1843, Barham broke with Bentley,[20] and on 13 June threw in his lot with Colburn and Hood.

The change-over was effected in June. Barham's last legend in the *Miscellany* appeared in May, his first in the *New Monthly* in July. At some time, between 26 May and 13 June, Hood wrote to Barham asking his decision:

17 Elm Tree Road
St John's Wood
Monday.

My dear Sir

Is there any hitch in Marlboro Street? I have had a note thence, today, implying that you are "making up your mind." I hope you will do so before I make up the Magazine, & so that we may both jingle in the same team.

My stiff Knee is relaxing, so that I shall be ready to unbend in your society, as Colburn proposes, whatever day & hour may be fixed.

I am
My dear Sir
Yours very truly
Thos. Hood[21]

Revd. R. Barham.

Barham's decision was made in time for the two humorists, so much alike and yet so distinctively individual, to jingle in the same team in the July issue. In the autumn of that year, Hood gave up the editorship of the *New Monthly.*

Hood's break with Colburn is another in the all-too-familiar pattern of business quarrels which stain the records of author-publisher annals of the 1830's and 1840's. The Dickens-Bentley dispute, the Bentley-Cruikshank-Ainsworth quarrels, ironically the Barham-Bentley literary breach, to mention but three disputes involving only one publisher, are cases in point. The whole question is perhaps well stated and summarized in a letter of advice on this point from Robert Southey to Carolyn Bowles: "Booksellers are not the most liberal, nor the most amiable of men. They are necessarily *tradesmen*; and a constant attention to profit and loss is neither wholesome for the heart nor the understanding."[22]

The letter from Dickens to Hood of 12 September 1843, besides giving details of the matter, reveals the degree of vituperation in which the combatants would excoriate each other:

> There can be no doubt in the mind of any honourable man, that the circumstances under which you signed your agreement are of the most disgraceful kind, in so far as Mr. Colburn is concerned. There can be no doubt that he took a money-lending, bill-broking, Jew-clothes-bagging, Saturday-night-pawnbroking advantage of your temporary situation. There is little doubt (so I learn from Forster, who had previously given me exactly your version of the circumstances) that, like most pieces of knavery, this precious document is a mere piece of folly, and just a scrap of wastepaper wherein Mr. Schobe[r]l might wrap his Chity-snuff. But I am sorry, speaking with a backward view to the feasibility of placing you in a better situation with Colburn, that you flung up the Editorship of the magazine. I think you did so at a bad time, and wasted your strength in consequence.[23]

Dickens goes on to ask if Hood has determined not to accept Colburn's offer of thirty guineas a sheet. If so, he advises, Hood should try to get the editorship of Bentley's magazine. "For to any man, I don't care who he is," Dickens says, "the Editorship of a monthly magazine, on tolerable terms, is a matter of too much moment, in its pecuniary importance and certainty, to be flung away as of little worth."

In his letter to Dickens of 19 October 1843,[24] Hood protested again at the vague answers he was receiving from Ainsworth and Colburn relative to his rejoining the group as a contributor. He stated that Barham had told him "they placed a blank paper before him to fill up with his own terms." Hood was given no such generous handling. He concludes: "I have had it proposed to me by a man with means to start a new one. It is rather tempting for I have never had fair play in the N. M. M. & think I could do something—if left alone to do it." When Bentley was applied to by Hood concerning the supposedly vacant editorship, the publisher remembered an earlier instance of breach of contract to contribute by Hood and rejected him abruptly. Hood turned now to the plan to found a new periodical, one that should bear his own name.

Sometime after Christmas Hood moved from Elm Tree Road to New Finchley Road.[25] From the new address he again wrote Barham and sent along a copy of the first number of *Hood's Magazine*.

[Jan. 1844]

Office. 1 Adam Street Adelphi
                        and
Home. Devonshire Lodge
              New Finchley Road
                   St. John's Wood
     "Like a Bird in two places at once!"—

My dear Sir

Herewith you have a sample of the quality of our Magazine. We shall have rather an uphill fight for having no connexion with the trade, they are making a bit of a set against us. But we mean to "do or die"—& rather consider it a compliment to our prowess. Colburn, to begin [,] has thoroughly committed himself by refusing to take in letters addressed to me at Marlboro St. by strangers, sending them adrift endorsed "Not known to Mr Colburn". I am therefore relieved of all delicacy towards him, & beg to say at once, that should your time allow, & your inclination prompt you to give us your help, I think you would find the connexion a pleasant one in every respect.

A line from you, or a look in—at the office—if you will make an appointment will oblige

              My dear Sir
                   Yours very truly
                        Thos. Hood[26]

Revd. R. Barham

     Lines On Being **"Unknown to Mr Colburn."**[27]

For a couple of years in the columns of Puff
I was reckon'd a passable writer enough.
But alas! for the favours of Fame!
Since I quitted her seat in Great Marlboro Street,
My decline in repute is so very complete
That a Colburn don't know of my name!

Now a Colburn I knew in his person so small,
That he seem'd the *Half* Brother of no one at all,
Yet in spirit a Dwarf may be big;
But his mind was so narrow, his soul was so dim,
Where's the wonder if all I remember of him,
Is—a suit of boy's clothes & a Wig!

Seriously, the miscarriage of a letter might be of such vital importance to *third* parties, I cannot imagine *a Man* could be guilty of such an act as Colburn's towards his most mortal enemy.

[Hood to Doctor—]
[paper watermarked 1842]
                        Friday evening.
                        [n.p., n.d.]

Dear Doctor.

Altho the winter has not exactly set in, I have volunteered to break some ice, in which you have hitherto preserved a certain secret, & of which some mutual friends at Stratford have given us a hint.

Of course you have had your note of invitation for the 6th to Jane's party—She has already received promises from Dickens, Ainsworth, Miss Pardoe, Peter Priggins, Forster, & expects Procter, Ingoldsby—Sir C & Lady

Morgan—Poole (the Author of Paul Pry) & some others. If you know therefore of any young lady who would like to see a few of our literary lions & lionesses we should be most happy to see her, particularly if she should happen to be a namesake of Mrs *Hemans*—a word from you to *authorise* it will produce a regular *article* from Jane to that effect. I am glad to say the Stratford-not-upon-Avon Elliots are coming, with Manley Hopkins, & some of the Wards *out* of Chancery. What a pity the Barnes's are not within reach!—to be at our first bit of gaiety!

If the INFLUENZA will let you, *do* drop us a line by return post, & believe *us* x

> Dear Doctor (for self & Partner)
> Yours very heartily
> Tho Hood.[28]

x not editorially but domestically.

[n.p., n.d.]

Dear Lemon

I am much better tho not allowed yet or indeed able to leave my bed. About five weeks ago I was struck by a very cold wind in walking home from Landseer's, near here, where I dined. It proved to be inveterate influenza,—complicated by my heart being faulty, & an old marsh complaint, that made a periodical of it, with spasms. I lost my breath so once or twice I felt & looked I am told very like death. One comfort is my three doctors between them could not discover any really unsound place in my lungs. My breath is now lengthening, my cough all but gone—& my chief complaint is weakness—but that is gigantic. But I am notorious for rallying at the worst—so I hope in a day or two to be on my legs.

Last Punch's cuts very good. Chuny [?] capital—& Brummel ditto. When you think of a subject likely to suit *me* let me know.

I understand entre nous that the Puck people applied to Thackeray—but he said he was too well used in *Punch* to join them. The prop^{rs} [proprietors] are safe in that feeling which is general.

Give my kind regards to B & E. I hope to see them soon. The Mag. is going on very well—rose to 90 last No. & a good many advts. come in. I am

> Dear Lemon
> Yours very truly
> Thos. Hood[29]

There was a consultation of three
Doctors on Tuesday so for once
I suppose I have been *serious*.

III

The Royal Literary Fund[30] was founded in 1790 by David Williams (1738-1816). "Against so bold, so manly, and so able an advocate in behalf of civil and religious liberty, much malignity has occasionally been displayed; to deprecate such malignity, or defend him from the attacks of the enemies of such principles, would be superfluous, because it would be unnecessary. We leave the friend of Franklin, and Roland, to defend himself, whenever an assailant shall appear worthy of such a contest." So runs the account in *Public Characters of 1798-9* of "this extraordinary man."

The organization he founded became his own haven immediately; he is designated "Resident Visitor 1790-1816" in the current Reports. It is fitting that he could be so cared for. His institution has long proved a bulwark to scores of necessitous authors or their immediate dependents. From its inception to the end of 1958, it had distributed in grants £350,186.

John Gibson Lockhart, reviewing Southey's essay on "Uneducated Poets" and pleading "the cause of struggling genius," was moved to praise both the Fund and its manner of conducting its affairs in the *Quarterly Review,* XLIV (January, 1831), 82:

> We hope to be pardoned for taking this opportunity of bearing witness to the wise and generous method in which the Managers of the London Literary Fund conduct that admirable Charity. It may not be known in many parts of the empire that such an institution exists at all; and even this casual notice may be serviceable to its revenues. We have had occasion to observe the equal promptitude and delicacy with which its Committee are ever ready to administer to the necessities of the unfortunate scholar, who can satisfy them that his misery is not the just punishment of immoral habits. Some of the brightest names in contemporary literature have been beholden to the bounty of this Institution; and in numerous instances its interference has shielded friendless merit from utter ruin.

A representative list of supporters of the institution, besides nobility, would include many prominent authors and publishers: Colburn (1818-1855), £106; Thackeray (1847-1859), £57; Talfourd (1836-1850), £41; Moxon (1833-1858), £37; Dilke (1832-1845), £45; Lockhart (1830-1840), £31. As a rule, such men ceased their connection with the Fund only at their deaths.

Barham, also, was associated with the Fund from 1826 until his death, contributed over £20, and served as a member of the Council. In this capacity he was often called upon to help govern the affairs of the Fund, or to make intercession to it in the cause of needy persons. There is record, for example, of the appeal made to him by William C. Macready, the actor, supporting Haynes Bayly.[31] Or again, Barham was by letter of 14 February 1840 notified by Octavian Blewitt, the Secretary, that he was appointed to a committee "for the purpose of determining on the propriety of obtaining more eligible chambers for the Society."[32] Barham was therefore in a favorable position to help Hood when in January, 1841, the latter's desperate plight was made known to the Society.

Hood had returned from Germany and Belgium in the summer of 1840. Besides ill health and mental depression, he had to disturb him the drawn-out lawsuit with his publisher A. H. Baily.[33] As he was to write later to his good friend Dr. William Elliott, of Stratford, "My fortunes seem subject to *crises,* like certain disorders."[34] Such a time had now come. His case was proposed to the Literary Fund,[35] and the letters that constitute the record are more eloquent than any commentary, if one were needed, could be:

13 January 1841
8 South Terrace,
Camberwell New Road

Dear Sirs,

I will thank you to bring under the consideration of the Committee the case of Mr. Thos. Hood. The writer of the Comic Annual and other works. It is within my knowledge that he has been for months in extreme ill-health, and that about ten days ago he was so bad that for many hours his life was in danger. For several months too he has been in great pecuniary difficulties—and without entering further into painful particulars, I can certify that within these few days, he has been in want of even a few shillings. He has a wife and two children.

I am, Gentlemen,
Yours truly,
C. W. Dilke.

O. Blewitt, Esq.

[13/14 January 1841]

Sir,

At a Meeting of the General Committee of the R.L.F. held yesterday afternoon, it was represented to the Committee that you are unfortunately suffering under the pressure of adverse circumstances. The Committee has therefore directed me to assure you of their sympathy, and to request your acceptance of £50, with their best wishes for your restoration to health. I shall be obliged by your sending an acknowledgement of its receipt.

I am, Sir, etc.
O. Blewitt

* * *

14 January 1841

Mr Hood presents his Compts. to Mr Blewitt, and begs to acknowledge the receipt of his note and the enclosure—and will forward a letter to the Committee in the course of to-morrow—Friday.

Hood returned the £50 with a long explanatory letter that has been several times reprinted. To omit it here, however, would be to omit a characteristically heroic note that belongs in this correspondence. It is further needed to gauge the pathos of the retraction that Hood soon found necessary.

2 Union Place,
High Street,
Camberwell.
[15 January 1841]

Gentlemen,

I have to acknowledge the receipt of a letter from your secretary which has deeply affected me.

The adverse circumstances to which it alludes are unfortunately too well known from their public announcement in the Athenaeum by my precocious Executor and officious Assignee. But I beg most emphatically to repeat that the disclosures so drawn from me were never intended to bespeak the world's pity or assistance. Sickness is too common to Humanity, and Poverty too old a companion of my order, to justify such an appeal. The revelation was merely meant to show, when taunted with "my Creditors", that I had been striving in humble imitation of an illustrious literary example to satisfy all claims on me—and to account for my imperfect success. I am too proud of my Profession to grudge it some suffering. I love it still, as Lord Byron loved England, "with all its faults", and I should hardly feel as one of the Fraternity if I had not my portion of "the Calamities of an Author". More fortunate than many, I have succeeded not only in getting into print, but occasionally in getting out of it, and surely, a man who had overcome such formidable difficulties may hope and expect to get over the commonplace one of procuring bread and cheese.

I am writing sincerely, Gentlemen, although in a cheerful tone, partly natural and partly intended to relieve you of your kindly concern on my account. Indeed my position at present is an easy one compared with that of some eight months ago, when out of health and out of heart, helpless, spiritless, sleepless, childless. I have now a home in my own country, and my little ones sit at my hearth. I smile sometimes and even laugh. For the same benign Providence that gifted me with the power of amusing others, has not denied me the ability of entertaining myself. Moreover, as to mere worldly losses I profess a cheerful Philosophy which can jest "though China fall", and for graver troubles a Christian faith that consoles and supports me even in walking through something like the Valley of the Shadow of Death.

My embarrassments and bad health are of such standing that I am become, as it were, seasoned. For the last six years I have been engaged in the same struggle, without seeking, receiving or recognizing any pecuniary assistance whatever. My pen and pencil procured not only enough for my wants, but to form a surplus besides—a sort of Literary Fund of my own, which at this moment is "doing good by stealth" to a person not exactly of learning or genius,—but whom, according to the example of your excellent Society, I will forbear to name. To provide for similar wants there are the same means and resources, the same head, heart and hands, the same bad health—and may it only last long enough!—in short the same crazy vessel for the same foul weather, but I have not thought yet of hanging my ensign upside down.

Fortunately since manhood I have been dependant solely on my own exertions—a condition which has exposed and enured me to vicissitude; whilst it has nourished a pride which will fight on, and has yet some retrenchments to make ere it surrender.

I have now, Gentlemen, described circumstances and feelings which will explain and must excuse my present course. The honourable and liberal manner in which you have entertained an application—that a friend delicately concealed from me—is acknowledged with the most ardent gratitude. Your welcome sympathy is valued in proportion to the very great comfort and encouragement it affords me. Your kind wishes for my better health—my greatest want—I accept and thank you for with all my heart, but I must not and cannot retain your money, which at the first safe opportunity will be returned. I really do not feel myself to be a proper object for your bounty. And should I ever become so, I fear that such a crisis will find me looking elsewhere—to the earth beneath me for a final rest, and to the heaven above me for final justice.

Pray excuse my trespassing at such length on your patience, and believe that I am with the utmost respect,

> Gentlemen,
> Your much obliged and grateful servant,
> Thos. Hood.

However heartwarming the sentiments expressed, and however proud of his refusal Hood may have been—for so he expressed himself to Dr. Eliott[36]—his fortunes did not improve. All of the woes, personal and professional, continued. Shortly thereafter Hood was forced to lay his case before the Society a second time:

25 May 1841

Mr Hood presents his compliments to Mr Blewitt and requests him to have the kindness to lay the enclosed before the proper Meeting. Below is a new address:

> 2 Union Row,
> High Street,
> Camberwell.

To the Gentlemen of the Committee of the Literary Fund.

Gentlemen,

You may conceive the extreme pain with which I revoke my former decision. My views and feelings as then expressed are still unaltered, but unexpected circumstances have occurred which compel me for the sake of others to seek and accept the aid you so handsomely offered me.

> Gentlemen,
> Your most obedient Servant,
> Thos. Hood

Another grant of £50 was given to him on 9 June 1841, when next the Committee met. It was receipted for by his wife. For this kindness, Hood thanked them as follows:

To the Gentlemen of the Committee of the Literary Fund.

Gentlemen,

The feelings I endeavoured to express when you so generously tendered me your assistance have left me little to add on the actual receipt of your bounty. Pray accept, once more, my most grateful thanks for your kindness, and your continued goodwill towards me. It cannot but be gratifying to find that so many strangers are my friends, at a time when friends are proverbially apt to degenerate into acquaintance and acquaintance into strangers.

The present opportunity tempts me to explain why my former renunciation of the money should have been followed so speedily by an application so much at variance with my professions. There was, however, no affectation of independance—indeed, during the last twelve months my earning will cover my very economical expenditure. The truth is that an unforseen case occurred when the sum would be of a service so important as to overcome my scruples,—or rather it made their sacrifice a matter of duty towards others. But my former sentiments and views remained unaltered—for my vessel is no crazier, my clouds no blacker, and my 'sea of troubles' no rougher than before. It is true that I have heard from Leicestershire that I am in prison,—and from Brussels that I am insane—my difficulties have again been paragraphed in public journals—and my "destitution" has been cried about the Exchange, or rather in the neighbourhood of Cornhill. Nevertheless, I am happy to inform you, Gentlemen, that as yet, my only confinement has been my bed, and that my madness must have originated in some brain or at least Head.

It is not improbable that the unwarrantable publicity thus given to my private affairs may again provoke or compel me to further disclosures—But such a statement I repeat, will be purely explanatory. It will be in fact my humble contribution to Literary history, and serve to show that my present cruel position is not due to improvidence and careless habits as generally imputed to authors (for my proper pecuniary difficulties I could have overcome) but to the fraudulent practices of a dishonest agent.

> I have the honour to be,
> Gentlemen,
> Your very grateful and obedient servant,
> Thos. Hood.

Appended as a footnote to this correspondence is a cutting from *The Argus,* 7 February 1841:

THE LITERARY FUND.—A subscriber informs us that the old system of favouritism is adopted in relieving applicants, and that in one instance lately it has been carried to a most unwarrantable excess. We shall enquire into this: the donors must not be Hoodwinked.

Hood died peacefully at noon on Saturday, 3 May 1845. On the nineteenth of that month began another series of letters relevant to his dependents, his wife and two children.

> Devonshire Lodge,
> New Finchley Road,

St Johns Wood.
19 May 1845

My dear Sir,

As the Widow of Thos. Hood I beg through your kind representation to solicit aid from the Gentlemen who form the Council of the Literary Fund. By the death of my dear Husband I am left with two children to educate and provide for on a small pension, which ceases with my life. The expenses of nearly a six month severe illness—during three of which Mr Hood was quite incapable of making any exertion to maintain his family—with also the cost of the funeral, have sadly distressed and embarrassed me. And the Gentlemen of the Council will render me a most essential service by granting me their most kind and benevolent assistance under these truly painful circumstances.—

I am Sir,
Your obliged and grateful servant,
Jane Hood.

Barham, ill himself and escorting an invalid wife, had sought "retirement and change of air"[37] at Clifton on May 5, after suffering a relapse from the cold he had caught at a vestry meeting at St. Paul's on April 19. From Clifton he wrote to the Secretary enclosing Mrs. Hood's application, which, apparently, had been sent to him for his signature, and strongly supporting it.

9 Dowry Square,
Clifton Hotwells.

My dear Sir,

I beg to enclose Mrs Hood's application, signed by myself, and have written to Mr Phillips, from whom I have just had the Form to ask him to call on you for any advice or assistance on the subject which your known kindness on these occasions warrants him in the assistance you will gladly give him.

I am sorry to say the still inflamed state of my throat for which I have been sent here will prevent my being able personally to advocate poor Mrs Hood's case, but I regret it the less as I am sure there will be but one feeling on this occasion to do her all that can be done. She has I know a family, but the precise number of which it consists I am not altogether informed, this is one of the reasons why I wish Mr P. to see you as he can give details which should be supplied.

I am mending very slowly,

Yours most truly,
R. H. Barham.

O. Blewitt, Esq.

I regret to say that I much fear I shall have no chance of dining with the Society this year, the first I believe I have missed for many.

In a letter dated 18, May, David Salomons also strongly supported Mrs. Hood's appeal; Samuel Phillips forwarded it and the letter from Mrs. Hood to the Secretary on 19 May.[38]

Mrs. Hood thanked the Committee for its grant shortly thereafter.

Devonshire Lodge,
New Finchley Road,
St John's Wood,
23rd May 1845

My dear Sir,

Will you have the goodness to present to the Gentlemen who form the Council of the Literary Fund, my very grateful thanks for the benevolent and kind assistance they have afforded me in their handsome present of seventy five pounds.

I am my dear Sir,
Yours very truly,
Jane Hood

Barham's next letter, the last of the series, expresses both his pleasure at hearing of the grant and his dismay over the continuing attacks on Hood's case.

9 Dowry Square,
Clifton Hotwells.
May 25, 1845

My dear Sir,

Many thanks for your communication. I am very glad poor Mrs Hood has got the Grant as, between ourselves, I am sadly afraid Hood's necessities had induced her to anticipate more than one year of her pension to supply them, at least it has been so hinted to me but it will not do to talk about this as offence might be taken in a high quarter and possibly the allowance stopped for I know it is understood *not* to mortgage a pension.

I am very sorry to hear what you tell me of the attacks and the Quarters they proceed from. I could never have anticipated it from either. What *can* be the motive? I have not seen either of them for, confined as I am to the house here, I see and hear little of what is going on except from the ordinary channel of my own newspaper.

I am suffering severely from my attack in the throat and still more from the remedies applied, counter irritation is worse than irritation itself, but it is I *hope* going on well so I grin and bear it. . . .[39]

Believe me to be,
My dear Sir,
Yours very faithfully,
R. H. Barham.

As with Hood, literature and writing were solace and diversion for Barham; like Hood, he meant to grin and bear his misfortunes. Within less than a month, on 17 June, he died in London. Mrs. Hood died in November the following year, only eighteen months after her husband. The notes of mirth had been resolved in a chord of melancholy. But it is chiefly as humorists that we recall both Hood and Barham—and that is as it should be.

Notes

1. Important biographical material and correspondence appear in Leslie A. Marchand's, *Letters of*

Thomas Hood (New Brunswick, N. J., 1945), in which he prints the manuscripts of the Dilke Collection; and Alvin Whitley's, "Hood and Dickens: Some New Letters," *HLQ* [*Huntington Library Quarterly*] XIV (August, 1951), 385-413. Professor P. F. Morgan, University of Toronto, is preparing an edition of Hood's correspondence.

Hitherto unpublished material in my study is drawn from Hood manuscripts in the Harvard College Library (hereafter HCL) and from the files of the Royal Literary Fund. With great pleasure I acknowledge my indebtedness to Dr. William A. Jackson and the Harvard College Library for permission to publish the Harvard material and to Mr. G. W. Cottrell, Jr., the editor of the *Harvard Library Bulletin*. Mr. J. G. Broadbent, Secretary of the Royal Literary Fund, and his assistant, Mrs. Frances Minto-Cowen, have been unfailingly helpful and patient with my many questions. Mr. Paul Kaufman, Consultant in Bibliography at the Library of the University of Washington, called my attention to additional Hood manuscripts both in this country and England. Finally, I owe thanks for the award of an ACLS grant-in-aid which made possible several phases of my study.

In quoting letters and documents I have used the spelling and punctuation of the originals except as specified in notes 14 and 23, below.

2. *Memorials of Thomas Hood* (2 vols. Boston, 1860).

3. Malcolm Elwin, *Thackeray* (London, 1932), p. 393.

4. Jerrold's *Thomas Hood & Charles Lamb* (London, 1930) is based on Hood's Reminiscences. Three additional works are important: *The Papers of a Critic: Selected from the Writings of the Late Charles Wentworth Dilke* (2 vols. London, 1875); Henry C. Shelley, *Literary By-Paths in Old England* (Boston, 1906); K. J. Fielding, "The Misfortunes of Hood: 1841," *N&Q,* [*Notes & Queries*] CXCVIII (1953), 534-536.

5. My critical study of Barham's own work and reputation, "The Primitive Muse of Thomas Ingoldsby," may be found in *HLB* [*Harvard Library Bulletin*], XII (1958), Nos. 1 and 2. The only life of Barham is that by his son, R. H. Dalton Barham, *Life and Letters of the Rev. R. H. Barham* (2 vols. London, 1870). It appears also in a single-volume edition (1880). Both were published by the Bentley firm.

6. Royal A. Gettmann's "Colburn—Bentley and the March of Intellect," *Studies in Bibliography. Papers of the Bibliographical Society of the University of Virginia,* IX (1957), 197-213,

discusses the contribution made by the two publishers' novel series. The standard commentary is Michael Sadleir's, *XIX Century Fiction* (London, 1951), II. Gettmann's "Barham and Bentley," *JEGP* [*Journal of English and Germanic Philology*], LVI (July, 1957), 337-346, deals not only with relationships but also financial aspects of the *Ingoldsby Legends* as a Victorian best seller; see, also, his *A Victorian Publisher: A Study of the Bentley Papers* (Cambridge University Press, 1960). Marjorie Shaw, "Henry Colburn et la Littérature Française," *RLC* [*Revue de Littérature Comparée*], XXXIII (1959), 414-419, emphasizes Colburn's service in publishing a considerable number of French works in the original or in translation between 1812 and 1849.

7. A recent account (anonymous) is "Dickens and the Royal Literary Fund," *TLS* [*Times Literary Supplement*], 15 October 1954, p. 664. See, also, *The Dickensian,* XLVII (Sept., 1951), 181. Dickens commissioned Morley to write the article that appeared in *Household Words,* XIII (1856), 169-172.

8. Like his brother-in-law, Reynolds turned to Barham for literary aid. His unpublished letter of 3 April 1839 (HCL. Eng. 936. II, 69) regards publication of a manuscript, the authorship of which was to be kept a strict secret.

9. HCL. Lowell Autograph. The printed version in Shelley, pp. 338-342, is a careless handling of the manuscript. Its length precludes its inclusion in this article.

10. The long letter Hood wrote to Charlotte on 29 March 182[4?] is in the Keats Collection, HCL; it is published in Jerrold, *Life,* pp. 150-154, substantially correct.

11. Without raising the vexatious question of puns, it may be well to cite two informative comments about Hood's use of them: "Hood . . . used the pun to make a sentence or a sentiment especially pointed and clear" (G. K. Chesterton, *The Victorian Age in Literature* [Oxford, 1946], p. 105); Paul Elmer More has said that Hood's puns are sometimes mere sounds, "but more often there is a kind of accompanying twist in the situation itself, playful or grotesque, which raises the humor above the exasperation of sheer verbicide" ("Thomas Hood" in *Shelburne Essays,* Seventh Series, Boston, 1910, pp. 57-58). The validity of these statements may be checked with reference to several of the letters in my article.

12. For the connection of Ollier (1788-1859) with Keats, for example, see Hyder E. Rollins, *N&Q,* CXCVIII (March, 1953), 118.

13. HCL. Autograph File. The event referred to in the letter was the occasion for Charles Lamb's poem "On an Infant Dying as Soon as Born" (*Memorials,* I, 18). Jerrold, *Life and Times,* p. 213, quotes an undated letter to "Mrs. Hamerton" who was actually Mrs. Reynolds, the author of *Mrs. Leslie and Her Grandchildren,* as the "only letter of Hood's that is extant written from here. . . ." Hood mentions *Mrs. Leslie* in a postscript to his unpublished letter (postmarked 25 June 1822) to William Jerdan. HCL. Eng. 883, II, facing p. 53.

14. HCL. *46M-222, Keats Collection. I have substituted parentheses for slash marks in the original because their meaning is patent. Words deleted in MS are enclosed in brackets. Two accurate and substantially complete chronological tables of Hood's life and works are available: the first in Jerrold's Oxford edition of Hood's poems; another, based on that, in March and, *Letters,* pp. 101-104.

15. Samuel Bentley (1785-1868) was an exceptionally versatile and accomplished man, excelling as artist, musician, antiquarian, and printer. It is entirely reasonable to suppose that Barham was among those who helped him in his major professional work, the *Excerpta Historica.*

16. DNB [*Dictionary of National Biography*], II, 316.

17. Matthew W. Rosa, *The Silver-Fork School: Novels of Fashion Preceding Vanity Fair* (New York, 1936), p. 178.

18. Rosa, p. 184.

19. (London, 1905), II, 312.

20. An extended exchange of letters (unpublished: Henry W. and Albert A. Berg Collection, New York Public Library) developed between the two men, with Bentley, as in so many other cases, saying more in a sterner manner than he intended, and Barham patiently explaining that he was ready to call off the agreements whenever the publisher so desired. Bentley hastened to assure Barham that it was only because the sales of the *Miscellany* had dropped appreciably that the step was being considered. Barham's letter to Dr. Thomas Hume, a friend, of 22 July 1843, puts the case succinctly: "The Bentley affair lies in a nutshell—he has played with his mouse till he has lost it. No quarrel at all, but merely a question of Pounds Shillings and pence." I am indebted to the Trustees of NYPL and Dr. John D. Gordan, the Curator of the Berg Collection, for permission to quote from this unpublished letter.

Colburn's social note to Barham, dated 3 July 1843, is in HCL. fMS Eng. 936. II, 17. Dalton Barham's *Life* (II, 157) is well-nigh useless on the matter of the Bentley-Barham-Colburn negotiations.

21. HCL. fMS Eng. 936. I, 78.

22. Keswick, 28 May 1818. *Letters* (Oxford University Press, 1912), p. 288.

23. Shelley, p. 359. In *Letters of Charles Dickens,* ed. Walter Dexter (Nonesuch edition, Bloomsbury, 1938), I, 539, only an excerpt from this part of the letter is given.

24. Whitley, *HLQ,* XIV, 406-407.

25. *Memorials,* II, 173.

26. HCL. fMS Eng. 936. I, 77.

27. Hood sent the Lines to others also. They are printed (with minor variants) in Dilke, *Papers of a Critic,* I, 60. For Barham's more kindly poem on Colburn, written under adverse circumstances, see *The Ingoldsby Lyrics* (1881), pp. 274-278.

28. HCL. *46M-102.

29. HCL. fMS Eng. 870: the Locker-Lampson-Warburg-Grimson Album, 93B, p. 262. The same Album also contains (93A, p. 260) an undated letter to Wright concerning woodcuts and a projected ode. Another letter to Wright on this subject is in HCL, *AC85. St 317. 875 vm. I, Pt. 1, 74.

30. Early Annual Reports of the Fund are much fuller and of more literary importance than are those of the twentieth century. HCL has nine Reports for the years 1848, 1852, 1853, 1855, 1858, 1860, 1862, 1869, 1871. Information about Williams is readily available in *DNB*; of considerable interest and help are HCL's comparatively rare copies of the following works: *Annual Biography and Obituary, For the Year 1818* (London, 1819); *Public Characters of 1798-9. The Third Edition. Enlarged and Corrected to the 20th of April, 1801* (London, 1801); *An Account of the Institution of the Society for the Establishment of the Literary Fund: Constitution of the Society; the Anniversary Poems of the Present Year: A List of the Subscribers: and the Cash Accompt of the Fund to June 30, 1804* (London, 1804). E. V. Lucas, "The Founder of the Literary Fund," *Quarterly Review,* CCXXXI (April, 1919), 273-295, is reprinted as Part I of that author's *David Williams, Founder of the Royal Literary Fund* (London, 1920); Part II, "Oratory of the Literary Fund," consists of generous examples of speeches and remarks made at anniversary dinner meetings. The nine Reports referred to above contain full records of these matters for the years specified. Several names are conspicuously absent from the list of those who took the chair or spoke at the anniversary dinners: Dickens, Tennyson, Darwin, Carlyle, and Macaulay.

31. HCL. Eng. 936. II, 55, 56. See, also, William Jerdan's letter, in the same collection, I, 83.

32. HCL. Eng. 936. I, 64.

33. The lawsuit, not settled during his lifetime, dragged slowly on but was "finally successful, and that without any cost to the plaintiff, for, as Hood's children have recorded, Mr. Hook, his legal adviser, firmly and consistently declined all remuneration for his labours" (Jerrold, *Life and Times,* pp. 340-341).

34. Jerrold, *Life and Times,* p. 365.

35. Registered Case 1022. Fielding states that Barham presented Hood's case to the society, and that Dilke's letter, quoted below, is in support.

36. *Memorials,* II, 80.

37. *Life* (1870), II, 204.

38. Both letters are in the files of the Royal Literary Fund.

39. Barham's jocose treatment of his illness and the irritation of the remedies may be found in *Life* (1870), II, 211-219: "The Bulletin" and "To The Garrick Club." See, also, the letter to Mrs. Hughes (*Life,* II, 206-209).

John Clubbe (essay date 1968)

SOURCE: Clubbe, John. "Poet of the Poor." In *Victorian Forerunner: The Later Career of Thomas Hood,* pp. 137-67. Durham, N.C.: Duke University Press, 1968.

[*In the following excerpt, Clubbe discusses Hood's "moral" poetry, which covered such social issues as slavery, the exploited working class, and alcoholism.*]

Scotland came as a relief and a rest. Hood's three-week visit marked the first time since he had assumed responsibility for the *New Monthly* two years before that he had gotten away for an extended holiday. An "excellent" passage by steamer brought him, accompanied by young Tom, to Dundee on the morning of September 15. Upon leaving London he had felt "very much out of sorts," but the sea air had, as so often before, revived his spirits. "My father was received with open arms by the Scotch," wrote his son later, and "having a little Scotch blood in him, [he] was not slow in meeting their advances."[1] When he could overcome his shyness in strange company, the poet conquered everyone with his quiet warmth. While he had not kept up with the friends he had made during his youthful stay at Dundee, still he made every effort to look them up. But he had poor luck: one was away, another died during his visit.

Dundee itself he found "much altered." A small fishing port thirty years ago, it had since grown, "owing to the march of manufacture," into an industrial town. "To the east a remarkably fine crop of tall chimneys had sprung up in lieu of one,—all factories. But," added the author of "I remember, I remember," "I suspect they have been going [up] too fast." Dundee provided Hood with the change of air he greatly needed, and at the home of his Scottish aunt and uncle the cares of London seemed far away. "I have banished all thoughts of bookery," he wrote his wife, "and mean to take my swing of idleness, not always the root of all evil."[2] After a pleasant week, father and son left for Edinburgh.

Arriving in the Scottish capital during the Long Vacation, Hood had the ill luck to miss seeing several of its absent literary celebrities: "Wilson thirty miles off, Napier gone too." But he did go out to Craigcrook to meet Francis Jeffrey; and he saw the publisher Blackwood as well as William Chambers, brother of the Robert he knew. Another day he spent in animated conversation with D. M. Moir, *Blackwood's* "Delta." Besides his visits, Hood engaged in extensive sightseeing; "I am delighted with the city," he wrote Jane, "—it exceeds my expectations."[3] After a week to ten-days' stay, strength and confidence restored, he took his return passage.

The beginning of October found Hood once again in London, once again without definite plans. Desirous of securing the editorship of an established journal, he made enquiries of Cunningham and Mortimer, publishers of *Ainsworth's Magazine.* Three parties had assured him Ainsworth was no longer editor. On October 19, to his surprise, Ainsworth himself wrote him saying that, though still editor, he would welcome him as contributor; he offered "16 guineas per sheet—the highest terms the Magazine can afford, and higher than are given to any other contributor."[4] Hood apologized for his error, but refused the offer. "At any rate the terms won't do," he confided to Dickens, "& I do not like the aspect of things. . . . My *notion* is to see *Mortimer* tomorrow & know the rights of it—to decline the thing—& reopen an old arrangement with Bentley."[5] Supposing the editorship of *Bentley's Miscellany* open, Hood wrote on October 21 to Bentley. By the twenty-fifth Bentley had informed him, Hood told Dickens, not only that it was not, but that he had "not the remotest idea of making any alteration. . . ."[6] To Bentley's formal note Hood replied stiffly that had he known the editorship was filled, he would not have offered his services. "Under this impression, and having paid off Colburn, I took the opportunity of offering my cooperation,—the loss of which," he reminded Bentley, "you were once pleased to consider as a grievance."[7] Bentley no doubt remembered the occasion three years before when Hood had not kept a contract for contributions.

While simultaneously negotiating on two fronts, Hood toyed with the idea of starting his own magazine. Independence of any kind always tempted him. His own journal and a completely free editorial hand—such a prospect enchanted the poet, cramped for two years by Henry Colburn's dishonest ethics. Nor did it exclude other projects. One was for a separate edition of **"The Elm Tree,"** William Harvey doing the illustrations; another was for an edition of his German poems. Nothing came of either project; but by early November his plans—a frenzied paragraph to Dr. Elliot reveals them—had at last coalesced: "first, my two volumes from the 'New Monthly' [*Whimsicalities*] to prepare for the press, with tedious waitings on Colburn . . . & finally negotiations about to close for a new periodical! '*Hood's Magazine.*' to come out 1st January!!!"[8]

Despite his rupture with Colburn and the consequent ill-feelings, aggravated with the passing of each month, Hood prepared for press two volumes of his *New Monthly* contributions written while editor. With most of the illustrations by the well-known comic artist John Leech, they were published in December, 1843, (the volumes carry an 1844 imprint) by Colburn as *Whimsicalities, a Periodical Gathering. Whimsicalities,* the preface indicates, has didactic purpose. Hood disclaims, however, any attempt at profundity: "As usual, the Reader will vainly look in my pages for any startling theological revelations, profound political views, philological disquisitions, or scientific discoveries." But he will do what he has always done: "instruct." For each article he feels obliged to tell the reader precisely what didactic purpose he has in mind:

> My humble aim has been chiefly to amuse: but the liberal Utilitarian will, perhaps, discern some small attempts to instruct at the same time. He will, maybe, detect in "The Defaulter," a warning against rash and uncharitable judgments; in the **"Black Job,"** a "take care of your pockets, from the Pseudo-Philanthropists"; in **"Mr. Withering's Cure,"** a hint on Domestic Economy; in the **"Omnibus,"** a lesson on Prudery; and in the **"News from China,"** a satire on maternal over-indulgence, and the neglect of moral culture in the young. . . .[9]

The "some small attempts to instruct," rarely obvious upon a first reading, remind us that Hood often is, when apparently most "comic," in fact most "serious."

Among *Whimsicalities*' "moral" poems, **"A Black Job"** stands out. In it Hood satirizes both the excesses of Evangelical fervor and the willing credulity of those who give unquestioningly to utopian schemes. When "A knot of very charitable men / Set up a Philanthropical Society" to aid the Negro, Hood asks why:

> And what might be their aim?
>   To rescue Afric's sable sons from fetters—
> To save their bodies from the burning shame
>   Of branding with hot letters—
> Their shoulders from the cowhide's bloody strokes,
>   Their necks from iron yokes?

To end or mitigate the ills of slavery,
    The Planter's avarice, the Driver's knavery?

If not "To end or mitigate the ills of slavery," what then? Education?

> To school the heathen Negroes and enlighten 'em,
>   To polish up and brighten 'em,
> And make them worthy of eternal bliss?

Obviously not. A "Philanthropical Society" would never lower itself to such a practical "aim."

> Why, no—the simple end and aim was this—
> Reading a well-known proverb much amiss—
>   To wash and whiten 'em!

The whiter the Negroes were scrubbed, the "pseudo-Philanthropists" assumed, the more pure and blessed they would become in God's eyes. Purposely making their project absurd, Hood mocks their misguided charity. A more active interest in the Negro's physical welfare on earth, he implies, might well replace such an impractical aim. No efforts, of course, prevail to lighten their black skins, "Satan's livery." But the Society's Chairman, "the philanthropic man," insists that "Because Humanity declares we must!" the task must go on:

> "We've scrubb'd the negroes till we've nearly killed
>   'em,
> And finding that we cannot wash them white,
> But still their nigritude offends the sight,
>   *We mean to gild 'em!"*[10]

Hood attacked not only the fatuous "aim" of the "pseudo-Philanthropists" but also their assumption of racial superiority when he had them propose "To benefit the race of man, / And in particular that dark variety, / Which some suppose inferior. . . ."[11] His own egalitarian belief he stated in **"The Workhouse Clock"**: "For surely . . . men are all akin, / Whether of fair or sable skin, / According to Nature's scheme. . . ."[12] Though few contemporaries held this view, Hood always had. Another poem, **"Pompey's Ghost,"** a "pathetic ballad," questions—in the lines "You think because I'm black I am / The Devil, but I ain't!"—common acceptance of a stereotype. The motto from Cowper pinpoints the "moral": "Skins may differ, but affection / Dwells in white and black the same."[13] Color, Hood realizes, is arbitrary.

The Evangelical and Quaker campaign to abolish slavery in British possessions, he admitted, had done much good. But having attained its goal in 1833, Evangelical moral fervor in years after sought new outlets, and found them in schemes less laudatory:[14] schemes that to outsiders like Hood often appeared ridiculous. His prose introduction to **"The Doves and the Crows"** indicates that he was well aware that "Victory had brought with it a very embarrassing result. The Abolition, in annihilating Slavery," he writes, had also abolished the Abolitionists; and a vast stock of sensibility and sympathy, and zeal and humanity, which had heretofore found a vent in another hemisphere, was left quite a drug upon hand.

Identifying the abolition movement more with the Quakers than with other sects, Hood asks: "What will the Quakers do next?" And replies:

The most obvious answer was, that they ought to continue their patronage to the Emancipated; but the manner in which it should be done, was more difficult to indicate.

That Hood was unimpressed by either Evangelical "patronage" or "the manner in which it should be done" both poems, **"The Doves [Quakers] and the Crows [Negroes]"** and **"A Black Job,"** amply, if humorously, demonstrate. But he realized that the interest in reform abroad was, in effect, a refusal to look at the need for reform at home. "How the 'Sable sons of Africa,'" he ponders, "became so signally the favourites, the pets, the 'curled darlings,' of the sedate, sober, silent, serious, sad-coloured sect [the Quakers], overlooking the Factory Children, and other white objects of sympathy, is a moral mystery. . . ."[15] This "moral mystery" Hood never pretended to understand. Though he in no way denies that Negroes should receive help, he argues in, for example, the essay "The Black and White Question" and in the poem **"The Sweep's Complaint"** that problems at home demand first attention.

"You know [Edwin] Landseer's Doggish picture of 'Laying Down the Law,'" Hood wrote Hewlett, "well, I have written some dogrel verses to go with the print. . . ."[16] Addressing Landseer as "Thou great Pictorial Aesop," he asks him, "What is the moral of this painted fable?" And he answers his own question: the right of the poor to due process of the law. This, the poem **"Laying Down the Law"** demonstrates, "lay" beyond their resources. In this poem Hood has animals, as in *Le Roman de Renart,* protest against society and triumph over the "system." Belonging to a line of humorous moralists that uses animals to criticize society, a line that runs from Aesop to Boccaccio, from La Fontaine to James Thurber, Hood too felt no constraint about explicitly stating his "moral": "As human suitors have had cause to weep—/ For what is Law, unless poor Dogs can get it / Dog-cheap?"[17]

"The Elm Tree," subtitled "A Dream in the Woods," is one of Hood's few late romantic poems. Written in imitation of Keats's style, it deals too, in its serious preoccupation with death, with a subject about which Keats had profound understanding. Though on the surface a poem about the cutting down of a tree, it is actually more: an allegory of Life and Death, and of Death's eventual victory. The opening stanza's mysterious sound echoes throughout the poem. It is a sound

that "from a Tree . . . came to me," the "me" being the poem's "I," its persona—or Hood himself. Not a forest sound, however, it is rather "As if beneath the dewy grass / The dead began to groan." It is omnipresent:

But still the sound was in my ear,
　A sad and solemn sound,
That sometimes murmur'd overhead,
　And sometimes underground—
'Twas in a shady Avenue
　Where lofty Elms abound.[18]

This "sad and solemn sound," hovering about the tree and yet not of it, anticipates the coming of Death.

In Part II another sound interrupts the wailings of the dead: the "Woodman's" axe-blows crashing through the forest. As they banish "bird and beast" from around the elm, in poetry traditionally the tree of sorrow, silence makes more audible the "sad and solemn sound." The ancient "Woodman," a primeval figure, is but a deputy for Death, perhaps even for Him who determines when Death shall strike, God. His "sturdy arm and steady aim" fell the elm. This particular tree, "yonder blasted Elm that stands / So like a man of sin," is like he "Who, frantic, flings his arms abroad / To feel the Worm within," a man, in short, very much like the death-haunted Hood himself. The "Elm" (it is capitalized throughout the poem), which had "thrice the human span . . . stood erect as man," must be, "like mortal Man himself, / Struck down by the hand of God." At the close of Part II there is only silence. "The Echo sleeps."[19] Death has conquered.

And yet, Part III reveals, not wholly. Death itself, a "grisly Phantom," comes nigh. A note of social protest enters the poem. Death seeks high prey, but "haughty Peer and mighty King . . . Shall lodge . . . well" within an "oaken cell." The poor man, however, "he who never knew a home," shall find in the elm his last and only refuge:

"The tatter'd, lean, dejected wretch,
　Who begs from door to door,
And dies within the cressy ditch,
　Or on the barren moor,
The friendly Elm shall lodge and clothe
　That houseless man and poor!"

In Part I the poet, "As one who walks afraid," had looked "Beyond the green arcade," and seen the sky, a "glimpse of Heav'n."[20] But the houseless pauper of Part II is given no such promise of redemption.

Death vanishes, and the skies, overcast at his arrival, clear. Nature rejoices, bursts into life. Only "on my sadden'd spirit still / The Shadow leaves a shade." For Hood realizes that Death has come, not to fell elm or oak, but rather to fell "conscious, moving, breathing trunks / That throb with living blood"—in short, human beings. The "I" of the poem, obviously Hood, has a "secret, vague, prophetic gloom":

> As though by certain mark
> I knew the fore-appointed Tree,
> Within whose rugged bark
> This warm and living frame shall find
> Its narrow house and dark.[21]

Though possibly a death wish, it is more likely that when Hood espies the "mystic Tree" that will contain his mortal remains, he indicates an acceptance of his own death as near. Death had always been an axial theme of his poetry and the inseparable companion of his life, but never before had he faced it with such direct honesty.

On December 16, 1843, occurred an event of capital importance in the career of Thomas Hood. When *Punch*'s Christmas issue came out on that day, it contained two poems by him. One was **"The Pauper's Christmas Carol."** The other was **"The Song of the Shirt."**

Hood's first acquaintance with *Punch* went back to 1841 when, to his mild annoyance, he found his name listed without his permission among the contributors to the first number: "MR. T. HOOD, Professor of Punmanship, Begs to acquaint the dull and witless, that he has established a class for the acquirement of an elegant and ready style of punning." Vouching for the Professor's abilities, the magazine claimed that the "very worst hands are improved in six short and mirthful lessons."[22] The next year, 1842, Hood's old friends and printers of the *Comic Annuals*, Bradbury and Evans, acquired a two-thirds share in the magazine and at the end of the year took over full control. Given Hood's comic talent and the magazine's modest success, he was soon asked to become a contributor. "You will be glad to hear that I have made an arrangement with Bradbury to contribute to *Punch*," he wrote Dickens, "but that is a secret I cannot keep from you." His first contribution to a magazine whose type of humor so well accorded with his own was a caustic epigram on *Punch*'s then favorite butt of ridicule, Lord William Lennox, and over the next few months he scribbled off a dozen or two conundrums. In the same letter to Dickens he observed, "It will be light occasional work for odd times."[23] And so it was—for a while.

Hood's first serious contribution to *Punch*, **"A Drop of Gin,"** appeared on November 18, 1843. To depict the grotesque victims of drink, the "magnified monsters," he recalled the diabolical blacksmiths, the "brutal monsters" in Retzsch's engravings for Schiller's "Der Gang nach dem Eisenhammer":

> Gin! Gin! a drop of Gin!
> What magnified monsters circle therein!

> Ragged, and stained with filth and mud,
> Some plague spotted, and some with blood!
> Shapes of misery, shame, and sin!
> Figures that make us loathe and tremble,
> Creatures scarce human that more resemble
> Broods of diabolical kin,
> Ghosts of vampyre, demon and Jin!

Once lured into the "Palace of Gin," the weary wretches, past earthly salvation, soon go under:

> Gin! Gin! a drop of Gin!
> Oh! then its tremendous temptations begin,
> To take, alas!
> To the fatal glass;—
> And happy the wretch that does not win
> To change the black hue
> Of his ruin to "blue"—
> While angels sorrow, and demons grin—
> And lose the rheumatic
> Chill of his attic
> By plunging into the Palace of Gin![24]

As in Zola's *L'Assommoir,* the "Gin Palace"—Walter Jerrold surmises that it was Hood who popularized this expression[25]—exercises a magnetic attraction on those who have abandoned hope; once man has succumbed to gin's "tremendous temptations," no reprieve is possible. Yet Hood recognizes he must not judge: "we are neither Barebones nor Prynne"; or condemn: "Let Anger be mute, / And sweet Mercy dilute, / With a drop of pity, the drop of Gin!" Zola did not explicitly ask for pity, but Hood did: what can man do when, penniless, without food and deep in debt, "darkly, Adversity's days set in," when "time elopes / With all golden hopes"?[26] Only the misery of life forces man to gin.

With this poem Hood became a dedicated man. The concern for the poor and their welfare manifest in **"A Drop of Gin"** represents no radical change of direction, but had been, on the contrary, a major concern of his work after 1835. That Hood had before affirmed humanitarian views and that he had affirmed them with force is a point, however, that needs insisting upon, for recent critics of Hood, among them Professors Cuyler, Whitley, and Reid, insist otherwise. Thus Cornelius M. Cuyler, writing of Hood's interest in social problems, asserts: "the change came only at the end of 1843."[27] Thus Alvin Whitley: "Although Hood's present reputation is based almost entirely on his humanitarian verse, the major portion of his career was unconcerned with social or political problems, and only a pre-disposed eye could find evidence of them in any earlier work."[28] And thus also J. C. Reid: writing of Hood's "new social vein," he states: "he had done little more than glancingly refer to social matters in such poems as 'The Assistant Drapers' Petition' before 1843."[29]

This is simply not the case. As the "change" was not precipitate, no "pre-disposed eye" is needed. In late 1843, however, Hood's feelings did grow in intensity and they did cause a shift of emphasis in his poetry. He had long played moralist to society; he was—if such a being exists—a comic *homme engagé*. But once he realized in late 1843 that people did take him seriously when he wrote seriously, he felt more secure in throwing off his comic mantle. In the last year and a half of his life he wrote other poems that, without humor and without puns, show his desire to teach freed from the shackles, if such they were, of comic poetry.

"A Drop of Gin" marks this turning point: it begins a series of eight poems whose seriousness is unquestionable. With its publication, Hood's commitment to expose contemporary injustice and to help remedy it by his verse never faltered. These eight poems are, in order of publication, **"A Drop of Gin," "The Pauper's Christmas Carol," "The Song of the Shirt," "The Lady's Dream," "The Workhouse Clock," "The Bridge of Sighs," "The Lay of the Labourer,"** and **"Suggestions by Steam." "A Drop of Gin,"** in essence a sincere plea though containing several puns, serves as transition from the boisterous **"Miss Kilmansegg"** to the punless **"Bridge of Sighs."**

Punch's Christmas number, besides **"The Song of the Shirt,"** contains the often-overlooked **"Pauper's Christmas Carol."** A workhouse pauper finds incongruous only one day of "famous cheer" in "Two-and-fifty weeks of toil":

> Full of drink and full of meat,
> On our *Saviour's* natal day,
> *Charity's* perennial treat;
> Thus I heard a Pauper say:—
> "Ought not I to dance and sing
> Thus supplied with famous cheer?
> . . . . .
>
> "After labour's long turmoil,
> Sorry fare and frequent fast,
> Two-and-fifty weeks of toil,
> Pudding-time is come at last!
> But are raisins high or low,
> Flour and suet cheap or dear?
> . . . . .
>
> "Fed upon the coarsest fare
> Three hundred days and sixty-four
> But for *one* on viands rare,
> Just as if I wasn't poor!
> Ought not I to bless my stars,
> Warden, clerk, and overseer?"[30]

Each stanza ends with the ironic refrain: "Heigho! / I hardly know—/ Christmas comes but once a year." The pauper's wistful sadness does not cloak his—and Hood's—deep bitterness. Nor does the poem exist in a sentimental vacuum. In a factual article, "Christmas-Day in the Workhouses" (December 26, 1842), *The Times* reported the total number of inmates in each of the London workhouses and whether the number of "in-door" and "out-door" poor had increased or decreased since the year previous. This article, or one similar, Hood may well have recalled when he wrote his poem. For each workhouse the article reported, without ironic intention, of what consisted the annual "Christmas-day fare": portions, severely rationed by the authorities, of the "old English cheer" of—I take one sample fare— "roast beef [6 oz.], plum-pudding [1 pd.], and porter [1 pt.]. . . ." Such once-a-year regalement led Hood, with ironic intention, to have his pauper wonder: "But shall I ever dine again? / Or see another feast appear?"[31]

"I send the **"Song of the Shirt"**—Will it be too grave for **Punch**?" Hood queried Mark Lemon, the magazine's bright young editor; "if not there may be some more of it."[32] He accompanied the manuscript with a note that left it to Lemon's discretion whether to put it in the journal or in the "waste-paper basket."[33] Though the "London Charivari" protested—was not *Punch* intended to be comic?—Lemon put it in the journal, gave it a page to itself, and surrounded it with an incongruous comic border. Years later he recalled that Hood, not thinking highly of the poem, had told him that he had already sent it off to three other journals and that all three had rejected it. But not Jane Hood: "Now mind, Hood, mark my words, this will tell wonderfully. It is one of the best things you ever did!"[34] And it was.

The opening stanzas—showing a poverty-stricken seamstress at her work in a shabby, almost bare room— establish the scene:

> With fingers weary and worn,
> With eyelids heavy and red,
> A woman sat, in unwomanly rags,
> Plying her needle and thread—
> Stitch! stitch! stitch!
> In poverty, hunger, and dirt,
> And still with a voice of dolorous pitch
> She sang the "Song of the Shirt."
> . . . . .
>
> "Work—work—work
> Till the brain begins to swim;
> Work—work—work
> Till the eyes are heavy and dim!
> Seam, and gusset, and band,
> Band, and gusset, and seam,
> Till over the buttons I fall asleep,
> And sew them on in a dream!
>
> "Oh, Men, with Sisters dear!
> Oh, Men, with Mothers and Wives!
> It is not linen you're wearing out,
> But human creatures' lives!
> Stitch—stitch—stitch,
> In poverty, hunger and dirt,
> Sewing at once, with a double thread,
> A Shroud as well as a Shirt."

Death, the seamstress sighs, will come as a relief to such a life of inhuman misery. Hood inserts his *morali-*

tas in the fifth stanza: "Oh, God! that bread should be so dear, / And flesh and blood so cheap!"[35]

Stanza eight closes with the poem's one pun:

> While underneath the eaves
> 　The brooding swallows cling
> As if to show me their sunny backs
> 　And twit me with the spring.

While some critics have thought in bad taste a pun on "twit" in this intensely serious poem, I find that "twit," its laughter both irreverent and terribly cruel, accentuates the girl's bleak fate. Echoes of Wordsworth and of Hood's own lament of lost innocence, **"I remember, I remember,"** haunt her desire to escape her fate for "only one short hour" and wander at will in the countryside:

> "Oh! but to breathe the breath
> Of the cowslip and primrose sweet—
> 　With the sky above my head,
> And the grass beneath my feet,
> For only one short hour
> 　To feel as I used to feel,
> Before I knew the woes of want
> 　And the walk that costs a meal!"

But "No blessed leisure for Love or Hope" is permitted her, not even tears: they would hinder her from sewing. Hood closes with the wish that "the Rich" will hear her **"Song of the Shirt."**[36]

Throughout the Hungry Forties *The Times* fought one bitter campaign after another against intolerable working conditions and against the New Poor Law. It carried frequent accounts of the abject circumstances under which London seamstresses struggled for existence. Many of Hood's poems are close to his age and many have a journalistic origin—none more so than **"The Song of the Shirt."**[37]

The Times's police report of October 26, 1843, records the case of a poor widow, "a wretched-looking woman named Biddell, with a squalid, half-starved infant at her breast." She had contracted to sew trousers together for a slopseller named Henry Moses at 7*d.* the pair; out of this wage she had to supply her own needles and thread. To obtain "dry bread" for herself and her two young children, she pawned several articles of the material entrusted to her; unable to redeem the security she had given, she had been hauled into court. Forced to sew trousers together all day every day, she claimed overwork and near starvation as excuse for not fulfilling her contract. Moses's foreman maintained that, if "honest and industrious," she could earn a "good living." When pressed by the magistrate to state what he considered a "good living," he replied about "7*s.* a week."[38] The prisoner agreed, but "only if she were to work by night as well as by day." The magistrate,

observing that "the affair was one of very common occurrence in that part of the metropolis," was hesitant to sentence Biddell to the House of Correction; he sent her instead to the workhouse. In a second case on the same day a "smartly-dressed" woman demanded the arrest of a girl for pawning some shirts; the woman "said that her contract for the shirts was 1½*d.* each, and she gave them out to be done for 1¼*d.*" The magistrate, though he ordered the return of the shirts, refused a warrant.

The next day, October 27, *The Times* responded to these cases with a long leader and a supporting factual article, "The White Slaves of London," both of which expressed outrage at such conditions. According to the leader, for Biddell to earn "her cruelly miserable pittance" of 7*s.* she would have to work 96 hours a week, "16 hours every week-day, or nearly 14 hours every day, including Sunday." Savage against the rich who "are scandalously neglect[ing] their duty" and against slopsellers and middlewomen, it concluded that a London seamstress was from "every moral point of view, as much a slave as any negro who ever toiled under as cruel taskmasters in the West Indies."

On October 31 *The Times* published a "justification" of his work contracts from Henry Moses himself. In the same issue it published another letter, dated October 28, from "An American." He had read *The Times's* reports, wondered how true they were, and decided to find out for himself. When a ragged woman, "decent but infirm," accosted him and besought him to buy a spray of flowers, he asked her if he might see where she lived. She agreed, took him to her home, and

> ushered me into a mean and miserable apartment, about 10 feet square, which contained no other furniture than a crazy chair, without bottom, and one or two cooking utensils. By the light of a farthing candle I discovered two poor children, shivering with cold (for there was no fire in the grate), with scarce a whole, and certainly not a warm, garment on their backs. . . . In one corner of the room lay a parcel of shavings on the floor, covered by an old and battered baize, and this she said was their only bed.

Though common to many of the cases reported in *The Times,* details in this letter closely parallel those in Hood's poem: the letter's "crazy chair, without bottom" corresponds to the "broken chair" of the **"Song"**; the "scarce a whole, and certainly not a warm, garment on their backs" to "rags"; the "only bed" a "parcel of shavings on the floor" to "a bed of straw."[39] Hood undoubtedly saw this letter and the reports of the Biddell case in *The Times.* He may even have seen "Famine and Fashion" in the November 4th *Punch* and the sarcastic poem subjoined to the article, "Moses and Co." Every writer on Hood has assumed these cases provided the immediate inspiration for the composition of **"The Song of the Shirt."**

But the sad plight of London seamstresses had engaged Hood years before he read of the Biddell case. In **"Miss Kilmansegg"** he deplored the lot of women who "sit all day to hem and sew, / As females must—and not a few—/ To fill their insides with stitches!"[40] And in "The Defaulter" (*New Monthly,* January, 1843), he abruptly reproached a generic character, "Female Sensibility," for her misdirected sentiments. In details and in vocabulary—"stitches," "seam," and "gusset"—he clearly anticipates **"The Song of the Shirt."** "My dear young lady," Hood begins,

> I can appreciate your motives and do honour to your feelings. But before you go round with your book among relations, acquaintance, and strangers, soliciting pounds, shillings, and pence, from people of broad, middling, and narrow incomes, just do me the favour to look into yonder garret, exposed to us by the magic of the Devil on Two Sticks, and consider that respectable young woman, engaged at past midnight, by the light of a solitary rushlight, in making shirts at three-halfpence a piece, and shifts for nothing. Look at her hollow eyes, her withered cheeks, and emaciated frame, for it is a part of the infernal bargain that she is to lose her own health and find her own needles and thread. Reckon, if you can, the thousands of weary stitches it will require to sew, not gussets, and seams, but body and soul together: and perhaps, after all her hard sewing, having to sue a shabby employer for the amount of her pitiful earnings. Estimate, if you may, the terrible wear and tear of head and heart, of liver and lungs. Appraise, on oath, the value of youth wasted, spirits outworn, prospects blasted, natural affections withered in the bud, and all blissful hopes annihilated, except those beyond the grave.[41]

From this prose paragraph emerged Hood's hymn to injured Woman. While the Biddell case may well have decided him to prepare the **"Song"** for publication, the existence of this hitherto ignored prose "synopsis"—as close in its details to the **"Song"** as the three cases reported in *The Times*—a year before the publication of the poem strongly suggests that Hood may have conceived the poem before January, 1843. (It also makes more credible his telling Lemon that three journals had already rejected it.)[42] Not at all the kind of poem that would suit the *New Monthly*'s pages, Hood may have put a draft of the **"Song"** aside, then decided to capitalize on it when he saw the furor caused by the Biddell case. He came in time to consider it the key poem of his career.

The poem made history. In *The Age of Paradox* John Dodds cites it as "perhaps of all poems in the decade the one to make the deepest impact on the largest number of people."[43] As it stands, the **"Song"** has a unity that none of *The Times*'s cases has: of place—the bare room; of time—any and all time; of action—the woman speaks in and of her misery. Hood's seamstress, like Arnold's Wragg, is a symbol for nameless, uncounted thousands. In time the poem became, as

Richard Garnett noted, one of the "genuine *Volkslieder*" that had their birth in the nineteenth century's squalid industrialism.[44] Reprinted in many newspapers—*The Times, The Examiner,* and *The Sun* among them—it was soon hawked about the streets on ballad sheets; ladies wove Hood's lines onto "moral" pocket handkerchiefs; translations appeared in French, German, Italian, eventually in Russian. "But what delighted, and yet touched, my father most deeply," remembered his daughter Fanny, "was that the poor creatures, to whose sorrows and sufferings he had given such eloquent voice, seemed to adopt its words as their own, by singing them about the streets to a rude air of their own adaptation."[45] As the **"Song,"** published anonymously, "ran through the land like wild-fire," several persons had the audacity to claim they had written it. Hood was obliged to send a note to *The Sun* to acknowledge his authorship publicly, though Dickens, for one, had guessed it right away. Throughout the nineteenth century the **"Song,"** its didactic value unquestioned, ranked as the most popular of Hood's poems. People alive today remember learning it by heart as youngsters either at home or in school.[46]

While **"The Song of the Shirt"** carried his name from one end of England to the other, preparations for the first number of *Hood's Magazine* had moved forward rapidly. In December, 1843, Hood looked upon the establishment of a magazine bearing his name and under his editorship as the apex of his career, the deserved reward of a lifetime's labor. The situation portended well: seemingly solid financial backing; sufficient written material by him for a good start; as editor, he would have a free hand and need not truckle to publisher "puffing"; lastly, his health held out admirably. Christmas Day, 1843, indeed provided occasion for rejoicing. Soon afterwards Hood changed residences, moving within the same neighborhood to New Finchley Road; in honor of his erstwhile patron and dedicatee, he christened his new and last home "Devonshire Lodge."

Edward Gill Flight had first approached Hood in mid-October about editing a new magazine; he offered to provide financial backing. Rebuffed in his search for the editorship of an established journal, Hood proved receptive. *Hood's Magazine and Comic Miscellany,* a December letter to Hewlett announced, will be in "quantity . . . 7 sheets—2/6 price—& in each number we propose to give a very good plate or *a work of art.*" "Series or Continuations" he decided to avoid, for he realized he lacked the means to publish them afterwards in volume form; moreover, "There has grown up a strong prejudice from the badness of so many of them."[47] He later relaxed—inevitably—his ban against serials, notably in favor of his own novel *Our Family.* Free to choose the kind of articles he wished to publish, Hood opted for variety and quality: "We do not lay any stress on the signature," he wrote Charles Mackay, "if the stuff be good."[48]

The magazine's "Prospectus," written in December, reaffirmed his long-held editorial principles. The *Comic Miscellany* of the title implied he would provide "harmless 'Mirth for the Million,' and light thoughts, to a public sorely oppressed . . . by hard times, heavy taxes, and those 'eating cares' which attend on the securing of food for the day, as well as a provision for the future."[49] Hood promised, as he always did, not to raise a "maiden blush"; nor would he take a stand on the Tractarian controversy. Political subjects he thought to avoid entirely, though "his notorious aversion to party spirit" did not impede his protesting against social wrongs, as would demonstrate **"The Bridge of Sighs"** and **"The Lay of the Labourer."**

During the hectic week that preceded the publication of the first number of *Hood's Magazine* on January 1, the poet grew convinced that a trade combination had formed against him: "I expect to see ½ the trade arrayed against me, Colburn & all."[50] He found the supposed antagonism *"flattering* in one sense—as they fear us. They will neither hang up a board nor put the book in a window—nor take one they can help."[51] Whether Hood had cause for his fear, or whether his sensitivity to persecution, imagined or real, was aroused unnecessarily, remains difficult to say. He did, after all, have good reason to suspect that a trade combination wanted to strangle the new venture at birth: his longtime advocacy of improved copyright laws, his active part in the formation of the stillborn "Association for the Protection of Litterature," and his recent rupture with Colburn—all had put him in bad standing with Publisher's Row. Relations with his former publisher had now deteriorated completely; Colburn shabbily refused to accept letters for Hood addressed to Great Marlborough Street, *New Monthly* headquarters, and endorsed them "not known to Mr. Colburn."[52] Prompt reception of his mail being crucial, such pettifogging tactics naturally outraged Hood. He found "this . . . so dirty a trick" that he responded with a dozen savage **"Lines on being 'Unknown to Mr. Colburn.'"**[53] Thoroughly angered, Hood threatened, "And if he gives me any more cause I'll 'Rae Wilson' him."[54]

Trade combination against him or not, the success of the first number of *Hood's Magazine* surpassed its editor's fondest hopes. Upon receiving his copy, R. H. Barham wrote immediately to Hood's good friend Hewlett: "I like his first number much. **'The Haunted House'** is capital."[55] Other friends sent him their sincere congratulations; *Hood's Magazine,* during the short span its editor actually performed his functions, became a noteworthy periodical. "Its merit as a magazine of fiction," comments Walter Graham, "perhaps exceeded its

value as a 'comic miscellany.'"[56] Contributors included "Barry Cornwall," Mrs. Norton, Bulwer, Hewlett, Monckton Milnes, "Delta," Robert Browning, and Charles Dickens. Mrs. S. C. Hall offered to send "occasional sketches," "the payment to be 'the pleasure she will feel in assisting, however humbly, in the success of his periodical: as a tribute of veneration to the author of the **Song of the Shirt.**'"[57] Not only did the magazine sell 1,500 copies—an almost unprecedented sale, Blackwood assured him, for a first number—but it represented a distinct personal triumph for Hood himself. He had written over half of it: forty-six pages of poetry and prose and a further ten of reviews. Of the number's contents the first and most often praised item is **"The Haunted House."**

In his last years, Hood had become less and less able to make comic capital of the spectre of Death. *"Tout ce qui touche à la mort est d'une gaieté folle,"* once wrote Champfleury, and for most of his adult life Thomas Hood would have agreed. But by the time he came to write **"The Elm Tree"** and **"The Haunted House"** his understanding of death had deepened; now, with Keats, "Darkling" he listened, "half in love with easeful Death. . . ." Similar in atmosphere to **"The Elm Tree,"** **"The Haunted House"** resembles it too in its chief defect: lack of movement. Nothing quite happens. The pace of Hood's poems tends to run to extremes: very swift—**"The Desert-Born," "Miss Kilmansegg"**; or very slow—**"The Elm Tree," "The Haunted House."** Neither extreme wholly succeeds. In both latter poems an atmosphere of gloom, desolation, and death prevails; both poems focus on one central object—an elm tree, a haunted house; both poems, weak in plot, abound in carefully chosen details. Subtitled "A Romance," **"The Haunted House"** is meant to be considered, the poet implies, as a "dream." The familiar pattern repeats itself once more: through a dream Hood masks his unease before the supernatural, here before the reality of death itself. Purposely, the opening stanzas are ambiguous:

> Some dreams we have are nothing but dreams,
> Unnatural, and full of contradictions;
> Yet others of our most romantic schemes
> Are something more than fictions.
>
> It might be only on enchanted ground;
> It might be merely by a thought's expansion;
> But, in the spirit or the flesh, I found
> An old deserted Mansion.[58]

In Part I we stand in the garden, as deserted as the house, and confront the scene of desolation. In Hood's "wasteland"—Victorian literature has many such—nature is not stunted, as in Browning's "Childe Roland to the Dark Tower Came";[59] rather, it has grown rank and defeated man's efforts to impose his will upon it:

> With shatter'd panes the grassy court was starr'd;
> The time-worn coping-stone had tumbled after;

And thro' the ragged roof the sky shone, barr'd
With naked beam and rafter.

　　· · · · ·

The flow'r grew wild and rankly as the reed,
Roses with thistles struggled for espial,
And vagrant plants of parasitic breed
Had overgrown the Dial.

　　· · · · ·

But Echo never mock'd the human tongue;
Some weighty crime, that Heaven could not pardon,
A secret curse on that old Building hung,
And its deserted Garden.

　　· · · · ·

For over all there hung a cloud of fear,
A sense of mystery that spirit daunted,
And said, as plain as whisper in the ear,
The place is Haunted![60]

This last stanza, nine times repeated with minor variations, unifies the poem's atmosphere; it forces the reader
to wonder what mystery the house contains. As Hood
shifts the focus from one image of decay to the next,
the succession of static descriptions heightens the
atmosphere of death-in-life. No detail is so insignificant,
W. H. Hudson claims, that Hood "cannot wring from it
some fresh and horrible suggestion of doom, and ruin,
and utter devastation."[61] While valid, this observation
misses the point: details, however masterly, should have
a purpose beyond themselves. In other Victorian poems
the hero challenges the wasteland—Childe Roland; or
is conquered by it—Arthur in Tennyson's *Idylls of the
King*; but in Hood's "deserted Garden" no one rises to
confront the unnamed horror.

In Part II we enter the house itself, or do we? "Howbeit,
the door I push'd," writes Hood, "—or so I dream'd."[62]
Climbing the stairs, we see a "BLOODY HAND" on
banner, curtain, and casement window. But the heavy
suspense and the carefully wrought images of interior
decay lead to no climax; the poem ends with its mystery
unresolved. We are left asking the question: "What happened?" Indeed Hood even asks it for us: "What shrieking Spirit in that bloody room / Its mortal frame had
violently quitted?" The house is under a "secret curse"
because a murder has been committed, but we never
learn whose or why. The admittedly impressive accumulation of detail serves no purpose: Hood did not
know what to do with it. Having already implied that
his poem was a "dream," he could not, as so often
before, further shatter the dramatic illusion by letting
the reader wake up at the close. Nor could he make it
credible. It is a characteristic of romanticism in its
decline not to believe in the reality of the world created; Hood could establish and sustain an atmosphere
quite skilfully, but he could not make the world he created meaningful.

Another contribution to the January number, "A Dream
by the Fire," deserves recognition as one of Hood's
more unusual prose tales. In it he again shows his
reluctance to face the supernatural squarely as well as
his wish, through undercutting, to make it palatable to
his readers. The human warmth of the opening scene—a
crackling fireplace in an inn, old cronies singing songs,
ale and beef—recalls a jovial Lamb atmosphere. An unnamed stranger, the story's first-person narrator, finds in
a corner "my bosom friend, the friend of my soul, my
other self, old Mann—or old humanity as we used to
call him . . . for he had a large heart and a liberal
hand, loved everybody in the world but himself, and
deserved to be as largely loved in return." Not only is
"Mann" or "old humanity" a generic character, to some
extent symbolic, but the story itself is allegorical,
though, as we discover, inconsistently so. Mann may
even represent, Hood hints, the stranger's "other self."
After the two friends drink themselves into a stupor,
they drop off to sleep. Some time passes before the
stranger awakes to find the lamps out, the fire extinguished. "I never felt so cold and dreary in my life," he
exclaims; not seeing his friend, he calls out. Mann
replies "as from somewhere under the floor." As the
stranger creeps toward a "glimmer of light," he discovers he is in the inn's cellar. He comes upon Mann at
last, almost naked; lying in a gigantic coffin, he is picking at the black earth which envelopes him, "as if he
had been buried alive and was trying to break out. . . .
What a mystery it was! As if I and Mann had actually
passed, by death, from the upper world, its light, its
warmth, and human society, to the dark chambers of the
grave! And was it really so?"[63]

The tale proceeds eerily. The thought that death may
have come upon him unawares forces the stranger to
recognize the blessings of the earth now that they are
his to enjoy no longer. His companion too preoccupied
in his task to concern himself with another, he begins to
comprehend man's essential solitude. A haggard, wasted
creature approaches—Mann's wife, but without word or
glance from her husband, she passes on. "There was no
time *there*, then, even for love! My soul sank within
me. What an eternity was before me; dead even to
hope!" Two other forms struggle forth—a girl and a
boy, Mann's children, dragging the burden, like Bunyan's Christian, of their sins: "In years and size so
young, in face so carefully old, like pain-ridden
dwarfs! . . . But the father looked not at his children;
the children glanced not at their father."[64] Why, the
stranger asks himself, has such an awful destiny been
meted out upon "Mann" and his family; in sickness
patient, in poverty munificent, he seemed to have led an
exemplary life on earth.

The sense of his own worthlessness gnaws at the
stranger's conscience. "No self-deceit," he realizes, exists "in that pitch-black prison, the Condemned Cell of

the Soul." Pricked by remorse, he exchanges places with Mann; when he sees his own wife and children approaching, he is forced to contemplate "those dear young faces, so prematurely old, hunger-pinched, and puckered with cares—precociously informed of the woes of the world—children, without childhood." Unable to bear the sight he shrieks, "I am, I am in————"[65] He awakes; the fire roars still. It has been a bad dream.

Mann is Everyman. His companion, the "stranger," represents he who can partake in the lot of Everyman. But the implications of reality Hood undercuts in two ways: first, for the greater part of the story the stranger observes Mann, does not partake in his agony; second, the story is, as was probably **"The Haunted House,"** but a dream. The idea of spirits flitting past a sinner in agony Hood got from Dickens's "A Christmas Carol" (which he reviewed and warmly commended in this same January number), where the Christmas spirits cower a fearful Scrooge. The haggard women and children of Hood's story show a remarkable parallel to the last vision which the Ghost of Christmas Present shows an unrepentant Scrooge—two ragged, wolfish children glaring from beneath his mantle. "They are Man's," calls the Spirit. "And they cling to me, appealing from their fathers. This boy is Ignorance. This girl is Want. Beware them both, and all of their degree, but most of all beware this boy, for on his brow I see that written which is Doom, unless the writing be erased." When Scrooge inquires if they have no "refuge or resource," the Ghost echoes his words ironically: "Are there no prisons? . . . Are there no workhouses?"[66]

"A Christmas Carol" Edgar Johnson considers "unavowed allegory."[67] So, too, we may consider Hood's less successful, imitative story: an allegory of man's fate. No one—even those whom we think the best among us—escapes final tribulation. An indifferent Divine Being, Hood implies in this tale, rewards everyone equally miserably; a good life on earth has no bearing on the afterlife. Though critics have considered psychologically unsound Scrooge's rapid about-face from unrelenting, flintlike indifference toward humankind to generosity, not for psychological reasons did Hood choose to give Mann and the stranger neither redemption nor understanding. A dream ending, adumbrated in the title, would leave his readers feeling more comfortable; for this reason he kept the allegory unfocused, the point blurred. Because that which might provoke a strong reaction in his readers—or in himself—was alien to his temper, Hood steadfastly shied away from coming to terms with the great moral issues. In his dream-visions and in his supernatural tales he preferred to dissolve the reality created: he wished his readers to believe that all had been airy fabric. Only in some of his social and humanitarian writings did he let stand, increasingly as the years went by, the ultimate implications of his position.

Hood's Magazine surmounted the obstacles that faced most fledgling journals. "The Mag is going on well—capital notices," the editor wrote Hewlett in mid-January; "the difficulty is to get them to customers in Glasgow &c.—the people want them but the trade are wilfully *backward* in forwarding them."[68] Confident in "our resources of every kind," a relaxed Hood exuded to Bradbury: "We have almost all the public press at our back, & such notices as Booksellers cannot buy!"[69] The trade combination he thought he could beat, and he felt pride in the real success of his magazine.

When Hood learned at the end of January that Edward Flight had haggled with the printers, Bradbury and Evans, over payment for the first number, the first crack in the structure on which he had based his future hopes appeared. He had not previously entertained qualms about the probity of Flight and his brother, apparently a silent partner, T. Flight, but his remaining faith in their integrity soon vanished. Thus began for Hood three months of constant anxiety. More than once he prepared to throw up his hands and abandon hope, but each time, through a series of fortuitous circumstances, the magazine did come out. Convinced that his break with fate had come at last, he suffered greatly in the realization that his hopes and dreams were crumbling about him, vanishing in the wake of the Flights' chicanery.

Hood soon discovered that the Flights had paid neither contributors nor stationers. When he asked them why, they pleaded bankruptcy one day—and denied they had the next; in any event, they refused further support for the magazine. If hauled into court, they would, Hood claimed, attempt this ingenious solution: "T. Flight is to walk off with the assets," he wrote Hewlett, "& E. Flight is to take the debts. But I hardly think the Creditors will stand a dissolution of partnership just before the break, & after they had told Ward they should fail."[70] According to Jane Hood, the Flights had "engaged in the speculation without sufficient means to carry it on—having been tempted by the goodness of the speculation, and hoping to scramble through it."[71] They even denied they had promised to pay her husband anything for the editorship. "In short," concluded a weary Hood, engulfed by a sea of troubles, "a regular shuffle."[72]

He found it necessary to rid himself of the pair. *Hood's Magazine,* "having been well advertised, . . . does not now want much to carry it on; so there will be no difficulty in getting another partner."[73] Although the poet feared the disagreeable rupture with the Flights might make his beloved "Mag" lose ground, it continued to prosper despite all problems. "The thing promises capitally," he confided to Hewlett,

> contributors are flowing in & from various indications I am making a stir. So you had better send your paper *here* at once—for I have no doubt of going on, & am

preparing a number; with a new name, for a fresh start. My name never stood higher than it does now; I mean to have better terms & a share in the property. . . . For my own sake, as he has compromised me with the public I shall explain the whole thing in a New Prospectus & appeal to the support of the press.[74]

Voluntarily or under pressure the Flights left. When Dickens recommended to him Andrew Spottiswoode, the Queen's printer, as backer, Hood insisted upon assurances of his reliability. Time pressed. On March 24 he wrote a new friend, Frederick Oldfield Ward, "I have come to the conclusion that a number for 1 April cannot be brought out. . . . As there *must* be a break in the publication,—there *must* be a sort of new announcement for a fresh start, which might include a full explanation—Showing that in spite of a new title—the spirit of the work would be kept up by the same Editor & contributors."[75] Ward, who had volunteered to work as the magazine's unpaid subeditor and who in this capacity performed valiant service, calmed Hood's nerves by convincing him that the magazine could continue and that, despite the Flights' threats of legal retaliation, it could keep the same title. No time remained, Hood declared, to prepare a new issue, but Ward accomplished the impossible: he engaged Spottiswoode and the magazine had an April number. Hood told Dickens that when Ward asked Flight how he reconciled his actions with his conscience, Flight audaciously replied, "Conscience . . . Sir, I have lived too long in the world to be *a slave to my conscience!*" "Was not this capital?" demanded a stunned Hood.[76]

The poet had a conscience, however. The rupture with the Flights and the month-to-month uncertainty of the magazine's publication greatly heightened his mental anxiety. Moreover, an attack of influenza in March confined him to bed. Thus began Hood's final illness, a complication and aggravation of the half-dozen maladies he had suffered from for years; only intermittently in the less than fourteen months that remained to him did he summon up the energy to rise from his sickbed. April brought another relapse—and recovery: "my three doctors between them could not discover any really unsound place in my lungs," he wrote Mark Lemon. "My breath is now lengthening my cough all but gone—& my chief complaint is weakness—but that is gigantic. But I am notorious for rallying at the worst—so I hope in a day or two to be on my legs."[77]

"I am going to dine today with three M. P.'s," wrote Hood to Hewlett in March, "—a sign of the times."[78] Largely because of the overwhelming success of **"The Song of the Shirt,"** he had begun to receive a new kind of attention. Sir John Bowring, a friend from *London* days, recalled that "the anti-Corn Law league was desirous of making him their poet-laureate by engaging him in their service, and I invited Cobden,

Bright, and some others of the leaders of that formidable body to meet Hood at my table, but his death put an end to any such arrangement."[79] The meeting was arranged, Jane Hood thought, "to engage him to write songs for the League."[80] But since it took place in March, 1844, more than a full year before Hood's death, other factors determined his refusal. Most likely, as the "Prospectus" for *Hood's Magazine* had again professed neutrality, he did not want to compromise publicly his lifelong disavowal of partisan politics. He may also have felt he could do more by writing other poems in the vein of **"The Song of the Shirt,"** poems which, while free of political bias, could strongly condemn society's injustice. Moreover, when Bowring made his offer, cares and ill health burdened Hood; he could have done little to aid publicly a cause whose goals he had long applauded privately.

As Hood's physical condition worsened in May, he was compelled to hand over care of the magazine to Ward. "Disease of the heart, my Esculapians say," joked Hood to D. M. Moir, even in the face of death making light of his maladies, "aggravated by old marsh fever, [is] . . . producing a state similar to the ancient Sea Scurvy."[81] Both Elliots attended him constantly during three crucial weeks. That Dr. William Elliot, living ten miles off in Stratford, came daily to see him, Jane deemed "an extraordinary act of friendship."[82] She found her husband more seriously ill than at any time in the past, and the long strain began to tell on her nerves. A slight recovery in the middle of May prompted Hood to consider with optimism the prospects of getting out the June number of *Hood's Magazine.*[83] But on the twenty-first he suffered a relapse, brought on by the impossibility of getting a publisher, and despaired. Hood's physical health was always intimately tied in to his mental happiness: "Last night he fretted dreadfully," wrote Jane on the twenty-second to Elliot, "and, at one this morning, was seized so suddenly with short breathing, and fullness of the chest, I thought he could not live."[84]

Once again Ward came to the rescue and accomplished another miracle: he got H. Renshaw on the shortest notice to publish the June number. "The Echo," the magazine's answers-to-correspondents column, announced the gallant fight Hood was waging against the mortal disease that sapped him. If he hoped to live, the poet slowly realized, he must do what he had never before done: take a complete rest. Resigned to become editor only in name, he gave over effective direction of his magazine to Ward. He had done his best and he could do no more.

Notes

1. *Memorials* [*of Thomas Hood,* edited by His *Son and Daughter* (London, 1860)], II, 165.

2. *Ibid.,* p. 169.

3. *Ibid.,* p. 173.

4. Samuel M. Ellis, *William Harrison Ainsworth and His Friends* (London, 1911), II, 70.

5. [Alvin] Whitley, *HLQ* [*Huntington Library Quarterly*], p. 407. The terms offered Hood, 16 guineas a sheet, were half those offered by Colburn, but his offer of 30 guineas a sheet included the copyright. During the various negotiations Hood kept Dickens constantly informed. Every letter manifests a despairing want of confidence in himself.

6. *Ibid.,* p. 408. Hood quotes Bentley's reply.

7. ALS, Bodleian. Whitley, "Thomas Hood," p. 408.

8. Hood collection, Yale (a garbled version in *Memorials,* II, 178). In the letter *"Hood's Magazine"* is four times underlined.

The letter also indicates Hood was at last to "come to issue with Baily." While I have not seen the legal records, P. F. Morgan, who apparently has, supplies the following information: "In Chancery Hood's amended Bill had been submitted 12 March 1844, to be answered 1 May. An order of the Court appeared 16 January 1845, and Hood's replication concerning 'the manifest insufficiencies of Baily's answer' twelve days later. Perhaps it was this case which Hood's daughter says was unfinished at his death . . ." (Master's thesis, University of London, 1956), p. 410. Hood's correspondence, published and unpublished over the years 1840 to 1845, records various flurries of activity over the suits—two at least, one in Chancery, another in Common Pleas. J. H. Reynolds was Hood's advocate at the start, but a "Mr. Hook" soon took over the case—without remuneration. The Hood children praised his "skill and energy" (*Memorials,* II, 83). The suits tied up throughout this period profits from both *Hood's Own* and *Up the Rhine.* In addition to the expense to maintain them, his strength and peace of mind were taxed by what he called, in a letter to Hewlett, "the nervous uncertainties of the Case." Cf. also Rollins, *The Keats Circle,* II, 470-71; Lytton, *Life of Edward Bulwer,* II, 62-66; P. F. Morgan, "John Hamilton Reynolds and Thomas Hood," *K-SJ* [*Keats-Shelley Journal*], XI (Winter, 1962), 83-95; and William G. Lane, "A Chord in Melancholy: Hood's Last Years," *K-SJ,* XIII (Winter, 1964), 43-61. *The Times* of February 16, 1844, carried a report of a Hood-Baily trial. In his unpublished dissertation (University of London, 1937), R. E. Davies prints "The Order of Court" of "Tuesday the 16th day of January 1845 . . ." (pp. 312-13; no source given).

The "Case of Mr. Thomas Hood" (British Museum), a brief summary of Hood's career

prepared in July, 1844, in order to forward his claims for a pension, claims that "against Mr. Baily he has obtained a verdict at law." Presumably on the basis of this statement, Hood's most recent biographer, J. C. Reid, writes, "Hood's lawsuit against Baily was eventually settled in his favour" (*Thomas Hood,* p. 240). But oversimplifying a complex legal situation, he takes into account neither the various suits nor the Order of Court of 1845.

More likely Hood obtained a "verdict at law" in Common Pleas but did not receive compensation in his lifetime in the court of Chancery. The "verdict at law" was indeed, as Hood put it to F. O. Ward, "my barren verdict and yet costly" (*Life of Edward Bulwer,* II, 64).

9. *Works,* IX, 34-35. *Whimsicalities* failed to make a profit; or so Colburn claimed. Hood, sceptical, later cautioned Hewlett, planning to publish a novel with Colburn, of his tactics: "It is not unlikely he may only offer *to share profits* . . . & of course there will be none to share,—any more than in my 'Whimsicalities'" (Brooke collection). Profits or no, Colburn republished the volumes in 1846.

10. *Works,* VIII, 322, 323, 325, 329. First published, *New Monthly,* March, 1843.

Hood's poem has a basis in fact: several societies did indeed exist to improve the Negro's welfare. The most important, called the "African Civilization Society," was headed by Sir Fowell Buxton, M.P. *The Times* in an editorial of November 26, 1842 (all quotations from this source), exposed the absurdity of Sir Fowell's plans. He "had at last, in 1840," it reported, "discovered the true remedy for slavery, which was to *civilize Africa* by introducing among the natives spades, pickaxes, ploughs, potatoes, and political economy, upon the newest European principles. For this purpose, nothing more (he said) would be necessary, than just to send a couple of steamers up the Niger, make treaties with the native chiefs, invent a general language for the use of the African continent, compile and put into circulation a universal dictionary, buy model farms, settle upon them a few Scotch farmers and liberated negroes . . ." etc. In 1840 a "great meeting" was held at the Evangelical bastion, Exeter Hall; present were the Consort, Prince Albert, Sir Robert Peel, Lord John Russell, Daniel O'Connell, and Archdeacon Samuel Wilberforce. The upshot of the meeting was that "Government steamers, and English crews, and 60,000£ of English money from the public Treasury, were devoted by the Queen's then advisers to the purposes of Sir Fowell Buxton and his new society." *The Times* expressed amazement that "any man in England, with any pretense to reason, could seriously and believingly swallow down such drivelling absurdity."

The expedition, as *The Times* foresaw, failed utterly. Though "the only result of all his exertions . . . [was] to make the evil much worse than when he began," Sir Fowell insisted upon making another attempt. *The Times* could not believe that "not merely conceited enthusiasts, but practical statesmen of all parties in the present day, are capable of acting upon subjects of the highest moral and social importance" with such "extreme shallowness of view." Nor could Hood. In "A Black Job" he mocks both the Society's Chairman, "the philanthropic man" obviously based upon Sir Fowell, and all such utopian schemes. "Looking back upon this whole transaction," *The Times*'s leader asserted—and Hood would have wholeheartedly agreed,—"the facts appear so marvellous, that we doubt if a more incredible narrative is to be found in the pages of *Gulliver* or *Munchausen.*"

11. *Works,* VIII, 322.

12. *Ibid.,* IX, 200. First published, *Hood's Magazine,* April, 1844.

13. *Ibid.,* III, 215, 213. First published, *New Monthly,* Aug., 1840.

14. Noel Annan, *Leslie Stephen* (Cambridge, Mass., 1952), p. 11 and *passim.*

15. *Works,* VII, 321, 318. First published, *Comic Annual* for 1839. Hood also writes of the Negro in "Black, White, and Brown" (*ibid.,* I, 57-63); and he twice reviewed books about them: John Briggs, *The History of Jim Crow* (*ibid.,* VIII, 90-93), and Reverend Pascoe Grenfell Hill, *Fifty Days on Board a Slaver* (*ibid.,* IX, 153-59). To Dr. Elliot he wrote on March 11, 1840: "They have made me an honorary Vice-President of the African Institute at Paris" (*Memorials,* II, 55)—a statement I have not been able to corroborate.

16. Brooke collection.

17. *Works,* VIII, 308, and 311—the poem's last line. First published, *New Monthly,* June, 1843.

18. *Ibid.,* pp. 177, 178. First published, *New Monthly,* Sept., 1842. At this time Hood lived on "Elm Tree Road."

19. *Ibid.,* pp. 184, 186, 187, 188.

20. *Ibid.,* pp. 190, 192, 181.

21. *Ibid.,* pp. 194, 191, 194.

22. *Punch,* I (July 17, 1841), 2.

23. M. H. Spielmann, *The History of "Punch"* (New York, 1895), p. 330. Spielmann discusses Hood's contributions to *Punch* (pp. 330-36) and gives a complete list in "Thomas Hood and *Punch," Bookman* (New York), X (1899), 151-52; Tom Hood gives a slightly different list in *Memorials,* II, 181-82 n.

24. *Works,* IX, 24, 26. The poem was written in connection with two illustrations by Kenny Meadows, "The Water Drop" and "The Gin Drop," and a humorous temperance article by "Q" (Douglas Jerrold), "Father Mathews's Polly-Put-the-Kettle-on-Icon" (*Punch,* V, 220-23). Hood used the expression "brutal monsters" in "The Forge" (*Works,* VIII, 298).

25. Jerrold, p. 365. The *OED* gives, however, two earlier uses of "Gin Palace."

26. *Works,* IX, 24, 25.

27. Cuyler, p. 411.

28. Whitley, "Thomas Hood," p. 181.

29. Reid, pp. 214, 206.

30. *Works,* IX, 31.

31. *Ibid.,* p. 32.

32. Hood collection, UCLA.

33. Spielmann, p. 332.

34. *Memorials,* II, 182.

35. *Works,* IX, 27-28; *Punch,* V, 260. Lemon omitted one stanza (easily the weakest) from the original MS (published in *Works,* IX, 30), and Spielmann conjectured, plausibly in my opinion, that he did so as "simply a matter of make-up" of the page (p. 334).

36. *Works,* IX, 29, 30.

37. Cf. Alvin Whitley, "Thomas Hood and 'The Times,'" *TLS* [*Times Literary Supplement*], May 17, 1957, p. 309. Other Victorian poets wrote topical poems—or poems which, though topical and inspired by accounts of happenings in the daily press, have not been traced to their origins. One wonders how many such poems there are—some of them perhaps familiar, some even by major authors. *Quellenforschung* in Victorian newspapers and periodicals has scarcely begun.

38. In *The Condition of the Working Class in England* [in 1844] (1845) Friedrich Engels pointed out that seamstresses earned from 1 1/2*d.* per shirt up to a rarely attained maximum of 6*d.* Engels states that it took eighteen hours to sew together "fine or fancy shirts"; but it was possible for a seamstress

to sew together as many as three per day of the "ordinary" kind. If Biddell could, making trousers, earn 7s. a week, she was indeed, as Moses's foreman claimed, making a "good living." Cf. the recent translation of Engels's classic study by W. O. Henderson and W. H. Chaloner (London and New York, 1958), pp. 237-40, and also Emil Oswald, *Thomas Hood und die soziale Tendenzdichtung seiner Zeit* (Wien and Leipzig, 1904), p. 99.

39. Biddell's room, too, a person in the court observed, was the "very picture of wretchedness. It was almost without a vestige of furniture of any sort, and quite unfit for the residence of human beings" (*The Times,* Oct. 26).

40. *Works,* VII, 373.

41. *Ibid.,* VIII, 370.

42. Walter Jerrold, in a 1929 letter to Bertram Dobell (Hood collection, UCLA), points out that the MS of the "Song," unlike those of Hood's comic poems, is full of crossings-out and revisions. But cf. the *Eclectic Review* for March, 1846, p. 289.

The paragraph quoted from "The Defaulter" has little connection with the rest of the story. A guess would be that Hood inserted it at the last moment before sending the January *New Monthly* off to press. And a letter to Hewlett, dated "Dec 24th 1842," seems to confirm this guess: he mentions he had "written more than usual this month—an Etching Poem ["Etching Moralised"]—& The Defaulter, a prose story—& yet am done today as far as I am concerned!" (Brooke collection). In the story Hood mentions the woman's "perhaps . . . having to sue a shabby employer for the amount of her pitiful earnings," and that her plight was originally caused "by a breach of trust on the part of a banker" (*Works,* VIII, 370). He gives other details, so precise as to imply he had in mind a particular case, but after a search through *The Times* for November and December, 1842, I find none to which they fit exactly. The closest is an account, reprinted from the *Monthly Magazine,* in *The Times* of December 20, 1842, about a seamstress who earned "1 1/2d. for making a sailor's shirt"—the same price, apparently standard, that Hood's "respectable young woman" is paid. Further: "The price of the cheapest quartern loaf she can buy is 5 1/2d. A loaf of bread is 1d. dearer than her whole day's work."

43. P. 210. Dodds notes: "All sensitive people were shocked by the disclosures but no one knew quite what to do. The magistrate had given [the foreman of] Mr. Moses a bad half-hour, yet official action on the whole problem lagged. Sweated seamstresses continued to sew 'a shroud as well

as a shirt.' As late as 1859 the shirtmakers were receiving only 4s. 6d. a dozen" (p. 148). The "Song" did have one positive effect: "the initial meeting of the Society for the Protection and Employment of Distressed Needlewomen" (p. 149).

44. *DNB* [*Dictionary of National Biography*], "Hood, Thomas."

45. *Memorials,* II, 183.

46. My aunt, Mrs. Alice Gauterin of Churton, Cheshire, speaking for many of her generation, tells me it was required memorization work in school in the first decade of the century.

47. Brooke collection.

48. Manuscript Division, New York Public Library.

49. *Works,* IX, 37.

50. Brooke collection.

51. *Ibid.,* a different letter.

52. Whitley, *HLQ,* p. 410.

53. First published in Dilke, *The Papers of a Critic* (London, 1875), I, 60. MS, Harvard.

54. Brooke collection.

55. *Ibid.,* a different letter.

56. *English Literary Periodicals* (New York, 1930), pp. 365-66. Graham's judgment holds true for the magazine during its term of publication. For a writer usually identified with comic writing, Hood contributed surprisingly little humor; in *Hood's Magazine,* except for the epigrams, most written to fill out a page, only Hewlett's whimsical sketches (presumably) tickled readers's wits.

57. *Memorials,* II, 191.

58. *Works,* IX, 39-40.

59. Cf. Curtis Dahl, "The Victorian Wasteland," *CE* [*College English*], XVI (1955), 341-47; (reprinted in Austin Wright, ed., *Victorian Literature: Modern Essays in Criticism* [New York, 1961], pp. 32-41). Browning wrote that "Childe Roland" "came upon me as a kind of dream."

60. *Works,* IX, 40-42.

61. *A Quiet Corner in a Library* (Chicago, 1915), p. 45.

62. *Works,* IX, 45. J. Cousen's engraving, taken from a painting by Thomas Creswick and used as frontispiece for the January *Hood's Magazine,* either suggested or was specially engraved for "The Haunted House." A few months before Hood

had visited Edinburgh Castle; he may have recalled the mystery that surrounded the gory murder of Queen Mary's secretary, David Rizzio, and blurred it into the poem's "BLOODY HAND" and unnamed "weighty crime."

63. *Works,* IX, 133-34, 135, 136.

64. *Ibid.,* pp. 137, 138.

65. *Ibid.,* pp. 138, 139.

66. *Christmas Stories* (London, 1954), p. 57. New Oxford Illustrated Dickens. Hood's review of Dickens's story is in *Works,* IX, 93-103.

67. *Charles Dickens: His Tragedy and Triumph* (New York, 1952), I, 489.

68. Brooke collection.

69. ALS, University of Rochester Library, to the publishers Smith and Elder (dated "Tuesday" [February, 1844])—Whitley, "Thomas Hood," p. 417; Hood collection, UCLA.

70. Brooke collection.

71. *Memorials,* II, 195. On Hood's relations with the Flights, see also his unpublished correspondence with Ward at UCLA and in the Fitzwilliam Museum, Cambridge, as well as Hannah Lawrance's article in the *British Quarterly Review,* XLVI (Oct., 1867).

72. Brooke collection.

73. *Memorials,* II, 195. Amidst the various suits and threats of countersuits, Hood eventually entered an action against Flight for the amount he claimed was owed him—£100.

74. Brooke collection.

75. Hood collection, UCLA.

76. Whitley, *HLQ,* pp. 410-11.

77. Hood collection, Harvard.

78. Brooke collection.

79. *Autobiographical Recollections* (London, 1877), p. 63.

80. *Memorials,* II, 196. Cf. P. F. Morgan, *TLS,* June 7, 1957, p. 349, and the *Eclectic Review,* March, 1846, p. 290.

81. Hood collection, National Library of Scotland. Letter dated October 8, 1844.

82. *Memorials,* II, 226-27.

83. Hood collection, UCLA.

84. *Memorials,* II, 200.

Bibliography

1. MANUSCRIPT MATERIAL

I wish to acknowledge permission to quote from Hood letters held by the following libraries:

British Museum

California, University of, at Los Angeles

National Library of Scotland

New York Public Library, Manuscript Division and Henry W. and Albert A. Berg Collection

Oxford University, Bodleian Library

Private Collections: Jocelyn Brooke; Robert C. Cameron

Yale University

2. UNPUBLISHED MATERIAL

Cuyler, Cornelius M. "Thomas Hood: An Illustration of the Transition from the Romantic to the Victorian Era." Unpublished Ph.D. dissertation, the Johns Hopkins University, 1943.

Davies, R. E. "Thomas Hood: a Critical Study." Unpublished Ph.D. dissertation, University of London, 1937.

Whitley, Alvin. "Thomas Hood." Unpublished Ph.D. dissertation, Harvard University, 1950.

3. ARTICLES AND BOOKS

With the exception of a few works of general interest, I have limited this bibliography to the more important articles and books on Hood that I have consulted and found helpful. Contemporary periodicals are not listed, nor are all the works cited in the footnotes. The dissertation by Alvin Whitley, cited above, has a thorough bibliography to 1950 of secondary works relating to Hood, his contemporaries, and the age; briefer lists may be found in the *Cambridge Bibliography of English Literature* (1941), the *Supplement* (1955), and in J. C. Reid, *Thomas Hood* (1963). The yearly bibliographies of the romantic movement in *English Literary History* (1937-49), in *Philological Quarterly* (1950-64), and now in *English Language Notes* (1965-), as well as the "Current Bibliography" in the annual *Keats-Shelley Journal* are reasonably complete and mutually supplementing. That in *K-SJ* from July 1, 1950, to June 30, 1962, has been conveniently published in volume form, *Keats, Shelley, Byron, Hunt, and Their Circles,* ed. David Bonnell Green and Edwin Graves Wilson (Lincoln, Neb., 1964). Every student of Hood acknowledges with gratitude the nearly complete bibliography of editions of Hood's works assembled by Constance Goodrich in her dissertation cited above.

Annan, Noel Gilroy. *Leslie Stephen.* Cambridge, Mass., 1952.

Dodds, John W. *The Age of Paradox: A Biography of England 1841-1851.* New York, 1952.

Hood, Thomas. *The Complete Poetical Works of Thomas Hood,* ed. Walter Jerrold. London, 1906.

————. *Memorials of Thomas Hood,* edited by his Son [Tom Hood] and Daughter [Frances Freeling Broderip]. 2 vols. London, 1860.

————. *The Works of Thomas Hood,* edited by his Son and Daughter. 10 vols. London, 1869-73.

————. *Tylney Hall.* London, 1883.

Hudson, William Henry. *A Quiet Corner in a Library.* Chicago, 1915.

Jerrold, Walter. *Douglas Jerrold and "Punch."* London, 1910.

————. *Thomas Hood and Charles Lamb: The Story of a Friendship.* London, 1930.

————. *Thomas Hood: His Life and Times.* New York, 1909.

Johnson, Edgar. *Charles Dickens: His Tragedy and Triumph.* 2 vols. New York, 1952.

Lane, William G. "A Chord in Melancholy: Hood's Last Years." *Keats-Shelley Journal,* XIII (Winter, 1964), 43-61.

Lawrance, Hannah. *British Quarterly Review,* XLVI (October, 1867), 323-54.

Lytton, The Earl of. *The Life of Edward Bulwer.* 2 vols. London, 1913.

Marchand, Leslie A. *Letters of Thomas Hood, from the Dilke Papers in the British Museum.* New Brunswick, N.J., 1945.

Morgan, Peter F. "Thomas Hood." *Times Literary Supplement,* June 7, 1957, p. 349.

————. "John Hamilton Reynolds and Thomas Hood." *Keats-Shelley Journal,* XI (Winter, 1962), 83-95.

Oswald, Emil. *Thomas Hood und die soziale Tendenzdichtung seiner Zeit.* Wien and Leipzig, 1904.

Reid, J. C. *Thomas Hood.* London, 1963.

Rollins, Hyder E. *The Keats Circle: Letters and Papers.* 2 vols. Cambridge, Mass., 1948.

Spielmann, M. H. *The History of "Punch."* New York, 1895.

————. "Thomas Hood and 'Punch.'" *Bookman* (New York), X (1899), 151-52.

Whitley, Alvin. "Hood and Dickens: Some New Letters." *Huntington Library Quarterly,* XIV, 4 (August, 1951), 385-413.

Wright, Austin, ed. *Victorian Literature: Essays in Criticism.* New York, 1961.

Joy Flint (essay date 1992)

SOURCE: Flint, Joy. Introduction to *Thomas Hood, Selected Poems,* pp. 7-25. Manchester, England: Carcanet Press, 1992.

[*In the following introduction to Hood's poems, Flint discusses the poet's commitment to exposing social ills, as well as the influence of both Keats and Coleridge on his odes and sonnets.*]

Thomas Hood was remembered affectionately by his children:

> While in Germany,[1] he bought a small toy theatre for us, and then . . . drew, painted and cut out the characters and scenery for a tragedy (Paul and Virginia),[2] a spectacle (St George and the Dragon), and a pantomime. The figures were very clever, and the groups and procession capitally arranged—and the dragon *was* a dragon! . . . On high days and holidays this theatre used to be brought out and my father used to perform the pieces . . . He used to extemporise the dialogue . . . His stage management, properties, and machinery were capital, and I can still remember the agony with which I used to see the wreck in Paul and Virginia break up by degrees, and the bodies of the lovers washed in over the breakers. In addition to these means of evening entertainment he had a magic lantern, for which he painted a number of slides, some humorous and some pretty ones—a flight of doves and swallows with a hawk, and a little cottage in the snow, with a 'practicable'[3] regiment marching over a bridge.

There is much in this Victorian scene which is typical of Hood: domesticity; sociability; fun; skill—of hand and eye and tongue—fed by a fertile inventiveness and used to delight an audience. Characteristically, he appears as a versatile entertainer, responsive to shifting moods, to comedy and tragedy, alive to laughter and to the threat of the hawk and the terror of the dragon.

He was born into the London Book trade: in the heart of the City of London, in the Poultry, on 23 May 1799, the second son and third child of Thomas and Elizabeth Hood. His Scottish father was by this time an established bookseller and publisher, a partner in the firm of Vernor and Hood. His mother, Elizabeth Sands, came from a well-known family of engravers.

His father's early death, followed by that of his elder brother, left him with a widowed mother and four sisters. The family resources were limited and Hood's formal education came to an end when he was about fourteen and friends found a position for him as a counting-house clerk. He was, however, a voracious reader; in a sonnet he describes how he 'sat upon a lofty stool' and, under an indulgent master, enlivened his book-keeping by writing verses in imitation of the poets he read, succeeding in 'mingling poetic honey with trade wax'—as he was to do throughout his life. His health had always been poor and when he was advised to change his occupation he was apprenticed to his uncle, Robert Sands, to learn engraving; when it continued to cause concern, he was sent for an extended stay to his Scottish relations near Dundee. It would seem that in the two years he was there he continued to work at engraving and to write, sending contributions to local newspapers. He was also writing poetry: passages of a satire on Dundee society and a poem **'The Bandit'** with a Byronic hero, survive.

In the autumn of 1817 he returned home, greatly improved in health, to finish his apprenticeship and to practise as an engraver.[4] The whole process of engraving interested him: he invented a device to ease the labour of drawing lines, and left behind both a prose and a verse treatise on the art. At the same time he continued to write for his own amusement, becoming a member of his local literary society. His mother died in the summer of 1821 and he became responsible for the household; his letters reveal that he worked at home and that two of his sisters helped him in the arduous task of preparing the plates. Hood wrote delightful, spontaneous letters and in one written to a Scottish friend he describes his life about this time: 'Perhaps you will ask what I am doing. Why truly I am T. Hood Scripsit et sculpsit—I am engraving and writing prose and Poetry by turns—'.[5] This was to be the pattern of his future life. Few of his engravings survive but one, published in 1825, prompted Lamb to describe him as 'that half-Hogarth';[6] entitled *The Progress of Cant,* it had a characteristically satirical theme and illustrated a banner-waving procession of what Hood saw as the outstanding hypocrisies of the time. He never abandoned drawing but produced a constant supply of line-drawings and wood-cuts to illustrate his writing until the time of his death; often these have a crude cartoon vitality which highlights the serious intent beneath the comic surface of many of his poems.

Most importantly for his writing, the artist's observant eye and habitual interest in external detail never left him. For from the beginning of 1821 Hood had become more writer than engraver. John Taylor—of Taylor and Hessey, the publishers of Keats—who had once worked for Hood's father, offered him the position of editorial assistant on *The London Magazine.*[7] Hood was full of enthusiasm: 'I dreamt articles, thought articles, wrote articles . . . The more irksome parts of authorship, such as the correction of the press, were to me labours

of love.'[8] From this time onwards he was a professional author, earning his living by writing and editing.

The London Magazine brought this very young man into the heart of the literary scene of the time, into contact with Lamb, who became a close friend, and with the established figures of the Romantic Movement: Wordsworth, Coleridge, Scott, Hazlitt, de Quincey, Clare. Hood has left lively descriptions of them all in his *Literary Reminiscences.* It introduced him also to J. H. Reynolds, Keats's friend and correspondent. In 1825 Hood was to collaborate with Reynolds in a lightly satirical collection of **Odes and Addresses to Great People**; most of these were by Hood and the popularity of the volume helped to establish his reputation as a comic writer. In the same year he married Reynolds's sister Jane, to whom Keats had also written and sent copies of his poems.

Being so closely associated with a circle of the poet's former friends and so soon after his death, it was not surprising that Hood's own early serious poetry was deeply influenced by Keats. There are echoes of Keats's 1820 volume in poems written by Hood as early as 1821: he was the first disciple and known for many years as the last of the Romantics. But it is a misleading description. Even his physical appearance does not fit the popular image of the young Romantic poet, epitomized in Severn's portrait of Keats, book in hand, by the open window. Portraits of Hood as a young man, both actual and verbal, show a different, more typically Victorian figure:

> In outward appearance, Hood conveyed the idea of a clergyman. His figure slight and invariably dressed in black: his face pallid; the complexion delicate, and features regular; his countenance bespeaking sympathy by its sweet expression of melancholy and suffering.[9]

His was, as he described it himself, relishing the thought that appearances might well be deceptive, a 'Methodist face'.[10]

In the *Reminiscences* he recalled listening, as a young man by Lamb's fireside, to Lamb and Wordsworth discussing the 'promissory notes' left behind by the younger poets, Keats and Shelley. Hood himself was one of the few poets of this younger generation to live on into Victoria's reign. Towards the end of his own, not very long, life he gives an account in a letter of another occasion at which he was present—a dinner of the Literary Fund,[11] held in Greenwich to welcome Charles Dickens home from America. These two social engagements pinpoint Hood's place in the chronology of the nineteenth century literary world exactly. Hood was able to count both Lamb and Dickens among his friends and both valued him as a writer and as a man. 'What a fertile genius (and a quiet good soul withal) is Hood . . .'[12] wrote Lamb in a letter to a friend. And Dickens, when he heard that Hood was dying:

He . . . was a man of great power—of prodigious force and genius as a poet—and not generally known, perhaps, by his best credentials. When he was under the pressure of severe misfortune and illness, and I had never seen him, he went far out of his way to praise me; and wrote in the *Athenaeum* a paper on *The Curiosity Shop*; so full of enthusiasm and high appreciation, and so free from any taint of envy or reluctance to acknowledge me as a young man far more fortunate than himself, that I can hardly bear to think of it.[13]

Hood's career, therefore, spans the years which saw the Romantic imagination and temper develop into the Victorian. As a result, besides the intrinsic merit of much of his writing, Hood's work, even the hack-work, has an added dimension and interest: he was part of, and absorbed in, a rapidly expanding literary scene, 'an age of literary industry',[14] as he described it, and his writing reflects, sustains, and sometimes influences, changing public taste and concern.

He worked hard to satisfy the demands of the widening market of middle-class readers, constantly meeting deadlines as contributor to and editor of various periodicals and annuals. He produced, often single-handed, supplying both text and illustrations, a series of *Comic Annuals,* providing 'harmless amusement for the Christmas fireside'. In the last few months of his life he had embarked on the first issues of *Hood's Magazine,* which others carried on after his death.

In many ways he was a successful author, much in demand both as editor and contributor and among the best loved writers of his time; but his life, professional and private, was overshadowed by crippling bouts of ill-health and by financial insecurity. He was financially involved with a firm of engravers which failed and, in 1835, in an attempt to economise and clear his debts, he moved abroad with his young family, first to the Rhine, later settling in Antwerp. The self-imposed exile, though it cut his expenses and provided him with copy, proved disastrous to his health. When he returned to England in 1840 he was chronically sick and, increasingly, in pain. Hood died in 1845,[15] on 3 May, a few weeks before his forty-sixth birthday, after a lifetime wholly spent in writing for the literary magazines of the period.

Repeated misfortunes with publishers and booksellers cast some doubt on his business judgment. Again and again he seemed to put his trust in the wrong people, and, when disappointed, was inclined to litigation; he was often the victim of plagiarism; he made a number of impetuous decisions which proved financially disastrous for him—like the one to withdraw from his share in what became the highly profitable *Athenaeum.*[16] These experiences made him a tireless publicist of the injustices suffered by writers in the very volatile conditions then obtaining in the world of books and periodicals. He pleaded eloquently for 'the dignity of the craft' and, in the campaigning years which preceded the Copyright Bill of 1842, for the rights of the author: 'He writes for bread, and gets it short weight; for money and gets the wrong change; for the Present, and he is pirated; for the Future, and his children are disinherited for his pains.'[17] He exerted himself energetically on behalf of individual authors and actors who had fallen on hard times, and in his turn he commanded the loyalty and affectionate regard of his colleagues; many friends rallied to help him through his own difficulties, to petition for a loan for him from the Literary Fund, to help relieve the burden of editorship in his last years and, finally, through the good offices of Peel, to ensure the granting of a civil list pension to his wife.

His output was prodigious—daunting to anyone attempting a selection of his work. He was endlessly inventive and versatile. Amphibian, at home in both prose and verse and in many varieties of each, he ranges in scope from a comic epigram on the death of the giraffe at the London Zoo to a three-volume novel *Tylney Hall*. He reviewed exhibitions, plays and books—from the newest novels to cookery books and the first *Kelly's Directory*. He wrote sketches and pantomimes for the stage. He wrote travelogues, tales and legends, and humorous snatches of patter and dialogue—radio scripts before their time.

Much of Hood's verse was comic and humorous: he wrote comic ballads; he wrote topical light verse and stronger satire; he wrote children's verses full of a robust playground cruelty, in which animals do not escape the butcher's knife,

> And Ogres draw their cruel knives,
>   To shed the blood of girls and boys.

He wrote nonsense verses which can sound—as many of his comic illustrations look—like those of Edward Lear:

> *Krak kraziboo ban,*[18]
>   I'm the Lunatick Man
> Confined in the Moon since creation began—
>   *Sit muggy bigog,*
>   Whom except in a fog
> You see with a Lanthorn, a Bush, and a Dog.

In *Miss Kilmansegg and her Precious Leg* he wrote a bizarre, comic, harshly satirical poem in serial form. But he also wrote more conventional serious verse: street ballads, song lyrics and sentimental ballads; traditional sonnets; dramatic monologues; mythological narratives; and a handful of tender, controlled poems, some of which are among the best known in the language. He also wrote poems of social protest which touched the conscience of the nation.

All Hood's poetry should be seen in the context of its production. Most of the poems, even the most intimate, first appeared in popular periodicals; many were written expressly for them and with a specific audience of middle-class readers in mind. Many were written to meet a deadline or fill a vacant space with little time for revision or refinement. Yet even the most recognisably derivative work always bears some mark of originality and there is a competence about even the most obvious hack-work, of which there is plenty; there is no call to doubt his own assertion that he never wrote anything that did not please himself. This professional, working, journalistic background makes him a different kind of poet from most of his Romantic contemporaries. He was no less talented: he was perhaps in many ways more original and technically more gifted, with a facility and virtuosity that earned Auden's admiration,[19] but his sense of poetic vocation was less exalted, less dedicated, less single-minded than theirs. Temperament and circumstances made his view more modest and more commercial but, for all his relentless clowning, he was a serious poet.

When the authorship of the anonymously published *Odes and Addresses to Great People* became known—the quality of the puns caused Coleridge to attribute the volume to Lamb—Hood was quickly established in the minds of the public as a talented writer of comic verse and in his own lifetime it was as a humorist that he was best known, celebrated for his—to modern taste—deplorable puns. He became, as he said, 'lively Hood for a livelihood' and seems to have accepted his role as verbal clown philosophically: 'To make laugh is my calling. I must jump, I must tumble, I must turn language head over heels, and leap through grammar.'[20] He saw his role principally as an entertainer, himself as the literary equivalent of Joseph Grimaldi,[21] that favourite clown, whose portrait hung, alongside that of Lamb, on his study wall.

By all accounts Hood's punning appears to have been instinctive and compulsive and he defends its use: 'having taken out a certificate to "shoot folly as it flies"[22] I shall persist in using the double barrel as long as meanings will rise in coveys'; he insisted that 'A double meaning shows a double sense'. Nor is it 'altogether fool'; Hood is often, like King Lear's companion, 'a bitter fool' and his double meanings reflect on his principal theme, or, as in his play on 'twit' in **'The Song of the Shirt'**, cast a nervous sidelong glance at life's cruel practical jokes. The most brutal word-play in the ballads—in **'A Waterloo Ballad'**, for instance—has all the pungency of the parodies current in the trenches of the First World War:

> Alas! a splinter of a shell
>   Right in my stomach sticks;
> French mortars don't agree so well
>   With stomachs as French bricks.

> This very night a merry dance
>   At Brussels was to be;—
> Instead of opening a ball,
>   A ball has open'd me.

Hood the clown and Hood the serious poet were closer kin than is sometimes supposed. His work lacks the sustained fusion of the sinister and the laughable which characterizes Dickens's mature work but it is Dickens's crowded, kaleidoscopic imagination, that Hood's own, with its dark and comic side, most nearly resembles. Even as a person he often has the air of a character from Dickens; something of Wemmick's split personality dwells in him: the man of sober appearance, fascinated by crime and murder, as excited as his young son when, in Edinburgh they 'saw the shop where the rope was bought to hang Porteous',[23] can switch abruptly into the whimsical host firing a miniature cannon[24] across the lake to welcome friends to his home at Lake House, Wanstead. His patience in adversity recalls Tom Pinch;[25] it is not surprising to find him pleading with Dickens as the parts of *Martin Chuzzlewit* appeared, to 'make Tom Pinch turn author, and Pecksniff become a publisher . . .'.

Like Dickens and like Lamb he was a Londoner. His many pages of prose and verse are crowded with the life and sounds, people and miscellaneous personalities of London. Shops, theatres, pleasure gardens, Lord Mayor's Show, day trippers on the Thames, rogues, Members of Parliament, are all here. The author of Waverley, 'The Great Unknown', jostles alongside Madame Hengler, firework-maker to Vauxhall and the prison-reformer, Elizabeth Fry accompanies the theatre's most famous clown, Grimaldi; Mr Graham, the Aeronaut, looks down from his balloon on the capital's 'mob of little men . . . Like mites upon a cheese!'

It was not only the multi-faceted surface of contemporary life to which Hood was alert and sensitive. He was profoundly conscious of deeper undercurrents of change affecting the times in which he lived and quickly aware of the implications for ordinary people of the great technical and industrial advances of the century. He might write in comic vein of the plight of washerwomen in his **'Address to The Steam-Washing Company'** or imagine the thoughts of an Under-ostler on the coming of steam, but his concern was serious. Social awareness is obvious enough under the bantering tone and, no doubt irresistible, puns of his **'Friendly Epistle to Mrs Fry'**, urging her to teach the children of the prisoners outside the walls of the gaol:

> Come out of Newgate, Mrs Fry! Repair
>   Abroad, and find your pupils in the streets,
> O, come abroad into the wholesome air,
>   And take your moral place, before Sin seats
> Her wicked self in the Professor's chair.
>   Suppose some morals raw! the true receipt's

To dress them in the pan, but do not try
To cook them in the fire, good Mrs Fry!

But the voice of compassion and social conscience, the voice of the forerunner of Dickens, had been present in Hood's very earliest contribution to *The London Magazine,* which described, in the manner of Sterne, a walk from Islington to Waterloo Bridge, and it rings true: 'I hate the weeping-willow set, who will cry over their pug dogs and canaries, till they have no tears to spare for the real children of misfortune and misery.'

In 1826 and 1827 Hood published two collections of his pieces, in prose and verse, taken from periodicals, under the title **Whims and Oddities.** They contained a motley selection, largely popular ballads and lyrics. In 1827 also he made a collection of his more serious poems under the title **The Plea of the Midsummer Fairies.** The volume was not well received by the public and sales were poor; to the regret of his friends, who valued it more highly, Hood never attempted a similar collection. His reputation as a comic writer was by then so firmly established that when, in 1828, he issued a serious collection of *National Tales,* he felt it necessary to offer an explanation:

> Because I have jested elsewhere, it does not follow that I am incompetent for gravity . . . It is from none of the player's ambition, which has led the buffoon by a rash step to the tragic buskin, that I assume the sadder humour, but because I know from certain passages that such affections are not foreign to my nature. During my short lifetime, I have often been as 'sad as night', and not like the young gentlemen of France, 'merely from wantonness'. It is the contrast of such leaden and golden fits that lends a double relish to our days.

Chronic ill-health ensured that the double vision was always with him and the sadder humour often cast its shadow. An atmosphere of death and foreboding clings to much of Hood's writing, comic as well as serious. In the course of his career it takes many forms: a dream of water babies in **'The Sea of Death'**,

> And there were spring-faced cherubs that did sleep
> Like water-lilies on that motionless deep,
> How beautiful! with bright unruffled hair
> On sleek unfretted brows . . . ;

or the sub-aqueous light of **Hero and Leander**; or the intrusion of physical cruelty, even in his comic verses for children; or the reflective mood of personal sadness, as in 'I remember, I remember'; his fascination with murder and guilt; his concern for the suicides of Waterloo Bridge; or morbid attraction to the 'narrow house and dark' in **'The Elm Tree'**;[26] or saturation in an atmosphere of fear and foreboding in **'The Haunted House'**.

It is from the poems in **The Plea of the Midsummer Fairies** that Hood has been most commonly represented in standard anthologies and which are largely respon-sible for his reputation as a Romantic poet. The influence of Keats is apparent even in many of the titles: **'The Departure of Summer'**; **'Ode: to Autumn'**; **'To Fancy'**; **'Ode to Melancholy'**. There are others which are familiar to many readers: the song lyric, **'Fair Ines'**; **'Ruth'**; the sonnet, **'Silence'**; **'I remember, I remember'**.

Nearly all the longer narrative poems in the volume have, like those of Keats, a basis in myth and legend: **The Plea of the Midsummer Fairies** itself; **Hero and Leander**; **Lycus, the Centaur**; **The Two Peacocks of Bedfont**. All four of the myths are Hood's inventions. The title poem—dedicated to Lamb—is an elaborate allegory in which the figure of Shakespeare rescues the Midsummer Fairies from the scythe of Time; the Leander of Hood's poem is lured to his death by the sea-nymph, Scylla; **The Two Peacocks of Bedfont**—clipped in yew—is a homespun myth preaching a homily on the wages of Vanity and Pride. **Lycus, the Centaur** is often considered wholly imitative; it certainly owes debts to Keats, to Milton, perhaps to Mary Shelley, but there is some justification for Hartley Coleridge's[27] view that it is a work 'absolutely unique in its line' for the poem is original in several ways. Hood creates a myth to explain the origin of the Centaur, imagining the human Lycus, as victim of a Circean spell which is interrupted before the transformation is complete so that he remains half horse, half man—a Centaur. It is written as an interior monologue. Elsewhere, in his comic poems, with his adroit handling of the vernacular, Hood's use of the monologue looks forward to Browning, sometimes to Kipling; here he anticipates Tennyson. There are passages in this over-long poem, when, contemplating the plight of the beasts under Circe's spell, or Lycus's involuntary exclusion from domestic affection, Hood jars on nerves which Tennyson was to touch in 'Maud' or in 'Lucretius'.

Lycus is written in anapaests: an insensitive choice to many, but the galloping metre seems symptomatic of that nervous instinct which constantly drives Hood into black humour and brutal pun in the face of the unbearable. This is the case with another early poem, printed in **Whims and Oddities** in 1826, on a popular theme of the time, **'The Last Man'**. In its use of monologue and its emotional base it resembles **Lycus** but the style, texture and treatment could hardly be more different: **'The Last Man'** has all the crude vitality and pace of a street ballad, in which the anti-climax of the stark pun in the final line does not seem out of place.

It was inevitable that as a very young man Hood should have been seduced by Keats's style but **'The Last Man'** indicates the much deeper underlying influence, in both manner and substance, that had been exerted by *The Lyrical Ballads* of Wordsworth and Coleridge. It seems fitting that Hood should have been born at the turn of the century when Wordsworth was forming and articulating the perceptions of profound social change and social need which had given rise to *The Lyrical Ballads*. Nearly all of Hood's work, comic and serious, is firmly anchored in a deep conviction of the worth of 'the great and simple affections of our nature' and in his sense of his own common humanity. Even in so apparently Keatsian a poem as **'Ruth'**, Hood does not emphasize her grief, but, looking through the eyes of Boaz, records the compassionate impulse of the human heart:

> Sure, I said, heav'n did not mean,
> Where I reap thou shouldst but glean,
> Lay thy sheaf adown and come,
> Share my harvest and my home.

With hindsight it is not difficult to discern signs in Hood's early poems of an awakened humanitarian strain which was to strengthen as the century advanced and come to dominate his later poetry.

Coleridge's voice is clearly heard in the stanzas of **'The Last Man'**:

> My conscience began to gnaw my heart,
> Before the day was done,
> For other men's lives had all gone out,
> Like candles in the sun!—
> But it seem'd as if I had broke, at last,
> A thousand necks in one!

His influence is also strong in a poem first published in 1829, **'The Dream of Eugene Aram'**. Like 'The Ancient Mariner' the poem is a study in guilt and remorse but takes as its subject, not an imaginary, but a real crime and an actual criminal. More and more Hood's subject-matter was taken from 'incidents and situations from common life' and his writing, humorous and serious, related to the actual world in which he lived. He consciously turned away from legend, recognizing the inappropriateness of Gothic Romanticism in a rapidly industrialized world. He preferred caricature to what he called 'enthusimoosy' when he came to write the travel sketches in *Up the Rhine,* saying that modern steamboats associated awkwardly with feudal ruins and there had been 'enough of vapouring, in more senses than one, on the blue and castled river.'

His comic poetry had begun to address social and moral evils in a more openly satirical and serious way than the teasing, bantering tone adopted towards topical personalities in the *Odes and Addresses*. In 1837, stung by an unwarranted and personal attack, condemning the 'profaneness and ribaldry' of his work, he used a sharper voice to defend himself and to launch a general attack on hypocrisy and cant in his **'Ode to Rae Wilson'**.[28] The poem contains Hood's clearest statement of his philosophy of life:

> Well!—be the graceless lineaments confest!
> I do enjoy this bounteous beauteous earth;
>   And dote upon a jest
> 'Within the limits of becoming mirth';—
> No solemn sanctimonious face I pull,
> Nor think I'm pious when I'm only bilious—
> Nor study in my sanctum supercilious
> To frame a Sabbath Bill or forge a Bull.
> I pray for grace—repent each sinful act—
> Peruse, but underneath the rose, my Bible;
> And love my neighbour, far too well, in fact,
> To call and twit him with a godly tract
> That's turn'd by application to a libel.
> My heart ferments not with the bigot's leaven,
> All creeds I view with toleration thorough,
> And have a horror of regarding heaven
>   As anybody's rotten borough.

In September 1840 the *New Monthly Magazine*[29] began serialisation of Hood's most grotesque poetic production, *Miss Kilmansegg and her Precious Leg*; it continued to appear in monthly parts until the middle of 1841. This 'golden legend' had as its target the increasing materialism and acquisitiveness of the society he found around him on his return from the continent. The energetic buffoonery is typical of Hood's comic verse but the frenetic pace of its verbal and comic invention—manic punning and accumulation of detail—sustained for so long on a single theme, betray a very serious moral purpose and social message: the 'Methodist face' was not wholly deceptive. Both target and accumulative method in *Miss Kilmansegg* anticipate Dickens's portrayal of the Veneerings in *Our Mutual Friend*.

The humanitarian strain always present in Hood's writing—early in his career he spoke out against slavery—became more pronounced as the century advanced; in the last few years of his life he pleaded directly for the poor and unfortunate victims of the affluent Victorian society he had attacked in *Miss Kilmansegg.* **'The Song of the Shirt'** and **'The Pauper's Christmas Carol'** reminded well-fed Christmas readers of *Punch* in 1843 of the sweated labour of the seamstresses who produced their finery and of the plight of those in the hated workhouses. Hood was always sympathetic to the hardship and injustice suffered by many women in his society; most poignantly, with a tenderness similar to that which he brought to personal sorrow in 'We watch'd her breathing through the night', he wrote in **'The Bridge of Sighs'** of the many suicides who fell to their deaths from Waterloo Bridge.

These poems of social protest were widely circulated and widely influential, voicing and stimulating the awakening moral conscience of the middle classes. Readers in the earlier half of the twentieth century, considering the poems out of their immediate context and forgetting their urgent didactic purpose, found them over-sentimental. But Hood was in tune with the mood of his public: most of the poems were written in response to reports in daily newspapers which had touched his own heart and common humanity. The extent to which he felt for and with these unknown strangers can be gauged from his response to the case of Gifford White, an eighteen-year-old agricultural labourer, desperate for work, who had been sentenced to transportation for life for threatening—no more—to set fire to local farms. The case preyed on Hood's mind in his final illness; he petitioned Members of Parliament on White's behalf and he wrote **'The Lay of the Labourer'**,[30] haunted, as he said, by the phantom 'of a real person, a living breathing man, with a known name . . . .'.

It is typical of Hood that when he pleads for life's anonymous unfortunates, he thinks of the individual personality, of the 'living breathing man, with a known name'. A single seamstress sings the **'The Song of the Shirt'**; 'Every soul,' crowding 'in a very torrent of Man' in time to **'The Workhouse Clock'**, is as distinct as a Lowry figure; the homeless, nameless suicide, lifted up so tenderly from the Thames is 'one more Unfortunate' in a drab world but Hood asserts her individuality with striking economy of detail:

> Loop up her tresses
> Escaped from the comb,
> Her fair auburn tresses;

His instinct to focus on the suffering of a particular individual had always been strong: in his early work it led him to voice the anguish of Lycus and, writing of guilt and remorse, to tell the story, not of any strange and emblematic Ancient Mariner but of an actual criminal 'with a known name'—Eugene Aram, executed in 1759 for a real crime of murder.

What moves Hood most throughout his career is the thought of those men and women cut off from the sympathy and love of their fellow creatures, deprived of domestic affection, by their own actions, by circumstance, or by economic necessity and man's inhumanity to man. He was devoted to his own wife and children, a daughter and a son; his domestic life, in spite of the loss in infancy of their first child—the subject of Lamb's poem 'On an Infant dying as soon as born'—in spite of precarious finances and his own and Jane's ill-health, was a happy one. 'I feel strongly that my domestic happiness has kept me so long alive', he wrote in a letter in 1843. Elsewhere he noted with regret that there were few examples of 'domestic poetry'[31] in English, as there were in Scottish, poetry. When he expresses personal emotion directly in his poetry it is of these intimate domestic feelings that he writes: of his love for his wife and children, or of the memories or deaths of those he loved. Here he is self-effacing, unassuming, unsentimental; these poems, sparse, tender and restrained, carry with them the assurance that Hood's

more demonstrative cries on behalf of the poor and oppressed are founded securely on genuine feeling and understanding.

Hood's darkest poetry springs from his dread of losing all that is essentially dear to him. **'The Haunted House'** is a nightmare projection of this blankness, 'where Love, domestic Love, no longer nestles':

> A residence for woman, child, and man,
> A dwelling-place—and yet no habitation;
> A House,—but under some prodigious ban
> Of excommunication.

The vision of blank desertion, of a complete absence of life and affection had recurred throughout his life: it is there in the fragment **'The Sea of Death'**; or in the sonnet **'Silence'**; it is the horror felt by **'The Last Man'**, by Lycus and by Eugene Aram, the void sensed at the heart of *Miss Kilmansegg*. The compassion which informs all his writing—even the blackest humour of the stinging puns—springs from an anguished apprehension of a life severed from domestic care and love. It prompts him to plead directly to the general reading public in **'The Bridge of Sighs'**:

> Touch her not scornfully
> Think of her mournfully,
> Gently and humanly;

and to reflect, in that supposedly moral Victorian society:

> Alas! for the rarity
> Of Christian charity
> Under the sun!
> Oh! it was pitiful!
> Near a whole city full,
> Home she had none!

Hood wrote for a living, to please a public and to pay his debts and therefore his estimate of his role as poet was a modest one but he never lost sight of 'the dignity of the craft'[32] and its moral obligations. At the lowest level, in his *Comic Annuals*, by 'humbly contributing to the greatest entertainment of the greatest number', he hoped 'to be of use' to his countrymen; it was a matter of pride to him that, in spite of his addiction to the double meaning, 'the reproach of impurity has never been cast upon me by my judges'. As entertainer his aim was to spread 'a cheerful philosophy', to foster the domestic virtues and at the same time, as he did fearlessly throughout his career, to expose hypocrisy wherever he found it and to alert the conscience of society to the plight of the poor in their midst. He never failed, as he wrote of Dickens, to remind 'wealth of the claims of want, the feasting of the fasting'.[33]

It was not surprising that Hood should have been quick to identify the young Dickens as a kindred spirit and to realize that the Romantic humanitarian impetus had begun to find a new channel of literary expression in the novel. Writing of Boz in 1839 he recognized that 'his drift is a natural one: along with the great human currents and not against them'.[34] Much in Hood anticipates the social concern and moral stance of the mid-century reforming novelists: Dickens, Eliot and Gaskell. The diversity and scope of his work, its wide distribution and popularity, demonstrates very clearly both the continuity of the Romantic tradition and the way in which those ideas and sensibilities filtered through into popular literature, pervading and influencing the consciousness of an avid and widening, predominantly urban, reading public.

Reviewing Hood's total output, appreciating his technical virtuosity, openness to new influences and willingness to experiment, his keen awareness of social and cultural change, acknowledging also the imaginative power and independent achievement of some of his poems, it is tempting to think that he had been constrained by illness and poverty to waste his talents. Many of his contemporaries thought so, Thackeray among them:

> Here is a man with a power to touch the heart almost unequalled, and he passes days and years in writing, "Young Ben he was a nice young man," and so forth . . . "You great man, you good man, you true genius and poet," I cry out, as I turn page after page. "Do, do, make no more of these jokes, but be yourself, and take your station."[35]

Hood knew himself better; it is unlikely that he would have agreed. His was essentially a quicksilver temperament, thoughtful but not contemplative, diverted and fascinated by every aspect of life, trivial or grave, restlessly finding outlet and expression in many different forms.

One of the incidental pleasures of reading widely in Hood's work is the frequency with which the ear catches tones and cadences, not merely echoes of past voices, but anticipations also of many differing writers who came after him. Most modern readers know Hood only from anthologies—a few of the shorter serious poems, or one of his light verses, or a poem of social protest. He is a much more coherent poet than reading him in this piecemeal fashion suggests. All that he writes springs from delight in and concern for his fellow creatures, whether he wishes to move them to laughter, to tears, or to action; he commands both affection and respect.

At heart Hood is a serious and moral poet—the shadow of the hawk always darkened his sky, the dragon *was* a dragon—but he never forgot the value of pantomime, toy theatre and magic lantern, recognizing the need for fantasy in the face of harsh reality. Like his own Lycus he remains a hybrid creature: half-clown, half-preacher; light-hearted but gravely haunted; Romantic and Victorian; terse one moment, garrulous the next; illustrator, journalist, and poet.

Notes

1. '*While in Germany . . .*': Extract from *Memorials of Thomas Hood*, F. F. Broderip (Hood's daughter), 1860. A note by his son, Tom Hood, to a letter from Jane Hood to Mrs Elliot, 29 Oct. 1836.

2. *Paul and Virginia*: from the French *Paul et Virginie* by Bernadin de St Pierre, which Hood claimed to have translated; the translation has not been traced.

3. '*practicable*': a theatrical term, indicating parts of the scenery capable of actual use in the play.

4. *as an engraver*: Hood appears to have worked as a free lance, executing topographical work for one of the le Keux brothers.

5. '*Perhaps you will ask . . .*': Letter to George Rollo, October 1821, *Memorials*, op.cit. *The Letters of Thomas Hood* have been edited by Peter F. Morgan, Edinburgh, 1973.

6. '*that half-Hogarth . . .*': Lamb's review was for *The New Monthly Magazine*, XVI, February 1826. The cartoon, in The British Museum, is reproduced in John Clubbe, *Victorian Forerunner*, Duke University Press, 1968.

7. *The London Magazine*: was founded in 1820 in opposition to Blackwood's; it was bought by Taylor and Hessey in 1821 on the death in a duel of its first editor, John Scott.

8. '*I dreamt articles . . .*': from *Literary Reminiscences*, printed in *Hood's Own*, 1839.

9. '*In outward appearance . . .*': A recollection in *Pen and Pencil* by Mrs Balmanno, New York, 1858; quoted in the *Memorials*, op.cit.

10. '*Methodist face*': Letter to Philip de Franck, January 1838, *Letters*, ed. Morgan, p 348.

11. *The Literary Fund*: The Royal Literary Fund was established in 1790 for the relief of authors in financial difficulties.

12. '*What a fertile genius . . .*': in a letter to Bernard Barton, *Letters of Charles Lamb*, ed. E. V. Lucas, London, 1935.

13. *He . . . was a man of great power*: writing to Angela Burdett-Coutts, March 1845.

14. '*an age of literary industry*': Prospectus to *Hood's Own*, Jan. 1838

15. *Hood died in 1845 . . .*: he was buried in Kensal Green Cemetery. Some time after his death, a monument, paid for by public subscription, was

raised over the grave. It remains—but the bust of the poet and the decorative panels illustrating his poems are missing.

16. *the Athenaeum*: a literary review founded in 1828; it was at its most successful when owned and edited by Hood's friend, Charles Wentworth Dilke. Hood continued to write for it after ending his financial involvement.

17. *He writes for bread*: Letter to *The Athenaeum*, Hood *Works*, 1862, Vol VI, p. 114.

18. *Krak kraziboo ban*: from 'A Flying Visit', *Comic Annual*, 1839.

19. *Auden's admiration*: 'When Hood (whom *I*, by the way, consider a major poet) . . . is writing as a comic poet, he is like nobody but himself and serious in the true sense of the word.' *Introduction to Nineteenth Century British Minor Poets*, 1966, p. 17.

20. *To make laugh is my calling*: quoted from the *Memorials* by Thackeray in *Roundabout Papers*, 'On a Joke I once heard from the Late Thomas Hood'.

21. *Grimaldi*: See note on page 122 below.

22. *to shoot folly as it flies*: Preface, *Comic Annual*, 1834.

23. *Porteous*: leader of the Porteous riots of 1736, described by Scott in *The Heart of Midlothian*.

24. *cannon*: Hood's miniature cannon may have suggested this detail in Dickens's description of Wemmick's 'castle' in *Great Expectations*.

25. *Tom Pinch*: Letter to Dickens, 4 December 1843. *Letters*, ed. Morgan, p. 577.

26. *'The Elm Tree'*: is not included in this selection. As in 'The Haunted House' Hood builds up an atmosphere of foreboding as the speaker voices his premonition that a particular elm will furnish the timber for his coffin.

27. *Hartley Coleridge*: letter to Hood, 1831 quoted by Tom Hood, *Works*, 1862, Vol I, p. 86 n.

28. *Ode to Rae Wilson*: published in *The Athenaeum*, 12 August 1837. Rae Wilson (1772-1849), a Scot of narrow Protestant views, repeatedly attacked Hood for irreligion, from the publication of Hood's etching *The Progress of Cant* onwards.

29. *New Monthly Magazine*: founded in 1814, took the place of *The London Magazine* when this declined. Hood was an occasional contributor and became editor in 1841 on the death of Theodore Hook.

30. *'The Lay of the Labourer'*: in *Hood's Magazine*, November 1844 was a plea, largely in prose, on behalf of the agricultural labourer. It contained a 'lay' with the refrain 'A spade! a rake! a hoe! and the message:

> 'Ay, only give me work,
>   And then you need not fear
> That I shall snare his worship's hare,
>   Or kill his grace's deer;'

31. *'domestic poetry'*: Preface, *Comic Annual*, 1837.

32. *the dignity of the craft*: from Hood's first letter to *The Athenaeum*, 1837, on the subject of *Copyright and Copywrong*.

33. *'wealth of the claims of want . . .'*: from Hood's review of *The Chimes*, *Hood's Magazine*, 1845.

34. *'his drift . . .'*: Letter to C. W. Dilke, November 1839. *Letters*, ed. Morgan, p. 396.

35. *Here is a man . . .*: see note to p. 14.

Robert D. Butterworth (essay date fall 2005)

SOURCE: Butterworth, Robert D. "Hood's Stanzas ('Farewell, Life . . .')." *Explicator* 64, no. 1 (fall 2005): 30-32.

[*In the following essay, Butterworth explores Hood's poetic persona as a dying person in "Stanzas ('Farewell Life . . .')"—a departure from his usual approach to death featuring a third-person narrator.*]

> Farewell, Life! My senses swim;
> And the world is growing dim;
> Thronging shadows cloud the light,
> Like the advent of the night,—
> Colder, colder, colder still
> Upward steals a vapour chill—
> Strong the earthly odour grows—
> I smell the Mould above the Rose!
>
> Welcome, Life! the Spirit strives!
> Strength returns, and hope revives;
> Cloudy fears and shapes forlorn
> Fly like shadows at the morn,—
> O'er the earth there comes a bloom—
> Sunny light for sullen gloom,
> Warm perfume for vapour cold—
> I smell the Rose above the Mould!

Thomas Hood's **"Stanzas ('Farewell, Life . . .')"** completes a circle. Having written about death during his career from every standpoint, from that of a third-person narrator impersonally relating an event (as in, for instance, **"Faithless Nelly Gray"**) to that of a relative watching a loved one die (**"The Death-Bed"**), the process is completed as Hood now writes about death, or at least about dying, from the perspective of the person dying. The poem hinges on a particularly telling deployment of a device Hood has long used, the antithesis and related forms of contrast and reversal. The parallelisms of "Farewell, Life" (1) and "Welcome, Life" (9) and the last lines of each stanza hold the verses in tension and prevent us from seeing the poem as a narrative of a man apparently dying who then recovers. The parallelisms suggest, rather, that these are alternating states that reverse into one another. Anyone who has cared for a person chronically ill or slowly dying will be familiar with the pattern that the patient has good days and bad days. On bad days, the person may well appear to be sinking and to be bidding "Farewell, Life"; on good days, spirits revive and hopes are entertained, by the patient and his or her loved ones, of recovery, after all. It is this fluctuation and alternation of moods and perceptions with which the poem deals. In the course of the poem, Hood notably explores one of his other favorite preoccupations, the complex role delusions play in human life. In a number of Hood's poems the psychological needs of the characters make them cling to delusions in the face of evidence. In **"A Parental Ode to My Son, Aged Three Years and Five Months,"** for instance, the "happy, happy elf" (1) of the father's imagination needs his tears wiped away in reality, and though described as "idol of thy parents," the boy is immediately afterward the object of one parent's irritation ("Drat the boy!" 17) for spilling his ink. The boy's father needs the lad out of the way both physically—so that he can concentrate to write—and psychologically, to sustain his idealized account of childhood, a version plainly at odds with the evidence staring him in the face: "(I'll tell you what, my love, / I cannot write, unless he's sent above)" (56-57).

Faced with untidy reality, far from modifying his ideas, he has the disturbing evidence removed from his sight. Even when, as in **"Moral Reflections on the Cross of St. Paul's,"** a true perspective would help avoid effort and struggle, the man with "Ambition" is not interested in a perspective that would make ambitious striving irrelevant and pointless: "Oh me! hence could I read an admonition / To mad Ambition! / But that he would not listen to my call" (45-47).

In **"Stanzas,"** it would seem that delusion is at work. It may be that the speaker is being self-dramatizing about his illness, with his rhetorical cry, "Farewell, Life"; perhaps the condition is not fatal. More likely, perhaps, is that the notion that a day's rallying gives grounds for hope of recovery ("hope revives" 10) is a delusory hope to which he desperately clings. That the hope is a delusion is hinted at in the image of the rose and its perfume, both of which will fade, and eventually become part of the "Mould" (16). The speaker's delusional state of mind is reflected, too, in the use of pathetic fallacy in "sullen gloom" (14); and this in turn casts into perspective his eager seizing, with questionable confidence, on the apparently reassuring omen of

"sunny light" (14). (The absence of pathetic fallacy in this phrase underlines his genuine belief, superseding a half-acknowledged earlier delusion, in his incipient recovery at this point; but although the "sunny light" is real and objective enough, the significance he attaches to it is highly subjective.) But, such is human nature, and it is observed as such from Hood's self-aware and laconic viewpoint. Humans, being psychologically dependent on delusions, their dying (no less than their living) involves the sustaining of such delusions, and the speaker is caught helplessly between hope and resignation, as his physical condition varies day by day.

In **"Stanzas,"** Hood uses the artistic devices in his armory with particular effectiveness. He often employs antithesis or reversal incidentally, for effects ranging from humor, as in **"Faithless Sally Brown,"** in which the rejected lover "then began to eye his pipe, / And then to pipe his eye" (59-60), and following whose death "They went and told the sexton, and / The sexton toll'd the bell (67-68) to poignancy, as in **"The Death-Bed,"** where it is used to convey the emotional confusion of those keeping vigil: "Our very hopes belied our fears / Our fears our hopes belied" (9-10).

Here, however, it becomes structural. Pathetic fallacy, which Hood elsewhere employs straightforwardly, again, as in **"The Death-Bed,"** in which appropriate weather—"the morn came dim and sad—/ And chill with early showers" (13-14)—accompanies the loved one's death, is here used in a subtly ironic way.

Work Cited

Hood, Thomas. *The Complete Poetical Works of Thomas Hood.* Oxford edition. Ed. Walter Jerrold. London: Henry Frowde, 1906.

Bryan Rivers (essay date September 2006)

SOURCE: Rivers, Bryan. "'Tenderly' and 'With Care': Thomas Hood's 'The Bridge of Sighs' and the Suicide of Harriet Shelley." *Notes & Queries* 53, no. 3 (September 2006): 327-29.

[*In the following essay, Rivers discusses Hood's poem "The Bridge of Sighs" and its later citation by Henry George Davis to comment on the suicide of Harriet Shelley.*]

Kenneth Neill Cameron, in his discussion of documents relating to the suicide of Harriet Shelley, includes the following brief extract from Henry George Davis' local history, *The Memorials of the Hamlet of Knightsbridge* (1859), concerning a famous, demolished London landmark, the Fox and Bull tavern:

The 'Fox and Bull' was for many years the receiving house of the Royal Humane Society; and here was brought the poor frame of the first wife of the poet Shelley, who had drowned herself in the Serpentine. She had lodged in Hans Place, a short time before, and was known to the landlord's daughter, Miss Mary Ann Phillips; hence, her remains were treated 'tenderly', and laid out 'with care'. An inquest was held, and a verdict returned, which saved her the revolting burial then awarded to the suicide.[1]

Cameron notes that this account was listed as a 'Reminiscence of the Compiler' in the Table of Contents, and obviously 'based on material gathered in Knightsbridge from people who knew what had happened'. Cameron emphasizes that Davis was the first author to document that Harriet lived in Hans Place, that her body was taken to the Fox and Bull, and that the name of the landlord was Phillips.[2] Clearly, Davis diligently collected important original details, and Cameron rightly values his research as a significant contribution to our knowledge of events immediately following Harriet's suicide.

However, what seems to have escaped Cameron's attention is that Davis did not limit himself simply to retailing facts, but also entered, albeit discreetly, into the contentious posthumous Victorian debate regarding Harriet's moral character, and the wider, disquieting issue of who was ultimately to blame for her suicide. To fully appreciate the implications of Davis's account it is important to note his distinctive use of quotation marks when describing how Harriet's recovered body was: 'treated "tenderly" and laid out "with care"'. Initially, this punctuation gives the somewhat misleading impression that Davis is directly citing Miss Phillips, or other eyewitnesses whom he had interviewed. However, Davis was actually quoting from Thomas Hood's popular poem, **'The Bridge of Sighs'**. Those Victorian readers who recognized the quotation would immediately have understood the charged nuances associated with Davis's source, and the attendant negative imputations regarding both Harriet's moral character and the true cause of her suicide.

Hood's poem, published in 1844, was 'enormously popular and influential'.[3] It describes the recovered body of a prostitute who has committed suicide by drowning, and Davis cites the narrator's well-known instructions to onlookers to: 'Take her up tenderly, / Lift her with care / Fashion'd so slenderly / Young, and so fair!' (5-8).[4] This famous quatrain was repeated verbatim by Hood at lines 80-3; it soon became a Victorian catch-phrase, succinctly expressing the prevalent, sentimentalized view that suicide by drowning constituted an act of spiritual and social atonement for 'fallen' women. Indeed, the poem so perfectly captured popular opinion on this issue that Robert Browning declared **'The Bridge of Sighs'** to be 'alone in its generation'.[5] In his biographical study of Hood, Walter Jerrold noted: 'it has been declared that "in all the wide range of the poetry of our own country, and of all other countries, there is nothing more profoundly pathetic" than these lines on the poor suicide, which have taken their place among our familiar quotations'[6]; so familiar, in fact, that Bernard Shaw, in his *Preface* to *Mrs. Warren's Profession,* could even quote the lines sarcastically, without acknowledging their source, confident that they would be instantly recognized. Shaw complained of the de facto censorship involved in the general refusal to discuss the issue of prostitution in Victorian society; particularly by those: 'who are smitten with a sentimental affection for our fallen sister, and would "take her up tenderly, lift her with care, fashioned so slenderly, young, and *so* fair"'.[7]

The imputation behind Davis's citation from Hood's popular poem is clear: Harriet Shelley was a 'fallen' woman whose suicide was the tragic consequence of her immoral behaviour. At the inquest into Harriet's death, held on 11 December 1816, serious efforts were made to throw a veil of discrete silence over potentially scandalous facts. At the time of her death Harriet had been missing for over a week; she had also been living under the pseudonym of 'Smith', and was in an advanced state of pregnancy, out of wedlock. Simultaneously, Percy Bysshe Shelley, still legally her husband, was openly cohabiting with Mary Godwin.[8] Cameron argues that the inquest was a 'hushed-up procedure' which 'bears the marks of outside influence'. The true identity of the deceased was never revealed. Harriet's family, the Westbrooks, who lived locally and were well known, did not come forward to claim the body, and witnesses, who obviously knew the real identity of the deceased, preserved the fiction of her pseudonym, 'Harriet Smith'. No reference to her advanced state of pregnancy was made in the coroner's official report, and no account of the inquest was contained in the newspapers, although 'such inquests were commonly reported'.[9] The official verdict omitted any mention of prostitution or suicide, opting instead for the factually precise and morally neutral finding of 'Found dead in the Serpentine River'.[10] At the time of Harriet's death, serious efforts were obviously made to ensure that her indiscretions, as well as her drowned body, were carefully veiled from close public scrutiny.

In 1859, forty-eight years later, the deafening silence of the coroner's inquest was cleverly nullified by the adroit ambiguity of Davis's narrative strategy which, while apparently reporting eye-witness accounts sympathetically, actually, by the allusion to Hood's poem, impugned Harriet's character through guilt by association with the legion of anonymous London prostitutes who drowned themselves each year. For Davis's readers, the implied parallel between Harriet Shelley, and the nameless drowned prostitute who is the subject of Hood's poem, would have been clearly understood.

Moreover, once the parallel was established, the imputations were no longer solely limited to Harriet. The allusion to Hood's poem also enabled Davis to implicitly raise the wider and equally disquieting issue of the potential culpability of her husband, and her own family, in the sequence of events leading to her tragic suicide. The narrative voice in **'The Bridge of Sighs'** asks a battery of questions regarding the nameless drowned prostitute:

> Who was her father?
> Who was her mother?
> Had she a sister?
> Had she a brother?
> Or was there a dearer one
> Still, and a nearer one
> Yet, than all other?
>
> 　　　　　　　　　　　　(36-42)[11]

The answer to such questions, at least from Percy Bysshe Shelley's somewhat biased perspective, were contained in a letter he wrote to Mary Godwin, dated 16 December 1816, just five days after the coroner's inquest. He declared:

> It seems that this poor woman—the most innocent of her abhorred & unnatural family—was driven from her father's house, & descended the steps of prostitution until she lived with a groom of the name of Smith, who deserting her, she killed herself—There can be no question that the beastly viper her sister, unable to gain profit from her connection with me—has secured to herself the fortune of the old man—who is now dying—by the murder of this poor creature.[12]

The views expressed in this private letter may be seen as an attempt by Shelley to eschew personal blame, or to protect Mary, as the 'other woman', from any sense of guilt regarding Harriet's suicide; certainly, they were never intended for public scrutiny. However, as the nineteenth century unfolded, Shelley's growing posthumous reputation inevitably led to increasing public interest in the somewhat sensational details of his private life; consequently, the apparent failure of those closest to Harriet to care for her during a time of personal crisis became the subject of much partisan debate and accusation. Depending on the leanings of different nineteenth-century Shelley biographers, Harriet's father, John Westbrook, her older and dominating sister, Eliza, or her philandering husband, Percy Bysshe Shelley, were variously depicted as morally responsible either for provoking, or failing to prevent her suicide.[13]

By citing the well-known lines from Thomas Hood's **'The Bridge of Sighs'** in connection with Harriet Shelley's death, Davis creatively exploited literary allusion to discreetly imply that she had resorted to prostitution,

and also to question why, seemingly, those closest to her had not come to her aid. Davis's remarks regarding Harriet are of particular interest since they were not made within the context of a discussion of Shelley's life, but as a passing aside in a local history of Knightsbridge, where Davis lived his entire life. As such, his comments provide valuable insight into the sentiments of local residents regarding the tragic events surrounding Harriet's death. Furthermore, the fact that he chose not to comment openly on Harriet's apparent recourse to prostitution, but instead to employ a strategy of oblique imputation through citation from Hood's well-known poem, necessarily reflects his perception, as a Victorian writer, of the limited possibilities for public discourse on such an inherently controversial subject. As a meticulous historian, Davis seems ultimately to have chosen the route of compromise; discreetly hinting at the truth, but leaving readers to decide for themselves whether Harriet's posthumous reputation, like her 'poor frame', should be treated 'tenderly' and 'with care'.

Notes

1. Kenneth Neill Cameron, *Shelley and His Circle, 1773-1822,* vol. IV (Cambridge, MA: Harvard University Press, 1970), 779.

2. Cameron, 779.

3. Barbara T. Gates, *Victorian Suicide: Mad Crimes and Sad Histories* (Princeton University Press, 1988), 135.

4. *Selected Poems of Thomas Hood,* ed. John Clubbe (Cambridge, MA: Harvard University Press, 1970), 317-20. All citations are from this edition.

5. Cited in Walter Jerrold, *Thomas Hood: His Life and Times* (London: Alston Rivers, 1907), 379.

6. Jerrold, 379.

7. *Bernard Shaw: Complete Plays With Prefaces,* vol. III (New York: Dodd, Mead & Co., 1963), 6.

8. Details abstracted from Cameron, 769-801.

9. Cameron, 782 and 797.

10. Cameron, 778.

11. Harriet had no brother. Her mother, Mrs Westbrook, was 'apparently quite ineffective' and 'seems to have played no active role in the household' (Cameron, 795).

12. Cited in Cameron, 785-6.

13. For information regarding the politics driving biographies of Shelley in the nineteenth century, and the various positions which they took regarding the death of Harriet, see the Introduction, and notes to: *Lives of the Great Romantics By Their Contemporaries,* vol. I, *Shelley,* ed. John Mullan

(London: William Pickering, 1996), and Valeria Tinkler-Villani, 'Victorian Shelley: Perspectives on a Romantic Poet', *Configuring Romanticism: Essays Offered to C. C. Barfoot,* ed. Theo D'haen *et al.,* (Amsterdam: Rodopi, 2003), 89-104.

FURTHER READING

Biography

Bennett, Hannaford. "Biographical Introduction." In *Humorous Poems,* pp. 7-13. London: John Long, 1907.

  Brief overview of Hood's life and writing career.

Criticism

Brander, Laurence. "Thomas Hood." In *Thomas Hood,* pp. 7-44. London: Longmans, Green, 1963.

  Discusses the various phases of Hood's development as a writer, contending that his most memorable poems were those devoted to the social and economic injustices associated with industrialization.

Clubbe, John. Introduction to *Selected Poems of Thomas Hood,* pp. 1-31. Cambridge, Mass.: Harvard University Press, 1970.

  Suggests that Hood's poetry was misunderstood—both in his own time and in the years since—and insists that Hood was far more versatile than has been commonly assumed.

Edgecombe, Rodney Stenning. "Martin Chuzzlewit and Hood's 'Dream of Eugene Aram.'" *Dickensian* 99, Part 2, no. 460 (summer 2003): 153-55.

  Considers Hood's poem as a possible inspiration for the character of Jonas Chuzzlewit in Dickens's novel.

Henkle, Roger B. "Comedy as Commodity: Thomas Hood's Poetry of Class Desire." *Victorian Poetry* 26, no. 3 (autumn 1988): 301-18.

  Suggests that Hood's poetry—particularly the comic verse filled with puns and given to grotesque imagery—has gone out of fashion; however, the critic claims that Hood remains an important figure in literary history as a voice of the impoverished working class.

Lodge, Sara. "Hood, Clare, and the 'Mary' Chain." *Notes & Queries* 45, no. 2 (June 1998): 205-08.

  Considers Hood's "A Lay of Real Life" as a response to John Clare's "My Mary."

Morgan, Peter. "John Hamilton Reynolds and Thomas Hood." *Keats-Shelley Journal* 11 (winter 1962): 83-95.

  Discusses the friendship and professional relationship of Hood and Reynolds

Reeves, James. "Thomas Hood (1799-1845)." In *Five Late Romantic Poets,* edited by James Reeves, pp. 146-50. London: Heinemann, 1974.

  Provides a brief description of Hood's life and career as a poet, contending that Hood's poetry suffers in comparison to the Romantic poets of the earlier generation.

Thorogood, Peter. "Thomas Hood: A Nineteenth-Century Author and his Relations with the Book Trade to 1835." In *Development of the English Book Trade, 1700-1899,* edited by Robin Myers and Michael Harris, pp. 106-72. Oxford, England: Oxford Polytechnic Press, 1981.

  Examines the publication history of Hood's poems and his relationships with magazine editors and publishing houses.

Wolfson, Susan J. "Representing Some Late Romantic-Era, Non-Canonical Male Poets: Thomas Hood, Winthrop Mackworth Praed, Thomas Lovell Beddoes." *Romanticism on the Net* 19 (August 2000): http://users.ox.ac.uk/~scat0385/19hood.html.

  Contends that Hood's "relentlessly inventive punning" often dealt with the frailties of the human body and the misery associated with poverty.

Additional coverage of Hood's life and career is contained in the following sources published by Gale: *British Writers,* **Vol. 4;** *Dictionary of Literary Biography,* **Vol. 96;** *Literature Resource Center;* *Nineteenth-Century Literature Criticism,* **Vol. 16; and** *Reference Guide to English Literature,* **Ed. 2.**

X. J. Kennedy
1929-

(Pseudonym of Joseph Charles Kennedy) American poet, editor, translator, and anthologist.

INTRODUCTION

An award-winning author of numerous volumes of poetry and children's verse, Kennedy adheres to traditional principles of rhyme and meter, and is best known for light, unpretentious verse and a satiric, self-deprecating poetic persona.

BIOGRAPHICAL INFORMATION

Kennedy was born August 21, 1929, in Dover, New Jersey, to Joseph Francis and Agnes Kennedy. Kennedy has described his Depression Era upbringing as "working-class, white-collar proletarian." He graduated Phi Beta Kappa from Seton Hall College with a B.Sc. in 1950, and earned a Master's degree from Columbia University in 1951. While serving the next four years in the U.S. Navy as a journalist, Kennedy adopted the pseudonym X. J., primarily to distinguish himself from Joseph Kennedy, then United States Ambassador to England and father of the future president, John F. Kennedy. After his discharge, he studied for two years at the Sorbonne, his enrollment funded through the G.I. Bill. From 1956-62, Kennedy studied and worked as a teaching fellow at the University of Michigan in Ann Arbor where he became associated with a circle of poets that included W. D. Snodgrass, Donald Hall, and John Heath-Stubbs. It was also in Ann Arbor that Kennedy met fellow poet Dorothy Mintzlaff, who became his wife in 1962. The Kennedys have five children—Kathleen Anna, David Ian, Matthew Devin, Daniel Joseph, and Joshua Quentin—and six grandchildren.

Kennedy left the University of Michigan without completing his doctorate in 1962. After teaching for a year at the University of North Carolina, he secured a position at Tufts University that he would hold until 1979. That year, he decided to leave his tenured position at Tufts to become a full-time writer. He has served as visiting professor at Wellesley College, the University of California, Irvine, and the University of Leeds. In addition he and his wife founded and co-edited *Counter/Measures,* a journal devoted to the principles of formalist poetry; Kennedy also served as Poetry Editor of the *Paris Review.*

Kennedy began producing poetry during his time in the Navy, where his official workload was light and he had plenty of time to devote to writing. With his characteristic self-deprecating humility, Kennedy claimed that his early verse, as well as the daily newspaper he produced aboard ship, were well received by the members of the crew simply because the men were so starved for entertainment. He began selling his poetry near the end of his stint in the service, with an initial contribution of two poems to the *New Yorker.* He received further encouragement from the members of the expatriate community of writers and editors in Paris during the time he spent at the Sorbonne. In 1961, his first published book of poetry, *Nude Descending a Staircase,* won the prestigious Lamont Award of the Academy of American Poets.

In addition, Kennedy's poetry has received such notable awards as the University of Michigan's Avery Hopwood Award (1959); a grant from the National Council on the Arts and Humanities (1967-68); a Guggenheim fellowship (1973); and the *Los Angeles Times* book award for poetry (1985) for *Cross Ties: Selected Poems.* Kennedy's children's poetry has been similarly honored by a number of organizations and publications, among them the National Council for Teachers of English, the *New York Times Book Review,* the New York Public Library, the American Library Association, and *Hornbook* magazine. Kennedy has earned honorary degrees from Lawrence University, Adelphi University, and Westfield State College, and has served as original judge of the Texas Review Press poetry prize that bears his name. He is a member of the Poetry Society of America, the Modern Language Association, the National Council of Teachers of English, PEN, the Authors Guild, the John Barton Wolgamot Society, and Phi Beta Kappa. He and his wife currently reside in Lexington, Massachusetts.

MAJOR WORKS

Kennedy's first volume of poetry was the award-winning *Nude Descending a Staircase,* which appeared in 1961; it remains one of his most celebrated books. It consists primarily of poems that are humorous, although Kennedy himself prefers to classify them as witty. There are exceptions, however, such as "At the Stoplight by the Paupers' Grave" and "Little Elegy," each featuring a serious tone and subject matter. His next collection, published eight years later, was *Growing into Love,* featuring poems that are remarkably similar, both thematically and stylistically, to those of his first volume. In 1970, Kennedy turned to more strident satirical poems with the publication of *Bulsh,* whose title character is an anti-Christ figure and whose target is traditional Christian dogma. The poems of the first three volumes, along with seven previously unpublished pieces, comprise *Breaking and Entering,* which appeared in 1971. Three years later, Kennedy produced *Emily Dickinson in Southern California,* consisting of poems written in Dickinson's style, and *Celebrations after the Death of John Brennan,* a long poem far more serious than much of Kennedy's previous work, dedicated to the memory of a former student who had committed suicide. *Cross Ties: Selected Poems,* published in 1985, contains much of Kennedy's earlier work along with twenty-eight new poems. The poems collected here run the gamut from serious poetry to light verse and poems for children. His most recent collections include *The Lords of Misrule, Poems 1992-2001* (2002) and *In a Prominent Bar in Secaucus: New and Selected Poems, 1955-2007* (2007). Kennedy also selected and translated the twelve poems in *French Leave: Translations* (1983), many of which are connected by themes of anger and cynicism.

In addition to his adult poetry, Kennedy is also a prolific writer of children's verse and children's novels. His best-known poetry books for children include: *One Winter Night in August and Other Nonsense Jingles* (1975); *Did Adam Name the Vinegarroon?* (1982); *Brats* (1986); *Fresh Brats* (1990); *The Kite That Braved Old Orchard Beach: Year-Round Poems for Young People* (1991); and *Drat These Brats!* (1993). Kennedy has also published a number of college-level textbooks that have been widely used, among them *An Introduction to Poetry* (1966); *Literature: An Introduction to Fiction, Poetry, and Drama* (1976); and *The Bedford Reader* (1982), which he co-edited with his wife.

CRITICAL RECEPTION

Kennedy is often dismissed as a purveyor of light verse rather than a serious poet. Poems such as "B Negative" and "Epitaph for a Postal Clerk" are offered as evidence of Kennedy's commitment to entertaining readers with his playful tone and fanciful subject matter. Bernard E. Morris surveys the critical response to every volume of Kennedy's poetry from *Nude Descending a Staircase* to *The Lords of Misrule* and finds that many critics acknowledge Kennedy's "quick and clever wit" but are unimpressed with his work as a whole, considering it superficial and whimsical. Even—or perhaps especially—when the poems deal with weighty issues, they are often denigrated because such elaborate and

sophisticated wordplay seems to be employed in a manner that insufficiently respects the despair inherent in the situations described. One critic contends that the serious subject matter of "Solitary Confinement" was handled with "facetiousness" and the effect was to leave the reader "ill at ease." Another, commenting on "Little Elegy," complains of "woefully inadequate language" resulting in "a stultifying cuteness." Kennedy himself acknowledges to some extent the accuracy of the charges but challenges the dichotomy between serious poetry and light verse, claiming that they are not mutually exclusive; he believes that it is possible to produce something between "so-called light verse and so-called heavy poetry."

Many critics concur with Kennedy's assertion and believe that the poet has produced poems that successfully reside in the "country in between" the light and the serious. R. S. Gwynn (see Further Reading), in his review of *The Lords of Misrule,* contends that the volume "contains poems that successfully inhabit the narrow ledge halfway down from the frosty summit of Arnoldian high seriousness and halfway up from the balmy veil of outright light verse." Michael J. Collins notes that "the deft balance of the serious and the playful and the skillful use of rhyme and meter are the distinct and consistent qualities of Kennedy's best poems." According to Morris, the poem "Ars Poetica" "encapsulates Kennedy's acerbic wit and epitomizes his gift for combining serious and playful expression to the advantage of each." He claims that throughout Kennedy's career, he has produced works whose tone is "irreverent, impatient with authority yet obedient to it, wayward, recalcitrant, witty, playful, yet profoundly serious."

Kennedy's subject matter is very often serious. The poems of the first two sections of *Growing into Love,* according to Morris, "offer images of a modern American landscape blighted by industrialism or tourism" inhabited by "unheroic people trapped by materialism and greed." Collins maintains that "the world [Kennedy] characteristically writes about is the ordered, diminished, undifferentiated urban world in which most Americans these days make their home and live out lives of quiet desperation." The long poem *Celebrations after the Death of John Brennan* is especially somber, dealing as it does with the suicide of a former student, and critics generally agree that Kennedy handles the material with the seriousness and respect it deserves.

Many critics comment on Kennedy's fairly strict observance of traditional forms of rhyme and meter, which often set him in opposition to the trend of contemporary American poetry. Morris reports that "because of his persistent use of rhyme, meter, and stanzaic regularity, Kennedy was regarded by many critics as an anachronism and was set upon by those who took offense at his use of traditional forms." Indeed, such terms as iconoclastic, archaic, and unfashionable have often been used when referring to Kennedy's poetic output by those who believe that open form is more appropriate for modern times. Some critics, however, find that the discipline of traditional forms led Kennedy to produce poems characterized by order and unity and Kennedy himself claims that he likes the challenge of conforming to the contraints of traditional forms.

In the end, Kennedy's literary legacy may be determined more by his work as a textbook author and as a successful writer of children's books than by his production of poetry for adults. Although some of his children's verse has been described as "dark," for the most part, it is humorous—but lightheartedness and playfulness are terms not typically used pejoratively by critics when referring to verses written for children.

PRINCIPAL WORKS

Poetry

Nude Descending a Staircase: Poems, Songs, A Ballad 1961

Growing Into Love 1969

Bulsh 1970

Breaking and Entering 1971

Celebrations after the Death of John Brennan 1974

Emily Dickinson in Southern California 1974

One Winter Night in August and Other Nonsense Jingles 1975

Three Tenors, One Vehicle [with James Camp and Keith Waldrop] 1975

The Phantom Ice Cream Man: More Nonsense Verse 1979

Did Adam Name the Vinegarroon? 1982

French Leave: Translations [translator and compiler] 1983

Missing Link 1983

Hangover Mass 1984

Cross Ties: Selected Poems 1985

Brats 1986

Fresh Brats 1990

Winter Thunder 1990

The Kite That Braved Old Orchard Beach: Year-Round Poems for Young People 1991

Dark Horses: New Poems 1992

Drat These Brats! 1993

Jimmy Harlow 1994

Elympics 1999

Elefantina's Dream 2002

The Lords of Misrule: Poems, 1992-2001 2002

In a Prominent Bar in Secaucus: New and Selected Poems, 1955-2007 2007

Other Major Works

An Introduction to Poetry (textbook) 1966

Pegasus Descending: A Book of the Best Bad Verse [editor, with James Camp and Keith Waldrop] (anthology) 1971

Literature: An Introduction to Fiction, Poetry, and Drama (textbook) 1976

Tygers of Wrath: Poems of Hate, Anger and Invective [editor] (anthology) 1981

The Bedford Reader [editor, with Dorothy M. Kennedy] (anthology) 1982

Knock at a Star: A Child's Introduction to Poetry [compiler, with Dorothy M. Kennedy] (anthology) 1982

Talking Like the Rain: A Read-to Me Book of Poems [compiler, with Dorothy M. Kennedy] (anthology) 1992

Knee-Deep in Blazing Snow: Growing up in Vermont [compiler, with Dorothy M. Kennedy] (anthology) 2005

CRITICISM

Michael J. Collins (essay date winter 1987)

SOURCE: Collins, Michael J. "The Poetry of X. J. Kennedy." *World Literature Today* 61, no. 1 (winter 1987): 55-58.

[*In the following essay, Collins provides a general overview of Kennedy's poetry, focusing on several individual poems from different stages of Kennedy's career. Collins describes the tone of many of Kennedy's best poems as simultaneously playful and serious, and offers several examples of the poet's technical skill.*]

X. J. Kennedy, who was born Joseph Charles Kennedy in Dover, New Jersey on 21 August 1929, published his first volume of poetry, **Nude Descending a Staircase**, in 1961. After more than twenty years it remains, in at least two important ways, a distinct, highly individual collection. Like most of Kennedy's subsequent work, the poems are written in rhyme and meter and for the most part stand delicately balanced between the serious and the playful. As Dennis Lynch put it in a brief commentary on Kennedy's poetry, "**Nude Descending a Staircase** remains one of the most remarkable first volumes of poetry written by a 20th-century author."[1]

"**Little Elegy,**" "for a child who skipped rope," one of the best poems in the volume, suggests the strengths, if not the diversity, of the entire collection.

> Here lies resting, out of breath,
> Out of turns, Elizabeth
> Whose quicksilver toes not quite
> Cleared the whirring edge of night.
>
> Earth whose circles round us skim
> Till they catch the lightest limb,
> Shelter now Elizabeth
> And for her sake trip up Death.[2]

While the double or triple puns ("resting," "out of breath," "out of turns") bring a playful tone to the first two lines, they also evoke an image of the little girl at play, and together tone and image make the next two lines, with their recollection (in "quicksilver toes") of the little girl's lovely vitality, profoundly sad. At the same time, the falling rhythms of the entire poem (with three and a half trochaic feet in each line) gently reinforce the tone of sadness. The use of *quite* to rhyme with *night* and the stress the rhythm puts on the word both intensify the irony, the absurdity of the child's death.

In the second stanza, with a traditional elegiac turn, the poem widens its vision to those who live within earth's whirling circles of night and day. While "lightest limb" suggests (in part through alliteration) the loveliness of the living child, it also recalls our own fragile hold on life. The poem here playfully imagines each of us skipping, like Elizabeth, over the diurnal circles of the earth. The last two lines, a prayer for Elizabeth and for all the living, in part through the final rhythmic shift to three consecutive stressed syllables, end the poem with a sad, almost bitter repudiation of death in a lovely, fragile world.

"**Little Elegy,**" which Kennedy put "through a couple of dozen re-writes,"[3] is a beautiful, effective, carefully written poem, and it represents, in little, X. J. Kennedy at the top of his craft. The skillful rhythmic movements, the rhyme, the deft balance of the serious and playful all combine to make "**Little Elegy**" a moving and memorable poem that contains, to use T. S. Eliot's words, "an alliance of levity and seriousness . . . by which the seriousness is intensified."[4]

During a reading of his poetry at Fordham University on 28 November 1978, Kennedy rejected the attempt of criticism to make a clear distinction between light and serious verse: "I confess . . . I'm not too sure what the difference is between so-called light verse and so-called heavy poetry, and it seems to me there's a country in between. Some of my favorite poems inhabit that country in between—Marvell's 'To His Coy Mistress' or some of Yeats's ballads. Are they serious or are they light? I think it's hard to tell." "**Little Elegy**" too inhabits the "country in between," and much of its success is a result of its peculiar geography.

The deft balance of the serious and the playful and the skillful use of rhyme and meter are the distinct and consistent qualities of Kennedy's best poems. One of the most recent, "**To Dorothy on Her Exclusion from the *Guinness Book of World Records*,**" is a love sonnet whose playful tropes suggest an easy intimacy between the speaker and the woman and provide an effective context for the simple, unadorned compliment that ends the poem.

> Not being Breedlove, whose immortal skid
> Bore him for six charmed miles on screeching brakes;
> Not having whacked from Mieres to Madrid
> The longest-running hoop; at ducks and drakes
> The type whose stone drowns in a couple of ships
> Even if pittypats be counted plinkers;
> Smashing of face, but having launched no ships;
> Not of a kidney with beer's foremost drinkers;
>
> Fewer the namesakes that display your brand
> Than Prout has little protons—yet you win
> The world with just a peerless laugh. I stand
> Stricken amazed: you merely settle chin
> Into a casual fixture of your hand
> And a uniqueness is, that hasn't been.

After the first two examples, which seem among the silliest in the *Guinness Book of World Records,* create a playful tone, the octave becomes more personal: the speaker's teasing of the woman about her failures at skimming stones and drinking beer suggest some of the small, domestic joys they have shared. The first two lines of the sestet continue momentarily the tone and rhythm of the octave; but then the poem sounds suddenly serious as the meter gives way to the irregular rhythms of colloquial speech ("yet you win / The world with just a peerless laugh"), and the lines break out of the familiar sonnet form to celebrate, in unconventional rhythms, the unique loveliness of the woman. As the poem moves toward its close, the irregular rhythms continue to the middle of the last line. Then, with the long pause after "is," the poem returns to the familiar iambic meter, which, with the assonance (of "is" and "been") and the audible closing rhyme, makes the last line a deft and elegant compliment to the lady and, through its distinct harmonies, affirms her loveliness. "**To Dorothy**" is one of Kennedy's best poems, again largely as a result of his careful balance of the playful and the serious and his skillful use of rhyme and meter.

The playfulness that marks so much of Kennedy's work is as evident in his choice of subject as in the characteristic tone of his poetry. He has written poems (e.g., "**In a Prominent Bar in Secaucus One Day**") to be sung to the tunes of popular songs, and he has published two books of comic poems for children: *One Winter Night* *in August* (1975) and *The Phantom Ice Cream Man* (1979). One of his latest poems, **"The Death of Professor Backwards,"** is an elegy for James Edmondson, who, as Professor Backwards, made a nightclub act of his ability to say things backwards.

> Three hot-eyed kids hard on a fix's heels,
> Enraged at the cash he had, few bills and small,
> Did in James Edmondson, famed vaudeville's
> Professor Backwards. Three slugs through the skull
> Closed his great act: the Gettysburg Address
> About he'd switch and back-to-front deliver.
> Transposed perfectly them at back hurl he'd
> Out called crowd the in hecklers any whatever.
>
> More than clashed glass in Vegas clubs fell still
> That night his heart backpaddled to a stop:
> Unheard lay songs that once with dazzling skill
> His brainpan's funhouse mirror used to flop.
> A listening Sennett, applause his to command,
> Why had it to be him, so lean of purse,
> Felled like a dog in an alley when his blind
> Fate shot back like a truck parked in reverse
> To hurl him backwards, trailing gory clouds?
>
> The world will little note and long forget
> How any watcher in whole spellbound crowds
> Would light the wrong end of a cigarette.

While Kennedy plays with metaphors of reversal and comically transposes words, phrases, and (at the end of the first stanza) whole lines, the poem is finally an effective elegy for its murdered subject. The last stanza, which first alters some familiar words from the Gettysburg Address, becomes, through the gentle rhyme and falling rhythm with which it ends, a playfully appropriate tribute to Professor Backwards that quietly and movingly celebrates his idiosyncratic achievements and makes clear the elegy's traditional affirmation of life in the presence of sorrow and death. If the talents of Professor Backwards are finally small and even absurd, he nonetheless brought them to a kind of perfection all too rare in this fallen world.

The poem on Professor Backwards recalls one that had appeared a few years earlier in *Breaking and Entering.* Balanced deftly between the serious and the playful, the poem, **"Consumer's Report,"** celebrates the bizarre integrity of John Dowd, who sold horseradish "made from cream and home-ground roots."

> At meat, or hearing you deplore
>   How fast things break, my mind salutes
> John Dowd, who'd bring by rolling store
> Horse radish to our kitchen door
>   He'd make from cream and home-ground roots.
>
> My God. The heat of it would burn
>   Holes through your beef and knock your tongue
>   out.
> Once, for a snowsuit I'd outgrown,
> Came so much free stuff in return
>   It smoldered down and ended flung out.

> Why did he sport that look of pain
>   Strangely, although his trade kept thriving?
> They say the fumes get to your brain.
> One day he came round with a cane
>   And someone else to do the driving,
>
> But ground right on with open eyes
>   And, grinding, stared straight at his killer.
> I bet theirs takes them by surprise
> Though they can see, today-type guys,
>   The guys who use white turnip filler.

The bounding regularity of the tetrameter lines and the insistent rhymes (particularly "tongue out" and "flung out") of the first three stanzas help create an essentially comic tone. In the last stanza, however, the stressed syllables side by side in the first two lines slow the poem down and give "stared straight at his killer" an unexpectedly serious connotation. The perverse integrity of John Dowd, affirmed by the emphatic rhythms of the second line, becomes the norm against which we see the compromises of the other horseradish makers. The heavier stress on the words of the sequence "white turnip filler" in the last lines closes the poem with a tone of quiet contempt that, through the rhythm, evokes assent. Although the poem at first seems something of a humorous parody of small-town American values, the rhythmic shifts in the last stanza unexpectedly broaden its vision and persuade us to take its conclusion seriously. John Dowd the horseradish maker seems, like Professor Backwards, worthy of celebration, because in the shoddy, temporizing world that is modern America, he is true to his craft and does well the job he has to do.

These two poems, on Professor Backwards and John Dowd, deftly poised between the serious and the playful, celebrating the bizarre achievements of two essentially comic figures, suggest one of the persistent themes of X. J. Kennedy's poetry. Kennedy is a poet of contemporary middle-class America. The world he characteristically writes about is the ordered, diminished, undifferentiated urban world in which most Americans these days make their home and live out lives of quiet desperation. If he celebrates Professor Backwards and John Dowd in his poetry, it is because each has, in a different way, distinguished himself from the mass of men who will never hold whole crowds spellbound or stare straight at their killers with open eyes. In Kennedy's world of dull conformity and dreary mediocrity, idiosyncratic achievement is honored.

In a well-known essay he wrote in 1961, "Who Killed King Kong?," Kennedy tried to account for the enduring popularity in America of a B-grade movie about a great ape made in 1933. After suggesting that part of King Kong's appeal was the impulse "in the heart of urban man . . . to fling a bomb . . . to see the downtown express smack head-on into the uptown local,"[5] he concluded the essay with these words:

> Everyday in the week on a screen somewhere in the world, King Kong relives his agony. Again and again he expires on the Empire State Building, as audiences of the devout assist his sacrifice. We watch him die, and by extension kill the ape within our bones, but these little deaths of ours occur in prosaic surroundings. We do not die on a tower, New York before our feet, nor do we give our lives to smash a few flying machines. It is not for us to bring a momentary standstill to the civilization in which we move. King Kong does this for us. And so we kill him again and again, in much-spliced celluloid, while the ape in us expires from day to day, obscure in desperation.
>
> (1052)

In the ordered, urban world of our own time, we need King Kong to release us momentarily from the dull conformity that hides individual desperation.

In one of his best-known poems, the sonnet **"Nothing in Heaven Functions As It Ought,"** Kennedy's characteristic fusion of the serious and playful and his witty use of rhythm and rhyme combine to produce a superb comic indictment of the efficient, corporate conformity that marks the modern world.

> Nothing in Heaven functions as it ought:
> Peter's bifocals, blindly sat on, crack;
> His gates lurch wide with the cackle of a cock,
> Not turn with a hush of gold as Milton had thought;
> Gangs of the slaughtered innocents keep huffing
> The nimbus off the Venerable Bede
> Like that of an old dandelion gone to seed;
> And the beatific choir keep breaking up, coughing.
>
> But Hell, sleek Hell hath no freewheeling part:
> None takes his own sweet time, none quickens pace.
> Ask anyone, *How come you here, poor heart?*—
> And he will slot a quarter through his face,
> You'll hear an instant click, a tear will start
> Imprinted with an abstract of his case.

The broken rhythms, the half rhymes, the cacophony of the octave give way in the sestet to full rhymes, harmonious sounds, and a perfect iambic meter. The sonnet is a skillfully written satire of a society that, to take only one example, mindlessly extols the impersonal, mechanistic efficiency that computers of the future will make possible. The vision of Hell in the sestet recalls Kennedy's description of the world of urban man in "Who Killed King Kong?": "Machines speed him to the scene of his daily grind. . . . IBM comptometers ('freeing the human mind from drudgery') enable him to drudge more efficiently once he arrives" (1050-51). The same theme appears in different terms in **"Sex Manual,"** one of the many epigrams Kennedy has written over the years: "By the cold glow that lit my lover's eye / I could read what page eight had said to try."

Diminished lives in the bland, urban world of contemporary America appear in some of Kennedy's best poems. One of the earliest, **"Solitary Confinement,"** looks at a dull and monotonous marriage from the wife's point of view.

> She might have stolen from his arms
> Except that there was nothing left
> To steal. There was the crucifix
> Of silver good enough to hock
> But how far could she go on it
> And what had he left her to pack
> And steal away with and lay down
> By someone new in a new town?
>
> She put the notion back
> And turned her look up where the clock,
> Green ghost, swept round its tethered hand
> That had made off with many nights
> But no more could break from its shelf
> Than she could quit this bed where breath
> By breath these years he'd nailed her fast
> Between two thieves, him and herself.

Except for the pun on *stolen* and *steal* in the opening lines, the poem has little of Kennedy's characteristic playfulness, and it achieves much of its success through its apparently direct and simple language. The metric regularity, which suggests both the ticking of the clock and the unbroken monotony of the woman's life, continues almost to the end of the poem. In the last line, however, the pause and the rhythmic shift (in "him and herself") slow the poem down and underscore the irony of its closing words. The crucifix, which at first recalls their wedding, becomes, by the end of the poem, an image of the woman's married life which she herself helped to shape.

More recently, in a poem very different in tone and manner, **"At the Last Rites for Two Hotrodders,"** Kennedy satirizes, in comic allegory, one of America's fundamental values.

> Sheeted in steel, embedded face to face,
> They idle now in feelingless embrace,
> The only ones at last who had the nerve
> To meet head-on, not chicken out and swerve.
>
> Inseparable, in one closed car they roll
> Down the stoned aisle and on out to a hole,
> Wheeled by the losers: six of fledgling beard,
> Black-jacketed and glum, who also steered
> Toward absolute success with total pride,
> But, inches from it, felt, and turned aside.

Written, ironically, in heroic couplets, the poem describes the ludicrous funeral of two hotrodders fused and killed in a head-on collision neither would chicken out to avoid. In the last two lines, however, the vision of the poem widens, and the two hotrodders come to represent all who are dehumanized and destroyed by their single-minded pursuit of success. The last line, with its two distinct pauses, slows the poem down and brings it to a thoughtful, gently sad conclusion which suggests the price that success-ridden Americans pay to live their lives in what is often called, without a bit of irony, "the fast lane."

One of Kennedy's most ambitious poems, **"Golgotha,"** from a sequence called **"West Somerville, Mass.,"** sets the ordered, suburban world of the speaker, a teacher of writing in some New England college, against the chaos of war in Vietnam. It begins by describing a construction site on campus: once the dormitory is completed, the "cleared" hill will be restored, the brick sprayed to fit unobtrusively with the older buildings on campus, and the land planted and landscaped. Even in winter, man's orderly, efficient work goes forward to provide housing for a new generation of students. In the second stanza, set in the speaker's basement workroom where he is trying to read his students' papers, more good work is being done. The hearth, the bed sheets in the dryer, the old edition of Keats place the speaker in a settled, civilized community.

One of the papers, however, evokes images of war. Suddenly, the torn-up hill on campus and the defoliation of the jungle are joined as destruction in the apparent service of good. While the dormitory nears completion, the students who would live in it are drafted for service in Vietnam. The sprayed bricks and the repaired landscape seem now just a façade to affirm that all is well, to hide the evil that blights the apparently civilized world. The speaker's tired comment on one of his papers, "Interesting idea," seems itself an evasion, a façade, a pretense, like the environment in which he lives and works, that chaos and evil have been overcome, that rational discourse can be conducted in a civilized world. While the child's stuffed lion, rattling in the dryer, may sound like shots, it recalls again the disparity, in this ordered American suburb, between what seems and what is.

In the final stanza, the speaker leaves reading papers to take out trash in the rain.

> I take out trash, not to read more—
> Torn gift wraps, Christmas-tree rain—
> Lift can-cover on a white horde
> Writhing. Lean rain
> Blown to bits by the murderous wind
> Has it in for you, finger and face,
> Drives through every hole to your brain,
> Taking over the place
> As though it had been here before,
> Had come back in its own hour,
> Snow gaining ground in the dark yard,
> The mad in absolute power.

The torn Christmas wrapping, another reminder of the disparity between the appearance of suburban Mas-

sachusetts and the reality of Southeast Asia, suggests also the failure of the Christian world to bring about the peace and goodwill it celebrates and prays for at Christmas. The last lines, which in a frantic crescendo move the poem to its close, see the savage rain and accumulating snow as images of the destructive chaos that is once again engulfing the world. While a façade of civilized order is still maintained by the college with its new lawn and dormitory, by the community, and, to some extent, by the troubled speaker with his Keats and his papers to grade, our fragile hold on that order is now inescapably clear, for madness holds "absolute power." Although **"Golgotha"** refers to a specific moment in American history, it transcends the particulars of time and place and suggests even now the continuing gulf between America's bright appearance and its dark realities, between the civility of the suburbs and the chaos of the inner city, between affluent success and quiet desperation.

"Golgotha" seems to me one of Kennedy's most accomplished poems, largely because in it he brings his considerable skills as a poet to a complex and compelling meditation on significant human experience. Although the poem seems remarkably direct—a simple, unadorned narrative—its four stanzas, skillfully linked and intricately reflexive, offer a rich and resonant vision of contemporary America. As **"Golgotha"** suggests, X. J. Kennedy is a distinguished, highly individual poet whose work reflects and comments with rare insight on the settled urban world in which most Americans these days make their homes.

Notes

1. *Contemporary Poets,* 2d ed., James Vinson, ed., London, St. James, 1975, p. 829.

2. X. J. Kennedy, *Cross Ties: Selected Poems,* Athens, Ga., University of Georgia Press, 1985; for a review, see *WLT* [*World Literature Today*] 60:3 (Summer 1986), p. 473. All citations of Kennedy's poetry are taken from this edition.

3. Kennedy made this statement during his reading at Fordham University on 28 November 1978.

4. T. S. Eliot, "Andrew Marvell," in his *Selected Essays,* new ed., New York, Harcourt, Brace, 1950, p. 255.

5. X. J. Kennedy, "Who Killed King Kong?," *Dissent,* Spring 1960; reprinted in Arthur M. Eastman et al., *The Norton Reader,* 6th ed., New York, Norton, 1983, pp. 1050-51. Subsequent citations are indicated by page numbers of the Norton volume.

Daniel L. Darigan (essay date January 2001)

SOURCE: Darigan, Daniel L. "NCTE Poetry Award Recipient X. J. Kennedy." *Language Arts* 78, no. 3 (January 2001): 295-99.

[*In the following essay, Darigan presents an overview of Kennedy's life and works, touching on Kennedy's anthologies, textbooks, and children's verse in addition to his adult poetry.*]

Throughout his long and illustrious career, poet and author X. J. Kennedy has cut a wide literary swath. He has informed tens of thousands of college students about poetry and literature in his many editions of *An Introduction to Poetry* (1997, in its 9th edition), *Literature: An Introduction to Fiction, Poetry, and Drama* (1998), and his *Bedford Reader* (1999), all academic texts. His adult poetry, which includes **Nude Descending a Staircase: Poems, Songs, Ballad** (1995) and **Dark Horses: New Poems** (1992), has won many national awards including a Guggenheim fellowship. His anthologies of poetry for children and his own volumes of original poems range from realistic to nonsensical and are tempered in between by his hilarious **Brats** series that portrays mischievous children in many a domestic squabble. It is for the latter, his great contribution to children's poetry, that the NCTE Selection Committee has honored him with the prestigious National Council of Teachers of English Award for Poetry for Children. This award, presented once every three years, is bestowed on a given poet for his or her distinguished body of work sustained over a period of years (Cullinan, 1996, p. ix). I was able to interview X. J. Kennedy in June of 2000.

X. J. Kennedy, born Joseph Charles Kennedy, decided to use that pen name at the end of his hitch in the United States Navy. After being chided for his seeming relationship with the then U.S. Ambassador to England, Joseph Kennedy—also father to the future president John F. Kennedy and brothers Robert and Ted—he decided that adding an X to his name was far more to his liking. X. J. Kennedy, poet, sounded best.

Born in Dover, New Jersey, just before the stock market crash of 1929, Kennedy was raised in a nurturing working-class family. His father, a timekeeper and paymaster at the local boiler works, kept the family fed and provided Kennedy with his first exposure to poetry. His father would recite poems he himself had learned as a student. More book-oriented than athletic, Kennedy was forever scribbling out his own comics, patterning these after the *Marvel Comics* series. His growing interest in science fiction led him to publish two "fanzines" of national circulation while still in high school.

His parents surprised him by insisting that he go on to college, not a common occurrence for most of his peers. After four years at Seton Hall College and a year at Columbia University, Kennedy's interest in science fiction waned, but his love for poetry blossomed. He then enlisted in the U.S. Navy and over the next four years he was allowed an abundant amount of time to write. About his poetic influences Kennedy says:

> The biggest influence that I ever felt was William Butler Yeats. In fact, when I was a sailor in the Navy I used to carry Yeats' collected poems around in my sea bag and pore over them. The problem, of course, is that you learn from whomever you love. And Yeats is, in a way, a dangerous influence because he is so very good that you can never hope to equal him. You can only trot after him in dumb, dog-like admiration. I think I also picked up a lot from reading William Blake and the Medieval ballads, not to mention Wallace Stevens, Thomas Hardy, and Emily Dickinson.

After studying for a year at the Sorbonne in Paris, Kennedy was accepted to the University of Michigan and began his doctoral studies. Spending six years in Ann Arbor allowed Kennedy the opportunity to meet with a variety of writers and poets, two with whom he would later collaborate and one whom he would subsequently marry. Along with Kennedy, James Camp, and Keith Waldrop compiled the hilarious *Pegasus Descending: A Book of the Best Bad Verse (1971).* This book has gone out of print. The writer he met and married at Michigan was Dorothy Mintzlaff[1] (also a poet) who is still very much "in print"; so far, the marriage has lasted 38 years.

In 1962, Kennedy taught for a year at the Woman's College of the University of North Carolina, then went on to teach at Tufts University as well as to serve as a visiting lecturer at Wellesley College and the University of California at Irvine. During this time, he continued to write in earnest for ardent, adult, poetry aficionados.

Interestingly, his book **Nude Descending a Staircase** contained two poems appropriate for children. It was the notice of these that led him to editor Margaret McElderry in New York City who, upon seeing his talent, signed him for his first book of poetry for children, **One Winter Night in August and Other Nonsense Jingles** in 1975. This was the beginning of Kennedy's career in children's poetry. Following his **The Phantom Ice Cream Man: More Nonsense Verse** (1979), he and his wife put together the enormously successful children's poetry anthology *Knock at a Star: A Child's Introduction to Poetry* (1982). Kennedy says:

> We wanted to produce a book that you could just place in a child's hands without any adult interference, and just turn the kid loose to read the poems with brief remarks about their elements. In first putting together *Knock at a Star* we went against much received advice that you don't dare analyze poetry with children. But we thought that since children love to inspect things close up, like machines, animals, birds, and plants, they might not mind looking closely at poems as well. So

we tried to do that without overburdening the kids with a heavy weight of analysis, but just to help them see what makes poems go.

For example, at the beginning of a section in *Knock at a Star* called "What's Inside a Poem?" they discuss some images children may meet in their reading with a short three-paragraph introduction. They write:

> When a poet tries to capture in words . . . how something looks, tastes, smells, feels, or sounds, those descriptions are called images. Images can even help us imagine heat or cold. When John Keats wants us to sense how cold it is on a bitter evening, he writes: "The hare limped trembling through the frozen grass"—a line that almost makes you want to go *brrr-r-r!*

> (Kennedy, 1982, p. 42)

These short descriptions prompt the child reader to see, perhaps for the first time, elements of poetry that would have possibly gone unnoticed. The poems that follow each introduction are superb examples of their point. In this section on "images" for instance, they refer to "My Fingers" by Mary O'Neill, "September" by John Updike, and "Snowy Benches," by Aileen Fisher.

Recently, *Knock at a Star* was reissued with new illustrations by Karen Lee Baker, and it included 75 new poems. Of the new collection, Kennedy says:

> *Knock at a Star* has continuously been in print since 1982 and when we suggested that we'd like to update it, John Keller, publisher at Little, Brown kindly subscribed to this notion. Children's poetry doesn't stand still and in the eighteen years since the book originally came out many excellent new poets have emerged, and a number of new tendencies that we wanted the book to reflect. In the new edition we have introduced poets such as Sandra Cisneros, Barbara Juster Esbensen, and Constance Levy who have burst onto the poetry scene.

> Further, one of our strong concerns was that children be introduced to ways of life and patterns of culture other than their own. We have a section now in answer to our question, "What do poems do?", in *Knock at a Star* called "Help You Understand People" which, without being blatantly politically correct, I hope, suggests that there are many different kinds of Americans.

In that section, the authors include new poems such as Charles Reznikoff's "Puerto Ricans in New York," Karama Fufuka's "The Park People," Ashley Bryan's "Mama's Bouquets," and Gwendolyn Brooks' "Narcissa."

In 1992, the Kennedy's embarked on a variation on *Knock at a Star* aimed at a primary school audience. The finished product was *Talking Like the Rain: A First Book of Poems* (1992). Kennedy speaks of the process of publishing this collection:

Having done our book, *Knock at a Star*, which introduced kids from 8-12 to poetry, Dorothy and I always wanted to go back and hit the littler guys. It seemed clear that pre-readers need a bright, colorful book that they can observe while sitting on an adult's lap. *Talking Like the Rain* seemed to be the way to go. We had collected poems for a long time for this book and again propositioned Little, Brown and John Keller who had accepted *Knock at a Star*. He, along with Maria Modugno, Little, Brown's children's book Editor-in-Chief, were very encouraging.

The book, of course, owes its colorfulness to illustrator, Jane Dyer. Jane spent about two years doing the watercolors for this book and Dorothy and I did not see the results of this effort until publication was imminent. We were invited into Little, Brown in Boston to behold the results of Jane's labors. We were ushered into this big room where all of Jane's illustrations were laid out on an immense table. We walked around and around this table "ooh-ing" and "ahh-ing" with glee when we saw what she had done. To our amazement, Jane had worked in the actual size that the watercolors were to be reproduced in the book. I was amazed at all this fine detail in watercolor. When I asked her how she accomplished this, she replied, "I had a magnifying glass."

Talking Like Rain is oversized and filled with a wide range of poets, such as Langston Hughes, Eve Merriam, and Christina Rossetti. The book is divided into sections dealing with the early childhood years; "Play," "Families," "Rhymes and Songs," and "Magic and Wonder," are but a sampling of the sections available to the young child. Kennedy says:

> We hope this book will offer kids a taste of outstanding poetry. Our conviction is that it is possible to give kids good poems that they will like. Those two qualities do not always go together. Take, for example the poems of Milton or Shakespeare, who are included in many anthologies for children. No doubt they are great poems, but will children find them likeable? Perhaps they are included only because they are in the public domain and therefore don't require permissions fees.

Another very successful foray into children's poetry came with Kennedy's series of three books, *Brats* (1986), *Fresh Brats* (1990), and *Drat These Brats* (1993). Kennedy described his own influences:

> Little Willie, and the many poems about him, was one of my early admirations. I loved all those anonymous poems about this pathetic brat who had terrible things happen to him. I hope that my Brats poems are not so sadistic and nasty as the Little Willie poems:

> Little Willie from the mirror
> Licked the mercury quite off.
> Thinking in his childish error
> It would cure the whooping cough.
> At the funeral, weeping mother
> Sadly said to Mrs. Brown,
> "Twas a chilly day for Willie
> When the mercury went down."

This, of course, is really adult verse. But I had a lot of fun with the brats poems. I love poems that are brief and that tell stories. One hope is to show children that poems need not be solemn and that they can be fun. Humor is, of course, a way to hook kids, especially skeptical boys, to poetry. Of course, the expectation is that they will go on to read other things as well.

Kennedy's humor is evident in every selection. Take for example this poem from *Brats*:

> Snickering like crazy, Sue
> Brushed a pig with Elmer's Glue
> And, to set Aunt Effie squealing,
> Stuck it to the kitchen ceiling.
> Uncle, gawking, spilled his cup.
> "Wow!" he cried. "Has pork gone up!"
>
> (Kennedy, 1990, p. 32)

His use of alliteration and assonance only heightens the enjoyment of these quirky verses:

> On a factory tour, Will Gossage,
> Watching folks make bratwurst sausage,
> Jumped into the meat feet-first,
> Brats are bad, but Will's the wurst.
>
> (Kennedy, 1993, p. 43)

More recently, Kennedy has written a collection of poems featuring elephants, oddly enough, engaged in the Olympics. His *Elympics* (1999) came about this way:

> The seed of *Elympics* came initially from the illustrator Graham Percy, an English artist who has done many children's books. He had, I think for his own pleasure, done a series of drawings of elephants taking part in sports, throwing the javelin and one thing and another. Patricia Lee Gauch, Senior Editor at Philomel Books had seen some of Graham's elephant work and recognized that there must be a book in this. But for it to be just right she envisioned some verse to go with it. So the original idea came from Graham and Patti, and I was enlisted to supply the poems.

Elympics includes both summer and winter games, in which elephants are seen sprinting, balancing on the beam, high jumping, and, of course, skiing, figure skating, and playing ice hockey. All of Kennedy's strengths seem to be put into play in this book. As in *Brats,* he uses the basic lyric form, adds his offbeat humor, and combines it with his great facility with wordplay to conjure verses, like this one from **"Bobsled"**:

> Swift as the wind, Eileen and Trish,
> Two tusky girls in goggles,
> Take a bobsled ride down a slippery slide
> All bumps and wiggle-woggles.
>
> (Kennedy, 1999)

This charming book has proved so enjoyable that Kennedy decided to go even further:

> *Elympics* has led to a sequel, which is now nearing completion. The sequel is called *Elefantina's Dream.* It takes one of the characters from *Elympics,* the little figure skater, and tells how she learned to skate. She goes on to become an Olympic champion, which is quite a feat because if you're an elephant living in the jungle, there is a paucity of ice. She managed it by using the icehouse in her village, where big blocks were stored, and begins her training on these frozen lumps.

With Kennedy's great experience in poetry, both as an academic and a writer for adults and children, he has some important insights into the genre and draws a distinct line between poetry and verse:

> I think of *verse* as anything in rhyme and meter, which may or may not be poetry. For it to be poetry it has to go a little bit deeper than the mere piece of verse like, "Thirty days hath September." Poetry leaves you wondering and perhaps finding something else when you return to it that you haven't seen the first time around.
>
> I think that much of the poetry for children that we care most to remember has been written by poets who also wrote for adults; from Robert Louis Stevenson and Christina Rossetti to us petty moderns. I first got interested in poetry for children because I saw contemporary poets writing it. People like William Jay Smith and Randall Jarrell, John Ciardi, Theodore Roethke, and Richard Wilbur were writing for kids and not apologizing for so doing. And, to this day, we still find many poets that write for adults who also care to write for children, as well, and this has been a lovely thing. Nancy Willard and Naomi Nye among others are great examples of these.

When asked to give his assessment of the health of poetry today, Kennedy, in his wry way, stated:

> I'll try and polish up my crystal ball. At the moment, poetry for children suddenly seems in a healthy state. Publishers, again, seem more willing to take risks on poetry collections. Certainly the impact of poetry in the schools has been felt more and more in the last ten or fifteen years since the California Reading Initiative encouraged the return of poetry to textbooks. It clearly is very popular with today's teachers.
>
> As for the future of poetry, a lesson might be learned from the adult world, for it seems it is in the process of changing. And by that I mean through the media by which poetry reaches its readers. Nowadays you find more poetry first published on the Internet and listened to in the poet's own voice. No doubt this will affect children's poetry too. I am a book person and do not believe that books will ever be obsolete—indeed they seem to be holding their own—I do think that the computer world is going to impinge even more upon poetry and perhaps make it more widespread and more easily available.
>
> For example, there are magazines of poetry on the Internet that enable you to hear the poet reading his or her own poems. I know the *Atlantic Monthly,* a big magazine, has had a website for some time that enables you to hear the poets themselves.

As for the "Bill of Health" and future of poet X. J. Kennedy, the NCTE Award for Poetry is but another manifestation of this man's great contribution to poetry and children's literature. The real test is what children think of his work, and, in that, they give two thumbs up. His topics are timely and accessible, his use of the language sophisticated, and his humor leads children and adoring adults into a genre that often gets overlooked and ignored. Children who read his collections as well as his anthologies will receive a better understanding of what poetry is and the joys it holds for them.

Note

1. Mintzlaff and Kennedy have collaborated on both the *Bedford Reader* (2000) and the *Bedford Guide for College Writers* (1999).

References

Cullinan, B. (1996). *A jar of tiny stars: Poems by NCTE award-winning poets.* Honesdale, PA: Boyds Mills.

Kennedy, X. J. (1975). *One winter night in August and other nonsense jingles.* New York: McElderry.

Kennedy, X. J. (1979). *The phantom ice cream man: More nonsense verse.* New York: McElderry.

Kennedy, X. J. (1986). *Brats.* New York: McElderry.

Kennedy, X. J. (1990). *Fresh brats.* New York: McElderry.

Kennedy, X. J. (1992). *Talking like the rain.* Boston: Little, Brown.

Kennedy, X. J. (1993). *Drat these brats.* New York: McElderry.

Kennedy, X. J. (1995). *Nude descending a staircase: Poems, songs, a ballad* (reprint edition). Pittsburgh: Carnegie-Mellon University Press.

Kennedy, X. J. (1998). *Dark horses: New poems.* Baltimore: Johns Hopkins University Press.

Kennedy, X. J. (1999). *Elympics.* New York: Philomel.

Kennedy, X. J., Camp, J., & Waldrop, K. (1971). *Pegasus descending: A book of the best bad verse.* New York, Collier/Macmillan.

Kennedy, X. J., & Gioia, Dana. (1997). *An introduction to poetry* (9th ed.). New York: Addison Wesley.

Kennedy, X. J., & Gioia, Dana. (1998). *Literature: An introduction to fiction, poetry, and drama* (7th ed.). New York: Longman.

Kennedy, X. J., Kennedy, D. M., & Aaron, J. E. (2000). *The Bedford reader* (7th ed.). New York: Bedford/St. Martin's.

Kennedy, X. J., Kennedy, D. M., & Holladay, S. A. (1999). *The Bedford guide for college writers* (5th ed.). New York: Bedford/St. Martins.

Kennedy, X. J., & Kennedy, D. M. (1999). *Knock at a star: A child's introduction to poetry.* (Rev. ed.). Boston: Little, Brown.

Bernard E. Morris (essay date 2003)

SOURCE: Morris, Bernard E. "The Poetry Collections." In *Taking Measure: The Poetry and Prose of X. J. Kennedy,* pp. 51-91. Selinsgrove, Penn.: Susquehanna University Press, 2003.

[*In the following essay, Morris presents a comprehensive overview of the contents and style of each of Kennedy's major books of original poetry.*]

Like other poets, Kennedy published many of his poems separately in various magazines and periodicals before accumulating enough to put them into a single volume. In doing so, he was able to select only those he felt were worthy of reprinting and to make changes in some of them. On the whole, these changes are minor, but they do show a penchant for revising even work that has been published. He confesses that the temptation to revise finished work is dangerous. He has told the story of an early misjudgment in this regard. After one of his poems had been accepted by the prestigious *Poetry* magazine, Kennedy had second thoughts: "I began toying with the accepted poem, rewrote the last lines, loused them up, but took a notion that my later inspiration was superior. . . . I rushed the new draft to Mr. Rago [then editor of *Poetry*], begging him to substitute it. Another silence followed, and then a gentle letter explaining that he thought the original version much better, that he himself was often prone to second thoughts, but that in this case I had best leave well enough alone. . . . I now know that Henry Rago wasn't willful, but wise. (The poem, **"Nude Descending a Staircase,"** unmuddied by my later worryings, appeared in *Poetry* in January 1960.)"[1]

By 1960, while still in graduate school, Kennedy had already published poetry in the *New Yorker, Poetry, Paris Review,* and other prestigious magazines, including *The Cornhill Magazine* in England. At the urging of Naomi Burton, a literary agent with Curtis Brown Limited, Kennedy assembled thirty-four poems into a book and called it *Nude Descending a Staircase,* which appeared in 1961 and promptly won the Lamont Award from Academy of American Poets, which only first books by American poets may receive. This was an impressive beginning for the young poet. The book's title recalls a series of photographs with the same name created by Gustaf Marley in the 1880s. The series depicts a nude woman walking down stairs. This visual representation does with photography what Kennedy aimed to do in his own poems with language and poetic form. Kennedy would also have in mind the famous painting by Marcel Duchamps that caused some stir when exhibited in 1913. The painting transforms Marley's photographic idea into a Cubist vision that looks like, as one critic put it, an explosion of shingles. Both the photographs and the painting express the idea of sequence and introduce motion into a static form, suggesting to Kennedy that what was done in film and paint could be done in language on paper. He may also have wanted to associate his first book of poems with works of art that looked at experience in a new and sensational way. He therefore designed his first book to suggest that poetry is performance, a visual, musical potpourri that takes the reader through individual "acts" or scenes, the poet performing in various ways and creating various meanings, both serious and playful. Like the nude descending a staircase, the book would offer frames of static meaning set in motion by reading, and the result would be provocative, daring, and inviting. Performance is the key feature of the book's design, reflecting Kennedy's desire for the reader to see that poetry is both an aural and a visual experience, a desire that has fueled his career-long involvement in public readings of his work. This first book of poems also marked Kennedy as a traditionalist of impressive technical skill, represented by the ballad, elegy, sonnet, epigram, with a heavy emphasis on the quatrain, and some verse for children. His mastery of form drew immediate praise and serious attention from many reviewers.

Clearly, Kennedy wanted to present the range of his poetic interests. His subjects in his first collection include the classical past, religious authority, and the modern condition. **"Leave of Absence"** reflects his academic experience, and several poems indicate an interest in and knowledge of French poetry (**"Rondeau," "Ladies Looking for Lice," "Where Are the Snows of Yesteryear?"**). All the poems together set the tone of Kennedy's whole career: irreverent, impatient with authority yet obedient to it, wayward, recalcitrant, witty, playful, yet profoundly serious. As a first collection, it shows remarkable maturity and polish in the handling of form and tone.[2] Though the product of a relatively young poet, it bears few marks of youth and inexperience. As his worldly experience grew and his mind sifted it, his attention would dwell more often on human types, human relationships, and human conditions. Children would receive greater attention; death would become a larger presence; and thoughts regarding the future, or fate, of humankind would invade his mind. Kennedy's development in his first collection was so sophisticated, however, that only the retrospect of nearly forty years would highlight these changes.

Among the critics, *Nude Descending a Staircase* established Kennedy as a poet of considerable skill in the use of conventional forms. His impressive weapons included metaphysical wit and Augustan satire, although his achievements in this area did not impress some critics favorably. John Simon saw Kennedy as "a curious cross between the *boulevardier* and the Metaphysical: he believes in the well-made, witty but significant poem, donning its top hat and its Donne. When this blend comes off . . . the effect is rousing. But when the wit fizzles or the elegance gets creased, things look sorry indeed. Even a relatively successful poem like **"Solitary Confinement"** can leave us ill at ease, because so serious a subject is handled with a facetiousness under which one looks in vain for a deeper humanity or profounder pessimism."[3] Nor did Forrest Read have much patience with Kennedy in this regard. He admired "the quick and clever wit for which Kennedy has been properly singled out," but he regretted that Kennedy "allows himself to become bedazzled by his own virtuosity."[4] Nevertheless, others saw much to be praised. Theodore Holmes noted some of Kennedy's trademark skills, an "incomparable mastery of pun" and an eye for the "fragmentation, impersonality unto death, and the disintegration of human values."[5] This laudatory assessment is remarkable for a young poet's first slim collection.

Because of his persistent use of rhyme, meter, and stanzaic regularity, Kennedy was regarded by many critics as an anachronism and was set upon by those who took offense at his use of traditional forms. More than one critic saw Kennedy's use of rhyme and meter as a weakness. One of them asserted: "He relies heavily on end rhyme and the four-stressed line, a form that lends itself to recitation rather than reading. The jaunty sound often carries the verse; that is, the sentiment or image may be nothing more than a commonplace dignified by rhyme . . . many of Kennedy's poems are funny, rhythmic, and interesting, but they are often superficial."[6] This same critic thought he had found the key to Kennedy's art, saying that "The clue to reading Kennedy comes as early as the table of contents in *Nude Descending a Staircase,* where readers find the book divided into three parts and an **'Intermission with Peanuts.'** Kennedy's metaphor is a good one; his poems are usually entertaining sidelights or intermissions."[7] Forrest Read thought Kennedy's ballads had "only shaky voices. They remain too close to untransmuted jargon and sometimes descend nearly to doggerel." Read cannot praise Kennedy without heavy qualification: "In his poems on remembered subjects (a partial list: Jonson, Donne, Lewis Carroll, Waller, Rimbaud, Villon), he is far better than in the songs and ballad. But even there he is best at wry, oblique comment on the established and traditional, as by a witty and sharply perceptive scholar; he misses the note of compelling currency, of insight into modernity which would make even the traditional come alive. He looks back at the images of the past, and doesn't often enough live now, in this place, with them."[8] Read is impressed by Kennedy's "great skill with charged words, unexpected and surprising phrases, juxtapositions and overlays," and his "brilliant phrasing . . . has light, but it lacks fire."[9] Despite these snipes and misreadings, this first collection introduced several of Kennedy's most praised and enduring poems, including the title poem, **"B Negative," "In a Prominent Bar in Secaucus One Day," "The Man in the Manmade Moon,"** and others, particularly **"Solitary Confinement,"** about which Theodore Holmes said, "For its size, what more could anyone expect of poetry . . . ?"[10]

In the same year that *Nude Descending a Staircase* was published, 1961, poems by Kennedy and several of his friends—Donald Hall, Keith Waldrop, and W. D. Snodgrass, were collected in a chapbook titled *The Wolgamot Interstice.*[11] Of Kennedy's five poems, four were taken from *Nude Descending a Staircase.* His selection shows that he wanted a variety of moods. **"Little Elegy,"** written "for a child who skipped rope" and in whose play Kennedy discovers circles of significance, added poignancy. Critic David Harsent objected to **"Little Elegy"** for its "woefully inadequate language" that produces a "stultifying cuteness," but he admired Kennedy's "economical, near vernacular line: by turns acerbic, lilting, or racy. . . ."[12] The boisterous **"Satori,"** not in *Nude* and not in later collections, mocks beatniks and their lifestyle. **"In a Prominent Bar in Secaucus One Day"** showcases his interest in the musical aspects of poetry, especially in combination with bawdy humor and raucous goings-on in low places. The two-line **"Overheard in the Louvre"** again illustrates his gift for aphorism: "Said the Victory of Samothrace, / What winning's worth this loss of face?" He had already demonstrated this quality in *Nude* with **"Ars Poetica,"** one of his most well-known and most appreciated poems:[13]

> The goose that laid the golden egg
> Died looking up its crotch
> To find out how its sphincter worked.
>
> Would you lay well? Don't watch.

The poem also serves as a testament to Kennedy's conviction that rhyme and meter have a place in modern poetry. The message in this succinct statement is timeless, as is all good poetry, Kennedy would say. **"Ars Poetica"** encapsulates Kennedy's acerbic wit and epitomizes his gift for combining serious and playful expression to the advantage of each. Kennedy ends his contribution to *The Wolgamot Interstice,* however, on a more serious note with **"Leave of Absence,"** whose academic subject would suit this college production. In all, the five poems reflect Kennedy's conviction that poetry can be playfully wicked as well as serious.

In 1965 Anchor Books included five poems by Kennedy in its volume of poems *A Controversy of Poets: An Anthology of Contemporary American Poetry,* edited by Paris Leary and Robert Kelly. Though Kennedy's work shared space with the poems of Denise Levertov, Robert Lowell, Galway Kinnell, and other distinguished poets, it received little critical attention. Nevertheless, the poems again showcase the range of his subjects and moods, a range that includes serious intent and social consciousness as well as an irrepressible comic spirit. **"A Water Glass of Whisky"** depicts a slice of the American landscape where the inhabitants are connected to the outside world only by television. **"Song to the Tune of 'Somebody Stole My Gal'"** is a comical lament bemoaning the absence of classical myths in modern times. **"Down in Dallas,"** already published in a collection devoted to the death of John F. Kennedy, transforms the assassination into an image of the Crucifixion and works toward a sense of harmony, balance, and compensation.[14] **"Hearthside Story"** treats of a young man's visit to a prostitute and his attempt to put the experience into perspective. The last poem, **"Cross Ties,"** shows a remarkable sophistication and maturity early in Kennedy's career. Kennedy thought well enough of this poem to include it in all his major collections and to use its title for his award-winning collection.

In 1969 Kennedy again collected several years' worth of poems and published *Growing into Love,* his second major collection, this one published in hardcover. More substantial in terms of number of poems than *Nude Descending a Staircase,* it contains fifty-three poems, divided into three sections. Fifty of the poems are newly collected, and forty-two of them would find their way into later collections. Unlike *Nude Descending a Staircase,* the book contains no ballads or songs and lacks an "Intermission" containing light verse and epigrams. The poems, particularly in the first two sections, "Experiences" and "Countrymen," offer images of a modern American landscape blighted by industrialism or tourism. Unheroic people, trapped by materialism and greed and alienated from one another and from heaven, fall into madness or retreat into an alcoholic blur. In this world, men are lost and women are contemptuous of the failure of men to find enrichment and fulfillment. The middle section closes with the gloomy image of an army of modern men, all failures, twitching in death. One reviewer, Steven Tudor, understating the case, saw the poems of the first two sections as "rather negative," adding that "While art itself is an affirmation, the occasions for these poems seem bitter, even petulant."[15] The third section, **"Growing into Love,"** injects a note of hope, however. Tudor believed the poems in this part of the book "mainly celebrate various dimensions of love."[16] The dozen poems in this section speak of man's rescue from his worst conditions and qualities. Though salvation is not attained, endurance is noted. In their journey, humans may be improving. **"Growing into Love,"** for Kennedy at least, suggests emotional growth and reflects a broader understanding of his personal experience and public vision.

Not surprisingly, reviewers of this collection spoke of Kennedy's characteristic intellectual intensity, inventiveness, and laughter.[17] Peter Simpson saw in the new collection an "ability to see oneself grappling sheepishly—yet with a kind of sustained grace—with the large and the small challenges of the human condition. . . ." He regarded this ability as one of Kennedy's "most engaging qualities. . . ."[18] John Leggett noted these same qualities and found "a pair of triumphs in the collection," the poems **"Cross Ties"** and **"Ant Trap."**[19] On the other hand, reviewer John Demos echoed earlier complaints, that Kennedy's word play and "sophisticated wit" and "metaphors under glass mar what otherwise would have been straight but good poems." When "wit and passion meet, this poet can be brilliantly wonderful." Demos also finds Kennedy's language "verbally sensuous," particularly in lines such as "O Lukewarm spew, you, stir yourself and boil," from **"West Somerville, Mass."**[20] This poem represents the volume's serious elements, which critic Alan Brownjohn singled out for comment, saying that "under the confident surfaces lurk numerous worries about sin, war, religion . . ." Recalling Kennedy's first collection, Brownjohn said that *Growing into Love* is "less overtly humorous"; it seemed that Kennedy "really wants to do something grave and substantial with this flair for polished, elaborate, zanily conceited writing." To Brownjohn, Kennedy is "one of a diminishing band of American academic poets who are still fettering these topics in punctilious metrics," but Brownjohn thinks that Kennedy is improving: "he is beginning to turn to a kind of eloquent irony that is all his own, especially where the social detail succeeds (**'Poets'** and **'Pottery Class'**), or where he goes in for grim, pointless narrative. **'Artificer,'** a poem of insolent, ingenious extravagance, succeeds beautifully."[21] Knute Skinner also believed that this collection "shows a deepening seriousness of purpose. The comic poems turn serious and the serious poems reflect a mind grappling with aspiration and doubt at one and the same time."[22]

Growing into Love further established Kennedy as a practitioner of traditional forms. In a review of this collection, Skinner refers to Kennedy as "a marvelous, if unfashionable, poet," then sets out to defend his use of rhyme and meter by instancing **"Reading Trip,"** which Skinner considered "a tour de force narrative in heroic sestets. . . ."[23] Thomas Tessier began his review of the collection by saying that "Kennedy's techniques are conventional—his rhymes and stanza forms date back centuries—but he is always in control and never uses the forms for mere convenience."[24] Though Kennedy

was still considered "academic" for his efforts, at least one critic was able to see that traditional forms were a source of his excellence:[25] "His adherence to stricter forms never hampers the verve and forcefulness of his writing, nor the acuteness of his irony. On the contrary, his poems demonstrate the great value of traditional devices in giving shape and muscle to imaginative vision. While it is all the rage these days to make poems discontinuous and open-ended, Kennedy's work can stand as a sturdy reminder of what can be accomplished by order and unity. His new book is refreshing and delightful."[26] Tessier agrees that Kennedy's "rhythms are often subtle and clever, and would . . . sound very musical if the poems were to be read aloud." Tessier also senses "powerful and potentially explosive passions smoldering beneath the surface" of the book's final poem, **"The Shorter View."**[27]

In his review of *Growing into Love,* James Carroll saw Kennedy's use of form in a positive light, saying Kennedy "takes form seriously and bothers to work hard at it. He is master of an unself-conscious rhyme," and his "disciplined expression allows him to achieve control and flexibility." Carroll believed that this volume would establish Kennedy "as one of our country's formidable poets."[28] This prediction has proven correct. Reviewer Henry Taylor appreciated Kennedy's skills with light verse, "which he is able to raise above the usual level." Taylor was especially impressed by Kennedy's "astonishing ability to absorb and revivify the flat rhythms and colloquialisms of contemporary American speech."[29] He cites the language of **"O'Riley's Late-Bloomed Little Son,"** a poem on the death of a child who had been frostbitten and then died from croup: "in their arms he just went stiff" (l. 6). The bland finality of this statement and the sorrow inherent in its meaning poignantly balance ordinary speech and fresh poetic insight and expression. Perhaps it is in instances like this one that a critic like Louis Martz sees Kennedy's "admirable taciturnity"[30] as well as the revivication of ordinary speech.

Thomas Tessier refers to one of the few very personal poems Kennedy has written. In **"The Shorter View,"** the final poem in *Growing into Love,* Kennedy returns to the theme that is developed in the book's first poem, **"Cross Ties,"** the theme of procreation and generation and of futurity. Kennedy develops **"The Shorter View"** on two levels, in literal and metaphorical terms: the wife and husband are in bed, and she falls asleep reading while he is thinking of birth, death, and the future of their family. He imagines she is seeing them both in their old age: "seeing how in space / Stars in old age will stagger, drop, and burst, / throwing out far their darknesses and dust." Kennedy's ambivalence is evident in the contrasting meanings of these lines: they are stars, but they shall become decrepit and die; they will have offspring, but their children are "darknesses and dust." His ambivalence extends to what his wife thinks of him, or will think of him, when he is old. When the wife "lets her book fall with stricken face," stricken because she has not thought of dying: "She'd thought tomorrow set and rooted here, / And people" (ll. 5-6). She also sees "through me to an earth / Littered with ashes, too dried-up to bear" (ll. 9-10). The vision, in which the old husband and the earth are one and the same, causes her to see little point in giving birth, and her despair casts a shadow over their marriage bed and over the future. Making children takes place in "our dark bed," and giving birth is a growing burden, more so in light of these dark thoughts. The wife, "Her arms drawn shut," appears to retreat from her husband, his love making, his lack of concern: "What the Hell," he tells her, "we won't be there" (l. 11). She knows their descendant will be, and this conviction makes her obstinate in the face of his indifference: "this night will not give / One inch of ground for any shorter view" (ll. 15-16). The poem returns full circle—even the language makes it so, "Her eyes" opening the poem and "view" closing it—back to the wife's vision, only by the close of the poem, her arms are closed, contrasting with her "outstretched" eyes at the beginning, and his ambivalence turns into her obduracy.

At the time he was having doubts about parental responsibility, Kennedy looked at the issue from a different perspective in **"One-Night Homecoming."** Though not collected in *Growing into Love,* the poem grew out of the same stage of his poetic development and shows that he had more than a passing interest in this theme.[31] The poem records the disillusionment that occurs when one returns to the parental home and discovers change. Parents get old: the father cannot quite lift the son's suitcase, "Breathes hard, mounting stairs," and the mother "doesn't notice yolk stuck to the dishes / Nailheads arising from the kitchen chairs" (ll. 2-4). The son cannot endure his mother's "persistent needling," which "hurts without intending to, like sleet" (ll. 7-8). The parents' physical deterioration is reflected in images of deterioration in the house itself, symbol of the child's world:

> From childhood's bed I follow in the ceiling
> The latest progress of each crack I know,
> But still the general cave-in hangs suspended,
> Its capillary action running slow,
>
> And the huge roof I used to think unchanging
> Gives with each wind.
>
> (ll. 9-14)

Kennedy sees the speaker's discovery as part of a generational sequence: "It's my turn now to fall / Over strewn blocks, stuffed animals on staircases, / My turn to read the writing crayoned on the wall" (ll. 14-16). The decline runs through the generations, perhaps all the way from Eden—the use of the word "fall" suggests this idea. The poem's tone is pessimistic; children are viewed as clutterers whose crayon markings on the wall forecast decline and symbolize destruction. Parents are seen as deteriorated beings, and with advancement into adulthood comes sight enough to see the human predicament, which is dismal.

Growing into Love showed Kennedy at his most personal. Many critics again focused on his use of traditional forms, overlooking the many poems in which he turns the light directly onto his own experience. **"Cross Ties"** opens the collection, as if to signal to the reader that the book's focus shall be on aspects of the poet's life. This poem is immediately followed by **"Snapshots,"** which includes two parts, **"Birth Report"** and **"The Nineteen-thirties,"** both of which deal with Kennedy's first days of infancy. The first poem, **"Birth Report,"** likens the poet's conception to a foot race: "When blam! My father's gun began the dash / Of fifty thousand tadpoles for one egg . . ." (ll. 1-2). From the start, Kennedy sees his life as a struggle, and it did not get any better: "And then my mother in a nest my aunt / Had paid for let me down" (ll. 5-6). Although the baby's delivery is a "letting down," Kennedy's primary meaning here is that his mother disappointed him somehow, perhaps by simply bringing him into this world. The second poem of this pair, **"The Nineteen-thirties,"** reinforces the idea that the poet was brought into a horrible place: "Wall Street swallowed brokers whole," in the Midwest "dust clouds chased their tails like dogs" (ll. 1-2), and the Holocaust raged while the infant, "Not knowing who'd been let to live / Or who'd been herded in and gassed" (ll. 5-6), slept. The pair of memories ends on another catastrophe: "The sky's bough broke. Down fell / The Hindenburg's big blue hornet's nest" (ll. 7-8). Kennedy saw himself brought into the world of unspeakable horrors for which he was not responsible. By placing these two "snapshots" together, Kennedy suggests that the larger context follows from and creates a context for the smaller one and that somehow they cannot be disconnected from each other, only from heaven. Both are the result of a separation: the poet was let down, the world fell down. Together, they go down.

In **"The Shorter View,"** in addition to its picture of marriage, Kennedy offers a vision of his own child's future that reminds one of his view of his own infancy: his child shall inherit "an earth / Littered with ashes, too dried-up to bear." It is undoubtedly these images that trouble his mind whenever he considers his role in continuing the generations, as he does in **"Cross Ties"** and in later poems, such as **"Last Child"** and **"One-Night Homecoming"** (all three collected in *Cross Ties*). In **"Cross Ties"** he senses something "Bearing down Hell-bent from behind my back" (l. 4), and he believes the world might be ruled by both God and the devil. In **"Last Child"** he has begun to see that the babies themselves may be part of the problem: "Your fingers writhe: inane anemones / A decent ocean ought to starve" (ll. 9-10).

The last section of *Growing into Love* contains poems that reveal perhaps more than any other group of poems Kennedy's ambivalent attitude toward not only his own children but his wife. They are among his most personal poems and probably the last ones of this kind he would publish. Several poems in the collection show that he views his own infancy with mixed feelings, mainly negative. **"First Confession,"** in *Nude Descending a Staircase,* is the first poem that deals with Kennedy's troubled relations with the church. In **"At the Stoplight by the Paupers' Graves,"** another poem from *Nude,* the poem's protagonist is stopped at a traffic light thinking of the dead in a nearby cemetery. He wants to have faith, but he has "no heart to wait with them all night / That would be long to tense here for a leap. . . ." (ll. 10-11). Kennedy uses the same image in **"Cross Ties"** to characterize a similar feeling, this one associated with his own parenthood: "I go safe, / Walk on, tensed for a leap, unreconciled / To a dark void all kindness" (ll. 12-14). The later poems in *Growing into Love* cannot let go of his ambivalence. **"Transparency"** begins with conflict: "Love was the woman I loved, / A grave, inhuman woman . . . ," (ll. 1-2), and it ends with mixed feelings about his wife:

> She'd turn to me dim lips
> Held next my lips by will—
> Yet, as we thinned to sleep,
> Even through gorged eyes,
> I could see through her skull.
>
> (ll. 11-15)

The central image of **"Mean Gnome Day"** (so far collected only in *Growing into Love*) is that of a dwarf-like creature who lives underground and guards treasure. Both the tone and theme of the poem are established in a definition placed at the head of the poem: "LOST MO-TION: Looseness / which allows movement / between mating parts / supposed to turn in unison / *The Machinist Dictionary.*" The poem opens with unattractive images of the husband and wife and their day:

> The day comes limping in as though a hump
> Stood on its back and bowed it. As we fall
> Apart in bed, each to a separate lump,
> We do not speak. Our thoughts are shrunk to dwarfs
> Whose piggish eyeballs glitter as they curl
> About to stoke their privates.
>
> (ll. 1-6)

In this life, "There is small remedy, no, none in gin" (l. 7). At dinner, the turkey pies reflect the couple themselves, who are "Frozen" and "deformed." As night approaches, "Something in us begins to yield" (l. 20), but the two are likened to the "matted form of some

Neanderthal" frozen in a glacier. They are chipped free and "boated south, / There to be thawed, there to bestir numb arms, / To try ripe fruit with unfamiliar mouth" (ll. 25-27). Their lives have so deformed them physically and emotionally that they can scarcely manage physical contact. Kennedy suggests that a marriage can come to this, a frigid confinement in which warmth and love have vanished and which turns husband and wife into lumps, "blurred but alive."

"Two Apparitions," which is placed right after **"Mean Gnome Day"** in *Growing into Love,* returns to the worry Kennedy has at this point in his marriage: growing old in a way that turns the couple into monsters. Lying beside his wife in bed, he sees the two of them misshapen by old age, and Kennedy transforms the moon-June cliché into an image of fairy-tale magic that casts a haunting glow over the frightened pair:

> Another man's hand, not mine,
>
> A scaled hand, a lizard's blotched over with bile,
>   Every knuckle a knot on a stick,
> And in her cheek, dug there, a crone's wan smile.
>   I shuddered. Wild-eyed she woke,
>
> Then in the next moment, the moon's white rise
>   Cast the two of us smooth once more
> And we fell to each other with timid cries,
>   Backs turned on what lay in store.

In the second part of this poem, the moon itself is drained of spirit, "Having had to look on / In diseased old age" (ll. 7-8). The prospect of a diseased, impotent old age and parenthood darkens these two poems, but the volume as a whole is rescued from pessimism not only by the few poems in it that express genuine love and appreciation for the child and the wife but by the understanding that the poet is a young man looking ahead, expressing doubt about his ability to measure up. As the title of this section and of the whole volume suggests, the future entails a growing, which represents for Kennedy a promise and a challenge.

For critic Louis Martz, *Growing into Love* marked a shift in American poetry: the younger poets at the time tended to "work very close to the land or the city of our time. Mythology, the past, plays little part. The effort is, I think, to move out of the interior world and to place concretely before us the world we know. . . . If the past exists, even its crises stand as a witty memory of something that hardly touches the new consciousness."[32] If Martz sees in Kennedy's poetry an absence of the "confessional" impulse associated with the open-verse poetry of the recent past, his remarks certainly apply to Kennedy, and one does see that in his second major volume of poetry, Kennedy looks increasingly at the world around him, producing, in Martz's opinion, his best work to date. Nevertheless, Martz missed the mark widely if he means that Kennedy has begun to exclude the past from his repertoire of subjects or poetic consciousness. In *Growing into Love* the past in one form or another plays a part in many poems, including **"The Korean Emergency," "Creation Morning," "Nothing in Heaven Functions as It Ought,"** and **"Golgotha,"** not to mention elements of the past implicit in the formal aspects of the poems. Kennedy's later collections would continue to show that the past, expressed either in subject or form, is essential to understanding the present and to capturing its essential nature.

For Kennedy, the past offers a context in which the present is measured. As he shows in the final part of **"Inscriptions After Fact,"** the theater of Dionysus is a stage for a young sailor to find his part. Kennedy elaborates the contrast between a heroic past and a diminished future in **"The Korean Emergency,"** which he placed in the first part of *Growing into Love.* His tour of duty in the Mediterranean provided him with a number of opportunities to contrast the bookish world of epic characters and events with modern reality. **"The Korean Emergency"** elaborates the experiences of a young sailor on liberty, this time in Sicily. Most of the poem's forty-five lines are taken up with vivid description of what the young sailor experiences ashore:

> Let loose,
> The lira leaking out of your dress blues,
> You'd wander, up for grabs,
> Through droves of boys who'd feel you up and pluck,
> Or, if it were your will
> Down on the beach or under some dark arch,
> Nurse or give suck.
>
> (ll. 33-39)

In lines such as these, Kennedy derives from language extraordinary descriptive power. The phrase "Let loose," in light of the sexual implications of the whole passage, suggests not only pent-up desire, but pent-up animals wild with the desire for freedom and other stimulants. The image in the next line describes both the way money flows from sailors on liberty and the consequence of unbridled sexual indulgence, this idea reinforced by the rhyming of *crab's* and *grabs* in the same stanza. In such a rich context, words and phrases take on meaning that, in a more innocent, more wholesome place, would not occur to the reader, "Down on the beach" among them. Another rhyme in this group of lines, *pluck* and *suck,* is especially well placed to capture the young sailor's sensual sense of the experience, and the final line suggests in its brevity and lack of qualification neither approval nor condemnation.

The poem contrasts three environments, each unattractive. The ship's world is replete with foul language, impatient officers, and ponderous duty; it is set in a sickly sea: "Swelling a moment only to subside, / Hesitant as breath from an injured lung" (ll. 10-11). Disease mingles with animal energy. The final five lines capture the sailor's perspective with marvelous force and precision:

> Who'd hate a thirst that held him in its sway
> When the deep wine dish of the Mediterranean lay
> Within his hands? Once more
> We steamed back home. To meet us on the dock
> Sat Gene's Dry Cleans.
>   Emergency, not war.
>
> (ll. 40-45)

Reflecting on his shoreside experiences, the young sailor is reminded of Odysseus lured by the Sirens, who held the men in their sway, and the line "the deep wine dish of the Mediterranean lay / Within his hands" recalls the epic metaphors of Homer, even as it combines the sailor's sexual memories. "We steamed back home" forecasts the dry cleaning the sailors will get back home and suggests their angry state of mind, angry for having been plucked from Sicilian pleasures. Although the Roman theater in Syracuse is "some crab's / Picked gutted shell," at home the sterile cleanliness of "Gene's Dry Cleans" is just as repellant to the young sailor. Given a choice, he would clearly choose the unwholesome to the wholesome, for this is an "Emergency, not war."

Two years after *Growing into Love* appeared, Kennedy brought out his third major collection of poems, *Breaking and Entering* (1971), published in England by Oxford University Press. On its title page appears a quotation from T. S. Eliot:

> The chief use of the 'meaning' of a poem,
> in the ordinary sense, may be . . . to satisfy
> one habit of the reader, to keep his mind
> diverted and quiet, while the poem
> does its work upon him . . . [.]

Kennedy said that Eliot's metaphor gave him his title. In his explanation, he reveals one of his artistic motives: "A remark of Eliot's has stuck with me: his comparison of the meaning of a poem—the prose sense of it—to the burglar's bit of meat. There in the darkened house sits the mind of the reader, a house-dog given a kidney to keep him quiet, while the rest of the poem stalks about its business: making off with the first editions and the silver gravy-boat."[33] Perhaps because he was having difficulty with the creative process, only eight of the forty-five poems in this collection are new.[34] Fifteen are reprinted from *Nude Descending a Staircase* and twenty-two from *Growing into Love.* He rearranged some of the poems, as he would continue doing through his most recent collection, and he added lighter poems, including the seriocomic *Bulsh* and more than a dozen epigrams, one of his favorite forms. The epigrams make fun of such subjects as the Teutonic scholar, the literary anthologist, marriage, death, and a young poet. These light, satirical pieces help to dissipate the somber mood that dominated *Growing into Love,* though several poems show that Kennedy continued to be interested in religious subjects and the grimmer aspects of the modern American scene. Modern domestic relationships received attention, including his own in **"Cross Ties"** and **"Last Child"** (dedicated to his son Daniel).

The new volume brought increased attention to Kennedy, this time from England as well as America, and his work won praise on both sides of the Atlantic. A reviewer for the *Times Literary Supplement* noted the "humour, wit, elaborate figures and technical mastery [that were] demonstrated by his first book," features that by now had become widely accepted as Kennedy's best and most characteristic. In this third collection, however, the reviewer found that "Mr[.] Kennedy has steadily infused a moral energy independent of religion and dark with ambivalence. His art and articulateness, the evidence of his control over his rhetoric, add power to the wry insights."[35] Alan Brownjohn, as he had done with *Growing into Love,* mingles praise with criticism. Calling Kennedy "a fantastic" and "one of the most bizarrely resourceful practitioners of the earlier style," meaning traditional forms, Brownjohn considers Kennedy's wit "uneasy, abrasive. Archaic phraseology is made to bite with energetic technical accomplishment, and irony"; Kennedy's performance is "skillful and alarming, if not often moving," but the "extraordinary wit and energy startles and hurts rather than touches."[36] The new poems showed Kennedy experimenting with formal features in new ways, with the refrain in **"Drivers of Diaper-Service Trucks Are Sad"** and with tag lines in **"Song: Great Chain of Being."**[37] On the whole, he wanted to give the reader a taste of the full range of his poetic skills—he said that this collection "offers the gist of me,"[38] though absent are poems for children.

In 1974 Kennedy's fourth collection, *Emily Dickinson in Southern California,* appeared. It contained fifteen poems and two series of epigrams, comprising fifteen couplets. Fourteen of the poems had not been collected before, and three were from *Breaking and Entering.*[39] Twelve of the poems, with revisions, would be reprinted in *Cross Ties.* Five of the poems appear in only this collection. Kennedy's interest in form is given prominence in one of his longer poems, **"Emily Dickinson in Southern California,"** which is sustained for one hundred and four lines. It is unusual for Kennedy to write poems of this length; only a handful exceed fifty lines. In this collection, for example, only one other poem reaches thirty lines, and most of the poems are under twenty lines, with several under ten.

The volume received very little critical notice, although it was, in the words of one reviewer, a "charming book, made even more attractive as the first volume in David

R. Godine's new, beautifully printed and handsomely bound Chapbook series."[40] The book's principal poem, **"Emily Dickinson in Southern California,"** is remarkable for reasons more important than length, of course; it brings together Kennedy's skill in infusing a new vision in an established form, his skill in imitating the idiosyncratic style of another poet, his interest in the modern condition in America, and his skill in sustaining a narrative through many lines. Ignoring the poem's subject, one reviewer thought this poem "skillfully done" but "not much more than high pastiche—nine Dickinsonian essays in the cryptic-ecstatic. . . ."[41]

In this collection of poems, Kennedy's interest in the past remains in evidence, both as an ideal of wit and polish and, in the four-line **"At Colonus,"** as a context for suggesting that in ancient Greece, mankind has been abandoned by the gods of antiquity. The idea of abandonment turns into a sense of futility in a two-line poem, **"Protest,"** that ends the book: "On marble stairs under the bloated dome of time / Everyone living sets himself on fire." Such a sentiment is offset by Kennedy's continued interest, and seeming faith, in parenthood, the family, and the flow of generations. A degree of skepticism is evident in his treatment of poetry and poets and in the value of writing. His relations with church authority are replete with disillusionment, disapproval, even contempt—*Bulsh* may be fun to read, but it has a sharp edge of bitterness. In his personal remarks, Kennedy has said that his religious faith weakened early in his life and that he abandoned it soon after.[42] His poems dealing with church authority reflect this personal shift, and his faith in literary pursuits seems to be strong but ambivalent. Meanwhile, he is increasingly interested in the family, children in particular, including his own. In this collection he reprints **"Last Child,"** and would reprint it again in *Cross Ties.* The poem shows a father filled with disgust and loathing as he looks upon this "Small vampire" and wonders whether he and his generation will be the ones to break "earth's back." Joseph Parisi sees a "curious mixture of resentment and tenderness"[43] in the father's attitude, but it is difficult to find the tenderness.

In this same year as *Emily Dickinson in Southern California,* Kennedy published *Celebrations after the Death of John Brennan* in a limited edition of 326.[44] As a student of Kennedy's, Brennan had made a deep impression on his professor. The young man's suicide inspired this poem, one of Kennedy's most personal expressions, which throughout is somber, dignified, and restrained. Despite Kennedy's growing popularity, the book received little critical notice. David Shapiro reviewed it along with three other collections in *Poetry* two years after the poem appeared, and though he admired the poem, Shapiro spends more space on its alleged flaws than on its genuine merits. He objects to some overwriting, slang, "archaic diction" (as in

Kennedy's phrase, "fugitive songs"), and some "clotted melodrama." Shapiro was also "appalled" by the "abstract genitive" in the line "Churned by the wind, the iceberg of his death / Slowly revolves. . . ."[45] On the positive side, Shapiro found that Kennedy's use of "interpolated quotes from the student's own poetry enhance this book and give it a formally interesting dramatic structure."[46]

As a deeply personal and intensely felt poem, it bears close scrutiny and deserves more attention than it has received. The poem begins with Kennedy approaching the place where the public celebration of John Brennan is to be held, and at the end of the poem, Kennedy brings the reader back to the celebration as it is ending. Between these two points, Kennedy recalls moments from Brennan's life along with some of their encounters, all arranged in chronological order, taking Brennan through his college days. Kennedy broadens the scope of the elegy by drawing a parallel between his relationship with Brennan and his relationship with his own sons and father. In the middle part of the poem, Kennedy wrestles with powerful, entangled feelings that have been exposed by the younger man's death:

> I'd not aspire to be your father, John.
> I meant only to copyread your words.
> Hard enough now—four blood sons of my own
> Trussing me too
> In dried umbilical cords.
>
> (7:ll. 7-11)

Kennedy's characteristic wit and playfulness are absent here; he is entirely serious, relying almost exclusively on the sound effects and rhythms to convey the depth of his emotions. The effect is to amplify both. The *I*s in the first two lines sound like cries of anguish, and the alliteration in the fourth and fifth lines is aided by the imagery "blood sons" opposed by "dried umbilical cords." In the next stanza, part 8, the thought shifts to Kennedy's father:

> "Well, most of me's still here," my old man said
> After the surgeon pared him, hospitaled. . . .
> Still hanging on. John gone.
>
> (ll. 1-2, 5)

The poem, reprinted in *Cross Ties,* reveals more about Kennedy himself than Brennan and represents an important step in Kennedy's psychological and artistic development. It demonstrates clearly the breadth of his poetic skills, which are capable of the most sensitive expressions of feeling and subtleties of thought in forms exceedingly suitable to both. The poem's candor is as striking as its depth of feeling and maturity.

In 1975 Kennedy teamed with James Camp and Keith Waldrop to publish *Three Tenors, One Vehicle: A Book of Songs.* Twelve poems by Kennedy are listed in the table of contents, although the last poem in the list, **"If You Got a Notion,"** is not wholly Kennedy's.[47] Of the eleven that are entirely his, three are set to tunes. One of them, **"Ultimate Motel,"** is a "hymn in common meter," and two are in dialect. Kennedy's characteristic playfulness is predominant in three of the poems, in which he mocks the individual who mourns the loss of mythical beliefs (**"Song to the Tune of 'Somebody Stole My Gal'"**), the poet who gives up poetry for booze (**"Uncle Ool's Song against the Ill-Paid Life of Poetry"**), and the masochist (**"Flagellant's Song"**). Several poems deal with a familiar subject, the loss of some ideal, whether it be classical myth or biblical tradition, or the loss of a past that gave the individual a certain order, beauty, and certitude. When Kennedy looks at the world around him, as he does in several of the poems, he sees a loss of order and faith, an ugly landscape peopled by disenchanted, confused lost souls who appear to have given up the struggle for truth and beauty. The poems also show a variety of forms, including some poems in which elements of the folk ballad are used. The poems in dialect explore the possibilities inherent in adopting a variety of voices, and the structural diversity evident in all of the poems suggests that Kennedy is experimenting. In **"Great Chain of Being,"** for example, each stanza ends with a repeated refrain:

> Drinking smooth wine in a castle or digging potatoes
>   knee-deep in dung,
> Everybody in creation knew just how high or how
>   low he hung
> On that ladder with Lord god at the top and dumb
>   mud at the bottom rung,
>   *Great Chain of Being,*
>   *Great Chain of Being.*[48]
>
> (ll. 1-5)

"Sentimentalist's Song, or Answers for Everything," set to the tune of "Deutschland über Alles," represents an ironic commentary on present-day existence; its short rhymed lines mock the poem's subject:

> Strife-torn city?
> What a pity!
> Tint it pretty,
>   Pop rose pills.
> Air pollution?
> Quick solution!
> Evolution,
>   Smog-breathing gills.
>
> (ll. 1-8)

Throughout the series of poems, entire stanzas are italicized, and although rhyme occurs in all the poems, the lines vary widely in length within several of the poems and from poem to poem. It seems as though Kennedy is as interested in how his poems look and sound as in what they are saying. Technical exploration is the theme of his contributions to this slim volume as he skips from the serious to the playful, from heaven to earth in locale, from the ironic and mocking to the more serious and reflective.

For several years after this publication, Kennedy continued to explore different ways to express his ideas, even turning from his own ideas to those of others, thereby relinquishing self-expression for the benefits of trying new forms. In 1983, eight years after the publication of **Three Tenors, One Vehicle,** he published **French Leave,** a volume of twelve translations from the works of eight French poets, whose dates range from the sixteenth to the twentieth century. Kennedy's attraction to these French authors may be due to their anger, their cynicism mingled with a weariness of the world, their *doleur,* their interest in male-female relationships, and their sophistication and intellectuality. Formally, they offered him a chance to manipulate language into tight structures and to use language under the pressure of formal demands, including the challenge of capturing from another language such difficult elements as tone and image.

"Sonnet for Hélène" by Pierre de Ronsard is a poignant expression by the poet who complains to his mistress for having rejected him. He exhorts her to read his lines when she is old, when her beauty is "long gone by." With that prospect in mind, he pleads, "delay no longer. Gather ye / From this day forth the roses of To Be" (ll. 13-14). The sentiments of this graceful sonnet no longer suit the modern sensibility, but Kennedy expresses the ideas in such subtle, fresh ways that the old seems new. How he manages may be seen in the use of the rose, a traditional symbol both of woman's beauty and romantic love, in the poem's final line: "From this day forth the roses of To Be." By giving the image an existential twist, Kennedy saves the symbol from being simply a cliché and fuses the old with the new, tossing in a clever reference to Hamlet's soliloquy as well.

Kennedy translated three poems by Charles Baudelaire. **"Epigraph for a Banned Book"** tells the reader to "Throw down this book, it's steeped in bile, / Cocked for an orgy, melancholic" (ll. 3-4). The pun on "Cocked" cleverly illustrates the kind of material the reader will find in "this book." In the final two lines, the poet imagines the self-righteous would-be reader, and scornfully tells him to "Run along. Chase your perfect whole" (l. 13). The parting pun is classic Kennedy, in the vein of **"Ars Poetica."** The second poem, **"Abyss,"** is a dolorous, self-absorbed expression of the poet's feeling of emptiness. The chasm within himself is "seductive space," a "gaping pit / Oozing with spooks . . ." (ll. 9-10). The human intellect is suspended above this fathomless chasm. The third poem, **"Conformity,"** is a four-line satirical attack on the Belgians for being conformists and for drinking "to drench / Their draw-

ers." The sardonic wit of the final line appeals to Kennedy's affection for the sting and brevity of aphorism: when the Belgians catch syphilis, "They'll double-dose, to be twice French."

"Pierrot's Soliloquy" by Jules LaForgue laments the famous clown's desire for immortality in a quatrain as graceful as it is succinct:

> All I am is a clown in the moon
> Plunking pebbles in fountain pools with
> No particular hope, no design
> Except one: to make myself myth.

> (ll. 1-4)

Paul Verlaine's **"Fall Song"** continues the melancholic mood. The poem's short lines suggest the speaker's enervation, and Kennedy's use of image and sound plays fully to the speaker's mood:

> I go away
> Any old way
>   Ill winds drive—
> Here, there—off
> Like a leaf
>   Once alive.

> (ll. 13-15)

Thinking of the "Olden days" he cries, envisioning himself driven like a leaf by autumn's ill winds, and, like the leaf, he will die.

In the translation of **"Pont Mirabeau"**[49] by Guillaume Apollinaire, Kennedy returns to the theme of the lover and his beloved, symbolized by the Seine and the bridge on which the lover stands, reminiscing about the past and the "flow" of time. The poem is a marvelous creative effort on Kennedy's part that bears close scrutiny.[50] Kennedy uses wide spaces and other structural and grammatical features to express the disjunction the lover feels between himself and his beloved and between the past and present:

> Under Pont Mirabeau glides the Seine
>   And loves of ours
>   Must I think back to when
> Joy always followed in the wake of pain
>
>   Sound the hour   night draw near
>   The days go running   I stay here.[51]

The final line of the first stanza begins with "Joy" and ends with "pain," balanced at opposite ends by the opposite states of the poet's remembered love. Contrast, too, is evident in the opposition of movement and stasis, which the refrain expresses in a balanced line: "Sound the hour [space] night draw near." This refrain seems to freeze time on a stroke of the clock, an impression reinforced by the heavy stresses on *Sound* and *hour.* After the wide medial caesura, suggestive of the poet's meditative pause and of the wide and long separation of the lovers and of the poet's present and past times, the line continues: "night draw near." The image here is of motion, a contrast to the abrupt sound of the hour. Grammatically, the line suggests that the poet is addressing night, asking it to "draw near," to bring to the poet forgetfulness, death, sorrow, the inability to see. The second line of the refrain continues the idea of motion: "The days go running." The poet's sense of time's quick passage contrasts with the first line, which ends with a spondee that emphasizes movement toward closure and finality. But this motion is brought to an abrupt halt by the second half of the line: "I stay here." These contrasting ideas and images suggest the poet's painful dilemma: he wants to die, to forget, and to escape his painful memories and sense of loss, but he is mindful too of the fact that time swiftly distances him from his "loves." Paradoxically, ever in the moment, he finds that he does not move, however; he is always in sorrow and pain, for he is always in the moment. Every sounding of the hour reminds him that he is fixed in the moment. Time passes swiftly but he does not move: "I stay here." By not closing this line with a period, Kennedy suggests that his dilemma and sorrow are endless; ironically, he is fixed in endless time and is ever moving with it, but is ever fixed in the moment.

The second quatrain continues the poet's recollection of his time with his beloved by the Seine, under Pont Mirabeau. The image is of the lovers embracing, hand in hand, face to face, but the poet is looking for support too: "Hand in my hand stand by me face to face" (l. 7). The Seine lends counterpoint to the freshness of the lovers' joy: "Weary of everlasting looks the slow wave passes" (l. 10). Again, contrast expresses the poet's dilemma: to the river, the lovers are a wearisome sight, but for the lovers, the experience is fresh and joyful. The third quatrain returns to the idea that time passes swiftly by, like the river, only now the poet connects time and the river to love in an image, "Love flows away as running water went" (l. 13), and his sense of fixedness and entrapment returns in the next line: "As life is indolent" (l. 15). Contrast plagues his mind, for life is "indolent," yet "Hope is violent." The violence is caused by the poet's emotions as he hopes for a return of his love, yet he knows that time at every moment distances him from his loves, and, fixed in the moment, he can only suffer violent emotions, sorrow, and a sense of entrapment and helplessness. The final stanza states the poet's dilemma emphatically, repeating in the first line the sense of movement in time, "Though days run on [space] though days and weeks run on . . ." (l. 19). He knows, however, that "No time gone by / No love comes back again . . ." (ll. 20-21). Like the river, what flows away is gone forever. The final refrain, "The days

go running [space] I stay here . . . ," (l. 24), underscores the poet's sorrow and the painful dilemma that, like the line that lacks a period, continues without end.

"Pont Mirabeau" appealed to Kennedy for several reasons. Through it, he could express the kind of sorrow that his own experience probably lacked, and the poem's expression of love-sick suffering offered emotional, if vicarious, fulfillment. The poem also represented an artistic challenge beyond the difficulties of translation. The quatrain, one of Kennedy's favorite forms, is in this poem often "sprung" by spacing, and the lines vary in length. He was also challenged to capture not only the mood of the original poem but the imagery, which expresses complex feelings and paradoxical ideas about time. The poem is ostensibly about romantic love, but underneath the surface, as it were, Kennedy addresses the concept of flowing, structurally, emotionally, and philosophically. His success may be gauged by how he changed the opening line from the way it was printed in *French Leave.* His first attempt states the idea of the river's movement thus: "Underneath Pont Mirabeau flows the Seine." By the time he printed the poem in *Dark Horses,* he had honed his mastery of both form and idea to a point where he could with the slightest modification shift the emphasis from the preposition, *Underneath,* to the bridge, Pont Mirabeau, whose vowel sounds establish the poem's mood. Kennedy's impeccable ear for sound and exquisite taste told him also not to retain *flow,* which repeats the same vowels sounds as *Pont Mirabeau;* rather, he opened the sound somewhat with the word *glide,* which also suggests swift motion somewhat better than the original *flow* and shifts the sound from *o* sounds to the *s* sounds in *glides* and *Seine,* which suggest the idea of water slipping by. By shortening *Underneath,* he not only rids the line of the unnecessary sound and meaning of *neath* but also creates a better balance between the *n* sound in *Seine.* Thus altered, the new line reads: "Under Pont Mirabeau glides the Seine."

Kennedy next turned to Apollinaire's collection of animal portraits in *The Bestiary,* from which he translated six, each given four lines. This work resembles Kennedy's book for children, *Did Adam Name the Vinegarroon?* which was published a year before *French Leave* and which consists of portraits of natural and supernatural animals. The premise of the poems from Apollinaire's work is to draw parallels between the animal addressed and some aspect of humanity. In **"Hare,"** for example, the animal offers an example for the human addressed by the poem's speaker of how to conduct himself in his love making. Instead of leaping for cover "Like buck hare shacking up with lover," one should let his mind "obscenely lie / Like fat doe hare and fructify." In **"Grasshopper"** a connection is drawn between the grasshopper, "The diet of Saint John," and the poet's verses, which are exhorted to be like the grasshopper, "What the best folk nibble on." In **"Sirens"** the poet sees in the "discontent" of the Sirens a reflection of his own. It is not much of a leap from Kennedy's own bestiary to these French poems.

Robert Desnos is represented by two short poems. The first one, **"Sun,"** addresses the sunflower as the "Sun in the earth" and draws a parallel between the poet and the moon, "For round ourselves we go round / Like madmen in a pound." Desnos's **"Last Poem"** plays on the idea that the poet is a shade dreaming of the shade of his beloved. He is "A hundred times more shade than shade" (l. 7). In the final image the poet sees himself cast "into your sun-transfigured life" (l. 9). This final burst of poetic light demonstrates Kennedy's skill with imagery, even when he is bound by the ideas of another poet.

Kennedy's attraction to the poetry of despair in the French poets he admires drew him to Robert Sabatier's **"Mortal Landscape,"** which is somber, despairing. The speaker opens with a sense of anticipation, and the prospect is dark: "The bird is flown, the monster not yet born," and the world is "demolished." He lies with someone "in position on our deaths, / . . . in decrepit light / Weary of walking to encounter dawns" (ll. 3-5). Life is also brief, "A hairsbreadth crack"; even the stars "sink teeth in worlds," while he plants "the stolen dagger of my cry / Into that breast where Godhead walks its rounds" (ll. 7-10). The final stanza repeats the statement that opens the poem, "The bird is flown," and the poet seeks "a dirt hole where [he] can sleep." Death seems attractive to him, but that prospect disquiets him, too, for "so many bodies dreamless lie / That what in man is man has had to die / And even words at last make meals on lips" (ll. 18-20).[52] In the end, the speaker remains suspended in a bleak world with few options, none of them inviting—murder or peace—or death, wherein none dream—and in that state, "what in man is man" dies.

The last poem in the series, **"Central Heat"** by Pierre Reverdy, develops through a series of impressionist images that express disillusionment in unrelenting expressions of despair:

> Utter nought
> Dead fire a man relights that goes back out
> I've had enough of the wind
> I've had enough of the sky
> Deep down whatever we look at is a lie
> Even your lips. . . .
>
> (ll. 10-15)

The poem's dominant metaphor is that of a furnace and its attendant features, principally light and heat. The speaker's problem is that he suffers a "Short circuit in the heart / Engine that won't start . . ." (ll. 6-7). By the middle of the final stanza, it becomes clear that the speaker is the light in the furnace who responds to the presence of the woman. The poem becomes a revelation of the meaning of the "central heat" of the title: it is the fire of sexual arousal, and for the male, the "Light's led here on a leash of copper wire," whereas her heart is "of the same stuff as the sun's fire" (ll. 24-25).

Kennedy's interest in translation did not begin, and would not end, with this small volume. He would go on to translate some German poems as well as, most recently, Aristophanes' *Lysistrata,* but early in his career, when French poetry was still fresh in his mind, *French Leave* offered him an opportunity to concentrate on those sentiments that reflected his own mood and offered him a rewarding challenge.[53]

In the same year that *French Leave* was published, 1983, the self-published chapbook *Missing Link* appeared, containing eighteen adult poems and four children's poems collected under a single title, **"For Children, If They'll Take 'Em."**[54] Kennedy sets the tone of this slim volume with an overblown subtitle: *"Being a Retrospective of Twenty-two Songs, Poems, Epigrams, and Verses That the Author Now Considers among his Least Unsuccessful and Contemptible, Including Several Long out of Print in This Country, and Offered as a Freeby to a Patient Listener, in Thankfulness, by X. J. Kennedy."* In collecting his poems for *Cross Ties,* he omits seven of these poems. The front cover is illustrated by a drawing of a giant hairy paw wrapped around a young man dressed in eighteenth-century attire, including a wig. On the monster's wrist is a shackle with a broken link. Kennedy was having fun with this volume. Some of the poems appear to have been snipped out of previous books and simply pasted into this one. Some titles are typed above their respective poems, and different typewriters were used to type the poems, too. All of this informality is consistent with the poems Kennedy selected to reprint here, including a handful of his best serious poems—**"First Confession," "Nude Descending a Staircase," "Cross Ties"** (in its fourth collection so far) and a few others. Despite the presence of some serious poems, the emphasis is on playfulness and lightness of spirit.[55] He also advertises on the back cover five books of his poetry for children and his anthology, *Tygers of Wrath.* Perhaps the link that Kennedy felt had been missing was this lightness of spirit.

Hangover Mass, another chapbook, appeared in 1984. The collection included fourteen poems. All but **"A Word from Hart Crane's Ghost"**[56] are reprinted a year later in *Cross Ties.* The excellent quality of the printing of this volume, published by Bits Press, makes the book remarkably different from *Missing Link.* The text and paper are first-rate, and the pages are stitched between a soft cover. The selection of poems has a characteristic range. Five of the poems have religious elements or themes, and the first one, **"Hangover Mass,"** combines a father, booze, a saloon atmosphere, and the Catholic religion, all in five quatrains. None has the rebellious spirit of **"First Confession"** and satirical attacks of **Bulsh,** yet Kennedy's attitude toward religion remains irreverent. Although the spirit is more often serious than light-hearted, the volume is never grim, and it contains none of Kennedy's satiric epigrammatic attacks on human types and conditions, his sense of futility, or his gloomy assessment of conditions in the modern world.

For all his efforts and continued publication, Kennedy's poetry did not attract much critical attention from **Breaking and Entering** (1971) to **Cross Ties** (1985). His collections consisted of skimpy chapbooks and shared space with other poets, and when he did produce a collection, many of the poems were taken from earlier collections and would appear in later ones. Perhaps Kennedy's heart and mind lay with the children's literature he was publishing in this interim, four volumes of verse and a novel.

Another contributing factor to the paucity of Kennedy's output and public notice during these years may be discerned in the public notice of the publication of **Hangover Mass,** in which Peter Wild declares that "Writing in meter and rhyme leads to sure artistic disaster, if not psychic disorder,"[57] for "The more hidebound proponents [of open forms] would have all measured poetry swept into the dustbin." Kennedy, however, has "stuck with the poetry world despite the uneasy ride, writing all the while and iconoclastically in metered, rhymed verse." According to Wild, the evidence that Kennedy has survived is **Hangover Mass,** "an elegantly printed offering of a mere fourteen pieces, but its length serves as a testimony to Kennedy's demands of the quality of what he prints."[58] The reason for Kennedy's slight public showing over the previous fifteen years has been, it seems, his insistence on quality, on not releasing a poem until it has matured in his mind. Whatever the reason, Kennedy's next collection brought his poetry once again to the attention of a host of critics, who recognized him as a poet of the first rank and effectively answered those critics who seemed unable to see beyond Kennedy's puns, playfulness, and technical virtuosity.

Cross Ties: Selected Poems was published in 1985 and promptly won the Los Angeles Times Book Award.[59] It represented Kennedy's most important collection to date. The book's back cover says the book contains "every poem that the poet cares to save . . . ," although Kennedy has revised this claim. In the book's notes he explains the arrangement of the poems: "For a reader who might care to trace the progress of my work, or its deterioration, I have sorted these poems into five sections; then, within each section, arranged things from early to late, following the order in which they first appeared. In between these five acts, each section called an Intermission offers light refreshment. Like each act, each intermission also follows a chronology—one that begins as early as 1955 and ends as late as 1984, since it displays the kind of verse I have been writing off and on all this while." Curiously, Kennedy had earlier given a different opinion of arrangements. "Me, when I read a book, I don't give a hoot about how the poems are arranged; all that counts is: are there a few good poems in it? Auden once twitted this fallacy by arranging his *Collected Poems* by titles, in alphabetical order."[60] In any case, the book's design follows that of his three major previous collections, **Nude Descending a Staircase** (1961), **Growing into Love** (1969), and **Breaking and Entering** (1971). Of the one hundred twenty-two poems in **Cross Ties,** twenty-eight had not been collected before, and, like **Nude Descending a Staircase** and **Missing Link,** the book contains light verse, serious poetry, and verse for children. As in **Nude,** the sections of light verse are titled "Intermissions," giving the whole collection a theatrical connection. Though this framework remains more abstract than felt as one reads, it nevertheless illustrates how Kennedy sees his poetry and his relationship with readers.

Cross Ties shows clearly that throughout his career Kennedy is aware of the diversity of his literary heritage, seeing in it an opportunity to weave new patterns, richer for the diversity. His skill in journeying into hazardous waters is remarkably present in poems that find in traditional subjects and forms new directions. He is so astute in his handling of subjects that the old or familiar comes forth entirely fresh, freshened not only by his imagery and form but also by the meaning that emerges from his choices. Without the appearance of great compression, lines can express a great deal, both seen and felt, because the poems work on many levels simultaneously. What appears first in the collection is a series of poems whose subjects reflect Kennedy's early interest in what other poets have done, from medieval (**"Faces from a Bestiary"**) to modern (**"Ladies Looking for Lice / after Rimbaud"**). Kennedy's interest in popular (or folk) subjects and rhythms is evident in **"Song to the Tune of 'Somebody Stole My Gal'"** and **"In a Prominent Bar in Secaucus One Day."** These serio-comic exercises prominently display the importance to Kennedy of rhythm and playful wit and suggest that he is exploring the relation of ideas to rhythms that have that "swing." This interest leads in two directions: into poetry for children and into the serious poems. The more one reads these latter poems, the more one sees that play is basic to Kennedy's poetic craft, most evident in his many puns, in his recurrent ambivalence, and in his irrepressible humor and irony, all complementary expressions of his creative impulses and vision.

Although *Cross Ties* is laid out like a five-act play, the poet journeying, not unlike Odysseus, from one time period, or act, to the next, the poems may be viewed also as discrete expressions strung on a different string, depending on which thematic trail one follows.[61] When asked whether there is "a single thematic thread running through *Cross Ties,*" Kennedy replied, "Ex-Catholicism,"[62] but many themes tie the poems together, actually. The theme found in **"The Sirens,"** for instance, surfaces again in **"Two Views of Rhyme and Meter."** The sound Odysseus hears "in his loins" echoes in the later poem's definition of meter as "the thrust rest thrust of loins." Many of the poems explore the creative process. Kennedy mocks the writer's self-scrutiny in a reprint of his famous epigram—"Would you lay well? Don't watch"—but elsewhere he is serious about the origin of the creative impulse. In **"Creation Morning"** he likens God's impulse to that of boys wanting to leave their mark in wet cement and to the bridegroom's urge to make something grow from effort (sexual). In his final poem Kennedy resorts to the poet's traditional **"Envoi,"** sending his book into the world with a hope that it enjoys good fortune. Typically, though, Kennedy's version ends on self-effacement. Addressing his "slothful book," he tells it to go forth and sing to the one who "will care / Should words with a rhythm align" (ll. 6-7) and to sing to lovers. They will soon have other interests, however, and will abandon his book, which then "Crash-lands."

In several poems the advance of generations plays a major role. The interweaving of generations is especially pronounced in Kennedy's old companion, **"Cross Ties,"** in which the speaker sees his child as the recipient of his own entwined loyalties. **"Last Child"** and **"The Shorter View"** also deal with generational sequence from the perspective of Kennedy's personal experience. Seeing lineage in **"Dirty English Potatoes"** makes the poet realize how far the new world has taken him from the land: "I want / Unreal meals risen from sheer mist." Kennedy is not despairing, however. Perhaps his faith in the benefits of artful play and in regeneration keeps him balanced between the light of blind faith and the darkness of despair. The individual may reach the end of the line, but the generations advance.

Kennedy's interest in people is also a main feature in the collection. His songs capture the spirit and comical character of the raucous denizens of saloons; his epigrams skewer ignorance and pretense; and several poems portray the aged, the isolated, and the disturbed. Some early and middle poems address the despoliation of the American landscape by industry and neglect.

"No Neutral Stone" takes a pessimistic view of human worth and the value of beauty and love. Summer passion generally turns into "Starved sod . . . and ashen / Leaves . . . ," symbols of decline of flesh and spirit and of death. John Keats used the stars and planets to characterize human love and beauty, he reminds us, but today "Venus thus invoked / Scrapes dog dung from her soles and comes indoors." The world consists of "debris," which "Sprawls formless" until a passing poet, using "an electromagnet of emotion," collects material from this formless heap of debris to create a "whole mess." The junk parts that the poet misses in his sweep meanwhile lie "in the rejected world's trash heap," pelted by incessant rain. One of these rejected parts, a "rusting wheel or gearshift lever," asks, "Am I not what Hardy must have felt, / Alone, after Tryphena slammed her thighs?"[63] This closing image, reminiscent of the talkative earthen jars in the *Rubaiyat of Omar Khayyám,* suggests that the poet's depiction of human love and beauty leaves something out, the aftermath of passion, the "junk" that would show what the lover feels after the act of sex, passion, or love. The poem suggests that human passion, love, and beauty occur in a world where frost holds sway, a world that is a junkyard, which provides poets the material for creating images of beauty, love, and passion. The poem also suggests that "No Neutral Stone" exists, this stone being a magnet that draws from the junk heap random pieces to form its own vision, or version, of the "truth." Inevitably, though, pieces are left out; no one perspective, not even the poet's, is wholly true.

This is Kennedy at his bitterest, and he seems convinced that nature and humans are too often at odds, nature being the universal spirit that runs through all things as well as the visible parts of our existence that are not made by humans. He seems also convinced that humans lack the ability to understand how nature works. He makes this point in **"Categories,"** which focuses on the puzzles found in nature and in man's condition. "Nothing stays put" is the opening statement; today "Species collide like fast tailgating cars . . . ," (l. 3), and the century "Collapses through the mind's pained hourglass" (l. 11). These changes are illogical and beyond human comprehension; they are also unpredictable. Understanding natural phenomena challenges the human intellect almost beyond limit: "Was it Rimbaud, that trader of tusks, who said / You don't begin to understand / Till through the tip of your tongue you hear bright red?" (ll. 12-14). The poem ends on a story about "that master in Kyoto who began / 'To seize on what had been left out before' . . ." (ll. 15-16). This bit of wisdom is counterpointed by a novice monk's demonstration that "you can / If you have hatched from names, or lack clean plates, / Serve cake on a shut fan" (ll. 18-20). If one can understand the monk's demonstration, one can perhaps understand nature and man's condition. The inability to understand is proof that one lacks the insight or wisdom needed to understand the puzzle of nature and human behavior. The poem puts the reader in the poet's place, faced with a conundrum that leaves one stymied.

Kennedy believes that as long as humans assault the environment, it will retaliate, and that in the end nature will prevail. Its great trump card, of course, is death, and throughout his career Kennedy shows an interest in death, increasingly in his own. One of the intermissions in this volume, in fact, is subtitled, "Epigrams and Epitaphs."[64]

The changes in Kennedy's thoughts regarding mortality and other abiding concerns may be attributed in part to his maturing. Early poems argue that the ancient gods abandoned humankind, and in later poems nature seems to have taken their place. Religion offers Kennedy no solace or hope, but nature does, in close, personal ways. The accumulation of snow, the falling of a leaf, the fresh earth, all seem to comfort Kennedy. **"Epiphany,"** the book's penultimate poem, helps to explain a profound shift in his vision of the world. Lying on the floor one day, he regards a simple chair: "For days I'd gone on trudging, too far dulled / To take mere things in" (ll. 5-6). Astounded, he finally sees "how they joined—the legs and rungs of chairs." His position is symbolic: he is "Floored now, freed from airs / Of uprightness . . ." (ll. 6-7). He could be speaking of his entire career, during which he has been "too far dulled / To take mere things in."[65] He also could be speaking of humans in general: when they are "freed from airs / Of uprightness . . . ," they can see that focusing on what is near and basic can bring an understanding of their relation to the Everything.

Five years after *Cross Ties* was published, Kennedy came out with another chapbook, *Winter Thunder* (1990), consisting of fifteen poems, though two poems, **"City Churchyard"** and **"Epigrams,"** contain individual poems under their titles. Six of the poems were originally intended for another collection.[66] The poems are often negative in their treatment of parenthood, the writer's lot, and death. The two longest poems add considerable weight to the darker mood of the selection. **"Pileup,"** which is reprinted in *The Lords of Misrule,* depicts in forty-one lines the scene of a traffic accident on a modern freeway, littered with wrecks and mangled bodies. In seventeen quatrains, **"Invitations to the Dance"** shows a nursing home where the dying inhabitants fight despair. Someone shouts, "'For what in God's name do we cling to living?'" Mabel offers a grim alternative to passivity and futility: "'Why, I'm dancing,' said Mabel, 'to keep from dying'" (l. 61). Ironically, Mabel's desperate effort to coax some liveliness out of her peers takes place on Easter morning. The final poem, **"Ambition,"** shows another protagonist frustrated by forces out of his control. In the poem's concluding quatrain, the entanglements that impede human effort are expressed in images that depict nature as the human's antagonist:[67]

> I'd be glad to go out on a limb with those
> Who can live with whatever a wind bestows

> Were it not for these roots, dug in deep to bear
> Never being done grasping for light and air.

> (ll. 9-12)

Two years later, in 1992, Kennedy published another major collection, *Dark Horses,* containing forty-three poems in three sections. Despite the "New Poems" printed on the book's cover, nine of the poems had already appeared in *Winter Thunder,* and **"Pont Mirabeau,"** here heavily revised, had been printed in *French Leave.* The title, *Dark Horses,* suggests that each of the poems in the collection is a "dark horse," an unlikely success, expressing Kennedy's characteristic modesty in presenting his own poetry. The title also has an apocalyptic sound, suggesting that Kennedy intended a significance beyond the individual meanings of each poem. In this sense the book contains Kennedy's vision of the times, and of the future. The implication is that the human race is in for a rough ride.[68]

One of the fundamental qualities of the poetry in *Dark Horses* is Kennedy's particular brand of wit, which was quickly noted by one of the book's reviewers, who appreciated its importance: "Although some of the New Formalists have published amusing formal epigrams, wit in the Jacobean or Augustan sense is not central to the work of most of them. For Kennedy, an older formalist, it is; every poem he writes is at least touched and sometimes profoundly shaped by it. As a feature of style his wit manifests itself in verbal sleight-of-hand, often in the interest of satire. As a quality of thought it brings notice, as Doctor Johnson said of Metaphysical poetry, to 'occult resemblances' between apparently disparate things, yielding a complex overview of existence."[69]

By placing **"Woman in Rain"** at the beginning of *Dark Horses,* Kennedy establishes a connection between it and **"Nude Descending a Staircase,"** the title poem in his first collection. It is no coincidence that both poems employ structure to depict the literal and metaphorical motions of a woman. Both poems suggest how much and in what ways Kennedy has and has not changed in the intervening thirty years. He has developed a clearer focus on the relationship of humankind to nature and remains concerned mainly with contemporary scenes and figures, often in a context reminiscent of prior ages—the epigraph of **"The Woodpile Skull"** is a line from *Hamlet,* for example, and Hamlet is alluded to in the poem itself. Though his range is wide, Kennedy looks deeply at the world we live in, keenly aware, as Robert Frost was, of the menacing aspects of man's physical environment. This theme runs throughout *Dark Horses*: "The wind last night kept breaking into song / Beautiful only if you heard it wrong," he writes in **"Twelve Dead, Hundreds Homeless."** The wind can be a weapon, delivering "A note so high / Removed an ear that listened."

Kennedy believes that the future depends on a synthesis of what has been and what is. In **"The Woodpile Skull,"** for instance, we find the speaker confronted by "a black ant's severed head." Remembering a similar scene in Robert Burns's "To a Field Mouse," the reader is intrigued: what will the poet do with this familiar theme? Kennedy brings a modern perception, of course:

> Wind wedges through my woodpile. But this chill
> Comes from a sense that, blindly, I can kill
> And can be killed. Bemused and metaphoric,
> I stand, ham Hamlet to a formic Yorick.

> (ll. 29-30)

The speaker's dilemma is contemporary. The past gives him cause to ruminate anew on his relationship to higher forces. Though he may feel like a "ham Hamlet," the playfulness of the expression suggests that he is not entirely uncomfortable in his predicament, chilled, perhaps, but finally bemused because he can be metaphoric, and formic. Poetry may be a means to keep the chill off. The final stanza of **"The Woodpile Skull,"** like the entire collection, reflects a view of the human condition that is neither bleak nor sentimental. It is often just commonsensical, as he says in **"Christmas Abrupted,"** where he explains the "common sense in stripping bare" the tree that fixes children in fantasy.

Still, many poems take a gloomy view of the human condition, and Kennedy ends the volume with a series of them. In **"Staring into a River Till Moved by It,"** a bridge breaks from its supports and sweeps two people away. They barely make it back to land. The title suggests that the couple would be emotionally "Moved" by the river, but the poem gives an ironic twist, turning the river into a hazard barely survived. In another poem, the speaker nearly drowns; in another, a leopard in a painting is "crouched to leap / Upon a bathing beauty sound asleep." This poem, **"Black Velvet Art,"** claims that the stars "at the final dawn" will vanish, and God—in a rare poetic appearance—will command "Even the last black hole, *Get off My Hands.*" In **"Winter Thunder"** cell mates hear "the widening crack of thunder" and their "jailblock breaks and falls." Finally, the speaker in **"Ambition"** wonders whether he has wasted his summer indoors. Speaking perhaps for Kennedy himself, he suggests that he is rooted in earth, and though these roots provide an anchor in "whatever the wind bestows," they also leave him "grasping for light and air." If Kennedy late in his career feels the heaviness of years accumulating in an indifferent universe, poetry gives him a means for recording his predicament. Poetry may not promise happy times ahead, but it offers an activity that has long sustained him. Both *Winter Thunder* and *Dark Horses* end with the same two poems, **"Winter Thunder"** and **"Ambition,"** suggesting that Kennedy wants to leave readers with a dark view of the modern predicament. He does not reprint in *Dark Horses* the more boisterous **"Invitation to the Dance,"** although this poem's rollicking spirit underlies many of his poems.[70] When one thinks of Kennedy's poetry, the voice that rises above all others, it is hoped, is Mabel's, and she is shouting, "This world is the worse for too little dancing."

In recent collections, Kennedy has focused on epigrams.[71] The all-Kennedy number of *The Epigrammatist,* published in 1994, collects forty-six poems of various lengths, none more than eight lines and most only two or four lines long. The dedication to Donald Hall, "master of the art of making each word matter," befits the ensuing series of epigrams, in which each word matters and which features the best of Kennedy's epigrammatic skills: wit, grace, and verbal dexterity. The ironic voice gives Kennedy a distance from his subject that suits his poetic temperament, and the formal brevity of the epigram allows him to deflate, deride, and denounce and have fun doing so. The poems include Kennedy's favorite targets in his epigrams: hypocrisy, pretense, and folly. Three of the four sections are titled "Literati," "Sexual Combat," and "Epitaphs," and one section lacks a title.

The Minimus Poems (1996) continues in the same vein as *The Epigrammatist,* offering satirical epigrams on favorite subjects. It differs from all of Kennedy's publications, however, in its format. Each epigram is printed on a separate card, each is about the size of a postcard, and each is printed in a different typeface. Some are illustrated with graphics or simple drawings. None is numbered, so readers may arrange the poems in whatever order they wish, even use them as greeting cards, sending them to friends. The title of this little production may be a playful poke at Charles Olson, the poet-guru who inspired legions of free-verse writers and who titled his poetry collection of 1960 *Maximus Poems.* If so, Kennedy's epigrams contain features that would be anathema to Olson—rhyme, meter, regularity, balance—and the expectations and demands of preconceived form. The effectiveness with which Kennedy uses these elements makes his twitting of the opposition all the more fun.

The Minimus Poems represents one of Kennedy's main features: a willingness and ability to remain fluid. His maturity as a poet is reflected in his treatment of such subjects as mankind's relation to the world at large, and if he has grown pessimistic about the fate of mankind and if he remains less than rosy about the role good poetry will play in the future, he seems unable to sustain a bitter attitude for long. Perhaps the epigram helps him to diffuse the pessimism. In any case, he can continue to experiment, to be challenged, and to see the past not as a burden but as a kind of anchor. Perhaps, he would say, the past is almost all we have left, and writing about it and learning from it may be the best we can do for our future.

Kennedy has remarked that he seems to come out with a new collection about every ten years. If we scan the list of his major publications, we find that he is not far off the mark. *Nude Descending a Staircase* appeared in 1961, *Breaking and Entering,* in 1971, *Growing into Love,* in 1969, *Cross Ties,* in 1985, *Dark Horses,* in 1992, and *The Lords of Misrule,* in 2002. He sends poems first to magazines, where they incubate until a collection is offered or until he feels ready to give them another burnishing, and out they come. Each collection represents not only the accumulation of a decade of thinking and maturing but a fresh opportunity to stage a new presentation, to put on a new show. *Nude Descending a Staircase* was designed both as a confession and as an introduction, Kennedy the poet descending the staircase and baring all in tantalizing artfulness. *Breaking and Entering* was an attempt to burglarize the reader's mind; *Growing into Love* offered a mature poet's exploration of love's emotions and commitments, and in *Cross Ties,* Kennedy tied together twenty years of writing poetry for adults and gave it all a dramatic structure. He was not altogether pleased with *Dark Horses,* for it lacked his characteristic light verse and epigrammatic sorties into contemporary manners, morals, and moronic behavior. He made up for the omission partly by publishing a series of epigrams in *The Epigrammatist* and *The Minimus Poems,* just prior to *The Lords of Misrule,* which contains only one epigram (**"Epitaph Proposed for the Headstone of S. R. Quiett"**) but several comic poems.[72] The book's title also calls attention to the book's premise: traditional forms control the riotous spirits of poetic creativity.[73] Kennedy may have intended a sly dig at the free-verse poets by casting his **"Invocation"** in unrhymed stanzas of irregular length and, in that same invocation, by giving some of the elements of traditional poetry a living presence: "Come then, sweet Meter, / Come, strict-lipped Stanza, / Regulate the revels / Of these half-crocked lines" (ll. 16-19). These spirits overlook the "revels" that follow, and the poems themselves are a blend of celebration and reflection.

In the absence of stinging satire, Kennedy has turned his mind to reflecting and recollecting scenes and people from his own past. The first two poems set the tone of the whole book, a somewhat bemused, somewhat nostalgic, looking back. Time is on the poet's mind first. **"'The Purpose of Time Is to Prevent Everything from Happening at Once'"** conflates into a sonnet a series of remembered moments: "Suppose you crash / Your car, your marriage—toddler laying waste / A field of daisies, schoolkid, zitfaced teen / With lover zipping up your pants in haste / Hearing your parents' tread downstairs—all one" (ll. 4-8). The next poem, and several after it, turns to a childhood memory in portraying a relative who died of cancer, still present in a series of images: "But here you are with your invented toy, / This empty cup suspended in midair, / Arms uplifted,

sunlight drifting through your hair, / Your upturned face still wreathed with utter joy" (ll. 13-16). The quatrains condense into vivid images years of life and intense emotion. In portraits of Jimmy Harlow and Naomi Trimmer, Kennedy recalls former companions in fond detail, and the ten quatrains of **"Five-and-Dime, Late Thirties"** offer images that remind one of a Norman Rockwell painting, the youth savoring the aroma of "frying franks' / Salt pungent odor" and giving thanks "For shreds of turkey strung / On a mound of stuffing doled / With icecream scoop, lone spoon / Of gray canned peas, one cold / Roll, cranberry half-moon" (ll. 4-8). The painter, however, gives way to the poet who has seen what the youth cannot or will not see and what the poet cannot forget:

> nightly, hordes of rats
> Shat in the licorice lace
>
> Until one day the Board
>   Of Health padlocked the door.
> As sure as FDR
>   Had kept us out of war,
>
> Brown Shirts were just a show,
>   Hitler a comic wraith
> Far off. What you don't know
>   Won't hurt had been our faith.
>
> (ll. 27-36)

The following poem, **"Sailors with the Clap,"** captures a theme that runs through all Kennedy's collections, that revelry has a sharp edge to it. The sailors' venereal disease is symbolic punishment for the sins of the flesh: "each man smokes thoughtfully, / Counting his shots, those daily penances, like beads told on a cast-iron rosary" (ll. 6-8). Kennedy the ex-Catholic recalls his navy days with the poet's ironic perspective shaping the memory in a sonnet as smoothly made as the sailors' rosary bead.

The underlying pattern in these early poems in *The Lords of Misrule* reflects one of the reasons Kennedy turns to the sonnet, the epigram, and the rhymed stanza: each is shaped by opposition, point and counterpoint. The yin-yang of his vision provides the swing he looks for in poetry: as he has said, "it don't mean a thing if it ain't got that swing," the swing from bright hope to gloom, from resplendence to tawdriness, from one perspective to another, which often undermines the previous idea or qualifies it in some way. This pattern is seen in **"Salute Sweet Deceptions."** This eight-line unrhymed poem, like the epigram and the sonnet, establishes a thought, and an image: "At break of morning / How the brick firehouse / Seems carved from amber . . ." (ll. 3-6). The image stays in the mind across the space that separates the two stanzas and comes to rest on another image that contrasts sharply with the previous one: "Beer cans in river / Mime stars dissolving / A seedpearl necklace / Of rain wears phone-wires" (ll. 5-8). Like the collagist, Kennedy creates an arresting beauty out of details that in themselves are unattractive or unremarkable. His poem unfolds in layers of meaning and effect, one thought or image opposed by another, yet together they form an attractive whole. Without the second image, the first would be un-redeemed ugliness or commonplace; without the first, the second would be sight without insight. Together, for Kennedy, they form a striking vision that comes out of his experience.

Kennedy has spoken of the tension derived from working with traditional forms, such as the sonnet or couplet, and the poems in his latest collection are rife with this kind of tension, as **"Salute Sweet Deceptions"** demonstrates. He favors, too, the quatrain, which allows him to vary the rhyme scheme and, in that way, vary the tension and the poem's yin-yang swing. Two dozen of these poems employ the quatrain, which are unrhymed, or have varying rhymes, *abba, abab,* or *aabb*. The sonnets, of course, are made up of two quatrains in the octave and another in the sestet, and five of the poems use the sonnet form. The metric base of the lines, too, can vary from five stresses in each line to an alternate pattern of three and two. The **"Epitaph Proposed for the Headstone of S. R. Quiett,"** for example, consists of one quatrain, each line having five accents:

> Born with loud cries but carried off in quiet,
>   I lie, the stillest of the Quiett boys.
> Death sang a song so sweet I had to try it.
>   I might have known. It's only empty noise.

Subjects characteristic of Kennedy's earlier collections are represented here as well. He especially likes to portray tourists confronted by unsettling places, as he does in **"Fat Cats in Egypt,"** where "One thin barefoot girl / Nibbles from empty fingers. Given cash, / She yells—and we're surrounded in a flash . . ." (ll. 16-18). A street scene is revisited in **"Street Moths,"** where "Grown boys at night before the games arcade / Wearing tattoos that wash off in the sink / Accelerate vain efforts to get laid" (ll. 2-4). An airport lounge, a bus station where "People lip cupfuls of coffee," a police court, a motel, or a "funky pizza parlor," all remind us that Kennedy has kept a keen eye on humans shuffling about. What people have made of themselves and their world is the subject of many of these poems, a pileup on the freeway and commuter's experience symbolizing the loss of roots in the earth. The television screen, for Kennedy, symbolizes another shift in the human condition, which fixes the individual in front of a "beaming face" that "for a moment . . . obscures / The stares of unforgiving stars" (**"Covering the Massacre"**). It all makes the poet occasionally long for the good old days, as he does in **"Then and Now,"** which opens with a forthright statement: "I half long for those crappy days

again, / When babies used to be produced by sex. . . ." Sometimes he is simply tired: "I'm sick of old perplexities. Sweet Jaysus, / Give us a patch of clarity instead" (**"Perplexities"**).

For Kennedy, who is fond of singing **"In a Prominent Bar in Secaucus One Day"** and other rollicking ballads to audiences and friends, song has offered a way of enduring whatever in a fallen world blocks out the stars, and he restates his credo—and this book's major theme—in a brief poem that also acknowledges the loss of an audience for poetry these days:

> How odd that verse that's song
> Should so displease the young.
> They are so serious.
> They hate all artifice
> As standing in the way
> Of mind's insistent say.
> But to my mind what counts
> Is language that surmounts
> The message it must bear,
> Steps back without a care
> And, stone blind, yields the day
> To bloodstream's reckless play.

Old people, children, death, these subjects, too, are given ample space in these poems, and all leave images that represent Kennedy at his best, where all the elements of his art combine, and where sound and sight form music and insight. Two poems that best illustrate this kind of poetic moment deal with very different experiences, but each is exceedingly private and intensely felt. Together they place Kennedy at the peak of his achievement and show how he finds stability in a world that has lost its center. **"Close Call"** stops time for an instant as the poet catches a sudden insight:

> How suddenly she roused my ardor,
> That woman with wide-open car door
> Who, with a certain languid Sapphic
> Grace into brisk rush-hour traffic
> Stepped casually. I tromped the brake.
> Her lips shaped softly, "My mistake."
> Then for a moment as I glided
> By, our glances coincided
> And I drove off, whole rib cage filled
> With joy at having not quite killed.

The joy of this moment is generated, partly, by the realization that this near collision has brought together two strangers into an intimacy that would not have occurred otherwise. The poem becomes a paradigm of the experience itself, for it brings together sound and sense in a momentary coincidence, fixing disparate elements forever in a single unity—"ardor" and "car door," for example, or "Sapphic" and "traffic"—in a flawless, surprising intimacy. The humor of the expression is as light as the moment and their relationship are fleeting.

We realize the exchange is sexual when we read, "Her lips shaped softly, 'My mistake,'" but their encounter is too accidental, brief, and unphysical to be other than innocent.

A different world is evoked in the book's final poem, **"September Twelfth, 2001,"** which eschews words of outrage and does not attempt to describe the horror of a terrorist attack in photographic detail; rather, Kennedy has condensed both outrage and horror into an image that expresses more than a thousand pictures could: "Two caught on film who hurtle / From the eighty-second floor, / Choosing between a fireball / And to jump holding hands . . ." (ll. 1-4). The absence of rhyme in this quatrain strips the moment down to its bare elements, floor, fireball, hands. Kennedy, with exquisite taste, lets the image carry the unbearable lightness of his being still alive:

> Alive, we open eyelids
> On our pitiful share of time,
> We bubbles rising and bursting
> In a boiling pot.

He shows how imagery can make the heart burst. His latest collection shows how strong are his principles, how keen his mind, how sharp his eye, and how honed are his skills.

Notes

1. X. J. Kennedy, "Comment," *Poetry* 151, nos. 1-2 (October-November 1987), 215-16.

2. Lachlan Mackinnon noted this remarkable quality twenty-five years later, saying that although *Cross Ties* "contains poems written from 1955 to 1984, it is impossible to tell early Kennedy from late[;] . . . like Frost, whose voice he deliberately takes on in a light poem, [Kennedy] demonstrates the virtues of consistency." ("High Fidelity," *Times Literary Supplement* 4303 [September 20, 1985]: 1039).

3. John Simon, "More Brass Than Enduring," *Hudson Review* 15 (autumn 1962), 464-65.

4. Forrest Read, "Notes, Reviews & Speculations," *Epoch* 11 (winter 1962): 257.

5. Theodore Holmes, "Wit, Nature, and the Human Concern," *Poetry* 100, no. 5 (August 1962): 321.

6. Thomas Goldstein, "X. J. Kennedy," *Dictionary of Literary Biography,* s.v. 5: 394. Goldstein contributed one of the longer reviews of Kennedy's career up to 1975, yet he clearly does not think much of Kennedy or his poetry. In addition to the attacks already quoted, he says that "Kennedy's poetry is often pugnacious," that "Another recurrent theme is a strident atheism"—he instances

"First Confession" as one of the examples—and to a critic who referred to Kennedy's poetry as "'irreverent speculations' on a variety of themes," Goldstein replies: "when Kennedy turns to religion, his poems become more intolerant than irreverent. Rather than satirize the organization of religion, he often questions the authenticity of people's religious beliefs." Of *Breaking and Entering,* Goldstein says, "The title page contains a portentous quotation from T. S. Eliot. . . . Yet the seven new poems do not transcend, in either theme or scope, those of the previous books. It is difficult to imagine in what manner such a poem as 'In a Secret Field' may divert the mind." Goldstein is even less taken with *Emily Dickinson in Southern California,* in which Kennedy, "Rather than interpret the mayhem of Southern California as though through the ironic, cryptic, and refined sensibility of Emily Dickinson . . . is content to imitate her verse. The similarity gets no closer, however, than the frequent use of the dash, because Kennedy mocks the combination of depth of vision and teasing playfulness characteristic of Dickinson's verse. Ultimately, his poems only look like hers on the page." Goldstein thinks Kennedy's "most successful verse to date" may be found in *Celebrations after the Death of John Brennan* because "his subject . . . gives the poem direction and poignancy." (5: 396-97).

7. Ibid., 394.

8. Forrest Read, "Notes, Reviews & Speculations," 258.

9. Ibid., 259.

10. Holmes, "Wit, Nature, and the Human Concern," 321.

11. Kennedy identifies this work as a "brochure of poems by poets associated in Ann Arbor and Detroit, published by Burning Deck (at the time run by Donald C. Hope). The volume includes poems by James Camp, Donald Hall, D. C. Hope, John Heath-Stubbs, X. J. Kennedy, W. D. Snodgrass, and Bernard Keith Waldrop" (private correspondence with the author). W. D. Snodgrass adds that Kennedy and Keith Waldrop "—also a grad student—were joint heads of the John Barton Wolgamot Society. This organization, dedicated to the Principles of the Truly Awful and intended to offset the rigid propriety and stodginess of Michigan's English Department, was named for the worst poet they had yet discovered" ("Remembering Joe Kennedy," *Paintbrush* 25 [autumn 1998], 136).

12. David Harsent, "Poetae Sepulchrum," *Spectator* (February 12, 1972). Harsent is not alone on this point; sixteen years later, Moore Moran felt that in

Cross Ties Kennedy's "cleverness sometimes borders on the cute. Or that such a large swallow of traditional (and predictable) verse forms tires the palate a bit prematurely. But these are venial [sic] sins" ("X. J. Kennedy, *Cross Ties*," *Prairie Schooner* 60, no. 4 [winter 1986]: 113-14).

13. David Harsent is not favorably impressed by this widely praised epigram, saying that "it is always a pleasure to watch a craftsman at work—but it can become a questionable virtue when used for little more than a five-finger exercise, as in 'Ars Poetica'" ("Poetae Sepulchrum").

14. Kennedy would not reprint this poem in later collections, perhaps because his emotional ties to the poem's central event, the assassination of President John F. Kennedy, diminished over time.

15. Stephen Tudor, *"Growing into Love," Spirit* 37 (spring 1970): 38.

16. Ibid.

17. John Leggett, *Boston Globe,* 24 August 1969, 73.

18. Peter L. Simpson, "The Candor of Poetry," *St. Louis Post-Dispatch,* 7 December 1969, 16M.

19. Leggett, "Poems with a Temper of Mind," 73.

20. John Demos, "A Review of *Growing into Love,* by X. J. Kennedy," *Library Journal* 94, no. 15 (September 1, 1969): 2929.

21. Alan Brownjohn, "Dark Forces," *New Statesman* 28, no. 2009 (September 12, 1969): 347.

22. Knute Skinner, "Good Measures," *Northern Review,* XII, 95. Douglas Dunn also believed that this collection shows that Kennedy's "wit gets chronologically darker and sharper." *Encounter,* May 1972, 77.

23. Skinner, *Review* XII, 94. Thomas Goldstein says that the poem characterizes all those involved in such reading trips, including Kennedy himself, as "phony and culpable," adding that "his willingness to acknowledge his own part in the sanctimonious behavior of high literary circles does not exonerate him from the self-conscious cuteness that characterizes much of the poetry in this volume." *Dictionary of Literary Biography,* s.v. "Kennedy, X. J.," 396.

24. Thomas Tessier, "X. J. Kennedy's Poetry," *The New Haven Register,* 1969.

25. P. J. Ferlazzo is so struck by Kennedy's use of traditional forms, as evidenced in *Cross Ties,* that he says, "Not since the 18th century has one seen such a commitment to traditional forms," and although he admires Kennedy's "clear, sensible intelligence at work and at play on the page," Ferlazzo thinks that Kennedy has limited his audience: "He is writing essentially for the college crowd—readers, for example, who have studied the college textbooks he and his wife (Dorothy M. Kennedy), have edited and written over the years. Perhaps, one is tempted to say, he is writing for English majors. In sum, if Kennedy is an academic poet, he is one of the best" ("Kennedy, X. J. *Cross Ties*: Selected Poems," *Choice* 23 [October 1985:296]). This comment is surprising in a review of *Cross Ties,* which appeared in 1985, by which time Kennedy was long past being considered an "academic" poet. For some readers, apparently, old—and outmoded—labels are difficult to put aside. Nevertheless, the belief persisted. Mark McCloskey ends his long review of *Cross Ties* on the same idea: "The range of poets to whom he alludes is wide . . . These and various allusions to such bookish things as Greek mythology and the Great Chain of Being tend to confine the focus of his work (notwithstanding the down-to-earth tone behind it) to an academic audience. All in all, though, Kennedy's work is first-rate within its confinement" (*"Cross Ties: Selected Poems,"* in *Magill's Literary Annual,* ed. Frank N. Magill. [Englewood Cliffs, N.J.: Salem Press, 1986] 1: 203. R. S. Gwynn probably sensed that Kennedy's reputation as an academic poet would be an issue when *Cross Ties* was published, for in his review of it, he sought to put the issue to rest: "Those who favor neat schisms in their -isms would call him an 'academic' poet, though Kennedy's ties to the university are now limited to guest lectures and readings and the continued success of *Literature,* one of the most popular of freshman textbooks ever" ("Swans in Ice," *Sewanee Review* 43, no. 4 [fall 1985]: lxxviii).

26. Ralph J. Mills, Jr., "Three Established Poets and a New One," *Chicago Sun-Times Book Week,* 19 October 1969, 10. Douglas Dunn, speaking of *Breaking and Entering,* also believes that Kennedy may seem "dry and academic" because he "writes carefully, usually in polished stanzas in which a dexterous technique complements a cultured wit and balanced sense of narrative episode, but the fineness of craft is never offensively obtrusive as the only reason for having written . . . and he prefers the mystery of feelings to showing off in metre." *Encounter,* May 1972, 77. Edward Lucie-Smith relegates Kennedy to the "academic wing of contemporary American poetry" and considers him to be, essentially, "an extremely witty lightweight, a poet with a cunning ear and a deft hand with rhyme and off-rhyme" (*Contemporary Poets,* 2nd edition, 1975).

27. Tessier, "X. J. Kennedy's Poetry."

28. James Carroll, "Blossoming Poet," a review of *Growing into Love,* by X. J. Kennedy, *Catholic World,* January, 1970, 183.

29. Henry Taylor, "'Singing to Spite This Hunger,'" *The Nation* 210 (2 February 1970): 122-24.

30. Louis L. Martz, "Recent Poetry: The End of an Era," *Yale Review* 59 (winter 1970): 265.

31. This poem is not collected before *Cross Ties,* but Kennedy places it among the poems written between 1978 and 1984.

32. Martz, "Recent Poetry," 264.

33. X. J. Kennedy, "X. J. Kennedy Writes," *Poetry Book Society Bulletin* 71 (Christmas 1971).

34. The table of contents designates the last seven poems as "New poems"; the poem preceding these seven did not appear in a previous collection and is listed thus: *Bulsh* (1970). In "X. J. Kennedy Writes," Kennedy adds that he has been writing song lyrics while would-be poems remain obstinate.

35. "No Shortage of Satisfactions," *The Times Literary Supplement* 3643, 24 December 1971, 1602.

36. Alan Brownjohn, "Light Fantastic," *New Statesman,* 52-53.

37. When Kennedy reprinted this poem in *Cross Ties,* he revised it so that each of the tag-lines is repeated. Another poem in *Breaking and Entering,* "To a Young Poet," would be reprinted in *Emily Dickinson in Southern California* three years later without its first four lines because, as Kennedy explained in a note to the author, the editor, Jan Schreiber, suggested that they be omitted, and Kennedy agreed.

38. X. J. Kennedy, "X. J. Kennedy Writes."

39. The three poems are "Last Child," *Japanese Beetles* (a sequence of epigrams), and *Last Lines.* In the earlier collection, *Last Lines* is part of *Japanese Beetles.* All three of these poems are reprinted in *Cross Ties* as well. In a note to the author, Kennedy says that this volume "Contains a couple of things not in *Cross Ties*—like 'A Little Night Music.' (Embarrassed to discover it in *Emily*: when I printed it lately in *New York Quarterly* as 'Sensual Music,' I thought I hadn't ever printed it before!)[.]"

40. Joseph Parisi, "Coming to Terms," *Poetry,* 124 (September 1974): 348.

41. "Reserves of Energy," *The Times Literary Supplement,* 30 August 1974, 932.

42. In an interview, Kennedy describes the history of his religious affiliation: "I sort of drifted out of the Church at the time I was thirteen. My old man was a Catholic, my mother was a Methodist and around adolescence the two sort of blanked each other out. Then I went to a Catholic college and took twenty credits of Scholastic philosophy and that really killed my faith altogether, so weak and namby-pamby a thing it was. Still, you can't pass through the Catholic Church, even nominally, without—Oh it sounds so crass and trite to say it!—without picking up a lot of useful symbols along the way. It does provide one with some important things to care about." Jim Svejda, "The Funniest Poet Alive: An Interview with X. J. Kennedy," *Syracuse Guide,* 26.

43. Joseph Parisi, *Poetry* 348.

44. The collection was printed by The Penmaen Press without a Table of Contents. The poem is divided into ten numbered sections, one section per page, and the collection is illustrated with three wood engravings by Michael McCurdy. In the notes at the end of the book, Kennedy says, in part: "These notes are offered for readers who did not know the subject of this poem and his circumstances. John Michael Brennan was born in 1950 in Denver and died in Denver in February 1973. He had been a student at Tufts University, located on a hill in Medford, Massachusetts, where I am a teacher. About a year before his death, John Brennan had dropped out of school to make a journey alone through England and Ireland. He returned home and in the summer of 1972 self-published his only book, *Air is,* a collection of poems, drawings, and photographs. In my poem, italics indicate quotations from that book."

45. David Shapiro, "Into the Gloom," *Poetry* 128, no. 4 (July 1976): 227.

46. Ibid., 226.

47. At the end of this poem is the note, "Translated by X. J. Kennedy and Keith Waldrop." The note does not indicate which parts Kennedy has written.

48. R. S. Gwynn asks rhetorically, "What other poet would even *think* of mourning the loss of a world-view, the collapse of the 'Great Chain of Being,' in the folk-measures of a chain-gang song?" *Sewanee Review,* lxxix.

49. Kennedy reprinted "Fall Song" in *Cross Ties* and "Pont Mirabeau" in *Dark Horses* along with another translation of Apollinaire's work, "Churchbells." Besides being an incorrigible reviser of his already published poems, Kennedy is very particular when it comes to choosing which of his poems to reprint. One measure of his opinion of a poem is to see whether he reprints it and how often. His poem "Cross Ties," for example, is printed in five

of his collections, whereas "Down in Dallas" and other quite accomplished poems are printed in only one collection.

50. Above this poem in the author's copy, Kennedy wrote, "Worked on since 1955-56 in Paris and rewritten once more & I hope laid to rest in *Dark Horses.*"

51. In *French Leave,* these two lines are: "Evening come [space] be sounded hour," and the next line reads, "The days go running [space] I stand here." Several other relatively minor changes have been made. This discussion quotes from the version printed in *Dark Horses.*

52. In the author's copy of this poem, Kennedy draw a vertical line in the margin beside these three lines and wrote, "The best lines."

53. The dedication of this collection reads: "For Mary V. Toye, professeur de français extraordinaire." In the margin of the author's copy, Kennedy adds: "My high school French teacher, 86 years old in '92, & with whom I'm still in touch."

54. Kennedy explained that this "booklet of poems" was self-published "to give away at readings" since all books of his adult poetry were out of print. Private correspondence with the author.

55. Thomas Goldstein considered the theme of "First Confession" to be "strident atheism." *Dictionary of Literary Biography,* s.v. "Kennedy, X. J.," 396.

56. For a discussion of Crane's influence on Kennedy's work, see Appendix A.

57. Peter Wild, *Arizona Quarterly,* 279.

58. Ibid., 279-80.

59. A few years later, Kennedy said that he experienced great joy getting the *Los Angeles Times* Book Award for *Cross Ties.* Barbra Nightingale, "X. J. Kennedy: Poet for All Ages," *The South Florida Poetry Review,* 38.

60. "A Selection of Notebook Entries," *The Poet's Notebook,* ed. Stephen Kuusisto, Deborah Tall, and David Weiss (New York: W. W. Norton, 1995): 121-33.

61. Loxley Nichols says that "The mere structure of the book gives an inkling of the precision with which Kennedy writes. Not just an odd lot of poems left over or recycled, *Cross Ties* is a carefully constructed entity itself, a drama of sorts, wherein the poems, arranged chronologically over a span of thirty years, are divided into five sections, or acts, of major poems." "Facing the Gorgon," *National Review* 38, no. 13 (18 July 1986): 55.

62. X. J. Kennedy, "Interview with X. J. Kennedy: Keeping Merriment on the Boil," by Bruce Morgan, *Boston Literary News* 1, no. 6 (1986), 2. R. S. Gwynn, reviewing *Cross Ties,* sees vestiges of Kennedy's Catholicism: "Even the title *Cross Ties* cleverly puns on the persistence of a Catholic upbringing in the mind of an adult who is badly, to put it mildly, lapsed." "Swans on Ice," lxxviii.

63. In a note Kennedy says that this poem (or its title) "refers to Thomas Hardy's early lyric 'Neutral Tones.' Some think Hardy depicts the aftermath of his unsuccessful courtship of his cousin Tryphena Sparks."

64. Michael Collins concludes that Kennedy writes about the "ordered, diminished, undifferentiated urban world in which most Americans these days make their home and live out lives of quiet desperation." "The Poetry of X. J. Kennedy," *World Literature Today* 61 (winter 1987): 55-58.

65. R. S. Gwynn knows Kennedy's career well enough to be able to say that in his poems, Kennedy does not "look away from modern life; indeed [his poems] often describe such ubiquitous horrors as family violence . . . despair and suicide in nascent genius . . . and night-thoughts of a future where all is night . . . Through all this one never loses the sense that Kennedy has managed to strike a fair bargain between absolute pessimism and sheer escape." "Swans in Ice," lxxviii-lxxix.

66. In a note to the author at the front of the book, Kennedy writes: "Items checked ($\sqrt{}$) were faces on the cutting-room floor when John Irwin pared down the manuscript for *Dark Horses.* The Belli sonnet & "Pacifier" are dear to me, and I hope to work them into a future book." The following poems have been checked: "A Penitent Giuseppe Belli Enters Heaven," "Pacifier," "Pileup," "Sisyphus: A Parable of the Writer's Lot," "Invitation to the Dance," and "Epigrams." Among these, only "Pacifier" and "Pileup" made it into *Lords of Misrule.*

67. Kennedy says that this poem is "supposed to celebrate work and striving: the speaker chooses to endure, like a tree that keeps putting out leaves" (Note to the author).

68. Reviewer Bruce Bennett said of the collection, "Ultimately, despite its pervasive wit and verve, *Dark Horses* is a somber and unsettling book." *Harvard Review,* no. 3 (winter 1993), 192.

69. Robert B. Shaw, "*Dark Horses.* (book reviews)," *Poetry* 158, no. 1 (October 1993): 42.

70. As noted in a previous reference, the decision to omit the poem from *Dark Horses* was not Kennedy's.

71. David Middleton discusses epigrams in general and some of Kennedy's epigrams in particular in "Stingers: X. J. Kennedy at Epigrams," *Paintbrush* 25 (autumn 1998): 92-99. Richard Moore adds his keen insights as well in "The Decline of Satire and the Specialist Society: Some Thoughts on the Poetry of X. J. Kennedy." *Light* 3 (autumn 1993): 31-34, and in "Lyrics of Wit." *Sewanee Review* 101, no. 1 (winter 1993): lxiii-xliv.

72. In a note to the author, Kennedy explains: "It may strike you that, unlike *Dark Horses,* this book has a number of comic poems in it—'Then and Now,' 'The Blessing of the Bikes,' 'A Curse on a Thief,' 'Horny Man's Song.' That's one reason I like this book better than *Dark Horses.*" The reason for the comic poems, he adds, is that "This time, John Irwin [editor at Johns Hopkins University Press] and I saw practically eye to eye, and he let me keep everything that I thought really mattered."

73. Kennedy explains that "The Lords of Misrule were those officials who presided over Christmas revels in England in the late Middle Ages, their job being to keep revelers from getting too obnoxious. In the **'Invocation,'** a new poem to stand at the front of the book, I take the lords as a metaphor for strict form in poetry, which does a similar job—a force presiding over riotous emotions. (The riotous emotions had better be there, though, or the result isn't poetry.) By happy accident, in an earlier item, 'For Allen Ginbsberg,' I call Ginsberg 'misrule's lord' (private correspondence with the author). Kennedy may be having further fun by going to England, to medieval England no less, for his spirits, going as far from the spirits of contemporary free verse as decency would allow. If Robert Bly, echoing Walt Whitman, believes that traditional forms are alien to the American poetic spirit, here is Kennedy's answer, in part. For more of Bly's argument, see Robert Bly, "Reflections on the Origins of Poetic Form," *Field* 10 (spring 1974): 32.

Works Cited

Adamo, Ralph. "Poetry." *The New Orleans Review* 2, no. 1 (1970): 88-90.

Basho, Matsuo. *The Essential Basho: Matsuo Basho.* Translated by Sam Hamill. Boston and London: Shambhala, 1999.

Bennett, Bruce. "*Dark Horses* by X. J. Kennedy." *Harvard Review* 3 (winter 1993): 191-92.

———. "X. J. Kennedy's Poetry for Children: A User's Guide." *Paintbrush* 25 (autumn 1998): 111-18.

Benthall, R. A. "The Kneeling Ox: Catholicism in the Poems of X. J. Kennedy."

Bjork, Robert E. "Kennedy's 'Nothing in Heaven Functions as It Ought.'" *The Explicator* 40, no. 2 (winter 1982): 6-7.

Bly, Robert. "Reflections on the Origins of Poetic Form." *Field* 10 (spring 1974): 31-35.

Brownjohn, Alan. "Dark Forces." *New Statesman* 78, no. 2009 (September 12, 1969): 346-47.

———. "Light Fantastic." *New Statesman* 83, no. 2130 (January 14, 1972): 52-53.

Carroll, James. "Blossoming Poet." Review of *Growing into Love,* by X. J. Kennedy. *Catholic World,* January 1970, 183.

Clark, Marden J. "Liberating Form." In *Liberating Form: Mormon Essays on Religion and Literature,* 1-15. Salt Lake City, Utah: Aspen Books, 1992.

Collins, Michael J. "The Poetry of X. J. Kennedy." *World Literature Today* 61 (winter 1987): 55-58.

———. "X. J. Kennedy. *Cross Ties.*" *World Literature Today* 60 (summer 1986): 473.

"X. J. Kennedy." *Contemporary Authors Autobiography Series,* vol. 9. Edited by Mark Zadrozny. Detroit: Gale Research, 1989: 73-88.

Copeland, Jeffrey S., ed., *Speaking of Poets: Interviews with Poets Who Write for Children and Young Adults.* Urbana, Ill.: National Council of Teachers of English, 1993.

"*Dark Horses,* by X. J. Kennedy." *Publishers Weekly* 239, no. 49 (November 9, 1992): 79.

Demos, John. Review of *Growing into Love,* by X. J. Kennedy. *Library Journal* 94, no. 15 (September 1, 1969): 2929.

Dunn, Douglas. "A Bridge in Minneapolis." *Encounter* 38, no. 5 (May 1972): 77.

Ferlazzo, P. J. *Choice* 23 (October 1985): 296.

Goldstein, Thomas. S. V. "X. J. Kennedy." *Dictionary of Literary Biography.* Vol. 5: American Poets since World War II. Detroit: Gale Research, 1980.

Gordon, John. "Never Trust a Guy Whose First Name Is a Letter." *Boston Review of the Arts* 2, no. 4 (July 1972): 11-17, 77.

Grosholz, Emily. "Poetry Chronicle." *The Hudson Review* 46 (autumn 1993): 570-78.

Gwynn, R. S. "Swans in Ice." *Sewanee Review* 93, no. 4 (fall 1985): lxxviii-lxxix.

Harsent, David. "Poetae Sepulchrum." *Spectator* (February 12, 1972).

Heath-Stubbs, John. *Aquarius* 5 (1972): 91.

Hofmannsthal, Hugo von. "Die Beiden." Trans. Robert Bly and X. J. Kennedy. *Counter/Measures* 3 (1974): 174-75.

Holmes, Theodore. "Wit, Nature, and the Human Concern." *Poetry* 100, no. 5 (August 1962): 319-24.

"Kennedy, Joseph Charles." *Contemporary Authors: New Revision Series,* vol. 30. Edited by James G. Lesniak. Detroit: Gale Research, 1990: 212-14.

Kennedy, X. J. "After the Bombs Subside." Review of *American Free Verse: The Modern Revolution in Poetry,* by Walter Sutton. *Counter/Measures* 3 (1974): 186-87.

———. "Comment." *Poetry* 151, nos. 1-2 (October-November 1987): 215-16.

———. "*Counter / Measures*: X. J. Kennedy on Form, Meter, and Rime." By John Ciardi. *Saturday Review* 4 (May 20, 1972): 14, 19.

———. "The Funniest Poet Alive: An Interview with X. J. Kennedy." By Jim Svejda. *Syracuse Guide* 9 (May 1976): 14-17, 26.

———. "An Interview with X. J. Kennedy." By William Baer. *The Formalist* 11 (2000): 19-34.

———. "An Interview with X. J. Kennedy." By Jill Scherer. *Lodestar* 5 (1984): 49-50.

———. "Interview with X. J. Kennedy: Keeping Merriment on the Boil." By Bruce Morgan. *Boston Literary News* 1, no. 6 (1986): 2-3.

———. "Old Wine, New Wrinkles." *Counter/Measures* 3 (1974): 200.

———. "The Poet in the Playpen." Three reviews. *Poetry* 105, no. 3 (1964): 190-91.

———. "The Poetry: Form and Informality." In *Miller Williams and the Poetry of the Particular.* Edited by Michael Burns. Columbia, Mo.: University of Missouri Press, 1991: 43-53.

———. "A Self-Demanding Englisher." Review of *Sappho to Valery: Poems in Translation,* by John Frederick Nims. *Counter/Measures* 2 (1973): 193-94.

———. "Staying Human." A review of *When You Are Alone / It Keeps You Capone, an Approach to Creative Writing with Children,* by Myra Cohn Livingston. *Counter/Measures* 3 (1974): 190.

———. "Talking with X. J. Kennedy." By Jack Prelutsky. *Instructor* 102, no. 2 (September 1992): 26.

———. "X. J. Kennedy: An Interview." By Foster Mancini. *Paintbrush* 25 (autumn 1998): 12-22.

Leggett, John. "Poems with a Temper of Mind." *Boston Globe,* August 24, 1969, 73.

Lucie-Smith, Edward. *Contemporary Poets.* 2d ed. New York: St. Martin's Press, 1975.

Mackinnon, Lachlan. "High Fidelity." *Times Literary Supplement* 4303, September 20, 1985, 1039.

Martz, Louis L. "Recent Poetry: The End of an Era." *Yale Review* 59 (winter 1970): 252-67.

McCloskey, Mark. *"Cross Ties: Selected Poems."* In *Magill's Literary Annual,* edited by Frank N. Magill. Englewood Cliffs, N.J.: Salem Press, 1986. 1: 199-203.

McGann, Jerome. "Poetry and Truth." *Poetry* 117, no. 3 (December 1970): 195-203.

Middleton, David. "Stingers: X. J. Kennedy at Epigrams." *Paintbrush* 25 (autumn 1998): 92-99.

Middleton, Francine K. "Introduction of X. J. Kennedy as the 1996 Fletcher Lecturer at Nicholls State University, Thibodaux, Louisiana, 11 April 1996." *Paintbrush* 25 (autumn 1998): 103-4.

Mills, Jr., Ralph J. "Three Established Poets and a New One." *Chicago Sun-Times Book Week,* 19 October 1969, 10.

Milosz, Czeslaw. "The Writing Life." By Nathan Gardels. *Los Angeles Times,* 25 July 1999.

Mitchell, Roger. "Nine Poets." *Poetry* 147, no. 4 (January 1986): 232-34.

Moore, Richard. "The Decline of Satire and the Specialist Society: Some Thoughts on the Poetry of X. J. Kennedy." *Light* 3 (autumn 1993): 31-34.

———. "Lyrics of Wit." *Sewanee Review* 101, no. 1 (winter 1993): xliii-xliv.

Moran, Moore. "*Cross Ties*: X. J. Kennedy." *Prairie Schooner* 60, no. 4 (winter 1986): 112-14.

Nichols, Loxley. "Facing the Gorgon." *National Review* 38, no. 13 (18 July 1986): 55-56.

Nightingale, Barbra. "X. J. Kennedy: Poet for All Ages." *The South Florida Poetry Review* 7, no. 3 (1990): 33-39.

"No Shortage of Satisfactions." *The Times Literary Supplement* 3643, 24 December 1971, 1602.

Oliver, Raymond. "X. J. Kennedy's Poems Revel in Humor, Humanity." *Christian Science Monitor* 77, August 7, 1985, 21-22.

Orth, Ghita. "Rich in Discipline." *New England Review* 16 (spring 1994): 168-73.

Parisi, Joseph. "Coming to Terms." *Poetry* 124 (September 1974): 343-52.

Ray, David. "Heroic, Mock-Heroic." *New York Times Book Review* 90, 24 November 1985, 28.

Read, Forrest. "Notes, Reviews and Speculations." *Epoch* 11 (winter 1962): 257-60.

"Reserves of Energy." *Times Literary Supplement,* 30 August 1974, 932.

Review of *Dark Horses,* by X. J. Kennedy. *Publishers Weekly* 239, no. 49 (November 9, 1992): 79.

Rice, William. "A Conversation with X. J. Kennedy." *Sparrow* 62 (1995): 48-57.

Rilke, Rainer Marie. "Wie der Wachter in den Weingelanden." Trans. Robert Bly and X. J. Kennedy. *Counter/Measures* 3 (1974): 160-61.

Rosenthal, M. L. "Poetic Power—Free the Swan!" *Shenandoah* 24, no. 1 (fall 1972): 88-91.

A Selection of Notebook Entries. In *The Poet's Notebook,* edited by Stephen Kuusisto, Deborah Tall, and David Weiss, 121-33. New York: W. W. Norton, 1995.

Senick, Gerard J., ed. *Children's Literature Review,* vol. 27. Detroit, Mich.: Gale Research, 1992.

Shapiro, David. "Into the Gloom." *Poetry* 128, no. 4 (July 1976): 226-27.

Sharp, Ronald A. "Kennedy's 'Nude Descending a Staircase.'" *Explicator* 37, no. 3 (spring 1979): 2-3.

Shaw, Robert B. "*Dark Horses* (book reviews)." *Poetry* 163, no. 1 (October 1993): 42-44.

Simon, John. "More Brass Than Enduring." *Hudson Review* 15 (autumn 1962): 455-68.

Simpson, Peter L. "The Candor of Poetry." *St. Louis Post-Dispatch,* December 7, 1969, 1-16M.

Skinner, Knute. *Northern Review* 12, no. 2 (spring 1972): 94-96.

Snodgrass, W. D. "Remembering Joe Kennedy." *Paintbrush* 25 (autumn 1998): 136-38.

Sullivan, Nancy. "Perspective and the Poetic Process." *Wisconsin Studies in Contemporary Literature* 6, no. 1 (winter-spring 1965): 114-31.

Taylor, Henry. "*Growing into Love.*" In *Magill's Literary Annual,* edited by Frank N. Magill. Englewood Cliffs, N.J.: Salem Press, 1970. 1: 154-57.

———. "'Singing to Spite This Hunger.'" *The Nation* 210 (February 2, 1970): 122-24.

Tessier, Thomas. "X. J. Kennedy's Poetry." *New Haven Register,* 1969.

True, Michael. *Contemporary Poets,* 6th ed. Detroit: St. James Press, 1996.

Tudor, Stephen. "*Growing into Love.*" *Spirit* 37 (spring 1970): 36-39.

Vinson, James, ed., *Contemporary Poets.* 2d ed. London: St. Martin's Press, 1975.

Wakeman, John, ed. *World Authors, 1950-1970.* New York: H. W. Wilson, 1975.

Waldrop, Bernard Keith. "Squibs." *Burning Deck* 2 (spring 1963): 92.

Who's Who in America. 54th ed. S. V. "Kennedy, X. J." New Providence, N.J.: Marquis, 2000. 1: 2576-77.

Wild, Peter. *Arizona Quarterly* 41 (autumn 1985): 279-80.

Wright, G. T. "Pulse and Breath." *The North Stone Review* 11 (1993): 63-64.

"X. J. Kennedy." *American Poets Since World War II.* Detroit: Gale Research Company, 1980.

"X. J. Kennedy." *Contemporary Authors Autobiography Series,* vol. 9. Edited by Mark Zadrozny. Detroit: Gale Research, 1989: 73-88.

Elizabeth Lund (essay date 18 April 2006)

SOURCE: Lund, Elizabeth. "A Poet Who Celebrates the Joy of Verse." *The Christian Science Monitor* (18 April 2006): 13+.

[*In the following essay, Lund presents a picture of Kennedy as a lifelong ambassador for poetry, discussing Kennedy's textbooks and compilations as well as the accessibility of his verse.*]

When X. J. Kennedy flies somewhere, he doesn't tell seatmates that he is a poet. If he's interested in chatting, he'll say he writes books for children. If not, "I write textbooks" is his conversation killer. "I don't think anybody is a poet 24/7," he says, "only in those rare moments when a person is producing a poem."

That perspective might seem odd, given that Mr. Kennedy has won a Lamont Award from the Academy of American Poets, a Guggenheim, and a Los Angeles Book Award, among other prestigious prizes. Yet even during National Poetry Month—when many poets actively promote the genre—Kennedy plays down the fact that he has had a profound effect on generations of readers.

His "An Introduction to Poetry," now in its 11th edition, is the bestselling college poetry textbook. His two anthologies for children have also been bestsellers.

And his poems, distinctive for their use of wit and rhyme, helped fuel a renewed interest in both formal and humorous work.

"He was the Billy Collins before there was a Billy Collins," says bg Thurston, a creative writing teacher at Lasell College in Newton, Mass. "He is a poet that the general audience easily connects with, but his ego doesn't seem to get in the way. He actively cares about promoting younger or unknown poets."

Such was the case at the Concord Free Public Library (Mass.) recently, where Kennedy opened with two children's poems by the late James Hayford, a little-known Vermont writer whose work was admired by Robert Frost.

Kennedy and his wife, Dorothy, sifted through 774 of Hayford's poems to find the 38 that appear in the book *Knee-Deep in Blazing Snow,* which was published at the end of last year.

"Goats in Pasture," he began, with the aplomb of a stage actor.

> Their bony heads untaxed by need of moving,
> Changing, repairing, laying by,
> Goats keep a comprehensive eye
> On the condition of the sky. . . .

The audience, many of whom had gray hair, chuckled. Then, moments later, they gave a collective sigh when Kennedy read,

> Time to plant trees is when you're young,
> So you will have them to walk among—
> So, aging, you can walk in shade
> That you and time together made.

The rhyme and meter of Hayford's work clearly pleased the crowd, as it did Kennedy, who says that the ghost of meter can been seen in everything he writes. "To me, a poem that's in rhyme and meter is the difference between watching a film in full color and watching a film in black and white," he says. "Not that a few black and white films aren't wonderful. So are certain successful pieces of free verse."

His college students didn't always agree with that assessment, especially when they used rhyme for the first time. Kennedy, who has taught at Wellesley College, Leeds University in England, and the universities of Michigan, North Carolina (Greensboro), and California (Irvine) often heard the same response:" 'Oh I hate this. It won't let me say what I want to say.' But I'd tell them that is a tremendous advantage. 'Now you will discover something you didn't want to say, and that's where it gets really deep and fascinating.'"

Kennedy began his own process of discovery when, as a full professor at Tufts University in Boston, he decided to write *An Introduction to Poetry* as a "summer project."

Instead, the book took three years to complete. (Dana Gioia joined as coauthor with the eighth edition.)

He wrote more textbooks after that, and in 1977, he made some big decisions. Days before the start of the fall semester, Kennedy, a father of five, told his wife he didn't want to continue teaching.

She supported his decision, saying, "Maybe you'll get more writing done for yourself." The couple lived off their credit cards for two years.

Eventually, though, Kennedy's writing provided the family with a steady income. To date he has penned 16 children's books, coedited three, and written seven books of poems for adults. He also edited poetry for *The Paris Review* and started, with Dorothy, a little magazine of poetry called *Counter/Measures.*

"I like poems where you don't really know whether to laugh or cry when you read them," he says. "I like what Auden said once, that poetry is the clear expression of mixed feelings."

At the Concord Library, listeners did sense the complex emotions in his poetry.

"Kennedy knows how to use traditional poetic forms to give us both joyful and truthful observations about the human condition," says Glenn Mitchell, coordinator of the Friends of the Concord Library's poetry reading series. "His sketches of people and experiences combine playful irreverence with language full of sound and rhythm, and refreshing bites of irony."

Such comments might gratify the teacher who viewed himself as "a tour guide through the murky forest of poetry. Most college students have read [poetry] rather sporadically, spottily, and I was out to show them where the good stuff is. I'm the guy with the pointer and flashlight saying, 'Hey, look at this.' My goal was to make people see that poems can give us joy."

That's one reason Kennedy adds a dash of humor to his textbooks—"humor leavens life"—yet he encourages even young readers to understand how poems are constructed.

"The attitude that poetry should not be analyzed is prevalent among many who consider themselves experts on children's literature. But I suspected that kids like to look closely at things and figure out what makes them go. Without talking a poem to death, why couldn't you look closely and see what some of its elements are, what's going on in the language? Do you have metaphors, colorful figures of speech, musical sound effects?"

This approach has become popular in recent years. (The current US poet laureate, Ted Kooser, has both a book and a weekly newspaper column in which he encourages adults to do close reading.)

But Kennedy doesn't worry about being trendy. Nor does he agree with some of the ideas poets have about themselves.

"I get uneasy with people who say poets are the unacknowledged legislators of the world," he says. "If poets were the legislators of the world, the world would be even worse off. What poet can you think of that you'd like to vote for for president?"

Instead, he focuses on doing his work well, which at readings includes signing copies of his books, both the newer ones and dog-eared copies of *An Introduction to Poetry*.

He also answers listeners' questions about everything from his choice of tie—green and white stripes in Concord—to his lively reading style. "A poetry reading, whether anybody likes it or not, is inevitably a theatri-cal experience," he says. "Why not face that fact and be the least boring performer you are able to?"

FURTHER READING

Criticism

Gwynn, R. S. "The Grey Disguise of Years." *Hudson Review* 56, no. 1 (spring 2003): 208-16.
    Favorably describes Kennedy's poetry as inhabiting a middle ground between "high seriousness" and light verse.

Scarf, Michael. Review of *The Lords of Misrule*. *Publishers Weekly* 249, no. 49 (9 December 2002): 78.
    Characterizes the poetry of Kennedy's *The Lords of Misrule* as stylistically familiar while occasionally dealing with surprisingly serious subject matter.

Additional coverage of Kennedy's life and career is contained in the following sources published by Gale: *American Writers Supplement*, Vol. 15; *Children's Literature Review*, Vol. 27; *Contemporary Authors*, Vols 1-4R, 201; *Contemporary Authors Autobiography Series*, Vols. 9, 201; *Contemporary Authors New Revision Series*, Vols. 4, 30, 40; *Contemporary Literary Criticism*, Vols. 8, 42; *Contemporary Poets*, Eds. 1, 2, 3, 4, 5, 6, 7; *Dictionary of Literary Biography*, Vol. 5; *Literature Resource Center*; *Major Authors and Illustrators for Children and Young Adults*, Ed. 2; *Major Authors and Illustrators for Children and Young Adults Supplement*, Ed. 1; *Something About the Author*, Vols. 14, 86, 130; *Something About the Author Autobiography Series*, Vol. 22; and *St. James Guide to Children's Writers*, Ed. 5.

John Greenleaf Whittier
1807-1892

American poet, essayist, editor, critic, journalist, novelist, and short story writer.

INTRODUCTION

A well-known abolitionist and social reformer, Whittier is remembered for his passionate commitment to social justice and his vivid descriptions of New England life. Much of his poetry is now considered overly-didactic and dated, yet he remains an important figure in nineteenth-century American literary history.

BIOGRAPHICAL INFORMATION

Whittier was born December 17, 1807, near Haverhill, Massachusetts, on a modest farm that had been in the family since the seventeenth century. His parents, John and Abigail (Hussey) Whittier, were devout Quakers, hard working and devoted to family life. Although Whittier had little formal education, he was schooled in New England history and folklore through stories and legends recounted around the family fireplace on wintry evenings. He briefly attended a local school during the years 1814-1815, and later spent a year at the Haverhill Academy (1828-1829), but was unable to continue because of his financial situation. For a time he supported himself by teaching and shoemaking, and in 1829 he assumed the editorship of the *American Manufacturer,* a position obtained for him by the abolitionist William Lloyd Garrison. The following year, Whittier became editor of the *Haverhill Gazette,* a post he held for only six months before taking over as editor of the prestigious *New England Review.* Late in 1831, Whittier gave up editorial work and returned to Haverhill because of the death of his father and his own poor health. A year later, encouraged by Garrison, who had just begun publishing his anti-slavery journal the *Liberator,* Whittier took up the cause of abolition. He joined the anti-slavery party, published the essay *Justice and Expediency,* and began writing anti-slavery poetry. The subject dominated all of his writing—both poetry and prose—for more than a decade. Abolition was at that time an unpopular cause in New England, however, and Whittier paid a heavy price for his convictions. He was all but cut off from the mainstream literary world and support for his poetry waned, making it difficult to publish any new work.

In 1835, Whittier was elected to the Massachusetts state legislature, where he lobbied extensively against slavery. He continued to write on the subject as well, publishing in both the *Liberator* and the *Essex Gazette,* a paper he also edited. In 1836 Whittier, his mother, and sister moved to Amesbury, Massachusetts, but by the following year Whittier was working in the Anti-Slavery Society's New York office, and in 1838 he took over as editor of the *Pennsylvania Freeman,* headquartered in Philadelphia. In the spring of that year, his office was attacked and burned by an angry mob. By some accounts, Whittier was lucky to get out alive. Whittier published a number of poetry volumes throughout the 1840s and 1850s, but his work was not commercially successful until after the Civil War. He moved to Danvers, Massachusetts, in 1876, where he lived for the rest of his life. He continued to write until his death on September 7, 1892; he is buried in Amesbury, Massachusetts.

MAJOR WORKS

Whittier began writing poetry around 1821, but his first published poem was "The Exile's Departure," which appeared in Garrison's *Newburyport Free Press* in 1826. During the two year period following that publication, Whittier published more than eighty poems in various local newspapers, and in 1831 published his first volume of stories and poetry, *Legends of New England in Prose and Verse.* Two years later, he began concentrating on the abolition issue and in 1837 his friends published, without his consent, *Poems Written during the Progress of the Abolition Question in the United States, Between the Years 1830 and 1838* (1837). Whittier revised and republished his own version a year later as *Poems.* Many of the anti-slavery poems were overly didactic, written strictly as political propaganda, and literary merit was often sacrificed in the process. In addition to attacking the institution of slavery and slave-owners, some poems, such as "Clerical Oppressors," criticized clergymen in both the North and the South for supporting slavery.

Far more successful, with both readers and critics, are Whittier's representations of New England life, a subject to which he returned in 1843 with the publication of *Lays of My Home, and Other Poems.* The collection features poems based on the New England landscape, local history, and folklore; it includes such poems as "The Ballad of Cassandra Southwick" and "The Merrimack." Whittier published another volume of anti-slavery poems, *Voices of Freedom,* in 1846, and although it was his last collection on the subject, he continued to produce and publish individual pieces devoted to the cause. "Ichabod" (1850), considered one of his finest poems, was written in response to Daniel Webster's support of the Compromise Laws of 1850, which included concessions to Southern slave states.

Throughout the 1850s, Whittier published a number of poetry collections, among them *Songs of Labor and Other Poems* (1850), *The Chapel of the Hermits and Other Poems* (1853), and *The Panorama and Other Poems* (1856). The following year, Whittier began contributing to the newly-founded *Atlantic Monthly;* some of his most highly-acclaimed poems appeared in the magazine, particularly "Telling the Bees" and "Skipper Ireson's Ride," both based on New England legends he had heard in his youth. The latter involves the tarring and feathering of a sea captain by a group of grieving Marblehead women. According to the legend, Ireson had bypassed the crew of a sinking fishing vessel, leaving the men—the husbands, fathers, and brothers of the Marblehead women—to drown.

Also among Whittier's best-remembered individual poems are "The Barefoot Boy," (1855) featuring a forerunner of Huck Finn as the main character, and its companion poem "Maud Muller," preferred by critics but not as well received by the public. His 1864 collection of civil war poetry, *In War Time and Other Poems,* includes his most famous ballad, "Barbara Frietchie," supposedly inspired by an incident involving an old woman in Frederick, Maryland, who waved a Union flag from her window as the Confederate troops passed through the town. The poem contains the line once memorized by American schoolchildren: "Shoot, if you must, this old grey head, / But spare your country's flag." The historical accuracy of the incident was questioned by many after the poem's publication, but Whittier believed that "in its main outlines, it was substantially historical," according to William Henry Hudson.

Snow-Bound: A Winter Idyl (1866) was Whittier's longest poem and is considered his best by most critics. It was enormously popular with contemporary readers and proved so successful that its returns afforded the poet financial security for the remainder of his life. *Snow-Bound* presents a nostalgic look at the comfort and protection offered by family life on the farm, but is coupled with a deep sense of loss. According to Lewis Leary, the poem's powerful emotions "are primarily developed by a series of contrasts: of fire and snow, past and present, people and elements—which combine to form the larger theme of love and immortality struggling against pain and death." *The Tent on the Beach*

and Other Poems, published in 1867, was also a commercially successful book, as were the remaining volumes Whittier produced from that point on. They include *Among the Hills, and Other Poems* (1868); *Ballads of New-England* (1870); *The Pennsylvania Pilgrim, and Other Poems* (1872); and *At Sundown* (1890).

CRITICAL RECEPTION

The popular reception of Whittier's poetry was tempered by the unpopularity of his commitment to the anti-slavery cause. Until the publication of the very successful *Snow-Bound* at the end of the Civil War, sales of Whittier's poetry collections were only moderate at best. Today, *Snow-Bound* is one of the few poems of Whittier's that does not appear out of date and is still praised by critics. Contributing to the current critical notion that much of Whittier's poetry is irrelevant today is the didactic nature of his abolitionist poetry, although many scholars praise the passion and zeal with which he approached the subject of slavery. According to W. Sloane Kennedy, "the slavery poems are full of moral stamina and fiery indignation at oppression." The historical significance of Whittier's anti-slavery poems has been studied by Osborn T. Smallwood, who finds that they were an important part of pre-Civil War protest literature that effectively turned public opinion against slavery, as well as a reflection of abolitionist attitudes toward pro-slavery clergymen. Additionally, claims Smallwood, "they point to the eminence of Whittier as a fighter for freedom." Brenda Wineapple disagrees with the notion that Whittier's poetry is outdated or of interest only to literary historians. "Revisited now, Whittier appears fresh, honest, even flinty and practical," she insists; "his diction is easy, his detail rich and unassuming, his emotion deep."

A number of critics have commented on elements of Orientalism in Whittier's poetry. Arthur Christy notes that such themes are to be expected in the literary efforts of the Transcendentalist Ralph Waldo Emerson, but constitute an anomaly in the work of Whittier, a devout Quaker. Yet, reports Christy, Whittier wrote "more poems on Oriental themes, more paraphrases of Oriental maxims and more imitations of Oriental models than may be found in Emerson's verse." Christy also discusses the differences in each poet's use of the theme of Brahma, believing that Whittier essentially Christianized the Oriental material he employed. Christy cites as an example the poem "Disarmament," which "commences with Christ's injunction, 'Put up the sword!' and concludes with a Buddhist birth-story."

Another contemporary issue that Whittier embraced was the rights of women. Joseph M. Ernest, Jr. has traced the assistance Whittier extended to a number of women writers and credits him with greatly increasing the number of women in American literary life during the mid-nineteenth century. James E. Rocks, in his analysis of *Snow-Bound,* concedes that Whittier's representation of women in the poem reflects "the sentimental tradition" of his time, but notes that "his views, in that poem, as well as in his letters, transcend the purely patriarchal and reflect his strong Quaker principle of human rights."

Robert Penn Warren contends that Whittier's early poetry "lacked content, and it lacked style," and believes that Whittier did not produce a "really fine" poem until 1850, when he wrote "Ichabod." The critic also praises "Telling the Bees," calling it a "little masterpiece." Assessing Whittier's poetry as a whole, Kennedy maintains that Whittier produced "very simple and unoriginal" poetry, and while some of his work has merit, much of it is "merely an echo of that of the English Lake School." The critic concedes, however, that at its best, the ballads and lyrics are reminiscent of the sincerity and simplicity of Wordsworth, while the reform pieces capture Byron's sense of indignation, and the religious poems evoke Cowper's piety. Leary observes that Whittier "is a poet of phrases or of a few lines or stanzas. He can be made to sound better in quotation or parts than in reproductions of complete poems." Nonetheless, the critic acknowledges that "few poets have written as successfully as Whittier of nature without man in it," and considers him a precursor of Robert Frost in that respect.

PRINCIPAL WORKS

Poetry

Legends of New England in Prose and Verse (short stories and poems) 1831

Moll Pitcher and the Minstrel Girl 1832; revised 1840

Mogg Megone 1836

Poems Written during the Progress of the Abolition Question in the United States, Between the Years 1830 and 1838 1837; also published as *Poems* [revised edition] 1838

Lays of My Home, and Other Poems 1843

Voices of Freedom (poetry and essays) 1846

The Supernaturalism of New-England (poetry and prose) 1847

Old Portraits and Modern Sketches (poetry and biographical sketches) 1850

Songs of Labor, and Other Poems 1850

The Chapel of the Hermit, and Other Poems (poetry) 1853

The Panorama, and Other Poems 1856

The Poetical Works of John Greenleaf Whittier, 2 vols. 1857

Home Ballads and Poems 1860

In War Time, and Other Poems 1864

Snow-Bound: A Winter Idyl 1866

The Tent on the Beach, and Other Poems 1867

Among the Hills, and Other Poems 1868

Ballads of New England 1870

Child-Life: A Collection of Poems [editor; with Lucy Larcom] 1872

The Pennsylvania Pilgrim, and Other Poems 1872

The Complete Works of John Greenleaf Whittier 7 vols. (poetry, legends, essays, tales, biographical sketches, and historical sketches) 1876

The Vision of Echard, and Other Poems 1878

The King's Missive, and Other Poems 1881

The Bay of Seven Islands, and Other Poems 1883

At Sundown 1890

The Complete Poetical Works of John Greenleaf Whittier 1894

Other Major Works

Justice and Expediency; or, Slavery considered with a View to Its Rightful and Effectual Remedy, Abolition (essay) 1833

The Stranger in Lowell (criticism) 1845

Leaves from Margaret Smith's Journal in the Province of Massachusetts Bay (novel) 1849

Child Life in Prose [editor; with Lucy Larcom] 1874

Whittier on Writers and Writing: The Uncollected Critical Writings of John Greenleaf Whittier (criticism) 1950

The Letters of John Greenleaf Whittier (letters) 1975

CRITICISM

W. Sloane Kennedy (essay date 1883)

SOURCE: Kennedy, W. Sloane. "The Artist" and "Poems Seriatim." In *John Greenleaf Whittier: His Life, Genius, and Writings,* pp. 196-253. Boston: S. E. Cassino, 1883.

[*In the following excerpts, Kennedy discusses Whittier's poetic style and the way it evolved over the course of his literary career, from the fiery indignation of his early reform poetry to the more mellow tone of his later ballads and lyrical poems.*]

THE ARTIST

The title of this chapter is almost a misnomer; for the style, or technique, of the poet whose works we are considering is so very simple and unoriginal that he can hardly be said to have a distinctive style of his own,—unless a few persistent mannerisms establish a claim to it. His diction, however, is always pictorial, and glows with an intense Oriental fervor. Fused in this interior vital heat, his thoughts do not sink, like powerful Jinn, into the deep silence-sphere of the mind, to fetch thence sparkling treasures, rich and strange: rather, they run to and fro with lightning swiftness amid the million surface-pictures of the intellect; rearranging, recombining, and creatively blending its images, and finally pouring them out along the page to charm our fancy and feeling with old thoughts and scenes painted in fresh colors and from new points of view. There is more of fancy than of creative imagination in Whittier.

The artistic quality, or tone, of his mind is a fusion of that of Wordsworth and that of Byron. In his best ballads and other lyrics you have the moral sincerity of Wordsworth and the sweet Wordsworthian simplicity (with a difference); and in his reform poems you have the Byronic indignation, and scorn of Philistinism and its tyrannies. As a religious poet, he reveals the quiet piety and devoutness of Cowper; and his rural and folk poems show that he is a debtor to Burns.

He has been a diligent reader,—"a close-browed miser of the scholar's gains,"—and his writings are full of bookish allusions. But, if the truth must be told, his doctor's gown does not often sit gracefully upon his shoulders. His readers soon learn to know that his strength lies in his moral nature, and in his power to tell a story melodiously, simply, and sweetly. Hence it is, doubtless, that they care little for his literary allusions,—think, perhaps, that they are rather awkwardly dragged in by the ears, and at any rate hasten by them impatiently that they may inhale anew the violet-freshness of the poet's own soul. What has just been said about bookish allusions does not apply to the beautiful historical ballads produced by Whittier in the mellow maturity of his powers. These fresh improvisations are as perfect works of art as the finest Greek marbles. In them Whittier at length succeeds in freeing himself completely from the shackles of didacticism. Such ballads as **"The Witch's Daughter"** and **"Telling the Bees"** are as absolutely faultless productions as Wordsworth's "We are Seven" and his "Lucy Gray," or as Uhland's "Des Sänger's Fluch," or William Blake's "Mary." There is in them the confident and unconscious ease that marks the work of the highest genius. A shower of lucid water-drops falls in no truer obedience to the law of perfect sphericity than flowed from the pen of the poet these delicate creations in obedience to the law of perfect spontaneity. Almost all of Whittier's lyrics have evidently been rapidly written, poured forth in the first glow of feeling, and not carefully amended and polished as were Longfellow's works. And herein he is at fault, as was Byron. But the delicate health of Whittier, and his toilsome early days, form an excuse for his deficiency in this respect. His later creations, the product of his leisure years, are full of pure and flawless music. They have no harmony or rhythmic volume of sound, as in Tennyson, Swinburne, Milton, and Shakspere; but they set themselves to simple melodious airs spontaneously. As you read them, your feet begin to tap time,—only the music is that of a good rural choir rather than that of an orchestra.

The thought of each poem is generally conveyed to the reader's understanding with the utmost lucidity. There is no mysticism, no obscurity. The story or thought unfolds itself naturally, and without fatigue to our minds. A great many poems are indeed spun out at too great length; but the central idea to be conveyed is rarely lost sight of.

To the list of his virtues as an artist, it remains to add his frequent surprising strength. This is naturally most marked in the anti-slavery poems. When he wrote these, he was in the flush of manhood, his soul at a white heat of moral indignation. He is occasionally nerved to almost superhuman effort: it is the battle-axe of Richard thundering at the gates of Front de Bœuf. For nervous energy, there is nothing in the Hebrew prophets finer than such passages as these:—

> Strike home, strong-hearted man!
> Down to the root
> Of old oppression sink the Saxon steel.
>
> *To Ronge*

> Maddened by Earth's wrong and evil,
> 'Lord!' I cried in sudden ire,
> 'From thy right hand, clothed with thunder,
> Shake the bolted fire!'
>
> ***What the Voice Said***

> Hands off! thou tithe-fat plunderer! play
> No trick of priestcraft here!
> Back, puny lordling! darest thou lay
> A hand on Elliott's bier?
> Alive, your rank and pomp, as dust,
> Beneath his feet he trod:
> He knew the locust-swarm that cursed
> The harvest-fields of God.
>
> On these pale lips, the smothered thought
> Which England's millions feel,
> A fierce and fearful splendor caught,
> As from his forge the steel.
> Strong-armed as Thor,—a shower of fire
> His smitten anvil flung;

God's curse, Earth's wrong, dumb Hunger's ire,—
  He gave them all a tongue!

                Elliott.

And Law, an unloosed maniac, strong,
  Blood-drunken, through the blackness trod,
  Hoarse-shouting in the ear of God
The blasphemy of wrong."

             The Rendition.

All grim and soiled, and brown with tan,
  I saw a Strong One, in his wrath,
Smiting the godless shrines of man
  Along his path.

             The Reformer.

As Whittier has grown older, and the battles of his life have become (as he expressed it to the writer) like "a remembered dream," his genius has grown mellow and full of graciousness. His art culminated in **"Home Ballads," "Snow-Bound,"** and **"The Tent on the Beach."** He has kept longer than most poets the lyric glow; only in his later poems it is "emotion remembered in tranquillity."

If asked to name the finest poems of Whittier, would not the following instinctively recur to the mind: **"Snow-Bound," "Maud Muller," "Barbara Frietchie," "The Witch's Daughter," "Telling the Bees," "Skipper Ireson's Ride," "King Volmer and Elsie,"** and **"The Tent on the Beach"**?

To these one would like to add several exquisite hymns and short secular lyrics. But the poems mentioned would probably be regarded by most critics as Whittier's finest works of art. They merit this distinction largely because they are not disfigured (as most of his productions are) by homiletical tail-pieces, or morals, and by commonplace ejaculations of piety and inopportune religious aspirations.

The foregoing remark must be our cue for beginning to pass in review the artistic deficiencies of Whittier. He has three crazes that have nearly ruined the mass of his poetry. They are the reform craze, the religious craze, and the rhyme craze. Of course, as a man, he could not have a superfluity of the first of these; but, as a poet, they have been a great injury to him. We need not deny that he has taken the manlier course in subordinating the artist to the reformer and preacher; but in estimating his poetic merits we ought to regard his work from an absolute point of view. Let us not be misunderstood. It is gladly and freely conceded that the theory that great poetry is not necessarily moral, and that the aim of poetry is only to please the senses, is a petty and shallow one, and that the true function of the great poet is also to bear witness to the ideal and noble, to the moral

and religious. Let us heartily agree with Principal Shairp when he says that the true end of the poet "is to awaken men to the divine side of things; to bear witness to the beauty that clothes the outer world, the nobility that lies hid, often obscured, in human souls; to call forth sympathy for neglected truths, for noble but oppressed persons, for downtrodden causes, and to make men feel that through all outward beauty and all pure inward affection God himself is addressing them." We may admit all this, and yet find fault with the moralizations and homilies of Whittier. The poetry of Dante and Milton is full of ethical passion, and occasionally a little sermon is wedged in; yet they do not treat us to endless broadsides of preaching, as Whittier does in his earlier poems, and in some of his later ones. But there is this distinction: the moral in Dante and Milton and Shakspere and Emerson is so garnitured with beauty that while our souls are ennobled our imaginations are gratified. But in many of Whittier's poems we have the bare skeleton of the moral, without the rounded contour and delicate tints of the living body of beauty. His reform poems have been called stump-speeches in verse. His anti-slavery poems are, with a few exceptions, devoid of beauty. They should have been written in the manner he himself commends in a review of Longfellow's "Evangeline": he should have depicted the truth strongly and attractively, and left to the reader the censure and the indignation. Mr. Whittier seems to know his peculiar limitations as well as his critics. He speaks of himself as one—

           Whose rhyme
    Beat often Labor's hurried time,
  Or Duty's rugged march through storm and strife,

and he has once or twice expressed himself in prose in a way that seems to show that he recognizes the artistic mistake in the construction of his earlier poems. The omission of the moral *l'envoi* from so many of his maturer creations strengthens one in this surmise. In 1867 Whittier published the following letter in the New York *Nation*:

To the Editor of the Nation:

I am very well aware that merely personal explanations are not likely to be as interesting to the public as to the parties concerned; but I am induced to notice what is either a misconception on thy part, or, as is most probable, a failure on my own to make myself clearly understood. In the review of **"The Tent on the Beach"** in thy paper of last week, I confess I was not a little surprised to find myself represented as regretting my life-long and active participation in the great conflict which has ended in the emancipation of the slave, and that I had not devoted myself to merely literary pursuits. In the half-playful lines upon which this statement is founded, if I did not feel at liberty to boast of my anti-slavery labors and magnify my editorial profession, I certainly did not mean to underrate them, or express the shadow of a regret that they had occupied so large a share of my time and thought. The simple fact is that I cannot be sufficiently thankful to the Divine Providence that so early called my attention to the great interests of humanity, saving me from the poor ambitions and miserable jealousies of a selfish pursuit of literary reputation. Up to a comparatively recent period my writings have been simply episodical, something apart from the real object and aim of my life; and whatever of favor they have found with the public has come to me as a grateful surprise rather than as an expected reward. As I have never staked all upon the chances of authorship, I have been spared the pain of disappointment and the temptation to envy those who, as men of letters, deservedly occupy a higher place in the popular estimation than I have ever aspired to.

Truly thy friend, JOHN G. WHITTIER. AMESBURY, 9th, 3d mo., 1867.

One is reminded by this letter that Wordsworth once said to Dr. Orville Dewey, of Boston, that, "although he was known to the world only as a poet, he had given twelve hours' thought to the condition and prospects of society for one to poetry." In a letter read at the third decade meeting of the American Anti-Slavery Society in Philadelphia, Mr. Whittier said: "I am not insensible to literary reputation; I love, perhaps too well, the praise and good-will of my fellow-men; but I set a higher value on my name as appended to the Anti-Slavery Declaration of 1833 than on the title-page of any book."

In his earlier years our poet was wholly ignorant of the fact that an artist should love beauty for its own sake. The simple-hearted Quaker and Puritan farmer-youth thought it almost a sin to spend his time in the cultivation of the beautiful. In his dedication of the "Supernaturalism of New England" to his sister, he says:—

> And knowing how my life hath been
> A weary work of tongue and pen,
> A long, harsh strife with strong-willed men,
>   Thou wilt not chide my turning,
> To con, at times, an idle rhyme,
> To pluck a flower from childhood's clime,
> Or listen, at Life's noon-day chime,
>   For the sweet bells of Morning!"

"Poor fellow!" we say at first. And yet there is something refreshing and noble in such a spirit. It is with difficulty that the Germanic mind can bring itself to the study of the beautiful as something of co-equal worth with the moral. Let us leave that, says the Teuton, to the nation whose word for love of art is "virtue." How Whittier would have abhorred in his youth and early manhood the following sentiment by one of the Latin race:—

> The arts require idle, delicate minds, not stoics, especially not Puritans, easily shocked by dissonance, inclined to sensuous pleasure, employing their long periods of leisure, their free reveries, in harmoniously arranging, and with no other object but enjoyment, forms, colors, and sounds.
>
> (Taine's *English Literature,* II. 332.)

Or the following from the same work:—

> The Puritan destroys the artist, stiffens the man, fetters the writer, and leaves of artist, man, writer, only a sort of abstract being, the slave of a watchword. If a Milton springs up among them, it is because, by his wide curiosity, his travels, his comprehensive education, and by his independence of spirit, loftily adhered to even against the sectarians, Milton passes beyond sectarianism.
>
> (I. 397, 398.)

Here is another passage from Whittier which is very amusing. It is almost a pity to give it, since the author has apparently repudiated the sentiment by omitting the lines from his complete works. In the introduction to "Supernaturalism of New England" he says:—

> If in some few instances, like Burns in view of his national thistle, I have—
>
> 'Turned my weeding-hook aside,
>   And spared the symbol dear,'
>
> I have been influenced by the comparatively innocent nature and simple poetic beauty of the traditions in question; yet not even for the sake of poetry and romance would I confirm in any mind a pernicious credulity, or seek to absolve myself from that stern duty which the true man owes to his generation, to expose error whenever and wherever he finds it.

One more instance. In one of his sketches he is describing an old custom called "Pope Night," which has been kept up in the Merrimack Valley in unbroken sequence from the time of the Guy Fawkes plot. The plot is commemorated by bonfires and effigies of the Pope and others, and Whittier quotes these lines of a song which is sung on the occasion:—

> Look here! from Rome
> The Pope has come,
>   That fiery serpent dire;
> Here's the Pope that we have got,
> The old promoter of the plot;
> We'll stick a pitchfork in his back,
>   And throw him in the fire.

Whittier thinks it will never do to allow such a bloodthirsty sentiment as this to go unrebuked, and accordingly treats us to a long and solemn paragraph on the wickedness of religious hatred and intolerance as well as cruelty!

Another of Whittier's mannerisms consists in his pietistic effusions. He is a born preacher. But a preacher is not a poet; and when a poet carries religion to such a length that out of some five hundred poems he cannot write more than half a dozen that do not contain more or less (generally a profusion) of pious exhortation or allusion, it not only becomes disagreeable from its monotony, but reminds us of the sighs and groans of revivalists, or the Mahometan's wearisome refrain of "God is great, and Mahomet is his prophet." Many of Whittier's purely religious poems are the most exquisite and beautiful ever written. The tender feeling, the warm-hearted trustfulness, and the reverent touch of his hymns speak directly to our hearts. The prayer-hymn at the close of **"The Brewing of Soma"** ("Dear Lord and Father of mankind," etc.), and such poems as **"At Last"** and **"The Wish of To-day,"** are unsurpassed in sacred song. Some one has said that in Whittier's books we rarely meet with ideas expressed in such perfection and idiosyncrasy of manner that ever afterward the same ideas must recur to our minds in the words of this author and no other; that is to say, there are few dicta, few portable and universally-quoted passages in his writings. But exception must be made in favor of his best hymns. Their stanzas haunt the mind with their beauty, and you are obliged to learn them by heart before you can have peace. It is needless to say that it is not with these purely religious productions that we must quarrel; but it is with those other poems in which the secular theme seems to serve merely as a text for the preaching of a little sermon; it is to these that reference is made, as well as to those which might be classed under the general head of religious gush and sentimentality. The fault we are considering, like the faults of every other poet, seems more conspicuous when one peruses the entire bulk of Whittier's poetical productions in consecutive reading. Now, there is only one poet in the world whose works will not suffer by such reading, and that is Shakspere. Poetry should be read solely for the refreshment and elevation of the mind, and only when one's mood requires it. Unquestionably, when so read, the mannerisms of Whittier would not appear so conspicuous. Still, no poet needs more to have his work sifted, and the finest productions rescued from the mass of feeble writing in which they are swallowed up. This is pre-eminently the age of *réchauffé*, especially as regards imaginative literature of the pre-Darwinian era. Doubtless Mr. Whittier will have at some future time his Matthew Arnold.

Another of the mannerisms of our poet is his dead set toward the four-foot line with consecutive or alternate rhymes. Almost all of Burns's poetry is written as just described; and it is evident that the Whittier pendulum caught its tick and swing from that of Burns, his early favorite. But seesaw rhyme has become unendurable to a person whose ear has been educated by Tennyson and the other Victorian poets. To such a one the poetry of the Queen Anne school is torture. We are pleased when rhymes are so masked, so subtly intertwined, and parted by intervening lines, that each shall seem like a delicate echo of that which preceded it,—the assonance just remembered, and no more. In this art Tennyson is the master.

A minor mannerism of Whittier is his frequent use of the present participle in *ing* with the verb *to be*; "is flowing," "is shining," etc. We had become disgusted with this thing by its occurrence in the gush of innumerable poetasters, and had often wondered whence it came. After reading Whittier the mystery was solved: we had previously been reading his imitators. Perhaps it would not seem so odious if met with for the first time in his own writings. The jingle of the *ing* evidently caught Whittier's rhyme-loving ear, and sometimes it really has a very pretty effect.

As to the originality of our poet there is this to be said: He has a distinctively national spirit or vision; he is democratic in his feelings, and treats of indigenous subjects. But his vehicle, his poetic forms and handling, have no originality whatever. He is democratic, not so powerfully and broadly as Whitman, but more unaffectedly and sincerely. He has not the magnificent prophetic vision, or *Vorstellungskraft*, of Whitman, any more than he has the crushing mastodon-steps of Whitman's ponderous rhythm. But he has thrown himself, with trembling ardor and patriotism, into the life of his country. It is this fresh, New-World spirit that entitles him to be called original: he is non-European. He has not travelled much, nor mingled in the seething currents of Western and Southern life; but his strong sympathy has gone forth over the entire land. He also reflects faithfully the quiet scenes of his own Merrimack Valley. From his descriptions of these scenes we receive the impression of freshness and originality; but this is due rather to new combinations than to new creations. His descriptions are careful copies, but are not so transfused with his own soul as to have absolute originality.

But enough of this analysis. One almost regrets using a critical pen at all in discussing such a writer. It would be ungracious to call to a severe account one who places the most modest estimate upon his own work, and who has distinctly stated that, up to "about the year 1865, his writings were simply episodical, something apart from the real object and aim of [his] life." It is hard to criticise severely one who is unjust to himself through excess of diffident humility. In the exquisite Proem to his complete poems he would fain persuade us that he cannot breathe such notes as those of—

> The old melodious lays
> Which softly melt the ages through,
> The songs of Spenser's golden days,
> Arcadian Sidney's silvery phrase,
> Sprinkling our noon of time with freshest morning
> dew.

But not so, O gentle minstrel of Essex! There are poems of thine which thousands prefer to the best of Spenser's or Sidney's, and which will continue to exist as long as beauty is its own excuse for being. Thou too hast been in Paradise, to fetch thence armfuls of dewy roses for our delight; not mounting thither by the "stairway of surprise," but along the common highway of daily duty and noble endeavor, unmindful of the dust and heat and chafing burdens, but singing aloud thy songs of lofty cheer, all magically intertwined with pictures of wayside flowers, and the homely beauty of lowliest things.

* * *

POEMS SERIATIM.

Among the three or four critical papers on Whittier that have up to this time been published, there is one that is marked by exceptional vigor; namely, the admirable philosophical analysis by Mr. David A. Wasson, published in the *Atlantic Monthly* for March, 1864. The author gladly acknowledges his indebtedness to this paper for several things,—chiefly for its keen *aperçu* into the nature of Whittier's genius, and the proper psychological grouping of his poems. Mr. Wasson's classification can hardly be improved upon in its general features. He divides the literary life of the poet into three epochs,—The Struggle for Life, The Culture Epoch, and The Epoch of Poetic Realism; and between each of these he places transitional periods. The lines of his classification, however, are too sharply drawn, and the epochs seem too minutely subdivided. Moreover, the present writer would add an introductory or preparatory period; in other respects it seems to him that the grouping is as correct as such mathematical measurements of a poet's development can be. Suppose we group and name the poet's mental epochs as follows:—

First Period.—Introductory. 1830-1833.

During this quiet, purely literary epoch, Whittier published **"Legends of New England"** and **"Moll Pitcher,"** and edited the "Literary Remains of Brainard."

Second Period.—Storm and Stress. 1833-1853.

The beginning of this period was marked by the publication of "Justice and Expediency," and during its continuance were written most of the anti-slavery productions, the Indian poems, many legendary lays and prose pieces, religious lyrics, and **"Songs of Labor."** The latter, being partially free from didacticism, leads naturally up to the third period.

Third Period.—Transition. 1853-1860

This Mr. Wasson calls the epoch of culture and religious doubt, the central poems of which are **"Chapel of the Hermits"** and **"Questions of Life."** We now begin to see a love of art for art's sake, and there are fewer moral stump-speeches. The indignation of the reformer is giving place to the calm repose of the artist. And

such ballads as **"Mary Garvin"** and **"Maud Muller"** form the introduction to the culminating (or fourth) epoch in the poet's creative life.

Fourth Period.—Religious and Artistic Repose. 1860-

During this time have been written nearly all the author's great works, namely, his beautiful ballads, as well as **"Snow-Bound"** and **"The Tent on the Beach."** The literary style is now mature. The beautiful is sought for its own sake, both in nature and in lowly life. It is a season of trust and *naïve* simplicity.

The works produced during the Introductory period have already been discussed in the biographical portion of this volume.

Before passing rapidly in review some of the more important detached poems of the three latter periods (reserving a number of poems for consideration by groups), we must be allowed to offer a few criticisms on the earlier poems in general, meaning by this the ones published previous to the **"Songs of Labor"** in 1850. These earlier productions are to be commended chiefly for two things: (1) the subjects are drawn from original and native sources, and (2) the slavery poems are full of moral stamina and fiery indignation at oppression. There are single poems of great merit and beauty. But the style of most of them is unoriginal, being merely an echo of that of the English Lake School. Whittier's poetical development has been a steady growth. His genius matured late, and in his early poems there is little promise of the exquisite work of his riper years, unless it is a distinct indication of his rare power of telling a story in verse. It must be remembered that when Whittier began to write, American literature had yet to be created. There was not a single great American poem, with the exception of Bryant's "Thanatopsis." The prominent poets of that time—Percival, Brainard, Trumbull, Joel Barlow, Hillhouse, Pierpont, Dana, Sprague—are all forgotten now. The breath of immortality was not upon anything they wrote. A national literature is a thing of slow growth. Every writer is insensibly influenced by the intellectual tone of his neighbors and contemporaries. Judged in the light of his early disadvantages, and estimated by the standard of that time, Whittier's first essays are deserving of much credit, and they have had a distinct æsthetic and moral value in the development of American literature and the American character. But their deficiencies are very grave. There is a good deal of commonplace, and much extravagance of rhetoric. There are a great many "Lines" called forth by circumstances not at all poetical in their suggestions. Emotion and rhyme and commonplace incident are not enough to make a poem. One cannot embalm the memory of all one's friends in verse. In casting about for an explanation of the circumstance that our poet has so often chosen tame and uninspiring themes for his poems, we reach the conclusion that it is due to his solitary and uneventful life, and to the subdued and art-chilling atmosphere of his Quaker religion. You get, at any rate, the impression of intellectual flaccidity from many of the productions of the period we are considering: the theme is too weak to support the poetical structure reared upon it. The poems and essays are written by one untoughened and unvitalized by varied and cheerful intercourse with men and affairs. There is occasional bathos, also. The poet enters upon the treatment of a slight facetious theme with all the earnestness and dignity of historical illustration that we have been used to find in his serious poems,—when, bump! we stumble upon a pumpkin, or Fox's leathern breeches, or washing-day, or something similarly bathetic.

A minor fault of this period is the too frequent interruption of explanatory notes. We find the same blemish in Longfellow's early work. A prose explanation of a poem always injures it.

At the opening of the complete poetical works of Whittier stand two long Indian poems, with their war-paint and blood,—like scarlet maples at the entrance of an aboriginal forest. The first of these poems, **"Mogg Megone,"** is every way inferior to the second, or **"The Bridal of Pennacook." "Mogg Megone"** was published in 1836, and **"The Bridal of Pennacook"** in 1848. Mr. Whittier half apologizes for retaining the former of these in his complete works. It is a pity that he spared it. Its strength is frenzy; its rhetoric, fustian and extravaganza; its juvenility unredeemed by anything except a certain fresh and realistic diction, or nomenclature. It is picturesque, in portions somewhat dramatic, and as thrilling as a play by Buffalo Bill and his troupe of stage braves. In style it is an echo of Scott's "Lady of the Lake" or "Marmion." The bathos of the toothache scene is very ludicrous.

In **"The Bridal of Pennacook"** we have an Indian idyl of unquestionable power and beauty, a descriptive poem full of the cool, mossy sweetness of mountain landscapes, and although too artificial and subjective for a poem of primitive life, yet saturated with the imagery of the wigwam and the forest. A favorite article of food with the Indians of Northern Ohio was dried bear's-meat dipped in maple syrup. There is a savor of the like ferity and sweetness in this poem. It is almost wholly free from the melodrama and fustian of **"Mogg Megone,"** and (that test of all tests) it is pleasant reading. Its two cardinal defects are lack of simplicity of treatment, and tenuity or triviality of the subject, or plot. The story is lost sight of in a jungle of verbiage and description. In contrasting such a poem with "Hiawatha," we see the wisdom of Longfellow in choosing an antique vehicle, or rhythmic style. Aborigines never talk as do Whittier's sachems. The sentences of an

Indian brave are as abrupt and sharp as the screams of an eagle. The set speeches of the North American Indians are always full of divers stock metaphors about natural scenery, wild animals, totems, and spirits, and are so different from those of civilized life that an expert can instantly detect a forgery or an imitation. The incongruity of the poem in attributing the complex and refined emotions of civilized life to the savage is so ludicrous as seriously to mar the pleasure of the reader.

In plan the poem is like the "Decameron," the "Princess," the "Canterbury Tales," and "Tales of a Wayside Inn." The different portions are supposed to be related by five persons,—a lawyer, a clergyman, a merchant and his daughter, and the poet,—who are all sight-seeing in the White Mountains. The opening description, in blank verse, conveys a vague but not very powerful impression of sublimity. The musical nomenclature of the red aborigines is finely handled, and such words as Pennacook, Babboosuck, Contoocook, Bashaba, and Weetamoo chime out here and there along the pages with as silvery a sweetness as the Tuscan words in Macaulay's "Lays." At the wedding of Weetamoo we have—

> Pike and perch from the Suncook taken,
> Nuts from the trees of the Black Hills shaken,
> Cranberries picked from the Squamscot bog,
> And grapes from the vines of Piscataquog:
>
> And, drawn from that great stone vase which stands
> In the river scooped by a spirit's hands,
> Garnished with spoons of shell and horn,
> Stood the birchen dishes of smoking corn.

The following stanza on the heroine, Weetamoo, is a fine one:—

> Child of the forest!—strong and free,
>   Slight-robed, with loosely flowing hair,
> She swam the lake, or climbed the tree,
>   Or struck the flying bird in air.
> O'er the heaped drifts of winter's moon
>   Her snow-shoes tracked the hunter's way;
> And, dazzling in the summer noon,
> The blade of her light oar threw off its shower of spray!

The **"Song of Indian Women,"** at the close of **"The Bridal of Pennacook,"** is admirable for melody, weird and wild beauty, and naturalness. It is a lament for the lost Weetamoo, who, unfortunate in her married life, has committed suicide by sailing over the rapids in her canoe:—

> The Dark Eye has left us,
>   The Spring-bird has flown;
> On the pathway of spirits
>   She wanders alone.
> The song of the wood-dove has died on our shore,—
> *Mat wonck kunna-monee!*—We hear it no more!

O mighty Sowanna!
  Thy gateways unfold,
From thy wigwams of sunset
  Lift curtains of gold!
Take home the poor Spirit whose journey is o'er,—
Mat wonck kunna-monee!—We see her no more!

There are two minor Indian poems by Whittier that
have the true ring; namely, the **"Truce of Piscataqua"**
and **"Funeral Tree of the Sokokis."** The latter well-
known poem is pitched in as high and solemn a key as
Platen's "Grab im Busento," a poem similar in theme to
Whittier's:—

They heave the stubborn trunk aside,
The firm roots from the earth divide,—
The rent beneath yawns dark and wide.

And there the fallen chief is laid,
In tasselled garbs of skins arrayed,
And girded with his wampum-braid.

Whittier

In der wogenleeren Höhlung wühlten sie empor die
  Erde,
Senkten tief hinein den Leichnam, mit der Rüstung
  auf dem Pferde.
Deckten dann mit Erde wieder ihn und seine stolze
  Habe.

Platen

In the empty river-bottom hurriedly they dug the
  death-pit,
Deep therein they sank the hero with his armor and
  his war-steed,
Covered then with earth and darkness him and all his
  splendid trappings.

When the reader, who has worked gloomily along
through Whittier's anti-slavery and miscellaneous
poems, reaches the **"Songs of Labor,"** he feels at once
the breath of a fresher spirit,—as a traveller who has
been toiling for weary leagues through sandy deserts
bares his brow with delight to the coolness and shade
of a green forest through whose thick roof of leaves the
garish sunlight scarcely sifts. We feel that in these
poems a new departure has been made. The wrath of
the reformer has expended itself, and the poet now
returns, with mind elevated and more tensely keyed by
his moral warfare, to the study of the beautiful in native
themes and in homely life. **"The Shipbuilders," "The
Shoemakers," "The Fishermen,"** and **"The Huskers"**
are genuine songs; and more shame to the craftsmen
celebrated if they do not get them set to music, and
sing them while at their work. One cannot help feeling
that Walt Whitman's call for some one to make songs
for American laborers had already been met in a goodly
degree by these spirited **"Songs of Labor."** What work-

man would not be glad to carol such stanzas as the following, if they were set to popular airs?

Hurrah! the seaward breezes
  Sweep down the bay amain;
Heave up, my lads, the anchor!
  Run up the sail again!
Leave to the lubber landsmen
  The rail-car and the steed:
The stars of heaven shall guide us,
  The breath of heaven shall speed.

The Fishermen

Ho! workers of the old time styled
  The Gentle Craft of Leather!
Young brothers of the ancient guild,
  Stand forth once more together!
Call out again your long array,
  In the olden merry manner!
Once more, on gay St. Crispin's day,
  Fling out your blazoned banner!

Rap, rap! upon the well-worn stone
  How falls the polished hammer!
Rap, rap! the measured sound has grown
  A quick and merry clamor.
Now shape the sole! now deftly curl
  The glossy vamp around it,
And bless the while the bright-eyed girl
  Whose gentle fingers bound it!

The Shoemakers

The publication of **"The Chapel of the Hermits"** and
"Questions of Life," in 1853, marks (as has been said)
the period of culture and of religious doubt,—doubt
which ended in trust. In this period we have such
genuine undidactic poems as **"The Barefoot Boy."**

Blessings on thee, little man,
Barefoot boy, with cheek of tan!
With thy turned-up pantaloons,
And thy merry whistled tunes;
With thy red lip, redder still
Kissed by strawberries on the hill;
With the sunshine on thy face,
Through thy torn brim's jaunty grace.

Also, such fine poems as **"Flowers in Winter"** and
"To My Old Schoolmaster," as well as the excellent
ballads, **"Maud Muller," "Kathleen,"** and **"Mary
Garvin."**

The period in Whittier's life from about 1858 to 1868
we may call the Ballad Decade, (The beginning of this
decade nearly coincides with the fourth or final period
in our classification, upon the consideration of which
we shall now enter.) for within this time were produced
most of his immortal ballads. We say immortal, believing that if all else that he has written shall perish, his
finest ballads will carry his name down to a remote
posterity. **"The Tent on the Beach"** is mainly a series

of ballads; and **"Snow-Bound,"** although not a ballad, is still a narrative poem closely allied to that species of poetry, the difference between a ballad and an idyl being that one is made to be sung and the other to be read: both narrate events as they occur, and leave to the reader all sentiment and reflection.

The finest ballads of Whittier have the power of keeping us in breathless suspense of interest until the *dénouement* or the catastrophe, as the case may be. The popularity of **"Maud Muller"** is well deserved. What a rich and mellow translucence it has! How it appeals to the universal heart! And yet **"The Witch's Daughter"** and **"Telling the Bees"** are more exquisite creations than **"Maud Muller"**: they have a spontaneity, a subtle pathos, a sublimated sweetness of despair that take hold of the very heart-strings, and thus deal with deeper emotions than such light, objective ballads as **"Maud Muller"** and **"Skipper Ireson's Ride."** But the surface grace of the two latter have of course made them the more popular, just as the "Scarlet Letter" finds greater favor with most people than does "The House of the Seven Gables," although Hawthorne rightly thought the "Seven Gables" to be his finest and subtlest work.

Mark the Chaucerian freshness of the opening stanzas of **"The Witch's Daughter"**:—

> It was the pleasant harvest time,
>   When cellar-bins are closely stowed,
>   And garrets bend beneath their load,
>
> And the old swallow-haunted barns—
>   Brown-gabled, long, and full of seams
>   Through which the moted sunlight streams.
>
> And winds blow freshly in, to shake
>   The red plumes of the roosted cocks,
>   And the loose hay-mow's scented locks—
>
> Are filled with summer's ripened stores,
>   Its odorous grass and barley sheaves,
>   From their low scaffolds to their eaves.

A companion ballad to **"The Witch's Daughter"** is **"The Witch of Wenham,"** a poem almost equal to it in merit, and like it ending happily. These ballads do not quite attain the almost supernatural simplicity of Wordsworth's "Lucy Gray" and "We are Seven"; but they possess an equal interest, excited by the same poetical qualities. **"Telling the Bees,"** however, seems to the writer as purely Wordsworthian as anything Wordsworth ever wrote:—

> Stay at home, pretty bees, fly not hence!
>   Mistress Mary is dead and gone!

How the tears spring to the eyes in reading this immortal little poem! The beehives ranged in the garden, the sun "tangling his wings of fire in the trees," the dog whining low, the old man "with his cane to his chin,"—we all know the scene: its every feature appeals to our sympathies and associations.

"The Double-headed Snake of Newbury" is a whimsical story, in which the poet waxes right merry as he relates how—

> Far and wide the tale was told,
> Like a snowball growing while it rolled.
> The nurse hushed with it the baby's cry;
> And it served, in the worthy minister's eye,
> To paint the primitive serpent by.
> Cotton Mather came galloping down
> All the way to Newbury town,
> With his eyes agog and his ears set wide,
> And his marvellous inkhorn at his side;
> Stirring the while in the shallow pool
> Of his brains for the lore he learned at school,
> To garnish the story, with here a streak
> Of Latin, and there another of Greek:
> And the tales he heard and the notes he took,
> Behold! are they not in his Wonder-Book?

A word about Whittier's **"Prophecy of Samuel Sewall."** It seems that old Judge Sewall made the prophecies of the Bible his favorite study. One of his ideas was that America was to be the site of the New Jerusalem. Toward the end of his book entitled "Phenomena Quædam Apocalyptica; . . . or . . . a Description of the New Heaven as it makes to those who stand upon the New Earth" (1697), he gives utterance to the triumphant prophecy that forms the subject of Whittier's poem. His language is so quaint that the reader will like to see the passage in Sewall's own words:—

> As long as Plum Island shall faithfully keep the commanded post, notwithstanding all the hectoring words and hard blows of the proud and boisterous ocean; as long as any salmon or sturgeon shall swim in the streams of Merrimac, or any perch or pickerel in Crane Pond; as long as the sea-fowl shall know the time of their coming, and not neglect seasonably to visit the places of their acquaintance; as long as any cattle shall be fed with the grass growing in the meadows, which do humbly bow down themselves before Turkey Hill; as long as any sheep shall walk upon Old-Town Hills, and shall from thence pleasantly look down upon the River Parker, and the fruitful marshes lying beneath; as long as any free and harmless doves shall find a white oak or other tree within the township, to perch, or feed, or build a careless nest upon, and shall voluntarily present themselves to perform the office of gleaners after barley-harvest; as long as Nature shall not grow old and dote, but shall constantly remember to give the rows of Indian corn their education by pairs; so long shall Christians be born there, and being first made meet, shall from thence be translated to be made partakers of the inheritance of the saints in light.

Moses Coit Tyler, in his "History of American Literature," II., p. 102 (note), says: "Whittier speaks of Newbury as Sewall's 'native town,' but Sewall was born at

Horton, England. He also describes Sewall as an 'old man,' propped on his staff of age when he made this prophecy; but Sewall was then forty-five years old."

There are two or three other ballads in which Whittier is said to have made historical blunders. It really does not seem of much importance whether he did or did not get the precise facts in each case. The important point is that he made beautiful ballads. But it will be right to give, in brief, the objections that have been brought against **"Skipper Ireson's Ride"** and **"Barbara Frietchie."** **"The King's Missive"** will be discussed in another place.

Apropos of Skipper Ireson, Mr. John W. Chadwick has spoken as follows in *Harper's Monthly* for July, 1874:—

> In one of the queerest corners of the town [Marblehead], there stands a house as modest as the Lee house was magnificent. So long as he lived it was the home of 'Old Flood Oirson,' whose name and fame have gone farther and fared worse than any other fact or fancy connected with his native town. Plain, honest folk don't know about poetic license, and I have often heard the poet's conduct in the matter of Skipper Ireson's ride characterized with profane severity. He unwittingly departed from the truth in various particulars. The wreck did not, as the ballad recites, contain any of 'his own town's-people.' Moreover, the most of those it did contain *were* saved by a whale-boat from Provincetown. It was off Cape Cod, and not in Chaleur Bay, that the wreck was deserted; and the desertion was in this wise: It was in the night that the wreck was discovered. In the darkness and the heavy sea it was impossible to give assistance. When the skipper went below, he ordered the watch to lie by the wreck till 'dorning'; but the watch wilfully disobeyed, and afterward, to shield themselves, laid all the blame upon the skipper. Then came the tarring and feathering. The women, whose *rôle* in the ballad is so striking, had nothing to do with it. The vehicle was not a cart, but a dory; and the skipper, instead of being contrite, said, 'I thank you for your ride.' I asked one of the skipper's contemporaries what the effect was on the skipper. 'Cowed him to death,' said he, 'cowed him to death.' He went skipper again the next year, but never afterward. He had been dead only a year or two when Whittier's ballad appeared. His real name was not Floyd, as Whittier supposes, but Benjamin, 'Flood' being one of those nicknames that were not the exception, but the rule, in the old fishing-days. For many years before his death the old man earned a precarious living by dory-fishing in the bay, and selling his daily catch from a wheelbarrow. When old age and blindness overtook him, and his last trip was made, his dory was hauled up into the lane before his house, and there went to rot and ruin. . . . The hoarse refrain of Whittier's ballad is the best-known example of the once famous Marblehead dialect, and it is not a bad one. To what extent this dialect was peculiar to Marblehead it might be difficult to determine. Largely, no doubt, it was inherited from English ancestors. Its principal delight consisted in pronouncing *o* for *a,* and *a* for *o.*

> For example, if an old-fashioned Marbleheader wished to say he 'was born in a barn,' he would say, 'I was barn in a born.' The *e* was also turned into *a,* and even into *o,* and the *v* into *w.* 'That vessel's stern' became 'that wessel's starn,' or 'storn.' I remember a schoolboy declaiming from Shakspere, 'Thou little walliant, great in willany.' There was a great deal of shortening. The fine name Crowninshield became Grounsel, and Florence became Flurry, and a Frenchman named Blancpied found himself changed into Blumpy. Endings in *une* and *ing* were alike changed into *in.* Misfortune was misfartin', and fishing was always fishin'. There were words peculiar to the place. One of these was planchment for ceiling. Crim was another, meaning to shudder with cold, and there was an adjective, crimmy. Still another was *clitch,* meaning to stick badly, surely an onomatopoetic word that should be naturalized before it is too late. Some of the swearing, too, was neither by the throne nor footstool, such as 'Dahst my eyes!' and 'Godfrey darmints.' The ancient dialect in all its purity is now seldom used. It crops out here and there sometimes where least expected, and occasionally one meets with some old veteran whose speech has lost none of the ancient savor.

Now for **"Barbara Frietchie."** The incident of the poem was given to Whittier by the novelist, Mrs. E. D. E. N. Southworth. The philanthropist, Dorothea Dix, investigated the case in Frederick, and she says that Barbara did wave the flag, etc. An army officer also made affidavit of the truth of the lines. A young Southern soldier has declared that he was present, and that his was one of the shots that hit the flagstaff!

On the other side are Samuel Tyler and Jacob Engelbrecht, the latter an old and greatly respected citizen of Frederick, and living directly opposite Barbara's house. Jacob wrote to the Baltimore *Sun,* saying that Stonewall Jackson's corps marched through another street, and did not approach Dame Frietchie's house at all. Lee's column did pass it, he says; but he, who stood watching at his window, saw no flag whatever at *her* window. He says that when ten days later General McClellan passed through the town she did exhibit a flag.

Finally, General Jubal Early comes upon the witness stand, and testifies that as the Southern troops passed through Frederick, there were only two cases of waving of Union flags; one of these was by a little girl, about ten years old, who stood on the platform of a house and waved incessantly a little "candy flag," and cried in a dull, monotonous voice: "Hurrah for the Stars and Stripes! Down with the Stars and Bars!" No one molested her. The other case was that of a coarse, slovenly-looking woman, who rushed up to the entrance of an alley and waved a dirty United States flag.

Such is the testimony *In re* **"Barbara Frietchie,"** and if the reader thinks it worth while to puzzle over the matter, he has before him all the *criteria* he is likely to get.

"The Pipes at Lucknow" is a poem full of martial fire and lyric rush,—the subject a capital one for a poet. A little band of English, besieged in a town in the heart of India, and full of despair, hear in the distance the sweetest sound that ever fell upon their ears, *i. e.,* the shrill pibroch of the MacGregor Clan; and—

> When the far-off dust-cloud
> To plaided legions grew,
> Full tenderly and blithesomely
> The pipes of rescue blew!

Another group of ballads comprises **"Cobbler Keezar's Vision," "Amy Wentworth,"** and **"The Countess."** In the first of these, old Cobbler Keezar, of the early Puritan times, by virtue of a mystic lapstone, sees a vision of our age of religious tolerance, and wonders greatly thereat:—

> Keezar sat on the hillside
> Upon his cobbler's form,
> With a pan of coals on either hand
> To keep his waxed-ends warm.
>
> And there, in the golden weather,
> He stitched and hammered and sung;
> In the brook he moistened his leather,
> In the pewter mug his tongue.

The ballad of **"Amy Wentworth"** treats of the same subject as **"Among The Hills,"** namely, a superior woman, of the white-handed caste, falling in love with and marrying a broad-shouldered, brown-handed hero, with a right manly heart and brain.

Many and many a poem of Whittier's is spoiled by its too great length,—a thing that is fatal in a lyric. The long prelude to **"Amy Wentworth"** should have been omitted.

The scene of the lovely poem entitled **"The Countess"** is laid in Rocks Village, a part of East Haverhill, and lying on the Merrimack, where—

> The river's steel-blue crescent curves
> To meet, in ebb and flow,
> The single broken wharf that serves
> For sloop and gundelow.
>
> With salt sea-scents along its shores
> The heavy hay-boats crawl,
> The long antennæ of their oars
> In lazy rise and fall.
>
> Along the gray abutment's wall
> The idle shad-net dries;
> The toll-man in his cobbler's stall
> Sits smoking with closed eyes.

Whittier dedicates his poem to his father's family physician, Elias Weld, of Rocks Village. The story which forms the subject of the poem is a romantic one, and

exquisitely has our poet embalmed it in verse. From a sketch by Rebecca I. Davis, of East Haverhill, the following facts relating to the personages that figure in the poem have been culled:—

The Countess was Miss Mary Ingalls, daughter of Henry and Abigail Ingalls, of Rocks Village. She was born in 1786, and is still remembered by a few old inhabitants as a young girl of remarkable beauty. She was of medium height, had long golden curls, violet eyes, fair complexion, and rosy cheeks, and was exceedingly modest and lovable. It was in the year 1806 that a little company of French exiles fled from the Island of Guadaloupe on account of a bloody rebellion or uprising of the inhabitants. Among the fugitives were Count Francis de Vipart and Joseph Rochemont de Poyen. The company reached Newburyport. The two gentlemen just mentioned settled at Rocks Village, and both married there. Mary Ingalls was only a laborer's daughter, and of course her marriage with the count created a sensation in the simple, rustic community. The count was a pleasant, stately man, and a fine violinist. The bridal dress, says Miss Davis, was of a pink satin, with an overdress of white lace; her slippers also were of white satin. The count delighted to lavish upon her the richest apparel, yet nothing spoiled the sweet modesty of her disposition. After one short year of happy married life the lovely wife died. Assiduous attention to a sick mother had brought on consumption. In the village God's-acre her gray tombstone is already covered with moss.

The count returned to his native island overwhelmed with grief. In after years, however, he married again. When he died he was interred in the family burial-place of the De Viparts at Bordeaux. He left several children.

Mr. Stedman, in his fine synthetic survey of American poetry, published in *The Century,* has remarked that most of our early poetry and painting is full of landscape. The loveliest season in America is the autumn, when, as Whittier beautifully says, the woods "wear their robes of praise, the south winds softly sigh,"—

> And sweet, calm days in golden haze
> Melt down the amber sky.

We have plenty of idyls of autumn color, like Buchanan Read's "Closing Scene," and portions of Longfellow's "Hiawatha." But American winter landscapes are as poetical as those of autumn.[1] It is probable that the scarcity of snow-idyls hitherto is due to the supposed cheerlessness of the snow. But with the rapid multiplication of winter comforts, our nature-worship is cautiously broadening so as to include even the stern beauty of winter. There are already a good many signs of this in literature. We have had, of late, lovely little snow-and-winter vignettes in prose by John Burroughs of New York, and Edith Thomas of Ohio; and there is plenty of room for further study of winter in other regions of the United States. The most delicate bit of realistic winter poetry in literature is Emerson's "Snow-Storm." Mr. Whittier is an ardent admirer of that writer—as what poet is not?—and his own productions show frequent traces of Emersonianisms. He has prefixed to **"Snow-Bound"** a quotation from the "Snow-Storm," and there can scarcely be a doubt that to the countless obligations we all owe Emerson must be added this: that he inspired the writing of Whittier's finest poem, and the best idyl of American rural life. It is too complex and diffusive fully to equal in artistic purity and plastic proportion the "Cotter's Saturday Night" of Burns; but it is much richer than that poem in felicitous single epithets, which, like little wicket doors, open up to the eye of memory many a long-forgotten picture of early life.

"Snow-Bound" was published in 1860, and was written, Mr. Whittier has said, "to beguile the weariness of a sick-chamber." The poet has obeyed the canon of Lessing, and instead of giving us dead description wholly, has shown us his characters in action, and extended his story over three days and the two intervening nights,—that is to say, the main action covers that time: the whole time mentioned in the poem is a week. It is unnecessary to give here any further account of the idyl than has already been furnished in the account of Whittier's boyhood.

"The Tent on the Beach" is a cluster of ballads. In accordance with a familiar fiction, they are supposed to be sung, or told, by several persons, in this case three, namely, the poet himself, "a lettered magnate" (James T. Fields), and a traveller (Bayard Taylor). All of the poems are readable, and many of them are to be classed among Whittier's best lyrics. **"The Wreck of Rivermouth," "The Changeling,"** and **"Kallundborg Church"** are masterpieces in the line of ballads. In **"The Dead Ship of Harpswell"** we have the fine phrase,—

> O hundred-harbored Maine!

Whittier has now become almost a perfect master of verbal melody. Hearken to this:—

> "Oho!" she muttered, "ye're brave to-day!
> But I hear the little waves laugh and say,
> 'The broth will be cold that waits at home;
> For it's one to go, but another to come!'"

There is a light and piquant humor about some of the interludes of the **"Tent on the Beach."** The song in the last of these contains a striking and original stanza concerning the ocean:—

> Its waves are kneeling on the strand,
> As kneels the human knee,

> Their white locks bowing to the sand,
> The priesthood of the sea!

"Among the Hills" is a little farm-idyl, or love-idyl, of the New Hampshire mountain land, and bearing some resemblance to Tennyson's "Gardener's Daughter." It is an excellent specimen of the poems of Whittier that reach the popular heart, and engage its sympathies. In the remotest farm-houses of the land you are almost sure to find among their few books a copy of Whittier's Poems, well-thumbed and soiled with use. The opening description of the prelude to **"Among the Hills"** could not be surpassed by Bion or Theocritus. In this poem a fresh interest is excited in the reader by the fact that the city woman falls in love with a manly farmer, thus happily reversing the old, old story of the city man wooing and winning the rustic beauty. The farmer accuses the fair city maid of coquetry. She replies:

> "Nor frock nor tan can hide the man;
>   And see you not, my farmer,
> How weak and fond a woman waits
>   Behind this silken armor?

> "I love you: on that love alone,
>   And not my worth, presuming,
> Will you not trust for summer fruit
>   The tree in May-day blooming?"

> Alone the hangbird overhead,
>   His hair-swung cradle straining,
> Looked down to see love's miracle,—
>   The giving that is gaining.

In **"Lines on a Fly-Leaf,"** the author of **"Snow-Bound"** gives in his hearty adherence to that movement for the elevation of woman, and the securing of her rights as a human being, which is perhaps the most significant and important of the many agitations of this agitated age.

The poem **"Miriam,"** like **"The Preacher,"** is one of those long sermons, or meditations in verse, which Whittier loves to spin out of his mind in solitude. It contains in **"Shah Akbar"** a fine Oriental ballad.

The narrative poem called **"The Pennsylvania Pilgrim,"** published in 1872, has no striking poetical merit, but is valuable and readable for the pleasant light in which it sets forth the doings of the quaint people of Germantown and the Wissahickon, near Philadelphia, nearly two hundred years ago. It introduces us to the homes and hearts of the little settlements of German Quakers under Francis Daniel Pastorius, the Mystics under the leadership of Magister Johann Kelpius, and the Mennonites under their various leaders. **"The Pennsylvania Pilgrim"** is a poem for Quakers, for Philadelphians who love their great park and its Wissahickon drives, and for antiquarian historical students.

We may regret, if we choose, that the poet has not succeeded in embalming the memory of the Germantown Quakers in such felicitous verse as other poets have sung the virtues and ways of the Puritans, but we cannot deny that he has garnished with the flowers of poetry a dry historical subject, and so earned the gratitude of a goodly number of students and scholars.

In **"The King's Missive, and Other Poems,"** published in 1881, the most notable piece is **"The Lost Occasion,"** a poem on Daniel Webster, finer even than the much-admired **"Ichabod,"** published many years previously. **"The Lost Occasion"** is pitched in a high, solemn, and majestic strain. It is a superb eulogy, full of magnanimity and generous forgiveness. Listen to a few stanzas:—

Thou
Whom the rich heavens did endow
With eyes of power and Jove's own brow,
With all the massive strength that fills
Thy home-horizon's granite hills,

. . . . .

Whose words, in simplest home-spun clad,
The Saxon strength of Caedmon had,

. . . . .

Sweet with persuasion, eloquent
In passion, cool in argument,
Or, ponderous, falling on thy foes
As fell the Norse god's hammer blows,

. . . . .

Too soon for us, too soon for thee,
Beside thy lonely Northern sea,
Where long and low the marsh-lands spread,
Laid wearily down thy august head.

The poem of **"The King's Missive"** calls for such extended discussion that a brief chapter shall be devoted to it.

Note

1. What is the subtle fascination that lurks in such bits of winter poetry as the following, collected by the writer out of his reading?

Yesterday the sullen year
Saw the snowy whirlwind fly.

—*Gray*

All winter drives along the darkened air.

—*Thomson*

High-ridged the whirled drift has almost reached
The powdered keystone of the churchyard porch;
Mute hangs the hooded bell; the tombs lie buried.

—*Grahame*

Alas! alas! thou snow-smitten wood of
Troy, and mountains of Ida.

—*Sophocles*

O hard, dull bitterness of cold.

—*Whittier*

And in the narrow house o' death
Let winter round me rave.

—*Burns*

The mesmerizer, Snow,
With his hand's first sweep
Put the earth to sleep.

—*Robert Browning*

And the cakèd snow is shuffled
From the plough-boy's heavy shoon.

—*Keats*

BIBLIOGRAPHY

PUBLISHED WORKS TO DATE

LEGENDS OF NEW ENGLAND. Hartford: Hanmer & Phelps. 1831.

THE LITERARY REMAINS OF J. G. C. BRAINARD. [Edited.] Hartford: P. B. Goodsell. 1832.

MOLL PITCHER. 1831 or 1832.

A poem on the famous witch of Nahant.

JUSTICE AND EXPEDIENCY; OR, SLAVERY CONSIDERED WITH A VIEW TO ITS RIGHTFUL AND EFFECTUAL REMEDY, ABOLITION. Haverhill: C. P. Thayer & Co. 1833.

MOGG MEGONE. Boston: Light & Stearns, No. 1 Cornhill. 1836.

There is a copy of this tiny 32mo of 69 pages in the Harvard College Library. It was presented to the Library in 1847 by the Massachusetts Anti-Slavery Society of Boston.

VIEWS OF SLAVERY AND EMANCIPATION; from "Society in America," by Harriet Martineau. [Edited.] New York: Piercy & Reed, Printers, No. 7 Theatre Alley. 1837.

LETTERS FROM JOHN QUINCY ADAMS TO HIS CONSTITUENTS. [Edited.] Boston: Isaac Knapp. 1837.

LAYS OF MY HOME, and Other Poems. 1843.

THE STRANGER IN LOWELL. Boston: Waite, Pierce & Co., No. 1 Cornhill. 1845.

THE SUPERNATURALISM OF NEW ENGLAND. New York and London: Wiley & Putnam. 1847.

THE BRIDAL OF PENNACOOK. 1848.

LEAVES FROM MARGARET SMITH'S JOURNAL, IN THE PROVINCE OF MASSACHUSETTS BAY, 1678-9. Boston: Ticknor, Reed & Fields. 1849.

THE VOICES OF FREEDOM. Philadelphia: Mussey & Co. 1849. Illustrations by Billings.

SONGS OF LABOR, and Other Poems. Boston: Ticknor, Reed & Fields. 1850.

OLD PORTRAITS AND MODERN SKETCHES. Boston: Ticknor, Reed & Fields. 1850.

These sketches first appeared in the *National Era,* a Washington literary and anti-slavery paper, in the columns of which Mrs. Stowe's "Uncle Tom's Cabin" first appeared.

LITTLE EVA; UNCLE TOM'S GUARDIAN ANGEL. Boston and Cleveland. 1852. 4to, pp. 4. "Words by J. G. Whittier; music by Emilio Manuel."

The poem now appears in Whittier's complete works under the title "Eva."

THE CHAPEL OF THE HERMITS. Boston: Ticknor, Reed & Fields. 1853.

A SABBATH SCENE. Boston: John P. Jewett & Co. 1854.

A slender volume, illustrated by Baker, Smith, and Andrew.

LITERARY RECREATIONS AND MISCELLANIES. Boston: Ticknor & Fields. 1854.

THE PANORAMA, and Other Poems. Boston: Ticknor & Fields. 1856.

HOME BALLADS, and Other Poems. Boston: Ticknor & Fields. 1860.

IN WAR TIME, and Other Poems. Boston: Ticknor & Fields. 1863.

SNOW-BOUND. A Winter Idyl. Boston: Ticknor & Fields. 1866.

THE TENT ON THE BEACH, and Other Poems. Boston: Ticknor & Fields. 1867.

AMONG THE HILLS, and Other Poems. Boston: Fields, Osgood & Co. 1868.

MIRIAM, and Other Poems. Boston: Fields, Osgood & Co. 1870.

CHILD-LIFE: A Collection of Poems. [Edited.] Boston: Houghton, Mifflin & Co. 1871.

THE PENNSYLVANIA PILGRIM, and Other Poems. Boston: James R. Osgood & Co. 1872.

THE JOURNAL OF JOHN WOOLMAN. [Edited.] Boston: James R. Osgood & Co. 1873.

CHILD-LIFE IN PROSE. [Edited.] Boston: Houghton, Mifflin & Co. 1873.

Contains, among its stories of the childhood of eminent people, a little narrative by Mr. Whittier about "A Fish I Didn't Catch."

MABEL MARTIN. Boston. Illustrated. 1874.

HAZEL BLOSSOMS. Boston: James R. Osgood & Co. 1875.

SONGS OF THREE CENTURIES. [Edited.] Boston: James R. Osgood & Co. Illustrated. 1875.

This is a rich and careful selection of lyrics and hymns of the last three centuries.

THE VISION OF ECHARD, and Other Poems. Boston: Houghton, Osgood & Co. 1878.

THE KING'S MISSIVE, and Other Poems. Boston: Houghton, Mifflin & Co. 1881.

LETTERS OF LYDIA MARIA CHILD. [Edited.] Boston: Houghton, Mifflin & Co. 1882.

Introduction by Whittier; appendix by Wendell Phillips.

The first collection of Whittier's poems was published by Joseph Healy, Philadelphia, 1838. The volume is dedicated to Henry B. Stanton. It contains twenty-four anti-slavery poems and twenty-six poems of a miscellaneous nature, mostly religious. On the title-page appear the following noble words of Samuel T. Coleridge: "'There is a time to keep silence,' saith Solomon; but when I proceeded to the first verse of the fourth chapter of the Ecclesiastes, 'and considered all the oppressions that are done under the sun, and beheld the tears of such as were oppressed, and they had no comforter; and on the side of the oppressors there was power'; I concluded this was *not* the time to keep silence; for Truth should be spoken at all times, but more especially at those times when to speak Truth is dangerous." A copy of this first collection may be seen in the Newburyport Public Library.

The first complete edition of the poems was published in Boston in 1857. Houghton, Mifflin & Co. now publish seven complete editions. The complete prose works were published at Boston in two volumes in the year 1866. *Editions de luxe* of "The River Path" and of "Mabel Martin" have been published. In 1881 Elizabeth S. Owen published a "Whittier Birthday Book." "Barbara Frietchie" has been translated into German by J. J. Sturtz [Berlin, 1865]. "The Cry of a Lost Soul" has been translated into Portuguese by Dom Pedro II., Emperor of Brazil. "Snow-Bound" has been translated in the "Zwei Amerikanische Idyllen" of Karl Knortz of New York, under the title "Eingeschneit."

William Henry Hudson (essay date 1917)

SOURCE: Hudson, William Henry. "IV." In *Whittier and His Poetry*, pp. 41-73. London: George G. Harrap, 1917.

[*In the following excerpt, Hudson recounts Whittier's literary work in support of abolitionism, noting that as a Quaker, the poet hated war as much as he hated slavery, and was profoundly disturbed by the outbreak of the Civil War brought on by the crisis over the slavery issue.*]

Notwithstanding the reputation which he was gaining as a poet, Whittier himself meanwhile regarded the writing of verses only as work by the way. His real interest at the time was not in literature. He was looking forward rather to a political career. His success as a journalist in Boston and Hartford had naturally turned his thoughts in this direction, while it had also marked him out as a young man of promise in the so-called Whig party—the party of which Henry Clay was the leader—to which he then belonged. At twenty-five, as prospective candidate for Congress at the forthcoming elections, he already had his foot on the first rung of the ladder. Only his fragile health, which made it doubtful whether he would ever prove equal to the strain and excitement of public life, seemed to stand for the moment between him and the realization of his dearest wishes. Then suddenly came a great change in his circumstances and prospects. He deliberately turned his back upon his ambitions and set aside all thought of the prizes which would otherwise have been within his reach, by throwing himself heart and soul into an unpopular cause.

The curse of negro slavery was at that time the one great blot on the young American democracy. The doctrine of the constitution—that all men are born free and equal—was saddled with the proviso that their skins must be white: a proviso tacitly accepted by all political parties. Abolitionist views had indeed long been held by individuals here and there, and notably by the Society of Friends. But till the end of the twenties of the nineteenth century no emphatic protest against slavery had yet been made. No statesman had ventured to attack it. Even the Church was silent; indeed, when the great crusade against it began many of the prominent official exponents of Christianity triumphantly appealed to the Bible in defence of what they regarded as a divinely appointed institution.

The history of the anti-slavery movement really begins on the day in 1831 when Lloyd Garrison, then a young man of twenty-four, established himself in Boston and started his "Liberator." He had no capital; he had no subscription list; he had no regular body of contributors; his office was one dark little room, his "only visible helper" a negro boy. But, hopeless as his enterprise must necessarily have appeared to any one less resolute than himself, he set out like David to slay the giant Philistine. From that dark little room of his he sent his voice abroad in imperious demand for the immediate and total destruction of slavery throughout the United States. He brought to his task abilities of a high order, and, what counted even more than abilities, the terrible earnestness of the fanatic. He realized that outside New England nearly the whole American public was against him, and that even in New England he would have to contend with apathy, if not with active opposition. Yet he was determined that his challenge should be heard. His early labours, carried on for the most part single-handed, brought him little but hatred and persecution. For several years letters poured in upon him, threatening him with bodily harm, and even with assassination. The State of Georgia offered a reward of 500 dollars to any one who would secure his conviction under the libel laws and so close his mouth. Even in Boston, the boasted home of enlightenment and liberty, he was hooted by angry mobs, and once he was dragged through the streets with a rope round his neck, narrowly escaping death at the hands of a rabble led by "men of property and standing." But he stuck to his post undaunted. "I will not equivocate, I will not excuse, I will not retreat a single inch, and I will be heard"— such was his ultimatum. Presently friends gathered about him—Sumner, Wendell Phillips, Theodore Parker, to name only a few of the most famous. Little by little all New England was aroused; the agitation spread thence throughout the country; and before long the tremendous national conflict was precipitated which was to be waged for many years with ever-growing bitterness, and was ultimately to culminate in the great Civil War. All this time Garrison himself continued to work with unabated enthusiasm, and when, after thirty-five years of strenuous activity, he brought the issue of "The Liberator" to an end, it was only because its purpose had at last been accomplished and its mission fulfilled.

Love of liberty and hatred of cruelty and oppression were part of the inheritance of Whittier's Quaker blood. He was thus prepared to sympathize with the Abolition movement from the moment of its inception. But it was the influence of Garrison which turned his sympathy from merely sentimental into practical channels. Convinced by his friend of the importance not only of moral effort but also of organized political action, he made a careful study of the whole slavery question under all its aspects, and as a result of his deliberations produced in the spring of 1833 a pamphlet entitled "Justice and Expediency." This pamphlet he had to publish at his own expense, paying the cost of the first small edition out of his modest savings. But it was soon reprinted and widely read; in the North it produced a very strong impression; while something of the feeling with which it was received in the South may be inferred from the fact that a physician in Washington was imprisoned for circulating it: an incident to which Whittier himself made reference many years afterward in a poem celebrating the abolition of slavery in the district of Columbia:

> Beside me gloomed the prison cell
>   Where wasted one in slow decline
>   For uttering simple words of mine,
> And loving freedom all too well.[1]

The writing of "Justice and Expediency" was for Whittier the parting of the ways. Deeply interested in the subject, and carried forward from point to point by the irresistible pressure of his own argument, he finished it without pausing to reflect on the effect which it would almost certainly have upon his own career. It was only on the very eve of its publication that this personal aspect of the matter occurred to him. Then followed a brief period of moral conflict and some sleepless nights. But, as his biographer says, "a decision to follow the path of duty at all hazards ended the struggle, and the decision was never regretted, although it crowded his life with hardships for many years, and ended all his dreams of political preferment."[2]

It is important for us to emphasize the fact that when he thus cast in his lot with the anti-slavery party Whittier knew perfectly well what he was about. Young as he was, he was no raw enthusiast. He was not blinded by his moral zeal to the magnitude of the evil he was to help to combat, and he foresaw quite clearly the sacrifices which he would himself have to make. Despite his poetic temperament and the intensity of his feelings, his relations with the great cause to which he gave the best energies of the best years of his life were characterized from first to last by extraordinary sanity and common sense. There were many among the reformers who at the outset believed that success would soon crown their labours. Whittier did not share their sanguine views. He realized that the struggle would be long and bitter. Nor was he ever swept by mere passion into any of those fanatical excesses by which the Abolitionists at times damaged their cause. He was cautious as well as determined, discreet as well as courageous. No one was more insistent than he on the supremacy of the fundamental moral issues which were at stake: it was part of his poetic mission to drive these issues home upon the consciences of his countrymen and to make the whole nation alive to their significance. But all through he perceived that the question of Abolition was not only a moral but also a practical one—that slavery was a concrete reality which had to be attacked by practical means. While in his verse he always struck the highest note of religious and patriotic idealism, he none the less recognized to the full that in the world as it actually exists the spirit of idealism can accomplish its purpose only when it is united with persistent and well-directed efforts toward specific ends. There was therefore nothing visionary about his own work for the Abolition cause. On the contrary, he carried into it a clear, steady brain and the sagacity of the trained politician. "He took men as he found them," we are told, "and encouraged them to go part way with him," even if they were unwilling to go farther; and he was ready to join with "any party that was marching in his general direction, even if he could not keep step with all its music." "Hast thee found many saints or angels in thy dealings with either political party?" he once asked a friend. "Do not expect too much of human nature." When divisions broke out in the anti-slavery ranks on minor points of theory and practice, he was always anxious to act as peacemaker. He had, moreover, "a genius for coalitions," and did not hesitate on occasion to "accept assistance from unfriendly sources"—though never, it is scarcely necessary to add, by any sacrifice of principle. He used to advantage the political machinery which he found ready to his hand. "His was a familiar figure in the lobby of the State House for many years. He was a shrewd judge of men, knew how to touch their weak points, and scrupled not to reach their consciences along the line of least resistance. His keen sense of the ridiculous kept him from being in the least 'cranky' in his philanthropy."[3] Filled as he was with all the zeal and fire of the old Hebrew prophets, he yet understood that in these days of modern warfare the walls of Jericho will not fall before any trumpet-blast, but must be undermined by slow and skilful engineering operations. For these reasons he was to the very end of the struggle a great practical help to the party of reform, his direct influence upon the destinies of which was, indeed, far more considerable than has been commonly supposed.

His activity at first took the form of miscellaneous literary work, of executive work of one and another sort in connexion with societies and conventions, and of general political effort. For a short time he even sat in the legislature of his State. But by taste and training he was a journalist, and it was through journalism, as he properly felt, that he could make his powers most widely effective. Accordingly in the autumn of 1837 he accepted a call to the editorship of "The National Enquirer" (afterward "The Pennsylvania Freeman"), which he retained till 1840, when the condition of his health, which meanwhile had repeatedly given cause for grave alarm, became so serious that he was obliged to resign his post and retire to the quiet of his Amesbury home. His eight years of incessant labour for the anti-slavery movement had, indeed, tried him severely. The constant stress and anxiety of his work had in themselves proved too much for his strength, while, to make matters worse, he had more than once been involved in scenes of wild excitement when popular passion against the reformers had run high, and like his friends he had stood in danger of indignity and even of outrage. He was assaulted in a riot at Concord in 1835, and again at Newburyport two years later; and in May 1838, during a most disgraceful outburst of mob violence in Philadelphia—an outburst which the city authorities made no attempt to check—he saw the offices of his journal destroyed in the burning of Pennsylvania Hall. Such experiences were the common lot of the Abolitionists at the time, and Whittier took his share of them with placid courage. But though he made light of them, they added in some measure at least to the general nervous strain under which he presently broke down.

His retirement to Amesbury, though it relieved him of burdens which he was physically unfit to bear, did not interfere with his industry in the cause which he had at heart. He continued to contribute to anti-slavery papers, edited for a short time "The Middlesex Standard" in Lowell, Massachusetts, and for a couple of years was virtually in control of the local organ of the "Liberty" party, "The Essex Transcript." All this time he was dependent upon his pen not only for his own support, but also for that of his mother and sister, and his earnings thus far had been so very meagre that it was only with the utmost care that he contrived to keep out of debt. He was therefore glad when in 1847 he was invited to join the regular staff of the then just founded "National Era"—the paper in which a few years later "Uncle Tom's Cabin" first appeared as a serial. This new connexion was eminently satisfactory because it was profitable, because it gave him a wide audience, and because it still allowed him to do his work at home. Henceforth for some ten years the "Era" was both his financial mainstay and the principal channel for his exertions. For it he wrote poems, reviews, sketches, and articles on various subjects outside slavery. In it also he first published his one long essay in prose fiction— "Leaves from Margaret Smith's Journal"—a work which, though without value as fiction, gives a vivid and faithful picture of New England life and character in the old colonial days. Another opening came in 1857 with the establishment of "The Atlantic Monthly," of which I shall have more to say presently.

When a little later than this the anti-slavery agitation reached its crisis, and the country was plunged into the fearful war for the Union, Whittier, like other prominent Abolitionists belonging to the Society of Friends, was profoundly disturbed by this great shock to his religious principles. As a Quaker he hated slavery. But as a Quaker he also hated war, which he regarded as absolutely and essentially opposed to that law of love which is the great rule of the Christian life. Yet deeply as he deplored the appeal to the sword, he was firmly convinced that in the circumstances it was inevitable—a view also taken in a letter to him by the great English Quaker, John Bright. The war with all its monstrous evils he looked upon, in fact, as the terrible price which had to be paid for the country's long connivance in sin;

and while his simple religious philosophy taught him that it was God's stern way of punishing men for their wrongdoing, it also inspired him with the confidence that divine providence would in the end overrule all things for good. This thought is brought out in one of his poems *In War Time,* entitled **"Thy Will be Done"**:

> We see not, know not; all our way
> Is night,—with Thee alone is day:
> From out the torrent's troubled drift,
> Above the storm our prayers we lift,
>   Thy will be done!
>
> The flesh may fail, the heart may fain
> But who are we to make complaint,
> Or dare to plead, in times like these
> The weakness of our love of ease?
>   Thy will be done!
>
> We take with solemn thankfulness
> Our burden up, nor ask it less,
> And count it joy that even we
> May suffer, serve, or wait for Thee,
>   Whose will be done!
>
> Though dim as yet in tint and line,
> We trace Thy picture's wise design,
> And thank Thee that our age supplies
> Its dark relief of sacrifice.
>   Thy will be done!
>
> And if, in our unworthiness,
> Thy sacrificial wine we press;
> If from Thy ordeal's heated bars
> Our feet are seamed with crimson scars,
>   Thy will be done!
>
> If, for the age to come, this hour
> Of trial hath vicarious power,
> And, blest by Thee, our present pain,
> Be Liberty's eternal gain,
>   Thy will be done!
>
> Strike, Thou the Master, we Thy keys,
>   The anthem of the destinies!
> The minor of Thy loftier strain,
> Our hearts shall breathe the old refrain,
>   Thy will be done!

One of his chief concerns, therefore, was to guide and help his co-religionists in the solution of those problems of conscience by which they now found themselves beset. In a circular letter which he addressed to the Society of Friends in January 1861, he thus gave them a lead:

> We have no right to ask or expect an exemption from the chastisement which the Divine Providence is inflicting upon the nation. Steadily and faithfully maintaining our testimony against war, we owe it to the cause of truth to show that exalted heroism and generous self-sacrifice are not incompatible with our pacific principles. Our mission is at this time to mitigate the sufferings of our countrymen, to visit and aid the sick and the wounded, to relieve the necessities of the widow

and the orphan, and to practise economy for the sake of charity. Let the Quaker bonnet be seen by the side of the black hood of the Catholic Sister of Charity in the hospital ward. Let the same heroic devotion to duty which our brethren in Great Britain manifested in the Irish famine and pestilence be reproduced on this side of the water in mitigating the horrors of war and its attendant calamities. What hinders us from holding up the hands of Dorothea Dix in her holy work of mercy at Washington? Our society is rich, and of those to whom much is given much will be required in this hour of proving and trial.

These counsels he repeated in a poem which in 1863 he read at the annual gathering of the Friends' Meeting School in Newport, Rhode Island:

> Our path is plain; the war-net draws
>   Round us in vain,
> While, faithful to the Higher Cause,
> We keep our fealty to the laws
>   Through patient pain.
>
> The levelled gun, the battle-brand,
>   We may not take;
> But, calmly loyal, we can stand
> And suffer with our suffering land
>   For conscience' sake.
>   . . . . .
>
> Thanks for the privilege to bless,
>   By word and deed,
> The widow in her keen distress,
> The childless and the fatherless,
>   The hearts that bleed.
>   . . . . .
>
> And we may tread the sick-bed floors
>   Where strong men pine,
> And, down the groaning corridors,
> Pour freely from our liberal stores
>   The oil and wine.
>
> Who murmurs that in these dark days
>   His lot is cast?
> God's hand within the shadow lays
> The stones whereon His gates of praise
>   Shall rise at last.

Such in bare outline is the story of Whittier's otherwise uneventful life in the thirty years during which, as he himself expressed it, he laid his best gifts on the shrine of freedom. Absorbed as he was all this time in his labours for abolition—

> Making his rustic reed of song
> A weapon in the war with wrong[4]

—he none the less found frequent relief in the production of poetry having little or nothing to do with the burning questions of the hour. But, as a matter of convenience, we will for the moment disregard this part of his work and confine our attention to what is represented by the division entitled "Anti-Slavery Poems" in the collective edition of his writings.

The place of these poems in the history of the anti-slavery movement and in Whittier's own life must first be recognized. Valuable as was his work in other directions, it was through these that he contributed most effectively to the progress of the cause. His *Voices of Freedom* rang, in Lloyd Garrison's phrase, "from Maine to the Rocky Mountains," and their influence upon the country was, as Bryant said, like that of a trumpet calling to battle. From the outset he stepped to the front as the acknowledged poet laureate of the party of reform, and as year by year he sent his message far and wide, the immense power of his verse in stirring the feelings of his countrymen and shaping public opinion became more and more apparent. "From the heart of the onset upon the serried mercenaries of every tyranny," wrote Lowell, "the chords of his iron-strung lyre clang with a martial and triumphant cheer; and where Freedom's Spartan few maintain their inviolable mountain pass against the assaults of slavery, his voice may be heard, clear and fearless, as if the victory were already won."[5] When at length the victory was really won, Whittier's share in it was universally recognized, and as his principles had now triumphed he found himself in popular estimation one of America's greatest men. He had taken up the work of righteousness never dreaming of reward; yet in the end reward came to him without his seeking. Hence the point of his advice, given late in life to a boy of fifteen: "My lad, if thou wouldst win success, join thyself to some unpopular but noble cause." He had lived long enough to prove out of his own experience the truth for which he had contended in his early pamphlet—that justice is the highest form of expediency.

Yet great as was the influence, both on the world and on himself, of Whittier's anti-slavery poems, there are very few of them which are entitled to rank with his enduring contributions to literature. Their vigour and fire, the force of their simple and direct appeal to the hearts and consciences of their readers, their unwavering faith in God, their deep and passionate love of man, their withering denunciation of vested interests, their manly contempt for the coward and the time-server— all these qualities combined to make them, as even now we can easily understand, tremendously effective while the issues with which they dealt were vital and urgent. But their power has necessarily faded with the abuses which they helped to destroy. The excitement long since over, the issues in question buried and forgotten, the critical mood naturally asserts itself; and though in reading them to-day we are still impressed by their moral and religious fervour, and agree with an American critic that as Anglo-Saxons we must rejoice that such poems were written,[6] we feel that for the most part they are splendid rhetoric rather than essential poetry. Many of them were occasional in the narrowest sense of the term: that is, they were inspired by incidents which were pregnant with significance at the moment, but are now remembered only by those to whom all the details of the emancipation movement are familiar; while even those of a more general character are frequently over-weighted by their specific didactic intention. It has been said that Whittier really found his voice in these anti-slavery poems; that in them he for the first time displayed powers which had hardly been so much as suggested by the smooth but quite colourless verses of his earlier years. This is quite true. Yet the stress of im-mediate purpose was often fatal to the technical quality of such work. Whittier wrote at the moment for the mo-ment, careless of fame, indifferent to the claims of art; there were times when his emotions were so strong that they almost choked his utterance; but his one object was to make men listen to him, and if he succeeded in this he was satisfied. Hence, while he had flashes of re-ally great inspiration, he was often diffuse, declamatory, and even prosaic.

Whittier himself was under no misapprehension on these points. His final judgment of his anti-slavery poetry as a whole was thoroughly sound. He thus records it in his introduction to the collective edition of his works published in 1887:

> Perhaps a word of explanation may be needed in regard to a class of poems written between 1832 and 1865. Of their defects from an artistic point of view it is not necessary to speak. They were the earnest and often vehement expression of the writer's thought and feel-ing at critical periods in the great conflict between Freedom and Slavery. They were written with no expectation that they would survive the occasions which called them forth; they were protests, alarm signals, trumpet-calls to action, words wrung from the writer's heart, forged at white heat, and of course lack-ing the finish and careful word-selection which reflec-tion and patient brooding over them might have given. Such as they are, they belong to the Anti-Slavery move-ment, and may serve as way-marks of its progress.

I do not think it necessary to linger long over the more directly propagandist of these poems. I will give one of them complete by way of illustration. As the one I select belongs to the general rather than to the occasional class, no introduction to it is required.

The Farewell

of a Virginia Slave Mother to Her Daughters

Sold into Southern Bondage

Gone, gone,—sold and gone,
  To the rice-swamp dank and lone.
Where the slave-whip ceaseless swings,
Where the noisome insect stings,
Where the fever demon strews
Poison with the falling dews,
Where the sickly sunbeams glare
Through the hot and misty air.
   Gone, gone,—sold and gone,

   To the rice-swamp dank and lone,
   From Virginia's hills and waters,—
   Woe is me, my stolen daughters!

Gone, gone,—sold and gone,
  To the rice-swamp dank and lone.
There no mother's eye is near them,
There no mother's ear can hear them;
Never, when the torturing lash
Seams their back with many a gash,
Shall a mother's kindness bless them,
Or a mother's arms caress them.
   Gone, gone,—sold and gone,
   To the rice-swamp dank and lone,
   From Virginia's hills and waters,—
   Woe is me, my stolen daughters!

Gone, gone,—sold and gone,
  To the rice-swamp dank and lone.
Oh, when weary, sad and slow,
From the fields at night they go,
Faint with toil, and racked with pain,
To their cheerless homes again,
There no brother's voice shall greet them,—
There no father's welcome meet them.
   Gone, gone,—sold and gone,
   To the rice-swamp dank and lone,
   From Virginia's hills and waters,—
   Woe is me, my stolen daughters!

Gone, gone,—sold and gone,
  To the rice-swamp dank and lone.
From the tree whose shadow lay
On their childhood's place of play;
From the cool spring where they drank,
Rock, and hill, and rivulet bank;
From the solemn house of prayer
And the holy counsels there,—
   Gone, gone,—sold and gone,
   To the rice-swamp dank and lone,
   From Virginia's hills and waters,—
   Woe is me, my stolen daughters!

Gone, gone,—sold and gone,
  To the rice-swamp dank and lone,—
Toiling through the weary day,
And at night the spoiler's prey.
Oh that they had earlier died,
Sleeping calmly, side by side,
Where the tyrant's power is o'er,
And the fetter galls no more!
   Gone, gone,—sold and gone,
   To the rice-swamp dank and lone,
   From Virginia's hills and waters,—
   Woe is me, my stolen daughters!

Gone, gone,—sold and gone,
  To the rice-swamp dank and lone.
By the holy love He beareth,—
By the bruisèd reed He spareth,—
Oh, may He, to whom alone
All their cruel wrongs are known,
Still their hope and refuge prove,
With a more than mother's love.
   Gone, gone,—sold and gone,
   To the rice-swamp dank and lone,

From Virginia's hills and waters,—
Woe is me, my stolen daughters!

This poem may be taken as a fair representative of its class, and if in reading it we remember that at the time of its publication the evils which it exposes were living facts, we can still feel something of its original power. There are, however, other poems belonging to the same large division of Whittier's work which, though inspired by the circumstances of the time, are not so specifically didactic or topical in character, and deserve somewhat closer attention on account of their greater permanent interest and value.

One of these is the famous **"Barbara Frietchie."** The story upon which this stirring little ballad was founded was afterward the subject of a good deal of controversy, but Whittier had it from what he regarded as a thoroughly trustworthy source, and while he admitted that his own version was probably incorrect in details, he believed that in its main outlines it was substantially historical. This, however, is a matter of comparatively slight importance. It is the quality of the poem as such which concerns us. Whittier was by nature and instinct a born ballad-writer, and as a ballad-writer he holds his place in the front rank of American poets. The present example, as will be seen, is marked in a high degree by the simplicity, directness, vividness, and force which are essential to great achievement in this particular kind of narrative poetry.

"Barbara Frietchie"

Up from the meadows rich with corn,
Clear in the cool September morn,

The clustered spires of Frederick stand
Green-walled by the hills of Maryland.

Round about them orchards sweep,
Apple and peach tree fruited deep,

Fair as the garden of the Lord
To the eyes of the famished rebel horde,

On that pleasant morn of the early fall
When Lee marched over the mountain-wall,—

Over the mountains winding down,
Horse and foot, into Frederick town.

Forty flags with their silver stars,
Forty flags with their crimson bars,

Flapped in the morning wind: the sun
Of noon looked down, and saw not one.

Up rose old Barbara Frietchie then,
Bowed with her fourscore years and ten;

Bravest of all in Frederick town,
She took up the flag the men hauled down;

In her attic window the staff she set,
To show that one heart was loyal yet.

Up the street came the rebel tread,
Stonewall Jackson riding ahead.

Under his slouched hat left and right
He glanced: the old flag met his sight.

"Halt!"—the dust-brown ranks stood fast.
"Fire!"—out blazed the rifle blast.

It shivered the window, pane and sash;
It rent the banner with seam and gash.

Quick, as it fell, from the broken staff
Dame Barbara snatched the silken scarf.

She leaned far out on the window-sill,
And shook it forth with a royal will.

"Shoot, if you must, this old grey head,
But spare your country's flag," she said.

A shade of sadness, a blush of shame,
Over the face of the leader came;

The nobler nature within him stirred
To life at that woman's deed and word:

"Who touches a hair of yon grey head
Dies like a dog! March on!" he said.

All day long through Frederick street
Sounded the tread of marching feet:

All day long that free flag tost
Over the heads of the rebel host,

Ever its torn folds rose and fell
On the loyal winds that loved it well;

And through the hill-gaps sunset light
Shone over it with a warm good-night.

Barbara Frietchie's work is o'er,
And the Rebel rides on his raids no more.

Honour to her! and let a tear
Fall, for her sake, on Stonewall's bier.

Over Barbara Frietchie's grave,
Flag of Freedom and Union, wave!

Peace and order and beauty draw
Round thy symbol of light and law;

And ever the stars above look down
On thy stars below in Frederick town!

As fine in its own way, though very different in character, is the grave and majestic poem in which Whittier gave voice to his grief over the defection of Daniel Webster from the Abolition cause. That great orator had long been the idol of New England, and the reformers had hoped much from him, despite his increasing tendency to temporize and compromise on the question of slavery. It was therefore a cruel shock to them when, in his famous speech in the Senate on March 7, 1850, he openly threw the weight of his influence on the side of the South. They were, indeed, astonished and enraged by what they believed to be a cynical sacrifice of principle to personal ambition. Whittier shared their amazement, but his own feelings, as his poem shows, were of sorrow rather than of anger. His note to the poem clearly defines his position:

> This poem was the outcome of the surprise and grief and forecast of evil consequences which I felt on reading the seventh of March speech of Daniel Webster in support of the "compromise" and the Fugitive Slave Law. No partisan or personal enmity dictated it. On the contrary my admiration of the splendid personality and intellectual power of the great Senator was never stronger than when I laid down his speech, and, in one of the saddest moments of my life, penned my protest. I saw, as I wrote, with painful clearness its sure results—the Slave Power arrogant and defiant, strengthened and encouraged to carry out its scheme for the extension of its baleful system, or the dissolution of the Union, the guarantees of personal liberty in the Free States broken down, and the whole country made the hunting ground of slave-catchers. In the horror of such a vision, so soon fearfully fulfilled, if one spoke at all, he could only speak in tones of stern and sorrowful rebuke.

The poem is, indeed, a little masterpiece of "stern and sorrowful rebuke." As a rule a tendency to diffuseness was one of Whittier's besetting sins. **"Ichabod"** is the more powerful and impressive because of its marked concentration and restraint.

"Ichabod"!

So fallen! so lost! the light withdrawn
    Which once he wore!
The glory from his grey hairs gone
    For evermore!

Revile him not,—the Tempter hath
    A snare for all;
And pitying tears, not scorn and wrath,
    Befit his fall!

Oh, dumb be passion's stormy rage,
    When he who might
Have lighted up and led his age
    Falls back in night.

Scorn! would the angels laugh, to mark
    A bright soul driven,
Fiend-goaded, down the endless dark,
    From hope and heaven!

Let not the land once proud of him
    Insult him now,
Nor brand with deeper shame his dim,
    Dishonoured brow.

But let its humbled sons, instead,
    From sea to lake,
A long lament, as for the dead,
    In sadness make.

Of all we loved and honoured, naught
    Save power remains,—
A fallen angel's pride of thought,
    Still strong in chains.

All else is gone; from those great eyes
    The soul has fled:
When faith is lost, when honour dies,
    The man is dead!

Then, pay the reverence of old days
    To his dead fame;
Walk backward, with averted gaze,
    And hide the shame!

We do not wonder that Webster himself was more deeply affected by this noble and sad remonstrance than by all other criticisms and attacks put together.

It will be remembered that while the war for the Union was being fought out on the bloody battle-fields of the South, Whittier was living quietly in his little cottage at Amesbury. Often during those dark and critical days he sought solace for his soul in the peace of the familiar landscape which he loved so well. But nature then as always offered to him something more than a temporary refuge from the tragedy of human life. Such was his simple, steady religious faith that to him it seemed full of the oracles of God. The following beautiful little poem will show us how he read its divine message.

"The Battle Autumn of 1862"

The flags of war like storm-birds fly,
    The charging trumpets blow;
Yet rolls no thunder in the sky,
    No earthquake strives below.

And, calm and patient, Nature keeps
    Her ancient promise well,
Though o'er her bloom and greenness sweeps
    The battle's breath of hell.

And still she walks in golden hours
    Through harvest-happy farms,
And still she wears her fruits and flowers
    Like jewels on her arms.

What mean the gladness of the plain,
    This joy of eve and morn,
The mirth that shakes the beard of grain
    And yellow locks of corn?

Ah! eyes may well be full of tears,
    And hearts with hate are hot;
But even-paced come round the years,
    And Nature changes not.

She meets with smiles our bitter grief,
  With songs our groans of pain;
She mocks with tint of flower and leaf
  The war field's crimson stain.

Still, in the cannon's pause, we hear
  Her sweet thanksgiving-psalm;
Too near to God for doubt or fear,
  She shares the eternal calm.

She knows the seed lies safe below
  The fires that blast and burn;
For all the tears of blood we sow
  She waits the rich return.

She sees with clearer eye than ours
  The good of suffering born,—
The hearts that blossom like her flowers,
  And ripen like her corn.

Oh, give to us, in times like these,
  The vision of her eyes;
And make her fields and fruited trees
  Our golden prophecies!

Oh, give to us her finer ear!
  Above this stormy din,
We too would hear the bells of cheer
  Ring peace and freedom in.

This poem was written in the early days of the war, and while the Southern generals, Robert Lee and 'Stonewall' Jackson, were engaged in a successful campaign against the Federal forces in the East. It needed faith at such a moment to hear in anticipation "the bells of cheer ring peace and freedom in." Three years later—on January 31, 1865—Whittier was one of a small gathering in the Friends' Meeting House at Amesbury. The occasion was the regular Fifth Day meeting of the Society. Within all was silent, for no one in the company was moved to speak. But outside the bells were ringing and the guns booming to celebrate the passage of the Constitutional Amendment abolishing slavery throughout the United States. And Whittier, as he sat with bowed head, remembering his thirty years' struggle for a cause which at first had seemed hopeless, and knowing that all over the country the music of bells and guns was even then proclaiming victory, was inspired with a great song of jubilation, in which he poured out his heart in praise and thanks to God Who had brought this mighty thing to pass. "It wrote itself," he said of the following poem, "or rather sang itself while the bells rang"; and the throb and swing of the bells are in its verses. Never did Whittier strike a higher note than in this magnificent lyric. It forms a fitting close to his long labours for humanity and righteousness. Even to-day it is impossible to read it without a thrill.

"Laus Deo"!

It is done!
  Clang of bell and roar of gun
Send the tidings up and down.

How the belfries rock and reel!
  How the great guns, peal on peal,
Fling the joy from town to town!

Ring, O bells!
  Every stroke exulting tells
Of the burial hour of crime.
  Loud and long, that all may hear,
  Ring for every listening ear
Of Eternity and Time!

Let us kneel:
  God's own voice is in that peal,
And this spot is holy ground.
  Lord, forgive us! What are we,
  That our eyes this glory see,
That our ears have heard the sound!

For the Lord
  On the whirlwind is abroad;
In the earthquake He has spoken;
  He has smitten with His thunder
  The iron walls asunder,
And the gates of brass are broken!

Loud and long
  Lift the old exulting song;
Sing with Miriam by the sea,
  He has cast the mighty down;
  Horse and rider sink and drown;
"He hath triumphed gloriously!"

Did we dare,
  In our agony of prayer,
Ask for more than He has done?
  When was ever His right hand
  Over any time or land
Stretched as now beneath the sun?

How they pale,
  Ancient myth and song and tale,
In this wonder of our days,
  When the cruel rod of war
  Blossoms white with righteous law,
And the wrath of man is praise!

Blotted out!
  All within and all about
Shall a fresher life begin;
  Freer breathe the universe
  As it rolls its heavy curse
On the dead and buried sin!

It is done!
  In the circuit of the sun
Shall the sound thereof go forth.
  It shall bid the sad rejoice,
  It shall give the dumb a voice,
It shall belt with joy the earth!

Ring and swing,
  Bells of joy! On morning's wing
Send the song of praise abroad!
  With a sound of broken chains
  Tell the nations that He reigns,
Who alone is Lord and God!

Notes

1. "Astræa at the Capitol," 1862.

2. Pickard [Samuel T. Pickard, *Life and Letters of John Greenleaf Whittier* (Boston: Houghton Mifflin Co., 2 vols., 1894)], p. 126.

3. Pickard, pp. 189-191.

4. "The Tent on the Beach": Prelude.

5. Prefatory note to the poem "Texas" when first published in "The Boston Courier," April 1844.

6. W. C. Bronson, "Short History of American Literature" [Boston: D. C. Heath, 1919], p. 235.

Arthur Christy (essay date November 1933)

SOURCE: Christy, Arthur. "The Orientalism of Whittier." *American Literature* 5, no. 3 (November 1933): 247-57.

[*In the following essay, Christy examines the influence of the* Bhagavadgita *on some of Whittier's poems, among them "Miriam," "The Preacher," and "The Over-Heart."*]

Whittier is so provincial a poet that it is somewhat surprising, perhaps, to find him sharing the contemporary interest in Orientalism. But of his share in the current enthusiasm there are abundant proofs, many of which I must pass by for lack of space. I must omit mention of poems in the manner of Leigh Hunt's "Abou Ben Adhem," which indeed do not indicate the direct use of Oriental material,[1] and I must pass over the noticeable influence on Whittier of the Brahmo Somaj.[2] The **"Oriental Maxims,"** composed chiefly of Whittier's paraphrases of moral sentiments found in English translations of Hindu classics, I have discussed in a previously published article.[3] Whittier's relations to Bayard Taylor and the results of their friendship upon the former's work might well be a chapter in the completely definitive study of the Quaker poet which still remains to be written. Such a chapter would be a unique contribution to the study of the Oriental tale in America.[4]

In examining Whittier's library, I found that the Oriental books were mostly of a secondary nature; they afforded him general expositions of Asiatic life and culture. W. R. Alger's *Poetry of the Orient* and Lydia Maria Child's[5] *The Progress of Religious Ideas* were on the shelves, as were R. H. Stoddard's *The Book of the East,* C. D. Warner's *In the Levant,* Evariste Huc's *Journey through the Chinese Empire,* a work entitled *Biography and Letters of Chinese Gordon,* and R. S. Watson's *A Journey to Wazan, the Sacred City of Morocco.* But Whittier's personal library does not indicate the full extent of the

sources of his Orientalism. His writings reveal that he made extensive use of other works on the East.[6] Of the English Orientalists, he knew Max Müller and Monier-Williams. He knew well the *Laws of Menu,* probably in Sir William Jones's translation, two works by the Orientalist John Muir, *Religious and Moral Sentiments from Sanskrit Writers,* and the *Metrical Translations,* W. H. Drew's *The Cural of Tiruvalluvar* and N. E. Kendersley's *Specimens of the Hindu Theatre.* It is clear also that he read in the files of *The Journal of the Asiatic Society of Bengal,* that he knew Hafiz, the Zoroastrian scriptures,[7] the *Koran,*[8] the *Arabian Nights,* Samuel Lee's translation of the *Travels of Ibn Batuta,* and the Sufi poets in general. His writings also indicate that he had acquired considerable information in Buddhist lore, and that he was much interested in Near-Eastern or Biblical themes. But, most important of all, he read the *Bhagavadgita,* the great religious classic of the Hindus. It is with this last work that we shall be primarily concerned in this article.

The catholicity of Whittier's Oriental interests is well indicated by an obituary which he wrote for a fellow-townsman, Henry Taylor, in *The Villager* of Amesbury. In it Whittier described his friend as a simple, unassuming, unlettered working-man who gave no outward evidence of the depth of his meditative life. Upon lending him a volume of Plato, Whittier learned that his friend had no idea such a man ever lived. The book was returned by Taylor with the simple remark that he saw "that Plato had got hold of some of his own ideas." "He was Oriental in his cast of mind," wrote Whittier, "he would have been quite at home with Chinese benzes, Buddhist priests, Mohammedan dervishes, and Christian monks of Mt. Athos. . . . He had somehow reached the state of absolute quietude—a region of ineffable calm, blown over by no winds of hope or fear. All personal anxieties and solicitudes were unknown. The outward world was phantasmal and unreal—he was utterly beyond its common temptations, and looked with simple wonder upon the struggle for wealth and place, the strifes and ambitions of sects and parties about him." As Whittier continues the exposition of Henry Taylor's mysticism, he incidentally discloses one of the sources of his own information in Buddhist lore: "He used to quote with much intensity of meaning, the words which Prof. Plumptre attributes to the founder of Buddhism, on reaching the condition of absolute rest. It was a description of his own state, in which the Nirvana of the Buddhist, the mystic suicide and self-abnegation of the Moslem Sufi, the absorption into the Divine will of the Christian mystics, and 'the rest which remaineth for the people of God,' seemed to him but different names for the same spiritual experience."[9]

Another bit of unnoticed Whittieriana worthy of recalling is a contribution by Ellen E. Dickinson to *The Churchman,* an account of Whittier's comments on her report of a conversation on spiritualism with Longfellow a few months before his death. "'And for myself,' said Whittier, 'I have felt but very slightly that closeness and nearness of the unseen of which you speak.' After a few moments, in the progress of our talk, he remarked: 'Life is a mystery, death is a mystery. I am like the Chinese philosopher, Confucius, who, when he was asked, What is death? answered, Life is such a mystery that I do not seek to penetrate what is beyond it.'"[10]

Whittier's most significant uses of Oriental thought will be found in his poems **"Miriam," "The Preacher,"** and **"The Over-Heart."** Even a brief examination of these poems will indicate the essential nature of his interest in the ancient faiths of the East and the extent of his acceptance of the basic principles of the Vedanta.

In **"Miriam"** the discussion between the poet and a friend, after they had left the Quaker meeting-house in a somber Sabbath mood, turned to the question of God's essential nature and responsibility to humanity, and Whittier declares:

> Truth is one;
> And, in all lands beneath the sun,
> Whoso hath eyes to see may see
> The tokens of its unity.[11]

In support of his reasoning, the poet insists that in what he calls "Vedic verse" and "the dull Koran," in the thoughts of "our Aryan sires" and "the slant-eyed sages of Cathay," is evidence that they "read not the riddle all amiss." Whittier defends his latitudinarianism by insisting that the gospel of Jesus is not rendered less precious by recognizing in it echoes of ancient truths, and continues:

> We come back laden from our quest,
> To find that all the sages said
> Is in the Book our mothers read.[12]

This wholesale finding of the teachings of the Oriental sages in the Bible, and the inclusion of the Brahman, Mohammedan, and Confucian, if only by implication, in the "all-embracing Fatherhood" of God, indicates a liberalism that owes, no doubt, a good deal to Emerson.[13] How much is suggested by other lines from **"Miriam"**:

> Each, in its measure, but a part
> Of the unmeasured Over-Heart.[14]

The suggestive resemblances between Whittier's **"Over-Heart"** and Emerson's "Over-Soul," likewise the echo of Emerson's familiar doctrine of man being "part and parcel of God" in Whittier's lines, would seem to place his thought well beyond the bounds of contemporary sectarian conceptions of deity. Whittier's explanation was that he welcomed from every source the tokens of the Primal Force,

> Beneath whose steady impulse rolls
> The tidal wave of human souls;
> Guide, comforter, and inward word,
> The eternal spirit of the Lord![15]

Obviously, such lines are too pantheistic to be Christian and too Christian to be good pantheism.

The poem **"Miriam"** concludes with a paraphrase from the *Bhagavadgita* to illustrate Christ's precept of forgiveness. Whittier ends his verses, which have an entirely Christian theme and setting, with a description of an Oriental ascetic:

> . . . sitting in his place,
> Motionless as an idol and as grim,
>
> . . . . .
>
> Under the court-yard trees, (for he was wise,
> Knew Menu's laws, and through his close-shut eyes
> Saw things far off, and as an open book
> Into the thoughts of other men could look,)
> Began, half chant, half howling to rehearse
> The fragment of a holy Vedic verse;
> And thus it ran: "He who all things forgives
> Conquers himself and all things else, and lives
> Above the reach of wrong or hate or fear,
> Calm as the gods, to whom he is most dear."[16]

It does not require insight into Oriental systems to realize that Whittier in this context indicated his blindness to the distinctions between the Christian principle of forgiveness and the Oriental's desireless striving for Brahma-realization or the Nirvana.

The poem entitled **"The Over-Heart"** was based on the Pauline text, "For of Him, and through Him, and to Him are all things, to whom be glory forever." In the lines which develop this passage Whittier incorporates Neo-Platonic, Quaker, and Hindu mysticism. The second stanza is as follows:

> And India's mystic sang aright
> Of the One Life pervading all,—
> One Being's tidal rise and fall
> In soul and form, in sound and sight,—
> Eternal outflow and recall.[17]

Emerson might well have written these lines, as the title itself, **"The Over-Heart,"** suggests. It is significant indeed that Whittier is not only in agreement with Emerson in the concept of the Over-Soul as the substrate of the universe, but the last line—"Eternal outflow and recall"—also indicates anything but a Hebraic-Christian concept of cosmology. God, for Whittier, was immanent in the world and constantly emanating in new forms. This is surprisingly good Brahman doctrine.

But even more significant than either the poems **"Miriam"** or **"The Over-Heart"** as a curious harborage of Whittier's Orientalism, is the poem entitled **"The**

Preacher," written in celebration of George Whitefield. Here the theme is not one of questioning reverie but one of militant hatred of the slave-trade, with lines that allude to the fervor of the Moslem in his holy wars. The passage

> But he is greatest and best who can
> Worship Allah by loving man![18]

expresses the sentiment which reaches a climax in Whittier's anomalous paraphrase, in 1859, of the identical passage in the *Bhagavadgita* which had served Emerson as one of the sources of his famous poem "Brahma" in 1857. Emerson's poem is too familiar to need quotation. The following are the *Gita*-inspired lines of Whittier:

> In the Indian fable Arjoon hears
> The scorn of a god rebuke his fears:
> "Spare thy pity!" Krishna saith;
> "Not in thy sword is the power of death!
> All is illusion,—loss but seems;
> Pleasure and pain are only dreams;
> Who deems he slayeth doth not kill;
> Who counts as slain is living still.
> Strike, nor fear thy blow is crime;
> Nothing dies but the cheats of time;
> Slain or slayer, small the odds
> To each, immortal as Indra's gods!"[19]

Now, Whittier's use of the *Bhagavadgita* was characteristically different from Emerson's. Emerson borrowed from its lines to epitomize his own philosophy, to crystallize his personal beliefs regarding the character of the Over-Soul and the veil of Maya, or illusion, behind which God lurks. On the other hand, Whittier's paraphrase was used in an attempt to impale religious sanction of the slave-trade. The context was an attempted *reductio ad absurdum* of the minds for whom heaven seems so large that the things of earth are forgotten, and in which there is inherent the belief that since God is all, man is nothing. In this temper, runs the argument, there is complete misunderstanding of the adage that the love of God and man are the same. Whittier the humanitarian, not Whittier the mystic with occasional speculative tendencies, then paraphrases the *Bhagavadgita* to illustrate the idealist's doctrine of identity and to launch into an attack on the religious indifference which permitted the building of the churches of Christ with cement mixed with negro blood.

The problem of evil, as has often been said, is the stumbling-block to all religious philosophies that more or less identify the phenomenal world with God. Emerson got around the problem with his doctrine of Compensation. When Whittier applied the philosophy of identity to life, he realized that it would be, as he expressed it, the wings of the Holy Ghost that fanned the sails of the slave ships as they passed from coast to coast. To Whittier, this was repugnant heresy indeed!

Thus we find the theme of Brahma in both Emerson and Whittier, but put to how different uses!

Whittier's Christianizing of Oriental material is nowhere better illustrated than in the poem **"Disarmament,"** which commences with Christ's injunction, "Put up the sword!" and concludes with a Buddhist birth-story to illustrate the efficacy of the Christian principle of love. Thus run Whittier's lines:

> There is a story told
> In Eastern tents, when autumn nights grow cold,
> And round the fire the Mongol shepherds sit
> With grave responses listening unto it:
> Once, on the errands of his mercy bent,
> Buddha, the holy and benevolent,
> Met a fell monster, huge and fierce of look,
> Whose awful voice the hills and forests shook.
> "O son of peace!" the giant cried, "thy fate
> Is sealed at last, and love shall yield to hate."
> The unarmed Buddha looking, with no trace
> Of fear or anger, in the monster's face,
> In pity said: "Poor fiend, even thee I love."
> Lo! as he spake the sky-tall terror sank
> To hand-breadth size; the huge abhorrence shrank
> Into the form and fashion of a dove;
> And where the thunder of its rage was heard,
> Circling above him sweetly sang the bird:
> "Hate hath no harm for love," so ran the song;
> "And peace unweaponed conquers every wrong!"[20]

Whatever may have been Whittier's sources for these lines, whether from a version of the *Jataka* tales which happened to come to him, or a reading of the Buddhist *Dhammapada,* or merely from his own gift of poetic invention, they may be taken as the most characteristic illustration of his method of isolating unique passages in Oriental books from their contexts and adapting them to his own purposes.[21]

We may conclude with several generalizations. The Orientalism which sprang up in New England was the result of varying causes and found a different emphasis in each writer affected. At times, it was the mere expression of a love of far-fetched quotations; at others, it was the broad recognition of identical ideas and the use of these ideas in bolstering faith in the transcendent. Just as Henry Taylor, Whittier's village friend, thought "that Plato had got hold of some of his own ideas," in somewhat the same temper the New Englanders read the Oriental books, always with the privilege of personal interpretation and without benefit of rishi. Neither Whittier nor his Transcendentalist contemporaries can be studied in a purely belles-lettristic sense. The scholar is obliged to recognize, as we have done, that a philosophy of religion was an integral part of their lives and work. This is the crucial distinction between the Orientalism of the American and the Orientalism of the English Romanticists. Another fact we must ever consider is that New England Orientalism was the result of a synthesis between old ideas and the new civilization of nineteenth-century America, which was anything but one of quietism, of stagnation and uniformity, or of finding in the Nirvana the summum bonum. Neither the mysticism of Sankara of India, nor of Plotinus of Alexandria, could have been transplanted to New England unless it made a great concession. As Emerson once pointed out, Orientalism had long thought it majestic to do nothing. The modern majesty consists in work.

Notes

1. The outstanding poems of this type composed by Whittier are "Rabbi Ishmael," "The Khan's Devil," "The Two Rabbins," and "Requital." These poems probably had no more Oriental a source than the one by Leigh Hunt or Browning's "Rabbi Ben Ezra." The present article will deal only with poems that indicate Whittier's Quaker affinities with Oriental monism and general parallels between his beliefs and the Vedanta.

2. Whittier's enthusiastic endorsement of the Brahmo Somaj and the work of Protap Chunder Mozoomdar in particular suggests that interesting parallels could also be drawn between his theism and the theism of the Hindu movement.

3. "Orientalism in New England: Whittier," *American Literature,* I, 372-92 (Jan., 1930). This article contained the results of an attempt to trace the sources of poems by Whittier which were paraphrases of unique passages in books on Oriental folk-lore that had passed through his hands or interesting moral sentiments in Hindu poetry.

4. *Cf.* Mrs. James T. Fields, *Whittier: Notes of His Life and of His Friendships* (New York, Harper, 1893), p. 83: "No sketch of Whittier, however slight, should omit mention of his friendship for Bayard Taylor. Their Quaker parentage helped to bring the two poets into communion; and although Taylor was so much the younger and more vigorous man, Whittier was also to see him pass, and to mourn his loss. . . . Certainly no one knew Taylor's work better, or brought a deeper sympathy into his reading of it." In his poem entitled "Bayard Taylor" (*Works,* IV, 141, Riverside Edition, from which all citations will be taken) Whittier tells of his friend in these words:

> He brought us wonders of the new and old;
> We shared all climes with him. The Arab's tent
> To him its story-telling secret lent.
> And, pleased, we listened to the tales he told.

Again, in "The Tent on the Beach" (*Works,* IV, 231) Bayard Taylor appears:

> And one, whose Arab face was tanned
> By tropic sun and boreal frost,
> So travelled there was scarce a land
> Or people left him to exhaust,
> In idling mood had from him hurled
> The poor squeezed orange of the world,
> And in the tent-shade, as beneath a palm,
> Smoked, cross-legged like a Turk, in Oriental calm.

In the light of Mrs. Fields's statement and the descriptions of Bayard Taylor, it may be profitable to note the former's opinion of Whittier's foreign interests (*op. cit.,* pp. 98-99): "As a traveller, too, he is unrivalled, giving us, without leaving his own garden, the fine fruit of foreign lands. In reading his poems of the East, it is difficult to believe that he never saw Palestine, nor Ceylon, nor India; and the wonder is no less when he writes of his own wide country."

5. Of Lydia Maria Child, Whittier wrote (*Works,* VI, 293): "Her great work, in three octavo volumes, *The Progress of Religious Ideas* . . . is an attempt to represent in a candid, unprejudiced manner the rise and progress of the great religions of the world, and their ethical relations to each other. . . . If, in her desire to do justice to the religions of Buddha and Mohammed . . . she seems at times to dwell upon the best and overlook the darker features of those systems, her concluding reflections should vindicate her from the charge of undervaluing the Christian faith."

6. Reference to my discussion of Whittier in *American Literature* will indicate the uses he made of the translations of Orientalists as well as the specific editions of their works which passed through his hands. General reference to the Orientals will be found readily through even a casual inspection of Whittier's writings.

7. Whittier's insight into Zoroastrianism is indicated by his essay on "The Agency of Evil" (*Works,* VII, 249-266) in which he discusses the interpretation of evil as personified by Ahriman.

8. Apropos of Whittier's interest in the *Koran,* note his words in Mrs. James T. Fields, *op. cit.,* pp. 54-55, which record an experience when a circus visited Amesbury: "I was in my garden when I saw an Arab wander down the street, and by-and-by stop and lean against my gate. He held a small book in his hand, which he was reading from time to time when he was not occupied with gazing about him. Presently I went to talk with him, and found he had lived all his life on the edge of the Desert until he had started for America. He was very homesick, and longed for the time of his return. He had hired himself for a term of years to the master of the circus. He held the Koran in his hand, and was delighted to find a friend who had also read his sacred book."

9. Whittier's obituary of Henry Taylor was reprinted from *The Villager* of Amesbury in *The Index,* III, 415 (Dec. 28, 1872). The Buddhist verses alluded to are those of Edward Hayes Plumptre, entitled "Sakya Mouni at Bodhimanda," which appeared in *The Contemporary Review,* V, 114-116 (May-Aug., 1867). The poem contained fifteen stanzas, of which I quote two to indicate the nature of Henry Taylor's surprising recitations:

> But, oh, the raptured deep
> Of that entrancèd sleep,
> When Wisdom's self has 'numbed the thrice-blest soul.
> When every sound is hushed,
> And o'er each sense have rushed
> The mighty waves that from Nirvana roll!

. . . . .

> Yes, the true Wisdom's way,
> The only perfect day,
> Is pure Not-being, Nothing absolute;
> The dark abyss profound,
> Where comes nor light nor sound,
> And the vast orb lies motionless and mute.

10. Ellen E. Dickinson, "A Morning With the Poet Whittier," *The Churchman,* XLV, 609 (June 3, 1882). The Confucian reference is to *Analects,* XI. 11.

11. Whittier, *Works,* I, 293.

12. *Ibid.,* I, 294.

13. An illuminating passage dealing with Whittier's relations to his contemporaries, and Emerson in particular, will be found in Mary B. Claflin, *Personal Recollections of John G. Whittier* (New York, Crowell, 1893), pp. 22-25: "In the companionship of his friends the poet found the keenest pleasure of his lonely life. Mr. Emerson, Mr. Sumner, Edna Dean Proctor, Harriet Beecher Stowe, Elizabeth Stuart Phelps, Lydia Maria Child. . . . With Mr. Emerson he discussed the great problems of human needs, and the great mysteries of eternity. . . . With Miss Proctor he talked of poetry, and especially of Oriental poetry and religion, which had a wonderful fascination for him; of Egypt and the East; of the Mohammedans and their worship; and of the imposing ceremonies of the Greek Church in Russia."

14. Whittier, *Works,* I, 295.

15. *Ibid.*

16. Whittier, *Works,* I, 302-303. There are numerous passages in the *Bhagavadgita* that might have served Whittier as a model for these lines. I believe the most likely are those found in the twelfth chapter, rendered in J. Cockburn Thomson's translation, *The Bhagavad-Gita* (Hertford, 1855), pp. 83-84 as follows: "He who is free from aversion, well-disposed towards all beings, and also compassionate, unselfish and unconceited, the same in pain and pleasure, patient, contented, always devotional, self-governed, firmly resolute, who directs his heart and thoughts to me (only), and worships me, is dear to me; and he from the world receives no emotions, and who receives no emotions from the world, who is free from the emotions of joy, envy, and fear, is dear to me. . . . He who neither rejoices, nor hates, nor grieves, nor loves, who has no interest in good or bad, and is full of devotion, is dear to me."

17. Whittier, *Works,* II, 249-250.

18. *Ibid.,* I, 222.

19. Whittier, *Works,* I, 223. The source will be found in *Bhagavadgita,* II. 19. A very similar passage, used by Emerson for "Brahma," will be found in *Katha Upanishad,* II. 19. In Whittier's lines the evidence of the names of the participants in the dialogue conclusively proves that the *Gita* was the probable exclusive source. The translation by J. Cockburn Thomson, *op. cit.,* pp. 10-12, follows: "Thou hast grieved for those who need not be grieved for. . . . The wise grieve not for dead or living. . . . But the contact of the elements, O son of Kunti! which bring cold and heat, pleasure and pain, which come and go, and are temporary. . . . There is no existence for what does not exist, nor is there any non-existence for what exists. . . . He who believes that this spirit can kill, and who thinks that it can be killed, both of these are wrong in judgment. It neither kills, nor is killed."

20. Whittier, *Works,* III, 365-366.

21. A possible source is T. Rogers, *Buddhaghosha's Parables . . . with an Introduction containing Buddha's Dhammapada . . . translated from Pali by F. Max Müller* (London, Trübner, 1870). This work was known to Alcott and his Concord associates; see Arthur Christy, *The Orient in American Transcendentalism* (Columbia University Press, 1932), p. 300. Since Whittier's poem was written in 1870, there is the chronological possibility that Rogers's book was the basis of the adaptation; this surmise is further supported by the fact the book contains both *Jataka* tales and the *Dhammapada,* the combination suggested in Whittier's lines. I do not find the familiar Occidental dove of peace in the Buddhaghosha pages; the figure seems to me clearly Whittier's invention. But his lines would seem a not too distant echo of *Dhammapada,* I. 5: "For hatred does not cease by hatred at any time: hatred ceases by love, this is an old rule"; and IX. 124: "He who has no

wound on his hand, may touch poison with his hand; poison does not affect one who has no wound; nor is there evil for one who does not commit evil." Without doubt the outstanding instance of Whittier's confusion of Buddhist teaching and the moral injunctions of his own Quaker heritage appears in the two lines of the poem "Miriam" which read (*Works,* I, 299): "He who forgiveth not shall, unforgiven, Fail of the rest of Buddha." The Christian principle of forgiveness, so emphasized in the Lord's Prayer, is not a part of the Buddhist "way." Nirvana is reached by seclusion from the entire phenomenal world.

John A. Pollard (essay date 1949)

SOURCE: Pollard, John A. "First Writings." In *John Greenleaf Whittier: Friend of Man,* pp. 36-59. Boston: Houghton Mifflin, 1949.

[*In the following excerpt, Pollard examines Whittier's poems written between 1823 and 1833, when he produced the essay* Justice and Expediency *and embraced the abolitionist cause. During this early period, according to Pollard, Whittier was "a verse-maker, and not yet a poet."*]

Whittier matured slowly as a whole man. He came early to spiritual grace but late to literary culture, and it was not until 1833 that he welded these elements into a nearly balanced character. Meanwhile, from the time of his first experiments with verse until he wrote the prose tract *Justice and Expediency* in 1833, he spent the most trying period of his life, roughly ten years, in anxious pursuit of an uncertain end. During this interlude he was a stranger to his essential being:

> . . . over restless wings of song,
> His birthright garb hung loose.[1]

He was not a complete Quaker, and was just beginning to be a man; he was a verse-maker, and not yet a poet. For a decade of imitation his half-formed intellect guided his wavering course. He got his true bearing on life only when his heart fully reasserted itself and when, like a true Quaker, he embraced a cause.

1

Whittier early put himself to the hard school of writing by the forcing method. Like most literary aspirants, he knew books before he had had any direct experience of life, and books were inevitably his first source of inspiration. He had delved in Doctor Weld's library before 1820, but his introduction to Burns in 1821-22 was the fillip which set him to writing. At the age of fourteen or fifteen he scribbled on his slate, to the amusement of his schoolfellows. In turn he amused himself at the family's fireside, after chores were finished in the evening, not by doing the conventional sums on his slate but by composing rhymes. Almost the only survival of these youthful effusions shows with sufficient clarity the bent of his mind at this time:

> And must I always swing the flail,
> And help to fill the milking pail?
> I wish to go away to school;
> I do not wish to be a fool.[2]

What Whittier himself considered his first exercise in versification was written in 1823 or 1824, a rhymed list, thirty-four lines long, of the books in his father's library. Two aspects of the verse are of passing interest: it is written in rhymed octosyllabics, favorite measure of the mature Whittier, and in its way it is autobiographical, like many of his later writings. First and last, these were virtually a "song of myself," and they constituted Whittier's diary. Like his quietistic forebears, who appear to have left no written records whatever, he did not have the diarist's habit of mind. He attempted a journal only once, on his mother's suggestion and in a notebook fashioned by her out of foolscap. Greenleaf made just one entry.[3]

From his matter-of-fact father, product of three generations of Yankee yeomen, Whittier probably received scant encouragement in his literary tendencies. Greenleaf, too, would be a farmer, his father doubtless assumed. Uncle Moses would more likely have understood and sympathized with Greenleaf's literary endeavors; but Uncle Moses was killed by the fall of a tree which he was cutting down, on January 23, 1824. This was the first death in the boy's family circle, and for him it was a serious loss. However, Whittier's mother approved of his course, despite the Quakers' ban upon poetry, and his sister Mary actively abetted his versifying.[4]

This was at best tentative and awkward although, even without criticism, Whittier had progressed measurably by 1823. He had left doggerel behind and was now embarked upon his prolonged period of imitation—imitation less of word or phrase than of style and subject and atmosphere. Now and for a decade, Whittier dwelt with all too much of Byronic melancholy upon the transiency of life, counterpoised by the benediction of lasting friendship.

Inevitably bookish and derivative as the burden of his early writing was, there was yet something of his own personality and place at its core. The play of a developing talent between literary and native materials is shown clearly in a group of unpublished manuscript verses.[5] **"The Martyr"** told the story of the Quaker William Leddra's execution at Boston in 1659 for returning from banishment by the Puritans. To the story of Canute and the ocean, Whittier added a moral tag. **"Lafayette"** praised the French nobleman for having fought and bled in the American Revolution, and **"Montgomery's Return"** sounded a patriotic tocsin for one "who a tyrants encroachments so nobly prevented." Together these two poems looked forward to Whittier's frank admiration, in later years, of General "Chinese" Gordon—admiration tempered by regret for the means he employed. For Whittier, as a Quaker, always disapproved of war, a fact of which **"The Wounded Soldier,"** dated June, 1824, was perhaps the earliest record.

That poem of ninety-two lines was heavily charged with sentimentalism. So, too, was **"The Brothers,"** dated October, 1825, and written in blank verse. One of the longest poems attempted by the youthful Whittier, this was a curious composition, containing among its 166 lines hints of Milton and suggestions in theme and treatment of Wordsworth's "Michael." Twenty of the lines prefigured interestingly the vision of God in nature to which Whittier in 1876 gave choice expression in **"Sunset on the Bearcamp."**

Under equally obvious influence, Whittier sounded the romantics' praise of the poet in **"To the Memory of Chatterton, Who Died Aged 17"**—probably Whittier's own age when he wrote the poem. The twenty-four lines were extremely sentimental, but chiefly notable was the complaint, in the third stanza, which Whittier was soon to voice for himself:

> But ill thy haughty soul could bear
>   To meet disdain and cold neglect
> To see those hopes which promis'd fair
>   So early by misfortune check'd [.]

Still more significant was Whittier's first appreciation of Byron. This manly tribute, not too much marred by the wholly moral considerations which determined Whittier's final rejection of the apostle of freedom whom Goethe called the greatest talent of the century, was contained in an extract of a **"New Year's Address"** written on December 31, 1824. It could be wished that Whittier had left this judgment final:

> One bright, bold star has fallen on thy coast
>   Byron, renown'd on Albions classic page
> A master spirit of the times, the boast
>   The pride, the shame, the wonder of his age [.]
> But peace to him, let deep oblivion shade
>   The memory of his wanderings, for there was
> A spirit in him which has oft display'd
>   Its pure devotion to the sacred cause
> Of freedom; let this serve to palliate
>   His numerous errors, for the generous mind
> That mourns the loss of genius mourns the fate
>   Of him whose haughty form is now reclin'd
> Where Pindus lifts itself.[6]

In his interest in the remote, it will be seen, Whittier was always a romantic but never a traveler. His inherited feeling for place, plus Burns' example, taught him to look for poetic subjects in life and nature close at hand. In **"To Nahant,"** for example, Whittier delighted in the physical charm and the contemporary fame of the Essex County seashore resort, which later was much frequented by celebrated New Englanders.[7] These lines were dated August 20, 1825.

Somewhat earlier, in his first rhyming period, Whittier had written the poem **"Superstition,"** which clearly was based upon the eery beliefs then still current in rural New England. Also at about this time Whittier penned **"The Midnight Scene (A tradition from the banks of the Merrimac),"** a prophecy of the *Legends of New England* which he brought together, in 1831, in his first published volume.

In the train of these and other snatches of verse—"the work of intervals, a ploughboy's lore,"[8] written oftentimes by hearthlight when the day's work was done—two years brought to Whittier some increase of facility. There was wanting only an audience to encourage the eighteen-year-old boy's rhetorical efforts, and by a play of favorable circumstance it came to him through William Lloyd Garrison, who crossed his path now for the first time. Garrison was only two years older than Whittier, but he had been better favored in his early education, in relatively populous Newburyport, and he had early learned the printing trade. On March 16, 1826, he acquired the year-old *Essex Courant* and renamed it the *Newburyport Free Press.* Garrison at once gave the newspaper a humanitarian character, and won as a subscriber John Whittier.[9]

An important part of the newspaper of that day was its poetical column. Garrison promptly filled his with verse by the reigning favorites, people now mostly forgotten, who included Bernard Barton, Felicia Hemans, Letitia E. Landon, James Montgomery, John Pierpont, Lydia H. Sigourney, and Nathaniel Parker Willis. On their verse, no rich pabulum, the popular taste of the day was nourished.[10] Whittier was merely like his fellows in approving the sentimentalism which made Mrs. Hemans probably the most popular writer whose verses appeared in the American newspapers of that time. Certainly Garrison thought well of her; in the *Free Press* of May 4, 1826, he called her "this wonderful and extraordinary woman." Of this sentiment there was an echo in Whittier's reference, in the *Haverhill Gazette* of March 1, 1828, to "the gifted Felicia Hemans."

It was with such models before him in 1825-26 that Whittier practised assiduously the arts of imitation. Mary Whittier rightly believed that his outpourings were as publishable as the effusions which Garrison and other editors were currently printing as poetry. From among Greenleaf's productions she therefore selected, as most likely to be accepted, **"The Exile's Departure."**

He had written it in 1825, but she posted it to Garrison with the date "Haverhill, June 1, 1826" and with the signature "W."[11]

Garrison was glad enough to have new talent drop free into his copy basket. In the issue of June 8 he published Whittier's poem of thirty-two lines, and he said in editorial appreciation, "If 'W.' at Haverhill, will continue to favor us with pieces, beautiful as the one inserted in our poetical department of today, we shall esteem it a favor." Whittier, who had known nothing of Mary's action, was confounded with pleasure when he saw a copy of the weekly, with his verses placed above both Byron's "To Thyrza" and an excerpt from Mrs. Hemans' work.[12]

For Whittier, of course, Garrison's request amounted to a deal. Here was Greenleaf's opportunity to be heard, and he met it better than half way. Sixteen more of his poems appeared in the columns of the *Free Press* during the remainder of 1826, nine of them in unbroken weekly succession during July and August. Whittier's first response to Garrison's invitation was **"The Deity,"** written in 1825, which the *Free Press* published on June 22. It was based on I Kings, xix, 11-12, and was the first in the long series of poems published by the youthful Whittier on biblical themes. Garrison now gave him even stronger encouragement: "The author of the following graphic sketch (which would do credit to riper years) is a youth of only *sixteen,*[13] who, we think, bids fair to prove another *Bernard Barton,* of whose persuasion he is. His poetry bears the stamp of true poetic genius, which, if carefully cultivated, will rank him among the bards of his country."[14]

Garrison did more. Directed by the postrider, he drove, in company with a woman friend, the fourteen miles from Newburyport to the Whittiers' rural retreat. His visit was not unwelcome flattery to Greenleaf, and yet was an embarrassment. Garrison was himself just past twenty years of age, but he had polish and presence; Whittier, at their first meeting, had neither. He was burrowing for eggs under the barn when his sister Mary summoned him to meet his visitors from the city. Despite a quick—and unlucky—change of clothing, he was saved from extreme uneasiness only by Garrison's ready social tact.[15]

In person, Garrison now enlarged upon his belief expressed in the *Free Press,* that Whittier's gift deserved the discipline of a formal education. What the future reformer discovered by this visit he related later, on April 11, 1828, in the *National Philanthropist.*

> He indulged his propensity for rhyming with so much secrecy, (as his father informed us,) that it was only by removing some rubbish in the garret, where he had concealed his manuscripts, that the discovery was made. This bent of his mind was discouraged by his parents: they were in indigent circumstances, and unable to give him a suitable education, and they did not wish to inspire him with hopes which might never be fulfilled. . . . We endeavored to speak cheeringly of the prospects of their son; we dwelt upon the impolicy of warring against nature . . .—and we spoke too of fame—"Sir," replied the father with an emotion which went home to our bosom like an electric shock, "poetry will not give him *bread.*"[16]

It is true that the Whittiers' financial position held no promise of a college education for Greenleaf, yet he himself wrote Garrison in 1859 that his father had not opposed his destined course—had in fact been proud of his verses. His mother, evidently, always encouraged Greenleaf.[17]

At any rate, Garrison's visit brought Whittier no immediate relief from the dull tyranny of farm work. Greenleaf nevertheless continued as before to read and write, mainly with a romantic eye for the remote or the adventurous. Likewise he shaped Quaker beliefs and history into verse. He deplored the Crusaders; they served not Christ but earthly pride. In contrast, he inscribed two paeans of praise to William Penn for his idealism and his fair dealing with the Indians. **"To the Memory of David Sands"** was Whittier's encomium to another Quaker messenger of peace.[18] And since most of what Whittier then wrote was a calm distillation of his reading, he praised equally the power of memory itself. In his lines—

> . . . Memory can lead
> The harass'd mind back to the scenes it lov'd
> In years departed; . . .

there was a plain forecast of *Snow-Bound,* written in 1865 out of a mind harassed by the death of Elizabeth Whittier in the previous year; and the conclusion of the poem prefigured the Chaucerian portrait-painting of Whittier's family in his New England idyll:

> Fancy can bring th' enchanting vision near,
> The sister's playful smile, the brother's laugh,
> The mother's anxious look, the father's tale
> Of other days, and all the dear delights
> Felt by youth's hopeful bosom, when the tho't
> Of evil hours, and manhood's wasting cares,
> No blight has flung upon the spring of Hope.[19]

Life itself, its meaning and end, equally engaged Whittier's early meditations. The poet Gray taught him something of the transiency of human affairs. The beliefs of the Friends settled Whittier's conviction that the world's philosophy of "getting ahead" was a sham; that position without honor was a false aim.[20] And Whittier now became convinced that life without liberty is without meaning. In **"The Emerald Isle,"** a sonorous appreciation of Ireland's one-time greatness and a lament for her fallen state, he trumpeted a Quaker's love of freedom.[21]

For Byron's daring, dash, and grandiosity Whittier had no liking, but for his championship of liberty, the utmost admiration. When Whittier was just outgrowing his style of farmer boy, Byron, then two years in his grave, strongly influenced American literary thought. Inevitably Whittier read and seemingly reread him, and in **"Byron. Written after a perusal of his works,"** the young Quaker balanced the "living fire" of Byron's "never-dying strain," along with his "soul-enchanting lays to beauty's power," over against the "detested vice" which soured "his tuneful numbers." Whittier ended with this characteristic tribute to Byron:

> Farewell departed minstrel,
>   Where'er is freedom's clime,
> There shall thy laurels be preserv'd,
>   And greener grow with time.[22]

2

At the end of 1826 Whittier lost one sounding board and gained another. When Garrison removed to Boston and the *Newburyport Free Press* was suspended, Whittier placed his wares on the home market. During January, 1827, the *Haverhill Gazette & Essex Patriot* published four of his poems, two of which were plagiarized in a Philadelphia magazine later that year. **"Ocean"** was in fact widely copied by the press of the country. Within the year, thanks to this free circulation, Whittier came to have a measure of poetical reputation.

He was known, in the first place, as a shoemaker poet. It appears that he had already determined to earn his way through Haverhill Academy, for the editor of the *Gazette,* in printing **"Ocean"** and **"Micah"** on January 13, described him as "an Apprentice to the Shoemaking business." From a hired man on the farm Whittier had learned the not uncommon winter trade of making a simple type of women's slipper which was sold at retail for twenty-five cents a pair. Of this sum the craftsman received eight cents. During the winter of 1826-27 Whittier saved enough money from his earnings to pay for a term of six months at the Academy.[23]

It was Whittier's misfortune that some well-to-do Friend did not, in accordance with a general precept of the Society, take a special interest in his education.[24] A kind fate might have sent him to the Moses Brown School, which the Quakers reopened in 1819 at Providence. Nevertheless, Whittier had good fortune of a kind in the opportune opening of Haverhill Academy in 1827.[25]

If there had remained any lingering doubt of Whittier's attending the Academy, Abijah Wyman Thayer[26] removed it by urging upon John Whittier, as Garrison had done, a classical education for the young poet. Thayer was one of the several able men who touched Greenleaf's life significantly. He became editor and publisher of the *Haverhill Gazette*[27] in February, 1827,

and gratefully printed the poems which came in a flood from Whittier's pen. Thayer had indeed such an extravagantly high opinion of Greenleaf's verses that his enthusiasm must have had some weight with John Whittier. He, then in his sixty-seventh year, at length saw reason in Greenleaf's having the rudiments of a classical education. The boy's injury, two years previously, made it unlikely that he would ever be able to manage the heavy work of the farm, which had already undermined his constitution. To the Academy, then, it was agreed that Greenleaf should go, when it was opened in May.[28]

Whittier was now aflame with ambition. "Few guessed beneath his aspect grave," as he wrote, "what passions strove in chains." Fame he would have, and that quickly. He sought it by means of quantity production—and in the ripeness of years he rued this boyish rush into print. In subject and manner his youthful bagatelles were almost wholly conventional; they had in them almost no music; they were subjected to little revision, and they had almost none of the mature Whittier's felicitous touch. Hard schooling alone gave him that.

During 1827 fifty of Whittier's poems were published for the first time, in the *Haverhill Gazette,* and he achieved also the dignity of his first publication in Boston. Nathaniel Greene appropriated for the *Boston Statesman* from May to July three of "W.'s" poems which appeared in the *Gazette.* So encouraged, Whittier sent to Greene a manuscript which was published in the *Statesman* of July 19. N. P. Willis, whom Whittier seemed then to read with the most respectful attention, was co-editor of the *Recorder and Telegraph* in 1827, and on August 17 he published Whittier's poem **"Loneliness."** All this writing betokened a prodigious industry, which won for Whittier much untempered praise.

However slender these accomplishments were, the publicity given to Whittier in the newspaper press of the country had sent echoes of his reputation back to Haverhill, with the result that he was hailed as a prodigy when he finally entered the Academy. Here he was, after perhaps a dozen years' attendance at the district school, entering at the age of nearly twenty upon what would roughly correspond to a freshman course in a high school of today. For him the day was significant indeed, and it was no less memorable for Haverhill. Whittier for the first and last time entered the "grove of Academe," where he was to study for half of 1827 and half of 1828.

The manner of his entrance recalled the good estate of poets in ancient times, for he and Robert Dinsmoor, an aged Scottish rhymester of Windham, New Hampshire, had been appointed to march together at the head of Haverhill's academic procession, with which the dedicatory exercises were begun. Both had been requested to write poems for the occasion of April 30, 1827, and Whittier carried off his part with honor. Yet his ode, **"Hail, Star of Science!"** addressed to the eternal spirit in the Greek sense, was somewhat incongruously styled after the rhetorical Moore. A Haverhill man sang the aspiring three verses to the air, **"Pillar of Glory."**[29]

3

A bashful youth, made perhaps the more self-conscious by his Quaker dress, Whittier nevertheless quickly won his place, both with fellow students and with faculty. Twice previously he had come under the tutelage of able Dartmouth men, and here he met another graduate of that college, Oliver Carlton.[30] At the Academy, moreover, Whittier for the first time knew students from other localities. Sixteen of the one hundred students came from outside of Massachusetts—twelve from New Hampshire, two from Louisiana, and one each from Maine and New York—and a faint air of cosmopolitanism was imparted to the school by the seven who were enrolled from Boston.[31]

As his mother had requested, Whittier was enabled to live with the Thayers, to whose son, Professor James B. Thayer, he wrote in 1877: "I never think of thy mother without feelings of love and gratitude. She and thy father were my best friends in the hard struggle of my schooldays."[32] Every Friday night Whittier walked home to spend the week end with his family. But he was not forgotten by his schoolmates, then or later. Mrs. Thayer, too, retained a clear remembrance of his schoolboy character: of his impeccable appearance, "the liveliness of his temper, his ready wit, his perfect courtesy and infallible sense of truth and justice." Whittier's character, along with his poetic reputation, made him socially sought after, and the youthful gatherings counted heavily upon his presence—especially at the teas over which young belles of school and village presided.[33]

Easily the clearest contemporary picture of Whittier during and just after his Academy days was that drawn by Harriet Minot Pitman, who wrote in part:

> . . . He was tall, slight, and very erect; a bashful youth, but *never awkward,* my mother said, who was a better judge than I of such matters.
>
> He went to school awhile at Haverhill Academy. There were pupils of all ages, from ten to twenty-five. My brother, George Minot, then about ten years old, used to say that Whittier was the best of all the big fellows, and he was in the habit of calling him "Uncle Toby." Whittier was always kind to children, and under a very grave and quiet exterior there was a real love of fun, and a keen sense of the ludicrous. In society he was embarrassed, and his manners were, in consequence, sometimes brusque and cold. With intimate friends he talked a great deal, and in a wonderfully interesting

manner; usually earnest, often analytical, and frequently playful. He had a great deal of wit. It was a family characteristic. The study of human nature was very interesting to him, and his insight was keen. He liked to draw out his young friends, and to suggest puzzling doubts and queries.

> When a wrong was to be righted, or an evil to be remedied, he was readier to act than any young man I ever knew, and was very wise in his action,—shrewd, sensible, practical. The influence of his Quaker bringing-up was manifest. I think it was always his endeavor
>
> > "To render less
> > The sum of human wretchedness."[34]
>
> This, I say, was his steadfast endeavor, in spite of an inborn love of teasing. He was very modest, never conceited, never egotistic.
>
> One could never flatter him. I never tried, but I have seen people attempt it, and it was a signal failure. He did not flatter, but told very wholesome and unpalatable truths, yet in a way to spare one's self-love by admitting a doubt whether he was in earnest or in jest.
>
> The great questions of Calvinism were subjects of which he often talked in those early days. He was exceedingly conscientious. He cared for people—quite as much for the plainest and most uncultivated, if they were original and had something in them, as for the most polished.
>
> He was much interested in politics, and thoroughly posted. I remember, in one of his first calls at our house, being surprised at his conversation with my father [Judge Stephen Minot] upon Governor Gerry and the Gerry-mandering of the State, or the attempt to do it, of which I had until then been wholly ignorant.
>
> He had a retentive memory and a marvellous store of information on many subjects. I once saw a little commonplace book of his,—full of quaint things, and as interesting as Southey's.
>
> . . . . .
>
> I have said nothing of Whittier in his relations to women. There was never a particle of coxcombry about him. He was delicate and chivalrous, but paid few of the little attentions common in society. If a girl dropped her glove or handkerchief in his presence, she had to pick it up again, especially if she did it on purpose. *; *. *.[35]

Whittier's eyes, if they probably were not blinded by the richness of the Academy's offerings, were yet filled with new visions. As it turned out, his choice rested not upon the Classical department but upon the English. For instruction in its several branches during each of his two periods of twenty-six weeks at the Academy he paid eight dollars, and four dollars additional for lessons in French. Likewise he gave himself practical lessons, of lasting benefit, in bookkeeping. At the end of his first six months of study he had left in his pocket precisely the twenty-five cents upon which he had calculated, after having prepared in advance an exact budget of every allowable expense. This lesson was useful to Whittier long after his school days were past. Until 1866 his income in no year was much more than five hundred dollars, but he was never seriously in debt.[36]

Scholastically, Whittier's benefits came from composing in prose, under criticism, and in wider reading. This, it appears from his current writings, was mainly in history and literature. His first "theme" was read incredulously by Carlton, but succeeding compositions convinced the twenty-six-year-old master of the ability of his nearly twenty-year-old student, and soon established a friendly and equal plane between the two.[37] This relationship seems to have typified others which Whittier now enjoyed in the village, where—

> . . . homes of wealth and beauty, wit and mirth,
> By taste refined, by eloquence and worth,
> Taught and diffused the intellect's high joy,
> And gladly welcomed e'en a rustic boy.[38]

Whittier thus had access to the few private libraries in Haverhill, and, above all, to James Gale's circulating library. Of this windfall Whittier later wrote: ". . . it was the opening of a new world of enjoyment to me. I can still remember the feeling of mingled awe and pleasure with which I gazed for the first time on his crowded bookshelves."[39]

One other profit Whittier derived from attending the Academy: an acquaintance with young ladies from outside his own family. As it happened, the males at the Academy were outnumbered three to two by the females; and to at least two of these Whittier, as a sensitive human being, was quite naturally attracted. In a letter of about 1840 he stated precisely what his cousin Mary Emerson Smith meant to him:

> For myself, I owe much to the kind encouragement of female friends. A bashful, ignorant boy, I was favored by the kindness of a lady who saw, or thought she saw, beneath the clownish exterior something which gave promise of intellect and worth. The powers of my own mind, the mysteries of my own spirit, were revealed to myself, only as they were called out by one of those dangerous relations called cousins, who, with all her boarding-school glories upon her, condescended to smile upon my rustic simplicity. She was so learned in the to me more than occult mysteries of verbs and nouns, and philosophy, and botany, and mineralogy, and French, and all that, and then she had seen something of society, and could talk (an accomplishment at that time to which I could lay no claim), that on the whole I looked upon her as a being to obtain whose good opinion no effort could be too great. I smile at this sometimes,—this feeling of my unsophisticated boyhood,—yet to a great degree it is still with me.[40]

Whittier had known his cousin before Academy days, at the Haverhill home of her grandfather, Captain Nehemiah Emerson. He, who had been an officer in

Washington's army at Valley Forge and at Saratoga, married a cousin of Whittier's father. Greenleaf called her "Aunt Mary," and for a while, in his 'teens, he lived at her house while attending school. Mary Emerson Smith as a young girl passed much of her time at her grandparents' home,[41] and she was the "beautiful and happy girl" of **"Memories,"** which Greenleaf wrote in 1841.

Differences alike of creed and of station would have prevented any stronger attachment between them than friendship, as Whittier clearly recognized.[42] Besides, he was still a minor when he left the Academy in 1828, and early marriage would have clashed both with his family's tradition and his own financial prudence. He measured clearly, however, the depth of his boyhood affection by placing **"Memories"** first among "Poems Subjective and Reminiscent" in his collected writings. Like any normal boy he may have been an "enraptured young noodle," but he was always a person of deep, unselfish, and lasting affections.[43] Their friendship did not end with his cousin's marriage to a Covington, Kentucky, judge. In her widowhood, late in life, Mrs. Thomas spent the summer months in New England, and she occasionally saw Whittier in the White Mountains. To the end of his days they enjoyed a friendly correspondence.[44]

Evelina Bray,[45] of Marblehead, was Whittier's other special favorite among the young ladies of the Academy, and with her also he formed an enduring friendship. She attended the Academy with Whittier only in 1828, and afterward they met seldom. Fate had set them, also, on divergent roads; the two were of different faiths, and she was, relatively, a social aristocrat. To have married any one "out of meeting" would have led to Whittier's disownment as a Friend—and that would have been intolerable to him.[46]

None the less, after Academy days Whittier maintained communication with Evelina. In the early summer of 1829, while editing the *American Manufacturer* in Boston, he attended with his mother a Quarterly Meeting of the Friends, in Salem. Before breakfast one morning he walked the two or three miles to Marblehead, and called on Evelina. She could not so early in the day receive him in the house, so they walked to the old fort, then in ruins, and sat looking out over the harbor,[47] reputed birthplace of the United States Navy. As his habit was, Whittier banked this incident in his memory. In 1874 he described the meeting in the first three stanzas of the song in **"A Sea Dream."**[48]

In February, 1839, Whittier posted to Evelina a book of his poems, probably a copy of the 1838 edition, and with maidenly reticence she acknowledged it on May 1, 1840.[49] About 1849 she became the wife of an English evangelist, William Downey, and a widow in 1889, three years before Whittier died. She corresponded with him occasionally, and at his suggestion she attended the reunion of his Academy classmates at Haverhill in 1885.[50]

4

The realization that by the world's standard he was not "eligible" was undoubtedly wormwood to a sensitive youth already well aware of his intrinsic worth; but Whittier's experience with these young ladies filled a gap, which he acknowledged, in his upbringing. If there followed now a period of brooding, Whittier, like any other youth becoming adjusted to life, was naturally destined to go through it. As late as 1832 this mood seems to have been intermittently upon him, but Whittier's religion and inner strength saved him from any danger of wasting in despair. Besides, there was work to be done, and it soon beguiled away what melancholy Whittier may honestly have felt.

His religion was unquestionably one of the stays of Whittier's life, if not the chief one. On February 3, three months before entering the Academy, he contributed a prose article, "Sacred Music," to the *Haverhill Gazette,* and stated a strictly Quaker position from which he never retreated. The subject of sacred music was in controversy in 1827, for Governor Levi Lincoln of Massachusetts had refused to sign an act incorporating the Mozart Association, which he considered merely one more useless organization.[51] In contrast, Whittier objected to sacred music almost wholly on religious grounds.

Whittier was very proud to be a Quaker, but sensitive to the world's ridicule of his "peculiar people" for their nonconformity in dress. Yet he adhered steadfastly all his life to eighteenth-century Quaker drab and cut; most New England Friends abandoned it. As Carlyle in 1833-34 specifically lauded George Fox's simplicity of dress, in *Sartor Resartus,* so Whittier in 1827 championed the typical Friend:

> Beware my good friend and revile not too rashly
> A person you know not, because of his dress;
> For, believe me, the man you have pictur'd so harshly,
> Does many a noble endowment possess.
>
> True, he has not deck'd out his humble exterior
> In those fast varying fashions, of vanity born—
> To such idle allurements his heart is superior;
> 'Tis his mind, not his person, he seeks to adorn.[52]

Often in his later work Whittier sounded this chord—in poems such as **"Cassandra Southwick," "The Exiles," "The King's Missive," "The Meeting," "The Old South,"** and **"The Quaker Alumni."**

Seeds of another of Whittier's lifelong interests showed close to the surface of his 1827 output. He lyricized freedom romantically in **"The Switzer's Song,"** based upon the bloodless revolution of 1306 which relieved Switzerland of the Austrian yoke; and he championed liberty in **"Montezuma,"** which seared Cortez for having pretended to advance the cause of religion by his military barbarity.[53]

In addition to these inherited strains, Whittier's reading at the Academy was echoed in his contemporary verses. He read "Paradise Lost" with immediate and lasting appreciation, and took Milton's moral kingdom to be his own.[54] On the other hand, he seems to have considered Spenser's arena of moral knighthood as alien territory. In **"Proem"**[55] he later wrote that "I love . . . the songs of Spenser's golden days," but he seldom manifested this love. For Chaucer, unfortunately, Whittier cared little. Byron continued to fascinate and to perplex him,[56] while stimulating him to train one of the best gifts of his later writing: that of recreating distant places in his imagination. In time this talent became—almost—a compensation for his inability to travel.

Significantly, Whittier's interest in his native scene survived all the press of new enthusiasms growing out of the opportunities for wider reading which the Academy provided. With a faint promise of his future narrative skill, he told the story of a young Indian who scoffed at the tribal tradition that supernatural beings resided in the White Mountains, and lost his life in a storm conjured up by "spectral forms" which "stood above the rushing mountain flood." Whittier experimented further with native material in **"The Pawnee Brave,"** which exhibited a marked increase in narrative skill.[57]

Beyond his reading, the social climate of the day also helped to bring Whittier's young talent to the budding stage. There were already stirring, in the nation, currents which soon eddied around Whittier and which he was later to help direct in their courses. On July 4, 1827, slavery was abolished in New York State, as it had already been regulated elsewhere.[58] Moreover, the anti-aristocratic forces which contributed to the election of Andrew Jackson as President in 1828 were already reflected in the newspapers of the day. As a Quaker and a Jeffersonian Democrat by birthright, Whittier had a natural alliance with these forces, and in two poems of 1827 he made clear his sympathy with them.[59]

Only one break occurred during 1827 in Whittier's intensive program of education and writing, and the occasion of it was his trip to Boston.[60] Harriet Beecher Stowe has described the fervor of mind with which a rural New Englander of that day made his first trip to the metropolis,[61] and into the pattern of that picture the known facts of Whittier's first visit to Boston fit well. On Whittier's part there were distinctive preparations; he was groomed by all the sartorial resources of his family. His new homespun suit of clothes was equipped with "boughten buttons," which the boyish Whittier conceived as measuring the difference between urban and rural dress. In addition, Aunt Mercy made for him, out of pasteboard, a broad-brim Quaker hat covered with drab velvet. Finally, in good Quaker style,[62] Whittier's mother gave him moral preparation for the journey by advising him strongly against attending the theater.

On the six-hour trip from Haverhill to Boston, Whittier rode in a stagecoach for probably the first time. He went to the city on the invitation of Mrs. Nathaniel Greene, who occasionally visited the Whittiers in East Haverhill. In 1827 Nathaniel Greene was postmaster of Boston and editor of the *American* (later the *Boston*) *Statesman,* forerunner of the *Boston Post* of today. He knew of the young poet's work, and during the year he published in the *Statesman* four of his poems.

Whittier slipped unnoticed into Boston, then a busy commercial city of nearly sixty thousand inhabitants. Through the confusing maze of streets he found his way alone to the Greenes' home, probably at 65 Congress Street, and there he was affectionately received. He promised to return for tea, and then, with characteristic independence, set forth to do his own exploring.

> "I wandered up and down the streets," he used to say. "Somehow it wasn't just what I expected, and the crowd was worse and worse after I got into Washington Street; and when I got tired of being jostled, it seemed to me as if the folks might get by if I waited a little while. Some of them looked at me, and so I stepped into an alleyway and waited and looked out. Sometimes there didn't seem to be so many passing, and I thought of starting, and then they'd begin again. 'Twas a terrible stream of people to me. I began to think my new clothes and the buttons were all thrown away. I stayed there a good while." (This was said with great amusement.) "I began to be homesick. I thought it made no difference at all about my having those boughten buttons."[63]

This excursion was disappointing, but at tea time Whittier had his reward. Among Mrs. Greene's guests whom he had been invited to meet there were several gay and friendly ladies who appear to have found, beneath his quaint Friend's garb, the quick wit and drollery which his handsome eyes must have betrayed. Whittier's apparent favorite among these ladies, eager to contribute to the pleasure of such an engaging youth's first visit to Boston, invited him to attend the theater that evening. She was herself the leading player of the company appearing there.

Poor Whittier's conflict of emotions may be easily imagined. Here was feminine company of the pleasantest, and it bore no marks of the wickedness imputed to stage-players by the Puritans and the Quakers. Moreover, Whittier had a natural affinity for the company of attractive women. Yet as always his Quaker scruples prevailed over his emotions of delight. That night an uneasy spirit, aggravated by homesickness, hindered his sleep and decided him to return to Haverhill the next morning. His projected visit of one week had lasted one day. Of his encounter with the actress he spoke no word to his surprised family. Neither, in all probability, did he mention the copy of Shakespeare which he had bought.[64]

5

References to this book soon appeared in Whittier's writing, although from November 19, 1827, he was for twelve weeks chiefly occupied with books of another kind. Into this period was crowded his only experience of schoolteaching, an occupation which gave him no pleasure but which enabled him to attend Haverhill Academy for six months more. The committee of three men appointed to engage a master for School District Five in West Amesbury (now Merrimac) desired in him only neat handwriting. Whittier's fine eighteenth-century script won him the position, although he distrusted his general qualifications for the post.[65]

Once he had assumed the rôle of tutor, Whittier's training in mathematical subjects at the Academy did him good service, for the larger boys in the school plagued him with puzzles in "figures." He solved these, in his conscientious way, but only at the cost of sleepless nights. To this general experience he later alluded, as editor of the *New England Weekly Review,*[66] by writing of his friend Frederick A. P. Barnard's *New Treatise on Arithmetic*: "The confusion of ideas resulting from the use of technical terms before the pupil is capable of comprehending them, has been judiciously guarded against, in this treatise." Nevertheless, Whittier's patience survived twelve weeks of teaching, and in February he was paid forty-five dollars for his labors.[67]

While he was in Merrimac, Whittier lost none of his interest in Haverhill and its affairs. His concern was, in fact, so lively as to lead to the familiarity of unwonted satire, and to embarrassment. On January 5, 1828, his **"New Year's Address to the Patrons of the Essex Gazette"** appeared in that newspaper.[68] To the extent of thirty-five stanzas, without the benefit of a light touch, Whittier satirized the civic foibles of Haverhill. He even rallied himself for having pictured the Indians "with the glowing fancy of a poet." When a tribe of them in their birch canoes, he said, visited Haverhill in the autumn of 1827,

> I went, and saw them, all alive and real,
> And the plain truth destroy'd my *beau ideal.*

For one rollicking moment he ceased being the sweet singer of native songs, the reverent versifier of biblical tales. For his materials he went directly to life, and it taught him a practical lesson—one which he later chose to forget when he dedicated himself to the cause of abolition.

> An unlucky New Year's Address [he wrote to Doctor Weld on March 5, 1828] publish'd in the Ess. Gaz. has call'd down upon me the anathemas of some half a dozen, who *felt* that they or their follies were alluded to. I have learn'd, however, that it is an unthankful task to lash vice and prejudice. . . .

This experience, useful to Whittier, opened a second full year of intensive writing which further disciplined his mind and his hand. Nothing which he then wrote had any other value. Yet amid the ephemeral interests bred by his avid reading there were prefigurings of Whittier the reformer. On January 19, 1828, for instance, he contributed to the *Haverhill Gazette* a poem, **"The Drunkard to His Bottle,"** which he wrote in Scottish dialect. In the Society of Friends Whittier had long heard testimonies against the use of intoxicating spirits, but in A. W. Thayer he met a militant moralist who had the means to oppose them publicly. Under his editorship the *Gazette* was reputedly the first political newspaper in the United States, and the second periodical anywhere, to advocate total abstinence from intoxicating liquors.[69]

When in 1827 the movement for temperance in Haverhill was started, there were between twenty and thirty places in the village of fewer than four thousand people where liquor was sold. It was served at funerals as well as at marriages, farmers and mechanics drank it at work, and not uncommonly it was tendered as a gift to clergymen. In courageously leading the movement for temperance in Haverhill, Thayer suffered temporary misfortune. His bearing was perhaps exemplary for young Whittier. His convictions only deepened by opposition, Thayer held resolutely to his course, and remained long enough in Haverhill to see the village become almost tinder-dry.[70]

Whittier was undoubtedly drawn by Thayer toward prohibitionism. From the time **"The Drunkard to His Bottle"** appeared, Whittier's interest in the movement developed to the extent that in 1833 he was nominated a delegate from Haverhill to the convention, at Worcester, of the Massachusetts Society for the Suppression of Intemperance.[71] From that year, however, he devoted himself almost wholly to the abolition of slavery.

The year 1828 was still too early a time for Whittier to have discovered his real interests. No theme dominated his sixty-eight or more poems published that year. He was still an author in search of his literary character; and he was still seeking an education.

To both these ends Thayer sought to help him by proposing, in the *Haverhill Gazette* of January 19, 1828, the publication of "The Poems of Adrian." The required five hundred subscriptions were not forthcoming, however, and by this fact Whittier was in two ways unfortunately affected. His formal education ended by necessity with the second term of six months which he began at Haverhill Academy at the end of April 1828, and a sense of neglect in him soon made the melancholy seem real which previously he had been simulating.

On balance, it was fortunate that "Adrian's" poems did not achieve the permanency of a collected edition. Whittier was so embarrassed by his first book, *Legends of New England* (1831), that he later bought and destroyed all discoverable copies of it.[72] In February, 1828, it sufficed that his first poem to appear within the covers of a book or under his own name found a place in *Incidental Poems, Accompanied with Letters . . .* , by Robert Dinsmoor, the "Rustic Bard."[73] The composition, which was entitled **"J. G. Whittier to the 'Rustic Bard,'"** was published also in the *Haverhill Gazette* of February 16.

Frustrate for the moment, Whittier still felt the whip of ambition—ambition blended of desire for literary fame and for success in love—and the melancholy resulting from its fancied thwarting begot in him great confusion of mind. Melancholy now appeared, at least, to be his governing mood, occasionally offset by a note of jocular satire. Inevitably his work improved in the wrong way. In **"The Confessions of a Bachelor,"**[74] an effusion of 304 lines, Whittier's stanzas lost their run and form and became "the very false gallop of verses." He seems to have been deservedly censured, for in the *Gazette* of September 13, 1828, appeared **"Lines, Written on Being Told There Was Too Much of Levity in My Later Writings."** This piece was a marvel of self-revelation and self-defense, and resembled nothing else that Whittier ever wrote. With defiant pride he proclaimed: "I can feel a consciousness of slumbering power."

It was, of course, no discredit to him that he did not then know what he desired in life. The passing of time was the specific needed to bring order and clarity to his thinking and to his purposes. Meanwhile, his verses were a vent—a useful and necessary one—out of which he passed the mild poisons of youthful love and ambition.

His topics he found where his reading led him. Two untitled poems based respectively on passages in Job and in Mark invite notice here.[75] The first of them (**"When, like the cloud before the sun"**) constituted one of Whittier's earliest expressions of belief in the eternal life, and the second contained one of his first references to the Inner Light. The poem ended with this significant stanza, one of the few Quaker touches in a year of frenzied writing:

> O, thou! whose power could rule the sea,
> Extend thine influence e'en to me!

> Control my will, and lay to rest
> The stormy passions of my breast;
> Check there, each wild discordant mood,
> And grant an humble quietude,
> To list, amid earth's jarring din,
> The teachings of *thy voice within.*

Most significantly of all, in his lines **"Night steals upon the world,"**[76] written in blank verse, Whittier rose for a moment above mere rhyming, and caught the true accent of poetry. This poem was unquestionably one of the best which he had so far written upon nature.

But logically, in this year of intensive reading, Whittier looked less to the native scene for literary materials than he did both earlier and later. During 1828 he appears to have written only one poem of merit which had a New England background, and this, **"To the Merrimack,"** Garrison published in the *National Philanthropist* of June 6, 1828, with the remark: "We trust that this is only the commencement of a series of favors from our esteemed friend W———. Our poetical department has been lamentably deficient in original pieces, and needs to be replenished. This invitation, however, is made to *poets,* and to only such as deserve that name."

Before the year was past, Whittier began indeed to lay some claim to the title of poet; in the last three months of 1828 his grasp seemed for the first time nearly equal to his reach. It is of note that in two poems of conservative cast—**"The Times"** and **"The Days Gone By"**[77]—he began to find himself. "And yet I love the vanished past," he confessed, and so revealed again the core of his conservatism, the will to save the best in his environment, which lay at the heart of his whole life's work.

By October, too, Whittier had gained enough confidence in his work to give it in public the seal of his own name. In the *Haverhill Gazette* of October 25, 1828, **"The Outlaw"** was published as "By J. G. Whittier." Thenceforth, whenever Whittier's label was on his verses, it was usually represented by his name, his initials, or by "W." Earlier in the year he had continued to be "Adrian," "Donald," or "W.," but he soon called himself also "Nehemiah," "Timothy," "Ichabod," and "Micajah."

6

In many directions a young experimenter in verse, Whittier was possibly even more of an experimenter in prose, of which he wrote a prodigious amount during his years of literary apprenticeship. In 1828, his voluminous output of prose bore a direct and obvious relation to his reading at the Academy.

Little concerning this period, May to November, need be related. Presumably Whittier continued the studies which he had begun in the previous year. Certainly his economic habits were the same. To help pay his Academy expenses he posted the ledgers of a Haverhill merchant.[78] His abhorrence of educational debt was, indeed, a main factor in his inability to go on to college.[79] If, however, he frequently deplored the lack of books in his youth, Whittier seems never to have regretted the want of college training. He had warm respect for self-education, and in a letter written to a youth who requested financial help toward his schooling, Whittier said:

> I am sorry for the circumstance of thy condition for I have known what it is to be without money, & to live by hard labor. But, as to education, use thy leisure in *educating thyself.* Read & study a little every day, and before thee art 20 years of age, thee will find that a school is not needed. I regret that I cannot help all who ask help, as my means are limited & I have several dependent upon me. I enclose $5.00 with good wishes.[80]

As his previous habit was, Whittier during his second term at the Academy read with a catholic taste. Primarily, he was drawn to Milton even more strongly than before, and praised him heartily in an article which the *Haverhill Gazette* published on May 24, 1828. The strong early impression became permanent, for in 1866 Whittier wrote: "Milton's prose has long been my favorite reading. My whole life has felt the influence of his writings."[81] Whittier also conceived a lasting admiration for Milton as a man, and later, in "The Training," he wrote: "Blind Milton approaches nearly to my conception of a true hero."[82] By 1828 Whittier had also formed an enduring attachment to the works of Burns, whom he praised in two brief critiques in the *Gazette.* In that weekly he likewise devoted short notices to Shakespeare and others.

Meanwhile, amid all these excitements, Whittier's Quaker heart beat quietly on. On August 9 and 30, 1828, the *Gazette* published two editorials by him on war. Whittier invoked scholarship in aid of his firm, calm arguments, and he cited ancient examples of Christian testimony against the barbarity of armed conflict.

Very different was a short introductory article, breathless with awe, which in the *Gazette* of September 27 prefaced five thousand words of translation, which Whittier had read, from Johann August Apel's *Der Freischütz; or the Magic Balls.* Another strange fancy of Whittier's was reflected in an article, "Spectral Illusions," which the *Gazette* published on November 22. This prose piece manifested Whittier's wide acquaintance with the literature of the subject.

By that time Whittier had ended his studies at the Academy. In keeping with his literary thrift he commented upon the fact in an unsigned article, "Haverhill Academy," which appeared in the *American Manufacturer* of November 28. (Garrison had already procured from his former employer, the Reverend William Collier, an offer of the editorship of the *Manufacturer.*)[83]

The year 1828 was thus pivotal in Whittier's early development. During these twelve months he rose from his position as a schoolboy to the station of a steady contributor to Boston periodicals, in both verse and prose. His pedestrian pace was beginning to quicken into a running rhythm. It is true that he had not yet found his *métier,* but signs of it, moral as well as musical, were gradually appearing in his spate of verse. This served merely, in Browning's phrase, to "arrest Soul's evanescent moods." Yet it won for Whittier intermittent praise and encouragement which he needed.

Garrison, significantly, continued to keep his helpful hand and somewhat paternal eye upon the friend two years his junior. In the *National Philanthropist* of April 11 Whittier was the subject of his long editorial, "A Word for Indigent Merit."[84] Moreover, after Garrison had relinquished the editorship of that sheet on July 4 and had gone to Bennington, he continued to be interested in Whittier. This interest was reciprocal, for when Garrison started the *Journal of the Times* Whittier "wrote him a letter commending his views upon Slavery, Intemperance and War, and assuring him that he was destined to do great things."[85] Finally, in November, Garrison provided Whittier with his first editorial opportunity, in Boston.

It is important to remember that Garrison's broadening of social interests during 1828 was in the tide of humanitarian impulses then slowly swelling in the young nation. The American Peace Society, for example, was founded in 1828. Furthermore, on July 16 of that year the *Yankee,* edited by John Neal, who was of Quaker parentage, was early in the field with a forceful editorial on "Anti-Slavery Societies." Neal argued the futility of the American Colonization Society and urged New England to busy herself with constructive measures to meet the problem of slavery, if she wished longer "to be heard in the councils of the free."

Whittier, around whom incitements to social usefulness were perceptibly on the increase, was not yet quite ready to make himself heard in those councils.

Notes

1. "My Namesake," *Poetical Works,* II, 119.

2. Pickard, 43.

3. *Ibid.,* 44.

4. *Ibid.,* 46-47.

5. These are in the Henry E. Huntington Library, San Marino, Calif., and in vol. I of the Oak Knoll Collection, Essex Institute, Salem, Mass.

6. See Mordell, 10. Byron died in April, 1824.

7. Summer residents in Whittier's day included Louis Agassiz, Longfellow (whom Whittier visited), John Lothrop Motley, William Hickling Prescott,

and Daniel Webster. Nahant was sufficiently celebrated to attract there Harriet Martineau, who gave an appreciative description of the place in *Retrospect of Western Travel* (London, 1838), III, 140-147.

8. "A Retrospect," *Whittier-Land,* 35.

9. See John J. Currier, *History of Newburyport, Mass., 1764-1905* (Newburyport, 1906), I, 512-513. In *Prose Works,* III, 189, Whittier wrote (1879): "My father was a subscriber to his first paper, the *Free Press,* and the humanitarian tone of his editorials awakened a deep interest in our little household, which was increased by a visit which he made us."

10. In a note on "Early and Uncollected Verses" published as an Appendix to *Poetical Works,* IV, 301, Whittier said: "I suppose they should have died a natural death long ago, but their feline tenacity of life seems to contradict the theory of the 'survival of the fittest.' I have consented, at my publishers' request, to take the poor vagrants home and give them a more presentable appearance, in the hope that they may at least be of some interest to those who are curious enough to note the weak beginnings of the graduate of a small country district school, sixty years ago. That they met with some degree of favor at that time may be accounted for by the fact that the makers of verse were then few in number, with little competition in their unprofitable vocation, and that the standard of criticism was not discouragingly high."

11. It is printed in *Poetical Works,* IV, 301-302. The Quakers refrain from using the conventional names for the days and the months, on the ground that they have a pagan or a mythological basis unsanctioned by Scripture. Whittier habitually dated his letters in the Quaker style, as, e.g., that of "28th of 11th mo., 1828," to A. W. Thayer. See Pickard, 67.

12. Pickard, 47-48, tells how Whittier received the news of his first appearance in print: "The paper came to him when he was with his father mending a stone wall by the roadside, picking up and placing the stones in position. As they were thus engaged, the postman passed them on horseback, and tossed the paper to the young man. His heart stood still a moment when he saw his own verses. Such delight as his comes only once in the lifetime of any aspirant to literary fame. His father at last called to him to put up the paper, and keep at work. But he could not resist the temptation to take the paper again and again from his pocket to stare at his lines in print. He has said he was sure that he did not read a word of the poem all the time he looked at it."

13. At that time Whittier was in his nineteenth year.

14. Cf. Pickard, 48.

15. The full story of Garrison's visit is told in Pickard, 48-49, and in *Whittier-Land*, 36-37.

16. Cf. *William Lloyd Garrison: The Story of His Life, Told by His Children* (New York, 1885), I, 67-68; Pickard, 1894 ed., I, 52.

17. *Ibid.*

18. *Newburyport Free Press*, Dec. 2, Aug. 3, Nov. 18, July 27, 1826.

19. *Ibid.*, Sept. 7, 1826.

20. *Ibid.*, Aug. 10, July 13, and Nov. 18, 1826.

21. *Ibid.*, Aug. 31, 1826.

22. *Ibid.*, Dec. 2, 1826.

23. Whittier was sensitive upon this score. In a letter from Amesbury dated Feb. 28, 1871, a photostat of which is in the Essex Institute, he said, ". . . I did not work at shoe-making except [for] some few experiments in the winter between 16 & 18." But the evidence is conclusive that he did make women's slippers, in a typical small shoe-shop on the farm. Pickard mentioned the circumstances of that work (p. 51), as did the earliest biographer, W. S. Kennedy (1), 49. Kennedy's authority was Moses Emerson, one of Whittier's former teachers in the district school. F. H. Underwood, whose biography was written with Whittier's approval, also spoke (p. 68) of his shoe-making. Likewise, Rebecca I. Davis, in *Gleanings from Merrimac Valley*, Sheaf Number Two (Haverhill, 1886), 15-16, reported these remarks of her uncle, who was foreman of the shop for which Whittier did piecework: "Upon his first entrance I was strongly attracted by his honest, open countenance and manly bearing, and as the employer was somewhat loth to give out work to beginners, I took special pains to make every suggestion of improvement in my power, and he obtained employment as long as he wished."

24. *Rules of Discipline of the Yearly Meeting, Held on Rhode Island, for New England*, 127: "It is the renewed concern of this meeting, to recommend a care for the offspring of parents, whose earnings or income are so small, as to render them incapable of giving their children a suitable and guarded education. . . ."

25. In 1826 two maiden ladies of the town gave a half acre of land on the north side of what is now Winter Street as the site for an academy. Other interested citizens provided the money for the erection of the building. Chase, *History of Haverhill*, 496; *Haverhill Gazette*, Jan. 6, 1827.

26. See Appendix C.

27. The *Haverhill Gazette* was first issued on Jan. 6, 1821. On Feb. 1, 1823, it absorbed the old Democratic *Essex Patriot*, which had been started by Nathaniel Greene. He was later postmaster of Boston and he founded the *American* (Boston) *Statesman*, forerunner of the present-day *Boston Post*. After several changes of title, the *Haverhill Gazette* resumed that title on Jan. 7, 1837, and retains it today. I have used the name uniformly in this book.

28. Pickard, 50.

29. Albert L. Bartlett, *Some Memories of Old Haverhill* (Haverhill, 1915), 88-89; *Haverhill Gazette*, May 5, 1827; *Whittier-Land*, 7. In a letter of March 17, 1890, addressed to Mr. Bartlett and now in the possession of HPL, Whittier said: "I do not know where a copy of the Ode referred to can be found, and I feel very sure it would poorly repay any effort to recover it. My impression is that it would not add to the honorable record of the Academy."

   The dedicatory address at the exercises was made by the Honorable Leverett Saltonstall (Harvard 1802), of Salem, a lawyer and a member of Congress.

30. See Appendix C.

31. From a broadside *Catalogue of the Officers and Students of Haverhill Academy* (Haverhill, 1827), now owned by HPL.

32. Pickard, 50, 54-55.

33. Kennedy (2), 52-53; Underwood, 73-74.

34. Whittier, *Poetical Works*, II, 105. The first line correctly should read, "Where deed or word hath rendered less."

35. Quoted in Underwood, 75-78.

36. *Catalogue of Officers & Students of Haverhill Academy*; Pickard, 51.

37. Underwood, 73; Kennedy (2), 50 ff.

38. "A Retrospect," *Whittier-Land*, 35.

39. In a letter of Nov. 10, 1875, now in the possession of the HPL, addressed to Mayor Alpheus Currier of Haverhill on the occasion of the dedication of the HPL.

40. Quoted in Pickard, 57-58.

41. *Whittier-Land*, 66.

42. *Poetical Works*, II, 95-98.

43. The Connecticut Historical Society has a letter from Whittier to Lydia H. Sigourney dated Jan. (11?) 1833, in which he says: "I have warm &

deep & kind feelings. I believe there is not a particle of mysanthropy in my disposition: and I am more at peace with the whole world than myself, not that *I & myself* are much in the habit of quarrelling. But, I believe in the holy realities of friendship—pure—lofty—intellectual,—a communion of kindred affinities—of mental similitudes,—a redemption from the miserable fetters of human selfishness—a practical obedience to the beautiful injunction of our Common Friend—*'Love thy neighbor as thyself.'* I believe too, that the pure love which we feel for our friends, is a part & portion of that love which we owe & offer to our Creator, and is acceptable to him, inasmuch as it is offered not to the decaying elements of humanity, but to those brighter & holier attributes, which are of themselves the emanations of the Divinity,—to those pure emotions of the heart & those high capacities of the soul in which that Divinity is most clearly manifested;—and that, in proportion as we draw men to each other in the holy communion & unforbidden love of earthly friendship, we lessen the distance between our spirits and their Original Source,—just as the radii of a circle in approaching each other approach also their common centre."

44. *Whittier-Land,* 66.

45. See Appendix C.

46. *Rules of Discipline of the Yearly Meeting, Held on Rhode Island, for New England,* 65: "This meeting having deliberately considered the great exercise brought upon our society, by divers in profession with us, who are joined in marriage contrary to our known principles, and the wholesome discipline established among us, with persons either of our own or other persuasions, doth earnestly advise that all friends use their utmost endeavors to prevent such marriages, whensoever the parties' inclinations may come to their knowledge.

"And it is the sense and judgment of this meeting, that where any do marry, contrary to the established rules of the society, they should be dealt with in a spirit of Christian love and tenderness, agreeably to our known discipline."

47. *Whittier-Land,* 69.

48. *Poetical Works,* II, 69.

49. Oak Knoll Collection, V, 25.

50. *Whittier-Land,* 70-71.

51. Despite Governor Lincoln, the Association came into being, and took rank with the Handel and Haydn Society, which dated from 1815 in Boston. *Grove's Dictionary of Music and Musicians* (London, 3rd ed., 1927), I, 425.

52. *Haverhill Gazette,* March 17.

53. *Ibid.,* April 28, and May 5.

54. *Ibid.,* May 12, 1827.

55. *Poetical Works,* I, 11.

56. *Haverhill Gazette,* May 19, 1827.

57. *Ibid.,* July 28 and Sept. 29, 1827.

58. Ulrich Bonnell Phillips, *American Negro Slavery* (New York, 1918), 118-121.

59. *Haverhill Gazette,* July 7 and Aug. 4, 1827.

60. Fields, 24-29, and *Harper's New Monthly Magazine,* LXXXVI, 344 ff. (Feb. 1893).

61. *Oldtown Folks,* p. 321: "In the eyes of the New England people, it [Boston] was always a sort of mother-town,—a sacred city, the shrine of that religious enthusiasm which founded the States of New England. There were the graves of her prophets and her martyrs,—those who had given their lives through the hardships of that enterprise in so ungenial a climate."

62. *Rules of Discipline of the Yearly Meeting, Held on Rhode Island . . . ,* 52: ". . . it is advised that a watchful care be exercised over our youth, to prevent their going to stage-plays, horse-races, entertainments of music and dancing, or any such vain sports and pastimes. . . ."

63. Fields, 26.

64. Pickard, 41-42.

65. Manuscript records of the Committee of School District No. 5, West Amesbury. The school over which Whittier presided was accommodated in a house on Birch Meadow Road. Remodeled, the house is now occupied by Mr. Willard T. Kelly.

66. Aug. 23, 1830.

67. Manuscript records of the Committee of School District No. 5.

68. It was republished in *A New Year's Address to the Patrons of the Essex Gazette, 1828, With a Letter Hitherto Unpublished, by John G. Whittier* (Boston, 1903).

69. Chase, *History of Haverhill,* 634-635.

70. *Ibid.,* 498-499.

71. Whether or not he attended was not reported at the time.

72. Pickard, 92.

73. Mordell's statement that Whittier edited Dinsmoor's poems and wrote the preface to the book is open to doubt. The matter is covered in detail in J. A. Pollard, *Whittier's Early Years, 1807-1836* (Yale Ph.D. dissertation, 1937), 119-120.

74. *Boston Statesman,* May 1 and 3, June 14, 1828.

75. *Haverhill Gazette,* July 12 and Feb. 9, 1828.

76. *Ibid.,* Aug. 30, 1828.

77. *Ibid.,* Oct. 4 and 11, 1828.

78. Pickard, 64.

79. *Ibid.,* 67-68

80. Oak Knoll Collection, IV, 74. The letter is dated "28th Sept." from Danvers, and so is obviously of the year 1876 or later. It is addressed simply to "My friend."

81. Pickard, 506.

82. *Prose Works,* I, 348.

83. Pickard, 67.

84. See 41.

85. Carpenter, 300. Garrison, who was soon responsible for Whittier's entering anti-slavery work, was himself brought into it by the Quaker editor, Benjamin Lundy. See Garrison's editorial, Dec. 12, 1828, in the Bennington *Journal of the Times.*

Works Cited

Books frequently referred to in the following notes, under short titles only, are:

BENNETT: Whitman Bennett, *Whittier, Bard of Freedom* (Chapel Hill: University of North Carolina Press, 1941).

CARPENTER: George Rice Carpenter, *John Greenleaf Whittier.* American Men of Letters (Boston: Houghton Mifflin Co., 1903).

CLAFLIN: Mary B. Claflin, *Personal Recollections of John G. Whittier* (New York: Thomas Y. Crowell & Co., 1893).

CURRIER: Thomas Franklin Currier, *A Bibliography of John Greenleaf Whittier* (Cambridge: Harvard University Press, 1937).

FIELDS: Mrs. James T. Fields, *Whittier, Notes of His Life and of His Friendships* (New York: Harper & Bros., 1893).

HIGGINSON: Thomas Wentworth Higginson, *John Greenleaf Whittier.* English Men of Letters (New York: The Macmillan Co., 1902).

KENNEDY (1): W. Sloane Kennedy, *John Greenleaf Whittier: His Life, Genius, and Writings* (Chicago: The Werner Co., 1895 ed.). First issued in Boston, 1882.

KENNEDY (2): William Sloane Kennedy, *John G. Whittier, The Poet of Freedom.* American Reformers (New York: Funk & Wagnalls Co., 1892).

MORDELL: Albert Mordell, *Quaker Militant: John Greenleaf Whittier* (Boston: Houghton Mifflin Co., 1933).

PICKARD: Samuel T. Pickard, *Life and Letters of John Greenleaf Whittier* (Boston: Houghton Mifflin Co., 2 vols., 1894). The authorized biography. Unless otherwise indicated, reference is made to the 1-vol. 1907 revised edition.

POETICAL WORKS: Riverside Edition, *The Writings of John Greenleaf Whittier* (Boston: Houghton Mifflin Co., 1888).

PROSE WORKS: Vols. 1-4 include *Poetical Works*; vols. 5-7 the *Prose Works.*

SPARHAWK: Frances Campbell Sparhawk, *Whittier at Close Range* (Boston: The Riverdale Press, 1926).

UNDERWOOD: Francis H. Underwood, *John Greenleaf Whittier* (Boston: James R. Osgood Co., 1884).

WHITTIER-LAND: Samuel T. Pickard, *Whittier-Land, A Handbook of North Essex* (Boston: Houghton Mifflin Co., 1904).

WOODMAN: Mrs. Abby J. Woodman, *Reminiscences of John Greenleaf Whittier's Life at Oak Knoll* (Salem: The Essex Institute, 1908).

Short titles for libraries or collections most frequently referred to in the notes are as follows:

HPL: Whittier Collection, Haverhill (Mass.) Public Library.

HUL (Houghton): Collections, including the Pickard-Whittier papers, in Houghton Library, Harvard University.

OAK KNOLL COLLECTION: Special papers in the library of the Essex Institute, Salem, Mass.

Osborn T. Smallwood (essay date April 1950)

SOURCE: Smallwood, Osborn T. "The Historical Significance of Whittier's Anti-Slavery Poems as Reflected by their Political and Social Background." *Journal of Negro History* 35, no. 2 (April 1950): 150-73.

[*In the following essay, Smallwood discusses Whittier's contributions to the anti-slavery movement as a poet and journalist, but also as a militant activist in the abolitionist cause.*]

The fame of John Greenleaf Whittier as an abolitionist is based as much on the poems which he published attacking the evils of slavery as upon his physical labors with anti-slavery organizations. However, a thorough analysis of the poems with special reference to the political and social events which evoked them has heretofore been neglected. Such an analysis is the objective of this paper and is unusually rewarding, as the succeeding pages will show, in revealing the unique contribution to the cause of freedom made by this militant Quaker who combined in one person the qualities of agitator, journalist, politician, and poet.

I

John Greenleaf Whittier was a politician. Of that there can be no doubt. Mordell feels that he was "one of the ablest and shrewdest politicians we have ever had."[1] His political sagacity held him in good stead during his early work as an abolitionist, when he did not have a strong political party behind him. Pickard puts it this way: "Although a third party man and in a small minority until the Republican party came to power, his constant effort was to secure the election of either a Whig or Democrat, it mattered not which, from whom he could obtain a pledge of at least partial support of anti-slavery demands."[2] The problems which he faced as an abolitionist in seeking through political power to bring about the release of the slaves from their shackles gave him first hand information on the struggles of the abolitionists and formed the incentive for a number of the poems under consideration.

Prior to 1840 the abolitionists were not united on the matter of making abolition an issue in politics, but in this year the American Anti-Slavery Society was disrupted in New York, and a new organization, The American and Foreign Anti-Slavery Society, which favored political action, was formed. Whittier, as would be expected, was wholeheartedly in favor of the methods of this group. He had realized the necessity for political action years before, as can be seen from the poems which he wrote vigorously condemning the efforts that were being made to suppress free speech on the slavery issue. **"Stanzas for the Times,"** written in 1835, is such a poem. Whittier states that the **"Times"** referred to were those evil times of the pro-slavery meeting in Faneuil Hall, August 21, 1835, in which a demand was made for the suppression of free speech, lest it should endanger the foundation of commercial society. The poem was a caustic protest against this demand. The poet expressed the idea that it would be the worst thing imaginable for free men to remain quiet while the Negro was under the yoke:[3]

> Shall tongue be mute, when deeds are wrought
> Which might shame extremest hell?
> Shall freemen lock the indignant thought?
> Shall Pity's bosom cease to swell?
> Shall honor bleed?—shall Truth succumb?
> Shall pen, and press, and soul be dumb?

He concluded by bringing out that the free speech of the northerner will not be restricted to make slavery secure. Addressing the members of the meeting, he said,

> Rail on, then, brethren of the South,
> Ye shall not hear the truth the less;
> No seal is on the Yankee's mouth,
> No fetter on the Yankee's press!
> From our Green mountains to the sea,
> One voice shall thunder, we are free!

In the next year he again found it necessary to combat this threat. Upon the adoption of H. L. Pinkney's Resolution in the House of Representatives 'to the effect that Congress had no right to interfere with slavery in the United States, and ought not to interfere with it in the District of Columbia, and that, therefore, all resolutions which meant interference with slavery should be tabled without printing' together with John C. Calhoun's Resolution, which made it unlawful for a postmaster to deliver anti-slavery material in states where their circulation was forbidden, Whittier felt that it was necessary to protest again. He did so in **"A Summons."** In this poem he called upon the people of New England to fight and protest the action of Congress; and not henceforth ask as favors rights which were their own. He held that to remain silent at such a time was a crime, and pleaded with them to send forth their voices so that

> The millions who are gazing
> Sadly upon us from afar shall smile,
> And unto God devout thanksgiving raising
> Bless us the while.

About this same time another effort was made to obstruct the progress of the abolitionists when President Jackson delivered his message denouncing the abolitionists and calling for laws to restrain their activities.[4] When southern governors then made demands upon the governors of the North to punish the abolitionists in their states through new legislations, Governor Ritner of Pennsylvania courageously refused, and evoked Whittier's **"Ritner,"** in which he praises the Governor as a friend of freedom whose "lip is still free," and who refused to bow to the tyrants of the South. How sensitive Whittier was on the subject of the denial of the right of petition is shown in his lines on **"The New Year,"** addressed to the subscribers of the *Pennsylvania Freeman* in 1839. Atherton of New Hampshire had introduced a rule which the house had passed to the effect that all petitions relative to slavery should be received but neither read nor referred. To this act the poet alluded as he wrote:

> And he, the basest of the base,
> The vilest of the vile, whose name
> Embalmed in infinite disgrace,
> Is deathless in its shame![5]

As he depicted the struggles of the abolitionists, Whittier was particularly caustic in his condemnation of the clergymen and religious organizations who contributed toward intensifying those struggles. In one of his editorials entitled "The Methodist Church and Slavery" he pointed out that a conference of the Methodist Church condemned an abolitionist minister as a heretic. The journalist made it very clear that the clergyman was condemned "solely for his principles."[6] Toward the latter part of July, 1844, through an editorial in the *Middlesex Standard* entitled "Slavery and the Church," he attacked the clergymen who opposed abolition. He said, "Men who maintain the doctrine that slaveholding is a divine institution, and consistent with the holy attributes of the Deity, have no more claim to the character of Christian than the worshippers of the Scandinavian Odin, or the devotees of Brahma and Vishnu." He then charged them with worshipping a false god, "not the God of the Bible," but "a monster not outwardly fashioned of wood and stone, but a moral abomination originating in the mind of a slave-holding priesthood."[7] This disdain for religionists who upheld slavery is shown in a number of his poems dealing with various events, as will be shown later; but when, in September, 1835, he noticed an article in the Charleston, South Carolina, *Courier* to the effect that the clergy of all denominations had attended in a body a celebrated pro-slavery meeting in that city, "lending their sanction to the proceedings and adding by their presence to the impressive character of the scene,"[8] he was constrained to make a direct poetical attack upon them. **"Clerical Oppressors"** was the result. The contempt which the poet felt is expressed as he called these clergymen "paid hypocrites" who "preach and kidnap men:"

> How long, O Lord! how long
> Shall such a priesthood barter truth away,
> And in Thy name, for robbery and wrong
> At Thy own altars pray?

He concluded by calling a curse down on such a clergy and prayed God to

> Speed the moment on
> When wrong shall cease, and Liberty and Love
> And Truth and Right throughout the earth be known
> As in their home above.

The poems reflecting the struggles of the abolitionists occasionally took the form of personal tributes in which Whittier expressed his admiration for those who were working with him in the cause of freedom. One of the outstanding of such was his tribute to William Lloyd Garrison, which was read at the convention that formed the American Anti-Slavery Society in Philadelphia in 1833. He addressed Garrison as

> Champion of those who groan beneath
> Oppression's iron hand,

and encouraged him to continue his fearless stand against the advocates of slavery until

> The fetter's link be broken.

He expressed his love and admiration for the great abolitionist, and stated that his faith in Garrison was too strong to permit him to believe slanderers who said that Garrison was not sincere but was only seeking after fame. Whittier, therefore, concluded:

> Then onward with a martyr's zeal;
> And wait thy sure reward
> When man to man no more shall kneel,
> And God alone be Lord.

In 1834, besides being attacked by politicians and clergymen, the abolitionists were persecuted by the orators of the American Colonization Society, who were demanding that the free Negroes should be sent back to Africa and opposing emancipation unless expatriation followed. This opposition caused Whittier to write **"The Hunters of Men,"** in which he depicted the members of that organization as pseudo-philanthropists who were hypocritically more concerned about their own interests than about securing freedom for the slaves.

One of the first problems attacked by the abolitionists was the outlawing of slavery in the District of Columbia. In January, 1837, while he was living in Haverhill, Whittier decided to visit Washington to assist in the movement there, but on the way he learned that a new "gag" rule had been applied, and ended his journey at Philadelphia. From here he wrote to John Quincy Adams, commending him for bravely presenting a group of petitions against slavery in the District of Columbia. He also promised to get the "representatives of Massachusetts to enter their solemn and united protest" against the encroachments that had been made on the right of free speech. When President Martin Van Buren, in his Inaugural address took the position that he was definitely opposed to the abolishing of slavery in the District, Whittier prepared to go to Boston to use his influence to get the Legislature to pass resolutions in favor of abolition in the District. After his arrival he spent the whole month of March engaged in lobbying. He was successful in this effort because of the influence he had with old friends.[9] It was these efforts of his which he had in mind, no doubt, as he penned his **"At Washington,"** which was suggested by a visit to the city in December, 1845. He contrasted the fashionable dress of the Washingtonians with the misery of the slaves, and concluded with an exhortation that his countrymen should eradicate their misery. Unfortunately the objective of Whittier and his associates was not achieved until the country had been plunged into war. When, as the result of a series of measures due to the war, the slaves were freed, Whittier wrote his **"Astrea at the Capital"** in which he expressed this fact:

> Not as we hoped, in calm of prayer,
> The message of deliverance comes,
> But heralded by roll of drums
> On waves of battle troubled air.

Nevertheless, he called upon the friends of freedom to rejoice as

> Above our broken dreams and plans
> God lays, with wiser hand than man's
> The corner-stones of liberty.

In the midst of the agitation for the emancipation of the slaves of Washington the impulse of abolition was felt in Delaware, and the Legislature of that state, during the winter of 1846 and 1847, discussed a bill for the abolition of slavery. Whittier encouraged them to pass the bill with his **"To Delaware,"** in which he assured Delaware that the free states would be happy to welcome her into their number, and would sing,

> Glory and praise to God!
> Another State is free!

II

It was a principle of the abolitionists not only to seek to destroy slavery where it already existed in the Union, but to resist any attempt to spread the institution into the new territories that were being added to the country in the forties and the fifties. With this in mind one can easily see how the Texas question and its consequence, the Mexican War, presented a formidable problem to those in this struggle. Whittier was very quick to size up the situation and bring to bear his political shrewdness in an effort to prevent the admission of Texas into the Union as a slave state. A letter written by him in 1845, in the heat of the Anti-Texas campaign, illustrates his shrewdness as a politician. He saw the uselessness of contending against the admission of Texas as a territory, and would narrow the contest to the question of its coming in as a slave state. He wrote, "Let us not attempt impossibilities, but take our stand not against the *territory* of Texas, but its *slavery*. Let us confine ourselves to a simple remonstrance against the admission of Texas as a *slave state* into the Union. With this we can go before the people and, in spite of the office holders, we can carry them with us."[10] Mordell says that Whittier "feared a double calamity by the entrance of Texas into the Union—a victory for the cause of slavery and a war with Mexico."[11] The reformer used every means at his disposal—including lobbying and circulating petitions—to prevent annexation. In 1845 he turned his attention completely toward the Texas question and wrote a large number of editorials in which he called on the people to protest vigorously in conventions. Even after the cause was lost, and Texas was finally annexed in March, 1846, he sent an article which he had written to Alden Morse, of Essex County, "to circulate it with a petition for signatures against the admission of Texas as a slave state."[12]

When the Mexican war resulted from the annexation of Texas as Whittier had feared, he expressed his disapproval of the war in an editorial entitled "The Mexican War—Massachusetts," in which he commended Edward L. Keyes, Esq. of Dedham for introducing a resolution in the House of Representatives of Massachusetts to the effect that the Mexican war was being "waged, by a powerful nation against a weak neighbor, unnecessarily and without just cause, at immense cost of treasure and life, for the dismemberment of Mexico, and for the conquest of a portion of her territory, from which slavery has already been excluded, with the triple object of extending slavery, of strengthening the 'slave power,' and of obtaining the control of the free States, under the Constitution of the United States." The resolutions condemned the war, secondly, as a "war against freedom, against humanity, against justice . . . and *against the free States*." Thirdly, it was resolved that "our attention is directed anew to the wrong and 'enormity' of slavery, and to the tyranny and usurpation of the 'slave power' as displayed in the history of our country, particularly in the annexation of Texas and the present war with Mexico . . ." Whittier commented that these were "sound and honest resolutions expressive of the *real* feeling of the state on the subject."[13]

That the Quaker poet intended to use his pen in the battle to prevent the annexation of Texas as a slave state is shown in the letter which he wrote to Professor Wright in 1845. He said, "For one, so long as I can wield a pen, or lift a voice, I am willing to work; and if Texas comes in red with slavery, it shall not be my fault."[14] This resolution coupled with his political activities resulted in his writing a series of poems on the Texas question and the Mexican War. The first and foremost of these was **"Texas,"** written in 1844. In this poem he called upon all the lovers of freedom in the North to speak at this time and fight the spreading of slavery to Texas. With one voice they were to tell the South that patience was almost exhausted. He then warned the southerners that a continuance of slavery might

> Make our Union-bond a chain,
> Weak as tow in Freedom's strain
> Link by link shall snap in twain.

When that time came, the South would regret slavery:

> And when vengeance clouds your skies,
> Hither shall ye turn your eyes,
> As the lost on Paradise.

When a meeting of the citizens of Massachusetts, without distinction of party, who were opposed to the annexation of Texas, was called at Faneuil Hall in 1844 for the purpose of beginning decisive action against slavery, the poet wrote **"To Faneuil Hall"** to encourage the citizens to attend the meeting. He appealed to the members of all parties to forget party ties and come to Faneuil Hall to lend their voices to those who were protesting against slavery. He closed it:

Up, your banner leads the van,
Blazoned, "Liberty for all!"
Finish what your sires began!
Up, to Faneuil Hall!

In the same year he wrote his **"To Massachusetts"** appealing to the state to lend her influence to prevent the spread of slavery.

Shall thy line of battle falter,
With its allies just in view?
Oh, by Hearth and holy altar,
My fatherland, be true!
Fling abroad thy scrolls of Freedom!
Speed them onward far and fast!

At times Whittier used the activities of an enemy as an excuse for writing a poem on the question. Such a production was his **"To a Southern Statesman,"** written in dishonor of John C. Calhoun in 1846. Whittier also wrote a number of editorials on Calhoun. One of these in which he gave his estimate of the man was written as early as 1838. He depicted Calhoun as an individual of "mighty intellect" who had unfortunately given himself to the support of slavery. He said, "It is a mournful consideration that talents so extraordinary, and capabilities so vast, as those of John C. Calhoun should be almost exclusively devoted to the support of a system of slavery as cruel and as mean as ever existed in any part of the earth. . . . He has overcome all scruples—he has crucified his conscience—his humanity is dead within him—cold, stern, abstracted,—almost unearthly, he ministers at the altar of oppression—the High Priest of Slavery. . . ."[15] He showed this antipathy toward Calhoun in the poem. The South Carolina senator had objected to the government's acquiring the free territory of Oregon, because he feared foreign complications; but he had strongly urged the extension of slave territory by the annexation of Texas, even if it would involve a war with England. Whittier asserted that this Texas attitude of Calhoun's had become his nemesis which had now come back upon his own head, and might result in the acquiring of so much free territory in the West that this section together with the North would be able to destroy the evil of slavery in the Union.

After the annexation of Texas had precipitated the Mexican War, which ended in the acquiring of new lands from Mexico, Whittier again fired his cannon against the expansion of slave territory with **"The Crisis."** He pointed out in this poem that the country faced a crisis in having to decide whether the newly acquired land should be free or slave. He called upon his countrymen to renounce slavery as a crime of the old world and hasten the day when

The mighty West shall bless the East, and sea shall
answer sea,

And mountain unto mountain call, Praise God, for we
are free!

He continued:

Is this, O countrymen of mine, a day for us to sow
The soil of new-gained empire with slavery's seeds of
woe?
To feed with our fresh life-blood the Old World's
cast-off crime,
Dropped, like some monstrous early birth, from the
tired lap of time?
To run anew the evil race the old lost nations ran,
And die like them of unbelief of God, and wrong of
man?

III

The conflict over slavery had not only its two extremes, the abolitionists and the pro-slavery groups, but there were also persons, particularly statesmen, who were interested in bringing about compromises between both groups. The Fugitive Slave law of 1850 was a part of the efforts of such compromisers in Congress to placate the South and prevent secession. The law was calculated to assist southern slave owners to recapture runaway slaves. One historian, in giving its stipulations, says, "For the speedy capture of fugitives special federal commissioners were provided, and the United States Marshals and their deputies were injoined to aid; the procedure was simply proving the identity of the asserted slave to the satisfaction of the commissioner by *ex parte* evidence, excluding any testimony of the Negro whose freedom was at stake; the decision of the commissioner was final; and all good citizens were liable to be called upon to aid in enforcing the law under heavy penalties for refusal or for aiding the fugitive." This authority further states that the law was denounced in the North as "unconstitutional, immoral, unchristian, and abhorrent to every instinct of justice and religion."[16] Hundreds of protest meetings were held throughout the free states expressing this sentiment, and demanding its repeal. There were previous fugitive slave laws in force before this one was passed, but this one, which was introduced by Henry Clay, gave the South a more stringent law than ever before.

The acridity of Whittier's attitude toward fugitive laws had manifested itself in earlier poetic efforts. One of his earliest was **"Massachusetts to Virginia,"** written in 1843. In his introduction Whittier says that he wrote the poem on "reading an account of the proceedings of the citizens of Norfolk, Virginia, in reference to George Latimer, the alleged fugitive slave, who was seized in Boston without warrant at the request of James B. Grey, of Norfolk, claiming to be his master. The case caused great excitement north and south, and led to the presentation of a petition to Congress signed by more than fifty thousand citizens of Massachusetts, calling for such laws and proposed amendments to the Constitution as should relieve the Commonwealth from all further participation in the crime of oppression. George Latimer himself was finally given free papers for the sum of four hundred dollars."[17] In the poem the state of Massachusetts was pictured as a portion of the Union which was remaining true to the principles of freedom for which the Revolutionary War was fought while Virginia was not doing so, but was showing her "gallant ancestry." Then was brought out the fact that it was the voice of the free sons and daughters of Massachusetts which rose up in protest when "the prowling man-thief" sought to re-enslave Latimer. Whittier concluded by telling Virginia that slavery may be wrestled with down there,

> But for us and for our children, the vow which we
>   have given
> For freedom and humanity is registered in heaven;
> No slave hunt in our borders,—no pirate on our strand
> No fetters in the Bay State,—no slave upon our land.

Taking advantage of another incident to attack this law in 1846, the poet wrote **"The Branded Hand,"** in which he eulogized Captain Jonathan Walker of Massachusetts, who had been branded on his right hand with the letters "S. S." (slave-stealer) when he was assisting several fugitive slaves to escape. Whittier pictured him as a brave heroic seaman who suffered for the cause of freedom, and expressed the idea that the brand would become a prophecy of the freedom of the slaves.

> Lift that manly right-hand, bold ploughman of the
>   wave!
> Its branded palm shall prophesy, "Salvation to the
>   Slave!"

The Fugitive Slave Law of 1850 thus only served to intensify a resentment that had already been burning within the bosom of this enemy of slavery.

The bitterness of Whittier's attitude against the law can be seen from the fact that in 1850 he could have become State Senator, for the Democrats wanted to nominate him on the eventually victorious coalition ticket then being formed between them and the Free Soilers against the Whigs, but refused to run for any office on the grounds that as a public official he would have to support the new obnoxious law.[18] In declining the nomination he expressed his uncompromising opposition to the bill. He wrote, "Since the passage of the Fugitive Slave Law by Congress, I find myself in a position with respect to it, which, I fear, my fellow citizens generally are not prepared to justify. So far as that law is concerned, *I am a nullifier.* By no act or countenance or consent, of mine, shall that law be enforced in Massachusetts."[19] To create hostile sentiment against the bill and thereby possibly prevent it from becoming law, Whittier wrote **"A Sabbath Scene,"** a powerful poem,

in which he showed the cruelty that resulted from the compliance with the old law by the clergy. The scene of the poem is in a church. The parson is on his way to the pulpit when a fugitive girl, pursued by her master, runs into the church seeking safety. The minister calls on the deacon to trip her with the heavy Bible, and when she stumbles, and falls, he himself ties the knots to bind her. He then defends his course with Biblical texts, citing the return of Onesimus by Paul to his master, but he does not drown out the cries of the girl, as they can be clearly heard as she is led away. The poet expressed his abhorrence at this scene and said:

> My brain took fire: "Is this," I cried,
> "The end of prayer and preaching?
> Then down with pulpit, down with priest,
> And give us Nature's teaching."

As he observed the freedom of the birds and the flowers, nature's interpretation of God's word was brought home to his mind.

> For to my ear methought the breeze
> Bore freedom's blessed word on;
> Thus saith the Lord: Break every yoke,
> Undo the heavy burden!

When this effort failed, and the bill became law, Whittier took advantage of every opportunity to show his opposition. Daniel Webster had supported Henry Clay's bill in his Seventh-of-March speech, and at the same time denounced the abolitionists, censured all who did not admit the binding force of the law, and declared that "no man is at liberty to set up or affect to set up his own conscience above the law."[20] For this bit of oratory he earned the distinction of becoming the hero in Whittier's **"Ichabod."** Written in 1850 when Whittier was under the full force of the surprise and grief which he felt at the actions of the senator from Massachusetts, the poem castigated Webster as a man who had so disgraced, and dishonored himself that he was deserving of pity and should be lamented as dead:

> All else is gone; from those great eyes
> The soul has fled;
> When faith is lost, when honor dies,
> The man is dead!
> Then, pay the reverence of old days
> To his dead fame;
> Walk backward, with averted gaze,
> And hide the shame!

"The Rendition" was written when, in 1854, Anthony Burns, a fugitive slave from Virginia, was paraded down State Street in Boston to be returned to slavery. As thousands observed the humiliating spectacle, Whittier's heart was filled with disgust, and, as he says in the poem, it seemed to him that

> Liberty
> Marched handcuffed down that sworded street.

He closed **"The Rendition"** by calling upon the State of Massachusetts as the "Mother of Freedom" to rise with her strength and make right this wrong. However, his appeal appeared useless:

> Ah me! I spake but to the dead;
> I stood upon her grave.

When the following year the State of Massachusetts passed a bill to protect the rights and liberties of the people of the state against the Fugitive Slave Act, Whittier felt that the "Mother of Freedom" had arisen to the occasion, and **"Arisen at Last"** flowed from his pen. To his home state he said,

> Once more thy strong maternal arms
> Are round thy children flung,—
> A lioness that guards her young!

He retained the same attitude toward the state, when in 1857 he wrote **"Moloch in State Street."** In this poem he represented the public of Boston as persons who were making a human sacrifice to Moloch, in taking a fugitive slave, Thomas Sims, from a marshal and returning him to slavery. He places the sin at the door of the officers, not at that of the State of Massachusetts, which he exalts as a land of freedom:

> The brave old blood, quick flowing yet,
> Shall know no check,
> Till a free people's foot is set
> On Slavery's neck.

The same spirit of compromise which had prompted members of Congress to pass Henry Clay's fugitive slave bill motivated their passing the Kansas-Nebraska bill in 1854. When the bill became law, and thus provided for the entrance of the Kansas-Nebraska territory into the Union after it became a state "with or without slavery," Stephen C. Douglas introduced his "Popular Sovereignty." Southerners welcomed this as assurance that Kansas would come in as a slave state because of the heavy influx of immigrants from Missouri, the lower Mississippi Valley, Kentucky, and Tennessee. Thus they felt that the balance of power would be maintained. However, the anti-slavery men of the North were intent on preventing this, and a struggle for Kansas began. These Northerners, led by Eli Thayer of Worcester and supported by many of the wealthiest and most prominent men of Massachusetts, organized the New England Emigrant Society the purpose of which was "to assist the emigration of genuine settlers . . . who were unwilling to see Kansas made into a slave state; the society did not enlist men as recruits, but was ready to assist applicants by loaning capital for mills and hotels and by furnishing supplies and transportation." The first band of northern settlers reached Kansas in the summer of 1854, and others followed soon after. This organized immigration aroused indignation in the South and a strong feeling of antagonism developed between the two groups. The result was frequent bloodshed which almost brought on civil war in Kansas.[21]

These occurrences formed the background for a number of poetic expressions from Whittier's pen dealing with the problem. When the popular movement for emigration to Kansas began in 1854, he wrote **"The Kansas Emigrants,"** a poem in which he represented the emigrants as pioneers who were going to Kansas, the West, to make it the land of the free just as the Pilgrims had crossed the sea to make the East

> The Homestead of the free!

In the same year he wrote his **"Letter from a Missionary of the Methodist Episcopal Church, South, in Kansas, to a Distinguished Politician."** This poem is a satire on the ministers who defended slavery on a Christian basis. In the letter the minister puts the stamp of his blessing on slavery, praises God for converts who, in showing their Christianity,

> Have purchased Negroes and are settling down as
> sober Christians.

The abolitionists who are trying to break down "our institutions" are condemned. From its concluding lines, the tenor of the letter can be seen:

> You, I hear,
> Are on the eve of visiting Chicago,
> To fight with the wild beasts of Ephesus,
> Long John, and Dutch Free-Soilers. May your arm
> Be clothed with strength, and on your tongue be found
> The sweet soil of persuasion. So desires
> Your brother and co-laborer. Amen!

The skirmishes and bloodshed which the friction between the two groups brought about in Kansas was not unexpressed in Whittier's verse. The shooting of Thomas Barber, a Free Soiler, on December 6, 1855, near Lawrence, Kansas, was one of the incidents which evoked a poem from the militant Quaker's pen. In 1856, the following year, he wrote his **"Burial of Barber,"** in which he portrayed Barber as a martyr, and pleaded with the friends of freedom to have patience, as their suffering would lead to the freedom of the slaves. To these Free Soilers, he said,

> Lay him down in hope and faith,
> And above the broken sod,
> Once again, to Freedom's God,
> Pledge ourselves for life or death,
> That the State whose walls we lay,
> Shall be free from bonds of shame,
> And our goodly land untrod

By the feet of Slavery, shod
With cursing as with flame!

Two years later a group of Free Soilers, unarmed and unoffending, were massacred in Southern Kansas near the Marais du Cygne of the French *Voyageurs.* **"La Marais du Cygne"** resulted from this occurrence. In this poem the poet pictures the brutality of the massacre, and states that these persons did not die in vain as,

> On the lintels of Kansas
> That blood shall not dry;
> Henceforth the Bad angel
> Shall harmless go by;
> Henceforth to the sunset,
> Unchecked on her way,
> Shall Liberty follow
> The march of the day.

IV

The passing of the Kansas-Nebraska bill and the repeal of the Missouri Compromise so incensed the anti-slavery men of the North that they began a cry for a new party. The result was that "in Michigan a state mass convention at Jackson nominated on July 6, 1854, a mixed ticket of Whigs, Democrats, and Free Soilers, and adopted a new name, that of Republicans. Their resolutions . . . placed the new body squarely on an anti-slavery basis by declaring slavery a 'moral, social, and political evil,' and denouncing the repeal of the Missouri Compromise." The party also demanded the repeal of the Kansas-Nebraska Act and the Fugitive Slave Law.[22] The organization and growth of this party which was devoted to the cause of freedom served as the inspiration for Whittier's verse, just as the events which brought it into being had done. When the new party was conducting its first campaign under the candidacy of John C. Fremont, Whittier wrote **"A Song of the Time"** as one of his efforts to secure votes. In the poem he expressed the belief that those who refused to join the Free Soilers were slaves to those who oppose freedom as much as the slaves. He felt that the Free Soilers would win, because

> Wrong is so weak, and Right is so strong.

He, therefore, exhorted voters to

> Come forth all together! Come old and come young,
> Freedom's vote in each hand, and her song on each
>   tongue;
> Truth naked is stronger than Falsehood in mail;
> The Wrong cannot prosper, the Right cannot fail!

After the campaign ended with the election of Buchanan, but had shown the gains which the Free Soil party had made, Whittier wrote **"A Song Inscribed to the Fremont Clubs."** He exulted in the gains made by the party, and praised God for them. Envisioning the success of the party in 1860, he ended each stanza with the refrain:

> If months have well-nigh won the field,
> What may not four years do?

The dreams of the Quaker poet were realized in 1860 with the election of Abraham Lincoln. In 1861, Secretary of State William H. Seward made in the Senate a speech which was supposed to outline the policy of the Lincoln administration. It had not given entire satisfaction to the more radical wing of the anti-slavery party, and yet Whittier felt that it was as much as could be expected, considering the difficulties of the situation. Immediately following the address he wrote his sonnet, **"To William H. Seward."** He expressed confidence that Seward's speech was nobly meant even though he tried not to offend the South. Assurance was given to Seward that he would be forever blessed if he could thus

> Without damage to the sacred cause of Freedom,

save the Union from a "baptism of blood." To assure himself that Seward would not weaken, on February 1, 1861, Whittier wrote to W. S. Thayer, Washington correspondent of the *New York Evening Post*: "Tell Mr. Seward I have bound him to good behavior in my verse—and that if he yields the ground upon which the election was carried and consents to the further extension of slavery, he will 'compromise' *me* as well as the country."[23]

With the election of Lincoln the South realized that further compromise on the question of slavery was impossible, and one by one the slave states began to secede from the Union. Whittier felt that if they were willing to go that far to maintain their institution of human bondage, then they should be permitted to go in peace.[24] In January, 1861, he expressed his position in **"A Word for the Hour."** This poem suggested that if the South insisted on having slavery, it should be permitted to get out of the Union, and that the states should not go to war to prevent it.

> They break the links of Union; shall we light
> The fires of hell to weld anew the chain
> On that red anvil where each blow is pain?

He concluded,

> The golden cluster on our brave old flag
> In closer union, and, if numbering less,
> Brighter shall shine the stars which still remain.

A month after he wrote this poem, he was invited to attend a mass meeting in Boston to consider the political situation. In response he wrote to F. H. Underwood, "As to fighting, in any event to *force back* the seceders, I see no sense in it. Let them go with their mad experiment."[25] As it became evident that the Union would not consent to let the slave states secede peacefully, and the threatening dark cloud of the war hovered over the country, Whittier was inspired to pen **"Thy Will Be Done,"** in which he expressed the willingness to make the sacrifices which a civil war would demand, if God willed that such sacrifices had to be made for the cause of freedom.

> If, for the age to come, this hour
> Of trial hath vicarious power,
> And, blest by Thee, our present pain
> Be Liberty's eternal gain,
> Thy will be done!

It apparently was God's will, for the war came. Then Whittier felt that it was necessary to reassure his countrymen that the cause was worthy of the sacrifices demanded, and wrote **"Ein feste Burg ist unser Gott."** He told the fighters for freedom that God does not recast a nation painlessly. However, they were to realize that slavery was the threat to the life of the Union, and, therefore, all should cry,

> Let slavery die!

He assured them no sacrifice was too great to eradicate this curse. As the war progressed, the poet was given the occasion for another poem. General John C. Fremont issued his premature declaration in 1861 freeing the slaves of rebel slave owners in the State of Missouri. When his proclamation was countermanded by President Lincoln, Whittier comforted the General in **"To John C. Fremont"** by assuring him that he had simply acted

> A brave man's part, without the statesman's tact.

However, he concluded, the effort was not wasted, as it would act as a prophecy of the emancipation which was to come. As the fall of the second year of the war rolled around, the poet wrote **"The Battle Autumn of 1862,"** as he observed that nature sent the seasons as regularly as in peace time. He attributed nature's calmness in the midst of cannon fire to the fact that

> She sees with clearer eye than ours
> The good of suffering born—

and, therefore, he prayed,

> Oh, give to us her finer ear!
> Above this stormy din,
> We too would hear the bells of cheer
> Ring peace and freedom in.

The issuance of the Emancipation Proclamation on January 1, 1863, called forth **"The Proclamation"** from Whittier's pen. The poet here likened the emancipated slaves to Saint Patrick, who while escaping from slavery and finding his freedom, prayed that God would pardon his master. The slave later became a saint

> And, dying, gave
> The land a saint that lost him as a slave.

Whittier would have the emancipated slaves likewise to go forth and heap "coals of prayer" upon their oppressors' heads:

> Go forth, like him! Like him return again,
> To bless the land whereon in bitter pain
> Ye toiled at first,
> And heal with freedom what your slavery cursed.

Thirty days after the proclamation was given out by the President, the eradication of slavery from the land was completed by the passage of the Thirteenth Amendment, which abolished slavery. The ultimate goal of the abolitionists was represented in this amendment, and thus it occasioned Whittier's immortal **"Laus Deo."** The poem was suggested as he sat in the Friends' Meeting-House in Amesbury, and listened to the bells and the cannon which proclaimed the passage of the amendment. The poem expresses Whittier's recognition of the fact that the abolition of slavery was a work of God, and gives the sensations which he felt as he listened to the bells.

> It is done!
> Clang of bell and roar of gun
> Send the tidings up and down.
> How the belfries rock and reel!
> How the great guns, peal and peal,
> Fling the joy from town to town!
> Let us kneel:
> God's own voice is in that peal,
> And this spot is holy ground.
> Lord, forgive us! What are we,
> That our eyes this glory see,
> That our ears have heard the sound?

In the same year he wrote his **"Hymn for the Celebration of Emancipation at Newburyport,"** in which he recounted the struggle for freedom of the slaves, expressed the idea that the fight was motivated by the love of the country, and gave praise and glory to God for the accomplishment.

By the end of April, 1865, the war was over and the question as to how the rebel states were to be treated was the chief topic of discussion. In that year the Thirty-Ninth Congress was convened to consider the great question of reconstruction, and the status of those who had taken up arms against the Union. Whittier expressed his opinion in **"To the Thirty-Ninth Congress."** He encouraged Congress not to exact "conqueror's terms of shame," but to treat the vanquished southerners like a "rebel son," and demand that they

> Make all men peers before the law,
> Take hands from off the Negro's throat,
> Give black and white an equal vote.

He suggested that the South be told to forget the woes of the war, and the past,

Then shall the Union's mother heart
Her lost and wandering ones recall,
Forgiving and restoring all . . .

Whittier's anti-slavery poems had as their background the struggles of the abolitionists during the thirty years preceding the convening of the Thirty-Ninth Congress in 1865. These included the political activities which revolved around the Texas question and the Mexican War, the outrages of the fugitive slave laws, the Kansas-Nebraska struggle, the growth of the Republican party, the Civil War, the Emancipation Proclamation, and the passage of the Thirteenth Amendment to the Constitution. Viewed against this background, the poems possess a threefold significance. First, they represent an important contribution to that great body of protest literature which preceded emancipation and which was so effective in molding the public opinion that finally produced the election of the Republicans in 1860. Secondly, they reflect the attitude of abolitionists toward historical developments and toward the opinions of pro-slavery religious groups during the thirty years preceding emancipation. Thirdly, they point to the eminence of Whittier as a fighter for freedom.

Notes

1. A. Mordell, Preface, *Quaker Militant John Greenleaf Whittier* (Boston, 1933), p. xvi.

2. S. T. Pickard, *Whittier As a Politician* (Boston, 1900), pp. 2f.

3. All poems are quoted from *The Complete Poetical Works of John Greenleaf Whittier.* Cambridge ed. (Boston [cop. 1894]).

4. Mordell, *op. cit.,* p. 81.

5. J. Albree (ed.), Introduction, *Whittier Correspondence from the Oak Knoll Collections, 1830-1892* (Salem [Mass.], 1911), pp. 20-21.

6. *Pennsylvania Freeman,* April 26, 1838.

7. Quoted in Mordell, *op. cit.,* p. 135.

8. *Cf.* introduction to "Clerical Oppressors," *Poems, op cit.,* p. 272.

9. Mordell, *op. cit.,* pp. 85f.

10. Pickard, *op. cit.,* pp. 33f. Letter to Prof. Elizar Wright, October 10, 1845.

11. *Op. cit.,* p. 142.

12. *Ibid.,* pp. 142f.

13. *The National Era,* May 13, 1847.

14. Pickard, *op. cit.,* p. 35.

15. *Pennsylvania Freeman,* April 19, 1838.

16. T. C. Smith, *Parties and Slavery, 1850-1859* (New York [cop, 1906]), pp. 14-17.

17. *Poems, op. cit.,* pp. 287f.

18. Mordell, *op. cit.,* p. 158.

19. Allbree, *op. cit.,* pp. 113f.

20. Smith, *op. cit.,* p. 17.

21. *Ibid.,* pp. 94-108, 121-135.

22. *Ibid.,* pp. 110f. 161-173.

23. S. T. Pickard, *Life and Letters of John Greenleaf Whittier* (Boston, 1894), II, 435.

24. *Ibid.,* p. 436.

25. *Ibid.*

Joseph M. Ernest, Jr. (essay date May 1956)

SOURCE: Ernest, Jr., Joseph M. "Whittier and the 'Feminine Fifties.'" *American Literature* 28, no. 2 (May 1956): 184-96.

[*In the following essay, Ernest discusses Whittier's support and encouragement of contemporary female poets.*]

The fact that women writers in America were few before about 1840 and plentiful after about 1850 has been discussed at length in a book by Fred Lewis Pattee entitled *The Feminine Fifties.*[1] An additional fact, apparently never before clearly recognized, is that John Greenleaf Whittier, the saintly bachelor of Quakerdom, is due substantial credit for this phenomenon. To be sure, Whittier was not the only male member of the writing profession who was willing upon occasion to give a friendly word, a boost, and a cheer to the writing ladies. On the contrary, the chivalric Poe sometimes praised the books of Mrs. Sigourney, Mrs. Amelia Welby, and Mrs. R. S. Nichols in the 1830's and '40's;[2] Emerson gave some support to his friend Emma Lazarus;[3] and Lowell, in *A Fable for Critics*, praised Mrs. Child.[4] But the men in general felt that the "females" were encroaching upon a domain that did not belong to them. The attitude of some is implied in Dr. Holmes's disgusted query at the end of a too-discursive letter: "Am I a woman, that I should fill eight pagelets with less than nothing?"[5] Still more ungallantly, Hawthorne, astounded by the torrent of books produced by the authoresses in 1855, referred to the new writers as "a d———d mob of scribbling women."[6]

In contrast to most of his contemporaries during the 1850's and '60's, the very time when more and more women were devoting themselves to writing, Whittier stands out as a guide, philosopher, and friend to a number of the struggling neophytes. His appreciation of the intellectual and artistic talents of women came from the Quakers, who were leaders in the belief that both man and woman had access to spiritual inspiration, or the Inner Light. One remembers that in Quaker meetings the women are as free as the men to stand and testify when moved by the spirit. The Quaker woman—reserved, self-possessed, strong, but gentle, guided by calm faith and wisdom—is a well-known type. Whittier's household throughout most of his life consisted of his mother and his youngest sister, Elizabeth, both typical Quaker women. Elizabeth it was who read and criticized all of her brother's poems until her death in 1864. The poet not only counted heavily upon her approval of his work, but also encouraged her in the exercise of her own limited poetic talent. From his own home and his own religious denomination, he extended the boundaries of his interest outward to include the literary work of women in general.

The women, in turn, greatly appreciated Whittier, in more ways than one. The poet's biographers have always been impressed by his never-ending appeal to the other sex. First, his lithe, quick body, straight as a pine, his piercing black eyes and astonishing black eyebrows, which made a pleasing contrast in old age with a snow-white beard, and his frosty reserve, which melted into a wonderful smile, attracted all women. Second, these admirable characteristics were capped by the moral rectitude, the very aura of a Hebrew prophet. Third, and very important, Whittier could always "understand" women, or at least they thought he could. And last, Whittier was in a position to offer help in a very material way to beginning writers. His practical experience as a newspaper editor, his connection from 1847 until 1860 with the *National Era,* his wide-spread and ever-increasing popularity as a poet, and his considerable influence with editors and publishers (especially after the great financial success of his tremendously popular ***Snow-Bound*** in 1866) enabled him to be very useful to the women writers.

An authoress had only to request his help to obtain it, provided that he considered the general influence of the applicant and her work morally wholesome. From the 1830's to the 1890's he gave liberal encouragement and practical help to a great many female writers, including over a third of the forty-four women who, according to Pattee, gave a feminine cast to mid-nineteenth-century America.[7] To authoresses in all parts of the country, Whittier gave the much-needed appreciation of an intelligent and responsive reader; he complied with their requests for sympathetic criticism; and he aided them in finding publishers. He was not only ready to lend his own aid, but also willing, if possible, to enlist that of his friends, including Thomas Wentworth Higginson, Bayard Taylor, and, later, William Dean Howells.[8]

In order to determine the nature and the extent of Whittier's assistance to the bluestockings, I have read, in addition to the pertinent published material, several thousand letters to and by Whittier. These are scattered widely in libraries and private collections, the largest deposits being in the Houghton Library, Harvard; the Essex Historical Institute, Salem, Massachusetts; and the Henry E. Huntington Library.

Whittier began offering encouragement to women writers when he was a young newspaper editor in Boston and Hartford in 1829 and the early 1830's. He wrote letters praising the works of Mrs. Sigourney, Mrs. Hale, Mrs. Child, and Miss Sedgwick. No doubt his appreciation was pleasing to these established writers, but as an unknown young man he exerted slight influence upon them. Apparently the first of the many that he specifically helped was Lucy Hooper, a young poetess of abolitionist sympathies whom he met in Brooklyn in 1837. Declaring that her poems were superior to those of the famous Mrs. Sigourney, he urged her to more extensive efforts.[9] As editor of the *Pennsylvania Freeman* he published some of her work in 1838 with friendly editorial comment. Her volume published posthumously in 1848 was appreciatively reviewed by Whittier in the *National Era.*[10]

In the period 1840-1880 Whittier stood godfather to the works of a number of other poetesses. Just before the middle of the century he introduced to the reading public many of the early poems of Alice and Phoebe Cary, two young farm girls from Ohio, by opening to them the columns of the *National Era.* Their poems were collected in a volume in 1849. In his review Whittier proudly stated that he had been "one of the first to recognize the rare and delicate gifts of its young authors"; and he "cheerfully commend[ed] them and their volume to the public favor."[11] In 1850 the Cary sisters accepted his invitation to visit at Amesbury[12] and thereafter were his close personal friends. He introduced them to Longfellow and other literary people of Boston.[13] To anthologist Rufus Griswold[14] and to publisher James T. Fields, Whittier praised Alice's prose *Clovernook Sketches* and Phoebe's poems. The former volume Whittier boosted enthusiastically in the *Era* in 1851, predicting for it "a wide popularity" because it bore the "true stamp of genius";[15] the latter, he finally persuaded Fields to publish in 1853.[16] To help the poems along, Whittier also asked his friend Bayard Taylor to commend the book.[17] By interchanges of visits and by correspondence, Whittier continued to keep a fatherly eye upon the Carys, even after they had established a home in New York which became a gathering place for the literati.[18] Whittier's **"The Singer,"** written on the death of Alice Cary, mentions his early encouragement.

A true protégée was Lucy Larcom, a Massachusetts girl who, under his encouragement, turned author also in the 1840's. Miss Larcom had admired Whittier ever after coming across a volume of his poems while she was employed in a textile mill. The poet later had visited her place of employment and roused her ambition by commending some of her writing in the *Lowell Offering*.[19] She forsook the mill to become a teacher in Illinois, whence in the late 1840's she sent some of her poems to Whittier for publication in the *Era.* These were printed, with his editorial praise. In 1853 he succeeded in persuading Fields to publish her early pieces in a volume, entitled *Similitudes from the Ocean and the Prairie*,[20] which Whittier praised in the *Era.*[21]

Thereafter, Miss Larcom, at Whittier's insistence, sent her manuscripts to him for revision. Her pride finally rebelled, however, and she wrote, "You have taught me all that I ought to ask. . . . Why should I always write with you holding my hand?"[22] Nevertheless, he remained her advisor. Their extensive extant correspondence[23] indicates that she sought his advice about her stories, poems, books, and financial affairs. They exchanged visits often. He encouraged her to write, praised her work, and urged Fields to publish other volumes of her poems. After repeated attempts,[24] Whittier was successful in this endeavor in 1868, and a volume appeared with an advertising leaflet that he wrote himself.[25] To further insure the favorable reception of this foster child, the Quaker poet asked T. W. Higginson to review the book sympathetically.[26]

To other people also Whittier boosted Miss Larcom's work; Harriet Minot Pitman, William Dean Howells, Oliver Wendell Holmes, and Celia Thaxter received his letters of praise for her various poems and books.[27] Houghton, Mifflin published collected editions of her verse again in 1881 and 1885. The Library of Congress now has at least seventeen volumes bearing her name, including miscellaneous books which she edited. For a number of years she worked with J. T. Trowbridge as an editor of *Our Young Folks.* And it is to her credit that Whittier chose her as his only literary partner; she helped him with his two collections known as **Child Life** in 1871 and 1873 and his **Songs of Three Centuries** in 1875. Whatever mark she made in the literary world, however, in due to Whittier himself.[28] Today she is known as "a lesser Whittier."[29]

Still other poetesses encouraged and supported by Whittier, though to a somewhat lesser extent, were Julia Ward Howe, Edna Dean Proctor, Harriet McEwen Kimball, Annie Adams Fields, and Nora Perry. Publicly and privately he commended Mrs. Howe's initial volume, *Passion Flowers* (1853). Emerson and others received this book well, but nobody more enthusiastically than Whittier. He wrote, "It is a great book; it has placed thee at the head of us all."[30] He also praised the book in letters to Fields and Bayard Taylor. Whittier asked Taylor to "say a good word" for it.[31]

With Miss Proctor, Whittier initiated a correspondence, praising enthusiastically her poems, which were beginning to appear in the *Independent* in the early 1860's. It is said that he considered her perhaps the best poetess of her day.[32] Once when she had not published anything for a time, he wrote, "I wonder thee does not write more, and how thee can keep so good a pen as thine still, I cannot conjecture."[33] Again he queried, "Why don't thee write more? That little clover blossom in the 'Youth's Companion' was a perfect gem."[34] With his permission she printed in a New York newspaper his epistolary praise of her poem "El Mahdi," and at her request he seems to have used his influence with Houghton, Mifflin Company to effect the publication of the first of several volumes of her poetry and prose.[35] One of her poems, "The Morning Star," is addressed to him.[36]

In regard to Miss Kimball, Whittier forwarded several of her poems to Fields for the *Atlantic* in the 1860's. He was well acquainted with her and knew that she was too shy to send them herself.[37] When a volume of her verses, entitled *Hymns,* was published at the close of the war, Whittier wrote, "To me it is better than anything of Vaughn [*sic*] or Herbert, excepting a very few pieces of the latter."[38] Eventually she produced half a dozen volumes of verse.

Simultaneously with Miss Kimball, Mrs. Fields, the wife of the publisher, was entering the writing field with a poem now and then in the *Atlantic*. Whittier was a close friend of Mr. and Mrs. Fields for many years and often visited in their elegant Boston home. He was always an appreciative reader of his hostess's poems and usually quick to praise them. A voluminous extant correspondence at the Huntington Library (Fields papers)[39] attests Whittier's warm encouragement and her reverent appreciation for it. Her literary output was large; the Library of Congress now has twelve volumes of her verse and prose. She was not, however, as clearly indebted to Whittier for assistance as were several others.

Nora Perry was already publishing poems and stories in 1869 when Whittier praised her verses "After the Ball" and urged her to write more poems like it. She gladly complied, and he read and criticized several of her subsequent efforts. She asked in 1872 that he recommend to the J. R. Osgood Company the publication of her poetry. Apparently he did so, for in 1873 she and Mr. Osgood came to Whittier's house to discuss the forthcoming book (*After the Ball and Other Poems*, 1875). She requested Whittier's permission to dedicate it to him and also asked him to review it. But Howells wrote the desired review, for which Whittier thanked him.[40] Afterwards she sent copies of her other books—there were over a dozen—and he consistently praised them. Just before his death she wrote him this testimony, which expresses well the general attitude of Whittier's neophytes to their mentor:

I remember years ago from the first, I had the most perfect feeling of ease and confidence with you—a feeling that I could say anything to you, & you would never, that you couldn't, misunderstand. As the years have gone on this feeling has been the same under all conditions. . . .[41]

In addition there were several of Whittier's literary protégées who devoted themselves largely to essays or prose sketches, including Mary Abigail Dodge ("Gail Hamilton"), Sara Jane Clarke Lippincott ("Grace Greenwood"), and Celia Thaxter. Perhaps "protégée" is not quite the word for Miss Dodge, a witty and vivacious newspaper woman. She was undeniably in love with Whittier but took great delight in laughing at his unresponsive, dignified reserve. Her delightful letters contain much baby talk and many terms of endearment, all of which were humorously incongruent to the frosty old bachelor. She called him "dear little darling," "My dear Sheikh," etc. He admired her books, which were collections of essays, political and otherwise, and praised them year after year, from first acquaintance in the 1850's onward. But she was self-reliant and her mind was her own; probably Whittier had little influence upon her career,[42] as he implied in his poem written on the flyleaf of one of her volumes.[43]

By contrast, Mrs. Lippincott, another of the essayists, testified in 1851 that Whittier's influence on both her literary life and her private life was stronger than that of any other person except her mother.[44] This testimony throws light upon Whittier's relationship to the "feminine fifties" in general, for Mrs. Lippincott is considered by Pattee so typical of the decade that he uses a full-page portrait of her as the frontispiece of his book. She also was an abolitionist. As early as 1848 Whittier's notices in the *Era* warmly praised some of her works, including the poem "Ariadne." Before publication she consulted him in regard to the title of her best book, *Greenwood Leaves* (1850), a volume of sketches that he later praised enthusiastically in the *Era*. Other books by Mrs. Lippincott appeared in the early 1850's and received in their turn his editorial boosts—*History of My Pets, Greenwood Leaves* (second series), *Haps and Mishaps of a Tour in Europe*.[45] In letters to Mrs. Fields several years later, Whittier praised Mrs. Lippincott's *Records of Five Years* and urged that Mrs. Fields ask her publisher husband to accept for the *Atlantic Monthly* a poem by the physically ailing authoress.[46] For forty years Mrs. Lippincott enjoyed "cozy visits" with Whittier and discussed with him her writing. From the first she considered him her ideal poet, "one who might answer to all I required of the poet of to-day."[47]

Somewhat less outspokenly responsive, perhaps, but even more a protégée was Celia Thaxter, who wrote numerous volumes of both prose and verse. When Whit-tier met her in 1863 she had already begun to publish sketches, verse, and children's stories in periodicals. He immediately urged her to write more, declaring that she had genius and it was her destiny to become an author. He sent copies of her books to such people as Paul Hamilton Hayne and Elizabeth Stuart Phelps.[48] Ten years after their first meeting Whittier wrote Mrs. Thaxter: "Everybody now reads thy poems. Thee have become famous, and I am glad to have had the public confirm my early impressions." Again, "More and more I congratulate myself on my share in urging thee to 'exercise thy gift,' as we Friends say. . . ."[49] Though she had already "become famous," he continued urging her to greater literary activity. Over a period of years she sent a number of her poems to him for criticism. He always responded with sympathetic and helpful comments. Without his prodding, one of her best books, a collection of prose sketches entitled *Among the Isles of Shoals* (1873), would probably never have been written. In 1869, thinking that her long letters to him describing her home on the Isles of Shoals were interesting enough to warrant publication, he suggested that she send some of them to the *Atlantic*. She said later that he gave her no peace until she began a series of such articles in 1870. During the serial publication of the articles he encouraged her with praise, once referring to a recent paper as "one of the most delicious bits of prose writing I have ever seen." Following his suggestion in 1871 to publish the series as a volume, she sent the proof sheets for his criticism. The book was duly published, and Whittier recommended it to his friends, including Mrs. Fields and Mr. Howells. He asked the latter to "say a good word for it," adding, "It has all the charm of Thoreau and White of Selborne."[50] It is no wonder that Mrs. Thaxter considered Whittier's interest and help "perfectly invaluable" to her writing.[51]

No less was Whittier a friend to some of the women who wrote fiction. One of the first of all the struggling "females" to be befriended by the poet was a teacher, Mrs. E. D. E. N. Southworth, whom he met in Washington about 1847.[52] After reading several of her first manuscripts, Whittier recommended to Dr. Bailey, editor of the *National Era,* with which Whittier himself was connected, that she be employed for a weekly contribution to the paper.[53] In a review of her book *Retribution, or The Vale of Shadows* in 1849, Whittier compared the book favorably to *Jane Eyre* and the work of Charles Brockden Brown. He then advised her to forsake school teaching in favor of full-time novel writing, a step which she took.[54] In 1856 he wrote an appreciative review of her novel *India, or The Pearl of Pearl River.* As a guest in her Washington home in 1863 he offered helpful criticism of the plot of *Ishmael,* another story upon which she was working. She later declared that this book owed much of its success to his criticism.[55] It is said that she ultimately wrote fifty or sixty novels in which, following Whittier's advice, she made her virtuous characters uniformly successful in their endeavors.[56]

A close friend of Whittier's for many years was Elizabeth Stuart Phelps, who wrote fiction of the imaginative and religious cast most likely to appeal to the old Quaker. He met her in 1868, when his warm letter of congratulation upon her first story in the *Atlantic* elicited the response, "There is nobody in the world—except my father—whom I would rather have like my little story than you."[57] The old poet and the young story writer soon found that they had various things in common: interest in reform and religion, trouble with insomnia, and love of literature. For many years she sent work to Whittier for criticism and each time received a sympathetic response. He said that she had genius and brought her work to the attention of other literary people. Once he asked Lucy Larcom to write a favorable review of one of Miss Phelps's books.[58] The quality of Whittier's enthusiastic reception is illustrated by this statement from his letter in regard to her book *Sealed Orders*: "No volume of the kind since Hawthorne's *Twice-Told Tales* can compare with thine—and morally and spiritually thine is far better than his."[59] Miss Phelps said later that Whittier's friendship was "one of the inspirations" of her life.[60]

The chief woman writer of fiction and also the most important authoress whose career was advanced by Whittier's friendship, however, was his last real protégée, Sarah Orne Jewett. Whittier had the privilege of being, as he said, "one of the first to discover her."[61] Meeting in Boston about 1877, after she had written her first book, they formed a comradeship that lasted until his death fifteen years later. He found her "fresh, natural, lovable."[62] Old enough to be her grandfather, he enjoyed referring to her in fun as his "adopted daughter."[63] She returned his affection, declaring, "I really belong to you more lovingly every year."[64]

She spent part of her time in leisurely visits with her close friend Mrs. Fields. By interchanges of letters and visits, and through Mrs. Fields, Whittier always maintained contact with "dear Sarah."[65] An example of his constant interest is his poem **"Godspeed,"**[66] a farewell to her and Mrs. Fields on their departure for a trip abroad in 1882.

Whittier was a great admirer of Miss Jewett's work. Her first book, *Deephaven,* so appealed to him that he admitted having read it half a dozen times.[67] Her most treasured letter among the congratulations received upon the publication of this book was from Whittier. In it he stated, "I know of nothing better in our literature of the kind, though it recalls Miss Mitford's 'Our Village' and 'The Chronicles of Carlingford.' I heartily congratulate thee on thy complete success. . . ."[68] He sent copies of her books to some of his correspondents.[69] At his

favorite summer boarding places in New Hampshire, he liked to sit under the pines with friends while someone read aloud from Sarah's latest story.[70] As soon as Sarah finished one story Whittier would be after her to begin a new one. He was sure to appreciate each story for the best qualities she tried to put into it. His unflagging interest and praise served to cheer her out of occasional moods of despondency.[71]

Some of her works owed their existence directly to Whittier. Her story "The Courting of Sister Wisby" was developed from a suggestion of Whittier's.[72] She said that he was the inspiration of her book *The King of Folly Island* and that it owed even its title to him; therefore she dedicated it to him.[73]

Conscious of the enviable position she occupied as Whittier's protégée during the years of his greatest influence, she did what she could to express her appreciation for the "help" that he had been in all her "story-writing years."[74] She pleased him by declaring that their bonds of affection were growing stronger year by year.[75] She offered to nurse him when he was ill.[76] Near the end of his life, she expressed regret at her inability to be "what [she had] wished to be" to Whittier.[77] She wrote a fifty-six-line poem to him, entitled "The Eagle Trees," praising his character and his poetic genius. This poem is built around the metaphor of great pines which tower into the heavens but yet are deeply rooted in their native soil.[78] She voiced the same idea again in a prose tribute to Whittier in the Boston *Journal* on the occasion of his eighty-fourth birthday:

> The joy is ours of being sure that . . . he is growing yet, like one of our noblest forest trees, some great pine. . . . The roots of the great landmark cling fast to the strong New England ledges, but its green top, where singing birds come and go, is held high to the sunshine and winds in clearest air.[79]

This emphasis upon the local-color quality of the poet points up the essential correspondence between his literary genius and hers; for her best book, *The Country of the Pointed Firs,* published five years later, is an outstanding example of New-England local-color writing. Who can doubt that when she gave this title to her masterpiece four years after Whittier's death she was inspired again by her conception, twice expressed previously, of the sturdy New England poet of the "Eagle Trees"?

The women named above are only a few of the many who profited by Whittier's friendship. To a lesser degree numerous others owed a measure of literary success to his good will: Lydia Maria Child, Julia C. R. Dorr, Charlotte Forten, Mrs. A. D. T. Whitney, Miss E. C. Wingate ("Feärn Gray"), Mrs. Elizabeth L. Kinney, Frances C. Sparhawk, Mary E. Pratt, Laura S. Haviland, Harriet Maxwell Converse, Frances E. Willard,

Jessie Fremont, Ina Coolbrith, and others. For some, he gained access to the pages of the august *Atlantic Monthly*; to others he gave generous criticism and encouragement; for still others, he wrote advertisements to advance the sale of their books. Without Whittier, indeed, the "Feminine Fifties" would not have been so feminine, nor the sixties, seventies, and eighties either.

Notes

1. (New York, 1940).

2. See Edgar Allan Poe, *Complete Works,* ed. James A. Harrison (New York, 1902), VIII, 122; IX, 146; XI, 275; XII, 110, etc.

3. See *The Letters of Ralph Waldo Emerson,* ed. Ralph L. Rusk (New York, 1939), VI, 90; VI, 144, etc.

4. See James Russell Lowell, *Writings,* Riverside Ed. (Boston, 1895), IX, 74-78.

5. Fred Lewis Pattee, *The Feminine Fifties,* pp. 99-100.

6. *Ibid.,* p. 110.

7. *Ibid., passim.*

8. See Whittier's letters to Higginson, Oct. 20, 1868 (MS, Huntington Library); to Taylor, in S. T. Pickard, *Life and Letters of John Greenleaf Whittier* (Boston, 1894), I, 367; and to Howells, May 12, 1873, and Nov. 24, 1874 (MSS, Harvard Library). To simplify the numerous citations of letters hereafter, I have used the following formulae: "W" means a letter by Whittier, "T" means a letter by Thaxter (used only in the section devoted to Thaxter), etc. Following the initial will be the date or the letters "n.d." for "no date given" (dates supplied by the present writer are enclosed in brackets). Third is the library where the letter may be seen, abbreviated as follows: "H" for Huntington, "HU" for Harvard, and "E" for Essex Historical Institute, Salem, Mass. Thus, "W 8-1-68 H" indicates a letter by Whittier dated Aug. 1, 1868, in the Huntington Library.

9. See W 8-27-37, in A. S. W. Rosenbach, *A Catalogue of the Books and Manuscripts of Harry Elkins Widener* (Philadelphia, 1918), II, 272. A collection of Whittier-Hooper correspondence appears in Albert Mordell, "Whittier and Lucy Hooper," *New England Quarterly,* VII, 316-325 (June, 1934).

10. See the review in *Whittier on Writers and Writing: The Uncollected Critical Writings of John Greenleaf Whittier,* ed. E. H. Cady and H. H. Clark (Ithaca, 1950), p. 139.

11. *Ibid.,* pp. 156-157.

12. Frances C. Sparhawk, *Whittier at Close Range* (Boston, 1925), pp. 65-66; and T. W. Higginson, *John Greenleaf Whittier* (New York, 1926), pp. 108-109.

13. W 8-12-52 Longfellow House, Cambridge; W 8-12-52 N. Y. Pub. Lib.

14. Clara P. Marcy, "The Literary Criticism of John Greenleaf Whittier," unpubl. diss., Boston Univ., 1946, p. 281.

15. *Whittier on Writers and Writing,* p. 185.

16. W 1-8-53 H; Fields 1-9-53 E.

17. Pickard, *Life,* I, 367.

18. Albert Mordell, *Quaker Militant: John Greenleaf Whittier* (Boston, 1933), p. 272. See also Higginson, *Life,* p. 98, and Higginson 8-1-71 HU.

19. Lucy Larcom, *A New England Girlhood Outlined from Memory* (Boston, 1889), *passim.*

20. Mrs. James T. Fields, "Whittier: Notes of His Life and of His Friendships," *Harper's Magazine,* LXXXVI, 341 (Feb., 1893).

21. *Whittier on Writers and Writing,* p. 213.

22. D. D. Addison, *Lucy Larcom: Life, Letters, and Diary* (Boston, 1897), p. 68.

23. The chief collection is at Harvard.

24. W 10-8-60 H, W 12-28-66 H, W 2-15-67 H, W 8-20-68 H, etc.

25. T. F. Currier, *A Bibliography of John Greenleaf Whittier* (Cambridge, 1937), p. 110.

26. W 10-20-68 H.

27. W 11-24- and 11-30-68 C. Marshall Taylor Coll., N. Y. (photostats); W 11-24-74 HU; W 11-14-80 Addison, *Lucy Larcom,* p. 198; W 1-18-81 HU.

28. His fatherly care may be seen in the fact that when she became poverty-stricken and ill in the 1880's he solicited donations from friends in order to establish an annuity for her. See Mrs. Fields 9-19-83 HU; H. M. Pitman 11-2-83 HU; S. Maria Parsons 12-17-83 HU; and George W. Childs 1-31-87 HU.

29. Stanley J. Kunitz and Howard Haycraft, eds., *American Authors, 1600-1900: A Biographical Dictionary of American Literature* (New York, 1938), *s.v.* "Larcom, Lucy."

30. Laura E. Richard and Maude Howe Elliott, *Julia Ward Howe, 1819-1910* (Boston, 1925), p. 67.

31. W n.d. H (to Fields), and Pickard, *Life,* I, 367 (to Taylor).

32. Mordell, *Quaker Militant,* pp. 238-240.

33. Pickard, *op. cit.,* II, 605.

34. W 4-26-78 New Hampshire Hist. Soc.

35. P n.d. [Apr. 1884] HU; P 4-19- [84] HU; P 3-7-[87] HU.

36. The manuscript of this poem is at Harvard, among the Pickard-Whittier papers.

37. K 6-2-62 HU; W n.d. H (to Fields).

38. Pickard, *op. cit.,* II, 486.

39. See also Mrs. Fields' reminiscences, above, n. 20.

40. W 11-24-74 HU (to Howells).

41. P 5-27-92 HU. See also her correspondence with Whittier 1869-1892 in Essex Inst and Harvard; and Nora Perry, "A Personal Sketch of Whittier," in F. H. Underwood *John Greenleaf Whittier: A Biography* (Boston, 1892).

42. See a collection of her sparkling letters to Whittier in the *Ladies' Home Journal,* XVII, 7-8 (Dec., 1899), 9-10 (Jan., 1900). An account of their relationship emphasizing the love interest is contained in Mordell, *Quaker Militant,* pp. 225-235. See also Pickard, *op. cit.,* II, 573, 577, 630, and 645-646, for Whittier's references to her political articles, to which he mildly objected.

43. *The Complete Writings of John Greenleaf Whittier,* Amesbury Ed. (Boston, 1894), IV, 114-117.

44. L 9-24-51 E.

45. See L 4-11-49 E and *Whittier on Writers and Writing,* pp. 157-162, 180-181, 187-188, 213.

46. W 2-15-67 H, W n.d. H.

47. The term "cozy" in reference to her visits is used by Whittier in a letter to his friend Elizabeth Nicholson, Feb. 4, 1853, in Edward D. Snyder, "Whittier Returns to Philadelphia after a Hundred Years," *Pennsylvania Magazine of History and Biography,* LXII, 157 (April, 1938). See also L 2-18-50 E and L 9-24-51 E.

48. See W n.d. H (to Mrs. Fields); W 5-21-72 HU (to Mrs. Thaxter); W 2-5-73 Duke Univ. Lib. and W 12-5-73 Duke (to Hayne); and W 2-26-72 C. Marshall Taylor Coll., N. Y. (to Miss Phelps).

49. W 9-26-74 HU; and W 3-?-75 in Pickard, *op. cit.,* II, 600.

50. W 4-28-[69] HU; W n.d. [1870] HU; W 5-12-71 HU; W 3-30-72 H; W 5-12-73 HU; and Pickard, *op. cit.,* II, 520, 564.

51. T 4-1-72 HU.

52. Regis Louise Boyle, *Mrs. E. D. E. N. Southworth: Novelist* (Washington, 1939), p. 8.

53. See Pickard, *op. cit.,* I, 344, and Marcy, *op. cit.,* p. 192.

54. See *Whittier on Writers and Writing,* p. 153; and Pattee, *op. cit.,* p. 123.

55. Boyle, *op. cit.,* pp. 16, 58.

56. Marcy, *op. cit.,* p. 192.

57. Elizabeth Stuart Phelps, *Chapters from a Life* (Boston, 1896), pp. 92-93. See also P 3-13-68 HU.

58. W 3-7-79 C. Marshall Taylor Coll.; W 12-18-78 H. See also Pickard, *op. cit.,* II, 563.

59. Marcy, *op. cit.,* p. 284.

60. Phelps, *op. cit.,* p. 160.

61. W 7-25-82 HU.

62. W n.d. H (to Mrs. Fields).

63. See his letters to Mrs. Fields in Huntington Library.

64. J n.d. HU.

65. See the Fields papers, Huntington Library.

66. *The Complete Writings,* IV, 218-219.

67. Pickard, *op. cit.,* II, 654.

68. Francis O. Matthiessen, *Sarah Orne Jewett* (Boston, 1929), p. 56.

69. See, for example, W 12-25-79 Yale University Library, and W 6-28-85 H.

70. Pickard, II, 688.

71. See Mrs. Fields n.d. [Oct. 1886?] HU.

72. See W 4-21-[87] H.

73. See J 5-27-[88] HU.

74. *Ibid.*

75. J n.d. HU.

76. J n.d. [Oct. 1889?] HU.

77. J 12-13-90 HU.

78. First published in Carl J. Weber, "Whittier and Sarah Orne Jewett," *New England Quarterly,* XVIII, 403-404 (June, 1945).

79. *Ibid.,* p. 405.

Lewis Leary (essay date 1961)

SOURCE: Leary, Lewis. "The Vanished Past" and "Flemish Pictures." In *John Greenleaf Whittier,* pp. 117-71. New York: Twayne, 1961.

[*In the following excerpts, Leary discusses Whittier's poems based on New England history and legends of the past, as well as those of New England life in his own time.*]

I love the vanished past—love to listen when
The legend of its stirring times is told by aged men—
The hunter's tale of forest deeds—the struggle with
*   the storm—*
His battle with the savage bear, a cougar's fearful
*   form.*

I love the spell that lendeth to each familiar stream,
The dimness and incoherence of some mysterious
*   dream.*
That linketh supernatural things to native hill and
*   glen,*
And blendeth with the present view a glimpse of what
*   has been.*

—"The Days Gone By"

Whittier responded to legendary lore because he liked good stories similar to those which were told when he and his family and their visitors gathered about the great kitchen fire in his boyhood home. He thrilled to tales of adventure in trapper's hut and Indian camp, of the merry whirl of dancing among red-capped French Canadians to the north, of fishing off Boar's Head or among the rocky waters about the Isle of Shoals, of old-time chowder-parties and clambakes. He was held spellbound by blood-curdling accounts of Indian raids and listened enrapt to stories of the red man's stoic bravery. He responded with enthusiasm to the rich and picturesque unrhymed poetry, he said, of simple life and country living—its huskings and sleigh-rides and apple-bees, its woodcraft mysteries and prodigies of rod and gun. So much of the romance of New England seemed to him to be past. The countryside was disturbed no longer, he lamented in **"An Extract from 'A New England Legend,'"** by the Indian's wizard yell nor by witches, ghosts, or goblins:

> The cautious goodman nails no more
> A horseshoe on his outer door,
> Lest some unseemly hag should fit
> To his own mouth the bridle bit;
> The goodwife's churn no more refuses
> Its wonted culinary uses
> Until, with heated needle burned,
> The witch has to her place returned!

He heard with pride of the courage of his ancestors, both Puritan and Quaker, and of the wrath and violence suffered patiently by those among them who strove for freedom to worship or believe as their conscience urged. He learned to recognize harshness and bigotry among the first settlers of New England who sought enforcement of righteousness with sword and scourge, but he found others among them blessed with charity. They were often simple people, like the sea captains who befriended the persecuted Quaker maiden, Cassandra Southwick; or the Boston man who bought, then freed, the Irish girl, Kathleen. For history had usefulness other than the charm of story. Reaching through the past, Whittier found instances fit to inform countrymen of his day of continuing error, but also of inherited humble virtues.

USES OF TIMES PAST

Musing beside the Merrimack, he could forget, he said, the hum and bustle of workaday life, its waste of sin and woe, while simple things—a stone, a mound of earth, a giant tree left standing, a roofless house, decayed, deserted—reminded him of other times when other men lived among these hills and valleys. Remembering was a kind of resurrection. Man owed tremendous debts of gratitude to that within him which allowed him thus to raise the dead past to life. His gift of re-creation through memory or imagination brought man as close as he could approach to God's redemptive power. Retrieving what had been in order to wrest from it what was good was, therefore, a responsibility. These things had once existed and should not die; for, properly remembered, they witnessed to the extent and wisdom of a divine plan. Their restoration, translated to words which other men could understand, could be a service not only to man but to God.

Whittier's notion of the poet's task seldom allowed him to tell a tale for story alone. Even the early **"Moll Pitcher"** and **"Mogg Megone"** contain instructive commentary about the inevitable consequences of evil. Seldom, even as a young man, did he submit to the notion that art needed no sanction other than "beauty for its own fair sake"; it owed allegiance also to goodness and eternal truth. The result, in his narrative verse, is a simplified goodness and a simplified truth, measured, he said, "by the breadth of Christian liberty." His bad people seem irredeemably bad and his good unquestionably good. He seldom probed, as Melville or Hawthorne did, toward sources or explanations for evil. It is simply present, susceptible of being flushed away by goodness, which is also there and is patiently awaiting its inevitable recognition.

Not only the New England past was brought to life in Whittier's narrative verse; many subjects came from his reading in European history or in accounts of saints and martyrs everywhere. **"The Legend of St. Mark,"** for example, was inspired by a picture in a book of sacred and legendary art: Tintoretto's sketch for his painting of a tortured Christian slave saved by the intervention of the saint at whose altar he had worshiped. **"Barclay of Ury"** is a tale of a Quaker's fortitude in Scotland. **"Rabbi Ismael"** recounts the story of an Israelite priest who, within the Holy of Holies, looked upon the face of his Lord and found it, not stern, but tenderly merciful. **"King Volmer and Elsie"** was adapted from a Danish writer, Christian Winter; **"The Dead Feast of the Kol-Folk"** derived from reading in the *Journal of*

Asiatic Culture; **"The Chapel of the Hermits"** from Bernardin Henri Saint-Pierre's *Etudes de la Nature*; and **"The Khan's Devil,"** from a Middle Eastern story.

"Miriam," with Islamic setting, tells a tale "not found in printed books,—in sooth A fancy, with slight hint of truth," written to demonstrate that differing faiths, Moslem and Christian, "agree In one sweet law of charity." **"King Solomon and the Ants"** is from a legend of the ruler so wise that he "knew The languages of all The creatures great or small That trod the earth or flew"; when his horse was about to step on an ant-hill, Solomon heard the insects speak resignedly of their fate; and, he turned aside in spite of suggestions from his companion, the Queen of Sheba ("comely but black withal"), that such vile creatures should be honored to be stamped to death by so great a man. Recognizing finally the secret of the wise king's worthiness, the dusky Ethiopian queen remarks: "Happy must be the State Whose ruler heedeth more The murmurs of the poor Than flatteries of the great." Few of the early narratives are as clumsily rhetorical as this quotation, but in each a story simple told is capped with a similar enunciation of some noble or pious attitude.

Perhaps best among the poems derived from Whittier's reading is **"The Cypress-Tree of Ceylon,"** which recounts a legend told by Batuba, a Moslem traveler of the fourteenth century, about a sacred tree whose leaves fell seldom; but, when fallen and found and eaten, they had power like the water of Ponce de Leon's fountain to restore youth and vigor. Whittier pictures pious men sitting beneath the tree through weary nights and lingering days, their eyes dimmed to the beauties of nature and the bustle of the world around them as they wait the falling of the restorative leaf. Shall we, he asked, who sit beneath a better tree, whose healing leaves are shed in answer to Christian prayer, be less patient than they? Must the stir of outward things distract us from our vigil? How sternly does the godly man rebuke his erring brother! How easy to wield the sword, as Peter did, to enforce righteousness!

> But oh! we shrink from Jordan's side,
>   From waters which alone can save;
> And murmur for Abana's banks
>   And Pharpar's brighter wave.

Yet eyes need not be dimmed nor the world's work left undone. The poem ends with a prayer addressed to the Saviour who rose from redeeming death to wake his slumbering disciples:

> Bend o'er us now, as over them,
>   And set our sleep-bound spirits free,
> Nor leave us slumbering in the watch
>   Our souls should keep with Thee!

Whittier's popularly effective sermonic manner is here illustrated. An old tale, this time of pagan belief, is used to underscore—to typify, Whittier might have said—the better efficacy of Christian faith. Yet beneath its simplicity of rhyme and line are complexities over which the reader will linger. To understand the first quatrain quoted above, he must recall how Naaman, captain of the host of the King of Syria, a mighty man in valor but a leper, was prepared to do "some great thing" to rid himself of his disease; but how he balked when Elisha instructed him simply to bathe in the waters of Jordan: "Are not Abana and Pharpar, rivers of Damascus, better than all the waters of Israel?" he asked. "May I not wash in them and be clean?"

Meanings then begin to flutter through the poem, which is never completely precise, any more than the symbolism of the tale of Naaman in II Kings 5 is precise. Jordan's water seems to represent simple faith and the rivers which irrigate Damascus' fertile plain worldliness; but the implications of the lines suggest more— not only the proud man humbled, but also the fate of Gehazi who tried to profit from Elisha's healing gift, and how he was punished. So throughout the poem there are intimations of meaning which probe beyond what is said directly. Is it better to remain so blind to everything but faith that the sweet song of birds, the bloom of flowers, and the lithesome dance of maidens go unnoticed? Should concern with personal salvation distract one from noticing the passing gleam of battle flag, or from girding himself to rebuke his erring brethren? What is the relation between pious waiting and instructive action? Whittier suggests answers; first this, then that, but he presents no solution which can be simply paraphrased. It may be suspected that he did not know these answers; and, in this instance, the friction of one question against the other has produced a poem. Like Thoreau, he pleads for wakefulness, for use of man's perceptive power: Let us not slumber. But on the responsibilities of the waking man he is, though less compelling, equally as elusive as the man who lived beside Walden Pond. He has left something for the reader to do.

This imprecision of Whittier, perhaps because linked to the familiarly affective imprecisions of Christian scripture, is less effective than that of Thoreau, or even of Melville who used biblical lore more sacrilegiously. **"The Cypress Tree of Ceylon"** is a poem which invites to dedication. Its intention is to inspire. Its counters are ideas, arranged one against the other. More important than the tree, which is never described, or the men who wait beneath it, grim, grey with age and an unidentified sickness, are the abstractions which each signifies. The slumber to be avoided suggests failure to respond to conventional symbols—a bird's sweet song, the thunder of a tropic storm, or the unnamed wrongs pursued by anonymous men. Words are not attached to things, but to generalities. The poem fails finally to please, not because it lacks the complexity of ambiguity, but because it is thus unnecessarily obscure.

Sometimes Whittier's narrative has no identifiable setting, in place or time. **"The New Wife and the Old"** is the kind of tale which Poe told better: a dead woman intrudes to the marriage bed of her husband and his young second wife to prove that the dead do not forget nor are forgotten, as

> From their solemn homes of thought,
> Where the cypress shadows blend
> Darkly over foe and friend,
> Or in love or sad rebuke,
> Back upon the living look.

But the story is badly managed. The triumph over the proud strength of the man and his jewel-bedecked bride by the work-torn, meekly suffering former wife may be psychologically sound. The memory of her so fills the bridegroom with the cowardice of sin that he shrinks from the whiteness of his young wife's arms. But something goes amiss, even in regard to symbolic effectiveness, when the spotless first wife steals the jewels which her husband has given as a wedding gift to her fair successor. So mild and long-suffering, yet so rapacious? Whittier's point that even in death the meek do inherit good things of the earth might have been better made.

Another arresting poem is **"Kathleen,"** written skillfully in the measure and spirit of old English balladry:

> There was a Lord of Galaway,
>   A mighty lord was he;
> And he did wed a second wife,
>   A maid of low degree.
>
> But he was old, and she was young,
>   And so, in evil spite,
> She baked the black bread for his kin,
>   And fed her own with white.

The lord had a fair daughter whom her stepmother, in the manner of traditional story, treated cruelly:

> She clipped her glossy hair away,
>   That none her rank might know,
> She took away her gown of silk,
>   And gave her one of tow,
>
> And sent her down to Limerick town
>   And to a seaman sold
> This daughter of an Irish lord
>   For ten good pounds of gold.

Discovering this betrayal, the lord offered all his riches and his lands to whoever would bring Kathleen back to him. A handsome young page responded that he would find her, but that he desired no reward other than her hand in marriage. He traveled far and long in search, until finally he discovered the fair maid in Boston, a bond servant to a worthy man who refused to accept money for her ransom, but gave her freely to the young man. They return to Ireland to live happily ever afterwards by Galway's shore. Though a Protestant and, in the eyes of Kathleen and her lover, a heretic, the good American proved that mercy and loving kindness know neither sect nor creed.

For it was native demeanor and native places and people that Whittier was most fond of remembering or inventing tales about. He read widely in the chronicles of New England: for history, Edward Winslow's *Relation,* Edward Johnson's *Wonder-Working Providence of Sion's Saviour,* William Bradford's *History of Plymouth Plantation,* Thomas Morton's brash *New English Canaan,* and John Jocelyn's *New England's Rarities;* for stories of witchcraft or persecution, Cotton Mather's *Wonders of the Invisible World* or his giant *Magnalia Christi Americana*; and for Indian lore, Roger Williams' *A Key into the Languages of America.* A complete listing of Whittier's reading would provide a useful bibliography of colonial history. His best known prose narrative, *Margaret Smith's Diary,* is so filled with facts drawn from ancient records that most readers have difficulty knowing where history leaves off and fiction begins. One of the puzzles confronting students of colonial poetry, for example, is the authenticity of the remarkable poem about Lake Champlain, beginning "This lonesome lake, like to a sea, among the mountains lies"; Whittier attributes it to Edward Johnson, but the source has not been found among colonial archives.

Indian lore and Indian tales attracted Whittier as a young man, either as he read of them in books or as he heard recitations like those recalled in **"Haverhill"** of

> The terror of the midnight raid,
> The death-concealing ambuscade,
> The winter march, through deserts wild,
> Of captive mother, wife, and child.

But Whittier's poems about Indians are not among his most successful. Because he seems to have known them only in story, they remain the Indians of colonial tradition, interpreted through the rosy haze of nineteenth-century sentimentality. Like Mogg Megone, who historically was a sachem among the savage Sacos at the time of King Philip's wars, they were brave but cruel; quick with knife and gun, quicker with tomahawk; and proud of the number of scalps "from the Yenkees torn" which hung from their belts. Fenimore Cooper's red men were not more alert than Whittier's to the "faintest shiver of leaf and limb" which betrayed an enemy's presence. But like Cooper's aged Chingachgook, Whittier's Indians were prey also to the white man's firewater; and they sometimes lay unmanly and helpless in drunken slumber. They are either good Indians, stern but just, and friendly to the white men, as Squanto was; or they are cruel, treacherous, and proud. Hardly any woman in Whittier's chivalrous opinion was ever evil, and his Indian maidens were not exceptions.

"The Bridal of Pennacook" tells a tearful tale of female fidelity, as Weetamoo, lovely daughter of the great chief Passaconaway, whose hunting grounds stretch from the White Mountains eastward to the sea, is given in marriage to proud Winnepurkit, leader of a northern tribe. She is a child of the forest, strong and free, graceful and lithe, "slight robed, with loosely flowing hair," a creature of love and laughter:

> Unknown to her the rigid rule,
>   The dull restraint, the chiding frown,
> The weary torture of a school,
>   The taming of wild nature down.
> Her only lore, the legends told
>   Around the hunter's fire at night;
> Stars rose and set, and seasons rolled,
>   Flowers bloomed and snow-flakes fell,
>   unquestioned in her sight.

In contrast, her father is a stern, lone man who melts only to the innocent warmth and grace of his daughter's joyous being. A chief among chiefs, at whose command lesser sachems gather their tribes for the warpath, he rules in regal splendor from his lodge beside the Merrimack near what is now Concord in New Hampshire:

> There his spoils of chase and war,
> Jaw of wolf and black bear's paw,
> Panther's skin and eagle's claw,
>   Lay beside his axe and bow;
> And, adown the roof-pole hung,
> Loosely on a snake-skin strung,
> In the smoke his scalp-locks swung
>   Grimly to and fro.

Weetamoo, her father's only solace, reminds him of his dead wife, her mother, in memory of whom, because of the stoic tradition in which Indians are bred, he could shed no tear:

> The Indian heart is hard and cold,
>   It closes darkly o'er its care,
> And formed in Nature's sternest mould,
>   Is slow to feel and strong to bear.

In greater contrast is Winnepurkit, the bridegroom who takes Weetamoo to the wind-swept ledges, cavernous hillsides, and icy waters of his northern home among the Saugus. In him "no warmth of heart, no passionate burst of feeling" ever responds to her smile or wifely ministrations. When she expresses a wish to pay a summer visit to her father in the fairer lands about the Merrimac, her husband allows her to go; but he will not receive her back unless her father sends presents of wampum with her. This the proud chief of Pennacook will not do, and Weetamoo remains at her father's lodge in "home-bound grief and pining loneliness" through weary months of autumn and winter. When spring comes, the "still faithful wife" leaves "her father's door, To seek the wigwam of her chief once more." Her loyalty as a woman, however, exceeds her Indian sagac-ity; and she disappears beneath the waters of the Merrimack when the frail canoe in which she set out alone is dashed to pieces among the rocks and swirling ice-floes of the swollen stream. Her death is mourned in a funeral song which sorrowful Indian women sing:

> The Dark eye has left us
>   The Spring-bird has flown;
> On the pathway of spirits
>   She wanders alone,
> The song of the wood-dove has died on our shore:
>   *Mat wonck kunna-monee!* We hear it no more!

Probably because he realized that such sentimentalized devotion was closer to the tradition of European romance than to the truth about Indian ways, Whittier pretended that the story of **"The Bridal of Pennacook"** was told by a group of travelers resting at an inn at Conway after a climb of Mt. Washington. Finding among the landlord's books an old chronicle of border wars, each in turn set to verse part of the story told there of the marriage of Weetamoo. Which traveler—the city lawyer, the student of theology, the shrewd merchant or his lovely daughter, or the unnamed narrator who can be supposed to be Whittier—told which portions of the tale cannot be distinguished, any more than in the later *The Tent on the Beach* a reader can in every instance determine which of the vacationing narrators is responsible for which poems there presented. Whittier's conception of the proper use of history as parable justified such imaginative reconstruction by men and women who filled bare outlines of fact with soft coloring. Faithfulness was faithfulness, even in primitive times. Amid harshness and pride and greed, love however loyal can be destroyed. Thus re-created, the vanished past had messages for people of a later day.

History Retold

Whittier probably treated history most effectively in prose, and especially well in *Margaret Smith's Diary,* a quietly instructive story, filled with sound sense and authentic anecdote rather than with excitement. Certainly one of Whittier's writings which should not be forgotten, it is discovered anew in every generation by a fortunate few who are charmed by Whittier's rendering of a young English girl's account of a visit to New England, where, she said, "I was kindly cared for and entertained, and where I have seen so many strange things." During her year in the colony Margaret met many of the great men of Massachusetts: John Eliot, who tutored the Indians; Simon Bradstreet and his wife who wrote poetry; the learned Nathaniel Ward with whom her brother studied at Agawam; Samuel Sewall, who worried because the selling of beer and strong drink was on the increase in the colony; and Michael Wigglesworth, who spoke against "the gay apparel of the young women of Boston, and their lack of plainness and modesty in the manner of wearing their hair."

Frightened at the sight of her first Indian, Margaret was pleased to see how acquiescent and friendly Indians became after a gift of Jamaica rum. She visited their wigwams and felt pity for their solemn-faced squaws; but she also heard stories of Indian captivity, even from the lips of a young man who was shortly to die because of hardships and cruelty he had suffered at the hands of the red men. Traveling through the countryside, she discovered many fine things about the western world—that maple syrup was quite as good as treacle, how skillful fishermen were in cutting quids of tobacco with their jack-knives, how fond the Irish were of strong drink, and how filled with superstition colonial country-men were.

When journeying to the frontier outpost of Strawberry Bank, she stayed overnight with a widow and her three daughters. "I made a comfortable supper of baked pumpkin and milk," said Margaret, "and for lodgings I had a straw bed on the floor, in a dark loft, which was piled well nigh full with corn-ears, pumpkins, and beans, besides a great deal of old household trumpery, wool, and flax, and the skins of animals." In her sleep she inadvertently struck her foot against one of the pumpkins, "which set it rolling down the stairs, bumping hard on every step as it went." The noise awoke the landlady and her daughters who "came fleeing into the corn-loft, the girls bouncing upon my bed and hiding under the blanket, and the old woman praying and groaning, and saying that she did believe it was the spirit of her poor husband" which had gone thumping down the stairs. "As soon as I could speak for laughing," said Margaret, "I told the poor creature what it was that so frightened her; at which she was greatly vexed; and, after she went to bed again, I could hear her scolding me for playing tricks upon honest people."

In such anecdotes Whittier managed a simple, colloquial language not greatly different from what Mark Twain was to use. The humor is straight-faced; even the irony is masked. There was in Salem, reported Margaret, a poor woman named Goody Morse, who was condemned as a witch because she was said to have been seen "flying about in the sun, as if she had been cut in twain, or as if the Devil did hide the lower half of her." Even her daughter turned against her, saying that inasmuch as her mother had "sold herself to the Devil, did she owe her no further love nor service, for as she had made her bed, so must she lie." When the poor creature's sentence was set aside by the governor, "many people, both men and women, coming in from the towns about to see the hanging, be sore disappointed, and vehemently condemn the Governor therein."

No more than Huckleberry Finn, who was to travel through American villages almost two hundred years later, did Margaret moralize often about what she saw. Her brother fell in love with a Quaker girl and suffered for it. Margaret herself was not sure she liked Quakers: "although I do judge them to be a worthy and pious people, I like not their manner of worship, and their great gravity and soberness do little accord with my natural temper and high spirits." She was sorry for them because they were persecuted, so great a number, both men and women, whipped and put into the stocks. "And I once," she said, "beheld two of them, one a young and the other an aged woman, on a cold day in winter, tied to the tail of a cart, going through Salem Street, stripped to their waists, as naked as they were born, and their backs all covered with red whip marks." Drunken Boggs or the Grangerfords did not have their stories more directly told.

Whittier does not seem to have known that poetry must be as well written as prose. When he told the same story of Quakers whipped, half-naked, at the cart-tail in **"How the Women Went from Dover,"** he underlined it then as a tale "of an evil time, When souls were fettered and thought was a crime," and he introduced a brave good man who reproved the constable whose "torturing whip . . . the bare flesh stung." The language is different: it has become literary, inverted, unnatural. The incident is recounted as a reminder to modern women, "at ease in these happier days," that they may "forbear to judge" of their sister's ways. Translated to prose, the words perhaps might speak more clearly, but their meaning would be little different. Poetry, some people have said, is that which is lost in translation. In this instance, very little is lost.

Most ambitious of Whittier's later poems is **"The Pennsylvania Pilgrim,"** written in 1872 as a tribute to colonial Quakers of Philadelphia and particularly to Francis Daniel Pastorius who in 1663, at the invitation of William Penn, brought a colony of his countrymen to Pennsylvania and settled them in what is now called Germantown. Whittier thought it "as good as (if not better than) any long poem I have written." He hoped that it could appear in a volume by itself, as *Snow-Bound* had; for he sometimes thought it more successful than that profitable poem. At first he wanted to call it "The Germantown Pilgrim." James T. Fields suggested instead "Pastorius of Pennsylvania," which Whittier did not like. After some correspondence, they settled together on **"The Pennsylvania Pilgrim,"** Whittier finding in that title "a rather pleasant sounding alliteration."

Perhaps that is what must be said of **"The Pennsylvania Pilgrim"**: it is a pleasant-sounding poem. Whittier filled it with the trappings of an epic; and in the invocation—not to the gods, but to posterity or to the descendants of the patient, valiant men who settled the New World—he asked that new generations never forget the trials and fears which these ancestors had encountered as they hewed homesteads from wild forest lands. Then a prelude begins, in epic fashion,

> I sing the Pilgrim of a softer clime
>   And milder speech than those brave men who
>   brought
> To the ice and iron of our winter time
>   A will as firm, a creed as stern . . .

The measure chosen for the body of the poem, perhaps with Dante's example vaguely in mind, was a three-line rhymed stanza in iambic pentameter—a meter in which Whittier was seldom conspicuously successful. In spite of attempts to run the sense from one stanza to another, each was so bound within itself by triple-rhyme that the narrative often stumbles forward by jerks and starts and lacks the natural transitions which Whittier managed well in prose.

But Whittier's high estimate of **"The Pennsylvania Pilgrim"** is understandable. It celebrates a man who was both wise and good, a convert to the Quaker faith and among the first in colonial America to speak openly against slavery:

> Whatever legal maze he wandered through,
> He kept the Sermon on the Mount in view,
> And justice always into mercy grew.

The poem absorbs, as George Arms has observed,[1] everything which Whittier wished to pack into it: homely humor, antiquarian detail, rebukes to New England harshness, and the inception of the antislavery movement. But that is not to say that it is packed well. Whittier explains that free men in that waking time dropped their buckets deep to bring up hidden waters; but he himself, strolling leisurely through Pennsylvania kitchens and woodlands, seems awkwardly a stranger who brings to an unfamiliar scene only what he had learned before. Pennsylvania, that is to say, becomes a suburb of New England, distinguished only because its men enjoyed freedoms denied those who settled amid the ice and iron of Puritan lands. If Whittier drank from the buckets which Pennsylvanians dropped deeply down, the water must have tasted little different from that in the well-house at Amesbury.

What does distinguish **"The Pennsylvania Pilgrim"** and makes it superior to Whittier's other discursive narrative is the metaphor of seed, sowing, flowering, and harvest which is introduced first in the prelude and then repeated again at intervals throughout the poem. Seed planted in seventeenth-century Germantown promised bright blossoms for men who followed. Like the century plant given William Penn by John Evelyn in England, slowly "year by year its patient leaves unfold." In the last stanzas a glance is directed toward the late eighteenth century, when it is asked of the century plant

>   if it flowered at last
> In Bartram's garden, did John Woolman cast
> A glance upon it as he meekly passed?

And, seeing it, was Quaker John Woolman possessed of a "secret sympathy" which lent him hope, strength, and patience? The plant perhaps is mythical, a symbol provided by nature to remind man that "no seed of truth is lost" and that, because of the planting by pious Quakers of Pennsylvania, "from sea to sea such flowers of freedom bloom."

Patient readers will find the narrative sustained, bound together by the strands of imagery of seed and harvest which Whittier wove through it. They will delight in a sprinkling of sedate humor and a muted, calm assurance that these simple things of which the poet speaks are good. But the argument is finally greater than the poetry; of it one must inevitably say what Whittier said of Pastorius' equally aspiring verse: it is native and homely, nourishing

>   like the hash
> Of corn and beans in Indian succatash;
> Dull, doubtless, but with here and there a flash
>
> Of wit and fine conceit,—the good man's play
> Of quiet fancies.

Among those in history whom Whittier liked best to remember were people like Goody Morse, accused of witchcraft. For purposes of poetry he remembered them, not as old, but as young and attractive and thus the more to be pitied. **"The Witch of Wenham"** tells in ballad measure the story of a gentle maiden imprisoned as a witch until her lover comes riding in the night to rescue her. Verse form and story were both of a kind with which Whittier was most familiar. Simply told, pathos alternating with hints of peril, but lightened by colloquialism and humor, **"The Witch of Wenham"** is as successful in its kind as anything Whittier attempted. "She chains him with her great blue eyes," says the young man's mother. "She binds him with her hair." Like the Lorelei of German legend,

> She weaves her golden hair; she sings
>   Her spell-song low and faint;
> The wickedest witch in Salem jail
>   Is to that girl a saint.

Captured, shut up in the garret of an old farmhouse to wait trial, then helped to escape by the young man who caught her as she dropped, Tom Sawyer-like, from the sloping shingled roof outside her window, she mounted the saddle behind her rescuer and rode away:

>   Her arms around him twined;
> And noiseless, as if velvet-shod,
>   They left the house behind.

Through wild wood's paths and bridgeless streams they fled, till they came to the Merrimack, where an ancient ferryman rowed them to safety on the other side. Charmed by the youth and happiness of the runaway couple, he gave them his benediction as they left him:

"God keep thee from the evil eye,
    And harm of witch!" he cried.

The maiden laughed, as youth will laugh
    At all its fears gone by;
"He doesn't know," she whispered low,
    "A little witch am I!"

Perhaps Whittier should have stopped here, but he could not. Seven concluding stanzas tell of the young people's reception among Quakers who welcomed them gladly and with whom they lived happily,

Until from off its breast the land
    The haunting horror threw,
And hatred born of ghastly dreams,
    To shame and pity grew.

Again the words limp to find syntax which will fit the rhyme, to clip on a moral which, if it had not been before happily implicit in the ballad, now becomes a nuisance.

Favorite among anthologists of Whittier's most characteristic verse is **"The Prophecy of Samuel Sewall,"** which recounts New England's cherished story of the Puritan judge's penitential recantation of sentences which he had passed on people who had appeared before his court accused as witches. Much of the poem is preparatory, telling the history of the wise old man, a "poet who never measured rhyme," and a "seer unknown to his dull-eared time," who placed the law of divine justice above the laws of man and who late in life even condemned human slavery:

Honor and praise to the Puritan
Who the halting step of his age outran,
And, seeing the infinite worth of man
In the priceless gift the Father gave,
In the infinite love that stooped to save,
Dared not brand his brother a slave!

Musing on the example of Samuel Sewall, Whittier then wrote the judge's prophecy in words to which generations of Yankee patriots have responded with pride and declaimed with earnest dedication:

"As long as Plum Island, to guard the coast
As God appointed, shall keep its post;
As long as salmon shall haunt the deep
Of Merrimac river, or sturgeon leap;
As long as pickerel swift and slim,
Or red-backed perch, in Crane Pond swim;
As long as the annual sea-fowl know
Their time to come and their time to go;
As long as cattle shall roam at will
The green grass meadows by Turkey Hill;
As long as sheep shall look from the side
Of Oldtown Hill on marshes wide,
And Parker River, and salt-sea tide;
As long as wandering pigeons shall search
The fields below from his white-oak perch,

When the barley-harvest is ripe and shorn,
And the dry husks fall from the standing corn;
As long as Nature shall not grow old,
Nor drop her work from her doting hold,
And her care for the Indian corn forget,
And the yellow rows in pairs to set;—
So long shall Christians here be born,
Grow up and ripen as God's sweet corn!—
By the beak of bird, by the breath of frost,
Shall never a holy ear be lost,
But, husked by Death in the Planter's sight,
Be sown again in the fields of light!"

Caught up by the spirit of the prophecy, Whittier concludes:

The Island still is purple with plums,
Up the river the salmon comes,
The sturgeon leaps, and the wild-fowl feeds
On hillside berries and marish seeds,—
All the beautiful signs remain,
From spring-time sowing to autumn rain
The good man's vision returns again!
And let us hope, as well we can,
That the Silent Angel who garners man
May find some grain as of old he found
In the human cornfield ripe and sound,
And the Lord of the Harvest deign to own
The precious seed by their father's sown!

Legend into Verse

Whittier, however, may be at his best when, unhampered by history, he remade legend into verse, as he did in **"Mabel Martin, a Harvest Idyll,"** which was written almost ten years after his sister's death in memory of her who "loved with us the beautiful and old." Again in simple measure, he tells of the daughter of a woman executed as a witch; she lives unhappily alone, rejected or mocked by her neighbors until she finds protection within the arms of a strong man who loves her. It is an idyll, nothing more; but as one it is softly compelling. At its end, when moonlight falls through great elm boughs onto the pair, secure at last in love, each reader is likely to agree with what the night wind then whispered: "It is well."

Equally effective is **"The Double-Headed Snake of Newbury"** which derives from contemplation of the serpent which the Rev. Christopher Toppan described to Cotton Mather as having "really two heads, one at each end; two mouths, two stings or tongues." To those who would scoff at the tale, Whittier warned:

Thou who makest the tale thy mirth,
Consider that strip of Christian earth
On the desolate shore of a sailless sea,
Full of terror and mystery,
Half redeemed from the evil hold
Of wood so dreary, and dark, and old,
Which drank with its lips of leaves the dew
When Time was young, and the world was new,
And wove its shadows with sun and moon,

Ere the stones of Cheops were squared and hewn.
Think of the sea's dread monotone,
Of the mournful wail from the pine-wood blown,
Of the strange, vast splendors that lit the North,
Of the troubled throes of the quaking earth,
And the dismal tales the Indian told,
Till the settler's heart at his hearth grew cold,
And he shrank from the tawny wizard boasts,
And the hovering shadows seemed full of ghosts,
And above, below, and on every side,
The fear of his creed seemed verified;—
And think, if his lot were now thine own,
To grope with terrors nor named nor known
How laxer muscle and weaker nerve
And a feebler faith thy need might serve;
And to own to thyself the wonder more
That the snake had two heads, and not a score!

This excellent light verse is well phrased, well rhymed, written with good-humored sense. No wonder then that

Cotton Mather came galloping down
All the way to Newberry town,
With his eyes agog and his ears set wide,
And his marvelous inkhorn at his side;
Stirring the while in the shallow pool
Of his brains for the lore he learned in school,
To garnish the story, with here a streak
Of Latin, and there another of Greek:
And the tales he heard and the notes he took,
Behold! are they not in his Wonder-Book?

Seldom has bumptious Cotton Mather been more soundly given his come-uppance, or his portentous volume of supernatural lore, *Wonders of the Invisible World,* been more expertly ticked off. But the stories which he told "like dragon's teeth are hard to kill," so that still in New England far beyond Mather's time

whenever husband and wife
Publish the shame of their daily strife,
And, with mad cross-purpose, tug and strain
At either end of the marriage chain,

Then people say, "Look! . . . One in body and two in will," the double-headed snake is living still.

Whittier never did so well with legend as in **"Skipper Ireson's Ride,"** a story told him as true by a schoolmate at Haverhill Academy. He is said to have begun putting it to verse as early as 1828, but almost thirty years passed before he completed it and sent it off to James Russell Lowell for the *Atlantic Monthly* in 1857. He described it then as "a bit of Yankee ballad, the spirit of which pleases me more than the execution." Yet it is the execution—precise, graphic and dramatic, without a wasted word—which allows some readers to consider this poem Whittier's masterpiece and the best American ballad of the nineteenth century. It begins, as many well-told tales do, with the action under way. Old Floyd Ireson, because of his hard heart, has been tarred and feathered and is being carried on a cart by the women of Marblehead.

That is all the reader is told, except that the narrator thinks that Floyd's ride was the strangest since the birth of time. Now, dripping with feathers, "ruffled in every part," the unfortunate Floyd looks like the "Body of turkey" with "head of owl," with his "wings a-droop like a rained-on fowl," while "scores of women, old and young, Strong of muscle and glib of tongue" push and pull the cart in which he stands; they move it steadily up the rocky Salem road, while they shout and sing the shrill refrain, which this time is not written as it had been at the end of the first stanza in the smoothly correct accents of the narrator, but in Marblehead dialect:

Here's Flud Oirson, fur his horrd horrt,
Torr'd an' futherr'd an' corr'd in a corrt
        By the women of Morble'ead!

What a pack of women they were: "wrinkled scolds with hands on hips," young girls "in bloom of cheek and lips,"

Wild-eyed, free-limbed, such as chase
Bacchus round some antique vase,
Brief of skirt, with ankles bare,
Loose of kerchief and loose of hair.

Whittier calls them Maenads, sea-nymphs, singing to the accompaniment of "conch-shells blowing and fish-horns' twang."

Only with the fourth stanza does the reader learn the reason for the riot. The narrator then interrupts the procession to explain that Floyd Ireson was a sea captain, a native of Marblehead, who had sailed his vessel away from a sinking ship manned by his own townspeople and had left them to drown amid the fog and rain of stormy Chaleur Bay. Why he had done it is not revealed. It can be suspected that the crew of the stricken ship had done better than he on some former fishing expedition; for, in the one bit of dialect in these two expository stanzas, Ireson is reported to have shouted,

"Sink or swim!
Brag of your catch of fish again!"

Whittier is seldom so succinct or so successful. He approaches pathos, but only for a moment, when he thinks of the mothers, sisters, wives, and daughters of the sailors so cruelly deserted. They watch "over the moaning rainy sea . . . For the coming that might not be." And not only they, but the whole town—"sharp-tongued spinsters, old wives grey," and "sea-worn grandsires"—join the mob around the cart in which Floyd Ireson rode, dishonored. They shook

head, and fist, and hat, and cane
And croaked with curses the hoarse refrain.

And the refrain is again in the dialect of Marblehead, harsh and bitterly recriminating.

Then suddenly the mood of the poem changes, as the beauty of orchard and lilac beside the Salem road contrasts with the grim spectacle of hatred and revenge. Floyd Ireson speaks for the first time: "Hear me neighbors!" He speaks as one of them, a fellow-townsman, a neighbor still, though held in contempt and made to appear less than human by his garment of feathers and tar. Humiliated and degraded, he is still a man. What, he asks,

> What is the shame that hides the skin
> To the nameless horror that lives within?

Awake or asleep, he remembers that dreadful scene at sea. He is haunted by the cries of the sailors he had callously deserted to certain death. His crime was the crime of any man who turned away from his suffering fellows. "Hate me and curse me," he cries,

> "I only dread
> The hand of God and the face of the dead."

Touched by his words, half in pity, half in contempt, the women set him free. They gave him a cloak to cover the shame which they had smeared on him, and then left him alone: "God has touched him!" they said, "Why should we!" The punishment which fitted his crime was not to be provided by human hands.

The wild anger of the women is moderated to compassion mixed with scorn. It is not they but the narrator who transforms their mad, revengeful refrain to contemplative commentary. No longer is it "Old Floyd Ireson," but "Poor Floyd Ireson" who is carried on the cart by the women of Marblehead. The ballad succeeds because of its effective dramatic structure, its handling of details of locale and character, and its balance of colloquial with traditional literary diction. Of all the rides "told in story or sung in rhyme," this, said the narrator, was the strangest. What begins in a spirit of mockery, compared lightly to Apuleius' "Golden Ass" and "one-eyed Calender's horse of brass," suddenly becomes drama, filled with movement, noise and shouting. Just as suddenly it then moves toward a climax in which action ceases, to be replaced by realization that Floyd Ireson's brief ride in Marblehead can in truth be compared with fabled "rides since the birth of time." The refrain which ends each stanza becomes at last, as John Pickard has said so well, a mournful dirge forever accusing and dooming poor Floyd Ireson who lives on when his story is ended—a tragic figure who "towers over the drama, acting without apparent justification, and then vanishing to live alone with his shame and remorse."[2] No tag of moral is needed; because suggestions of meaning are organic to the poem, they inevitably emerge without obtrusive prodding by the narrator.

Historians of Marblehead have complained that the legend is distorted, that it was not Captain Ireson, but someone of quite another name who was punished by his townspeople, and not in just this manner. But Whittier was not writing history, any more than he was in *Margaret Smith's Diary,* or than Melville was in *Israel Potter* or than Hawthorne was in "The Maypole of Merrymount" or *The Scarlet Letter.* Equally unimportant is knowledge that in the *Arabian Nights* it was not "one-eyed Calender" who had a horse of brass; it is also insignificant that Lowell contributed importantly to **"Skipper Ireson's Ride"** by correcting the refrain, as it appears in all but the first and the last two stanzas, to give it the peculiar accent of Marblehead speech. For whatever aid he received or however his imagination amended facts of history or legend, Whittier perhaps for the first time and at the age of fifty made a poem which was organically whole. He was sometimes to do as well again, but seldom better.

Twenty years later in **"The Henchman"** he produced a narrative ballad of courtly love which Winfield Townley Scott is correct in placing also among Whittier's best: "His purity of line, its chaste control of the art of lyric singing make it truly beautiful."[3] The first stanza and the last give some impression of the whole; but the poem should be read entire as an illustration of how Whittier, when he forgot his preachments, could write with simple effectiveness of matters which strike close to the heart:

> My lady walks her morning round,
> My lady's page her fleet greyhound,
> My lady's hair the fond winds stir,
> And all the birds make songs for her.
>
> . . . . .
>
> No lance have I, in joust or fight,
> To splinter in my lady's sight;
> But at her feet, how blest were I
> For any need of hers to die!

> * * *

> *But my thoughts are full of the past and old,*
> *I hear the tales of my boyhood told;*
> *And the shadows and shapes of early days*
> *Flit dimly by in the veiling haze,*
> *With measured movement and rhythmic chime,*
> *Weaving like shuttles my web of rhyme.*
>
> **—"The Prophecy of Samuel Sewall"**

As much as he loved the New England of history and legend, Whittier loved best the New England of his own time, especially of his youth. Like Stephen Vincent Benét, he was charmed by the sound of old American names, and decorated his verses with them: Moosehillock. Kearsarge, Sunapee, Winnepisogee, Pemigewasset, Monadnock. He liked native ways of saying words, rhyming "lion" with "iron," "Martha" with "swarthy" and "worthy," "calling" with "broiling," "shadows" with "meadows" and "ladders," "timbers" with "embers." He found reminders of romance in the sight of boatmen on the river, the sound of huntsmen among the woods or meadowlands, in the clang of anvil or the creak of water-wheel. He liked to recall the chatter of wild geese, the laugh of the loon, the lonely plaint of the whippoorwill. He thought of beaver cutting timber with patient teeth, of minks that were fish-wards, of crows as surveyors of highways. His verses are densely planted with birches and scarlet maples, hemlock, oak, and lilac. Wild grapes border his brooks, lilies blossom in his ponds, brown nuts and violets are scattered over his hills. He recalled the sumptuous fare of old-time feasts:

> small wild hens in the reed-snares caught
> From the banks of Sondagardee brought;
> Pike and perch from the Suncock taken,
> Nut from the trees of the Black Hills shaken,
> Cranberries picked in the Squanscot bog,
> And grapes from the vines of Piscataquog.

PRECURSOR OF ROBERT FROST

Few poets have written as successfully as Whittier of nature without man in it. "With the sureness that plain simple vision gives to the imperfect craftsman," John Macy has said, "he made pictures of his landscape that are unsurpassed, if not unsurpassable."[4] His wistfully tender verses of place are as indigenous as the trees and wildflowers and harvests which they describe. His genius, said Francis Parkman, drew its nourishment from native soil.[5] Not until Robert Frost began to write of birches and stone walls and snow-filled New Hampshire woods was another to do as well. When Whittier's poems of countryside are no longer read with pleasure, then, it has been said, the last Yankee will have died.

Sometimes, as in **"The Fruit-Gift,"** written late when his language was maturely under control, Whittier contemplated the lush and clustered sweetness of nature's product,

> Full-orbed and glowing with the prisoned beams
> Of summery suns, and rounded to completeness
> By kisses of the south-wind . . . ,

to find in it reminders of finer and even fuller beauties which man once knew in Eden but which now must be imagined through analogy. Musing over the gift of fruit—grapes, perhaps, or an ear of golden corn—which had been sent to him,

> I said, "This fruit beseems no world of sin.
> Its parent vine, rooted in Paradise,
> O'ercrept the wall, and never paid the price
> Of the great mischief—an ambrosial tree,
> Eden's exotic, somehow smuggled in,

> To keep the thorns and thistles company."
> Perchance our frail, sad mother plucked in haste
> A single vine-slip as she passed the gate,
> Where the dread sword alternate paled and burned,
> And the stern angel, pitying her fate,
> Forgave the lovely trespasser, and turned
> Aside his face of fire; and thus the waste
> And fallen world hath yet its annual taste
> Of primal good, to prove of sin the cost,
> And show by one gleaned ear the mighty harvest lost.

For Whittier's descriptive verse, no more than Robert Frost's, was not written simply for description's sake. His landscape had people in it; and, usually good people, their activities were meant to supply meaning to the scene. In the Prelude to **"Among the Hills,"** composed in 1869 at the peak of his late-maturing powers, Whittier spoke of himself as

> a farmer's son
> Proud of field-lore and harvest-craft, and feeling
> All their fine possibilities, how rich
> And restful even poverty and toil
> Become when beauty, harmony, and love
> Sit at their humble hearth.

He remembered, however, that among New England's stone-filled farmlands toil was often wearisome, that bodies tired and hearts were starved even among the plenitude of nature. Like Hawthorne and William Faulkner, he invoked images of nature untended which irresistibly overcame the husbandry of man. Looking back over half a century, he recalled

> old homesteads where no flower
> Told that the spring had come, but evil weeds,
> Nightshade and rough-leaved burdock in the place
> Of the sweet doorway greeting of the rose
> And honeysuckle, where the house walls seemed
> Blistering in sun, without a tree or vine
> To cast the tremulous shadow of its leaves
> Across the curtainless windows, from whose panes
> Fluttered the signal rags of shiftlessness.

Part of the poverty of New England was poverty of the spirit. Many of its strongest people had adventured westward to new lands and less rocky fields. But New England was not desolate; only its people were. Amid rich woodlands and half-tilled fields they lived a pinched, bare, and comfortless existence. Within the farmhouses of New England

> the cluttered kitchen floor, unwashed
> (Broom-clean I think they called it); the best room
> Stifling with cellar-damp, shut from the air
> In hot midsummer, bookless, pictureless
> Save the inevitable sampler hung
> Over the fireplace, or a mourning piece,
> A green-haired woman, peony-cheeked, beneath
> Impossible willows; the wide-throated hearth
> Bristling with faded pine-boughs half concealing
> The piled-up rubbish at the chimney's back;
> And, in sad keeping with all things about them,

> Shrill querulous women, sour and sullen men,
> Untidy, loveless, old before their time,
> With scarce a human interest save their own
> Monotonous round of small economies
> Or the poor scandal of the neighborhood.

Blind to beauty everywhere about them, these people lived crippled lives as prisoners, cramped and starved, Whittier said, while Nature spread a feast of joy and wonder all about them. This should not be:

> Our yeoman should be equal to his home
> Set in fair, green valleys, purple walled,
> A man to match his mountains, not to creep
> Dwarfed and abased below them.

Like Emerson and Thoreau, each of whom years before had spoken similar words, perhaps more effectively, Whittier would invite his countrymen to look freshly on their world with their eyes and hearts to feel the "beauty and the joy within their reach." He would recall the simple pleasures of "Home and home loves, and the beatitudes Of nature." His ministering gift to them and to all people was to remind them of what they had been and might be, to help them recognize in nature the

> outward types and signs
> Of the eternal beauty which fulfills
> The one great purpose of creation, Love.

Yet no matter how often Whittier cautioned himself that in the "beautiful present the past is no longer needed," he seemed as he grew older increasingly to find in nature mementos of the passing of time. In **"The Last Walk in Autumn"** he told of wandering through hilly woodlands beneath bare boughs outstretched as if pleading with the leaden skies. Beside the Merrimack he saw that

> The withered tufts of asters nod;
> And trembles on its arid stalk
>   The hoar plume of the goldenrod,
> And on the ground of sombre fir,
>   And azure-studded juniper,
> The silver birch its buds of purple shows,
> And scarlet berries tell where bloomed the sweet
>   wild-rose.

As he walked, he thus looked about to see, much as Thoreau had, each fair embodiment of nature clearly; but he did not write about his observations so well as the Concord walker. Whittier often allowed adjectives to do too much of his descriptive work for him; but, in these lines and in others like them, he captured something of the grey bleakness of approaching winter in New England, which reminded him of the approaching winter of his life. Living quietly now in Amesbury, with books and friends, he remembered visits from Emerson, "who might Plato's banquet grace," and Longfellow, the "gentle pilgrim troubadour, Whose songs have girded half the earth." He knew not, he said, "how in

other lands The changing seasons come and go." New England brought him happiness enough:

> Here dwells no perfect man, sublime,
>   Nor women winged before their time,
> But with the faults and follies of the race,
> Old home-bred virtues hold their not unhonored place.

Remembering these home-bred virtues, he would sing, not the harsh songs of persuasion which he formerly had sung, but simpler melodies; and he hoped that they might reach the homes and hearths, he said, even of those who had disagreed with his partisan verses. In **"Mountain Pictures"** he wrote of a "brown old farmhouse like a bird's-nest hung" upon the side of Mount Monadnock:

> The bucket plashing in the cool, sweet well,
> The pasture bars that clattered as they fell;
> Dogs barked, fowls fluttered, cattle lowed; the gate
> Of the barnyard creaked beneath the merry weight
> Of sun-brown children, listening while they swung,
> The welcome sound of supper-call to hear;
> And down the shadowy lane, in tinklings clear,
> The pastoral curfew of the cow-bell rung.

If recollection of Samuel Woodworth's "Old Oaken Bucket" and Oliver Goldsmith's "The Deserted Village" both intrude between many readers and complete appreciation of these lines, the lines nonetheless succeed in setting forth, even in the faded colors of an old daguerreotype, a picture which evokes quiet emotion. Against such backgrounds of forest or hillside or farm were to be set the New England pastorals which Whittier had called for many years before and which now, as he approached fifty, he would attempt seriously to produce.

DEMOCRATIC PASTORALS

Sentimentality was to tint almost all of those later genre sketches done from observation or memory of incidents of everyday life. Even when he wrote of them in prose, as in "Schoolday Remembrances" or in reminiscence of "The Fish I Didn't Catch" or of carefree "Yankee Gypsies" who roamed the countryside of his youth, they were colored with an almost doleful assurance that these things which once were and which he knew and loved were now gone and would not return. What distinguishes them all is that they were drawn from scenes and models which Whittier had known. He did not now, like Longfellow or even Lowell, attempt to elevate the taste of his contemporaries by presenting them with home-made copies of style or subject imported from other lands. Winfield Townley Scott is correct in suggesting that in this "lay his chief differences from the countrymen with whom he is mostly closely connected—Longfellow, Lowell, Holmes; and here, too, the mainspring of his superiority over them. Where they were often wooden, he was natural."[6] There is something clear and authentic about Whittier, Ludwig Lewisohn once said, "something of brooks and trees rather than of horse-hair furniture and antimacassars."[7] Whittier produced, said another commentator, "the sort of verse which appealed, first of all, to his neighbors."[8]

In that sense he can be thought of, even more than the self-conscious Whitman, as a democratic poet. He was the kind of poet, descended from simple ballad singers of all time, who made the kinds of verse which his listeners wanted to hear. Though the voice of the people may be loud and in many matters undoubtedly finally right, its ear is often faulty, its senses lulled by what it wishes to feel. **"The Barefoot Boy,"** which is perhaps after **"Barbara Frietchie"** Whittier's best-remembered poem, represents an example of just this point. Though twenty years older than Tom Sawyer, Whittier's little man with turned-up pantaloons has appealed to much the same kind of sentimental reconstruction of past days as Mark Twain's ragged urchin. Either barefoot boy, fishing pole on shoulder, scuffling carefree through the dust of summer, might have sat model for the other; and which is more sentimentally realized would be difficult to determine. There are differences, of course; and these are explained, in part, by differences in the total experience of Whittier and Samuel Clemens and, in greater part, by the circumstance that in his book Mark Twain built parts more skillfully into an organic whole. But the dissimilarities are probably also as correctly explained by the differences between what appealed to people in 1855, when **"The Barefoot Boy"** first appeared, and what appealed to another generation which applauded Tom Sawyer with an appreciation not unsimilar to that which even later greeted the hard-bitten sentimentality of Holden Caulfield in *The Catcher in the Rye*. Each work—or each youth—reproduced in terms of its time what readers best wanted to recall of certain superiorities which boyhood offered. In its way, each celebrated the "clouds of glory" which Wordsworth had said surround the child who with sad inevitability is father to the man.

Hedged about by moral restrictions, Whittier in the 1850's narrowed and intensified the focus of his imagination. If once he had thought of poetry as an end in itself and had asked in youthful prayer that his soul be quickened by "fancy's pure imaginings," he was now certain that, when not grounded solidly on the rock of humanitarian ethics, "Art builds on sand." But he had also discovered that, even dedicated to the service of man, poetry could be dangerous and difficult to control: it could lead men toward war, as his militant verses seemed to. As he grew older, Whittier appears to have distrusted imagination, especially those "bolder flights that know no check." It was better, he said in **"The Tent on the Beach,"**

> to use the bit then throw
> The reins all free on fancy's neck.

> The liberal range of Art should be
> The breadth of Christian liberty,
> Restrained alone by challenge and alarm
> When its charmed footsteps tread the border land of harm.

Invention was dangerous, art was suspect, for the most sincerely made contrivance of man failed to encompass the largeness of the divine, eternal plan. How impious and audacious of man to believe that he could create! Perhaps the best he could do, Whittier thought, was to remember and to reproduce—as Wordsworth had suggested—simple emotions recollected now in mature tranquility. Memory was indeed a kind of imagination, and reconstruction of scenes and events and people recalled from his past a poet's legitimate task. Late in life Whittier confessed, "If not the wisest, it appears to me the happiest people in the world are those who still retain something of the child's creative faculty of imagination, which makes atmosphere and color, sun and shadow, and boundless horizons, out of what seems to prosaic wisdom most inadequate material."[9]

In **"The Barefoot Boy"** Whittier spelled this out with direct simplicity: the "painless play," the "laughing day" of boyhood, the "Health that mocks the doctor's rules" and "Knowledge never learned in schools"

> Of the wild bee's morning chase,
> Of the wild-flower's time and place,
> Flight of fowl and habitude
> Of the tenants in the wood;
> How the tortoise bears his shell,
> How the woodchuck digs his cell,
> And the ground-mole sinks his well;
> How the robin feeds her young,
> How the oriole's nest is hung;
> Where the whitest lilies blow,
> Where the freshest berries grow,
> Where the ground-nut trails its vine,
> Where the wood-grape's clusters shine;
> Of the black wasp's cunning way,
> Mason of his walls of clay,
> And the architectural plans
> Of gray hornet artisans.

The poem does not probe deeply. Until its final twenty lines, it is simply a remembrancer: "From my heart I give thee joy,—I was once a barefoot boy." Then the mood changes:

> Cheerily, then, my little man,
> Live and laugh, as boyhood can!

All too soon those bare feet must be shod, imprisoned by adult pride, threatened by treacherous sands of sin. How simply it is said, yet nothing in the poem is fresh or new, except the buoyant boyhood memories! The moral thrust at the end becomes bathos. At just about this time Walt Whitman was contemplating a childhood reminiscence of another barefoot boy who walked and talked with nature as cheerily as Whittier's did; but he became the man who produced in "Out of the Cradle Endlessly Rocking" one of America's few great poems. It was at this time also that Whittier is said to have thrown a copy of Whitman's *Leaves of Grass* in disgust into the fire.

Published in the same year as **"The Barefoot Boy,"** Whittier's companion tale—and a better poem—of "the barefoot maiden," **"Maud Muller"** has not fared so well with readers. The story is well formulated and told with an economy of phrase unusual in Whittier; Wordsworth at his lowliest seldom managed meter better. The first thirty-four lines are straight, objective narrative: they tell of the Judge, an urbane man, riding his chestnut mare through the countryside, where

> Maud Muller on a summer's day
> Raked the meadow sweet with hay.

Stopping for a cup of water from the spring that flows through the meadow, he gallantly compliments and honestly admires the "simple beauty and rustic health" of the country girl; and she, forgetting her bashfulness, talks to him of simple, country things. Then the narrative pauses for thirty lines in which the reader is allowed to hear the thoughts which pass through the minds of each. After the Judge has ridden away, Maud says to herself:

> "Ah me!
> That I the Judge's bride might be!
>
> "He would dress me up in silks so fine,
> "And praise and toast me at his wine.
>
> "My father would wear a broadcloth coat;
> "My brother should sail a painted boat.
>
> "I'd dress my mother so grand and gay,
> "And the baby should have a new toy each day."

And the Judge, as he returns to his duties in the town, also ponders about the simple joys which might ensue if

> "she were mine, and I to-day,
> "Like her a harvester of hay."

Years then pass; and, in a third section, the Judge is pictured as successful in every worldly way—the owner of a fine house, a leader among men, and wedded to

> a wife of the richest dower,
> Who lived for fashion, as he for power,

while Maud remained a country woman, a household drudge married to

> a man unlearned and poor,
> And many children played round her door.

Yet often at the end of a weary day, he, before his marble fireplace, and she, spinning beside her humble hearth, recall their brief meeting; each vaguely wonders whether his life might have been happier if he had succumbed to the romantic impulse which had held him then. Finally, the story told, Whittier takes over to comment with choked voice:

> God pity them both! and pity us all,
> Who vainly the dreams of youth recall.
>
> For of all sad words of tongue or pen,
> The saddest are these: "It might have been!"

It may be, as George Arms has suggested, that the sadness of these lines "points as much to the thoughtless reader's wish fulfillment as to Maud's recrimination."[10] Their soft sentiment, however, is capped by a pious benediction which even to discriminating readers of Whittier's time must have made the poem seem to end in a whimper. The poet sighs as he finishes the tale—as if in an aside, he suggests that perhaps we all in some future life will discover the happiness which has eluded us on earth:

> Ah, well! for us some sweet hope lies
> Deeply buried from human eyes;
>
> And, in the hereafter, angels may
> Roll this stone from its grave away.

Why does a poem which presents so simple a story of a not uncommon human predicament seem to fail so utterly? Sentiment is not of itself destructive; for as managed by Wordsworth or Tennyson, or even by Scott Fitzgerald or Sherwood Anderson, it can surround a subject with an evanescent glow of tenderness. But this subtle mood is difficult beyond all others to maintain; it must withstand the brighter light of logic if it is not to tumble into grotesque caricature of itself. The mawkishness of **"Maud Muller"** is nowhere more effectively exposed than in the parody-sequel which Bret Harte wrote sixteen years later in "Mrs. Judge Jenkins." In this retelling of the story the Judge returns to see his country maid.

> And ere the languid summer died,
> Sweet Maud became the Judge's bride.
>
> But on the day that they were mated,
> Maud's brother Bob was intoxicated;
>
> And Maud's relations, twelve in all,
> Were very drunk at the Judge's hall.
>
> And when the summer came again,
> The young bride bore him babies twain;
>
> And the Judge was blest, but thought it strange
> That bearing children made such a change;

For Maud grew broad and red and stout,
And the waist that his arm once clasped about

Was more than he now could span; and he,
Sighed as he pondered ruefully,

How that which in Maud was native grace
In Mrs. Jenkins was out of place;

And thought of the twins, and wished that they
Looked less like the men who raked the hay

On Muller's farm, and dreamed with pain
Of the day he wandered down the lane.

Bret Harte was not so good a man as Whittier, nor had he such good intentions. His verses are languid and his phrasing not so perfected as that of the older man; but, even though leaning on what Whittier had done, he wrote a better poem, ending it with slashing finality:

If, of all words of tongue or pen
The saddest are, "It might have been,"
More sad are these we daily see:
"It is, but hadn't ought to be."

Only two years after his pair of barefoot poems, Whittier reached close to the height of his poetic achievement with **"Skipper Ireson's Ride"** and a few months later, with **"Telling the Bees."** Both derived from legends he had heard as a younger man and both are included in his collected edition among the "Narrative and Legendary Poems"; but there is a tone of personal involvement in the second poem which makes it seem more proper to consider it, at least in part, as a reconstruction of experience which Whittier had known. **"Telling the Bees"** is among the few of Whittier's better poems written in the first person; and is almost the only poem written with the simple directness characteristic of his best prose. The opening lines have the same quality of quiet conversation which Robert Frost was later to manage so well in such a poem as "Stopping by Woods on a Snowy Evening." The scene which Whittier describes is in almost every detail that of the farmyard of the house in Haverhill in which he had lived as a boy:

Here is the place; right over the hill
    Runs the path I took;
You can see that gap in the old wall still,
    And the stepping stones in the shallow brook.

There is the house, with gate red-barred
    And poplars tall;
And the barn's brown length, and the cattle-yard,
    And white horns tossing above the wall.

The background is thus set forth in simple impressionistic strokes, with adjectives economically and expertly placed. Permanence and solidity pervade the scene, as if it had always been just this way and always

would be. The bee hives stand in a row beneath the sun as they had always stood. Only down by the brook is there any change; there the pansies and daffodils, roses and pinks are overrun with weeds; why the reader does not know, except that they are described as "her poor flowers." Who "she" is is not revealed. A year has passed, and slowly, since something had happened,

And the same rose blows, and the same sun glows,
    And the same brook sings of a year ago.

There's the same sweet clover-smell in the breeze;
    And the June sun warm.

The mood hints of sadness, but also of serenity. The linkage of sound in assonance and controlled alliteration and the repetition of the word "same," which re-enforces the atmosphere of solid permanence, and the slowing of cadence achieved in the line about the June sun contribute toward the creation of sentiment unspoiled by excess.

The narrator then remembers how a year before he had come courting to that place, carefully brushing the burrs from his best coat, smoothing his hair, and refreshing himself—the reader supposes after a dusty walk through the hot summer countryside—at the brook which flowed beside the farmyard gate. He had not been there for a month, but little was changed since his last visit. Sunlight slanted through the leaves; her roses bloomed as they had bloomed a month before. But the bee hives were different—passing among them walked a young servant girl, draping each hive with black and crooning softly to the bees. The narrator knew enough of Essex custom to realize the significance of this action. Someone had died, and local superstition required that the bees be informed immediately to keep them from swarming from their hives to seek a new home. His heart went out to Mary, named now for the first time as the young lady he had come to see. He thought of her unhappiness, weeping as she must be over the death of a loved one, perhaps her aged grandfather. But then he heard her dog whining and, looking more closely toward the farmhouse, saw that

            on the doorway sill,
    With his cane to his chin,
The old man sat; and the chore-girl still
    Sung to the bees stealing out and in.

Only with the last stanza does the reader surely know the cause of the young man's quietly modulated grief, held close and almost inarticulate, as a countryman's grief can be:

And the song she was singing ever since
    In my ear sounds on:—
"Stay at home pretty bees, fly not hence!
    Mistress Mary is dead and gone!"

No more than in **"Skipper Ireson's Ride"** or **"The Henchman"** is a moral appended, or needed. The solemn elegiac tone, the emotional control, the serene knowledge that beyond the permanence of personal grief is the permanence of memory and custom and place are effectively, even artlessly present, without need for underlining statement. Some readers find that the final stanzas fall below the standard set by the first, that the grief of the narrator is too muted and unrelieved to be convincing. To others, narrative and mood move hand in hand to produce the one flawless poem which Whittier wrote. Most will agreed with John Pickard that **"Telling the Bees"** succeeds "because of the utter simplicity of its prose-like phrasing and ballad meter, and because of its firm structural unity created by the progression from assurance to fear and then surprise."[11] Whittier himself wondered whether what he thought of as simplicity in the poem might not be interpreted as silliness by others.

Allied in theme to **"Telling the Bees"** is **"My Playmate,"** which Tennyson is reported to have called "a perfect poem"—and to have added in prophecy that "in some of his descriptions of scenery and wild flowers" Whittier would rank with Wordsworth.[12] But the beauty of the commonplace set forth in colloquial directness to create the mood of quiet submission characteristic of Whittier's best work is smothered in this second poem by the bathos of its theme which simply restates the familiar plaint of lonesome lovers: "Now that we have parted, do you ever think of me?" Even the wild grapes, the brown nuts, the violets, the dark pines, and the summer roses of New England woven through the tapestry of retrospective narrative succeed only briefly in supplying color to its irresponsible formlessness of design.

For all his crying down of art, Whittier succeeded only when, consciously or not, he provided some kind of structural foundation for his poems, as he had in **"Ichabod,"** in **"Telling the Bees,"** and in **"Skipper Ireson's Ride."** In many of his attractive poems, he is a poet of phrases or of a few lines or stanzas. He can be made to sound better in quotation of parts then in reproductions of complete poems. The familiar hymn which begins "Immortal love, forever full, Forever flowing free" is a reduction to five of the thirty-three stanzas of **"Our Master,"** the poem from which it is taken. Most of his poems are too long for what they have to say. Even his most devoted admirers must often skip judiciously if they are to make him appear at his best.

THE WINTER IDYL

Yet by almost unanimous consent, his longest poem is his best. *Snow-Bound: A Winter Idyl* has been described as "the greatest nineteenth-century poem of its type," a "composite of Yankee vignettes all mounted on one mat."[13] It has been compared, not always with excellent

reason, to Robert Burns's "The Cotter's Saturday Night" and to Oliver Goldsmith's "The Deserted Village." Bliss Perry found it "notable, not so much for sensuous beauty or for any fresh ways of thought, as for its vividness, its fidelity to homely detail, its unerring feeling for the sentiment of the hearthside."[14] Edmund C. Stedman thought it superior to "Hermann and Dorothea," "Enoch Arden," or even "Evangeline"; for these poems, "memorable for beauty of another kind, leave the impression that each of their authors said, as Virgil must have, 'And now I will write an idyl.' Whittier found his idyl already pictured for him by the camera of his own heart."[15] The poet himself was more modest; he spoke of *Snow-Bound* as a collection of "Flemish pictures of old days" or, more simply, as "a picture of an old-fashioned farmer's fireside in winter—and if it were not mine," he added with as much whimsicality as guile, "I should call it pretty good."[16]

Most of these statements about *Snow-Bound* are probably true. The poem is a sublimation of the subjective, written with lyrical intensity in tender memory, as Whittier stated in its dedication, of the household which it describes. He had first thought of dedicating it to his brother, the only other surviving member of the Whittier family and also, except for the poet, the only member of the family not seen in the poem sitting about the family fire. He and his brother were the anonymous boys of *Snow-Bound* who watched enchanted as the storm swept through the farmyard, who dug a tunnel through the snow toward the barn, who listened—unseen to the reader—by the fire, and who in bed that night dreamed summer dreams. They alone of all the family later went out into the world. But more than this, *Snow-Bound* was written in 1865, soon after the death not only of Whittier's sister but of their mother; and, in the truest sense, the poem was a memorial to them and to the quiet happiness which their presence and that of other members of the family who were now gone had once brought.

The theme of *Snow-Bound* turns, as John Pickard has explained, "on the nostalgic recall of the love and protection which the Whittier family once gave the poet, emphasizing the powerful sense of present loss and hope for spiritual comfort. These emotions are primarily developed by a series of contrasts: of fire and snow, past and present, people and elements—which combine to form the larger theme of love and immortality struggling against pain and death." He suggests that a touchstone for interpreting the poem is the symbolic development of the wood fire, the physical comforts derived from its brightness and warmth compared to the emotional and spiritual warmth of family love.[17]

These things are in *Snow-Bound,* and they are woven together securely by the familiar unities of time, place, and mood; but it is not a static poem. Time moves steadily on—that is another of the things which the poem is about. After a night and a day of steady snowfall, the family sat snug beside its fire—"Shut from all the world without"—for an evening of companionship and story; the next morning, members of the family were wakened by the shout of teamsters clearing the highway; but it is a week before they have full contact with the world again. Within this simple pattern much is packed, just as Thoreau crammed into the cycle of a single year the experience of two years' residence beside Walden Pond. The remembered evening by the fire is filled with more tales than could possibly be told between sundown and a farm-boy's bedtime. Memories of many years are distilled to produce an essence more purely characteristic than any single evening could have been. Because it is thus compacted of a lifetime of feeling focused upon a single experience and what led up to it and what followed, *Snow-Bound* develops naturally through a pattern in which chronology and theme are intricately interwoven. Only when Whittier indulges himself by speaking, not in reminiscence, but of present thoughts, is the pattern broken. But even these personal interludes become part of an integral whole.

Depth of feeling and finely etched vignettes of people and place had characterized many of Whittier's earlier poems. Occasionally, as in **"Skipper Ireson's Ride"** and **"Telling the Bees,"** these qualities had found coherence within patterns which have insured preservation to these poems—not because of the single excellence of any part, but through their wholeness as constructed entities. *Snow-Bound,* whether Whittier planned it so or not, is expertly patterned. It begins with a prelude made up of two quotations with which the poem is prefaced. The body of the poem is divided into three sections, each of which in turn is divided into parts. Each section is separated from the other by an interlude; and the whole is ended with a postlude which picks up, develops, and extends the theme suggested by the prelude at the beginning. The first section presents a mood of isolation; the second, of love and companionship; and the third, one created by the inevitable impingement of the world upon the quiet of wintry, rural solitude.

The introductory quotations set forth what seems at the beginning to have been considered its theme: the first from Agrippa's *Occult Philosophy* testifies to the superior power of light over darkness, even in the instance of "our common wood-fire" which, no less than the divine light of the sun, can drive away dark spirits; the second from Emerson's poem "The Snow Storm" speaks of housemates sitting about a radiant fireplace in a "tumultuous privacy of storm." Then the first section of the poem, lines 1-178, is introduced by thirty lines which describe the advent of the storm, the dark, circled sun, the steady east wind, and the hurry of the farm household in preparation for the coming of the snow. With line 31 comes "the whirl-dance of the blinding storm" which, as darkness fell quickly, piled white drifts against the window-frame; and for the next one hundred and twenty-four lines the storm is described: the marvelous shapes the snow took as it piled on corncrib, well-curb, or garden wall; the activities of the family in digging a path to the barn and caring for livestock there; the preparation of the evening fire, described in explicit detail:

> We piled with care our nightly stack
> Of wood against the chimney back—
> The oaken log, green, huge, and thick,
> And on its top the stout back-stick;
> The knotty forestick laid apart
> And filled between with curious art
> The ragged brush.

Outside the house, the whiteness of the snow, like the whiteness of Melville's whale or the encompassing whiteness which engulfs the climax of Poe's *Narrative of Arthur Gordon Pym,* is awesome and large with implications better felt than understood. All through this storm section the prevailing tone, beyond that of muted wonder at the strange beauty and fearsome menace of wind and snow and sleet, is of isolation:

> Beyond the circle of our hearth
> No welcome sound of toil or mirth
> Unbound the spell, and testified
> Of human life and thought inside.

Yet the section ends with thirty-four lines of quiet exhilaration, the family about the fire with house-dog and cat beside them, with cider simmering on the hearth and apples sputtering in a row. As so often in Hawthorne's tales, the cavernous hearth can be thought of as a symbol of the human heart which, when warmed by fires of love, is protected from all else besides:

> Blow high, blow low, not all its snow
> Could quench our hearth-fire's ruddy glow.

The second, longest, and central portion of the poem, lines 212-613, is separated from the first by an interlude of thirty-three lines in which Whittier comments on time and change; he recalls that his own hair now is as grey as his father's was on that winter evening long ago—

> How strange it seems, with so much gone
> Of life and love, to still live on!

Any life beyond this seemed no certainty, "yet love will dream, and Faith will trust" that somewhere, somehow, loved ones would meet again. Whittier pitied those

> Who hath not learned, in hours of faith,
> The truth to flesh and sense unknown,

> That Life is ever lord of Death,
>   And Love can never lose its own!

Then for more than four hundred lines the evening by the fire is recalled, the yarns which were spun, the puzzles and riddles proposed, the schoolwork stammered through. The father's tales are remembered—of trapper's hut and Indian camp; of Norman village dances, fishing and clambakes; and of witchcraft—and then the mother's tales are recalled. Neither is described as a person except through the stories they told; but the bachelor uncle—innocent of books, simple, guileless, childlike—and the maiden aunt, the sweetest woman ever withheld from marriage by a perverse fate, are described in more detail; and so is the elder sister, impulsive, earnest, but ultimately unhappy. The younger sister, recently dead, said nothing; she only sat quietly with large, sweet, asking eyes. At the thought of her Whittier breaks into a thirty-eight line elegiac interlude, lines 400-437, which concludes the first part of the second section. Though isolated within by cold and snow, the family is firmly bound and protected by bonds of love.

The theme of the second part of the second section, lines 438-589, moves from recollection of family love to memory of widened horizons brought to the family group by the companionship of visitors from the world outside. The stories told about the fire in the first part had been of native experience or of local legend. In the second part, the schoolmaster brings lore from books; and the woman visitor brings an aura of tempestuous romance from a world quite beyond that known to any of the family. All of the best of life is there, centered about the homestead hearth. Isolated but compact, the universe was what they made it, these people by the blazing wood-fire, as their minds ranged in reminiscence over what they knew or had seen. Among the best of Whittier's character sketches, worthy of a place beside the portraits of ladies later done by Edwin Arlington Robinson, T. S. Eliot, and Ezra Pound, is that of Harriet Livermore, the eccentric and high-minded adventurer, battered by rebuffs in her attempts at reform:

> A woman tropical, intense
> In thought and act, in soul and sense,
> She blended in a like degree
> The vixen and the devotee,
> Revealing with each freak or feint
> The temper of Petruchio's Kate,
> The raptures of Sienna's saint.
> Her tapering hand and rounded wrist
> Had facile power to form a fist;
> The warm, dark languish of her eyes
> Was never safe from wrath's surprise.
> Brows saintly calm and lips devout
> Knew every change of scowl and pout;
> And the sweet voice had notes more high
> And shrill in social battle-cry.

The second section ends when at bedtime, nine o'clock, the uncle covered the fire with ashes—an action perhaps too undisguisedly symbolic—and the mother offered a brief prayer of gratitude "For food and shelter, warmth and health, And love's contentment." A brief interlude, lines 614-628, then introduces the third section, as the brothers lay abed listening to the wind roaring about the gables, loosening clapboards, sometimes beating with such force against the house that "our very bedsteads rock." But the peace of sleep came finally to them, so like the peace of death which was to take away every other member of the family. Whittier seldom wrote with more delicate suggestion:

> But sleep stole on, as sleep will do
> When hearts are light and life is new;
> Faint and more faint the murmurs grew,
> Till in the summer-land of dreams
> They softened to the sound of streams,
> Low stir of leaves, and dip of oars,
> And lapsing waves on quiet shores.

The third section, lines 629-714, opens with the coming of a second morning and the arrival of teamsters clearing the highway of snow. It was a community project, each farmer in turn lending his oxen and his labor to the task. Then came the village doctor on his sleigh, requiring neighborly assistance in the care of the sick. Work and duty call members of the family from the quiet comfort of their fireside. Finally, a week later, the local newspaper arrived; and the world was suddenly with them again—and all its practicality in measuring the depth, not the awesome beauty, of the snow; with its cold, pragmatic record of marriage, death, or imprisonment; with its quest and celebration of profit. The pulse of life about them seemed now to melt the "chill embargo of the snow," which had not really been chill at all; for it had provided the warmth of love and companionship. A careless reading can overlook the ironic ambiguity of the lines with which Whittier ends the section:

> Wide swing again our ice-locked door,
> And all the world was ours once more!

In conclusion, lines 715-759, the poet speaks in his present, lonely voice of that "spectral past" when the brightness of a wood-fire drove away black spirits, when beside a radiant hearth happiness was found in spite of the tumult of the storm. *Snow-Bound* becomes then a parable of the life of any man, drawn by duty from the comfort of home ties; it becomes particularly a parable of Whittier's life, containing within it all for which he most had cared—a treasure chest crammed full of the people and the place, the kinds of legends of the past, and the lore of country life which formed the core of his existence. The fireside represented the kind of "insular Tahiti" of which Melville had spoken fifteen years earlier—a place of peaceful contentment to which, once having left it, no man could, nor indeed should, return. Here in comfort Whittier might have stayed, except that

> Importunate hours that hours succeed
> Each clamorous with its own sharp need,
>   And duty keeping pace with all.
> Shut down and clasp the heavy lids;
> I hear again the voice that bids
> The dreamer leave his dream midway
> For larger hopes and graver fears:
> Life threatens in these later years,
> The century's aloe flowers today!

This summons is not something which Whittier had not said before or would not say again. What distinguishes its statement in *Snow-Bound* beyond its statement almost anywhere else is that, though the words are not greatly better nor the feeling more intense than at other times, here it is firmly secured within a form which holds it firm as more than statement. What poetry has to say is not said alone by words which, as T. S. Eliot has explained,

> Crack and sometimes break under the burden,
> Under the tension, slip, slide, perish,
> Decay with imprecision. . . .

Only by the form—the pattern into which they are placed so that they play one upon another to suggest meanings beyond what is said—do they blend to become a poem. For this reason *Snow-Bound* becomes more than another exercise in nostalgic memory or a call for resolution in meeting the demands of duty; it shimmers with other suggestions. The past is good and beautiful and warm, like the wood-fire's blaze; and, in quiet moments, the benediction of memory is solace and joy; but life greatens when the present calls. In the last line quoted above, Whittier uses a favorite image of the century plant to say what Goethe said at the close of *Wilhelm Meister,* that America is here and now—and what T. S. Eliot meant when he said in "Burnt Norton"

> What might have been and what has been
> Point to one end, which is always present.

This comparison is not to imply that Whittier was a poet like T. S. Eliot or anyone else, or that he was a better or worse poet. What can be said is that occasionally he was a poet, and that his personal goodness and piety and gentleness contributed to and shine through that poetry. By themselves these qualities, whatever their excellence otherwise, can make a literary man a bore. Because goodness is a recognizable and eternal thing, what he says has so often been said, that one's answer to it is often a shrug—or an eye cocked for brighter, less hackneyed diversion. When the message is subdued, however, to the demands of art with its formal requirement of a beginning, a middle, and an end; when, without obtrusive intervention of the artist,

one part is linked to another through image and extension of theme; and when self and art and moral are merged to one as they do merge in *Snow-Bound* but in so few of Whittier's other writings—then the poem becomes an entity which, once read, remains.

THE HIGHEST REWARD

Whittier composed many more lines during the next quarter century, but most of them were about subjects of which he had written better before. In **"The Tent on the Beach"** and the prelude to **"Among the Hills"** he spoke again with simple directness of his poetic creed and his hopes for humanity. **"The Pennsylvania Pilgrim,"** though tediously long and repetitious, thought Barrett Wendell,[18] rang as wondrously free as ever in description of nature. Sarah Orne Jewett admired the nostalgic charm of **"The Homestead,"** especially the "line about the squirrel in the house."[19] Matthew Arnold is said to have considered **"In Schooldays"** as "one of the perfect poems that must live"; and Oliver Wendell Holmes wept on first reading it—"the most beautiful schoolboy poem," he said, "in the English language." Some months later, in the fall of 1878, Holmes wrote his old friend: "I thank God that He has given you the thoughts and feelings which sing themselves as naturally as the wood-thrush rings his silver bell—to steal your own exquisitely descriptive line. Who has preached the gospel of love to such a mighty congregation as you have preached it? Who has done so much to sweeten the soul of Calvinistic New England? You have your reward here in the affection with which all our people, who are capable of loving anybody, regard you. I trust you will find a still higher, in that world the harmony of which finds an echo in so many of your songs."[20]

Although most of the poems after *Snow-Bound* were echoes, many of them were also portents of kinds of poetry to be written by other New England men who were boys during these latter years when Whittier lived quietly in his village home. If in his vignettes of country life, Whittier's simple colloquialism and instinctive fidelity to local scene reveal him as a literary ancestor of Robert Frost, his portraits of people suggest him equally an ancestor of Edwin Arlington Robinson who in "Miniver Cheevy," "Luke Havergal," and "Richard Cory" sketched character with no less insight but with more expert strokes. Robinson was fifteen when Whittier in 1884 wrote **"Abram Morrison"** as part of his contribution toward support of a charitable fair in Amesbury. The boy in Maine might even then have struck out several of the stanzas in which the more loquacious, older poet recorded his memory of an idiosyncratic Irish Quaker whom he had known long ago; but he certainly would have enjoyed some of them:

> Midst the men and things which will
> Haunt an old man's memory still,

Drollest, quaintest of them all,
With a boy's laugh I recall
  Good old Abram Morrison.

. . . . .

Wandering down from Nutfield woods
With his household and its goods,
Never was it clearly told
How within our quiet fold
  Came to be a Morrison.

. . . . .

Simple-hearted, boy o'ergrown,
With a humour quite his own,
Of our sober-stepping ways,
Speech and look and cautious phrase,
  Slow to learn was Morrison.

Much we loved his stories told
Of a country strange and old,
Where the fairies danced till dawn,
And the goblin Leprecaun
  Looked, we thought, like Morrison.

Or wild tales of feud and fight,
Witch and troll and second sight
Whispered still where Stornoway
Looks across the stormy bay,
  Once the home of Morrisons.

. . . . .

On his well-worn theme intent,
Simple, child-like, innocent,
Heaven forgive the half-checked smile
Of our careless boyhood, while
  Listening to Friend Morrison.

. . . . .

Gone forever with the queer
Characters of that old year!
Now the many are as one;
Broken is the mould that run
  Men like Abram Morrison.

And broken perhaps is the mold also which produced the boy who became the man who remembered him.

Of the more than five hundred poems which Whittier included in his collected edition, perhaps only a dozen can be counted as surely successful. The following twelve seem to me Whittier's best, poems which might be included without apology in any Selected Edition of his writings: *Snow-Bound,* **"Skipper Ireson's Ride," "Telling the Bees," "Ichabod," "Proem," "Prelude"** to **"Among the Hills," "Massachusetts to Virginia," "Letter from a Missionary . . . ," "The Henchman," "Laus Deo," "The Fruit Gift,"** and **"Monadnock from Wachusett."** Another group contains excellent poetry, but in poems more impressive when quoted in part than when read entire: **"Mabel Martyn," "Kathleen," "The Witch of Wenham," "The Double-Headed Snake of Newbury," "The Prophecy of Samuel Sewall," "The Tent on the Beach," "The**

Panorama," "The Brewing of Soma," "The Waiting," "The Cypress Tree of Ceylon," "A Summer Pilgrimage," "The Last Walk in Autumn," "The Homestead," "The Old Burying Ground," "Abraham Davenport," and **"Abram Morrison."** No selection from Whittier would be representative, however, without some among the following more sentimental favorites: **"Maud Muller," "The Barefoot Boy," "In Schooldays," "Barbara Frietchie," "Official Piety,"** and **"Our Countrymen in Chains."**

George Arms, in presenting a "new view" of Whittier in *The Fields Were Green,* defends and reprints **"Birchbrook Hill," "The Pennsylvania Pilgrim," "Ichabod," "Skipper Ireson's Ride," "Maud Muller," "Barbara Frietchie,"** and *Snow-Bound.* Walt Whitman's friend William Sloane Kennedy—having made an appreciative bow toward *Snow-Bound* and **"Ichabod"**—named as "Whittier's best ballads": **"Telling the Bees," "Maud Muller," "Barbara Frietchie," "Skipper Ireson's Ride," "The Witch's Daughter,"** and **"The Witch of Wenham."** These only, he said, were "free from the disfigurement . . . of so many of Whittier's descriptive pieces; namely, the moral at the end."[21]

Hyatt Waggoner is more generous. "The following poems," he says, "seem to me to offer the best basis for a defense of Whittier's achievement as a poet. They are at any rate the ones I have had chiefly in mind in making the claim that a significant number of his poems are still rewarding to read. It seems to me that many of the least known are better than those most commonly anthologized." He lists them then in the order which Whittier gave them in his final arrangement: **"Telling the Bees," "The Double-Headed Snake of Newbury," "Mabel Martyn," "The Prophecy of Samuel Sewall," "Among the Hills"** (the whole poem, but especially the "Prelude"), **"The Pennsylvania Pilgrim," "The Fruit Gift," "The Old Burying Ground," "Monadnock from Wachusett," "A Summer Pilgrimage," "Ichabod," "The Tent on the Beach," "Massachusetts to Virginia," "The Christian Slave," "Lines from the Portrait . . . ," "The Panorama," "On a Prayer-Book," "My Namesake,"** *Snow-Bound,* **"Laus Deo," "Trust," "Trinitas,"** and **"Our Master."**[22]

In these listings, only *Snow-Bound* and **"Ichabod"** stand out as unanimous choices. Perhaps it is by these two that Whittier will finally be remembered, along with **"Telling the Bees"** and **"Skipper Ireson's Ride,"** both of which have attracted enthusiastic admirers. Each reader must finally make his own choice, for critics are notoriously better at finding faults than in recognizing superiority. To select so few of his poems as excellent is not however, to suggest that many others among his verses—phrases, lines, often whole stanzas—will not continue to appeal to the emotion or imagination of many readers. "This," he once said, "is, after all, the highest reward of a writer, to know that suffering and sad hearts have been made happier by his words." Whittier never made high claims for his verses. "I am not one of the master singers," he confessed, "and don't pose as one. By the grace of God I am only what I am, and don't wish to pose as more."[23]

A dozen poems—or even four—is a generous legacy from any poet. Few among his countrymen have contributed more. Whittier was wrong when once, in a moment of despondency, he wrote: "We shall perish and verily *our works will follow us.* The hearts which now know us and love us will also cease to beat, and with them our memories will die. The utilitarian of the twentieth century will not heed whether, in treading on our graves, he shakes the dust of prose or poetry from his feet."[24] For Whittier does live on, recognized both as a courageous and a gentle man and as a gifted minor poet whom his countrymen may well remember with gratitude and pride. His limits are plainly marked, and by none more honestly than by himself.

Few poets are more comfortable to be with, for Whittier seldom makes any demand on readers other than to ask them to recognize with him that God is good, that nature is radiant with beauty, and that love is man's single shield against meanness and despair. Neither subtle nor complicated, and rarely perplexed either by sophistication or compromise, he speaks often of matters so radically profound that they require simplest statement. Late in life he wrote of **"A Summer Pilgrimage"** which took him once again to New England mountains amid whose untroubled quiet man and nature seemed momentarily at peace: behind the veils which beauty wove, man and mountain, lake, stream, and wood stood "witness to the Eternal Good." What the poet saw or felt or heard was an imperfect representation:

> A holier beauty overbroods
> These fair and faint similitudes.

Only undisturbed, familiar, and quiet words might reach toward truths which every man knew, and not in vain would be the reaching, though it failed to find its goal, for

> not unblest is he who sees
> Shadows of God's realities
> And knows beyond this masquerade
> Of shape and color, light and shade,
> And dawn and set, and wax and wane,
> Eternal verities remain.

Whittier's honesty and gentleness, his humility, and his quick anger at injustice certify him a good man, serene in faith which no experience could corrupt. His own life, as Whitman might have said, was his best poem, and **Snow-Bound** caught much of its essence. The

journeyman verses excoriating slavery are part of the history of his time, testimonies to the purity of his intentions. Except occasionally, as in **"Telling the Bees"** and **"Skipper Ireson's Ride,"** his narrative gift was not great. What seems most satisfactorily to survive are his portraits of people and his sketches of New England countryside—the vignettes, the pastorals, the idyls, the genre pieces, evocative of scene and character and mood. Though outlines are sometimes blurred with sentiment, the central portions usually stand clear, with trees, mountains, flowers, and people distinctly drawn. When he thus looked at objects and found words to reveal them, then he was a poet.

The goodness was always there, a precious possession, underlying and directing everything he wrote, and sometimes intruding. Without it, Whittier would have been someone else, a lesser man. To find the proper words and their necessary order, the artist's task, required discipline of a kind which neither Whittier's temperament nor time consistently provided. The wonder is that, unrestrained by criticism and unchallenged by effective competition, he should so often have done so well. That even in a few poems he surmounted his obvious shortcomings seems a miracle, as if Whittier, a rhymster by trade, was a poet by accident. Because poetry derives both from miracle and discipline, the point need not be labored. Whittier's achievement, small but unmistakably genuine, presents sufficient proof that on more than one occasion he submitted to both.

Notes

1. [George Arms] *The Fields Were Green: A New View of Bryant, Whittier, Holmes, Lowell, and Longfellow* (Stanford, California, [1953]), pp. 38-39.

2. [John B. Pickard] "Whittier's Ballads: The Maturing of an Artist," *Essex Institute Historical Collections,* XCVI (January, 1960), 56-72; see also Mr. Pickard's *The Artistry of Whittier,* unpublished University of Wisconsin doctoral dissertation, 1954.

3. [Winfield Townley Scott] "Poetry in America: A New Consideration of Whittier's Poetry," *New England Quarterly,* VII (June, 1934), 259.

4. [John May] *The Spirit of American Literature* (New York, 1913), p. 121.

5. Quoted in Edmund Clarence Stedman, *The Poets of America* (Boston and New York, 1885), p. 604.

6. "Poetry in America," *op. cit.,* p. 273.

7. [Ludwig Lewisohn] *Expression in America* [(New York, 1932)], p. 127.

8. [Samuel T.] Pickard, *Life* [*Life and Letters of John Greenleaf Whittier* (Boston and New York, 1899)], II, 364.

9. *Ibid.,* II, 593.

10. *The Fields Were Green,* p. 6.

11. "Whittier's Ballads," *op. cit.,* p. 68.

12. Pickard, *Life,* II, 428, 453.

13. John A. Pollard, *John Greenleaf Whittier: Friend to Man* (Boston, 1949), p. 265.

14. [Perry, Bliss] *John Greenleaf Whittier: A Sketch of His Life* (Boston, 1907), p. 28.

15. *Poets of America,* p. 117.

16. Pickard, *Life,* II, 497-98.

17. [John B. Pickard] "Imagistic and Structural Unity in 'Snow-Bound,'" *College English,* XXI (March, 1960), 34-50. Mr. Pickard discovers a structure in *Snow-Bound* somewhat simpler than the one which I outline; his treatment of the whole poem, however, is the most expert and sympathetic which I have seen.

18. [Barrett Wendall] "John Greenleaf Whittier," *Stelligeri and Other Essays Concerning America* (New York, 1893), pp. 166-67.

19. Quoted in Pickard, *Life,* II, 718-19. Whittier admired Miss Jewett's writings also. In 1879 he wrote to her: "I have read 'Deephaven' over half a dozen times, and always with gratitude to thee for such a book—so simple, pure, and so true to nature. And 'Old Friends and New' I shall certainly read as often. When tired and worried I resort to thy books and find rest and refreshing. I recommend them to everybody, and everybody likes them. There is no dissenting opinion; and already thousands whom thee have never seen love the author as well as her books" (Pickard, *Life,* II, 654).

20. Pickard, *Life,* II, 644.

21. *John Greenleaf Whittier,* p. 221.

22. "What I Had I Gave," *op. cit.,* p. 40n.

23. Quoted in Jay B. Hubbell, *American Life in Literature* (New York, 1949), I, 565.

24. Quoted in Scott, "Poetry in America," *op. cit.,* p. 274-75.

Selected Bibliography

WHITTIER'S WORKS

The most complete edition of Whittier's writings, edited by Horace E. Scudder, with Whittier's assistance, is *The Writings of John Greenleaf Whittier* (Boston and New York: Houghton Mifflin Company, 1888-89), 7 vols., reissued, 1904; see Eleanor M. Tilton, "Making Whittier Definitive," *New England Quarterly,* XII (June, 1939), 281-84. This edition forms the basis of Scudder's one-volume Cambridge Edition, *The Complete Poems of John Greenleaf Whittier* (Boston and New York: Houghton Mifflin Company, 1894). An excellently edited text is Harry Hayden Clark's *John Greenleaf Whittier: Representative Selections, with Introduction, Bibliography, and Notes* (New York: American Book Company, 1935).

Bibliographically, Whittier is exhaustively explained in Thomas Franklin Currier, *A Bibliography of John Greenleaf Whittier* (Cambridge: Harvard University Press, 1937). For later periodical writings concerning him, see Lewis Leary, ed., *Articles on American Literature, 1900-1950* (Durham, North Carolina: Duke University Press, 1954), pp. 316-19.

SECONDARY SOURCES

The following selective list includes biographical and critical writings useful to the student of Whittier.

ARMS, GEORGE. *The Fields Were Green: A New View of Bryant, Whittier, Holmes, Lowell, and Longfellow, with a Selection of Their Poems.* Stanford, California: Stanford University Press (1953).

KENNEDY, WILLIAM SLOANE. *John Greenleaf Whittier: The Poet of Freedom.* New York: Funk and Wagnalls Company, 1892.

PERRY, BLISS. *John Greenleaf Whittier: A Sketch of His Life.* Boston and New York: Houghton Mifflin Company, 1907.

PICKARD, JOHN B. "Imagistic and Structural Unity in 'Snow-Bound,'" *College English,* XXI (March, 1960), 338-42.

———. "Whittier's Ballads: The Maturing of an Artist," *Essex Institute Historical Collections,* XCVI (January, 1960), 56-73.

PICKARD, SAMUEL T. *Life and Letters of John Greenleaf Whittier.* Boston and New York: Houghton Mifflin Company, 1894.

POLLARD, JOHN A. *John Greenleaf Whittier: Friend to Man.* Boston: Houghton Mifflin Company, 1949.

SCOTT, WINFIELD TOWNLEY. "Poetry in America: A New Consideration of Whittier's Poetry," *New England Quarterly,* VII (June, 1934), 258-75.

WAGGONER, HYATT H. "What I Had I Gave: Another Look at Whittier," *Essex Institute Historical Collections,* XVI (January, 1959), 32-40.

John B. Pickard (essay date 1961)

SOURCE: Pickard, John B. "The Ballads" and "Genre Poetry." In *John Greenleaf Whittier: An Introduction and Interpretation,* pp. 59-100. New York: Barnes and Noble, 1961.

[*In the following excerpts, Pickard discusses two groups of Whittier's poems, contending that together they represent his finest achievement as a poet.*]

Excluding his genre poems, Whittier's ballads probably represent his finest poetic achievement and the best re-creation of native folklore and legend written in the nineteenth century. His ballads, especially, express his lifelong interest in New England history and wide knowledge of local customs and superstitions. Still the formation of these ballads was a tortuous process which reveals how slowly Whittier's artistry matured and how tardily he recognized his own abilities. Only when dealing with material that was intimately associated with his Quaker beliefs, rural background, humanitarian interests, and Essex region could Whittier produce poetry of artistic quality and enduring merit.

In general Whittier's ballads remain remarkably true to the characteristics of traditional folk balladry. Like Sir Walter Scott, Whittier was genuinely responsive to the spirit of folk narrative, having the background knowledge necessary to embody popular feeling and legend in narrative song. His best ballads are realistic and direct, centralizing on dramatic action and developing one main theme. As in traditional ballads the tragic overtones of the theme evolve from the basic emotions of love, hate, loyalty, and betrayal with particular emphasis on an individual rebellion against society. Whittier's diction is usually sparse and simple, while his images are commonplace and filled with folk expression. Even so, lyric and pastoral effects often hinder dramatic action and mar the objectivity so necessary for good balladry. Nor do the ballads escape his habitual "moral squint."

Though many American poets wrote ballads in the nineteenth century, only Whittier and Longfellow attempted to narrate folk and native material in a large number of their verses. Most of Longfellow's ballads utilize European folk tales or chivalric romances to glorify the past and create an atmosphere of melancholy. Some of them, such as his longer narratives "Evangeline" and "The Song of Hiawatha," do employ native material and are polished attempts to create beauty and romance in the American scene. His most famous ballad, "The Wreck of the Hesperus," dramatizes a moment of action that is purely American, the wreck of a schooner near Gloucester in 1839, or actually the wrecks of several ships there during a severe storm. The form is faultless, the story's movement is light and

smooth, and the idiom remains simple. The structure is good, building to the disaster with the warning of the old sailor and its scornful dismissal by the confident captain. However, the storm and the captain's fears for his daughter are melodramatically and sentimentally presented. Also noticeable is the lack of realistic setting and definite locale, for Longfellow does little more than refer to the "reef of Norman's woe." In contrast is Whittier's ballad **"The Wreck of Rivermouth,"** which also suffers from an excess of melodrama and moralizing, but in Whittier's poem the unreality of the actual situation is bulwarked by a realistic account of the storm and the story is inseparably tied to the New England coastline by a concrete description of the locale.

Most of Longfellow's ballads are far from the spirit of traditional ones. Their conscious poetic devices and sentimental handling of narrative destroy drama, while the subjects used have little relation to his own experience. The dream world of the past when culled from foreign sources is hardly conducive to the production of typical American ballads. It is precisely on this point of realism and local atmosphere that Whittier displays superiority to Longfellow, for he produced ballads which typified the American heritage and expressed its values. Whittier lived his life in the main currents of his age as editor, Abolitionist, and politician; he knew and loved his generation; and by background, religious training, and study he could sympathize with the previous ones. As a Quaker, Whittier's earliest readings and instructions had been from the journals and histories of the Friends, which contained accounts of the persecutions endured by the original Quaker settlers. Whittier grew up revering Quakers such as Margaret Brewster and Samuel Shattuck who suffered for their beliefs, and admiring those who resisted intolerance such as Thomas Macy and Cassandra Southwick, while his later researches into Colonial history gave him a sympathetic insight into the nature of the Puritan theocracy and the reasons for the persecutions. Then his isolated rural upbringing made him completely dependent on his family and the surrounding district for intellectual growth and emotional maturity, and the close ties formed by years of permanent association with one place instilled in him a love of locality and all the traditions connected with it. His imaginative, responsive mind never forgot the tales told around the Whittier fireplace about Essex County witches, popular superstitions, or local personages such as Floyd Ireson and Mary Ingalls. It was from these sources that Whittier obtained the material for some of his best ballads.

* * *

Fortunately for Whittier, his earliest literary influences were the poems of Burns, which glorified rural life and local customs, and the romances of Scott, which centered on the heroism of Scottish warriors. His imitations of these two men, or at least his use of their themes as he saw them reflected in his own life, were the most promising verses of his early years. His first collection of poems and tales, *Legends of New England,* dealt entirely with local traditions and superstitions. The verses are marred by digressions and extravagant romantic phrasing and employ the typical Gothic devices of doomed lovers, ghostly ships, and hidden horrors. However, one ballad, **"The Black Fox,"** has a sure poetic beat and adapts its subject and content to the ballad tradition of simplicity. The introduction to the poem recreates the atmosphere of a winter's evening in rural New England with a clearness of language and simplicity of diction that indicate Whittier's ballad capabilities. The grandmother is an excellent choice as narrator with her homespun descriptions and superstitious nature, while her account of the mysterious activities of the black fox effectively conveys a rural delight in the supernatural. Though the story is artificial, even sentimental in parts, it minimizes Gothic horror and eliminates moralizing—a marked advance over Whittier's other ballad attempts.

Another early ballad is **"The Song of the Vermonters"** (1833). Its theme, a rallying cry for all patriotic Vermonters to defend their state during the Revolutionary War, is an obvious imitation of Scott's border romances; its form, rhyming couplets with a basic anapestic beat, gives a martial ring to the whole:

> He—all to the borders! Vermonters, come down,
> With your breeches of deerskin and jackets of brown;
> With your red woolen caps, and your moccasins,
>   come,
> To the gathering summons of trumpet and drum.

The poem's local color descriptions of the countryside, boastful praise of Vermont's qualities, and defiant challenge to "all the world" are conscious attempts to present the song as an authentic ballad. In fact, Whittier predated the poem 1779. Despite its rhetorical air, characteristic moralizing, and poetic language, many sections do accord with good ballad presentation. This poem indicates how close Whittier was to having the right medium for expressing his deep-rooted feelings about the New England past.

During the next fifteen years, Whittier only intermittently followed the path marked out by these pioneer pieces, as his Abolitionist work demanded his full attention. Still, some of his anti-slavery poems show the experiments that he was making with ballad technique. **"The Hunters of Men"** (1835) is a caustic satire on the newest southern amusement, the tracking down of escaped slaves. Opening his poem in the best chivalric manner, Whittier establishes the atmosphere of a medieval chase with his invitation for all to come hunting:

> Have ye heard of our hunting, o'er mountain and glen,
> Through cane-brake and forest—the hunting of men?
> The lords of our land to this hunting have gone,
> As the fox-hunter follows the sound of the horn;
> Hark! the cheer and hallo! the crack of the whip.

The archaic words, the courtly adjectives, and the titling of the hunters as "lords" are all devices of olden romances; while the use of a refrain, "the hunting of men," and the conscious repetitions of similar phrases and sound patterns are part of established ballad technique. These gracious phrases and romantic images are ironically contrasted with the inhuman purpose of the hunt—the killing of men. With heavy-handed satire Whittier continues this romantic pretense crying out: "Gay luck to our hunters" and "Oh, goodly and grand is our hunting to see." The irony fails when Whittier depicts priests, politicians, mothers, and daughters merrily hunting the slaves; he had not yet learned the restraint and understatement necessary for finished satiric art and true ballad creation.

* * *

One of his first real ballads is **"The Exiles,"** written in 1841. It shows how a decade of Abolitionist work had matured him, and, conversely, how far he had yet to go for poetic maturity. Certainly his antislavery writing had enlarged his sense of the dramatic, developed his awareness of emotional appeal, and taught him the necessity of direct statement. The plot of **"The Exiles"** is aptly suited to ballad demands for an exciting, realistic narrative, since it is the tale of Thomas Macy's flight down the Merrimack River to escape persecution for harboring a Quaker. Its theme, the dramatic struggle of one man against existing injustice, stresses the value of inner principle over outward law. Everything was within the range of Whittier's talents and interests, for he had grown up in the Merrimack Valley and had spent the greater part of his life fighting for freedom and resisting intolerance. Yet he failed to develop the poem artistically. It is overly long (sixty stanzas) and greatly weakened by numerous digressions and pious interjections, while its labored comparisons and sentimental tone ignore the realism of good balladry. Over half the poem deals with a wordy description of the fleeing Quaker and his eventual capture—all of which distract from the central drama of Macy's courage and flight.

However, there is a fine ballad meter, and touches in the story demonstrate how naturally Whittier could portray characters and how realistically he could sketch in background settings. The inner serenity of the old Quaker is described as the covering of "autumn's moonlight," while the frustrated priest is seen with his "grave cocked hat" gone and his dishevelled wig hanging behind him "like some owl's nest . . . upon a thorn." The flight of Macy down the Merrimack is simply presented through selected scenes of nearby communities:

The fisher wives of Salisbury—
    The men were all away—
Looked out to see the stranger oar
    Upon their waters play.

Deer Island's rocks and fir-trees threw
    Their sunset-shadows o'er them,
And Newbury's spire and weathercock
    Peered o'er the pines before them.

* * *

"Cassandra Southwick," written in 1843, shows a considerable advance over **"The Exiles"** in dramatic structure and presentation. Here, too, the incident is one culled from the history of Quaker persecutions; but instead of relating the complete story behind Cassandra's imprisonment, Whittier concentrates on the fears and doubts of the girl as she waits to be sold into slavery. The early section of the poem, though overlong and rhetorical, probes the nature of Cassandra's fears and near despair. Her simple, trusting spirit is prey to all the distorted visions that the night and the unknown can bring. Torturedly she contrasts her past rural childhood, her shy hopes of romance, and her open delight in nature against her present imprisonment for following the "crazy fancies" of the Quakers. Fearfully she imagines the insults and pain that her gentle feminine nature will soon be subject to. Though her language is platitudinous and filled with biblical allusions, it fits her religious spirit and farm background. Finally prayer and her recollections of other martyrs dispel the nightmarish terrors. Once dawn breaks, the movement is swift and dramatic as she is led to the wharves. Whittier pauses briefly to show her dazed response to the bright sunlight, the idle laughter of the crowd, and the rough handling by the sheriff. Her shame under the glare of the curious onlookers and her pathetic cry for God's aid increase the tenseness of the scene. As she approaches the docks, Whittier conveys the atmosphere of a sea town with the briefest possible detail:

We paused at length, where at my feet the sunlit waters
    broke
On glaring reach of shining beach, and shingly wall of
    rock;

The merchant-ships lay idly there, in hard clear lines
    on high,
Tracing with rope and slender spar their network on
    the sky.

And there were ancient citizens, cloak-wrapped and
    grave and cold,
And grim and stout sea-captains with faces bronzed
    and old.

All the characters, including the clerk Rawson and Governor Endicott, are generalized—only briefly seen by the hesitant glances of the young girl. Under the taunts of the sheriff, Cassandra defends her innocence,

while her passionate outcry and complete helplessness win the sympathy of the crowd. The captains remain silent as the sheriff repeatedly calls for a volunteer to sell Cassandra into slavery. Finally, one answers:

Pile my ship with bars of silver, pack with coins of
    Spanish gold,
From keel-piece up to deck-plank, the roomage of her
    hold,
By the living God who made me!—I would sooner in
    your bay
Sink ship and crew and cargo, than bear this child
    away!

An aroused crowd now roars its approval and turns on Endicott and his followers. As they leave, Cassandra is freed; unfortunately the denouement is prolonged by Cassandra's fervent thanksgiving to God. Still the nucleus of the story is well told and it does have a swift dramatic movement. Whittier's use of the first person narrative gives an immediacy to the action and deepens the tale by an examination of her mental fears and religious doubts. The heavy religious imagery and allusions strengthen the underlying theme—that God protects his own. Throughout, the repetition of key words, the series of "and" connectives, and the parallelisms of adjectives and nouns create a definite folk flavor. The descriptive imagery is of the simplest kind: Rawson's cheek is "wine-empurpled," the captain growls back his answer like "the roaring of the sea," and Endicott looks at the disapproving crowd with a "lion glare." Though the poem is overlong and didactic, it is a long step from the discursive and dramatically weak **"The Exiles."** Whittier had found his proper subject matter and was now approaching surety of presentation.

* * *

Another ballad of the same year, **"The New Wife and the Old,"** deals with a local superstition which Whittier had heard as a child about the power of dead spirits. Though its consciously set mood of terror and suspense is somewhat reminiscent of Gothic narrative, its excellent style holds the reader's interest:

Dark the halls, and cold the feast,
Gone the bridemaids, gone the priest.
All is over, all is done.

. . . . .

Hushed within and hushed without,
Dancing feet and wrestlers' shout;
Dies the bonfire on the hill;
All is dark and all is still.

The repetitions of similar verb patterns and the balance of phrases with their recurrence in later stanzas establish a mood of waiting and anxiety. The resulting drama does not quite live up to this effective introduction as the young bride has her wedding ring and bracelet melodramatically stolen by the ghost of a former wife. Near the end of the story, interest switches from the terror and wonder of the new bride to an examination of the sinful conscience of the older husband. Also Whittier upsets the unity of the story by musing on the supernatural reasons for the dead wife's action. Still, the ballad technique is sure and the story concentrates on the one main incident without undue moralizing.

* * *

During the next ten years the pressures of editorial and journalistic duties caused Whittier to write mainly prose; consequently he neglected his ballads. Two ballads of this period merit attention, however, **"Barclay of Ury"** and **"Kathleen,"** "Barclay of Ury" (1847) expands the general theme of **"Cassandra Southwick"** in dealing with the indignities heaped upon an old warrior for joining the Quakers. Again the story turns on the conflict of inner conviction versus outward ridicule with the added irony that Barclay's former friends now abuse him, feeling that he betrayed their trust. The simple diction and unadorned tone are in perfect keeping with ballad objectivity and directness, while the religious note is intimately connected with Barclay's character. As he slowly rides through his native town, secure in the strength of the Inner Light, his dignity is contrasted with the emotional outbursts of the surrounding mob. The slow deliberate beat of the verse echoes the measured pace of his horse, indicating his unflinching religious confidence and determination to pursue his Quaker course despite all threats. The climax of the poem occurs when a former comrade rushes to his defense and pleads with Barclay to fight the crowd. His bewilderment when Barclay refuses to fight re-echoes the mob's previous betrayal, while his pity moves Barclay as violence never could. This meeting serves as the dramatic introduction to Barclay's simple testament of faith. He contrasts past glory and acclaim with his present debasement and admits that it is hard to lose friends, to be humiliated, and "to learn forgiving"; but, realizing that "God's own time is best," he can endure all—so he goes his own way, completely alone. Whittier should have ended the ballad with this moving speech which grew organically out of a definite dramatic situation. Instead he tagged on a moral of four stanzas which marred an otherwise fine ballad. Still the portrait of Barclay is Whittier's first successful investigation of those reserved, stiff figures whose utter simplicity and tenacious faith reveal a sense of elemental power.

The other ballad of this period, **"Kathleen"** (1849), shows Whittier's complete mastery of ballad technique. Purporting to be a tale of old Ireland sung by a wandering Irish scholar, the poem does not have a local theme, but its content and style are handled in traditional ballad manner. The story relates the selling of a beautiful Irish girl to the American colonies by her cruel stepmother, a later rescue by a young lover, and a safe return to her sorrowing father. The first stanzas immediately begin the narrative with the marriage of the "mighty lord" of "Galaway" to another wife; the second stanza marks out the conflict in the ballad, the new wife's favoring of her own child to the neglect of Kathleen. A few stanzas later, Kathleen is introduced and warning is given of her coming doom. In traditional ballad fashion, dialogue is used throughout to convey feeling and action: no motivation is given for the stepmother's sudden decision to sell Kathleen; and there is no plausible explanation for her triumph over the old lord's love for his daughter. The art in these following stanzas is a thing of the utmost simplicity:

> Oh, then spake up the angry dame,
> 　"Get up, get up," quoth she,
> "I'll sell ye over Ireland,
> 　I'll sell ye o'er the sea!"
>
> She clipped her glossy hair away,
> 　That none her rank might know,
> She took away her gown of silk,
> 　And gave her one of tow,
>
> And sent her down to Limerick town
> 　And to a seaman sold
> This daughter of an Irish lord
> 　For ten good pounds in gold.

This objective tone is preserved throughout and the scholar's final summation, in perfect keeping with his function as a wandering minstrel, provides the desired happy ending. Noticeable too is the absence of sophisticated imagery; only the most conventional descriptions are given: the girl is "fair" and "the flower of Ireland"; her arm is "snowy-white" and her hand "snow-white"; and the stepmother is seen as "angry" and "evil." This ballad readily illustrates the progress Whittier had made from his early uneven, discursive ballads.

* * *

Whittier was now at the height of his poetic powers and the next twenty years were to witness the writing of his best ballads. In 1828 Whittier first heard from a schoolmate at Haverhill Academy the song of Skipper Ireson's being tarred and feathered by the women of Marblehead. It was a typical folk song known to all the inhabitants of the town—perfect material for a poet who knew the locale and understood the mentality of the people. At that time Whittier tried writing it down, but it was not to be finished until nearly thirty years later. This gestation period proved valuable, for when Whittier finally wrote **"Skipper Ireson's Ride"** he created the best American ballad of the nineteenth century.

The ballad opens slowly, almost incongruously, as the strangeness of Ireson's ride out of Marblehead is compared to other famous rides of story and rhyme.

The reference to Apuleius' journey after his transformation into an ass, to Mohammed's flight on the back of a strange winged, white mule, and to the Tartar king's ride on a magical horse of brass, are purposefully outlandish and, as George Arms has pointed out, set a grotesque, grimly humorous tone for the opening stanzas. The refrain, which is repeated with slight variations in every stanza, gives the essence of the story, though it does not tell why the skipper is being punished. The second and third stanzas put the reader immediately *in medias res* as we watch the tarred and feathered captain driven through the streets of Marblehead by the enraged populace. The descriptions are exaggerated, even ludicrous, for Floyd's dishevelled condition is mocked as "Body of turkey, head of owl, / Wings a-droop like a rained-on fowl" and later on as "an Indian idol glum and grim." The crowd, strangely consisting of women, responds to his plight with raucous cries and violent jostling which travesty the underlying seriousness of the scene. Their wild actions create a half-mad, half-comic mood which catches the chaos and confusion of mob action. Again the comparisons follow a classical pattern as the recklessness of the girls in the crowd is portrayed:

> Wild-eyed, free-limbed, such as chase
> Bacchus round some antique vase,
> Brief of skirt, with ankles bare,
> Loose of kerchief and loose of hair,
> With conch-shells blowing and fish-horns' twang,
> Over and over the Maenads sang.

The reference to the frenzied antics of Bacchus' women followers links Ireson's present misery to the ancient accounts of males being torn to pieces during the orgies of the Maenads. From another aspect it also ridicules the pathetic figure of Ireson who is far from being the jovial god of wine and farther from enjoying the rite now being performed in his honor.

The tone changes in the fourth and fifth stanzas as the reasons for the punishment are revealed. He had sailed away from a sinking ship that was filled with his own townspeople; he had betrayed his own kin. The brief dialogue in stanza four gives the crucial moment of the tragedy, as the drowning crew called out for Ireson to save them, only to receive his heartless reply, "Sink or swim! / Brag of your catch of fish again!" Only this and nothing more. We never know his motivation, nor is the event further elaborated. One can surmise from the tone of fragmentary conversation that there was a deep-rooted enmity between Floyd and the crew over a catch of fish, and for this he wrathfully allowed them to die. The horror of his act is enlarged upon by the pathetic picture of the women of Marblehead, looking "for the coming that might not be." Now we know why the women pursue the old skipper—they are the dead men's wives, mothers, sisters, and daughters, trying to wring some measure of revenge for the senseless death of their loved ones. Now we can understand why their actions are such a curious blend of humor and hate, for their disorder and emotional confusion symbolize their own broken lives. All these things are but touched upon as the story moves quickly back to the original scene and Ireson's shameful ride. Stanza six returns to the savage humor of the opening, rising to a climax with this description of the old men who join the women:

> Sea-worn grandsires, cripple-bound,
> Hulks of old sailors run aground,
> Shook head, and fist, and hat, and cane,
> And cracked with curses the hoarse refrain.

Part of Whittier's achievement is seen in these lines. The shipwreck images echo Ireson's betrayal and ridicule the pitiful attempts of the old sailors to obtain revenge, while their feeble, cracking voices make the refrain childish and meaningless. The crippled quality of their acts and the female character of the mob indicate the complete failure of the townspeople to obtain any measure of satisfaction that equals their loss.

Suddenly the mood shifts, and in contrast to the harsh voices of the turbulent mob in the narrow winding streets is the peace and serenity of the road leading to nearby Salem:

> Sweetly along the Salem road
> Bloom of orchard and lilac showed.
> Little the wicked skipper knew
> Of the fields so green and the sky so blue.

As the physical setting changes for artistic contrast, so does the psychological tone. For the first time the skipper is allowed to dominate the scene. Here again the action is presented through dialogue, rather than through author-narration, to preserve dramatic intensity. The outward scene fades, along with the ignominy of the ride and tarring, when the inward soul of the skipper cries out wretchedly:

> What to me is this noisy ride?
> What is the shame that clothes the skin
> To the nameless horror that lives within?

The transition is sudden and complete, surprising the reader who is engrossed in the outward narrative and making him startlingly aware of the poem's chief theme—the torture and remorse of a man after his crime. Though the hate of the mob and his present physical disfigurement will pass with time, his own terrible awareness of the sin will not. The image of the material clothes of shame (the tar and feathers) is contrasted with his mental revulsion for the crime, which covers or clothes his soul; the external suffering becomes insignificant when compared to the torments of conscience. Ireson's unexpected admission of guilt is perhaps unmotivated, but the change from hate to remorse is in keeping with the shifting pattern of the poem, its mixture of humor, pathos, and cruelty—all ironic paradoxes which highlight the irrationality of mob action and revenge. The crowd's response to Ireson's outcry attests to the validity of the skipper's comments; in accord with their New England religious heritage their vengeful yells turn to sorrowful murmurings. In "half scorn, half pity" they turn him loose and with a fine ironic echo of the clothes image give him a cloak to hide in. The final refrain changes "Old" Floyd Ireson to "Poor" Floyd Ireson and so becomes a mournful dirge forever accusing and dooming the man as well as emphasizing the hollowness remaining in the lives of the townspeople. The ballad makes Ireson live as an essentially tragic figure, a man who has betrayed the loyalties of his home and the manly traditions of the sea. He towers over the drama, coming from the sea, acting without apparent justification, and then vanishing to live alone with his shame.

The ballad succeeds because of its dramatic structure, sure handling of tone, definite localization, simplicity of diction, and knowledge of the psychology indigenous to New England. The whole poem centralizes on one incident, Skipper Ireson's ride from Marblehead. Like "Sir Patrick Spens," the well-known old English ballad, the story is based on a conflict of loyalties and gives no description of the central incident; the sinking of the ship is merely indicated by a brief dialogue, while its effects are seen in the actions of the townspeople. The tone is a unique blend of grim exaggeration, farfetched allusion, and genuine pathos which captures perfectly the swirl of conflicting emotions resulting from deep pain and sudden loss. Throughout, the author is impersonal, employing terse dialogue to keep the action objective and straightforward. And there is no moral attached, for it is organic within the story itself. The variations in the ballad, from the outward crowd scene to the flashback, then to the crowd again, and to the final sudden psychological twist, masterfully sustain interest. Whittier was to write other fine ballads—some more famous—but none were to equal the harmony of content and form which he achieved here.

* * *

At last Whittier had attained the artistry to express his feelings for the New England scene, its history, customs, and deeper psychological traditions. And so in rapid succession followed the gems of his maturity: the lyric drama **"Telling the Bees"**; the pastoral romance ballads **"Amy Wentworth," "The Countess,"** and **"The Witch of Wenham"**; the hardier ballads of history and superstition **"The Wreck of Rivermouth," "The Garrison of Cape Ann,"** and **"The Palatine"**; and his later dramatic ballads of Quaker persecution **"The King's Missive"** and **"How the Women Went from Dover."** Francis B. Gummere states in his introduction to *Old*

English Ballads that spontaneity is one of the virtues of the ballad, that ballads never give "poetry for poetry's sake, but are born of an occasion, a need; they have as little subjectivity as speech itself." Whittier's most famous ballad, **"Barbara Frietchie,"** exemplifies this phase of ballad approach. The incident—the courage of an old lady in waving a Union flag before the conquering rebel troops—was supposedly a true one. The poem was written in the heat of the crucial battle year of 1863 and embodied Whittier's passionate belief that fundamentally many southern rebels loved the Union as he did. His years of Abolitionist work had centered around a peaceful solution to the problem, but when the war came Whittier resigned himself to waiting and enduring its horrors. He knew that the Union must be preserved, and this poem was his spontaneous expression of that feeling. He saw in the image of Barbara Frietchie's holding the stars and stripes a symbol of all who loved the Union and were willing to die for it.

The story is told in the simplest of all verse forms, rhyming couplets of four beats a line, separated into stanzas. The rhythm has a biblical cadence and also catches the tramp of heavy boots as the rebels advance upon the town. The stage for the drama is set by the few suggestive details, evoking the environs of Frederick town and the luxuriant land, ripe both for the actual crop harvest and for the one of blood and destruction: "meadows rich with corn," and "apple and peach tree fruited deep." The action proper begins with the entrance of the "famished rebel horde" into the town and the disappearance of the Union flags:

> Forty flags with their silver stars,
> Forty flags with their crimson bars,
>
> Flapped in the morning wind: the sun
> Of noon looked down, and saw not one.

These lines have a perfect ballad movement, and a continuing economy of detail sweeps the drama along: the ranks of soldiers are "dust-brown"; and their leader, Stonewall Jackson, is characterized by his "slouched hat" and impetuous order to shoot the last flag down. Barbara Frietchie's act in waving the torn flag and her address to the rebels, "Shoot if you must this old grey head, / But spare your country's flag," are melodramatic, as are Jackson's blush of shame and order to his troops to spare the woman. Yet this unpolished and highly emotional presentation is in keeping with the manner of true balladry, where subtlety is a thing unknown. The theatrical nature of Barbara Frietchie's and Jackson's acts heightens the climax and pointedly illustrates the theme. Her successful defense of the flag is underscored by Whittier's picture of it waving over the heads of the rebel host and leads to the ending tribute, "Flag of Freedom and Union, wave!" The final couplets tightly bind the drama together as the stars of evening shine over the graves of the protagonists, the town, and the

Union itself, suggesting nature's full approval of the battle for "peace and order and beauty" represented in the flag. By means of this simple story, Whittier echoed the thoughts and emotions of an entire country. No other Civil War poem, save Walt Whitman's "O Captain! My Captain!" and Julia Ward Howe's "Battle Hymn of the Republic," was so definitely the product of the hour and so quickly recognized by the people as an expression of their feelings.

* * *

Whittier's mature ballads show many interesting variations. **"Amy Wentworth,"** like many others, is more a genre piece than a ballad, since it lacks dramatic action. The poem mainly portrays a tradition-reared Amy Wentworth who defies her rank to love a common sea captain. Its sentimental theme, the power of true love, is saved by the fine imagistic development of the poem. Amy's background is portrayed by the material objects which surround her, the beautiful piano, her silken dress, the stately stairway, the ancestral portraits in the hall, and the English ivy curving about the coat of arms. These externals are contrasted with her inner determination to love as she desires, not as the artifacts of tradition direct. Her physical beauty and the spirit of her love are captured by a series of sea images. The ballad opens with a graceful image of her fragile, delicate appearance and then continues with a more evocative sea image:

> Her fingers shame the ivory keys
> They dance so light along;
> The bloom upon her parted lips
> Is sweeter than the song.
> . . . . .
>
> Her heart is like an outbound ship
> That at its anchor swings;
> The murmur of the stranded shell
> Is in the song she sings.

The images in the second stanza thus center on the sea concept, the straining of an anchored ship and the helplessness of a washed-up shell. Like the shell, Amy is caught (stranded) by her ancestral background which forbade marriage outside its class, and she can only weakly murmur until her lover (the sea) sweeps her back into his grasp. The whole situation in the poem is summed up by the two words "stranded" and "murmur," which carry the subtle undertones of her longing and wistfulness. Throughout, this sea imagery is contrasted with the physical heaviness of her ancestral home and its precise refinement. Also her lover's voice, unlike hers, is sounded in the "clanging cry" of the white gulls and his rough jerkin gives a strength to her delicate silken gown. Striving to bring her absent lover closer, she imagines the house's gallery as his deck and finds pebbles and sand more attractive than her family's garden. The whole poem preserves this air of fragile romantic beauty so rarely found in Whittier's poems.

* * *

Sections of **"The Witch of Wenham"** and **"How the Women Went from Dover"** contain some of Whittier's best rendering of Colonial customs and illustrate his complete understanding of the psychology of witchcraft and local superstition. However, overlong digressions and sentimental touches mar the graphic descriptions and rustic phrases—indicating again how badly Whittier's art suffered from a lack of selection. **"The Palatine"** also catches the grim and foreboding atmosphere of past days in recording the legend of a spectre ship. Throughout there is swiftness of narrative and the ending remarks avoid Whittier's usual moralizing to hint at the complexity existing between the physical and spiritual worlds. In the ending conceit Whittier wonders if the return of the ship to haunt those who wrecked it isn't nature's grim comment on our past actions:

> Do the elements subtle reflections give?
> Do pictures of all the ages live
> On Nature's infinite negative,
>
> Which, half in sport, in malice half,
> She shows at times, with shudder or laugh,
> Phantom and shadow in photograph?

Two of Whittier's less well known ballads also merit attention. **"The Sisters"** is based on a traditional ballad theme—the rivalry of two sisters for the same man—and bears a close resemblance to the original Scottish ballad "The Twa Sisters" in form and presentation. The action of the story is concentrated on a single stormy night as the sisters sleep. Annie, the younger, awakens and hears a voice calling to her. From here the narrative drives forward without a pause. The love conflict and the impending tragedy are hinted at by Rhoda's scornful attitude toward the voices and by her derisive remarks about Annie's failure to have a lover. Ironically, she hits upon the truth of the situation when she ridicules Annie's insistence that she does hear the voice of Estwick Hall, Rhoda's fiancé. When Annie claims to hear the voice again calling her name, the now enraged sister cries out:

> "Thou liest! He would never call thy name!
>
> "If he did, I would pray the wind and sea
> To keep him forever from thee and me!"

Again Rhoda unwittingly keynotes the approaching tragedy, for Hall is dead. Only Annie, with her lover's insight, knows the truth, and in his death she triumphs as she never could have had he lived. She faces her sister and for the first time reveals her feelings:

> "Life was a lie, but true is death.
> . . . . .

But now my soul with his soul I wed;
Thine the living, and mine the dead!"

The whole narrative is done in dialogue with none of the before-or after-events included. Only the one scene is given, the resulting effects of the tragedy, and the reader himself must fill in the details. The presentation is bare, almost harsh, in its simplicity. Still, the story is definitely tied up with the New England coast, not as in so many literary ballads situated in the land of romance: the storm which drowns Hall is a typical New England northeaster; the waves lash Cape Ann's rocky coast; and the girls' dialogue has a New England flavor, for Hall's boat is the "tautest schooner that ever swam" and Rhoda's trousseau is "bridal gear."

Another of Whittier's later pieces, **"The Henchman"** (1877), also demonstrates his mastery of ballad techniques. Like **"The Sisters,"** it has no moral, but it is entirely different in tone and presentation. The poem is a love song, chanted exultantly and hopefully by the lover in praise of his lady. The imagery centralizes on the joyous things of spring and summer, birds, flowers, sun, and wind, and makes the lady superior to them all.

My lady walks her morning round,
My lady's page her fleet greyhound,
My lady's hair the fond winds stir,
And all the birds make songs for her.

. . . . .

The hound and I are on her trail,
The wind and I uplift her veil;
As if the calm, cold moon she were,
And I the tide, I follow her.

The repetition of certain phrases and syntactical patterns conveys the reverence of the lover's devotion with a litany of praise. The action of the ballad is slight, though there is an undercurrent of conflict—his adoration versus her proud disdain. However, this is never developed and the lyric and decorative effects dominate.

This type of ballad is the exception rather than the rule for most of Whittier's later pieces. Some of his mature ballads, such as **"The Brown Dwarf of Rügen,"** **"King Volmer and Elsie,"** and **"Kallundborg Church,"** also convey the charm of a foreign land and create a fairy tale atmosphere by the techniques used in **"The Henchman"**; in general, however, Whittier's later ballads tend to take a concrete historical incident or some local tradition and dramatize it, using actual locale for realistic background setting. These tales fit in perfectly with his critical belief that there is romance underlying the simplest of incidents and that the writer should utilize the materials within his own experience.

* * *

"The Wreck of Rivermouth" is typical. The story is based on the historical character of Goody Cole of Hampton, who was persecuted for being a witch in the latter half of the seventeenth century. Many of the exploits attributed to her were probably superstitions based on unfounded popular traditions; yet they were common in Whittier's youth. The setting is laid precisely, with an eye for picturesque detail:

And fair are the sunny isles in view
East of the grisly Head of the Boar,
And Agamenticus lifts its blue
Disk of a cloud the woodlands o'er;
And southerly, when the tide is down,
'Twixt white sea-waves and sand-hills brown,
The beach-birds dance and the gray gulls wheel
Over a floor of burnished steel.

The ballad proper begins with the boat full of "goodly company," sailing past the rocks for fishing outside the bay. The idyllic atmosphere of the summer's day is conveyed by the picture of the mowers in the Hampton meadows, who listen to the songs coming from the passing boat and who longingly watch the joyous young girls. As the boat rounds the point where Goody Cole lives, the laughing group taunts her and sails on, but only after she answers their jibes with a bitter proverb: "'The broth will be cold that waits at home; / For it's one to go, but another to come!'" Ironically her prophecy proves true, as a sudden storm sweeps upon the ship, driving it to destruction on Rivermouth Rocks. In one brief moment all are lost, and the next stanzas mournfully re-echo their previous happiness; the mower still looks up from the peaceful meadows and the sea is clear, but

The wind of the sea is a waft of death,
The waves are singing a song of woe!
By silent river, by moaning sea,
Long and vain shall thy watching be:
Never again shall the sweet voice call,
Never the white hand rise and fall!

A stunned and broken Goody Cole is left behind, pathetically cursing the sea for fulfilling her wish. Her tragedy, like Skipper Ireson's, is an inner thing—the torment she will have for the rest of her life, wondering if her angry words actually caused the death of the group. The final scene in church highlights the community's silent condemnation of those who dare to live outside its conventions. This scene is overlong and weakened by the needless introduction of another outcast, Reverend Stephen Bachiler, and by the heavy moral tone of the conclusion, "Lord, forgive us! we're sinners all!"

The poem illustrates Whittier's successes and failures in ballad presentation. The story itself is typical and probable, and Whittier's handling of it is realistic. He places it exactly in Hampton, New Hampshire, by employing details characteristic of that locale: fishing for haddock and cod, the scent of the pines of nearby Rye, the mowing of salted grass, and Goody Cole's use of familiar native proverbs. There is a keynote of drama in the situation and a direct narrative appeal that fit ballad presentation, for Whittier allows us to view a most human Goody Cole, an old woman tragically destroyed by a village's narrow hate. Yet, like so many of Whittier's ballads, this one needs more concentration, especially in ending before the dramatic effect is lost. Also, there is a touch here of his overreaching for sentimental and melodramatic effects, a fault clearly seen in **"The Changeling"** and **"How the Women Went from Dover."**

* * *

On the whole, Whittier's ballads demonstrate his pioneer work in the development of native American ballads. He understood the true function of balladry and refused to write ballads based on European themes. Whittier took moments from American history and local legends and presented them in a realistic manner that was strengthened by his wide knowledge of past times and his lifelong familiarity with the locale. In these ballads Whittier attained the rank of one of America's finest creators of historical and traditional narrative.

* * *

The distinction between Whittier's sectional or genre poems and his ballads is often nonexistent. Many poems such as **"Telling the Bees"** (discussed in chapter five), **"Amy Wentworth"** (discussed in chapter six); and **"Maud Muller"** can be handled either as ballads or genre poems. Usually the genre verses differ from the ballads in their lack of drama and objectivity; they are personal and subjective, fully revealing the poet and his ideas. Their subject matter deals with the life and manners of common people, a recollection of a past agrarian society or a nostalgic remembrance of boyhood experiences. Often they are longer, employing description and decorative imagery which minimize physical action and narrative pace, and the tone of wistful longing and romantic reminiscence replaces the impersonality and directness of the ballad. The best genre poems realistically portray the particular scenes, customs, traditions, and personages of nineteenth-century rural New England: the fields, drab and bare on a sleety winter day or green and growing under a summer sun; the plain Colonial houses with their massive cross beams, wide fireplaces, and rustic furniture; the barns filled with harvest or the excitement of a husking party; the isolation and narrowness of a small town with its delight in superstitions, eccentric wanderers, and local poets; the emotional effect of evangelical preaching on a farm populace; the traditional folk tales of stern "Yankee" forebears—the list is seemingly endless, a complete

social history of the period. These genre poems most vividly exemplify Whittier's belief that the best materials for poetry lie in the commonplace objects of familiar experience.

Whittier's achievement in these poems goes beyond that of the mere local colorist who emphasizes regional peculiarities and the strangely picturesque or who produces folklore sketches and antiquarian pieces. Of course Whittier depends on his home territory for the images and situations of his genre art, but in his best Essex County poems the life of the region becomes the medium for his expression of universal insights and attitudes. His genre poems illustrate the validity of Frederick Jackson Turner's remark that "American literature is not a simple thing, but the choral song of many sections." This regional diversity not only preserves a section's own characteristics and history, but gives vitality and flavor to the nation's literature.

* * *

"Maud Muller" shows Whittier's genre art at its most typical. The story is an unpretentious account of the popular American belief in romantic love, set in a quaint rural background; yet Whittier pauses in the poem to examine realistically this trust and to question its validity. The poem's narrative sparseness and ironic undertones avoid his usual sentimentality and overelaboration. The occasion for the poem was Whittier's recollection of a trivial event—his meeting with a young farm girl and her shame at her torn attire and bare feet. To this matter-of-fact incident Whittier added an unadorned story of the appearance of a wealthy judge and the effect of this meeting upon their lives. The surface theme illustrates the belief that instinctive romantic love is the only basis for happiness, but for once Whittier undercuts excessive sentiment by ironic development of the theme and realistic presentation of the action. The structure of the poem is built upon a series of contrasts, of reality versus the dream and of action versus thought. As George Arms has pointed out, the opening stanzas prepare for an objective treatment of the romance. Whittier has the "mock-bird" echoing Maud's daydreams, and the town she gazes at, the symbol of her romantic aspirations, is "far-off" and only causes her "vague unrest" and unhappiness. The judge appears seated on his horse, while Maud blushingly offers him a cup of water. This simple placement of figures quietly indicates their basic, unreconcilable differences. After her meeting with him, Maud sighs wistfully, "Ah, me! / That I the Judge's bride might be" and naively dreams of the fine dresses and social benefits that would derive from the marriage. The judge is also considering marriage with her but from an entirely different aspect, wishing that he might live the simple life of a farmer, close to nature without the problems of his present social position. Each desires what the other one has, and each is temporarily affected by the power of the wish: the judge hums a tune in court and Maud leaves the hay unraked. However, their dreams fade in the hard light of reality. The judge marries within his own class, though he constantly remembers and idealizes the former meeting. As he drinks a glass of wine, he longs for Maud's cool drink. Maud fares even worse. Instead of living in a fine house with the handsome judge for her husband, she dwells in a cramped hovel as the wife of a poor, coarse farmer; yet she refuses to let the past die and continually relives the meeting, envisioning her unattractive kitchen walls as "stately halls." The concluding moral grows directly out of the story; it is the quiet musing of the author as he looks back on the dreams of all youths and realizes that "of all sad words of tongue or pen, / The saddest are these: 'It might have been!'" As viewed within the context of the poem, the "sadness" of this tale lies not in their failure to marry, but in their refusal to confront reality. The imaginative hopes of the judge and Maud reflect the sentiments of the "rags to riches" saga and trust in romantic love; yet the poem warns that, although one may believe in and cherish the dream, reality and life usually prove different. The ending remarks probe deeper as Whittier points out that only in heaven may our human dreams be realized (and even here the subjunctive "may" indicates his doubt that heaven would consist of such romantic fulfillment) and that only a final spiritual goal provides consolation, not vain regrets. Rather than asking for a sentimental response to the story, Whittier indicates his doubts and asks the question, "Who knows what is best after all?" —and therewithin lie the pathos and universality of the tale.

The extreme plainness of the poem's diction is most noticeable. The words are mainly monosyllables, while the imagery is commonplace and undeveloped. The girl is portrayed by the most conventional terms: her eyes are long-lashed and innocent; she has a graceful air, a fair form, and a sweet face; the only touch of imagery in her description, her glowing with the "*wealth* / Of simple beauty and rustic health" (italics mine) provides an ironic reflection on her impossible dreams. Characterization of the judge, too, is kept vague; the single adjective applied to him is "manly." Both the judge and Maud are types, symbols of the dreams of all mankind. Still the structure of the story is firmly ribbed with realistic setting, probable attitudes, and plausible action. The girl's dreams are the naive, unaffected ones of a farmer's daughter: she longs for fine dresses, jewels, and rich furnishings—her unsophisticated view of what wealth implies; characteristically, she would help all her relatives and give money to the poor. Her conversation with the judge revolves around the everyday things of her life—birds, trees, the haying, and the weather. Also the ending section on Maud's poverty-stricken existence discloses all the drabness and bitterness of her life.

The poem is a classic of its kind in simplicity, for Whittier manipulates theme and story into an organic whole to keep sentiment at a distance.

* * *

Just as he captured the naive aspirations of his age, Whittier also preserved the memories of the old order and the history of the local scene. His rustic anecdotes, "Yankee" character sketches, and humorous satires of legends and superstitions have been almost completely neglected by critics; yet they rank with his finest poetic achievements. His fanciful handling of Cotton Mather's history of a fabled two-headed snake in **"The Double-Headed Snake of Newbury"** is a minor comic triumph. Whittier ridicules Mather's credulous account of the "wonder workings of God's providence" by thoroughly reworking the tale with appropriate exaggeration and a mock-heroic tone that satirizes the Puritan delight in superstition and moralizing. The section on the townspeople opens with a description of the ancient gossips who, "shaking their heads in their dreary way," humorously parallel the coiling of the snake. The passage reaches a climax with Whittier's caricature of Cotton Mather's entrance:

> Cotton Mather came galloping down
> All the way to Newbury town,
> With his eyes agog and his ears set wide,
> And his marvelous inkhorn at his side;
> Stirring the while in the shallow pool
> Of his brains for the lore he learned at school,
> To garnish the story, with here a streak
> Of Latin and there another of Greek.

Even the ending of the poem preserves the burlesque mood as Whittier records the present-day life of the snake in a native proverb dealing with the quarreling of husband and wife: "One in body and two in will, / The Amphisbaena is living still." This poem is the best among a group including **"The Preacher," "Birchbrook Mill,"** and **"The Prophecy of Samuel Sewall."**

* * *

Whittier never had notable success with characterization, but in a few anecdotes of historical figures that strikingly foreshadow the work of Robert Frost and Edwin Arlington Robinson he did capture the essential characteristics of the New England mind. **"Abraham Davenport"** shows Whittier's genre art at its most realistic and enjoyable. The "old preaching mood" of the poem is at once dryly humorous and honestly respectful. Whittier pictures Davenport's granite-like determination and shrewd common sense as he calmly goes about his legislative duties amidst the fear and religious hysteria occasioned by an eclipse of the sun, the famous dark day of 1780. The poem opens with a laconic observation on the present age's slackness:

In the old days (a custom laid aside
With breeches and cocked hats) the people
Sent their wisest men to make the public laws.

The terror of the day, lampooned by the overdrawn setting and the farfetched comparisons, conveys the still strong Calvinist belief in a wrathful God and the presence of the supernatural in physical occurrences. As Howard Mumford Jones notes, the style with its "fusion of low relief with salient observations" keeps this formal description from being melodramatic.

Birds *ceased* to sing, and all the barn-yard fowls
Roosted; the cattle at the pasture bars
Lowed, and *looked* homeward; bats on leathern wings
Flitted abroad; the sounds of labor *died*;
Men *prayed,* and women *wept*.

(Italics mine.)

The humorous urgency of the verbs and the incongruity of such insignificant details only ridicule the total solemnity of the event to make the ending human prayers and tears outrageously anti-climactic. Emphasizing the lawgivers, "dim as ghosts," trembling beneath their formal legislative robes, the next section evokes the image of these men in their winding sheets and provides an ironic contrast with the previous picture of the wrathful God and his "inexorable Law." Their decision to adjourn introduces Abraham Davenport who rises, "slow cleaving with his steady voice / The intolerable hush." In a common sense blend of faith and realism he advises them: "'Let God do His work, we will see to ours. / Bring in the candles.' And they brought them in." The simple repetition of the thought again puts a humorous, yet authentic, perspective on the whole scene. So, by the flickering candlelight the apprehensive legislators debate "an act to amend an act to regulate / The shad and alewive fisheries." The complete incongruity of the bill with the scene is reinforced by the monotonous phrasing and repetition. Whittier can even afford a pun as he pictures his hero speaking "straight to the question, with no figures of speech / Save the ten Arab signs." In the midst of this scene Davenport stands as a figure of awe and grandeur:

Erect, self-poised, a rugged face, half seen
Against the background of unnatural dark,
A witness to the ages as they pass,
That simple duty hath no place for fear.

The concluding lines again echo the failure of the present day to develop such men.

* * *

"Cobbler Keezar," "The Sycamores," and **"Abram Morrison"** also exemplify Whittier's facility in rustic character sketches. All three employ a ballad form and might well be classified as such. Two of the poems contrast song- and wine-loving immigrant outsiders, a German cobbler and an Irish workman, with the grim, repressed existence of the early Puritan settlers; and **"Abram Morrison"** follows the career of an Irish Quaker well known in Whittier's youth. All three poems are filled with Whittier's native wit and dry turn of phrase. One other characterization, **"A Spiritual Manifestation,"** reveals a most human Roger Williams who laconically depicts the mob of dissenters and religious cranks who formerly descended upon his colony:

I hear again the snuffled tones,
I see in dreary vision
Dyspeptic dreamers, spiritual bores,
And prophets with a mission.

. . . . .

I fed, but spared them not a whit;
I gave to all who walked in
Not clams and succotash alone,
But stronger meat of doctrine.

I proved the prophets false, I pricked
The bubble of perfection,
And clapped upon their inner light
The snuffers of election.

The burlesque tone is heightened by Whittier's feminine rhymes and dialect associations such as "assorter-water" and "braggarts-fagots." Unfortunately, he did not let Williams' monologue stand by itself but apologized for his "light" treatment of the reformer—once again illustrating Whittier's distressing lack of artistic control and inability to condense. These failings are also evident in **"To My Old Schoolmaster"** and **"The Prophecy of Samuel Sewall,"** where realistic genre touches, shrewd social comment, and character insight are obscured by didactic passages and digressive material.

* * *

More and more Whittier turned to the memories of his own youth for poetic material, typifying and idealizing the barefoot days, the district school days, and lost childhood romances. Throughout all these poems run the strains of his sentimental longing for the simplicity of a past social order. **"The Barefoot Boy," "In School-Days," "My Playmate," "Memories,"** and **"A Sea Dream"** captured the romantic aspirations of a wide reading public and were enshrined as part of traditional Americana along with Longfellow's verses, the songs of Stephen Foster, and Emanuel Leutze's painting of "Washington Crossing the Delaware." Though **"The Barefoot Boy"** displays Whittier's most obvious artistic flaws, it also indicates why his verses were so popular. The introduction is sentimental and unreal, depending on hackneyed imagery and conventional poetic diction. The boy is styled "little man," wears "pantaloons," has lips "kissed by strawberries on the hill," and is pompously addressed as "Prince." These generalizations reveal nothing about a real boy or his background; rather they show how responsive Whittier was to the Currier and Ives's approach to local color. The central section of the poem does realistically examine the world and interests of a small boy. Forgetting the idealized little man, Whittier identifies himself with the scene:

> I was rich in flowers and trees,
> Humming-birds and honey-bees;
> For my sport the squirrel played,
> Plied the snouted mole his spade;
> For my taste the blackberry cone
> Purpled over hedge and stone.
>
> . . . . .
>
> All the world I saw or knew
> Seemed a complex Chinese toy,
> Fashioned for a barefoot boy!

The last stanzas return to the platitudes of the opening as Whittier concludes with the pious hope that the boy's bare feet will never sink in the "quick and treacherous sands of sin." And yet this poem became a national tradition, symbolizing a romantic phase of America's past. Its companion piece, **"In School-Days,"** is correctly considered a poem for children, though its first four stanzas do contain some of Whittier's best local color description. **"My Playmate"** is the best of the three love lyrics which nostalgically recall the bittersweet pain of young love. Its blend of memory and reality, symbolized by the moaning pines and falling blossoms, artistically portrays an older man's sense of regret and longing.

* * *

One of Whittier's most neglected poems, **"The Pennsylvania Pilgrim,"** shows how accurately and realistically he could recreate the past. His portrait of the seventeenth-century Quaker Pastorius fully explores the varied nature of that settler, while the mood and imagistic development of the poem convey Pastorius' quiet, secure personality. The "Prelude" establishes the poem's contemplative mood with its emphasis on Pastorius as a pilgrim of "a softer clime / And milder speech" who lives completely by the "white" radiance of the Inner Light. Its concluding lines introduce the other principal image of sowing and reaping.

Employing a style similar to Jonathan Edwards' *Personal Narrative* with its insistent repetition of certain phrases, Whittier connotes the presence of the Inner Light in Pastorius. Throughout the poem terms such as peace, mild, meek, simple, tender, sober, mystical, and others are continually enlarged upon and reechoed. Decorative, pastoral similes pervade the whole poem and create a quiet, almost dreamlike, atmosphere. Rarely did Whittier achieve a more artistic fusion of his own interests and those of the actual story than in the following lines:

> Fair First-Day mornings, steeped in summer calm,
> Warm, tender, restful, sweet with woodland balm,
> Came to him, like some mother-hallowed psalm
>
> . . . . .
>
> There, through the gathered stillness multiplied
> And made intense by sympathy,
>
> . . . . .
>
> Or, without spoken words, low breathings stole
> Of a diviner life from soul to soul,
> Baptizing in one tender thought the whole.

In the descriptions of Pastorius' silence as "soul-sabbath" or his reading the Bible by the "Inward Light," Whittier movingly and thoughtfully symbolizes the guiding force of Pastorius' Quaker faith. The climax to this light image comes with Whittier's paraphrase of Ezekiel's strange vision of the wheels, which is introduced:

> The Light of Life shone round him; one by one
> The wandering lights, that all-misleading run,
> Went out like candles paling in the sun.

Balancing this light image are references to planting, sowing, reaping, and blossoming which signify Pastorius' attempts to transplant Old World culture in the New, his cultivation of religious tolerance, and his work to free the slaves. In particular the image of the aloe or legendary plant that supposedly bloomed every hundred years evokes the slow, patient efforts of Pastorius to make the Quakers renounce slavery. Whittier notes how this "seed of truth" does finally blossom under the hands of Woolman and other Quakers. The poem not only depicts Pastorius as the saint figure, but humanizes him by portraying the tender relationship between Pastorius and his wife, his tenacious fight for tolerance and abolishment of slavery, his speculative interests in science and religion, his monumental verse writings in "Dutch, English, Latin, like the hash / Of corn and beans in Indian succotash," his nostalgic recollection of music-filled Christmases in Germany, his love of local superstition and Indian lore, and his achievement in transferring "the Old World flowers to virgin soil." The portrait leaves the reader with a full impression of a complex, idealistic, and learned Quaker who was at the same time a simple, tolerant, and humble man.

* * *

The most famous of Whittier's genre poems, and undoubtedly his masterpiece, is **"Snow-Bound."** Written a few months after the end of the Civil War, it was Whittier's memorial to the two women who were closest to him during his life—his mother, who had died eight years before, and his sister Elizabeth, who had died the previous year. The loss of his favorite companion, Elizabeth, left Whittier a lonely man, and the outcome of the Civil War completed the one great work of his life. In this mood of sorrow and isolation, Whittier turned to the happy past when the family was intact at the Haverhill birthplace, and constructed this winter idyl to express his feelings for the section and family which had produced and molded him. Its theme, the value of family affection, had always been deepest in his heart; and its locale, the homestead during a snowstorm, was one he knew intimately. Nowhere in Whittier's work, outside of some of his ballads, had the material so suited his capabilities and interest.

Relying on Whittier's comment that **"Snow-Bound"** portrays "Flemish pictures of old days," most critics have examined it as a loosely connected montage which quaintly evokes the atmosphere of rural New England in the 1800's.[1] Such comment accords value to Whittier's graphic rendering of physical details, to his authentic delineation of family figures, and to his fidelity to actual experience. But the poem, "old, rude-furnished" like the house, does burst "flower-like, into rosy bloom" and this artistic fruition is not a chance occurrence. The imagistic development of the poem, use of appropriate symbols, and closely organized structure provide a satisfying artistic framework for these rustic scenes. An examination of these aspects indicates a genuine literary value far beyond local or historical interest.

The theme turns on the poet's nostalgic recalling of the love and protection which his family once gave him, emphasizing his painful sense of present loss and hope for spiritual consolation. These emotions are primarily developed by a series of contrasts: of fire and snow, past and present, people and elements—which combine to form the larger theme of love and immortality struggling against pain and death.

Perhaps the touchstone for interpreting the poem is the symbolic development of the wood fire. The poem is headed by a quotation from Agrippa's *Occult Philosophy*: "As the Spirits of Darkness be stronger in the dark, so Good Spirits, which be Angels of Light, are augmented not only by the Divine light of the Sun, but also by our common Wood Fire: and as the Celestial Fire drives away dark spirits, so also this our Fire of Wood doth the same." Also a second epigraph from Emerson's "The Snow-Storm" re-emphasizes the importance of the "radiant" fire. In the poem, fire is associated not only with brightness, relaxation, and physical comfort, but with the emotional and spiritual warmth of family love, with "the genial glow" of community brotherhood, and with divine protection against the evil spirits of nature and time. Artistically delayed by the description of the "unwarming" storm, the initial lighting of the fire introduces the Whittier household, and its blaze symbolizes the reality of family love. Throughout the central section, particularly, Whittier associates the vigor and happiness of family talk, games, and interests with the color and sparkle of the glowing logs; and unites the close bond of family love with the red heat of the fire. For example, the uncle's simple tales are "warming" and cause the listeners to forget "the outside cold, / The bitter wind." Also Whittier weaves into the fire pattern the sunny richness, ripe crops, blooming hillsides, and full greenness associated with summer. Finally, the dying fire indicates the end of the evening's activities, while also symbolizing the eventual crumbling of the security and protection of the family group.

By contrast, the storm evokes sensations of fear and awe and illustrates the terrible anonymity of nature and death. It dominates the entire first section of the poem, transforming its principal antagonist, the sun, into a cheerless, dark, snowblown wanderer, and enforcing on the family a "savage" isolation which obtains no comfort from "social smoke." The storm's assault on the house is likened to the later attack of death on its individual members as Whittier recalls "the chill weight of the winter snow" on Elizabeth's grave. Conversely, the storm's magical power changes a dull, commonplace farm into a wintry fairyland of beauty and wonder.

A second major contrast deals with the past versus the present. Whittier imaginatively re-creates the past, while echoing his present-day feelings of loneliness. Four main interpolations deal with this problem of time and change, contrasting past happiness with present pain and concluding with the hope for future social progress and spiritual consolation. For example, the first interpolation (lines 179-211) appropriately comes when the fire is lighted and the storm's force seems abated. As if lost in the scene he has recalled, Whittier cries: "What matter how the night behaved? / What matter how the north-wind raved?" But immediately the knowledge of "Time and Change" stop him; for what the elements failed to do that night death has since accomplished. These stark reflections are contrasted with the strength of Whittier's faith as the section ends with his defiant affirmation that spiritual life is the "lord of Death," for a soul's love remains an eternal force. These major contrasts are further expanded by an increasing depth of images and a movement from concrete physical description to an investigation of personality and emotions, with a final return to realistic depiction. All these aspects are blended into the total theme—the strength and bond of family love.

Yet the underlying unity of the poem is developed by a time cycle—the two days' snowfall; the third day's activity and family gathering that night; the fourth day's visit of the teamsters and the doctor; and finally, after a week, the arrival of the newspaper, completely breaking the isolation. However, within this framework is a more ordered threefold division which pits the forces of nature against the family group. The first section of the poem (to line 178) presents the physical domination of the storm and concludes with a view of the inner house and the lighting of the fire. The emphasis throughout is on exact physical detail and on the primitive forces of nature. In the second section the storm is forgotten, for human love and companionship have exorcised the raging spirits of the night. The images become more complex and introspective as loneliness and nostalgia overwhelm the poet. The dying embers of the fire and dreams of summer open the third section (line 629) with a return to the outside physical world; correspondingly, the images also become more concrete. Here the theme of family strength is widened to the larger bond of community union. The final interpolation emphasizes the "larger hopes and graver fears" of social responsibility that can finally unite all mankind, just as the bond of personal love and Quaker Inner Light had once securely linked the Whittier family. This section closes with a hope that art will also preserve some of the more valued aspects of the family group.

A closer analysis of each section reveals the skillful interweaving of the theme with structure and its artistic expansion from major imagistic contrasts. The poem opens with a description of the approaching storm and its complete domination over the "Divine light of the Sun," which is darkly circled, barely able to diffuse a sad "light." Still, as a portent, the sun briefly foreshadows the coming fire of the hearth which does temporarily defeat the storm. A sense of unusual expectation grips the early lines and the cold checks the "circling race / Of lifeblood"—suggesting the eventual triumph of death over the family life. A following description of nightly chores deepens this mood by emphasizing the helplessness of all animate beings before the elements. Then the full fury of the storm breaks to create a chaos of whirling, blinding snow which destroys man's order and intelligent control. On the second morning:

> The old familiar sights of ours
> Took marvelous shapes; strange domes and towers
> Rose up where sty or corn-crib stood.
>
> . . . . .
>
> The bridle-post an old man sat
> With loose-flung coat and high cocked hat;
> The well-curb had a Chinese roof;
> And even the long sweep, high aloof,
> In its slant splendor, seemed to tell
> Of Pisa's leaning miracle.

The condensed details of pure fancy, clever allusion, and purposeful exaggeration evoke a childlike wonder and convey a panoramic view of the transforming power of the storm. Once more human activity intrudes as the father and boys cut through "the solid whiteness" to reach the barn, but now even labor is a delight, for their finished tunnel resembles the dazzling crystal of Aladdin's cave. These pleasing aspects of the storm are immediately counterbalanced by a piercing wind which creates a "savage" world of terror and sunlessness, eliminates "social smoke," and deadens Christian sounds.

When the snowblown and still helpless sun sets that afternoon, loving hands gather the wood and brush necessary to kindle the fire. The "curious art" displayed in these simple tasks suggests a ritual-like significance in their performance. The first red blaze metamorphoses the kitchen into "rosy bloom," but an even greater miracle occurs as the snowdrifts outside reflect the inner fire with their own mimic flame. For the first time the fire controls and the snow receives its burning imprint. Yet the outer elements are not so easily conquered and the moon that night reveals an eerie half-world of "dead white" snows and "pitchy black" hemlocks suffused by an "unwarming" light. Once more the fire's "tropic heat" asserts its power and the glowing light reveals a mug of simmering cider, rows of apples, and a basket of nuts—objects closely associated with the inner world of personality and life.

Though the second section of the poem opens with an emphatic defiance of the elements, this confidence is soon undercut by the painful realization that time has finally conquered. For the faces "lighted" by love and the warmth of the fire are no longer alive ("in the sun they cast no shade"). Ironically, this realization occurs just as the fire does finally dominate the outside elements. Still, forcing these melancholy thoughts from mind by utilizing the fire-snow contrast, Whittier insists that the light of breaking day will play across the mournful marbles of the tomb—that love and faith will find spiritual happiness. This consolation provides an uneasy truce which allows the poet to describe the personalities of the family. The father, mother, and uncle are fittingly characterized by warm summer days, outdoor fishing and haying, ripening corn, steaming clambakes, and sunny hillsides. Also their plain childlike natures and interests are perfectly echoed by the quaint couplet rhythm, the rough unpolished lines, and the vernacular "Yankee" rhymes. To follow these three innocent characters, Whittier introduces another group of three, the aunt and two sisters, whose more complex natures reflect some measure of life's pain, sacrifice, and loneliness. Similarly, the tone becomes more introspective and the images more expansive and thoughtful. The aunt's still youthful charm and virgin freshness are expressed in a delicate summer figure of clouds and dew:

> Before her still a cloud-land lay,
> The mirage loomed across her way;
> The morning dew, that dries so soon
> With others, glistened at her noon.

The elder sister's death is described as an entrance "beneath the low green tent / Whose curtain never outward swings." Significantly her death is not snow-filled or chilling; rather it is the casual lifting of a tent-flap with the later discovery that this light opening has now been closed with the heavy weight of "low green" sod. A following passage on Elizabeth, "our youngest and our dearest," introduces the second interpolation (lines 400-437). Once again Whittier's faith struggles with the brutal reality of death as the chilling snows of the grave cover the summer charm and violet beauty of Elizabeth's nature. Finally the poet asks:

> Am I not richer than of old?
> Safe in thy immortality,
> What change can reach the wealth I hold?

At first glance the figure appears paradoxical, for how can Elizabeth's death make the poet "richer" and "safe"? On one level his rich memories of her vibrant personality and spiritual perfection are now "safe," secured forever from realistic tarnish and inexorable change; but also her "immortality" secures him, since it illuminates his final spiritual goal and provides him with a standard for judging all his future acts.

The following two characterizations portray the visiting schoolmaster and the "not unfeared, half-welcome guest" (Harriet Livermore), while also introducing the third interpolation. The realistic sketch of the schoolmaster's entertaining knowledge of the classics and rural games, his boyish humor, and self-reliant, yet humble, nature is a fine genre portrait that matches the earlier ones of the father and uncle. Indeed the schoolmaster's close intimacy with the family is underscored by the lines that introduce him as one who "held at the fire his favored place, / Its warm glow lit a laughing face." His further delineation as one of "Freedom's young apostles" completes Whittier's portrait of the fearless young leader whose moral strength will destroy social injustice such as slavery and open a new era of peace and progress. At the same time the expansion of these optimistic ideas on the power of education and reform, in the third interpolation (lines 485-509), displays the thinness of Whittier's social thought; and its abstract, hackneyed imagery ("War's bloody trail," "Treason's monstrous growth") contrasts unfavorably with the concrete detail of other sections. The final figure, Harriet Livermore, presents an interesting variation of the fire imagery as she combines characteristics of both the spirits of light and blackness. Her warm and lustrous eyes flash light, but also hold "dark languish" and wrath; her brows are "black with night" and shoot out a "dangerous light." This tortured nature warps and twists the "Celestial Fire," for she enters the family group without sharing its close affection or receiving the warm benefits of love from the wood fire. Her complex characterization is appropriately climaxed by the uneasy observation that in some natures the line between "will and fate" is indistinguishable. Structurally these two outsiders represent the contrast-

ing "warm-cold" aspects of a forgotten external world. The schoolmaster offers the warmth of companionship, the balance of learning, and eventual hope for social responsibility, while Harriet Livermore reveals the chill of fanaticism and the failure of personal, emotional efforts to correct injustice. Also their intrusion foreshadows the unavoidable demands that society is soon to make upon the secure family group.

Appropriately, the second section concludes when the family disbands for bed and the now dull fire is extinguished. As the family falls asleep, the snow sifts through the loosened clapboards and the storm re-enters the poem (though significantly the snow no longer has the power to disturb their dreams of summer). The ending of the night's activities carefully reworks the fire image:

> At last the great logs, crumbling low,
> Sent out a dull and duller glow,
> The bull's-eye watch that hung in view,
> Ticking its weary circuit through,
> Pointed with mutely warning sign
> Its black hand to the hour of nine.
> That sign the pleasant circle broke:
> My uncle ceased his pipe to smoke,
> Knocked from its bowl the refuse gray,
> And laid it tenderly away;
> Then roused himself to safely cover
> The dull red brands with ashes over.

The crumbling of the once great logs hints of nature's eventual triumph over the family unit, while the ominous black watch, like a living spirit of darkness, also specifies that time has run out. When the uncle knocks the ashes from his pipe, he deepens the suggestion of the burned-out logs and echoes the clock's warning. Even the halting verse pattern with its awkward inversions reflects the fumbling slowness and plodding, careful manner of the uncle.

The final section briefly returns to the physical world of the opening stanzas, as the teamsters and plows now control the effects of the storm, while the children find sport, instead of terror, in its whiteness. Signalizing the larger social union which radiates from the smaller family bond, the visiting doctor utilizes the mother's nursing skill to aid a sick neighbor. So love joins his "mail of Calvin's creed" with her Quaker "inward light." Finally, the local newspaper arrives and the family broadens its interests to other communities and "warmer" zones. Now the storm's isolation is completely broken and the section ends with the joyful cry, "Now all the world was ours once more."

While this seems to be the logical conclusion for the poem, it disregards the troubling theme of time's ultimate victory. So, in a final interpolation (from line 715) Whittier asks the "Angel of the backward look" to close the volume in which he has been writing. With difficulty he shakes off this mood of regret and nostalgia to respond to present-day demands (much as he had pictured the young schoolmaster doing) and employs the image of the century-blooming aloe to dramatically portray the successful flowering of his Abolitionist's aim to eradicate slavery. The ending lines further console Whittier with the hope that his "Flemish" artistry has truly re-created "pictures of old days" and that others might gather a similar spiritual and emotional comfort from them by stretching the "hands of memory forth / To warm them at the wood-fire's blaze!" A final summer image completes the poem as the thought of future readers enjoying his efforts refreshes him as odors blown from unseen meadows or the sight of lilies in some half-hidden pond. These lines reflect the inner serenity and imperturbable peace which offer final solace. The dread of time and change is assuaged by the confidence that social reform will improve the future, by the knowledge that art often outlasts time's ravages, and by the certainty that spiritual immortality does conquer it completely. So the poem moves in artistic transitions from the physical level of storm and fire to the psychological world of death and love, utilizing the wood fire as the dominant symbol. It is for this skillful fusing of form and theme that Whittier deserves that future readers send him "benediction of the air."

The interwoven theme and structure are enhanced by some of Whittier's finest genre touches. His descriptions of the homestead's kitchen, the fireplace, and his bedroom are imperishable vignettes which typify the thousands of similar New England farm houses. Throughout the poem there is an abundance of local color. The hake-broil on the beach and the chowder served with clam shells were part of a traditional New England clambake. The games of cross pins, forfeits, riddles, and whirling plate as well as the skating parties and husking bees were common rural practices. The family's activities and interests, fishing off the Isles of Shoals, hunting for teal and loon, trips to Salisbury and far-off Canada, tales of Indian raids, and delight in the almanac and weekly newspaper, were intimately connected with the New England scene. Even more particularized were the Quaker traits and practices detailed in the poem: their reading from Quaker journals, their practice of the Quaker doctrines of tolerance and spirituality, and their Quaker injunctions against slavery. If the Whittiers' interests and outlooks were those of an Essex County family in the early nineteenth century, from their definite local characteristics comes a broader picture of all New England and, indeed, all rural America at that time.

* * *

Like **"Snow-Bound"** the best of Whittier's genre poetry reflected the ideals and attitudes of the majority of the American public. His genre pieces captured their romantic dreams, belief in the value of the passing social order, deep-rooted religious faith, nostalgic recollection of childhood, and instinctive attachment to one locale. Throughout all these poems ran a distinctive local coloring in use of situation, description of scenery, and manner of expression, which made the themes concrete and probable. As Emerson embodied the philosophic thought of America in his poems, Whittier incorporated its common ideals and traditions in his. By being scrupulously true to his own experience, conscious of the beauty of the commonplace, and responsive to the popular sentiments of domesticity, piety, and freedom he was "the people's poet" in a sense that the educated and cultured genteel poets could never be.

Note

1. One notable exception is George Arms's excellent essay on Whittier. This analysis has utilized Arms's comments on the fire symbol, the antislavery theme, and the meaning of the "century's aloe" and has been further expanded by his personal criticism.

Selected Bibliography

WHITTIER'S CHIEF WORKS

Legends of New England. Hartford: Hanmer and Phelps, 1831.

Justice and Expediency. Haverhill, Mass.: C. P. Thayer, 1833.

Poems. Philadelphia: Joseph Healy, 1838.

Lays of My Home, and Other Poems. Boston: W. D. Ticknor, 1843.

Voices of Freedom. Philadelphia: T. S. Cavender, 1846.

Leaves From Margaret Smith's Journal. Boston: Ticknor, Reed, and Fields, 1849.

Songs of Labor, and Other Poems. Boston: Ticknor, Reed, and Fields, 1850.

Home Ballads and Poems. Boston: Ticknor and Fields, 1860.

In War Time, and Other Poems. Boston: Ticknor and Fields, 1864.

Snow-Bound. Boston: Ticknor and Fields, 1866.

The Tent on the Beach, and Other Poems. Boston: Ticknor and Fields, 1867.

The Pennsylvania Pilgrim, and Other Poems. Boston: J. R. Osgood, 1872.

The Vision of Echard, and Other Poems. Boston: Houghton, Osgood, 1878.

The King's Missive, and Other Poems. Boston: Houghton Mifflin, 1881.

The Bay of Seven Islands, and Other Poems. Boston: Houghton Mifflin, 1883.

ADDITIONAL WORKS

A Study of Whittier's Apprenticeship as a Poet: Dealing with Poems Written between 1825 and 1835 not Available in the Poet's Collected Works by Francis Mary Pray. Bristol, N. H.: Musgrove Printing House, 1930.

Whittier on Writers and Writing: The uncollected critical writings of John Greenleaf Whittier, eds. Edwin Harrison Cady and Harry Hayden Clark. Syracuse: Syracuse University Press, 1950.

LETTERS

Life and Letters of John Greenleaf Whittier, ed. Samuel T. Pickard. 2 vols. Boston: Houghton Mifflin, 1894. [The main source for Whittier's letters.]

Whittier as a Politician, Illustrated by His Letters to Professor Elizur Wright, Jr., now first published, ed. Samuel T. Pickard. Boston: Charles E. Goodspeed, 1900.

Whittier Correspondence from the Oak Knoll Collection, ed. John Albree. Salem: Essex Book and Print Club, 1911.

Whittier's Unknown Romance, ed. Marie V. Denervaud. Boston: Houghton Mifflin, 1922.

Elizabeth Lloyd and the Whittiers. A Budget of Letters, ed. Thomas Franklin Currier. Cambridge: Harvard University Press, 1939.

COLLECTED WORKS

The Writings of John Greenleaf Whittier. 7 vols. Boston: Houghton Mifflin, 1888-1889. (Riverside Edition)

The Complete Poetical Works of John Greenleaf Whittier, ed. Horace E. Scudder. Boston and New York: Houghton Mifflin, 1894. (Cambridge Edition)

[There is a recent paperbound selection of Whittier's poems, edited by Donald Hall in the Dell Laurel Poetry Series.]

BIBLIOGRAPHY

Currier, Thomas Franklin. *A Bibliography of John Greenleaf Whittier.* Cambridge: Harvard University Press, 1937. [The complete, indispensable guide to Whittier bibliography up to 1937.]

Spiller, Robert E. et al. *Literary History of the United States,* Vol. III, *Bibliography.* New York: Macmillan, 1948. *Supplement,* ed. Richard M. Ludwig. New York: Macmillan, 1959.

BIOGRAPHY

WRITTEN BY RELATIVES AND ASSOCIATES

Claflin, Mrs. Mary B. *Personal Recollections of John G. Whittier.* New York: Thomas Crowell, 1893.

Fields, Mrs. James T. *Whittier, Notes of His Life and Friendships.* New York: Harper, 1893.

Kennedy, William Sloane. *John G. Whittier, The Poet of Freedom.* New York: Funk & Wagnalls, 1892.

Pickard, Samuel T. *Life and Letters of John Greenleaf Whittier.* 2 vols. Boston: Houghton Mifflin, 1894. [The authorized biography and still the primary source book.]

Underwood, Francis H. *John Greenleaf Whittier; a Biography.* Boston: J. R. Osgood, 1884.

WRITTEN BY LATER AUTHORS

Bennett, Whitman. *Whittier, Bard of Freedom.* Chapel Hill: University of North Carolina Press, 1941. [Most readable.]

Perry, Bliss. *John Greenleaf Whittier; a Sketch of His Life, with Selected Poems.* Boston: Houghton Mifflin, 1907.

Pollard, John A. *John Greenleaf Whittier, Friend of Man.* Boston: Houghton Mifflin, 1949. [Probably the definitive account of Whittier's life, though it completely neglects the poet.]

CRITICAL AND INTERPRETATIVE STUDIES FRAMED AS BIOGRAPHIES

Carpenter, George Rice. *John Greenleaf Whittier.* Boston: Houghton Mifflin, 1903. (American Men of Letters Series) [Still the best account of the man and poet.]

Higginson, Thomas Wentworth. *John Greenleaf Whittier.* New York: Macmillan, 1902. (English Men of Letters Series)

Mordell, Albert. *Quaker Militant: John Greenleaf Whittier.* Boston: Houghton Mifflin, 1933. [Highly partisan and slanted by a Freudian interpretation.]

SPECIALIZED STUDIES

Eastburn, Iola Kay. *Whittier's Relation to German Life and Thought.* Philadelphia: University of Pennsylvania Press, 1915.

Pickard, Samuel T. *Whittier-Land, A Handbook of North Essex.* Boston: Houghton Mifflin, 1904.

Stevens, James Stacy. *Whittier's Use of the Bible.* Orono, Maine: University of Maine Press, 1930. (The Maine Bulletin, Vol. XXXIII)

Williams, Cecil Brown. *Whittier's Use of Historical Material in Margaret Smith's Journal.* Chicago: University of Chicago Libraries, 1936.

Analysis and Criticism

Allen, Gay W. "John Greenleaf Whittier," *American Prosody*. New York: American Book Company, 1935.

Arms, George. "Whittier," *The Fields Were Green*. Stanford: Stanford University Press, 1953. [The most revealing and appreciative of all recent essays on Whittier.]

Clark, Harry Hayden (ed.). "Notes," *Major American Poets*. New York: American Book Co., 1936.

Jones, Howard Mumford. "Whittier Reconsidered," *Essex Institute Historical Collections* (October, 1957).

McEuen, Kathryn Anderson. "Whittier's Rhymes," *American Speech* (February, 1945).

Scott, Winfield Townley. "Poetry in American; a New Consideration of Whittier's Verse," *New England Quarterly* (June, 1934).

Waggoner, Hyatt H. "What I Had I Gave; Another Look at Whittier," *Essex Institute Historical Collections* (January, 1959).

Wells, Henry W. "Cambridge Culture and Folk Poetry," *The American Way of Poetry*. New York: Columbia University Press, 1943.

Robert Penn Warren (essay date January-March 1971)

SOURCE: Warren, Robert Penn. "Whittier." *Sewanee Review* 79 (January-March 1971): 86-135.

[*In the following essay, Warren traces Whittier's development as a poet, moving from his early poorly-organized work, to his abolitionist propaganda, and finally, to the more successful poems he produced after 1850, such as "Ichabod," "Telling the Bees," and* Snow-Bound.]

The first Whittier, Thomas, arrived in Massachusetts in 1638. He was a man of moral force, as is attested by the fact that, a generation before the family had any connection with Quakerdom, he took grave risks in protesting against the persecution of the sect. Though willing to espouse a dangerously unpopular cause, he still had influence in his little world, and was a holder of office. He was, too, a physical giant, and vigorous enough to begin, at the age of sixty-eight, in Haverhill, to hew the oak timbers for a new house, the solid two-story structure in which, on December 17, 1807, the poet, his great-great-grandson, was to be born.

There John Whittier, the father of John Greenleaf, worked a farm of 185 indifferent acres, and saw to it that his sons did their share. John Greenleaf loved the land, but loathed the work on it. For one thing, he was

frail, and at the age of fifteen suffered an injury from overexertion; for another thing, he early had a passion for study. His verses began early, too, and one of them sets forth the intellectual ambition that was to dominate his youth:

> And must I always swing the flail,
> And help to fill the milking pail?
> I want to go away to school,
> I do not want to be a fool.

In the light of these verses, Whittier's boyhood circumstances, and his admiration for Burns, certain critics have been tempted to think of Whittier as a "peasant poet". Nothing could be more wide of the mark. The Whittiers were farmers, certainly; and if they were not, in relation to time and place, exactly poor, they were not rich. But to think of them as peasants is to fail to realize that what makes a peasant is a psychological rather than an economic fact. When Jefferson thought of his independent farmer he was not thinking of a peasant; he was thinking of a type central to a whole society. And when the poet Whittier looked backward on the family past, he saw the "founding fathers" of a whole new world—a whole society—and if anything characterized his early manhood, it was an almost pathological ambition to take his "rightful" place in that whole society.

The house of the Quaker farmer at Haverhill had books, and, after absorbing them, the son reached out for others, for Milton, who was to become a personal rather than a poetic model, and for such un-Quakerish works as the stage plays of Shakespeare. By the age of fourteen, Whittier had already heard a Scot, "a pawky auld carle", singing songs of Robert Burns at the kitchen hearth of the Whittiers, and in the same year the schoolmaster Joshua Coffin sat in the same spot and read from a volume of Burns. "This was the first poetry I ever read," Whittier was to say, "with the exception of the Bible (of which I was a close student) and it had a lasting influence upon me. I began to make rhymes myself, and to imagine stories and adventure." It was thus by Burns that Whittier's eyes, according to a later account in the poem **"Burns"**, were opened to the land and life around him as the substance of poetry:

> I matched with Scotland's heathery hills
>   The sweetbrier and the clover;
> With Ayr and Doon, my native rills,
>   Their wood-hymns shouting over.

But it was not only to nature that Burns opened the boy's eyes. He was already steeped in the legends and folklore of his region, which he had absorbed as naturally as the air he breathed, but Burns interpreted what the boy had naturally absorbed and showed that it was the stuff of poetry. So Whittier, as early as Hawthorne, and earlier than Longfellow, was to turn to the past of New England for subject matter, and by 1831, in a poem called **"New England"**, was expressing his ambition to be the poet of his region. His first volume, a mixture of eleven poems and seven prose pieces, published in 1831, in Hartford, was called *Legends of New England.*

To return to Whittier's literary beginnings, Milton and Burns were not the only models he proposed to himself. There was the flood of contemporary trash, American and English, from writers like Felicia Hemans, Lydia Sigourney, N. P. Willis, the elder Dana, Lydia Maria Child, Bernard Barton, and John Pierpont. The marks of their incorrigible gabble remained in Whittier, except for his happiest moments, more indelibly than those made by the work of even the idolized Burns; and it is highly probable that Whittier, in spite of the fact that he was to deplore "the imbecility of our poetry", could not nicely distinguish the poetic level of Burns from that of, say, Lydia Sigourney, the "sweet singer of Hartford", who was his friend. He could write, too, of Longfellow's "A Psalm of Life": "These nine simple verses are worth more than all the dreams of Shelley, Keats, and Wordsworth. They are alive and vigorous with the spirit of the day in which we live—the moral steam enginery of an age of action." Whenever "moral steam enginery" came in the door, whatever taste Whittier did happen to have went precipitously out the window.

But, in addition to all the other poets good and bad whom Whittier read, there was, inevitably, Byron. In fact, it was under the aegis of Byron that Whittier, with a poem called **"The Exile's Departure"**, written when he was eighteen, first found his way into print. His sister Mary had secretly sent the poem, with only the signature "W", to the *Free Press,* the newspaper at Newburyport. There, on June 8, 1826, it was published—not only published but accompanied by the hope of the editor that "W" would continue to favor him with pieces equally "beautiful".

This editor was William Lloyd Garrison, then only twenty-one, destined not only to become the most intransigent and famous of the Abolitionists, but also to have a lasting effect on the shape of Whittier's life. The most immediate effect came, however, when Garrison, having discovered the identity of "W", drove fifteen miles to the Whittier farm, burst in upon the family, and lectured John Whittier on his duty to give the son "every facility for the development of his remarkable genius". To this oratory of a beardless youth, old John Whittier replied: "Sir, poetry will not give him bread."

Nevertheless, the father did allow his son to enroll, one year and some fifty poems later, as a freshman—that is, as a freshman in high school—in the Haverhill Academy, just then established. For two sessions, broken by a stint at schoolmastering, Whittier managed to support himself at the Academy, and this was the end of his formal education. By this time his poetry, which issued in a swelling stream, had been published in distant places like Boston, Hartford, and Philadelphia (in the *Saturday Evening Post*), and was being widely reprinted by newspaper editors. Whittier was something of a local celebrity, had friends and admirers (whose efforts to raise money for his continuing his education at college came to nothing), and was inflamed with ambition and the ignorant confidence that the world was his for the reaching out. He could write that he felt "a consciousness of slumbering powers".

While in Haverhill, Whittier had already had some experience in the office of the local newspaper, and it was to be in journalism that he entered the great world and became a writer—a pattern very common in America in the nineteenth century but, for various reasons, now rare. Whittier, anxious to take a hand in the "moral steam enginery" of the age, aspired to the editorship of the *National Philanthropist,* of Boston, the first prohibition paper in the country, which Garrison was then editing. Alcohol, however, had not proved a worthy challenge to Garrison's mettle, and now he was resigning the post to establish, in Bennington, Vermont, the *Journal of the Times,* which was to take as its twin targets slavery and war. Meanwhile, Garrison was sponsoring his protegé as successor in the crusade for prohibition. This did not work out, but the Collier family, owners of the *Philanthropist,* published two other papers, the *American Manufacturer* and the *Baptist Minister,* and, presumably out of respect for their resigning employee, made Whittier the editor of the first.

The *Manufacturer* was a weekly dedicated to the support of Henry Clay and the Whig Party, especially to the policy of the high protective tariff. But Whittier, who, while still hoping for the editorship of the *Philanthropist,* had written to a friend that he would "rather have the memory" of a reformer "than the undying fame of a Byron", promptly grafted the cause of prohibition on to that of a high tariff, and the first poem he wrote for his editorial column was an un-Byronic ditty entitled **"Take Back the Bowl!"**.

In spite of this and other reformist excursions in the *Manufacturer,* Whittier knew his duty to the Tariff of Abominations and the "American System" of the Whigs. As one of Whittier's biographers, John A. Pollard, has pointed out, Whittier, in spite of the fact that he had been raised in the tradition of Jeffersonian democracy, failed to grasp the relation of the tariff and Whig capitalism to his own inherited principles, and assumed that what was good for New England loommasters was good for New England in general, and, in fact, for the human race at large. Whittier's Quaker pacifism made him regard Jackson, a soldier and duelist, as the "blood-thirsty old man at the head of our government", and blinded him to some of the economic and social implications of Jacksonian democracy.

Meanwhile, Whittier helped in preparing a campaign biography of Clay, and came to edit two other pro-Clay papers, the *Gazette* of Haverhill and the *New England Weekly Review* of Hartford. He had made something of a reputation as a partisan editor, with a prose of biting sarcasm and a sense of political strategy. Though the poems continued in unabated flow, his personal ambitions were more and more political. It is hard to believe that at this stage in his life Whittier was really committed to poetry. The conclusion is almost inevitable that he was using his facility in verse as a device for success rather than using poetry as a way of coming to grips with experience. He wrote poems by the bushel and got himself extravagantly praised for them—and why not? He had become a master of the garrulous vapidity which was in general fashion.

But poetry was not enough. The joy of discovery and composition was not enough, nor even the recognition he was receiving. Whittier wanted more than recognition; he wanted some great, overwhelming, apocalyptic success, a success that he probably could not, or dared not, define for himself, a success that would be the very justification for life. "I would have fame visit me *now*, or not at all," he wrote to Lydia Sigourney. Again, in a most extraordinary essay, "The Nervous Man", in 1833, he speaks through his character:

> 'Time has dealt hardly with my boyhood's muse. Poetry has been to me a beautiful delusion. It was something woven of my young fancies, and reality has destroyed it. I can, indeed, make rhymes now, as mechanically as a mason piles one brick above another; but the glow of feeling, the hope, the ardor, the excitement have passed away forever. I have long thought, or rather the world hath *made* me think, that poetry is too trifling, too insignificant a pursuit for the matured intellect of sober manhood. . . .'

With some rational sense of his own limitations (he knew that what he knew was how to pile the bricks) was paradoxically coupled a self-pity and an air of grievance against the world that had not adequately rewarded the poet, by the age of twenty-five, with that overwhelming, life-justifying, undefinable, and apocalyptic success. So he wrote Lydia Sigourney that politics was "the only field now open". He turned to politics for the prize, not merely by clinging to Clay's coattails, to which he pinned wildly adulatory effusions such as "Star of the West", which became an effective campaign item, but by trying to run for office himself. In this period he made at least two unsuccessful attempts, and a letter soliciting support is significant.

Again, this letter emphasizes the *now*: "It [the election to Congress] would be worth more to me *now*, young as I am, than almost any office after I had reached the

meridian of life." And the letter, which, in fact, was related to some rather dubious maneuvering, shows that Whittier, who had been outraged at Jackson and the Spoils System, had secretly learned something—a "something" to which he now must give the moral disguise of unselfishness and loyalty:

> . . . If I know my own heart, I am not entirely selfish. I have never yet *deserted a friend,* and I never will. If my friends enable me to acquire influence, it shall be exerted for *their benefit.* And give me once an opportunity of exercising it, my first object shall be to evince my gratitude by exertions in behalf of those who had conferred such a favor upon me. . . .

Which, translated, means: you scratch my back and I'll scratch yours.

For the moment, nothing came of Whittier's political projects, and nothing came of the love affairs that belong to the same period of his attempt to enter the great world. Whittier, in spite of a certain frailty, was tall, handsome, and attractive to women; and he himself was greatly attracted to women, and was rather inclined to insist on the fact. But he remained a bachelor. In the series of love affairs, in the period before 1833, one pattern seems to run. The girls were non-Quaker, good-looking, popular, and above Whittier's station, both financially and socially; that is, the choice of sweethearts seems to have been consistent with his worldly and un-Quakerish ambitions. Some biographers take at its face value Whittier's statement, made late in life, that he refused matrimony because of "the care of an aged mother, and the duty owed to a sister in delicate health", but the facts apparently do not quite square with this explanation. The girls, with one possible exception, seem to have turned him down. As an index to wounded self-esteem, frustrated ambition, and a considerable talent for boyish self-dramatization, we have this passage, which, though it dates back to 1828, cannot be without significance in relation to more than poetry:

> . . . *I will quit poetry and everything else of a literary nature,* for I am sick at heart of the business. . . . Insult has maddened me. The friendless boy has been mocked at; and years ago, he vowed to triumph over the scorners of his boyish endeavors. With the unescapable sense of wrong burning like a volcano in the recesses of his spirit, he has striven to accomplish this vow, until his heart has grown weary of the struggle. . . .

There is no way to be sure what went on in Whittier's soul or in his romances. In 1857, in a poem called **"My Namesake"**, looking back on his youth, he said of himself:

> His eye was beauty's powerless slave,
>   And his the ear which discord pains;
> Few guessed beneath his aspect grave
>   What passions strove in chains.

Though Whittier was aware of the existence of the "chains", we cannot know exactly what they were. It may even be that Whittier, consciously choosing girls that fitted his "passions" and his vaulting ambition, was unconsciously choosing girls who would be certain to turn him down, and to get whom, if they refused his Quakerism, he would have to violate his training by marrying "outside of meeting".

But what was to prevent him from seeking some pretty Quaker girl—or even a pretty Quaker girl who happened to be rich? The thought of a Quaker sweetheart did cross his mind, for in 1830, in the middle of his love affairs, he wrote a poem to a **"Fair Quakeress"**, and praised her, whether she was real or imagined, for being "unadorned save for her youthful charms", and stated his conviction that beneath the "calm temper and a chastened mind" a "warmth of passion" was awaiting the "thrilling of some kindly touch"; but that was, for the time being, as far as he got along this particular line of thought. Whittier did, it is true, have a protracted, complex relationship with one Quaker lady, Elizabeth Lloyd, to whom we shall recur. But this was after he had given up his worldly ambitions and had made his commitment to Abolitionism as a way of life. The change in the way of life may have made some difference in the kind of girl Whittier, in this second phase, found congenial: poetesses, dabblers in art, Abolitionists, hero-worshippers, and protegés. But the pattern of behavior did not change. We have already mentioned "The Nervous Man". In the same period Whittier had written another remarkable piece of undeclared self-analysis called "The Male Coquette". This predicted the rôle he was doomed to play until the end.

In any case, there was some deep inner conflict in Whittier, with fits of self-pity and depression, breakdowns and withdrawals from the world, violent chronic headaches and insomnia. A breakdown sent Whittier from Hartford and his editorship back to Haverhill, and to such farming as his health permitted. Here, again, Garrison appeared. Already he had done a hitch in a Baltimore jail (unable to pay a judgment for libelously accusing a shipmaster of carrying a cargo of slaves), had founded, in January, 1831, the *Liberator,* the most famous of Abolitionist papers, and had written the pamphlet "Thoughts on African Colonization"; and these things had already had an effect on Whittier. Now, in the spring of 1833, Garrison wrote Whittier a direct appeal: "The cause is worthy of Gabriel—yea, the God of hosts places himself at its head. Whittier, enlist!— Your talent, zeal, influences—all are needed."

When, a few weeks later, Garrison came to Haverhill and spoke at the Quaker meeting-house, Whittier was ready, as he put it, to knock "Pegasus on the head, as a tanner does his barkmill donkey, when he is past service". Years later, after the Civil War, in the poem

"The Tent on the Beach", Whittier wrote, with something less than full historical accuracy, of his shift in direction:

> And one there was, a dreamer born,
>   Who, with a mission to fulfill,
> Had left the Muses' haunts to turn
>   The crank of an opinion mill,
> Making his rustic reed of song
> A weapon in the war with wrong. . . .

A more candid account appears in a letter to E. L. Godkin, the editor of the *Nation*: "I cannot be sufficiently grateful to the Divine Providence that so early called my attention to the great interests of humanity, saving me from the poor ambitions and miserable jealousies of a selfish pursuit of literary remuneration. And from," he added, "the pain of disappointment and the temptation to envy." Whittier had, apparently, already suffered enough from those things, as well as from other wounds to ego and ambition.

In spite of the fact that many Quakers had been slave-holders and some, especially the sea-going Quakers of the southwest of England, had been in the slave trade (one of the most famous slave ships of the eighteenth century was *The Willing Quaker*), the tradition that Whittier directly inherited was that of Benjamin Lay and John Woolman, whose anti-slavery writings were fundamental documents in the history of anti-slavery thought. It was a tradition of brotherhood understood in quite simple and literal terms, and so his entrance into the Abolition movement was a natural act, as was his repudiation of ambition and the reduction of poetry.

Whittier began his career as a militant in 1833, by writing, and publishing out of his own thinly-furnished pocket, a carefully-studied and well-argued pamphlet, "Justice and Expediency", in which he expressed the conviction that the "withering concentration of public opinion upon the slave system is alone needed for its total annihilation." At the end of that year, he attended the convention in Philadelphia that founded the American Anti-Slavery Society, and himself drew up the platform, which disavowed all violence and any attempt to foment servile insurrection. All his life it was a point of pride for him that he had been one of the original signers of this "Declaration".

From this time on, Whittier was constantly engaged in the cause of Abolitionism, as a writer of both prose and verse, as a member, briefly, of the lower house of the Massachusetts legislature, as an editor of a series of anti-slavery papers, and as an organizer and speaker. He came to know contumely, the odor of rotten eggs, mob violence, and the struggle against physical fear. He also came to know the formidable wrath and contempt of Garrison.

Whittier had become more and more firm in his belief in political action—that is, in his belief that man is, among other things, a member of society. For instance, in a letter to his publisher, J. T. Fields, he rejected the radical individualism of Thoreau's *Walden,* which he called "capital reading, but very wicked and heathenish", and added that the "moral of it seems to be that if a man is willing to sink himself into woodchuck he can live as cheaply as that quadruped; but after all, for me, I prefer walking on two legs." Whittier saw man among men, in his social as well as in other dimensions, and as the proper object of appeal to reason rather than the target for contumely; and nothing could more infuriate the radical Garrison, who was publicly to accuse Whittier of being a traitor to principle. In fact, Whittier, as a good Quaker, spent much of his energy, as we have said, in trying to mediate among factions of the movement, an effort that came to little. In the end the "political" wing of the original American Anti-Slavery Society split off to form the American and Foreign Anti-Slavery Society, and to this Whittier, in spite of his depression over the schism and estrangement from his old friend and benefactor, devoted his energies for some years as an editor, propagandist, and political manipulator. In the last rôle, his great triumph was to get Charles Sumner to Washington, as a senator from Massachusetts.

As the tensions mounted during the 1850's, Whittier held to his principles of institutional reform and political action—and to his Quaker pacifism. He never compromised on the question of slavery, but he steadily insisted on viewing the question in human and institutional contexts, as, for instance, in the poem **"Randolph of Roanoke"**:

> He held his slaves; yet kept the while
>   His reverence for the Human;
> In the dark vassals of his will
>   He saw but Man and Woman!
> No hunter of God's outraged poor
>   His Roanoke valley entered;
> No trader in the souls of men
>   Across his threshold ventured.

When the news of John Brown's raid on Harper's Ferry broke, Whittier wrote an article in which he expressed his "emphatic condemnation" of "this and all similar attempts to promote the goal of freedom by the evil of servile strife and civil war", and at the same time analyzed the danger which the South created for itself by trying to maintain and justify the internal contradiction between freedom and slavery in its system. In other words, on this test matter of Brown, Whittier agreed with Lincoln and not with Emerson, Thoreau, Garrison, or the "Secret Six", the gentlemen who had provided John Brown with money and encouragement for his project.

There is, in fact, a general similarity between Whittier's views and those of Lincoln. As early as 1833, in his "Justice and Expediency", Whittier pointed out the internal contradiction created by the presence of slavery in the United States, and declared: "Liberty and slavery cannot swell in harmony together." He saw the psychological and economic issues raised by this co-existence of free and slave labor. He held the view that Christianity and civilization had placed slavery "on a moral quarantine": in other words, he agreed with Lincoln that if the extension of slavery were stopped, it would die out in the slave states without forceful intermeddling. Though on the question of the annexation of Texas Whittier had toyed with the idea of disunion, he fundamentally saw the union as necessary to Abolition. He also held very early the view that the problem was to "give effect to the spirit of the Constitution"—a notion which may be taken to describe the social history of the United States to the present time.

When the Civil War was over, Whittier saw, as many could not, or would not, see, that the war had not automatically solved the problem of freedom. Though rejoicing in the fact of emancipation, he could write, in a letter to Lydia Maria Child, that the "emancipation that came by military necessity and enforced by bayonets, was not the emancipation for which we worked and prayed."

When Whittier, at the age of twenty-six, came to knock "Pegasus on the head", the creature he laid low was, indeed, not much better than the tanner's superannuated donkey. In giving up his poetry he gave up very little. Looking back on the work he had done up to that time, we can see little achievement and less promise of growth. He had the knack, as he put it in "The Nervous Man", for making rhymes "as mechanically as a mason piles one brick above another", but nothing that he wrote had the inwardness, the organic quality, of poetry. The stuff, in brief, lacked content, and it lacked style. Even when he was able to strike out poetic phrases, images, or effects, he was not able to organize a poem; his poems usually began anywhere and ended when the author got tired. If occasionally we see a poem begin with a real sense of poetry, the poetry gets quickly lost in some abstract idea. Even a poem as late as **"The Last Walk in Autumn"** (1857) suffers in this way. It opens with a fine stanza like this:

> O'er the bare woods, whose outstretched hands
>   Plead with the leaden heavens in vain,
>   I see beyond the valley lands,
>   The sea's long level dim with rain,
>   Around me, all things, stark and dumb,
>   Seem praying for the snows to come,
> And for the summer bloom and greenness, gone,
> With winter's sunset lights and dazzling morn atone.

But after five stanzas, the poem dies and the abstractions take over for some score of stanzas.

For a poet of natural sensibility, subtlety, and depth to dedicate his work to propaganda would probably result in a coarsening of style and a blunting of effects, for the essence of propaganda is to refuse qualifications and complexity. But Whittier had, by 1833, shown little sensibility, subtlety, or depth, and his style was coarse to a degree. He had nothing to lose, and stood to gain certain things. To be effective, propaganda, if it is to be more than random vituperation, has to make a point, and the point has to be held in view from the start; the piece has to show some sense of organization and control, the very thing Whittier's poems had lacked. But his prose had not lacked this quality, nor, in fact, a sense of the biting phrase; now his verse could absorb the virtues of his prose. It could learn, in addition to a sense of point, something of the poetic pungency of phrase and image, and the precision that sometimes marked the prose. He had referred to his poems as "fancies", and that is what they were, no more. Now he began to relate poetry, though blunderingly enough, to reality. The process was slow. It was ten years—1843—before Whittier was able to write a piece as good as **"Massachusetts to Virginia"**. This was effective propaganda; it had content and was organized to make a point.

Whittier had to wait seven more years before, at the age of forty-three, he could write his first really fine poem. This piece, the famous **"Ichabod"**, came more directly, and personally, out of his political commitment than any previous work. On March 7, 1850, Daniel Webster, senator from Massachusetts, spoke on behalf of the more stringent Fugitive Slave Bill that had just been introduced by Whittier's ex-idol Henry Clay; and the poem, which appeared in March in the *Washington National Era*,[1] a paper of the "political" wing of the Abolition movement, deals with the loss of the more recent and significant idol. "This poem," Whittier wrote years later, "was the outcome of the surprise and grief and forecast of evil consequences which I felt on reading the Seventh of March Speech by Daniel Webster. . . ." But here the poet remembers his poem, which does dramatically exploit surprise and grief, better than he remembers the facts of its origin; he could scarcely have felt surprise at Webster's speech, for as early as 1847, in a letter to Sumner, Whittier had called Webster a "colossal coward" because of his attitude toward the annexation of Texas and the Mexican War.

Here is the poem:

> So fallen! so lost! the light withdrawn
>   Which once he wore!
> The glory from his gray hairs gone
>   Forevermore!
>
> Revile him not, the Tempter hath
>   A snare for all;
> And pitying tears, not scorn and wrath,
>   Befit his fall!

Oh, dumb be passion's stormy rage,
  When he who might
Have lighted up and led his age,
  Falls back in night.

Scorn! would the angels laugh, to mark
  A bright soul driven,
Fiend-goaded, down the endless dark,
  From hope and heaven!

Let not the land once proud of him
  Insult him now,
Nor brand with deeper shame his dim,
  Dishonored brow.

But let its humbled sons, instead,
  From sea to lake,
A long lament, as for the dead,
  In sadness make.

Of all we loved and honored, naught
  Save power remains;
A fallen angel's pride of thought,
  Still strong in chains.

All else is gone; from those great eyes
  The soul has fled;
When faith is lost, when honor dies,
  The man is dead!

Then, pay the reverence of old days
  To his dead fame;
Walk backward, with averted gaze,
  And hide the shame!

The effectiveness of **"Ichabod"**, certainly one of the most telling poems of personal attack in English, is largely due to the dramatization of the situation. At the center of the dramatization lies a division of feeling on the part of the poet: the poem is not a simple piece of vituperation, but represents a tension between old trust and new disappointment, old admiration and new rejection, the past and the present. The Biblical allusion in the title sets this up: "And she named the child Ichabod, saying, the glory is departed from Israel" (*I Samuel* 4:21). The glory has departed, but grief rather than rage, respect for the man who was once the vessel of glory rather than contempt, pity for his frailty rather than condemnation—these are the emotions recommended as appropriate. We may note that they are appropriate not only as a generosity of attitude; they are also the emotions that are basically condescending, that put the holder of the emotions above the object of them, and that make the most destructive assault on the ego of the object. If Webster had been motivated by ambition, then pity is the one attitude unforgivable by his pride.

The Biblical allusion at the end offers a brilliant and concrete summary of the complexity of feeling in the poem. As Notley Sinclair Maddox has pointed out (*Explicator*, April, 1960), the last stanza is based on

Genesis 9:20-25. Noah, in his old age, plants a vineyard, drinks the wine, and is found drunk and naked in his tent by his youngest son, Ham, who merely reports the fact to his brothers Shem and Japheth. Out of filial piety, they go to cover Noah's shame, but "their faces were backward, and they saw not their father's nakedness." Ham, for having looked upon Noah's nakedness, is cursed as a "servant to servants" to his "brethren".

The allusion works as a complex and precise metaphor: The great Webster of the past, who, in the time of the debate with Robert Young Hayne (1830), had opposed the slave power and thus established his reputation, has now become obsessed with ambition (drunk with wine) and has exposed the nakedness of human pride and frailty. The conduct of Shem and Japheth sums up, of course, the attitude recommended by the poet. We may remember as an ironical adjunct that the Biblical episode was used from many a pulpit as a theological defense of slavery; Ham, accursed as a "servant to servants", being, presumably, the forefather of the black race.

We may look back at the first stanza to see another complex and effective metaphor, suggested rather than presented. The light is withdrawn, and the light is identified, by the appositive construction, with the "glory" of Webster's gray hair—the glory being the achievement of age and the respect due to honorable age, but also the image of a literal light, an aureole about the head coming like a glow from the literal gray hair. This image fuses with that of the "fallen angel" of line 27 and the dimness of the "dim, / Dishonored brow" in lines 19 and 20. In other words, by suggestion, one of the things that hold the poem together (as contrasted with the logical sequence of the statement) is the image of the angel Lucifer, the light-bearer, fallen by excess of pride. Then in lines 29 and 30, the light image, introduced in the first stanza with the aureole about the gray hair, appears as an inward light shed outward, the "soul" that had once shone from Webster's eyes (he had remarkably large and lustrous dark eyes). But the soul is now dead, the light "withdrawn", and we have by suggestion a death's-head with the eyes hollow and blank. How subtly the abstract ideas of "faith" and "honor" are drawn into this image, and how subtly the image itself is related to the continuing play of variations of the idea of light and dark.

From the point of view of technique this poem is, next to **"Telling the Bees"**, Whittier's most perfectly controlled and subtle composition. This is true not only of the dramatic ordering and interplay of imagery, but also of the handling of rhythm as related to meter and stanza, and to the verbal texture. For Whittier, in those rare moments when he could shut out the inane gabble of the sweet singers like Lydia Sigourney, and of his own incorrigible meter-machine, could hear the true voice of feeling. But how rarely he heard—or trusted—the voice of feeling. He was, we may hazard, afraid of feeling. Unless, of course, a feeling had been properly disinfected.

In the "war with wrong", Whittier wrote a number of poems that were, in their moment, effectively composed, but only two (aside from **"Ichabod"**) that survive to us as poetry. To one, **"Song of Slaves in the Desert"**, we shall return; but the other, **"Letter from a Missionary of the Methodist Episcopal Church South, in Kansas, to a Distinguished Politician"**, not only marks a high point in Whittier's poetic education but may enlighten us as to the relation of that education to his activity as a journalist and propagandist.

The **"Letter"**, as the full title indicates, grew out of the struggle between the pro-slavery and the free-state forces for the control of "Bleeding Kansas". Though the poem appeared in 1854, four years after **"Ichabod"**, it shows us more clearly than the earlier piece how the realism, wit, and irony of Whittier's prose could be absorbed into a composition that is both polemic and poetry. The polemical element is converted into poetry by the force of its dramatization—as in the case of **"Ichabod"**: but here specifically by an ironic ventriloquism, the device of having the **"Letter"** come from the pen of the godly missionary:

> Last week—the Lord be praised for all His mercies
> To His unworthy servant!—I arrived
> Safe at the Mission, *via* Westport; where
> I tarried over night, to aid in forming
> A Vigilance Committee, to send back,
> In shirts of tar, and feather-doublets quilted
> With forty stripes save one, all Yankee comers,
> Uncircumcised and Gentile, aliens from
> The Commonwealth of Israel, who despise
> The prize of the high calling of the saints,
> Who plant amidst this heathen wilderness
> Pure gospel institutions, sanctified
> By patriarchal use. The meeting opened
> With prayer, as was most fitting. Half an hour,
> Or thereaway, I groaned, and strove, and wrestled,
> As Jacob did at Penuel, till the power
> Fell on the people, and they cried "Amen!"
> "Glory to God!" and stamped and clapped their hands;
> And the rough river boatmen wiped their eyes;
> "Go it, old hoss!" they cried, and cursed the niggers—
> Fulfilling thus the word of prophecy,
> "Cursed be Canaan."

By the ventriloquism the poem achieves a control of style, a fluctuating tension between the requirements of verse and those of "speech", a basis for the variations of tone that set up the sudden poetic, and ironic, effect at the end:

> P.S. All's lost. Even while I write these lines,
> The Yankee abolitionists are coming
> Upon us like a flood—grim, stalwart men,

Each face set like a flint of Plymouth Rock
Against our institutions—staking out
Their farm lots on the wooded Wakarusa,
Or squatting by the mellow-bottomed Kansas;
The pioneers of mightier multitudes,
The small rain-patter, ere the thunder shower
Drowns the dry prairies. Hope from man is not.
Oh, for a quiet berth at Washington,
Snug naval chaplaincy, or clerkship, where
These rumors of free labor and free soil
Might never meet me more. Better to be
Door-keeper in the White House, than to dwell
Amidst these Yankee tents, that, whitening, show
On the green prairie like a fleet becalmed.
Methinks I hear a voice come up the river
From those far bayous, where the alligators
Mount guard around the camping filibusters:
"Shake off the dust of Kansas. Turn to Cuba—
(That golden orange just about to fall,
O'er-ripe, into the Democratic lap;)
Keep pace with Providence, or, as we say,
Manifest destiny. Go forth and follow
The message of our gospel, thither borne
Upon the point of Quitman's bowie-knife,
And the persuasive lips of Colt's revolvers.
There may'st thou, underneath thy vine and fig-tree,
Watch thy increase of sugar cane and negroes,
Calm as a patriarch in his eastern tent!"
Amen: So mote it be. So prays your friend.

Here quite obviously the ventriloquism is what gives the poem a "voice", and the fact instructs us as to how Whittier, less obviously, develops through dramatization a voice in **"Ichabod"**. The voice of a poem is effective—is resonant—insofar as it bespeaks a life behind that voice, implies a dramatic issue by which that life is defined. We have spoken of the complexity of feeling behind the voice of **"Ichabod"**, and in the present case we find such a complexity in the character of the missionary himself. At first glance, we have the simple irony of the evil man cloaking himself in the language of the good. But another irony, and deeper, is implicit in the poem: the missionary may not be evil, after all; he may even be, in a sense, "good"—that is, be speaking in perfect sincerity, a man good but misguided; and thus we have the fundamental irony of the relation of evil and good in human character, action, and history. Whittier was a polemicist, and a very astute one, as the **"Letter"** in its primary irony exemplifies. But he was also a devout Quaker, and by fits and starts a poet, and his creed, like his art, would necessarily give a grounding for the secondary, and deeper, irony, an irony that implies humility and forgiveness.

What we have been saying is that by repudiating poetry Whittier became a poet. His image of knocking Pegasus on the head tells a deeper truth than he knew; by getting rid of the "poetical" notion of poetry, he was able, eventually, to ground his poetry on experience. In the years of his crusade and of the Civil War, he was, bit by bit, learning this, and the process was, as we have said, slow. It was a process that seems to have been by fits and starts, trial and error, by floundering, rather than by rational understanding. Whittier was without much natural taste and almost totally devoid of critical judgment, and he seems to have had only a flickering awareness of what he was doing—though he did have a deep awareness, it would seem, of his personal situation. As a poet he was trapped in the automatism and compulsiveness that, in **"Amy Wentworth"**, he defined as the "automatic play of pen and pencil, solace in our pain"—the process that writing seems usually to have been for him. Even after a triumph, he could fall back for another fifty poems into this dreary repetitiveness.

The mere mass of his published work in verse between 1843 and the Civil War indicates something of this. In 1843 appeared *Lays of My Home,* in 1848 what amounted to a collected edition, in 1850 *Songs of Labor,* in 1853 *The Chapel of the Hermits, and Other Poems,* in 1856 *The Panorama, and Other Poems,* in 1857 the *Political Works,* in two volumes, and in 1860, *Home Ballads, Poems and Lyrics.*

But in this massive and blundering production there had been a growth. In 1843 even poems like **"To My Old Schoolmaster"**, **"The Barefoot Boy"**, **"Maud Muller"**, **"Lines Suggested by Reading a State Paper"**, and **"Kossuth"** would have been impossible, not to mention **"Skipper Ireson's Ride"**, which exhibits something of the élan of traditional balladry and something of the freedom of living language of **"Ichabod"** and the **"Letter"**. But nothing short of miracle, and a sudden miraculous understanding of Wordsworth and the traditional ballad, accounts for a little masterpiece like **"Telling the Bees"**. There had been the technical development, but something else was happening too, something more difficult to define; Whittier was stumbling, now and then, on the subjects that might release the inner energy necessary for real poetry.

There was, almost certainly, a deep streak of grievance and undischarged anger in Whittier, for which the Abolitionist poems (and editorials) could allow a hallowed—and disinfected—expression; simple indignation at fate could become "righteous indignation", and the biting sarcasm was redeemed by the very savagery of the bite. But there was another subject which released, and more deeply, the inner energy—the memory of the past, more specifically the childhood past, nostalgia, shall we say, for the happy, protected time before he knew the dark inward struggle, the outer struggle with "strong-willed men" (as he was to put it in **"To My Sister"**) to which he had to steel himself, the collapses, and the grinding headaches. Almost everyone has an Eden time to look back on, even if it never existed and he has to create it for his own delusion; but for Whittier the need to dwell on this lost Eden was more marked than is ordinary. If the simple indignation against a fate that had deprived him of the security of childhood could be transmuted into righteous indignation, both could be redeemed in a dream of Edenic innocence. This was the subject that could summon up Whittier's deepest feeling and release his fullest poetic power.

Furthermore, if we review the poems after 1850, we find a subsidiary and associated theme, sometimes in the same poem. In poems like **"Maud Muller"**, **"Kathleen"**, **"Mary Garvin"**, **"The Witch's Daughter"**, **"The Truce of Piscataqua"**, **"My Playmate"**, **"The Countess"**, and **"Telling the Bees"**, there is the theme of the lost girl, a child or a beloved, who may or may not be, in the course of a poem, recovered. Some of these poems, notably **"Maud Muller"** and **"Kathleen"**, raise the question of differences of social rank, as do **"The Truce of Piscataqua"** if we read "blood" for *social difference,* and **"Marguerite"** and **"Mary Garvin"** if we read the bar of religion in the same way. This last theme, in fact, often appears; we have it in **"Amy Wentworth"**, **"The Countess"**, and **"Among the Hills"**, all of which belong to the mature period of Whittier's work, when he was looking nostalgically backward. But this theme of the lost girl, especially when the loss is caused by difference in social rank or the religious bar, even though it clearly repeats a theme enacted in Whittier's personal life, never really touched the spring of poetry in him except in **"Telling the Bees"**, where it is crossed with the theme of childhood to reduce the pang of the sexual overtones. The theme of the lost girl, taken alone, belonged too literally, perhaps, to the world of frustration. In life Whittier had worked out the problem and had survived, by finding the right kind of action for himself, a "sanctified" action, and this action could, as we have seen, contribute to some of his best poetry; but, more characteristically, his poetic powers were released by the refuge in assuagement, the flight into Eden, and this was at once his great limitation and the source of his success.

For the poems specifically of nostalgia for childhood, we have **"To My Old Schoolmaster"**, **"The Barefoot Boy"**, **"The Playmate"**, **"The Prelude"** (to **"Among the Hills"**), **"To My Sister, with a Copy of 'The Supernaturalism of New England'"**, **"School-Days"**, **"Telling the Bees"**, and, preeminently, *Snow-Bound*. It is not so much the number of poems involved that is significant, but the coherent quality of feeling and, by and large, the poetic quality in contrast to the other work. As Whittier puts it in **"The Prelude"**, he was more and more impelled to

> . . . idly turn
> The leaves of memory's sketch-book, dreaming o'er
> Old summer pictures of the quiet hills,
> And human life, as quiet, at their feet.

He was, as he shrewdly saw himself in **"Questions of Life"**, an "over-wearied child", seeking in "cool and shade his peace to find", in flight

> From vain philosophies, that try
> The sevenfold gates of mystery,
> And, baffled ever, babble still,
> Word-prodigal of fate and will;
> From Nature, and her mockery, Art
> And book and speech of men apart,
> To the still witness in my heart.

As a young man hot with passion and ambition, and later as a journalist, agitator, and propagandist, he had struggled with the world, but there had always been the yearning for the total peace which could be imaged in the Quaker meeting-house, but more deeply in childhood, as he summarized it in **"To My Sister"**:

> And, knowing how my life hath been
> A weary work of tongue and pen,
> A long, harsh strife with strong-willed men,
> 　　Thou wilt not chide my turning
> To con, at times, an idle rhyme,
> To pluck a flower from childhood's clime,
> Or listen, at Life's noonday chime,
> 　　For the sweet bells of Morning!

The thing which he fled from but did not mention was, of course, inner struggle, more protracted and more bitter than the outer struggle with "strong-willed men".

"To My Old Schoolmaster", which appeared in 1851, just after Whittier's great poetic break-through with **"Ichabod"**, is the germ of *Snow-Bound,* the summarizing poem of Whittier's basic impulse. It can be taken as such a germ not merely because it turns back to the early years, but because Joshua Coffin, the schoolmaster, was a person associated with certain of Whittier's rites of passage, as it were. It was Coffin who, when Whittier was a boy of fourteen, sat by the family fire and read aloud from Burns. It was Coffin who was with Whittier at the founding of the American Anti-Slavery Society in Philadelphia, in 1833. Furthermore, Coffin early encouraged Whittier's historical and antiquarian interests (a fact that explains certain passages in the poem), and shared in his religious sense of the world; and in this last connection it is logical to assume that when, late in life, Coffin, a sweet-natured and devout man, fell prey to the conviction that he was not among the "elect" and would be damned, the fact would stir the aging Whittier's deepest feelings about the meaning of his own experience. Be that as it may, when Coffin died, in June, 1864, just before the death of Whittier's sister Elizabeth, which provoked *Snow-Bound,* Whittier felt, as he said in a letter, that he had lost "one of the old landmarks of the past". This bereavement would be absorbed into the more catastrophic one about to occur, just as the figure of Coffin would be absorbed into that of the schoolmaster in the poem that is ordinarily taken to refer, as we shall see, to a certain George Haskell.

We have remarked that **"To My Old Schoolmaster"**, composed shortly after **"Ichabod"**, may in one sense be taken also as contributing to *Snow-Bound.* But an even earlier poem, **"Song of the Slaves in the Desert"** (1847), indicates more clearly the relation of the poems inspired by Whittier's "war on wrong" to the poems of personal inspiration. The **"Song"** is, as a matter of fact, the best poem done by Whittier up to that time; and here the homesickness of the slaves gives a clear early example of the theme of nostalgia. Furthermore, since the slaves are, specifically, female, here is the first example of the theme of the lost girl:

> Where are we going? where are we going,
>   Where are we going, Rubee?
>
> Lord of peoples, lord of lands,
> Look across these shining sands,
> Through the furnace of the noon,
> Through the white light of the moon.
> Strong the Ghiblee wind is blowing,
> Strange and large the world is growing!
> Speak and tell us where we are going,
>   Where are we going, Rubee?
>
> Bornou land was rich and good,
> Wells of water, fields of food,
> Dourra fields, and bloom of bean,
> And the palm-tree cool and green:
> Bornou land we see no longer,
> Here we thirst and here we hunger,
> Here the Moor-man smites in anger:
>   Where are we going, Rubee?
>
> When we went from Bornou land,
> We were like the leaves and sand,
> We were many, we are few;
> Life has one, and death has two:
> Whitened bones our path are showing,
> Thou All-seeing, thou All-knowing!
> Hear us, tell us, where are we going,
>   Where are we going, Rubee?
>
> Moons of marches from our eyes
> Bornou land behind us lies;
> Stranger round us day by day
> Bends the desert circle gray;
> Wild the waves of sand are flowing,
> Hot the winds above them blowing,—
> Lord of all things! where are we going?
>   Where are we going, Rubee?
>
> We are weak, but Thou art strong;
> Short our lives, but Thine is long;
> We are blind, but Thou hast eyes;
> We are fools, but Thou art wise!
> Thou, our morrow's pathway knowing
> Through the strange world round us growing,
> Hear us, tell us where are we going,
>   Where are we going, Rubee?

The relation of **"Ichabod"** to the theme of nostalgia is somewhat more indirect and complex, but we may remember that, as the title declares, the theme is a la-ment for departed glory. Literally the glory is that of Webster, who has betrayed his trust, but also involved is the "glory" of those who trusted, who had trailed their own clouds of glory, not of strength and dedication, but of innocence, simplicity, and faith. The followers are betrayed by their natural protector, for, as the Biblical reference indicates, they are the sons of the drunken Noah. In the massiveness of the image, however, the father betrays the sons not only by wine but by death, for it is a death's-head with empty eye-sockets that is the most striking fact of the poem. Here the evitable moral betrayal is equated, imagistically, with the inevitable, and morally irrelevant, fact of death. But by the same token, as a conversion of the proposition, the fact of death in the morally irrelevant course of nature is, too, a moral betrayal. The child, in other words, cannot forgive the course of nature—the fate—that leaves him defenseless.

In connection with this purely latent content of the imagery, we may remark that Whittier, in looking back on the composition of the poem, claimed that he had recognized in Webster's act the "forecast of evil consequences" and knew the "horror of such a vision". For him this was the moment of confronting the grim actuality of life. It was, as it were, a political rite of passage. Here the protector has become the betrayer—has "died". So, in this recognition of the isolation of maturity, we have the beginning of the massive cluster of poems of the nostalgia of childhood.[2]

Let us glance at a later poem, **"The Pipes of Lucknow: An Incident of the Sepoy Mutiny"**, that seems, at first glance, even more unrelated to the theme of childhood than does **"Ichabod"**. But as **"Ichabod"** is associated with **"To My Old Schoolmaster"**, a more explicit poem of childhood, so **"Lucknow"** is associated with **"Telling the Bees"**. If we translate **"Lucknow"**, we have something like this: The Scots have left home (*i.e.*, grown up) and are now beleaguered.

> Day by day the Indian tiger
>   Louder yelled, and nearer crept;
> Round and round the jungle-serpent
>   Nearer and nearer circles swept.

The "Indian tiger" and the "jungle-serpent" are melodramatic versions of the "strong-willed men" and other manifestations of the adult world that Whittier had steeled himself to cope with, and had turned from, as the Scots turn now, on hearing the pipes, to seek assuagement in the vision of home. As another factor in this equation, we may recall that Whittier had early identified his father's rocky acres with the Scotland of Burns, and so the mystic "pipes o' Havelock" are the pipes of Haverhill.

With one difference: the pipes of Havelock announce not merely a vision of assuagement but also a vengeful carnage to be wrought on all those evil forces and persons that had robbed the child of "home", on the "strong-willed men" and the "Indian tiger" and the "jungle-serpent". Furthermore, since in the inner darkness, where its dramas are enacted, desire knows no logic or justice beyond its own incorrigible nature, we may see distorted in the dark face of the "Indian tiger" and the "jungle-serpent" the dark faces of those poor slaves in Dixie—for it was all their fault; they were the enemy—if it had not been for them Whittier would never have been drawn forth from the daydreams and neurotic indulgences of his youth into the broad daylight of mature and objective action.[3]

Whittier recognized in himself an appetite for violence. "I have still strong suspicions," he would write in the essay **"The Training"**, "that somewhat of the old Norman blood, something of the grim Berserker spirit, has been bequeathed to me." So, paradoxically, but in the deepest logic of his being, this strain of violence is provoked against these forces that would threaten the "peace" of childhood, and it is to the "air of Auld Lang Syne", rising above the "cruel roll of war-drums", that the vengeful slaughter is released and the gentle Quaker poet breaks out in warlike glee in such lines as:

> And the tartan clove the tartan
>   As the Goomtee cleaves the plain.

"Lucknow", in fact, seems nearer to Kipling than to the saint of Amesbury, the Abolitionist, and the libertarian poet who, in this very period, was writing poems deeply concerned with the freedom of Italians (**"From Perugia"**, 1858, and **"Italy"**, 1860), if not with that of Sepoys. But it is no mystery that in 1858, the year of **"Lucknow"**, Whittier should have written the gentle little masterpiece of nostalgia **"Telling the Bees"**, for both would seem to have been conditioned by the same traumatic event: the death of Whittier's mother, which occurred in December, 1857.

On February 16, 1858, Whittier sent **"Telling the Bees"** to James Russell Lowell, at the *Atlantic Monthly*, saying, "What I call simplicity may be only silliness." It was not silliness. It was a pure and beautiful little poem informed by the flood of feeling that broke forth at the death of his mother.

> Here is the place; right over the hill
>   Runs the path I took;
> You can see the gap in the old wall still,
>   And the stepping-stones in the shallow brook.
>
> There is the house, with the gate red-barred,
>   And the poplars tall;
> And the barn's brown length, and the cattle-yard,
>   And the white horns tossing above the wall.
>
> There are the beehives ranged in the sun;
>   And down by the brink
> Of the brook are her poor flowers, weed-o'errun,
>   Pansy and daffodil, rose and pink.

> A year has gone, as the tortoise goes,
>   Heavy and slow;
> And the same rose blows, and the same sun glows,
>   And the same brook sings of a year ago.
>
> There's the same sweet clover-smell in the breeze;
>   And the June sun warm
> Tangles his wings of fire in the trees,
>   Setting, as then, over Fernside farm.
>
> I mind me how with a lover's care
>   From my Sunday coat
> I brushed off the burrs, and smoothed my hair,
>   And cooled at the brookside my brow and throat.
>
> Since we parted, a month had passed,—
>   To love, a year;
> Down through the beeches I looked at last
>   On the little red gate and the well-sweep near.
>
> I can see it all now,—the slantwise rain
>   Of light through the leaves,
> The sundown's blaze on her window-pane,
>   The bloom of her roses under the eaves.
>
> Just the same as a month before,—
>   The house and the trees,
> The barn's brown gable, the vine by the door,—
>   Nothing changed but the hives of bees.
>
> Before them, under the garden wall,
>   Forward and back,
> Went drearily singing the chore-girl small,
>   Draping each hive with a shred of black.
>
> Trembling, I listened: the summer sun
>   Had the chill of snow;
> For I knew she was telling the bees of one
>   Gone on the journey we all must go!
>
> Then I said to myself, "My Mary weeps
>   For the dead to-day:
> Haply her blind old grandsire sleeps
>   The fret and the pain of his age away."
>
> But her dog whined low; on the doorway sill,
>   With his cane to his chin,
> The old man sat; and the chore-girl still
>   Sung to the bees stealing out and in.
>
> And the song she was singing ever since
>   In my ear sounds on:—
> "Stay at home, pretty bees, fly not hence!
>   Mistress Mary is dead and gone!"

The setting of the poem is a scrupulous re-creation of the farmstead where Whittier spent his youth. The poem was composed almost thirty years after Whittier had gone out into the world, and some twenty-two years after he had sold the home place and moved the family to Amesbury. Not only is the same nostalgia that informs *Snow-Bound* part of the motivation of this poem, but also the same literalism. But more than mere literalism seems to be involved in the strange fact that Whittier keeps his sister Mary—or at least her name—in the poem, and keeps her there to kill her off; and there is, of course, the strange fact that he cast a shadowy self—the "I" of the poem—in the rôle of the lover of Mary, again playing here with the theme of lost love, of the lost girl, but bringing the story within the family circle, curiously coalescing the youthful yearning for sexual love and the childhood yearning for love and security within the family circle. And all this at a time when Mary was very much alive.

Just as the shock of his mother's death turned Whittier's imagination back to the boyhood home and released the energy for **"Telling the Bees"**, so the death of his sister Elizabeth lies behind *Snow-Bound.* The relation of Whittier to this sister, who shared his literary and other tastes, who herself wrote verses (often indistinguishable in their lack of distinction from the mass of her brother's work), who was a spirited and humorous person, and who, as a spinster, was a companion to his bachelorhood, was of a more complex and intimate kind than even that of Whittier to his mother. She was "dear Lizzie, his sole home-flower, the meek lily-blossom that cheers and beautifies his life"—as was observed in the diary of Lucy Larcom, a poetess of some small fame and one of the ladies who, along the way, was in love, to no avail, with the poet himself. When Elizabeth died, on September 3, 1864, Whittier said, "The great motive of my life seems lost."

Shortly before Elizabeth's death there had been another crisis in Whittier's life, the end of his second and final romance with Elizabeth Lloyd, whom we have already mentioned. The relation with that lady was something more than merely one among his numerous frustrated romances. He had known her for some twenty-five years, from the time when he was thirty. She was good-looking, wrote verses, painted pictures, believed ardently in Abolition, and was a Quaker to boot. What could have been more appropriate? She even fell in love with him, if we can judge from the appeals in her letters toward the end of the first connection with her: "Spirit, silent, dumb and cold! What hath possessed thee?" Or: "Do come, Greenleaf! I am almost forgetting how thee looks and seems." But Greenleaf was beating one of his strategic retreats; so she cut her losses, got to work and made a literary reputation of sorts, married a non-Quaker, and got "read out of meeting".

After her husband's death, however, Elizabeth Lloyd, now Howell, reappeared in Whittier's life. They became constant companions. Both suffered from severe headaches, but they found that if they caressed each other's hair and massaged each other's brows, the headaches would go away. Or at least Whittier's headache would, and he proposed to her. She refused him, but not definitively, and the dalliance went on.

Even a quarrel about Quakerism did not end it. But it did end; or perhaps it merely petered out. In any case, in later years the lady nursed a grievance, and spoke bitterly of the old sweetheart.

So in spite of Elizabeth Howell's healing hands, Whittier again took up his solitude, and if he still clung to the explanation that his bachelorhood had been due to "the care of an aged mother, and the duty owed a sister in delicate health", the last vestige of plausibility was, ironically enough, now to be removed by the sister's sudden death. He was now truly alone, with no landmarks left from the Edenic past except those of memory.

Before the end of the month in which Elizabeth died, Whittier sent to the *Atlantic* a poem which he said had "beguiled some weary hours". It was **"The Vanishers"**, based on a legend he had read in Schoolcraft's famous *History, Condition, and Prospects of the American Indians* about the beautiful spirits who fleetingly appear to beckon the living on to what Whittier calls "The Sunset of the Blest". To the Vanishers, Whittier likens the beloved dead:

> Gentle eyes we closed below,
>   Tender voices heard once more,
> Smile and call us, as they go
>   On and onward, still before.

The poem is, in its basic impulse, a first draft of *Snow-Bound.*

In a very special way *Snow-Bound* summarizes Whittier's life and work. The poem gives the definitive expression to the obsessive theme of childhood nostalgia. As early as 1830, in **"The Frost Spirit"**, we find the key situation of the family gathered about a fire while the "evil power" of the winter storm (and of the world) goes shrieking by. Already, too, Whittier had long been fumbling toward his great question of how to find in the contemplation of the past a meaning for the future. In **"My Soul and I"**, (1847), the soul that turns in fear from the unknown future to seek comfort in the "Known and Gone" must learn that

> The past and the time to be are one,
>   And both are now.

The same issue reappears in **"The Garrison of Cape Ann"**:

> The great eventful present hides the past; but through
>   the din
> Of its loud life hints and echoes from the life behind
>   steal in;
> And the lore of home and fireside, and the legendary
>   rhyme,
> Make the task of duty lighter which the true man owes
>   his time.

And it appears again in **"The Prophecy of Samuel Sewall"** (1859).

As for the relation to the poet's personal life, ***Snow-Bound*** came after another manifestation of the old inhibition that forbade his seeking solace from Elizabeth Lloyd's healing hands (and this as he neared the age of sixty, when the repudiation of the solace must have seemed more nearly and catastrophically final). It came after the death of the sister had deprived him of the motive of his life. And it came, too, toward the end of the Civil War, when he could foresee the victory of the cause to which he had given his energies for more than thirty years and which had, in a sense, served as his justification for life, and as a substitute for other aspects of life. Now the joy of victory would, necessarily, carry with it a sense of emptiness. Furthermore, the victory itself was in terms sadly different, as Whittier recognized, from those that he had dreamed.

Snow-Bound is, then, a summarizing poem for Whittier; but it came, also, at a summarizing moment for the country. It came when the country—at least all the country that counted, the North—was poised on the threshold of a new life, the world of technology, big industry, big business, finance capitalism, and urban values. At that moment, caught up in the promises of the future, the new breed of American could afford to look back on his innocent beginnings; and the new breed could afford to pay for the indulgence of nostalgia—in fact, in the new affluence, paid quite well for it. Whittier's book appeared on February 17, 1866,[4] and the success was immediate. For instance, in April, J. T. Fields, the publisher, wrote to Whittier: "We can't keep the plaguey thing quiet. It goes and goes, and now, today, we are bankrupt again, not a one being in crib." The first edition earned Whittier ten thousand dollars—a sum to be multiplied many times over if translated into present values. The poor man was, overnight, modestly rich.

The scene of the poem, the "Flemish picture", as Whittier calls it, the modest genre piece, is rendered with precise and loving care, and this scene had its simple nostalgic appeal for the generation who had come to town and made it, and a somewhat different appeal, compensatory and comforting no doubt, for the generation that had stayed in the country and had not made it. But the poem is not simple, and it is likely that the appeals would have been far less strong and permanent if Whittier had not set the "idyl" in certain "perspectives" or deeper interpretations. In other words, it can be said of this poem, as of most poetry, that the effect does not depend so much on the thing looked at as on the way of the looking. True, if there is nothing to look at, there can be no looking, but the way of the looking determines the kind of feeling that fuses with the object looked at.

Before we speak of the particular "perspectives" in which the poem is set, we may say that there is a preliminary and general one. This general perspective, specified in Whittier's dedicatory note to his **"Winter Idyl"**,[5] denies that the poem is a mere "poem". The poem, that is, is offered as autobiography with all the validation of fact. In other words, the impulse that had appeared in **"The Vanishers"** as fanciful is here given a grounding in the real world, and in presenting that world the poem explores a complex idea—how different from the vague emotion of **"The Vanishers"**—concerning the human relation to Time.

The literalness of that world is most obviously certified by the lovingly and precisely observed details: the faces sharpened by cold, the "clashing horn on horn" of the restless cattle in the barn, the "grizzled squirrel" dropping his shell, the "board nails snapping in the frost" at night. The general base of the style is low, depending on precision of rendering rather than on the shock and brilliance of language or image; but from this base certain positive poetic effects emerge as accents and point of focus. For instance:

> A chill no coat, however stout,
> Of homespun stuff could quite shut out,
> A hard, dull bitterness of cold,
> That checked, mid-vein, the circling race
> Of life-blood in the sharpened face,
> The coming of the snow-storm told.
> The wind blew east; we heard the roar
> Of Ocean on his wintry shore,
> And felt the strong pulse throbbing there
> Beat with low rhythm our inland air.

Associated with this background realism of the style of the poem we find a firm realism in the drawing of character. Three of the portraits are sharp and memorable, accented against the other members of the group and at the same time bearing thematic relations to them: the spinster aunt, the schoolmaster, and Harriet Livermore.

The aunt, who had had a tragic love affair but who, as the poem states, has found reconciliation with life, bears a thematic relation to both Elizabeth Whittier and Whittier himself. The schoolmaster, whose name Whittier could not remember until near the end of his life, was a George Haskell, who later became a doctor, practiced in New Jersey and Illinois, and died in 1876 without even knowing, presumably, of his rôle in the poem; but as we have pointed out, there are echoes here, too, of Joshua Coffin. As for Harriet Livermore, Whittier's note identifies her. The fact that the "warm, dark languish of her eyes" might change to rage is amply documented by the fact that at one time, before the scene of ***Snow-Bound,*** she had been converted to Quakerism, but during an argument with another Quaker on a point of doctrine she asserted her theological view by laying out with a length of stove wood the man who was her antagonist. This action, of course, got her out of the sect. In her restless search for a satisfying religion, she represents one strain of thought in nineteenth-century America, and has specific resemblances to the characters Nathan and Nehemiah in Melville's *Clarel*. As a "woman tropical, intense", and at the same time concerned with ideas and beliefs, she is of the type of Margaret Fuller, the model for Zenobia in the *Blithedale Romance* of Hawthorne.

To return to the structure of the poem, there are three particular "perspectives"—ways in which the material is to be viewed—that can be localized in the body of the work. These perspectives operate as inserts that indicate the stages of the dialectic of this poem. The first appears in lines 175 to 211, the second in lines 400 to 437, and the third in lines 715 to the end.

The first section of the poem (up to the first perspective) presents a generalized setting: the coming of the storm, the first night, the first day, and the second night. Here the outside world is given full value in contrast to the interior, especially in the following passage, which is set between two close-ups of the hearthside, that Edenic spot surrounded by the dark world:

> The moon above the eastern wood
> Shone at its full; the hill-range stood
> Transfigured in the silver flood,
> Its blown snows flashing cold and keen,
> Dead white, save where some sharp ravine
> Took shadow, or the sombre green
> Of hemlocks turned to pitchy black
> Against the whiteness at their back.
> For such a world and such a night
> Most fitting that unwarming light,
> Which only seemed where'er it fell
> To make the coldness visible.

The setting, as we have said, is generalized; the individual characters have not yet emerged, the father having appeared in only one line of description and as a voice ordering the boys (John and his only brother, Matthew) to dig a path, with the group at the fireside only an undifferentiated "we". This section ends with the very sharp focus on the mug of cider simmering between the feet of the andirons and the apples sputtering—the literal fire, the literal comfort against the threat of literal darkness and cold outside.

Now the first perspective is introduced:

> What matter how the night behaved?
> What matter how the north-wind raved?
> Blow high, blow low, not all its snow
> Could quench our hearth-fire's ruddy glow.

But immediately, even as he affirms the inviolability of the fireside world, the poet cries out:

> O Time and Change!—with hair as gray
> As was my sire's that winter day,
> How strange it seems, with so much gone
> Of life and love, to still live on!

From this remembered scene by the fireside only two of the participants survive, the poet and his brother, who are now as gray as the father at that snowfall of long ago; for all are caught in Time, in this less beneficent snowfall that whitens every head, as the implied image seems to say. Given this process of the repetition of the pattern of Time and Change, what, the poet asks, can survive? The answer is that "love can never lose its own."

After the first perspective has thus grafted a new meaning on the scene of simple nostalgia by the fire, the poem becomes a gallery of individual portraits, the father, the mother, the uncle, the aunt, the elder sister (Mary), and the younger (Elizabeth), the schoolmaster, and Harriet Livermore. That is, each individual brings into the poem a specific dramatization of the problem of Time. In the simplest dimension, they offer continuity and repetition: they, the old, were once young, and now, sitting by the fire with the young, tell of youth remembered against the background of age. More specifically, each of the old has had to try to come to terms with Time, and their portraits concern this past.

When the family portraits have been completed, the second perspective is introduced; this is concerned primarily with the recent bereavement, with the absent Elizabeth, and with the poet's personal future as he walks toward the night and sees (as an echo from **"The Vanishers"**) Elizabeth's beckoning hand. Thus out from the theme of Time and Change emerges the theme of the Future, which is to be developed in the portraits of Haskell and Harriet Livermore.

The first will make his peace in Time, by identifying himself with progressive social good (which, as a matter of fact, George Haskell had done by 1866). Harriet Livermore, though seeking, by her theological questing, a peace out of Time, has found no peace in Time, presumably because she cannot seek in the right spirit; with the "love within her mute", she cannot identify herself with the real needs of the world about her (as Aunt Mercy can and George Haskell will); she is caught in the "tangled skein of will and fate", and can only hope for a peace in divine forgiveness, out of Time. After the portrait of Harriet Livermore, we find the contrast in the mother's attitude at the goodnight scene: unlike Harriet she finds peace in the here-and-now, "food and shelter, warmth and health" and love, with no "vain prayers" but with a willingness to act practically in the world—an idea that echoes the theme of **"My Soul and I"**, which we have already mentioned. And this is followed with the peace of night and the "reconciled" dream of summer in the middle of the winter.

With dawn, the present—not the past, not the future—appears, with its obligations, joys, and promises. Here there is a lag in the structure of the poem. When the snow-bound ones awake to the sound of "merry voices high and clear", the poem should, logically, move toward its fulfilment. But instead, after the gay and active intrusion of the world and the present, we have the section beginning "So days went on", and then the dead "filler" for some twenty lines. Whittier's literalism, his fidelity to irrelevant fact rather than to relevant meaning and appropriate structure of the whole, here almost destroys both the emotional and the thematic thrust, and it is due only to the power of the last movement that the poem is not irretrievably damaged.

The third "perspective" (lines 715-759), which ends the poem, is introduced by the eloquence of these lines:

> Clasp, Angel of the backward look
>   And folded wings of ashen gray
>   And voice of echoes far away,
> The brazen covers of thy book . . .

Then follow certain new considerations. What is the relation between the dream of the past and the obligations and actions of the future? The answer is, of course, in the sense of continuity of human experience, found when one stretches the "hands of memory" to the "wood-fire's blaze" of the past; it is thus that one may discover the meaningfulness of obligation and action in Time, even as he discovers in the specific memories of the past an image for the values out of Time. The "idyl" is more than a "Flemish picture"; it is an image, and a dialectic, of one of life's most fundamental questions that is summed up in the haunting simplicity of the end:

> Sit with me by the homestead hearth,
> And stretch the hands of memory forth
>   To warm them at the wood-fire's blaze!
> And thanks untraced to lips unknown
> Shall greet me like the odors blown
> From unseen meadows newly mown,
> Or lilies floating in some pond,
> Wood-fringed, the wayside gaze beyond;
> The traveller owns the grateful sense
> Of sweetness near, he knows not whence,
> And, pausing, takes with forehead bare
> The benediction of the air.

As a corollary to the third "perspective" generally considered, Whittier has, however, ventured a specific application. He refers not merely to the action in the future, in general, in relation to the past, but also, quite clearly, to the Civil War and the new order with its "larger hopes and graver fears"—the new order of "throngful city ways" as contrasted with the old agrarian way of life and thought. He invites the "worldling"—the man who, irreligiously, would see no meaning in the shared experience of human history, which to Whittier would have been a form of revelation—to seek

in the past not only a sense of personal renewal and continuity, but also a sense of the continuity of the new order with the American past. This idea is clearly related to Whittier's conviction, which we have already mentioned, that the course of development for America should be the fulfilling of the "implied intent" of the Constitution in particular, of the American revelation in general, and of God's will. And we may add that Whittier, by this, also gives another "perspective" in which his poem is to be read.

If we leave *Snow-Bound,* the poem, and go back again to its springs in Whittier's personal story, we may find that it recapitulates in a new form an old issue. The story of his youth is one of entrapments—and of his failure to break out into the world of mature action. In love, politics, and poetry, he was constantly being involved in a deep, inner struggle, with the self-pity, the outrage, the headaches, the breakdowns. He was, to no avail, trying to break out of the "past" of childhood into the "future" of manhood—to achieve, in other words, a self.

The mad ambition that drove him to try to break out of the entrapments, became in itself, paradoxically, another entrapment—another dead hand of the past laid on him. He cried out, "Now, now!"—not even knowing what he cried out for, from what need, for what reality. But nothing worked out, not love, nor politics, nor even poetry, that common substitute for success of a more immediate order. In poetry, in fact, he could only pile up words as a mason piles up bricks; he could only repeat, compulsively, the dreary clichés; his meter-making machine ground on, and nothing that came out was, he knew, real: his poems were only "fancies", as he called them, only an echo of the past, not his own present. And if he set out with the declared intention of being the poet of New England, his sense of its history was mere antiquarianism, mere quaintness—no sense of an abiding human reality. Again he was trapped in the past. All his passions strove, as he put it, "in chains". He found release from what he called "the pain of disappointment and the temptation to envy" only in repudiating the self, and all the self stood for, in order to save the self. He could find a cause that, because it had absorbed (shall we hazard?) all the inner forces of the "past" that thwarted his desires, could free him into some "future" of action.

So much for the story of the young Whittier.

But what of the old?

He had, in the end, fallen into another entrapment of the past. All action—and the possibility of action and continuing life—had been withdrawn: the solacing hands of Elizabeth Lloyd, the "great motive of . . . life" that the other Elizabeth represented, old friends such as Joshua Coffin, even the "cause" to which he had given his life and which had given his life meaning. Only memory—the past—was left. To live—to have a future—he had to re-fight the old battle of his youth on a new and more difficult terrain. He had to find a new way to make the past nourish the future.

It could not be the old way. The old way had been, in a sense, merely a surrender. By it, Whittier had indeed found a future, a life of action. But the victory had been incomplete, and the cost great; for we must remember that the grinding headaches continued and that the solacing hands of Elizabeth Lloyd had been, in the end, impossible for him.

The new way was more radical. That is, Whittier undertook to see the problem of the past and future as generalized rather than personal, as an issue confronting America, not only himself: furthermore, to see it *sub specie aeternitatis,* as an aspect of man's fate. And he came to see—how late!—that man's fate is that he must learn to accept and use his past completely, knowingly, rather than to permit himself to be used, ignorantly, by it.

Having struggled for years with the deep difficulties of his own life, Whittier at last found a way fruitfully to regard them, and **Snow-Bound** is the monument of this personal victory. No, it may be the dynamic image of the very process by which the victory itself was achieved. But there is another way in which we may regard it. It sets Whittier into relation to an obsessive and continuing theme in our literature, a theme that most powerfully appears in Cooper, Hawthorne, Melville, and Faulkner: what does the past mean to an American?

The underlying question is, of course, why a sense of the past should be necessary at all. Why in a country that was new—was all "future"—should the question have arisen at all? Cooper dealt with it in various dramatizations, most obviously in the figures of Hurry Harry and the old pirate in *Deerslayer* and of the squatter in *The Prairie,* who are looters, exploiters, and spoilers of man and nature: none of these men has a sense of the pride and humility that history may inculcate. How close are these figures to those of Faulkner's world who have no past, or who would repudiate the past, who are outside history—for example, the Snopeses (descendants of bushwhackers who had no "side" in the Civil War), Popeye of *Sanctuary,* Jason and the girl Quentin of *The Sound and the Fury* (who repudiate the family and the past), and of course poor Joe Christmas of *Light in August,* whose story is the pathetic struggle of a man who, literally, has no past, who does not know who he is or his own reality. Whittier, too, understood the fate of the man who has no past—or who repudiates his past. This is his "worldling" of **Snow-Bound** (whom

we may also take as an image of what the past might have been had the vainglorious dreams of his youth been realized), whom he calls to spread his hands before the warmth of the past in order to understand his own humanity, to catch the sweetness coming "he knows not where", and the "benediction of the air".

But, on the other side of this question, Whittier understood all too well the danger of misinterpreting the past—in his own case the danger of using the past as a refuge from reality. Faulkner, too, fully understood this particular danger and dramatized it early in *Sartoris* and later in **"The Odor of Verbena"**. But the theme appears more strikingly and deeply philosophized in characters like Quentin Compson in *The Sound and the Fury,* and Hightower in *Light in August.* But Faulkner understood other kinds of dangers of misinterpretation. Sutpen, with his "design" and no comprehension of the inwardness of the past, suggests, in spite of all differences, a parallel with Cooper's squatter in *The Prairie,* whose only link with the past is some tattered pages from the Old Testament that serve, in the end, to justify his killing of the brother-in-law (the pages having no word of the peace and brotherhood of the New Testament). But Faulkner's most complex instance of the misinterpretation of the past occurs with Ike McCaslin, who, horrified by the family crime of slavery and incest, thinks he can buy out simply by refusing his patrimony: he does not realize that a true understanding of the past involves both an acceptance and a transcendence of the acceptance.

If we turn to Melville, we find in *Pierre, or The Ambiguities* the story of a man trapped, as Whittier was, in the past and desperately trying to free himself for adult action, just as we find in *Battle-Pieces,* in more general terms, the overarching ironical idea of the vanity of human action set against man's need to validate his life in action. And, for a variation, in *Clarel* we find the hero (who has no "past"—who is fatherless and has lost his God, and who does not know mother or sister) seeking in history a meaning of life, this quest occurring in the Holy Land, the birthplace of the spiritual history of the Western World; and it is significant that Clarel finds his only answer in the realization that men are "cross-bearers all"—that is, by identifying himself with the human community, in its fate of expiatory suffering—an answer very similar to, though in a different tonality from, that of **Snow-Bound.**

With Hawthorne the same basic question is somewhat differently framed. We do not find figures with rôles like those of Hurry Harry, the squatter, Joe Christmas, Hightower, or Clarel, but we find, rather, a general approach to the meaning of the past embodied in Hawthorne's treatment of the history of New England. Nothing could be further than his impulse from the antiquarian and sentimental attitude of Whittier in his

historical pieces or from that of Longfellow. What Hawthorne found in the past was not the quaint charm of
distance but the living issues of moral and psychological definition. What the fact of the past meant to him
was a perspective on the present which gives an
archetypal clarity and a mythic force. The sentimental
flight into an assuagement possible in the past was the
last thing he sought. He could praise the ancestors, but
at the same time thank God for every year that had
come to give distance from them. In his great novel and
the tales the underlying theme concerns "legend" as
contrasted with "action", the "past" as contrasted with
the "future", as in the works of Cooper, Melville, and
Faulkner; and sometimes, most obviously in "My Kinsman, Major Molyneux", with this theme is intertwined
the psychological struggle to achieve maturity, with the
struggle seen as a "fate".

Whittier, though without the scale and power of Cooper,
Hawthorne, Melville, and Faulkner, and though he was
singularly lacking in their sense of historical and
philosophic irony, yet shared their deep intuition of
what it meant to be an American. Further, he shared
their intuitive capacity to see personal fate as an image
for a general cultural and philosophic situation. His star
belongs in their constellation. If it is less commanding
than any of theirs, it yet shines with a clear and
authentic light.

Whittier lived some twenty-five years after *Snow-
Bound* and wrote voluminously. But, as always, the
flashes of poetry were intermittent: **"Abraham Davenport"**, **"The Prelude"**, **"The Hive at Gettysburg"**,
"The Pressed Gentian", **"At Last"**, and **"To Oliver
Wendell Holmes"**. To these might be added the elegy
on Conductor Bradley ("A railway conductor who lost
his life in an accident on a Connecticut railway, May 9,
1873"), which may claim immortality of a sort scarcely
intended by the poet—as a work of grotesque humor
and unconscious parody and self-parody. The world
would be poorer without this accidental triumph of
inspired bathos, which begins:

> Conductor Bradley, (always may his name
> Be said with reverence!) as the swift doom came,
> Smitten to death, a crushed and mangled frame,
>
> Sank, with brake he grasped just where he stood
> To do the utmost that a brave man could,
> And die, if needful, as a true man should.
>
> Men stooped above him; women dropped their tears
> On that poor wreck beyond all hopes and fears,
> Lost in the strength and glory of his years.
>
> What heard they? Lo! the ghastly lips of pain,
> Dead to all thought save duty's, moved again:
> "Put out the signals for the other train!"

Whittier had lived into a world totally strange to him.
The world of industrialism and finance capitalism, of

strikes and strike-breaking, meant nothing to him. When
a man like William Dean Howells saw the Haymarket
case as a crucial test of justice, Whittier simply could
not understand the issue. But his fame was world-wide:
the Abolitionist, the hero, the humorist (for he was that,
too, in his way), and, to top it all, a sort of minor saint
in outmoded Quaker dress.

The house at Amesbury had long since become a point
of pilgrimage and many of the pilgrims were female,
and often marriageable, or fancied themselves so. In
Whittier's continuing bachelorhood, with a series of
female friends and admirers, there ran a strain of
flirtatiousness that more than one lady seems to have
taken too seriously. The old fierce ambition had now
shrunk to a small vanity that gratified itself in an excessive number of sittings for photographs and some devious tricks of self-advertisement, such as writing an
interview with himself and disguising the identity of the
interviewer, or doing the laudatory entry under his name
in an encyclopedia of biography. So, too, the old passion that had striven "in chains" now flickered on in
these little erotic charades. His ego needed these things
even at the time when he had long since won the real
battle against himself, and even now when he could
turn his basic feelings and imagination to the safe past
of the child by the fireside. Or perhaps now, as age
drew on, even with all of his humor, self-humor, self-
knowledge, self-discipline, and real humility, he needed
this old charade more than ever.

Whittier died September 7, 1892, after a brief period of
illness and a paralytic stroke. Toward the end, he was
often heard to murmur, "Love—love to all the world."
As he was dying, one of his relatives present by the
bedside quoted his poem "At Last". He was buried in
the section of the cemetery at Amesbury reserved for
Friends. The grave was lined with fern and goldenrod,
and the coffin was lowered to rest on a bed of roses.
Nearby were the graves of the members of the family
who had sat at the fireside of *Snow-Bound.*

Notes

1. In which Whittier's only novel—or near-novel—
   Margaret Smith's Journal, had appeared the previous year, and in which *Uncle Tom's Cabin* was to
   appear.

2. "Ichabod" has thematic parallels with Hawthorne's
   great story "My Kinsman, Major Molyneux". Both
   concern the degrading of a "father", Noah-as-
   Webster in his drunkenness and the Major at the
   hands of the mob. Both concern the son's involvement in the degrading: Whittier repudiates Webster even as Robin joins the mob in repudiating
   Molyneux. Both works concern a betrayal by the
   father: Webster of his political trust, and Molyneux, less precisely, in being an agent of the King

and not of the colonists (*i.e.,* children). Both concern what Hawthorne calls a "majesty in ruins", and in this connection involve deep ambivalences of the son toward the father. And in both the son is thrown back upon his own resources, Whittier as is implied in his comment on the poem, and Robin quite specifically when he is offered the chance of going home or staying in Boston to "rise" by his own "efforts".

There is probably one great difference between the two works. It is hard not to believe that Hawthorne was conscious of what is at stake in his work, and it is hard to believe that Whittier was not unconscious of certain implications in "Ichabod".

3. The poem may be taken as a kind of racist nightmare, like that of Isaac McCaslin in Faulkner's story "Delta Autumn", when he lies shaking with horror at his vision of the wilderness ruined to make room for a world of "usury and mortgage and bankruptcy and measureless wealth, where a breed of Chinese and African and Aryan and Jew all breed and spawn together until no man has time to say which one is which nor cares". Needless to say, Whittier's nightmare, like Ike's, was conquered.

4. Melville's book of poems on the Civil War, *Battle-Pieces,* appeared almost simultaneously, and was a crashing failure. As *Snow-Bound* seemed to dwell merely on the simplicity of the past, *Battle-Pieces* analyzed some of the painful complexities of the War and the present, and recognized some of the painful paradoxes in the glowing promises of the future: not what the public wanted to hear.

5. Here is the beginning of the prefatory note: "The inmates of the family at the Whittier homestead who are referred to in the poem were my father, mother, my brother and two sisters, and my uncle and aunt, both unmarried. In addition, there was the district schoolmaster, who boarded with us. The 'not unfeared, half-welcome guest' was Harriet Livermore, daughter of Judge Livermore, of New Hampshire, a young woman of fine natural ability, enthusiastic, eccentric, with slight control over her violent temper, which sometimes made her religious profession doubtful. She was equally ready to exhort in school-house prayer-meetings and dance in a Washington ball-room, while her father was a member of Congress. She early embraced the doctrine of the Second Advent, and felt it her duty to proclaim the Lord's speedy coming. With this message she crossed the Atlantic and spent the greater part of a long life in traveling over Europe and Asia. She lived some time with Lady Hester Stanhope, a woman as fantastic and mentally strained as herself, on the slope of Mt. Lebanon, but finally quarrelled with her in regard to two white horses with red marks on their backs which suggested the idea of saddles, on which her titled hostess expected to ride into Jerusalem with the Lord. A friend of mine found her, when quite an old woman, wandering in Syria with a tribe of Arabs, who, with the Oriental notion that madness is inspiration, accepted her as their prophetess and leader. At the time referred to in *Snow-Bound* she was boarding at the Rocks Village, about two miles from us."

Elsewhere, in a prefatory note to another poem, "The Countess", Whittier identifies the "wise old doctor" of *Snow-Bound* as Dr. Elias Weld of Haverhill, "the one cultivated man in the neighborhood", who had given the boy the use of his library.

Karl Keller (essay date 1971)

SOURCE: Keller, Karl. "John Greenleaf Whittier: Criticism." In *Fifteen American Authors Before 1900: Bibliographic Essays on Research and Criticism,* edited by Robert A. Rees and Earl N. Harbert, pp. 372-86. Madison, Wisc.: University of Wisconsin Press, 1971.

[*In the following excerpt, Keller provides an overview of criticism on Whittier's poetry, finding that the body of criticism available is less than satisfactory in terms of the poetry itself, although he concedes that there is adequate coverage of the biographical elements of the poet's work as well as its historical and social contexts.*]

The shape of Whittier criticism from the middle of the nineteenth century to the middle of this century has been discussed by Lewis E. Weeks, "Whittier Criticism Over the Years" (*EIHC* [*Essex Institute Historical Collections*], July 1964). Weeks has found two phases in the critical fortunes of Whittier. The first phase (up to Whittier's death in 1892) is characterized by a double attitude: he is the kindly, honest Quaker and the dreaded, vigorous abolitionist; he is violently loved (because he is loyally American, domestic, public, and a simple, earnest, sincere writer) and violently hated (because he is an anarchist, an overpassionate libertarian, overweeningly didactic, and a poet without adequate technique or range). Beginning in mistrust, the criticism becomes increasingly elegiac toward the end of the century. But because Whittier was such a personal force, there was difficulty in assessing his work esthetically. The second phase (the twentieth century) is concerned mainly with placing Whittier in perspective. The result by and large is a minor rank for him, yet not obscurity. His morality is worth rescuing but not his moralizing, his courage but not his voice, his passion for writing but not the poems that he wrote passionately. Our concern has therefore turned in this century from his substance to his reputation.

Although Whittier was noticed almost everywhere during his lifetime, only a few of the notices now seem very important. One of the earliest serious assessments of Whittier was Rufus Griswold's *Poets and Poetry of America* (Philadelphia, 1842). Whittier's **Supernaturalism of New England** appeared in 1847 and it was one of literary history's "shocks of recognition" when Hawthorne reviewed it in *The Literary World* (reprinted in *NEQ*[*New England Quarterly*], Sept. 1936); Hawthorne saw Whittier as too practical-minded to "believe his ghost-story while he is telling it," too pedantic and fussy, too far removed from the folk life from which New England legends spring; Whittier, Hawthorne said, "did not care much for literature." Orestes Brownson, in a review of Whittier's **Songs of Labor** in *Brownson's Quarterly Review* (Oct. 1850), went further and saw Whittier as the devil incarnate; to Brownson, Whittier sought to undermine faith, eradicate loyalty, break down authority, and establish the reign of anarchy: "He is a Quaker, an infidel, an abolitionist, a philanthropist, a peace man, a Red Republican, a nonresistant, a revolutionist, all characters we hold in horror and detestation, and his poems are the echo of himself." In contrast, David Wasson, representative of the period's Transcendentalists, thought of Whittier as a kind of Biblical poet-prophet (*AM* [*American Mercury*], Mar. 1864); like a prophet, Whittier spoke plainly to plain men, had a firm "moral sentiment," and was a reformer of the world around him.

Near the end of his life and immediately following his death, as Currier and Pulsifer have noted in the Whittier bibliography, discussions of Whittier, most of them by Friends and friends, ran into the hundreds. Harriet Prescott Spofford's is typical of these (*HM* [*Harper's Magazine*] Jan. 1884); because he is democratic, simple, rustic, moral, a man of broad interests and natural esthetic sense, Whittier is promoted as the ideal American poet, the nation's poet laureate. Edmund Gosse's *Portraits and Sketches* (London, 1912) is also typical; like Gosse, many found his personality "sweet" and "Quakerly" but his verse "primitive" and "redundant." Yet interestingly enough, the first assessment of Whittier from a nearly esthetic point of view was not made until 1881 when Richard Henry Stoddard wrote *The Homes and Haunts of Our Elder Poets* (New York) and until 1885 when Edmund C. Stedman wrote *Poets of America* (Boston). Both found that the power of Whittier's poetry comes not from the man so much as from his background (the Colonial past, the injustices in the society around him) and yet both also attempt to account for his failings as a poet: he is too naive, too

moralistic, too simplistic. Unfortunately, most of the critical comments on Whittier at his death serve better as nostalgia than as literary criticism.

Whittier's reputation in America during his lifetime has been discussed by T. W. Higginson, "The Place of Whittier among the Poets" (*Reader*, Feb. 1905), and his reputation abroad by John A. Pollard, "Whittier's Esteem in Great Britain" (*BFHA* [*Bulletin of the Friends Historical Association*], Spring 1949). A brief note on Whittier's reputation is C. Marshall Taylor, "The 1849 Best Seller" (*BFHA*, Autumn 1950). The problem of keeping Whittier's reputation alive is discussed by C. Waller Barrett, "John Greenleaf Whittier: The 100th Anniversary of His Birth" (*American Antiquarian Society Proceedings*, 1957) and by Donald C. Freeman, "The History of the Haverhill Whittier Club" (*ESQ* [*Emerson Society Quarterly*], First Quarter 1968).

As Weeks has mentioned, almost all of the Whittier criticism since the turn of the century is concerned essentially with Whittier's reputation, rather than with his thought or art. Three attempts to account for Whittier's universal appeal in the nineteenth century but neglect in the twentieth are Rica Brenner, *Twelve American Poets before 1900* (New York, 1932); Desmond Powell, "Whittier" (*AL* [*American Literature*], Nov. 1937); and W. Harvey-Jellie, "A Forgotten Poet" (*Dalhousie Review*, Apr. 1939).

There are almost formidable problems in reading Whittier in the twentieth century. Stanley Kunitz has articulated best, in *American Authors, 1600-1900* (New York, 1938), how invalid Whittier's assumptions about life and art and how irrelevant his writings now seem. He was "the voice of the middle nineteenth-century New England farmer and small town dweller," but ours is a different world. In *The Fields Were Green* (Stanford, Calif., 1953), George Arms, while defending him as a poet, sees Whittier's single-mindedness as the central problem in reading him today. To Arms, Whittier was a personal poet, a poet of personal experience, who tended to have only one motif, the Quaker view of man, even going so far as to identify English Romanticism with Quaker cosmology. As a result Whittier was uneasy as a poet; he could not accept art as an essential expression of life. Like Arms, Howard Mumford Jones, in "Whittier Reconsidered," in his *History and the Contemporary* (Madison, Wis., 1964), bemoans the inattention given Whittier's values and Christian gentlemanliness in our own time, but sees that the central problems for us are the superficiality of Whittier's indignation and his monotony and sentimentality.

Yet for all the problems in reading Whittier, much of the Whittier criticism has attempted to find what is redeemable in the man and his art. One of the most balanced early views is that by John Vance Cheney, *That*

Dome in Air (Chicago, 1895); Cheney feels that though Whittier is stiff and provincial, what he has left to generations after him is the idea of the poet as lover of man. Like this view is Paul Elmer More's, in *Shelburne Essays, Third Series* (Boston, 1906): for all Whittier's faults of taste, he had an indisputable, simple grace. To More, Whittier is the poet who brought the quiet affections of the home into our literature; his poetry is unmatched in the genre of "poetry of the hearth." Bliss Perry, in "Whittier for Today" (*AtM* [*Atlantic Monthly*], Dec. 1907), explains Whittier's relevance on other grounds—his courage and humanity, his involvement in social affairs. To Perry, there are two issues on which Whittier is always right: his insistence that there must not be any race issue and his demand for international peace. An extension of Perry's claim for Whittier is Ernest D. Lee's argument, in "John Greenleaf Whittier" (*The Westminister Review,* Jan. 1908), that Whittier should be preserved as an example of the phenomenon of a national poet.

Winfield Townley Scott, in his excellent essay "A New Consideration of Whittier's Verse" (*NEQ,* June 1934) and in his poem "Mr. Whittier," deplores the schoolroom use to which Whittier has been put and argues that Whittier can be restored to eminence if emphasis is placed on the poetry written after the Civil War, especially the religious verse. Hyatt H. Waggoner, in his *American Poets from the Puritans to the Present* (Boston, 1967) and in "What I Had I Gave: Another Look at Whittier" (*EIHC,* Jan. 1959), also finds Whittier's religious verse that which should recommend him to our own time. Waggoner shows how Whittier moved from moralizing and propagandizing to symbolizing and spiritualizing the world as he knew it, making him one of our literature's few Christian poets. To Waggoner there is value in relearning how to read Whittier; his contemporaries read him as a religious poet, as a poet of universal and humane causes, as a poet documenting God's part in the progress of The American Dream, and we must do so too.

Yet to read Whittier today, as Donald Hall has argued in "Whittier" (*Texas Quarterly,* Autumn 1960), requires an effort of the historical imagination. To Hall it is the nineteenth-century themes of goodness and optimism that give Whittier a firm place in our literary history. George E. Woodberry, in his essay on Whittier in *Makers of Literature* (New York, 1901), was one of the first to see how representative Whittier was of his time. John Macy, in *The Spirit of American Literature* (New York, 1913), saw Whittier as the poet who best represents the crudeness, banality, and prejudices, but also the idealism and exaltation, of the nineteenth century. To William M. Payne, writing in *CHAL* [*Cambridge History of American Literature*], Whittier was the representative man of "the epic days" preceding the war. Yet as Daniel W. Smythe has pointed out in "Whit-

tier and the New Critics" (*ESQ,* First Quarter 1968), Whittier continues to suffer disparagement under contemporary critical methods.

Whittier's development as an artist has been discussed best by H. H. Clark, J. B. Pickard, and Edward Wagenknecht. Clark, in an essay, "The Growth of Whittier's Mind" (*ESQ,* First Quarter 1968), assigns Whittier's work to the three conventional phases of his life: up to 1833, Whittier was interested mainly in sensational local legend; from 1833 to 1857 his mind was preoccupied with outward reformism; and from 1857 until his death he turned to the inward life. Pickard, in the critical essays in *John Greenleaf Whittier: An Introduction and Interpretion* (New York, 1961), sees his growth not so much in subject matter as in movement between genres, that is, from folk forms to protest forms and finally to nature poems and religious lyrics. Wagenknecht, on the other hand, sees, in *John Greenleaf Whittier: A Portrait in Paradox,* the growth of Whittier's mind in terms of coming to grips with the contradictions in his thinking; that is, the resolution of his fears, his pride, his senses (all of which conflicted with his otherworldly interests) into a sense of grace.

The earliest work on Whittier's esthetics and literary theory was done by Samuel T. Pickard, "Whittier's Literary Methods" (*Independent,* Sept. 1897) and by Harry H. Clark, in his notes on Whittier in *Major American Poets.* J. B. Pickard's work on the artistry of Whittier (especially in an essay, "Poetic Creed and Practice," in his *John Greenleaf Whittier*) shows that Whittier's views on art and beauty are dominated by a conflict between the lure of external natural beauty and the strict plainness of the Quaker life-style. Confusing religion with esthetics, Whittier's view of the purpose of art remained obscured throughout his life. Edward Wagenknecht's life, like Pickard's, is mainly a concern for Whittier's esthetics, and like Pickard he finds Whittier torn between regarding beauty as grace and beauty as a snare. Wagenknecht's discussion of Whittier's worship of nature, "The Light That Is Light Indeed," is excellent in reconciling Whittier's regard for art with his regard for religion. Lewis Leary, in his *John Greenleaf Whittier,* finds Whittier's literary principles centered around the idea of "the beauty of holiness, of purity, of that inward grace which passeth show," as opposed to the idea of the holiness of beauty of his Romantic contemporaries. Like Emerson, he felt that a high seriousness made language poetic, and though he lacked that esthetic education which might have provided the literary counterbalance to the moralist in him, he compensated for it with sincerity, devotion, humor, and stinging words. Though Leary is often more interested in Whittier's performance than in his poetics, he does demonstrate how a sense of the past, a consciousness of life being lived, and the meditating on one's own pride and humility were to Whittier more important parts of the poet's esthetics than his prosody or imagery. Roy Harvey Pearce, in discussing the esthetics of the Fireside Poets in *The Continuity of American Poetry* (Princeton, N.J., 1961), distorts Whittier in arguing that his literary principles were dominated by a fantasy principle, that is, by the belief that the poet has special access to the common man's dreams and fantasies. Whittier's poems, Pearce maintains, are therefore dominated by visions, dreams, nostalgia, idealistic indulgence, romanticizing of the past, and blind faith in the future.

With regard to Whittier's literary theory, what is lacking in the criticism is an extended discussion of Whittier's concern for form. We have Gay Wilson Allen's discussion of rhythm and stanza form in his *American Prosody* (New York, 1935) and two notes on "Whittier's Rhymes" by Kathryn A. McEuen and S. T. Byington (*AS* [*American Speech*], Feb. 1945; Feb. 1946), but Whittier's use of conventions and his many innovations have gone largely unexplored.

Whittier himself promoted the popular legend that he was not a well-read man, but scholars have gone to great pains to prove otherwise. The closest we have to a list of Whittier's reading is "The Library of John G. Whittier" (*ESQ*, First Quarter 1964). Alwin Thaler, in "Whittier and the English Poets" (*NEQ*, Mar. 1951; *ESQ*, First Quarter 1968), lists all of the British writers that Whittier knew. Thaler persuasively argues Whittier's wide reading and frequent use of his reading in his poems, especially Elizabethan and Romantic writings.

Whittier's legend also excluded the problem of literary influence, but the writers who influenced Whittier the most are revealed in an unpublished dissertation, Joseph M. Ernest's "Whittier and the American Writers" (Tennessee, 1952). As with other New England writers of the period, some of the strongest influences on Whittier were Elizabethan, German, and Oriental—all of which Whittier in his strict Quaker orthodoxy was able largely to resist. Iola K. Eastburn shows Whittier's catholic interests and wide reading in *Whittier's Relation to German Life and Thought* (Philadelphia, 1915); though Whittier was interested in German legends and reform movements, the German influence on him was not strong. Whittier was not a mystic, either, not a promoter of faith in the transcendent, and yet his Oriental interests were strong. Arthur E. Christy, "The Orientalism in Whittier" (*AL*, Jan. 1930; Nov. 1933), found that what appealed to the orthodox Quaker was mainly the moral tone and the general ethical principles of Eastern thought; Whittier's was not a spiritual and philosophical affinity with the Orient like Emerson's, for he was blind to distinctions between Christian and Oriental principles.

That Whittier was a borrower from his readings is shown by J. Chesley Matthews's study of "Whittier's

Knowledge of Dante" (*Italica*, 1957), by Jack Stillinger's notice of "Whittier's Early Imitation of Thomas Campbell" (*PQ* [*Philological Quarterly*], Oct. 1959), by Theodore Garrison's account of "The Influence of Robert Ginsmore ['the Rustic Bard of Windham, N. H.'] upon Whittier" (*ESQ*, First Quarter 1968), and by Nelson F. Adkins, "Sources of Some of Whittier's Lines" (*NEQ*, June 1933).

As a critic, as Edwin H. Cady and H. H. Clark show in their collection *Whittier on Writers and Writing*, Whittier was much more interested in the moral, the sublime, the antiquarian, and that which would reform society than he was in technical skill. The best discussions of Whittier's critical principles are two unpublished dissertations: C. P. Marcy, "The Literary Criticism of John Greenleaf Whittier" (Boston University, 1945) and J. M. Ernest, "Whittier and the American Writers." Marcy outlines the formative influences on Whittier's critical thought—his homelife, his education, his religion and politics—and finds Whittier most concerned with a writer's morality, the sensitivity of his response to nature, and the functionality of his imagination. Marcy's conclusion is that Whittier was not a discriminating critic of literature, and what limited him most severely was his idea that literature should conform to the conventions of a society controlled by Quaker tenets of morality and simplicity. Ernest, on the other hand, is interested mainly in showing how Whittier was one of the great promoters of American literature. He had a deep interest in seventeenth-century American writings and he kept abreast of the literary movements of his time by meeting and corresponding with, reading and reviewing most of the authors of his day. But as a critic, because his interests were primarily ethical rather than esthetic, he did not usually consider the work as distinct from the author. Not until he was older did his esthetic sense outgrow his crusading zeal.

Whittier's relationships with writers who were his contemporaries have been taken up separately to show what John J. McAleer calls "Whittier's Selective Tolerance" (*ESQ*, First Quarter 1968). McAleer finds Whittier both consoling and severe in his work with other writers. While the relationship between Whittier and Tennyson, as William J. Fowler (*Arena*, Dec. 1892) and Alwin Thaler (*PQ*, Oct. 1949) have both found, was one of mutual admiration, Whittier's regard for Carlyle, discussed by Roland H. Woodwell in *ESQ* (First Quarter 1968), was one of growing disgust because of Carlyle's refusal to support humanitarian causes important to Whittier.

The regard that Whittier and Bryant had for one another is discussed by Charles D. Deshler, *Afternoon with the Poets* (New York, 1879), and by Charles I. Glicksberg, "Bryant and Whittier" (*EIHC*, Apr. 1936); what they had in common was the cause of human freedom and an ardent patriotism. Longfellow's indebtedness to Whittier is discussed by Frank B. Sanborn, "Whittier and Longfellow Compared as Poets of New England" (*Boston Evening Transcript,* 24 July 1902), and by O. S. Coad, "The Bride of the Sea" (*AL,* Mar. 1937). His indebtedness to Bayard Taylor is discussed by Joseph M. Ernest in *Friend's Intelligencer* (Sept. 1952). Ernest has also documented Whittier's influence on American women writers in the latter half of the century in "Whittier and the 'Feminine Fifties'" (*AL,* May 1956). Ernest gives credit to Whittier for the phenomenon of so many women writers in the period; more than anyone else, Whittier gave them practical help and encouragement in their liberal causes. This important influence is documented further by Rudolph Kirk, "Whittier and Miss Piatt" (*JRUL* [*Journal of the Rutgers University Library*], June 1944), and by Carl J. Weber, "Whittier and Sarah Orne Jewett" (*NEQ,* Sept. 1945).

Whittier's thorniest relationship was with Whitman. Joseph M. Ernest, in "Whittier and Whitman: Uncongenial Personalities" (*BFHA,* Autumn 1953), blames Whittier for this. Whittier threw his copy of *Leaves of Grass* into the fire, would not mention Whitman's name, and then publicly denounced him in 1885. Lewis E. Weeks's documentation of the relationship, "Whittier and Whitman" (*ESQ,* First Quarter 1968), finds great similarity between them but also inevitable incompatibility.

Whittier is one of the pioneer regionalists in our literature. The attention to nation, region, land, and folk called for by Emerson was already appearing, though from a different, less self-conscious, less programmatic perspective than Emerson's, in the writings of Whittier. Mamoru Ohmori has written of this in "J. G. Whittier and American National Literature" in his *Essays in English and American Literature* (New York, 1961). The causes that led Whittier to use folk materials in his poems are discussed by George C. Carey, "Whittier's Place in New England Folklore" (*ESQ,* First Quarter 1968) and "Whittier's Roots in a Folk Culture" (*EIHC,* Jan. 1968). Carey shows that Whittier was the product of a folk milieu, born and raised in the context of rural New England story-telling. So where most of the writers of the time were patricians, Whittier was a new phenomenon to our literature, the peasant poet. Henry W. Wells, in "Cambridge Culture and Folk Poetry," in his *The American Way of Poetry* (New York, 1943), sees Whittier as a type—"the New England Quaker," a role Whittier played so well that he gave us a form of folk poetry. In "Whittier's Ballads: The Making of an Artist" (*EIHC,* Jan. 1960), J. B. Pickard discusses Whittier's ballads as the best re-creation of native folklore and legend written in the nineteenth century. A special study of a folktale type is Harry Oster, "Whittier's Use of the *Sage* in His Ballads," in *Studies in American Literature,* edited by Waldo McNeir and Leo B. Levy (Baton Rouge, La., 1960).

The attention to New England folk ways and history resulted in an early if sometimes awkward and sentimental form of regional writing, as has been shown by Albert Mordell in his biography *Quaker Militant* and by Theodore R. Garrison in a dissertation, "John Greenleaf Whittier: Pioneer Regionalist and Folklorist" (Wisconsin, 1960). The use to which Whittier put New England history is given general treatment by Thomas F. Waters, "Whittier, the Poet, as Historian" (*Massachusetts Magazine,* Jan. 1908) and M. Jane Griswold, "American Quaker History in the Works of Whittier, Hawthorne, and Longfellow" (*Americana,* 1940). How willing a contributor to the Puritan legend Whittier was—and in this regard as a forerunner of Hawthorne and Melville—is discussed by Louis C. Schaedler, "Whittier's Attitude toward Colonial Puritanism" (*NEQ,* Sept. 1948). Though Whittier's attitude turned initially from impartiality to hostility, the more he dealt with Puritan materials the more appreciative he became. Cecil B. Williams, in a work devoted entirely to Whittier's regionalism, *Whittier's Use of Historical Material in "Margaret Smith's Journal"* (Chicago, 1936), shows the care with which Whittier used colonial records and New England historians in the construction of his prose legend. The quality of Whittier's imagination is seen in his use of the legend genre to turn historical material into protest literature. This approach inspired much of the local color writing toward the end of the century. The skillful construction of this work is discussed further by Lewis Leary, "A Note on Whittier's Margaret Smith" (*ESQ,* First Quarter 1968).

The best argument against Whittier as being merely a regionalist is Cora Dolbee, "Kansas and 'The Prairied West' of John G. Whittier" (*EIHC,* Oct. 1945). Although intended as a survey of Whittier's contribution to freedom in Kansas, from 1827 to 1891, the discussion demonstrates Whittier's ability to deal with local issues and local color of areas outside New England.

Discussions of individual works by Whittier are for the most part attempts either at checking Whittier's facts and sources or making one aware of Whittier's values. Whittier's poem **"Barbara Frietchie"** and his poems on John Brown (**"Brown of Ossawatomie"**) and Daniel Webster (**"Ichabod"**) are cases in point. As early as 1875, historians began questioning Whittier's use of the Revolutionary War story of Barbara Frietchie; see especially Jubal Early, "**Barbara Frietchie**: The Poet's Base of Facts" (*Boston Daily Advertiser,* 8 May 1875) and "Letter on the Barbara Frietchie Myth" (*Southern Historical Society Papers,* 1879), and Henry M. Nixdorff, *Life of Whittier's Heroine, Barbara Frietchie* (Frederick, Md., 1887). Others, however, have rushed to Whittier's defense with information from Maryland history: Caroline H. Dall, *Barbara Frietchie, a Study* (Boston, 1892); R. M. Cheshire, "More About Barbara Frietchie" (*Book of the Royal Blue,* July 1903); D. M.

and W. R. Quynn, "Barbara Frietchie," *Maryland Historical Magazine,* Sept. 1942; Dec. 1942).

In the case of the John Brown poem, Cecil D. Eby has tried to prove the accuracy of Whittier's information, first in "Whittier's **'Brown of Ossawatomie'**" (*NEQ,* Dec. 1960) and then in **"John Brown's Kiss"** (*Virginia Cavalcade,* May, 1961). In the case of the Webster poem, two brief notes have tried to show the features of Webster's life and personality that Whittier uses in his poem: Margaret H. Gangewer, "Whittier's Poem **'Ichabod'**" (*AN&Q* [*American Notes & Queries*], Mar. 1889) and Motley S. Maddox, "Whittier's **'Ichabod'**" (*Expl,* Apr. 1960).

Even with more explicable poems like **"Skipper Ireson's Ride"** and **"Snow-Bound,"** the critical comments have had more to do with historical and biographical background than with art. There are a number of notes identifying the characters in **"Snow-Bound"** and these show how personal the poem was: Nathaniel L. Sayles, "A Note on Whittier's **'Snow-Bound'**" (*AL,* Nov. 1934); Helen L. Drew, "The Schoolmaster in **'Snow-Bound'**" (*AL,* May 1937); Elizabeth F. Hoxie, "Harriet Livermore: 'Vixen and Devotee'" (*NEQ,* June 1945); W. Gary Groat, "Harriet Livermore: A Whittier Recollection" (*AN&Q,* May 1966). But there are two long discussions of the poem (the only two real explications among all of the comments on Whittier's individual poems) which are excellent: J. B. Pickard, "Imagistic and Structural Unity in **'Snow-Bound'**" (*CE* [*College English*], Mar. 1960), and Elizabeth V. Pickett, "**'Snow-Bound'** and the New Critics" (*ESQ,* First Quarter 1968). These two essays show that the greatest need in Whittier criticism is for full discussions of individual poems.

Most Whittier criticism has had to deal in one way or another with Whittier's faith, which was important personally and culturally. "In Whittier," wrote Whitman, "lives the zeal, the moral energy that founded New England." Whittier's place in American religious literature in the nineteenth century is explored by Augustus H. Strong, *American Poets and Their Theology* (Philadelphia, 1916), and Elmer J. Bailey, *Religious Thought in the Greater American Poets* (Boston, 1922). Whittier's Quaker contribution to our literature is examined by Howard W. Hintz, *The Quaker Influence in American Literature* (New York, 1940). Three essays in Howard H. Brinton's *Byways in Quaker History* (Wallinford, Pa., 1944) are a good introduction to the three major concerns about Whittier's faith. Rufus M. Jones, in "Whittier's Fundamental Religious Faith," agrees that Whittier's faith leaned neither to the orthodox nor to the unitarian side of nineteenth-century American Quakerism, but as the result of the influence of Coleridge and Emerson, it was unique in its strong Platonism, and as such is the finest expression of Quaker beliefs in American life. Henry J. Cadbury, in

"Whittier as Historian of Quakerism," shows how Whittier found in historic Quakerism the full expression of his social philosophy and therefore tried to protect it from misrepresentation or abuse. C. Marshall Taylor, in "Whittier, the Quaker Politician," shows Whittier's faith as the main force behind his interest in social reform.

The broad religious interests of Whittier—Biblical, Quaker, Oriental—are discussed in a dissertation by Charles R. Tegen, "The Religious Poetry of John Greenleaf Whittier" (Central Wesleyan, 1968). Whittier's specific principles are discussed by Luella Wright, "Whittier on the Dignity of Man" (*The Friend,* Dec. 1945) and by Elfriede Fecalek in an unpublished work, "Die Wertwelt John Greenleaf Whittiers" (Vienna, 1946). His general morality is commented on by C. M. Severance, F. M. Larkin, and J. C. Carr in a Whittier symposium in *Pacific Monthly* (Spring 1891).

Whittier was seen, by Friends and others, as an important religious force in his time. Early comments like Henry Blanchard's "The Theology of Whittier" (*The Friend,* May 1866) and G. R. Baker's "John Greenleaf Whittier" (*Friends Quarterly Examiner,* Oct. 1871), show how important he was to Quakers on both sides of the Atlantic as a purveyor of the faith. Estimates like those of Mrs. James T. Fields, "The Inner Life of John Greenleaf Whittier" (*The Chautauquan,* Nov. 1899), and Oliver Wendell Holmes, "Whittier's Religion" (*Unity,* Dec. 1892), show how important he was to writers of the time as a sustainer of Christian thought. Other brief comments emphasizing how much Whittier's Quaker ancestry, environment, and faith meant to him are John W. Chadwick, "Whittier's Spiritual Career" (*New World,* Mar. 1893); William H. Savage, "Whittier's Religion" (*Arena,* July 1894); and Will D. Howe, "Whittier," in *American Writers on American Literature,* edited by John Macy (New York, 1931).

A number of the separate titles on Whittier are merely Quaker tracts, in which the Quaker life is celebrated as much as Whittier's orthodoxy: Julius W. Atwood, *The Spiritual Influence of John Greenleaf Whittier* (Providence, R.I., 1894); Ernest E. Taylor, *John Greenleaf Whittier, the Quaker* (New York, 1954); and Benjamin F. Trueblood, *The Faith of John Greenleaf Whittier* (Amesbury, Mass., 1957). The significance of Whittier's poetry in transmitting Quaker ideas to the common man is emphasized by T. T. Munger, "The Religious Influence of Whittier" (*Christian Union,* 24 September 1892), and by Frederick M. Meek, "Whittier the Religious Man" (*ESQ,* First Quarter 1968).

Yet for all of the faith in Whittier's faith, a battle has raged over whether he was really orthodox. His leanings toward New England Puritanism are discussed by James Mudge in "The Quaker Laureate of Puritanism" (*Methodist Review,* Jan. 1908) and by M. E. Kingsley in

"A Quaker Poet in Puritan New England" (*Poet-Lore,* Oct. 1910). On the other side of the nineteenth-century Quaker spectrum, it is argued that Whittier inclined toward Unitarianism, an accusation Whittier fought all his life. Richard H. Thomas, "Was Whittier Unitarian?" (*Friends' Review,* 17 November 1892), and Edward D. Snyder, "Whittier and the Unitarians" (*BFHA,* Autumn 1960), attempt to show that though he was not Unitarian, Whittier had mild pro-Unitarian feelings that made him a man of interdenominational good will. Lewis H. Chrisman argues, in "The Spiritual Message of Whittier" (in his *John Ruskin, Preacher and Other Essays,* Cincinnati, Ohio, 1921), that Whittier's fundamentalism was a reaction against the popularity of a nebulous Unitarianism.

Other defenses of Whittier's orthodoxy have been made on the basis of the principle of the Inner Light. Chauncey J. Hawkins, in *The Mind of Whittier: A Study of Whittier's Fundamental Religious Ideas* (New York, 1904), shows how Whittier's faith depended on the concept of the immanence of God; hope and humanitarianism were to Whittier man's main courses of action, but both spring from the conviction of immanence in self and others. Edward Wagenknecht, in "Whittier and the Supernatural—a Test Case" (*ESQ,* First Quarter 1968), is also able to defend Whittier's orthodoxy on the basis of his belief in immanence; Whittier survived nineteenth-century religious currents because he took the Inner Light, rather than the Bible, tradition, or superstition, as the supreme authority in his life.

This does not mean, however, that Whittier was a mystic, as some have carelessly labeled him: S. M. Crothers, "Whittier the Mystic" (*Unity,* Dec. 1892); Rufus M. Jones, "Whittier the Mystic" (*American Friend,* Dec. 1907); and Lyman Abbott, "John G. Whittier, Mystic" (*Outlook,* Jan. 1921). The role of nature in Whittier's religious outlook is discussed by Norman Foerster, *Nature in American Literature* (New York, 1923), a role disputed by Percy H. Boynton, *American Poetry* (New York, 1921). As Arthur E. Christy has shown in his discussions of Whittier's Oriental interests in "The Orientalism in Whittier," Whittier was not so much resistant to other religious systems as he was selective of those values from them which coincided with his own.

Still, Whittier has been looked at from a wide variety of sectarian positions, perhaps indicating the universality of his values. For a Roman Catholic view, see John L. Spalding, "John Greenleaf Whittier" (*Catholic World,* Jan. 1877); for a Universalist view, W. T. Stowe, "Whittier" (*University Quarterly,* July 1867); for a Presbyterian view, A. MacLeod, "The Great Poets of America: Whittier" (*Catholic Presbyterian,* July 1882); for a Unitarian view, Edward Everett Hale, "Curtis, Whittier, and Longfellow" (in his *Five Prophets of To-day,*

Boston, 1892); for a Methodist view, Camden M. Cobern, "The Religious Beliefs of John Greenleaf Whittier" (*Methodist Review,* Mar. 1895); for a Congregational view, J. W. Buckham, "Whittier Face to Face" (*Congregational Quarterly,* Sept. 1935); and for a Disciples of Christ view, Henry J. Cadbury, "Whittier's Religion" (*Christian Century,* 5 February 1958).

There are two studies of Whittier and the Bible: S. Trevena Jackson, "Whittier's Use of the Bible" (*Christian Advocate,* Dec. 1907) and James S. Stevens, *Whittier's Use of the Bible* (Orono, Maine, 1930), both showing Whittier to be a literalist. This literal use resulted in a large body of religious verse, as Edward D. Snyder had pointed out in "Whittier's Religious Poetry" (*Friends Quarterly Examiner,* Apr. 1934). Whittier as a writer of religious verse for hymns has been discussed by William C. Gannett, "Whittier in Our Hymn Books" (*Unity,* Dec. 1892), and by C. Marshall Taylor, "Whittier Set to Music" (*EIHC,* Jan. 1952).

Unfortunately, most of the commentary on Whittier's faith deals with the phenomenon of Quaker theology and says little about Whittier himself in this regard. Two studies that are enlightening on the religious Whittier are by Philip C. Moon and Perry Miller. Moon, in "Observations on the Religious Philosophy and Method of Whittier in *Voices of Freedom*" (*EIHC,* Oct. 1957), demonstrates that it was the influence of Garrison, not Quakerism, that gave Whittier his messianic humanitarianism, his conscientious devotion, and his religious-reformist zeal. But Miller, in "John Greenleaf Whittier: The Conscience in Poetry" (*Harvard Review,* Spring 1964), identifies Whittier's Quaker role as a method of self-defense, a convenience, a life-long act; beneath his quietism was a ferocity that characterized the real Whittier.

The regard for Whittier as abolitionist could not have been higher in his lifetime. As Samuel J. May put it, in *Some Recollections of Our Anti-Slavery Conflict* (Boston, 1869), "Of all our American poets, John G. Whittier has from first to last done most for the abolition of slavery. All my anti-slavery bretheren, I doubt not, will unite with me to crown him our laureate." The anti-slavery movement and Whittier's place in it are discussed effectively in Gilbert H. Barnes, *The Anti-Slavery Impulse* (New York, 1933), and in *The Anti-Slavery Vanguard,* edited by Martin Duberman (Princeton, N.J. 1965). Whittier's part in the reconciliation of North and South after the war is discussed in Paul H. Beck, *The Road to Reunion* (Boston, 1937).

Many other contemporaries celebrated Whittier as a poetic prophet of the movement—David V. Barlett, *Modern Agitators* (New York, 1855); William Lloyd Garrison II, *John Greenleaf Whittier* (Brooklyn, N.Y., 1892); T. W. Higginson, "Whittier as a Combatant"

(*Book News Monthly,* Dec. 1907); Frank B. Sanborn, "Whittier as Man, Poet, and Reformer" (*Biblia Sacra,* Apr. 1908). Seldom did anyone take issue, as William Dean Howells did in his *Literary Friends and Acquaintance* (New York, 1900), with those who considered him a great reformer. The most extensive treatment of Whittier's antislavery ideas and activities is an unpublished work, Siegfried Krugmann's "John Greenleaf Whittiers Kampf gegen die Sklaverei" (Erlangen, 1953).

However, Whittier's abolition poetry, roughly one-third of the canon, has seldom been discussed critically. Most comments are like John V. Cheney's "Whittier" (*Chautauquan,* Dec. 1892), arguing that Whittier is the ideal poet for democracy and that his antislavery poems are central to that position, or like Alfred Kreymborg's "A Rustic Quaker Goes to War" in his *Our Singing Strength* (New York, 1928), arguing that Whittier's poetry is autobiographical and that his best poetry resulted from his abolition work. The only discussion of artistic qualities of the poetry is in J. B. Pickard's "Whittier's Abolitionist Poetry" (*ESQ,* First Quarter 1968). "At best," Pickard concludes, "their earnest simplicity and religious intensity redeemed their topical nature, simplified their digressive tendency, and toughened their derivative phrasing."

The wide range of Whittier's social conscience has been celebrated best by V. L. Parrington, *Main Currents in American Thought* (New York, 1927), but many others have cited his historical significance for liberalism. J. Wilfred Holmes shows this wide range in his collection, *Whittier's Prose on Reforms Other than Abolition* (Pittsburgh, Pa., 1945). Whittier's work against capital punishment is discussed in David Brion Davis, "The Movement to Abolish Capital Punishment in America, 1787-1861" (*AHR,* Oct. 1957). His concern for laborers and labor conditions is discussed in Thomas F. Currier, "Whittier and the Amesbury-Salisbury Strike" (*NEQ,* Mar. 1935), and John A. Pollard, "Whittier on Labor Unions" (*NEQ,* Mar. 1939). That Whittier belongs to the tradition of Hawthorne and Melville in reacting against the advance of technology is argued by Richard Olson, "Whittier and the Machine Age" (*ESQ,* First Quarter 1968); in the conflict, Whittier preferred the garden, that is, the idyllic and humane, to the machine.

Whittier's relationships with other reformers, political or abolitionist, reveal the uniqueness and limitations of his thinking. His political idealism resulted in an intimate friendship like that with Charles Sumner, as J. Wilfred Holmes claims in "Whittier and Sumner: A Political Friendship" (*NEQ,* Mar. 1957), though a number of differences were dictated by Whittier's Quakerism. The same is true of his relation with Thomas Clarkson, as C. Marshall Taylor notes (*BFHA,* Autumn 1954). The relation with William Lloyd Garrison was more of a test, however. Philip C. Moon, in

"Observations on the Religious Philosophy and Method of Whittier in *Voices of Freedom,*" argues that Garrison was the main creative influence in Whittier's life, and Cecil B. Williams, in "Whittier's Relation to Garrison and the *Liberator*" (*NEQ,* June 1952), shows how Garrison helped Whittier's career as poet and journalist. T. W. Higginson's was perhaps the earliest serious comparison of the two, "Garrison and Whittier" (*Independent,* Dec. 1905); to him the men complemented each other. C. Marshall Taylor's comparison, "Whittier vs. Garrison" (*EIHC,* July 1946), though heavily biased in favor of Whittier's pacifism, patience, idealism, and faith, identifies the cause of their differences in Whittier's heavy sense of sin. Other discussions of Whittier as an editor of abolitionist periodicals are Bertha-Monica Stearns, "John Greenleaf Whittier, Editor" (*NEQ,* June 1940), and Thomas F. Currier, "Whittier and the *New England Weekly Review*" (*NEQ,* Sept. 1933).

The Negro view of Whittier as an abolitionist is shown by Beatrice J. Fleming, "John G. Whittier, Abolition Poet" (*Negro History Bulletin,* Dec. 1942). J. Wilfred Holmes, in "Whittier's Friends among the Lowly" (*ESQ,* First Quarter 1968), discusses Whittier's association with and attitude toward Negroes. Even though he finds Whittier's poems to have been evoked more by specific events than by humanitarian values, Osborn T. Smallwood, in "The Historical Significance of Whittier's Anti-Slavery Poems as Reflected in Their Political and Social Background" (*Journal of Negro History,* Apr. 1950), recognizes that Whittier's poems are an important part of the protest literature that molded public opinion and finally elected Lincoln.

Whittier's abolitionist influence extended to the Midwest, where through his correspondence he worked to keep new states free; these were among his most successful political moves. Whittier's influence on affairs in Iowa and Nebraska is discussed by Charles A. Hawley in *IJHP* (Apr. 1936) and in *BFHA* (Autumn 1939; Spring 1941). Whittier's concern over freedom abroad is discussed by Livio Jannattoni, "Whittier e la Beecher Stowe d'accordo su Garibaldi" (*La Fiera Letteraria,* Oct. 1951), and by Francis B. Dedmond, "A Note on Whittier and Italian Freedom" (*BFHA,* Autumn 1951).

In conclusion it must be said that, in depth, the Whittier criticism leaves much to be desired. Though Whittier does not fit easily into any mode of criticism, he has been dealt with honestly (and it is a temptation to say excessively) if not fully. In the criticism, we have much of Whittier's life, mind, soul, and times, but not yet all of the life and liveliness that may be hidden in the poetry itself.

Key to Abbreviations

AH: American Heritage

AHR: American Historical Review

AL: American Literature

ALR: American Literary Realism

AM: American Mercury

AN&Q: American Notes & Queries

AQ: American Quarterly

Archiv: Archiv für das Studium der Neueren Sprachen und Literaturen

ArQ: Arizona Quarterly

AS: American Speech

ASch: American Scholar

AtM: Atlantic Monthly, Atlantic

AWS: American Writers Series

BAL: Bibliography of American Literature

BB: Bulletin of Bibliography

BFHA: Bulletin of the Friends Historical Association

BJRL: Bulletin of the John Rylands Library

BNYPL: Bulletin of the New York Public Library

Bookman: Bookman (U.S.)

BuR: Bucknell Review

BUSE: Boston University Studies in English

Caliban: Caliban (Toulouse)

Carrell: Journal of the Friends of the U. of Miami (Fla.) Library

CE: College English

Century: Century Illustrated Monthly Magazine

CH: Church History

CHAL: Cambridge History of American Literature

CLAJ: College Language Association Journal

CMHS: Collections of the Massachusetts Historical Society

Col: Colophon

DA: Dissertation Abstracts

DAB: Dictionary of American Biography

Daedalus: Daedalus (Proceedings of the American Academy of Arts and Sciences)

DN: Delaware Notes

DVLG: Deutsche Viertel jahrsschrift für Literatur Wissenschaft und Giestesgeschichte

EA: Études Anglaises

EAL: Early American Literature

EALN: Early American Literature Newsletter

EIHC: Essex Institute Historical Collections

EJ: English Journal

ELH: Journal of English Literary History

ELN: English Language Notes

ESQ: Emerson Society Quarterly

Expl: Explicator

ForumNY: Forum (New York)

FR: French Review

The Friend: The Friend: A Quaker Weekly Journal

HLB: Harvard Library Bulletin

HLQ: Huntington Library Quarterly

HM: Harper's Magazine, Harper's New Monthly Magazine, Harper's Monthly Magazine, Harper's

HTR: Harvard Theological Review

IJHP: Iowa Journal of History and Politics

JA: Jahrbuch für Amerikastudien

JAmS: Journal of American Studies

JEGP: Journal of English and Germanic Philology

JFI: Journal of the Franklin Institute

JHI: Journal of the History of Ideas

JRUL: Journal of the Rutgers University Library

KR: Kenyon Review

LHJ: Ladies' Home Journal

LHUS: Literary History of the United States

MagA: Magazine of Art

MF: Midwest Folklore

MFS: Modern Fiction Studies

MissQ: Mississippi Quarterly

MLA: Modern Language Association

MLN: Modern Language Notes

MLQ: Modern Language Quarterly

MLR: Modern Language Review

Monatshefte: Monatshefte für Deutschen Unterricht, Deutsche Sprache und Literatur (Wisconsin)

MP: *Modern Philology*

N&Q: *Notes and Queries*

NAR: *North American Review*

NCF: *Nineteenth-Century Fiction*

NDQ: *North Dakota Quarterly*

NEHGR: *New England Historical and Genealogical Register*

NEM: *New England Magazine*

NEQ: *New England Quarterly*

NR: *New Republic*

NYH: *New York History*

NYHTBR: *New York Herald Tribune Book Review*

NY Review of Books: *New York Review of Books*

NYTBR: *New York Times Book Review*

Outlook: *Outlook* (U.S.)

PAAS: *Proceedings American Antiquarian Society*

PAPS: *Proceedings American Philosophical Society*

PBSA: *Papers of the Bibliographical Society of America*

PHR: *Pacific Historical Review*

PMASAL: *Papers of the Michigan Academy of Science, Arts, and Letters*

PMHB: *Pennsylvania Magazine of History and Biography*

PMHS: *Proceedings of the Massachusetts Historical Society*

PMLA: *Publications of the Modern Language Association of America*

PNJHS: *Proceedings of the New Jersey Historical Society*

PQ: *Philological Quarterly*

QH: *Quaker History: Bulletin of the Friends' Historical Association*

RR: *Romanic Review*

SAQ: *South Atlantic Quarterly*

SatR: *Saturday Review*

SB: *Studies in Bibliography: Papers of the Bibliographical Society of the University of Virginia*

SCraneN: *Stephen Crane Newsletter*

SELit: *Studies in English Literature* (Eng. Literary Soc. of Japan, U. of Tokyo)

SN: *Studia Neophilologica*

SoR: *Southern Review*

SP: *Studies in Philology*

SR: *Sewanee Review*

SSF: *Studies in Short Fiction*

Sym: *Symposium: A Quarterly Journal in Modern Foreign Literature*

TLS: *Times Literary Supplement* (London)

TSE: *Tulane Studies in English*

TSL: *Tennessee Studies in Literature*

TSLL: *Texas Studies in Literature and Language*

TUSAS: Twayne's United States Authors Series

UKCR: *University of Kansas City Review*

UMPAW: University of Minnesota Pamphlets on American Writers

VQR: *Virginia Quarterly Review*

WHR: *Western Humanities Review*

WMQ: *William and Mary Quarterly*

YR: *Yale Review*

YULG: *Yale University Library Gazette*

Leonard M. Trawick (essay date spring 1974)

SOURCE: Trawick, Leonard M. "Whittier's *Snow-Bound*: A Poem about the Imagination." *Essays in Literature* 1, no. 1 (spring 1974): 46-53.

[*In the following essay, Trawick discusses Whittier's most successful poem, contending that* Snow-Bound *is a traditional Romantic poem since it celebrates the power of the imagination to transcend the limits of the physical universe.*]

The preoccupation with the nature and powers of the imagination that characterizes much British Romantic poetry entered into the assumptions of nineteeth-century American writers so pervasively that its effects sometimes go unrecognized where they are most profound. The Romantic orientation is often clear enough, for instance, in Poe, Emerson, and Whitman. It is not so obvious in John Greenleaf Whittier's **Snow-Bound,** which is still most often praised as a charmingly nostalgic record of New England farm life. Yet, as Robert Penn Warren recently observed, the powerful effect of **Snow-Bound** "does not depend so much on the thing looked at as on the way of the looking."[1] Warren goes on to argue that Whittier's attempt to come to terms with the past resembles similar efforts made by Cooper, Hawthorne, Melville, and Faulkner. In this essay I would like to pursue Warren's suggestion in a different direction, and relate Whittier to a broader tradition: *Snow-Bound* continues to occupy its unassailable, if modest, niche among the famous poems in English precisely because of its complex yet coherent development of a Romantic epistemology.

At the end of *Snow-Bound* "the worldling,"

> Dreaming in throngful city ways
> Of winter joys his boyhood knew

(ll. 743-44),[2]

is very much like the Wordsworth in "Tintern Abbey" who "oft, in lonely rooms, and 'mid the din / Of towns and cities," recalls the "beauteous forms" along the River Wye (ll. 22-28). Wordsworth, reflecting the eighteenth-century associationists' theories of the imagination, discovers a significant relation between his inner self and external physical phenomena, "the heavy and the weary weight / Of all this unintelligible world" (ll. 39-40); and the same process of imagination which lightens this "burthen of the mystery" also allows him to rise above the changes which time inevitably works. Wordsworth consistently stresses the active power of the mind to infuse life and meaning into—indeed, to "half create"—the natural world around him. The "spots of time" in Book XII of *The Prelude,* for example, are valuable to Wordsworth because they give

> Profoundest knowledge to what point, and how,
> The mind is lord and master—outward sense
> The obedient servant of her will.

(ll. 221-23)

In *Snow-Bound* Whittier, in a similar manner, confronts a dead external world, "mindless," "blind," and "unmeaning," and pits against it the creations of the human imagination, symbolized through most of the poem by fire. The exuberant imagination of the farm boy turns the dead, snowy "world unknown" into a "wonder," full of "marvellous shapes" of Chinese roofs, leaning towers, and Aladdin's caves (ll. 54-65). At the same time that he celebrates this youthful joy and laments its loss, Whittier also finds some consolation in the continuation of the same faculty that once cast the aura of wonder over the world; the "woodfire's blaze" of his homely imagination still brings him a bit of warmth in the midst of the cold "throngful city." In "Tintern Abbey," the "Immortality Ode," and other poems, Wordsworth traces a similar loss of youthful zest, and regrets the passing of "the glory and the dream," which made "The earth, and every common sight" seem "Apparelled in celestial light"; and, like Whittier, he finds "Strength in what remains behind" and solace in the thought that though time brings change, the memories of the joys of youth as well as those of the present provide "life and food / For future years."[3] For both Wordsworth and Whittier,

the imagination, feeding on the stores of memory, can bridge the gulf that time interposes between oneself and one's childhood and loved ones.

Although Whittier's response to the depredations of time is simpler than Wordsworth's, there are close similarities between the problems which the two poets face, and between the resolutions which they find. Whittier undoubtedly absorbed some of his ideas directly from Wordsworth, but I have not been drawing the parallel between the two poets merely to prove that Wordsworth is a "source": similar attitudes may be found in Coleridge, Shelley, and Keats. My main point is that *Snow-Bound* can be most fully appreciated when read not just as a bit of American local color, but as a poem reflecting in a profound way the Romantic preoccupation with perception and imagination. *Snow-Bound* does more than simply "memorialize a way of life" or even "memorialize life that is always lost to death," as one of the poem's principal interpreters has concluded.[4] More that this, it is a poem about the way the mind comes to grips with privations that are uniquely human because they are implicit in the human quality of consciousness.

Snow-Bound is complicated by Whittier's own ambivalent attitude toward imagination. His particular upbringing and the American society that he knew led him to suspect art as an immoral escape from the duties of real life.[5] Of Longfellow's "Psalm of Life" he could assert, "These nine simple verses are worth more than all the dreams of Shelley, and Keats, and Wordsworth. They are alive and vigorous with the spirit of the day in which we live—the moral steam enginery of an age of action."[6] This rejection of Romantic "dreams" actually links him further with the British Romantic poets, whose apotheosis of imagination is often balanced with distrust. Wordsworth's "Elegiac Stanzas" on Peele Castle, for example, bid farewell to "the heart that lives alone / Housed in a dream, at distance from the Kind!" (ll. 53-54); and Keats's *The Fall of Hyperion* contrasts weak "dreaming" poets with humanitarians who "Labor for mortal good" (l. 159). At times, of course, Whittier spoke highly of the Romantic poets.[7] In *Snow-Bound* Whittier's ambivalence culminates at the conclusion, which I will discuss later. But from its opening description of the dull cold before the storm, the poem develops a consistent structure of imagery which carries out the theme of living mental power opposed to a dead external world of space and time.

Readers have always recognized the opposition in *Snow-Bound* between the cold, lifeless snow and the glowing hearth, heart of the family circle and symbol of human love. Lewis Leary identifies the whiteness of the snow in the poem with "the whiteness of Melville's whale or the encompassing whiteness which engulfs the climax of Poe's *Narrative of Arthur Gordon Pym.*"[8] Indeed,

Whittier seems to be carefully emphasizing the feeling that the snow is not so much inimical as indifferent-a feeling important in *Moby-Dick,* and familiar in many writings of Americans who face a nature unmarked with comforting hedgerows or melancholy ruins. On that day of "dull bitterness of cold" with which ***Snow-Bound*** begins, the ocean throbbing "with low rhythm" sounds like the sea described by the Autocrat of the Breakfast Table, which "drowns out humanity and time," and "has no sympathy with either; for it belongs to eternity, and of that it sings its monotonous song forever and ever."⁹ Human "life-blood" is "checked"; the solitude is "made more intense" by

> The shrieking of the mindless wind,
> The moaning tree-boughs swaying blind,
> And on the glass the unmeaning beat
> Of ghostly [i.e., dead] finger-tips of sleet.

(ll. 102-05)

Even the brook, to which fancy had given "an almost human tone," is silenced.

The snowstorm not only represents the loss by human beings of a feeling of kinship with nature; it also represents the separation of man from man. Literally the snow cuts off the farm family from the rest of the world—a deprivation which Whittier strongly feels. The church-bell, proclaimer of a human community of spirit, is silenced, and

> No welcome sound of toil or mirth
> Unbound the spell, and testified
> Of human life and thought outside.

(ll. 107-09)

Whittier highly values all means of overcoming "the chill embargo of the snow" (l. 711) on social commerce: the village newspaper, the "quick wires of intelligence" which will eventually unite the country, even "the snowball's compliments" which are actually "missives" to the girls instead of missiles (ll. 654-55).

The snow represents a third kind of alienation, the separation of loved ones by time. Whittier thinks of his youngest sister's recent death:

> The chill weight of the winter snow
> For months upon her grave has lain.

(ll. 405-06)

In its contrast of the cold, lifeless out-of-doors with the warm glow of the hearth, ***Snow-Bound*** evokes two of the most familiar metaphors for death—night and winter.¹⁰ The basic contrast is not between black and white, but between the "colorless all-color" of these two and the bright hues of summer. A whiteness reminiscent of the snow is sometimes associated with the metaphor of night or the dark shadows of the cypress: the dead sister welcomes the poet with a hand "white against the evening star" (l. 436), and the flowers beneath the "mournful cypresses" are "white amaranths" (l. 728). More earthly flowers and greenery are the images of life: contrasted with the sister's snow-covered grave are the violets and brier-roses that the poet can still see, and the hills that "stretch green, to June's unclouded sky" (l. 417). Heavenly immortality is "the unfading green" of Paradise. The "green hills of life" (l. 725) at the end of the poem slope toward a death which is not defined, but which is obviously neither green nor flowery.

For all three kinds of alienation which he treats—the loss of a sense of kinship with nature, and the separation from other human beings by space and by time—Whittier finds a remedy in the activities of the imagination, which he symbolizes in the central image of the fire. The two epigraphs make clear enough Whittier's poetic intentions. The first, from Cornelius Agrippa, opposes fire to darkness: "as the Celestial Fire [the sun] drives away dark spirits, so also this our Fire of VVood doth the same." The second, from Emerson's "The Snow-Storm," opposes it to snow:

> . . . the housemates sit
> Around the radiant fireplace, enclosed
> In a tumultuous privacy of storm.

Fire of course does suggest the warm family love which critics usually see in ***Snow-Bound***; but the image—especially at the time when Whittier was writing—carries additional connotations of dreams, revery, and fancy. Cowper in Book IV of *The Task* watches the fire and lets his fancy present

> a waking dream of houses, tow'rs,
> Trees, churches, and strange visages, express'd
> In the red cinders, while with pouring eye
> I gaz'd, myself creating what I saw.

(ll. 287-90)

Coleridge, staring at the "stranger" in "Frost at Midnight," similarly experiences a poetic visitation. And in the nineteenth century the image of the open fire would arouse even more complex associations than it would to the modern reader. Light, of course, traditionally suggests not only life but consciousness, knowledge, imagination, poetry—the attributes of Phoebus Apollo. But firelight is not the spontaneous warmth and brightness of the sun, which God sheds on all without their asking; the wood must be sawed, "piled, with care" and laid "with curious art" (ll. 120-25). The wood fire, suggesting the mental warmth and light that comes from individual human effort, is indeed a good emblem of the New England mind, with its strenuous acceptance of personal responsibility. In Whittier himself the Quaker inner light is hardly more obvious than the Puritan gloom against which it glows.¹¹

The replacement in the nineteenth century of the open fireplace by the more economical closed stove inspired a whole literature in praise of the open fire, the most common defense being its ability to stimulate the fancy. Such a piece is Hawthorne's little essay "Fire Worship," in which, as Roy R. Male, Jr., has pointed out, the "fire . . . would seem to symbolize the imaginative creative spirit."[12] In "The Courtin'," Lowell reminds the reader that "There warn't no stoves (tell comfort died)," and goes on to describe the romantic light which the flames throw over the room (ll. 9.16). Popular books and magazines abounded in "Fireside Essays" and "Fireside Reminiscences," and one of the most popular American books of the mid-century, *Reveries of a Bachelor* by Ik Marvel (Donald G. Mitchell), begins with a series of fantasies evoked by a country wood fire, and then proceeds with city reveries which bituminous and anthracite fires inspire.

The image which Whittier constantly sets against the snow and darkness would thus immediately suggest to the first readers of the poem not only coziness and love but imagination. From the beginning of the poem, life, warmth, and comfort are projected from the human mind onto the cold, dead externals, rather than residing in nature and being absorbed by man. As I have already suggested, it is nothing in the snow itself, but the exuberant fancy of the boys, stimulated by novelty, which casts a spell over the blank world outside; their own perceptions figuratively "cut the solid whiteness through" (l. 73), making from it something "marvellous," "wondrous." They wish for Aladdin's lamp, not realizing that the "supernal powers" of their own minds achieve just as great a magic. Even the farm animals, seen in a moment of heightened imagination, take on an exotic air: the cock has a "speckled harem" and the "horned patriarch of the sheep" suggests "Egypt's Amun" (ll. 83-92). Descriptions that in another context might seem affectedly cute here become articulate means of conveying the boys' mental excitement.

With the approach of the third night and the building of the fire, Whittier moves into the heart of his poem. The fire blazes a warm red, and sends over the colorless, whitewashed room a "gleam," a word that after *Intimations of Immortality* could probably not be used without suggesting Wordsworth's "visionary gleam." Contrasting with the fire is the "dead white" of the moonlit snow, against which the hemlocks seem "pitchy black," having lost even the "sombre green" which they showed in the daytime (ll. 143-50). To complete this introduction of his main opposing images, Whittier relates them in the striking symbol of the "witches' tea" (ll. 132-42), the reflection in the window panes which makes the fire on the hearth seem to be burning outside in the dark.[13] This illusion throws all that follows it into a new and equivocal light. Of all the loved ones around the hearth, the descriptions of whom form the core of the poem,

only the poet and his brother are left alive. The past happiness is as dead and cold as the snow and shadows outside the window pane:

> Look where we may, the wide earth o'er
> Those lighted faces smile no more.

(ll. 189-90)

The happy memories are projected by the mind upon a past which is actually dead, just as the reflected fire is projected upon the cold, dark snow. Whittier seems to waver between an indulgence in the pleasant memories, and a realization that the memories are, after all, only an "unwarming light."

The illusion which forms the framework of the poem—that is, the poet's imaginatively recreated memory of his childhood hearth—contains within it the same illusion, recessed in the past. As in Coleridge's "Frost at Midnight," the fire inspires a series of memories within memories. For the tales told around the hearth are themselves recollections of even earlier years; the children recapture by imagination the childhood of the older generation, which Whittier again connects with summer images of warmth and color. The father recalls the "green prairies of the sea," and we glimpse a vista of memories extending over the generations, as he describes another group assembled around "driftwood coals," and makes his own children hear again "tales of witchcraft old" (ll. 241-48). The mother's memories again make the children vividly relive the past, and the uncle, too, the coals of his imagination "warming with the tales he told," forgets "the outside cold" (ll. 337-38) and relives in momentary illusion the bright days of the past. The happiness of the aunt is also an illusion which she projects upon "all the poor details / And homespun warp of circumstance" (ll. 363-64), like the flames reflected in the window pane.

Whittier himself is consoled by pleasing "fancies" as he thinks of his dead sisters in the next two sections, which parallel in the present the earlier reminiscences of his elder relatives. The older sister's "low . . . tent" is at least "green" (l. 390) and the younger lives in a Paradise of "unfading green" (ll. 398-99). But Whittier's conceptions of life beyond death, unlike those other fancies of his father, mother, uncle, and aunt, are projected into the future, or at least into another world, and do not suffer from the direct contradiction of experience. Reinforced by religious faith, this exercise of imagination is more satisfying than the "unwarming light" of old memories would be by themselves:

> And yet, dear heart! remembering thee,
>   Am I not richer than of old?
> Safe in thy immortality,
>   What change can reach the wealth I hold?

(ll. 422-25)

From this serious center of the poem, Whittier returns to a somewhat lighter pursuit of his re-creations of the past. The descriptions of the two visitors in the household carry out the basic metaphor of the poem. The schoolmaster uses the light of his mind to "Scatter . . . darkness" (ll. 491-92) and establish communication between all parts of the country until it "shall own the same electric thought" (l. 505). Harriet Livermore's unnatural energies are described in metaphors of unwholesome heat or dangerous light, especially lightning, and these images are linked with words suggesting a disordered imagination.

As the great fire sinks to coals on the hearth, the boys go to sleep, and once more escape the cold and snow in dreams—dreams of summer and green leaves. Now the high point of the poem is past, and with the coming of the teams and other members of the community, the family is no longer "bound" by the snow. Yet imagination continues to help overcome the separation of men. The "curious eyes of merry girls" read in the snowballs the "charm with Eden never lost" (ll. 652-56); and a more literary "reading" of the scant supply of books and the village newspaper is the means of establishing broader connections. The children participate in the events of the paper just as completely as they did in the uncle's reminiscences: "We saw marvels that it told";

> We felt the stir of hall and street,
> The pulse of life that round us beat.
>
> (ll. 709-10)

The newspaper carries them to "warmer zones," and, like the fireplace, creates a "genial glow" of sympathetic imagination which melts the "ice-locked door" to the world.

The concluding section of *Snow-Bound* is a sort of envoy in which the poet draws back for a more detached appraisal of his poem. Here the symbolism that has been operating throughout the poem becomes more explicit. The "characters" or letters in the palimpsest of memory "pale and glow" just like the human "characters" who have glowed and faded in the poet's own imagination:

> The dear home faces whereupon
> That fitful firelight paled and shone.[14]

But Whittier now rejects these memories as mere dreaming. The voice of duty calls him to the real world where "the century's aloe" (l. 739)—the bitterness that culminated in the Civil War—is more intense than ever; and he tells the "Angel of the backward look" (l. 715) to shut the book of memory. The past is "spectral," the glow of memory a false, unwarming light like that reflected in the window pane at the witches' tea. Even the wings of the Angel are not flames of imagination but burnt-out coals, "ashen grey."

In the final twenty lines Whittier changes his mind again and says he might indulge his dreams if there is ever a "lull of life" when practical philanthropy can enjoy a respite in its struggles. Then the rekindled imagination will once more bring the rustic past to life, and the poet and his friends will

> stretch the hands of memory forth
> To warm them at the wood-fire's blaze!
>
> (ll. 749-50)

Whittier speaks of his reminiscences first as of interest only to himself and old friends. But he is also a public poet, and he recognizes that his memories will refresh readers unknown to him. Just as in the body of the poem the primary image of the winter fire modulates, in the adults' stories and the boys' dreams, into the warmth and greenery of summer, so in these last lines the image of the "wood-fire's blaze" shifts, with Whittier's description of his unknown reader, into summer odors of water lilies and a new-mown meadow. We are left with the impression that the flame of the imagination may not be altogether artificial, but may be related, after all, to God's own warmth and light, and hence be able to convey a valid "benediction."

All that Whittier claims for his poem is the merit of "Flemish pictures": small, photographically detailed descriptions of homely subjects. But more important than this immediate subject matter is the preoccupation, gradually emerging through the whole poem, with the act itself of transcending the limitations of time and space through imagination. It is this concern that makes *Snow-Bound* more than just good descriptive verse, and that also marks it as a poem firmly in the Romantic tradition.

Notes

1. "Whittier," *Sewanee Review,* 79 (1971), 122. A slightly different version of this essay is printed in Warren's book, *John Greenleaf Whittier's Poetry: An Appraisal and a Selection* (Minneapolis: Univ. of Minnesota Press, 1971).

2. The text of *Snow-Bound* used is from *The Works of John Greenleaf Whittier* (Boston: Houghton, 1892), II, 134-59.

3. Lewis Leary suggests the similarity of Whittier's and Wordsworth's celebration of the "clouds of glory" which surround the child who "is father to the man," in *John Greenleaf Whittier* (New York: Twayne, 1961), p. 149.

4. George Arms, *The Fields Were Green* (Stanford: Stanford Univ. Press, 1953), p. 47.

5. For a recent commentary on the clash of pragmatic and aesthetic impulses in Whittier see the chapter entitled "Beauty as Grace and Snare" in Edward

Wagenknecht's *John Greenleaf Whittier: A Portrait in Paradox* (New York: Oxford Univ. Press, 1967), pp. 91-156. Perry Miller also discusses these inner conflicts in "John Greenleaf Whittier: The Conscience in Poetry," *Harvard Review,* 2, No. 2 (1964), 8-24, rpt. in *Memorabilia of John Greenleaf Whittier,* ed. John B. Pickard (Hartford, Conn.: Emerson Society, 1968), pp. 128-42.

6. Quoted by John B. Pickard, *John Greenleaf Whittier* (New York: Barnes & Noble, 1961), p. 48.

7. In his preface to *Songs of Three Centuries,* for example, Whittier wrote, "There can be little doubt that the critical essayist of the twentieth century will make a large advance upon the present estimate, not only of Cowper and Burns, but of Wordsworth, Coleridge, Shelley, Keats, Browning, Tennyson, and Emerson." In the same essay he approvingly quotes Shelley's *Defence of Poetry* and says that Wordsworth has touched for his age "the key note of the thoughtful harmonies of natural and intellectual beauty." *Whittier on Writers and Writing,* ed. Edwin Harrison Cady and Harry Hayden Clark (Syracuse, N. Y.: Syracuse Univ. Press, 1950), pp. 202-03, 205.

8. Leary, p. 160.

9. Oliver Wendell Holmes, *Complete Works* (Boston: Houghton, 1891), I, 264.

10. Elizabeth A. C. Akers uses snow and darkness with similar associations in a poem, "Snow," which appeared about two years before Whittier wrote *Snow-Bound* and which may have influenced him (*Atlantic Monthly,* 13 [February 1864], 200). She describes the snow falling much as Whittier does:

> And all the air is dizzy and dim
> 　　With a whirl of dancing, dazzling snow.

But soon it becomes a symbol of death:

> Night and darkness are over all:
> Rest, pale city, beneath their pall!
> 　　Sleep, white world, in thy winding sheet!

In her last stanza she opposes, like Whittier, the power of the imagination to the snow outside: she finds warmth and life in a picture of Rome which is on her wall.

11. John B. Pickard's article, "Imagistic and Structural Unity in *Snow-Bound,*" *College English,* 21 (1960), 338-43, outlines the fire and snow imagery in the poem, but does not develop the psychological implications which are the concern of the present essay. For further treatment of light and fire as symbols for imagination, see M. H. Abrams, *The Mirror and the Lamp* (New York: Oxford Univ. Press, 1953), especially Chap. III, "Romantic Analogues of Art and Mind," pp. 47-69.

12. Male, "Criticism of Bell's 'Hawthorne's "Fire Worship": Interpretation and Source,'" *American Literature,* 25 (1953), 86-87. A related use of the stove image occurs in a September 1802 entry in Coleridge's notebooks: "Socinianism moonlight—Methodism a Stove! O for some Sun to unite heat & Light!" (*The Notebooks of Samuel Taylor Coleridge,* I [Text], ed. Kathleen Coburn [London: Routledge, 1957], entry 1233). For the New Englander the open fire replaces sunlight.

13. It is interesting that Coleridge notices the same phenomenon in *Notebooks,* I (Text), entry 1737.

14. These lines (185-86) occur about a third of the way through the poem. It is perhaps worth noticing that up to that point the fire has been described in positive terms: it has a "ruddy glow" that makes the old white-washed room "burst, flower-like, into rosy bloom"; and the "great throat of the chimney" laughs merrily. Only when the poet begins to think of "Time and Change," and his own imaginative resurrection of the past falters, does the remembered firelight become "fitful."

Shirley Marchalonis (essay date 1988)

SOURCE: Marchalonis, Shirley. "A Model for Mentors?: Lucy Larcom and John Greenleaf Whittier." In *Patrons and Protégées: Gender, Friendship, and Writing in Nineteenth-Century America,* edited by Shirley Marchalonis, pp. 94-121. New Brunswick, N.J.: Rutgers University Press, 1988.

[*In the following essay, Marchalonis examines the relationship between Whittier and his literary protegé, Lucy Larcom.*]

Biographers of John Greenleaf Whittier have dealt competently with his abolitionism, his Quaker background, and his poetry. They have been less comfortable in portraying his relationships with his "protégées"—the women writers in whom he took a real and active interest. A variety of biographical approaches seem to avoid the questions that these relationships raise.[1]

Although treatments of the protégées vary according to each biographer's thesis or perspective, they reduce all the women to the status of objects existing only in relation to Whittier. Alice and Phoebe Cary, Lucy Larcom, Gail Hamilton, Elizabeth Stuart Phelps, Celia Thaxter, Sarah Orne Jewett, and others are usually treated as a lump of women writers whose careers Whittier somehow encouraged.

Naturally a biographer concentrates on his subject; however, by presenting the protégées as if they were paper cutouts, the scholar finally projects an incomplete, if not false, picture. These women, all very popular and widely read in their day, were a part of the literary world of the latter half of nineteenth-century America; without consideration of them and their work, the account is not complete.

Furthermore, failure to examine these relationships closely leaves unanswered a great many questions about Whittier himself. In crudest terms, what did he get out of his role as mentor to talented, aspiring young women? What led to his interest in them and their needs? Was his reward a sense of power and the enjoyment of the admiration, sometimes verging on adoration, that he received? Was it a trade-off for the sexual life he apparently denied himself? Was his behavior an extension of the Quaker beliefs that led him almost to sacrifice his poetic career in the abolitionist cause? Were these relationships love affairs, or was he simply the too-kind-hearted victim of women's importunities? On the other side of the picture, what did it mean to be a Whittier protégée? What effect did he have on the career of any one writer?

Whittier and the very popular poet Lucy Larcom had a personal and professional friendship that lasted nearly fifty years.[2] Larcom, usually identified as a "former mill girl," appears in most of the biographies; her adult status as a well-known magazine editor and a leading poet is seldom mentioned. She is the recipient of letters (Pollard), a languishing lady (Warren), or a lovesick idiot (Mordell). Seldom is she presented as a person with her own identity.

From almost any study of Whittier, one thing is very clear. He liked women, was comfortable in their company, and enjoyed their admiration of him. His biographers often claim that his Quaker upbringing taught him to see women as equals; in reality, he treated his protégées as daughters, over whom he had some paternal control that permitted him to tell them what to do and how to do it. That attitude hardly reflects equality, but it is more enlightened than the then-prevailing patriarchal attitudes toward women writers. Whittier never told talented women that their real work was to marry and produce young.

Whittier's warm relationships with women began at home. He was extremely close to his mother and his sister Elizabeth, both of whom supported and encouraged him through the years of near-poverty, ill health, and the intense dedication to the abolitionist cause that dominated much of his life. Their Quaker moderation did not inhibit the free use of intelligence and expression of ideas, and Whittier respected their opinions. Visitors to Amesbury, Larcom among them, commented on the beauty of the intense love between brother and sister. However a more psychologically oriented age interprets the kind or degree of such a relationship, it

did exist, and it served to educate him to women's identities and talents. His own youthful career was encouraged by the famous poet, Lydia Sigourney.

Whittier and Larcom first met in the spring of 1844 at Lowell, and it is important to understand the status of each at the time. He came to Lowell as the editor of the Free-Soil and abolitionist *Middlesex Standard*. While he had a reputation as a poet, he was far better known as an antislavery activist and writer. Everything—career, health, sexual energy—had been repressed and channeled into the abolitionist cause. He had dedicated, perhaps sacrificed, his pen to the cause; editors without the abolitionist commitment feared his work. His income from editing jobs, articles, and poems was barely enough to support him, his mother, and his sister. One of the reasons he gave in later years for not marrying when young was his extreme poverty and his responsibility for his dependents. At thirty-five he was, according to both male and female contemporaries, strikingly handsome, tall and spare and dark, with a rather bony face dominated by intense dark eyes, which glowed and burned and shot fire and pierced like an eagle's when his emotions were evoked.[3]

The romantic attachments of his young manhood, differentiated from the protégées, were certainly inhibited by his poverty, poor health, and the intensity of his commitment. Letters to them often seem to attract and then repel, but his behavior can be more simply explained as normal attraction that had to be limited by physical and financial circumstances.

By the time he came to Lowell, his image was that of a crusader. Among the mill girls, who were strongly abolitionist in their sentiments (perhaps because the cotton mill owners were so definitely not), he was a hero. He spoke for the bright, well-read, and upright farm girls whose recruitment made the Lowell experiment internationally famous.[4] Most of them could recite, for example, his poem, **"The Yankee Girl,"** about a lovely Northern girl who rejects a marriage proposal and a life of luxury with a Southern plantation owner. She tosses back "the dark wealth of her curls, / With a scorn in her eye which the gazer could feel," and orders, "Go back, haughty Southron!":

> Full low at thy bidding thy negroes may kneel,
> With the iron of bondage on spirit and heel;
> Yet know that the Yankee girl sooner would be
> In fetters with them, than in freedom with thee.

One evening Harriet Farley, a neighbor of Whittier's, brought him to a meeting of the Improvement Circle that produced the monthly magazine called the *Lowell Offering*. The girls in their white dresses were awed at the poet's visit; Larcom, a major although very youthful contributor to the magazine, was embarrassed to have her verses read aloud. When he came to talk to her, she could barely speak.[5]

For a long time awe overshadowed friendship, for Larcom was never very self-confident. Her secure, happy childhood in Beverly, Massachusetts, dominated by her remote, austere, but loving father, ended when his death sent the family to Lowell, where Mrs. Larcom became a boardinghouse keeper. Larcom went to work as a doffer at eleven. She loved school, but financial pressures sent her back to the mill; at about thirteen she was exhausted and ill and was sent to stay with a married sister in Beverly. When she came back to Lowell, her brilliant older sister Emeline's friends, Harriet Farley and Harriott Curtis, had started the *Lowell Offering*; Larcom, although she was much younger than the others, began to write for it. She was an avid reader, had written verses since she was seven, and took every opportunity Lowell offered to educate herself.

At twenty she was a tall, stately young woman, attractive rather than beautiful, with rich light brown hair and bright blue eyes that, according to one of her friends, seemed always to be laughing.[6] She was a compulsive reader with an insatiable love of learning, a talent for verse making, and no real goal for the future. She had a curiously divided personality: cheerful, outgoing and affectionate among friends; reserved, diffident, and barely able to assert herself among strangers.

Larcom called once or twice at the Whittier home, but in 1846 she went west, at that time the Illinois prairie, with her sister Emeline, Emeline's husband, and her brother-in-law, Frank, to whom Larcom was engaged. For them, as for many young people, the west seemed to offer the future.

Larcom took with her from eleven years in the mills the habit of reading and study, a great deal of unfocused knowledge gained from books and lectures and unrelated courses—when she could not find any way of learning English literature, for example, she went to the Lowell library and read and outlined her way through the canon—the self-discipline to make herself work even when she did not want to, and an accompanying belief in the sanctity of work. She also took a hatred of crowds and noise that was almost pathological, and the seeds of disease.[7] Although diffident outside her circle of friends, she had confidence in her ability to take care of herself.

The west was disappointing, but she remained for six years. She acquired an excellent education at Monticello Seminary under its remarkable headmistress, Philena Fobes, and she made some close friends in a family of transplanted New Englanders who encouraged her writing and study, but there were few other positive elements. She watched her brilliant sister Emeline abandon all her talents for a life that seemed to consist of dirt, drudgery, and dead babies. (Emeline bore twelve children altogether, of whom three reached adulthood.) Prairie marriage disgusted the younger sister; she was

careful not to say so, but the poems she sent back to the *New England Offering,* successor to the *Lowell Offering,* cannot conceal under their humor her consistently negative feelings.

Larcom described her childhood self as stubborn rather than aggressive; she could never confront, but she developed protective strategies to evade what she did not want. One of the things she managed to evade for the moment was her own marriage.

It was on her return to Massachusetts in 1852 that her real friendship with the Whittiers began. She had called at their home several times while she still lived in Lowell, and after she went west had occasionally written to Elizabeth. Whittier, now corresponding editor for the *National Era,* the Washington, D.C., abolitionist newspaper, once or twice reprinted some of her essays from the *Offering,* like her amusing but rueful account of a district teacher's life. The *Era* published a poem of hers called "The Burning Prairie," in which the sudden prairie fires are compared to the fire in the nation's soul that would burn away slavery, and Whittier wrote a biographical and critical introduction praising her work. He probably recommended her to Rufus W. Griswold, for two of her poems appeared in the 1850 edition of *Female Poets of America,* with Whittier's biographical sketch.

By 1852 Whittier was approaching the point in his career when he was beginning to move away from his role as political activist to become more and more the poet. His belief in the antislavery cause had not changed, but he was forty-five, and most of his energies up to this point had gone into his abolitionist efforts. It was, as J. B. Pickard says, time now for younger men to take over, and for him to concentrate on poetry that celebrated nature, goodness, and the New England past.[8]

His initiative in developing their friendship was one of the bright spots of Larcom's return; she herself was still far too diffident to do more than make the proper formal call on his family. He visited her in Beverly, and gave cordial invitations, backed up by his mother and sister, to visit in Amesbury. His interest in her writing made it more valuable in her eyes, for it never occurred to her to doubt his judgment; she still regarded him with awe. He was as dynamic and compelling as ever, and to have some of that intensity directed on her and her work was flattering; if he chose to set himself up as mentor, she was too dazzled to respond with anything but happiness and gratitude. He was the Master and she the humble pupil—in both their eyes.

Obviously, there were other grounds for compatibility. They were both great readers and shared their love of books, especially poetry. They had the same dry, straight-faced New England humor.[9] Both of them had a love of the natural world—landscape, flowers, trees, water—and this love of nature is reflected in her letters to him. They shared the same morality and background. The early years of Larcom's life as she described them in *A New England Girlhood,* though spent in a village rather than on a farm, resemble the world that Whittier was to evoke in **Snow-Bound** in both the mechanics of daily living and the strong family orientation. Their values—work, honesty, duty, love of God—were rooted in the same New England past.

In none of Larcom's letters and journals is there the slightest hint that she ever expected any more of him than friendship. No relationship between complex people is ever simple, and there was certainly a romantic element in their friendship. But it was the romance of hero worship rather than of sex; he was for years the glorious Mr. Great-Heart of *Pilgrim's Progress* and her ideals, and in that sense she remained a little in love with him all her life. The approval of her and her work, the attention and concern from this commanding older man, satisfied something in her that had ached since her father died. She was happy to write as he suggested, and not for many years did she grow restless and uncomfortable with his guidance. The relationship was so much that of master and pupil that she was more comfortable with his sister and saw herself as Elizabeth's friend who was also Whittier's protégée.

Five of her poems were published in the *National Era* in 1853, but Whittier urged her to do more than verses. She had, ever since her days in Lowell, written short essays that she called "Similitudes": a child, in a beautifully described natural setting, learns a religious truth. Whittier was enthusiastic when he read them, and decided that they should be published as a book. He began by urging his own publishers, Ticknor and Fields, to accept them, writing about the "unique and beautiful little book" that "I am quite sure that if it was an *English* book of equal merit and beauty, it would not lack republication here at once."[10] Fields felt that it was not for his house (Larcom herself had been modestly horrified at the idea of submitting her book to the most prestigious of all publishers), but Whittier kept on; a few weeks later he wrote her, "I have seen J. P. Jewett and he is quite ready to publish it. . . . I am certain he is the best publisher for it. He will make a handsome little volume of it."[11]

The book, called *Similitudes: From the Ocean and the Prairie,* came out in autumn and sold for fifty cents (fifty-eight in gilt). Larcom was quietly proud of it, and it had comfortable sales; Whittier, of course, gave it favorable reviews in the *Era.*

Once the book was out, Whittier had other ideas for his protégé:

> When ever I take up *Similitudes,* or read a letter of thine, I am impressed with the notion that thou shouldst write a story of sufficient length for a book by itself. It vexes me to see such a work as *The Lamplighter* [by Maria S. Cummins] having such a run, when you cannot remember a single sentence or idea in it after reading it. I am sure thee could do better—give plesaure to thy old friends and make a thousand new ones—and "put money in thy purse" if I may be permitted to speak after the manner of a Yankee. Pray think of it—study thy plan well and go ahead.[12]

Although Larcom dutifully thought about a novel, or a long story, as they both called it, it is unlikely that she did much more than that at this point. She certainly did not think of herself as a writer, as a letter to an intimate friend shows:

> Writing gets a poor remuneration in "lucre" unless one can create a sensation by some sudden flash, which I, with my disposition to peace and quietness, will never do. Mr. Arthur [the editor of *Arthur's Home Magazine*] wishes to pay me for all I write for him; but he feels poor and I suppose has met with many reverses.[13]

This solicitude for the welfare of a publisher is hardly characteristic of a professional writer. She liked to write her poems, and she was grateful for the ability; expressing her feelings in verse brought great satisfaction. But it might be unladylike to thrust oneself in the public eye, and she did not see herself as a writer, although she did expect her verses to be read seriously for their message. It would, indeed, be hard to see oneself as a writer when payment was usually gratitude, a magazine subscription, or at most one or two dollars a poem.

Larcom had evaded a decision about her marriage, and the question was still undecided when in December 1854 she took a position at Wheaton Seminary, a fine school for young ladies in Norton, Massachusetts. It was a temporary measure, she thought; actually, she stayed there for nine years, the most difficult time of her life.

The whole period at Wheaton was full of interlocking conflicts, which, although they are specific to Larcom's life, are representative of what intelligent and talented women of the time went through if they attempted to use their brains or themselves for anything beyond the accepted role of women. Simply, the question for these women was, What did God want them to do with their lives?[14] Victorian women's roles were clearly (male) defined; a woman was to be the queen of her home, to give up self to the nurture of others—her family, or, if she had none, perhaps other women's children. Woman in her purity, piety, submission, and obedience was a quiet force for good.[15] Out of the world she would remain untouched—and, of course, uncompetitive. Her role was to be invisible and silent.

Although Larcom always gave lip service to this view, her own life quietly contradicted it. When she went to Wheaton she was just beginning to face the problem of marriage or possible alternatives. There was always the picture of her sister, diminished to household drudge, before her. Teaching was an acceptable substitute nurturing, but, as hard as she tried and as much as her pupils praised her, she disliked the life. Even on the prairie she had distinguished between teaching and "keeping school"; at Wheaton the latter meant living among the girls and being a kind of surrogate mother: noise, bustle, constant interruptions, and lack of privacy. What she really loved to do, although she hesitated to confess it, was to read books, write her verses, go for long walks and talk to friends.

Her background was so different from that of the average middle-class woman that it was doubly difficult for her to disappear into a stereotype, no matter how much she might want to. From age eleven she had contributed to the family income or supported herself, experience that gave her an unusual independence. Her mind had been challenged and developed during the Lowell years, when young women were distinguishing themselves by their intelligence and participation—there had even been Lowell girls who had bank accounts of their own! The west, with its comparative openness and newness, had standards and rules of propriety for women, but Larcom rejected some of them and could stay detached from the rest. Monticello Seminary, whose curriculum then sounds comparable to today's small liberal arts colleges, widened her mind, taught her to use it more efficiently, and gave her a great deal of confidence in her own intelligence. All of these environments had created a young woman of independence, but at Wheaton (in what she called sedate New England) her confidence in herself weakened.

For several years she was greatly influenced and her problems were intensified by a strange young woman named Esther Humiston, who carried womanly silence and invisibility to an extreme. Humiston, who was probably tubercular, had taken to her bed and her room to wait for death, refusing to see anyone except her family and an assortment of ministers. Apparently she and Larcom met only once, but their correspondence lasted from 1856 to 1860 (she died in 1861). Humiston preached resignation, self-effacement, contempt for the world, piety, and other saintly attitudes. All Larcom's religious belief and much of her early conditioning supported these views, although her temperament and experience did not, and her letters to Humiston were tortured and morbid as she tried to force herself into a life she did not want. Intensifying the difficulties was the fact that she could no longer mindlessly accept the Calvinism into which she had been born; she was moving toward a kind of Christian transcendentalism, reflected in so much of her poetry, but to reject orthodoxy was terrifying. Much of her reading was theological as she attempted to give her feelings legitimacy.

All these conflicts showed themselves in a variety of ways: wide extremes of mood from exhilaration when her naturally cheerful temperament was in control to dark and morbid depression, restlessness, and dissatisfaction with her physical surroundings; increasing bouts of psychosomatic illness characterized by a heavy pain in her head accompanied by almost total apathy; and finally a near nervous breakdown and briefly a questioning of her own sanity.

Through all this mental turbulence, Whittier was, consciously or not, a steady voice that repeated that she and what she had to say were important. At a very bad point in her life he wrote, "I see nothing of thine lately. I am sure thou must have found something to say in thine own clear simple and beautiful way during this long winter. Does not the voice say to thee as formerly to the Exile of Patmos, *Write!*"[16]

She never did stop writing, although in her worst moments she could do little, and then her inability increased her illness. To be fanciful, Whittier and Humiston are like two allegorical figures: a light angel and a dark angel fighting for a soul. His praise and belief in her was an enormous source of strength; her visits to Amesbury when she and Elizabeth and "Greenleaf" sat before the fire and talked or stared into the flames, or the walks she and the poet took in the natural world they both loved, were shining and serene moments in a troubled existence. Elizabeth's friendship and encouragement was as important as her brother's; Larcom's place in their home and family gave her more confidence in herself. She was pleased, for example, that she was invited to use Whittier's family name, Greenleaf. She described Whittier and Elizabeth to Esther Humiston:

> He was never married; that perhaps is one reason why there is such depth to his poetry, for if ever a man was capable of love stronger than death, it must have been he. One cannot help feeling that he has been through the deep waters, through the furnace-heat, and so is cleansed and purified. The calmness of some great self-conquest rests upon his life. Lizzie seems like a meek, timid bird that one would brood under motherly wings, and yet she has much mental and moral strength and is a most lovely character.[17]

Paradoxically, Whittier's support and encouragement deepened her conflict. When she went to Wheaton she was working on the "long story" he had suggested in the leisurely way in which she liked to do things; to her horror, he announced in the *Era* that Miss Larcom would soon produce a long American story. "I wonder if you can guess how frightened I was when I saw the announcement in the *Era,* that a book of mine would be published this season!" she wrote him. "I had begun to count it among the impossibilities, my time is so completely broken into little bits here. But when I saw that notice, I said, 'Now it *must* be done.' Will it be a 'breach of promise' if I shouldn't succeed in finishing it?"[18]

To her friend Harriet Hanson Robinson she wrote much more emotionally, "How that book is ever going to get written I don't know. I could have cried, when I saw that Mr. Whittier had mentioned it, in the paper; for I had given it up in discouragement, myself. And then I didn't mean to have my name to it. Indeed, I should not have dreamed that I could write a long story, if Mr. Whittier had not told me I could, and advised me to try."[19] The pressure of attempting to live up to Whittier's expectations for her, adjusting to a new world that she did not really like, trying to find time to do any writing at all, and other personal problems plunged her into mental turmoil at the very beginning of her time at Wheaton. In fact, the book that was to outdo the best-selling *Lamplighter* eventually dwindled into *Lottie's Thought Book,* letters from a young girl to her mother—similitudes in another form.

Clearly Whittier felt that he had every right to tell her what and how to write; there is never a hint of apology as he suggests corrections in words or lines. Nor in these early days did Larcom mind. If he wanted to correct her poems and send them to editors without asking her first, she did not feel herself in a position to object. "I received a few days ago, the poem 'Across the River,' with a 'respectfully declined' from the new Maga.," she wrote him, referring to the *Atlantic Monthly.* "I was not at all surprised, only that I did not certainly know that you had sent it. With all deference to the gentlemen editors, I think it is quite a decent little poem, with the changes you made."[20] Comments in both their letters indicate that for years she sent him copies of her poems, and he approved or edited them to fit his moral vision of poetry. Perhaps the most extreme example is the following letter from Whittier:

> "On the Beach" is admirable in conception and so very felicitous in some of its lines and verses that I wanted to have thee work it over until it took a perfect shape. I have ventured to alter the copy sent me, by way of hint of what I think would tersely and clearly express the idea: and I send the marred manuscript back to do with as pleases thee best. Even as it stands it is one of thy best poems, and should go to the *Atlantic* for the Nov. number, before it comes out in the book.
>
> There are lines in it that will live always: "The bands of green and purple light" *"The broad refreshment of the sea"* "My thoughts *o'er float these murmurous miles"* "They add to tenderness divine / Unto this tremulous sea." But the last verse rises into sublimity and is worth fifty pages of ordinary verse.
>
> I don't quite like the line, "Around us daylight gently dies." It seems common-place as compared with the verbal felicities of the poem. The "gently dies" don't suit me. It would be better to say "Around us slow the daylight dies," perhaps. . . .
>
> In the Prelude to thy book, when thee get the proof-sheet of it, see if "Its pines are tennanted" is quite the thing. Squirrels and crows run and roost in the pines,

and suggest *themselves* at once as their *tennants* But I must let criticism alone. I'm not able to correct my own verses.[21]

Ironically, the person to whom the letter was sent was no longer a novice poet but a magazine editor (to whom writers submitted their work) and a poet with an established reputation of her own. In spite of her personal crises through the 1850s, she had produced four small books and a steady stream of poetry that usually had no trouble in finding a publisher. She appeared often in the *Crayon,* a prestigious but short-lived journal of the arts (1855-1861) whose editors liked her work and paid well; less prestigious (and less well-paying) outlets were newspapers and some of the "family" magazines like *Arthur's Home Magazine.*

The kind of fame that makes one's name a household word came, unexpectedly, early in 1858, when the *Crayon* published a poem of hers called "Hannah Binding Shoes." Its appearance was followed almost at once by charges of plagiarism from the *New York Tribune.* Larcom was able to defend herself by telling a story that illustrates the perils of midcentury publication: She had sent the poem to that paper four years earlier, with a letter requesting payment if the paper used it. When she never heard from them, she assumed the poem had not been accepted. Years later she pulled it out of her files and sent it to the *Crayon,* only to discover that the paper had published it (under the pseudonym "Mercy More") and neither paid nor informed her.

The controversy called attention to the poem, which became instantly popular, surprising no one more than its author. It was a story poem, picturing a scene thoroughly familiar in the fishing and shipping villages of the New England coast: a young woman waiting faithfully for her sailor husband who would never return. It was set to music and became a concert song; several paintings represented Hannah at her window, waiting for the ship that never came. Hannah had all the womanly virtues: love, fidelity, quiet uncomplaining courage. William Dean Howells thought of it as a great poem, one that could confer immortality on its writer.[22] The poem followed her all her life, when she would much rather have been judged by more important and more characteristic work.[23]

The poem opened editorial doors for her, as well as calling forth a great deal of fan mail. For a small but regular salary she became unofficial poetry editor of the *Congregationalist,* a denominational paper with a wide circulation. The patriotic verses she wrote as the Civil War approached also gained attention, and in 1861 she had her first acceptance from the *Atlantic Monthly.*

It was still the *Atlantic*'s custom to publish poems anonymously and not to reveal authors until the yearly index came out. This practice made a pleasant guessing game for the literati; Larcom's poem "The Rose Enthroned" (June 1861), involving evolution, the growth and perfectability of the human race, and the horror of civil war, was briefly attributed to Lowell, but then firmly given to Emerson. The poem added prestige to Larcom's fame; it also brought her to the attention of James and Annie Fields, who promptly made her part of the literary world that they dominated. There were other *Atlantic* poems, including the much-anthologized "A Loyal Woman's No" (December 1863).

Whittier was not, however, the only person from whom she sought advice. She frequently sent her verses to William S. Robinson, political activist, writer, editor, later clerk of the Massachusetts House of Representatives, and husband of her friend Harriet Hanson.[24] He liked her work and published it in whatever paper he happened to be editing at the time. He was temporarily a reader for the *Atlantic* when she sent him "The Rose Enthroned," and he promptly showed it to the editor, James Russell Lowell, who accepted it. Nor did Whittier see "A Loyal Woman's No" before publication. That poem was written in Wisconsin and sent directly to Annie Fields: "Will you care to look at the enclosed, as you have glanced at other verses of mine? They can be returned to Beverly if not the thing for the Maga.—I wrote from a sudden feeling of how I wished some women would feel."[25]

In 1863, as a result of some personal and family tragedies that caused a real examination of her life, Larcom finally broke away from Wheaton. A year later she became one of the editors of *Our Young Folks Magazine,* whose first issue came out in January 1865. The magazine was one of the new projects that Fields launched when Ticknor's death gave him control of the firm, and it was set up in a way that could not work unless Fields himself were involved.[26] There were three editors who apparently never saw one another. Larcom did most of her work at home; the tempestuous Gail Hamilton (Mary Abigail Dodge) wrote for the magazine and occasionally gave advice; John Townsend Trowbridge was sent off almost at once to travel through the South and write about Civil War battlefields. Howard Ticknor was the office manager, and apparently Fields made all final decisions about what went into the magazine. At the end of two years, Hamilton left, to begin the controversy with Fields that would drag on for several years and end with her *Battle of the Books* (1869) and Fields's retirement from publishing in 1871.[27] Larcom became the sole editor in 1868 and remained so for two years, although Trowbridge's name remained on the title page, and he took over for the last years of the magazine's life.

As an editor Larcom had financial security, time, and a recognized position in the literary world. Fields could call on the best writers of the day; Larcom met them, of course, and her circle of friends widened.

The kinds of new friends she made are significant. Her chief model for a writer was Whittier; now she began to meet women who wrote. She corresponded with Lydia Maria Child, as one editor to another; she met and enjoyed talking with Harriet Beecher Stowe, who greatly admired her work; Grace Greenwood (Sara Lippincott) spent time with her when the latter visited in Boston. Best-selling novelist Adeline Dutton Train Whitney and the author of the *William Henry Letters,* Abby Morton Diaz, who had grown up at Brook Farm and as part of an antislavery activist family, became her close friends. Mary Bucklin Claflin, wife of a governor and herself influential in the establishment of women's degrees at Boston University, was another good friend at whose gracious home Larcom was a frequent visitor. These women—busy, active, and yet "ladies"—provided new models for Larcom; it would be hard, if not impossible, for her to go back to pupil status, even if she wanted to.

Whittier's letter (quoted above) concerned selections from her published verses for Larcom's first collection, called *Poems* (1868); the poem he talks about, which referred to Elizabeth Whittier, appeared in the collection, although probably nowhere else. Whittier has been given credit for having her book published; how much influence he had cannot be determined (he had certainly tried twice before).[28] If there was a motive for its publication beyond the fact that the public liked Larcom's poems and therefore a book of them would sell, it is more likely that James and Annie Fields wanted to reward her for her loyalty during the controversy that Gail Hamilton was now creating. Harriet Hanson Robinson's journal records Larcom's confidence that she still had never received any money from Fields for her devotional book, *Breathings of a Better Life* (1866), although it had steady sales and several revisions.[29]

At some point Larcom stopped sending copies of her poems to Whittier, and he wrote her wondering why. Anxious not to hurt his feelings, but clearly wanting to go her own way now, she wrote back, tactfully, "But you have taught me all that I ought to ask: why should I remain a burden on you? Why should I always write with you holding my hand? My conscience and my pride rebel. I will be myself, faults and all."[30]

Although his mentorship was ended, Whittier remained supportive. After the publication of her third book of poems, *Wild Roses of Cape Ann* (1880), a book with strong local color and Essex Country flavor, he wrote to Oliver Wendell Holmes, "Has thee seen Miss Larcom's *Cape Ann*? I like it, and in reading it I thought thee would also. Get it and see if she has not a right to stand with the rest of us."[31]

Just as their professional relationship changed over the years, so did the quality of their friendship. Until Elizabeth Whittier's death in 1864, the primary relationship was that of mentor and pupil. Larcom herself had gone through a heartbreaking year in 1863, and the death of Elizabeth the following summer was another deep hurt, but one she shared with Whittier, who turned to the people his sister had loved. She visited Amesbury as often as she could during the autumn, and they read "In Memoriam" together.

Larcom's job as editor allowed her to organize her life as she wanted it: she rented an "apartment" in Beverly Farms, the first home of her own that she had ever had; she spent the winter in "rooms" in Boston where she could enjoy her fill of exhibitions, concerts, and social life and give some time to the North End Mission and various working-girls' clubs; spring and early summer she spent at home in Beverly, and in August, just before her hay fever arrived, she left for New Hampshire, taking her work with her and sometimes staying well into November. Generally her stay included Bearcamp (a small hotel in West Ossipee that Whittier and his friends virtually took over for a few weeks each summer), various resorts, and a quiet farmhouse where she could relax and write. Mountains came to mean a great deal to her, for themselves and for their symbolic closeness to God. The years at *Our Young Folks* were the happiest and most productive of her life.

She wrote the kind of poems she had established as hers, with the theme of nature's beauty leading to God and celebrating a kind of Christian transcendentalism. She also wrote poems about children, most of them for her own magazine, and collected as *Childhood Songs* (1875), and for a while some poems about women and marriage. Although she had long since rejected her engagement and the kind of life it offered, circumstances now forced her into defining her position as an unmarried woman; the poem "Unwedded" (*Poems*) justifies her choice. It grew out of her own feelings and a conversation on the subject with Harriet Beecher Stowe. She was a regular contributor now to the *Independent,* a nominally Congregationalist newspaper with great prestige and circulation; it published all the "great" writers and paid them very well.

James T. Fields retired from publishing in 1871, leaving the firm in the hands of the charming but not very competent Osgood, who ran into more and more trouble until eventually he was rescued and eased out by Henry O. Houghton.

Osgood sold *Our Young Folks* to Scribner's in 1873. Larcom was not at first worried; she had money in the bank and sources of income from her writing. As time passed, however, she missed the dependable income, and she went to Osgood to ask that some kind of editorial position be found for her. She had had seven years of experience, and of living the kind of life that truly satisfied her; she dreaded the thought of going back to

teaching but feared dependence on her writing. Osgood, unmarried and very much "one of the boys" responded with a letter of charming callousness, cheerfully suggesting that of course she could teach and write at the same time.[32] Somewhat grimly, she took a teaching job at Bradford Academy. She lasted only one dreadful year; she hated it, her teaching was bad, and all the symptoms of illness that had virtually disappeared when she left Wheaton returned. After that year she never again had a steady position or a secure income, but it is clear that she would have preferred dependence on her family or starvation to another regular teaching job.

She had money from her poems, and from another source: beginning in 1870, she and Whittier had collaborated on three anthologies for Osgood, *Child Life* (1871), *Child Life in Prose* (1873), and *Songs of Three Centuries* (1875). The division of labor can be pieced together from her letters: Whittier, whose name was given as editor, made the final choice of poems, wrote the preface, was paid for his work, and received all the royalties; Larcom read, found poems, copied them out, discussed the choice with Whittier, then made copies of the poems, dealt with the publisher, and read and corrected proof. For this she was paid a flat sum, either three hundred or five hundred dollars. At first the inequality did not matter; it was a pleasure to work with Whittier and she was still in the editorial offices anyway. The second collaboration was not quite so easy.

In *Child Life* she was acknowledged in the preface by name as a kind friend "who has given him the benefit of her cultivated taste and very thorough acquaintance with whatever is valuable in the poetical literature of *Child Life.*" In the second collaboration her name was not mentioned at all.

"*The Hearth and Home*'s notice of 'C. L. in Prose' gives me all the credit for this last volume. I deferred to what I thought was thy wish in not directly using thy name in the Preface, but I ought in justice to both of us to have given it," Whittier wrote her.[33] Earlier, however, he had written: "I've got the sheets of our *Child-Life* and like it hugely. But I think now I shall take all the credit to myself. If it had not looked nice and good, I should have shirked it, and left it all on thy shoulders."[34]

However Larcom felt about the omission of her name, she said nothing to Whittier. The return to teaching and anonymity seemed to negate all she had achieved. Her health did not improve, and she may have been suffering the discomforts of menopause as well. Anxiety about her finances drove her to work harder than she should have. As pressures increased, so did her tense, nervous state and the bouts of illness.

The third collaborative volume, *Songs of Three Centuries,* was more elaborate than the former ones. It contained about five hundred fifty poems, ranging through three hundred years of English and American literature. Larcom and Whittier planned on doing the final selection of material during their stay at Bearcamp House. Before her delayed arrival there, however, she wrote a friend, "I have scarcely walked to the beach this summer,—for why? I have been so busy about a book, Mr. Whittier's book—a compilation of English poetry which Mr. Osgood wished him to make and which he agreed to do with my help. It is to be published this fall, and there is the hurry and fatigue of it; my head has been nearly used up, through the warm weather. If I had supposed it would be one third as hard, I would have refused to do it, without a year's time. . . . I have lost the beauty of the summer, poring over books."[35] Knowing that Whittier was enjoying himself at Bearcamp did not help her mental state.

That there was some kind of quarrel is confirmed by two letters from Whittier, apologizing and blaming "the matter" on his "nervous excitability."[36] The other letter, undated, says they were both to blame and ends, "I dare say I was a fool, but that's no reason thee should make thyself one, by dwelling on it. Lay it all to dyspepsia, Ben Butler, or anything else than intentional wrong on the part of thy old friend. We have known each other too long, and done each other too many kind offices, to let it disturb us."

Larcom's valuable suggestions and aid were noted in the preface, and Whittier assigned her half the copyright and royalties; he received the money directly, however, then gave her her share. Although on the surface everything was patched up, and the following summer found the Whittier circle again happily at Bearcamp House, the relationship was never the same.

It is difficult to understand what comes across as an incredible piece of exploitation, except to assume that, regardless of Larcom's gentle attempts to break away from the role, he still regarded her as his protégée long after she stopped seeing herself that way. Her work on the books was both decision-making and secretarial drudgery, with neither money nor credit enough to reward her for her task, and was done under pressure from her own precarious financial situation, her illness, and the unsympathetic Osgood, who saw her only as the person who could keep Whittier working.

It is also difficult to understand Whittier's miserliness, since it extends in some directions and not in others. For fifty-eight years he lived close to poverty until the publication of **Snow-Bound** in 1866 brought the popularity that made all subsequent volumes sell, and made him rich. Like a canny New Englander, of course, he kept quiet about money in the bank, but he was quite generous to his nieces, and he tried, as Larcom told Lizzie Whittier Pickard years later, many times to pay her expenses in the mountains. Her pride would

never let her accept the offers, of course, and besides, "I thought he was as poor as I was."[37]

Yet the flat sums paid her certainly do not reflect the proportion of work she did, and while the second and third volumes were being done, she had no steady income. Whittier must have known that; there is a curious blindness and insensitivity in his failure to make sure that she was adequately and fairly paid and credited.

Perhaps the breach would have been healed sooner, but other circumstances intervened. In the spring of 1876, his niece and housekeeper, Lizzie Whittier, married Samuel T. Pickard and moved to Portland, Maine. After a delightful stay at Bearcamp,[38] Whittier left Amesbury to live with cousins in Danvers.

There are conflicting reports about Oak Knoll and Whittier's residence there. Some of his friends found him less accessible and the atmosphere less welcoming. He did, perhaps, need protection from all the strangers who felt they had the right to visit this venerable institution—Whittier called them the Pilgrims—but an account from Edmund Gosse, British critic and scholar, suggests that the protection may have been overdone.

Gosse describes the place as "sinister. . . . After a long pause the front door opened slightly, and a very unprepossessing dog emerged, and shut the door (if I may say so) behind him." After a few tense minutes assuring the dog that they were friends, he rang again. The door was "slightly opened, and a voice of no agreeable timbre asked what we wanted." He explained an appointment with Whittier, and the door was closed again. "But at length a hard-featured woman grudgingly admitted us, and showed us, growling as she did it, into a parlor."[39]

Friends saw him only in the most formal way. Larcom wrote Lizzie Pickard that she had been to tea at Oak Knoll and had seen Whittier again at the Claflins:

> Sometimes I wish the old times could come back, as when I used to be so at home with you all at Amesbury, and saw him so often,—for you know how I value his friendship. But he almost never calls on me now, and I never was one who could run after even my best friends, when they seemed to be having a better time without me. . . . The spirit of anything good can never be lost, so I shall always be grateful for that pleasant share of mine in the Amesbury life, in your Aunt Lizzie's time, and after.[40]

After a while, however, Whittier began spending more time away from Oak Knoll, going back often to Amesbury, which was still his legal residence, staying with his Cartland cousins in Newburyport, visiting friends like Mrs. Claflin in Newtonville or Annie Fields in

Manchester, or staying in Boston. Gradually he sought out his old friends, and several of Larcom's letters in the 1880's mention having met him, usually by arrangement, at friends' houses.

Not until 1877 did Larcom feel well again, although she worked steadily. Learning from the collaboration with Whittier that anthologies paid, she edited two small books designed to accompany the traveler: *Roadside Poems for Summer Travelers* (1876) and *Hillside and Seaside in Poetry* (1877). Another book, *Landscape in American Poetry* (1879), was a commission; it is a handsome art book for which she wrote the text. She frequently taught classes for schools or private groups; she worked up several lectures, mostly on literature or women in literature, which she gave to women's groups or lyceums and for which she was paid twenty-five dollars (men were paid more); she wrote a commissioned article for the *Atlantic* on the Lowell mill girls (November 1881); she wrote a newsletter for Samuel Pickard's *Portland Transcript.* In 1881 she published her collection of local-color poetry called *Wild Roses of Cape Ann* and the new firm, Houghton Mifflin (in the break between Osgood and Houghton, she had wisely gone with the latter) brought out a *Household Edition* of her poems in 1884. At their request she wrote what is undoubtedly her best work, *A New England Girlhood* (1889). That was followed by three very popular small devotional books in which she tried to sum up and communicate all that she had learned about life and religion. From 1875 on, her letters to her Houghton Mifflin editors show no sign of the amateurishness that had characterized her earlier dealings with publishers; they are pleasant but firm, and concerned with typeface, arrangement, texture of paper, color of covers, price, advertising, and availability in bookstores—the letter of a professional regarding the details of her career.[41]

Nevertheless, life was precarious. Her ability to write depended entirely on her health. When she was seriously ill in the autumn of 1883, Whittier immediately set about raising money for her. Many of their common friends contributed, but it all had to be done very quietly for, as Harriet Minot Pitman, a close friend of both, wrote Whittier, everyone knew that Lucy was too proud and independent to accept charity.[42]

They met fairly often, but the mentorship was long past. In the late 1870s, at the time when Larcom felt that Whittier was turning away from his old friends, she met Phillips Brooks, the young rector of Trinity Church, Boston, famous for his superb preaching as well as for his nondogmatic Christianity. The two became very close friends; he was the last of the father figures in her life, although their relationship was not so much that of mentor and pupil as of friends who shared a religious vision.

Her last three books were dedicated to the three people she felt had most influenced her life: Philena Fobes (her headmistress at Monticello), her sister Emeline, and Whittier. The dedication to Whittier in *The Unseen Friend* (1891) calls him "Most beloved and most spiritual of American poets whose friendship has been to me almost a life-long blessing." In June 1892 came news of her sister's death, and in September of the same year, Whittier died. She hurried back from the mountains to be an honorary pallbearer, along with Elizabeth Stuart Phelps, Mary Bucklin Claflin, and Alice Freeman Palmer, at his funeral.[43] He left an estate of over one hundred thirty thousand dollars; to Larcom he left five hundred dollars and the copyrights of their three collaborations. "I am very glad he left me the copyrights of the books I compiled with him," she wrote Lizzie Pickard, "and indeed, it was only right, as I worked hard on them. The *Songs of Three Centuries* nearly cost me my health, the publishers rushed it so. I was good for nothing for three or four years after, as far as writing went. But he never knew the cause."[44]

Samuel Pickard was Whittier's literary executor, and he set to work at once to collect material and find a suitable biographer, finally deciding, with the approval of friends, to do the job himself. He and Larcom corresponded about the project:

> Mr. Whittier many times said to me—apparently in earnest and jest both—"Don't *thee* ever go to writing about me!" It used to hurt me a little, as if I *would* parade his friendship for me in any way! I could not do after he died what I would not when he was alive—unless I knew he was willing—and he never hinted any wish of the kind, certainly. I have already been asked to furnish "Recollections" for two periodicals, and have declined. I may be over-particular in this matter, but I do feel a delicacy about it—almost as if I had not the right.[45]

Her delicacy also meant a financial sacrifice, since she would have been paid well for her memories, and she seems to be the only one of Whittier's women friends who did not write about him. But she offered Pickard letters and all the help she could give him.

> I think Mr. Whittier had a wish that just a straight-forward story should be written about him, the plain facts of his life, and he put the material into your hands as the person he could be surest of, to tell just the truth. He may have feared that his women-friends idealized him too much,—and some of his men-friends, too. At any rate, he did want you to write his life, and he knew you so well that he knew what to expect of you. I think he was wise in his choice, and the book will be better for being entirely yours.—But if, by talking things over with you, I can help, I shall be glad to do so. I shall look up his letters soon.[46]

Larcom had very little time to help or to profit by the royalties. In the autumn of 1892 she was ill with heart disease; she recovered and, refusing to rest, went back to Boston to get on with her work. Her illness returned in the winter, and after the sudden death of Phillips Brooks in January 1893, she seemed to give up. Her last weeks were spent in Boston, where her window looked out to Trinity Church, and she was cared for by family, loving friends, and a number of former students from Wheaton. She died 17 April 1893. After a memorial service in Boston, attended by personal friends and most of the literary world, her body was taken home to Beverly for burial.

The two-column headline in the *Boston Globe* announcing her death called her "The Best of Our Minor Poets." Her poems continued to be anthologized. In 1924 the *Boston Evening Transcript* did a half-page article on her life and work, and in the 1930s a Lowell paper asked in its headlines whether Lucy Larcom would have approved the strike then going on. When Whittier and the other nineteenth-century giants were swept from poetic eminence, Larcom went with them.

During the years of her fame—from 1858 to 1893—she, like Whittier, spoke in a voice that appealed to a wide public. Even in the last years, when they were beginning to be old-fashioned, they somehow retained their popularity. She was usually classed with him as a New England poet, and the classification was a logical one up to a point. They wrote on many of the same themes and out of the same moral vision. Both were deeply religious, and both wrote public poetry.

Technically, she was a better craftsman than he. She is far more consciously experimental about verse form, using everything from the sonnet and Spenserian stanza to ballad meter and the unfortunate fourteener. Her lines are more consistently metrical. She wrote from a coherent theory of what poetry should be: "I believe in but one Beauty, the twin of truth, and the subtle essence of all that is sweet and deep and noble, in letters, morals, religion, and everyday life. I think that poetry would lose its very soul, if it ceased to breathe out *moral* lessons; though, of course, no one wants it to be *'preachy.'*"[47] This moral vision of poetry (and, indeed, of art in general), was one she shared with other poets of her time, and certainly with Whittier, who had, after all, used his poetry as a weapon in the abolitionist cause. Her ideas are not in themselves original; they were part of the intellectual climate in which she lived. Her work and ideas were acceptable because, for the most part, they did not deviate from the patriarchal tradition; she was a part, if a minor one, of the nineteenth-century literary establishment of New England.

Even when she writes about women, few of her poems are gender marked; her subjects are women in a patriarchal world. Like Hannah, binding her shoes and faithfully waiting, they celebrate the male-defined womanly virtues: fidelity, patience, quiet suffering, and enduring love. Even in "A Loyal Woman's No" the attack is not against men and marriage, but against one kind of man and one kind of marriage, and the poem assumes that the "right" man should lead a woman to the sublimity of the mountains, not keep her in the valleys. (There is a bit of subversion here in the implication that if a man does not lead her to the mountains, she will get there by herself.) "Unwedded," about a woman who chooses to remain single, justifies that choice to a patriarchal system, as later poems, "Woman's Christmas" and "Woman's Easter," justify woman's importance in Christianity.

Yet there are a few hints of dissatisfaction, as if suppressed feeling occasionally burst out of her. The poems that show this feeling stem from her experience on the prairie, the same experience that set her permanently against marriage. One often-repeated theme is loss of identity: in some very early verses and in "Sylvia" (*Atlantic Monthly,* 1873) the subject becomes, after marriage, "Old Woman" or "Wife." In Sylvia's case, the loss of her identity weakens and destroys her; not until she is dying does her husband again think of her as a person with a name of her own.

Probably her most antiestablishment poem appears, surprisingly, in her *Childhood Songs.* Called "A Little Old Girl," it is the tale of Prudence, who is taught to bake, sweep, sew, milk, plant, and go to school and meeting. She is also taught to fear the beauty and magic of nature, which might distract her from work. Her reward is the approval of her elders: "What a good wife she will make!"

A contemporary review of *Childhood Songs* calls this poem a light and pleasant picture of childhood; I find it the most cynical poem Larcom wrote. Given her own free and happy childhood and her concern as an adult for young girls, her love of freedom, and above all, her belief that it is through the perception of natural beauty that we grow in our souls and toward God, it is clear that the inhibiting of the child's instinctive playfulness and attraction to beauty will result in a wasted life and an unhappy woman.

Larcom did not think of herself as a "woman poet." In fact, it was being a woman that first kept her from thinking of herself as a writer and then, during the time at Wheaton, caused so much conflict. Even late in her life she rejected the word *career.*[48] It was here, I think, that she owes her greatest debt to Whittier; his influence slowly turned her into a professional.

As a young woman she was far too unsure of herself, and far too buried in the tradition of womanliness to bring herself deliberately to public notice. Like so many women writers, she used pseudonyms or initials to sign her poems; "Angelina Abigail" or "L. L." wrote the light verses, essays, and stories she sent back from Illinois to the *Offering*; "Culma Croly," an anagram of her name, wrote for *Arthur's Magazine*; "L. L." sent material to newspapers. Her *Era* poems are signed; Whittier used her full name. He knew the value of public familiarity with a specific name while Larcom was still picturing herself as a person who liked to write verses. When she did use her own name she was amused to find that many people assumed it was a pen name (like Grace Greenwood, Fanny Fern, and other alliterative women); once she moved into the literary world in 1865, name and identity came together. By the end of her career her name had become important to her on her own terms; in 1884, when the Houghton Mifflin Household Edition of *Larcom's Poetical Works* was published, she was horrified. "I feel naked without my prefix," she wrote her editors. "It makes me sound like one of 'them literary fellows'—and I'm not."[49] Later editions are of *Lucy Larcom's Poems*.

A single woman who wrote for a living could stay womanly by a life of service to others. Larcom came to believe, and letters from her admirers supported her belief, that her verses were her contribution, that by using the talents given her to tell her readers what she knew about life and nature and religion, she was indeed doing what God wanted her to do with her life.

Beyond that she could not go. Although she was committed to the abolitionist movement, and a great many of her early poems are propaganda pieces for it, she could never allow herself to be involved with the struggle for women's rights. Her friend Harriet Hanson Robinson was an active feminist, and there are several letters in which Larcom refuses to help the cause. Her excuses are that she has no time, or is working on something else, or, finally, that she had not made up her mind what was right, or whether women were ready for such a responsibility as the vote. She was certainly in favor of education for women. Perhaps because her own happy childhood had been so sharply curtailed and she had never had a "girlhood," she felt and showed a strong interest in young women, but that interest did not overtly include voting rights. The end of *A New England Girlhood* has a long passage directed to girls, telling them to prepare themselves for their futures, since as women they will be the upholders of morals, goodness, and truth for future generations.

The paradox is, of course, that she had rejected the very womanly role that she praised and supported. She could disguise herself, however, under her support and her womanly behavior. Aside from the fact that earning a living took most of her time and energy, women's activism was threatening; her hold on the place she had won for herself and the life she so enjoyed was at all times precarious. Because she had no strong base other than her own efforts, she was vulnerable to public disapproval. Whatever her deep feelings, she had to remain within the establishment to be safe.

Her need for security also explains her writing of verse. Having read all her published work and as much of her unpublished writing as is available (letters, journals, rough drafts), I feel a sense of regret for a lost vocation. She was most comfortable with the length and shape of the essay, and her prose is better than her verse. Her style is clear, direct, and unadorned; it flows smoothly and with some elegance to its point. *A New England Girlhood,* although it suffers to many modern readers from its messages about religion, is still a book that can enchant. She had a gift for making pictures for the reader, perhaps because she was also a painter and a lover of painting. Her visual imagination and her perception of natural detail make the beauty she describes very real. She enjoyed writing articles and stories, spending time lovingly crafting her prose—and that fact made the writing of prose a luxury that she literally could seldom afford.

Her verses had brought her approval as a child, even from her awesome father, and brought her approval as an adult, for it was perfectly acceptable for women to write poems. The inspirational messages of these sweet singers were, indeed, womanly. Larcom's poems were as much a guide as was Agnes's lamp.

To return finally to the question with which this study began, What was the nature and extent of Whittier's influence on her and her work? She did not, even though her poetry is like his, imitate his content and themes. She herself, in fact, named as the chief influence on her poetry not Whittier, but William Cullen Bryant; they all wrote within one tradition of nineteenth-century poetry that connected man and God and nature. Nor did she learn the techniques of poetry writing from him; she was a far better crafter than he was.

Nevertheless, Whittier made her a writer, not so much by editing her work and submitting it to publishers as by building up her confidence in herself and her abilities, by giving his approval to the image of Lucy Larcom as a writer, by forcing her to act as a professional. In that way he was the most important figure in Larcom's life, and she never stopped being grateful to him, even after she eased away from his guidance. Perhaps the other protégées benefited in the same way, getting from the poet not so much the tinkering with their work that he liked to do, but the confidence to see themselves as writers through the approval of the institution that Whittier had come to be and represent.

Notes

1. Most of the information on which this paper is based comes from letters: Whittier's from John B. Pickard, ed., *The Letters of John Greenleaf Whit-*

tier, 3 vols. (Cambridge: Harvard University Press, 1975); and Larcom's from various manuscript collections (see note 2 below). I also use Samuel T. Pickard, *Life and Letters of John Greenleaf Whittier,* 2 vols. (Boston: Houghton Mifflin, 1895); and idem, *Whittier-Land* (Boston: Houghton Mifflin, 1904). Whittier letters quoted here are from J. B. Pickard and identified by date, unless otherwise noted. Other biographies mentioned are John A. Pollard, *John Greenleaf Whittier: Friend of Man* (Boston: Houghton Mifflin, 1949); Robert Penn Warren, *John Greenleaf Whittier's Poetry* (Minneapolis: University of Minnesota Press, 1971); Edward Wagenknecht, *John Greenleaf Whittier: A Portrait in Paradox* (New York: Oxford University Press, 1967); and Albert Mordell, *Quaker Militant: John Greenleaf Whittier* (Boston: Houghton Mifflin, 1933). For an excellent account of Whittier biographers and critical attitudes, see Jayne Kribbs, introduction to *Critical Essays on John Greenleaf Whittier* (Boston: G. K. Hall, 1980).

2. Nearly two thousand letters, some autobiographical writings, and contemporary personal reminiscences are my sources of information about Lucy Larcom. Frequently statements in published works are modified by comments in letters; when that happens, I follow the letters. Location and dates of letters are given in the notes; I would like to thank the various libraries for permission to quote from their holdings.

Larcom's own autobiography, *A New England Girlhood* (Boston: Houghton Mifflin, 1889), is an obvious source of information, although it is impressionistic rather than factual. I have not used the only biography, Daniel Dulany Addison, *Lucy Larcom: Life, Letters, and Diary* (Boston: Houghton Mifflin, 1894), except when he quotes material not available anywhere else; Addison allows his thesis to shape his selection and interpretations.

Since I am working from a background of much research, and since this is a short paper, I have not traced all my steps to the conclusions I have reached. They will be available in the biography of Larcom on which I am working.

3. All Whittier's biographers talk about his eyes; the adjectives I use here are typical.

4. Benita Eisler, *The Lowell Offering* (New York: Lippincott, 1977), is the best modern account of the mill girls and has a bibliography of important works in the subject. Contemporary accounts are Harriet Hanson Robinson, *Loom and Spindle* (New York: Thomas Y. Crowell, 1896); Larcom's *A New England Girlhood*; and her "Among Lowell Mill-Girls," *Atlantic Monthly* 48 (1881): 593-612.

5. Larcom, *Girlhood,* 254-255.

6. Robinson, *Loom,* 109.

7. She had scrofula, a form of tuberculosis also called the king's evil, and probably had a susceptibility to respiratory ailments.

8. J. B. Pickard, *Letters of Whittier,* 2:207-208.

9. Both Larcom and Whittier have been accused of being humorless, a charge that S. T. Pickard, Elizabeth Stuart Phelps, and other contemporaries deny.

10. J. B. Pickard, *Letters of Whittier,* 2:221, 8 July 1853.

11. Ibid., 2:222, 28 July 1853.

12. Ibid., 2:256-257, 14 May 1854.

13. Lucy Larcom to Ann Spaulding and Rebecca Danforth, 15 May 1854, Lucy Larcom Papers (7006-b), Clifton Waller Barrett Library, University of Virginia, Charlottesville.

14. Elaine Showalter, *A Literature of Their Own: British Women Novelists from Brontë to Lessing* (Princeton: Princeton University Press, 1977), 24. Showalter is talking about British women, but American women certainly felt the same question of vocation.

15. Barbara Welter, "The Cult of True Womanhood, 1820-1860," *American Quarterly* 18 (1966):151-174.

16. J. B. Pickard, *Letters of Whittier,* 2:323, 20 February 1857.

17. Larcom to Esther Humiston, 1 May 1859; quoted by permission of the Massachusetts Historical Society, Boston.

18. Larcom to John Greenleaf Whittier, 22 February 1855; quoted by permission of the Wheaton College Library, Norton, Mass.

19. Larcom to Harriet Hanson Robinson, 16 February 1855; quoted by permission of the Arthur and Elizabeth Schlesinger Library, Radcliffe College, Cambridge, Mass.

20. Larcom to John Greenleaf Whittier, 30 October 1857; quoted by permission of the Wheaton College Library.

21. J. B. Pickard, *Letters of Whittier,* 3:178, 22 August 1868. For evidence that Larcom was not the only poet with whose work Whittier "tinkered," see S. T. Pickard, *Life of Whittier,* 2:535.

22. William Dean Howells, *Literary Friends and Acquaintance: A Personal Retrospect of American Authorship* (New York: Harper and Brothers, 1900), 123.

23. The Beverly, Massachusetts, Historical Society has the journal of Sarah Trask, whose story is like Hannah's; it was almost a commonplace in coastal towns. See also Mary Blewett, "'I Am Doom to Disappointment': 1849-51," *Essex Institute Historical Collections* 117 (1981): 191-212.

24. The story of Harriet Hanson and William S. Robinson is told in Claudia Bushman, *A Good Poor Man's Wife* (Hanover, N.H.: University Press of New England, 1981). Her journal is in the Schlesinger Library, Radcliffe College, Cambridge, Mass.

25. Larcom to Annie Adams Fields, 11 September 1863; quoted by permission of the Houghton Library, Harvard University, Cambridge, Mass. Whittier wrote James T. Fields, asking, "Who wrote 'A Loyal Woman's No!'—Was it Lucy Larcom? I though it might be" (J. B. Pickard, *Letters of Whittier,* 3: 54-55, 25 December 1863).

26. My statement contradicts Warren S. Tryon, *Parnassus Corner: A Life of James T. Fields, Publisher to the Victorians* (Boston: Houghton Mifflin, 1963), 290, but everything I have read in the letters leads me to believe that Fields and Annie Fields kept firm control over the magazine.

27. See Tryon, *Parnassus Corner*; and James C. Austin, *Fields of the "Atlantic Monthly": Letters to an Editor, 1861-1870* (San Marino, Calif.: Huntington Library Press, 1953), for accounts of the controversy from Fields's point of view.

28. Generally scholars have mixed up Larcom's first book, *Similitudes*, 1853, with her first book of poems, 1868; usually they add that the earlier book was published by Ticknor and Fields, when the publisher was in fact John P. Jewett.

29. Robinson journal, 8 November 1868.

30. Addison, *Lucy Larcom,* 68. He gives no date; I assume the letter was written after 1868 because there are no more editing letters from Whittier and because Larcom's attitude about her work changed at this time.

31. Ibid., 198. The letter was written by Whittier to Oliver Wendell Holmes; Holmes quoted the passage in a letter of congratulations to Larcom.

32. James R. Osgood to Larcom, 25 July 1873; by permission of the Massachusetts Historical Society. The letter, pleasant enough in tone, is very patronizing; it also reveals Osgood's belief that only Larcom could get Whittier involved in these anthologies, and it suggests plans for further books by Larcom.

33. J. B. Pickard, *Letters of Whittier,* 3:307-308, 19 November 1873.

34. S. T. Pickard, *Life of Whittier,* 2:575; the letter is dated November 1871.

35. Larcom to Mary B. Claflin, 25 August 1875; quoted by permission of the Rutherford B. Hayes Presidential Center Library, Fremont, Ohio.

36. J. B. Pickard, *Letters of Whittier,* 3:338-339, 22 September 1875; the undated letter is given in a note on the same page.

37. Larcom to Elizabeth Whittier Pickard, 16 October 1892; quoted by permission of the Houghton Library.

38. S. T. Pickard, *Whittier-Land,* 110-118.

39. Gosse is quoted in Edwin Watts Chubb, *Stories of Authors* (New York: Macmillan, 1926), 317-318. For the more usual view, see Richard P. Zollo, "Oak Knoll—Whittier's Hermitage," *Essex Institute Historical Collections* 117 (1981): 27-42.

40. Larcom to Elizabeth Whittier Pickard, 19 April 1877; quoted by permission of the Houghton Library.

41. Most of this active correspondence is in the Houghton Library.

42. Harriet Minot Pitman to John Greenleaf Whittier, 13 October and 2 November 1883; quoted by permission of the Houghton Library.

43. Elizabeth Stuart Phelps (Ward), "The Bearer Falls," *Independent,* 4 May 1893.

44. Larcom to Elizabeth Whittier Pickard, 16 October 1892; quoted by permission of the Houghton Library.

45. Larcom to Samuel T. Pickard, 11 November 1892; quoted by permission of the Houghton Library.

46. Larcom to S. T. Pickard, 21 November 1892; quoted by permission of the Houghton Library.

47. Larcom to John Greenleaf Whittier, 30 October 1857; quoted by permission of the Wheaton College Library.

48. Larcom, *Girlhood,* 274.

49. Larcom, to Frank Garrison, 13 November 1884, and to Henry O. Houghton, 11 November 1884; quoted by permission of the Houghton Library.

James E. Rocks (essay date 1993)

SOURCE: Rocks, James E. "Whittier's *Snow-Bound*: 'The Circle of Our Hearth' and the Discourse on Domesticity." In *Studies in the American Renaissance,* edited by Joel Myerson, pp. 339-53. Charlottesville, Va.: The University Press of Virginia, 1993.

[*In the following essay, Rocks maintains that Snow-Bound, in its affirmation of the comforts and protection of family life, offered a war-weary nation the consolation it so desperately needed in the years immediately following the Civil War.*]

When John Greenleaf Whittier's younger sister Elizabeth, the companion of his mature years, died on 3 September 1864, he suffered a loss no less severe than if a wife of many years had died. More sociable than her shy brother, Elizabeth had been at the center of his life, the person whose support had helped nurture a public career of considerable success and fame and a private domestic life of exceptional warmth and security. Writing to his wide circle of friends, particularly to Gail Hamilton, Grace Greenwood, and Lydia Maria Child, he expressed the profound depression that her death had induced, but also his acceptance of the will of God that had determined the course of his sister's illness and death. To Annie Fields, his publisher's wife and among his closest women friends, he wrote: "I find it difficult even now to understand and realize all I have lost. But I sorrow without repining, and with a feeling of calm submission to the Will which I am sure is best."[1]

While acceptance of the divine ways distinguishes Whittier's letters to his consoling friends, Elizabeth's death brought about a major transition in his life. One consequence of this change was a temporary failure with language; the glib pen that had composed dozens of poems on national, political, and social topics was unable to express this personal loss. To Theodore Tilton, a New York journalist who supported abolition and women's rights, Whittier expressed his speechlessness in a terse, poetic line: "I cannot now write anything worthy of her memory."[2] Responding to his friends' condolences was painful but necessary; expressing the meaning of his sister's life as his companion and the domestic order and tranquility which she, like their parents before her, had sustained for him was far more difficult. Within a year the Civil War concluded, and one of his last, and best, anti-slavery poems **"Laus Deo"** put some finality on a lifetime of combatting slavery. And by October 1865 he finished the work that was "worthy of her memory." Published in February 1866, **Snow-Bound** became Whittier's most popular and famous—and his best—work, one of the important autobiographical writings of the nineteenth century. It was, as Robert Penn Warren has aptly called it, a "summarizing poem,"[3] because in it Whittier discovered the power of language again—the very weapon against the destructive, frightening natural world that his solitary family employs in the charmed circle around the hearth—and because the poem articulated the domestic

and gender ideology of Whittier's time to an audience ready to be healed after the schism of the Civil War and responsive to a philosophy that linked home, hearth, and heaven into one vision of a unified past and future.

Readings of **Snow-Bound** have generally not placed the poem in the context of Whittier's whole life—why the poem came to be at a critical time in his personal life, his public career, and the post-Civil War period of anticipated reconciliation and the reuniting of the "house divided." Studies have recognized the complexity of his personality and the interrelationship of his work and his times and, more recently, his advocacy of women in the literary marketplace, but they have not examined sufficiently the domestic and gender ideological issues that give the poem its considerable relevance as a coalescence of the discourses on domestic economy during the first half of the nineteenth century. **Snow-Bound** deserves to be reread for the wealth of its connections to the important discussions of the time on family and home. Whittier's definition of the masculine and the feminine in the poem reveals his long-held beliefs about his own gender identity, at a time when male writers often felt insecure about their masculinity in a commercial world, and discloses his traditional values regarding the family and women's role, which was defined in the writings of, among others, Catharine Beecher and her sister Harriet Beecher Stowe, as that of the dominant moral authority of society. While his portrayal of women in **Snow-Bound** does partake of the sentimental tradition of the time, his views in that poem, as well as in his letters, transcend the purely patriarchal and reflect his strong Quaker principle of human rights.

In an essay on the Scottish poet William Burleigh in the 9 September 1847 issue of the *National Era,* the anti-slavery paper of which he was for fifteen years a contributing editor and in which most of his literary works appeared until the founding of the *Atlantic Monthly* in 1857, Whittier described a poetic country very like the one he would create in **Snow-Bound.** The charm of the poetry of Scotland, he wrote, was "its simplicity, and genuine, affected sympathy with the common joys and sorrows of daily life. It is a home-taught, household melody." He also lamented that the poetry of home, nature, and the affections was lacking in America; there were no songs of American domestic life, "no Yankee pastorals."[4] By the time Whittier accomplished in **Snow-Bound** his call for a native form of the antique genre, there were already major examples of the pastoral, but by the mid-1860s the genre was rather played out (except of course for Whitman), and much of the appeal of **Snow-Bound** was its backward glance to a simpler world, to a time prior to the social and political upheaval of the 1830s to 1860s. Whittier's readers had always valued him for what James Russell Lowell, in the *North American Review* of January 1864, called his "intense home-feeling." Later, in a review of

Snow-Bound, Lowell expressed the effect of the poem's nostalgia on a sentimental audience: "It describes scenes and manners which the rapid changes of our national habits will soon have made as remote from us as if they were foreign or ancient."[5] Lowell was correct in his assessment of the poem's appeal, but his future verb tense was mistaken; by the time of the publication of Whittier's major poem, those rapid social changes had already made the scenes and manners of the world of Whittier's boyhood farm remote and quaint for many of his readers.[6]

In *Snow-Bound* Whittier returned to his youthful past for two immediate, compelling, yet contradictory reasons. He wanted his niece Lizzie to know the family portrait, and he needed the money that a longer poem about the rural past could earn. But there were also other reasons, perhaps not so easily identified, that inspired his "winter idyl." Creating this poem would bring further healing to the recovery from his loss of Elizabeth and, unaware as he might have been of another consequence, it would contribute in a small way to the public appeals for national reconciliation after the Civil War. And most importantly *Snow-Bound* would characterize a domestic ideology of home and hearth that, dated as it might have seemed to some readers in Whittier's time, was, however, a representation of the principal values that had defined the American family in the nineteenth century. Whittier's desire to recreate his home life served both his own practical and emotional needs and those of a nation seeking order once again; for Whittier the time could not have been more favorable.

On the flyleaf of a first edition of *Snow-Bound,* Whittier wrote some lines in 1888 expressing the faith and peace of his old age (he would die within two years). Thinking of the time when he composed his pastoral, he wrote about his sorrow then: "Lone and weary life seemed when / First these pictures of the pen / Grew upon my page."[7] The general dispiritedness and lack of confidence in his poetic ability, exacerbated by and contributing to his chronic ill health, are reflected in the letters he wrote, primarily to James T. Fields, during the several months (August to October 1865) while he was composing and revising the poem. Because Whittier tended to be self-effacing in his correspondence—and particularly so to other writers and his publisher—he refers to his manuscript only as "tolerably good" or "pretty good."[8] To Lucy Larcom, a close friend of Elizabeth and one of his "pupils" among the women authors he knew, Whittier wrote in a postscript to a letter in January 1866, a month before the poem's publication: "I'm not without my misgivings about it."[9] On the other hand, reading proofs of it in December 1865, he wrote Fields that he agreed with him and his wife Annie that the poem was "good"; furthermore, he took a particular interest in its physical make-up, engravings,

and date of publication (a December distribution would make it a timely gift-book, he suggested), and fussed over some last-minute revisions. His anxieties were groundless: within two months of the February publication, *Snow-Bound* had sold 10,000 copies and by midsummer 20,000 copies. Ultimately Whittier earned $10,000 from this one volume; its success provided him economic security and reaffirmed his poetic reputation.[10]

Whittier's uncertainty about the worth of his poem was typical of his general insecurity as a writer throughout his career; later, despite the critical and financial success of *Snow-Bound,* he would say that subsequent poems, however less inspired, were better. Scholars of Whittier's writings have always noted his lack of a keen critical insight, into both his own and others' writings, although he was an unpatronizing advocate and support of the many women authors who wrote and visited him with accounts of their craft. This uncertainty about his own vocation—at once liking and not liking his compositions—is an example of the pattern of oppositions and contradictions that critics have found in his own life and in the imagery and themes of *Snow-Bound.* Whittier was torn between the quiet study and the fretful political scene, and his life can best be defined as an oscillation between the public and the private—a pattern of outside and inside that dominates the theme of *Snow-Bound,* as John B. Pickard and other critics have demonstrated, and reveals its autobiographical dimensions. Because Whittier identified an old teacher from his Haverhill past as the source of the character of the schoolmaster, scholars have not recognized an important autobiographical connection between the schoolmaster and an idealized young Whittier. The schoolmaster can be read as an artistic representation of the adolescent Whittier, because the schoolmaster depicts the youthful artist-thinker, comfortable near the hearth but anxious to go outside into the world where he can make a reputation if not achieve fame. Manliness, for Whittier, as it was for many male writers during this period, could be experienced in the making of strong poetic verse, crafted in the cause of social and political change. The anxiety of manhood was overcome in the world outside the home, which was defined and controlled by women as a place of refuge from the active world of material gain and political turmoil.

Writing in 1882, Whittier looked back on his shy youth as a time of "vague dreams and ambitions and fancies interweaving with [his] common-place surroundings."[11] In an early poem, written in his teens, Whittier stated that he needed to seek out an education because he did not want to grow up a "fool."[12] Whittier's own statements—both early and late in his writings—confirm his commitment to a life that alternates action with repose, the life of the scholar in rhythm with that of the man of political and social involvement. Whenever he returned to the farm in the early decades of his life, he did so out of the necessity of family responsibility, money, or the too-intense activity of his political, journalistic, and abolitionist work. And when he came to write *Song-Bound,* his poem of reconciliation with the past and future, he put himself into it not only as the first-person narrator but also as the schoolmaster, who was the man Whittier had hoped to become and the man who would guide the country into a new era of peace and renewal. Whittier's young schoolmaster characterizes the ideal blend of the artistic and the scholarly with masculine athleticism; like Whittier himself he was nurtured in the domestic setting and yet, through books and experience, went out to meet the future. The schoolmaster's father, exactly like Whittier's, was a yeoman who worked the land for a meager but adequate livelihood: "By patient toil subsistence scant, / Not competence and yet not want."[13] In the tradition of schoolmasters in American literature, Whittier's is a jovial, sociable type, attracted like Whittier to vivacious and charming women; also he is independent and self-reliant, one who combines the practical and abstract in clear-sighted balance: he "[c]ould doff at ease his scholar's gown / To peddle wares from town to town" (454-55). As a storyteller he could domesticate the antique and the exotic, bringing to the realm of the commonplace the great scenes of the historical past and interpreting for his audience those moments in terms it could easily associate with the homely and everyday: "dread Olympus at his will / Became a huckleberry hill" (478-79).

A major reason for the popularity of *Snow-Bound,* and one which critics have not adequately emphasized, is the poem's rhetoric of reconciliation and consolation for a future in which all wrongs will be righted and freedom will replace slavery. The schoolmaster is just such a man for that task, and in a major section of the poem (480-510) Whittier envisions the new America, a land that will be led by young apostles like the schoolmaster, who will eliminate pride, ignorance, prejudice, and treason, and restore wisdom, learning, equality, and peace. These powerful lines reveal Whittier's hope for the restoration of the American promise, and they look back to his own past when he envisioned his career committed to the abolition of slavery: "Large-brained, clear-eyed, of such as he / Shall Freedom's young apostles be" (485-86). The schoolmaster is the leader of a future America, reconciling the opposites of Yankee and Southerner, working inside and outside the family and uniting rural and urban. In the character of the schoolmaster Whittier defined some important traits of masculinity in the self-reliant scholar-poet, values of male gender ideology among writers of his time that he attempted to demonstrate in his own behavior and writing.[14]

Snow-Bound is as deeply connected to the period after the Civil War as it is to the time of Whittier's boyhood, because it offers consolation not only for the poet, who had lost a close relative, but also for the nation at large, which had lost many family members. The deaths of one million soldiers during the war required this need for reconciliation, which was reflected in the popular works of the time, among them, for example, *The Gates Ajar* (1868) by Elizabeth Stuart Phelps, another close friend among the many women writers Whittier mentored.[15] The sense of having survived so much loss after the war is pondered in a major passage of the poem as Whittier reflects on the change that comes with the passage of time. With everyone in his family dead except his brother, he thinks of how strange it seems "with so much gone / Of life and love, to still live on!" (181-82). Even though his sentiment refers to the changes in his own family, it opens out to include the whole American nation, which had suffered such a collective loss but still continued to live and needed to find through memory and faith the connections to a meaningful past and a hopeful future. Just as during the war, in popular songs and poems, the image of the home as a haven of comfort and escape was kept alive for the homeless soldiers, so after the war the idea of home as a place of order and permanence—and as a setting for the remembrance of deceased family members and friends—took on for Americans an even more potent meaning. In the connections between the Civil War and domestic ideology, *Snow-Bound* reunites the "house divided" and sanctifies the "holy hearth" (Whittier's description in the poem **"To My Sister"**) as an anticipation of heaven.[16]

In the prominent passage on time and change Whittier states that the once living family members have left the familiar premises: "No step is on the conscious floor!" (199). The home, especially the farm, as a setting of familial love, connectedness, and identity is central to the ideology and imagery of the whole poem and especially to that important, if traditional, consolation section. To Whittier's readers during the first half of the nineteenth century, engaged as they were by the rhetoric of domesticity, the definition of home was a foremost cultural and social issue. The discourse on domesticity engaged a wide and important number of commentators, among them some of the women authors whom Whittier counted as his best friends and correspondents—Lydia Sigourney is a major example—not to mention a considerable group of both men and women authors whose works he did not necessarily know first hand (we have no evidence in his essays or letters, for instance) but whose ideology was so pervasive in the thinking of the time that it had at least an indirect influence on his own conceptualization of domestic values. As he was deeply involved in the anti-slavery discourse of the time, with its accompanying feminist commentaries on women's political rights, he was quite aware of the discussions on domestic ideology that characterized much of the writing of his peers. *Snow-Bound* brings together, and helps us to understand, the varied discourses on domesticity and gender during the first half of the century.

Whittier's Quaker upbringing and the life-long practice of his family faith engendered his fervent abolitionism, and they also explain the profound belief in domestic values that runs through his writings. The famous Quaker family scene in Chapter XIII of *Uncle Tom's Cabin* works an important intertextuality with *Snow-Bound* because in it Stowe characterizes the domestic economy that slavery destroyed; for Stowe black women needed and deserved the same domestic authority that white women could achieve.[17] Whittier was deeply moved by Stowe's novel, published in the *National Era* from June 1851 to April 1852, while he was a corresponding editor of the paper. In a letter to William Lloyd Garrison he called the novel "glorious" and twice after it was published he wrote his praises to Stowe in equally religious terms, rhetoric that is rare in Whittier's often laudatory expressions of literary judgment or political commentary: "Ten thousand thanks for thy immortal book!"; "I bless God for it, as I look with awe and wonder upon its world moving mission."[18] The power of Stowe's novel resided in, among other ideas and images, the ideal domestic order in which each family member contributed to the general economic good, with no one segment of the human family subservient to another and denied the domestic circle.

Although the Quaker settlement depicted by Stowe is more sentimentalized than Whittier's boyhood home in *Snow-Bound,* it represents the domestic ideal of the time expounded in the popular handbooks on house design and on the nurturing ministrations of the capable wife, all of which were familiar to Whittier's audience. The opening paragraph of Chapter XIII describes the perfect kitchen design, neat, orderly, and comfortable, and features the "motherly," "persuasive," and "honest" rocking chair where Eliza sits, which like the Quaker mother Rachel's old rocker is the central symbol of this domestic paradise. Such possessions of the material culture, like the tea kettle, "a sort of censer of hospitality and good cheer," or the knives and forks, which "had a social clatter as they went on to the table," define and unite the home and the homemaker and are given human attributes; they make music to accompany Rachel's "loving words, and gentle moralities, and motherly loving kindness."[19] Rachel is the ideal Quaker mother, quite like Whittier's own mother and her representation in *Snow-Bound*; she is beautiful in her maturity and adept at all domestic and culinary tasks, both a healer of ills and a bringer of harmony and good fellowship. Most important, she is the maker of a home, a concept that George Harris, as a deracinated slave, has never been able to comprehend. Stowe's portrait of the home in this chapter emphasizes the Christian definition that prevailed during these antebellum

decades; her language shares the rhetoric of Whittier's tributes to Stowe in his letters and reflects Whittier's own description of the family circle in *Snow-Bound.*

To combat slavery, alcoholism, and women's disenfranchisement, reform movements in the early nineteenth century sought support from the institution of the family, which was often defined in terms of the domestic economy represented in Stowe's famous novel and by the architecture and decoration of the houses wherein the family resided. Clifford E. Clark, Jr., summarizes this social phenomenon: "[The] influence of the temperance and anti-slavery movements together with the new outlook of Protestantism, the reaction against the pace of social change, the need for new housing, the expansion of the cities, and the vogue of romanticism all served to give the advocates of domestic housing reform an unprecedented influence on the American public."[20] The number of handbooks that recommended house design and argued for the rural home as a place of seclusion from the activities of a material economy demonstrates the significance of appropriate housing as a key component in the discussions on domestic economy. Sara Josepha Hale, in *Godey's Lady's Book,* for example, wrote often about the ideal home, as did Andrew Jackson Downing, in *The Architecture of Country Houses,* and Catharine Beecher, in *Treatise on Domestic Economy,* two works that provide an important background to understanding the timely success of Whittier's pastoral poem on domestic and gender ideology.

Downing's essay on rural architecture first appeared in 1850 and went through nine printings and sold 16,000 copies by the end of the Civil War. Among the many such treatises and handbooks that were widely read in the period of the 1840s to the 1860s, Downing's popularized the current ideology of the house as a civilizing, moral force for the betterment of the genius and character of the family. For Downing, as for most of these writers, the rural cottage and farm house, closely connected to the soil, of an ample, solid design and built of enduring material, were the best environments for nurturing family values. The farmer's dwelling, he wrote, "ought to suggest simplicity, honesty of purpose, frankness, a hearty, genuine spirit of goodwill, and a homely and modest, though manly and independent, bearing in his outward deportment."[21] Although Whittier was not familiar, so far as we can determine, with Downing's popular book, these sentiments on the farmhouse might well have been his own, phrased in language he would have used, especially the notion of the manliness of the house and its resident farmer.

Snow-Bound celebrates Downing's sturdy rural cottage, in a setting of pastoral harmony, that conforms to the landscape and unites the inner world of the hearth with the outer world of the barns, lands, and farm animals. In the essay cited earlier on the Scottish poet William Burleigh, Whittier commented on the numerous "great, unshapely, shingle structures, glaring with windows, which deform our landscape."[22] He recognized the need for an attractive, yet functional house, such as Downing and other commentators described, wherein the family could live harmoniously and communicate openly. Although Whittier's childhood home at Haverhill was built in the late seventeenth century, it possessed the qualities which later theorists on house design would advocate, in part to recapture the nostalgia of an earlier pioneer time, when the family unit was even stronger. Many of the writers on farmhouse architecture emphasized the need for sight lines from house to barn so that the farmer and his wife could keep watch over the activities of the whole farm. In those sections of *Snow-Bound* in which Whittier describes the barn activities during the snowstorm (19-30, 81-92)—passages which Robert Penn Warren mistakenly calls "dead filler"[23]— Whittier is connecting the inner and outer worlds in a rhythm that defines his own personal ideology of retreat from and action in society. His farm setting epitomizes the ideal rural home as fashioned and advocated by Downing and other popular writers on the architectural design of the time.[24]

Whittier was acquainted with probably the most popular of these writers on family values, Harriet Beecher Stowe. Her sister, Catharine Beecher, was the author of several works on female hegemony and the culture of the home, one of them co-authored with Stowe, *The American Woman's Home* (1869). *Treatise on Domestic Economy,* which first appeared in 1841 and was reprinted almost every year from 1841 to 1856, gained Beecher the reputation, as her biographer Kathryn Kish Sklar states, "as a national authority on the psychological state and the physical well-being of the American home."[25] Like *Uncle Tom's Cabin* Beecher's writing contextualizes Whittier's poem, because it expounds the female ideal portrayed in *Snow-Bound*: the wife who acquires her status and identity by creating the home setting that nurtures children and draws a circle of repose for the enterprising husband. In order to fulfill herself, argued Beecher, a woman must put the needs of others before her own desires; as Sklar writes, "Self-sacrifice, more than any other concept, informed both the triumph and tensions of nineteenth-century womanhood, and Catharine Beecher was its major theoretician."[26] She believed that the general good of society required women to be the moral foundation of a democratic society and the healer of social conflict, and in this role women could gain authority. Never could she be on an equal footing politically with men but her role as domestic ideologue would give her identity in a society dominated by men and commerce. "A woman, who is habitually gentle, sympathizing, forbearing, and cheerful," Beecher wrote, "carries an atmosphere about her, which imparts a soothing and sustaining influence, and renders it easier for all to do right, under her administration, than in any other situation."[27] Beecher attributed to women the responsibility for Christian nurture in the home, thus serving, ultimately, the welfare of the state by integrating domestic values with a reformed social and political morality.

Catharine Beecher's doctrine of female influence did not admit of true equality between the sexes but defended women's superior role as mistress of the household, wherein the family could attain Christian faith and moral rectitude. Because of his Quaker background, Whittier believed that women as well as men possessed the capacity for inner light, and throughout his career he appreciated and supported the intellectual and artistic talents of many women friends. On the other hand, however, Whittier never actively supported women's right to enfranchisement and political equality, and accepted the belief of Beecher and other writers that women's domestic tasks were her first and principal duties, although he demonstrated repeatedly in his letters that women could strive for literary recognition and economic prosperity. Furthermore, Whittier tended to accept the conventional notion that men's and women's responsibilities were distinctly separate.[28] In Stowe's Quaker family Rachel and Simeon Halliday respect one another as equals in a Christian family, but Stowe's chapter clearly portrays them as master and mistress of separate spheres, she of the kitchen and he of the political world outside. What gives Rachel her ultimate authority, as Beecher and Whittier would have it, is her capacity to inculcate Christian morality into her children so that they may make the right judgments in the complex moral dilemmas they will face in the political world outside the protection of the home.

Catharine Beecher's treatise and Stowe's Rachel define the model woman by what was then understood and has come to be known as the angel of the house, a metaphor that appropriates the religious rhetoric permeating all these domestic discourses during the nineteenth century. Of central interest to a reading of *Snow-Bound* is Whittier's treatment of the female gender ideology of the period in his portraits of the women of his childhood home; more than the men, even the schoolmaster with his future-oriented vision, they represent the central morality of a poem that drew a sizable audience because of its ideological resonances. Although the descriptions of the women of his family comprise only about twenty percent of the lines of the poem, the importance of these portraits is considerably greater than the proportion of lines assigned to them. These women define the benign piety and ministering goodness of the angel, particularly in the character of Whittier's mother, Abigail Whittier, from her first appearance in the poem turning her spinning wheel to one of the last references to her as an aid to and healer of the sick, the "Christian pearl of charity" (673), desiring that no one during those dark nights of "mindless wind" (102) and "[d]ead white" snow (147) will lack warmth and security. Whittier's mother universalizes the meaning of home in her story-telling; as a maker of words while spinning her thread, she casts a poet's spell of fact and fantasy to conquer nature's "spell" of fearsome weather. She defines a "simple life and country ways" (265) and unifies the home of the past with the homes of the present, her own and those of the readers' real and imagined homes: "She made us welcome to her home; / Old hearths grew wide to give us room" (267-68).[29] Abigail Whittier is the angel of light described in Cornelius Agrippa's occult writings, a passage of which serves as one epigraph to the poem; these angels come alive in the presence of the wood fire of the hearth, the earthly counterpart to the celestial fire of heaven, and transform the temporal home into a holy place.

Whittier's unmarried aunt, his mother's sister, Mercy Evans Hussey, is described as "homeless" (354) because, as Whittier expresses it, a "Fate / Perverse" (352-53) had denied her a husband. While she never had her own home, she, like so many unmarried women of her time, found a place of security and identity in her family's home. "[W]elcome wheresoe'er she went" (356), she epitomizes Beecher's code of female selflessness and represents an untarnished innocence and virginity which Whittier praises even though her spinsterhood is out of the natural scheme of things, as he defines a woman's life. Like all of the women in the poem, except of course Harriet Livermore, his aunt is the angel whose "presence seemed the sweet income / And womanly atmosphere of home" (358-59). Domestic economy, represented in the play on the word "income," derives not only from the farmer in the field but from the woman at the hearth. Whittier admonishes the reader strongly not to judge ill of her innocence, as if to defend the single person, like himself, who can keep the ideal in an imperfect, changing world. Self-sacrifice as an attribute of feminine behavior is reflected even more fully in Mary Whittier, the oldest child, who had been an active support of her brother's poetic career but whose own domestic career failed for want of a happy marriage. A truthful, just, trusting, and impulsive woman, she "let her heart / Against the household bosom lean" (393-94). Whittier sees in her death the only consolation possible for a life of bitter regret; in this conventional response he acknowledges society's judgment of the irrevocable effects of a bad marriage on a woman's life and concedes only one option for his elder sister, a return to the first home and duty to the original family hearth.

Whittier's final portrait of the women in his youthful household is of Elizabeth, whom he remembers as an adult, not as a childhood contemporary. The poetic theme of the permanence of memory is represented in Elizabeth, whose death brought a "loss in all familiar things" (420) but a gain in the richness of a remembered past. He recognizes his own mortality more acutely and anticipates a reunion with her in paradise. The angel of their house has become an "Angel of the backward look" (715), or the spirit of memory, lately transformed into an angel of heaven. She is a guide, with her large eyes as beacons, leading the elder Whittier, known all his life for his own intense and penetrating eyes, from his earthly home to his divine home. The summer vision beginning with line 407 to the end of that section (437) articulates Whittier's religious philosophy, in a passage of traditional, yet intensely felt, Christian rhetoric of the hoped-for afterlife.

Although each of the women in Whittier's family—Elizabeth most fully—exemplifies the type of the nineteenth-century angel, Harriet Livermore contrasts dramatically with that ideal and sits outside the family circle. She may be characterized as the spirit of darkness in Cornelius Agrippa's polarity of light and darkness; isolated in the farmhouse because of the weather, her "darkness" is not lightened by the wood fire of the family circle. She combines an uneasy mix of light and dark, her light described paradoxically as "dangerous" (527) and "sharp" (528). The portrait of Livermore is one of the longest in the poem and is separated from the portraits of the other family members by the highly autobiographical description of the schoolmaster, to whom she is more akin. Her delineation works a notable opposition to the values of the domestic ideology in the poem and complicates Whittier's depiction of the world outside, which the men must enter for their self-definition. Although clearly womanly in her appearance—one thinks of Hawthorne's Zenobia, who is at once more beguiling and less daunting—Livermore possesses traits that the ideology of the time would define as masculine. Whittier describes her passionate, bold, self-centered, wilful temperament combined with her womanly shape: "Her tapering hand and rounded wrist / Had facile power to form a fist" (538-39). Her personality and appearance define her contradictory nature, and because she can never join a conventional domestic circle, she succumbs to eccentric religious beliefs and fitful rambling. Whittier acknowledges his compassion for her solitary wanderings, her unrequited love, and her "outward wayward life" (565), which contrasts with the inward domestic life he celebrates. The "tumultuous privacy of storm" which rages outside in Emerson's "The Snow-Storm" (the second epigraph) describes the emotional turbulence of her unorthodox, antisocial behavior and her "unbent will's majestic pride" (518). The character of Harriet Livermore adds depth and complexity to *Snow-Bound* and compares with that of the schoolmaster, likewise an "outward" person. In Whittier's conceptualization of gender identities the schoolmaster has the privilege (indeed the necessity) to venture outside, but his quintessential self has been formed within the domestic circle and as a man he has the right to seek his individuality. Livermore's religious eccentricities are cause and effect of her drawing a circle around herself and excluding all others from those bounds. Because she possesses traits that are distinctly masculine according to the gender ideology of the time, she fails to live up to the eternal feminine and suffers accordingly.[30]

Whittier's interest in Harriet Livermore reveals a curious fascination with an unconventional woman who sacrifices her domestic role and becomes, by circumstance and choice, a homeless wanderer, the dreaded result of rejecting the charmed circle. Whittier's other women, who fulfill the responsibilities allotted to them by the ideology of the time, are never homeless; in fact, they define the place of their existence and sanctify it. Through the ministrations of women, the home, as the paradigm of a democratic society, fosters traditional values in children and tempers commercial and political assertiveness in men, thereby moving American society toward a higher realm of virtue. In **Snow-Bound** Whittier affirms the domestic economy of his time and the personal values and family history of his Quaker heritage and defines the redeemed American family, lately broken apart by the Civil War but now ready for consolation and renewal. In the poem he recreates his younger self in the schoolmaster, a healer no less than Whittier's mother Abigail, who is the maternal ideal for the schoolmaster as she was for her own son. The merit of **Snow-Bound** resides in its fusion of public philosophy and private creed; written at a timely moment both for the poet and his society, the poem unites the many discourses of its age into an intricate pattern of theme and metaphor.

Notes

1. *The Letters of John Greenleaf Whittier,* ed. John B. Pickard, 3 vols. (Cambridge: Harvard University Press, 1975), 3:78.

2. *Letters,* 3:77. Tilton became famous for his disastrous suit against Henry Ward Beecher for allegedly committing adultery with Tilton's wife. Whittier found it difficult not to support Beecher.

3. *John Greenleaf Whittier: An Appraisal and a Selection* (Minneapolis: University of Minnesota Press, 1971), p. 47.

4. *Whittier on Writers and Writing,* ed. Edwin Cady and Harry Hayden Clark (Syracuse: Syracuse University Press, 1950), p. 121.

5. *Critical Essays on John Greenleaf Whittier,* ed. Jayne Kribbs (Boston: G. K. Hall, 1980), pp. 40, 42.

6. Roland Woodwell, Whittier's most recent biographer, explains the effect on the reader in 1866 of Whittier's reminiscence of a moribund culture:

"Deep in the American mind was a real or imagined love for the farm, often strongest in those who had never lived on a farm nor had their ancestors since the settlement of North America. Sitting in their warm homes, in the new luxury of a hot-air furnace and flaring gas chandeliers, they let their imagination give them a nostalgic delight in a life they had never known" (*John Greenleaf Whittier* [Haverhill, Mass.: Trustees of the John Greenleaf Whittier Homestead, 1985], p. 338) V. L. Parrington speaks of *Snow-Bound*'s "homely economy long since buried under the snows of forgotten winters." Whittier's economics, he says, have no relationship with "a scrambling free-soilism or a rapacious capitalism" (from his *Main Currents in American Thought* [1927-30], reprinted in *Critical Essays on Whittier,* p. 105). This is precisely the economic reality that domestic ideology in the nineteenth century was attempting to isolate; the home provided a haven from the marketplace. Whittier himself seemed to realize that he was dealing with a distant past when he wrote to Fields in August 1865 that he was creating a "homely picture of *old* New England times" (*Letters,* 3:99).

7. *The Complete Poetical Works of John Greenleaf Whittier* (Boston: Houghton, Mifflin, 1895), p. 525.

8. *Letters,* 3:99, 102.

9. *Letters,* 3:117. Whittier's long and complex half-century friendship with Lucy Larcom is chronicled in Shirley Marchalonis, "A Model for Mentors?: Lucy Larcom and John Greenleaf Whittier," in *Patrons and Protégées: Gender, Friendship and Writing in Nineteenth-Century America,* ed. Marchalonis (New Brunswick: Rutgers University Press, 1988), pp. 94-121.

10. *Letters,* 3:113, and Woodwell, *John Greenleaf Whittier,* p. 337.

11. *Letters,* 3:444.

12. *John Greenleaf Whittier's Poetry,* p. 4. Warren emphasizes Whittier's "almost pathological ambition" to find his position in the new American society of the nineteenth century. In one of his later poems, "My Namesake," Whittier speaks of the dichotomy of past and future that defines his career: "He reconciled as best he could / Old faith and fancies new" (*Complete Poetical Works,* p. 393).

13. Lines 450-51; further line numbers will appear in the text; the 1895 *Complete Poetical Works* is the source.

14. Whittier's portrait of Uncle Moses reveals an interesting treatment of male gender ideology; like Thoreau, his uncle was a student of nature and

woodcraft, who lived only within his own parish. "Content to live where life began" (325), he was the opposite type of Whittier and the schoolmaster, and possessed characteristics that are more like feminine gender values than the male behavior Whittier characterizes in his father and the schoolmaster.

15. Ann Douglas, "Heaven Our Home: Consolation Literature in the Northern United States, 1830-1880," in *Death in America,* ed. David E. Stannard (Philadelphia: University of Pennsylvania Press, 1975), p. 50.

16. In "To My Sister," Whittier speaks of their childhood home as a sanctified place, an image that implies an anticipation of the final home in heaven. Frances Armstrong, in *Dickens and the Concept of Home* (Ann Arbor: UMI Research Press, 1990), writes of the connection between the past and future home; the childhood home is "the place to which one can return to die, sure of an acceptance and foregiveness which will act as an encouraging preliminary to or even substitute for entry to heaven" (p. 2).

17. Gillian Brown, in *Domestic Individualism: Imagining Self in Nineteenth-Century America* (Berkeley: University of California Press, 1990), discusses the idea that in slavery the economic and personal status are never differentiated. She writes, concerning *Uncle Tom's Cabin:* "The call to the mothers of America for the abolition of slavery is a summons to fortify the home, to rescue domesticity from shiftlessness and slavery" (p. 16).

18. *Letters,* 2:191, 201, 213.

19. *Uncle Tom's Cabin,* in *Harriet Beecher Stowe: Three Novels,* sel. Kathryn Kish Sklar (New York: Library of America, 1982), pp. 162, 163, 165, 170.

20. "Domestic Architecture as an Index to Social History: The Romantic Revival and the Culture of Domesticity in America, 1840-1870," *Journal of Interdisciplinary History,* 7 (Summer 1976): 47.

21. *The Architecture of Country Houses* (New York: Dover, 1969 [1850]), p. 139.

22. *Whittier on Writers and Writing,* ed. Cady and Clark, p. 121. In a letter several years before his death, Whittier commented that in the life of the farmer the best gains could be made in the creation of pleasant homes (*Letters,* 3:563).

23. Warren, *John Greenleaf Whittier's Poetry,* p. 53.

24. The extensive writing on the flourishing discourse on domestic architecture during the nineteenth century includes the following excellent essays and books: Clifford Edward Clark, Jr., *The American Family Home, 1800-1960* (Chapel Hill: University of North Carolina Press, 1986); Oscar P. Handlin, *The American Home: Architecture and Society, 1815-1915* (Boston: Little, Brown, 1979); Dolores Hayden, *The Grand Domestic Revolution: A History of Feminist Designs for American Homes, Neighborhoods, and Cities* (Cambridge: MIT Press, 1981); Sally McMurray, *Families and Farmhouses in Nineteenth-Century America: Vernacular Design and Social Change* (New York: Oxford University Press, 1988); Maxine Van de Wetering, "The Popular Concept of 'Home' in Nineteenth-Century America," *Journal of American Studies,* 18 (April 1984): 5-28; and Gwendolyn Wright, *Building the Dream: A Social History of Housing in America* (New York: Pantheon, 1981). Wright states: "To the majority of citizens in the early republic, the ideal American home was an independent homestead, attractive enough to encourage family pride yet unpretentious and economical" (p. 73). Gaston Bachelard's *The Poetics of Space* (trans. Maria Jolas [New York: Orion, 1964]) offers valuable commentary on the felicitous space of old houses, where dreams and the imagination invigorate memories of the past, particularly during a winter storm. Bachelard's discussion on the dialectic of outside and inside the house has significance to a reading of *Snow-Bound.*

25. *Catharine Beecher: A Study in American Domesticity* (New Haven: Yale University Press, 1973), p. 151.

26. *Catharine Beecher,* p. xiv.

27. *Treatise on Domestic Economy for the Use of Young Ladies at Home and at School* (New York: Harpers, 1848), pp. 148-49.

28. Gail Hamilton (the pen name of Mary Abigail Dodge) was one of his most ardent, humorous, and lively correspondents, frequently playing the coy role almost of a beloved. In a letter to him in October 1865, she writes about his "household idyls, in which I know there will be serving and women doing daintily all manner of pretty feminine doings" (*Letters,* 3:103).

29. Thomas Wentworth Higginson confirmed Whittier's characterization of his mother as Beecher's ideal woman: "Mrs. Whittier was placid, strong, sensible, an exquisite housekeeper and 'provider'; it seems to me that I have since seen no whiteness to be compared to the snow of her table cloths and napkins" (quoted in Samuel T. Pickard, *Whittier-Land: A Handbook of North Essex* [Cambridge: Riverside Press, 1956 (1904)], p. 78). Mrs. Whittier's housekeeping talents are compa-

rable to Rachel Halliday's in *Uncle Tom's Cabin*. Eliza looks in on supper preparations and sees the table with its "snowy cloth" (p. 168); all these references to white connect with the dreamy state of Eliza's post-sleep languor to suggest the power of domesticity, defined curiously in language with racial overtones.

30. In a letter in 1879, Whittier recounted the subsequent history of Harriet Livermore and his later contacts with her; he states he did not exaggerate her personality in his poem and in this letter he describes her in more positive terms as "a brilliant darkeyed woman—striking in her personal appearance, and gifted in conversation." He does indicate, in a typical stereotyping of the time, that her peculiar behavior and fanaticism were "the result of a failed love affair" (*Letters*, 3:412-13).

Angela Michele Leonard (essay date summer 1995)

SOURCE: Leonard, Angela Michele. "The Topography of Violence in John Greenleaf Whittier's 'Antislavery Poems.'" *American Journal of Semiotics* 12, nos. 1-4 (summer 1995): 41-58.

[*In the following essay, Leonard examines "The Slave-Ships," "The Christian Slave," "Toussaint L'Ouverture," and other anti-slavery poems, contending that they are characterized by violent characters, settings, language, and actions.*]

The inspiration and source material of John Greenleaf Whittier's "Antislavery Poems" came from newspaper articles, contemporary literature, and historical accounts of chattel slavery. He heard and read about the "Middle Passage," southern plantations, auction blocks, proslavery evangelicals, Northern abolitionists, fugitive slaves as well as slave revolters. Whittier borrowed these images and other topics from the discourse of American slavery to produce a substantial canon of protest poetry that collectively inscribes a single vision of slavery—a topography of violence. Violence of catastrophic and grotesque dimensions permeates Whittier's antislavery verses because the very domain they describe—the reality of ante-bellum slavery—is an intrinsically violent one. Slavery, as Whittier demonstrates, is a Protean reality which even breeds violence in moral characters, like the infamous Haitian slave revolutionary Toussaint L'Ouverture, who reacted violently as a consequence of previous violence meted against him and his people.

Whittier's protest poems not only share, ideologically, an antislavery attitude, but also a consistent topographical rhetoric of violence: violence of place, language, and action, in addition to the violence of character just

mentioned above. This essay will sample a few of Whittier's poems, including **"The Slave-Ships"** (1834), **"The Christian Slave"** (1843), and **"Toussaint L'Ouverture"** (1833), to demonstrate how the topographical references produce this unmistakable impression of slavery as simply "hell on earth." Activity in the poems (e.g. the transformation of African captives into American slaves), place names, and character portrayal reinforce this vision of captivity as a 'hellish' reality of darkness, mayhem, and death. In fact, a semiotic survey of poetical settings, for example, "a slave-cursed land," "the valley of death," "heathen wilderness," "nether hell," and "soil of sin"—contain scriptural terms that buttress the idea of slavery as "hell on earth"; in fact, the phrase "Slavery's hateful hell" practically summarizes the reality. These references show an attachment to the historical record as well as the plethora of topothetic references that Whittier enlists to package his ideological stance. The catalogue of topoi contains a varied list of commercial/urban ("market-place," "trader's cell," and "prison-cell"), agricultural/rural ("low rice-swamp" and "fields of cane"), oceanic ("slaver"—meaning a ship of slaves, "slave-ship" and "ship's dark bosom"), and even geographically indefinite locations ("land of slaves" and "land of chains"). Most of these references establish a system of metonymies that extends the range of Whittier's topographical rhetoric throughout his antislavery verse and prose, and the historical contextualization of the descriptions reinforce Whittier's critique of slavocracy.

VIOLENCE OF PLACE AND ACTION: "THE SLAVE-SHIPS"

The single poem **"The Slave-Ships"** capitulates nearly all of the delineated settings mentioned above. In **"The Slave-Ships,"** Whittier reconstructs the account of the French ship Le Rôdeur in which twenty-two crew members and one hundred and sixty Negro slaves were stricken by a contagious disease culminating in blindness and death (Whittier 1834 [1969], 3:19-24):

> All ready?' cried the captain;
> 'Ay, Ay!' the seamen said;
> 'Heave up the worthless lubbers,—
> The dying and the dead.'
> Up from the slave-ship's prison
> Fierce, bearded heads were thrust:
> 'Now let the sharks look to it,—
> Toss up the dead ones first!'
> Corpse after corpse came up,—
> Death had been busy there;
> Where every blow is mercy,
> Why should the spoiler spare?
> Corpse after corpse they cast
> Sullenly from the ship,
> Yet bloody with the traces
> Of fetter-link and whip.
> Gloomily stood the captain,
> With his arms upon his breast,
> With his cold brow sternly knotted,

And his iron lip compressed.
'Are all the dead dogs over?'
Growled through the matted lip;
The blind ones are no better,
Let's lighten the good ship.'

                                        (lines 1-24)

In the above stanzas of **"The Slave-Ships,"** death, dying and the related term, corpse, appear a total of nine times. If one adds "worthless lubbers" which refers to dead bodies of slaves, as well as "the blind ones [who] are no better" than the dead, the count grows by two. Even the living in this setting assume a deadly persona. The captain, "with the cold brow, sternly knotted," and "iron lip compressed" is the very sight of an embalmed specimen, preserved by formaldehyde, or "cold" ice. Whereas the living are deathly, the dead are doubly dead. As the corpses are brought above deck, we learn that the slaves were nearly beaten to death before the disease assaulted them, since some bodies are "bloody with the traces / Of fetter-link and whip" (lines 15-16). Fundamentally, we learn in these two lines that a hellish reality preceded the onslaught of this massively fatal disease. The word "hell" (a central motif in Whittier's poetry) first appears in the fourth stanza, but the weight of the death (as suggested by the captain's desire to "lighten the good ship") and the image of gore in a world below deck—"the slave-ship's prison"—establishes a pre-existent state of hell. Phrase exchanges occur continuously between stanzas: "dead ones" in stanza one becomes "corpses" in stanza two; in stanzas four and five, "prison" becomes "the ship's dark bosom," and "death" above becomes "darkness" below. Nevertheless, in each instance, the circumstances remain the same:

Hark! from the ship's dark bosom,
The very sounds of hell!
The ringing clank of iron,
The maniac's short, sharp yell!
The hoarse, low curse, throat-stifled;
The starving infant's moan,
The horror of a breaking heart
Poured through a mother's groan.
Up from that loathsome prison
The stricken blind ones came:
Below, had all been darkness,
Above, was still the same.
Yet the holy breath of heaven
Was sweetly breathing there,
And the heated brow of fever
Cooled in the soft sea air.

                                        (lines 25-40)

Imagistically, "hell" is a motif that describes the historical contexts of many of Whittier's poems. Hell is right now, right here on earth. **"Slave-Ships"** vividly and emphatically dramatizes the presentness of this reality with the seaman's steady preoccupation with hauling "up" the dead and dying from a place of darkness, to a

world "Above, [which] was still the same" (line 36). The physical mutilation of the slaves below deck is matched by the "unsated shark" and by the vulturistic quality of the captain's vicarious consumption of the "blind ones" as he orders them fed to the sea.

In stanza seven, the poetic voice will engage in a dialogue with God, but a spiritual presence first appears in stanza five as "The holy breath of heaven / . . . sweetly breathing there" (lines 37-38). Yet this stanza responds to the sounds enumerated in stanza four:

God of the earth! what cries
Rang upward unto Thee?
Voices of agony and blood,
From ship-deck and from sea.
The last dull plunge was heard,
The last wave caught its stain,
And the unsated shark looked up
For human hearts in vain.

                                        (lines 49-56)

Stanza four gives a litany of sounds which are summarized as "cries" and "voices of agony and blood" in stanza five. This compression of a motley of tones: clanking iron, "maniac's short, sharp yell," "hoarse, low curse," "starving infant's moan" and "mother's groan" is not unlike the poet's suggestion that all "slave-ships"—noted by the title's plurality—are alike; all are hellish.

Thomas Braga, in his comparative study of the Brazilian poet "Castro Alves and the New England Abolitionist Poets," fails to recognize the propagandistic value of Whittier's "hellish" poetic settings. Instead, he contends that the rhetorical effect is minimized "by not couching the slave-trade in a national setting as [Antonio de] Castro Alves so effectively succeeded in doing" in "O navio negreiro" (1868, translated 'The Slaver: Tragedy at Sea') (Braga 1984: 586-87). However, the title of Whittier's poem **"The Slave-Ships"** directly challenges Braga's conclusion, for the ignominy of this particular setting is presented as exemplary of all "middle passages." If the poet had only one slave voyage in mind, presumably, the salient linguistic article in the title would be the indefinite "a" rather than the definitive "the." The different poetic audiences (slavers, slaves, and the narrator) in a single piece, as indicated by the shifting poetic voice, suggest a very large landscape of geographically indefinite territories (like "land of chains," "land of slaves," or "a slave-cursed land"), one in which the poet can traverse up and down and back and forth. In other words, the speaker in Whittier's verse compresses both mortal and immortal beings, and mundane and transcendent realities all into a single poem; the speaker, therefore, connects heaven to hell on earth. Heaven, a trope for God and spirit/uality, finds a way like the "breath of Heaven" that comes unexpect-edly and emerges illogically into an inhumane and demonic situation in the last stanza of **"The Slave-Ships."**

Slavery, itself, the legally and socially constructed institution in which Whittier's oppressed are formally and strategically contained, is an all-consuming "night of moral death" (**"The New Year"**—Whittier 1839 [1969], 3:63-69). Other descriptive and topographical images, such "valley of the dead" or "a slave-cursed land" in Whittier's **"The Watchers"** (1862 [1969], 3:223-26) and **"Mithridates at Chios"** (1863 [1969], 3:228-29), respectively, reek of finality and destruction and, thereby, metaphorically link slavery to violence. Equating slavery with death, dying, deadness or finality is quite common, and Whittier plays with this idea. Orlando Patterson calls it a state of "social death" by which he does not mean actual death but the equation of the absolute and total powerlessness of the slaves with death (Patterson 1982: 1-7; 10-13).

MANIPULATION OF LANGUAGE: "THE
CHRISTIAN SLAVE"

Whittier's poems give a panoramic view and history of the mercantilist institution of American slavery, prob-ably because many originate from news reports. Yet each piece takes us into a hellish realm. For example, the poem **"The Christian Slave"** at first leads one to assume, by virtue of its title, that the subject is a good Samaritan voluntarily doing "God's work" on earth. Yet this poem, ironically, Whittier based on "a description of a slave auction at New Orleans at which the auctioneer recommended the woman on the stand as A GOOD CHRISTIAN!'" Certainly the historical gloss on **"The Christian Slave"** makes evident that there is a depth and complexity in some of Whittier's antislavery poems which is not always obvious by a seemingly deceptively simple title. We come to realize that, in actuality, the "Christian slave" is in the service of men who are committed to sustaining and perpetuating an institution of bonded laborers. The first line of this poem introduces another tremulous institutional contriv-ance of chattel slavery, the slave auction, and simulta-neously—as expressed almost verbatim in **"Clerical Oppressors"** (Whittier 1836)—raises a major theme which persists in other antislavery verses by Whittier, for example, **"A Summons"** (1836), **"The Pastoral Letter"** (1837), and **"Pennsylvania Hall"** (1838): the ambiguity of the word "Christian." Let us consider first how Whittier reconstructs a slave auction (1843 [1969]:86-89):

> A CHRISTIAN! going, gone!
> Who bids for God's own image? for His
> grace,

> Which that poor victim of the market-
> place
> Hath in her suffering won?

(lines 1-4)

From the outset, Whittier introduces another hell that he mentions or recreates in many of his poems—e.g. **"Ex-postulation"** (1834), **"The New Year"** (1839), **"Daniel Neall"** (1846), **"Lines on the Portrait of a Celebrated Publisher"** (1850), and **"The Panorama"** (1856). This first stanza of **"The Christian Slave"** establishes hell as the slave market. An inverted and secularized use of the word "CHRISTIAN" transforms the context atmo-spherically, environmentally and ideologically. Spoken with force and volume, the ideological notion of "CHRISTIAN" is put forth as the society's professed ideal. But as soon as the traditional signification of the label becomes a figment of the past ("going, gone!"), the Christian becomes objectified ("who bids for . . . that poor victim of the market-place"). The economic construct abruptly pushes into the past and cancels out both the word "CHRISTIAN" as an idea or a person, and any notions of this as a place of / with Christians/ity. As a consequence of the sudden alteration of a pervasive form of consciousness, the entire scene is af-fected. Mimicking an auctioneer's cant (or rant), the very first line identifies not only the item sold, but also a departure from an ideological state signified by "CHRISTIAN."

Throughout Whittier, topographical rhetoric is employed to suggest how deeply moral concepts are couched in the language of men. Whittier frequently uses his skill to expose and exploit those who have no sense of their own moralizing language, like the auctioneer in **"The Christian Slave."** The idea of Christianity is constantly placed in opposition to the hellish reality constructed. Whereas the first line—"A CHRISTIAN! going, gone"—announces the departure of a Christian presence or religious ambiance, the second line—poised as a query—escorts us into the world of commerce. Signifi-cantly, though, this world of economic materiality is also a world of unreality, of intangibles, at least initially, since the poet displays his own resistance to the auction by asking "who bids for God's own image? for His grace . . .", rather than "who bids for the slave."[1] With the allusion to "poor victim" in **"The Christian Slave"** coupled with the pronominal reference to "her suffering," we are finally forced to confront the poetic context as a market in human flesh, where slaves have been "trampled down" and beaten into submission like cattle for sale. In a single stanza, then, the slave completely loses her humanity ('God-image'), becomes an object, and ultimately a commodity.

As stated above, the very first line of **"The Christian Slave"** underscores the slave's pitiless state of bondage. In fact, the closeness of "going, gone"—the juxtaposi-tion of the active and the passive—suggests the inescapable fate of the auction block and the defenselessness of the "poor victim." The only reward for "her suffering" is "His grace"—an intangible that is distinguished from its rhyme "place" by its immateriality. Moreover, just as "death" seemed antecedent to the wake of the disease aboard "the slaveships", "suffering" is posited as a precondition to the hellish, dehumanizing experience of the slave auction, as suggested by the pastness in "her suffering won". What the slave has won, however, is not the power to determine their legal and physical status, but instead a power with only inner, self-accessibility. The poet implies, then, that even in the midst of a hellish topos, the slave successfully endures because real strength resides within.

> My God! can such things be?
> Hast Thou not said that whatsoe'er is
> done
> Unto Thy weakest and Thy humblest
> one
> Is even done to Thee?
> In that sad victim, then,
> Child of Thy pitying love, I see Thee
> stand;
> Once more the jest-word of a mocking
> band,
> Bound, sold, and scourged again!
>
> (lines 5-12)

Like the slave ship captain, the damnable auctioneers in **"The Christian Slave"** exert economic, legal, verbal and physical power over their victims within the context of the poem through language: "Once more the jest-word of a mocking band, / Bound, sold, and scourged again!" (lines 11-12). The same action, however, which empowers slave dealers renders slaves speechless as demonstrated in a very similar passage from **"Expostulation"** (Whittier 1834 [1969], 3: 24-28):

> What! God's own image bought and
> sold!
> Americans to market driven,
> And bartered as the brute for gold!
> Speak! shall their agony of prayer
> Come thrilling to our hearts in vain? . . .
> Say, shall these writhing slaves of wrong
> Plead vainly for their plundered Right?
>
> (lines 22-26, 31-32)

Slaves only adopt a consistently verbal discourse after emancipation. When they speak as slaves, they communicate in agonizing or irregular sounds. But to the poet's rhetorical demands above, the slaves are mute, suggesting that the painful commodification, dehumanization, and de-christianizing experiences robbed them of all speech. Their pain is all of the body indicated by the description "writhing slaves of wrong."

The environmentally situated and institutional violence descriptive of slavery in Whittier's verse receive reinforcement in the form of overt physical acts (Whittier 1843 [1969], 3: 86-89):

> A Christian up for sale!
> Wet with her blood your whips, o'ertask
> her frame,
> Make her life loathsome with your wrong
> and shame,
> Her patience shall not fail!
> A heathen hand might deal
> Back on your heads the gathered wrong
> of years:
> But her low, broken prayer and nightly
> tears,
> Ye neither heed nor feel.
>
> (lines 13-20)

In stanza four of **"The Christian Slave"**, signs of physical violence, which reappear throughout Whittier's poetry, become more pronounced as the poet addresses a different audience, indicated by "your whips," and "your wrong and shame." Physical abuse is often introduced by the coupling of the words "blood" and "whip," as we note above in line 14 and as observed in **"The Slave-Ships"**—"Yet bloody with the traces / Of fetter-link and whip" (lines 14-15; Whittier 1834 [1969], 3: 19-24). However, stanza five suggests that physical cruelty takes a toll on both victim and oppressor. The oppressor loses emotional receptivity; numbed senses paralyze and destroy one's ability to respond to sensitive situations and to sensations. Inhumanity and violence, which overtakes the oppressors, as much as it "o'ertask [the slave's] frame," consumes their souls such that the victim's "low, broken prayer, and nightly tears / ye [They] neither heed nor feel" (lines 19-20; Whittier 1843 [1969], 3: 89). In **"Stanzas For the Times,"** sons of Revolutionary fathers "cease to feel" empathy for the persecuted or admonish priests who stand mute "when deeds are wrought / Which well might shame extremest hell" (lines 13, 25-26; Whittier 1835 [1969], 3: 35-38). Because of his own unyielding commitment to "the old Pilgrim Spirit," and unwavering faith in democratic "traditions dear and old," Whittier speaks harshly of those who breach what he perceives as their patriotic "fields of duty" (**"Anniversary Poem"**—Whittier 1863 [1969], 3: 241-45). He writes, you "shame your gallant ancestry . . . By watching round the shambles where human flesh is sold . . ." (**"Massachusetts to Virginia,"** lines 49-50; Whittier 1843 [1969], 3: 80-86). The worst wrong of all, however, he exclaims, is refusal to speak out against human atrocities: "Silence is crime!" (**"A Summons,"** line 9; Whittier 1836 [1969], 3: 40-43).

In Whittier, violence pervades the entire landscape making victims of all under its cloud. Slavery's accomplices become linked to slaveholders who are inherently tied to slaves. This chain of culpability and suffering Whittier details in **"Song of the Negro Boatmen"** (Whittier 1862 [1969], 3: 230-33):

> That laws of changeless justice
> bind

Oppressor with oppressed;
And, close as sin and suffering joined
We march to Fate abreast.

(lines 97-100)

Slavery, "the one cause of all the races / Holds both in tether" (**"Howard at Atlanta"**—Whittier 1869 [1969], 3: 264-66), locks black and white to a common fate of either freedom or bondage; "Guilty or guiltless, all within its range / Feel the blind justice of its sure revenge" (**"The Panorama"**—Whittier 1856 [1969], 3: 193-210).

VIOLENCE IN HUMAN FORM: CHARACTER INVERSION

Whittier uses language instrumentally to recast the contemporary literary image of the slave. He abandons typical stereotypes and literary conventions. Whittier's slaves, though a collective subject (except memorialized individuals), are not black criminalized stereotypes nor literary symbols like the "noble savage" alluded to by Thomas Braga, nor superior [nor inferior] to whites in Christian virtues as depicted by "romantic racialists" (Frederickson 1971: 97-129). In Whittier's antislavery poems, blacks appear typically as a collective identity (usually as a slave), but not as the traditional racialized stereotypes with names like Pompey, Mammy, George and Sambo. According to Thomas Braga, in much white Puritan abolitionist verse "slaves lack an individualized personality, appearing frequently as bodiless profiles incarnating a desire for freedom but nothing more." When they are not "Christ like figures" made in God's own image, like Whittier's **"Christian Slave,"** they "are postured in a Rousseauistic noble savage pastoral fashion such as Longfellow's "The Slave's Dream"" (Longfellow 1842; Braga 1984: 590):

Beside the ungathering rice he lay,
His sickle in his hand;
His breast was bare, his matted hair
Was buried in the sand.

Conversely, Whittier inverts the latter tradition in his tribute to Toussaint L'Ouverture. He writes (Whittier 1833 [1969], 3: 11-19):

. . . round the white man's lordly hall,
Trod, fierce and free, the brute he made;
And those who crept along the wall,
And answered to his lightest call
With more than spaniel dread,
The creatures of his lawless beek,
Were trampling on his very neck!

(lines 84-90)

According to Wylie Sypher, "The noble Negro, begot by primitivism and fostered by sensibility, is a creature ill-fitted to humanitarian purposes in any century but the eighteenth." While semiotically this symbol seems to be available in Whittier, in actuality it is inverted because Whittier blames whites for the slaves' infrequent outbursts of 'brutish' behavior. Instead of the "noble savage" who is "born of Nature's wild and vigor," the "brute" is a product of his social environment, a consequence of the dehumanizing conditions and physical torture suffered in slavery (Sypher 1969:155).[2] In **"Toussaint L'Ouverture"** the poet pulls to the surface that which is repressed in anti-black discourse: that blacks emotionally dwell in a state of powerlessness which may eventually lead to violence. Whittier's poetry constructs a world of violence in which slaves are driven ultimately to respond violently—orally and physically—as an act of protest against the oppressive political ideology which subjugates and dehumanizes them. Violence seems the consequence of previous violence, e.g. inhumane treatment of Africans aboard slave ships provokes slave mutinies and the massacre of a ship's crew. And the latter violence even results from previous violence, namely, the actual deception, purchase, trapping, and seizure of Africans for export, sale and enslavement.

In the introductory pages of his study on the roots of violence, Rollo May attributes violent outburst to feelings of powerlessness:

As we make people powerless, we promote their violence rather than its control. Deeds of violence . . . are performed largely by those trying to establish their self-esteem, to defend their self-image, and to demonstrate that they, too, are significant. Regardless of how derailed or wrongly used these motivations may be or how destructive their expression, they are still the manifestations of positive interpersonal needs. We cannot ignore the fact that, no matter how difficult their redirection may be, these needs themselves are potentially constructive. Violence arises not out of superfluity of power but out of powerlessness

(May 1972: 23).

Vividly and graphically detailed in **"Toussaint L'Ouverture,"** Haitian slaves, battered into a state of legal and social submission, eventually explode violently, retaliating by murdering their oppressors and risking their own lives (Whittier 1833 [1969, 3: 11-19):

. . . despair itself grew strong,
And vengeance fed its torch from wrong?
Now, when the thunderbolt is speeding;
Now, when oppression's heart is bleeding;
Now, when the latent curse of Time
Is raining down in fire and blood,
That curse which, through long years of crime,
Has gathered, drop by drop, its flood,—
Why strikes he not, the foremost one,
Where murder's sternest deeds are done?

(lines 103-12)

William Stanage would describe this behavior as "constructive violence," meaning "violence committed by a person or persons and employed toward creative, positive ends" (Stanage 1975: 217-18). Whittier's poems not only justify violent acts by blacks but they frequently substantiate Stanage's notion of "constructive violence." In **"The Watchers"** (1862 [1969], 3: 223-26) Whittier transforms Freedom from an abstraction into a speaking human. With this technique, Whittier in a circuitous way empowers the slaves—for the goal of constructive violence by the slave is given a voice to justify the means used by the slave:

> . . . Freedom sternly said: 'I shun
> No strife nor pang beneath the sun,
> When human rights are staked and won.'
>
> (lines 28-30)

According to the poet, even the Haitian revolt, through liberation sought and won through bloodshed, produced positive (i.e. "constructive") results.

On a superficial level, a world of lawlessness and blacks as subhuman reappears in a scene from **"The Panorama"** (Whittier 1856 [1969], 3: 193-210):

> Look once again! The moving canvass shows
> A slave plantation's slovenly repose,
> Where, in rude cabins rotting midst their weeds,
> The human chattel eats, and sleeps, and breeds;
> And, held a brute, in practice, as in law,
> Becomes in fact the thing he's taken for.
>
> (lines 156-63)

An initial reading of this passage connects Whittier to primitivism and to his white poetic contemporaries who "commented on slaves' accommodations to oppressive conditions" while black poets "shared their reactions to bondage with their readers and described slave survival techniques."[3] However, the above scene is embedded with irony; it is not one of repose but of lawlessness and psychological violence that transforms the human as commodity—from "chattel" (a thing), to a powerful monstrous animal, a "brute". Indeed, the psychological violence of the "slave plantation's slovenly repose" further reduces the slave from "human chattel" to "brute . . . the thing he's taken for." The slave's degradation clearly violates natural and human rights which is in contradiction to the semblance of order denoted by reference to "law." These conditions are essentially "lawless" since they violate "righteousness" and bear marks of primitivism. Hence, this scene loosely resembles the emphatic "lawless" nature of the previous quote from **"Toussaint L'Ouverture."** Moreover, these states of lawlessness overshadow inferences to power and class inscribed in both quotes. For example, power is linked to residence (the white man lives in a "lordly hall" and the slave "in rude cabins rotting midst their weeds"), and accompanies class which is associated with race.

The lawless state reverses positions of power. Force executed by the slave as brute registers attention because in this context only "brutishness" is power. Other significations of power—"law" and a sense of "orderedness" like the slave's routinized lot—are deemphasized. In fact, the very sense of a routine compresses the shock value of this scenario. Yet this very type of inhumane reality eventually unleashes the brute who "tramples on the very neck" of those slavocratic tyrants and lords, and reaches its peak with the Haitian rebellion. Characteristic in Whittier, though, the slave is not defined solely by his actions (language does not reflect reality). For in Whittier's verse, brutes are usually pedestaled as heroic, virtuous men: "praised for every instinct which / rebels against a lot / where the brute survives the human, and / man's upright form is not" (**"The Slaves of Martinique"**—1848 [1969], 3: 136-41). A similar chord resonates in the closing comments directed to the one immortalized in **"Toussaint L'Ouverture"** (Whittier 1833 [1969], 3: 11-19):

> Be mine the better task to find
> A tribute for thy lofty mind,
> Amidst whose gloomy vengeance shone
> Some milder virtues all thine own,
> Some gleams of feeling pure and warm,
> Like sunshine on a sky of storm,
> Proofs that the Negro's heart retains
> Some nobleness amid its chains,—
> That kindness to the wronged is never
> Without its excellent reward,
> Holy to human-kind and ever
> Acceptable to God.
>
> (lines 235-46)

Whittier uses a strategy of linguistic and semantic inversion and reversibility which also appears in his redefinition of the ideological concept "Christian" in **"The Christian Slave"** and of the word "brute" found in **"Toussaint L'Ouverture"** (1833), **"The New Year"** (1839), **"The Branded Hand"** (1846), **"Slaves of Martinique"** (1848), and **"The Panorama"** (1856). In the above quote, the poet indirectly challenges the church. Disempowering linguistic authority through language subsequently and ultimately demonstrates that definitions belong to the defined and not to the definers. Hence, Whittier's reversal and inversion of the previous sign "Christian" and now "brute"—who is heroic and virtuous—upends the power relationship established in language by linguistic authoritarians. One recalls from **"The Branded Hand"** (Whittier 1846 [1969], 3:111-15) that those who violate slave statutes gain "mercy, but "woe to him who crushes the SOUL with chain and rod."

Whittier thus inverts the noble savage literary symbol later discussed by Wylie Sypher in *Guinea Captive Kings* (1969), and presents black characterization that responds to the ante-bellum black-authored depictions of black subjectivity in both **"Toussaint L'Ouverture"** and **"Panorama."** Whittier employs, therefore, a strategy of semantic reversibility that rescues a repressed portrait of another identity of the slave in elitist, white discourse of Negro colonization, namely the proud and moral black. Although few of Whittier's characters have distinct personalities and identities, his break from logocentrism results in the redefinition and the reconstruction of black subjectivity.

Conclusion

Concomitant with the nation's progress towards the manumission of slaves are shifts in Whittier's topographical rhetoric. Whittier's rhetorical progression is traceable in the language he gives the slaves. Initially, as previously mentioned, Whittier empowers the slaves with a resistive language, a preverbal / non-literary communicative system of sounds—cries, moans, groans, shrieks, and infrequently of "broken Saxon words" (**"Song of the Negro Boatmen"**), rendering a "tragic chorus of the baleful wrong" (**"The Panorama,"** line 187-1856 [1969], 3: 193-210). But once freed, the slaves speak a language of liberation, and thereby introduce a second pattern of language. With emancipation, the freedmen take to words but this does not mean they assume the language of the dominate, of their oppressors. The freedmen's discourse graphematically resembles the language of the mind or of words but is superior to it, because it embodies the spirit: "the words of Jesus . . . the songs of David," and emanates from spiritually transformed "bones of the prophet's vision" that were previously "dumb lips" and "blind eyes" (**"Howard at Atlanta,"** lines 11-12; 1869 [1969], 3: 264-66). The language of liberation transcends the language of the dominant because it represents the reunification of the body and the mind through the spirit—through the constancy of the slaves' belief in an other-worldly power; this freedmen's discourse symbolizes a "soul waking."

In addition to empowering bonded blacks with orality, Whittier constructs an image of blacks with semantic reversals that unwrite anti-black, pro-slavery discourse. Whittier appropriates language from the discourse of slavery to emphasize its violent historical reality. The result is a body of poetry that presents a pervasive topography of violence that informs the slave's reality on every level, and implicitly and resoundingly challenges whites who blame the black criminal element for society's ills. Indeed, Whittier's poems, like **"Toussaint L'Ouverture,"** justify violence by blacks as the slave's aggressive expression of apathy, frustration, and utter powerlessness. Interior accounts of these poems show violence as the witness of the unheard and inarticulate. And in several of Whittier's poems, the very historical nature of the titles gives us a hint of the poem's tone and content, as well as indicates Whittier's moral center—a belief in freedom and equality for all.

John Greenleaf Whittier's topography of violence is always at the service of his moral imperative—i.e. the abolition of slavery. In his own words, he exclaimed that the true measure of one's success was determined by joining "thyself to some unpopular but noble cause." In an April 16, 1831 letter to Mrs. L. C. Tuthill, he wrote: "If my life is spared, the world shall know me in a loftier capacity than as a writer of rhymes. There—is not that boasting? But I have said it with a strong pulse and a swelling heart, and I shall strive to verify it" (Whittier 1831; Pickard [1894b], 1: 122, 56). Over ninety poems (including some of his early ballads, narratives, hymns, and occasional pieces) may be classified as anti-slavery. He published two individual volumes of these poems before the Civil War: in 1837, ***Poems Written during the Progress of the Abolition Question in the United States,*** and in 1846, ***Voices of Freedom.*** Several titles from these works fill the expanded group of "Antislavery Poems" which Whittier personally arranged for publication in ***The Poetical Works of Whittier,*** printed two years after his death in 1894. Whittier's "Antislavery Poems"—poems of an uncompromising, oppositional consciousness, poems of a violent slave reality—were intended to disturb, to challenge, to at least bring about a change of desire.

Just before the Civil War Whittier turned to political abolitionism because he realized immediate emancipation required more than William Lloyd Garrison's "moral suasion"; more than evangelizing to ambiguous hypocritical Christians; more than rhetoric. Whittier envisioned a nation of racial harmony and equality and this is realized in **"Howard at Atlanta"** (Whittier 1869 [1969], 3: 264-66). This vision dims, though, in his post-Civil War poems which offer no firm sign of progress towards racial democracy. Writing as late as 1880, in a tribute to **"The Jubilee Singers"** (Whittier 1869 [1969], 3: 268),, Whittier conveys, by implication, his awareness that blacks, by the end of Reconstruction, had lost all the legal victories they had won in a ten-year period. Instead, they were being forced to confront now a state of neoslavery made possible by segregationist Jim Crow legislation:

> Voice of a ransomed race, sing on
> Till Freedom's every right is won,
> And slavery's every wrong undone!

> (lines 16-18)

In spite of Whittier's dashed dreams, this poem ends with the recognition of the need for a faith far greater than the power of statutes designed to maintain white supremacy. Whittier extends the abolitionist mission and the range of the slaves' sounds of liberation by reaffirming the "ransomed race's" a-temporal, interiorized power as that spiritual force which has always sustained these people and will continue to do so until all of their citizenship "rights" are "won," and all vestiges of legal and social oppression are "undone."

Notes

*; All citations of John Greenleaf Whittier's "Anti-Slavery Poems" are from the 1894 reprint of *The Poetical Works of John Greenleaf Whittier,* Vol. III. Only poems actually quoted are listed in the references; all other poems are listed only with date of composition in parentheses the first time mentioned.

1. In "Stanzas for the Times," the poet also uses the interrogative rhetorically, but his sense of spiritual duty to his fellow man, who is made in "The image of a common God" is more explicit:

> What! shall we guard out neighbor still,
> While woman shrieks beneath his rod,
> And while he tramples down at will
> The image of a common God?

(lines 31-46)

2. According to Sypher, "The noble Negro is born of Nature's wild vigor; the humanity of the eighteenth century speaks the jargon of primitivism, and the royal slave-Nature's outcast child-takes his place beside Ossian and Cannassatego" (1969: 103).

3. See Ada, "the Slave," *Liberator* 7 (11 March 1837): 44; A. Gibbs Campbell, "the Prayer of the Bondmen," *National Anti-Slavery Standard* 19 (9 April 1859).

Works Cited

BRAGA, Thomas. 1984. "Castro Alves and the New England Abolitionist Poets", *Hispania: A Journal Devoted to the Interest of the Teaching of Spanish and Portuguese* 67 (Dec.): 586-87.

FREDRICKSON, George M. 1971. "Uncle Tom and the Anglo-Saxons: Romantic Racialism in the North" in *The Black Image in the White Mind: The Debate on Afro-American Character and Destiny, 1817-1914* (New York: Harper & Row).

LONGFELLOW, Henry Wadsworth. 1842. *The Complete Works of Longfellow,* Cambridge edition (Boston: Houghton, Mifflin & Co., 1922); reprinted in Braga.

MAY, Rollo. 1972. *Power and Innocence: A Search for the Sources of Violence* (New York: W. W. Norton & Company, Inc.).

PATTERSON, Orlando. 1982. *Slavery and Social Death: A Comparative Study* (Cambridge: Harvard University Press).

STANAGE, Sherman. 1975. "Violatives: Modes and Themes of Violence" in *Reason and Violence* (Totowa: Rowman & Littlefield).

SYPHER, Wylie. 1969. *Guinea's Captive Kings: British Anti-Slavery Literature of the XVIIth Century* (New York: Octagon Books).

WHITTIER, John Greenleaf. 1831. Letter to Mrs. L. C. Tuthill of April 16, cited in 1894b, below, 56.

———. 1833-1880. *The Poetical Works of John Greenleaf Whittle* r. Vol. 3: Antislavery Poems, Songs of Labor and Reform. Cambridge edition (Boston: Houghton, Mifflin & Co., 1894, 3 vols.); reprinted as *The Complete Writings of John Greenleaf Whittier* (NY: AMS Press, 1969, 7 vols.).

———. 1894b. *Life and Letters of John Greenleaf Whittier,* ed. Samuel T. Pickard. (Boston and New York: Houghton, Mifflin and Co., 3 vols.).

David Grant (essay date fall 1996)

SOURCE: Grant, David. "'The Unequal Sovereigns of a Slaveholding Land': The North as Subject in Whittier's 'The Panorama.'" *Criticism* 38, no. 4 (fall 1996): 521-49.

[*In the following essay, Grant discusses the political poetry Whittier aimed at Northerners who compromised with Southern slave-owners, focusing in particular on "The Panorama," which combines an attack on Northern hypocrisy with anti-slavery rhetoric.*]

Although it is probably unprofitable to draw too sharp a distinction between Whittier's anti-slavery poetry and his political poetry, one basic criterion for isolating the latter may be that Northern compromisers stand out as the primary object of attack. Such bitingly satirical poems as **"The Haschish"** or **"Lines on the Portrait of a Celebrated Publisher"** deal not with slavery at all but with the apostasy or hypocrisy of the Northern elites. It is therefore all the more significant that Whittier's most important political poem, **"The Panorama"** of 1855, contains prominent anti-slavery passages.[1] Indeed, out of this combination grows the true force of the work: its ability to coordinate and confound the contemporary political dispute with the larger questions of political economy raised by the crisis over the fate of the territories. Eric Foner's influential thesis—that the ideology of the Republican party in the pre-Civil War period can be summed up as an attachment to a society based on free labor—has recently been challenged by an historian who assigns greater significance to the Republican fear of the Slave Power as a more narrowly political threat.[2] Whittier's poem, however, indicates the interdependence of these two mainsprings of Republican growth by placing the slave system itself at the root of the threats to the North.

"The Panorama"'s achievements along these lines reveal how Whittier, as a poet long recognized and perhaps discounted by mid-century Americans as a member of the political anti-slavery vanguard, could help to solidify Republican rhetoric in the crucial years 1854-56, when the new party took full advantage of its best chance to define the terms of political debate in a newly uncertain environment. Those terms, if they were to carry the North beyond the unsustainable outrage over the Kansas-Nebraska Act that had spawned the party, needed to rest on a discourse that bound slavery as a socio-economic institution to those specific Southern infringements on Northern rights which seemed of most immediate concern to the public. Strategies available within the American political tradition made poetry in some respects a more suitable mode than political prose for forging one link in this chain: both the popular poetry of the American revolution[3] and much of the anti-extensionist verse of the 1840s called for the people to assert their "manhood" or fall inevitably into the role of the political slave, a metaphor that grew more compelling in the mid 1850s while the violence against Northern settlers in Kansas seemed to take on apocalyptic dimensions. Also, the verse jeremiad, by hinging the fate of the nation on the spiritual health of the individual even more absolutely than its prose equivalents, offered another tradition friendly to the kind of metaphorical associations found in many Republican poems, **"The Panorama"** included.[4] There is a more immediate reason, however, for the Republican movement to have turned to poetry in general, and to Whittier in particular, when setting out to attribute the North's powerlessness to slavery itself.

The aim of Republican discourse was not so much to win over the North as to *bring about* the North, to create an historical subject that had not yet come into existence. From this victory all others would follow. The sense that the North needed to be constructed before it could be called to action grew partly from the problem of the doughface, the Northern politician who, far from hiding his limitless compliance to Southern demands, trumpeted that compliance as a proof of his patriotism. That the American people tolerated such figures as their representatives pointed to a collective failure to grasp the North's community of interest in the face of a completely united, and ruthless, Southern oligarchy.[5] Within this context simply to assert the unity that Republicans wished to foster was one of the tasks assigned to campaign poetry: hence, "The North is Discovered!," the very first piece in *The Republican Campaign Songster* of 1856, transformed the party's presidential candidate, John Fremont, from the explorer of California to the founder of the North: "She's of age, and her guardians can no more enslave / The *free North,* protected by Fremont the brave!"[6] Yet if the North was truly to find itself through a proper understanding of its position as a collectivity, only a long narrative poem could undertake the difficult discursive task of locating precisely the obstacles in the way of achieving the kind of subjecthood that "The North is Discovered!" blithely

takes for granted. And for those obstacles to be understood as a product specifically of the slave system itself, only an author with solid credentials as an analyst of slavery could go beyond, on the one hand, the timidity of Republican politicians not wishing to be tarred with the abolitionist brush, and on the other the false bravado of the shorter propaganda poems, in order to construct an ideological vision built upon the subject positions that any narrative maps out from its raw materials. Whittier, then, was in the perfect position to show that slavery itself, and not simply its political manifestations, robbed the North of its status as a functioning agent in the world. By affirming a homology between the slave as subject and the North as subject, **"The Panorama"** drew out the implications, and thus contributed to the maturation, of Republican discourse.

This homology can emerge thanks to the poem's structure. The poem is divided into two major parts, the first a Showman's revelation of his vision of two possible futures for the West, alternately free or slave, the second the same Showman's lecture to the North on how it could avoid the dystopian future and bring about the utopian one were it only to mend its ways. Because the Showman couches his warning to the North in terms that inevitably recall his earlier visions of the West's future, the poem invites the reader to see the future itself as already latent in the two tendencies within the Northern subject. By means of this strategy, the poem can enter into the contemporary political debate by addressing the two ideals exploited by the Republicans' Democratic and conservative opponents—sovereignty and Union. By exposing how the Northern subject is in danger of mirroring in its own position the perversities of the Southern social system, the poem subverts the misuse of these ideals, showing their complicity in the power of property. Analysing **"The Panorama"** with a view to tracing the relations between its two parts is thus the best way to reconstruct the poem's original intervention in the political crisis of the 1850s and its role in establishing a triumphant Republican worldview.

1

One point of entry into the individuality of **"The Panorama"** is to notice in it those features either missing or highly underplayed that are prominent in many of Whittier's other works. Two elements in particular seem to be virtually absent, presumably because they would, as subjects in their own right, dilute the emphasis on the Northern subject: God and History. Of course, no poem by Whittier could entirely put aside his Quaker belief in divine agency, but **"The Panorama"**'s relative lack of insistence on this force has particular significance, especially given that the extremely time-specific, political concerns of the poem cannot in and of themselves account for the situation. When Whittier can take to be the work of Nemesis something so mundane as the decisions of the hopelessly pro-Compromise Whig and Democratic conventions of 1852,[7] it is clear that no feature on the political landscape automatically escapes his broader perspective. Yet the particular polemical stance adopted by **"The Panorama"** requires it to minimize the agency of God for the same reason that it must also incapacitate History.

Before he unveils the West's two possible futures, the Showman reveals why both subjects missing from the poem must be diminished and incorporated into the realm of human choice: "present time is but the mould wherein / We cast the shapes of holiness and sin."[8] In such phrases the Showman implicitly challenges the notion of historical inevitability upheld by Whittier elsewhere and closely linked to his belief in God's agency. To the demand by the "shrewd onlooker" that he describe a single future, the Showman more directly responds:

> . . . He who grieves
> Over the scattering of the Sibyl's leaves
> Unwisely mourns. Suffice it, that we know
> What needs must ripen from the seed we sow.
>
> (6)

There was, of course, a very immediate reason for the poem to reject the onlooker's notion of the past simply obeying the future,[9] of the future simply coming of History's own accord independently of human action, for the Northern Democratic argument against sectional agitation took advantage of just such confidence that geographical and historical conditions would of themselves keep the territories free. Thus, later, the poem stands on its head the argument that the Kansas-Nebraska Act opened the Middle West to slavery only on paper when the line "If the dark face of Slavery on you turns" is immediately rephrased as "If the mad curse its paper barrier spurns" (13). Far from a token concession to a human agency substantively powerless against larger historical forces, political measures ("paper") are in fact the North's sole fragile defence against the will of a South that has already "spurned" the Missouri Compromise and thus indirectly affirmed the importance of legal restraints. In order, therefore, to sidestep a facile belief in progress, the Showman strips his projections in advance of any validity that History as a power in itself could accord them. The two futures become not prophesies but the alternate dystopian and utopian extrapolations of the *present* or soon to be present condition of the Northern subject.

The two visions are thus able to focus on opposing labor systems and yet remain integrated with the political diatribe in the second half of the poem. Indeed, the stanza linking the two parts of the poem—the fulcrum of the argument—makes the linking analogy explicit:

> Oh friends! . . . in this poor trick of paint
> You see the semblance, incomplete and faint,
> Of the two-fronted Future, which, to-day,
> Stands dim and silent, waiting in your way.
> *To-day, your servant, subject to your will;*
> *To-morrow, master, or for good or ill.*
>
> (12, my italics)

In this image the Showman at once accepts and subverts the onlooker's conceit of the past obeying the future by inserting a particular "master"—either the North *or* the future—that bifurcates the continuous line of the historical process and grounds the image of obedience in a collective human subject. History is master only of the already-done, and an acceptance of the demands of slavery would be a submission to what in **"The Issue"** Whittier calls the tired lap of Time's "monstrous early birth" before its mastery over the present has been enshrined—in effect giving up one's sovereign will at the only stage in the process when that will can sustain the power of choice.[10]

The analogy drawn in this part of the poem is the key to the larger policy of equating what Lydia Maria Child called "the servile submission of the North"[11] with the coerced submission of the slave—a common equation in political discourse throughout the 1850s. Indeed, the North as slave is precisely the aspect of Republican rhetoric that the latest crop of revisionist historians emphasize, usually with the implication that it somehow represented a turning away from the anti-slavery program of the Radicals.[12] In fact, however, no one embraced the metaphor more enthusiastically than figures such as Whittier and Child whose anti-slavery motivation cannot be questioned. Thus, in **"A Song for the Time,"** written for the 1856 campaign, Whittier lays out a program for those who refuse to join the Republican ranks:

> Let him join that foe's service, accursed and abhorred!
> Let him do his base will, as the slave only can, . . .
> Let him go . . .
> Where the black slave shall laugh in his bonds, to behold
> The White Slave beside him, self-fettered and sold![13]

The notion of being self-sold resonates strongly in **"The Panorama,"** where the slave's sudden and permanent loss of his labor-power is transmuted, when applied to the North, into a gradual depletion over time, brought on by an unreciprocated surrender or selling of the self's attributes. More generally, however, **"A Song for the Time"** depicts a breakdown in the mechanisms of willed action that helps to explain how, within the discursive context of contemporary political debate, **"The Panorama"** manages to equate the North's capabilities with those of the slave. In terms that also register a breakdown in the subject's narrative capacity, an 1855 Congressional attack on slavery reveals how closely

Whittier's appeal to the North's pride is affiliated with one aspect of the traditional socio-economic argument against slavery. According to one minor figure in the new anti-Nebraskan coalition, George Dunn, each man, as his own "subject," "is entitled to have and ought to have secured to him *free will* and *free action.*" Under slavery "how shall he answer for his deeds who has no government of himself?"[14] The theological support for Dunn's argument does not detract from its narratological, and fundamentally ideological, underpinnings, invoking as it does the most fundamental unit from which a capitalist economy is meant to emerge: the freely chosen action of each individual. Whittier's depiction of this same distortion in reference to the North suggests that, however much the Republicans exalted free labor in their braver hours, they also sensed in the North's submissions to Southern pressure an incipient weakness underlying free society as a political subject and preventing the North, like the slave, from having true "government of itself."

Despite all that we in literary studies have been taught over the last twenty-five years to make us despise the so-called autonomous bourgeois subject, at a time when that subject was under a much graver threat than all our theoretical speculations could ever put it, one upholder of the notion, **"The Panorama,"** shows itself to be quite without illusions about the constitution of the individual. So far as slavery itself is concerned the poem makes no sentimental claims as to the integrity of a fully insulated unit merely enchained by circumstances, but insists instead upon the social construction of the self: the slave, "held a brute, in practice, as in law, / Becomes in fact the thing he's taken for" (10). Once again the political and structural imperatives of the poem rather than Whittier's particular beliefs, which themselves affirmed each individual's immutable reflection of the divine, dictate this representation. For, in fact, the poem refuses to work with theological or other notions of the "self," choosing to focus instead on the subject: the ultimate significance of the obliteration of the slave's status as an acting, self-directing subject is the analogy with the North. (Thus, from now on in this paper "self" will be used only as a convenient synonym for "subject.") This analogy is possible because, as Rush Welter has shown,[15] Americans in mid century viewed collective self-government as arising organically from the self-government of the individual. By drawing parallels with a system, namely slavery, in which the mechanisms of action have been completely curtailed, the poem can focus Northerners' attention on their own position without letting them forget the broader socio-economic source of their loss of power.

This strategy illuminates the poem's replacement of History with narrative, where, as in Greimassian semiotics for instance, acts are contingent on the construction of a competent subject, whether collective or individual, anthropomorphised or abstract, who alone can undertake those performances which will change the current state of affairs. Both the possibility of constructing such a subject and the obstacles in the way dominate the second half of the poem. Against the warnings to the North stand those explicit calls for Northern unity in action—depending on the construction of a properly regulated and thus powerful subject—which follow upon the more vitriolic passages. Yet these two parts of the second half of the poem ultimately gain their meaning from their parallels to the Showman's alternate visions of the future—the dystopian vision illuminating the case of the depleted Northern subject, the utopian vision the case of the North aroused to unity and action. Hence, it is only *after* his visual presentation ends, immediately before his long lecture to the North, that the Showman evolves from a mere projector into a prophet, hearing the "footsteps of the things to be" (12) in the very current duality within the North that he proceeds to delineate.

2

For the analogy between the brutalized slave and the North to be convincing **"The Panorama"** must reject a soothing commonplace found in anti-slavery poetry over the previous twenty years: the distinction between the doughface and the Northerner true to freedom's principles. Were the poem simply to endorse, at too early a stage, the banishment of doughfaces from the North, the polemical purpose undergirding its argument would collapse. Only by first insisting on the indivisibility of the Northern subject, with the conflict over doughface and freedom-lover occurring within the self, can the poem drive home its call for action and eventually subvert the Union-fetishizing rhetoric of the Republicans' opponents. This process begins at the poem's turning-point, when the Showman turns from friendly sympathizer to accuser:

> If the world granary of the West is made
> The last foul market of the slaver's trade,
> Why rail at fate? The mischief is your own.
> Why hate your neighbor? Blame yourselves alone!
>
> (13)

Although the Showman goes on to describe the North's inherent strength ("Your thews united could, at once, roll back / The jostled nation to its primal track" [13]), this affirmation soon yields to a description of the debilitating effects of the North's complicity in the operation of slavery's already existing "foul market": the North could only realize its potential power "[i]f stainless honor outweighed in [its] scale / A codfish quintal or a factory bale" (13).

The image of a scale that places on the same level personal attributes and marketable products prepares for the poem's continual return to the figure of the

Northerner selling components of himself for immediate gain, "bartering rights for broth," relinquishing his eternal "manhood" to the economic or political needs of the moment.[16] This ambiguously individual and collective process falls between two parallel exchanges depicted in the poem. At the strictly individual end of the scale stands the marketing of the slave, with all of his or her personal components: in the second of the Showman's alternate futures the slaver never scruples to "Sell all the virtues with his human stock, / The Christian graces on his auction-block" (10). At the opposite end of the individual/collective spectrum, but equally important to this network of meaning, stand the political agreements reached over the years between the North and the South, agreements in which the North was "[o]'erreached in bargains with her neighbour made, / When selfish thrift and party held the scales / For peddling dicker, not for honest sales" (15). Whereas the individual process is all too efficacious, thanks to the unilateral power relationship that frames it, the collective process betrays a failure of the ideal version of exchange, a failure which can ultimately be laid at the doorstep of the Northern "self-sold knaves of gain and place" (23), whose ongoing participation in the process leads to the growing debility of the collective Northern subject. The South, on the other hand, is marked by the absence of a contagion that could threaten its role within an exchange. Though freedom-lovers survive below the Mason-Dixon line, for all practical purposes the South presents a perfect model for the unhindered action of a unified subject: "the braggart Southron," the poem asserts in frankly admiring terms, is "open in his aim, / And bold as wicked, crashing straight through all / That bars his purpose, like a cannon-ball" (15). To see why the South, despite being inherently "weak and poor" (13), produces such a transparent and powerful subject at the political level, and thus to delve further into the significance of the parallel exchanges depicted by the Showman, one needs to venture outside the text for a moment to take a closer look at what the poem itself refers to in passing as "Seward's words of power" (14).

In 1856 William Seward—described by historians as the intellectual leader of the Republican movement—gave a clear articulation to what had for years been the basis of Northern distrust of Southern political power,[17] and his analysis of the problem pinpoints the same source as does the Showman in **"The Panorama,"** published a few months earlier. In "The Dominant Class in the Republic" Seward contends that the new Republican party aims to readjust the imbalance in the nation caused by property's inherent advantage of common self-interest—owners of slave property having the will to combine and perform as a collective agent that the North, composed of individuals with discrete interests, conspicuously lacks: "Property . . . derives power to oppress from its own nature, the watchfulness of its possessors, and the ease with which they can combine.

Liberty is exposed to the danger of such oppression by means of the inconsiderateness and the jealousies which habitually prevail among subjects or citizens. In every state all the property classes sympathize with each other, through the force of common instincts of fear, cupidity and ambition, and are easily marshalled under the lead of one which becomes dominant and represents the whole."[18] Neither Seward nor Whittier has any doubt as to which property class has currently become dominant and representative of the whole: **"The Panorama"** itself investigates the complicity of Northern property interests in the slave system. In another sense, however, the claim that only property can manifest itself in representation serves to explain the success of the South in the exchanges that take place at the national political level. Even without the "effective sympathy of other property classes,"[19] the slaveocracy has an engrained ability to marshall its forces; should the North ever choose to follow suit, it would need to do so on an entirely different basis, a basis suited to a free economy not dominated by concentrations of property in a few hands.

While Seward's analysis of the slaveholders' unity seems implicit in Whittier's poem (and will be considered in greater depth later in this paper), more important to **"The Panorama"** is the anxiety Seward evinces over the dynamics of interest in a society based on freely acting individuals. Elsewhere Seward claims that the same agent, namely self-interest, that has brought the situation to such a perilous point will ultimately induce the North to assert itself,[20] but the Showman has no such confidence that taking the logic of interest one step further can direct the North into united action. For the primary force pulling against a united Northern subject is precisely individual interest itself, that "lust of gold [and] strife for place and power" (6) which tempts individual Northerners to concede principles to the South while taming the North. The only possible return these figures can give to the investments made in them by Southern property is, as with the slave, their own internal qualities. Because one of these qualities is their political inheritance from the "fathers," the gradual diminution of the self-sold knave microcosmically reflects the losses increasingly suffered by the North as a whole.

The two visions of the future present alternate descriptive models for the later discursive political analysis of the North's position. In both futures the role of individual self-interest within a larger social whole enters into the picture, leading to representations of two very different kinds of unity within diversity. Whether the context is worship or work, in the utopian future the capitalist ideal of separately chosen activities blending magically into a larger harmony finds expression in the metaphor of music, which both introduces and concludes the brief depiction of a free West:

Then [the curtain rises], with a burst of music, touch-
   ing all
The keys of thrifty life. . . .
Of diverse sects and differing names the shrines,
One in their faith, whate'er their outward signs,
Like varying strophes of the same sweet hymn.

                          (7-8)

Although the second half of the poem by no means
disavows this ideal (true national unity is figured as a
"chorus" or "refrain"), it must first assert the parallels
between the North's current position and the different
kind of unity found in the slave South. Whereas the
utopian vision is predicated on a union within which
each element retains its distinctness while contributing
to the larger whole,[21] the dystopian vision portrays a
sinister interblending and drawing together of all forces
within a society ostensibly more stratified and hierarchi-
cally divided than the North. Self-interest's concentration in and subsequent diffusion from the individual
owner collapses the boundaries essential to a healthy,
and truly unified, social structure. Here the implicit
paradigm, borrowed from abolitionist critiques of the
South, is that of incest and miscegenation: the Showman puts the popular notion of immorality within a
plantation household to the service of a broader
analysis. The spread of "vice" on the slaveowner's
estate, however vaguely delineated, gives concrete form
to the more abstract bond of sin congealing the slave
world into a totality:

There, all the vices, which, like birds obscene,
Batten on slavery loathsome and unclean,
From the foul kitchen to the parlor rise,
Pollute the nursery where the child-heir lies . . .
So swells from low to high, from weak to strong,
The tragic chorus of the baleful wrong;
Guilty or guiltless, all within its range
Feel the blind justice of its sure revenge.

                          (11)

This picture of sinister unity, using the same metaphor
of the "chorus" as the positive version, then extends
further to include the nation as a whole. As the Showman broadens his perspective spatially and temporally
to depict the inexorable spread of slavery, the verse-
paragraph concludes, for the one and only time in the
poem, not with the standard couplet but with a triplet
that serves to suggest the incorporation of the whole
country within a single unified structure: "A belt of
curses on the New World's zone!" (12). The interest of
the slaveholder, which begins by making the powerless
its surrogate in work, ends by making the nation a
scarred reflection of its diffused force. This diffusion's
point of origin has its parallel at the national political
level: in the same way that the initial displacement of
the individual slaveowner's self-interest into the labor-
power of the slave weakens both parties and enervates
the entire Southern social system, so the circular efforts

of the Slave Power's surrogates in the North debilitate
the collective Northern subject, robbing it of the
potential advantages of the free labor system.

                          3

As if to disarm the hysterical anti-Republican warnings
against the dangers to the Union, the second half of the
poem implicates American political unity in that vicious
interblending of elements within slave society which
inevitably results from the concentration of power and
interest in a single figure: in the North figurative incest
and abstract disinheritance threaten the same consequences as their more concrete equivalents in the South.
In both cases this process begins with disinheritance: in
the case of the slave, the absorption into "Slavery's
sphere of sin" is made possible by the rupture of
original family ties, leaving "sad-eyed Rachels" to
"weep for their lost ones sold and torn away" (10); in
the case of the North, this same absorption depends
upon the willful abandonment of "the faith [America's]
fathers left in trust" (13), leaving the North as vulnerable to the controlling force of Southern property as the
individual slave. (In the heroic simile equating the
Northern compromiser with a convert to Islam the
former is portrayed as "some poor wretch, whose lips
no longer bear / The sacred burden of his mother's
prayer" [20].) Deprived of the frameworks within which
identity and difference could be regulated, both worlds
suffer a collapse of oppositions that signals, in the case
of the North especially, a blurring of semantic boundaries. On the plantation, because the lodgings fail to offer refuge and comfort, the place of work outside the
home stands "loose-scattered like a wreck adrift" (11),
neither demarcating a realm of necessity from which
the home is a retreat nor establishing an ideal of thrift
by which the "slovenly" tendencies of the home (both
the slave's and the master's) could be counteracted. An-
nulling difference, the master's home is simply "in
shabby keeping with his half-tilled lands" (10). This
merging sets the stage for the eventual violation of
boundaries *within* the home, involving in part the
premature externalization of youthful sexual passion, a
process which, as a particular failure of self-regulation,
mirrors the broader dynamics of social interaction
within the plantation. In the North the collapse of differences that issues from disinheritance manifests itself
more abstractly but with similar effect: doughfaces
"[c]onfound all contrasts, good and ill. . . . And lose
thenceforth from their perverted sight / The eternal difference 'twixt the wrong and right" (18). For Northerners, therefore, "real danger lies" not in some demon-
ized, far-away Other from the South but "beneath [their]
very eyes, / By hearth and home" (20). Since the "profusion" the Southern master both commands and falls
subject to on his plantation leads inevitably to the sexual
immorality by which the poem dramatizes the conver-
gence of elements within slave society, it is appropriate

that the metaphor of embracing should be employed to explain the North's own incorporation into the slave system: Northern traitors can be defined as those who form their ideals from institutions "within / The fell embrace of Slavery's sphere of sin" (17).[22] Whether in the North or in the South, the within / without opposition, which dominates the poem's imaginative topography and is the key to its eventual resolution, weakens and breaks down under the force of the slave system. Only by drawing a new line, one which replaces that spurious boundary between the slave and the free states which Democratic politicians use to assuage Northern fears, can the nation reassert the power of difference in shaping a genuine social harmony. But a different kind of unity already prevails in the North.

Although those passages in the second half of the poem which condemn institutional and commercial complicity in the slave system certainly contribute to the overall anatomy of collective interest, the focus of this part of the poem remains on the "party felon" who, even without any direct commercial interest in the preservation of slavery, sets the conditions for unity on such terms as to emasculate the collective Northern subject. When carried into the North the sinister interconnection of elements within the plantation becomes a kind of turning in upon the self that makes union the trigger for ongoing debilitation and corporealizes the rights of property in the bonds of self-composure. The personal condition of doughfaces thus duplicates at a higher level their own implicit ideology: "To them the Law is but the iron span / That girds the ankles of imbruted man" (18).[23] Such images of enchainment run throughout the Showman's depiction of the condition and procedures of the typical compromiser. The scars of the brutalized slave become in his person badges of honour: receiving the satirical punishment from critics such as Whittier, the party felon "[l]ooks from the pillory of his bribe of place, / And coolly makes a merit of disgrace" (17). More importantly, the doughfaces' immediate calls for the preservation of the Union the moment the ideal of freedom is introduced into the body politic make their own bondage a requisite for the survival of the nation:

> Such are the patriots, self-bound to the stake
> Of office, martyrs for their country's sake:
> Who fill themselves the hungry jaws of Fate,
> And by their loss of manhood save the State.
> In the wide gulf themselves like Curtius throw,
> And test the virtues of cohesive dough;
> As tropic monkeys, linking heads and tails,
> Bridge o'er some torrent of Ecuador's vales!
>
> (18)

These four parallel images accomplish more than an invocation of the traditional American distrust of an entrenched political class. The Showman has already made the point that the compromisers' survival depends on the very agitation they condemn: when true union between the states is one day achieved "Some Northern lip will drawl the last dissent, / Some Union-saving patriot of your own / Lament to find his occupation gone" (15). Now in his mock-heroic images the Showman goes further to suggest a more direct homology between the personal constitution of the doughface and the structure of the Union: both are founded on restraint and debilitation. In the course of expressing this homology the Showman inverts the standard call for republican virtue through a description of the ways in which the doughfaces in fact test their mettle. These figures give up their manhood not to a strengthened Union but to Fate itself: staving off the outcome they fear involves their own castration, which frees them to break their chains and rush headlong into self-defeating effort. Confronted then with the need to fuse the gap their concessions have done nothing but widen, they have no tool left but the substance of their own now weakened constitutions—i.e., dough—to throw into the task of rescuing the nation from division. In other words, the loss of potency that tempts the South to raise the stakes in sectional conflict also produces the very material for the new basis of union, so that the downward spiralling process hinges on an ever-weakened North's attempts at sacrifice. The trigger of this process—the doughface's "instinctive dread" (18)—inevitably calls to mind the fear that drives the slave to work even while it destroys his capacity to make that work productive,[24] in the process validating the initial alienation from his labor-power that had set the machine of decline into motion. Like the slave, whose fear has also become instinctive, the Slave Power's Northerner inevitably incorporates into the very structure of his being the qualities required by "compromise," so that the process of concession becomes self-perpetuating, built into the system: hence Northern Senators "yield up to Slavery all it asks, *and more*" (21, my italics). The doughface as subject eventually becomes nothing more than the temporary union he has generated, just as the Union itself becomes nothing more than the embodiment of the doughface's incapacity. For all practical purposes this Union only binds together *the North* into a single body which assumes increasingly ridiculous and dehumanizing poses in a desperate attempt to form a line of connection to the ever-drifting, still potent South: in the final image the monkeys can bridge the gulf only by turning their individual body parts—the last remaining vestiges of their ability to act—into indistinguishable and interchangeable objects whose original functions have been lost in the panic to unite. Once again the doughfaces are tied up, only now by and with each other. This picture of unity in effort both inverts the interdependence of work and social cohesion displayed in the utopian free West and mirrors the binding dominance of slavery represented in the dystopian slave West.

4

It is clear, then, that at the crux of the North's position is the collapse of the mechanisms of sovereignty that ideally operate within a political subject. The term sovereignty, so dear to Northern Democrats, is never used in the poem, but an implicit critique of its misappropriation shines through nonetheless, and that critique relates to a matter this paper has as yet only briefly touched on: the inability of free labor to express itself through representation. The Showman figures this inability at first through a general depiction of Northern incapacity.

In the poem's analysis of sovereignty the two extremes are as usual exemplified by the slaveholder and the slave, although in the end the former's enhanced and the latter's diminished sovereignty both become absorbed within a universally deautonomizing system. More important as a point of reference for the depiction of Northern leaders are their direct counterparts: the defenders of Southern rights. In these figures we find sovereignty not so much compromised as running rampant: the Missourian border ruffians shift "their drunken franchise . . . from scene to scene, / As tile-beard Jourdan did his guillotine!" (17). As in this instance, Southern representatives tend to be figured in the poem through images of movement and mobility, often in contrast to the transfixed and self-immobilized doughface,[25] the former shooting out like a cannonball to impose their demands while the latter stands "chin-buried in some foul offence" (16); the former crossing over into Kansas while the latter "looks from the pillory of his bribe of place" (17); the former lynching from his stump while the latter "imitate[s]" that action "upon [the law's] cushion plump" (21). This last example suggests that even when the doughfaces do stir themselves to action, the performances amount to nothing more than secondary, unoriginal gestures that merely take up the call of the master. For this reason, in the poem's topography Northerners are constantly *behind,* either "dragged in the slime of Slavery's loathsome trail" (18) or more actively following in attendance:

> The prophet's Word some favored camel bears,
> The marked apostate has his place assigned
> The Koran-bearer's sacred rump behind,
> With brush and pitcher following, grave and mute,
> In meek attendance on the holy brute!
>
> (20)

The figure of the apostate governs this simile because the North's estrangement from the heritage of the fathers accounts for both the form and the content of the doughfaces' present attempts at conservation: for the form, in that they work by following rather than leading and thus hold historical progress back; for the content, in that they work to preserve the shell of Union rather than the substance that makes that Union worth preserving. In the light of this falling away from a previous ideal and of the ease with which the South's representatives move forward, the most important flaw in Democratic rhetoric can be located; within the context of intersectional politics the Democratic valorization of sovereignty evades the kind of relationship between the individual and the collectivity necessary for the exercise of a truly democratic will.

An early Whittier propaganda piece, written some twenty years before **"The Panorama,"** invoked the principle of popular sovereignty to justify abolition: "Let the awful sovereignty of the people, a power which is limited only by the sovereignty of Heaven, arise and pronounce judgement against the crying iniquity. Let each individual remember that upon himself rests a portion of that sovereignty; a part of the tremendous responsibility of its exercise."[26] It is in terms of this interdependence between the sovereignty of the individual and of the collectivity that **"The Panorama"**'s anatomy of the threats to the North as subject can best be understood. For in the actual process of political representation individual Northerners hand over their portion of sovereignty to figures whose own powers have been compromised by a different kind of collective interest—the kind analysed by Seward. In the South the relationship works the other way: proxies represent the interests of property with a kind of vitality and intensity unavailable to the actual slave-owner. "Doubly armed with vote and gun" (17), the border ruffian is the emblem for the perfect fusion of sovereignty and raw power in the South's displacement of authority from its narrow, degraded source. On the other hand, the inherent power of the free laborer is eventually dispersed in political representation. Each Northerner's necessary and voluntary surrender of will becomes so distorted by the interventions of property's interest that, by the end-point of the process of delegation, he too falls victim to those dynamics of disinheritance which already infect the slave system and the self-sold knave. As a perversion of the larger process by which the faith of the fathers is "left in trust" (13) to their descendants, each Northerner's "loftiest outlooks" are *"h[e]ld"* by the politicians, who, despite the substance of their actions, continue to act "in [the] name" of their constituents (21). For their own protection these doughfaces must keep the rhetoric of sovereignty alive even while they undermine its practice; a debased discourse is the only surviving trace of the free laborer's original power.[27]

Once again a continuum, with the slave at one end, builds a larger framework for this disjunction between speech and meaning and thus for the Northerner's dispossession: the black boatman "redeems the jargon of his senseless song" with "a wild pathos borrowed of his wrong" (9); the salesman "mingles the negro-driving

bully's rant / With pious phrase and democratic cant"
(9); finally, the doughface's "cant the loss of principle
survives, / As the mud-turtle e'en its head outlives"
(16). Thus, at one extreme intrinsically meaningless
discourse is filled up by the integrity of the speaker's
expressive process, while at the other intrinsically potent
discourse is severed from the speaker's actions and as a
result drained of meaning, becoming cant. It is appropriate that in the middle example the salesman uses his
hybrid language to open the way to severing the slave's
family ties, for the rhetoric of the doughface serves to
disguise the squandering of not only the individual
sovereignty handed over by each citizen but also the
collective sovereignty handed down by the fathers.
(Significantly, Republicans restore the link to the past
and reintegrate language and meaning at one stroke:
"Seward's words of power, and Sumner's fresh renown,
/ Flow from the pen that Jefferson laid down!" [14])
Neither the individual Northerner nor the collective
North holds true sovereignty because the mechanisms
of delegation, like the mechanisms of inheritance, have
broken down. Conferring sovereignty on a small collective unit, the territorial settlers, covers up the Douglas
Democrats' real aim: to deny power to Congress, the
people's representatives and hence a force potentially
large enough to counterbalance the magnetic force of
property. Thus, the Showman's structural analysis, as is
so often the case in the poem, has affiliations with a
specific political argument prevalent at the time: one
common anti-Nebraskan objection to the Democratic
program of popular sovereignty for the territories was
that once slaves were admitted into a region, the
interests of those few holding them would override any
abstractly conceived popular will. In drawing attention
to the distorting medium through which the sovereignty
of the individual tries to realize itself as a collective
force on the national scene, the Showman subverts the
rhetoric of the Republicans' opponents.

5

At the poem's climax the contradiction between the
cohesive force of common individual interest and the
truly collective force of the Northern subject comes to
the fore. Following the poem's established strategy of
citing at the same time particular events and general
trends, this climax alludes to the scheme of certain
Northern merchants to work together to help enforce
the Fugitive Slave Law. The Showman places this joint
action within the larger context of political collusion
with the Slave Power in order to point up the futility of
the North's outrage over Bleeding Kansas:

> While truth and conscience with your wares are sold,
> While grave-browed merchants band themselves to
>   aid
> An annual man-hunt for their Southern trade,

> What moral power within your grasp remains
> To stay the mischief on Nebraska's plains?

(21)

All of the poem's themes converge at this point. Here
at last the Showman addresses definitively the problem
that has informed his analysis all along: Why can't the
North act? The answer can be found in the two seemingly dissimilar, yet mutually reinforcing, processes that
set the stage for the rape of Kansas: on the one hand,
there is the dispersal of collective force through the
selling by individuals of the attributes whose pooling
alone could produce a united Northern subject; on the
other, there is a strengthening of collective ties by a
group of individuals whose own property interests have
become assimilated into that larger network which
indeed holds the nation together but at the same time
curbs its power *as* a nation. The choice facing the North,
therefore, is not between collective will and popular
sovereignty but between a collective will shaped by the
bonds of property and one that reasserts the "moral
power" of resistance to private interest's encroachments
by fostering a true property *in the self.* Having so
framed the choices, the Showman can proceed to
describe the kind of self-regulation that a revitalized
North will have to practise if it means to reflect in its
collective body the conditions of an integrated,
responsible, and powerful subject.

By the time the Showman begins to explain what virtues
"Freedom's cause demands" (22) from each Northerner,
his syntax has already circumscribed this prescription
within a call for self-control that appropriates all that is
effective from the doughfaces' program for the nation.
Because the model for self-composure can be taken as
easily from the positive capitalist ideal of the free West
as from the negative example of the doughface, the
solution to the taming of the North lies not in some
impassioned release from the bonds of Union but rather
in a cooperative channelling of energies that reapplies
the former model at the level of political action. The
degraded ideals of union and restraint can be redeemed
in the person of the regulated collective Northern
subject. In this new context those who "temper and
restrain / The o'erwarm heart" (23) of a liberated North
aim not to sap its power but to redirect passion into
purposeful action, forestalling the premature release of
energies that characterizes the immoral life of the slave
plantation.[28] Even the shameful arrangement whereby
the doughface followed his master in attendance now
takes on a positive form in the North's coordination of
all temperaments in the movement toward the shared
goal of freedom: for this task Providence has "assigned
/ To each his part,—some forward, some behind" (22).
In so marshalling the different kinds of energies available in a diverse body politic the North will redefine
unity—the Union will depend not on homogeneity and
restraint but on difference and control. As a result, the

North as subject will move from mirroring the collapsed world of the slave plantation to realizing the ideal of diversity within unity of the free West.[29] At the same time the proper relationship between the individual and the collective, with the latter harnessing the power of the former, will finally prevail. Only with this transformation assumed can the Showman take back his earlier point that the North must be judged as a whole. Secure in the knowledge that cooler heads will act as a "well-meant drag" upon the North's "hurrying wheel," he can now make a more traditional call for purging the North of its debilitating elements: "Cast out the traitors who infest the land" (23).

The Showman's ultimate solution rests on the premise that only by reshaping the Northern subject can the South itself be changed. Turning on its head the dough-face argument that the North must show restraint to keep the South in line, he insists that the inevitable consequence of the North's claiming ownership of itself will be the South's parallel release from self-bondage,[30] leading in turn to a positive exertion of the force that up to that point she had used solely to coerce her underlings in Washington:

> till the Southron, who, with all his faults,
> Has manly instincts, in his pride revolts, . . .
> . . . lifts, self-prompted, with his own right hand,
> The vile incumbrance from his glorious land!
>
> (24)

In this spontaneous emancipation the Showman resolves the paradox of his own answer to the Union-Savers: that Union between the South and the North cannot exist precisely because the two sections are not truly separate. For Union to be possible the South must first be isolated: just as the end of slavery will one day release the owner from the degradation of control of the other, so too the liberation of the North will allow the South to apply its natural virtue to self-control. Simply to prepare the field by changing the North is already to have won the battle, a position later echoed by Seward when he claimed that a simple political victory for the Republicans would alone accomplish the revolutionary task of overthrowing the nation's dominant class.

In its concern for the Northern subject the Showman's program does not put aside the question of the territories. On the contrary, having set down his prescription for the North, the Showman can return to the future precisely because a free West must first be built in the collective soul of the North before it can be transported to the territories:

> So, wheresoe'er our destiny sends forth
> Its widening circles to the South or North, . . .
> There shall Free Labor's hardy children stand
> The equal sovereigns of a slaveless land.
>
> (24)

Equal sovereigns will reign in the American empire only because they reign first in the nation as a political body; Free Labor's children must first be made hardy before they can be made conquerors. The Showman's two visions of the distant future turn out to have been visions of the immediate future as defined by the two choices open to the North.

The final utopian vision of America's future also recalls the dramatic situation with which the poem opened. Before the Showman had begun his presentation, the difficulties facing any call for Northern action were already indicated by the demeanor of his audience, with its "blank indifference and . . . curious stare." As the poem progresses we learn why the crowd's "restless cane-tap and impatient foot," its "general din," had left the Showman feeling "half sad, half scornful" (3): such failure to live up to the ideal of the chorus represents that larger failure of the North to unite its diverse elements into a focused, coordinated body of freemen. The Showman's final words, however, show that both close attention and perfect coordination will frame America, once it is sufficiently liberated from the constraints of property to expand into an empire not regulated by the "belt of curses" that held the continent together in the dystopian vision. In its new unity America becomes its own audience:

> The Eastern sea shall hush his waves to hear
> Pacific's surf-beat answer Freedom's cheer,
> And one long rolling fire of triumph run
> Between the sunrise and the sunset gun!
>
> (25)

Whereas the Showman's last words hark back to the opening of the poem by way of contrast, the speaker's final words suggest how his own questionable audience (represented by the Showman's fictional audience) can transform itself by applying the Showman's lessons and thereby realize his final optimistic forecast. At the end of the epilogue Whittier employs the convention of asserting poetic inadequacy to return to the issue of the relation between speech and action: "Forget the poet, but his warning heed, / And shame his poor word with your nobler deed" (26). If the North has permitted language to supplant action, the verbal call for a readjustment can itself be supplanted by a non-verbal assertion of Northern force. The poem can fade away as its ideal audience renders its alternatives redundant and replaces its vision of debility with the reality of power.

6

The objection that can so easily be raised against taking **"The Panorama"** as representative of Republican thought—that Whittier's anti-slavery commitment preceded the birth of the new party and was stronger than that of most of his fellow Republicans—itself suggests how the poem can address the persistent traditionalist/revisionist debate in American political history of the 1850s. For the latest version of revisionism relies heavily on making a rigid and absolute distinction between opposition to slavery and opposition to Southern power; indeed, the article that inaugurated the new tack builds this distinction into its very title.[31] Perhaps because Gara's distinction took its prominent place in the debate as a quite explicit (and successful) attempt to revive a dying revisionism—one replacing the charge of Northern fanaticism with that of Northern selfishness—it has somehow fostered the view, even among some traditionalists,[32] that denunciations of the Slave Power constituted a particularly conservative appeal. That Whittier so fully integrated the two sides of the complaint against the South stands as a useful reminder that the construct of the Slave Power, after all, came originally from the Radicals and was meant to bolster, not attenuate, a broader anti-slavery ideology.

Yet whatever the intrinsic validity of distinguishing between the Republicans' two objections to the South, doing so tends to occlude what mediates between them: the anatomy of the North's position as a subject. Insofar as this anatomy represents a view of the world and the possibilities of action within it, while also pointing up the inherent dangers of a complacent democratic security, it may in fact be the most essential facet of Republican ideology, the element without which neither the critique of Southern society nor the distrust of Southern power could bear their full weight. Considered in this light, Radical participation in the Republican strategy of emphasizing Northern rights ceases to appear a cloak under which the North could be hoodwinked into accepting an anti-slavery program and becomes instead the honest assertion that such a program would be empty and meaningless without a world-view that made Northern action more than simply a means to a greater end. As Seward stresses again and again in his prewar speeches, the primary moral responsibility of the North is to roll back the demoralization it has allowed itself to suffer at the hands of the Slave Power. One of the most apocalyptic of the poems written for the Fremont campaign reveals in capsule form the catalytic role of the critique of the emasculated Northern subject in reconciling an ideology of world freedom and a narrow jealousy of Southern power. "Have you counted up the cost?" of a Republican defeat, the poem asks:

> Lost—desert of manly worth
> Lost—the right you had by birth
> Lost, lost—*Freedom for the earth.*[33]

What this short poem asserts discursively **"The Panorama"** builds into its imaginative world. Yet **"The Panorama"** goes further still in drawing the strands of Republican ideology together: by representing the depletion of the Northern subject in terms which recall its own description of the slave system, the poem breaks down the boundaries that allow each Northerner to separate his fate from the fate of the slave. This strategy—and not the straw-man of some pure, disinterested "moral" opposition to slavery—represents the truly radical approach in that it infuses an examination of the North's position with the ideological critique of Southern society. Hence, to fully appreciate the achievement of the poem one must return to Eric Foner's demonstration of the social goals of the Republicans, their endorsement of a society based on free labor and condemnation of the Southern degradation of labor. If Northerners rebelled against allowing slavery into the territories largely because slavery both tarnished the idea of labor and debased each individual laborer, thereby setting the nation on a path of decline, then **"The Panorama"** makes the radical claim that such a development is forecast in the political degradation of the North as a political subject. For freedom to have a foothold it is not enough for free labor to flourish in the North or even in this or that territory: as a political subject the North can lose the battle without its ever being fought on the fields of Kansas by refusing to realize politically the potential strength that derives from a free economic system. This position undercuts the premise of all conservative calls for compromise much more thoroughly than could even the purest abolitionist argument by making the North's political position in relation to the South both a metaphor and a potential antidote for the nation's failure, under the pressure of property, to promote self-ownership. By insisting that the North regain mastery of itself, Republican rhetoric set up a chain of associations that could not help but be revolutionary in their effect, bringing the Northern view of the South to bear symbolically on the day-by-day decisions of the North and, by the same token, making the duty to defend Northern rights an integral part of the struggle to move the nation toward freedom.

If, then, Republican rhetoric was most productive in its positioning of the North as subject, and if poetry was one of the means by which this positioning was achieved, the question then arises as to whether the less overtly political poems of the American Renaissance join in **"The Panorama"**'s demand that the power of property yield to a property in the self. So much has been accomplished in recent years in the critical project of restoring to texts of the American Renaissance their proper political meanings that one hesitates to suggest that the more blatantly polemical poetry of the period has anything to contribute on this score. Yet *Leaves of Grass*, published the same year Whittier's poem was written and a year before Whitman's Republican (though nominally nonpartisan) propaganda sheet "The Eighteenth Presidency," is indeed illuminated by **"The Panorama."** In a general sense, Whitman's aim of producing an American character "strong, limber, [and] just," as he explained to Emerson,[34] is of course compatible with **"The Panorama"**'s goal of producing a powerful Northern subject. More specifically, both works set a deadening self-regulation based on unity up against the possibilities of a disciplined unity within diversity, and both works take the self as a model for the nation's realization of its promise by locating the future within a potential present.

As Betsy Erkkila has observed, "like the American republic, 'Song of Myself' is an experiment in self-governance that both tests and illustrates the capacity of a muscular and self-possessed individual for regulation from within."[35] Viewed in the context of the 1855 collection as a whole, this experiment offers an alternative to the kind of centralized deautonomization that "A Boston Ballad" sees lurking in the submission of "all orderly citizens" to the Fugitive Slave Law. According to this satirical response to the remanding of Anthony Burns into slavery, there can be only one consequence to the North's strictly formal devotion to its revolutionary heritage: a welcomed conquest from the East, as King George's patched up corpse arrives on the Boston shore to sanctify the reversion of democratic force to symbolic power, reflected both in the king's position and in his lifelessness (At the end of "The Eighteenth Presidency," Millard Fillmore and James Buchanan are also depicted as corpses hoping to preside over the nation like the dead hand of the past). To forestall this metaphorical Eastern invasion "Song of Myself," like **"The Panorama,"** inscribes the democratic spirit of the free West into a diffused and diverse, yet directed, self. In subsequent pre-war editions of *Leaves of Grass* Whitman made this function of the West more explicit in such additions as "For You O Democracy" and especially "Starting from Paumanok." Inasmuch as both Whitman's and Whittier's poems urge the nation to foster within itself the highest possibilities of a free West, they participate in a rhetorical strategy employed in various modes of Republican discourse—from a speech at the first Republican national convention to the concluding paragraph of William Phillips' propagandistic narrative *The Conquest of Kansas*.[36] By helping to bridge the gap between political discourse and the great literary works of the decade, Whittier, while falling neither within nor beneath the American Renaissance, can stand proudly beside it, shedding his light on some of its lasting achievements.

Notes

1. Perhaps this feature accounts for Robert Penn Warren's strange charge that the poem is "diffuse and not well organized" (*John Greenleaf Whittier's Poetry: An Appraisal and a Selection* [Minneapolis: University of Minnesota Press, 1971], 29). On the contrary, the poem is very precisely organized, though not, of course, along the same

lines as are Whittier's shorter polemical poems. "The Panorama" has certainly not been a favourite of Whittier scholars over the years. Whitman Bennett, for instance, calls it the "most tedious item in the collection" in which it was the title-poem (*Whittier: Bard of Freedom* [Chapel Hill: University of North Carolina Press, 1941], 247). An exception is Lewis Leary's study, which makes frequent reference to the poem and describes it accurately as "Whittier's longest, most comprehensive, and rhetorically most effective political poem" (*John Greenleaf Whittier* [New York: Twayne Publishers, 1961], 113).

2. Eric Foner, *Free Soil, Free Labor, Free Men: The Ideology of the Republican Party before the Civil War* (New York: Oxford University Press, 1970), 11-39; William E. Gienapp, *The Origins of the Republican Party: 1852-1856* (New York: Oxford University Press, 1987), 357. Elsewhere Foner himself has stressed the cohesive function of the image of the Slave Power (*Politics and Ideology in the Age of the Civil War* [New York: Oxford University Press, 1980], 49-50). For a less moderate version of Gienapp's position on the basis of the Republicans' strength, see Michael F. Holt's *The Political Crisis of the 1850s* (New York: John Wiley and Sons, 1978), 183-217. In this paper historians holding the views of Gienapp and Holt on this matter will henceforth be called revisionists.

3. A collection containing numerous examples of the metaphor (see, for instance, "The Parody Parodised, or the Massachusetts Liberty Song" and "A Song, 1776") was, coincidentally, published the year "The Panorama" was written: *Songs and Ballads of the American Revolution*, ed. Frank Moore (New York: D. Appleton and Company, 1855), 44-7, 118.

4. In his important study Sacvan Bercovitch shows how the jeremiad typically links individual salvation to national progress, "public to private identity" (*The American Jeremiad* [Madison: University of Wisconsin Press, 1978], xi). "The Panorama" is clearly in the tradition of the American jeremiad—its very frame structure, in which the warning voiced by a fictional character lies at the centre of a larger discourse by the speaker, recalls such works as Wigglesworth's "God's Controversy with New England." Republican political discourse has been analysed in its use of "the jeremiad's anxiety of crisis" by Kathleen Diffley ("'Erecting Anew the Standard of Freedom': Salmon P. Chase's 'Appeal of the Independent Democrats' and the Rise of the Republican Party," *Quarterly Journal of Speech* 74 [1988]: 409). The rhetoric of crisis that fixes

the present as an irrecoverable turning point represents "The Panorama"'s greatest debt to the tradition of the jeremiad.

5. David Brion Davis, *The Slave Power Conspiracy and the Paranoid Style* (Baton Rouge: Louisiana State University Press, 1969), 79.

6. *The Republican Campaign Songster* (New York: Miller, Orton and Mulligan, 1856), 3.

7. *The Letters of John Greenleaf Whittier*, 3 vols., ed. John B. Pickard (Cambridge: Harvard University Press, 1975), 2: 194.

8. *The Panorama and Other Poems* (Boston: Ticknor and Sons, 1856), 6. Further references to this edition will be noted parenthetically in the text. For the sake of simplicity I have omitted the quotation marks arguably required for passages technically "spoken" by the Showman.

9. Whittier's syntax is ambiguous here, but the image of the past anachronistically obeying the future seems as widespread in nineteenth century American political poetry as the more common-sense notion of the future obeying the past: see, for instance, Melville's "The Conflict of Convictions."

10. It is perhaps significant that a somewhat more radical anti-slavery (and later Republican) poet, William Henry Burleigh, uses just the opposite metaphor, making the people the subject of the present as monarch ("Today," *Poems*, ed. Celia Burleigh [New York: Hurd and Houghton, 1871], 199-201).

11. *Selected Letters, 1817-1880*, ed. Milton Meltzer and Patricia G. Holland (Amherst: The University of Massachusetts Press, 1982), 269.

12. See, for instance, Holt, *Political Crisis*, 189-90.

13. *The Poetical Works of John Greenleaf Whittier*, 4 volumes (Boston: Houghton, Mifflin and Company, 1892), 3: 189-90. See also Lydia Maria Child's "Free-Soil Song" (*New York Daily Tribune*, 22 Oct. 1856, 3, col. 4) and the anonymous "The Slave's Appeal," which addresses the North: "Ah! dastards and fools! our contempt you're beneath, . . . We are freer in soul than the slaves who would swerve / From the altar of Freedom this Belial [the Slave Power] to serve" (*The Republican Campaign Songster*, 87). This political use of the North/slave analogy must of course be distinguished from the "moral" point raised, for instance, by Lowell's "Stanzas on Freedom": "If ye do not feel the chain, / when it works a brother's pain, / Are ye not base slaves indeed, / Slaves unworthy to be freed?" (*Poems of James Russell Lowell* [London: Oxford University Press, 1912], 79).

14. *Congressional Globe*, 34th Congress, Ist session, Appendix, 38.

15. *The Mind of America: 1820-1860* (New York: Columbia University Press), 185.

16. Of course, Whittier did not give birth to this self-depleting Northerner, although his famous poems "Ichabod" and "Moloch in State Street" certainly helped to popularize it. The opportunistic Northerner became, in fact, a kind of stock figure, especially among the more radical elements of the Republican party. Murat Halstead, for instance, explained certain perversities of the 1856 Democratic convention by reminding his readers that "the politician is ever a trimmer—ever ready, by a sale of himself, to realize upon the capital he has acquired" (*Trimmers, Trucklers, and Temporizers*, ed. William B. Hesseltine and Rex B. Fisher [Madison: The State Historical Society of Wisconsin, 1961], 20).

17. John Mayfield, *Rehearsal for Republicanism: Free Soil and the Politics of Anti-Slavery* (Port Washington, N. Y.: Kennikat Press, 1980), 26.

18. *The Works of William H. Seward*, 5 vols., ed. George E. Baker (Boston: Houghton, Mifflin and Company, 1884), 4: 254.

19. Seward, *Works*, 4: 268.

20. Ibid., 359-60.

21. As Eric Foner shows, Republicans inherited the Whig "doctrine of the harmony of interests" (*Free Soil*, 20).

22. Sumner's "The Crime Against Kansas" was by no means the only piece of Republican propaganda to use sex as a metaphor for unholy interaction with the Slave Power. The image of the prostitute runs throughout the *New York Tribune's* descriptions of the candidates for the 1856 Democratic nomination, for instance. (See also Walt Whitman's "The Eighteenth Presidency," *Complete Poetry and Collected Prose* [New York: Library of America, 1982], 1309.) In "The Panorama" a verbal echo casts the same aspersion: the curse of slavery "from girlhood's instincts steal[s] the blush of shame" (11), forging a resemblance between the slave girl's demeanor and the "unblushing face" (17) of the Northern compromiser. At the other extreme, freedom-loving Southerners are like Lot in Sodom, resisting the ideological advances of the Slave Power and keeping "white and pure their chastity of soul" (13).

23. Bercovitch describes the conservative tradition behind the doughface program as Whittier presents it: Federalist jeremiads promised "millenial glory earned through a process of *taming, binding, curb-*

ing, restraint" (*American Jeremiad,* 136). The most famous of all American anti-slavery works also contains an implicit condemnation of this doughface call for restraint. In the scene in which Haley casually sells a child behind its mother's back, Stowe implicates the heartlessness of the slaver in the then dominant belief that slavery agitation must give way to Northern self-control: "You can get used to such things, too, my friend; and it is the great object of recent efforts to make our whole northern community used to them, for the glory of the Union." This danger is symbolically averted when the cold-hearted Ophelia, on learning of the plan to send Rosa to a whipper, at last feels the "strong New England blood of liberty rise to her cheeks," and yet is able to channel her new-found passion through traditional Yankee "prudence and self-control" (*Uncle Tom's Cabin* [New York: Penguin, 1981], 208, 460). Thus, as in Whittier's poem, deadening self-restraint is set against positive self-discipline and self-mastery. In dealing with the Showman's ultimate solution, this paper will return to this opposition.

24. In the third stanza of "Massachusetts to Virginia" Whittier indirectly affirms the superiority of free labor while he ostensibly does nothing more than assert by synecdoche his state's indifference to Virginia's threats: "not one brown, hard hand foregoes its honest labor here, / No hewer of our mountain oaks suspends his axe in fear." For Whittier the doughfaces do not simply betray the North's political interests: in cowering they symbolically relinquish the inherent strengths of free labor.

25. This pattern of imagery recurs in the Republican poetry for the 1856 campaign. In John Pierpont's "The Call of Kansas," for example, slavery stretches herself forth to violate the borders separating her from freedom while "Her perjured panders sit and smile, / On her high places, where they swore / That she should agitate no more" (*New York Daily Tribune* 30 July 1856, 4, col. 3). In response the poetry calls for a countervailing movement, a reaching out into the public domain of previously sequestered freemen to rescue the kidnapped government, as in, for instance, Charles S. Weyman's "Fremont and Victory" (*New York Daily Times* 13 Sept. 1856, 3, col. 1).

26. *The Prose Works of John Greenleaf Whittier,* 3 volumes (Boston: Houghton, Mifflin and Company, 1892), 3: 47-8.

27. This tendency alarmed Republicans throughout the prewar period. One propaganda piece for the 1860 campaign expresses this fear of the "perversion of language" directly, linking it to another concern of Whittier's poem, the collapse of

distinctions: "Names should represent things. If they do not, they are deceptive, and become a 'delusion and a snare.' To designate opposites by one and the same word, would be to confound distinctions, and confuse and perplex ordinary minds." (*The Republican Pocket Pistol, A Collection of Facts, Opinions and Arguments for Freedom,* ed. William Burleigh [New York: H. Dayton, 1860], 39). See also Emerson's "Speech on Affairs in Kansas": "Language has lost its meaning in the universal cant" (*Miscellanies* [Boston: Houghton, Mifflin and Company, 1883], 245).

28. Eric Foner gives some vital ideological context for the Showman's solution: "Many anti-slavery men believed in an ideal of human character which emphasized an internalized self-discipline. They condemned slavery as a lack of control over one's own destiny and the fruit of one's labor, but defined freedom as more than a simple lack of restraint. The only truly free man . . . was one who imposed restraints upon himself" (*Politics and Ideology,* 24-5).

29. On the practical political matter of the need for Republicans to conciliate nativists and other potential allies for the sake of victory, Whittier's liberal views were so well known that his dictum ("Forget, forgive, unite") was actually quoted at the 1856 Republican convention during an appeal to wavering Know-Nothings (*Proceedings of the First Three Republican National Conventions* [Minneapolis: Harrison and Smith, 1893], 32).

30. In an editorial perhaps written by Whittier, a contributing editor to the paper, but more likely written by Bailey, the *National Era* suggests why such release is necessary: "The individual members of an Oligarchy . . . are themselves bound by the will of the whole. . . . The Slaveholder is himself the slave of the Slave Power" (*National Era,* 16 Feb. 1854, 26).

31. Lany Gara, "Slavery and the Slave Power: A Crucial Distinction," *Civil War History* 15 (March, 1969): 5-18.

32. See, for instance, Richard H. Sewell, *Ballots for Freedom: Antislavery Politics in the United States 1837-1860* (New York: Oxford University Press, 1976), 305.

33. "A Battle-Song for Freedom," *New York Daily Tribune,* 3 Nov. 1856, 6, col. 1.

34. *Complete Poetry and Collected Prose,* 1336.

35. *Whitman the Political Poet* (New York: Oxford University Press, 1989), 103. In my subsequent discussion of *Leaves of Grass,* I follow standard critical practice in referring to poems by titles often not given by Whitman until well after the war.

36. *Proceedings of the First Three Republican National Conventions,* 73. *The Conquest of Kansas by Missouri and her Allies* (Boston: Phillips, Sampson and Company, 1856), 414.

Beverly Peterson (essay date 2000)

SOURCE: Peterson, Beverly. "Stowe and Whittier Respond in Poetry to the Fugitive Slave Law." *Resources for American Literary Study* 26, no. 2 (2000): 184-99.

[*In the following essay, Peterson compares Stowe's 1853 poem "Caste and Christ" with Whittier's 1850 poem "A Sabbath Scene," noting that the two poets shared religious and political beliefs that were apparent in the two poems, both of which chastised clergymen who advocated compliance with the Fugitive Slave Law.*]

Harriet Beecher Stowe's famous antislavery novel *Uncle Tom's Cabin* (1852), its follow-up called *A Key to Uncle Tom's Cabin* (1853), and *Dred* (1856) are undoubtedly Stowe's most important contributions to antislavery literature. But Stowe also wrote a long-forgotten poem that is thematically similar to one of John Greenleaf Whittier's better-known antislavery poems, **"A Sabbath Scene"** (1850). Stowe's "Caste and Christ" (1853) and Whittier's **"A Sabbath Scene"** encapsulate their authors' opposition to slavery on religious grounds and chide clergy who, in compliance with the Fugitive Slave Law, advised their congregations to return runaway slaves to their owners. An analysis of the poems and their contexts shows that these two authors wrote accessible, emotionally charged verses to promulgate their shared religious and political convictions. Incorporating biblical allusions, the poems stir up feelings of righteous indignation by inviting readers to identify with mistreated fugitive slaves. Like *Uncle Tom's Cabin,* the poems urge readers to trust their feelings—not pronouncements from received authorities such as the church and the state—to lead them to correct moral actions.

Stowe wrote "Caste and Christ" in 1852 in response to a request from the Rochester Ladies' Anti-slavery Society, which included the poem and Stowe's autograph in the 1853 *Autographs for Freedom* (3).[1] The poem has been out of print in this country since then.

"Caste and Christ"

He is not ashamed to call them brethren.

Ho! thou dark and weary stranger,
  From the tropic's palmy strand,
Bowed with toil, with mind benighted,
  What wouldst thou upon our land?

Am I not, O man, thy brother?
  Spake the stranger patiently,
All that makes thee, man, immortal,
  Tell me, dwells it not in me?

I, like thee, have joy, have sorrow,
  I, like thee, have love and fear;
I, like thee, have hopes and longings,
  Far beyond this earthly sphere.

Thou art happy,—I am sorrowing,
  Thou art rich, and I am poor;
In the name of our *one* Father,
  Do not spurn me from your door.

Thus the dark one spake, imploring,
  To each stranger passing nigh,
But each child and man and woman,
  Priest and Levite passed him by.

Spurned of men,—despised, rejected,
  Spurned from school and church and hall,
Spurned from business and from pleasure,
  Sad he stood, apart from all.

Then I saw a form all glorious
  Spotless as the dazzling light,
As He passed, men veiled their faces,
  And the earth, as heaven, grew bright.

Spake he to the dusky stranger,
  Awe-struck there on bended knee,
Rise! for *I* have call'd thee *brother,*
  I am not asham'd of thee.

When I wedded mortal nature
  To my Godhead and my throne,
Then I made all mankind sacred,
  Sealed all human for mine own.

By Myself, the Lord of ages,
  I have sworn to right the wrong,
I have pledged my word, unbroken,
  For the weak against the strong.

And upon my Gospel banner
  I have blazed in light the sign,
He who scorns his lowliest brother,
  Never shall have hand of mine.

Hear the word!—who fight for freedom!
  Shout it in the battle's van!
Hope! for bleeding human nature!
  Christ the *God,* is Christ the *man*!

Stowe's poem opens with an epigraph from the New Testament, Hebrews 2:11. The whole chapter of which that verse is a part is a reminder that Jesus became man in order to redeem and sanctify all men. The epistle ends with an exhortation to "let brotherly love continue," to entertain strangers, and to "[r]emember them that are in bonds, as bound with them" (13:1-3). Although neither the word *slave* nor the word *Negro* appears in "Caste and Christ," the "dark and weary stranger" who is "bowed with toil" and whose mind is "benighted" is clearly a slave. His request for aid from strangers, and especially his plea, "Do not spurn me from your door," strongly suggest that he is a fugitive.

"Caste and Christ" depicts Christ's behavior if he were to encounter a slave who had been excluded from human sympathy and barred from participating in social institutions, including the church. The slave patiently explains to all he meets that he is human and possesses an immortal soul that hopes for heaven. In other words, he rebuts the notion that race is a justification for turning a man into a commodity, a thing. (The original subtitle of *Uncle Tom's Cabin* was not *Life Among the Lowly,* but "The Man Who Was a Thing.") In the poem, children, men, women, and even clergy are indifferent to the slave's request for refuge. But Christ ("a form all glorious / Spotless as the dazzling light") appears and reminds those present that, in taking on human nature, he redeemed humankind. He not only advocates for the weak and the poor, but also disowns those who turn their backs on the downtrodden. "Caste and Christ" underscores the fact that Stowe's strongest objections to slavery stemmed from her religious beliefs. Central to those beliefs was the conviction that Christ taught by example, making it possible to deduce the right course to follow regarding slavery, even though the New Testament does not record any words spoken by Christ to denounce the institution.

"Caste and Christ" is reminiscent of Stowe's "The Freeman's Dream; A Parable," which appeared in the *National Era* of 1 August 1850. In that sketch, a farmer refuses to give food to a fugitive slave family and then falls asleep and dreams of Judgment Day, when he will be turned away from heaven by an angry God who says, "I was an hungered, and ye gave me no meat" (1; Matt. 25:42). Once again, it is Christ's example—not New Testament pronouncements interpreted so as to seem to overturn Old Testament law—that undergirds Stowe's religious opposition to the institution of slavery.

"Caste and Christ," like Stowe's chapters on Senator Bird and the Quaker settlement in *Uncle Tom's Cabin,* focuses on the theme of free people's responsibilities to a fugitive slave. John Greenleaf Whittier is one of those who commented that the passage of the Fugitive Slave Law impelled Stowe to write *Uncle Tom's Cabin,* which appeared serially in the antislavery weekly *National Era* during his tenure as corresponding editor. In May 1852, Whittier wrote to William Lloyd Garrison: "What a glorious work Harriet Beecher Stowe has wrought. *Thanks* for the Fugitive Slave Law! Better for slavery that law had never been enacted, for it gave occasion for 'Uncle Tom's Cabin'" (*Letters* 2: 191).

Whittier's poem **"A Sabbath Scene"** (*Poems* 312-13), also written as a direct response to the Fugitive Slave Law and published on 27 June 1850 in the *National*

Era, offers the same conclusion as that presented in Stowe's works. In its focus on construing what Christ would do rather than what the Bible says or what the clergy teach, **"A Sabbath Scene"** resembles Stowe's "Caste and Christ." In twenty-six four-line stanzas, **"A Sabbath Scene"** tells a story of a fugitive slave woman who runs into a church on a Sunday, begging sanctuary against the slave hunter who follows close behind. Unlike Stowe's poem, in which the slave's pleas immediately fall on deaf ears, Whittier's poem shows men, women, and a pastor who instinctively move to protect the runaway. However, they are quickly persuaded to turn her over to her master once he identifies himself and claims, "[I have] law and gospel on my side." The pastor orders the deacon to throw down the holy book to trip the slave, and then the pastor himself ties her up while reciting scriptural texts that justify slavery. The slave's cries are smothered by the altar cloth, and in vain "she turned from face to face, / For human pity seeking!"

The speaker of the poem, an outraged witness, declares:

> My brain took fire: "Is this," I cried,
>   "The end of prayer and preaching?
> Then down with pulpit, down with priest,
>   And give us Nature's teaching!
>
> "Foul shame and scorn be on ye all
>   Who turn the good to evil,
> And steal the Bible from the Lord,
>   To give it to the Devil!"

The justification for this outburst is not Scripture, but higher law, or what the Quaker Whittier would have called "inner light." The speaker claims a "statute higher" than "garbled text or parchment law," adding, "God is true, though every book / And every man's a liar!" At that moment, he is seized, called an infidel by the priest, and accused of treason by the lawyer. Then he realizes that the clanging steeple bell is in reality a supper-bell; the horrific scene and the fiery challenge it elicited from him were a dream. It is as if the Quaker poet—who in real life had been stoned for his abolitionist activities, had been outraged when a physician was imprisoned for merely lending another man a copy of Whittier's *Justice and Expediency* (1833), and had seen his publishing house in Philadelphia burned to the ground by a mob of proslavery activists—preferred to distance himself from angry conflict by couching it in dream imagery.

A stanza that Whittier excised from later published versions of **"A Sabbath Scene"** alludes to the immediate political and theological circumstances that prompted him to write the poem:

> I woke, and lo! the fitting cause
>   Of all my dream's vagaries—

> Two bulky pamphlets, Webster's text
> With Stuart's Commentaries.

The references to Webster and Stuart, which in June 1850 would have been familiar to the reading public, require explanation today. On 7 March 1850, Daniel Webster, the senator from Whittier's home state of Massachusetts, delivered a passionate address before the U.S. Senate called "The Constitution and the Union" wherein he eloquently asserted that keeping the Union together was the most important consideration in the crisis over slavery. His speech began, "I wish to speak to-day, not as a Massachusetts man, nor as a Northern man, but as an American, and a member of the Senate of the United States. . . . I speak to-day for the preservation of the Union" (qtd. in Remini 669). Webster further asserted that, in the matter of a citizen's obligation to return runaway slaves, Southerners had the Constitution on their side. Reading "Webster's text" caused Whittier to experience, in his words, "one of the saddest moments of my life" (qtd. in Remini 677). Ralph Waldo Emerson, too, was dismayed. He called Webster's position "treachery" and decried Webster's use of the word *liberty*: "'Liberty! Liberty!' Pho! Let Mr Webster for decency's sake shut his lips once & forever on this word. The word *liberty* in the mouth of Mr Webster sounds like the word *love* in the mouth of a courtezan" (qtd. in Remini 677).

Later, on 3 June 1850, Webster threw his support behind the specific proposal that, when enacted in September, became known as the Fugitive Slave Law. So critical to its passage was Webster's support that Henry David Thoreau, in *Walden* (1854), referred to it as "Webster's Fugitive-Slave Bill" (232). "The Constitution and the Union" and passage of the Fugitive Slave Law were enough to cost Webster the support of many of his constituents and to confirm those with scruples against slavery in their belief that Webster was either morally blind or politically motivated. Whittier, who earlier in his life had supported Webster in his campaigns for the U.S. Senate and for president, had as early as 1846 come to see Webster as a "colossal coward" because he would not take an uncompromising stance against slavery (*Letters* 2: 38). **"Ichabod,"** another of Whittier's poems from 1850 concerning Daniel Webster, chronicles Webster's fall from grace among antislavery advocates. One stanza of **"Ichabod"** angrily expresses Whittier's sense of betrayal:

> Of all we loved and honored, naught
> Save power remains:
> A fallen angel's pride of thought,
> Still strong in chains.

> (***Poems*** 186-87)

Horace Mann, outraged at Webster's disregard for moral principles and human rights, read **"Ichabod"** to the House of Representatives (Remini 677).

The other person named in the stanza excised from **"A Sabbath Scene"** is Professor Moses Stuart of Andover Theological Seminary, one of the influential people who publicly endorsed Webster's reasoning. Then, in response to queries from those seeking "some way of Christian politics" to guide them in regard to the issue of fugitive slaves, Stuart wrote *Conscience and the Constitution* (1850), his commentary on Webster's speech. In this work—bulky indeed at 119 pages—one finds the biblical scholar's troubling exegesis of Deuteronomy 23:15-16: "Thou shalt not deliver unto his master the servant which is escaped from his master unto thee. He shall dwell with thee, even among you, in that place which he shall choose, in one of thy gates, where it liketh him best; thou shalt not oppress him." Stuart explained that *thee* referred to the whole nation of Israel. A fugitive slave seeking refuge in Israel would have escaped a pagan master, not one owned by a fellow Hebrew. Since the United States was one nation and southern slave owners were Christian, he reasoned, the directive to shelter a fugitive slave did not apply to individual Americans in 1850 (Mitchell 139-43). Taking different tacks, political and theological, Webster and Stuart both stressed the importance of honoring and preserving the country as one community.

To Whittier, preserving the Union was less important than securing justice and freedom for all. He had no patience for those who espoused a gradual emancipation of slaves. The last five stanzas of **"A Sabbath Scene"** assert the superiority of the speaker's intuitive understanding of God's will over the understanding of the clergy who privilege scriptural text over "Nature's teaching." In these stanzas, the speaker discovers that he fell asleep at an open window while reading the Bible. He wakes to see the wind lifting the pages of the "good old Book" and blowing white blooms over it, "as if God's truth / And Mercy kissed each other." An oriole singing to the sun completes the peaceful imagery that contrasts with the violent dream scene. The poem concludes:

> As bird and flower made plain of old
> The lesson of the Teacher,
> So now I heard the written Word
> Interpreted by Nature!
>
> For to my ear methought the breeze
> Bore Freedom's blessed word on;
> Thus saith the Lord: Break every yoke,
> Undo the heavy burden!

The bird that Christ used to illustrate the heavenly Father's care for even the lowliest of his creatures was the sparrow, whose fall does not go unnoticed, and the flower was one that was even more gloriously arrayed than Solomon, that is, the lily of the field. Even the breeze in **"A Sabbath Scene"** carries an abolitionist message that the poet translates for a public he hoped to sway. With the oriole, the white blooms, and the breeze in the last two stanzas, Whittier portrays nature as literally continuing—not just illustrating—Christ's teaching.

"A Sabbath Scene" struck a chord with mid-nineteenth-century readers, at least those in the North who had not made up their minds that returning runaway slaves was their legal and moral duty. Although its fame never rivaled that of Whittier's 1834 poem beginning "Our fellow-countrymen in chains!"—which was widely distributed under the famous picture of a kneeling, chained slave rhetorically asking, "Am I not a man and a brother?"—"A Sabbath Scene" was reprinted in many Northern newspapers and issued as a broadside (Pickard, *Introduction* 33).[2]

"Caste and Christ" and "A Sabbath Scene" present dramatic encounters between free whites and fugitive slaves. In each narrative poem, sympathy lies with the slave; harsh judgment is reserved for insensitive or brutal whites. Both authors use familiar images and simple verse forms with regular rhyme and rhythm, making their poems accessible to a wide readership. Most strikingly, both poets presume to speak for Christ, though Stowe does so more boldly. Stowe's poem, which uses biblical diction throughout, with such word choices as *wouldst, spake,* and *thee,* actually presents a Christ who preaches a sermon not found in the New Testament. From the middle of the eighth stanza, where Christ says, "Rise! for *I* have called thee *brother,*" to at least the penultimate stanza, the alternately comforting and admonishing words are purportedly spoken by Christ. Although Whittier's more politically explicit poem has a more outraged tone, it is more modest when it comes to speaking for Christ. The speaker of the poem simply interprets Christ's message from signs in nature; the breeze only seems to the speaker to be paraphrasing Isaiah 58:6, "Is not this the fast that I have chosen? To loose the bands of wickedness, to undo the heavy burdens, and to let the oppressed go free, and that ye break every yoke?" In these poems, Stowe is more theologically daring, Whittier more politically daring.

Through popular literature, Stowe and Whittier participated in the great antebellum political and religious debates. They both sided with the group of clergy that Laura L. Mitchell calls "antirenditionists." In her study of northern ministers' reactions to the Fugitive Slave Law, Mitchell contrasts prorenditionists with antirenditionists. The former disapproved of both slavery and abolitionism, preferring gradual emancipation. They preached in favor of compliance with the law and relied on a literal interpretation of the Bible to justify their arguments. Antirenditionists opposed slavery and advocated noncompliance with the Fugitive Slave Law. They based their arguments on Christ's example of charity toward all and his command that people love one another and treat all as they would wish to be treated. Mitchell explains: "This understanding of the golden rule reflected a 'Christocentric' trend in nineteenth-century romantic religion. . . . Liberal theologians increasingly focused on Christ as the revealer of human possibilities and the leader of divine and human causes. . . . The fact that neither Christ nor the apostles ever condemned slavery verbally was therefore irrelevant" (157-58). Stowe's "Caste and Christ" and Whittier's "A Sabbath Scene" are clearly meant to advance that Christocentric trend. Whittier had written explicitly about the golden rule in the 24 February 1848 *National Era* article titled "The Eleventh Commandment." In the story, an English bishop chastises a young clergyman for speaking of an eleventh commandment. The young man defends himself, pointing out that the original ten had been augmented by one when Christ said, "Behold I give unto you a new commandment, love one another." Whittier commented on the story: "The conduct of too many of the clergy of all sects in our own country, on the question of slavery, can only be accounted for by the supposition that they have neither learned, or forgotten the *Eleventh* commandment."

A few months later, on 4 May 1848, Whittier again used the *National Era* to scold the American clergy, this time by contrasting them with eighteenth-century bishops in England who would pronounce a curse on anyone—even a king—who would violate any part of the Magna Carta. In "The Curse of the Charter-Breakers," Whittier condemned the antebellum American clergy with these words:

> Now too oft the priesthood wait
> At the threshold of the State—
> Waiting for the beck and nod
> Of its power as "law and God."

> (*Poems* 306-8)

Whittier challenges the clergy to be protectors of the moral way, not apologists for man-made law.

Whittier had used poetry to criticize the clergy on a number of occasions prior to the passage of the Fugitive Slave Law. In 1836, in response to a news article claiming that the clergy of Charleston, South Carolina, had attended a proslavery meeting and thereby given their support to slavery as an institution, Whittier wrote "Clerical Oppressors," a poem of twelve four-line stanzas. The tone is one of moral indignation; Whittier calls the southern clergy "[p]aid hypocrites," and he sarcastically enjoins them to

> Feed fat, ye locusts, feed!
> And, in your tasselled pulpits, thank the Lord
> That, from the toiling bondsman's utter need
> Ye pile your own full board.

If the earthly injustice of profiting from the labor of the needy is outrageous, worse yet is the southern proslavery clergy's perversion of God's teaching:

> Woe to the priesthood! woe
> To those whose hire is with the price of blood;
> Perverting, darkening, changing, as they go,
> The searching truths of God!

Then Whittier calls on God to

> . . . speed the moment on
> When Wrong shall cease, and Liberty and Love
> And Truth and Right throughout the earth be known
> As in their home above.

(Poems 272)

To Whittier, the immorality of slavery was self-evident, and clergy who defended it had to be hypocrites.

Northern clergy did not escape Whittier's censure. In 1837, the year after the publication of **"Clerical Oppressors,"** Whittier used a poem to skewer those who had attended a meeting of the General Association of Congregational Ministers. That meeting resulted in a pastoral letter enjoining congregations not to be forced into debates over slavery. The letter further warned against the present dangers that threatened "female character." The event that prompted this clerical response was a public lecture by Angelina and Sarah Grimké, women whom Whittier admired for their abolitionist activism. Whittier's poem **"The Pastoral Letter"** likens these clergymen to "parish Popes" and to their Puritan ancestors, whose intolerance led to many atrocities, including hanging a Quaker woman. The poem condemns the clergy for their intolerance and warns them against trying to suppress those who "claim the right of free opinion." It further asks for divine protection for "Carolina's high-souled daughters" who are bringing truth to "an evil land" (***Poems*** 276-78).

Whittier's condemnation of clergy who did not advocate the immediate abolition of slavery is far more vehement than Stowe's in "Caste and Christ." His deeply held Quaker convictions made it more natural for him to reject clerical authority. Stowe, daughter and sister of prominent Congregationalist clergymen and wife of a theologian, held out hope that the church would find and do its moral duty. In a letter that she wrote to Frederick Douglass while she was working on *Uncle Tom's Cabin,* Stowe defended the church: "[T]he strength and hope of your oppressed race does lie in the church. . . . The light will spread in churches, the tone of feeling will rise, Christians North and South will give up their testimony against slavery, and thus the work will be done" (qtd. in C. Stowe 153). In a similar vein, she wrote in 1854 to William Lloyd Garrison, who had pointed out her inconsistency in participating in worship services with the evangelical American clergy,

"nine-tenths" of whom, he estimated, believed that the Bible justified slavery. She responded, "Our field lies in the church as yet. I differ from you as to what *may* be done and hoped there" (qtd. in Hedrick 252).[3]

When Stowe wrote *A Key to Uncle Tom's Cabin,* she devoted the final fourth of the book to a discussion of religion and slavery. There she decries the gradually corrupting influence of the concessions to slave owners that opponents of slavery made early in our country's history. She examines the divisions that occurred as various denominations split into pro- and antislavery factions, and she tackles the thorny problem of the Bible and its teachings on slavery. Of the northern clergy, she writes that there is "an ever increasing hostility to slavery in a decided majority of ministers and church-members in free states, *taken as individuals.*" But the problem for them, she continues, is that "sincere opponents of slavery have been unhappily divided among themselves as to principles and measures, the extreme principles and measures of some causing a hurtful reaction in others" (216). Even the Congregationalists, she writes, have not done all they should do to bring an end to slavery in America. She wishes that all American churches had proceeded with the same fervor and to the same effect as the Quakers, and she mentions that Whittier planned to write a history of the Quakers' actions regarding slavery.[4]

By the time Stowe wrote *Dred,* she was ready to censure the clergy fully. Reverend Titmarsh, Reverend Packthread, Dr. Calker, Dr. Cushing, and Father Bonnie are guilty of everything from wishing to avoid a confrontation over slavery to bargaining for a good deal on a slave. Sarah D. Hartshorne writes that Stowe "probed and unmasked the weaknesses and the doubts of this cross-section of Christians" (295). Stowe's *Dred* has all the fire of Whittier's antislavery, anticlerical poems.

Stowe and Whittier shared what each believed to be a sacred mission, to rid the United States of the sin of slavery. Using literature for their polemical purpose brought them together in the pages of the *National Era* and the *Atlantic.* And Stowe's publisher, John P. Jewett, established another literary connection between Whittier and Stowe. Jewett commissioned Whittier to write a poem about the sentimental idol of *Uncle Tom's Cabin* and paid him fifty dollars for it (Hedrick 224). The poem was later set to music. In **"Eva,"** a poem of seven four-line stanzas, Whittier exhorts readers to "dry the tears for holy Eva," for she has gone to a "better home" where "tears are wiped, and fetters fall" (***Poems*** 218).

Stowe and Whittier admired each other. Of Whittier, Stowe wrote, "He is the true poet whose *life* is a poem. . . . His life has been a consecration, his songs an inspiration, to all that is highest and best" (qtd. in Kribbs xxiv). In January 1853, Whittier wrote to Stowe,

"I say nothing of thy book. It needs no words. I bless God for it, as I look with awe and wonder upon its world moving mission" (*Letters* 2: 213). On the occasion of her seventieth birthday celebration, he saluted her in **"A Greeting"** as one who,

> . . . in our evil time,
> Dragged into light the nation's crime
> With strength beyond the strength of men,
> And, mightier than their swords, her pen!
> To her who world-wide entrance gave
> To the log-cabin of the slave;
> Made all his wrongs and sorrows known,
> And all earth's languages his own. . . .

> (*Poems* 237-38)

Two previously unpublished letters written late in his life show that Whittier continued to hold Stowe in high esteem. In 1888, he acknowledged Stowe's greetings to him on his eightieth birthday with a postcard:

Oak Knoll Danvers 1st 1st Mo 1888

Dear Mrs. Stowe, How can I thank thee for so kindly remembering me as I reached the 80th milestone. No voice of greeting was more welcome than thine. I have sad reports of thy ill health, and was very glad to see thy old handwriting again. I have been in very feeble condition for some months, and at this time am afflicted with catarrhal inflammation and almost blinding neuralgia. But I have enjoyed the summer and beautiful autumn, more than ever. God has been good to me in so many ways. O dear friend! Standing with me on the verge of life we can trust our future to Him! Ever affectionately John G Whittier

I got thy beautiful ed. of Uncle Tom's Cabin and am reading it for the 20th time."[5]

Whittier's rereadings of *Uncle Tom's Cabin*—even after the Emancipation Proclamation was history—attest to his continued fondness for the book that made its debut in his *National Era*.

Other letters written around the same time also contain references to his birthday, his health, and his work for abolition. Apparently, his eightieth birthday had proved quite an ordeal for Whittier, whose health had never been strong. In a letter to Elizabeth Nell Gay written eleven days after his note to Stowe, Whittier claims:

I have been thronged with visitors and overwhelmed with letters and telegrams. The letters alone number 1000. I had been ill for a month before and a cold and severe neuralgia since have made it quite impossible to answer the mass of friendly missives which is piled under my desk. The whole affair was very distasteful to me. I have always tried to avoid notoriety and I am ashamed of this *fuss* about my birth-day.

> (*Letters* 3: 550)

Again to Gay he mentions his past abolitionist activities:

It almost seems impossible that I am 80 years old. Looking back it seems but a little while since I was at Joseph Healys editing the *Penna. Freeman*. Well for good or ill, my life is drawing to its close and I am waiting the call which is inevitable with patience and hope.

> (3: 550)

Another birthday token Whittier acknowledged came from two prominent black leaders in Washington, DC. One, Robert Heberton Terrell, was a black educator who later became a judge for the Washington municipal court. The other, George Washington Williams, was a Baptist clergyman who had been a colonel in the Civil War and the U.S. minister to Haiti. Terrell and Williams had sent Whittier the resolutions passed by what Whittier called "a great meeting of the colored citizens of the nation's capital," which Whittier heard "as the voice of millions of my fellow countrymen." He continues:

That voice was dumb in slavery when, more than half a century ago, I put forth my plea for the freedom of the slave.

It could not answer me from the rice swamp and cotton field; but now, God be praised, it speaks from your great meeting in Washington and from all the colleges and schools where the youth of your race are taught. I scarcely expected then that the people for whom I pleaded would ever know of my efforts in their behalf. I cannot be too thankful to the Divine Providence that I have lived to hear their grateful response.

> (*Letters* 3: 548)

Near the end of his life, Whittier recalled his efforts on behalf of abolition with a mixture of pride and humility. His reference to God and Divine Providence and to "waiting the call" to the hereafter attest to the deeply spiritual motives that had actuated his reformist efforts.

An 1890 letter (written just two years before he died) expresses Whittier's appreciation for the gift of Stowe's biography compiled by her son Charles. This letter, too, alludes to Whittier's belief that abolitionist activity was a response to a divine mandate:

Oak Knoll, Danvers, Mass

6th Mo 10 1890

My Dear Friend

Harriet Beecher Stowe,

From my heart I thank thee for thy book—the record of a noble and beautiful life and of the mighty work which God gave thee to do for thy country and humanity. I am glad, notwithstanding thy enfeebled health, thou has been able to take a part in the biography, which seems to me all that could be wished for.

I am now in my 83rd year, and in feeble health, with failing strength and sight. We are both of us "only waiting" the call from the world of time and sense. In

God alone is our hope, and our faith in His goodness and mercy is unlimited. God bless and comfort thee! I am gratefully and affectionately thy old friend,

John G Whittier

In Whittier's retrospective evaluation, "[T]he mighty work which God gave thee to do for thy country and humanity"—the work of abolition—was divinely prompted work with both political and humanitarian benefits. His sense of gratitude for her friendship must have been augmented by the sense of loss of the many other literary and abolitionist friends who had died. James Russell Lowell (died 1891), John Greenleaf Whittier (died 1892), Oliver Wendell Holmes (died 1894), and Harriet Beecher Stowe (died 1896) were the last survivors of a group that had used its literary talents for political and moral suasion on the issue of slavery. The bonds that united those in that group were stronger for the shared sense of indignation that abolitionists felt when they were attacked by keepers of the status quo, including prorendition ministers.

Whittier expressed his feeling of belonging to a besieged group in his positive review of Emerson's "An Address . . . in Concord . . . on 1st August, 1844, on the Anniversary of the Emancipation of the Negroes in the British West Indies," which was later titled "Emancipation in the British West Indies." Emerson, always reluctant to play the reformer's role, nevertheless came out in support of the slave's humanity and in opposition to the institution of slavery. In a review of Emerson's address printed in the 12 September 1844 *Middlesex Standard,* Whittier writes that he and many other abolitionists have "felt half indignant that, while we were struggling against the popular current, mobbed, hunted, denounced, from the legislative forum, cursed from the pulpit, sneered at by wealth and fashion and shallow aristocracy, such a man as Ralph Waldo Emerson should be brooding over his pleasant philosophies, writing his quaint and beautiful essays, in his retirement on the banks of the Concord, unconcerned and 'calm as a summer's morning'" (qtd. in Gougeon 91). Although Whittier here praises Emerson's newly articulated antislavery position, there is no mistaking the resentment he acknowledges having felt when he and other abolitionists were incurring the scorn of the public, political leaders, preachers, and the prosperous while Emerson was concerning himself with philosophical—not political—matters.

Whittier's poem **"Tent on the Beach"** (1867) presents his earlier appraisal of the way in which he had used his poetic talents from the 1830s through the 1850s. In it, he casts himself as one

Who, with a mission to fulfil,
Had left the Muses' haunts to turn
The crank of an opinion-mill,

Making his rustic reed of song
A weapon in the war with wrong.

(*Poems* 242-45)

As his letters to Stowe and others show, at the end of his life Whittier believed his decision to abandon the muses and use his literary talents for political purposes was a good one. The Christocentric basis of Whittier's and Stowe's antislavery convictions forged a lasting bond between two people of very different backgrounds and temperaments.

Although "Caste and Christ" and **"A Sabbath Scene"** are not the most important of Stowe's and Whittier's "weapon[s] in the war with wrong," they nevertheless help to elucidate the religious dimensions of the debates over the Fugitive Slave Law and the institution of slavery.

Notes

1. The poem, with slight variations in wording and punctuation, appears in two children's versions of *Uncle Tom's Cabin.* They are *A Peep Into Uncle Tom's Cabin,* by "Aunt Mary" (1853) and *Un Coup d'oeil dans la case de l'oncle Tom* (1853). The French version includes "Caste and Christ" in English and in a French translation.

2. A broadside bearing the heading "A Tract for the Times! / A Sabbath Scene. / By J. G. Whittier" and dated June 1850 retains the verse that mentions Webster and Stuart. But when the poem was included in *The Chapel of the Hermits, and Other Poems* (1853), that verse was dropped. See Currier (69, 335-36) for the publication history of "A Sabbath Scene."

3. See Hedrick (225-26) for a discussion of Stowe's quarrel with one member of the clergy, Dr. Joel Parker of Philadelphia. The quarrel resulted from Stowe's mentioning his name in a footnote in *Uncle Tom's Cabin* and his subsequent threat to charge her with libel.

4. Whittier never completed his planned article. He did give Stowe a little assistance as she was compiling *A Key to Uncle Tom's Cabin.* John B. Pickard, editor of *The Letters of John Greenleaf Whittier,* claims that Whittier "probably supplied materials" on Quakers that Stowe used in part 1, chapter 13 (ii, 202). Also, in October 1852, Whittier wrote to Stowe, first sending her "[t]en thousand thanks for thy immortal book" and then telling her where she could find information about Richard Dillingham, the Ohio Quaker who was jailed for trying to help fugitive slaves escape in 1848 (Whittier, *Letters* 2: 201). Furthermore, Whittier's poem "The Cross"—which had appeared in the *National Era* in February 1852, near

the end of that periodical's serial publication of *Uncle Tom's Cabin*—is reprinted in "The Quakers," a chapter in Stowe's *Key*. It celebrates Dillingham as a martyr because he died in a Nashville penitentiary before serving out his three-year sentence. Whittier apostrophizes Dillingham, telling him that his cross of suffering is really a staff supporting him in the Master's path and that his sacrifice will yield results in time. Stowe expresses the same ideals about sacrifice and martyrdom through the famous fictional suffering and death of Uncle Tom.

5. This postcard, along with the letter below dated "6th Mo 10, 1890," is from the private collection of Daphne Chapin of Cambridge, Massachusetts, and is used by permission. I wish to thank Brian Kirkpatrick, former owner of the Drawbridge Gallery in Mystic, Connecticut, for calling these materials to my attention.

Works Cited

"Aunt Mary." *A Peep into Uncle Tom's Cabin*. London: Sampson Low & Son; Boston: Jewett, 1853.

The Bible. King James Version. Nashville: Thomas Nelson, 1984.

Currier, T. F. *A Bibliography of John Greenleaf Whittier*. New York: Russell & Russell, 1937.

Emerson, Ralph Waldo. "Emancipation in the British West Indies." *The Complete Works of Ralph Waldo Emerson*. Ed. E. W. Emerson. Boston: Houghton Mifflin, 1903-4. 11: [97]-147.

Gougeon, Len. *Virtue's Hero: Emerson, Antislavery, and Reform*. Athens: U of Georgia P, 1990.

Hartshorne, Sarah D. "'Woe Unto You That Desire the Day of the Lord': Harriet Beecher Stowe and the Corruption of Christianity in *Dred, A Tale of the Great Dismal Swamp*." *Anglican and Episcopal History* 64 (1995): 280-99.

Hedrick, Joan D. *Harriet Beecher Stowe: A Life*. New York: Oxford UP, 1994.

Kribbs, Jayne K., ed. *Critical Essays on John Greenleaf Whittier*. Boston: G. K. Hall, 1980.

Mitchell, Laura L. "'Matters of Justice Between Man and Man': Northern Divines, the Bible, and the Fugitive Slave Act of 1850." *Religion and the Antebellum Debate over Slavery*. Ed. John R. McKivigan and Mitchell Snay. Athens: U of Georgia P, 1998. 134-65.

Pickard, John B. *John Greenleaf Whittier: An Introduction and Interpretation*. New York: Barnes & Noble, 1961.

———. "Whittier's Abolitionist Poetry." Kribbs 106-15.

Remini, Robert V. *Daniel Webster: The Man and His Time*. New York: Norton, 1997.

Rochester Ladies' Anti-Slavery Society. *Autographs for Freedom*. Boston: Jewett, 1853.

Stowe, Charles Edward. *Life of Harriet Beecher Stowe, Compiled from Her Letters and Journals*. Boston: Houghton Mifflin, 1889.

Stowe, Harriet Beecher. "Caste and Christ." *A Peep into Uncle Tom's Cabin*. London: Sampson Low & Son, 1853. 419-21.

———. "The Freeman's Dream; A Parable." *National Era* 1 Aug. 1850: 1.

———. *A Key to Uncle Tom's Cabin*. Boston: Jewett, 1853.

———. *Uncle Tom's Cabin*. Ed. Elizabeth Ammons. New York: Norton, 1994.

Stowe, Mme Henriette [sic] Beecher. *Un Coup D'oeil dans LaCase de L'Oncle Tom*. Toulouse: Société des livres religieux, 1869.

Stuart, Moses. *Conscience and the Constitution*. Boston: Crocker & Brewster, 1850.

Thoreau, Henry D. *Walden*. Ed. J. Lyndon Shanley. The Writings of Henry D. Thoreau. Princeton: Princeton UP, 1971.

Whittier, John Greenleaf. "The Eleventh Commandment." *National Era* 24 Feb. 1848: 1.

———. Letter to Harriet Beecher Stowe. 10 June 1890. Private collection of Daphne Chapin, Cambridge, MA.

———. *The Letters of John Greenleaf Whittier*. Ed. John B. Pickard. Vols. 2 and 3. Cambridge: Harvard UP, 1975. 3 vols.

———. *The Poems of Whittier*. Ed. Horace Scudder. Boston: Houghton Mifflin, 1894.

———. Postcard to Harriet Beecher Stowe. 1 Jan. 1888. Private collection of Daphne Chapin, Cambridge, MA.

Brenda Wineapple (essay date 2004)

SOURCE: Wineapple, Brenda. Introduction to *John Greenleaf Whittier: Selected Poems*, edited by Brenda Wineapple, pp. xi-xxvii.: The Library of America, 2004.

[*In the following introduction, Wineapple praises the fiery rhetoric of Whittier's anti-slavery poems and believes they deserve to be revisited by readers today.*]

Once upon a time the poetry of John Greenleaf Whittier was force-fed to generations of schoolchildren, myself among them, who suffered, claustrophobic, through the masterpiece **Snow-Bound,** never for a moment under-standing what we read. I was in the eighth grade, my family having recently returned to Haverhill, Mas-sachusetts, Whittier's birthplace (and my mother's), and I shuffled off to school—the John Greenleaf Whittier school, of course—where in the first confusing days, I was temporarily placed in a class instructed by a Fireside Teacher whom I hated on first sight. Whittier didn't help. It all seemed so, well, *local.*

Disaffected, I longed for the alienation **Snow-Bound** can't provide. I did not know and was not told that the Quaker poet I resented actually put his life and his verse on the line, writing poetry committed to the aboli-tion of slavery. At 12, I knew only **Snow-Bound** and could not care less about its "Flemish pictures of old days"; its gray-winged "Angel of the backward look" seemed as beside the point as its unbroken surface. Later I realized I had been too young for the poem, and now I suspect that all the schoolchildren subjected to Whittier's assurances are themselves too callow to understand, never mind care, how memory fends off the mindlessness of winter storm. After all, the highly descriptive and introspective **Snow-Bound** is not just about a moment of rural life, beautifully evoked and bygone; it's a lyrical, lovely, and all-too-fragile hedge against the "coldness visible" that turns the world to white.

"Sit with me by the homestead hearth," invites the poet near **Snow-Bound**'s end,

> And stretch the hands of memory forth
>   To warm them at the wood-fire's blaze!
> And thanks untraced to lips unknown
> Shall greet me like the odors blown
> From unseen meadows newly mown,
> Or lilies floating in some pond,
> Wood-fringed, the wayside gaze beyond;
> The traveller owns the grateful sense
> Of sweetness near, he knows not whence,
> And, pausing, takes with forehead bare
> The benediction of the air.

At an early age, Whittier worked the farm and roamed the woods or climbed Job's Hill, which rose almost directly out of the family garden. In the house, there was a Bible but few other books, and the only annual was an almanac. Whittier later said that whenever he heard of a biography or volume of travel, he'd walk miles, doubtless through snow, to borrow it. But when William Lloyd Garrison began his weekly paper, the *Free Press,* in nearby Newburyport, Whittier's father, impressed, canceled his subscription to the *Haverhill Gazette.*

Whittier is a poet of place, and his place is fundamen-tally New England, where generations of Whittiers, turned Quaker, had lived since the poet's great-great-grandfather Thomas came to America in 1638. Settling permanently in the village of Haverhill, he then built the old farmhouse in sight of no other home, just miles of woodland and, to the west, a pasture dotted with oaks and walnuts. The poet's father was a hardscrabble farmer, often in debt, and a town selectman with scant use for literature: "A prompt, decisive man, no breath / Our father wasted," Whittier would write of him in **Snow-Bound.**

Whittier's literary mentor was the schoolmaster, Joshua Coffin, who brought a volume of Robert Burns to the Whittier homestead to recite aloud. Whittier was mesmerized—and thrilled when Coffin loaned him the book. A sensitive child, the boy was already living a double life, hunting eggs hidden in the barn by day and secretly reading Walter Scott's *The Pirate* at night by candlelight while fantasizing about the adventures he early put into rhyme. In 1826, his elder sister Mary mailed one of her brother's poems to the *Free Press*; Garrison printed it and another one, then drove out to Haverhill to meet the 19-year-old contributor and urge his father to send the boy to school. "Sir, poetry will not get him bread," Whittier's father reportedly answered.

Unfazed, at least outwardly, Whittier learned how to sew ladies' slippers for eight cents a pair and pocketed enough money for a six-month stint at the Haverhill Academy. Unlike his peers Henry Wadsworth Longfel-low or James Russell Lowell, he did not attend college or teach at Harvard and was not, as poet Richard Howard said of Longfellow, "fatally fluent." Whittier was, in essence, a poor farmer's son, a poor man, and an autodidact, insecure but without pretension. "I am not a builder in the sense of Milton's phrase of one who could 'build the lofty rhyme,'" he once said of his work. "My vehicles have been of the humbler sort—merely the farm wagon and buckboard of verse."

Yet verse was his life. Conscious of his meager educa-tion and a modest man despite world-class ambitions, inversely proportional to his poverty, toward the end of his life Whittier scrupulously told a biographer to anticipate the criticism readers would no doubt continue heaping on his work. "Touch upon my false rhymes and Yankeeisms," he instructed. "Own that I sometimes choose unpoetical themes. Endorse Lowell's 'Fable for Critics,' that I mistake, occasionally, simple excitement for inspiration." For Lowell, in his 1848 send-up of contemporary writers, had echoed the popular view of Whittier:

> Let his mind once get head in its favorite direction,
> And the torrent of verse bursts the dams of reflection,
> While, borne with the rush of the metre along,
> The poet may chance to go right or go wrong,
> Content with the whirl and delirium of song;

Then his grammar's not always correct, nor his
  rhymes,
And he's prone to repeat his own lyrics sometimes,—
Not his best, though, for those are struck off at white-
  heats,
When the heart in his breast like a trip-hammer beats.

To a well-heeled versifier like Lowell, Whittier was a rustic. But Whittier was well-read and even fairly catholic in his taste. He quoted Laurence Sterne almost obsessively, loved the *Bhagavad-Gita,* Edmund Burke, Edmund Spenser, Dante, Cervantes, Lamartine, Shelley, and Coleridge. Among American authors he admired Lowell, Emerson, Longfellow, Hawthorne, and Oliver Wendell Holmes. He considered Poe an "extraordinary genius" but was less sure of Thoreau, of whom he wrote: "Thoreau's 'Walden' is capital reading but very wicked and heathenish. The practical moral of it seems to be that if a man is willing to sink himself into a woodchuck, he can live as cheaply as that quadruped; but after all, for me I prefer walking on two legs." Not surprisingly, he didn't know Dickinson, and he regarded Walt Whitman as a "tender" man who, alas, rode an "untamed, rough-jolting Pegasus." When asked to help purchase a horse and buggy for Whitman, then partially paralyzed, Whittier sent ten dollars though he fretted lest the public might think he endorsed the "sensual school" of literature.

Whitman acknowledged that he and Whittier "would not travel well harnessed to the same rig," but he recognized and respected Whittier's "out-cropping love of heroism and war, for all his Quakerdom[;] his verses at times [are] like the measur'd step of Cromwell's old veterans." Whittier understood this side of himself but thought that "Few guessed beneath his aspect grave / What passions strove in chains." Whitman wasn't the only one who sensed the fire sizzling under Quaker drab. A friend, Edna Dean Proctor, observed, "I have always been impressed by the mingled volcano and iceberg of your character."

Despite flirtations with various women, Whittier never married. Tall, dark, and good-looking, since youth he complained of an array of ailments: palpitations, headaches, neuralgia, eyestrain, back pain, and insomnia, maladies that released him, over time, from farm chores, unwanted visitors, solicitations, speaking engagements, and commitment. "I always did love a pretty girl," he wrote as if in retrospect at the age of 22, adding "the worst of it is—if I ever get married I must marry a Quakeress with her bonnet like a flour dipper, and a face as long as a tobacco yawl." Loyal to the religion of his birth, he was suggesting that it, along with his sundry complaints, stood between himself and marriage. Later he admitted to a friend, "I think I have left a great many roses in my life for fear of the thorns."

Emotionally, he had long been sustained by his mother, Abigail Hussey Whittier, whom the poet remembered as speaking "The common unrhymed poetry / Of simple life and country ways." And he remained devoted to his unmarried sister Elizabeth, with whom he lived until her death, seeming more comfortable with her and the long-term friendships, particularly with women, that didn't threaten his bachelorhood or meddle with his work. Yet he was generous and supportive to writers like Lucy Larcom, Celia Thaxter, and Sarah Orne Jewett, whom he considered an adopted daughter; he exchanged witticisms with the acerbic Gail Hamilton; and after the death of his beloved editor James T. Fields, who first published his non-abolitionist poetry, Whittier grew closer to Fields' wife, Annie. Today, little evidence links Whittier with much of an erotic attachment to woman or to man—despite a smart-alecky interpretation of his "barefoot boy, with cheek of tan!"—though he did develop close friendships with men such as William Lloyd Garrison, for a time, and Charles Sumner.

Above all, Whittier was ambitious. "I am not one to be easily turned aside from any undertaking," he told a friend in youth, and to another, after reading a biography of Byron, he vowed: "I would not depart from this sphere of trial without leaving behind me a name to be remembered when I am dust." His preoccupation with fame persisted, though it was shaken by the poor reception given his first book of prose and verse, *Legends of New England,* published in 1831 when he was 23. He subsequently tried to destroy all copies of the book, and salvaged his pride by announcing: "The world shall know me in a loftier capacity than as a writer of rhymes."

When not working the farm or composing verse, Whittier earned an income as an editor, first of the *American Manufacturer* in Boston (a position he had secured through Garrison), then of the *Haverhill Gazette,* and later of the *New England Weekly Review* in Hartford, Connecticut. As editor, he was consistently active in politics, supporting Henry Clay's bid for the presidency and throwing his increasing weight around in local elections. "Politics is the only field now open for me," he told the poet Lydia Sigourney. "The truth is, I don't care a fig for poetical reputation," he wrote to another friend, "and I had much rather be known as an ardent friend of republican principles." Of course, he was posturing. Whittier had no intention of giving up poetry but needed to square it with his Quaker conscience and a more sober assessment of his talent. Shaking off the influence of Burns, he began to write, without conflict, of the political issues near his heart. As he subsequently explained, he

    with a mission to fulfil
Had left the Muses' haunts to turn
The crank of an opinion-mill,
Making his rustic reed of song
A Weapon in the war with wrong.

"Although I am a Quaker by birthright and sincere convictions," he once said, "I am no sectarian in the strict sense of the term. My sympathies are with the Broad Church of Humanity." As a Quaker, Whittier had been educated to consider slavery the scourge of the country, and as early as 1833 he joined forces with the nascent anti-slavery movement spearheaded by Garrison (with whom he later broke rank). Whittier printed at his own expense the pamphlet *Justice and Expediency; or, Slavery considered with a view to its Rightful and Effectual Remedy, Abolition* (1833), and filled newspapers with a tough-fibered prose, pushing for complete emancipation and the eradication of all prejudice based on skin color. "The tremendous sin of our country, which lies at the bottom of Slavery," he wrote in 1835, was "Hatred of the Black Man." Again, seven years later: "I hate slavery in all its forms, degrees and influences," Whittier declared, "and I deem myself bound by the highest moral and political obligations not to let that sentiment of hate lie dormant and smouldering in my own breast, but to give it free vent and let it blaze forth, that it may kindle equal ardor through the whole sphere of my influence."

Attending the first national anti-slavery convention in Philadelphia and drafting its Declaration of Sentiments, Whittier had also been a delegate to the national Republican convention and a candidate for the Massachusetts legislature, though he was disqualified because of his young age: he was just short of 26. But he was, even then, a crack political operator who, if not exactly in the fray, pulled the levers behind the scenes. For many years, he held Massachusetts congressman Caleb Cushing's toes to the abolitionist fire; he conspired with John Quincy Adams, and believing that the cause would be served best by practical politics, he helped found the Liberty party, a precursor to the new Republican party, running for Congress on its anti-slavery ticket. In 1864, he was instrumental in convincing John C. Frémont not to split the party by opposing Lincoln.

For his pains, a mob in Concord, New Hampshire, pelted the Quaker abolitionist with stones and mud when he accompanied the British anti-slavery activist George Thompson on a lecture tour, and on another occasion he was battered by rotten eggs and sticks in Newburyport. (Hawthorne, a staunch anti-abolitionist, gently poked fun at Whittier, whom he characterized fancifully as "a fiery Quaker youth, to whom the muse had perversely assigned a battle-trumpet, and who got himself lynched, ten years ago, in South Carolina.") In the spring of 1838 when he was editor of *The Pennsylvania Freeman,* a paper of the Anti-Slavery Society, an angry rabble sacked his office in the basement of Pennsylvania Hall, which was burned beyond recognition as the crowd shouted "hang Whittier." The poet barely escaped with his life.

Among his earliest anti-slavery poems was **"Toussaint l'Ouverture"** (1833), about the 1794 slave uprising in Haiti which includes an account of the rape of a French planter's wife so brutal that the literary historian Perry Miller commented it was probably one of the least useful contributions to the abolitionist cause since it could be construed as an argument against, not for, emancipation. If the poem doesn't entirely succeed—despite stirring scenes, it's somewhat diffuse—we need to remember that to Whittier poems are not well-wrought urns. They were meant to be read, sung, shouted, or printed on broadsides, and they took their structure from ballads, hymns, slogans, folk tales, sermons, and vernacular speech. During the Civil War, when the Hutchinson family sang Whittier's ballad **"Ein feste Burg ist unser Gott,"** based on Luther's hymn, it created such a fuss that General McClellan forbade the family to sing it to the troops—until, that is, Lincoln heard the song and renewed the permit.

Whittier did not think his readers would always agree with him—they decidedly didn't—but he wanted to stir their emotions, raise their dander, let them know how he felt. He intended to inspire, not to belittle, and in the matter of abolition he aimed literally to create an audience. (One could say he was eventually successful.) His moral compass clear, his sensibility proudly undissociated, Whittier did not evade, sidestep, or vamp about his convictions. He used no self-irony. His satires were direct, his forms conventional, his narratives linear, his hand open. Angry and at times doubtful ("How little, after all do we *know*?") he offered readers not just the consolations of form but of belief. "What I had I gave," he writes in his long anti-slavery poem **"The Panorama."** He is no Prufrock.

In much of his verse, he could wield a language of forceful immediacy—the "blood-red sky" of **"Toussaint l'Ouverture"**—or make his rhythms pliant, as in **"The Farewell,"** where the Virginia slave mother cries, over and over, "Gone, gone—sold and gone." In **"The Hunters of Men,"** the ballad form and galloping rhythm work well to deride with grim humor anyone, white or black, female or male, cleric or banker, who collaborates in human debasement:

> So speed to their hunting, o'er mountain and glen,
> Through cane-brake and forest,—the hunting of men!

In **"Song of Slaves in the Desert,"** Whittier dramatizes the awestruck cry of a dispossessed people, who ask in refrain, "Where are we going, Rubee?" as the poem's five stanzas take them progressively farther from home. That they never relinquish hope, in their despair, renders the poem supple and heart-piercing.

> When we went from Bornou land,
> We were like the leaves and sand,—

We were many, we are few;
Life has one, and death has two:
Whitened bones our path are showing,
Thou All-seeing, thou All-knowing!
Hear us, tell us, where are we going,
    Where are we going, Rubee?

Whittier clearly felt that poetry could be—although did not have to be—socially engaged, but he never believed poetry should subordinate itself to political necessity or rank didacticism. "There is something inconsistent in the character of a poet & a modern politician," he remarked as early as 1832 as he set out to bring the two worlds together. But by 1840, the abolitionist poet was himself testy on the subject of abolitionist verse. "The thing is getting to be sadly over done," Whittier groused. "Everybody rhymes for them—as if an abolitionist must be ex-officio a rhymer, as one of the Shaking Fraternity must be a dancer,—a sort of philanthropic Della Cruscan Style in which 'slavery's night' jingles with 'Truth and Right'—and 'down-trodden slave' treads upon 'Freedom's grave.'"

A self-critical man to whom versifying came naturally, and sometimes too easily, Whittier valued a poetry, whether political or not, of imagination. He excelled at dramatic monologues, similar in genre to Browning's although different in purpose, and showed real fluidity in this line in his only novel—a good one—called *Leaves from Margaret Smith's Journal,* in which he impersonates a young English woman visiting Massachusetts Bay in 1678. Here, and in principle, Whittier knew the difference between resistance and harangue, faith and dry dogma. His chief gripe against Transcendentalist verse, for example, was that "its largest intent is ethical and religious and not artistic."

If the charge that he is overly didactic or merely topical is to be flung against Whittier, it doesn't stick to a rhetorically powerful, intricately allusive poem like **"Ichabod!"** in which he expresses his disillusionment with the once-mighty orator Daniel Webster. Webster had supported the Compromise of 1850 with its nefarious Fugitive Slave Bill (proposed by another of Whittier's former idols, Henry Clay), allowing slave owners to enter free states, seize runaway slaves—kidnap them, according to the abolitionists—and drag them back to the South. Whittier's response was a kind of eulogy, its anger muted into condescension:

When faith is lost, when honor dies
The man is dead!

Less complex lyrics, like **"A Sabbath Scene,"** are also affecting, as are satires like the **"Letter . . . from a Missionary of the Methodist Episcopal Church,"** with its offhand horrors made conversational. "Here, at the Mission, all things have gone well," writes the missionary,

The brother who, throughout my absence, acted
As overseer, assures me that the crops
Never were better. I have lost one negro,
A first-rate hand, but obstinate and sullen.
He ran away some time last spring, and hid
In the river timber. There my Indian converts
Found him, and treed and shot him. For the rest,
The heathens round about begin to feel
The influence of our pious ministrations
And works of love; and some of them already
Have purchased negroes, and are settling down
As sober Christians! Bless the Lord for this!

We did not read these poems, or **"The Haschish,"** in school.

True, not all of Whittier's work succeeds in showing off his imagination. At times he seems almost afraid of it, as if it really were that fat wheezing demon of his study, the subject of one of his earliest poems. Yet had we, years ago, read his poems about slavery, war, injustice, or any of his comic ballads and dramatic monologues, we wouldn't have run so fast from what appeared as—and could be—pat moralization or facile optimism. We may even have discovered that the easily parodied **"Maud Muller"** is shrewder than we thought, **"Telling the Bees"** more adroit, and Whittier's verse forms, overall, more varied. But my generation (the last, no doubt, to read Whittier under duress) assigned him to the backroom of literature, and we missed the jarring images—"white pagodas of the snow" or "moony breadth of virgin face. / By thought unviolated"—as well as the tender plea in a touching poem like **"The Eternal Goodness"**:

And Thou, O Lord! by whom are seen
    Thy creatures as they be,
Forgive me if too close I lean
    My human heart on Thee!

Whittier often wrote better, more courageously, and with more beauty than we knew.

Consider too the poems where despair almost shatters nature's benign casing. With simple grace, he describes outward circumstance and inner feeling, often both in the same poem. **"The Garrison at Cape Ann,"** for instance, begins as a reminiscence of his walking along the "breezy headlands" on a summer morning; it proceeds to finely etch the garrison house, near the "rude and broken coastline, white with breakers stretching north,—" and its occupants, those soldiers who amuse themselves through the night telling stories until, by spectral sounds, they load their muskets and fire into nothingness. Whittier concludes, in the penultimate stanza, that

Soon or late to all our dwellings come the spectres of
  the mind,
Doubts and fears and dread forebodings, in the darkness undefined;

Round us throng the grim projections of the heart and
  of the brain,
And our pride of strength is weakness, and the cunning hand is vain.

This is a poet who knows of desert spaces.

"The loneliness of life, under even its best circumstances, becomes, at times, appalling to contemplate,"
Whittier told a friend. "No one human soul ever fully
knew another; and an infinite sigh for sympathy is
perpetually going up from the heart of humanity." But,
like Emerson—or Wallace Stevens—Whittier has a
knack for recovery. "Doubtless this very unrest and
longing is the prophecy and guaranty of an immortal
destination," he continued. "Perfect content is stagnation and ultimate death."

After the Civil War, Whittier increasingly wrote
controlled poems of a reflective cast culminating in
Snow-Bound, which was prompted in part by the deaths
of Whittier's mother in 1857 and of his beloved sister
Elizabeth in 1864. Selling 20,000 copies in the first
months of its publication, *Snow-Bound* rocketed the
poet to fame. Reputedly, the poem's staggering success
had to do with America's desire to flee a complicated
present in the aftermath of war, taking refuge in a
child's world of blithe ignorance and family value. But
this reading violates the spirit of the poem. Not only
does Whittier keep beating the drum of reform, the
poem is less a work of escapism than a meditation on
the inevitable "loss in all familiar things."

> The sun that brief December day
> Rose cheerless over hills of gray, . . .

Whittier writes of the inexorability of the winter season
when snow falls fast, its white drifts resembling "tall
and sheeted ghosts." The air turns savage, the winds
shriek, and one little group—one among many—huddles
indoors to stave off its terror with stories. Much as the
poet does: he too, his own "hair as gray / As was my
sire's that winter day," takes comfort, small as it is, in
the mind that replenishes by recreating. Such is the
benediction, to him, of poetry: it transforms sorrow and
affliction into words that are poised, straightforward
and, in their unvarnished way, brave.

The somewhat romanticized portrait of rural life in
Snow-Bound was followed by the **"Prelude"** to *Among
the Hills* (1869), a poem that reveals Whittier at his
scrupulous best. Here he also presents in plain and
speechlike language, startling in its directness, and
without a trace of idealization, the rural world he knew
well:

> Within, the cluttered kitchen-floor, unwashed
> (Broom-clean I think they called it); the best room
> Stifling with cellar damp, shut from the air

> In hot midsummer, bookless, pictureless
> Save the inevitable sampler hung
> Over the fireplace, or a mourning-piece,
> A green-haired woman, peony-cheeked, beneath
> Impossible willows. . . .

Whittier was by now something of a public treasure,
with his birthdays celebrated nationally, and more than
a hundred hymns extracted from his poems. (The most
renowned of these was the last section, "Dear Lord and
Father of mankind," in the otherwise somewhat
incongruous poem, **"The Brewing of Soma."**) He
continued to be politically active, backing local office-
seekers, advocating full civil rights for all citizens, supporting woman suffrage, and protesting both the avarice
of the carpetbaggers and the atrocities of the Ku Klux
Klan.

His private life remained as sequestered as ever, and he
continued to plead poor health as a way of protecting
himself from the unsought requests of well-wishers and
fans. Now, though, his symptoms spelled mortality, and
with death stalking his friends from abolitionist days—
Horace Greeley, Charles Sumner, and then Garrison in
1879—Whittier grew more and more troubled. His literary world began to disappear: Fields died and then Emerson and Longfellow, leaving Whittier to remark to Oliver Wendell Holmes that "we seem to hear our roots
cracking."

Chills, fever, and insomnia notwithstanding, Whittier
continued to publish volumes of verse prolifically, issuing nine collections between 1870 and 1886. His last
book, the privately printed *At Sundown,* appeared
posthumously in 1892, and contained one of the last
poems he wrote, **"To Oliver Wendell Holmes."** The
terms in which he addresses his longtime friend might
well serve to introduce the old poet to a new reader:

> Life is indeed no holiday; therein
>   Are want, and woe, and sin,
> Death and its nameless fears, and over all
>   Our pitying tears must fall.
>
> Sorrow is real; but the counterfeit
>   Which folly brings to it,
> We need thy wit and wisdom to resist,
>   O rarest Optimist!
>
> Thy hand, old friend! the service of our days,
>   In differing moods and ways,
> May prove to those who follow in our train
>   Not valueless nor vain.

Revisited now, Whittier appears fresh, honest, even
flinty and practical. His diction is easy, his detail rich
and unassuming, his emotion deep. And the shale of his
New England landscape reaches outward, promising not
relief from pain but a glimpse of a better, larger world.

One more thing: Whitman also took another look. For
Whittier's 80th birthday, December 17, 1887, the good
gray poet, large and wise, celebrated a fellow traveler:

As the Greek's signal flame, by antique records told,
Rose from the hill-top, like applause and glory,
Welcoming in fame some special veteran, hero,
With rosy tinge reddening the land he'd served,
So I aloft from Mannahatta's ship-fringed shore,
Lift high a kindled brand for thee, Old Poet.

Carol Iannone (essay date spring 2005)

SOURCE: Iannone, Carol. "John Greenleaf Whittier's Civil War." *Modern Age* 47, no. 2 (spring 2005): 132-38.

[*In the following essay, Iannone discusses Whittier's place in American literary history, acknowledging that much of his verse has been forgotten—perhaps rightly so—but praising much of his religious and nature poetry.*]

The Library of America recently issued a volume of the poetry of John Greenleaf Whittier. This is fitting. While he will never be placed in the first rank of poets and even his admirers admit that he authored much dismissible verse, Whittier, who enjoyed wide, trans-Atlantic fame in his lifetime and whose eightieth birthday was a national event, has earned a lasting place in American letters. He can justifiably be called our "best religious poet," as one critic named him, and hymns adapted from his poems are still sung in many Protestant churches today. He is also the author of a number of memorable narrative poems, ballads, and lyrics.

Since he is possibly best known as an Abolitionist, it can come as a surprise to learn that during the Civil War years and their immediate aftermath, Whittier, in his maturity as both a man and a poet, is no longer writing the fiery verse propaganda in support of the cause that marked much of his earlier career, but has for some time been composing out of deeper inspiration and greater poetic resonance. His other poetic subjects apart from slavery—legend, history, nature, the past, and especially the spiritual life—come more to the fore, and even the poems he does write on the events of the day are often more skillful and fashioned with a broader scope.

Whittier was born of Quaker background in December 1807 on a farm near Haverhill, Massachusetts. He became an avid reader and, inspired by the work of Robert Burns, began to write poetry. He received only a little formal education, however, before embarking on a career in journalism. He edited newspapers in Boston, Haverhill, and Hartford, while continuing to write poems on a variety of subjects. In 1833 he became prominent in William Lloyd Garrison's Abolitionist movement, and participated in the first National Anti-

Slavery Convention in Philadelphia. In the ensuing years, Whittier edited an Abolitionist newspaper, *The Pennsylvania Freeman,* served a term in the Massachusetts legislature, wrote many anti-slavery poems, and gave speeches for the cause.

In 1840, he returned to his native state to live in Amesbury, not far from Haverhill, with his mother, Abigail, and his younger sister, Elizabeth. In 1842, believing that slavery could be ended through the political process, he broke with William Lloyd Garrison's radicalism and began writing more expansively. During the years 1857-1863, Abigail, Elizabeth, and Whittier's older sister Mary all died. This added to his reflectiveness, and the experience of loss and the potential for recovery and redemption become prominent in his poetry.

Whittier never regretted his part in the Abolitionist movement, and remarked later in his life in a letter to E. L. Godkin, editor of the *Nation,* "that I cannot be sufficiently grateful to the Divine Providence that so early called my attention to the great interests of humanity, saving me from the poor ambitions and miserable jealousies of a selfish pursuit of literary reputation." Nevertheless, his maturation as a poet came as he turned away from the "war on wrong," as he calls it in the preface to his collection ***The Tent on the Beach*** (1867), toward poetry built more on experience and inspiration. He describes his earlier work deprecatingly in that same preface as the result of having "left the Muses' haunts to turn / The crank of an opinion-mill," although, admittedly, it was for the purpose of "turn[ing] the soil for truth to spring and grow."

Home Ballads, Poems, and Lyrics, published in 1860, was comprised mostly of poems written during the previous decade, and scarcely touches on contemporary issues. Thus the most recent volume of Whittier's that readers had in hand at the time of the crisis precipitated by the election of Abraham Lincoln presented Whittier more as the "folk poet of New England," as Gay Wilson Allen calls him, than as the anti-slavery agitator of old. Many of the poems in this volume are based on the legends and history of New England. **"The Double Headed Snake of Newbury,"** for example, comes from seventeenth-century Puritan writer Cotton Mather's *Magnalia Christi Americana,* as the poem itself reveals, and uses a folk tale about a snake with two heads to make a humorous comment on marriage. **"The Prophecy of Samuel Sewall"** also comes from Mather. The widely anthologized **"Skipper Ireson's Ride"** is based on a true-life incident, but an author's note that prefaces the poem confesses that it is not historically accurate, inasmuch as the poet did not have all the facts at the time of the writing.

Nevertheless, **"Skipper Ireson's Ride"** bears the marks of a historical tale. Set in the New England seaboard town of Marblehead, seasoned with lines in local dialect, written in ballad form ideal for reading aloud, it tells the story of one Floyd Ireson, a sea captain who has been tarred and feathered by the women of Marblehead for sailing away from a sinking ship and abandoning its crew—"his own town's-people"—to the waves. The enraged women are the sisters, mothers, and wives of the drowned sailors. In Whittier's hand, the tale becomes one of vengeance, remorse, and, finally, forgiveness. The poem was judged "by long odds the best of modern ballads" by James Russell Lowell, another of New England's notable nineteenth-century poets and a friend of Whittier's.

"The Garrison of Cape Ann," based on a marvelous supernatural incident related in Mather, also reflects Whittier's belief in the power of spirit to heal and bless human life. The soldiers of the garrison are harassed by spectral apparitions. They turn to prayer, however, and find that the ghosts have vanished. This poem also reflects on the uses of the past, one of Whittier's major preoccupations. "I love the old melodious lays," Whittier had written in 1847 in the **"Proem"** that he chose to preface the Riverside edition of his collected works in 1888 and that is often anthologized today. And in **"The Garrison of Cape Ann"** he renders an evocatively dramatic sense of the presentness of the past:

> The great eventful Present hides the
>   Past; but through the din
> Of its loud life hints and echoes from the
>   life behind steal in;
> And the lore of home and fireside, and
>   the legendary rhyme,
> Make the task of duty lighter which the
>   true man owes his time.

Home Ballads features a number of lyrics in which Whittier gives voice to his sense of loss at the deaths in his family, but even this more personal sense is often set against a wider backdrop of landscape, legend, or the simple past. **"Telling the Bees,"** judged by Robert Penn Warren to be "a little masterpiece," was written in response to the death of the poet's mother, although the deceased of the poem has been transformed into the speaker's beloved "Mary." The poem is a lyric of restrained grief, evoking the rural New England custom of dressing the hives in black at the death of a member of the family in order to keep the bees from migrating to a new home. The speaker describes the farm where Mary lived with great specificity—indeed it is recognizable as the farm on which Whittier grew up—and lets the landscape itself convey his sense of loss a year after his beloved's death.

> Here is the place; right over the hill
> Runs the path I took;
> You can see the gap in the old wall still,
> And the stepping-stones in the shallow brook.
>   . . . . .

> A year has gone, as the tortoise goes,
> Heavy and slow;
> And the same rose blows, and the same sun glows,
> And the same brook sings of a year ago.

"My Playmate" is another poem on the "lost girl" theme. Here the speaker travels even further back into the past, into his childhood, to recover a memory of boyhood affection and to lament the changes that brought it to an end.

But in **"My Psalm,"** Whittier shows himself surmounting his sense of loss through deep religious faith as he declares, "I mourn no more my vanished years" and finds

> That all the jarring notes of life
> Seem blending in a psalm,
> And all the angles of its strife
> Slow rounding into calm.

And indeed, *Home Ballads* contains one of the poems that in adapted form has become a staple of many Protestant hymnals, **"The Shadow and the Light,"** with its gentle Quaker sense of the inner light: "Truth, which the sage and prophet saw, / Long sought without, but found within."

Although such blissful inner calm will increasingly mark Whittier's journey as a man, as a poet, and as a Quaker, he was by no means oblivious to the war. In 1863 he published *In War Time,* and a number of its poems directly address the conflict, its causes, its purpose, and its bloody execution. As a Quaker and pacifist Whittier had hoped that the slavery question would be resolved without violence, although he seemed not to be aware of how even his brand of non-violent Abolition could arouse extreme passion. Once the war broke out, however, he understood that it would have to be fought to resolution, and he even encouraged his fellow Quakers to join the effort in noncombatant roles.

True to form, as a devout Quaker, Whittier saw the conflict in moral, spiritual, and religious terms, as in the poem from *In War Time,* **"Ein feste Burg ist unser Gott,"** set to Luther's hymn and written at the outbreak of the war:

> We wait beneath the furnace-blast
> The pangs of transformation;
> Not painlessly doth God recast
> And mould anew the nation.

The hymn was considered incendiary enough to be banned by General George B. McClellan from concerts given in Union camps. A performance by the famous Hutchinson Family Singers had resulted in their being forcibly ejected by the soldiers, who understood themselves to be fighting only for union, and not to eliminate slavery. Lincoln overturned the ban, however, remarking at a cabinet meeting that the poem's sentiments were just the kind of thing he wanted the Union Army to hear. This was in late 1862, shortly before the Emancipation Proclamation began to alter the meaning of the war. The poem portrays both North and South as equally the victims of the "demon" of slavery, and exclaims, "Can ye not cry, / 'Let slavery die!' / And union find in freedom?"

Whittier had not always been concerned with the importance of preserving the union. His first response to the secession was **"A Word for the Hour,"** also among the poems of *In War Time.* Its dramatic opening lines seem a lament: "The firmament breaks up. In black eclipse / Light after light goes out." But the import of that poem is to question the need to bring back the seceding slave states. Rather, the poet says,

> . . . Let us press
> The golden cluster on our brave old flag
> In closer union, and, if numbering less,
> Brighter shall shine the stars which still remain.

Once the war had broken out, however, Whittier came to endorse Lincoln's determination that freedom and union were inextricably bound together. This is suggested in another of the *In War Time* poems, **"Barbara Frietchie,"** which does not touch on the subject of slavery but focuses on simple patriotism and loyalty to the flag of the United States as symbol of freedom for all.

"Barbara Frietchie" is based on what Whittier thought was a true story, but turned out to be only tangentially related to fact. Once again, however, Whittier evokes a sense of historical time and place. Rendered in rhymed couplets with a rhythmic martial beat suited to its subject, **"Barbara Frietchie"** became a grammar school staple and perhaps Whittier's most famous poem. Old Barbara Frietchie, though "Bowed with her four score years and ten," not only saves a tattered Union flag from the Confederate guns when the rebels march into "Frederick town," but chastens the Confederate general Stonewall Jackson in those famous lines, "Shoot if you must this old gray head, / But spare your country's flag, she said." The designation of the flag of the United States as belonging even to Stonewall Jackson indicates Whittier's agreement with Lincoln's view that there was only one country in the war, not two, fighting to preserve itself. And lines near the close of the poem tie the courageous old dame's action to the larger cause as the poet cries: "Over Barbara Frietchie's grave, / Flag of Freedom and Union, wave!" (On one of his visits to the United States, Winston Churchill recited this poem from memory as he and FDR motored past Frederick, Maryland.)

In addition to his devotion to union, Whittier never forgot the absolute, apodictical imperative to abolish slavery, nor its spiritual implications for all involved, including those enslaved. **"The Proclamation,"** from *In War Time,* written in response to the Emancipation Proclamation of January 1, 1863, encourages forgiveness on the part of the former slaves and exhorts them as only a Christian could, "To bless the land whereon in bitter pain / Ye toiled at first, / And heal with freedom what your slavery cursed."

When the war had ended and Whittier heard the bells announcing the passage of the Thirteenth Amendment outlawing slavery, he wrote a poem, **"Laus Deo,"** couched in powerful biblical imagery:

> For the Lord
> On the whirlwind is abroad;
> In the earthquake He has spoken;
> He has smitten with His thunder
> The iron walls asunder,
> And the gates of brass are broken!

Whittier's major part in the cause had been played out many years before, back in the 1830s, when he helped to foment the issue in the public consciousness, and it always remained of paramount importance to him. Now to see its final triumph contributed to the ever increasing serenity of his post-war work that many critics have noted.

Whittier's next major effort is thus a warm reflection on his boyhood and a tender recreation of the past. *Snow-Bound,* published in 1866, and considered by some critics to be his best work, is a poem of over 750 lines that became a great popular success and made the poet modestly wealthy for the first time in his life. Robert Penn Warren argues that its popularity was due to the need of America, having undergone the cataclysm of war and poised on the brink of a new identity as a nation of industry, business, and finance, to look back to simpler, more innocent times. Once the first flush of victory had worn off, Whittier acknowledged that Emancipation alone was not to create the world for which he and religious idealists like him had hoped, and he therefore saw a need to reconnect with what was good and virtuous in the past. Unlike present-day reformers who often disdain any positive reference to the past, before their reforms were enacted, Whittier is able to see his country whole, and to find what was good in pre-Civil War America.

Snow-Bound is Whittier's tribute to his boyhood, his family, his home, as well as to the sense of place and the particular history that created him, and that created, by extension, the America that many of his readers remembered. It takes place over a week's time, in which the snowed-in household lives in a kind of magical suspension which allows the poet to recreate the life of his boyhood. Whittier had loved the Haverhill farm of his youth, although not the backbreaking work (he was a somewhat frail young man), but in this poem he brings out all the good of the childhood world he knew. The landscape, the weather, the homestead, the books, the games and pastimes of the household, and above all the people of his past—his mother, father, brother, two sisters, aunt, uncle, boarder, and a visitor—are all brought to life, lovingly, yet realistically.

After he has completed his sketches of his cherished boyhood life, what he calls his "Flemish pictures," in an iambic tetrameter reminiscent of the twentieth-century New England poet, Robert Frost, Whittier offers his poem to future readers. They too, perhaps weary of "throngful city ways," may wish to recall the past and to "Sit with me by the homestead hearth, / And stretch the hands of memory forth / To warm them at the woods-fire blaze." And in the incomparable last lines, he suggests a kind of anonymous transcendent unity with these unknown readers grateful for the sweetness of such moments of memory and the link they provide to the shared experience of the better part of an older America. With this sense of communion across time he emerges into the morning after the storm and "takes with forehead bare / The benediction of the air."

1866 also saw the publication of a two-volume edition of Whittier's prose pieces, and of **"Our Master,"** which became the basis for several hymns still sung in churches today. The following year brought *The Tent on the Beach,* another hugely popular bestseller. This was a collection of poems previously published in the *Atlantic Monthly,* a magazine founded in 1857 with a liberal, anti-slavery philosophy that featured many prominent New England writers.

Tent is not generally considered among Whittier's better works. It offers more New England lore, such as **"The Wreck of Rivermouth,"** a poetic retelling of the story of a New England fishing vessel that went down off the coast of New Hampshire in colonial times. The one poem in this collection which is sometimes singled out for praise and has become something of a readers' favorite is **"Abraham Davenport."** It tells the true story of the famous Dark Day of New England, May 19, 1780, when the afternoon blackened inexplicably into night, a phenomenon since attributed to natural causes, but at the time seen by those descendents of Puritans as the onset of Judgment Day. The Connecticut state legislators, trembling in fear, are about to adjourn their regular session when the representative from Stamford, the stalwart Abraham Davenport, staunchly declares that "at the post / Where He hath set me in His providence, / I choose, for one, to meet Him face to face." The session that ensues is portrayed in a gently humorous way—Abraham reciting budget figures while the other worthies listen for the trumpet sounds of doom. The poem's narrator remarks approvingly "That simple duty hath no fear."

Whittier's career reached a peak with *Snow-Bound* followed by the success of *The Tent on the Beach,* and he would thereafter be a literary eminence, much in demand and much honored. He was to write many more poems but not, according to most of his critics, to develop much beyond the aesthetic achievements of these years. Still, his own increasing spiritual sense inspires many of these later works.

This is not to say that he ignored life's hardships. For example, his love of New England did not blind him to the darker side of its rural life, and the **"Prelude"** to *Among the Hills,* published in 1868, is often praised for its unflinching realism in acknowledging the kind of shrinkage of soul that the grind of struggle for sheer survival in a harsh landscape can produce. Still, the poet chides those who fail to see the opportunity for love and sweetness in a country so blessed with abundance of all kinds. He invites his readers to see and feel "The beauty and the joy within their reach,—/ Home, and home loves, and the beatitudes / Of nature free to all."

Though such didacticism is considered to have marred many of Whittier's poems, this impulse is characteristic of the folk poet. In his love of nature, he perhaps comes closest to uniting truth and beauty, inasmuch as to his Protestant soul, the beauty of the natural world is a source of spiritual exaltation. For example, **"The Pageant,"** a poem written in 1868, finds in the glories of nature a foretaste of heaven. **"The Clear Vision,"** also from 1868, recounts the poet's nearly ecstatic experience of seeing the marvels of the wintry landscape as if for the first time—"I never knew / What charms our sternest season wore. / Was never yet the sky so blue, / Was never earth so white before." He connects this new vision to a spiritual sense of freshness in his own advancing winter years:

> As Thou hast made thy world without,
> Make Thou more fair my world within;
> Shine through its lingering clouds of doubt;
> Rebuke its haunting shapes of sin;
> Fill, brief or long, my granted span
> Of life with love to thee and man;
> Strike when thou wilt the hour of rest,
> But let my last days be my best!

In 1870 Whittier, still the folk poet, collected some of his earlier poems under the title *Ballads of New England,* and also wrote **"My Triumph,"** which provides a fitting end point for this account of the decade. In this poem he feels his connection to the past and also to the future, to the "dear ones gone above me" and to the "joy of unborn peoples."

> I feel the earth move sunward,
> I join the great march onward,
> And take, by faith, while living,
> My freehold of thanksgiving.

The champion of Abolition became the champion of Freedom in a spiritual sense, of freedom from fear and doubt and regret and discontent. He rooted his themes not in abstractions, however, but in the local, the natural, the pre-political ties of family, friends, home, community, and faith. In works such as the poems of **Home Ballads,** he kept alive the ways of peace even within the horrors of war. After the war, especially in **Snow-Bound,** he helped forge the ties to the American past that could offer a sense of unity and peace. He appeals directly, earnestly, and straightforwardly to the minds and hearts of his readers, and with all his poetic shortcomings, he will never be excluded from the roster of American poets.

Paul Christian Jones (essay date 2007)

SOURCE: Jones, Paul Christian. "The Politics of Poetry: The *Democratic Review* and the Gallows Verse of William Wordsworth and John Greenleaf Whittier." *American Periodicals* 17, no. 1 (2007): 1-25.

[*In the following essay, Jones compares the views of Wordsworth and Whittier on capital punishment and the poetry they wrote expressing those views.*]

In March 1842, the *United States Magazine and Democratic Review* published a sixteen-page attack on William Wordsworth's most recent publication, *Sonnets upon the Punishment of Death,* a sequence that argued for the preservation of capital punishment in England as a necessity to social order. While critics on both sides of the Atlantic expressed disappointment that Wordsworth would have defended the gallows and saw his advocacy of the death penalty as a betrayal of the populist values that many had associated with his earlier work, the response to these poems by the *Democratic Review* was particularly outraged. Editor John O'Sullivan, the author of the review, expressed "a little surprise and no little pain" that Wordsworth "should have lent the aid of his genius and his moral influence to promote this unholy purpose" and then continues: "To behold [Wordsworth] take down the sacred lyre, and attune its chords to the harsh creaking of the scaffold and the clanking of the victim's chains, seems almost a profanation and a sacrilege—as though a harp of heaven were transported from its proper sphere and its congenial themes, to be struck by some impious hand to the foul and hideous harmonies of hell."[1] O'Sullivan's reaction to these sonnets did not depart greatly from the typical response displayed by contemporary readers in both England and America or even from that displayed by Wordsworth scholars in the twentieth century.[2] However, this review was only the beginning of the *Review*'s negative response to this work. Over the course of the next two years, the *Review*

would publish a series of pieces critical of Wordsworth, in what amounted to a campaign to vilify him as a failed poet and as an enemy of popular interest.

In this article, I consider the *Democratic Review*'s sustained attack on Wordsworth in two contexts: first, the debate about abolishing capital punishment that was occurring in New York (where the *Review* was published), and, second, the *Review*'s effort to encourage the creation and publication of literary work that advocated populist politics and reforms, including such initiatives as attempting to ban the death penalty. Based on this consideration, I argue that the vitriol expressed by the *Review* toward Wordsworth is not essentially about Wordsworth at all but instead is merely a facet of the *Review*'s larger argument about the social and political obligations of poetry. That is, Wordsworth becomes a device for the *Review* to escalate its claims that literature should advocate social causes of importance to the common man and to inspire a body of American literature that would become engaged in the reforms the periodical supported. In the early 1840s, the *Review* saw it as especially important to convince American writers that an opposition to the death penalty must be among the political values of any democratic poet. After an introduction setting up the context of the *Review*'s campaign, the following essay is composed of two sections. The first explores how the *Review* uses Wordsworth as a negative example, the antithesis of everything that writers—specifically poets—in a democratic America should aspire to be, because of the positions he holds on capital punishment, among numerous other shortcomings. The second section explores the *Review*'s corresponding project of celebrating writers who achieve its democratic standards for literature by focusing specifically on the journal's treatment of John Greenleaf Whittier, who is presented as a model for American writers, based on his attitude toward the death penalty as well as his larger democratic commitments.

Given the traditional view of the political commitments of the *Democratic Review,* offered to us by critics and historians like Perry Miller, John Stafford, and Edward Widmer, its response to the conservative, anti-reform stance of Wordsworth's sonnets is not surprising. Linked to the Young America movement that promoted a native literature that was different both formally and ideologically from European—specifically English—literature, the magazine was known for its "high-quality articles by authors with Democratic leanings, deep sympathy with popular movements around the world, antipathy toward elitism and exclusionary culture, [and] an eclectic mix of political and literary articles."[3] From its very beginning, the *Review* proudly proclaimed a populist agenda and encouraged writers to depart from the Anglophilic standard for literature advocated by elitist Whig editors of periodicals like the *Knickerbocker* and the *North American Review*. The editors considered the literary works published in the *Review* to be part of this agenda and selected pieces for publication that, among other things, challenged aristocratic visions of America, celebrated the values of the working class, and promoted reform movements of various sorts. In his editorial for the inaugural issue in 1837, O'Sullivan argued that "the vital principle of an American national literature must be democracy" and vowed that the *Review*'s goal was to infuse "the true glory and greatness of the democratic principle . . . into our literature." He continued by asserting that this can only happen when writers break from English tradition and values:

> Our mind is enslaved to the past and present literature of England. Rich and glorious as is that vast collection of intellectual treasure, it would have been far better for us had we been separated from it by the ocean of a difference of language, as we are from the country itself by our sublime Atlantic. Our mind would then have been compelled to think for itself and to express itself, and its animating spirit would have been our democracy. As it now is, we are cowed by the mind of England. We follow feebly and afar in the splendid track of a literature moulded on the whole . . . by the ideas and feelings of an utterly anti-democratic social system. We give back but a dim reflection—a faint echo of the expression of the English mind.[4]

Some conservative writers were annoyed by the *Review*'s equation of "American" and Democratic politics. For example, Henry Wadsworth Longfellow complained about what he called "a new politico-literary system," in which the editors of the *Review* "shout Hosanna to every *loco-foco* authorling, and speak coolly of, if they do not abuse, every other. They puff Bryant loud and long; likewise my good friend Hawthorne."[5] This "new politico-literary system" countered the conservative establishment's long hold on the publishing industry and its promotion of literature in an English vein, work that was suspicious of democratic impulses and radical reform.

In a recent article, Robert Scholnick has usefully challenged this standard view of the *Review* as reductively focused on its "progressive, democratic ethos," arguing that such a view neglects its support of politics that are far from progressive. Scholnick notes that "especially on issues of race, the *Democratic Review* was reactionary" and characterizes "its larger cultural work" as attempting "to legitimize and naturalize a social order that included slavery, Indian extermination, and territorial conquest."[6] In his study, Scholnick attempts to reconcile the *Review*'s reputation as a progressive and democratic voice (it certainly was a voice for the empowerment of the common man, or the common *white* man to be specific) with its commitments to support non-progressive projects, like slavery, Indian removal, and the war with Mexico. He does this by focusing on its argument for limited Federal govern-

ment, exemplified in its motto, "The best government is that which governs least." Scholnick explains how this issue ties together these seemingly contradictory threads of the *Review*'s politics: "Since the principle of limited government signified the capacity of individuals to manage their own affairs, it could be read as radically democratic, but it also appealed to the South since it removed the threat of Federal action aimed at eliminating or restricting the spread of slavery."[7] Interestingly then, this central principle placed the *Review* on both the progressive and conservative sides of the political spectrum, depending upon which issue was being addressed. The issue under discussion in this article, the abolition of capital punishment, shows the *Review* in its progressive mode, but it is a position, like those addressed by Scholnick, that is firmly grounded in the belief of limited government, the belief that individuals have the ability to govern themselves and should be allowed to do so rather than suffering under the tyranny of oppressive government.

O'Sullivan was one of the best-known advocates for the abolition of the death penalty, a movement that had a number of successes across the United States in the 1840s and 1850s, including reducing the number of crimes that were considered to be capital, ending public executions in most states, and abolishing capital punishment altogether in Rhode Island, Michigan, and Wisconsin.[8] O'Sullivan served two terms in the New York legislature (1841-1842), where his "top priority" was ending the death penalty in the state. He chaired a committee to consider reform of capital punishment laws, and his report to the legislature, *Report in Favor of the Abolition of the Punishment of Death by Law* (1841), was published to wide acclaim and "became the standard reference work on the topic for the next twenty years." Though his legislative efforts ultimately failed in New York, he remained a well-known advocate of the anti-gallows movement and engaged in a series of debates (in print and before audiences) with Reverend George Cheever, a Presbyterian minister and advocate of the death penalty.[9]

O'Sullivan and the other writers of the *Democratic Review* viewed the institution of capital punishment as another aspect of the "mind of England" that had to be rejected by democratic America. The *Review* labeled the gallows as a tool of anti-democratic states in an 1843 essay, which claimed that "Monarchies, and all oppressive forms of government—in addition to their natural instinct of all conservatism—cling with peculiar affection to the Death Punishment."[10] The *Review*'s view of capital punishment as a device employed by oppressive, non-democratic states to maintain power over their populaces is similar to positions expressed in twentieth- and twenty-first century critiques of the death penalty, perhaps most notably in the work of Michel Foucault.[11] Believing this tool for terrorizing citizens inconsistent with a democratic society's emphasis on individual self-government, O'Sullivan worked to encourage America's writers to take on this subject, using his influence as editor of the *Review* to publish material in favor of abolishing hangings and to promote a larger body of literature in opposition to the gallows.

The publication of Wordsworth's pro-gallows sonnets in the London *Quarterly Review* in December 1841 provided a perfect opportunity not only for O'Sullivan to rehearse his arguments against capital punishment again but also to propel his effort to encourage other literary figures to join the cause. Written during the years 1839 and 1840, when Parliament was debating capital punishment and even considering a complete abolition, these poems were Wordsworth's justification for the preservation of the punishment of death.[12] While the poet grants that "Tenderly do we feel by Nature's law / For worst offenders" (II, 1-2), he moves his reader beyond this initial, natural sympathy for the condemned through a series of arguments for the necessity of executions. Included among these arguments are that the State needs the fear aroused by the death penalty in order to have any authority or social control, that humans will not govern their baser impulses if there is no fear of punishment, and that lesser punishments—such as imprisonment or exile—will not lead a criminal to repentance but only to further crime. The crux of the sequence's argument is that the State absolutely depends on this power; in Sonnet V, Wordsworth argues that the "wise Legislator," who is "uncaught by processes in show humane," will see "how far the act [of abolition] would derogate / From even the humblest functions of the State; / If she, self-shorn of Majesty, ordain / That never more shall hang upon her breath / The last alternative of Life or Death" (4, 9-14). For Wordsworth, the anti-gallows reformers have become the actual threat to society: "if consistent in their scheme, / They must forbid the State to inflict a pain, / Making of social order a mere dream" (VII, 12-14).

O'Sullivan's review presents counter-arguments to each of Wordsworth's major claims—that the gallows is a deterrent to crime, that executions lead criminals to repentance, that the death sentence is more dreaded than life imprisonments—and provides statistics, examples, and even a chart to disprove the sonnets' assertions. For example, O'Sullivan argues that the death penalty does not deter crime but actually encourages it and notes that juries are increasingly less likely to convict accused criminals when the death penalty is involved because of "the unwillingness of parties to bring the stain of blood on their consciences."[13] He claims that "the practice of Capital Punishment is far *less* repressive of crime than that of severe and more certain imprisonment" (279). O'Sullivan asserts that "the executioner has been himself the very cause of a far greater number [of crimes] than he has ever punished

or avenged" (279) because "the bad moral influence of the punishment of death, as a suggestive example and sanction, . . . tend[s] to harden and brutalize the minds of men, and to familiarize them with the idea of the cold and deliberate taking of human life" (284). O'Sullivan is perhaps most troubled by the complete faith that the poet places in "the State," exemplified in this passage:

> What is a State? The wise behold in her
> A creature born of time, that keeps one eye
> Fixed on the statutes of Eternity,
> To which her judgments reverently defer.
> Speaking through Law's dispassionate voice the State
> Endues her conscience with external life
> And being, to preclude or quell the strife
> Of individual will, to elevate
> The grovelling mind, the erring to recall,
> And fortify the moral sense of all.
>
> (IX, 5-14)

Displaying his belief in limited government, O'Sullivan objects to the sonnets' equation of the State with God and argues that there must be limits to the State's power. He also asserts that punishment as a means of preventing future crime must be very cautiously dispensed: "The smallest measure of punishment adequate to this object is the limit beyond which society cannot rightfully go" (283). Questions about whose interests—the State's, the people's, or God's—are ultimately being served by capital punishment are commonly addressed by voices on both sides of this argument. According to O'Sullivan, it is Wordsworth's reverent privileging of the State, without questioning its intentions or the effects of its actions, that becomes one of the sonnets' major flaws.

The anti-gallows O'Sullivan was not the only activist to use the publication of the sonnets as an occasion to reassert his arguments; at least one of the gallows' supporters did so as well. In *Punishment by Death: Its Authority and Expediency* (1842), death penalty advocate Cheever celebrates "the great and venerable poet Wordsworth" who "has brought the wisdom of seventy years, the power of an illustrious name, and the undiminished fire of his imagination to the illustration of this subject."[14] Within his arguments for the necessity of capital punishment, Cheever quotes three of Wordsworth's sonnets in full, finding support for his own claims in Sonnet V's argument that the State relies upon the fear produced by the gallows to maintain order and Sonnets VI and VIII's claims that individuals need the threat of death ("well-measured terrors" planted "in the road / Of wrongful acts" [VIII, 4-5]) to assure they abide by their consciences and avoid unlawful acts. Of course, the *Democratic Review* seriously disagreed with Cheever's evaluation of Wordsworth's work. However, it is not merely the poet's argument that the *Review* contested; instead, in the next months and years, the primary question for its writers will become whether Wordsworth can be said to uphold his responsibilities as a poet at all. That is, as we shall see in the next section, the *Review*'s arguments moved beyond whether Wordsworth's pro-gallows position was valid or not to whether that position is one that should appear in verse.

VILIFYING WORDSWORTH AND DEFINING THE DEMOCRATIC POET

While most of O'Sullivan's essay on the sonnets is concerned with the logical arguments Wordsworth presents, he also expresses sincere trepidation about such arguments appearing in verse and frames his point-by-point debate of Wordsworth's positions with a larger theoretical discussion of the social obligation of poetry. His review opens, as mentioned previously, with an expression of despair that Wordsworth would use his "sacred lyre" for such an "unholy purpose" (273). Similarly, the review ends with an acknowledgement that O'Sullivan has not addressed the "poetical merits" of the sonnets, but charges that "the genius of Wordsworth has folded the stately and imposing drapery of his poetic diction and imagery" around "false arguments and false assumptions" (287). Like critics in the twentieth century, O'Sullivan finds little merit in the poetry of these sonnets, and laments that poetry itself (the "sacred lyre") would have been put to such a dubious use as supporting the State's power to kill its citizens. Following this accusation that Wordsworth's "genius" has been misused, O'Sullivan expresses hope that Wordsworth will eventually "regret . . . hav[ing] thus lent the influence of his muse, to retard the advent of that hour which is to witness the total abolition of this revolting, useless, and worse than useless barbarism from the statute-books of every people" (288). With these statements begins the *Review*'s project of articulating the "sacred" responsibility of the poet to fight for the "abolition" of "useless barbarism," a project in which Wordsworth serves as a case study.

At this point, we should consider Wordsworth's status in the United States in the 1840s to understand why he was a suitable target for the *Review*'s campaign. Wordsworth's American popularity began decades after the initial publication of *Lyrical Ballads* with the 1824 publication of *The Poetical Works of William Wordsworth,* after which American reviewers and readers responded strongly to his celebration of humble folk and his overall religious perspective.[15] By 1839, the *Boston Quarterly Review* characterized the positive critical response to the poet by noting that "Our brethren of the reviewing tribe seem to have conspired to elevate the said William Wordsworth to the throne of English poesy."[16] Much of the enthusiasm for the poet's work can be credited to readers finding a demonstration of Christian values in the poetry. For example, the *Methodist Magazine and Quarterly Review* asserted that "Wordsworth is emphatically a religious, nay, a Christian poet" and "when he looks upon his fellow-man, it is with the warm sympathy of Christian benevolence, elevated and refined by a far-seeing faith."[17] And, the *Western Messenger* argued that "It is, in truth, the Christianity, the love, faith, and humility which fills all the better of Wordsworth's poems, that makes him great."[18]

The poems in *Lyrical Ballads* could be, as Joel Pace has argued, read by American readers not only as Christian poems but also as consistent with democratic values, exemplifying "the liberty and equality on which the country was founded."[19] Because progressive arguments could be read in these early poems, Wordsworth was admired by and provided inspiration to many American reformers, including advocates for women's rights and the abolition of slavery.[20] Among his earliest poems is even one poem, "The Convict," that seems to be an argument against capital punishment: the narrator of the poem goes to a condemned man's cell "to share" the convict's sorrows "as a brother" and announces to him, "My care, if the arm of the mighty were mine, / Would plant thee where yet thou might'st blossom again."[21] Because a large portion of the American readership, including perhaps even some of the writers from the *Democratic Review,* viewed Wordsworth as a Christian reform writer and even as "in the highest degree democratic," his endorsement of capital punishment in the later sonnets would have seemed dangerous for the anti-gallows movement, which wanted to convince people that support for the death penalty was inconsistent not only with Christianity but also with democratic values.[22] In part, the campaign that the *Review* began against Wordsworth was intent upon clarifying that his positions were neither Christian nor democratic, an assertion that would ultimately raise the question of whether his work could even be considered literature by the definition the *Review* established.

Building upon its claim in its first issue that American literature must be a democratic literature, the *Review* more clearly articulated this expectation in "Democracy and Literature," an essay appearing a few months after the initial response to Wordsworth's sonnets. This piece, written by W. A. Jones, argues that "the spirit of Literature and the spirit of Democracy are one." Jones proposes that "letters are the best advocates of principles" because "Literature is not only the natural ally of freedom, political or religious; but it also affords the firmest bulwark the wit of man has yet devised, to protect the interests of freedom. It not only breathes a similar spirit,—it is imbued with the same spirit."[23] Because of this expectation that literature should and even must defend the interests of liberty and democracy, the *Review* evaluated literary works according to how well they served these interests. As John Stafford has explained in regard to the literary criticism of the *Review,* the approach employed by its reviewers to evaluating work was explicitly ideological, as they expected authors to be concerned with "the common man and reform" and with the ideas of "Democracy, Equality, Freedom, and Brotherhood." It was the opinion of these reviewers that "the spiritual ideal in poetry and other works of the imagination is not a conservative ideal"; instead "it is progressive and in harmony with the 'spirit of the age.'" It should also be noted that many of the more elitist periodicals, such as the *New York Review* and the *Whig Review,* were equally ideological in their criticism. As Stafford explains, "conservative politically, religiously, and socially, they tended to emphasize the conservative ideas which must be found in poetry: the idea symbolized, to state it bluntly, had better be traditional and orthodox, and preferably highly moral and religious."[24] Expressing the ideological expectations of the *Review,* Jones asserts, in "Democracy and Literature," that Wordsworth and his peers were once aligned with the populist spirit of the age but have since seriously strayed: "In the present century the Muse of Liberty inspired her freest strains into the youthful lyres of Coleridge, Southey, and Wordsworth, who apostatized from their early creed in maturer life."[25] Thus, Jones's article clarifies, in a general sense, how Wordsworth has failed in his role as a poet because he has failed to remain an advocate of democratic progress as he was in his earlier career and, more egregiously, he now acts as an obstacle to such progress in his poetry.

In subsequent issues, the *Review* expanded its campaign to cast Wordsworth as the prime example of the failed poet, as an author who squandered his poetic talents and betrayed the democratic politics of literature. In May 1842, the *Review* published James Russell Lowell's sonnets in response to Wordsworth's, in which Lowell expressed his dismay at the unfortunate turn the elder poet had taken: "always 'tis the saddest sight to see / An old man faithless in Humanity." Echoing some of the language of O'Sullivan's review, Lowell's sonnets argue that poets have "the glorious duty / Of serving Truth;" therefore "A poet cannot strive for despotism; / His harp falls shattered; for it still must be / The instinct of great spirits to be free, / And the sworn foes of cunning barbarism." Ultimately, Lowell proclaims that poetry must place its faith in "truth and love" rather than "lies and hate," which he implies Wordsworth has failed to do.[26]

The *Review's* criticism becomes more explicit in an article by W. A. Jones titled "Wordsworth's Sonnets to Liberty" (February 1843), which is the periodical's most extensive discussion of the poet's faults. The essay provides a broad framework for the *Review's* hostility toward the trajectory of Wordsworth's career. Jones's essay begins by establishing a political expectation for the genre of poetry specifically, arguing that "of all writers, the Poets are the most moral, the most metaphysical, and we may add, the most political." Jones asserts that "we might call all poetry political: for all truly inspired verse is the outpouring of the Spirit of Freedom, and the Spirit of Humanity. A similar love of freedom animates both the Poet and the Patriot."[27] Jones would have concurred with Percy Bysshe Shelley's assertion in *A Defence of Poetry* that "Poets are the unacknowledged legislators of the world," but might have clarified that this legislation should be done with the aim of democracy.[28] Jones cast the poet as a "popular philosopher" who "cannot avoid the propagation of free principles and liberal ideas." Wordsworth is pronounced a failure at meeting such moral and political expectations in his more recent work, most notably *The Excursion,* and Jones criticizes him for being "a zealous churchman" and "a loyal subject" and for his "respect for authority, for precedent, for an established church, and a settled Monarchy." Ultimately, the essay suggests that, even though his *Sonnets Dedicated to Liberty* (1807) celebrated popular revolution against tyranny, Wordsworth has been incorporated into the powerful oppressive system that he had once attacked and has assumed "the truly royal position . . . as Prince of living English Poets." Because of his new loyalties, the essay claims, Wordsworth no longer participates in the democratic agenda of poetry: "There is no democracy in his verse, nor do we suspect in his character. We rather incline to picture him as one of the modest and most benevolent of aristocrats, but still an aristocrat. . . . We are obliged, hence, to abandon the hope of adding this illustrious name to the list of democratic poets." Even though a different group of sonnets is the subject of this essay, Jones reminds his readers of the poet's pro-gallows sonnets: "We have purposely avoided saying anything in relation to the sonnets in defence of capital punishment. They are a blot upon the poetic escutcheon of our author, to be effaced only by the consideration, that they present the sole instance of his deficiency as a philanthropic and truly Christian poet. They are not to be defended on any grounds, and can only be forgotten."[29] It is interesting to note that, according to Jones, Wordsworth's previous offenses were against democratic values, but his support for the gallows becomes a violation of Christianity as well. As we shall see later, not all of the writers of the *Review* would make the distinction that Jones does, seeing instead Christianity and democracy as essentially interconnected and inseparable and seeing the gallows as a contradiction to both.

In another article, "Poetry for the People" (September 1843), Jones repeats his insistence that the genre of poetry should be particularly committed to democracy and populism: "It is in poetry especially that we must look for the purest expression of the popular feeling. It is in poetry that . . . the national spirit is most faithfully evolved. Poetry, forsaking the knight in his bower, the baron in his castle, has taken up her abode, 'for better for worse,' with the artificer and the husbandman, not restricting herself, to be sure, to such society, but including them in her wide province, and watching over them with affectionate care. The poor man, upright, sincere, earnest, with deep enthusiasm and vigorous self-reliance, he is the hero of our time." The rest of the article evaluates well-known poets based on these criteria. Not surprisingly, Jones again proclaims that Wordsworth has failed to be a populist poet because he "has preferred to rest content with the applause of sages and scholars, adopting the worldly schemes of churchmen and the defenders of the sacred rights of kings." The author accuses Wordsworth of "car[ing] little for the obscurer classes of society" and of being "altogether too mild with tyrants and the harpies of government." Jones continues to catalog Wordsworth's failures at being "the orator for the people": "He is the advocate of liberty, and yet allows abuses to exist unchallenged, that are hedged in by precedent and guarded by the arm of power. He would have his country free, her name great among the nations, yet he discovers slight sympathy with any popular movement or the intellectual advancement of the industrial class. He would keep men in fixed castes. In a word, he distrusts the popular sentiment, and dreads the evidence of the popular will. Is this true? Let his poetry answer—noble as it is—it is *not* Poetry for the People." While capital punishment is not explicitly mentioned here, Jones's notice of Wordsworth's failure to challenge "abuses . . . hedged in by precedent" is likely an allusion to the *Sonnets upon the Punishment of Death*.[30]

From this body of criticism, cataloging Wordsworth's political and poetical shortcomings, readers can glean the traits that the *Democratic Review* was looking for in its ideal poet, the "Poet for the People." First, the writing of this poet must be in line with what the *Review* has defined as democratic and Christian values, namely, liberty, justice, and equality—at least for all white men in the nation. Second, the work of this poet must privilege the interest of this common man over that of the State, the Church, or the upper class. And, third, the message of this poet must be in accord with popular sentiment. According to the writers in the *Review,* Wordsworth has failed on each of these counts in his sonnets supporting the gallows. However, this extensive denunciation of the "Prince of living English Poets" was intended as more than a condemnation of Wordsworth; it also acted as an invitation to American poets to succeed where their esteemed British contemporary had failed.

CULTIVATING THE ANTI-WORDSWORTH: THE
ANTI-GALLOWS POETRY OF WHITTIER

The *Democratic Review*'s search for a poetic alternative to Wordsworth's pro-gallows sonnets took place on a number of fronts. One of these included the search for poetry that would specifically challenge the position advocated in Wordsworth's poems by insisting that the abolition of the death penalty was not only in the public interest but also an essentially democratic and Christian principle. The journal's promotion of such verse had a slow start, within the initial review of the Wordsworth's sonnets, when O'Sullivan quoted in full "The Execution," an 1833 poem by Lydia Sigourney, to object to Wordsworth's position in his Sonnet XII that a death sentence will transform a murderer into "a kneeling Penitent / Before the Altar" because "the solemn heed the State hath given / Helps him to meet the last Tribunal's voice" (6-7, 11-12). Sigourney's poem depicts a hanging in which the convict remains unrepentant in the face of execution. In the final stanzas of the poem, the narrator pleads with the condemned man to use his final moments to "reveal thy hidden pain," to "give passage to one suppliant sigh [or] one prayer," or to "say 'Jesus, save me!'" Disappointing the narrator, the man instead goes to his death "unhumbled, unannealed, . . . with falsehood's sullen front, to dare the glance of God."[31] While Sigourney's poem does contradict Wordsworth's belief that the shock of impending death will inevitably drive criminals to salvation, its focus, which ultimately seems less a criticism of the gallows than of this stubborn criminal facing his demise without contrition, made it unsatisfactory for the *Review*'s political aims of using literature to affect reader attitudes on this issue. Unlike the poetry that the *Review* would eventually publish, Sigourney's poem seems concerned exclusively with the soul of the condemned; she does not raise questions about the power of the State, the troubling position of the clergy, or the consequences of capital punishment on the populace. That this was the best poem O'Sullivan could hold up in opposition to Wordsworth's writing reflects the scarcity of American writing on this issue at this time and the necessity of the *Review*'s effort to promote more effective writing against the gallows.

In the three years following the essay on Wordsworth's sonnets, the *Review* published a series of anti-gallows literary works, as well as frequent essays (often written by O'Sullivan) on the subject. These works approached the subject from a number of perspectives. Rh. S. S. Andros's sonnet "The Two Murderers" (October 1842) pointed out the contradiction in our justice system; a murderer is hanged while someone who lets a poor man starve in the street is not charged with any crime. Nathaniel Hawthorne's "The New Adam and Eve" (February 1843) depicted the new Adam and Eve shuddering at the sight of a gallows; in their innocence, they cannot conceive of its uses. Harry Franco's poem "Now and Then" (August 1843) featured a dialogue between "Now," who cannot comprehend executing a man arrested for stealing bread for his hungry family, and "Then," who defends it as absolutely necessary and just, to propose that in the future we may be similarly outraged about hanging murderers. Walt Whitman's "Revenge and Requital" (July/August 1845) tells the story of a murderer who escapes execution but who makes up for his crime by doing good works. Other anti-gallows works published in this period included John Quod's "Harry Blake: A Story of Circumstantial Evidence" (November 1842), the unsigned story "The Innocent Convict" (July/August 1845), and another Whitman piece, "A Dialogue" (November 1845).

The author who best answered the call to compose anti-gallows literature expressing democratic values was John Greenleaf Whittier, who published two scathing poetic attacks on the gallows in the *Review*, "**Lines, Written on Reading Several Pamphlets Published by Clergymen Against the Abolition of the Gallows**" (October 1842, later known by the shorter title "**The Gallows**") and "**The Human Sacrifice**" (May 1843).[32] A Quaker, best known at the time for his poems in opposition to slavery, Whittier had already been a vocal supporter, as a member of the Massachusetts legislature, of the failed efforts to abolish the death penalty in that state in the mid-1830s. These two poems were his first efforts to address this subject in verse, and perhaps they were motivated by the *Review*'s response to Wordsworth's pro-gallows poems and its assertion that aggressive arguments against the death penalty should be part of the work of democratic poetry. While they may have been, as Albert Mordell claims, only "indirectly a reply to Wordsworth's sonnets in favor of capital punishment," they represent exactly the kind of poetry O'Sullivan strove to encourage, a passionate and persuasive attack on the gallows and its supporters.[33] In this pair of poems, Whittier substantially expands on elements of the execution narrative barely mentioned in the earlier poem by Sigourney—specifically the participation of the "holy priest" and the spectacle's effect upon the "gathering throng"—in order to explore further the larger social, political, and spiritual ramifications of capital punishment.

Composed of five irregular stanzas, "**Lines**" makes a Christian argument for abolishing the death penalty and proposes that the clergy who have become the most strident defenders of the gallows are setting themselves up in opposition to Christ. It might seem odd to today's readers that Whittier would couch his attack on capital punishment in terms of a critique of the clergy, and we might even think that he is, as one twentieth-century critic argued, "not . . . really fac[ing] any of the fundamental issues involved in the debate over capital punishment."[34] However, while it differs from more familiar arguments about the death penalty in the twentieth and twenty-first centuries, the question of whether or not capital punishment had Biblical sanction was central to the debates of the 1840s. When O'Sullivan composed his *Report in Favor of the Abolition of the Punishment of Death by Law* for the New

York state legislature, he felt it necessary to devote almost a third of the legal document's 165 pages to a scriptural argument because he was aware of "how extensively the opinion is entertained . . . that the terrible practice under consideration has not alone the sanction, but even the express injunction of that inspired wisdom against which it is not for us to dare either criticism or murmur."[35] During O'Sullivan's legislative effort to abolish the gallows in New York, an effort that eventually failed by only four votes, a group of Presbyterian ministers rose up as his strongest opposition. These ministers lobbied the legislature, circulated petitions among their congregations, and published arguments (likely the pamphlets referred to in Whittier's title) in support of the gallows.[36] O'Sullivan would later blame—both in print and in private correspondence—these ministers and the pressure they exerted on lawmakers for killing his reform. In a letter to the governor, he expressed his disbelief that these ministers were "so anxious to choke their fellow-men to death for the love of God."[37]

Whittier's poem expresses similar frustration with clerical support of the death penalty.[38] While the first stanza argues that the current age is a Christian one, the second stanza expresses regret that some have incorrectly interpreted Christian beliefs: "How ill are His high teachings understood" (18). In this poem, Whittier presents Christ as a progressive as he delineates the conservative misunderstanding of Christian teachings, particularly by the clergy: "Where He hath spoken Liberty, the priest / At His own altar binds the chain anew; / Where He hath bidden to Life's equal feast, / The starving many wait upon the few; / Where He hath spoken Peace, His name hath been / The loudest war-cry of contending men" (19-24). Whittier's depiction of Christ as a democrat—as a voice of liberty, equality, and peace—coincided with O'Sullivan's description of Jesus in his *Report* on abolishing hanging, wherein O'Sullivan celebrated the "radically democratic spirit and direction of [Christ's] whole doctrine, and its inevitable tendency to level in the dust every political or social institution at variance with that spirit."[39] In the pages of the *Review* as well, Christianity and democracy were often equated. For example, in the first piece in its inaugural issue, the *Review* called the democratic principle "the sister spirit of Christianity" because its "pervading spirit" is "democratic equality among men."[40] In "Democracy and Literature," the *Review* argued that "the sincerest Christian should be the firmest democrat; for democracy is that creed which teaches peace on earth and good-will toward men, reverence for the innate worth of all humanity, and respect for the equal divinity and ultimate capability of all human souls."[41] By appealing to Christ's teachings in his poem, Whittier reveals a particular position in the religious debate over capital punishment. Supporters of the death penalty often prioritized the Old Testament, specifically the

Mosaic code, to justify executions as divinely-sanctioned retribution, while opponents emphasized the New Testament teachings of love and forgiveness.[42] Wordsworth's Sonnet VII, for example, asserts a preference for the Old Testament "precept eye for eye, and tooth for tooth" (3), over the teachings of Christ, "A Master meek," which have love as their end (5). Sharon Setzer has argued that Wordsworth's gallows sonnets offer readers an "implicit feminization of Christ," whose authority has been restricted to "the sphere of private life, a world apart from the public affairs of the State."[43] Consequently, Wordsworth warns, "lamentably do they err who strain / His mandates" of love so far that they restrain the killing power of the State (9-10).

In opposition to Wordsworth and the pro-gallows ministers, Whittier prioritizes Christian principles over Old Testament law. Thus, he portrays clerical defenders of the death penalty as engaging in a mockery of Christianity. In a particularly graphic sequence of the poem, he characterizes priests as sadistic and hypocritical torturers who

> . . . in His name who bade the erring live,
> And daily taught His lesson—to forgive!—
>   Twisted the cord and edged the murderous steel;
> And, with His words of mercy on their lips,
> Hung gloating o'er the pincer's burning grips,
>   And the grim horror of the straining wheel;
> Fed the slow flame which gnawed the victim's limb,
> Who saw before his searing eye-balls swim
>   The image of *their* Christ, in cruel zeal,
> Through the black torment-smoke, held mockingly to
>   him!
>
>   (29-38)

In the third stanza, these ministers' support of "New England's scaffold" (53) is placed into a wider context of crimes committed in the name of Christianity, including the Crusades, the murder of Jews, and the burning of heretics, all incidents when "Heaven's anthem blend[ed] with the shriek of Hell" (49). This stanza ends with an address to Christ, "Thou wronged and merciful One," in whose name "Earth's most hateful crimes" have been committed (57-58).

Despite the preachings of this misguided pastorate, Whittier argues that popular sentiment is opposed to the gallows: "Thank God! that I have lived to see the time / When the great truth begins at last to find / An utterance from the deep heart of mankind, / Earnest and clear, that ALL REVENGE IS CRIME!" (59-62). He continues to assert that "the beautiful lesson which our Saviour taught / . . . its way hath wrought / Into the common mind and popular thought" (67-69). Christ's words "have found an echo in the general heart / And of the public faith become a living part" (72-73). In these lines, Whittier casts the anti-gallows movement as a people's movement in accordance with the teachings

of Christ; consequently, the pro-gallows ministers become not only Christ's enemies in their attempt to "arrest this tendency" (74) and to "harden the softening human heart again," but also enemies of the people (75).[44]

The poem's final stanza compares capital hangings to pagan sacrifices of human beings. After cataloging other cultures that engaged in ritualistic human sacrifice, Whittier asks, "Will ye become the Druids of *our* time? / Set up your scaffold-altars in *our* land, / And, consecrators of Law's darkest crime, / Urge to its loathsome work the Hangman's hand?" (96-99). The poem closes by warning the nation that, if it continues to inflict capital punishment, out of a "cry for blood," it will be ranked "with those who led their victims round / The Celt's red altar and the Indian's mound, / Abhorred of Earth and Heaven—a pagan brotherhood!" (101-105). The poem's arc, beginning with Whittier's celebration of the United States as a piously Christian society and ending with its envisioned descent into a "pagan brotherhood," provides an opportunity to raise doubt in its readers' minds and perhaps to lead them to question their own ministers' position on the gallows as a potential threat to society as a whole.

While the Presbyterian ministers were victorious in swaying the 1842 vote in the New York legislature, the argument between religious supporters of the gallows and their equally religious opponents would continue throughout the 1840s.[45] O'Sullivan would contribute to the debate again in his 1843 essay, "The Gallows and the Gospel," wherein he concurred with Whittier's argument and portrayed the ministers as "at variance with the true spirit of Christianity." In their rabid defense of the gallows, O'Sullivan claims that the ministers "seemed ambitious to assume the function of the very Body-Guard of the Hangman."[46] Whittier's next contribution to this debate, the poem **"The Human Sacrifice,"** was written in disgust after the poet read a published letter of a clergyman who witnessed a hanging, a letter in which the minister, according to Whittier, described "the agony of the wretched being—his abortive attempts at prayer—his appeal for life—[and] his horror of a violent death," yet asserted that he was "more than ever convinced of [the gallows'] utility by the awful dread and horror which it inspired."[47] Outraged by this minister's position, Whittier went beyond his first poem in its attack on the pro-gallows clergy, this time casting them as the partners of the hangman.

"The Human Sacrifice" begins in a different manner than **"Lines"** with a sympathetic focus on a condemned man awaiting execution. The first stanza describes the pleasant dreams of the sleeping convict—as he recalls his "school-day joys" (10), fishing in a brook (9), his sister's smile (19), and placing his head on his mother's knee (21). The second stanza begins abruptly with the man waking up with the terrifying recollection of his impending execution. While these stanzas humanize the criminal facing execution, they more importantly challenge the belief—asserted in Wordsworth's sonnets and in the Presbyterian arguments—that the gallows was useful in leading otherwise irredeemable criminals to salvation. Whittier here describes the gallows as "A horror in God's blessed air—/ A blackness in His morning light—/ Like some foul devil-altar there / Built up by demon-hands at night" (35-38). Rather than being an instrument of God, the gallows is cast instead as a diabolical device that has detrimental effects on the criminal's soul. Daunted by the scaffold, the condemned is no longer in the proper mindset for redemption: "In vain he strove to breathe a prayer, / In vain he turned the holy Book," but "He only heard the Gallows-stair / Creak as the wind its timbers shook" (44-47). The death sentence, *"Blood for Blood!,"* stands "Between him and the pitying Heaven!" (50-51). Whittier strongly contests the notion that the death penalty can be a tool for any sort of positive change.

The rest of the poem shifts its focus onto the minister who presides over the execution, which is itself depicted as a crime. This figure is introduced in stanza three as "The Hangman's ghostly ally," who stands, "Blessing with solemn text and word / The Gallows-drop and strangling cord; / Lending the sacred Gospel's awe / And sanction to the crime of Law" (61-65). The unholy alliance between clergy and executioner is highlighted again at the end of stanza four, which describes what the doomed man sees awaiting him on the Gallows: "Two busy fiends attending there; / One with cold mocking rite and prayer, / The other, with impatient grasp, / Tightening the death-rope's strangling clasp!" (84-87). The poem avoids a description of the actual execution in order to proceed to its indictment of the clergyman's participation. Whittier proposes that anyone who has witnessed a capital execution would be likely to "uplift his earnest cries / Against the crime of Law" (104-105), but he depicts a very different reaction from this minister:

> The man of prayer can only draw
> New reasons for his bloody Law;
> New faith in staying Murder's hand
> By murder at that Law's command;
> New reverence for the Gallows-rope,
> As human nature's latest hope;
> Last relic of the good old time,
> When Power found license for its crime,
> And held a writhing world in check
> By that fell cord about its neck;
> Stifled Sedition's rising shout,
> Choked the young breath of Freedom out,
> And timely checked the words which sprung
> From Heresy's forbidden tongue;
> While in its noose of terror bound,
> The Church its cherished union found,

> Conforming, on the Moslem plan,
> The motley-colored mind of man,
> Not by the Koran and the Sword,
> But by the Bible and the Cord!

>   (119-138)

This passage is especially intriguing and must have pleased the *Review*'s editors greatly, as it moves away from the initial argument that the clergy are aligned against Christian values to charging that they are in opposition specifically to those radical democratic values that the *Review* has often attributed to Christ and Christianity. Anticipating Foucault's arguments in the twentieth century, Whittier positions himself against "Power" (the "State" that Wordsworth's sonnets defend) that holds "a writhing world in check" with a "fell cord about its neck." Understanding that this "Power" uses the death penalty, "its noose of terror," to maintain its control over its subjects, Whittier condemns the State's willingness to stifle "the young breath of Freedom" by charging it with sedition or heresy; likewise, he criticizes the Church's "cherished union" with this "Power." The final lines of this passage return—by a comparison to Islam—to the assertion that capital punishment is not in accordance with Christianity.

Whittier ends his poem by explicitly dealing with his title's assertion that capital execution is a form of human sacrifice. In stanza six, which is essentially a prayer, Whittier describes Christ as one whose "holy faith / Was love and life, not hate and death" (150-151). Yet, he points out the contradiction in those who claim that they are killing murderers in Christ's name: "Thy name is Love! What, then, is he / Who in that name the Gallows rears, / An awful altar built to Thee, / With sacrifice of blood and tears?" (156-159). Whittier asks Christ to help the pro-gallows clergyman to see his error: "let the light of Thy pure day / Melt in upon his darkened thought. / Soften his hard, cold heart, and show / The power which in Forbearance lies, / And let him feel that Mercy now / Is better than old sacrifice!" (162-167). In the concluding lines, Whittier imagines a more direct divine intervention to halt these sacrifices as he alludes to the Old Testament story of Abraham's attempted sacrifice of Isaac: "My brother man, Beware! / With that deep voice which from the skies / Forbade the Patriarch's sacrifice, / God's angel cries, FORBEAR!" (186-190).

O'Sullivan surely found much to admire in Whittier's poems. While he would have enjoyed the poet's efforts to turn Christian rhetoric against his Bible-bearing political opponents, he would have especially appreciated the larger political schema into which Whittier places the debate about the gallows, wherein this conflict becomes just another in the struggle between the power-hungry State and the common man. While popular sentiment is portrayed as supporting the destruction of the gallows, the State is seen as interested only in preserving its authority and in using its ally the Church to persuade the populace that it should invest the government with this power so that the government will be able to protect them. In his effort to expose the hypocritical, self-interested, and "unchristian" practices of the clergy to mislead the masses and to empower the State, Whittier takes what the *Review* had delineated as the work of a Poet for the People: defending the rights of the common man against oppression and injustice. The *Review* essentially bestowed this title upon him in the article "Poetry for the People" when it predicted which American poets might write truly populist verse and said, "Whittier, by pre-eminence, we should select for the poet to execute this task."[48] By 1845, there no longer seemed to be any question about the matter as the *Review* honored "Our gentle Whittier—true poet, true man, true American, true democrat, true Christian."[49] This praise suggests that Whittier had succeeded in all the ways that Wordsworth had previously failed, providing a stark contrast to the *Review*'s description of Wordsworth's "truly royal position" as "Prince of English Poets." Clearly, by this point, Whittier had become the *Review*'s anti-Wordsworth; through its praise the publication encouraged others to follow in Whittier's path rather than Wordsworth's.

Over the course of the decade of the 1840s, these poems by Whittier became the literary works most often associated with the movement to abolish capital punishment. Immediately upon publication the writers associated with the *Review* sang the praises of the poems. Lowell, for example, wrote to Whittier, "I am glad to see you down on the cassocked pleaders for murder in the 'Democratic Review.'"[50] And, in the *Review*'s essay on Wordsworth's *Sonnets Dedicated to Liberty,* Jones holds up Whittier's **"Lines"** as sufficient response to Wordsworth's pro-gallows verse: "We would add more upon this head, had we not fresh in our minds those admirable lines of Whittier, . . . which appeared in this journal last October. It is meet that such an one should assume an attitude of defence on this question, and with such an opponent."[51] The *Liberator* also celebrated the poems and directed the clergy "to the mirror here held up to them by Whittier—whom I thank, in humanity's behalf, for the service he has here done it." The review continues, "The poetry is great, and the doom of the carnivorous, cannibal priesthood finely pronounced. Let them read it, and beware."[52] By the end of the decade, the *National Era* would write of the poems, that they "in each instance, . . . possessed more counteracting influence and power than all [the ministers'] efforts combined, and doubtless helped on the reform of these evils far more than [the ministers] were able to retard it."[53] The response was not completely positive, however. In accordance with its own ideological biases, the *North American Review* found the poems to be flawed by "the violence of the partisan" and "deformed by harshness." The reviewer asked, "What right . . . has Mr. Whittier to speak in the virulent tone, which he sees fit to employ, against those clergymen who hold different opinions from his on the disputed question of capital punishment? There is no taste, no Christianity, and no poetry in all this: if Mr. Whittier supposes there is, he mistakes all three."[54] Interestingly, the charges that this reviewer makes against Whittier's verses—suggesting that poetry should not be a tool for certain political ideas—are very similar to those leveled by the *Democratic Review* in its critique of Wordsworth.

While Whittier's approach in these poems, asserting that the gallows was inconsistent with the Gospel, was only one of the ways that reformers attacked the death penalty, this argument became one of the most popular in the 1840s. Whittier's work was probably influential in aiding a shift in the culture's view of executions in terms of Biblical sanction. Earlier writers, as can be observed in Wordsworth's sonnets or the pamphlets of the Presbyterian ministers, defended the gallows as a Christian tool to lead the criminal to salvation. In Whittier's poems, not only was the murderer's soul not redeemed but also, in the poet's dark prophetic vision, a multitude of souls—those of the supportive clergy and their submissive flocks—risks eternal doom as a consequence of participating in and condoning hanging. In these poems, the clergy become satanic figures. They blend the "shriek of Hell" with "Heaven's anthem" (**"Lines"** 49), they stand upon the "foul devil-altar" built by "demon-hands" (**"Sacrifice"** 37-38), and they fiendishly conduct the condemned to "the everlasting rise and fall / Of fire-waves round the infernal wall" (**"Sacrifice"** 80-81). Not only are they leading the convicted murderers to their infernal fate, but these evil men in their divine disguise are guiding their followers from a Christian age back to a Pagan existence. "Ye most unhappy men!—who turn'd away / From the mild sunshine of the Gospel day" stand accused of leading their congregations—like the doomed convict—to damnation (**"Lines"** 78-79).

Notably, the charge that Whittier makes against the pro-gallows clergy parallels closely the condemnation that the *Review* expressed for poets who supported the gallows. And the writers in the *Review* did indeed equate poets and priests, seeing both as having similar responsibilities, a divine obligation to "propagat[e] free principles and liberal ideas" and to teach "peace on earth and good-will toward men, reverence for the innate worth of all humanity, and respect for equal divinity and ultimate capability of all human souls."[55] Both were expected to be true Christians and therefore true democrats. Because the poet's role was seen to be similar to that of the minister, the *Review* could cast a poet like Wordsworth, writing in support of the gallows, in the same vein as clergymen advocating executions, as "a profanation and a sacrilege," as the use of a "sacred lyre" for an "unholy purpose," and as an abuse of the "harp of heaven" to give music to "the foul and hideous harmonies of hell."[56] For the *Review,* the stakes were very high. By demonizing poets like Wordsworth who misused their talents and by valorizing poets like Whittier whose poetry engaged in the populist reform that it advocated, the *Review* actively attempted to create an army of activist poets that would subsequently affect not only the literary culture but also the political culture of the day. Ultimately, in terms of the issue of capital punishment, these efforts should be seen as successful, even if only moderately. While the literary efforts against the gallows never reached the levels of influence of writings promoting the abolition of slavery, prison reform, labor reform, or even temperance, the *Review* was effective in creating a body of literature that gave a persuasive voice to the anti-gallows cause and that must be credited, to some extent, with the limited successes that the movement achieved in the 1840s. The *Review*'s criticism of Wordsworth and encouragement of Whittier and other writers demanded poets who were moral philosophers and legislators actively engaged in improving society for the masses, a challenge that might also be usefully issued to the poets of the twentieth and twenty-first centuries who have been just as likely to pursue apolitical aestheticism or confessional solipsism as any form of real-world activism. For the editors of the *Review,* if poets were not defending the interests of the common man and standing up for the powerless against the engines of power, they, like Wordsworth, could be considered guilty of committing a "profanation and a sacrilege," of misusing the "harp of heaven" to play the "hideous harmonies of hell."

Notes

1. "Wordsworth's Sonnets on the Punishment of Death," *Democratic Review* 10 (March 1842): 272-73. Though this essay, like many pieces in the *Review,* is unsigned, it has been attributed to John O'Sullivan, the *Review*'s editor at the time. See John Stafford, *The Literary Criticism of "Young America"* (New York: Russell & Russell, 1967), 100. Like Stafford, I believe that the author of this review was O'Sullivan, rather than a literary critic like W. A. Jones, because the review is less interested in evaluating the sonnets as verse than it is in arguing substantively against Wordsworth's positions about the death penalty in terms that are very similar to those included in O'Sullivan's *Report in Favor of the Abolition of the Punishment of Death by Law* (2nd ed., 1841; New York: Arno Press, 1974).

2. Almost immediately upon the sonnets' publication, Wordsworth noted that "An outcry, as I expected, has been raised against me by weak-minded humanitarians," *Letters of William and* *Dorothy Wordsworth,* ed. Ernest de Selincourt (Oxford: Clarendon, 1967), 7:292. Friends and reviewers also objected to the work; for example, Samuel Taylor Coleridge's son Hartley wondered "Is Sonnet a very good vehicle wherein to exhibit the Gallows?" (*Letters of Hartley Coleridge,* ed. Grace Evelyn Griggs and Earl Leslie Griggs [Oxford: Oxford University Press, 1937], 258), and Thomas Carlyle could muster only an exclamation in German—*"ach Gott!"*—in response to the sonnets (*Collected Letters of Thomas and Jane Welsh Carlyle,* ed. Charles Richard Sanders [Durham, NC: Duke University Press, 1970], 14:11). In America, an essay very similar in tone to the *Review*'s chastised Wordsworth as the "laureate of the gallows" and asserted that "thirty years ago, Wordsworth would never have thought of setting his muse about such sanguinary work" ("The Poetry of Hanging," *Liberator,* July 1, 1842, 103). Even Ralph Waldo Emerson, a supporter of Wordsworth's work, expressed disappointment with the sonnets but "very willingly forgave the poet for writing against the abolition of capital punishment, for the sake of the self-respect and truth to his own character, which the topic and the treatment evinced" (*Dial* 3 [July 1842]: 135).

One response to these sonnets was the writing of sonnets in opposition to them. As Wordsworth commented in a letter to a friend: "my penal Sonnets . . . have excited the wrath of an anonymous quarrelsome Admirer of mine—who had inflicted upon me no less than 19 of his—in refutation, and abuse" (*Letters,* 7:285). However, the impulse to write oppositional sonnets was not unique to this "quarrelsome Admirer," and Wordsworth on another occasion admits that "another sonneteer has had a solitary shot at me from Ireland" (7:292). This impulse appeared even in America, where in 1846, William Gilmore Simms offered the editors of the *Democratic Review* "a series of Sonnets against the punishment of death & in reply to Wordsworth" (*Letters of William Gilmore Simms,* ed. Mary Simms Oliphant, Alfred Taylor Odell, and T. C. Duncan Eaves [Columbia: University of South Carolina Press, 1953], 2:142).

Wordsworth scholarship has primarily maintained what Sharon Setzer has called a "dismissive silence" in regard to these sonnets ("Precedent and Perversity in Wordsworth's *Sonnets upon the Punishment of Death*" *Nineteenth-Century Literature* 50 [1996]: 428). Scholars who do acknowledge them almost always do so with regret. For example, Mary Moorman argues that the sequence is "not distinguished" as poetry and that Wordsworth "might have said it all as forcibly in a prose pamphlet" (*William Wordsworth: A Biography* [Oxford: Clarendon Press, 1957], 2:535). William Galperin labels the sonnets "notorious" and "failures" (*Revision and Authority in Wordsworth: The Interpretation of a Career* [Philadelphia: University of Pennsylvania Press, 1989], 217, 236). Annabel Newton claims that "little can be said in defense" of the poems as "the hangman is an inappropriate hero for a sonnet" (*Wordsworth in Early American Criticism* [Chicago: University of Chicago Press, 1928], 106-107). The scholarly distaste for these poems appears to be based on their content rather than their technical merit. As Galperin notes, there has been "a tendency to read these sonnets as arguments rather than as poems" (236). And the arguments contained in the sonnets have disappointed many readers; Margaret Drabble, for instance, expresses frustration that "such a passionate believer in social equality could ever have brought himself to write sonnets in praise of landed gentry, the death penalty and the Church of England" (*Wordsworth* [London: Evans, 1966], 131).

3. Edward Widmer, *Young America: The Flowering of Democracy in New York City* (Oxford: Oxford University Press, 1999), 65. Widmer provides the best recent study of the Young America movement. See also Miller's *The Raven and the Whale: Poe, Melville, and the New York Literary Scene* (1956; Baltimore: Johns Hopkins University Press, 1997) for a discussion of this group within the context of the antebellum publishing milieu of New York.

4. "Introduction," *Democratic Review* 1 (October 1837): 14, 15.

5. *The Letters of Henry Wadsworth Longfellow,* ed. Andrew Hilen (Cambridge: Harvard University Press, 1966), 2:162.

6. Robert Scholnick, "Extermination and Democracy: O'Sullivan, the *Democratic Review,* and Empire, 1837-1840," *American Periodicals* 15 (2005): 124-25. While I generally concur with Scholnick's characterization of the *Review,* its support for well-known abolitionist poet Whittier, discussed in the last segment of this essay, should complicate our understanding of the *Review*'s politics even further. Scholnick's essay addresses this complication somewhat in his survey of the "distinct periods of the periodical's life" as he describes the period between 1841 and 1844 (the period when most, but not all, of the *Review*'s praise for Whittier occurs) as one in which the *Review* was "[f]reed from the necessity of supporting a sitting administration" and "became somewhat more open to diverse voices" (129).

7. Scholnick, "Extermination and Democracy," 133.

8. The best histories of the American movement to abolish the death penalty in the antebellum period can be found in Louis Masur, *Rites of Execution: Capital Punishment and the Transformation of American Culture, 1776-1865* (New York: Oxford University Press, 1989), and in Stuart Banner, *The Death Penalty: An American History* (Cambridge: Harvard University Press, 2002).

9. Robert D. Sampson, *John L. O'Sullivan and His Times* (Kent: Kent State University Press, 2003), 96, 101. The most thorough account of O'Sullivan's anti-gallows activism can be found in Philip Mackey, *Hanging in the Balance: The Anti-Capital Punishment Movement in New York State, 1776-1861* (New York: Garland, 1982).

10. "Capital Punishment," *Democratic Review* 12 (April 1843): 424.

11. In *Discipline & Punish,* for instance, Foucault argues that executions serve a "juridico-political function," "an emphatic affirmation of power" intended "to make everyone aware, through the body of the criminal, of the unrestrained presence of the sovereign." Foucault asserts that public executions "did not re-establish justice" but instead "reactivated power." Michel Foucault, *Discipline & Punish: The Birth of the Prison,* trans. Alan Sheridan (1977, New York: Random House, 1995), 48-49.

12. *The Poetical Works of William Wordsworth,* ed. Ernest de Selincourt (Oxford: Clarendon, 1967), 4:135-41. References to these sonnets will be cited parenthetically within the text by sonnet and line number.

13. "Wordsworth's Sonnets on the Punishment of Death," 280. Subsequent quotations from this essay will be cited parenthetically within the text. Most of the arguments made by this review were frequently made by anti-gallows activists. See Masur, *Rites of Execution* and Banner, *The Death Penalty* for detailed discussions of these arguments.

14. George B. Cheever, *Punishment by Death: Its Authority and Expediency* (New York: M. W. Dodd, 1842), 115.

15. See Newton, *Wordsworth in Early American Criticism,* for the most thorough study of the American reception of Wordsworth. Other useful works on this topic are David Simpson, "Wordsworth in America," *The Age of William Wordsworth,* ed. Kenneth Johnston and Gene Ruoff (New Brunswick, NJ: Rutgers University Press, 1987), 276-90; Lance Newman, "Wordsworth in America and the Nature of Democracy," *New England Quarterly* 72 (1999): 517-38; Joel Pace, "Wordsworth and America: Reception and Reform," *The Cambridge Companion to Wordsworth,* ed. Stephen

Gill (Cambridge: Cambridge University Press, 2003), 230-45; and the essays in Joel Pace and Matthew Scott, eds., *Wordsworth in American Literary Culture* (New York: Palgrave, 2005).

16. Anonymous review of *The Poetical Works of William Wordsworth, Boston Quarterly Review* 2 (April 1839): 137.

17. Anonymous review of *The Complete Poetical Works of William Wordsworth, Methodist Magazine and Quarterly Review* 21 (October 1839): 457.

18. J. H. P., "Wordsworth's Poetry," *Western Messenger* 1 (January 1836): 462.

19. Pace, "Wordsworth and America," 233.

20. See Pace, who argues that among other writers Whittier was directly inspired by Wordsworth's early poems. He notes that Whittier acknowledged that Wordsworth's sonnet to the abolitionist leader Toussaint L'Ouverture provided the model for his own poem, "Toussaint L'Ouverture" (239).

21. "The Convict," *The Poetical Works of William Wordsworth*, ed. E. de Selincourt (Oxford: Clarendon, 1952), 1:312. Even though this poem was removed from the second British edition of *Lyrical Ballads* and never included by Wordsworth in subsequent collections, it did appear in the first American edition of *Lyrical Ballads* in 1802, and thus might have been known to American readers. See L. A. Fisher, "The First American Reprint of Wordsworth," *Modern Language Notes* 15 (1900): 39-42.

22. This assertion of Wordsworth's democratic nature comes from an anonymous review of *Complete Poetical Works of William Wordsworth, North American Review* 59 (October 1844), which noted that because "Wordsworth is considered a champion of monarchy and aristocracy, . . . there may be opinions expressed in his writings which can be forced to bear a construction inimical to political liberty; still if we consider the tendency of his whole works, we shall find them in the highest degree democratic" (383).

23. "Democracy and Literature," *Democratic Review* 11 (August 1842): 196. This unsigned essay has been attributed to Jones, the most frequent contributor of literary criticism to the review. See Stafford, *The Literary Criticism of "Young America,"* 67, Miller, *The Raven and the Whale,* 111-12 and Sampson, *John L. O'Sullivan and His Times,* 129.

24. Stafford, *The Literary Criticism of "Young America,"* 56, 60, 55-56.

25. "Democracy and Literature," 199.

26. "Sonnets," *Democratic Review* 10 (May 1842): 479-80. Because these poems were published merely with the title "Sonnets," Lowell believed they "were most unintelligible by the fact not being stated" that they "were written on reading Wordsworth in favor of bloodshed," causing many readers to miss their critique of the poet, Samuel Pickard, *Life and Letters of John Greenleaf Whittier* (Boston: Houghton Mifflin, 1894), 1:290. As a corrective to this ambiguity, all subsequent publications of these sonnets have been titled "On Reading Wordsworth's Sonnets in Defence of Capital Punishment."

27. "Wordsworth's Sonnets to Liberty," *Democratic Review* 12 (February 1843): 158. This unsigned article has been attributed to W. A. Jones. See Stafford, *The Literary Criticism of "Young America,"* 67.

28. "A Defense of Poetry," *Shelley's Prose,* ed. David Lee Clark (New York: New Amsterdam, 1988), 297. In contrast to Wordsworth, Shelley was praised by the *Review* for the democratic tone of his verse: "[T]he political principles of Shelley were democratic. . . . He was friendly to every reform, by which freedom was to be extended, or the condition of the multitude of men improved. . . . In all the efforts of the masses to shake off the intolerable tyranny of the aristocratic classes, he felt the strongest sympathy. . . . The noblest fires of his spirit were kindled by every cry of the oppressed against the oppressor. The purest strains of poesy were evoked from their hidden cells, when he struck the lyre in the cause of human progress" ("Percy Bysshe Shelley," *Democratic Review* 13 [December 1843]: 618).

29. "Wordsworth's Sonnets to Liberty," 158, 159, 163.

30. "Poetry for the People," *Democratic Review* 13 (September 1843): 267, 268, 269. This unsigned article has been attributed to W. A. Jones. See Miller, *The Raven and the Whale,* 111-12 and Sampson, *John L. O'Sullivan and His Times,* 131.

31. Sigourney's poem is quoted in full in "Wordsworth's Sonnets on the Punishment of Death," 286.

32. Before the appearance of these two poems, Whittier had already published his work in the *Review*; ultimately he published over two dozen pieces in the periodical. Many of these works express sentiments similar to the editorial positions of the *Review*. See, for example, "Democracy," a poem that considers democratic government to be "the immortal gift of God" (*Democratic Review* 9 [December 1841]: 528), and "To the Reformers of England," written to highlight the "struggle in

Great Britain between the People and the Aristocracy—between liberal, republican principles and class legislation" (*Democratic Review* 12 [January 1843]: 15).

33. Albert Mordell, *Quaker Militant, John Greenleaf Whittier* (Boston: Houghton Mifflin, 1933), 131.

34. Edward Wagenknecht, *John Greenleaf Whittier: A Portrait in Paradox* (New York: Oxford University Press, 1967), 67.

35. *Report in Favor of the Abolition of the Punishment of Death by Law,* 8. O'Sullivan, an Episcopalian, argued against the relevance of the Mosaic Law, which he asserted had been replaced by the New Testament "law of Mercy and Love" (20). He spends much of his report examining the Biblical passages frequently cited in defense of the gallows and arguing that they should not be read as divine sanction of capital punishment. For example, Genesis 9:6 ("Whoso sheddeth man's blood, by man shall his blood be shed") is read not as a command for state-inflicted death penalty but rather as a prophetic statement predicting the ends of violence.

36. A number of pro-gallows arguments were published by Presbyterian ministers in the months before the appearance of Whittier's poem. These include Cheever, *Punishment by Death*; William Patton, *Capital Punishment Sustained by Reason of the Word of God* (New York: Dayton and Newman, 1842); John McLeod, *The Capital Punishment of the Murderer: An Unrepealed Ordinance of God* (New York: Robert Carter, 1842); and Albert Dod, "Capital Punishment," *Biblical Repertory and Princeton Review* 14 (April 1842): 307-46.

37. Quoted in Mackey, *Hanging in the Balance,* 164. That the Presbyterian ministers were the primary opposition to reform is noted by many writers of the time. For example, the novelist and reformer Lydia Maria Child, who had been recruited into anti-gallows activism by O'Sullivan, wrote in 1843: "Curse the Presbyterians! I'll match 'em for energy this session" (*Lydia Maria Child: Selected Letters, 1817-1860,* ed. Milton Meltzer and Patricia Holland [Amherst: University of Massachusetts Press, 1982], 182).

38. "Lines, Written on Reading Several Pamphlets Published by Clergymen against the Abolition of the Gallows" (*Democratic Review* 11 [October 1842]: 374-75). References to this poem will be cited parenthetically within the text by line number.

39. *Report in Favor of the Abolition of the Punishment of Death by Law,* 21. It should be noted that Whittier's politics were not the same as the editors of the *Review,* and when he argued for liberty and equality, he certainly would have included the slave population as part of these ideas. The writers of the *Review* clearly understood this conflict. In "P.'s Correspondence," Nathaniel Hawthorne jokingly surveys the state of American verse and describes Whittier as "a fiery Quaker youth, to whom the muse had perversely assigned a battle-trumpet, and who got himself lynched, ten years agone, in South Carolina" (*Democratic Review* 16 [April 1845]: 344). For an example of how the *Review* reconciled the poet's anti-slavery stance (for which the South has already "lynched" him critically) with its own pro-slavery position, see "Whittier in Prose," *Democratic Review* 17 (July/August 1845): 115-25. The *Review* recommends that its southern readers get over their prejudices about Whittier and read his work, which will lead them to "rejoice in his genius as a bright jewel in the casket of our country's literature, and personally love and revere him as one nobly worthy of all their love and reverence" (116).

40. "Introduction," 7-8.

41. "Democracy and Literature," 197.

42. Masur argues that this division could be explained along denominational lines; Unitarians, Universalists, and Quakers were usually gallows opponents, and the more orthodox Calvinist churches—the Congregationalist, Presbyterian, and Dutch Reform churches—were its strongest defenders (*Rites of Execution,* 152).

43. Setzer, "Precedent and Perversity," 446-47. The editors of the *Review* would likely agree with Setzer's view of these sonnets: "Although it is conventional to say that religion came to overshadow Wordsworth's revolutionary politics, his sonnets in defense of capital punishment offer compelling justification for stating the case in exactly the opposite way. Indeed, I think it is fair to say that Wordsworth's political ideology thoroughly overshadowed his Christian theology" (447). That is, in Setzer's view, it is Wordsworth's conservative loyalty to the State that compromises his religious beliefs.

44. This claim of popular support was frequently made by anti-gallows activists, but there is little evidence to support this claim. Petition drives often produced tens of thousands of signatures, but, as Banner writes, "abolishing capital punishment for murder was probably never as popular as its proponents believed. . . . The era was thick with reform movements, and like many of them, . . . abolition [of the death penalty] may have been a cause favored primarily by educated elites," (*The Death Penalty,* 135). The only time

that the abolition of the gallows went before voters (rather than legislators) in the 1840s (in New Hampshire, 1844) the vote went almost 2 to 1 against abolition.

45. Cheever, for instance, would address the topic again in *Capital Punishment: The Argument of Rev. George B. Cheever in Reply to J. L. O'Sullivan* (New York: Saxton and Miles, 1843) and *A Defence of Capital Punishment* (New York: Wiley and Putnam, 1846). Biblical attacks on the gallows included Henry Christmas's *Capital Punishments Unsanctioned by the Gospel and Unnecessary in a Christian State* (London: Smith, Elder, 1846) and *The Bible against the Gallows* (New York: E. Walker, 1845) by "Presbuteros" (an orthodox minister writing under a pseudonym).

46. "The Gallows and the Gospel," *Democratic Review* 12 (March 1843): 227.

47. "The Human Sacrifice," *Democratic Review* 12 (May 1843): 475. References to this poem will be cited parenthetically within the text by line number.

48. "Poetry for the People," 279.

49. "Whittier in Prose," 115.

50. Quoted in Pickard, *Life and Letters of John Greenleaf Whittier,* 1: 290.

51. "Wordsworth's Sonnets to Liberty," 163.

52. "Whittier's Lines on the Gallows-Defence of the Clergy," *Liberator,* October 21, 1842, 166.

53. J. G. Forman, "Whittier's Poems," *National Era,* February 1, 1849, 17.

54. C. C. Felton, Review of *Lays of My Home, and Other Poems* by John Greenleaf Whittier, *North American Review* 57 (October 1843): 509.

55. "Wordsworth's Sonnets to Liberty," 158, and "Democracy and Literature," 197.

56. "Wordsworth's Sonnets on the Punishment of Death," 272.

FURTHER READING

Bibliography

von Frank, Albert J. *Whittier: A Comprehensive Annotated Bibliography.* New York: Garland, 1976, 273 p.
Complete, annotated listing of the standard editions of Whittier's work, as well as biographical studies, criticism, and guides to manuscripts.

Criticism

Budick, E. Miller. "The Immortalizing Power of Imagination: A Reading of Whittier's *Snow-Bound.*" *ESQ* 31, no. 2 (2nd Quarter 1985): 89-99.
Contends that in *Snow-Bound,* Whittier poses the power of the imagination as a counter-force to time and change.

Christy, Arthur. "Orientalism in New England: Whittier." *American Literature* 1, no. 4 (January 1930): 372-92.
Examines the influence of Orientalism on many of Whittier's poems, dividing them into those with pseudo-Oriental themes or settings, and those whose models were translations of Oriental texts.

Kribbs, Jayne K. *Critical Essays on John Greenleaf Whittier.* Boston: G. K. Hall, 1980, 228 p.
Collection of contemporary reviews of Whittier's writings as well as a number of essays by twentieth-century critics.

Moskal, Jeanne. "John Greenleaf Whittier and Ebenezer Elliott." *Resources for American Literary Study* 20, no. 1 (1994): 37-44.
Examines Whittier's admiration for English social reformer and poet Ebenezer Elliott.

Wagenknecht, Edward. "A Side to Face the World With." In *John Greenleaf Whittier: A Portrait in Paradox,* pp. 10-47. New York: Oxford University Press, 1967.
Discusses Whittier's public persona, his poetic self-portraits, his literary friendships, and his attitude towards music, art, and religion.

Additional coverage of Whittier's life and career is contained in the following sources published by Gale: *American Writers Supplement,* Vol. 1; *Concise Dictionary of American Literary Biography; Dictionary of Literary Biography,* Vols. 1, 243; *Literature Resource Center; Nineteenth-Century Literature Criticism,* Vols. 8, 59; and *Reference Guide to American Literature,* Ed. 4.

How to Use This Index

The main references

> **Calvino, Italo**
> 1923-1985 .... CLC 5, 8, 11, 22, 33, 39,
> 73; SSC 3, 48

list all author entries in the following Gale Literary Criticism series:

AAL = *Asian American Literature*
BG = *The Beat Generation: A Gale Critical Companion*
BLC = *Black Literature Criticism*
BLCS = *Black Literature Criticism Supplement*
CLC = *Contemporary Literary Criticism*
CLR = *Children's Literature Review*
CMLC = *Classical and Medieval Literature Criticism*
DC = *Drama Criticism*
FL = *Feminism in Literature: A Gale Critical Companion*
GL = *Gothic Literature: A Gale Critical Companion*
HLC = *Hispanic Literature Criticism*
HLCS = *Hispanic Literature Criticism Supplement*
HR = *Harlem Renaissance: A Gale Critical Companion*
LC = *Literature Criticism from 1400 to 1800*
NCLC = *Nineteenth-Century Literature Criticism*
NNAL = *Native North American Literature*
PC = *Poetry Criticism*
SSC = *Short Story Criticism*
TCLC = *Twentieth-Century Literary Criticism*
WLC = *World Literature Criticism, 1500 to the Present*
WLCS = *World Literature Criticism Supplement*

The cross-references

> See also CA 85-88, 116; CANR 23, 61;
> DAM NOV; DLB 196; EW 13; MTCW 1, 2;
> RGSF 2; RGWL 2; SFW 4; SSFS 12

list all author entries in the following Gale biographical and literary sources:

AAYA = *Authors & Artists for Young Adults*
AFAW = *African American Writers*
AFW = *African Writers*
AITN = *Authors in the News*
AMW = *American Writers*
AMWR = *American Writers Retrospective Supplement*
AMWS = *American Writers Supplement*
ANW = *American Nature Writers*
AW = *Ancient Writers*
BEST = *Bestsellers*
BPFB = *Beacham's Encyclopedia of Popular Fiction: Biography and Resources*
BRW = *British Writers*
BRWS = *British Writers Supplement*
BW = *Black Writers*
BYA = *Beacham's Guide to Literature for Young Adults*
CA = *Contemporary Authors*
CAAS = *Contemporary Authors Autobiography Series*
CABS = *Contemporary Authors Bibliographical Series*
CAD = *Contemporary American Dramatists*
CANR = *Contemporary Authors New Revision Series*
CAP = *Contemporary Authors Permanent Series*
CBD = *Contemporary British Dramatists*
CCA = *Contemporary Canadian Authors*
CD = *Contemporary Dramatists*
CDALB = *Concise Dictionary of American Literary Biography*

CDALBS = *Concise Dictionary of American Literary Biography Supplement*
CDBLB = *Concise Dictionary of British Literary Biography*
CMW = *St. James Guide to Crime & Mystery Writers*
CN = *Contemporary Novelists*
CP = *Contemporary Poets*
CPW = *Contemporary Popular Writers*
CSW = *Contemporary Southern Writers*
CWD = *Contemporary Women Dramatists*
CWP = *Contemporary Women Poets*
CWRI = *St. James Guide to Children's Writers*
CWW = *Contemporary World Writers*
DA = *DISCovering Authors*
DA3 = *DISCovering Authors 3.0*
DAB = *DISCovering Authors: British Edition*
DAC = *DISCovering Authors: Canadian Edition*
DAM = *DISCovering Authors: Modules*
   DRAM: Dramatists Module; **MST:** *Most-studied Authors Module;*
   MULT: *Multicultural Authors Module;* **NOV:** *Novelists Module;*
   POET: *Poets Module;* **POP:** *Popular Fiction and Genre Authors Module*
DFS = *Drama for Students*
DLB = *Dictionary of Literary Biography*
DLBD = *Dictionary of Literary Biography Documentary Series*
DLBY = *Dictionary of Literary Biography Yearbook*
DNFS = *Literature of Developing Nations for Students*
EFS = *Epics for Students*
EXPN = *Exploring Novels*
EXPP = *Exploring Poetry*
EXPS = *Exploring Short Stories*
EW = *European Writers*
FANT = *St. James Guide to Fantasy Writers*
FW = *Feminist Writers*
GFL = *Guide to French Literature,* Beginnings to 1789, 1798 to the Present
GLL = *Gay and Lesbian Literature*
HGG = *St. James Guide to Horror, Ghost & Gothic Writers*
HW = *Hispanic Writers*
IDFW = *International Dictionary of Films and Filmmakers: Writers and Production Artists*
IDTP = *International Dictionary of Theatre: Playwrights*
LAIT = *Literature and Its Times*
LAW = *Latin American Writers*
JRDA = *Junior DISCovering Authors*
MAICYA = *Major Authors and Illustrators for Children and Young Adults*
MAICYAS = *Major Authors and Illustrators for Children and Young Adults Supplement*
MAWW = *Modern American Women Writers*
MJW = *Modern Japanese Writers*
MTCW = *Major 20th-Century Writers*
NCFS = *Nonfiction Classics for Students*
NFS = *Novels for Students*
PAB = *Poets: American and British*
PFS = *Poetry for Students*
RGAL = *Reference Guide to American Literature*
RGEL = *Reference Guide to English Literature*
RGSF = *Reference Guide to Short Fiction*
RGWL = *Reference Guide to World Literature*
RHW = *Twentieth-Century Romance and Historical Writers*
SAAS = *Something about the Author Autobiography Series*
SATA = *Something about the Author*
SFW = *St. James Guide to Science Fiction Writers*
SSFS = *Short Stories for Students*
TCWW = *Twentieth-Century Western Writers*
WLIT = *World Literature and Its Times*
WP = *World Poets*
YABC = *Yesterday's Authors of Books for Children*
YAW = *St. James Guide to Young Adult Writers*

Literary Criticism Series
Cumulative Author Index

20/1631
See Upward, Allen

A/C Cross
See Lawrence, T(homas) E(dward)

A. M.
See Megged, Aharon

Abasiyanik, Sait Faik 1906-1954
See Sait Faik
See also CA 123; 231

Abbey, Edward 1927-1989 .... **CLC 36, 59; TCLC 160**
See also AAYA 75; AMWS 13; ANW; CA 45-48; 128; CANR 2, 41, 131; DA3; DLB 256, 275; LATS 1:2; MTCW 2; MTFW 2005; TCWW 1, 2

Abbott, Edwin A. 1838-1926 .... **TCLC 139**
See also DLB 178

Abbott, Lee K(ittredge) 1947- .... **CLC 48**
See also CA 124; CANR 51, 101; DLB 130

Abe, Kobo 1924-1993 ...... **CLC 8, 22, 53, 81; SSC 61; TCLC 131**
See also CA 65-68; 140; CANR 24, 60; DAM NOV; DFS 14; DLB 182; EWL 3; MJW; MTCW 1, 2; MTFW 2005; NFS 22; RGWL 3; SFW 4

Abe Kobo
See Abe, Kobo

Abelard, Peter c. 1079-c. 1142 ..... **CMLC 11, 77**
See also DLB 115, 208

Abell, Kjeld 1901-1961 .... **CLC 15**
See also CA 191; 111; DLB 214; EWL 3

Abercrombie, Lascelles
1881-1938 .... **TCLC 141**
See also CA 112; DLB 19; RGEL 2

Abish, Walter 1931- ... **CLC 22, 246; SSC 44**
See also CA 101; CANR 37, 114, 153; CN 3, 4, 5, 6; DLB 130, 227; MAL 5; RGHL

Abrahams, Peter (Henry) 1919- .... **CLC 4**
See also AFW; BW 1; CA 57-60; CANR 26, 125; CDWLB 3; CN 1, 2, 3, 4, 5, 6; DLB 117, 225; EWL 3; MTCW 1, 2; RGEL 2; WLIT 2

Abrams, M(eyer) H(oward) 1912- ... **CLC 24**
See also CA 57-60; CANR 13, 33; DLB 67

Abse, Dannie 1923- .... **CLC 7, 29; PC 41**
See also CA 53-56; CAAS 1; CANR 4, 46, 74, 124; CBD; CN 1, 2, 3; CP 1, 2, 3, 4, 5, 6, 7; DAB; DAM POET; DLB 27, 245; MTCW 2

Abutsu 1222(?)-1283 .... **CMLC 46**
See also Abutsu-ni

Abutsu-ni
See Abutsu
See also DLB 203

Achebe, Albert Chinualumogu
See Achebe, Chinua

Achebe, Chinua 1930- .... **BLC 1:1, 2:1; CLC 1, 3, 5, 7, 11, 26, 51, 75, 127, 152; SSC 105; WLC 1**
See also AAYA 15; AFW; BPFB 1; BRWC 2; BW 2, 3; CA 1-4R; CANR 6, 26, 47, 124; CDWLB 3; CLR 20; CN 1, 2, 3, 4, 5, 6, 7; CP 2, 3, 4, 5, 6, 7; CWRI 5; DA; DA3; DAB; DAC; DAM MST, MULT, NOV; DLB 117; DNFS 1; EWL 3; EXPN; EXPS; LAIT 2; LATS 1:2; MAICYA 1, 2; MTCW 1, 2; MTFW 2005; NFS 2; RGEL 2; RGSF 2; SATA 38, 40; SATA-Brief 38; SSFS 3, 13; TWA; WLIT 2; WWE 1

Acker, Kathy 1948-1997 .... **CLC 45, 111; TCLC 191**
See also AMWS 12; CA 117; 122; 162; CANR 55; CN 5, 6; MAL 5

Ackroyd, Peter 1949- .. **CLC 34, 52, 140, 256**
See also BRWS 6; CA 123; 127; CANR 51, 74, 99, 132, 175; CN 4, 5, 6, 7; DLB 155, 231; HGG; INT CA-127; MTCW 1, 2; MTFW 2005; RHW; SATA 153; SUFW 2

Acorn, Milton 1923-1986 .... **CLC 15**
See also CA 103; CCA 1; CP 1, 2, 3, 4; DAC; DLB 53; INT CA-103

Adam de la Halle c. 1250-c.
1285 .... **CMLC 80**

Adamov, Arthur 1908-1970 .... **CLC 4, 25; TCLC 189**
See also CA 17-18; 25-28R; CAP 2; DAM DRAM; DLB 321; EWL 3; GFL 1789 to the Present; MTCW 1; RGWL 2, 3

Adams, Alice 1926-1999 .... **CLC 6, 13, 46; SSC 24**
See also CA 81-84; 179; CANR 26, 53, 75, 88, 136; CN 4, 5, 6; CSW; DLB 234; DLBY 1986; INT CANR-26; MTCW 1, 2; MTFW 2005; SSFS 14, 21

Adams, Andy 1859-1935 .... **TCLC 56**
See also TCWW 1, 2; YABC 1

Adams, (Henry) Brooks
1848-1927 .... **TCLC 80**
See also CA 123; 193

Adams, Douglas 1952-2001 .... **CLC 27, 60**
See also AAYA 4, 33; BEST 89:3; BYA 14; CA 106; 197; CANR 34, 64, 124; CPW; DA3; DAM POP; DLB 261; DLBY 1983; JRDA; MTCW 2; MTFW 2005; NFS 7; SATA 116; SATA-Obit 128; SFW 4

Adams, Francis 1862-1893 .... **NCLC 33**

Adams, Henry (Brooks)
1838-1918 .... **TCLC 4, 52**
See also AMW; CA 104; 133; CANR 77; DA; DAB; DAC; DAM MST; DLB 12, 47, 189, 284; EWL 3; MAL 5; MTCW 2; NCFS 1; RGAL 4; TUS

Adams, John 1735-1826 .... **NCLC 106**
See also DLB 31, 183

Adams, John Quincy 1767-1848 .. **NCLC 175**
See also DLB 37

Adams, Mary
See Phelps, Elizabeth Stuart

Adams, Richard (George) 1920- ... **CLC 4, 5, 18**
See also AAYA 16; AITN 1, 2; BPFB 1; BYA 5; CA 49-52; CANR 3, 35, 128; CLR 20, 121; CN 4, 5, 6, 7; DAM NOV; DLB 261; FANT; JRDA; LAIT 5; MAICYA 1, 2; MTCW 1, 2; NFS 11; SATA 7, 69; YAW

Adamson, Joy(-Friederike Victoria)
1910-1980 .... **CLC 17**
See also CA 69-72; 93-96; CANR 22; MTCW 1; SATA 11; SATA-Obit 22

Adcock, Fleur 1934- .... **CLC 41**
See also BRWS 12; CA 25-28R; 182; CAAE 182; CAAS 23; CANR 11, 34, 69, 101; CP 1, 2, 3, 4, 5, 6, 7; CWP; DLB 40; FW; WWE 1

Addams, Charles 1912-1988 .... **CLC 30**
See also CA 61-64; 126; CANR 12, 79

Addams, Charles Samuel
See Addams, Charles

Addams, (Laura) Jane 1860-1935 . **TCLC 76**
See also AMWS 1; CA 194; DLB 303; FW

Addison, Joseph 1672-1719 .... **LC 18, 146**
See also BRW 3; CDBLB 1660-1789; DLB 101; RGEL 2; WLIT 3

Adichie, Chimamanda Ngozi
1977- .... **BLC 2:1**
See also CA 231

Adler, Alfred (F.) 1870-1937 .... **TCLC 61**
See also CA 119; 159

Adler, C(arole) S(chwerdtfeger)
1932- .... **CLC 35**
See also AAYA 4, 41; CA 89-92; CANR 19, 40, 101; CLR 78; JRDA; MAICYA 1, 2; SAAS 15; SATA 26, 63, 102, 126; YAW

Adler, Renata 1938- .... **CLC 8, 31**
See also CA 49-52; CANR 95; CN 4, 5, 6; MTCW 1

Adorno, Theodor W(iesengrund)
1903-1969 .... **TCLC 111**
See also CA 89-92; 25-28R; CANR 89; DLB 242; EWL 3

Ady, Endre 1877-1919 .... **TCLC 11**
See also CA 107; CDWLB 4; DLB 215; EW 9; EWL 3

A.E. TCLC 3, 10
See Russell, George William
See also DLB 19

Aelfric c. 955-c. 1010 .... **CMLC 46**
See also DLB 146

Aeschines c. 390B.C.-c. 320B.C. .... **CMLC 47**
See also DLB 176

Aeschylus 525(?)B.C.-456(?)B.C. .. **CMLC 11, 51, 94; DC 8; WLCS**
See also AW 1; CDWLB 1; DA; DAB; DAC; DAM DRAM, MST; DFS 5, 10; DLB 176; LMFS 1; RGWL 2, 3; TWA; WLIT 8

Aesop 620(?)B.C.-560(?)B.C. .... **CMLC 24**
See also CLR 14; MAICYA 1, 2; SATA 64

Affable Hawk
See MacCarthy, Sir (Charles Otto) Desmond

Africa, Ben
See Bosman, Herman Charles

Afton, Effie
See Harper, Frances Ellen Watkins

Agapida, Fray Antonio
See Irving, Washington

Agee, James (Rufus) 1909-1955 ...... **TCLC 1, 19, 180**
See also AAYA 44; AITN 1; AMW; CA 108; 148; CANR 131; CDALB 1941-1968; DAM NOV; DLB 2, 26, 152; DLBY 1989; EWL 3; LAIT 3; LATS 1:2; MAL 5; MTCW 2; MTFW 2005; NFS 22; RGAL 4; TUS

A Gentlewoman in New England
See Bradstreet, Anne

A Gentlewoman in Those Parts
See Bradstreet, Anne

Aghill, Gordon
See Silverberg, Robert

Agnon, S(hmuel) Y(osef Halevi) 1888-1970 .... **CLC 4, 8, 14; SSC 30; TCLC 151**
See also CA 17-18; 25-28R; CANR 60, 102; CAP 2; DLB 329; EWL 3; MTCW 1, 2; RGHL; RGSF 2; RGWL 2, 3; WLIT 6

Agrippa von Nettesheim, Henry Cornelius 1486-1535 .... **LC 27**

Aguilera Malta, Demetrio 1909-1981 .... **HLCS 1**
See also CA 111; 124; CANR 87; DAM MULT, NOV; DLB 145; EWL 3; HW 1; RGWL 3

Agustini, Delmira 1886-1914 .... **HLCS 1**
See also CA 166; DLB 290; HW 1, 2; LAW

Aherne, Owen
See Cassill, R(onald) V(erlin)

Ai 1947- .... **CLC 4, 14, 69; PC 72**
See also CA 85-88; CAAS 13; CANR 70; CP 6, 7; DLB 120; PFS 16

Aickman, Robert (Fordyce) 1914-1981 .... **CLC 57**
See also CA 5-8R; CANR 3, 72, 100; DLB 261; HGG; SUFW 1, 2

Aidoo, (Christina) Ama Ata 1942- .... **BLCS; CLC 177**
See also AFW; BW 1; CA 101; CANR 62, 144; CD 5, 6; CDWLB 3; CN 6, 7; CWD; CWP; DLB 117; DNFS 1, 2; EWL 3; FW; WLIT 2

Aiken, Conrad (Potter) 1889-1973 .... **CLC 1, 3, 5, 10, 52; PC 26; SSC 9**
See also AMW; CA 5-8R; 45-48; CANR 4, 60; CDALB 1929-1941; CN 1; CP 1; DAM NOV, POET; DLB 9, 45, 102; EWL 3; EXPS; HGG; MAL 5; MTCW 1, 2; MTFW 2005; PFS 24; RGAL 4; RGSF 2; SATA 3, 30; SSFS 8; TUS

Aiken, Joan (Delano) 1924-2004 ...... **CLC 35**
See also AAYA 1, 25; CA 9-12R, 182; 223; CAAE 182; CANR 4, 23, 34, 64, 121; CLR 1, 19, 90; DLB 161; FANT; HGG; JRDA; MAICYA 1, 2; MTCW 1; RHW; SAAS 1; SATA 2, 30, 73; SATA-Essay 109; SATA-Obit 152; SUFW 2; WYA; YAW

Ainsworth, William Harrison 1805-1882 .... **NCLC 13**
See also DLB 21; HGG; RGEL 2; SATA 24; SUFW 1

Aitmatov, Chingiz 1928-2008 .... **CLC 71**
See Aytmatov, Chingiz
See also CA 103; CANR 38; CWW 2; DLB 302; MTCW 1; RGSF 2; SATA 56

Aitmatov, Chingiz Torekulovich
See Aitmatov, Chingiz

Akers, Floyd
See Baum, L(yman) Frank

Akhmadulina, Bella Akhatovna 1937- .... **CLC 53; PC 43**
See also CA 65-68; CWP; CWW 2; DAM POET; EWL 3

Akhmatova, Anna 1888-1966 ..... **CLC 11, 25, 64, 126; PC 2, 55**
See also CA 19-20; 25-28R; CANR 35; CAP 1; DA3; DAM POET; DLB 295; EW 10; EWL 3; FL 1:5; MTCW 1, 2; PFS 18, 27; RGWL 2, 3

Aksakov, Sergei Timofeevich 1791-1859 .... **NCLC 2, 181**
See also DLB 198

Aksenov, Vasilii (Pavlovich)
See Aksyonov, Vassily (Pavlovich)
See also CWW 2

Aksenov, Vassily
See Aksyonov, Vassily (Pavlovich)

Akst, Daniel 1956- .... **CLC 109**
See also CA 161; CANR 110

Aksyonov, Vassily (Pavlovich) 1932- .... **CLC 22, 37, 101**
See Aksenov, Vasilii (Pavlovich)
See also CA 53-56; CANR 12, 48, 77; DLB 302; EWL 3

Akutagawa Ryunosuke 1892-1927 ... **SSC 44; TCLC 16**
See also CA 117; 154; DLB 180; EWL 3; MJW; RGSF 2; RGWL 2, 3

Alabaster, William 1568-1640 .... **LC 90**
See also DLB 132; RGEL 2

Alain 1868-1951 .... **TCLC 41**
See also CA 163; EWL 3; GFL 1789 to the Present

Alain de Lille c. 1116-c. 1203 .... **CMLC 53**
See also DLB 208

Alain-Fournier TCLC 6
See Fournier, Henri-Alban
See also DLB 65; EWL 3; GFL 1789 to the Present; RGWL 2, 3

Al-Amin, Jamil Abdullah 1943- ...... **BLC 1:1**
See also BW 1, 3; CA 112; 125; CANR 82; DAM MULT

Alanus de Insluis
See Alain de Lille

Alarcon, Pedro Antonio de 1833-1891 .... **NCLC 1; SSC 64**

Alas (y Urena), Leopoldo (Enrique Garcia) 1852-1901 .... **TCLC 29**
See also CA 113; 131; HW 1; RGSF 2

Albee, Edward (III) 1928- ..... **CLC 1, 2, 3, 5, 9, 11, 13, 25, 53, 86, 113; DC 11; WLC 1**
See also AAYA 51; AITN 1; AMW; CA 5-8R; CABS 3; CAD; CANR 8, 54, 74, 124; CD 5, 6; CDALB 1941-1968; DA; DA3; DAB; DAC; DAM DRAM, MST; DFS 25; DLB 7, 266; EWL 3; INT CANR-8; LAIT 4; LMFS 2; MAL 5; MTCW 1, 2; MTFW 2005; RGAL 4; TUS

Alberti (Merello), Rafael
See Alberti, Rafael
See also CWW 2

Alberti, Rafael 1902-1999 .... **CLC 7**
See Alberti (Merello), Rafael
See also CA 85-88; 185; CANR 81; DLB 108; EWL 3; HW 2; RGWL 2, 3

Albert the Great 1193(?)-1280 .... **CMLC 16**
See also DLB 115

Alcaeus c. 620B.C.- .... **CMLC 65**
See also DLB 176

Alcala-Galiano, Juan Valera y
See Valera y Alcala-Galiano, Juan

Alcayaga, Lucila Godoy
See Godoy Alcayaga, Lucila

Alciato, Andrea 1492-1550 .... **LC 116**

Alcott, Amos Bronson 1799-1888 ... **NCLC 1, 167**
See also DLB 1, 223

Alcott, Louisa May 1832-1888 . **NCLC 6, 58, 83; SSC 27, 98; WLC 1**
See also AAYA 20; AMWS 1; BPFB 1; BYA 2; CDALB 1865-1917; CLR 1, 38, 109; DA; DA3; DAB; DAC; DAM MST, NOV; DLB 1, 42, 79, 223, 239, 242; DLBD 14; FL 1:2; FW; JRDA; LAIT 2; MAICYA 1, 2; NFS 12; RGAL 4; SATA 100; TUS; WCH; WYA; YABC 1; YAW

Alcuin c. 730-804 .... **CMLC 69**
See also DLB 148

Aldanov, M. A.
See Aldanov, Mark (Alexandrovich)

Aldanov, Mark (Alexandrovich) 1886-1957 .... **TCLC 23**
See also CA 118; 181; DLB 317

Aldhelm c. 639-709 .... **CMLC 90**

Aldington, Richard 1892-1962 .... **CLC 49**
See also CA 85-88; CANR 45; DLB 20, 36, 100, 149; LMFS 2; RGEL 2

Aldiss, Brian W. 1925- .. **CLC 5, 14, 40; SSC 36**
See also AAYA 42; CA 5-8R, 190; CAAE 190; CAAS 2; CANR 5, 28, 64, 121, 168; CN 1, 2, 3, 4, 5, 6, 7; DAM NOV; DLB 14, 261, 271; MTCW 1, 2; MTFW 2005; SATA 34; SCFW 1, 2; SFW 4

Aldiss, Brian Wilson
See Aldiss, Brian W.

Aldrich, Ann
See Meaker, Marijane

Aldrich, Bess Streeter 1881-1954 .... **TCLC 125**
See also CLR 70; TCWW 2

Alegria, Claribel
See Alegria, Claribel
See also CWW 2; DLB 145, 283

Alegria, Claribel 1924- .... **CLC 75; HLCS 1; PC 26**
See Alegria, Claribel
See also CA 131; CAAS 15; CANR 66, 94, 134; DAM MULT; EWL 3; HW 1; MTCW 2; MTFW 2005; PFS 21

Alegria, Fernando 1918-2005 .... **CLC 57**
See also CA 9-12R; CANR 5, 32, 72; EWL 3; HW 1, 2

Aleixandre, Vicente 1898-1984 .... **HLCS 1; TCLC 113**
See also CANR 81; DLB 108, 329; EWL 3; HW 2; MTCW 1, 2; RGWL 2, 3

Alekseev, Konstantin Sergeivich
See Stanislavsky, Constantin

Alekseyer, Konstantin Sergeyevich
See Stanislavsky, Constantin

Aleman, Mateo 1547-1615(?) .... **LC 81**

Alencar, Jose de 1829-1877 .... **NCLC 157**
See also DLB 307; LAW; WLIT 1

Alencon, Marguerite d'
See de Navarre, Marguerite

Alepoudelis, Odysseus
See Elytis, Odysseus
See also CWW 2

Aleshkovsky, Joseph 1929-
See Aleshkovsky, Yuz
See also CA 121; 128

Aleshkovsky, Yuz CLC 44
See Aleshkovsky, Joseph
See also DLB 317

Alexander, Barbara
See Ehrenreich, Barbara

Alexander, Lloyd 1924-2007 .... **CLC 35**
   See also AAYA 1, 27; BPFB 1; BYA 5, 6,
   7, 9, 10, 11; CA 1-4R; 260; CANR 1, 24,
   38, 55, 113; CLR 1, 5, 48; CWRI 5; DLB
   52; FANT; JRDA; MAICYA 1, 2; MAIC-
   YAS 1; MTCW 1; SAAS 19; SATA 3, 49,
   81, 129, 135; SATA-Obit 182; SUFW;
   TUS; WYA; YAW
Alexander, Lloyd Chudley
   See Alexander, Lloyd
Alexander, Meena 1951- .... **CLC 121**
   See also CA 115; CANR 38, 70, 146; CP 5,
   6, 7; CWP; DLB 323; FW
Alexander, Samuel 1859-1938 .... **TCLC 77**
Alexeiev, Konstantin
   See Stanislavsky, Constantin
Alexeyev, Constantin Sergeivich
   See Stanislavsky, Constantin
Alexeyev, Konstantin Sergeyevich
   See Stanislavsky, Constantin
Alexie, Sherman 1966- .... **CLC 96, 154;**
   NNAL; PC 53; SSC 107
   See also AAYA 28; BYA 15; CA 138;
   CANR 65, 95, 133, 174; CN 7; DA3;
   DAM MULT; DLB 175, 206, 278; LATS
   1:2; MTCW 2; MTFW 2005; NFS 17;
   SSFS 18
Alexie, Sherman Joseph, Jr.
   See Alexie, Sherman
al-Farabi 870(?)-950 .... **CMLC 58**
   See also DLB 115
Alfau, Felipe 1902-1999 .... **CLC 66**
   See also CA 137
Alfieri, Vittorio 1749-1803 .... **NCLC 101**
   See also EW 4; RGWL 2, 3; WLIT 7
Alfonso X 1221-1284 .... **CMLC 78**
Alfred, Jean Gaston
   See Ponge, Francis
Alger, Horatio, Jr. 1832-1899 .... **NCLC 8, 83**
   See also CLR 87; DLB 42; LAIT 2; RGAL
   4; SATA 16; TUS
Al-Ghazali, Muhammad ibn Muhammad
   1058-1111 .... **CMLC 50**
   See also DLB 115
Algren, Nelson 1909-1981 ..... **CLC 4, 10, 33;**
   SSC 33
   See also AMWS 9; BPFB 1; CA 13-16R;
   103; CANR 20, 61; CDALB 1941-1968;
   CN 1, 2; DLB 9; DLBY 1981, 1982,
   2000; EWL 3; MAL 5; MTCW 1, 2;
   MTFW 2005; RGAL 4; RGSF 2
al-Hamadhani 967-1007 .... **CMLC 93**
   See also WLIT 6
al-Hariri, al-Qasim ibn 'Ali Abu
   Muhammad al-Basri
   1054-1122 .... **CMLC 63**
   See also RGWL 3
Ali, Ahmed 1908-1998 .... **CLC 69**
   See also CA 25-28R; CANR 15, 34; CN 1,
   2, 3, 4, 5; DLB 323; EWL 3
Ali, Tariq 1943- .... **CLC 173**
   See also CA 25-28R; CANR 10, 99, 161
Alighieri, Dante
   See Dante
   See also WLIT 7
al-Kindi, Abu Yusuf Ya'qub ibn Ishaq c.
   801-c. 873 .... **CMLC 80**
Allan, John B.
   See Westlake, Donald E.
Allan, Sidney
   See Hartmann, Sadakichi
Allan, Sydney
   See Hartmann, Sadakichi
Allard, Janet **CLC 59**

Allen, Edward 1948- .... **CLC 59**
Allen, Fred 1894-1956 .... **TCLC 87**
Allen, Paula Gunn 1939-2008 . **CLC 84, 202;**
   NNAL
   See also AMWS 4; CA 112; 143; 272;
   CANR 63, 130; CWP; DA3; DAM
   MULT; DLB 175; FW; MTCW 2; MTFW
   2005; RGAL 4; TCWW 2
Allen, Roland
   See Ayckbourn, Alan
Allen, Sarah A.
   See Hopkins, Pauline Elizabeth
Allen, Sidney H.
   See Hartmann, Sadakichi
Allen, Woody 1935- .... **CLC 16, 52, 195**
   See also AAYA 10, 51; AMWS 15; CA 33-
   36R; CANR 27, 38, 63, 128, 172; DAM
   POP; DLB 44; MTCW 1; SSFS 21
Allende, Isabel 1942- ... **CLC 39, 57, 97, 170,**
   264; HLC 1; SSC 65; WLCS
   See also AAYA 18, 70; CA 125; 130; CANR
   51, 74, 129, 165; CDWLB 3; CLR 99;
   CWW 2; DA3; DAM MULT, NOV; DLB
   145; DNFS 1; EWL 3; FL 1:5; FW; HW
   1, 2; INT CA-130; LAIT 5; LAWS 1;
   LMFS 2; MTCW 1, 2; MTFW 2005;
   NCFS 1; NFS 6, 18; RGSF 2; RGWL 3;
   SATA 163; SSFS 11, 16; WLIT 1
Alleyn, Ellen
   See Rossetti, Christina
Alleyne, Carla D. **CLC 65**
Allingham, Margery (Louise)
   1904-1966 .... **CLC 19**
   See also CA 5-8R; 25-28R; CANR 4, 58;
   CMW 4; DLB 77; MSW; MTCW 1, 2
Allingham, William 1824-1889 ...... **NCLC 25**
   See also DLB 35; RGEL 2
Allison, Dorothy E. 1949- .... **CLC 78, 153**
   See also AAYA 53; CA 140; CANR 66, 107;
   CN 7; CSW; DA3; FW; MTCW 2; MTFW
   2005; NFS 11; RGAL 4
Alloula, Malek **CLC 65**
Allston, Washington 1779-1843 .... **NCLC 2**
   See also DLB 1, 235
Almedingen, E. M. **CLC 12**
   See Almedingen, Martha Edith von
   See also SATA 3
Almedingen, Martha Edith von 1898-1971
   See Almedingen, E. M.
   See also CA 1-4R; CANR 1
Almodovar, Pedro 1949(?)- .... **CLC 114, 229;**
   HLCS 1
   See also CA 133; CANR 72, 151; HW 2
Almqvist, Carl Jonas Love
   1793-1866 .... **NCLC 42**
al-Mutanabbi, Ahmad ibn al-Husayn Abu
   al-Tayyib al-Jufi al-Kindi
   915-965 .... **CMLC 66**
   See Mutanabbi, Al-
   See also RGWL 3
Alonso, Damaso 1898-1990 .... **CLC 14**
   See also CA 110; 131; 130; CANR 72; DLB
   108; EWL 3; HW 1, 2
Alov
   See Gogol, Nikolai (Vasilyevich)
al'Sadaawi, Nawal
   See El Saadawi, Nawal
   See also FW
al-Shaykh, Hanan 1945- .... **CLC 218**
   See also CA 135; CANR 111; CWW 2;
   DLB 346; EWL 3; WLIT 6
Al Siddik
   See Rolfe, Frederick (William Serafino
   Austin Lewis Mary)
   See also GLL 1; RGEL 2
Alta 1942- .... **CLC 19**
   See also CA 57-60
Alter, Robert B. 1935- .... **CLC 34**
   See also CA 49-52; CANR 1, 47, 100, 160

Alter, Robert Bernard
   See Alter, Robert B.
Alther, Lisa 1944- .... **CLC 7, 41**
   See also BPFB 1; CA 65-68; CAAS 30;
   CANR 12, 30, 51, 180; CN 4, 5, 6, 7;
   CSW; GLL 2; MTCW 1
Althusser, L.
   See Althusser, Louis
Althusser, Louis 1918-1990 .... **CLC 106**
   See also CA 131; 132; CANR 102; DLB
   242
Altman, Robert 1925-2006 .... **CLC 16, 116,**
   242
   See also CA 73-76; 254; CANR 43
Alurista **HLCS 1; PC 34**
   See Urista (Heredia), Alberto (Baltazar)
   See also CA 45-48R; DLB 82; LLW
Alvarez, A. 1929- .... **CLC 5, 13**
   See also CA 1-4R; CANR 3, 33, 63, 101,
   134; CN 3, 4, 5, 6; CP 1, 2, 3, 4, 5, 6, 7;
   DLB 14, 40; MTFW 2005
Alvarez, Alejandro Rodriguez 1903-1965
   See Casona, Alejandro
   See also CA 131; 93-96; HW 1
Alvarez, Julia 1950- .... **CLC 93; HLCS 1**
   See also AAYA 25; AMWS 7; CA 147;
   CANR 69, 101, 133, 166; DA3; DLB 282;
   LATS 1:2; LLW; MTCW 2; MTFW 2005;
   NFS 5, 9; SATA 129; WLIT 1
Alvaro, Corrado 1896-1956 .... **TCLC 60**
   See also CA 163; DLB 264; EWL 3
Amado, Jorge 1912-2001 ... **CLC 13, 40, 106,**
   232; HLC 1
   See also CA 77-80; 201; CANR 35, 74, 135;
   CWW 2; DAM MULT, NOV; DLB 113,
   307; EWL 3; HW 2; LAW; LAWS 1;
   MTCW 1, 2; MTFW 2005; RGWL 2, 3;
   TWA; WLIT 1
Ambler, Eric 1909-1998 .... **CLC 4, 6, 9**
   See also BRWS 4; CA 9-12R; 171; CANR
   7, 38, 74; CMW 4; CN 1, 2, 3, 4, 5, 6;
   DLB 77; MSW; MTCW 1, 2; TEA
Ambrose c. 339-c. 397 .... **CMLC 103**
Ambrose, Stephen E. 1936-2002 ... **CLC 145**
   See also AAYA 44; CA 1-4R; 209; CANR
   3, 43, 57, 83, 105; MTFW 2005; NCFS 2;
   SATA 40, 138
Amichai, Yehuda 1924-2000 .. **CLC 9, 22, 57,**
   116; PC 38
   See also CA 85-88; 189; CANR 46, 60, 99,
   132; CWW 2; EWL 3; MTCW 1, 2;
   MTFW 2005; PFS 24; RGHL; WLIT 6
Amichai, Yehudah
   See Amichai, Yehuda
Amiel, Henri Frederic 1821-1881 .... **NCLC 4**
   See also DLB 217
Amis, Kingsley 1922-1995 . **CLC 1, 2, 3, 5, 8,**
   13, 40, 44, 129
   See also AAYA 77; AITN 2; BPFB 1;
   BRWS 2; CA 9-12R; 150; CANR 8, 28,
   54; CDBLB 1945-1960; CN 1, 2, 3, 4, 5,
   6; CP 1, 2, 3, 4; DA; DA3; DAB; DAC;
   DAM MST, NOV; DLB 15, 27, 100, 139,
   326; DLBY 1996; EWL 3; HGG; INT
   CANR-8; MTCW 1, 2; MTFW 2005;
   RGEL 2; RGSF 2; SFW 4
Amis, Martin 1949- ... **CLC 4, 9, 38, 62, 101,**
   213; SSC 112
   See also BEST 90:3; BRWS 4; CA 65-68;
   CANR 8, 27, 54, 73, 95, 132, 166; CN 5,
   6, 7; DA3; DLB 14, 194; EWL 3; INT
   CANR-27; MTCW 2; MTFW 2005
Amis, Martin Louis
   See Amis, Martin
Ammianus Marcellinus c. 330-c.
   395 .... **CMLC 60**
   See also AW 2; DLB 211

Ammons, A.R. 1926-2001 .. **CLC 2, 3, 5, 8, 9, 25, 57, 108; PC 16**
  See also AITN 1; AMWS 7; CA 9-12R; 193; CANR 6, 36, 51, 73, 107, 156; CP 1, 2, 3, 4, 5, 6, 7; CSW; DAM POET; DLB 5, 165, 342; EWL 3; MAL 5; MTCW 1, 2; PFS 19; RGAL 4; TCLE 1:1

Ammons, Archie Randolph
  See Ammons, A.R.

Amo, Tauraatua i
  See Adams, Henry (Brooks)

Amory, Thomas 1691(?)-1788 .... **LC 48**
  See also DLB 39

Anand, Mulk Raj 1905-2004 ..... **CLC 23, 93, 237**
  See also CA 65-68; 231; CANR 32, 64; CN 1, 2, 3, 4, 5, 6, 7; DAM NOV; DLB 323; EWL 3; MTCW 1, 2; MTFW 2005; RGSF 2

Anatol
  See Schnitzler, Arthur

Anaximander c. 611B.C.-c. 546B.C. .... **CMLC 22**

Anaya, Rudolfo A. 1937- . **CLC 23, 148, 255; HLC 1**
  See also AAYA 20; BYA 13; CA 45-48; CAAS 4; CANR 1, 32, 51, 124, 169; CLR 129; CN 4, 5, 6, 7; DAM MULT, NOV; DLB 82, 206, 278; HW 1; LAIT 4; LLW; MAL 5; MTCW 1, 2; MTFW 2005; NFS 12; RGAL 4; RGSF 2; TCWW 2; WLIT 1

Anaya, Rudolpho Alfonso
  See Anaya, Rudolfo A.

Andersen, Hans Christian 1805-1875 .... **NCLC 7, 79; SSC 6, 56; WLC 1**
  See also AAYA 57; CLR 6, 113; DA; DA3; DAB; DAC; DAM MST, POP; EW 6; MAICYA 1, 2; RGSF 2; RGWL 2, 3; SATA 100; TWA; WCH; YABC 1

Anderson, C. Farley
  See Mencken, H(enry) L(ouis); Nathan, George Jean

Anderson, Jessica (Margaret) Queale 1916- .... **CLC 37**
  See also CA 9-12R; CANR 4, 62; CN 4, 5, 6, 7; DLB 325

Anderson, Jon (Victor) 1940- .... **CLC 9**
  See also CA 25-28R; CANR 20; CP 1, 3, 4, 5; DAM POET

Anderson, Lindsay (Gordon) 1923-1994 .... **CLC 20**
  See also CA 125; 128; 146; CANR 77

Anderson, Maxwell 1888-1959 .... **TCLC 2, 144**
  See also CA 105; 152; DAM DRAM; DFS 16, 20; DLB 7, 228; MAL 5; MTCW 2; MTFW 2005; RGAL 4

Anderson, Poul 1926-2001 .... **CLC 15**
  See also AAYA 5, 34; BPFB 1; BYA 6, 8, 9; CA 1-4R, 181; 199; CAAE 181; CAAS 2; CANR 2, 15, 34, 64, 110; CLR 58; DLB 8; FANT; INT CANR-15; MTCW 1, 2; MTFW 2005; SATA 90; SATA-Brief 39; SATA-Essay 106; SCFW 1, 2; SFW 4; SUFW 1, 2

Anderson, Robert (Woodruff) 1917- .... **CLC 23**
  See also AITN 1; CA 21-24R; CANR 32; CD 6; DAM DRAM; DLB 7; LAIT 5

Anderson, Roberta Joan
  See Mitchell, Joni

Anderson, Sherwood 1876-1941 ... **SSC 1, 46, 91; TCLC 1, 10, 24, 123; WLC 1**
  See also AAYA 30; AMW; AMWC 2; BPFB 1; CA 104; 121; CANR 61; CDALB 1917-1929; DA; DA3; DAB; DAC; DAM MST, NOV; DLB 4, 9, 86; DLBD 1; EWL

3; EXPS; GLL 2; MAL 5; MTCW 1, 2; MTFW 2005; NFS 4; RGAL 4; RGSF 2; SSFS 4, 10, 11; TUS

Anderson, Wes 1969- .... **CLC 227**
  See also CA 214

Andier, Pierre
  See Desnos, Robert

Andouard
  See Giraudoux, Jean(-Hippolyte)

Andrade, Carlos Drummond de CLC 18
  See Drummond de Andrade, Carlos
  See also EWL 3; RGWL 2, 3

Andrade, Mario de TCLC 43
  See de Andrade, Mario
  See also DLB 307; EWL 3; LAW; RGWL 2, 3; WLIT 1

Andreae, Johann V(alentin) 1586-1654 .... **LC 32**
  See also DLB 164

Andreas Capellanus fl. c. 1185- .... **CMLC 45**
  See also DLB 208

Andreas-Salome, Lou 1861-1937 ... **TCLC 56**
  See also CA 178; DLB 66

Andreev, Leonid
  See Andreyev, Leonid (Nikolaevich)
  See also DLB 295; EWL 3

Andress, Lesley
  See Sanders, Lawrence

Andrewes, Lancelot 1555-1626 .... **LC 5**
  See also DLB 151, 172

Andrews, Cicily Fairfield
  See West, Rebecca

Andrews, Elton V.
  See Pohl, Frederik

Andrews, Peter
  See Soderbergh, Steven

Andrews, Raymond 1934-1991 .... **BLC 2:1**
  See also BW 2; CA 81-84; 136; CANR 15, 42

Andreyev, Leonid (Nikolaevich) 1871-1919 .... **TCLC 3**
  See Andreev, Leonid
  See also CA 104; 185

Andric, Ivo 1892-1975 .... **CLC 8; SSC 36; TCLC 135**
  See also CA 81-84; 57-60; CANR 43, 60; CDWLB 4; DLB 147, 329; EW 11; EWL 3; MTCW 1; RGSF 2; RGWL 2, 3

Androvar
  See Prado (Calvo), Pedro

Angela of Foligno 1248(?)-1309 .... **CMLC 76**

Angelique, Pierre
  See Bataille, Georges

Angell, Roger 1920- .... **CLC 26**
  See also CA 57-60; CANR 13, 44, 70, 144; DLB 171, 185

Angelou, Maya 1928- ...... **BLC 1:1; CLC 12, 35, 64, 77, 155; PC 32; WLCS**
  See also AAYA 7, 20; AMWS 4; BPFB 1; BW 2, 3; BYA 2; CA 65-68; CANR 19, 42, 65, 111, 133; CDALBS; CLR 53; CP 4, 5, 6, 7; CPW; CSW; CWP; DA; DA3; DAB; DAC; DAM MST, MULT, POET, POP; DLB 38; EWL 3; EXPN; EXPP; FL 1:5; LAIT 4; MAICYA 2; MAICYAS 1; MAL 5; MBL; MTCW 1, 2; MTFW 2005; NCFS 2; NFS 2; PFS 2, 3; RGAL 4; SATA 49, 136; TCLE 1:1; WYA; YAW

Angouleme, Marguerite d'
  See de Navarre, Marguerite

Anna Comnena 1083-1153 .... **CMLC 25**

Annensky, Innokentii Fedorovich
  See Annensky, Innokenty (Fyodorovich)
  See also DLB 295

Annensky, Innokenty (Fyodorovich) 1856-1909 .... **TCLC 14**
  See also CA 110; 155; EWL 3

Annunzio, Gabriele d'
  See D'Annunzio, Gabriele

Anodos
  See Coleridge, Mary E(lizabeth)

Anon, Charles Robert
  See Pessoa, Fernando

Anouilh, Jean 1910-1987 ..... **CLC 1, 3, 8, 13, 40, 50; DC 8, 21; TCLC 195**
  See also AAYA 67; CA 17-20R; 123; CANR 32; DAM DRAM; DFS 9, 10, 19; DLB 321; EW 13; EWL 3; GFL 1789 to the Present; MTCW 1, 2; MTFW 2005; RGWL 2, 3; TWA

Ansa, Tina McElroy 1949- .... **BLC 2:1**
  See also BW 2; CA 142; CANR 143; CSW

Anselm of Canterbury 1033(?)-1109 .... **CMLC 67**
  See also DLB 115

Anthony, Florence
  See Ai

Anthony, John
  See Ciardi, John (Anthony)

Anthony, Peter
  See Shaffer, Anthony; Shaffer, Peter

Anthony, Piers 1934- .... **CLC 35**
  See also AAYA 11, 48; BYA 7; CA 200; CAAE 200; CANR 28, 56, 73, 102, 133; CLR 118; CPW; DAM POP; DLB 8; FANT; MAICYA 2; MAICYAS 1; MTCW 1, 2; MTFW 2005; SAAS 22; SATA 84, 129; SATA-Essay 129; SFW 4; SUFW 1, 2; YAW

Anthony, Susan B(rownell) 1820-1906 .... **TCLC 84**
  See also CA 211; FW

Antiphon c. 480B.C.-c. 411B.C. .... **CMLC 55**

Antoine, Marc
  See Proust, (Valentin-Louis-George-Eugene) Marcel

Antoninus, Brother
  See Everson, William (Oliver)
  See also CP 1

Antonioni, Michelangelo 1912-2007 .... **CLC 20, 144, 259**
  See also CA 73-76; 262; CANR 45, 77

Antschel, Paul 1920-1970
  See Celan, Paul
  See also CA 85-88; CANR 33, 61; MTCW 1; PFS 21

Anwar, Chairil 1922-1949 .... **TCLC 22**
  See Chairil Anwar
  See also CA 121; 219; RGWL 3

Anyidoho, Kofi 1947- .... **BLC 2:1**
  See also BW 3; CA 178; CP 5, 6, 7; DLB 157; EWL 3

Anzaldua, Gloria (Evanjelina) 1942-2004 .... **CLC 200; HLCS 1**
  See also CA 175; 227; CSW; CWP; DLB 122; FW; LLW; RGAL 4; SATA-Obit 154

Apess, William 1798-1839(?) .... **NCLC 73; NNAL**
  See also DAM MULT; DLB 175, 243

Apollinaire, Guillaume 1880-1918 .... **PC 7; TCLC 3, 8, 51**
  See Kostrowitzki, Wilhelm Apollinaris de
  See also CA 152; DAM POET; DLB 258, 321; EW 9; EWL 3; GFL 1789 to the Present; MTCW 2; PFS 24; RGWL 2, 3; TWA; WP

Apollonius of Rhodes
  See Apollonius Rhodius
  See also AW 1; RGWL 2, 3

Apollonius Rhodius c. 300B.C.-c. 220B.C. .... **CMLC 28**
  See Apollonius of Rhodes
  See also DLB 176

Appelfeld, Aharon 1932- ... **CLC 23, 47; SSC 42**
  See also CA 112; 133; CANR 86, 160; CWW 2; DLB 299; EWL 3; RGHL; RGSF 2; WLIT 6

Appelfeld, Aron
See Appelfeld, Aharon

Apple, Max (Isaac) 1941- .... **CLC 9, 33; SSC 50**
See also AMWS 17; CA 81-84; CANR 19, 54; DLB 130

Appleman, Philip (Dean) 1926- .... **CLC 51**
See also CA 13-16R; CAAS 18; CANR 6, 29, 56

Appleton, Lawrence
See Lovecraft, H. P.

Apteryx
See Eliot, T(homas) S(tearns)

Apuleius, (Lucius Madaurensis) c. 125-c. 164 .... **CMLC 1, 84**
See also AW 2; CDWLB 1; DLB 211; RGWL 2, 3; SUFW; WLIT 8

Aquin, Hubert 1929-1977 .... **CLC 15**
See also CA 105; DLB 53; EWL 3

Aquinas, Thomas 1224(?)-1274 ..... **CMLC 33**
See also DLB 115; EW 1; TWA

Aragon, Louis 1897-1982 .... **CLC 3, 22; TCLC 123**
See also CA 69-72; 108; CANR 28, 71; DAM NOV, POET; DLB 72, 258; EW 11; EWL 3; GFL 1789 to the Present; GLL 2; LMFS 2; MTCW 1, 2; RGWL 2, 3

Arany, Janos 1817-1882 .... **NCLC 34**

Aranyos, Kakay 1847-1910
See Mikszath, Kalman

Aratus of Soli c. 315B.C.-c. 240B.C. .... **CMLC 64**
See also DLB 176

Arbuthnot, John 1667-1735 .... **LC 1**
See also DLB 101

Archer, Herbert Winslow
See Mencken, H(enry) L(ouis)

Archer, Jeffrey 1940- .... **CLC 28**
See also AAYA 16; BEST 89:3; BPFB 1; CA 77-80; CANR 22, 52, 95, 136; CPW; DA3; DAM POP; INT CANR-22; MTFW 2005

Archer, Jeffrey Howard
See Archer, Jeffrey

Archer, Jules 1915- .... **CLC 12**
See also CA 9-12R; CANR 6, 69; SAAS 5; SATA 4, 85

Archer, Lee
See Ellison, Harlan

Archilochus c. 7th cent. B.C.- .... **CMLC 44**
See also DLB 176

Ard, William
See Jakes, John

Arden, John 1930- .... **CLC 6, 13, 15**
See also BRWS 2; CA 13-16R; CAAS 4; CANR 31, 65, 67, 124; CBD; CD 5, 6; DAM DRAM; DFS 9; DLB 13, 245; EWL 3; MTCW 1

Arenas, Reinaldo 1943-1990 .. **CLC 41; HLC 1; TCLC 191**
See also CA 124; 128; 133; CANR 73, 106; DAM MULT; DLB 145; EWL 3; GLL 2; HW 1; LAW; LAWS 1; MTCW 2; MTFW 2005; RGSF 2; RGWL 3; WLIT 1

Arendt, Hannah 1906-1975 .... **CLC 66, 98; TCLC 193**
See also CA 17-20R; 61-64; CANR 26, 60, 172; DLB 242; MTCW 1, 2

Aretino, Pietro 1492-1556 .... **LC 12**
See also RGWL 2, 3

Arghezi, Tudor CLC 80
See Theodorescu, Ion N.
See also CA 167; CDWLB 4; DLB 220; EWL 3

Arguedas, Jose Maria 1911-1969 .... **CLC 10, 18; HLCS 1; TCLC 147**
See also CA 89-92; CANR 73; DLB 113; EWL 3; HW 1; LAW; RGWL 2, 3; WLIT 1

Argueta, Manlio 1936- .... **CLC 31**
See also CA 131; CANR 73; CWW 2; DLB 145; EWL 3; HW 1; RGWL 3

Arias, Ron 1941- .... **HLC 1**
See also CA 131; CANR 81, 136; DAM MULT; DLB 82; HW 1, 2; MTCW 2; MTFW 2005

Ariosto, Lodovico
See Ariosto, Ludovico
See also WLIT 7

Ariosto, Ludovico 1474-1533 ... **LC 6, 87; PC 42**
See Ariosto, Lodovico
See also EW 2; RGWL 2, 3

Aristides
See Epstein, Joseph

Aristophanes 450B.C.-385B.C. .... **CMLC 4, 51; DC 2; WLCS**
See also AW 1; CDWLB 1; DA; DA3; DAB; DAC; DAM DRAM, MST; DFS 10; DLB 176; LMFS 1; RGWL 2, 3; TWA; WLIT 8

Aristotle 384B.C.-322B.C. .... **CMLC 31; WLCS**
See also AW 1; CDWLB 1; DA; DA3; DAB; DAC; DAM MST; DLB 176; RGWL 2, 3; TWA; WLIT 8

Arlt, Roberto (Godofredo Christophersen) 1900-1942 .... **HLC 1; TCLC 29**
See also CA 123; 131; CANR 67; DAM MULT; DLB 305; EWL 3; HW 1, 2; IDTP; LAW

Armah, Ayi Kwei 1939- . **BLC 1:1, 2:1; CLC 5, 33, 136**
See also AFW; BRWS 10; BW 1; CA 61-64; CANR 21, 64; CDWLB 3; CN 1, 2, 3, 4, 5, 6, 7; DAM MULT, POET; DLB 117; EWL 3; MTCW 1; WLIT 2

Armatrading, Joan 1950- .... **CLC 17**
See also CA 114; 186

Armin, Robert 1568(?)-1615(?) .... **LC 120**

Armitage, Frank
See Carpenter, John (Howard)

Armstrong, Jeannette (C.) 1948- .... **NNAL**
See also CA 149; CCA 1; CN 6, 7; DAC; DLB 334; SATA 102

Arnette, Robert
See Silverberg, Robert

Arnim, Achim von (Ludwig Joachim von Arnim) 1781-1831 .. **NCLC 5, 159; SSC 29**
See also DLB 90

Arnim, Bettina von 1785-1859 ...... **NCLC 38, 123**
See also DLB 90; RGWL 2, 3

Arnold, Matthew 1822-1888 ..... **NCLC 6, 29, 89, 126; PC 5; WLC 1**
See also BRW 5; CDBLB 1832-1890; DA; DAB; DAC; DAM MST, POET; DLB 32, 57; EXPP; PAB; PFS 2; TEA; WP

Arnold, Thomas 1795-1842 .... **NCLC 18**
See also DLB 55

Arnow, Harriette (Louisa) Simpson 1908-1986 ...... **CLC 2, 7, 18; TCLC 196**
See also BPFB 1; CA 9-12R; 118; CANR 14; CN 2, 3, 4; DLB 6; FW; MTCW 1, 2; RHW; SATA 42; SATA-Obit 47

Arouet, Francois-Marie
See Voltaire

Arp, Hans
See Arp, Jean

Arp, Jean 1887-1966 .... **CLC 5; TCLC 115**
See also CA 81-84; 25-28R; CANR 42, 77; EW 10

Arrabal
See Arrabal, Fernando

Arrabal (Teran), Fernando
See Arrabal, Fernando
See also CWW 2

Arrabal, Fernando 1932- ... **CLC 2, 9, 18, 58**
See Arrabal (Teran), Fernando
See also CA 9-12R; CANR 15; DLB 321; EWL 3; LMFS 2

Arreola, Juan Jose 1918-2001 .... **CLC 147; HLC 1; SSC 38**
See also CA 113; 131; 200; CANR 81; CWW 2; DAM MULT; DLB 113; DNFS 2; EWL 3; HW 1, 2; LAW; RGSF 2

Arrian c. 89(?)-c. 155(?) .... **CMLC 43**
See also DLB 176

Arrick, Fran CLC 30
See Gaberman, Judie Angell
See also BYA 6

Arrley, Richmond
See Delany, Samuel R., Jr.

Artaud, Antonin (Marie Joseph) 1896-1948 .... **DC 14; TCLC 3, 36**
See also CA 104; 149; DA3; DAM DRAM; DFS 22; DLB 258, 321; EW 11; EWL 3; GFL 1789 to the Present; MTCW 2; MTFW 2005; RGWL 2, 3

Arthur, Ruth M(abel) 1905-1979 ..... **CLC 12**
See also CA 9-12R; 85-88; CANR 4; CWRI 5; SATA 7, 26

Artsybashev, Mikhail (Petrovich) 1878-1927 .... **TCLC 31**
See also CA 170; DLB 295

Arundel, Honor (Morfydd) 1919-1973 .... **CLC 17**
See also CA 21-22; 41-44R; CAP 2; CLR 35; CWRI 5; SATA 4; SATA-Obit 24

Arzner, Dorothy 1900-1979 .... **CLC 98**

Asch, Sholem 1880-1957 .... **TCLC 3**
See also CA 105; DLB 333; EWL 3; GLL 2; RGHL

Ascham, Roger 1516(?)-1568 .... **LC 101**
See also DLB 236

Ash, Shalom
See Asch, Sholem

Ashbery, John 1927- ... **CLC 2, 3, 4, 6, 9, 13, 15, 25, 41, 77, 125, 221; PC 26**
See also AMWS 3; CA 5-8R; CANR 9, 37, 66, 102, 132, 170; CP 1, 2, 3, 4, 5, 6, 7; DA3; DAM POET; DLB 5, 165; DLBY 1981; EWL 3; GLL 1; INT CANR-9; MAL 5; MTCW 1, 2; MTFW 2005; PAB; PFS 11, 28; RGAL 4; TCLE 1:1; WP

Ashbery, John Lawrence
See Ashbery, John

Ashbridge, Elizabeth 1713-1755 .... **LC 147**
See also DLB 200

Ashdown, Clifford
See Freeman, R(ichard) Austin

Ashe, Gordon
See Creasey, John

Ashton-Warner, Sylvia (Constance) 1908-1984 .... **CLC 19**
See also CA 69-72; 112; CANR 29; CN 1, 2, 3; MTCW 1, 2

Asimov, Isaac 1920-1992 ..... **CLC 1, 3, 9, 19, 26, 76, 92**
See also AAYA 13; BEST 90:2; BPFB 1; BYA 4, 6, 7, 9; CA 1-4R; 137; CANR 2, 19, 36, 60, 125; CLR 12, 79; CMW 4; CN 1, 2, 3, 4, 5; CPW; DA3; DAM POP; DLB 8; DLBY 1992; INT CANR-19; JRDA; LAIT 5; LMFS 2; MAICYA 1, 2; MAL 5; MTCW 1, 2; MTFW 2005; RGAL 4; SATA 1, 26, 74; SCFW 1, 2; SFW 4; SSFS 17; TUS; YAW

Askew, Anne 1521(?)-1546 .... **LC 81**
See also DLB 136

Assis, Joaquim Maria Machado de
See Machado de Assis, Joaquim Maria

Astell, Mary 1666-1731 .... **LC 68**
See also DLB 252, 336; FW

Astley, Thea (Beatrice May)
1925-2004 .... **CLC 41**
See also CA 65-68; 229; CANR 11, 43, 78;
CN 1, 2, 3, 4, 5, 6, 7; DLB 289; EWL 3

Astley, William 1855-1911
See Warung, Price

Aston, James
See White, T(erence) H(anbury)

Asturias, Miguel Angel 1899-1974 .... **CLC 3,
8, 13; HLC 1; TCLC 184**
See also CA 25-28; 49-52; CANR 32; CAP
2; CDWLB 3; DA3; DAM MULT, NOV;
DLB 113, 290, 329; EWL 3; HW 1; LAW;
LMFS 2; MTCW 1, 2; RGWL 2, 3; WLIT
1

Atares, Carlos Saura
See Saura (Atares), Carlos

Athanasius c. 295-c. 373 .... **CMLC 48**

Atheling, William
See Pound, Ezra (Weston Loomis)

Atheling, William, Jr.
See Blish, James (Benjamin)

Atherton, Gertrude (Franklin Horn)
1857-1948 .... **TCLC 2**
See also CA 104; 155; DLB 9, 78, 186;
HGG; RGAL 4; SUFW 1; TCWW 1, 2

Atherton, Lucius
See Masters, Edgar Lee

Atkins, Jack
See Harris, Mark

Atkinson, Kate 1951- .... **CLC 99**
See also CA 166; CANR 101, 153; DLB
267

Attaway, William (Alexander)
1911-1986 .... **BLC 1:1; CLC 92**
See also BW 2, 3; CA 143; CANR 82;
DAM MULT; DLB 76; MAL 5

Atticus
See Fleming, Ian; Wilson, (Thomas) Woodrow

Atwood, Margaret 1939- . **CLC 2, 3, 4, 8, 13,
15, 25, 44, 84, 135, 232, 239, 246; PC 8;
SSC 2, 46; WLC 1**
See also AAYA 12, 47; AMWS 13; BEST
89:2; BPFB 1; CA 49-52; CANR 3, 24,
33, 59, 95, 133; CN 2, 3, 4, 5, 6, 7; CP 1,
2, 3, 4, 5, 6, 7; CPW; CWP; DA; DA3;
DAB; DAC; DAM MST, NOV, POET;
DLB 53, 251, 326; EWL 3; EXPN; FL
1:5; FW; GL 2; INT CANR-24; LAIT 5;
MTCW 1, 2; MTFW 2005; NFS 4, 12,
13, 14, 19; PFS 7; RGSF 2; SATA 50,
170; SSFS 3, 13; TCLE 1:1; TWA; WWE
1; YAW

Atwood, Margaret Eleanor
See Atwood, Margaret

Aubigny, Pierre d'
See Mencken, H(enry) L(ouis)

Aubin, Penelope 1685-1731(?) .... **LC 9**
See also DLB 39

Auchincloss, Louis 1917- ..... **CLC 4, 6, 9, 18,
45; SSC 22**
See also AMWS 4; CA 1-4R; CANR 6, 29,
55, 87, 130, 168; CN 1, 2, 3, 4, 5, 6, 7;
DAM NOV; DLB 2, 244; DLBY 1980;
EWL 3; INT CANR-29; MAL 5; MTCW
1; RGAL 4

Auchincloss, Louis Stanton
See Auchincloss, Louis

Auden, W(ystan) H(ugh) 1907-1973 . **CLC 1,
2, 3, 4, 6, 9, 11, 14, 43, 123; PC 1, 92;
WLC 1**
See also AAYA 18; AMWS 2; BRW 7;
BRWR 1; CA 9-12R; 45-48; CANR 5, 61,
105; CDBLB 1914-1945; CP 1, 2; DA;
DA3; DAB; DAC; DAM DRAM, MST,
POET; DLB 10, 20; EWL 3; EXPP; MAL
5; MTCW 1, 2; MTFW 2005; PAB; PFS
1, 3, 4, 10, 27; TUS; WP

Audiberti, Jacques 1899-1965 .... **CLC 38**
See also CA 252; 25-28R; DAM DRAM;
DLB 321; EWL 3

Audubon, John James 1785-1851 . **NCLC 47**
See also AAYA 76; AMWS 16; ANW; DLB
248

Auel, Jean M(arie) 1936- .... **CLC 31, 107**
See also AAYA 7, 51; BEST 90:4; BPFB 1;
CA 103; CANR 21, 64, 115; CPW; DA3;
DAM POP; INT CANR-21; NFS 11;
RHW; SATA 91

Auerbach, Berthold 1812-1882 .... **NCLC 171**
See also DLB 133

Auerbach, Erich 1892-1957 .... **TCLC 43**
See also CA 118; 155; EWL 3

Augier, Emile 1820-1889 .... **NCLC 31**
See also DLB 192; GFL 1789 to the Present

August, John
See De Voto, Bernard (Augustine)

Augustine, St. 354-430 .... **CMLC 6, 95;
WLCS**
See also DA; DA3; DAB; DAC; DAM
MST; DLB 115; EW 1; RGWL 2, 3;
WLIT 8

Aunt Belinda
See Braddon, Mary Elizabeth

Aunt Weedy
See Alcott, Louisa May

Aurelius
See Bourne, Randolph S(illiman)

Aurelius, Marcus 121-180 .... **CMLC 45**
See Marcus Aurelius
See also RGWL 2, 3

Aurobindo, Sri
See Ghose, Aurabinda

Aurobindo Ghose
See Ghose, Aurabinda

Ausonius, Decimus Magnus c. 310-c.
394 .... **CMLC 88**
See also RGWL 2, 3

Austen, Jane 1775-1817 ...... **NCLC 1, 13, 19,
33, 51, 81, 95, 119, 150; WLC 1**
See also AAYA 19; BRW 4; BRWC 1;
BRWR 2; BYA 3; CDBLB 1789-1832;
DA; DA3; DAB; DAC; DAM MST, NOV;
DLB 116; EXPN; FL 1:2; GL 2; LAIT 2;
LATS 1:1; LMFS 1; NFS 1, 14, 18, 20,
21, 28; TEA; WLIT 3; WYAS 1

Auster, Paul 1947- .... **CLC 47, 131, 227**
See also AMWS 12; CA 69-72; CANR 23,
52, 75, 129, 165; CMW 4; CN 5, 6, 7;
DA3; DLB 227; MAL 5; MTCW 2;
MTFW 2005; SUFW 2; TCLE 1:1

Austin, Frank
See Faust, Frederick (Schiller)

Austin, Mary (Hunter) 1868-1934 . **SSC 104;
TCLC 25**
See also ANW; CA 109; 178; DLB 9, 78,
206, 221, 275; FW; TCWW 1, 2

Averroes 1126-1198 .... **CMLC 7, 104**
See also DLB 115

Avicenna 980-1037 .... **CMLC 16**
See also DLB 115

Avison, Margaret 1918-2007 .... **CLC 2, 4, 97**
See also CA 17-20R; CANR 134; CP 1, 2,
3, 4, 5, 6, 7; DAC; DAM POET; DLB 53;
MTCW 1

Avison, Margaret Kirkland
See Avison, Margaret

Axton, David
See Koontz, Dean R.

Ayckbourn, Alan 1939- ...... **CLC 5, 8, 18, 33,
74; DC 13**
See also BRWS 5; CA 21-24R; CANR 31,
59, 118; CBD; CD 5, 6; DAB; DAM
DRAM; DFS 7; DLB 13, 245; EWL 3;
MTCW 1, 2; MTFW 2005

Aydy, Catherine
See Tennant, Emma

Ayme, Marcel (Andre) 1902-1967 ... **CLC 11;
SSC 41**
See also CA 89-92; CANR 67, 137; CLR
25; DLB 72; EW 12; EWL 3; GFL 1789
to the Present; RGSF 2; RGWL 2, 3;
SATA 91

Ayrton, Michael 1921-1975 .... **CLC 7**
See also CA 5-8R; 61-64; CANR 9, 21

Aytmatov, Chingiz
See Aitmatov, Chingiz
See also EWL 3

Azorin CLC 11
See Martinez Ruiz, Jose
See also DLB 322; EW 9; EWL 3

Azuela, Mariano 1873-1952 .. **HLC 1; TCLC
3, 145**
See also CA 104; 131; CANR 81; DAM
MULT; EWL 3; HW 1, 2; LAW; MTCW
1, 2; MTFW 2005

Ba, Mariama 1929-1981 ...... **BLC 2:1; BLCS**
See also AFW; BW 2; CA 141; CANR 87;
DNFS 2; WLIT 2

Baastad, Babbis Friis
See Friis-Baastad, Babbis Ellinor

Bab
See Gilbert, W(illiam) S(chwenck)

Babbis, Eleanor
See Friis-Baastad, Babbis Ellinor

Babel, Isaac
See Babel, Isaak (Emmanuilovich)
See also EW 11; SSFS 10

Babel, Isaak (Emmanuilovich)
1894-1941(?) . **SSC 16, 78; TCLC 2, 13,
171**
See Babel, Isaac
See also CA 104; 155; CANR 113; DLB
272; EWL 3; MTCW 2; MTFW 2005;
RGSF 2; RGWL 2, 3; TWA

Babits, Mihaly 1883-1941 .... **TCLC 14**
See also CA 114; CDWLB 4; DLB 215;
EWL 3

Babur 1483-1530 .... **LC 18**

Babylas 1898-1962
See Ghelderode, Michel de

Baca, Jimmy Santiago 1952- . **HLC 1; PC 41**
See also CA 131; CANR 81, 90, 146; CP 6,
7; DAM MULT; DLB 122; HW 1, 2;
LLW; MAL 5

Baca, Jose Santiago
See Baca, Jimmy Santiago

Bacchelli, Riccardo 1891-1985 .... **CLC 19**
See also CA 29-32R; 117; DLB 264; EWL
3

Bach, Richard 1936- .... **CLC 14**
See also AITN 1; BEST 89:2; BPFB 1; BYA
5; CA 9-12R; CANR 18, 93, 151; CPW;
DAM NOV, POP; FANT; MTCW 1;
SATA 13

Bach, Richard David
See Bach, Richard

Bache, Benjamin Franklin
1769-1798 .... **LC 74**
See also DLB 43

Bachelard, Gaston 1884-1962 ...... **TCLC 128**
See also CA 97-100; 89-92; DLB 296; GFL
1789 to the Present

Bachman, Richard
See King, Stephen

Bachmann, Ingeborg 1926-1973 ..... **CLC 69;
TCLC 192**
See also CA 93-96; 45-48; CANR 69; DLB
85; EWL 3; RGHL; RGWL 2, 3

Bacon, Francis 1561-1626 ..... **LC 18, 32, 131**
See also BRW 1; CDBLB Before 1660;
DLB 151, 236, 252; RGEL 2; TEA

Bacon, Roger 1214(?)-1294 ... **CMLC 14, 108**
See also DLB 115

Bacovia, George 1881-1957 .... **TCLC 24**
  See Vasiliu, Gheorghe
  See also CDWLB 4; DLB 220; EWL 3
Badanes, Jerome 1937-1995 .... **CLC 59**
  See also CA 234
Bage, Robert 1728-1801 .... **NCLC 182**
  See also DLB 39; RGEL 2
Bagehot, Walter 1826-1877 .... **NCLC 10**
  See also DLB 55
Bagnold, Enid 1889-1981 .... **CLC 25**
  See also AAYA 75; BYA 2; CA 5-8R; 103;
  CANR 5, 40; CBD; CN 2; CWD; CWRI
  5; DAM DRAM; DLB 13, 160, 191, 245;
  FW; MAICYA 1, 2; RGEL 2; SATA 1, 25
Bagritsky, Eduard TCLC 60
  See Dzyubin, Eduard Georgievich
Bagrjana, Elisaveta
  See Belcheva, Elisaveta Lyubomirova
Bagryana, Elisaveta CLC 10
  See Belcheva, Elisaveta Lyubomirova
  See also CA 178; CDWLB 4; DLB 147;
  EWL 3
Bailey, Paul 1937- .... **CLC 45**
  See also CA 21-24R; CANR 16, 62, 124;
  CN 1, 2, 3, 4, 5, 6, 7; DLB 14, 271; GLL
  2
Baillie, Joanna 1762-1851 ...... **NCLC 71, 151**
  See also DLB 93, 344; GL 2; RGEL 2
Bainbridge, Beryl 1934- ...... **CLC 4, 5, 8, 10,
  14, 18, 22, 62, 130**
  See also BRWS 6; CA 21-24R; CANR 24,
  55, 75, 88, 128; CN 2, 3, 4, 5, 6, 7; DAM
  NOV; DLB 14, 231; EWL 3; MTCW 1,
  2; MTFW 2005
Baker, Carlos (Heard)
  1909-1987 .... **TCLC 119**
  See also CA 5-8R; 122; CANR 3, 63; DLB
  103
Baker, Elliott 1922-2007 .... **CLC 8**
  See also CA 45-48; 257; CANR 2, 63; CN
  1, 2, 3, 4, 5, 6, 7
Baker, Elliott Joseph
  See Baker, Elliott
Baker, Jean H. TCLC 3, 10
  See Russell, George William
Baker, Nicholson 1957- .... **CLC 61, 165**
  See also AMWS 13; CA 135; CANR 63,
  120, 138; CN 6; CPW; DA3; DAM POP;
  DLB 227; MTFW 2005
Baker, Ray Stannard 1870-1946 .... **TCLC 47**
  See also CA 118; DLB 345
Baker, Russell 1925- .... **CLC 31**
  See also BEST 89:4; CA 57-60; CANR 11,
  41, 59, 137; MTCW 1, 2; MTFW 2005
Bakhtin, M.
  See Bakhtin, Mikhail Mikhailovich
Bakhtin, M. M.
  See Bakhtin, Mikhail Mikhailovich
Bakhtin, Mikhail
  See Bakhtin, Mikhail Mikhailovich
Bakhtin, Mikhail Mikhailovich
  1895-1975 .... **CLC 83; TCLC 160**
  See also CA 128; 113; DLB 242; EWL 3
Bakshi, Ralph 1938(?)- .... **CLC 26**
  See also CA 112; 138; IDFW 3
Bakunin, Mikhail (Alexandrovich)
  1814-1876 .... **NCLC 25, 58**
  See also DLB 277
Bal, Mieke (Maria Gertrudis)
  1946- .... **CLC 252**
  See also CA 156; CANR 99
Baldwin, James 1924-1987 ...... **BLC 1:1, 2:1;
  CLC 1, 2, 3, 4, 5, 8, 13, 15, 17, 42, 50,
  67, 90, 127; DC 1; SSC 10, 33, 98;
  WLC 1**
  See also AAYA 4, 34; AFAW 1, 2; AMWR
  2; AMWS 1; BPFB 1; BW 1; CA 1-4R;
  124; CABS 1; CAD; CANR 3, 24;
  CDALB 1941-1968; CN 1, 2, 3, 4; CPW;

DA; DA3; DAB; DAC; DAM MST,
  MULT, NOV, POP; DFS 11, 15; DLB 2,
  7, 33, 249, 278; DLBY 1987; EWL 3;
  EXPS; LAIT 5; MAL 5; MTCW 1, 2;
  MTFW 2005; NCFS 4; NFS 4; RGAL 4;
  RGSF 2; SATA 9; SATA-Obit 54; SSFS
  2, 18; TUS
Baldwin, William c. 1515-1563 .... **LC 113**
  See also DLB 132
Bale, John 1495-1563 .... **LC 62**
  See also DLB 132; RGEL 2; TEA
Ball, Hugo 1886-1927 .... **TCLC 104**
Ballard, J.G. 1930- .... **CLC 3, 6, 14, 36, 137;
  SSC 1, 53**
  See also AAYA 3, 52; BRWS 5; CA 5-8R;
  CANR 15, 39, 65, 107, 133; CN 1, 2, 3,
  4, 5, 6, 7; DA3; DAM NOV, POP; DLB
  14, 207, 261, 319; EWL 3; HGG; MTCW
  1, 2; MTFW 2005; NFS 8; RGEL 2;
  RGSF 2; SATA 93; SCFW 1, 2; SFW 4
Balmont, Konstantin (Dmitriyevich)
  1867-1943 .... **TCLC 11**
  See also CA 109; 155; DLB 295; EWL 3
Baltausis, Vincas 1847-1910
  See Mikszath, Kalman
Balzac, Honore de 1799-1850 ... **NCLC 5, 35,
  53, 153; SSC 5, 59, 102; WLC 1**
  See also DA; DA3; DAB; DAC; DAM
  MST, NOV; DLB 119; EW 5; GFL 1789
  to the Present; LMFS 1; RGSF 2; RGWL
  2, 3; SSFS 10; SUFW; TWA
Bambara, Toni Cade 1939-1995 ..... **BLC 1:1,
  2:1; CLC 19, 88; SSC 35, 107; TCLC
  116; WLCS**
  See also AAYA 5, 49; AFAW 2; AMWS 11;
  BW 2, 3; BYA 12, 14; CA 29-32R; 150;
  CANR 24, 49, 81; CDALBS; DA; DA3;
  DAC; DAM MST, MULT; DLB 38, 218;
  EXPS; MAL 5; MTCW 1, 2; MTFW
  2005; RGAL 4; RGSF 2; SATA 112; SSFS
  4, 7, 12, 21
Bamdad, A.
  See Shamlu, Ahmad
Bamdad, Alef
  See Shamlu, Ahmad
Banat, D. R.
  See Bradbury, Ray
Bancroft, Laura
  See Baum, L(yman) Frank
Banim, John 1798-1842 .... **NCLC 13**
  See also DLB 116, 158, 159; RGEL 2
Banim, Michael 1796-1874 .... **NCLC 13**
  See also DLB 158, 159
Banjo, The
  See Paterson, A(ndrew) B(arton)
Banks, Iain 1954- .... **CLC 34**
  See also BRWS 11; CA 123; 128; CANR
  61, 106, 180; DLB 194, 261; EWL 3;
  HGG; INT CA-128; MTFW 2005; SFW 4
Banks, Iain M.
  See Banks, Iain
Banks, Iain Menzies
  See Banks, Iain
Banks, Lynne Reid CLC 23
  See Reid Banks, Lynne
  See also AAYA 6; BYA 7; CN 4, 5, 6
Banks, Russell 1940- . **CLC 37, 72, 187; SSC
  42**
  See also AAYA 45; AMWS 5; CA 65-68;
  CAAS 15; CANR 19, 52, 73, 118; CN 4,
  5, 6, 7; DLB 130, 278; EWL 3; MAL 5;
  MTCW 2; MTFW 2005; NFS 13
Banks, Russell Earl
  See Banks, Russell
Banville, John 1945- .... **CLC 46, 118, 224**
  See also CA 117; 128; CANR 104, 150,
  176; CN 4, 5, 6, 7; DLB 14, 271, 326;
  INT CA-128

Banville, Theodore (Faullain) de
  1832-1891 .... **NCLC 9**
  See also DLB 217; GFL 1789 to the Present
Baraka, Amiri 1934- .. **BLC 1:1, 2:1; CLC 1,
  2, 3, 5, 10, 14, 33, 115, 213; DC 6; PC
  4; WLCS**
  See Jones, LeRoi
  See also AAYA 63; AFAW 1, 2; AMWS 2;
  BW 2, 3; CA 21-24R; CABS 3; CAD;
  CANR 27, 38, 61, 133, 172; CD 3, 5, 6;
  CDALB 1941-1968; CP 4, 5, 6, 7; CPW;
  DA; DA3; DAC; DAM MST, MULT,
  POET, POP; DFS 3, 11, 16; DLB 5, 7,
  16, 38; DLBD 8; EWL 3; MAL 5; MTCW
  1, 2; MTFW 2005; PFS 9; RGAL 4;
  TCLE 1:1; TUS; WP
Baratynsky, Evgenii Abramovich
  1800-1844 .... **NCLC 103**
  See also DLB 205
Barbauld, Anna Laetitia
  1743-1825 .... **NCLC 50, 185**
  See also DLB 107, 109, 142, 158, 336;
  RGEL 2
Barbellion, W. N. P. TCLC 24
  See Cummings, Bruce F(rederick)
Barber, Benjamin R. 1939- .... **CLC 141**
  See also CA 29-32R; CANR 12, 32, 64, 119
Barbera, Jack (Vincent) 1945- .... **CLC 44**
  See also CA 110; CANR 45
Barbey d'Aurevilly, Jules-Amedee
  1808-1889 .... **NCLC 1; SSC 17**
  See also DLB 119; GFL 1789 to the Present
Barbour, John c. 1316-1395 .... **CMLC 33**
  See also DLB 146
Barbusse, Henri 1873-1935 .... **TCLC 5**
  See also CA 105; 154; DLB 65; EWL 3;
  RGWL 2, 3
Barclay, Alexander c. 1475-1552 .... **LC 109**
  See also DLB 132
Barclay, Bill
  See Moorcock, Michael
Barclay, William Ewert
  See Moorcock, Michael
Barea, Arturo 1897-1957 .... **TCLC 14**
  See also CA 111; 201
Barfoot, Joan 1946- .... **CLC 18**
  See also CA 105; CANR 141, 179
Barham, Richard Harris
  1788-1845 .... **NCLC 77**
  See also DLB 159
Baring, Maurice 1874-1945 .... **TCLC 8**
  See also CA 105; 168; DLB 34; HGG
Baring-Gould, Sabine 1834-1924 ... **TCLC 88**
  See also DLB 156, 190
Barker, Clive 1952- .... **CLC 52, 205; SSC 53**
  See also AAYA 10, 54; BEST 90:3; BPFB
  1; CA 121; 129; CANR 71, 111, 133;
  CPW; DA3; DAM POP; DLB 261; HGG;
  INT CA-129; MTCW 1, 2; MTFW 2005;
  SUFW 2
Barker, George Granville
  1913-1991 .... **CLC 8, 48; PC 77**
  See also CA 9-12R; 135; CANR 7, 38; CP
  1, 2, 3, 4, 5; DAM POET; DLB 20; EWL
  3; MTCW 1
Barker, Harley Granville
  See Granville-Barker, Harley
  See also DLB 10
Barker, Howard 1946- .... **CLC 37**
  See also CA 102; CBD; CD 5, 6; DLB 13,
  233
Barker, Jane 1652-1732 .... **LC 42, 82; PC 91**
  See also DLB 39, 131
Barker, Pat 1943- .... **CLC 32, 94, 146**
  See also BRWS 4; CA 117; 122; CANR 50,
  101, 148; CN 6, 7; DLB 271, 326; INT
  CA-122
Barker, Patricia
  See Barker, Pat

Barlach, Ernst (Heinrich)
1870-1938 .... **TCLC 84**
See also CA 178; DLB 56, 118; EWL 3

Barlow, Joel 1754-1812 .... **NCLC 23**
See also AMWS 2; DLB 37; RGAL 4

Barnard, Mary (Ethel) 1909- .... **CLC 48**
See also CA 21-22; CAP 2; CP 1

Barnes, Djuna 1892-1982 .... **CLC 3, 4, 8, 11, 29, 127; SSC 3; TCLC 212**
See Steptoe, Lydia
See also AMWS 3; CA 9-12R; 107; CAD; CANR 16, 55; CN 1, 2, 3; CWD; DLB 4, 9, 45; EWL 3; GLL 1; MAL 5; MTCW 1, 2; MTFW 2005; RGAL 4; TCLE 1:1; TUS

Barnes, Jim 1933- .... **NNAL**
See also CA 108, 175, 272; CAAE 175, 272; CAAS 28; DLB 175

Barnes, Julian 1946- .... **CLC 42, 141**
See also BRWS 4; CA 102; CANR 19, 54, 115, 137; CN 4, 5, 6, 7; DAB; DLB 194; DLBY 1993; EWL 3; MTCW 2; MTFW 2005; SSFS 24

Barnes, Julian Patrick
See Barnes, Julian

Barnes, Peter 1931-2004 .... **CLC 5, 56**
See also CA 65-68; 230; CAAS 12; CANR 33, 34, 64, 113; CBD; CD 5, 6; DFS 6; DLB 13, 233; MTCW 1

Barnes, William 1801-1886 .... **NCLC 75**
See also DLB 32

Baroja, Pio 1872-1956 .... **HLC 1; SSC 112; TCLC 8**
See also CA 104; 247; EW 9

Baroja y Nessi, Pio
See Baroja, Pio

Baron, David
See Pinter, Harold

Baron Corvo
See Rolfe, Frederick (William Serafino Austin Lewis Mary)

Barondess, Sue K(aufman)
1926-1977 .... **CLC 8**
See Kaufman, Sue
See also CA 1-4R; 69-72; CANR 1

Baron de Teive
See Pessoa, Fernando

Baroness Von S.
See Zangwill, Israel

Barres, (Auguste-)Maurice
1862-1923 .... **TCLC 47**
See also CA 164; DLB 123; GFL 1789 to the Present

Barreto, Afonso Henrique de Lima
See Lima Barreto, Afonso Henrique de

Barrett, Andrea 1954- .... **CLC 150**
See also CA 156; CANR 92; CN 7; DLB 335; SSFS 24

Barrett, Michele CLC 65

Barrett, (Roger) Syd 1946-2006 .... **CLC 35**

Barrett, William (Christopher)
1913-1992 .... **CLC 27**
See also CA 13-16R; 139; CANR 11, 67; INT CANR-11

Barrett Browning, Elizabeth
1806-1861 ...... **NCLC 1, 16, 61, 66, 170; PC 6, 62; WLC 1**
See also AAYA 63; BRW 4; CDBLB 1832-1890; DA; DA3; DAB; DAC; DAM MST, POET; DLB 32, 199; EXPP; FL 1:2; PAB; PFS 2, 16, 23; TEA; WLIT 4; WP

Barrie, J(ames) M(atthew)
1860-1937 .... **TCLC 2, 164**
See also BRWS 3; BYA 4, 5; CA 104; 136; CANR 77; CDBLB 1890-1914; CLR 16, 124; CWRI 5; DA3; DAB; DAM DRAM;

DFS 7; DLB 10, 141, 156; EWL 3; FANT; MAICYA 1, 2; MTCW 2; MTFW 2005; SATA 100; SUFW; WCH; WLIT 4; YABC 1

Barrington, Michael
See Moorcock, Michael

Barrol, Grady
See Bograd, Larry

Barry, Mike
See Malzberg, Barry N(athaniel)

Barry, Philip 1896-1949 .... **TCLC 11**
See also CA 109; 199; DFS 9; DLB 7, 228; MAL 5; RGAL 4

Bart, Andre Schwarz
See Schwarz-Bart, Andre

Barth, John (Simmons) 1930- ... **CLC 1, 2, 3, 5, 7, 9, 10, 14, 27, 51, 89, 214; SSC 10, 89**
See also AITN 1, 2; AMW; BPFB 1; CA 1-4R; CABS 1; CANR 5, 23, 49, 64, 113; CN 1, 2, 3, 4, 5, 6, 7; DAM NOV; DLB 2, 227; EWL 3; FANT; MAL 5; MTCW 1; RGAL 4; RGSF 2; RHW; SSFS 6; TUS

Barthelme, Donald 1931-1989 ... **CLC 1, 2, 3, 5, 6, 8, 13, 23, 46, 59, 115; SSC 2, 55**
See also AMWS 4; BPFB 1; CA 21-24R; 129; CANR 20, 58; CN 1, 2, 3, 4; DA3; DAM NOV; DLB 2, 234; DLBY 1980, 1989; EWL 3; FANT; LMFS 2; MAL 5; MTCW 1, 2; MTFW 2005; RGAL 4; RGSF 2; SATA 7; SATA-Obit 62; SSFS 17

Barthelme, Frederick 1943- ...... **CLC 36, 117**
See also AMWS 11; CA 114; 122; CANR 77; CN 4, 5, 6, 7; CSW; DLB 244; DLBY 1985; EWL 3; INT CA-122

Barthes, Roland (Gerard)
1915-1980 .... **CLC 24, 83; TCLC 135**
See also CA 130; 97-100; CANR 66; DLB 296; EW 13; EWL 3; GFL 1789 to the Present; MTCW 1, 2; TWA

Bartram, William 1739-1823 .... **NCLC 145**
See also ANW; DLB 37

Barzun, Jacques (Martin) 1907- ..... **CLC 51, 145**
See also CA 61-64; CANR 22, 95

Bashevis, Isaac
See Singer, Isaac Bashevis

Bashevis, Yitskhok
See Singer, Isaac Bashevis

Bashkirtseff, Marie 1859-1884 .... **NCLC 27**

Basho, Matsuo
See Matsuo Basho
See also RGWL 2, 3; WP

Basil of Caesaria c. 330-379 .... **CMLC 35**

Basket, Raney
See Edgerton, Clyde (Carlyle)

Bass, Kingsley B., Jr.
See Bullins, Ed

Bass, Rick 1958- .... **CLC 79, 143; SSC 60**
See also AMWS 16; ANW; CA 126; CANR 53, 93, 145, 183; CSW; DLB 212, 275

Bassani, Giorgio 1916-2000 .... **CLC 9**
See also CA 65-68; 190; CANR 33; CWW 2; DLB 128, 177, 299; EWL 3; MTCW 1; RGHL; RGWL 2, 3

Bassine, Helen
See Yglesias, Helen

Bastian, Ann CLC 70

Bastos, Augusto Roa
See Roa Bastos, Augusto

Bataille, Georges 1897-1962 .... **CLC 29; TCLC 155**
See also CA 101; 89-92; EWL 3

Bates, H(erbert) E(rnest)
1905-1974 .... **CLC 46; SSC 10**
See also CA 93-96; 45-48; CANR 34; CN 1; DA3; DAB; DAM POP; DLB 162, 191; EWL 3; EXPS; MTCW 1, 2; RGSF 2; SSFS 7

Bauchart
See Camus, Albert

Baudelaire, Charles 1821-1867 . **NCLC 6, 29, 55, 155; PC 1; SSC 18; WLC 1**
See also DA; DA3; DAB; DAC; DAM MST, POET; DLB 217; EW 7; GFL 1789 to the Present; LMFS 2; PFS 21; RGWL 2, 3; TWA

Baudouin, Marcel
See Peguy, Charles (Pierre)

Baudouin, Pierre
See Peguy, Charles (Pierre)

Baudrillard, Jean 1929-2007 .... **CLC 60**
See also CA 252; 258; DLB 296

Baum, L(yman) Frank 1856-1919 .. **TCLC 7, 132**
See also AAYA 46; BYA 16; CA 108; 133; CLR 15, 107; CWRI 5; DLB 22; FANT; JRDA; MAICYA 1, 2; MTCW 1, 2; NFS 13; RGAL 4; SATA 18, 100; WCH

Baum, Louis F.
See Baum, L(yman) Frank

Baumbach, Jonathan 1933- .... **CLC 6, 23**
See also CA 13-16R; CAAS 5; CANR 12, 66, 140; CN 3, 4, 5, 6, 7; DLBY 1980; INT CANR-12; MTCW 1

Bausch, Richard 1945- .... **CLC 51**
See also AMWS 7; CA 101; CAAS 14; CANR 43, 61, 87, 164; CN 7; CSW; DLB 130; MAL 5

Bausch, Richard Carl
See Bausch, Richard

Baxter, Charles 1947- .... **CLC 45, 78**
See also AMWS 17; CA 57-60; CANR 40, 64, 104, 133; CPW; DAM POP; DLB 130; MAL 5; MTCW 2; MTFW 2005; TCLE 1:1

Baxter, George Owen
See Faust, Frederick (Schiller)

Baxter, James K(eir) 1926-1972 .... **CLC 14**
See also CA 77-80; CP 1; EWL 3

Baxter, John
See Hunt, E. Howard

Bayer, Sylvia
See Glassco, John

Bayle, Pierre 1647-1706 .... **LC 126**
See also DLB 268, 313; GFL Beginnings to 1789

Baynton, Barbara 1857-1929 . **TCLC 57, 211**
See also DLB 230; RGSF 2

Beagle, Peter S. 1939- .... **CLC 7, 104**
See also AAYA 47; BPFB 1; BYA 9, 10, 16; CA 9-12R; CANR 4, 51, 73, 110; DA3; DLBY 1980; FANT; INT CANR-4; MTCW 2; MTFW 2005; SATA 60, 130; SUFW 1, 2; YAW

Beagle, Peter Soyer
See Beagle, Peter S.

Bean, Normal
See Burroughs, Edgar Rice

Beard, Charles A(ustin)
1874-1948 .... **TCLC 15**
See also CA 115; 189; DLB 17; SATA 18

Beardsley, Aubrey 1872-1898 .... **NCLC 6**

Beattie, Ann 1947- ..... **CLC 8, 13, 18, 40, 63, 146; SSC 11**
See also AMWS 5; BEST 90:2; BPFB 1; CA 81-84; CANR 53, 73, 128; CN 4, 5, 6, 7; CPW; DA3; DAM NOV, POP; DLB 218, 278; DLBY 1982; EWL 3; MAL 5; MTCW 1, 2; MTFW 2005; RGAL 4; RGSF 2; SSFS 9; TUS

Beattie, James 1735-1803 .... **NCLC 25**
See also DLB 109

Beauchamp, Kathleen Mansfield 1888-1923
See Mansfield, Katherine
See also CA 104; 134; DA; DA3; DAC;
DAM MST; MTCW 2; TEA

Beaumarchais, Pierre-Augustin Caron de
1732-1799 .... **DC 4; LC 61**
See also DAM DRAM; DFS 14, 16; DLB
313; EW 4; GFL Beginnings to 1789;
RGWL 2, 3

Beaumont, Francis 1584(?)-1616 .. **DC 6; LC
33**
See also BRW 2; CDBLB Before 1660;
DLB 58; TEA

Beauvoir, Simone de 1908-1986 .... **CLC 1, 2,
4, 8, 14, 31, 44, 50, 71, 124; SSC 35;
WLC 1**
See also BPFB 1; CA 9-12R; 118; CANR
28, 61; DA; DA3; DAB; DAC; DAM
MST, NOV; DLB 72; DLBY 1986; EW
12; EWL 3; FL 1:5; FW; GFL 1789 to the
Present; LMFS 2; MTCW 1, 2; MTFW
2005; RGSF 2; RGWL 2, 3; TWA

**Beauvoir, Simone Lucie Ernestine Marie
Bertrand de**
See Beauvoir, Simone de

Becker, Carl (Lotus) 1873-1945 ..... **TCLC 63**
See also CA 157; DLB 17

Becker, Jurek 1937-1997 .... **CLC 7, 19**
See also CA 85-88; 157; CANR 60, 117;
CWW 2; DLB 75, 299; EWL 3; RGHL

Becker, Walter 1950- .... **CLC 26**

Becket, Thomas a 1118(?)-1170 .... **CMLC 83**

Beckett, Samuel 1906-1989 ... **CLC 1, 2, 3, 4,
6, 9, 10, 11, 14, 18, 29, 57, 59, 83; DC
22; SSC 16, 74; TCLC 145; WLC 1**
See also BRWC 2; BRWR 1; BRWS 1; CA
5-8R; 130; CANR 33, 61; CBD; CDBLB
1945-1960; CN 1, 2, 3, 4; CP 1, 2, 3, 4;
DA; DA3; DAB; DAC; DAM DRAM,
MST, NOV; DFS 2, 7; DLB 13, 15,
233, 319, 321, 329; DLBY 1990; EWL 3;
GFL 1789 to the Present; LATS 1:2;
LMFS 2; MTCW 1, 2; MTFW 2005;
RGSF 2; RGWL 2, 3; SSFS 15; TEA;
WLIT 4

Beckford, William 1760-1844 .... **NCLC 16**
See also BRW 3; DLB 39, 213; GL 2; HGG;
LMFS 1; SUFW

Beckham, Barry (Earl) 1944- .... **BLC 1:1**
See also BW 1; CA 29-32R; CANR 26, 62;
CN 1, 2, 3, 4, 5, 6; DAM MULT; DLB 33

Beckman, Gunnel 1910- .... **CLC 26**
See also CA 33-36R; CANR 15, 114; CLR
25; MAICYA 1, 2; SAAS 9; SATA 6

Becque, Henri 1837-1899 .... **DC 21; NCLC 3**
See also DLB 192; GFL 1789 to the Present

Becquer, Gustavo Adolfo
1836-1870 .... **HLCS 1; NCLC 106**
See also DAM MULT

Beddoes, Thomas Lovell 1803-1849 .. **DC 15;
NCLC 3, 154**
See also BRWS 11; DLB 96

Bede c. 673-735 .... **CMLC 20**
See also DLB 146; TEA

Bedford, Denton R. 1907-(?) .... **NNAL**

Bedford, Donald F.
See Fearing, Kenneth (Flexner)

Beecher, Catharine Esther
1800-1878 .... **NCLC 30**
See also DLB 1, 243

Beecher, John 1904-1980 .... **CLC 6**
See also AITN 1; CA 5-8R; 105; CANR 8;
CP 1, 2, 3

Beer, Johann 1655-1700 .... **LC 5**
See also DLB 168

Beer, Patricia 1924- .... **CLC 58**
See also CA 61-64; 183; CANR 13, 46; CP
1, 2, 3, 4, 5, 6; CWP; DLB 40; FW

Beerbohm, Max
See Beerbohm, (Henry) Max(imilian)

Beerbohm, (Henry) Max(imilian)
1872-1956 .... **TCLC 1, 24**
See also BRWS 2; CA 104; 154; CANR 79;
DLB 34, 100; FANT; MTCW 2

Beer-Hofmann, Richard
1866-1945 .... **TCLC 60**
See also CA 160; DLB 81

Beg, Shemus
See Stephens, James

Begiebing, Robert J(ohn) 1946- .... **CLC 70**
See also CA 122; CANR 40, 88

Begley, Louis 1933- .... **CLC 197**
See also CA 140; CANR 98, 176; DLB 299;
RGHL; TCLE 1:1

Behan, Brendan (Francis)
1923-1964 .... **CLC 1, 8, 11, 15, 79**
See also BRWS 2; CA 73-76; CANR 33,
121; CBD; CDBLB 1945-1960; DAM
DRAM; DFS 7; DLB 13, 233; EWL 3;
MTCW 1, 2

Behn, Aphra 1640(?)-1689 .. **DC 4; LC 1, 30,
42, 135; PC 13, 88; WLC 1**
See also BRWS 3; DA; DA3; DAB; DAC;
DAM DRAM, MST, NOV, POET; DFS
16, 24; DLB 39, 80, 131; FW; TEA;
WLIT 3

Behrman, S(amuel) N(athaniel)
1893-1973 .... **CLC 40**
See also CA 13-16; 45-48; CAD; CAP 1;
DLB 7, 44; IDFW 3; MAL 5; RGAL 4

Bekederemo, J. P. Clark
See Clark Bekederemo, J.P.
See also CD 6

Belasco, David 1853-1931 .... **TCLC 3**
See also CA 104; 168; DLB 7; MAL 5;
RGAL 4

Belcheva, Elisaveta Lyubomirova
1893-1991 .... **CLC 10**
See Bagryana, Elisaveta

Beldone, Phil ''Cheech''
See Ellison, Harlan

Beleno
See Azuela, Mariano

Belinski, Vissarion Grigoryevich
1811-1848 .... **NCLC 5**
See also DLB 198

Belitt, Ben 1911- .... **CLC 22**
See also CA 13-16R; CAAS 4; CANR 7,
77; CP 1, 2, 3, 4, 5, 6; DLB 5

Belknap, Jeremy 1744-1798 .... **LC 115**
See also DLB 30, 37

Bell, Gertrude (Margaret Lowthian)
1868-1926 .... **TCLC 67**
See also CA 167; CANR 110; DLB 174

Bell, J. Freeman
See Zangwill, Israel

Bell, James Madison 1826-1902 ..... **BLC 1:1;
TCLC 43**
See also BW 1; CA 122; 124; DAM MULT;
DLB 50

Bell, Madison Smartt 1957- ..... **CLC 41, 102,
223**
See also AMWS 10; BPFB 1; CA 111; 183;
CAAE 183; CANR 28, 54, 73, 134, 176;
CN 5, 6, 7; CSW; DLB 218, 278; MTCW
2; MTFW 2005

Bell, Marvin (Hartley) 1937- ...... **CLC 8, 31;
PC 79**
See also CA 21-24R; CAAS 14; CANR 59,
102; CP 1, 2, 3, 4, 5, 6, 7; DAM POET;
DLB 5; MAL 5; MTCW 1; PFS 25

Bell, W. L. D.
See Mencken, H(enry) L(ouis)

Bellamy, Atwood C.
See Mencken, H(enry) L(ouis)

Bellamy, Edward 1850-1898 ..... **NCLC 4, 86,
147**
See also DLB 12; NFS 15; RGAL 4; SFW
4

Belli, Gioconda 1948- .... **HLCS 1**
See also CA 152; CANR 143; CWW 2;
DLB 290; EWL 3; RGWL 3

Bellin, Edward J.
See Kuttner, Henry

Bello, Andres 1781-1865 .... **NCLC 131**
See also LAW

**Belloc, (Joseph) Hilaire (Pierre Sebastien
Rene Swanton)** 1870-1953 .... **PC 24;
TCLC 7, 18**
See also CA 106; 152; CLR 102; CWRI 5;
DAM POET; DLB 19, 100, 141, 174;
EWL 3; MTCW 2; MTFW 2005; SATA
112; WCH; YABC 1

Belloc, Joseph Peter Rene Hilaire
See Belloc, (Joseph) Hilaire (Pierre Sebastien Rene Swanton)

Belloc, Joseph Pierre Hilaire
See Belloc, (Joseph) Hilaire (Pierre Sebastien Rene Swanton)

Belloc, M. A.
See Lowndes, Marie Adelaide (Belloc)

Belloc-Lowndes, Mrs.
See Lowndes, Marie Adelaide (Belloc)

Bellow, Saul 1915-2005 ...... **CLC 1, 2, 3, 6, 8,
10, 13, 15, 25, 33, 34, 63, 79, 190, 200;
SSC 14, 101; WLC 1**
See also AITN 2; AMW; AMWC 2; AMWR
2; BEST 89:3; BPFB 1; CA 5-8R; 238;
CABS 1; CANR 29, 53, 95, 132; CDALB
1941-1968; CN 1, 2, 3, 4, 5, 6, 7; DA;
DA3; DAB; DAC; DAM MST, NOV,
POP; DLB 2, 28, 299, 329; DLBD 3;
DLBY 1982; EWL 3; MAL 5; MTCW 1,
2; MTFW 2005; NFS 4, 14, 26; RGAL 4;
RGHL; RGSF 2; SSFS 12, 22; TUS

Belser, Reimond Karel Maria de 1929-
See Ruysslinck, Ward
See also CA 152

Bely, Andrey PC 11; TCLC 7
See Bugayev, Boris Nikolayevich
See also DLB 295; EW 9; EWL 3

Belyi, Andrei
See Bugayev, Boris Nikolayevich
See also RGWL 2, 3

Bembo, Pietro 1470-1547 .... **LC 79**
See also RGWL 2, 3

Benary, Margot
See Benary-Isbert, Margot

Benary-Isbert, Margot 1889-1979 .... **CLC 12**
See also CA 5-8R; 89-92; CANR 4, 72;
CLR 12; MAICYA 1, 2; SATA 2; SATA-
Obit 21

Benavente (y Martinez), Jacinto
1866-1954 .... **DC 26; HLCS 1; TCLC 3**
See also CA 106; 131; CANR 81; DAM
DRAM, MULT; DLB 329; EWL 3; GLL
2; HW 1, 2; MTCW 1, 2

Benchley, Peter 1940-2006 .... **CLC 4, 8**
See also AAYA 14; AITN 2; BPFB 1; CA
17-20R; 248; CANR 12, 35, 66, 115;
CPW; DAM NOV, POP; HGG; MTCW 1,
2; MTFW 2005; SATA 3, 89, 164

Benchley, Peter Bradford
See Benchley, Peter

Benchley, Robert (Charles)
1889-1945 .... **TCLC 1, 55**
See also CA 105; 153; DLB 11; MAL 5;
RGAL 4

Benda, Julien 1867-1956 .... **TCLC 60**
See also CA 120; 154; GFL 1789 to the
Present

Benedict, Ruth 1887-1948 .... **TCLC 60**
See also CA 158; CANR 146; DLB 246
Benedict, Ruth Fulton
See Benedict, Ruth
Benedikt, Michael 1935- .... **CLC 4, 14**
See also CA 13-16R; CANR 7; CP 1, 2, 3, 4, 5, 6, 7; DLB 5
Benet, Juan 1927-1993 .... **CLC 28**
See also CA 143; EWL 3
Benet, Stephen Vincent 1898-1943 ..... **PC 64; SSC 10, 86; TCLC 7**
See also AMWS 11; CA 104; 152; DA3; DAM POET; DLB 4, 48, 102, 249, 284; DLBY 1997; EWL 3; HGG; MAL 5; MTCW 2; MTFW 2005; RGAL 4; RGSF 2; SSFS 22; SUFW; WP; YABC 1
Benet, William Rose 1886-1950 ..... **TCLC 28**
See also CA 118; 152; DAM POET; DLB 45; RGAL 4
Benford, Gregory 1941- .... **CLC 52**
See also BPFB 1; CA 69-72, 175, 268; CAAE 175, 268; CAAS 27; CANR 12, 24, 49, 95, 134; CN 7; CSW; DLBY 1982; MTFW 2005; SCFW 2; SFW 4
Benford, Gregory Albert
See Benford, Gregory
Bengtsson, Frans (Gunnar) 1894-1954 .... **TCLC 48**
See also CA 170; EWL 3
Benjamin, David
See Slavitt, David R.
Benjamin, Lois
See Gould, Lois
Benjamin, Walter 1892-1940 .... **TCLC 39**
See also CA 164; CANR 181; DLB 242; EW 11; EWL 3
Ben Jelloun, Tahar 1944- .... **CLC 180**
See also CA 135, 162; CANR 100, 166; CWW 2; EWL 3; RGWL 3; WLIT 2
Benn, Gottfried 1886-1956 .. **PC 35; TCLC 3**
See also CA 106; 153; DLB 56; EWL 3; RGWL 2, 3
Bennett, Alan 1934- .... **CLC 45, 77**
See also BRWS 8; CA 103; CANR 35, 55, 106, 157; CBD; CD 5, 6; DAB; DAM MST; DLB 310; MTCW 1, 2; MTFW 2005
Bennett, (Enoch) Arnold 1867-1931 .... **TCLC 5, 20, 197**
See also BRW 6; CA 106; 155; CDBLB 1890-1914; DLB 10, 34, 98, 135; EWL 3; MTCW 2
Bennett, Elizabeth
See Mitchell, Margaret (Munnerlyn)
Bennett, George Harold 1930-
See Bennett, Hal
See also BW 1; CA 97-100; CANR 87
Bennett, Gwendolyn B. 1902-1981 .... **HR 1:2**
See also BW 1; CA 125; DLB 51; WP
Bennett, Hal CLC 5
See Bennett, George Harold
See also CAAS 13; DLB 33
Bennett, Jay 1912- .... **CLC 35**
See also AAYA 10, 73; CA 69-72; CANR 11, 42, 79; JRDA; SAAS 4; SATA 41, 87; SATA-Brief 27; WYA; YAW
Bennett, Louise 1919-2006 .... **BLC 1:1; CLC 28**
See also BW 2, 3; CA 151; 252; CDWLB 3; CP 1, 2, 3, 4, 5, 6, 7; DAM MULT; DLB 117; EWL 3
Bennett, Louise Simone
See Bennett, Louise
Bennett-Coverley, Louise
See Bennett, Louise
Benoit de Sainte-Maure fl. 12th cent. - .... **CMLC 90**
Benson, A. C. 1862-1925 .... **TCLC 123**
See also DLB 98

Benson, E(dward) F(rederic) 1867-1940 .... **TCLC 27**
See also CA 114; 157; DLB 135, 153; HGG; SUFW 1
Benson, Jackson J. 1930- .... **CLC 34**
See also CA 25-28R; DLB 111
Benson, Sally 1900-1972 .... **CLC 17**
See also CA 19-20; 37-40R; CAP 1; SATA 1, 35; SATA-Obit 27
Benson, Stella 1892-1933 .... **TCLC 17**
See also CA 117; 154, 155; DLB 36, 162; FANT; TEA
Bentham, Jeremy 1748-1832 .... **NCLC 38**
See also DLB 107, 158, 252
Bentley, E(dmund) C(lerihew) 1875-1956 .... **TCLC 12**
See also CA 108; 232; DLB 70; MSW
Bentley, Eric 1916- .... **CLC 24**
See also CA 5-8R; CAD; CANR 6, 67; CBD; CD 5, 6; INT CANR-6
Bentley, Eric Russell
See Bentley, Eric
ben Uzair, Salem
See Horne, Richard Henry Hengist
Beolco, Angelo 1496-1542 .... **LC 139**
Beranger, Pierre Jean de 1780-1857 .... **NCLC 34**
Berdyaev, Nicolas
See Berdyaev, Nikolai (Aleksandrovich)
Berdyaev, Nikolai (Aleksandrovich) 1874-1948 .... **TCLC 67**
See also CA 120; 157
Berdyayev, Nikolai (Aleksandrovich)
See Berdyaev, Nikolai (Aleksandrovich)
Berendt, John 1939- .... **CLC 86**
See also CA 146; CANR 75, 83, 151
Berendt, John Lawrence
See Berendt, John
Beresford, J(ohn) D(avys) 1873-1947 .... **TCLC 81**
See also CA 112; 155; DLB 162, 178, 197; SFW 4; SUFW 1
Bergelson, David (Rafailovich) 1884-1952 .... **TCLC 81**
See Bergelson, Dovid
See also CA 220; DLB 333
Bergelson, Dovid
See Bergelson, David (Rafailovich)
See also EWL 3
Berger, Colonel
See Malraux, (Georges-)Andre
Berger, John 1926- .... **CLC 2, 19**
See also BRWS 4; CA 81-84; CANR 51, 78, 117, 163; CN 1, 2, 3, 4, 5, 6, 7; DLB 14, 207, 319, 326
Berger, John Peter
See Berger, John
Berger, Melvin H. 1927- .... **CLC 12**
See also CA 5-8R; CANR 4, 142; CLR 32; SAAS 2; SATA 5, 88, 158; SATA-Essay 124
Berger, Thomas 1924- .... **CLC 3, 5, 8, 11, 18, 38, 259**
See also BPFB 1; CA 1-4R; CANR 5, 28, 51, 128; CN 1, 2, 3, 4, 5, 6, 7; DAM NOV; DLB 2; DLBY 1980; EWL 3; FANT; INT CANR-28; MAL 5; MTCW 1, 2; MTFW 2005; RHW; TCLE 1:1; TCWW 1, 2
Bergman, Ernst Ingmar
See Bergman, Ingmar
Bergman, Ingmar 1918-2007 ..... **CLC 16, 72, 210**
See also AAYA 61; CA 81-84; 262; CANR 33, 70; CWW 2; DLB 257; MTCW 2; MTFW 2005
Bergson, Henri(-Louis) 1859-1941 . **TCLC 32**
See also CA 164; DLB 329; EW 8; EWL 3; GFL 1789 to the Present

Bergstein, Eleanor 1938- .... **CLC 4**
See also CA 53-56; CANR 5
Berkeley, George 1685-1753 .... **LC 65**
See also DLB 31, 101, 252
Berkoff, Steven 1937- .... **CLC 56**
See also CA 104; CANR 72; CBD; CD 5, 6
Berlin, Isaiah 1909-1997 .... **TCLC 105**
See also CA 85-88; 162
Bermant, Chaim (Icyk) 1929-1998 ... **CLC 40**
See also CA 57-60; CANR 6, 31, 57, 105; CN 2, 3, 4, 5, 6
Bern, Victoria
See Fisher, M(ary) F(rances) K(ennedy)
Bernanos, (Paul Louis) Georges 1888-1948 .... **TCLC 3**
See also CA 104; 130; CANR 94; DLB 72; EWL 3; GFL 1789 to the Present; RGWL 2, 3
Bernard, April 1956- .... **CLC 59**
See also CA 131; CANR 144
Bernard, Mary Ann
See Soderbergh, Steven
Bernard of Clairvaux 1090-1153 .. **CMLC 71**
See also DLB 208
Bernard Silvestris fl. c. 1130-fl. c. 1160 .... **CMLC 87**
See also DLB 208
Bernart de Ventadorn c. 1130-c. 1190 .... **CMLC 98**
Berne, Victoria
See Fisher, M(ary) F(rances) K(ennedy)
Bernhard, Thomas 1931-1989 ..... **CLC 3, 32, 61; DC 14; TCLC 165**
See also CA 85-88; 127; CANR 32, 57; CD-WLB 2; DLB 85, 124; EWL 3; MTCW 1; RGHL; RGWL 2, 3
Bernhardt, Sarah (Henriette Rosine) 1844-1923 .... **TCLC 75**
See also CA 157
Bernstein, Charles 1950- .... **CLC 142**
See also CA 129; CAAS 24; CANR 90; CP 4, 5, 6, 7; DLB 169
Bernstein, Ingrid
See Kirsch, Sarah
Beroul fl. c. 12th cent. - .... **CMLC 75**
Berriault, Gina 1926-1999 .... **CLC 54, 109; SSC 30**
See also CA 116; 129; 185; CANR 66; DLB 130; SSFS 7,11
Berrigan, Daniel 1921- .... **CLC 4**
See also CA 33-36R, 187; CAAE 187; CAAS 1; CANR 11, 43, 78; CP 1, 2, 3, 4, 5, 6, 7; DLB 5
Berrigan, Edmund Joseph Michael, Jr. 1934-1983
See Berrigan, Ted
See also CA 61-64; 110; CANR 14, 102
Berrigan, Ted CLC 37
See Berrigan, Edmund Joseph Michael, Jr.
See also CP 1, 2, 3; DLB 5, 169; WP
Berry, Charles Edward Anderson 1931-
See Berry, Chuck
See also CA 115
Berry, Chuck CLC 17
See Berry, Charles Edward Anderson
Berry, Jonas
See Ashbery, John
Berry, Wendell 1934- .... **CLC 4, 6, 8, 27, 46; PC 28**
See also AITN 1; AMWS 10; ANW; CA 73-76; CANR 50, 73, 101, 132, 174; CP 1, 2, 3, 4, 5, 6, 7; CSW; DAM POET; DLB 5, 6, 234, 275, 342; MTCW 2; MTFW 2005; TCLE 1:1

Berryman, John 1914-1972 ... **CLC 1, 2, 3, 4, 6, 8, 10, 13, 25, 62; PC 64**
See also AMW; CA 13-16; 33-36R; CABS 2; CANR 35; CAP 1; CDALB 1941-1968; CP 1; DAM POET; DLB 48; EWL 3; MAL 5; MTCW 1, 2; MTFW 2005; PAB; PFS 27; RGAL 4; WP

Bertolucci, Bernardo 1940- ...... **CLC 16, 157**
See also CA 106; CANR 125

Berton, Pierre (Francis de Marigny)
1920-2004 .... **CLC 104**
See also CA 1-4R; 233; CANR 2, 56, 144; CPW; DLB 68; SATA 99; SATA-Obit 158

Bertrand, Aloysius 1807-1841 .... **NCLC 31**
See Bertrand, Louis oAloysiusc

Bertrand, Louis oAloysiusc
See Bertrand, Aloysius
See also DLB 217

Bertran de Born c. 1140-1215 .... **CMLC 5**

Besant, Annie (Wood) 1847-1933 ..... **TCLC 9**
See also CA 105; 185

Bessie, Alvah 1904-1985 .... **CLC 23**
See also CA 5-8R; 116; CANR 2, 80; DLB 26

Bestuzhev, Aleksandr Aleksandrovich
1797-1837 .... **NCLC 131**
See also DLB 198

Bethlen, T.D.
See Silverberg, Robert

Beti, Mongo **BLC 1:1; CLC 27**
See Biyidi, Alexandre
See also AFW; CANR 79; DAM MULT; EWL 3; WLIT 2

Betjeman, John 1906-1984 ...... **CLC 2, 6, 10, 34, 43; PC 75**
See also BRW 7; CA 9-12R; 112; CANR 33, 56; CDBLB 1945-1960; CP 1, 2, 3; DA3; DAB; DAM MST, POET; DLB 20; DLBY 1984; EWL 3; MTCW 1, 2

Bettelheim, Bruno 1903-1990 .... **CLC 79; TCLC 143**
See also CA 81-84; 131; CANR 23, 61; DA3; MTCW 1, 2; RGHL

Betti, Ugo 1892-1953 .... **TCLC 5**
See also CA 104; 155; EWL 3; RGWL 2, 3

Betts, Doris (Waugh) 1932- ..... **CLC 3, 6, 28; SSC 45**
See also CA 13-16R; CANR 9, 66, 77; CN 6, 7; CSW; DLB 218; DLBY 1982; INT CANR-9; RGAL 4

Bevan, Alistair
See Roberts, Keith (John Kingston)

Bey, Pilaff
See Douglas, (George) Norman

Beyala, Calixthe 1961- .... **BLC 2:1**
See also EWL 3

Bialik, Chaim Nachman
1873-1934 .... **TCLC 25, 201**
See Bialik, Hayyim Nahman
See also CA 170; EWL 3

Bialik, Hayyim Nahman
See Bialik, Chaim Nachman
See also WLIT 6

Bickerstaff, Isaac
See Swift, Jonathan

Bidart, Frank 1939- .... **CLC 33**
See also AMWS 15; CA 140; CANR 106; CP 5, 6, 7; PFS 26

Bienek, Horst 1930- .... **CLC 7, 11**
See also CA 73-76; DLB 75

Bierce, Ambrose (Gwinett)
1842-1914(?) ..... **SSC 9, 72; TCLC 1, 7, 44; WLC 1**
See also AAYA 55; AMW; BYA 11; CA 104; 139; CANR 78; CDALB 1865-1917; DA; DA3; DAC; DAM MST; DLB 11, 12, 23, 71, 74, 186; EWL 3; EXPS; HGG; LAIT 2; MAL 5; RGAL 4; RGSF 2; SSFS 9; SUFW 1

Biggers, Earl Derr 1884-1933 .... **TCLC 65**
See also CA 108; 153; DLB 306

Billiken, Bud
See Motley, Willard (Francis)

Billings, Josh
See Shaw, Henry Wheeler

Billington, (Lady) Rachel (Mary)
1942- .... **CLC 43**
See also AITN 2; CA 33-36R; CANR 44; CN 4, 5, 6, 7

Binchy, Maeve 1940- .... **CLC 153**
See also BEST 90:1; BPFB 1; CA 127; 134; CANR 50, 96, 134; CN 5, 6, 7; CPW; DA3; DAM POP; DLB 319; INT CA-134; MTCW 2; MTFW 2005; RHW

Binyon, T(imothy) J(ohn)
1936-2004 .... **CLC 34**
See also CA 111; 232; CANR 28, 140

Bion 335B.C.-245B.C. .... **CMLC 39**

Bioy Casares, Adolfo 1914-1999 ... **CLC 4, 8, 13, 88; HLC 1; SSC 17, 102**
See Casares, Adolfo Bioy; Miranda, Javier; Sacastru, Martin
See also CA 29-32R; 177; CANR 19, 43, 66; CWW 2; DAM MULT; DLB 113; EWL 3; HW 1, 2; LAW; MTCW 1, 2; MTFW 2005

Birch, Allison **CLC 65**

Bird, Cordwainer
See Ellison, Harlan

Bird, Robert Montgomery
1806-1854 .... **NCLC 1, 197**
See also DLB 202; RGAL 4

Birdwell, Cleo
See DeLillo, Don

Birkerts, Sven 1951- .... **CLC 116**
See also CA 128; 133; 176; CAAE 176; CAAS 29; CANR 151; INT CA-133

Birney, (Alfred) Earle 1904-1995 .. **CLC 1, 4, 6, 11; PC 52**
See also CA 1-4R; CANR 5, 20; CN 1, 2, 3, 4; CP 1, 2, 3, 4, 5, 6; DAC; DAM MST, POET; DLB 88; MTCW 1; PFS 8; RGEL 2

Biruni, al 973-1048(?) .... **CMLC 28**

Bishop, Elizabeth 1911-1979 ..... **CLC 1, 4, 9, 13, 15, 32; PC 3, 34; TCLC 121**
See also AMWR 2; AMWS 1; CA 5-8R; 89-92; CABS 2; CANR 26, 61, 108; CDALB 1968-1988; CP 1, 2, 3; DA; DA3; DAC; DAM MST, POET; DLB 5, 169; EWL 3; GLL 2; MAL 5; MBL; MTCW 1, 2; PAB; PFS 6, 12, 27; RGAL 4; SATA-Obit 24; TUS; WP

Bishop, John 1935- .... **CLC 10**
See also CA 105

Bishop, John Peale 1892-1944 ..... **TCLC 103**
See also CA 107; 155; DLB 4, 9, 45; MAL 5; RGAL 4

Bissett, Bill 1939- .... **CLC 18; PC 14**
See also CA 69-72; CAAS 19; CANR 15; CCA 1; CP 1, 2, 3, 4, 5, 6, 7; DLB 53; MTCW 1

Bissoondath, Neil 1955- .... **CLC 120**
See also CA 136; CANR 123, 165; CN 6, 7; DAC

Bissoondath, Neil Devindra
See Bissoondath, Neil

Bitov, Andrei (Georgievich) 1937- ... **CLC 57**
See also CA 142; DLB 302

Biyidi, Alexandre 1932-
See Beti, Mongo
See also BW 1, 3; CA 114; 124; CANR 81; DA3; MTCW 1, 2

Bjarme, Brynjolf
See Ibsen, Henrik (Johan)

Bjoernson, Bjoernstjerne (Martinius)
1832-1910 .... **TCLC 7, 37**
See also CA 104

Black, Benjamin
See Banville, John

Black, Robert
See Holdstock, Robert

Blackburn, Paul 1926-1971 .... **CLC 9, 43**
See also BG 1:2; CA 81-84; 33-36R; CANR 34; CP 1; DLB 16; DLBY 1981

Black Elk 1863-1950 .... **NNAL; TCLC 33**
See also CA 144; DAM MULT; MTCW 2; MTFW 2005; WP

Black Hawk 1767-1838 .... **NNAL**

Black Hobart
See Sanders, (James) Ed(ward)

Blacklin, Malcolm
See Chambers, Aidan

Blackmore, R(ichard) D(oddridge)
1825-1900 .... **TCLC 27**
See also CA 120; DLB 18; RGEL 2

Blackmur, R(ichard) P(almer)
1904-1965 .... **CLC 2, 24**
See also AMWS 2; CA 11-12; 25-28R; CANR 71; CAP 1; DLB 63; EWL 3; MAL 5

Black Tarantula
See Acker, Kathy

Blackwood, Algernon 1869-1951 .... **SSC 107; TCLC 5**
See also AAYA 78; CA 105; 150; CANR 169; DLB 153, 156, 178; HGG; SUFW 1

Blackwood, Algernon Henry
See Blackwood, Algernon

Blackwood, Caroline (Maureen)
1931-1996 .... **CLC 6, 9, 100**
See also BRWS 9; CA 85-88; 151; CANR 32, 61, 65; CN 3, 4, 5, 6; DLB 14, 207; HGG; MTCW 1

Blade, Alexander
See Hamilton, Edmond; Silverberg, Robert

Blaga, Lucian 1895-1961 .... **CLC 75**
See also CA 157; DLB 220; EWL 3

Blair, Eric (Arthur) 1903-1950 .... **TCLC 123**
See Orwell, George
See also CA 104; 132; DA; DA3; DAB; DAC; DAM MST, NOV; MTCW 1, 2; MTFW 2005; SATA 29

Blair, Hugh 1718-1800 .... **NCLC 75**

Blais, Marie-Claire 1939- .... **CLC 2, 4, 6, 13, 22**
See also CA 21-24R; CAAS 4; CANR 38, 75, 93; CWW 2; DAC; DAM MST; DLB 53; EWL 3; FW; MTCW 1, 2; MTFW 2005; TWA

Blaise, Clark 1940- .... **CLC 29, 261**
See also AITN 2; CA 53-56, 231; CAAE 231; CAAS 4; CANR 5, 66, 106; CN 4, 5, 6, 7; DLB 53; RGSF 2

Blake, Fairley
See De Voto, Bernard (Augustine)

Blake, Nicholas
See Day Lewis, C(ecil)
See also DLB 77; MSW

Blake, Sterling
See Benford, Gregory

Blake, William 1757-1827 . **NCLC 13, 37, 57, 127, 173, 190, 201; PC 12, 63; WLC 1**
See also AAYA 47; BRW 3; BRWR 1; CDBLB 1789-1832; CLR 52; DA; DA3; DAB; DAC; DAM MST, POET; DLB 93, 163; EXPP; LATS 1:1; LMFS 1; MAICYA 1, 2; PAB; PFS 2, 12, 24; SATA 30; TEA; WCH; WLIT 3; WP

Blanchot, Maurice 1907-2003 .... **CLC 135**
See also CA 117; 144; 213; CANR 138; DLB 72, 296; EWL 3

Blasco Ibanez, Vicente 1867-1928 . **TCLC 12**
See Ibanez, Vicente Blasco
See also BPFB 1; CA 110; 131; CANR 81; DA3; DAM NOV; EW 8; EWL 3; HW 1, 2; MTCW 1

Blatty, William Peter 1928- .... **CLC 2**
See also CA 5-8R; CANR 9, 124; DAM
POP; HGG

Bleeck, Oliver
See Thomas, Ross (Elmore)

Blessing, Lee (Knowlton) 1949- .... **CLC 54**
See also CA 236; CAD; CD 5, 6; DFS 23

Blight, Rose
See Greer, Germaine

Blind, Mathilde 1841-1896 .... **NCLC 202**
See also DLB 199

Blish, James (Benjamin) 1921-1975 . **CLC 14**
See also BPFB 1; CA 1-4R; 57-60; CANR
3; CN 2; DLB 8; MTCW 1; SATA 66;
SCFW 1, 2; SFW 4

Bliss, Frederick
See Card, Orson Scott

Bliss, Gillian
See Paton Walsh, Jill

Bliss, Reginald
See Wells, H(erbert) G(eorge)

Blixen, Karen (Christentze Dinesen)
1885-1962
See Dinesen, Isak
See also CA 25-28; CANR 22, 50; CAP 2;
DA3; DLB 214; LMFS 1; MTCW 1, 2;
SATA 44; SSFS 20

Bloch, Robert (Albert) 1917-1994 .... **CLC 33**
See also AAYA 29; CA 5-8R, 179; 146;
CAAE 179; CAAS 20; CANR 5, 78;
DA3; DLB 44; HGG; INT CANR-5;
MTCW 2; SATA 12; SATA-Obit 82; SFW
4; SUFW 1, 2

Blok, Alexander (Alexandrovich)
1880-1921 .... **PC 21; TCLC 5**
See also CA 104; 183; DLB 295; EW 9;
EWL 3; LMFS 2; RGWL 2, 3

Blom, Jan
See Breytenbach, Breyten

Bloom, Harold 1930- .... **CLC 24, 103, 221**
See also CA 13-16R; CANR 39, 75, 92,
133, 181; DLB 67; EWL 3; MTCW 2;
MTFW 2005; RGAL 4

Bloomfield, Aurelius
See Bourne, Randolph S(illiman)

Bloomfield, Robert 1766-1823 ..... **NCLC 145**
See also DLB 93

Blount, Roy, Jr. 1941- .... **CLC 38**
See also CA 53-56; CANR 10, 28, 61, 125,
176; CSW; INT CANR-28; MTCW 1, 2;
MTFW 2005

Blount, Roy Alton
See Blount, Roy, Jr.

Blowsnake, Sam 1875-(?) .... **NNAL**

Bloy, Leon 1846-1917 .... **TCLC 22**
See also CA 121; 183; DLB 123; GFL 1789
to the Present

Blue Cloud, Peter (Aroniawenrate)
1933- .... **NNAL**
See also CA 117; CANR 40; DAM MULT;
DLB 342

Bluggage, Oranthy
See Alcott, Louisa May

Blume, Judy (Sussman) 1938- .... **CLC 12, 30**
See also AAYA 3, 26; BYA 1, 8, 12; CA 29-
32R; CANR 13, 37, 66, 124; CLR 2, 15,
69; CPW; DA3; DAM NOV, POP; DLB
52; JRDA; MAICYA 1, 2; MAICYAS 1;
MTCW 1, 2; MTFW 2005; NFS 24;
SATA 2, 31, 79, 142; WYA; YAW

Blunden, Edmund (Charles)
1896-1974 .... **CLC 2, 56; PC 66**
See also BRW 6; BRWS 11; CA 17-18; 45-
48; CANR 54; CAP 2; CP 1, 2; DLB 20,
100, 155; MTCW 1; PAB

Bly, Robert (Elwood) 1926- .... **CLC 1, 2, 5,
10, 15, 38, 128; PC 39**
See also AMWS 4; CA 5-8R; CANR 41,
73, 125; CP 1, 2, 3, 4, 5, 6, 7; DA3; DAM
POET; DLB 5, 342; EWL 3; MAL 5;
MTCW 1, 2; MTFW 2005; PFS 6, 17;
RGAL 4

Boas, Franz 1858-1942 .... **TCLC 56**
See also CA 115; 181

Bobette
See Simenon, Georges (Jacques Christian)

Boccaccio, Giovanni 1313-1375 ... **CMLC 13,
57; SSC 10, 87**
See also EW 2; RGSF 2; RGWL 2, 3; TWA;
WLIT 7

Bochco, Steven 1943- .... **CLC 35**
See also AAYA 11, 71; CA 124; 138

Bode, Sigmund
See O'Doherty, Brian

Bodel, Jean 1167(?)-1210 .... **CMLC 28**

Bodenheim, Maxwell 1892-1954 .... **TCLC 44**
See also CA 110; 187; DLB 9, 45; MAL 5;
RGAL 4

Bodenheimer, Maxwell
See Bodenheim, Maxwell

Bodker, Cecil 1927-
See Bodker, Cecil

Bodker, Cecil 1927- .... **CLC 21**
See also CA 73-76; CANR 13, 44, 111;
CLR 23; MAICYA 1, 2; SATA 14, 133

Boell, Heinrich (Theodor)
1917-1985 ..... **CLC 2, 3, 6, 9, 11, 15, 27,
32, 72; SSC 23; WLC 1**
See Boll, Heinrich (Theodor)
See also CA 21-24R; 116; CANR 24; DA;
DA3; DAB; DAC; DAM MST, NOV;
DLB 69; DLBY 1985; MTCW 1, 2;
MTFW 2005; SSFS 20; TWA

Boerne, Alfred
See Doeblin, Alfred

Boethius c. 480-c. 524 .... **CMLC 15**
See also DLB 115; RGWL 2, 3; WLIT 8

Boff, Leonardo (Genezio Darci)
1938- .... **CLC 70; HLC 1**
See also CA 150; DAM MULT; HW 2

Bogan, Louise 1897-1970 .... **CLC 4, 39, 46,
93; PC 12**
See also AMWS 3; CA 73-76; 25-28R;
CANR 33, 82; CP 1; DAM POET; DLB
45, 169; EWL 3; MAL 5; MBL; MTCW
1, 2; PFS 21; RGAL 4

Bogarde, Dirk
See Van Den Bogarde, Derek Jules Gaspard
Ulric Niven
See also DLB 14

Bogosian, Eric 1953- .... **CLC 45, 141**
See also CA 138; CAD; CANR 102, 148;
CD 5, 6; DLB 341

Bograd, Larry 1953- .... **CLC 35**
See also CA 93-96; CANR 57; SAAS 21;
SATA 33, 89; WYA

Boiardo, Matteo Maria 1441-1494 .... **LC 6**

Boileau-Despreaux, Nicolas 1636-1711 . **LC 3**
See also DLB 268; EW 3; GFL Beginnings
to 1789; RGWL 2, 3

Boissard, Maurice
See Leautaud, Paul

Bojer, Johan 1872-1959 .... **TCLC 64**
See also CA 189; EWL 3

Bok, Edward W(illiam)
1863-1930 .... **TCLC 101**
See also CA 217; DLB 91; DLBD 16

Boker, George Henry 1823-1890 . **NCLC 125**
See also RGAL 4

Boland, Eavan 1944- ... **CLC 40, 67, 113; PC
58**
See also BRWS 5; CA 143, 207; CAAE
207; CANR 61, 180; CP 1, 6, 7; CWP;
DAM POET; DLB 40; FW; MTCW 2;
MTFW 2005; PFS 12, 22

Boland, Eavan Aisling
See Boland, Eavan

Boll, Heinrich (Theodor) TCLC 185
See Boell, Heinrich (Theodor)
See also BPFB 1; CDWLB 2; DLB 329;
EW 13; EWL 3; RGHL; RGSF 2; RGWL
2, 3

Bolt, Lee
See Faust, Frederick (Schiller)

Bolt, Robert (Oxton) 1924-1995 ...... **CLC 14;
TCLC 175**
See also CA 17-20R; 147; CANR 35, 67;
CBD; DAM DRAM; DFS 2; DLB 13,
233; EWL 3; LAIT 1; MTCW 1

Bombal, Maria Luisa 1910-1980 .... **HLCS 1;
SSC 37**
See also CA 127; CANR 72; EWL 3; HW
1; LAW; RGSF 2

Bombet, Louis-Alexandre-Cesar
See Stendhal

Bomkauf
See Kaufman, Bob (Garnell)

Bonaventura NCLC 35
See also DLB 90

Bonaventure 1217(?)-1274 .... **CMLC 79**
See also DLB 115; LMFS 1

Bond, Edward 1934- .... **CLC 4, 6, 13, 23**
See also AAYA 50; BRWS 1; CA 25-28R;
CANR 38, 67, 106; CBD; CD 5, 6; DAM
DRAM; DFS 3, 8; DLB 13, 310; EWL 3;
MTCW 1

Bonham, Frank 1914-1989 .... **CLC 12**
See also AAYA 1, 70; BYA 1, 3; CA 9-12R;
CANR 4, 36; JRDA; MAICYA 1, 2;
SAAS 3; SATA 1, 49; SATA-Obit 62;
TCWW 1, 2; YAW

Bonnefoy, Yves 1923- . **CLC 9, 15, 58; PC 58**
See also CA 85-88; CANR 33, 75, 97, 136;
CWW 2; DAM MST, POET; DLB 258;
EWL 3; GFL 1789 to the Present; MTCW
1, 2; MTFW 2005

Bonner, Marita HR 1:2; PC 72; TCLC 179
See Occomy, Marita (Odette) Bonner

Bonnin, Gertrude 1876-1938 .... **NNAL**
See Zitkala-Sa
See also CA 150; DAM MULT

Bontemps, Arna(ud Wendell)
1902-1973 ..... **BLC 1:1; CLC 1, 18; HR
1:2**
See also BW 1; CA 1-4R; 41-44R; CANR
4, 35; CLR 6; CP 1; CWRI 5; DA3; DAM
MULT, NOV, POET; DLB 48, 51; JRDA;
MAICYA 1, 2; MAL 5; MTCW 1, 2;
SATA 2, 44; SATA-Obit 24; WCH; WP

Boot, William
See Stoppard, Tom

Booth, Martin 1944-2004 .... **CLC 13**
See also CA 93-96, 188; 223; CAAE 188;
CAAS 2; CANR 92; CP 1, 2, 3, 4

Booth, Philip 1925-2007 .... **CLC 23**
See also CA 5-8R; 262; CANR 5, 88; CP 1,
2, 3, 4, 5, 6, 7; DLBY 1982

Booth, Philip Edmund
See Booth, Philip

Booth, Wayne C. 1921-2005 .... **CLC 24**
See also CA 1-4R; 244; CAAS 5; CANR 3,
43, 117; DLB 67

Booth, Wayne Clayson
See Booth, Wayne C.

Borchert, Wolfgang 1921-1947 .... **TCLC 5**
See also CA 104; 188; DLB 69, 124; EWL
3

Borel, Petrus 1809-1859 .... **NCLC 41**
See also DLB 119; GFL 1789 to the Present
Borges, Jorge Luis 1899-1986 ... **CLC 1, 2, 3, 4, 6, 8, 9, 10, 13, 19, 44, 48, 83; HLC 1; PC 22, 32; SSC 4, 41, 100; TCLC 109; WLC 1**
See also AAYA 26; BPFB 1; CA 21-24R; CANR 19, 33, 75, 105, 133; CDWLB 3; DA; DA3; DAB; DAC; DAM MST, MULT; DLB 113, 283; DLBY 1986; DNFS 1, 2; EWL 3; HW 1, 2; LAW; LMFS 2; MSW; MTCW 1, 2; MTFW 2005; PFS 27; RGHL; RGSF 2; RGWL 2, 3; SFW 4; SSFS 17; TWA; WLIT 1
Borne, Ludwig 1786-1837 .... **NCLC 193**
See also DLB 90
Borowski, Tadeusz 1922-1951 .... **SSC 48; TCLC 9**
See also CA 106; 154; CDWLB 4; DLB 215; EWL 3; RGHL; RGSF 2; RGWL 3; SSFS 13
Borrow, George (Henry)
1803-1881 .... **NCLC 9**
See also BRWS 12; DLB 21, 55, 166
Bosch (Gavino), Juan 1909-2001 .... **HLCS 1**
See also CA 151; 204; DAM MST, MULT; DLB 145; HW 1, 2
Bosman, Herman Charles
1905-1951 .... **TCLC 49**
See Malan, Herman
See also CA 160; DLB 225; RGSF 2
Bosschere, Jean de 1878(?)-1953 ... **TCLC 19**
See also CA 115; 186
Boswell, James 1740-1795 ... **LC 4, 50; WLC 1**
See also BRW 3; CDBLB 1660-1789; DA; DAB; DAC; DAM MST; DLB 104, 142; TEA; WLIT 3
Bottomley, Gordon 1874-1948 ..... **TCLC 107**
See also CA 120; 192; DLB 10
Bottoms, David 1949- .... **CLC 53**
See also CA 105; CANR 22; CSW; DLB 120; DLBY 1983
Boucicault, Dion 1820-1890 .... **NCLC 41**
See also DLB 344
Boucolon, Maryse
See Conde, Maryse
Bourcicault, Dion
See Boucicault, Dion
Bourdieu, Pierre 1930-2002 .... **CLC 198**
See also CA 130; 204
Bourget, Paul (Charles Joseph)
1852-1935 .... **TCLC 12**
See also CA 107; 196; DLB 123; GFL 1789 to the Present
Bourjaily, Vance (Nye) 1922- .... **CLC 8, 62**
See also CA 1-4R; CAAS 1; CANR 2, 72; CN 1, 2, 3, 4, 5, 6, 7; DLB 2, 143; MAL 5
Bourne, Randolph S(illiman)
1886-1918 .... **TCLC 16**
See also AMW; CA 117; 155; DLB 63; MAL 5
Boursiquot, Dionysius
See Boucicault, Dion
Bova, Ben 1932- .... **CLC 45**
See also AAYA 16; CA 5-8R; CAAS 18; CANR 11, 56, 94, 111, 157; CLR 3, 96; DLBY 1981; INT CANR-11; MAICYA 1, 2; MTCW 1; SATA 6, 68, 133; SFW 4
Bova, Benjamin William
See Bova, Ben
Bowen, Elizabeth (Dorothea Cole)
1899-1973 . **CLC 1, 3, 6, 11, 15, 22, 118; SSC 3, 28, 66; TCLC 148**
See also BRWS 2; CA 17-18; 41-44R; CANR 35, 105; CAP 2; CDBLB 1945-1960; CN 1; DA3; DAM NOV; DLB 15,

162; EWL 3; EXPS; FW; HGG; MTCW 1, 2; MTFW 2005; NFS 13; RGSF 2; SSFS 5, 22; SUFW 1; TEA; WLIT 4
Bowering, George 1935- .... **CLC 15, 47**
See also CA 21-24R; CAAS 16; CANR 10; CN 7; CP 1, 2, 3, 4, 5, 6, 7; DLB 53
Bowering, Marilyn R(uthe) 1949- .... **CLC 32**
See also CA 101; CANR 49; CP 4, 5, 6, 7; CWP; DLB 334
Bowers, Edgar 1924-2000 .... **CLC 9**
See also CA 5-8R; 188; CANR 24; CP 1, 2, 3, 4, 5, 6, 7; CSW; DLB 5
Bowers, Mrs. J. Milton 1842-1914
See Bierce, Ambrose (Gwinett)
Bowie, David CLC 17
See Jones, David Robert
Bowles, Jane (Sydney) 1917-1973 ..... **CLC 3, 68**
See Bowles, Jane Auer
See also CA 19-20; 41-44R; CAP 2; CN 1; MAL 5
Bowles, Jane Auer
See Bowles, Jane (Sydney)
See also EWL 3
Bowles, Paul 1910-1999 ..... **CLC 1, 2, 19, 53; SSC 3, 98; TCLC 209**
See also AMWS 4; CA 1-4R; 186; CAAS 1; CANR 1, 19, 50, 75; CN 1, 2, 3, 4, 5, 6; DA3; DLB 5, 6, 218; EWL 3; MAL 5; MTCW 1, 2; MTFW 2005; RGAL 4; SSFS 17
Bowles, William Lisle 1762-1850 . **NCLC 103**
See also DLB 93
Box, Edgar
See Vidal, Gore
Boyd, James 1888-1944 .... **TCLC 115**
See also CA 186; DLB 9; DLBD 16; RGAL 4; RHW
Boyd, Nancy
See Millay, Edna St. Vincent
See also GLL 1
Boyd, Thomas (Alexander)
1898-1935 .... **TCLC 111**
See also CA 111; 183; DLB 9; DLBD 16, 316
Boyd, William 1952- .... **CLC 28, 53, 70**
See also CA 114; 120; CANR 51, 71, 131, 174; CN 4, 5, 6, 7; DLB 231
Boyesen, Hjalmar Hjorth
1848-1895 .... **NCLC 135**
See also DLB 12, 71; DLBD 13; RGAL 4
Boyle, Kay 1902-1992 .... **CLC 1, 5, 19, 58, 121; SSC 5, 102**
See also CA 13-16R; 140; CAAS 1; CANR 29, 61, 110; CN 1, 2, 3, 4, 5; CP 1, 2, 3, 4, 5; DLB 4, 9, 48, 86; DLBY 1993; EWL 3; MAL 5; MTCW 1, 2; MTFW 2005; RGAL 4; RGSF 2; SSFS 10, 13, 14
Boyle, Mark
See Kienzle, William X.
Boyle, Patrick 1905-1982 .... **CLC 19**
See also CA 127
Boyle, T. C.
See Boyle, T. Coraghessan
See also AMWS 8
Boyle, T. Coraghessan 1948- ..... **CLC 36, 55, 90; SSC 16**
See Boyle, T. C.
See also AAYA 47; BEST 90:4; BPFB 1; CA 120; CANR 44, 76, 89, 132; CN 6, 7; CPW; DA3; DAM POP; DLB 218, 278; DLBY 1986; EWL 3; MAL 5; MTCW 2; MTFW 2005; SSFS 13, 19
Boz
See Dickens, Charles (John Huffam)
Brackenridge, Hugh Henry
1748-1816 .... **NCLC 7**
See also DLB 11, 37; RGAL 4

Bradbury, Edward P.
See Moorcock, Michael
See also MTCW 2
Bradbury, Malcolm (Stanley)
1932-2000 .... **CLC 32, 61**
See also CA 1-4R; CANR 1, 33, 91, 98, 137; CN 1, 2, 3, 4, 5, 6, 7; CP 1; DA3; DAM NOV; DLB 14, 207; EWL 3; MTCW 1, 2; MTFW 2005
Bradbury, Ray 1920- ... **CLC 1, 3, 10, 15, 42, 98, 235; SSC 29, 53; WLC 1**
See also AAYA 15; AITN 1, 2; AMWS 4; BPFB 1; BYA 4, 5, 11; CA 1-4R; CANR 2, 30, 75, 125; CDALB 1968-1988; CN 1, 2, 3, 4, 5, 6, 7; CPW; DA; DA3; DAB; DAC; DAM MST, NOV, POP; DLB 2, 8; EXPN; EXPS; HGG; LAIT 3, 5; LATS 1:2; LMFS 2; MAL 5; MTCW 1, 2; MTFW 2005; NFS 1, 22; RGAL 4; RGSF 2; SATA 11, 64, 123; SCFW 1, 2; SFW 4; SSFS 1, 20; SUFW 1, 2; TUS; YAW
Braddon, Mary Elizabeth
1837-1915 .... **TCLC 111**
See also BRWS 8; CA 108; 179; CMW 4; DLB 18, 70, 156; HGG
Bradfield, Scott 1955- .... **SSC 65**
See also CA 147; CANR 90; HGG; SUFW 2
Bradfield, Scott Michael
See Bradfield, Scott
Bradford, Gamaliel 1863-1932 .... **TCLC 36**
See also CA 160; DLB 17
Bradford, William 1590-1657 .... **LC 64**
See also DLB 24, 30; RGAL 4
Bradley, David, Jr. 1950- ...... **BLC 1:1; CLC 23, 118**
See also BW 1, 3; CA 104; CANR 26, 81; CN 4, 5, 6, 7; DAM MULT; DLB 33
Bradley, David Henry, Jr.
See Bradley, David, Jr.
Bradley, John Ed 1958- .... **CLC 55**
See also CA 139; CANR 99; CN 6, 7; CSW
Bradley, John Edmund, Jr.
See Bradley, John Ed
Bradley, Marion Zimmer
1930-1999 .... **CLC 30**
See Chapman, Lee; Dexter, John; Gardner, Miriam; Ives, Morgan; Rivers, Elfrida
See also AAYA 40; BPFB 1; CA 57-60; 185; CAAS 10; CANR 7, 31, 51, 75, 107; CPW; DA3; DAM POP; DLB 8; FANT; FW; MTCW 1, 2; MTFW 2005; SATA 90, 139; SATA-Obit 116; SFW 4; SUFW 2; YAW
Bradshaw, John 1933- .... **CLC 70**
See also CA 138; CANR 61
Bradstreet, Anne 1612(?)-1672 .... **LC 4, 30, 130; PC 10**
See also AMWS 1; CDALB 1640-1865; DA; DA3; DAC; DAM MST, POET; DLB 24; EXPP; FW; PFS 6; RGAL 4; TUS; WP
Brady, Joan 1939- .... **CLC 86**
See also CA 141
Bragg, Melvyn 1939- .... **CLC 10**
See also BEST 89:3; CA 57-60; CANR 10, 48, 89, 158; CN 1, 2, 3, 4, 5, 6, 7; DLB 14, 271; RHW
Brahe, Tycho 1546-1601 .... **LC 45**
See also DLB 300
Braine, John (Gerard) 1922-1986 . **CLC 1, 3, 41**
See also CA 1-4R; 120; CANR 1, 33; CDBLB 1945-1960; CN 1, 2, 3, 4; DLB 15; DLBY 1986; EWL 3; MTCW 1
Braithwaite, William Stanley (Beaumont)
1878-1962 ...... **BLC 1:1; HR 1:2; PC 52**
See also BW 1; CA 125; DAM MULT; DLB 50, 54; MAL 5

Bramah, Ernest 1868-1942 .... **TCLC 72**
See also CA 156; CMW 4; DLB 70; FANT
Brammer, Billy Lee
See Brammer, William
Brammer, William 1929-1978 .... **CLC 31**
See also CA 235; 77-80
Brancati, Vitaliano 1907-1954 .... **TCLC 12**
See also CA 109; DLB 264; EWL 3
Brancato, Robin F(idler) 1936- .... **CLC 35**
See also AAYA 9, 68; BYA 6; CA 69-72;
CANR 11, 45; CLR 32; JRDA; MAICYA
2; MAICYAS 1; SAAS 9; SATA 97;
WYA; YAW
Brand, Dionne 1953- .... **CLC 192**
See also BW 2; CA 143; CANR 143; CWP;
DLB 334
Brand, Max
See Faust, Frederick (Schiller)
See also BPFB 1; TCWW 1, 2
Brand, Millen 1906-1980 .... **CLC 7**
See also CA 21-24R; 97-100; CANR 72
Branden, Barbara 1929- .... **CLC 44**
See also CA 148
Brandes, Georg (Morris Cohen)
1842-1927 .... **TCLC 10**
See also CA 105; 189; DLB 300
Brandys, Kazimierz 1916-2000 .... **CLC 62**
See also CA 239; EWL 3
Branley, Franklyn M(ansfield)
1915-2002 .... **CLC 21**
See also CA 33-36R; 207; CANR 14, 39;
CLR 13; MAICYA 1, 2; SAAS 16; SATA
4, 68, 136
Brant, Beth (E.) 1941- .... **NNAL**
See also CA 144; FW
Brant, Sebastian 1457-1521 .... **LC 112**
See also DLB 179; RGWL 2, 3
Brathwaite, Edward Kamau
1930- ..... **BLC 2:1; BLCS; CLC 11; PC
56**
See also BRWS 12; BW 2, 3; CA 25-28R;
CANR 11, 26, 47, 107; CDWLB 3; CP 1,
2, 3, 4, 5, 6, 7; DAM POET; DLB 125;
EWL 3
Brathwaite, Kamau
See Brathwaite, Edward Kamau
Brautigan, Richard (Gary)
1935-1984 .... **CLC 1, 3, 5, 9, 12, 34, 42;
TCLC 133**
See also BPFB 1; CA 53-56; 113; CANR
34; CN 1, 2, 3; CP 1, 2, 3, 4; DA3; DAM
NOV; DLB 2, 5, 206; DLBY 1980, 1984;
FANT; MAL 5; MTCW 1; RGAL 4;
SATA 56
Brave Bird, Mary
See Crow Dog, Mary
Braverman, Kate 1950- .... **CLC 67**
See also CA 89-92; CANR 141; DLB 335
Brecht, (Eugen) Bertolt (Friedrich)
1898-1956 ..... **DC 3; TCLC 1, 6, 13, 35,
169; WLC 1**
See also CA 104; 133; CANR 62; CDWLB
2; DA; DA3; DAB; DAC; DAM DRAM,
MST; DFS 4, 5, 9; DLB 56, 124; EW 11;
EWL 3; IDTP; MTCW 1, 2; MTFW 2005;
RGHL; RGWL 2, 3; TWA
Brecht, Eugen Berthold Friedrich
See Brecht, (Eugen) Bertolt (Friedrich)
Bremer, Fredrika 1801-1865 .... **NCLC 11**
See also DLB 254
Brennan, Christopher John
1870-1932 .... **TCLC 17**
See also CA 117; 188; DLB 230; EWL 3
Brennan, Maeve 1917-1993 ... **CLC 5; TCLC
124**
See also CA 81-84; CANR 72, 100
Brenner, Jozef 1887-1919
See Csath, Geza
See also CA 240

Brent, Linda
See Jacobs, Harriet A(nn)
Brentano, Clemens (Maria)
1778-1842 .... **NCLC 1, 191; SSC 115**
See also DLB 90; RGWL 2, 3
Brent of Bin Bin
See Franklin, (Stella Maria Sarah) Miles
(Lampe)
Brenton, Howard 1942- .... **CLC 31**
See also CA 69-72; CANR 33, 67; CBD;
CD 5, 6; DLB 13; MTCW 1
Breslin, James 1930-
See Breslin, Jimmy
See also CA 73-76; CANR 31, 75, 139;
DAM NOV; MTCW 1, 2; MTFW 2005
Breslin, Jimmy **CLC 4, 43**
See Breslin, James
See also AITN 1; DLB 185; MTCW 2
Bresson, Robert 1901(?)-1999 .... **CLC 16**
See also CA 110; 187; CANR 49
Breton, Andre 1896-1966 .. **CLC 2, 9, 15, 54;
PC 15**
See also CA 19-20; 25-28R; CANR 40, 60;
CAP 2; DLB 65, 258; EW 11; EWL 3;
GFL 1789 to the Present; LMFS 2;
MTCW 1, 2; MTFW 2005; RGWL 2, 3;
TWA; WP
Breton, Nicholas c. 1554-c. 1626 .... **LC 133**
See also DLB 136
Breytenbach, Breyten 1939(?)- .. **CLC 23, 37,
126**
See also CA 113; 129; CANR 61, 122;
CWW 2; DAM POET; DLB 225; EWL 3
Bridgers, Sue Ellen 1942- .... **CLC 26**
See also AAYA 8, 49; BYA 7, 8; CA 65-68;
CANR 11, 36; CLR 18; DLB 52; JRDA;
MAICYA 1, 2; SAAS 1; SATA 22, 90;
SATA-Essay 109; WYA; YAW
Bridges, Robert (Seymour)
1844-1930 .... **PC 28; TCLC 1**
See also BRW 6; CA 104; 152; CDBLB
1890-1914; DAM POET; DLB 19, 98
Bridie, James **TCLC 3**
See Mavor, Osborne Henry
See also DLB 10; EWL 3
Brin, David 1950- .... **CLC 34**
See also AAYA 21; CA 102; CANR 24, 70,
125, 127; INT CANR-24; SATA 65;
SCFW 2; SFW 4
Brink, Andre 1935- .... **CLC 18, 36, 106**
See also AFW; BRWS 6; CA 104; CANR
39, 62, 109, 133, 182; CN 4, 5, 6, 7; DLB
225; EWL 3; INT CA-103; LATS 1:2;
MTCW 1, 2; MTFW 2005; WLIT 2
Brinsmead, H. F(ay)
See Brinsmead, H(esba) F(ay)
Brinsmead, H. F.
See Brinsmead, H(esba) F(ay)
Brinsmead, H(esba) F(ay) 1922- ...... **CLC 21**
See also CA 21-24R; CANR 10; CLR 47;
CWRI 5; MAICYA 1, 2; SAAS 5; SATA
18, 78
Brittain, Vera (Mary) 1893(?)-1970 . **CLC 23**
See also BRWS 10; CA 13-16; 25-28R;
CANR 58; CAP 1; DLB 191; FW; MTCW
1, 2
Broch, Hermann 1886-1951 ... **TCLC 20, 204**
See also CA 117; 211; CDWLB 2; DLB 85,
124; EW 10; EWL 3; RGWL 2, 3
Brock, Rose
See Hansen, Joseph
See also GLL 1
Brod, Max 1884-1968 .... **TCLC 115**
See also CA 5-8R; 25-28R; CANR 7; DLB
81; EWL 3
Brodkey, Harold (Roy) 1930-1996 .. **CLC 56;
TCLC 123**
See also CA 111; 151; CANR 71; CN 4, 5,
6; DLB 130

Brodsky, Iosif Alexandrovich 1940-1996
See Brodsky, Joseph
See also CA 41-44R; 151; CANR
37, 106; DA3; DAM POET; MTCW 1, 2;
MTFW 2005; RGWL 2, 3
Brodsky, Joseph **CLC 4, 6, 13, 36, 100; PC 9**
See Brodsky, Iosif Alexandrovich
See also AAYA 71; AMWS 8; CWW 2;
DLB 285, 329; EWL 3; MTCW 1
Brodsky, Michael 1948- .... **CLC 19**
See also CA 102; CANR 18, 41, 58, 147;
DLB 244
Brodsky, Michael Mark
See Brodsky, Michael
Brodzki, Bella **CLC 65**
Brome, Richard 1590(?)-1652 .... **LC 61**
See also BRWS 10; DLB 58
Bromell, Henry 1947- .... **CLC 5**
See also CA 53-56; CANR 9, 115, 116
Bromfield, Louis (Brucker)
1896-1956 .... **TCLC 11**
See also CA 107; 155; DLB 4, 9, 86; RGAL
4; RHW
Broner, E(sther) M(asserman)
1930- .... **CLC 19**
See also CA 17-20R; CANR 8, 25, 72; CN
4, 5, 6; DLB 28
Bronk, William (M.) 1918-1999 .... **CLC 10**
See also CA 89-92; 177; CANR 23; CP 3,
4, 5, 6, 7; DLB 165
Bronstein, Lev Davidovich
See Trotsky, Leon
Bronte, Anne
See Bronte, Anne
Bronte, Anne 1820-1849 ..... **NCLC 4, 71, 102**
See also BRW 5; BRWR 1; DA3; DLB 21,
199, 340; NFS 26; TEA
Bronte, (Patrick) Branwell
1817-1848 .... **NCLC 109**
See also DLB 340
Bronte, Charlotte
See Bronte, Charlotte
Bronte, Charlotte 1816-1855 ...... **NCLC 3, 8,
33, 58, 105, 155; WLC 1**
See also AAYA 17; BRW 5; BRWC 2;
BRWR 1; BYA 2; CDBLB 1832-1890;
DA; DA3; DAB; DAC; DAM MST, NOV;
DLB 21, 159, 199, 340; EXPN; FL 1:2;
GL 2; LAIT 2; NFS 4; TEA; WLIT 4
Bronte, Emily
See Bronte, Emily (Jane)
Bronte, Emily (Jane) 1818-1848 ... **NCLC 16,
35, 165; PC 8; WLC 1**
See also AAYA 17; BPFB 1; BRW 5;
BRWC 1; BRWR 1; BYA 3; CDBLB
1832-1890; DA; DA3; DAB; DAC; DAM
MST, NOV, POET; DLB 21, 32, 199, 340;
EXPN; FL 1:2; GL 2; LAIT 1; TEA;
WLIT 3
Brontes
See Bronte, Anne; Bronte, (Patrick) Bran-
well; Bronte, Charlotte; Bronte, Emily
(Jane)
Brooke, Frances 1724-1789 .... **LC 6, 48**
See also DLB 39, 99
Brooke, Henry 1703(?)-1783 .... **LC 1**
See also DLB 39
Brooke, Rupert (Chawner)
1887-1915 .. **PC 24; TCLC 2, 7; WLC 1**
See also BRWS 3; CA 104; 132; CANR 61;
CDBLB 1914-1945; DA; DAB; DAC;
DAM MST, POET; DLB 19, 216; EXPP;
GLL 2; MTCW 1, 2; MTFW 2005; PFS
7; TEA
Brooke-Haven, P.
See Wodehouse, P(elham) G(renville)

Brooke-Rose, Christine 1923(?)- ..... **CLC 40, 184**
See also BRWS 4; CA 13-16R; CANR 58, 118, 183; CN 1, 2, 3, 4, 5, 6, 7; DLB 14, 231; EWL 3; SFW 4

Brookner, Anita 1928- . **CLC 32, 34, 51, 136, 237**
See also BRWS 4; CA 114; 120; CANR 37, 56, 87, 130; CN 4, 5, 6, 7; CPW; DA3; DAB; DAM POP; DLB 194, 326; DLBY 1987; EWL 3; MTCW 1, 2; MTFW 2005; NFS 23; TEA

Brooks, Cleanth 1906-1994 . **CLC 24, 86, 110**
See also AMWS 14; CA 17-20R; 145; CANR 33, 35; CSW; DLB 63; DLBY 1994; EWL 3; INT CANR-35; MAL 5; MTCW 1, 2; MTFW 2005

Brooks, George
See Baum, L(yman) Frank

Brooks, Gwendolyn 1917-2000 .... **BLC 1:1, 2:1; CLC 1, 2, 4, 5, 15, 49, 125; PC 7; WLC 1**
See also AAYA 20; AFAW 1, 2; AITN 1; AMWS 3; BW 2, 3; CA 1-4R; 190; CANR 1, 27, 52, 75, 132; CDALB 1941-1968; CLR 27; CP 1, 2, 3, 4, 5, 6, 7; CWP; DA; DA3; DAC; DAM MST, MULT, POET; DLB 5, 76, 165; EWL 3; EXPP; FL 1:5; MAL 5; MBL; MTCW 1, 2; MTFW 2005; PFS 1, 2, 4, 6; RGAL 4; SATA 6; SATA-Obit 123; TUS; WP

Brooks, Mel 1926-
See Kaminsky, Melvin
See also CA 65-68; CANR 16; DFS 21

Brooks, Peter 1938- .... **CLC 34**
See also CA 45-48; CANR 1, 107, 182

Brooks, Peter Preston
See Brooks, Peter

Brooks, Van Wyck 1886-1963 .... **CLC 29**
See also AMW; CA 1-4R; CANR 6; DLB 45, 63, 103; MAL 5; TUS

Brophy, Brigid (Antonia)
1929-1995 .... **CLC 6, 11, 29, 105**
See also CA 5-8R; 149; CAAS 6; CANR 25, 53; CBD; CN 1, 2, 3, 4, 5, 6; CWD; DA3; DLB 14, 271; EWL 3; MTCW 1, 2

Brosman, Catharine Savage 1934- ..... **CLC 9**
See also CA 61-64; CANR 21, 46, 149

Brossard, Nicole 1943- .... **CLC 115, 169; PC 80**
See also CA 122; CAAS 16; CANR 140; CCA 1; CWP; CWW 2; DLB 53; EWL 3; FW; GLL 2; RGWL 3

Brother Antoninus
See Everson, William (Oliver)

Brothers Grimm
See Grimm, Jacob Ludwig Karl; Grimm, Wilhelm Karl

The Brothers Quay
See Quay, Stephen; Quay, Timothy

Broughton, T(homas) Alan 1936- ..... **CLC 19**
See also CA 45-48; CANR 2, 23, 48, 111

Broumas, Olga 1949- .... **CLC 10, 73**
See also CA 85-88; CANR 20, 69, 110; CP 5, 6, 7; CWP; GLL 2

Broun, Heywood 1888-1939 .... **TCLC 104**
See also DLB 29, 171

Brown, Alan 1950- .... **CLC 99**
See also CA 156

Brown, Charles Brockden
1771-1810 .... **NCLC 22, 74, 122**
See also AMWS 1; CDALB 1640-1865; DLB 37, 59, 73; FW; GL 2; HGG; LMFS 1; RGAL 4; TUS

Brown, Christy 1932-1981 .... **CLC 63**
See also BYA 13; CA 105; 104; CANR 72; DLB 14

Brown, Claude 1937-2002 ..... **BLC 1:1; CLC 30**
See also AAYA 7; BW 1, 3; CA 73-76; 205; CANR 81; DAM MULT

Brown, Dan 1964- .... **CLC 209**
See also AAYA 55; CA 217; MTFW 2005

Brown, Dee 1908-2002 .... **CLC 18, 47**
See also AAYA 30; CA 13-16R; 212; CAAS 6; CANR 11, 45, 60, 150; CPW; CSW; DA3; DAM POP; DLBY 1980; LAIT 2; MTCW 1, 2; MTFW 2005; NCFS 5; SATA 5, 110; SATA-Obit 141; TCWW 1, 2

Brown, Dee Alexander
See Brown, Dee

Brown, George
See Wertmueller, Lina

Brown, George Douglas
1869-1902 .... **TCLC 28**
See Douglas, George
See also CA 162

Brown, George Mackay 1921-1996 ... **CLC 5, 48, 100**
See also BRWS 6; CA 21-24R; 151; CAAS 6; CANR 12, 37, 67; CN 1, 2, 3, 4, 5, 6; CP 1, 2, 3, 4, 5, 6; DLB 14, 27, 139, 271; MTCW 1; RGSF 2; SATA 35

Brown, James Wllie
See Komunyakaa, Yusef

Brown, James Wllie, Jr.
See Komunyakaa, Yusef

Brown, Larry 1951-2004 .... **CLC 73**
See also CA 130; 134; 233; CANR 117, 145; CSW; DLB 234; INT CA-134

Brown, Moses
See Barrett, William (Christopher)

Brown, Rita Mae 1944- .... **CLC 18, 43, 79, 259**
See also BPFB 1; CA 45-48; CANR 2, 11, 35, 62, 95, 138, 183; CN 5, 6, 7; CPW; CSW; DA3; DAM NOV, POP; FW; INT CANR-11; MAL 5; MTCW 1, 2; MTFW 2005; NFS 9; RGAL 4; TUS

Brown, Roderick (Langmere) Haig-
See Haig-Brown, Roderick (Langmere)

Brown, Rosellen 1939- .... **CLC 32, 170**
See also CA 77-80; CAAS 10; CANR 14, 44, 98; CN 6, 7

Brown, Sterling Allen 1901-1989 ...... **BLC 1; CLC 1, 23, 59; HR 1:2; PC 55**
See also AFAW 1, 2; BW 1, 3; CA 85-88; 127; CANR 26; CP 3, 4; DA3; DAM MULT, POET; DLB 48, 51, 63; MAL 5; MTCW 1, 2; MTFW 2005; RGAL 4; WP

Brown, Will
See Ainsworth, William Harrison

Brown, William Hill 1765-1793 .... **LC 93**
See also DLB 37

Brown, William Larry
See Brown, Larry

Brown, William Wells 1815-1884 ... **BLC 1:1; DC 1; NCLC 2, 89**
See also DAM MULT; DLB 3, 50, 183, 248; RGAL 4

Browne, Clyde Jackson
See Browne, Jackson

Browne, Jackson 1948(?)- .... **CLC 21**
See also CA 120

Browne, Sir Thomas 1605-1682 .... **LC 111**
See also BRW 2; DLB 151

Browning, Robert 1812-1889 . **NCLC 19, 79; PC 2, 61; WLCS**
See also BRW 4; BRWC 2; BRWR 2; CD-BLB 1832-1890; CLR 97; DA; DA3; DAB; DAC; DAM MST, POET; DLB 32, 163; EXPP; LATS 1:1; PAB; PFS 1, 15; RGEL 2; TEA; WLIT 4; WP; YABC 1

Browning, Tod 1882-1962 .... **CLC 16**
See also CA 141; 117

Brownmiller, Susan 1935- .... **CLC 159**
See also CA 103; CANR 35, 75, 137; DAM NOV; FW; MTCW 1, 2; MTFW 2005

Brownson, Orestes Augustus
1803-1876 .... **NCLC 50**
See also DLB 1, 59, 73, 243

Bruccoli, Matthew J. 1931-2008 .... **CLC 34**
See also CA 9-12R; 274; CANR 7, 87; DLB 103

Bruccoli, Matthew Joseph
See Bruccoli, Matthew J.

Bruce, Lenny CLC 21
See Schneider, Leonard Alfred

Bruchac, Joseph 1942- .... **NNAL**
See also AAYA 19; CA 33-36R; 256; CAAE 256; CANR 13, 47, 75, 94, 137, 161; CLR 46; CWRI 5; DAM MULT; DLB 342; JRDA; MAICYA 2; MAICYAS 1; MTCW 2; MTFW 2005; SATA 42, 89, 131, 176; SATA-Essay 176

Bruin, John
See Brutus, Dennis

Brulard, Henri
See Stendhal

Brulls, Christian
See Simenon, Georges (Jacques Christian)

Brunetto Latini c. 1220-1294 .... **CMLC 73**

Brunner, John (Kilian Houston)
1934-1995 .... **CLC 8, 10**
See also CA 1-4R; 149; CAAS 8; CANR 2, 37; CPW; DAM POP; DLB 261; MTCW 1, 2; SCFW 1, 2; SFW 4

Bruno, Giordano 1548-1600 .... **LC 27**
See also RGWL 2, 3

Brutus, Dennis 1924- ...... **BLC 1:1; CLC 43; PC 24**
See also AFW; BW 2, 3; CA 49-52; CAAS 14; CANR 2, 27, 42, 81; CDWLB 3; CP 1, 2, 3, 4, 5, 6, 7; DAM MULT, POET; DLB 117, 225; EWL 3

Bryan, C(ourtlandt) D(ixon) B(arnes)
1936- .... **CLC 29**
See also CA 73-76; CANR 13, 68; DLB 185; INT CANR-13

Bryan, Michael
See Moore, Brian
See also CCA 1

Bryan, William Jennings
1860-1925 .... **TCLC 99**
See also DLB 303

Bryant, William Cullen 1794-1878 . **NCLC 6, 46; PC 20**
See also AMWS 1; CDALB 1640-1865; DA; DAB; DAC; DAM MST, POET; DLB 3, 43, 59, 189, 250; EXPP; PAB; RGAL 4; TUS

Bryusov, Valery Yakovlevich
1873-1924 .... **TCLC 10**
See also CA 107; 155; EWL 3; SFW 4

Buchan, John 1875-1940 .... **TCLC 41**
See also CA 108; 145; CMW 4; DAB; DAM POP; DLB 34, 70, 156; HGG; MSW; MTCW 2; RGEL 2; RHW; YABC 2

Buchanan, George 1506-1582 .... **LC 4**
See also DLB 132

Buchanan, Robert 1841-1901 .... **TCLC 107**
See also CA 179; DLB 18, 35

Buchheim, Lothar-Guenther
1918-2007 .... **CLC 6**
See also CA 85-88; 257

Buchner, (Karl) Georg
1813-1837 .... **NCLC 26, 146**
See also CDWLB 2; DLB 133; EW 6; RGSF 2; RGWL 2, 3; TWA

Buchwald, Art 1925-2007 .... **CLC 33**
See also AITN 1; CA 5-8R; 256; CANR 21, 67, 107; MTCW 1, 2; SATA 10

Buchwald, Arthur
See Buchwald, Art

Buck, Pearl S(ydenstricker)
1892-1973 .... **CLC 7, 11, 18, 127**
See also AAYA 42; AITN 1; AMWS 2; BPFB 1; CA 1-4R; 41-44R; CANR 1, 34; CDALBS; CN 1; DA; DA3; DAB; DAC; DAM MST, NOV; DLB 9, 102, 329; EWL 3; LAIT 3; MAL 5; MTCW 1, 2; MTFW 2005; NFS 25; RGAL 4; RHW; SATA 1, 25; TUS

Buckler, Ernest 1908-1984 .... **CLC 13**
See also CA 11-12; 114; CAP 1; CCA 1; CN 1, 2, 3; DAC; DAM MST; DLB 68; SATA 47

Buckley, Christopher 1952- .... **CLC 165**
See also CA 139; CANR 119, 180

Buckley, Christopher Taylor
See Buckley, Christopher

Buckley, Vincent (Thomas)
1925-1988 .... **CLC 57**
See also CA 101; CP 1, 2, 3, 4; DLB 289

Buckley, William F., Jr. 1925-2008 ... **CLC 7, 18, 37**
See also AITN 1; BPFB 1; CA 1-4R; 269; CANR 1, 24, 53, 93, 133; CMW 4; CPW; DA3; DAM POP; DLB 137; DLBY 1980; INT CANR-24; MTCW 1, 2; MTFW 2005; TUS

Buckley, William Frank
See Buckley, William F., Jr.

Buckley, William Frank, Jr.
See Buckley, William F., Jr.

Buechner, Frederick 1926- ..... **CLC 2, 4, 6, 9**
See also AMWS 12; BPFB 1; CA 13-16R; CANR 11, 39, 64, 114, 138; CN 1, 2, 3, 4, 5, 6, 7; DAM NOV; DLBY 1980; INT CANR-11; MAL 5; MTCW 1, 2; MTFW 2005; TCLE 1:1

Buell, John (Edward) 1927- .... **CLC 10**
See also CA 1-4R; CANR 71; DLB 53

Buero Vallejo, Antonio 1916-2000 ... **CLC 15, 46, 139, 226; DC 18**
See also CA 106; 189; CANR 24, 49, 75; CWW 2; DFS 11; EWL 3; HW 1; MTCW 1, 2

Bufalino, Gesualdo 1920-1996 .... **CLC 74**
See also CA 209; CWW 2; DLB 196

Bugayev, Boris Nikolayevich
1880-1934 .... **PC 11; TCLC 7**
See Bely, Andrey; Belyi, Andrei
See also CA 104; 165; MTCW 2; MTFW 2005

Bukowski, Charles 1920-1994 ... **CLC 2, 5, 9, 41, 82, 108; PC 18; SSC 45**
See also CA 17-20R; 144; CANR 40, 62, 105, 180; CN 4, 5; CP 1, 2, 3, 4, 5; CPW; DA3; DAM NOV, POET; DLB 5, 130, 169; EWL 3; MAL 5; MTCW 1, 2; MTFW 2005; PFS 28

Bulgakov, Mikhail 1891-1940 .... **SSC 18; TCLC 2, 16, 159**
See also AAYA 74; BPFB 1; CA 105; 152; DAM DRAM, NOV; DLB 272; EWL 3; MTCW 2; MTFW 2005; NFS 8; RGSF 2; RGWL 2, 3; SFW 4; TWA

Bulgakov, Mikhail Afanasevich
See Bulgakov, Mikhail

Bulgya, Alexander Alexandrovich
1901-1956 .... **TCLC 53**
See Fadeev, Aleksandr Aleksandrovich; Fadeev, Alexandr Alexandrovich; Fadeyev, Alexander
See also CA 117; 181

Bullins, Ed 1935- ...... **BLC 1:1; CLC 1, 5, 7; DC 6**
See also BW 2, 3; CA 49-52; CAAS 16; CAD; CANR 24, 46, 73, 134; CD 5, 6; DAM DRAM, MULT; DLB 7, 38, 249; EWL 3; MAL 5; MTCW 1, 2; MTFW 2005; RGAL 4

Bulosan, Carlos 1911-1956 .... **AAL**
See also CA 216; DLB 312; RGAL 4

Bulwer-Lytton, Edward (George Earle Lytton) 1803-1873 .... **NCLC 1, 45**
See also DLB 21; RGEL 2; SFW 4; SUFW 1; TEA

Bunin, Ivan
See Bunin, Ivan Alexeyevich

Bunin, Ivan Alekseevich
See Bunin, Ivan Alexeyevich

Bunin, Ivan Alexeyevich 1870-1953 ... **SSC 5; TCLC 6**
See also CA 104; DLB 317, 329; EWL 3; RGSF 2; RGWL 2, 3; TWA

Bunting, Basil 1900-1985 ...... **CLC 10, 39, 47**
See also BRWS 7; CA 53-56; 115; CANR 7; CP 1, 2, 3, 4; DAM POET; DLB 20; EWL 3; RGEL 2

Bunuel, Luis 1900-1983 ... **CLC 16, 80; HLC 1**
See also CA 101; 110; CANR 32, 77; DAM MULT; HW 1

Bunyan, John 1628-1688 .. **LC 4, 69; WLC 1**
See also BRW 2; BYA 5; CDBLB 1660-1789; CLR 124; DA; DAB; DAC; DAM MST; DLB 39; RGEL 2; TEA; WCH; WLIT 3

Buravsky, Alexandr CLC 59

Burchill, Julie 1959- .... **CLC 238**
See also CA 135; CANR 115, 116

Burckhardt, Jacob (Christoph)
1818-1897 .... **NCLC 49**
See also EW 6

Burford, Eleanor
See Hibbert, Eleanor Alice Burford

Burgess, Anthony 1917-1993 . **CLC 1, 2, 4, 5, 8, 10, 13, 15, 22, 40, 62, 81, 94**
See also AAYA 25; AITN 1; BRWS 1; CA 1-4R; 143; CANR 2, 46; CDBLB 1960 to Present; CN 1, 2, 3, 4, 5; DA3; DAB; DAC; DAM NOV; DLB 14, 194, 261; DLBY 1998; EWL 3; MTCW 1, 2; MTFW 2005; NFS 15; RGEL 2; RHW; SFW 4; TEA; YAW

Buridan, John c. 1295-c. 1358 ...... **CMLC 97**

Burke, Edmund 1729(?)-1797 .... **LC 7, 36, 146; WLC 1**
See also BRW 3; DA; DA3; DAB; DAC; DAM MST; DLB 104, 252, 336; RGEL 2; TEA

Burke, Kenneth (Duva) 1897-1993 ... **CLC 2, 24**
See also AMW; CA 5-8R; 143; CANR 39, 74, 136; CN 1, 2; CP 1, 2, 3, 4, 5; DLB 45, 63; EWL 3; MAL 5; MTCW 1, 2; MTFW 2005; RGAL 4

Burke, Leda
See Garnett, David

Burke, Ralph
See Silverberg, Robert

Burke, Thomas 1886-1945 .... **TCLC 63**
See also CA 113; 155; CMW 4; DLB 197

Burney, Fanny 1752-1840 .... **NCLC 12, 54, 107**
See also BRWS 3; DLB 39; FL 1:2; NFS 16; RGEL 2; TEA

Burney, Frances
See Burney, Fanny

Burns, Robert 1759-1796 ... **LC 3, 29, 40; PC 6; WLC 1**
See also AAYA 51; BRW 3; CDBLB 1789-1832; DA; DA3; DAB; DAC; DAM MST, POET; DLB 109; EXPP; PAB; RGEL 2; TEA; WP

Burns, Tex
See L'Amour, Louis

Burnshaw, Stanley 1906-2005 ..... **CLC 3, 13, 44**
See also CA 9-12R; 243; CP 1, 2, 3, 4, 5, 6, 7; DLB 48; DLBY 1997

Burr, Anne 1937- .... **CLC 6**
See also CA 25-28R

Burroughs, Edgar Rice 1875-1950 . **TCLC 2, 32**
See also AAYA 11; BPFB 1; BYA 4, 9; CA 104; 132; CANR 131; DA3; DAM NOV; DLB 8; FANT; MTCW 1, 2; MTFW 2005; RGAL 4; SATA 41; SCFW 1, 2; SFW 4; TCWW 1, 2; TUS; YAW

Burroughs, William S. 1914-1997 . **CLC 1, 2, 5, 15, 22, 42, 75, 109; TCLC 121; WLC 1**
See Lee, William; Lee, Willy
See also AAYA 60; AITN 2; AMWS 3; BG 1:2; BPFB 1; CA 9-12R; 160; CANR 20, 52, 104; CN 1, 2, 3, 4, 5, 6; CPW; DA; DA3; DAB; DAC; DAM MST, NOV, POP; DLB 2, 8, 16, 152, 237; DLBY 1981, 1997; EWL 3; HGG; LMFS 2; MAL 5; MTCW 1, 2; MTFW 2005; RGAL 4; SFW 4

Burroughs, William Seward
See Burroughs, William S.

Burton, Sir Richard F(rancis)
1821-1890 .... **NCLC 42**
See also DLB 55, 166, 184; SSFS 21

Burton, Robert 1577-1640 .... **LC 74**
See also DLB 151; RGEL 2

Buruma, Ian 1951- .... **CLC 163**
See also CA 128; CANR 65, 141

Busch, Frederick 1941-2006 .. **CLC 7, 10, 18, 47, 166**
See also CA 33-36R; 248; CAAS 1; CANR 45, 73, 92, 157; CN 1, 2, 3, 4, 5, 6, 7; DLB 6, 218

Busch, Frederick Matthew
See Busch, Frederick

Bush, Barney (Furman) 1946- .... **NNAL**
See also CA 145

Bush, Ronald 1946- .... **CLC 34**
See also CA 136

Busia, Abena, P. A. 1953- .... **BLC 2:1**

Bustos, F(rancisco)
See Borges, Jorge Luis

Bustos Domecq, H(onorio)
See Bioy Casares, Adolfo; Borges, Jorge Luis

Butler, Octavia E. 1947-2006 .... **BLC 2:1; BLCS; CLC 38, 121, 230, 240**
See also AAYA 18, 48; AFAW 2; AMWS 13; BPFB 1; BW 2, 3; CA 73-76; 248; CANR 12, 24, 38, 73, 145, 240; CLR 65; CN 7; CPW; DA3; DAM MULT, POP; DLB 33; LATS 1:2; MTCW 1, 2; MTFW 2005; NFS 8, 21; SATA 84; SCFW 2; SFW 4; SSFS 6; TCLE 1:1; YAW

Butler, Octavia Estelle
See Butler, Octavia E.

Butler, Robert Olen, (Jr.) 1945- ...... **CLC 81, 162; SSC 117**
See also AMWS 12; BPFB 1; CA 112; CANR 66, 138; CN 7; CSW; DAM POP; DLB 173, 335; INT CA-112; MAL 5; MTCW 2; MTFW 2005; SSFS 11, 22

Butler, Samuel 1612-1680 .... **LC 16, 43**
See also DLB 101, 126; RGEL 2

Butler, Samuel 1835-1902 .... **TCLC 1, 33; WLC 1**
See also BRWS 2; CA 143; CDBLB 1890-1914; DA; DA3; DAB; DAC; DAM MST, NOV; DLB 18, 57, 174; RGEL 2; SFW 4; TEA

Butler, Walter C.
See Faust, Frederick (Schiller)

Butor, Michel (Marie Francois)
1926- .... **CLC 1, 3, 8, 11, 15, 161**
See also CA 9-12R; CANR 33, 66; CWW
2; DLB 83; EW 13; EWL 3; GFL 1789 to
the Present; MTCW 1, 2; MTFW 2005

Butts, Mary 1890(?)-1937 .... **TCLC 77**
See also CA 148; DLB 240

Buxton, Ralph
See Silverstein, Alvin; Silverstein, Virginia
B(arbara Opshelor)

Buzo, Alex
See Buzo, Alexander (John)
See also DLB 289

Buzo, Alexander (John) 1944- .... **CLC 61**
See also CA 97-100; CANR 17, 39, 69; CD
5, 6

Buzzati, Dino 1906-1972 .... **CLC 36**
See also CA 160; 33-36R; DLB 177; RGWL
2, 3; SFW 4

Byars, Betsy 1928- .... **CLC 35**
See also AAYA 19; BYA 3; CA 33-36R,
183; CAAE 183; CANR 18, 36, 57, 102,
148; CLR 1, 16, 72; DLB 52; INT CANR-
18; JRDA; MAICYA 1, 2; MAICYAS 1;
MTCW 1; SAAS 1; SATA 4, 46, 80, 163;
SATA-Essay 108; WYA; YAW

Byars, Betsy Cromer
See Byars, Betsy

Byatt, Antonia Susan Drabble
See Byatt, A.S.

Byatt, A.S. 1936- .... **CLC 19, 65, 136, 223;
SSC 91**
See also BPFB 1; BRWC 2; BRWS 4; CA
13-16R; CANR 13, 33, 50, 75, 96, 133;
CN 1, 2, 3, 4, 5, 6; DA3; DAM NOV,
POP; DLB 14, 194, 319, 326; EWL 3;
MTCW 1, 2; MTFW 2005; RGSF 2;
RHW; SSFS 26; TEA

Byrd, William II 1674-1744 .... **LC 112**
See also DLB 24, 140; RGAL 4

Byrne, David 1952- .... **CLC 26**
See also CA 127

Byrne, John Keyes 1926-
See Leonard, Hugh
See also CA 102; CANR 78, 140; INT CA-
102

Byron, George Gordon (Noel)
1788-1824 ..... **DC 24; NCLC 2, 12, 109,
149; PC 16; WLC 1**
See also AAYA 64; BRW 4; BRWC 2; CD-
BLB 1789-1832; DA; DA3; DAB; DAC;
DAM MST, POET; DLB 96, 110; EXPP;
LMFS 1; PAB; PFS 1, 14, 29; RGEL 2;
TEA; WLIT 3; WP

Byron, Robert 1905-1941 .... **TCLC 67**
See also CA 160; DLB 195

C. 3. 3.
See Wilde, Oscar

Caballero, Fernan 1796-1877 .... **NCLC 10**

Cabell, Branch
See Cabell, James Branch

Cabell, James Branch 1879-1958 .... **TCLC 6**
See also CA 105; 152; DLB 9, 78; FANT;
MAL 5; MTCW 2; RGAL 4; SUFW 1

Cabeza de Vaca, Alvar Nunez
1490-1557(?) .... **LC 61**

Cable, George Washington
1844-1925 .... **SSC 4; TCLC 4**
See also CA 104; 155; DLB 12, 74; DLBD
13; RGAL 4; TUS

Cabral de Melo Neto, Joao
1920-1999 .... **CLC 76**
See Melo Neto, Joao Cabral de
See also CA 151; DAM MULT; DLB 307;
LAW; LAWS 1

Cabrera Infante, G. 1929-2005 ... **CLC 5, 25,
45, 120; HLC 1; SSC 39**
See also CA 85-88; 236; CANR 29, 65, 110;
CDWLB 3; CWW 2; DA3; DAM MULT;
DLB 113; EWL 3; HW 1, 2; LAW; LAWS
1; MTCW 1, 2; MTFW 2005; RGSF 2;
WLIT 1

Cabrera Infante, Guillermo
See Cabrera Infante, G.

Cade, Toni
See Bambara, Toni Cade

Cadmus and Harmonia
See Buchan, John

Caedmon fl. 658-680 .... **CMLC 7**
See also DLB 146

Caeiro, Alberto
See Pessoa, Fernando

Caesar, Julius **CMLC 47**
See Julius Caesar
See also AW 1; RGWL 2, 3; WLIT 8

Cage, John (Milton), (Jr.)
1912-1992 .... **CLC 41; PC 58**
See also CA 13-16R; 169; CANR 9, 78;
DLB 193; INT CANR-9; TCLE 1:1

Cahan, Abraham 1860-1951 .... **TCLC 71**
See also CA 108; 154; DLB 9, 25, 28; MAL
5; RGAL 4

Cain, Christopher
See Fleming, Thomas

Cain, G.
See Cabrera Infante, G.

Cain, Guillermo
See Cabrera Infante, G.

Cain, James M(allahan) 1892-1977 .. **CLC 3,
11, 28**
See also AITN 1; BPFB 1; CA 17-20R; 73-
76; CANR 8, 34, 61; CMW 4; CN 1, 2;
DLB 226; EWL 3; MAL 5; MSW; MTCW
1; RGAL 4

Caine, Hall 1853-1931 .... **TCLC 97**
See also RHW

Caine, Mark
See Raphael, Frederic (Michael)

Calasso, Roberto 1941- .... **CLC 81**
See also CA 143; CANR 89

Calderon de la Barca, Pedro
1600-1681 . **DC 3; HLCS 1; LC 23, 136**
See also DFS 23; EW 2; RGWL 2, 3; TWA

Caldwell, Erskine 1903-1987 ... **CLC 1, 8, 14,
50, 60; SSC 19; TCLC 117**
See also AITN 1; AMW; BPFB 1; CA 1-4R;
121; CAAS 1; CANR 2, 33; CN 1, 2, 3,
4; DA3; DAM NOV; DLB 9, 86; EWL 3;
MAL 5; MTCW 1, 2; MTFW 2005;
RGAL 4; RGSF 2; TUS

Caldwell, (Janet Miriam) Taylor (Holland)
1900-1985 .... **CLC 2, 28, 39**
See also BPFB 1; CA 5-8R; 116; CANR 5;
DA3; DAM NOV, POP; DLBD 17;
MTCW 2; RHW

Calhoun, John Caldwell
1782-1850 .... **NCLC 15**
See also DLB 3, 248

Calisher, Hortense 1911- ..... **CLC 2, 4, 8, 38,
134; SSC 15**
See also CA 1-4R; CANR 1, 22, 117; CN
1, 2, 3, 4, 5, 6, 7; DA3; DLB
2, 218; INT CANR-22; MAL 5; MTCW
1, 2; MTFW 2005; RGAL 4; RGSF 2

Callaghan, Morley Edward
1903-1990 ..... **CLC 3, 14, 41, 65; TCLC
145**
See also CA 9-12R; 132; CANR 33, 73;
CN 1, 2, 3, 4; DAC; DAM MST; DLB
68; EWL 3; MTCW 1, 2; MTFW 2005;
RGEL 2; RGSF 2; SSFS 19

Callimachus c. 305B.C.-c.
240B.C. .... **CMLC 18**
See also AW 1; DLB 176; RGWL 2, 3

Calvin, Jean
See Calvin, John
See also DLB 327; GFL Beginnings to 1789

Calvin, John 1509-1564 .... **LC 37**
See Calvin, Jean

Calvino, Italo 1923-1985 .... **CLC 5, 8, 11, 22,
33, 39, 73; SSC 3, 48; TCLC 183**
See also AAYA 58; CA 85-88; 116; CANR
23, 61, 132; DAM NOV; DLB 196; EW
13; EWL 3; MTCW 1, 2; MTFW 2005;
RGHL; RGSF 2; RGWL 2, 3; SFW 4;
SSFS 12; WLIT 7

Camara Laye
See Laye, Camara
See also EWL 3

Camden, William 1551-1623 .... **LC 77**
See also DLB 172

Cameron, Carey 1952- .... **CLC 59**
See also CA 135

Cameron, Peter 1959- .... **CLC 44**
See also AMWS 12; CA 125; CANR 50,
117; DLB 234; GLL 2

Camoens, Luis Vaz de 1524(?)-1580
See Camoes, Luis de
See also EW 2

Camoes, Luis de 1524(?)-1580 . **HLCS 1; LC
62; PC 31**
See Camoens, Luis Vaz de
See also DLB 287; RGWL 2, 3

Camp, Madeleine L'Engle
See L'Engle, Madeleine

Campana, Dino 1885-1932 .... **TCLC 20**
See also CA 117; 246; DLB 114; EWL 3

Campanella, Tommaso 1568-1639 .... **LC 32**
See also RGWL 2, 3

Campbell, Bebe Moore 1950-2006 . **BLC 2:1;
CLC 246**
See also AAYA 26; BW 2, 3; CA 139; 254;
CANR 81, 134; DLB 227; MTCW 2;
MTFW 2005

Campbell, John Ramsey
See Campbell, Ramsey

Campbell, John W(ood, Jr.)
1910-1971 .... **CLC 32**
See also CA 21-22; 29-32R; CANR 34;
CAP 2; DLB 8; MTCW 1; SCFW 1, 2;
SFW 4

Campbell, Joseph 1904-1987 .... **CLC 69;
TCLC 140**
See also AAYA 3, 66; BEST 89:2; CA 1-4R;
124; CANR 3, 28, 61, 107; DA3; MTCW
1, 2

Campbell, Maria 1940- .... **CLC 85; NNAL**
See also CA 102; CANR 54; CCA 1; DAC

Campbell, Ramsey 1946- ... **CLC 42; SSC 19**
See also AAYA 51; CA 57-60, 228; CAAE
228; CANR 7, 102, 171; DLB 261; HGG;
INT CANR-7; SUFW 1, 2

Campbell, (Ignatius) Roy (Dunnachie)
1901-1957 .... **TCLC 5**
See also AFW; CA 104; 155; DLB 20, 225;
EWL 3; MTCW 2; RGEL 2

Campbell, Thomas 1777-1844 .... **NCLC 19**
See also DLB 93, 144; RGEL 2

Campbell, Wilfred **TCLC 9**
See Campbell, William

Campbell, William 1858(?)-1918
See Campbell, Wilfred
See also CA 106; DLB 92

Campbell, William Edward March
1893-1954
See March, William
See also CA 108

Campion, Jane 1954- .... **CLC 95, 229**
See also AAYA 33; CA 138; CANR 87

Campion, Thomas 1567-1620 . **LC 78; PC 87**
See also CDBLB Before 1660; DAM POET;
DLB 58, 172; RGEL 2

Camus, Albert 1913-1960 ...... **CLC 1, 2, 4, 9, 11, 14, 32, 63, 69, 124; DC 2; SSC 9, 76; WLC 1**
See also AAYA 36; AFW; BPFB 1; CA 89-92; CANR 131; DA; DA3; DAB; DAC; DAM DRAM, MST, NOV; DLB 72, 321, 329; EW 13; EWL 3; EXPN; EXPS; GFL 1789 to the Present; LATS 1:2; LMFS 2; MTCW 1, 2; MTFW 2005; NFS 6, 16; RGHL; RGSF 2; RGWL 2, 3; SSFS 4; TWA

Canby, Vincent 1924-2000 .... **CLC 13**
See also CA 81-84; 191

Cancale
See Desnos, Robert

Canetti, Elias 1905-1994 .. **CLC 3, 14, 25, 75, 86; TCLC 157**
See also CA 21-24R; 146; CANR 23, 61, 79; CDWLB 2; CWW 2; DA3; DLB 85, 124, 329; EW 12; EWL 3; MTCW 1, 2; MTFW 2005; RGWL 2, 3; TWA

Canfield, Dorothea F.
See Fisher, Dorothy (Frances) Canfield

Canfield, Dorothea Frances
See Fisher, Dorothy (Frances) Canfield

Canfield, Dorothy
See Fisher, Dorothy (Frances) Canfield

Canin, Ethan 1960- .... **CLC 55; SSC 70**
See also CA 131; 135; DLB 335; MAL 5

Cankar, Ivan 1876-1918 .... **TCLC 105**
See also CDWLB 4; DLB 147; EWL 3

Cannon, Curt
See Hunter, Evan

Cao, Lan 1961- .... **CLC 109**
See also CA 165

Cape, Judith
See Page, P(atricia) K(athleen)
See also CCA 1

Capek, Karel 1890-1938 .... **DC 1; SSC 36; TCLC 6, 37, 192; WLC 1**
See also CA 104; 140; CDWLB 4; DA; DA3; DAB; DAC; DAM DRAM, MST, NOV; DFS 7, 11; DLB 215; EW 10; EWL 3; MTCW 2; MTFW 2005; RGSF 2; RGWL 2, 3; SCFW 1, 2; SFW 4

Capella, Martianus fl. 4th cent. - .. **CMLC 84**

Capote, Truman 1924-1984 . **CLC 1, 3, 8, 13, 19, 34, 38, 58; SSC 2, 47, 93; TCLC 164; WLC 1**
See also AAYA 61; AMWS 3; BPFB 1; CA 5-8R; 113; CANR 18, 62; CDALB 1941-1968; CN 1, 2, 3; CPW; DA; DA3; DAB; DAC; DAM MST, NOV, POP; DLB 2, 185, 227; DLBY 1980, 1984; EWL 3; EXPS; GLL 1; LAIT 3; MAL 5; MTCW 1, 2; MTFW 2005; NCFS 2; RGAL 4; RGSF 2; SATA 91; SSFS 2; TUS

Capra, Frank 1897-1991 .... **CLC 16**
See also AAYA 52; CA 61-64; 135

Caputo, Philip 1941- .... **CLC 32**
See also AAYA 60; CA 73-76; CANR 40, 135; YAW

Caragiale, Ion Luca 1852-1912 ...... **TCLC 76**
See also CA 157

Card, Orson Scott 1951- .... **CLC 44, 47, 50**
See also AAYA 11, 42; BPFB 1; BYA 5, 8; CA 102; CANR 27, 47, 73, 102, 106, 133, 184; CLR 116; CPW; DA3; DAM POP; FANT; INT CANR-27; MTCW 1, 2; MTFW 2005; NFS 5; SATA 83, 127; SCFW 2; SFW 4; SUFW 2; YAW

Cardenal, Ernesto 1925- .... **CLC 31, 161; HLC 1; PC 22**
See also CA 49-52; CANR 2, 32, 66, 138; CWW 2; DAM MULT, POET; DLB 290; EWL 3; HW 1, 2; LAWS 1; MTCW 1, 2; MTFW 2005; RGWL 2, 3

Cardinal, Marie 1929-2001 .... **CLC 189**
See also CA 177; CWW 2; DLB 83; FW

Cardozo, Benjamin N(athan) 1870-1938 .... **TCLC 65**
See also CA 117; 164

Carducci, Giosue (Alessandro Giuseppe) 1835-1907 .... **PC 46; TCLC 32**
See also CA 163; DLB 329; EW 7; RGWL 2, 3

Carew, Thomas 1595(?)-1640 ..... **LC 13, 159; PC 29**
See also BRW 2; DLB 126; PAB; RGEL 2

Carey, Ernestine Gilbreth 1908-2006 .... **CLC 17**
See also CA 5-8R; 254; CANR 71; SATA 2; SATA-Obit 177

Carey, Peter 1943- .... **CLC 40, 55, 96, 183**
See also BRWS 12; CA 123; 127; CANR 53, 76, 117, 157; CN 4, 5, 6, 7; DLB 289, 326; EWL 3; INT CA-127; MTCW 1, 2; MTFW 2005; RGSF 2; SATA 94

Carey, Peter Philip
See Carey, Peter

Carleton, William 1794-1869 ... **NCLC 3, 199**
See also DLB 159; RGEL 2; RGSF 2

Carlisle, Henry (Coffin) 1926- .... **CLC 33**
See also CA 13-16R; CANR 15, 85

Carlsen, Chris
See Holdstock, Robert

Carlson, Ron 1947- .... **CLC 54**
See also CA 105, 189; CAAE 189; CANR 27, 155; DLB 244

Carlson, Ronald F.
See Carlson, Ron

Carlyle, Jane Welsh 1801-1866 ... **NCLC 181**
See also DLB 55

Carlyle, Thomas 1795-1881 ..... **NCLC 22, 70**
See also BRW 4; CDBLB 1789-1832; DA; DAB; DAC; DAM MST; DLB 55, 144, 254, 338; RGEL 2; TEA

Carman, (William) Bliss 1861-1929 ... **PC 34; TCLC 7**
See also CA 104; 152; DAC; DLB 92; RGEL 2

Carnegie, Dale 1888-1955 .... **TCLC 53**
See also CA 218

Carossa, Hans 1878-1956 .... **TCLC 48**
See also CA 170; DLB 66; EWL 3

Carpenter, Don(ald Richard) 1931-1995 .... **CLC 41**
See also CA 45-48; 149; CANR 1, 71

Carpenter, Edward 1844-1929 .... **TCLC 88**
See also BRWS 13; CA 163; GLL 1

Carpenter, John (Howard) 1948- ... **CLC 161**
See also AAYA 2, 73; CA 134; SATA 58

Carpenter, Johnny
See Carpenter, John (Howard)

Carpentier (y Valmont), Alejo 1904-1980 . **CLC 8, 11, 38, 110; HLC 1; SSC 35; TCLC 201**
See also CA 65-68; 97-100; CANR 11, 70; CDWLB 3; DAM MULT; DLB 113; EWL 3; HW 1, 2; LAW; LMFS 2; RGSF 2; RGWL 2, 3; WLIT 1

Carr, Caleb 1955- .... **CLC 86**
See also CA 147; CANR 73, 134; DA3

Carr, Emily 1871-1945 .... **TCLC 32**
See also CA 159; DLB 68; FW; GLL 2

Carr, John Dickson 1906-1977 .... **CLC 3**
See Fairbairn, Roger
See also CA 49-52; 69-72; CANR 3, 33, 60; CMW 4; DLB 306; MSW; MTCW 1, 2

Carr, Philippa
See Hibbert, Eleanor Alice Burford

Carr, Virginia Spencer 1929- .... **CLC 34**
See also CA 61-64; CANR 175; DLB 111

Carrere, Emmanuel 1957- .... **CLC 89**
See also CA 200

Carrier, Roch 1937- .... **CLC 13, 78**
See also CA 130; CANR 61, 152; CCA 1; DAC; DAM MST; DLB 53; SATA 105, 166

Carroll, James Dennis
See Carroll, Jim

Carroll, James P. 1943(?)- .... **CLC 38**
See also CA 81-84; CANR 73, 139; MTCW 2; MTFW 2005

Carroll, Jim 1951- .... **CLC 35, 143**
See also AAYA 17; CA 45-48; CANR 42, 115; NCFS 5

Carroll, Lewis **NCLC 2, 53, 139; PC 18, 74; WLC 1**
See Dodgson, Charles L(utwidge)
See also AAYA 39; BRW 5; BYA 5, 13; CD-BLB 1832-1890; CLR 2, 18, 108; DLB 18, 163, 178; DLBY 1998; EXPN; EXPP; FANT; JRDA; LAIT 1; NFS 27; PFS 11; RGEL 2; SUFW 1; TEA; WCH

Carroll, Paul Vincent 1900-1968 ...... **CLC 10**
See also CA 9-12R; 25-28R; DLB 10; EWL 3; RGEL 2

Carruth, Hayden 1921-2008 .... **CLC 4, 7, 10, 18, 84; PC 10**
See also AMWS 16; CA 9-12R; CANR 4, 38, 59, 110, 174; CP 1, 2, 3, 4, 5, 6, 7; DLB 5, 165; INT CANR-4; MTCW 1, 2; MTFW 2005; PFS 26; SATA 47

Carson, Anne 1950- .... **CLC 185; PC 64**
See also AMWS 12; CA 203; CP 7; DLB 193; PFS 18; TCLE 1:1

Carson, Ciaran 1948- .... **CLC 201**
See also BRWS 13; CA 112; 153; CANR 113; CP 6, 7; PFS 26

Carson, Rachel
See Carson, Rachel Louise
See also AAYA 49; DLB 275

Carson, Rachel Louise 1907-1964 .... **CLC 71**
See Carson, Rachel
See also AMWS 9; ANW; CA 77-80; CANR 35; DA3; DAM POP; FW; LAIT 4; MAL 5; MTCW 1, 2; MTFW 2005; NCFS 1; SATA 23

Cartagena, Teresa de 1425(?)- .... **LC 155**
See also DLB 286

Carter, Angela 1940-1992 ...... **CLC 5, 41, 76; SSC 13, 85; TCLC 139**
See also BRWS 3; CA 53-56; 136; CANR 12, 36, 61, 106; CN 3, 4, 5; DA3; DLB 14, 207, 261, 319; EXPS; FANT; FW; GL 2; MTCW 1, 2; MTFW 2005; RGSF 2; SATA 66; SATA-Obit 70; SFW 4; SSFS 4, 12; SUFW 2; WLIT 4

Carter, Angela Olive
See Carter, Angela

Carter, Martin (Wylde) 1927- .... **BLC 2:1**
See also BW 2; CA 102; CANR 42; CD-WLB 3; CP 1, 2, 3, 4, 5, 6; DLB 117; EWL 3

Carter, Nick
See Smith, Martin Cruz

Carter, Nick
See Smith, Martin Cruz

Carver, Raymond 1938-1988 ..... **CLC 22, 36, 53, 55, 126; PC 54; SSC 8, 51, 104**
See also AAYA 44; AMWS 3; BPFB 1; CA 33-36R; 126; CANR 17, 34, 61, 103; CN 4; CPW; DA3; DAM NOV; DLB 130; DLBY 1984, 1988; EWL 3; MAL 5; MTCW 1, 2; MTFW 2005; PFS 17; RGAL 4; RGSF 2; SSFS 3, 6, 12, 13, 23; TCLE 1:1; TCWW 2; TUS

Cary, Elizabeth, Lady Falkland 1585-1639 .... **LC 30, 141**

Cary, (Arthur) Joyce (Lunel) 1888-1957 .... **TCLC 1, 29, 196**
See also BRW 7; CA 104; 164; CDBLB 1914-1945; DLB 15, 100; EWL 3; MTCW 2; RGEL 2; TEA

Casal, Julian del 1863-1893 .... **NCLC 131**
See also DLB 283; LAW
Casanova, Giacomo
See Casanova de Seingalt, Giovanni Jacopo
See also WLIT 7
Casanova, Giovanni Giacomo
See Casanova de Seingalt, Giovanni Jacopo
Casanova de Seingalt, Giovanni Jacopo
1725-1798 .... **LC 13, 151**
See Casanova, Giacomo
Casares, Adolfo Bioy
See Bioy Casares, Adolfo
See also RGSF 2
Casas, Bartolome de las 1474-1566
See Las Casas, Bartolome de
See also WLIT 1
Case, John
See Hougan, Carolyn
Casely-Hayford, J(oseph) E(phraim)
1866-1903 .... **BLC 1:1; TCLC 24**
See also BW 2; CA 123; 152; DAM MULT
Casey, John (Dudley) 1939- .... **CLC 59**
See also BEST 90:2; CA 69-72; CANR 23,
100
Casey, Michael 1947- .... **CLC 2**
See also CA 65-68; CANR 109; CP 2, 3;
DLB 5
Casey, Patrick
See Thurman, Wallace (Henry)
Casey, Warren (Peter) 1935-1988 .... **CLC 12**
See also CA 101; 127; INT CA-101
Casona, Alejandro **CLC 49; DC 32; TCLC**
199
See Alvarez, Alejandro Rodriguez
See also EWL 3
Cassavetes, John 1929-1989 .... **CLC 20**
See also CA 85-88; 127; CANR 82
Cassian, Nina 1924- .... **PC 17**
See also CWP; CWW 2
Cassill, R(onald) V(erlin)
1919-2002 .... **CLC 4, 23**
See also CA 9-12R; 208; CAAS 1; CANR
7, 45; CN 1, 2, 3, 4, 5, 6, 7; DLB 6, 218;
DLBY 2002
Cassiodorus, Flavius Magnus c. 490(?)-c.
583(?) .... **CMLC 43**
Cassirer, Ernst 1874-1945 .... **TCLC 61**
See also CA 157
Cassity, (Allen) Turner 1929- .... **CLC 6, 42**
See also CA 17-20R; 223; CAAE 223;
CAAS 8; CANR 11; CSW; DLB 105
Cassius Dio c. 155-c. 229 .... **CMLC 99**
See also DLB 176
Castaneda, Carlos (Cesar Aranha)
1931(?)-1998 .... **CLC 12, 119**
See also CA 25-28R; CANR 32, 66, 105;
DNFS 1; HW 1; MTCW 1
Castedo, Elena 1937- .... **CLC 65**
See also CA 132
Castedo-Ellerman, Elena
See Castedo, Elena
Castellanos, Rosario 1925-1974 .... **CLC 66;**
HLC 1; SSC 39, 68
See also CA 131; 53-56; CANR 58; CD-
WLB 3; DAM MULT; DLB 113, 290;
EWL 3; FW; HW 1; LAW; MTCW 1, 2;
MTFW 2005; RGSF 2; RGWL 2, 3
Castelvetro, Lodovico 1505-1571 .... **LC 12**
Castiglione, Baldassare 1478-1529 ...... **LC 12**
See Castiglione, Baldesar
See also LMFS 1; RGWL 2, 3
Castiglione, Baldesar
See Castiglione, Baldassare
See also EW 2; WLIT 7
Castillo, Ana 1953- .... **CLC 151**
See also AAYA 42; CA 131; CANR 51, 86,
128, 172; CWP; DLB 122, 227; DNFS 2;
FW; HW 1; LLW; PFS 21

Castillo, Ana Hernandez Del
See Castillo, Ana
Castle, Robert
See Hamilton, Edmond
Castro (Ruz), Fidel 1926(?)- .... **HLC 1**
See also CA 110; 129; CANR 81; DAM
MULT; HW 2
Castro, Guillen de 1569-1631 .... **LC 19**
Castro, Rosalia de 1837-1885 ... **NCLC 3, 78;**
PC 41
See also DAM MULT
Castro Alves, Antonio de
1847-1871 .... **NCLC 205**
See also DLB 307; LAW
Cather, Willa (Sibert) 1873-1947 . **SSC 2, 50,**
114; TCLC 1, 11, 31, 99, 132, 152;
WLC 1
See also AAYA 24; AMW; AMWC 1;
AMWR 1; BPFB 1; CA 104; 128; CDALB
1865-1917; CLR 98; DA; DA3; DAB;
DAC; DAM MST, NOV; DLB 9, 54, 78,
256; DLBD 1; EWL 3; EXPN; EXPS; FL
1:5; LAIT 3; LATS 1:1; MAL 5; MBL;
MTCW 1, 2; MTFW 2005; NFS 2, 19;
RGAL 4; RGSF 2; RHW; SATA 30; SSFS
2, 7, 16; TCWW 1, 2; TUS
Catherine II
See Catherine the Great
See also DLB 150
Catherine, Saint 1347-1380 ..... **CMLC 27, 95**
Catherine the Great 1729-1796 .... **LC 69**
See Catherine II
Cato, Marcus Porcius
234B.C.-149B.C. .... **CMLC 21**
See Cato the Elder
Cato, Marcus Porcius, the Elder
See Cato, Marcus Porcius
Cato the Elder
See Cato, Marcus Porcius
See also DLB 211
Catton, (Charles) Bruce 1899-1978 . **CLC 35**
See also AITN 1; CA 5-8R; 81-84; CANR
7, 74; DLB 17; MTCW 2; MTFW 2005;
SATA 2; SATA-Obit 24
Catullus c. 84B.C.-54B.C. .... **CMLC 18**
See also AW 2; CDWLB 1; DLB 211;
RGWL 2, 3; WLIT 8
Cauldwell, Frank
See King, Francis (Henry)
Caunitz, William J. 1933-1996 .... **CLC 34**
See also BEST 89:3; CA 125; 130; 152;
CANR 73; INT CA-130
Causley, Charles (Stanley)
1917-2003 .... **CLC 7**
See also CA 9-12R; 223; CANR 5, 35, 94;
CLR 30; CP 1, 2, 3, 4, 5; CWRI 5; DLB
27; MTCW 1; SATA 3, 66; SATA-Obit
149
Caute, (John) David 1936- .... **CLC 29**
See also CA 1-4R; CAAS 4; CANR 1, 33,
64, 120; CBD; CD 5, 6; CN 1, 2, 3, 4, 5,
6, 7; DAM NOV; DLB 14, 231
Cavafy, C(onstantine) P(eter) **PC 36; TCLC**
2, 7
See Kavafis, Konstantinos Petrou
See also CA 148; DA3; DAM POET; EW
8; EWL 3; MTCW 2; PFS 19; RGWL 2,
3; WP
Cavalcanti, Guido c. 1250-c.
1300 .... **CMLC 54**
See also RGWL 2, 3; WLIT 7
Cavallo, Evelyn
See Spark, Muriel
Cavanna, Betty **CLC 12**
See Harrison, Elizabeth (Allen) Cavanna
See also JRDA; MAICYA; SAAS 4;
SATA 1, 30

Cavendish, Margaret Lucas
1623-1673 .... **LC 30, 132**
See also DLB 131, 252, 281; RGEL 2
Caxton, William 1421(?)-1491(?) .... **LC 17**
See also DLB 170
Cayer, D. M.
See Duffy, Maureen (Patricia)
Cayrol, Jean 1911-2005 .... **CLC 11**
See also CA 89-92; 236; DLB 83; EWL 3
Cela (y Trulock), Camilo Jose
See Cela, Camilo Jose
See also CWW 2
Cela, Camilo Jose 1916-2002 .... **CLC 4, 13,**
59, 122; HLC 1; SSC 71
See Cela (y Trulock), Camilo Jose
See also BEST 90:2; CA 21-24R; 206;
CAAS 10; CANR 21, 32, 76, 139; DAM
MULT; DLB 322; DLBY 1989; EW 13;
EWL 3; HW 1; MTCW 1, 2; MTFW
2005; RGSF 2; RGWL 2, 3
Celan, Paul **CLC 10, 19, 53, 82; PC 10**
See Antschel, Paul
See also CDWLB 2; DLB 69; EWL 3;
RGHL; RGWL 2, 3
Celine, Louis-Ferdinand **CLC 1, 3, 4, 7, 9,**
15, 47, 124
See Destouches, Louis-Ferdinand
See also DLB 72; EW 11; EWL 3; GFL
1789 to the Present; RGWL 2, 3
Cellini, Benvenuto 1500-1571 .... **LC 7**
See also WLIT 7
Cendrars, Blaise **CLC 18, 106**
See Sauser-Hall, Frederic
See also DLB 258; EWL 3; GFL 1789 to
the Present; RGWL 2, 3; WP
Centlivre, Susanna 1669(?)-1723 .... **DC 25;**
LC 65
See also DLB 84; RGEL 2
Cernuda (y Bidon), Luis
1902-1963 .... **CLC 54; PC 62**
See also CA 131; 89-92; DAM POET; DLB
134; EWL 3; GLL 1; HW 1; RGWL 2, 3
Cervantes, Lorna Dee 1954- ..... **HLCS 1; PC**
35
See also CA 131; CANR 80; CP 7; CWP;
DLB 82; EXPP; HW 1; LLW
Cervantes (Saavedra), Miguel de
1547-1616 ...... **HLCS; LC 6, 23, 93; SSC**
12, 108; WLC 1
See also AAYA 56; BYA 1, 14; DA; DAB;
DAC; DAM MST, NOV; EW 2; LAIT 1;
LATS 1:1; LMFS 1; NFS 8; RGSF 2;
RGWL 2, 3; TWA
Cesaire, Aime
See Cesaire, Aime
Cesaire, Aime 1913-2008 .... **BLC 1:1; CLC**
19, 32, 112; DC 22; PC 25
See also BW 2, 3; CA 65-68; 271; CANR
24, 43, 81; CWW 2; DA3; DAM MULT,
POET; DLB 321; EWL 3; GFL 1789 to
the Present; MTCW 1, 2; MTFW 2005;
WP
Cesaire, Aime Fernand
See Cesaire, Aime
Chaadaev, Petr Iakovlevich
1794-1856 .... **NCLC 197**
See also DLB 198
Chabon, Michael 1963- ... **CLC 55, 149, 265;**
SSC 59
See also AAYA 45; AMWS 11; CA 139;
CANR 57, 96, 127, 138; DLB 278; MAL
5; MTFW 2005; NFS 25; SATA 145
Chabrol, Claude 1930- .... **CLC 16**
See also CA 110
Chairil Anwar
See Anwar, Chairil
See also EWL 3

Challans, Mary 1905-1983
See Renault, Mary
See also CA 81-84; 111; CANR 74; DA3;
MTCW 2; MTFW 2005; SATA 23; SATA-
Obit 36; TEA

Challis, George
See Faust, Frederick (Schiller)

Chambers, Aidan 1934- .... **CLC 35**
See also AAYA 27; CA 25-28R; CANR 12,
31, 58, 116; JRDA; MAICYA 1, 2; SAAS
12; SATA 1, 69, 108, 171; WYA; YAW

Chambers, James 1948-
See Cliff, Jimmy
See also CA 124

Chambers, Jessie
See Lawrence, D(avid) H(erbert Richards)
See also GLL 1

Chambers, Robert W(illiam)
1865-1933 .... **SSC 92; TCLC 41**
See also CA 165; DLB 202; HGG; SATA
107; SUFW 1

Chambers, (David) Whittaker
1901-1961 .... **TCLC 129**
See also CA 89-92; DLB 303

Chamisso, Adelbert von
1781-1838 .... **NCLC 82**
See also DLB 90; RGWL 2, 3; SUFW 1

Chance, James T.
See Carpenter, John (Howard)

Chance, John T.
See Carpenter, John (Howard)

Chandler, Raymond (Thornton)
1888-1959 .... **SSC 23; TCLC 1, 7, 179**
See also AAYA 25; AMWC 2; AMWS 4;
BPFB 1; CA 104; 129; CANR 60, 107;
CDALB 1929-1941; CMW 4; DA3; DLB
226, 253; DLBD 6; EWL 3; MAL 5;
MSW; MTCW 1, 2; MTFW 2005; NFS
17; RGAL 4; TUS

Chang, Diana 1934- .... **AAL**
See also CA 228; CWP; DLB 312; EXPP

Chang, Eileen 1920-1995 .... **AAL; SSC 28;
TCLC 184**
See also CA 166; CANR 168; CWW 2;
DLB 328; EWL 3; RGSF 2

Chang, Jung 1952- .... **CLC 71**
See also CA 142

Chang Ai-Ling
See Chang, Eileen

Channing, William Ellery
1780-1842 .... **NCLC 17**
See also DLB 1, 59, 235; RGAL 4

Chao, Patricia 1955- .... **CLC 119**
See also CA 163; CANR 155

Chaplin, Charles Spencer
1889-1977 .... **CLC 16**
See Chaplin, Charlie
See also CA 81-84; 73-76

Chaplin, Charlie
See Chaplin, Charles Spencer
See also AAYA 61; DLB 44

Chapman, George 1559(?)-1634 . **DC 19; LC
22, 116**
See also BRW 1; DAM DRAM; DLB 62,
121; LMFS 1; RGEL 2

Chapman, Graham 1941-1989 .... **CLC 21**
See Monty Python
See also CA 116; 129; CANR 35, 95

Chapman, John Jay 1862-1933 .... **TCLC 7**
See also AMWS 14; CA 104; 191

Chapman, Lee
See Bradley, Marion Zimmer
See also GLL 1

Chapman, Walker
See Silverberg, Robert

Chappell, Fred (Davis) 1936- .... **CLC 40, 78,
162**
See also CA 5-8R, 198; CAAE 198; CAAS
4; CANR 8, 33, 67, 110; CN 6; CP 6, 7;
CSW; DLB 6, 105; HGG

Char, Rene(-Emile) 1907-1988 .... **CLC 9, 11,
14, 55; PC 56**
See also CA 13-16R; 124; CANR 32; DAM
POET; DLB 258; EWL 3; GFL 1789 to
the Present; MTCW 1, 2; RGWL 2, 3

Charby, Jay
See Ellison, Harlan

Chardin, Pierre Teilhard de
See Teilhard de Chardin, (Marie Joseph)
Pierre

Chariton fl. 1st cent. (?)- .... **CMLC 49**

Charlemagne 742-814 .... **CMLC 37**

Charles I 1600-1649 .... **LC 13**

Charriere, Isabelle de 1740-1805 .. **NCLC 66**
See also DLB 313

Chartier, Alain c. 1392-1430 .... **LC 94**
See also DLB 208

Chartier, Emile-Auguste
See Alain

Charyn, Jerome 1937- .... **CLC 5, 8, 18**
See also CA 5-8R; CAAS 1; CANR 7, 61,
101, 158; CMW 4; CN 1, 2, 3, 4, 5, 6, 7;
DLBY 1983; MTCW 1

Chase, Adam
See Marlowe, Stephen

Chase, Mary (Coyle) 1907-1981 .... **DC 1**
See also CA 77-80; 105; CAD; CWD; DFS
11; DLB 228; SATA 17; SATA-Obit 29

Chase, Mary Ellen 1887-1973 .... **CLC 2;
TCLC 124**
See also CA 13-16; 41-44R; CAP 1; SATA
10

Chase, Nicholas
See Hyde, Anthony
See also CCA 1

Chase-Riboud, Barbara (Dewayne Tosi)
1939- .... **BLC 2:1**
See also BW 2; CA 113; CANR 76; DAM
MULT; DLB 33; MTCW 2

Chateaubriand, Francois Rene de
1768-1848 .... **NCLC 3, 134**
See also DLB 119; EW 5; GFL 1789 to the
Present; RGWL 2, 3; TWA

Chatelet, Gabrielle-Emilie Du
See du Chatelet, Emilie
See also DLB 313

Chatterje, Sarat Chandra 1876-1936(?)
See Chatterji, Saratchandra
See also CA 109

Chatterji, Bankim Chandra
1838-1894 .... **NCLC 19**

Chatterji, Saratchandra **TCLC 13**
See Chatterje, Sarat Chandra
See also CA 186; EWL 3

Chatterton, Thomas 1752-1770 .... **LC 3, 54**
See also DAM POET; DLB 109; RGEL 2

Chatwin, (Charles) Bruce
1940-1989 .... **CLC 28, 57, 59**
See also AAYA 4; BEST 90:1; BRWS 4;
CA 85-88; 127; CPW; DAM POP; DLB
194, 204; EWL 3; MTFW 2005

Chaucer, Daniel
See Ford, Ford Madox
See also RHW

Chaucer, Geoffrey 1340(?)-1400 .. **LC 17, 56;
PC 19, 58; WLCS**
See also BRW 1; BRWC 1; BRWR 2; CD-
BLB Before 1660; DA; DA3; DAB;
DAC; DAM MST, POET; DLB 146;
LAIT 1; PAB; PFS 14; RGEL 2; TEA;
WLIT 3; WP

Chavez, Denise 1948- .... **HLC 1**
See also CA 131; CANR 56, 81, 137; DAM
MULT; DLB 122; FW; HW 1, 2; LLW;
MAL 5; MTCW 2; MTFW 2005

Chaviaras, Strates 1935-
See Haviaras, Stratis
See also CA 105

Chayefsky, Paddy **CLC 23**
See Chayefsky, Sidney
See also CAD; DLB 7, 44; DLBY 1981;
RGAL 4

Chayefsky, Sidney 1923-1981
See Chayefsky, Paddy
See also CA 9-12R; 104; CANR 18; DAM
DRAM

Chedid, Andree 1920- .... **CLC 47**
See also CA 145; CANR 95; EWL 3

Cheever, John 1912-1982 ..... **CLC 3, 7, 8, 11,
15, 25, 64; SSC 1, 38, 57; WLC 2**
See also AAYA 65; AMWS 1; BPFB 1; CA
5-8R; 106; CABS 1; CANR 5, 27, 76;
CDALB 1941-1968; CN 1, 2, 3; CPW;
DA; DA3; DAB; DAC; DAM MST, NOV,
POP; DLB 2, 102, 227; DLBY 1980,
1982; EWL 3; EXPS; INT CANR-5;
MAL 5; MTCW 1, 2; MTFW 2005;
RGAL 4; RGSF 2; SSFS 2, 14; TUS

Cheever, Susan 1943- .... **CLC 18, 48**
See also CA 103; CANR 27, 51, 92, 157;
DLBY 1982; INT CANR-27

Chekhonte, Antosha
See Chekhov, Anton (Pavlovich)

Chekhov, Anton (Pavlovich)
1860-1904 .... **DC 9; SSC 2, 28, 41, 51,
85, 102; TCLC 3, 10, 31, 55, 96, 163;
WLC 2**
See also AAYA 68; BYA 14; CA 104; 124;
DA; DA3; DAB; DAC; DAM DRAM,
MST; DFS 1, 5, 10, 12; DLB 277; EW 7;
EWL 3; EXPS; LAIT 3; LATS 1:1; RGSF
2; RGWL 2, 3; SATA 90; SSFS 5, 13, 14,
26; TWA

Cheney, Lynne V. 1941- .... **CLC 70**
See also CA 89-92; CANR 58, 117; SATA
152

Chernyshevsky, Nikolai Gavrilovich
See Chernyshevsky, Nikolay Gavrilovich
See also DLB 238

Chernyshevsky, Nikolay Gavrilovich
1828-1889 .... **NCLC 1**
See Chernyshevsky, Nikolai Gavrilovich

Cherry, Carolyn Janice **CLC 35**
See Cherryh, C.J.
See also AAYA 24; BPFB 1; DLBY 1980;
FANT; SATA 93; SCFW 2; SFW 4; YAW

Cherryh, C.J. 1942-
See Cherry, Carolyn Janice
See also CA 65-68; CANR 10, 147, 179;
SATA 172

Chesler, Phyllis 1940- .... **CLC 247**
See also CA 49-52; CANR 4, 59, 140; FW

Chesnutt, Charles W(addell)
1858-1932 .... **BLC 1; SSC 7, 54; TCLC
5, 39**
See also AFAW 1, 2; AMWS 14; BW 1, 3;
CA 106; 125; CANR 76; DAM MULT;
DLB 12, 50, 78; EWL 3; MAL 5; MTCW
1, 2; MTFW 2005; RGAL 4; RGSF 2;
SSFS 11, 26

Chester, Alfred 1929(?)-1971 .... **CLC 49**
See also CA 196; 33-36R; DLB 130; MAL
5

Chesterton, G(ilbert) K(eith)
1874-1936 . **PC 28; SSC 1, 46; TCLC 1,
6, 64**
See also AAYA 57; BRW 6; CA 104; 132;
CANR 73, 131; CDBLB 1914-1945;
CMW 4; DAM NOV, POET; DLB 10, 19,

34, 70, 98, 149, 178; EWL 3; FANT; MSW; MTCW 1, 2; MTFW 2005; RGEL 2; RGSF 2; SATA 27; SUFW 1

Chettle, Henry 1560-1607(?) .... **LC 112**
See also DLB 136; RGEL 2

Chiang, Pin-chin 1904-1986
See Ding Ling
See also CA 118

Chief Joseph 1840-1904 .... **NNAL**
See also CA 152; DA3; DAM MULT

Chief Seattle 1786(?)-1866 .... **NNAL**
See also DA3; DAM MULT

Ch'ien, Chung-shu 1910-1998 .... **CLC 22**
See Qian Zhongshu
See also CA 130; CANR 73; MTCW 1, 2

Chikamatsu Monzaemon 1653-1724 ... **LC 66**
See also RGWL 2, 3

Child, Francis James 1825-1896 . **NCLC 173**
See also DLB 1, 64, 235

Child, L. Maria
See Child, Lydia Maria

Child, Lydia Maria 1802-1880 .. **NCLC 6, 73**
See also DLB 1, 74, 243; RGAL 4; SATA 67

Child, Mrs.
See Child, Lydia Maria

Child, Philip 1898-1978 .... **CLC 19, 68**
See also CA 13-14; CAP 1; CP 1; DLB 68; RHW; SATA 47

Childers, (Robert) Erskine
1870-1922 .... **TCLC 65**
See also CA 113; 153; DLB 70

Childress, Alice 1920-1994 .... **BLC 1:1; CLC 12, 15, 86, 96; DC 4; TCLC 116**
See also AAYA 8; BW 2, 3; BYA 2; CA 45-48; 146; CAD; CANR 3, 27, 50, 74; CLR 14; CWD; DA3; DAM DRAM, MULT, NOV; DFS 2, 8, 14; DLB 7, 38, 249; JRDA; LAIT 5; MAICYA 1, 2; MAIC-YAS 1; MAL 5; MTCW 1, 2; MTFW 2005; RGAL 4; SATA 7, 48, 81; TUS; WYA; YAW

Chin, Frank (Chew, Jr.) 1940- .... **AAL; CLC 135; DC 7**
See also CA 33-36R; CAD; CANR 71; CD 5, 6; DAM MULT; DLB 206, 312; LAIT 5; RGAL 4

Chin, Marilyn (Mei Ling) 1955- .... **PC 40**
See also CA 129; CANR 70, 113; CWP; DLB 312; PFS 28

Chislett, (Margaret) Anne 1943- ...... **CLC 34**
See also CA 151

Chitty, Thomas Willes 1926- .... **CLC 11**
See Hinde, Thomas
See also CA 5-8R; CN 7

Chivers, Thomas Holley
1809-1858 .... **NCLC 49**
See also DLB 3, 248; RGAL 4

Choi, Susan 1969- .... **CLC 119**
See also CA 223

Chomette, Rene Lucien 1898-1981
See Clair, Rene
See also CA 103

Chomsky, Avram Noam
See Chomsky, Noam

Chomsky, Noam 1928- .... **CLC 132**
See also CA 17-20R; CANR 28, 62, 110, 132, 179; DA3; DLB 246; MTCW 1, 2; MTFW 2005

Chona, Maria 1845(?)-1936 .... **NNAL**
See also CA 144

Chopin, Kate **SSC 8, 68, 110; TCLC 127; WLCS**
See Chopin, Katherine
See also AAYA 33; AMWR 2; AMWS 1; BYA 11, 15; CDALB 1865-1917; DA; DAB; DLB 12, 78; EXPN; EXPS; FL 1:3; FW; LAIT 3; MAL 5; MBL; NFS 3; RGAL 4; RGSF 2; SSFS 2, 13, 17, 26; TUS

Chopin, Katherine 1851-1904
See Chopin, Kate
See also CA 104; 122; DA3; DAC; DAM MST, NOV

Chretien de Troyes c. 12th cent. - . **CMLC 10**
See also DLB 208; EW 1; RGWL 2, 3; TWA

Christie
See Ichikawa, Kon

Christie, Agatha (Mary Clarissa)
1890-1976 .. **CLC 1, 6, 8, 12, 39, 48, 110**
See also AAYA 9; AITN 1, 2; BPFB 1; BRWS 2; CA 17-20R; 61-64; CANR 10, 37, 108; CBD; CDBLB 1914-1945; CMW 4; CN 1, 2; CPW; CWD; DA3; DAB; DAC; DAM NOV; DFS 2; DLB 13, 77, 245; MSW; MTCW 1, 2; MTFW 2005; NFS 8; RGEL 2; RHW; SATA 36; TEA; YAW

Christie, Philippa **CLC 21**
See Pearce, Philippa
See also BYA 5; CANR 109; CLR 9; DLB 161; MAICYA 1; SATA 1, 67, 129

Christine de Pisan
See Christine de Pizan
See also FW

Christine de Pizan 1365(?)-1431(?) ...... **LC 9, 130; PC 68**
See Christine de Pisan; de Pizan, Christine
See also DLB 208; FL 1:1; RGWL 2, 3

Chuang-Tzu c. 369B.C.-c.
286B.C. .... **CMLC 57**

Chubb, Elmer
See Masters, Edgar Lee

Chulkov, Mikhail Dmitrievich
1743-1792 .... **LC 2**
See also DLB 150

Churchill, Caryl 1938- .... **CLC 31, 55, 157; DC 5**
See Churchill, Chick
See also BRWS 4; CA 102; CANR 22, 46, 108; CBD; CD 6; CWD; DFS 25; DLB 13, 310; EWL 3; FW; MTCW 1; RGEL 2

Churchill, Charles 1731-1764 .... **LC 3**
See also DLB 109; RGEL 2

Churchill, Chick
See Churchill, Caryl
See also CD 5

Churchill, Sir Winston (Leonard Spencer)
1874-1965 .... **TCLC 113**
See also BRW 6; CA 97-100; CDBLB 1890-1914; DA3; DLB 100, 329; DLBD 16; LAIT 4; MTCW 1, 2

Chute, Carolyn 1947- .... **CLC 39**
See also CA 123; CANR 135; CN 7

Ciardi, John (Anthony) 1916-1986 . **CLC 10, 40, 44, 129; PC 69**
See also CA 5-8R; 118; CAAS 2; CANR 5, 33; CLR 19; CP 1, 2, 3, 4; CWRI 5; DAM POET; DLB 5; DLBY 1986; INT CANR-5; MAICYA 1, 2; MAL 5; MTCW 1, 2; MTFW 2005; RGAL 4; SAAS 26; SATA 1, 65; SATA-Obit 46

Cibber, Colley 1671-1757 .... **LC 66**
See also DLB 84; RGEL 2

Cicero, Marcus Tullius
106B.C.-43B.C. .... **CMLC 3, 81**
See also AW 2; CDWLB 1; DLB 211; RGWL 2, 3; WLIT 8

Cimino, Michael 1943- .... **CLC 16**
See also CA 105

Cioran, E(mil) M. 1911-1995 .... **CLC 64**
See also CA 25-28R; 149; CANR 91; DLB 220; EWL 3

Cisneros, Sandra 1954- .... **CLC 69, 118, 193; HLC 1; PC 52; SSC 32, 72**
See also AAYA 9, 53; AMWS 7; CA 131; CANR 64, 118; CLR 123; CN 7; CWP; DA3; DAM MULT; DLB 122, 152; EWL 3; EXPN; FL 1:5; FW; HW 1, 2; LAIT 5;

LATS 1:2; LLW; MAICYA 2; MAL 5; MTCW 2; MTFW 2005; NFS 2; PFS 19; RGAL 4; RGSF 2; SSFS 3, 13; WLIT 1; YAW

Cixous, Helene 1937- .... **CLC 92, 253**
See also CA 126; CANR 55, 123; CWW 2; DLB 83, 242; EWL 3; FL 1:5; FW; GLL 2; MTCW 1, 2; MTFW 2005; TWA

Clair, Rene **CLC 20**
See Chomette, Rene Lucien

Clampitt, Amy 1920-1994 .... **CLC 32; PC 19**
See also AMWS 9; CA 110; 146; CANR 29, 79; CP 4, 5; DLB 105; MAL 5; PFS 27

Clancy, Thomas L., Jr. 1947-
See Clancy, Tom
See also CA 125; 131; CANR 62, 105; DA3; INT CA-131; MTCW 1, 2; MTFW 2005

Clancy, Tom **CLC 45, 112**
See Clancy, Thomas L., Jr.
See also AAYA 9, 51; BEST 89:1, 90:1; BPFB 1; BYA 10, 11; CANR 132; CMW 4; CPW; DAM NOV, POP; DLB 227

Clare, John 1793-1864 .. **NCLC 9, 86; PC 23**
See also BRWS 11; DAB; DAM POET; DLB 55, 96; RGEL 2

Clarin
See Alas (y Urena), Leopoldo (Enrique Garcia)

Clark, Al C.
See Goines, Donald

Clark, Brian (Robert)
See Clark, (Robert) Brian
See also CD 6

Clark, (Robert) Brian 1932- .... **CLC 29**
See Clark, Brian (Robert)
See also CA 41-44R; CANR 67; CBD; CD 5

Clark, Curt
See Westlake, Donald E.

Clark, Eleanor 1913-1996 .... **CLC 5, 19**
See also CA 9-12R; 151; CANR 41; CN 1, 2, 3, 4, 5, 6; DLB 6

Clark, J. P.
See Clark Bekederemo, J.P.
See also CDWLB 3; DLB 117

Clark, John Pepper
See Clark Bekederemo, J.P.
See also AFW; CD 5; CP 1, 2, 3, 4, 5, 6, 7; RGEL 2

Clark, Kenneth (Mackenzie)
1903-1983 .... **TCLC 147**
See also CA 93-96; 109; CANR 36; MTCW 1, 2; MTFW 2005

Clark, M. R.
See Clark, Mavis Thorpe

Clark, Mavis Thorpe 1909-1999 ...... **CLC 12**
See also CA 57-60; CANR 8, 37, 107; CLR 30; CWRI 5; MAICYA 1, 2; SAAS 5; SATA 8, 74

Clark, Walter Van Tilburg
1909-1971 .... **CLC 28**
See also CA 9-12R; 33-36R; CANR 63, 113; CN 1; DLB 9, 206; LAIT 2; MAL 5; RGAL 4; SATA 8; TCWW 1, 2

Clark Bekederemo, J.P. 1935- .... **BLC 1:1; CLC 38; DC 5**
See Bekederemo, J. P. Clark; Clark, J. P.; Clark, John Pepper
See also BW 1; CA 65-68; CANR 16, 72; DAM DRAM, MULT; DFS 13; EWL 3; MTCW 2; MTFW 2005

Clarke, Arthur
See Clarke, Arthur C.

Clarke, Arthur C. 1917-2008 .. **CLC 1, 4, 13, 18, 35, 136; SSC 3**
See also AAYA 4, 33; BPFB 1; BYA 13; CA 1-4R; 270; CANR 2, 28, 55, 74, 130; CLR 119; CN 1, 2, 3, 4, 5, 6, 7; CPW; DA3; DAM POP; DLB 261; JRDA; LAIT 5; MAICYA 1, 2; MTCW 1, 2; MTFW 2005; SATA 13, 70, 115; SATA-Obit 191; SCFW 1, 2; SFW 4; SSFS 4, 18; TCLE 1:1; YAW

Clarke, Arthur Charles
See Clarke, Arthur C.

Clarke, Austin 1896-1974 .... **CLC 6, 9**
See also CA 29-32; 49-52; CAP 2; CP 1, 2; DAM POET; DLB 10, 20; EWL 3; RGEL 2

Clarke, Austin C. 1934- .... **BLC 1:1; CLC 8, 53; SSC 45, 116**
See also BW 1; CA 25-28R; CAAS 16; CANR 14, 32, 68, 140; CN 1, 2, 3, 4, 5, 6, 7; DAC; DAM MULT; DLB 53, 125; DNFS 2; MTCW 2; MTFW 2005; RGSF 2

Clarke, Gillian 1937- .... **CLC 61**
See also CA 106; CP 3, 4, 5, 6, 7; CWP; DLB 40

Clarke, Marcus (Andrew Hislop)
1846-1881 .... **NCLC 19; SSC 94**
See also DLB 230; RGEL 2; RGSF 2

Clarke, Shirley 1925-1997 .... **CLC 16**
See also CA 189

Clash, The
See Headon, (Nicky) Topper; Jones, Mick; Simonon, Paul; Strummer, Joe

Claudel, Paul (Louis Charles Marie)
1868-1955 .... **TCLC 2, 10**
See also CA 104; 165; DLB 192, 258, 321; EW 8; EWL 3; GFL 1789 to the Present; RGWL 2, 3; TWA

Claudian 370(?)-404(?) .... **CMLC 46**
See also RGWL 2, 3

Claudius, Matthias 1740-1815 .... **NCLC 75**
See also DLB 97

Clavell, James 1925-1994 .... **CLC 6, 25, 87**
See also BPFB 1; CA 25-28R; 146; CANR 26, 48; CN 5; CPW; DA3; DAM NOV, POP; MTCW 1, 2; MTFW 2005; NFS 10; RHW

Clayman, Gregory CLC 65

Cleage, Pearl 1948- .... **DC 32**
See also BW 2; CA 41-44R; CANR 27, 148, 177; DFS 14, 16; DLB 228; NFS 17

Cleage, Pearl Michelle
See Cleage, Pearl

Cleaver, (Leroy) Eldridge
1935-1998 .... **BLC 1:1; CLC 30, 119**
See also BW 1, 3; CA 21-24R; 167; CANR 16, 75; DA3; DAM MULT; MTCW 2; YAW

Cleese, John (Marwood) 1939- .... **CLC 21**
See Monty Python
See also CA 112; 116; CANR 35; MTCW 1

Cleishbotham, Jebediah
See Scott, Sir Walter

Cleland, John 1710-1789 .... **LC 2, 48**
See also DLB 39; RGEL 2

Clemens, Samuel Langhorne 1835-1910
See Twain, Mark
See also CA 104; 135; CDALB 1865-1917; DA; DA3; DAB; DAC; DAM MST, NOV; DLB 12, 23, 64, 74, 186, 189; JRDA; LMFS 1; MAICYA 1, 2; NCFS 4; NFS 20; SATA 100; YABC 2

Clement of Alexandria
150(?)-215(?) .... **CMLC 41**

Cleophil
See Congreve, William

Clerihew, E.
See Bentley, E(dmund) C(lerihew)

Clerk, N. W.
See Lewis, C.S.

Cleveland, John 1613-1658 .... **LC 106**
See also DLB 126; RGEL 2

Cliff, Jimmy CLC 21
See Chambers, James
See also CA 193

Cliff, Michelle 1946- .... **BLCS; CLC 120**
See also BW 2; CA 116; CANR 39, 72; CD-WLB 3; DLB 157; FW; GLL 2

Clifford, Lady Anne 1590-1676 .... **LC 76**
See also DLB 151

Clifton, Lucille 1936- ..... **BLC 1:1, 2:1; CLC 19, 66, 162; PC 17**
See also AFAW 2; BW 2, 3; CA 49-52; CANR 2, 24, 42, 76, 97, 138; CLR 5; CP 2, 3, 4, 5, 6, 7; CSW; CWP; CWRI 5; DA3; DAM MULT, POET; DLB 5, 41; EXPP; MAICYA 1, 2; MTCW 1, 2; MTFW 2005; PFS 1, 14, 29; SATA 20, 69, 128; WP

Clinton, Dirk
See Silverberg, Robert

Clough, Arthur Hugh 1819-1861 .. **NCLC 27, 163**
See also BRW 5; DLB 32; RGEL 2

Clutha, Janet Paterson Frame
See Frame, Janet

Clyne, Terence
See Blatty, William Peter

Cobalt, Martin
See Mayne, William (James Carter)

Cobb, Irvin S(hrewsbury)
1876-1944 .... **TCLC 77**
See also CA 175; DLB 11, 25, 86

Cobbett, William 1763-1835 .... **NCLC 49**
See also DLB 43, 107, 158; RGEL 2

Coburn, D(onald) L(ee) 1938- .... **CLC 10**
See also CA 89-92; DFS 23

Cocteau, Jean 1889-1963 ... **CLC 1, 8, 15, 16, 43; DC 17; TCLC 119; WLC 2**
See also AAYA 74; CA 25-28; CANR 40; CAP 2; DA; DA3; DAB; DAC; DAM DRAM, MST, NOV; DFS 24; DLB 65, 258, 321; EW 10; EWL 3; GFL 1789 to the Present; MTCW 1, 2; RGWL 2, 3; TWA

Cocteau, Jean Maurice Eugene Clement
See Cocteau, Jean

Codrescu, Andrei 1946- .... **CLC 46, 121**
See also CA 33-36R; CAAS 19; CANR 13, 34, 53, 76, 125; CN 7; DA3; DAM POET; MAL 5; MTCW 2; MTFW 2005

Coe, Max
See Bourne, Randolph S(illiman)

Coe, Tucker
See Westlake, Donald E.

Coelho, Paulo 1947- .... **CLC 258**
See also CA 152; CANR 80, 93, 155

Coen, Ethan 1957- .... **CLC 108**
See also AAYA 54; CA 126; CANR 85

Coen, Joel 1954- .... **CLC 108**
See also AAYA 54; CA 126; CANR 119

The Coen Brothers
See Coen, Ethan; Coen, Joel

Coetzee, J.M. 1940- ...... **CLC 23, 33, 66, 117, 161, 162**
See also AAYA 37; AFW; BRWS 6; CA 77-80; CANR 41, 54, 74, 114, 133, 180; CN 4, 5, 6, 7; DA3; DAM NOV; DLB 225, 326, 329; EWL 3; LMFS 2; MTCW 1, 2; MTFW 2005; NFS 21; WLIT 2; WWE 1

Coetzee, John Maxwell
See Coetzee, J.M.

Coffey, Brian
See Koontz, Dean R.

Coffin, Robert P(eter) Tristram
1892-1955 .... **TCLC 95**
See also CA 123; 169; DLB 45

Cohan, George M. 1878-1942 .... **TCLC 60**
See also CA 157; DLB 249; RGAL 4

Cohan, George Michael
See Cohan, George M.

Cohen, Arthur A(llen) 1928-1986 ...... **CLC 7, 31**
See also CA 1-4R; 120; CANR 1, 17, 42; DLB 28; RGHL

Cohen, Leonard 1934- .... **CLC 3, 38, 260**
See also CA 21-24R; CANR 14, 69; CN 1, 2, 3, 4, 5, 6; CP 1, 2, 3, 4, 5, 6, 7; DAC; DAM MST; DLB 53; EWL 3; MTCW 1

Cohen, Leonard Norman
See Cohen, Leonard

Cohen, Matt(hew) 1942-1999 .... **CLC 19**
See also CA 61-64; 187; CAAS 18; CANR 40; CN 1, 2, 3, 4, 5, 6; DAC; DLB 53

Cohen-Solal, Annie 1948- .... **CLC 50**
See also CA 239

Colegate, Isabel 1931- .... **CLC 36**
See also CA 17-20R; CANR 8, 22, 74; CN 4, 5, 6, 7; DLB 14, 231; INT CANR-22; MTCW 1

Coleman, Emmett
See Reed, Ishmael

Coleridge, Hartley 1796-1849 .... **NCLC 90**
See also DLB 96

Coleridge, M. E.
See Coleridge, Mary E(lizabeth)

Coleridge, Mary E(lizabeth)
1861-1907 .... **TCLC 73**
See also CA 116; 166; DLB 19, 98

Coleridge, Samuel Taylor
1772-1834 ..... **NCLC 9, 54, 99, 111, 177, 197; PC 11, 39, 67; WLC 2**
See also AAYA 66; BRW 4; BRWR 2; BYA 4; CDBLB 1789-1832; DA; DA3; DAB; DAC; DAM MST, POET; DLB 93, 107; EXPP; LATS 1:1; LMFS 1; PAB; PFS 4, 5; RGEL 2; TEA; WLIT 3; WP

Coleridge, Sara 1802-1852 .... **NCLC 31**
See also DLB 199

Coles, Don 1928- .... **CLC 46**
See also CA 115; CANR 38; CP 5, 6, 7

Coles, Robert (Martin) 1929- .... **CLC 108**
See also CA 45-48; CANR 3, 32, 66, 70, 135; INT CANR-32; SATA 23

Colette, (Sidonie-Gabrielle)
1873-1954 .. **SSC 10, 93; TCLC 1, 5, 16**
See Willy, Colette
See also CA 104; 131; DA3; DAM NOV; DLB 65; EW 9; EWL 3; GFL 1789 to the Present; MTCW 1, 2; MTFW 2005; RGWL 2, 3; TWA

Collett, (Jacobine) Camilla (Wergeland)
1813-1895 .... **NCLC 22**

Collier, Christopher 1930- .... **CLC 30**
See also AAYA 13; BYA 2; CA 33-36R; CANR 13, 33, 102; CLR 126; JRDA; MAICYA 1, 2; SATA 16, 70; WYA; YAW 1

Collier, James Lincoln 1928- .... **CLC 30**
See also AAYA 13; BYA 2; CA 9-12R; CANR 4, 33, 60, 102; CLR 3, 126; DAM POP; JRDA; MAICYA 1, 2; SAAS 21; SATA 8, 70, 166; WYA; YAW 1

Collier, Jeremy 1650-1726 .... **LC 6, 157**
See also DLB 336

Collier, John 1901-1980 . **SSC 19; TCLC 127**
See also CA 65-68; 97-100; CANR 10; CN 1, 2; DLB 77, 255; FANT; SUFW 1

Collier, Mary 1690-1762 .... **LC 86**
See also DLB 95

Collingwood, R(obin) G(eorge)
1889(?)-1943 .... **TCLC 67**
See also CA 117; 155; DLB 262

Collins, Billy 1941- .... **PC 68**
See also AAYA 64; CA 151; CANR 92; CP 7; MTFW 2005; PFS 18

Collins, Hunt
See Hunter, Evan
Collins, Linda 1931- .... **CLC 44**
See also CA 125
Collins, Merle 1950- .... **BLC 2:1**
See also BW 3; CA 175; DLB 157
Collins, Tom
See Furphy, Joseph
See also RGEL 2
Collins, (William) Wilkie
1824-1889 .... **NCLC 1, 18, 93; SSC 93**
See also BRWS 6; CDBLB 1832-1890;
CMW 4; DLB 18, 70, 159; GL 2; MSW;
RGEL 2; RGSF 2; SUFW 1; WLIT 4
Collins, William 1721-1759 ...... **LC 4, 40; PC
72**
See also BRW 3; DAM POET; DLB 109;
RGEL 2
Collodi, Carlo **NCLC 54**
See Lorenzini, Carlo
See also CLR 5, 120; WCH; WLIT 7
Colman, George
See Glassco, John
Colman, George, the Elder
1732-1794 .... **LC 98**
See also RGEL 2
Colonna, Vittoria 1492-1547 .... **LC 71**
See also RGWL 2, 3
Colt, Winchester Remington
See Hubbard, L. Ron
Colter, Cyrus J. 1910-2002 .... **CLC 58**
See also BW 1; CA 65-68; 205; CANR 10,
66; CN 2, 3, 4, 5, 6; DLB 33
Colton, James
See Hansen, Joseph
See also GLL 1
Colum, Padraic 1881-1972 .... **CLC 28**
See also BYA 4; CA 73-76; 33-36R; CANR
35; CLR 36; CP 1; CWRI 5; DLB 19;
MAICYA 1, 2; MTCW 1; RGEL 2; SATA
15; WCH
Colvin, James
See Moorcock, Michael
Colwin, Laurie (E.) 1944-1992 .... **CLC 5, 13,
23, 84**
See also CA 89-92; 139; CANR 20, 46;
DLB 218; DLBY 1980; MTCW 1
Comfort, Alex(ander) 1920-2000 .... **CLC 7**
See also CA 1-4R; 190; CANR 1, 45; CN
1, 2, 3, 4; CP 1, 2, 3, 4, 5, 6, 7; DAM
POP; MTCW 2
Comfort, Montgomery
See Campbell, Ramsey
Compton-Burnett, I(vy)
1892(?)-1969 .... **CLC 1, 3, 10, 15, 34;
TCLC 180**
See also BRW 7; CA 1-4R; 25-28R; CANR
4; DAM NOV; DLB 36; EWL 3; MTCW
1, 2; RGEL 2
Comstock, Anthony 1844-1915 ...... **TCLC 13**
See also CA 110; 169
Comte, Auguste 1798-1857 .... **NCLC 54**
Conan Doyle, Arthur
See Doyle, Sir Arthur Conan
See also BPFB 1; BYA 4, 5, 11
Conde (Abellan), Carmen
1901-1996 .... **HLCS 1**
See also CA 177; CWW 2; DLB 108; EWL
3; HW 2
Conde, Maryse 1937- .... **BLC 2:1; BLCS;
CLC 52, 92, 247**
See also BW 2, 3; CA 110, 190; CAAE 190;
CANR 30, 53, 76, 171; CWW 2; DAM
MULT; EWL 3; MTCW 2; MTFW 2005
Condillac, Etienne Bonnot de
1714-1780 .... **LC 26**
See also DLB 313

Condon, Richard 1915-1996 ...... **CLC 4, 6, 8,
10, 45, 100**
See also BEST 90:3; BPFB 1; CA 1-4R;
151; CAAS 1; CANR 2, 23, 164; CMW
4; CN 1, 2, 3, 4, 5, 6; DAM NOV; INT
CANR-23; MAL 5; MTCW 1, 2
Condon, Richard Thomas
See Condon, Richard
Condorcet **LC 104**
See Condorcet, marquis de Marie-Jean-
Antoine-Nicolas Caritat
See also GFL Beginnings to 1789
Condorcet, marquis de
Marie-Jean-Antoine-Nicolas Caritat
1743-1794
See Condorcet
See also DLB 313
Confucius 551B.C.-479B.C. .... **CMLC 19, 65;
WLCS**
See also DA; DA3; DAB; DAC; DAM
MST
Congreve, William 1670-1729 ... **DC 2; LC 5,
21; WLC 2**
See also BRW 2; CDBLB 1660-1789; DA;
DAB; DAC; DAM DRAM, MST, POET;
DFS 15; DLB 39, 84; RGEL 2; WLIT 3
Conley, Robert J(ackson) 1940- .... **NNAL**
See also CA 41-44R; CANR 15, 34, 45, 96;
DAM MULT; TCWW 2
Connell, Evan S., Jr. 1924- .... **CLC 4, 6, 45**
See also AAYA 7; AMWS 14; CA 1-4R;
CAAS 2; CANR 2, 39, 76, 97, 140; CN
1, 2, 3, 4, 5, 6; DAM NOV; DLB 2, 335;
DLBY 1981; MAL 5; MTCW 1, 2;
MTFW 2005
Connelly, Marc(us Cook) 1890-1980 . **CLC 7**
See also CA 85-88; 102; CAD; CANR 30;
DFS 12; DLB 7; DLBY 1980; MAL 5;
RGAL 4; SATA-Obit 25
Connolly, Paul
See Wicker, Tom
Connor, Ralph **TCLC 31**
See Gordon, Charles William
See also DLB 92; TCWW 1, 2
Conrad, Joseph 1857-1924 ..... **SSC 9, 67, 69,
71; TCLC 1, 6, 13, 25, 43, 57; WLC 2**
See also AAYA 26; BPFB 1; BRW 6;
BRWC 1; BRWR 2; BYA 2; CA 104; 131;
CANR 60; CDBLB 1890-1914; DA; DA3;
DAB; DAC; DAM MST, NOV; DLB 10,
34, 98, 156; EWL 3; EXPN; EXPS; LAIT
2; LATS 1:1; LMFS 1; MTCW 1, 2;
MTFW 2005; NFS 2, 16; RGEL 2; RGSF
2; SATA 27; SSFS 1, 12; TEA; WLIT 4
Conrad, Robert Arnold
See Hart, Moss
Conroy, Pat 1945- .... **CLC 30, 74**
See also AAYA 8, 52; AITN 1; BPFB 1;
CA 85-88; CANR 24, 53, 129; CN 7;
CPW; CSW; DA3; DAM NOV, POP;
DLB 6; LAIT 5; MAL 5; MTCW 1, 2;
MTFW 2005
Constant (de Rebecque), (Henri) Benjamin
1767-1830 .... **NCLC 6, 182**
See also DLB 119; EW 4; GFL 1789 to the
Present
Conway, Jill K. 1934- .... **CLC 152**
See also CA 130; CANR 94
Conway, Jill Kathryn Ker
See Conway, Jill K.
Conybeare, Charles Augustus
See Eliot, T(homas) S(tearns)
Cook, Michael 1933-1994 .... **CLC 58**
See also CA 93-96; CANR 68; DLB 53
Cook, Robin 1940- .... **CLC 14**
See also AAYA 32; BEST 90:2; BPFB 1;
CA 108; 111; CANR 41, 90, 109, 181;
CPW; DA3; DAM POP; HGG; INT CA-
111

Cook, Roy
See Silverberg, Robert
Cooke, Elizabeth 1948- .... **CLC 55**
See also CA 129
Cooke, John Esten 1830-1886 .... **NCLC 5**
See also DLB 3, 248; RGAL 4
Cooke, John Estes
See Baum, L(yman) Frank
Cooke, M. E.
See Creasey, John
Cooke, Margaret
See Creasey, John
Cooke, Rose Terry 1827-1892 ...... **NCLC 110**
See also DLB 12, 74
Cook-Lynn, Elizabeth 1930- .... **CLC 93;
NNAL**
See also CA 133; DAM MULT; DLB 175
Cooney, Ray **CLC 62**
See also CBD
Cooper, Anthony Ashley 1671-1713 .. **LC 107**
See also DLB 101, 336
Cooper, Dennis 1953- .... **CLC 203**
See also CA 133; CANR 72, 86; GLL 1;
HGG
Cooper, Douglas 1960- .... **CLC 86**
Cooper, Henry St. John
See Creasey, John
Cooper, J. California (?)- .... **CLC 56**
See also AAYA 12; BW 1; CA 125; CANR
55; DAM MULT; DLB 212
Cooper, James Fenimore
1789-1851 .... **NCLC 1, 27, 54, 203**
See also AAYA 22; AMW; BPFB 1;
CDALB 1640-1865; CLR 105; DA3;
DLB 3, 183, 250, 254; LAIT 1; NFS 25;
RGAL 4; SATA 19; TUS; WCH
Cooper, Susan Fenimore
1813-1894 .... **NCLC 129**
See also ANW; DLB 239, 254
Coover, Robert 1932- .. **CLC 3, 7, 15, 32, 46,
87, 161; SSC 15, 101**
See also AMWS 5; BPFB 1; CA 45-48;
CANR 3, 37, 58, 115; CN 1, 2, 3, 4, 5, 6,
7; DAM NOV; DLB 2, 227; DLBY 1981;
EWL 3; MAL 5; MTCW 1, 2; MTFW
2005; RGAL 4; RGSF 2
Copeland, Stewart (Armstrong)
1952- .... **CLC 26**
Copernicus, Nicolaus 1473-1543 .... **LC 45**
Coppard, A(lfred) E(dgar)
1878-1957 .... **SSC 21; TCLC 5**
See also BRWS 8; CA 114; 167; DLB 162;
EWL 3; HGG; RGEL 2; RGSF 2; SUFW
1; YABC 1
Coppee, Francois 1842-1908 .... **TCLC 25**
See also CA 170; DLB 217
Coppola, Francis Ford 1939- ... **CLC 16, 126**
See also AAYA 39; CA 77-80; CANR 40,
78; DLB 44
Copway, George 1818-1869 .... **NNAL**
See also DAM MULT; DLB 175, 183
Corbiere, Tristan 1845-1875 .... **NCLC 43**
See also DLB 217; GFL 1789 to the Present
Corcoran, Barbara (Asenath)
1911- .... **CLC 17**
See also AAYA 14; CA 21-24R, 191; CAAE
191; CAAS 2; CANR 11, 28, 48; CLR
50; DLB 52; JRDA; MAICYA 2; MAIC-
YAS 1; RHW; SAAS 20; SATA 3, 77;
SATA-Essay 125
Cordelier, Maurice
See Giraudoux, Jean(-Hippolyte)
Corelli, Marie **TCLC 51**
See Mackay, Mary
See also DLB 34, 156; RGEL 2; SUFW 1

Corinna c. 225B.C.-c. 305B.C. ...... **CMLC 72**

Corman, Cid CLC 9
See Corman, Sidney
See also CAAS 2; CP 1, 2, 3, 4, 5, 6, 7;
DLB 5, 193

Corman, Sidney 1924-2004
See Corman, Cid
See also CA 85-88; 225; CANR 44; DAM
POET

Cormier, Robert 1925-2000 .... **CLC 12, 30**
See also AAYA 3, 19; BYA 1, 2, 6, 8, 9;
CA 1-4R; CANR 5, 23, 76, 93; CDALB
1968-1988; CLR 12, 55; DA; DAB; DAC;
DAM MST, NOV; DLB 52; EXPN; INT
CANR-23; JRDA; LAIT 5; MAICYA 1,
2; MTCW 1, 2; MTFW 2005; NFS 2, 18;
SATA 10, 45, 83; SATA-Obit 122; WYA;
YAW

Corn, Alfred (DeWitt III) 1943- .... **CLC 33**
See also CA 179; CAAE 179; CAAS 25;
CANR 44; CP 3, 4, 5, 6, 7; CSW; DLB
120, 282; DLBY 1980

Corneille, Pierre 1606-1684 .. **DC 21; LC 28,
135**
See also DAB; DAM MST; DFS 21; DLB
268; EW 3; GFL Beginnings to 1789;
RGWL 2, 3; TWA

Cornwell, David
See le Carre, John

Cornwell, David John Moore
See le Carre, John

Cornwell, Patricia 1956- .... **CLC 155**
See also AAYA 16, 56; BPFB 1; CA 134;
CANR 53, 131; CMW 4; CPW; CSW;
DAM POP; DLB 306; MSW; MTCW 2;
MTFW 2005

Cornwell, Patricia Daniels
See Cornwell, Patricia

Corso, Gregory 1930-2001 .... **CLC 1, 11; PC
33**
See also AMWS 12; BG 1:2; CA 5-8R; 193;
CANR 41, 76, 132; CP 1, 2, 3, 4, 5, 6, 7;
DA3; DLB 5, 16, 237; LMFS 2; MAL 5;
MTCW 1, 2; MTFW 2005; WP

Cortazar, Julio 1914-1984 .. **CLC 2, 3, 5, 10,
13, 15, 33, 34, 92; HLC 1; SSC 7, 76**
See also BPFB 1; CA 21-24R; CANR 12,
32, 81; CDWLB 3; DA3; DAM MULT,
NOV; DLB 113; EWL 3; EXPS; HW 1,
2; LAW; MTCW 1, 2; MTFW 2005;
RGSF 2; RGWL 2, 3; SSFS 3, 20; TWA;
WLIT 1

Cortes, Hernan 1485-1547 .... **LC 31**

Cortez, Jayne 1936- .... **BLC 2:1**
See also BW 2, 3; CA 73-76; CANR 13,
31, 68, 126; CWP; DLB 41; EWL 3

Corvinus, Jakob
See Raabe, Wilhelm (Karl)

Corwin, Cecil
See Kornbluth, C(yril) M.

Cosic, Dobrica 1921- .... **CLC 14**
See also CA 122; 138; CDWLB 4; CWW
2; DLB 181; EWL 3

Costain, Thomas B(ertram)
1885-1965 .... **CLC 30**
See also BYA 3; CA 5-8R; 25-28R; DLB 9;
RHW

Costantini, Humberto 1924(?)-1987 . **CLC 49**
See also CA 131; 122; EWL 3; HW 1

Costello, Elvis 1954- .... **CLC 21**
See also CA 204

Costenoble, Philostene
See Ghelderode, Michel de

Cotes, Cecil V.
See Duncan, Sara Jeannette

Cotter, Joseph Seamon Sr.
1861-1949 .... **BLC 1:1; TCLC 28**
See also BW 1; CA 124; DAM MULT; DLB
50

Couch, Arthur Thomas Quiller
See Quiller-Couch, Sir Arthur (Thomas)

Coulton, James
See Hansen, Joseph

Couperus, Louis (Marie Anne)
1863-1923 .... **TCLC 15**
See also CA 115; EWL 3; RGWL 2, 3

Coupland, Douglas 1961- .... **CLC 85, 133**
See also AAYA 34; CA 142; CANR 57, 90,
130, 172; CCA 1; CN 7; CPW; DAC;
DAM POP; DLB 334

Coupland, Douglas Campbell
See Coupland, Douglas

Court, Wesli
See Turco, Lewis (Putnam)

Courtenay, Bryce 1933- .... **CLC 59**
See also CA 138; CPW

Courtney, Robert
See Ellison, Harlan

Cousteau, Jacques-Yves 1910-1997 .. **CLC 30**
See also CA 65-68; 159; CANR 15, 67;
MTCW 1; SATA 38, 98

Coventry, Francis 1725-1754 .... **LC 46**
See also DLB 39

Coverdale, Miles c. 1487-1569 .... **LC 77**
See also DLB 167

Cowan, Peter (Walkinshaw)
1914-2002 .... **SSC 28**
See also CA 21-24R; CANR 9, 25, 50, 83;
CN 1, 2, 3, 4, 5, 6, 7; DLB 260; RGSF 2

Coward, Noel (Peirce) 1899-1973 . **CLC 1, 9,
29, 51**
See also AITN 1; BRWS 2; CA 17-18; 41-
44R; CANR 35, 132; CAP 2; CBD; CD-
BLB 1914-1945; DA3; DAM DRAM;
DFS 3, 6; DLB 10, 245; EWL 3; IDFW
3, 4; MTCW 1, 2; MTFW 2005; RGEL 2;
TEA

Cowley, Abraham 1618-1667 .. **LC 43; PC 90**
See also BRW 2; DLB 131, 151; PAB;
RGEL 2

Cowley, Malcolm 1898-1989 .... **CLC 39**
See also AMWS 2; CA 5-8R; 128; CANR
3, 55; CP 1, 2, 3, 4; DLB 4, 48; DLBY
1981, 1989; EWL 3; MAL 5; MTCW 1,
2; MTFW 2005

Cowper, William 1731-1800 ..... **NCLC 8, 94;
PC 40**
See also BRW 3; DA3; DAM POET; DLB
104, 109; RGEL 2

Cox, William Trevor
See Trevor, William

Coyne, P. J.
See Masters, Hilary

Coyne, P.J.
See Masters, Hilary

Cozzens, James Gould 1903-1978 . **CLC 1, 4,
11, 92**
See also AMW; BPFB 1; CA 9-12R; 81-84;
CANR 19; CDALB 1941-1968; CN 1, 2;
DLB 9, 294; DLBD 2; DLBY 1984, 1997;
EWL 3; MAL 5; MTCW 1, 2; MTFW
2005; RGAL 4

Crabbe, George 1754-1832 .... **NCLC 26, 121**
See also BRW 3; DLB 93; RGEL 2

Crace, Jim 1946- .... **CLC 157; SSC 61**
See also CA 128; 135; CANR 55, 70, 123,
180; CN 5, 6, 7; DLB 231; INT CA-135

Craddock, Charles Egbert
See Murfree, Mary Noailles

Craig, A. A.
See Anderson, Poul

Craik, Mrs.
See Craik, Dinah Maria (Mulock)
See also RGEL 2

Craik, Dinah Maria (Mulock)
1826-1887 .... **NCLC 38**
See Craik, Mrs.; Mulock, Dinah Maria
See also DLB 35, 163; MAICYA 1, 2;
SATA 34

Cram, Ralph Adams 1863-1942 ..... **TCLC 45**
See also CA 160

Cranch, Christopher Pearse
1813-1892 .... **NCLC 115**
See also DLB 1, 42, 243

Crane, (Harold) Hart 1899-1932 .... **PC 3;
TCLC 2, 5, 80; WLC 2**
See also AMW; AMWR 2; CA 104; 127;
CDALB 1917-1929; DA; DA3; DAB;
DAC; DAM MST, POET; DLB 4, 48;
EWL 3; MAL 5; MTCW 1, 2; MTFW
2005; RGAL 4; TUS

Crane, R(onald) S(almon)
1886-1967 .... **CLC 27**
See also CA 85-88; DLB 63

Crane, Stephen (Townley)
1871-1900 .... **PC 80; SSC 7, 56, 70;
TCLC 11, 17, 32; WLC 2**
See also AAYA 21; AMW; AMWC 1; BPFB
1; BYA 3; CA 109; 140; CANR 84;
CDALB 1865-1917; CLR 132; DA; DA3;
DAB; DAC; DAM MST, NOV, POET;
DLB 12, 54, 78; EXPN; EXPS; LAIT 2;
LMFS 2; MAL 5; NFS 4, 20; PFS 9;
RGAL 4; RGSF 2; SSFS 4; TUS; WYA;
YABC 2

Cranmer, Thomas 1489-1556 .... **LC 95**
See also DLB 132, 213

Cranshaw, Stanley
See Fisher, Dorothy (Frances) Canfield

Crase, Douglas 1944- .... **CLC 58**
See also CA 106

Crashaw, Richard 1612(?)-1649 .. **LC 24; PC
84**
See also BRW 2; DLB 126; PAB; RGEL 2

Cratinus c. 519B.C.-c. 422B.C. ..... **CMLC 54**
See also LMFS 1

Craven, Margaret 1901-1980 .... **CLC 17**
See also BYA 2; CA 103; CCA 1; DAC;
LAIT 5

Crawford, F(rancis) Marion
1854-1909 .... **TCLC 10**
See also CA 107; 168; DLB 71; HGG;
RGAL 4; SUFW 1

Crawford, Isabella Valancy
1850-1887 .... **NCLC 12, 127**
See also DLB 92; RGEL 2

Crayon, Geoffrey
See Irving, Washington

Creasey, John 1908-1973 .... **CLC 11**
See Marric, J. J.
See also CA 5-8R; 41-44R; CANR 8, 59;
CMW 4; DLB 77; MTCW 1

Crebillon, Claude Prosper Jolyot de (fils)
1707-1777 .... **LC 1, 28**
See also DLB 313; GFL Beginnings to 1789

Credo
See Creasey, John

Credo, Alvaro J. de
See Prado (Calvo), Pedro

Creeley, Robert 1926-2005 .... **CLC 1, 2, 4, 8,
11, 15, 36, 78; PC 73**
See also AMWS 4; CA 1-4R; 237; CAAS
10; CANR 23, 43, 89, 137; CP 1, 2, 3, 4,
5, 6, 7; DA3; DAM POET; DLB 5, 16,
169; DLBD 17; EWL 3; MAL 5; MTCW
1, 2; MTFW 2005; PFS 21; RGAL 4; WP

Creeley, Robert White
See Creeley, Robert

Crenne, Helisenne de 1510-1560 .... **LC 113**
See also DLB 327

Crevecoeur, Hector St. John de
See Crevecoeur, Michel Guillaume Jean de
See also ANW

Crevecoeur, Michel Guillaume Jean de
1735-1813 .... **NCLC 105**
See Crevecoeur, Hector St. John de
See also AMWS 1; DLB 37

Crevel, Rene 1900-1935 .... **TCLC 112**
See also GLL 2

Crews, Harry 1935- .... **CLC 6, 23, 49**
See also AITN 1; AMWS 11; BPFB 1; CA
25-28R; CANR 20, 57; CN 3, 4, 5, 6, 7;
CSW; DA3; DLB 6, 143, 185; MTCW 1,
2; MTFW 2005; RGAL 4

Crichton, John Michael
See Crichton, Michael

Crichton, Michael 1942-2008 .. **CLC 2, 6, 54,**
90, 242
See also AAYA 10, 49; AITN 2; BPFB 1;
CA 25-28R; CANR 13, 40, 54, 76, 127,
179; CMW 4; CN 2, 3, 6, 7; CPW; DA3;
DAM NOV, POP; DLB 292; DLBY 1981;
INT CANR-13; JRDA; MTCW 1, 2;
MTFW 2005; SATA 9, 88; SFW 4; YAW

Crispin, Edmund CLC 22
See Montgomery, (Robert) Bruce
See also DLB 87; MSW

Cristina of Sweden 1626-1689 .... **LC 124**

Cristofer, Michael 1945(?)- .... **CLC 28**
See also CA 110; 152; CAD; CANR 150;
CD 5, 6; DAM DRAM; DFS 15; DLB 7

Cristofer, Michael Ivan
See Cristofer, Michael

Criton
See Alain

Croce, Benedetto 1866-1952 .... **TCLC 37**
See also CA 120; 155; EW 8; EWL 3;
WLIT 7

Crockett, David 1786-1836 .... **NCLC 8**
See also DLB 3, 11, 183, 248

Crockett, Davy
See Crockett, David

Crofts, Freeman Wills 1879-1957 .. **TCLC 55**
See also CA 115; 195; CMW 4; DLB 77;
MSW

Croker, John Wilson 1780-1857 .... **NCLC 10**
See also DLB 110

Crommelynck, Fernand 1885-1970 .. **CLC 75**
See also CA 189; 89-92; EWL 3

Cromwell, Oliver 1599-1658 .... **LC 43**

Cronenberg, David 1943- .... **CLC 143**
See also CA 138; CCA 1

Cronin, A(rchibald) J(oseph)
1896-1981 .... **CLC 32**
See also BPFB 1; CA 1-4R; 102; CANR 5;
CN 2; DLB 191; SATA 47; SATA-Obit 25

Cross, Amanda
See Heilbrun, Carolyn G(old)
See also BPFB 1; CMW; CPW; DLB 306;
MSW

Crothers, Rachel 1878-1958 .... **TCLC 19**
See also CA 113; 194; CAD; CWD; DLB
7, 266; RGAL 4

Croves, Hal
See Traven, B.

Crow Dog, Mary (?)- .... **CLC 93; NNAL**
See also CA 154

Crowfield, Christopher
See Stowe, Harriet (Elizabeth) Beecher

Crowley, Aleister TCLC 7
See Crowley, Edward Alexander
See also GLL 1

Crowley, Edward Alexander 1875-1947
See Crowley, Aleister
See also CA 104; HGG

Crowley, John 1942- .... **CLC 57**
See also AAYA 57; BPFB 1; CA 61-64;
CANR 43, 98, 138, 177; DLBY 1982;
FANT; MTFW 2005; SATA 65, 140; SFW
4; SUFW 2

Crowne, John 1641-1712 .... **LC 104**
See also DLB 80; RGEL 2

Crud
See Crumb, R.

Crumarums
See Crumb, R.

Crumb, R. 1943- .... **CLC 17**
See also CA 106; CANR 107, 150

Crumb, Robert
See Crumb, R.

Crumbum
See Crumb, R.

Crumski
See Crumb, R.

Crum the Bum
See Crumb, R.

Crunk
See Crumb, R.

Crustt
See Crumb, R.

Crutchfield, Les
See Trumbo, Dalton

Cruz, Victor Hernandez 1949- ... **HLC 1; PC**
37
See also BW 2; CA 65-68, 271; CAAE 271;
CAAS 17; CANR 14, 32, 74, 132; CP 1,
2, 3, 4, 5, 6, 7; DAM MULT, POET; DLB
41; DNFS 1; EXPP; HW 1, 2; LLW;
MTCW 2; MTFW 2005; PFS 16; WP

Cryer, Gretchen (Kiger) 1935- .... **CLC 21**
See also CA 114; 123

Csath, Geza TCLC 13
See Brenner, Jozef
See also CA 111

Cudlip, David R(ockwell) 1933- .... **CLC 34**
See also CA 177

Cullen, Countee 1903-1946 ..... **BLC 1:1; HR**
1:2; PC 20; TCLC 4, 37; WLCS
See also AAYA 78; AFAW 2; AMWS 4; BW
1; CA 108; 124; CDALB 1917-1929; DA;
DA3; DAC; DAM MST, MULT, POET;
DLB 4, 48, 51; EWL 3; EXPP; LMFS 2;
MAL 5; MTCW 1, 2; MTFW 2005; PFS
3; RGAL 4; SATA 18; WP

Culleton, Beatrice 1949- .... **NNAL**
See also CA 120; CANR 83; DAC

Cum, R.
See Crumb, R.

Cumberland, Richard
1732-1811 .... **NCLC 167**
See also DLB 89; RGEL 2

Cummings, Bruce F(rederick) 1889-1919
See Barbellion, W. N. P.
See also CA 123

Cummings, E(dward) E(stlin)
1894-1962 .. **CLC 1, 3, 8, 12, 15, 68; PC**
5; TCLC 137; WLC 2
See also AAYA 41; AMW; CA 73-76;
CANR 31; CDALB 1929-1941; DA;
DA3; DAB; DAC; DAM MST, POET;
DLB 4, 48; EWL 3; EXPP; MAL 5;
MTCW 1, 2; MTFW 2005; PAB; PFS 1,
3, 12, 13, 19; RGAL 4; TUS; WP

Cummins, Maria Susanna
1827-1866 .... **NCLC 139**
See also DLB 42; YABC 1

Cunha, Euclides (Rodrigues Pimenta) da
1866-1909 .... **TCLC 24**
See also CA 123; 219; DLB 307; LAW;
WLIT 1

Cunningham, E. V.
See Fast, Howard

Cunningham, J(ames) V(incent)
1911-1985 .... **CLC 3, 31; PC 92**
See also CA 1-4R; 115; CANR 1, 72; CP 1,
2, 3, 4; DLB 5

Cunningham, Julia (Woolfolk)
1916- .... **CLC 12**
See also CA 9-12R; CANR 4, 19, 36; CWRI
5; JRDA; MAICYA 1, 2; SAAS 2; SATA
1, 26, 132

Cunningham, Michael 1952- .... **CLC 34, 243**
See also AMWS 15; CA 136; CANR 96,
160; CN 7; DLB 292; GLL 2; MTFW
2005; NFS 23

Cunninghame Graham, R. B.
See Cunninghame Graham, Robert
(Gallnigad) Bontine

Cunninghame Graham, Robert (Gallnigad)
Bontine 1852-1936 .... **TCLC 19**
See Graham, R(obert) B(ontine) Cunning-
hame
See also CA 119; 184

Curnow, (Thomas) Allen (Monro)
1911-2001 .... **PC 48**
See also CA 69-72; 202; CANR 48, 99; CP
1, 2, 3, 4, 5, 6, 7; EWL 3; RGEL 2

Currie, Ellen 19(?)- .... **CLC 44**

Curtin, Philip
See Lowndes, Marie Adelaide (Belloc)

Curtin, Phillip
See Lowndes, Marie Adelaide (Belloc)

Curtis, Price
See Ellison, Harlan

Cusanus, Nicolaus 1401-1464 .... **LC 80**
See Nicholas of Cusa

Cutrate, Joe
See Spiegelman, Art

Cynewulf c. 770- .... **CMLC 23**
See also DLB 146; RGEL 2

Cyrano de Bergerac, Savinien de
1619-1655 .... **LC 65**
See also DLB 268; GFL Beginnings to
1789; RGWL 2, 3

Cyril of Alexandria c. 375-c. 430 . **CMLC 59**

Czaczkes, Shmuel Yosef Halevi
See Agnon, S(hmuel) Y(osef Halevi)

Dabrowska, Maria (Szumska)
1889-1965 .... **CLC 15**
See also CA 106; CDWLB 4; DLB 215;
EWL 3

Dabydeen, David 1955- .... **CLC 34**
See also BW 1; CA 125; CANR 56, 92; CN
6, 7; CP 5, 6, 7

Dacey, Philip 1939- .... **CLC 51**
See also CA 37-40R, 231; CAAE 231;
CAAS 17; CANR 14, 32, 64; CP 4, 5, 6,
7; DLB 105

Dacre, Charlotte c. 1772-1825(?) . **NCLC 151**

Dafydd ap Gwilym c. 1320-c. 1380 ..... **PC 56**

Dagerman, Stig (Halvard)
1923-1954 .... **TCLC 17**
See also CA 117; 155; DLB 259; EWL 3

D'Aguiar, Fred 1960- ..... **BLC 2:1; CLC 145**
See also CA 148; CANR 83, 101; CN 7;
CP 5, 6, 7; DLB 157; EWL 3

Dahl, Roald 1916-1990 ...... **CLC 1, 6, 18, 79;**
TCLC 173
See also AAYA 15; BPFB 1; BRWS 4; BYA
5; CA 1-4R; 133; CANR 6, 32, 37, 62;
CLR 1, 7, 41, 111; CN 1, 2, 3, 4; CPW;
DA3; DAB; DAC; DAM MST, NOV,
POP; DLB 139, 255; HGG; JRDA; MAI-
CYA 1, 2; MTCW 1, 2; MTFW 2005;
RGSF 2; SATA 1, 26, 73; SATA-Obit 65;
SSFS 4; TEA; YAW

Dahlberg, Edward 1900-1977 . **CLC 1, 7, 14;**
TCLC 208
See also CA 9-12R; 69-72; CANR 31, 62;
CN 1, 2; DLB 48; MAL 5; MTCW 1;
RGAL 4

Daitch, Susan 1954- .... **CLC 103**
See also CA 161

Dale, Colin TCLC 18
See Lawrence, T(homas) E(dward)

Dale, George E.
See Asimov, Isaac

d'Alembert, Jean Le Rond
   1717-1783 .... **LC 126**
Dalton, Roque 1935-1975(?) ..... **HLCS 1; PC 36**
   See also CA 176; DLB 283; HW 2
Daly, Elizabeth 1878-1967 .... **CLC 52**
   See also CA 23-24; 25-28R; CANR 60; CAP 2; CMW 4
Daly, Mary 1928- .... **CLC 173**
   See also CA 25-28R; CANR 30, 62, 166; FW; GLL 1; MTCW 1
Daly, Maureen 1921-2006 .... **CLC 17**
   See also AAYA 5, 58; BYA 6; CA 253; CANR 37, 83, 108; CLR 96; JRDA; MAICYA 1, 2; SAAS 1; SATA 2, 129; SATA-Obit 176; WYA; YAW
Damas, Leon-Gontran 1912-1978 ... **CLC 84; TCLC 204**
   See also BW 1; CA 125; 73-76; EWL 3
Dana, Richard Henry Sr.
   1787-1879 .... **NCLC 53**
Dangarembga, Tsitsi 1959- .... **BLC 2:1**
   See also BW 3; CA 163; NFS 28; WLIT 2
Daniel, Samuel 1562(?)-1619 .... **LC 24**
   See also DLB 62; RGEL 2
Daniels, Brett
   See Adler, Renata
Dannay, Frederic 1905-1982 .... **CLC 11**
   See Queen, Ellery
   See also CA 1-4R; 107; CANR 1, 39; CMW 4; DAM POP; DLB 137; MTCW 1
D'Annunzio, Gabriele 1863-1938 ... **TCLC 6, 40**
   See also CA 104; 155; EW 8; EWL 3; RGWL 2, 3; TWA; WLIT 7
Danois, N. le
   See Gourmont, Remy(-Marie-Charles) de
Dante 1265-1321 .... **CMLC 3, 18, 39, 70; PC 21; WLCS**
   See Alighieri, Dante
   See also DA; DA3; DAB; DAC; DAM MST, POET; EFS 1; EW 1; LAIT 1; RGWL 2, 3; TWA; WP
d'Antibes, Germain
   See Simenon, Georges (Jacques Christian)
Danticat, Edwidge 1969- . **BLC 2:1; CLC 94, 139, 228; SSC 100**
   See also AAYA 29; CA 152, 192; CAAE 192; CANR 73, 129, 179; CN 7; DNFS 1; EXPS; LATS 1:2; MTCW 2; MTFW 2005; NFS 28; SSFS 1, 25; YAW
Danvers, Dennis 1947- .... **CLC 70**
Danziger, Paula 1944-2004 .... **CLC 21**
   See also AAYA 4, 36; BYA 6, 7, 14; CA 112; 115; 229; CANR 37, 132; CLR 20; JRDA; MAICYA 1, 2; MTFW 2005; SATA 36, 63, 102, 149; SATA-Brief 30; SATA-Obit 155; WYA; YAW
Da Ponte, Lorenzo 1749-1838 .... **NCLC 50**
d'Aragona, Tullia 1510(?)-1556 .... **LC 121**
Dario, Ruben 1867-1916 .... **HLC 1; PC 15; TCLC 4**
   See also CA 131; CANR 81; DAM MULT; DLB 290; EWL 3; HW 1, 2; LAW; MTCW 1, 2; MTFW 2005; RGWL 2, 3
Darko, Amma 1956- .... **BLC 2:1**
Darley, George 1795-1846 .... **NCLC 2**
   See also DLB 96; RGEL 2
Darrow, Clarence (Seward)
   1857-1938 .... **TCLC 81**
   See also CA 164; DLB 303
Darwin, Charles 1809-1882 .... **NCLC 57**
   See also BRWS 7; DLB 57, 166; LATS 1:1; RGEL 2; TEA; WLIT 4
Darwin, Erasmus 1731-1802 .... **NCLC 106**
   See also DLB 93; RGEL 2

Darwish, Mahmoud 1941-2008 .... **PC 86**
   See Darwish, Mahmud
   See also CA 164; CANR 133; MTCW 2; MTFW 2005
Darwish, Mahmoud -2008
   See Darwish, Mahmud
   See also CWW 2; EWL 3
Daryush, Elizabeth 1887-1977 ...... **CLC 6, 19**
   See also CA 49-52; CANR 3, 81; DLB 20
Das, Kamala 1934- .... **CLC 191; PC 43**
   See also CA 101; CANR 27, 59; CP 1, 2, 3, 4, 5, 6, 7; CWP; DLB 323; FW
Dasgupta, Surendranath
   1887-1952 .... **TCLC 81**
   See also CA 157
Dashwood, Edmee Elizabeth Monica de la Pasture 1890-1943
   See Delafield, E. M.
   See also CA 119; 154
da Silva, Antonio Jose
   1705-1739 .... **NCLC 114**
Daudet, (Louis Marie) Alphonse
   1840-1897 .... **NCLC 1**
   See also DLB 123; GFL 1789 to the Present; RGSF 2
Daudet, Alphonse Marie Leon
   1867-1942 .... **SSC 94**
   See also CA 217
d'Aulnoy, Marie-Catherine c.
   1650-1705 .... **LC 100**
Daumal, Rene 1908-1944 .... **TCLC 14**
   See also CA 114; 247; EWL 3
Davenant, William 1606-1668 .... **LC 13**
   See also DLB 58, 126; RGEL 2
Davenport, Guy (Mattison, Jr.)
   1927-2005 . **CLC 6, 14, 38, 241; SSC 16**
   See also CA 33-36R; 235; CANR 23, 73; CN 3, 4, 5, 6; CSW; DLB 130
David, Robert
   See Nezval, Vitezslav
Davidson, Avram (James) 1923-1993
   See Queen, Ellery
   See also CA 101; 171; CANR 26; DLB 8; FANT; SFW 4; SUFW 1, 2
Davidson, Donald (Grady)
   1893-1968 .... **CLC 2, 13, 19**
   See also CA 5-8R; 25-28R; CANR 4, 84; DLB 45
Davidson, Hugh
   See Hamilton, Edmond
Davidson, John 1857-1909 .... **TCLC 24**
   See also CA 118; 217; DLB 19; RGEL 2
Davidson, Sara 1943- .... **CLC 9**
   See also CA 81-84; CANR 44, 68; DLB 185
Davie, Donald (Alfred) 1922-1995 .... **CLC 5, 8, 10, 31; PC 29**
   See also BRWS 6; CA 1-4R; 149; CAAS 3; CANR 1, 44; CP 1, 2, 3, 4, 5, 6; DLB 27; MTCW 1; RGEL 2
Davie, Elspeth 1918-1995 .... **SSC 52**
   See also CA 120; 126; 150; CANR 141; DLB 139
Davies, Ray(mond Douglas) 1944- ... **CLC 21**
   See also CA 116; 146; CANR 92
Davies, Rhys 1901-1978 .... **CLC 23**
   See also CA 9-12R; 81-84; CANR 4; CN 1, 2; DLB 139, 191
Davies, Robertson 1913-1995 .. **CLC 2, 7, 13, 25, 42, 75, 91; WLC 2**
   See Marchbanks, Samuel
   See also BEST 89:2; BPFB 1; CA 33-36R; 150; CANR 17, 42, 103; CN 1, 2, 3, 4, 5, 6; CPW; DA; DA3; DAB; DAC; DAM MST, NOV, POP; DLB 68; EWL 3; HGG; INT CANR-17; MTCW 1, 2; MTFW 2005; RGEL 2; TWA
Davies, Sir John 1569-1626 .... **LC 85**
   See also DLB 172

Davies, Walter C.
   See Kornbluth, C(yril) M.
Davies, William Henry 1871-1940 ... **TCLC 5**
   See also BRWS 11; CA 104; 179; DLB 19, 174; EWL 3; RGEL 2
Davies, William Robertson
   See Davies, Robertson
Da Vinci, Leonardo 1452-1519 ..... **LC 12, 57, 60**
   See also AAYA 40
Davis, Angela (Yvonne) 1944- .... **CLC 77**
   See also BW 2, 3; CA 57-60; CANR 10, 81; CSW; DA3; DAM MULT; FW
Davis, B. Lynch
   See Bioy Casares, Adolfo; Borges, Jorge Luis
Davis, Frank Marshall 1905-1987 ... **BLC 1:1**
   See also BW 2, 3; CA 125; 123; CANR 42, 80; DAM MULT; DLB 51
Davis, Gordon
   See Hunt, E. Howard
Davis, H(arold) L(enoir) 1896-1960 . **CLC 49**
   See also ANW; CA 178; 89-92; DLB 9, 206; SATA 114; TCWW 1, 2
Davis, Hart
   See Poniatowska, Elena
Davis, Natalie Zemon 1928- .... **CLC 204**
   See also CA 53-56; CANR 58, 100, 174
Davis, Rebecca (Blaine) Harding
   1831-1910 .... **SSC 38, 109; TCLC 6**
   See also AMWS 16; CA 104; 179; DLB 74, 239; FW; NFS 14; RGAL 4; SSFS 26; TUS
Davis, Richard Harding
   1864-1916 .... **TCLC 24**
   See also CA 114; 179; DLB 12, 23, 78, 79, 189; DLBD 13; RGAL 4
Davison, Frank Dalby 1893-1970 ..... **CLC 15**
   See also CA 217; 116; DLB 260
Davison, Lawrence H.
   See Lawrence, D(avid) H(erbert Richards)
Davison, Peter (Hubert) 1928-2004 . **CLC 28**
   See also CA 9-12R; 234; CAAS 4; CANR 3, 43, 84; CP 1, 2, 3, 4, 5, 6, 7; DLB 5
Davys, Mary 1674-1732 .... **LC 1, 46**
   See also DLB 39
Dawson, (Guy) Fielding (Lewis)
   1930-2002 .... **CLC 6**
   See also CA 85-88; 202; CANR 108; DLB 130; DLBY 2002
Dawson, Peter
   See Faust, Frederick (Schiller)
   See also TCWW 1, 2
Day, Clarence (Shepard, Jr.)
   1874-1935 .... **TCLC 25**
   See also CA 108; 199; DLB 11
Day, John 1574(?)-1640(?) .... **LC 70**
   See also DLB 62, 170; RGEL 2
Day, Thomas 1748-1789 .... **LC 1**
   See also DLB 39; YABC 1
Day Lewis, C(ecil) 1904-1972 . **CLC 1, 6, 10; PC 11**
   See Blake, Nicholas; Lewis, C. Day
   See also BRWS 3; CA 13-16; 33-36R; CANR 34; CAP 1; CP 1; CWRI 5; DAM POET; DLB 15, 20; EWL 3; MTCW 1, 2; RGEL 2
Dazai Osamu SSC 41; TCLC 11
   See Tsushima, Shuji
   See also CA 164; DLB 182; EWL 3; MJW; RGSF 2; RGWL 2, 3; TWA
de Andrade, Carlos Drummond
   See Drummond de Andrade, Carlos
de Andrade, Mario 1892(?)-1945
   See Andrade, Mario de
   See also CA 178; HW 2
Deane, Norman
   See Creasey, John

Deane, Seamus (Francis) 1940- ...... **CLC 122**
  See also CA 118; CANR 42

de Athayde, Alvaro Coelho
  See Pessoa, Fernando

de Beauvoir, Simone
  See Beauvoir, Simone de

de Beer, P.
  See Bosman, Herman Charles

De Botton, Alain 1969- .... **CLC 203**
  See also CA 159; CANR 96

de Brissac, Malcolm
  See Dickinson, Peter (Malcolm de Brissac)

de Campos, Alvaro
  See Pessoa, Fernando

de Chardin, Pierre Teilhard
  See Teilhard de Chardin, (Marie Joseph) Pierre

de Crenne, Helisenne c. 1510-c. 1560 .... **LC 113**

Dee, John 1527-1608 .... **LC 20**
  See also DLB 136, 213

Deer, Sandra 1940- .... **CLC 45**
  See also CA 186

De Ferrari, Gabriella 1941- .... **CLC 65**
  See also CA 146

de Filippo, Eduardo 1900-1984 ... **TCLC 127**
  See also CA 132; 114; EWL 3; MTCW 1; RGWL 2, 3

Defoe, Daniel 1660(?)-1731 .... **LC 1, 42, 108; WLC 2**
  See also AAYA 27; BRW 3; BRWR 1; BYA 4; CDBLB 1660-1789; CLR 61; DA; DA3; DAB; DAC; DAM MST, NOV; DLB 39, 95, 101, 336; JRDA; LAIT 1; LMFS 1; MAICYA 1, 2; NFS 9, 13; RGEL 2; SATA 22; TEA; WCH; WLIT 3

de Gouges, Olympe
  See de Gouges, Olympe

de Gouges, Olympe 1748-1793 .... **LC 127**
  See also DLB 313

de Gourmont, Remy(-Marie-Charles)
  See Gourmont, Remy(-Marie-Charles) de

de Gournay, Marie le Jars 1566-1645 .... **LC 98**
  See also DLB 327; FW

de Hartog, Jan 1914-2002 .... **CLC 19**
  See also CA 1-4R; 210; CANR 1; DFS 12

de Hostos, E. M.
  See Hostos (y Bonilla), Eugenio Maria de

de Hostos, Eugenio M.
  See Hostos (y Bonilla), Eugenio Maria de

Deighton, Len CLC 4, 7, 22, 46
  See Deighton, Leonard Cyril
  See also AAYA 6; BEST 89:2; BPFB 1; CDBLB 1960 to Present; CMW 4; CN 1, 2, 3, 4, 5, 6, 7; CPW; DLB 87

Deighton, Leonard Cyril 1929-
  See Deighton, Len
  See also AAYA 57; CA 9-12R; CANR 19, 33, 68; DA3; DAM NOV, POP; MTCW 1, 2; MTFW 2005

Dekker, Thomas 1572(?)-1632 ..... **DC 12; LC 22, 159**
  See also CDBLB Before 1660; DAM DRAM; DLB 62, 172; LMFS 1; RGEL 2

de Laclos, Pierre Ambroise Franois
  See Laclos, Pierre-Ambroise Francois

Delacroix, (Ferdinand-Victor-)Eugene 1798-1863 .... **NCLC 133**
  See also EW 5

Delafield, E. M. TCLC 61
  See Dashwood, Edmee Elizabeth Monica de la Pasture
  See also DLB 34; RHW

de la Mare, Walter (John) 1873-1956 ..... **PC 77; SSC 14; TCLC 4, 53; WLC 2**
  See also CA 163; CDBLB 1914-1945; CLR 23; CWRI 5; DA3; DAB; DAC; DAM MST, POET; DLB 19, 153, 162, 255, 284; EWL 3; EXPP; HGG; MAICYA 1, 2; MTCW 1; MTFW 2005; RGEL 2; RGSF 2; SATA 16; SUFW 1; TEA; WCH

de Lamartine, Alphonse (Marie Louis Prat)
  See Lamartine, Alphonse (Marie Louis Prat) de

Delaney, Franey
  See O'Hara, John (Henry)

Delaney, Shelagh 1939- .... **CLC 29**
  See also CA 17-20R; CANR 30, 67; CBD; CD 5, 6; CDBLB 1960 to Present; CWD; DAM DRAM; DFS 7; DLB 13; MTCW 1

Delany, Martin Robison 1812-1885 .... **NCLC 93**
  See also DLB 50; RGAL 4

Delany, Mary (Granville Pendarves) 1700-1788 .... **LC 12**

Delany, Samuel R., Jr. 1942- .... **BLC 1:1; CLC 8, 14, 38, 141**
  See also AAYA 24; AFAW 2; BPFB 1; BW 2, 3; CA 81-84; CANR 27, 43, 116, 172; CN 2, 3, 4, 5, 6, 7; DAM MULT; DLB 8, 33; FANT; MAL 5; MTCW 1, 2; RGAL 4; SATA 92; SCFW 1, 2; SFW 4; SUFW 2

Delany, Samuel Ray
  See Delany, Samuel R., Jr.

de la Parra, (Ana) Teresa (Sonojo) 1890(?)-1936 .... **TCLC 185**
  See Parra Sanojo, Ana Teresa de la
  See also CA 178; HW 2

De La Ramee, Marie Louise 1839-1908
  See Ouida
  See also CA 204; SATA 20

de la Roche, Mazo 1879-1961 .... **CLC 14**
  See also CA 85-88; CANR 30; DLB 68; RGEL 2; RHW; SATA 64

De La Salle, Innocent
  See Hartmann, Sadakichi

de Laureamont, Comte
  See Lautreamont

Delbanco, Nicholas 1942- ..... **CLC 6, 13, 167**
  See also CA 17-20R, 189; CAAE 189; CAAS 2; CANR 29, 55, 116, 150; CN 7; DLB 6, 234

Delbanco, Nicholas Franklin
  See Delbanco, Nicholas

del Castillo, Michel 1933- .... **CLC 38**
  See also CA 109; CANR 77

Deledda, Grazia (Cosima) 1875(?)-1936 .... **TCLC 23**
  See also CA 123; 205; DLB 264, 329; EWL 3; RGWL 2, 3; WLIT 7

Deleuze, Gilles 1925-1995 .... **TCLC 116**
  See also DLB 296

Delgado, Abelardo (Lalo) B(arrientos) 1930-2004 .... **HLC 1**
  See also CA 131; 230; CAAS 15; CANR 90; DAM MST, MULT; DLB 82; HW 1, 2

Delibes, Miguel CLC 8, 18
  See Delibes Setien, Miguel
  See also DLB 322; EWL 3

Delibes Setien, Miguel 1920-
  See Delibes, Miguel
  See also CA 45-48; CANR 1, 32; CWW 2; HW 1; MTCW 1

DeLillo, Don 1936- ..... **CLC 8, 10, 13, 27, 39, 54, 76, 143, 210, 213**
  See also AMWC 2; AMWS 6; BEST 89:1; BPFB 1; CA 81-84; CANR 21, 76, 92, 133, 173; CN 3, 4, 5, 6, 7; CPW; DA3; DAM NOV, POP; DLB 6, 173; EWL 3; MAL 5; MTCW 1, 2; MTFW 2005; NFS 28; RGAL 4; TUS

de Lisser, H. G.
  See De Lisser, H(erbert) G(eorge)
  See also DLB 117

De Lisser, H(erbert) G(eorge) 1878-1944 .... **TCLC 12**
  See de Lisser, H. G.
  See also BW 2; CA 109; 152

Deloire, Pierre
  See Peguy, Charles (Pierre)

Deloney, Thomas 1543(?)-1600 .... **LC 41; PC 79**
  See also DLB 167; RGEL 2

Deloria, Ella (Cara) 1889-1971(?) ..... **NNAL**
  See also CA 152; DAM MULT; DLB 175

Deloria, Vine, Jr. 1933-2005 .... **CLC 21, 122; NNAL**
  See also CA 53-56; 245; CANR 5, 20, 48, 98; DAM MULT; DLB 175; MTCW 1; SATA 21; SATA-Obit 171

Deloria, Vine Victor, Jr.
  See Deloria, Vine, Jr.

del Valle-Inclan, Ramon (Maria)
  See Valle-Inclan, Ramon (Maria) del
  See also DLB 322

Del Vecchio, John M(ichael) 1947- .. **CLC 29**
  See also CA 110; DLBD 9

de Man, Paul (Adolph Michel) 1919-1983 .... **CLC 55**
  See also CA 128; 111; CANR 61; DLB 67; MTCW 1, 2

DeMarinis, Rick 1934- .... **CLC 54**
  See also CA 57-60, 184; CAAE 184; CAAS 24; CANR 9, 25, 50, 160; DLB 218; TCWW 2

de Maupassant, (Henri Rene Albert) Guy
  See Maupassant, (Henri Rene Albert) Guy de

Dembry, R. Emmet
  See Murfree, Mary Noailles

Demby, William 1922- ...... **BLC 1:1; CLC 53**
  See also BW 1, 3; CA 81-84; CANR 81; DAM MULT; DLB 33

de Menton, Francisco
  See Chin, Frank (Chew, Jr.)

Demetrius of Phalerum c. 307B.C.- .... **CMLC 34**

Demijohn, Thom
  See Disch, Thomas M.

De Mille, James 1833-1880 .... **NCLC 123**
  See also DLB 99, 251

Deming, Richard 1915-1983
  See Queen, Ellery
  See also CA 9-12R; CANR 3, 94; SATA 24

Democritus c. 460B.C.-c. 370B.C. . **CMLC 47**

de Montaigne, Michel (Eyquem)
  See Montaigne, Michel (Eyquem) de

de Montherlant, Henry (Milon)
  See Montherlant, Henry (Milon) de

Demosthenes 384B.C.-322B.C. ...... **CMLC 13**
  See also AW 1; DLB 176; RGWL 2, 3; WLIT 8

de Musset, (Louis Charles) Alfred
  See Musset, Alfred de

de Natale, Francine
  See Malzberg, Barry N(athaniel)

de Navarre, Marguerite 1492-1549 ... **LC 61; SSC 85**
  See Marguerite d'Angouleme; Marguerite de Navarre
  See also DLB 327

Denby, Edwin (Orr) 1903-1983 .... **CLC 48**
  See also CA 138; 110; CP 1

de Nerval, Gerard
  See Nerval, Gerard de

Denham, John 1615-1669 .... **LC 73**
  See also DLB 58, 126; RGEL 2

Denis, Julio
  See Cortazar, Julio

Denmark, Harrison
  See Zelazny, Roger
Dennis, John 1658-1734 .... **LC 11, 154**
  See also DLB 101; RGEL 2
Dennis, Nigel (Forbes) 1912-1989 ...... **CLC 8**
  See also CA 25-28R; 129; CN 1, 2, 3, 4;
  DLB 13, 15, 233; EWL 3; MTCW 1
Dent, Lester 1904-1959 .... **TCLC 72**
  See also CA 112; 161; CMW 4; DLB 306;
  SFW 4
De Palma, Brian 1940- .... **CLC 20, 247**
  See also CA 109
De Palma, Brian Russell
  See De Palma, Brian
de Pizan, Christine
  See Christine de Pizan
  See also FL 1:1
De Quincey, Thomas 1785-1859 ..... **NCLC 4,
  87, 198**
  See also BRW 4; CDBLB 1789-1832; DLB
  110, 144; RGEL 2
De Ray, Jill
  See Moore, Alan
Deren, Eleanora 1908(?)-1961
  See Deren, Maya
  See also CA 192; 111
Deren, Maya CLC 16, 102
  See Deren, Eleanora
Derleth, August (William)
  1909-1971 .... **CLC 31**
  See also BPFB 1; BYA 9, 10; CA 1-4R; 29-
  32R; CANR 4; CMW 4; CN 1; DLB 9;
  DLBD 17; HGG; SATA 5; SUFW 1
Der Nister 1884-1950 .... **TCLC 56**
  See Nister, Der
de Routisie, Albert
  See Aragon, Louis
Derrida, Jacques 1930-2004 ...... **CLC 24, 87,
  225**
  See also CA 124; 127; 232; CANR 76, 98,
  133; DLB 242; EWL 3; LMFS 2; MTCW
  2; TWA
Derry Down Derry
  See Lear, Edward
Dersonnes, Jacques
  See Simenon, Georges (Jacques Christian)
Der Stricker c. 1190-c. 1250 .... **CMLC 75**
  See also DLB 138
Desai, Anita 1937- .... **CLC 19, 37, 97, 175**
  See also BRWS 5; CA 81-84; CANR 33,
  53, 95, 133; CN 1, 2, 3, 4, 5, 6, 7; CWRI
  5; DA3; DAB; DAM NOV; DLB 271,
  323; DNFS 2; EWL 3; FW; MTCW 1, 2;
  MTFW 2005; SATA 63, 126
Desai, Kiran 1971- .... **CLC 119**
  See also BYA 16; CA 171; CANR 127; NFS
  28
de Saint-Luc, Jean
  See Glassco, John
de Saint Roman, Arnaud
  See Aragon, Louis
Desbordes-Valmore, Marceline
  1786-1859 .... **NCLC 97**
  See also DLB 217
Descartes, Rene 1596-1650 .... **LC 20, 35, 150**
  See also DLB 268; EW 3; GFL Beginnings
  to 1789
Deschamps, Eustache 1340(?)-1404 .. **LC 103**
  See also DLB 208
De Sica, Vittorio 1901(?)-1974 .... **CLC 20**
  See also CA 117
Desnos, Robert 1900-1945 .... **TCLC 22**
  See also CA 121; 151; CANR 107; DLB
  258; EWL 3; LMFS 2
Destouches, Louis-Ferdinand
  1894-1961 .... **CLC 9, 15**
  See Celine, Louis-Ferdinand
  See also CA 85-88; CANR 28; MTCW 1

de Tolignac, Gaston
  See Griffith, D.W.
Deutsch, Babette 1895-1982 .... **CLC 18**
  See also BYA 3; CA 1-4R; 108; CANR 4,
  79; CP 1, 2, 3; DLB 45; SATA 1; SATA-
  Obit 33
Devenant, William 1606-1649 .... **LC 13**
Devkota, Laxmiprasad 1909-1959 . **TCLC 23**
  See also CA 123
De Voto, Bernard (Augustine)
  1897-1955 .... **TCLC 29**
  See also CA 113; 160; DLB 9, 256; MAL
  5; TCWW 1, 2
De Vries, Peter 1910-1993 ..... **CLC 1, 2, 3, 7,
  10, 28, 46**
  See also CA 17-20R; 142; CANR 41; CN
  1, 2, 3, 4, 5; DAM NOV; DLB 6; DLBY
  1982; MAL 5; MTCW 1, 2; MTFW 2005
Dewey, John 1859-1952 .... **TCLC 95**
  See also CA 114; 170; CANR 144; DLB
  246, 270; RGAL 4
Dexter, John
  See Bradley, Marion Zimmer
  See also GLL 1
Dexter, Martin
  See Faust, Frederick (Schiller)
Dexter, Pete 1943- .... **CLC 34, 55**
  See also BEST 89:2; CA 127; 131; CANR
  129; CPW; DAM POP; INT CA-131;
  MAL 5; MTCW 1; MTFW 2005
Diamano, Silmang
  See Senghor, Leopold Sedar
Diamant, Anita 1951- .... **CLC 239**
  See also CA 145; CANR 126
Diamond, Neil 1941- .... **CLC 30**
  See also CA 108
Diaz, Junot 1968- .... **CLC 258**
  See also BYA 12; CA 161; CANR 119, 183;
  LLW; SSFS 20
Diaz del Castillo, Bernal c.
  1496-1584 .... **HLCS 1; LC 31**
  See also DLB 318; LAW
di Bassetto, Corno
  See Shaw, George Bernard
Dick, Philip K. 1928-1982 ... **CLC 10, 30, 72;
  SSC 57**
  See also AAYA 24; BPFB 1; BYA 11; CA
  49-52; 106; CANR 2, 16, 132; CN 2, 3;
  CPW; DA3; DAM NOV, POP; DLB 8;
  MTCW 1, 2; MTFW 2005; NFS 5, 26;
  SCFW 1, 2; SFW 4
Dick, Philip Kindred
  See Dick, Philip K.
Dickens, Charles (John Huffam)
  1812-1870 .... **NCLC 3, 8, 18, 26, 37, 50,
  86, 105, 113, 161, 187, 203; SSC 17, 49,
  88; WLC 2**
  See also AAYA 23; BRW 5; BRWC 1, 2;
  BYA 1, 2, 3, 13, 14; CDBLB 1832-1890;
  CLR 95; CMW 4; DA; DA3; DAB; DAC;
  DAM MST, NOV; DLB 21, 55, 70, 159,
  166; EXPN; GL 2; HGG; JRDA; LAIT 1,
  2; LATS 1:1; LMFS 1; MAICYA 1, 2;
  NFS 4, 5, 10, 14, 20, 25; RGEL 2; RGSF
  2; SATA 15; SUFW 1; TEA; WCH; WLIT
  4; WYA
Dickey, James (Lafayette)
  1923-1997 .... **CLC 1, 2, 4, 7, 10, 15, 47,
  109; PC 40; TCLC 151**
  See also AAYA 50; AITN 1, 2; AMWS 4;
  BPFB 1; CA 9-12R; 156; CABS 2; CANR
  10, 48, 61, 105; CDALB 1968-1988; CP
  1, 2, 3, 4, 5, 6; CPW; CSW; DA3; DAM
  NOV, POET, POP; DLB 5, 193, 342;
  DLBD 7; DLBY 1982, 1993, 1996, 1997,
  1998; EWL 3; INT CANR-10; MAL 5;
  MTCW 1, 2; NFS 9; PFS 6, 11; RGAL 4;
  TUS

Dickey, William 1928-1994 .... **CLC 3, 28**
  See also CA 9-12R; 145; CANR 24, 79; CP
  1, 2, 3, 4; DLB 5
Dickinson, Charles 1951- .... **CLC 49**
  See also CA 128; CANR 141
Dickinson, Emily (Elizabeth)
  1830-1886 ..... **NCLC 21, 77, 171; PC 1;
  WLC 2**
  See also AAYA 22; AMW; AMWR 1;
  CDALB 1865-1917; DA; DA3; DAB;
  DAC; DAM MST, POET; DLB 1, 243;
  EXPP; FL 1:3; MBL; PAB; PFS 1, 2, 3,
  4, 5, 6, 8, 10, 11, 13, 16, 28; RGAL 4;
  SATA 29; TUS; WP; WYA
Dickinson, Mrs. Herbert Ward
  See Phelps, Elizabeth Stuart
Dickinson, Peter (Malcolm de Brissac)
  1927- .... **CLC 12, 35**
  See also AAYA 9, 49; BYA 5; CA 41-44R;
  CANR 31, 58, 88, 134; CLR 29, 125;
  CMW 4; DLB 87, 161, 276; JRDA; MAI-
  CYA 1, 2; SATA 5, 62, 95, 150; SFW 4;
  WYA; YAW
Dickson, Carr
  See Carr, John Dickson
Dickson, Carter
  See Carr, John Dickson
Diderot, Denis 1713-1784 .... **LC 26, 126**
  See also DLB 313; EW 4; GFL Beginnings
  to 1789; LMFS 1; RGWL 2, 3
Didion, Joan 1934- . **CLC 1, 3, 8, 14, 32, 129**
  See also AITN 1; AMWS 4; CA 5-8R;
  CANR 14, 52, 76, 125, 174; CDALB
  1968-1988; CN 2, 3, 4, 5, 6, 7; DA3;
  DAM NOV; DLB 2, 173, 185; DLBY
  1981, 1986; EWL 3; MAL 5; MBL;
  MTCW 1, 2; MTFW 2005; NFS 3; RGAL
  4; TCLE 1:1; TCWW 2; TUS
di Donato, Pietro 1911-1992 .... **TCLC 159**
  See also CA 101; 136; DLB 9
Dietrich, Robert
  See Hunt, E. Howard
Difusa, Pati
  See Almodovar, Pedro
Dillard, Annie 1945- ...... **CLC 9, 60, 115, 216**
  See also AAYA 6, 43; AMWS 6; ANW; CA
  49-52; CANR 3, 43, 62, 90, 125; DA3;
  DAM NOV; DLB 275, 278; DLBY 1980;
  LAIT 4, 5; MAL 5; MTCW 1, 2; MTFW
  2005; NCFS 1; RGAL 4; SATA 10, 140;
  TCLE 1:1; TUS
Dillard, R(ichard) H(enry) W(ilde)
  1937- .... **CLC 5**
  See also CA 21-24R; CAAS 7; CANR 10;
  CP 2, 3, 4, 5, 6, 7; CSW; DLB 5, 244
Dillon, Eilis 1920-1994 .... **CLC 17**
  See also CA 9-12R; 182; 147; CAAE 182;
  CAAS 3; CANR 4, 38, 78; CLR 26; MAI-
  CYA 1, 2; MAICYAS 1; SATA 2, 74;
  SATA-Essay 105; SATA-Obit 83; YAW
Dimont, Penelope
  See Mortimer, Penelope (Ruth)
Dinesen, Isak CLC 10, 29, 95; SSC 7, 75
  See Blixen, Karen (Christentze Dinesen)
  See also EW 10; EWL 3; EXPS; FW; GL
  2; HGG; LAIT 3; MTCW 1; NCFS 2;
  NFS 9; RGSF 2; RGWL 2, 3; SSFS 3, 6,
  13; WLIT 2
Ding Ling CLC 68
  See Chiang, Pin-chin
  See also DLB 328; RGWL 3
Diodorus Siculus c. 90B.C.-c.
  31B.C. .... **CMLC 88**
Diphusa, Patty
  See Almodovar, Pedro
Disch, Thomas M. 1940-2008 .... **CLC 7, 36**
  See Disch, Tom
  See also AAYA 17; BPFB 1; CA 21-24R;
  274; CAAS 4; CANR 17, 36, 54, 89; CLR
  18; CP 5, 6, 7; DA3; DLB 8; HGG; MAI-

CYA 1, 2; MTCW 1, 2; MTFW 2005; SAAS 15; SATA 92; SCFW 1, 2; SFW 4; SUFW 2

Disch, Thomas Michael
See Disch, Thomas M.

Disch, Tom
See Disch, Thomas M.
See also DLB 282

d'Isly, Georges
See Simenon, Georges (Jacques Christian)

Disraeli, Benjamin 1804-1881 ... **NCLC 2, 39, 79**
See also BRW 4; DLB 21, 55; RGEL 2

Ditcum, Steve
See Crumb, R.

Dixon, Paige
See Corcoran, Barbara (Asenath)

Dixon, Stephen 1936- .... **CLC 52; SSC 16**
See also AMWS 12; CA 89-92; CANR 17, 40, 54, 91, 175; CN 4, 5, 6, 7; DLB 130; MAL 5

Dixon, Thomas, Jr. 1864-1946 ..... **TCLC 163**
See also RHW

Djebar, Assia 1936- .... **BLC 2:1; CLC 182; SSC 114**
See also CA 188; CANR 169; DLB 346; EWL 3; RGWL 3; WLIT 2

Doak, Annie
See Dillard, Annie

Dobell, Sydney Thompson 1824-1874 .... **NCLC 43**
See also DLB 32; RGEL 2

Doblin, Alfred TCLC 13
See Doeblin, Alfred
See also CDWLB 2; EWL 3; RGWL 2, 3

Dobroliubov, Nikolai Aleksandrovich
See Dobrolyubov, Nikolai Alexandrovich
See also DLB 277

Dobrolyubov, Nikolai Alexandrovich 1836-1861 .... **NCLC 5**
See Dobroliubov, Nikolai Aleksandrovich

Dobson, Austin 1840-1921 .... **TCLC 79**
See also DLB 35, 144

Dobyns, Stephen 1941- .... **CLC 37, 233**
See also AMWS 13; CA 45-48; CANR 2, 18, 99; CMW 4; CP 4, 5, 6, 7; PFS 23

Doctorow, Edgar Laurence
See Doctorow, E.L.

Doctorow, E.L. 1931- . **CLC 6, 11, 15, 18, 37, 44, 65, 113, 214**
See also AAYA 22; AITN 2; AMWS 4; BEST 89:3; BPFB 1; CA 45-48; CANR 2, 33, 51, 76, 97, 133, 170; CDALB 1968-1988; CN 3, 4, 5, 6, 7; CPW; DA3; DAM NOV, POP; DLB 2, 28, 173; DLBY 1980; EWL 3; LAIT 3; MAL 5; MTCW 1, 2; MTFW 2005; NFS 6; RGAL 4; RGHL; RHW; TCLE 1:1; TCWW 1, 2; TUS

Dodgson, Charles L(utwidge) 1832-1898
See Carroll, Lewis
See also CLR 2; DA; DA3; DAB; DAC; DAM MST, NOV, POET; MAICYA 1, 2; SATA 100; YABC 2

Dodsley, Robert 1703-1764 .... **LC 97**
See also DLB 95; RGEL 2

Dodson, Owen (Vincent) 1914-1983 .... **BLC 1:1; CLC 79**
See also BW 1; CA 65-68; 110; CANR 24; DAM MULT; DLB 76

Doeblin, Alfred 1878-1957 .... **TCLC 13**
See Doblin, Alfred
See also CA 110; 141; DLB 66

Doerr, Harriet 1910-2002 .... **CLC 34**
See also CA 117; 122; 213; CANR 47; INT CA-122; LATS 1:2

Domecq, H(onorio) Bustos
See Bioy Casares, Adolfo; Borges, Jorge Luis

Domini, Rey
See Lorde, Audre
See also GLL 1

Dominique
See Proust, (Valentin-Louis-George-Eugene) Marcel

Don, A
See Stephen, Sir Leslie

Donaldson, Stephen R. 1947- ... **CLC 46, 138**
See also AAYA 36; BPFB 1; CA 89-92; CANR 13, 55, 99; CPW; DAM POP; FANT; INT CANR-13; SATA 121; SFW 4; SUFW 1, 2

Donleavy, J(ames) P(atrick) 1926- .... **CLC 1, 4, 6, 10, 45**
See also AITN 2; BPFB 1; CA 9-12R; CANR 24, 49, 62, 80, 124; CBD; CD 5, 6; CN 1, 2, 3, 4, 5, 6, 7; DLB 6, 173; INT CANR-24; MAL 5; MTCW 1, 2; MTFW 2005; RGAL 4

Donnadieu, Marguerite
See Duras, Marguerite

Donne, John 1572-1631 ... **LC 10, 24, 91; PC 1, 43; WLC 2**
See also AAYA 67; BRW 1; BRWC 1; BRWR 2; CDBLB Before 1660; DA; DAB; DAC; DAM MST, POET; DLB 121, 151; EXPP; PAB; PFS 2, 11; RGEL 3; TEA; WLIT 3; WP

Donnell, David 1939(?)- .... **CLC 34**
See also CA 197

Donoghue, Denis 1928- .... **CLC 209**
See also CA 17-20R; CANR 16, 102

Donoghue, Emma 1969- .... **CLC 239**
See also CA 155; CANR 103, 152; DLB 267; GLL 2; SATA 101

Donoghue, P.S.
See Hunt, E. Howard

Donoso (Yanez), Jose 1924-1996 ... **CLC 4, 8, 11, 32, 99; HLC 1; SSC 34; TCLC 133**
See also CA 81-84; 155; CANR 32, 73; CDWLB 3; CWW 2; DAM MULT; DLB 113; EWL 3; HW 1, 2; LAW; LAWS 1; MTCW 1, 2; MTFW 2005; RGSF 2; WLIT 1

Donovan, John 1928-1992 .... **CLC 35**
See also AAYA 20; CA 97-100; 137; CLR 3; MAICYA 1, 2; SATA 72; SATA-Brief 29; YAW

Don Roberto
See Cunninghame Graham, Robert (Gallnigad) Bontine

Doolittle, Hilda 1886-1961 . **CLC 3, 8, 14, 31, 34, 73; PC 5; WLC 3**
See H. D.
See also AAYA 66; AMWS 1; CA 97-100; CANR 35, 131; DA; DAC; DAM MST, POET; DLB 4, 45; EWL 3; FW; GLL 1; LMFS 2; MAL 5; MBL; MTCW 1, 2; MTFW 2005; PFS 6, 28; RGAL 4

Doppo, Kunikida TCLC 99
See Kunikida Doppo

Dorfman, Ariel 1942- .... **CLC 48, 77, 189; HLC 1**
See also CA 124; 130; CANR 67, 70, 135; CWW 2; DAM MULT; DFS 4; EWL 3; HW 1, 2; INT CA-130; WLIT 1

Dorn, Edward (Merton) 1929-1999 .... **CLC 10, 18**
See also CA 93-96; 187; CANR 42, 79; CP 1, 2, 3, 4, 5, 6, 7; DLB 5; INT CA-93-96; WP

Dor-Ner, Zvi CLC 70

Dorris, Michael 1945-1997 .... **CLC 109; NNAL**
See also AAYA 20; BEST 90:1; BYA 12; CA 102; 157; CANR 19, 46, 75; CLR 58; DA3; DAM MULT, NOV; DLB 175; LAIT 5; MTCW 2; MTFW 2005; NFS 3; RGAL 4; SATA 75; SATA-Obit 94; TCWW 2; YAW

Dorris, Michael A.
See Dorris, Michael

Dorsan, Luc
See Simenon, Georges (Jacques Christian)

Dorsange, Jean
See Simenon, Georges (Jacques Christian)

Dorset
See Sackville, Thomas

Dos Passos, John (Roderigo) 1896-1970 ... **CLC 1, 4, 8, 11, 15, 25, 34, 82; WLC 2**
See also AMW; BPFB 1; CA 1-4R; 29-32R; CANR 3; CDALB 1929-1941; DA; DA3; DAB; DAC; DAM MST, NOV; DLB 4, 9, 274, 316; DLBD 1, 15; DLBY 1996; EWL 3; MAL 5; MTCW 1, 2; MTFW 2005; NFS 14; RGAL 4; TUS

Dossage, Jean
See Simenon, Georges (Jacques Christian)

Dostoevsky, Fedor Mikhailovich 1821-1881 .. **NCLC 2, 7, 21, 33, 43, 119, 167, 202; SSC 2, 33, 44; WLC 2**
See Dostoevsky, Fyodor
See also AAYA 40; DA; DA3; DAB; DAC; DAM MST, NOV; EW 7; EXPN; NFS 28; RGSF 2; RGWL 2, 3; SSFS 8; TWA

Dostoevsky, Fyodor
See Dostoevsky, Fedor Mikhailovich
See also DLB 238; LATS 1:1; LMFS 1, 2

Doty, Mark 1953(?)- .... **CLC 176; PC 53**
See also AMWS 11; CA 161, 183; CAAE 183; CANR 110, 173; CP 7; PFS 28

Doty, Mark A.
See Doty, Mark

Doty, Mark Alan
See Doty, Mark

Doty, M.R.
See Doty, Mark

Doughty, Charles M(ontagu) 1843-1926 .... **TCLC 27**
See also CA 115; 178; DLB 19, 57, 174

Douglas, Ellen 1921- .... **CLC 73**
See also CA 115; CANR 41, 83; CN 5, 6, 7; CSW; DLB 292

Douglas, Gavin 1475(?)-1522 .... **LC 20**
See also DLB 132; RGEL 2

Douglas, George
See Brown, George Douglas
See also RGEL 2

Douglas, Keith (Castellain) 1920-1944 .... **TCLC 40**
See also BRW 7; CA 160; DLB 27; EWL 3; PAB; RGEL 2

Douglas, Leonard
See Bradbury, Ray

Douglas, Michael
See Crichton, Michael

Douglas, Michael
See Crichton, Michael

Douglas, (George) Norman 1868-1952 .... **TCLC 68**
See also BRW 6; CA 119; 157; DLB 34, 195; RGEL 2

Douglas, William
See Brown, George Douglas

Douglass, Frederick 1817(?)-1895 .. **BLC 1:1; NCLC 7, 55, 141; WLC 2**
See also AAYA 48; AFAW 1, 2; AMWC 1; AMWS 3; CDALB 1640-1865; DA; DA3; DAC; DAM MST, MULT; DLB 1, 43, 50, 79, 243; FW; LAIT 2; NCFS 2; RGAL 4; SATA 29

Dourado, (Waldomiro Freitas) Autran 1926- .... **CLC 23, 60**
See also CA 25-28R; 179; CANR 34, 81; DLB 145, 307; HW 2

Dourado, Waldomiro Freitas Autran
See Dourado, (Waldomiro Freitas) Autran

Dove, Rita 1952- . **BLC 2:1; BLCS; CLC 50, 81; PC 6**
See also AAYA 46; AMWS 4; BW 2; CA 109; CAAS 19; CANR 27, 42, 68, 76, 97, 132; CDALBS; CP 5, 6, 7; CSW; CWP; DA3; DAM MULT, POET; DLB 120; EWL 3; EXPP; MAL 5; MTCW 2; MTFW 2005; PFS 1, 15; RGAL 4

Dove, Rita Frances
See Dove, Rita

Doveglion
See Villa, Jose Garcia

Dowell, Coleman 1925-1985 .... **CLC 60**
See also CA 25-28R; 117; CANR 10; DLB 130; GLL 2

Downing, Major Jack
See Smith, Seba

Dowson, Ernest (Christopher)
1867-1900 .... **TCLC 4**
See also CA 105; 150; DLB 19, 135; RGEL 2

Doyle, A. Conan
See Doyle, Sir Arthur Conan

Doyle, Sir Arthur Conan
1859-1930 ..... **SSC 12, 83, 95; TCLC 7; WLC 2**
See Conan Doyle, Arthur
See also AAYA 14; BRWS 2; CA 104; 122; CANR 131; CDBLB 1890-1914; CLR 106; CMW 4; DA; DA3; DAB; DAC; DAM MST, NOV; DLB 18, 70, 156, 178; EXPS; HGG; LAIT 2; MSW; MTCW 1, 2; MTFW 2005; NFS 28; RGEL 2; RGSF 2; RHW; SATA 24; SCFW 1, 2; SFW 4; SSFS 2; TEA; WCH; WLIT 4; WYA; YAW

Doyle, Conan
See Doyle, Sir Arthur Conan

Doyle, John
See Graves, Robert

Doyle, Roddy 1958- .... **CLC 81, 178**
See also AAYA 14; BRWS 5; CA 143; CANR 73, 128, 168; CN 6, 7; DA3; DLB 194, 326; MTCW 2; MTFW 2005

Doyle, Sir A. Conan
See Doyle, Sir Arthur Conan

Dr. A
See Asimov, Isaac; Silverstein, Alvin; Silverstein, Virginia B(arbara Opshelor)

Drabble, Margaret 1939- ...... **CLC 2, 3, 5, 8, 10, 22, 53, 129**
See also BRWS 4; CA 13-16R; CANR 18, 35, 63, 112, 131, 174; CDBLB 1960 to Present; CN 1, 2, 3, 4, 5, 6, 7; CPW; DA3; DAB; DAC; DAM MST, NOV, POP; DLB 14, 155, 231; EWL 3; FW; MTCW 1, 2; MTFW 2005; RGEL 2; SATA 48; TEA

Drakulic, Slavenka 1949- .... **CLC 173**
See also CA 144; CANR 92

Drakulic-Ilic, Slavenka
See Drakulic, Slavenka

Drapier, M. B.
See Swift, Jonathan

Drayham, James
See Mencken, H(enry) L(ouis)

Drayton, Michael 1563-1631 .... **LC 8**
See also DAM POET; DLB 121; RGEL 2

Dreadstone, Carl
See Campbell, Ramsey

Dreiser, Theodore 1871-1945 .... **SSC 30, 114; TCLC 10, 18, 35, 83; WLC 2**
See also AMW; AMWC 2; AMWR 2; BYA 15, 16; CA 106; 132; CDALB 1865-1917; DA; DA3; DAC; DAM MST, NOV; DLB 9, 12, 102, 137; DLBD 1; EWL 3; LAIT 2; LMFS 2; MAL 5; MTCW 1, 2; MTFW 2005; NFS 8, 17; RGAL 4; TUS

Dreiser, Theodore Herman Albert
See Dreiser, Theodore

Drexler, Rosalyn 1926- .... **CLC 2, 6**
See also CA 81-84; CAD; CANR 68, 124; CD 5, 6; CWD; MAL 5

Dreyer, Carl Theodor 1889-1968 ...... **CLC 16**
See also CA 116

Drieu la Rochelle, Pierre
1893-1945 .... **TCLC 21**
See also CA 117; 250; DLB 72; EWL 3; GFL 1789 to the Present

Drieu la Rochelle, Pierre-Eugene 1893-1945
See Drieu la Rochelle, Pierre

Drinkwater, John 1882-1937 .... **TCLC 57**
See also CA 109; 149; DLB 10, 19, 149; RGEL 2

Drop Shot
See Cable, George Washington

Droste-Hulshoff, Annette Freiin von
1797-1848 .... **NCLC 3, 133**
See also CDWLB 2; DLB 133; RGSF 2; RGWL 2, 3

Drummond, Walter
See Silverberg, Robert

Drummond, William Henry
1854-1907 .... **TCLC 25**
See also CA 160; DLB 92

Drummond de Andrade, Carlos
1902-1987 .... **CLC 18; TCLC 139**
See Andrade, Carlos Drummond de
See also CA 132; 123; DLB 307; LAW

Drummond of Hawthornden, William
1585-1649 .... **LC 83**
See also DLB 121, 213; RGEL 2

Drury, Allen (Stuart) 1918-1998 .... **CLC 37**
See also CA 57-60; 170; CANR 18, 52; CN 1, 2, 3, 4, 5, 6; INT CANR-18

Druse, Eleanor
See King, Stephen

Dryden, John 1631-1700 ..... **DC 3; LC 3, 21, 115; PC 25; WLC 2**
See also BRW 2; CDBLB 1660-1789; DA; DAB; DAC; DAM DRAM, MST, POET; DLB 80, 101, 131; EXPP; IDTP; LMFS 1; RGEL 2; TEA; WLIT 3

du Bellay, Joachim 1524-1560 .... **LC 92**
See also DLB 327; GFL Beginnings to 1789; RGWL 2, 3

Duberman, Martin 1930- .... **CLC 8**
See also CA 1-4R; CAD; CANR 2, 63, 137, 174; CD 5, 6

Dubie, Norman (Evans) 1945- .... **CLC 36**
See also CA 69-72; CANR 12, 115; CP 3, 4, 5, 6, 7; DLB 120; PFS 12

Du Bois, W(illiam) E(dward) B(urghardt)
1868-1963 .. **BLC 1:1; CLC 1, 2, 13, 64, 96; HR 1:2; TCLC 169; WLC 2**
See also AAYA 40; AFAW 1, 2; AMWC 1; AMWS 2; BW 1, 3; CA 85-88; CANR 34, 82, 132; CDALB 1865-1917; DA; DA3; DAC; DAM MST, MULT, NOV; DLB 47, 50, 91, 246, 284; EWL 3; EXPP; LAIT 2; LMFS 2; MAL 5; MTCW 1, 2; MTFW 2005; NCFS 1; PFS 13; RGAL 4; SATA 42

Dubus, Andre 1936-1999 ..... **CLC 13, 36, 97; SSC 15**
See also AMWS 7; CA 21-24R; 177; CANR 17; CN 5, 6; CSW; DLB 130; INT CANR-17; RGAL 4; SSFS 10; TCLE 1:1

Duca Minimo
See D'Annunzio, Gabriele

Ducharme, Rejean 1941- .... **CLC 74**
See also CA 165; DLB 60

du Chatelet, Emilie 1706-1749 .... **LC 96**
See Chatelet, Gabrielle-Emilie Du

Duchen, Claire CLC 65

Duck, Stephen 1705(?)-1756 .... **PC 89**
See also DLB 95; RGEL 2

Duclos, Charles Pinot- 1704-1772 .... **LC 1**
See also GFL Beginnings to 1789

Ducornet, Erica 1943-
See Ducornet, Rikki
See also CA 37-40R; CANR 14, 34, 54, 82; SATA 7

Ducornet, Rikki CLC 232
See Ducornet, Erica

Dudek, Louis 1918-2001 .... **CLC 11, 19**
See also CA 45-48; 215; CAAS 14; CANR 1; CP 1, 2, 3, 4, 5, 6, 7; DLB 88

Duerrenmatt, Friedrich 1921-1990 ... **CLC 1, 4, 8, 11, 15, 43, 102**
See Durrenmatt, Friedrich
See also CA 17-20R; CANR 33; CMW 4; DAM DRAM; DLB 69, 124; MTCW 1, 2

Duffy, Bruce 1953(?)- .... **CLC 50**
See also CA 172

Duffy, Maureen (Patricia) 1933- ...... **CLC 37**
See also CA 25-28R; CANR 33, 68; CBD; CN 1, 2, 3, 4, 5, 6, 7; CP 5, 6, 7; CWD; CWP; DFS 15; DLB 14, 310; FW; MTCW 1

Du Fu
See Tu Fu
See also RGWL 2, 3

Dugan, Alan 1923-2003 .... **CLC 2, 6**
See also CA 81-84; 220; CANR 119; CP 1, 2, 3, 4, 5, 6, 7; DLB 5; MAL 5; PFS 10

du Gard, Roger Martin
See Martin du Gard, Roger

Duhamel, Georges 1884-1966 .... **CLC 8**
See also CA 81-84; 25-28R; CANR 35; DLB 65; EWL 3; GFL 1789 to the Present; MTCW 1

du Hault, Jean
See Grindel, Eugene

Dujardin, Edouard (Emile Louis)
1861-1949 .... **TCLC 13**
See also CA 109; DLB 123

Duke, Raoul
See Thompson, Hunter S.

Dulles, John Foster 1888-1959 .... **TCLC 72**
See also CA 115; 149

Dumas, Alexandre (pere)
1802-1870 .... **NCLC 11, 71; WLC 2**
See also AAYA 22; BYA 3; CLR 134; DA; DA3; DAB; DAC; DAM MST, NOV; DLB 119, 192; EW 6; GFL 1789 to the Present; LAIT 1, 2; NFS 14, 19; RGWL 2, 3; SATA 18; TWA; WCH

Dumas, Alexandre (fils) 1824-1895 ...... **DC 1; NCLC 9**
See also DLB 192; GFL 1789 to the Present; RGWL 2, 3

Dumas, Claudine
See Malzberg, Barry N(athaniel)

Dumas, Henry L. 1934-1968 . **BLC 2:1; CLC 6, 62; SSC 107**
See also BW 1; CA 85-88; DLB 41; RGAL 4

du Maurier, Daphne 1907-1989 .. **CLC 6, 11, 59; SSC 18; TCLC 209**
See also AAYA 37; BPFB 1; BRWS 3; CA 5-8R; 128; CANR 6, 55; CMW 4; CN 1, 2, 3, 4; CPW; DA3; DAB; DAC; DAM MST, POP; DLB 191; GL 2; HGG; LAIT 3; MSW; MTCW 1, 2; NFS 12; RGEL 2; RGSF 2; RHW; SATA 27; SATA-Obit 60; SSFS 14, 16; TEA

Du Maurier, George 1834-1896 ..... **NCLC 86**
See also DLB 153, 178; RGEL 2

Dunbar, Paul Laurence
1872-1906 .... **BLC 1:1; PC 5; SSC 8; TCLC 2, 12; WLC 2**
See also AAYA 75; AFAW 1, 2; AMWS 2; BW 1, 3; CA 104; 124; CANR 79; CDALB 1865-1917; DA; DA3; DAC; DAM MST, MULT, POET; DLB 50, 54, 78; EXPP; MAL 5; RGAL 4; SATA 34

Dunbar, William 1460(?)-1520(?) .... **LC 20; PC 67**
See also BRWS 8; DLB 132, 146; RGEL 2

Dunbar-Nelson, Alice HR 1:2
See Nelson, Alice Ruth Moore Dunbar

Duncan, Dora Angela
See Duncan, Isadora

Duncan, Isadora 1877(?)-1927 .... **TCLC 68**
See also CA 118; 149

Duncan, Lois 1934- .... **CLC 26**
See also AAYA 4, 34; BYA 6, 8; CA 1-4R; CANR 2, 23, 36, 111; CLR 29, 129; JRDA; MAICYA 1, 2; MAICYAS 1; MTFW 2005; SAAS 2; SATA 1, 36, 75, 133, 141; SATA-Essay 141; WYA; YAW

Duncan, Robert 1919-1988 ... **CLC 1, 2, 4, 7, 15, 41, 55; PC 2, 75**
See also BG 1:2; CA 9-12R; 124; CANR 28, 62; CP 1, 2, 3, 4; DAM POET; DLB 5, 16, 193; EWL 3; MAL 5; MTCW 1, 2; MTFW 2005; PFS 13; RGAL 4; WP

Duncan, Sara Jeannette
1861-1922 .... **TCLC 60**
See also CA 157; DLB 92

Dunlap, William 1766-1839 .... **NCLC 2**
See also DLB 30, 37, 59; RGAL 4

Dunn, Douglas (Eaglesham) 1942- .... **CLC 6, 40**
See also BRWS 10; CA 45-48; CANR 2, 33, 126; CP 1, 2, 3, 4, 5, 6, 7; DLB 40; MTCW 1

Dunn, Katherine 1945- .... **CLC 71**
See also CA 33-36R; CANR 72; HGG; MTCW 2; MTFW 2005

Dunn, Stephen 1939- .... **CLC 36, 206**
See also AMWS 11; CA 33-36R; CANR 12, 48, 53, 105; CP 3, 4, 5, 6, 7; DLB 105; PFS 21

Dunn, Stephen Elliott
See Dunn, Stephen

Dunne, Finley Peter 1867-1936 ...... **TCLC 28**
See also CA 108; 178; DLB 11, 23; RGAL 4

Dunne, John Gregory 1932-2003 ..... **CLC 28**
See also CA 25-28R; 222; CANR 14, 50; CN 5, 6, 7; DLBY 1980

Dunsany, Lord TCLC 2, 59
See Dunsany, Edward John Moreton Drax Plunkett
See also DLB 77, 153, 156, 255; FANT; IDTP; RGEL 2; SFW 4; SUFW 1

Dunsany, Edward John Moreton Drax Plunkett 1878-1957
See Dunsany, Lord
See also CA 104; 148; DLB 10; MTCW 2

Duns Scotus, John 1266(?)-1308 ... **CMLC 59**
See also DLB 115

du Perry, Jean
See Simenon, Georges (Jacques Christian)

Durang, Christopher 1949- .... **CLC 27, 38**
See also CA 105; CAD; CANR 50, 76, 130; CD 5, 6; MTCW 2; MTFW 2005

Durang, Christopher Ferdinand
See Durang, Christopher

Duras, Claire de 1777-1832 .... **NCLC 154**

Duras, Marguerite 1914-1996 . **CLC 3, 6, 11, 20, 34, 40, 68, 100; SSC 40**
See also BPFB 1; CA 25-28R; 151; CANR 50; CWW 2; DFS 21; DLB 83, 321; EWL 3; FL 1:5; GFL 1789 to the Present; IDFW 4; MTCW 1, 2; RGWL 2, 3; TWA

Durban, (Rosa) Pam 1947- .... **CLC 39**
See also CA 123; CANR 98; CSW

Durcan, Paul 1944- .... **CLC 43, 70**
See also CA 134; CANR 123; CP 1, 5, 6, 7; DAM POET; EWL 3

d'Urfe, Honore
See Urfe, Honore d'

Durfey, Thomas 1653-1723 .... **LC 94**
See also DLB 80; RGEL 2

Durkheim, Emile 1858-1917 .... **TCLC 55**
See also CA 249

Durrell, Lawrence (George)
1912-1990 ..... **CLC 1, 4, 6, 8, 13, 27, 41**
See also BPFB 1; BRWS 1; CA 9-12R; 132; CANR 40, 77; CDBLB 1945-1960; CN 1, 2, 3, 4; CP 1, 2, 3, 4, 5; DAM NOV; DLB 15, 27, 204; DLBY 1990; EWL 3; MTCW 1, 2; RGEL 2; SFW 4; TEA

Durrenmatt, Friedrich
See Duerrenmatt, Friedrich
See also CDWLB 2; EW 13; EWL 3; RGHL; RGWL 2, 3

Dutt, Michael Madhusudan
1824-1873 .... **NCLC 118**

Dutt, Toru 1856-1877 .... **NCLC 29**
See also DLB 240

Dwight, Timothy 1752-1817 .... **NCLC 13**
See also DLB 37; RGAL 4

Dworkin, Andrea 1946-2005 ..... **CLC 43, 123**
See also CA 77-80; 238; CAAS 21; CANR 16, 39, 76, 96; FL 1:5; FW; GLL 1; INT CANR-16; MTCW 1, 2; MTFW 2005

Dwyer, Deanna
See Koontz, Dean R.

Dwyer, K.R.
See Koontz, Dean R.

Dybek, Stuart 1942- .... **CLC 114; SSC 55**
See also CA 97-100; CANR 39; DLB 130; SSFS 23

Dye, Richard
See De Voto, Bernard (Augustine)

Dyer, Geoff 1958- .... **CLC 149**
See also CA 125; CANR 88

Dyer, George 1755-1841 .... **NCLC 129**
See also DLB 93

Dylan, Bob 1941- .... **CLC 3, 4, 6, 12, 77; PC 37**
See also AMWS 18; CA 41-44R; CANR 108; CP 1, 2, 3, 4, 5, 6, 7; DLB 16

Dyson, John 1943- .... **CLC 70**
See also CA 144

Dzyubin, Eduard Georgievich 1895-1934
See Bagritsky, Eduard
See also CA 170

E. V. L.
See Lucas, E(dward) V(errall)

Eagleton, Terence (Francis) 1943- .. **CLC 63, 132**
See also CA 57-60; CANR 7, 23, 68, 115; DLB 242; LMFS 2; MTCW 1, 2; MTFW 2005

Eagleton, Terry
See Eagleton, Terence (Francis)

Early, Jack
See Scoppettone, Sandra
See also GLL 1

East, Michael
See West, Morris L(anglo)

Eastaway, Edward
See Thomas, (Philip) Edward

Eastlake, William (Derry)
1917-1997 .... **CLC 8**
See also CA 5-8R; 158; CAAS 1; CANR 5, 63; CN 1, 2, 3, 4, 5, 6; DLB 6, 206; INT CANR-5; MAL 5; TCWW 1, 2

Eastman, Charles A(lexander)
1858-1939 .... **NNAL; TCLC 55**
See also CA 179; CANR 91; DAM MULT; DLB 175; YABC 1

Eaton, Edith Maude 1865-1914 .... **AAL**
See Far, Sui Sin
See also CA 154; DLB 221, 312; FW

Eaton, (Lillie) Winnifred 1875-1954 .... **AAL**
See also CA 217; DLB 221, 312; RGAL 4

Eberhart, Richard 1904-2005 ...... **CLC 3, 11, 19, 56; PC 76**
See also AMW; CA 1-4R; 240; CANR 2, 125; CDALB 1941-1968; CP 1, 2, 3, 4, 5, 6, 7; DAM POET; DLB 48; MAL 5; MTCW 1; RGAL 4

Eberhart, Richard Ghormley
See Eberhart, Richard

Eberstadt, Fernanda 1960- .... **CLC 39**
See also CA 136; CANR 69, 128

Ebner, Margaret c. 1291-1351 ...... **CMLC 98**

Echegaray (y Eizaguirre), Jose (Maria Waldo) 1832-1916 .... **HLCS 1; TCLC 4**
See also CA 104; CANR 32; DLB 329; EWL 3; HW 1; MTCW 1

Echeverria, (Jose) Esteban (Antonino)
1805-1851 .... **NCLC 18**
See also LAW

Echo
See Proust, (Valentin-Louis-George-Eugene) Marcel

Eckert, Allan W. 1931- .... **CLC 17**
See also AAYA 18; BYA 2; CA 13-16R; CANR 14, 45; INT CANR-14; MAICYA 2; MAICYAS 1; SAAS 21; SATA 29, 91; SATA-Brief 27

Eckhart, Meister 1260(?)-1327(?) .. **CMLC 9, 80**
See also DLB 115; LMFS 1

Eckmar, F. R.
See de Hartog, Jan

Eco, Umberto 1932- .... **CLC 28, 60, 142, 248**
See also BEST 90:1; BPFB 1; CA 77-80; CANR 12, 33, 55, 110, 131; CPW; CWW 2; DA3; DAM NOV, POP; DLB 196, 242; EWL 3; MSW; MTCW 1, 2; MTFW 2005; NFS 22; RGWL 3; WLIT 7

Eddison, E(ric) R(ucker)
1882-1945 .... **TCLC 15**
See also CA 109; 156; DLB 255; FANT; SFW 4; SUFW 1

Eddy, Mary (Ann Morse) Baker
1821-1910 .... **TCLC 71**
See also CA 113; 174

Edel, (Joseph) Leon 1907-1997 .. **CLC 29, 34**
See also CA 1-4R; 161; CANR 1, 22, 112; DLB 103; INT CANR-22

Eden, Emily 1797-1869 .... **NCLC 10**

Edgar, David 1948- .... **CLC 42**
See also CA 57-60; CANR 12, 61, 112; CBD; CD 5, 6; DAM DRAM; DFS 15; DLB 13, 233; MTCW 1

Edgerton, Clyde (Carlyle) 1944- ...... **CLC 39**
See also AAYA 17; CA 118; 134; CANR 64, 125; CN 7; CSW; DLB 278; INT CA-134; TCLE 1:1; YAW

Edgeworth, Maria 1768-1849 ... **NCLC 1, 51, 158; SSC 86**
See also BRWS 3; DLB 116, 159, 163; FL 1:3; FW; RGEL 2; SATA 21; TEA; WLIT 3

Edmonds, Paul
See Kuttner, Henry

Edmonds, Walter D(umaux)
1903-1998 .... **CLC 35**
See also BYA 2; CA 5-8R; CANR 2; CWRI 5; DLB 9; LAIT 1; MAICYA 1, 2; MAL 5; RHW; SAAS 4; SATA 1, 27; SATA-Obit 99

Edmondson, Wallace
See Ellison, Harlan

Edson, Margaret 1961- ...... **CLC 199; DC 24**
See also AMWS 18; CA 190; DFS 13; DLB 266

Edson, Russell 1935- .... **CLC 13**
See also CA 33-36R; CANR 115; CP 2, 3, 4, 5, 6, 7; DLB 244; WP

Edwards, Bronwen Elizabeth
See Rose, Wendy

Edwards, G(erald) B(asil)
1899-1976 .... **CLC 25**
See also CA 201; 110
Edwards, Gus 1939- .... **CLC 43**
See also CA 108; INT CA-108
Edwards, Jonathan 1703-1758 .... **LC 7, 54**
See also AMW; DA; DAC; DAM MST;
DLB 24, 270; RGAL 4; TUS
Edwards, Sarah Pierpont 1710-1758 .. **LC 87**
See also DLB 200
Efron, Marina Ivanovna Tsvetaeva
See Tsvetaeva (Efron), Marina (Ivanovna)
Egeria fl. 4th cent. - .... **CMLC 70**
Eggers, Dave 1970- .... **CLC 241**
See also AAYA 56; CA 198; CANR 138;
MTFW 2005
Egoyan, Atom 1960- .... **CLC 151**
See also AAYA 63; CA 157; CANR 151
Ehle, John (Marsden, Jr.) 1925- ...... **CLC 27**
See also CA 9-12R; CSW
Ehrenbourg, Ilya (Grigoryevich)
See Ehrenburg, Ilya (Grigoryevich)
Ehrenburg, Ilya (Grigoryevich)
1891-1967 .... **CLC 18, 34, 62**
See Erenburg, Il'ia Grigor'evich
See also CA 102; 25-28R; EWL 3
Ehrenburg, Ilyo (Grigoryevich)
See Ehrenburg, Ilya (Grigoryevich)
Ehrenreich, Barbara 1941- .... **CLC 110**
See also BEST 90:4; CA 73-76; CANR 16,
37, 62, 117, 167; DLB 246; FW; MTCW
1, 2; MTFW 2005
Ehrlich, Gretel 1946- .... **CLC 249**
See also ANW; CA 140; CANR 74, 146;
DLB 212, 275; TCWW 2
Eich, Gunter
See Eich, Gunter
See also RGWL 2, 3
Eich, Gunter 1907-1972 .... **CLC 15**
See Eich, Gunter
See also CA 111; 93-96; DLB 69, 124;
EWL 3
Eichendorff, Joseph 1788-1857 .... **NCLC 8**
See also DLB 90; RGWL 2, 3
Eigner, Larry CLC 9
See Eigner, Laurence (Joel)
See also CAAS 23; CP 1, 2, 3, 4, 5, 6; DLB
5; WP
Eigner, Laurence (Joel) 1927-1996
See Eigner, Larry
See also CA 9-12R; 151; CANR 6, 84; CP
7; DLB 193
Eilhart von Oberge c. 1140-c.
1195 .... **CMLC 67**
See also DLB 148
Einhard c. 770-840 .... **CMLC 50**
See also DLB 148
Einstein, Albert 1879-1955 .... **TCLC 65**
See also CA 121; 133; MTCW 1, 2
Eiseley, Loren
See Eiseley, Loren Corey
See also DLB 275
Eiseley, Loren Corey 1907-1977 .... **CLC 7**
See Eiseley, Loren
See also AAYA 5; ANW; CA 1-4R; 73-76;
CANR 6; DLBD 17
Eisenstadt, Jill 1963- .... **CLC 50**
See also CA 140
Eisenstein, Sergei (Mikhailovich)
1898-1948 .... **TCLC 57**
See also CA 114; 149
Eisner, Simon
See Kornbluth, C(yril) M.
Eisner, Will 1917-2005 .... **CLC 237**
See also AAYA 52; CA 108; 235; CANR
114, 140, 179; MTFW 2005; SATA 31,
165
Eisner, William Erwin
See Eisner, Will

Ekeloef, (Bengt) Gunnar
1899-1976 .... **CLC 27; PC 23**
See Ekelof, (Bengt) Gunnar
See also CA 123; 25-28R; DAM POET
Ekelof, (Bengt) Gunnar 1907-1968
See Ekeloef, (Bengt) Gunnar
See also DLB 259; EW 12; EWL 3
Ekelund, Vilhelm 1880-1949 .... **TCLC 75**
See also CA 189; EWL 3
Ekwensi, C. O. D.
See Ekwensi, Cyprian
Ekwensi, Cyprian 1921-2007 .... **BLC 1:1;
CLC 4**
See also AFW; BW 2, 3; CA 29-32R;
CANR 18, 42, 74, 125; CDWLB 3; CN 1,
2, 3, 4, 5, 6; CWRI 5; DAM MULT; DLB
117; EWL 3; MTCW 1, 2; RGEL 2; SATA
66; WLIT 2
Ekwensi, Cyprian Odiatu Duaka
See Ekwensi, Cyprian
Elaine TCLC 18
See Leverson, Ada Esther
El Crummo
See Crumb, R.
Elder, Lonne III 1931-1996 .. **BLC 1:1; DC 8**
See also BW 1, 3; CA 81-84; 152; CAD;
CANR 25; DAM MULT; DLB 7, 38, 44;
MAL 5
Eleanor of Aquitaine 1122-1204 ... **CMLC 39**
Elia
See Lamb, Charles
Eliade, Mircea 1907-1986 .... **CLC 19**
See also CA 65-68; 119; CANR 30, 62; CD-
WLB 4; DLB 220; EWL 3; MTCW 1;
RGWL 3; SFW 4
Eliot, A. D.
See Jewett, (Theodora) Sarah Orne
Eliot, Alice
See Jewett, (Theodora) Sarah Orne
Eliot, Dan
See Silverberg, Robert
Eliot, George 1819-1880 ...... **NCLC 4, 13, 23,
41, 49, 89, 118, 183, 199; PC 20; SSC
72; WLC 2**
See Evans, Mary Ann
See also BRW 5; BRWC 1, 2; BRWR 2;
CDBLB 1832-1890; CN 7; CPW; DA;
DA3; DAB; DAC; DAM MST, NOV;
DLB 21, 35, 55; FL 1:3; LATS 1:1; LMFS
1; NFS 17, 20; RGEL 2; RGSF 2; SSFS
8; TEA; WLIT 3
Eliot, John 1604-1690 .... **LC 5**
See also DLB 24
Eliot, T(homas) S(tearns)
1888-1965 ...... **CLC 1, 2, 3, 6, 9, 10, 13,
15, 24, 34, 41, 55, 57, 113; DC 28; PC
5, 31, 90; WLC 2**
See also AAYA 28; AMW; AMWC 1;
AMWR 1; BRW 7; BRWR 2; CA 5-8R;
25-28R; CANR 41; CBD; CDALB 1929-
1941; DA; DA3; DAB; DAC; DAM
DRAM, MST, POET; DFS 4, 13; DLB 7,
10, 45, 63, 245, 329; DLBY 1988; EWL
3; EXPP; LAIT 3; LATS 1:1; LMFS 2;
MAL 5; MTCW 1, 2; MTFW 2005; NCFS
5; PAB; PFS 1, 7, 20; RGAL 4; RGEL 2;
TUS; WLIT 4; WP
Elisabeth of Schonau c.
1129-1165 .... **CMLC 82**
Elizabeth 1866-1941 .... **TCLC 41**
Elizabeth I 1533-1603 .... **LC 118**
See also DLB 136
Elkin, Stanley L. 1930-1995 ...... **CLC 4, 6, 9,
14, 27, 51, 91; SSC 12**
See also AMWS 6; BPFB 1; CA 9-12R;
148; CANR 8, 46; CN 1, 2, 3, 4, 5, 6;
CPW; DAM NOV, POP; DLB 2, 28, 218,
278; DLBY 1980; EWL 3; INT CANR-8;
MAL 5; MTCW 1, 2; MTFW 2005;
RGAL 4; TCLE 1:1

Elledge, Scott CLC 34
Eller, Scott
See Shepard, Jim
Elliott, Don
See Silverberg, Robert
Elliott, George P(aul) 1918-1980 .... **CLC 2**
See also CA 1-4R; 97-100; CANR 2; CN 1,
2; CP 3; DLB 244; MAL 5
Elliott, Janice 1931-1995 .... **CLC 47**
See also CA 13-16R; CANR 8, 29, 84; CN
5, 6, 7; DLB 14; SATA 119
Elliott, Sumner Locke 1917-1991 ..... **CLC 38**
See also CA 5-8R; 134; CANR 2, 21; DLB
289
Elliott, William
See Bradbury, Ray
Ellis, A. E. CLC 7
Ellis, Alice Thomas CLC 40
See Haycraft, Anna
See also CN 4, 5, 6; DLB 194
Ellis, Bret Easton 1964- ..... **CLC 39, 71, 117,
229**
See also AAYA 2, 43; CA 118; 123; CANR
51, 74, 126; CN 6, 7; CPW; DA3; DAM
POP; DLB 292; HGG; INT CA-123;
MTCW 2; MTFW 2005; NFS 11
Ellis, (Henry) Havelock
1859-1939 .... **TCLC 14**
See also CA 109; 169; DLB 190
Ellis, Landon
See Ellison, Harlan
Ellis, Trey 1962- .... **CLC 55**
See also CA 146; CANR 92; CN 7
Ellison, Harlan 1934- .... **CLC 1, 13, 42, 139;
SSC 14**
See also AAYA 29; BPFB 1; BYA 14; CA
5-8R; CANR 5, 46, 115; CPW; DAM
POP; DLB 8, 335; HGG; INT CANR-5;
MTCW 1, 2; MTFW 2005; SCFW 2;
SFW 4; SSFS 13, 14, 15, 21; SUFW 1, 2
Ellison, Ralph 1914-1994 .... **BLC 1:1, 2:2;
CLC 1, 3, 11, 54, 86, 114; SSC 26, 79;
WLC 2**
See also AAYA 19; AFAW 1, 2; AMWC 2;
AMWR 2; AMWS 2; BPFB 1; BW 1, 3;
BYA 2; CA 9-12R; 145; CANR 24, 53;
CDALB 1941-1968; CN 1, 2, 3, 4, 5;
CSW; DA; DA3; DAB; DAC; DAM MST,
MULT, NOV; DLB 2, 76, 227; DLBY
1994; EWL 3; EXPN; EXPS; LAIT 4;
MAL 5; MTCW 1, 2; MTFW 2005; NCFS
3; NFS 2, 21; RGAL 4; RGSF 2; SSFS 1,
11; YAW
Ellmann, Lucy 1956- .... **CLC 61**
See also CA 128; CANR 154
Ellmann, Lucy Elizabeth
See Ellmann, Lucy
Ellmann, Richard (David)
1918-1987 .... **CLC 50**
See also BEST 89:2; CA 1-4R; 122; CANR
2, 28, 61; DLB 103; DLBY 1987; MTCW
1, 2; MTFW 2005
Elman, Richard (Martin)
1934-1997 .... **CLC 19**
See also CA 17-20R; 163; CAAS 3; CANR
47; TCLE 1:1
Elron
See Hubbard, L. Ron
El Saadawi, Nawal 1931- ...... **BLC 2:2; CLC
196**
See also al'Sadaawi, Nawal; Sa'adawi, al-
Nawal; Sa'dawi, Nawal al-
See also CA 118; CAAS 11; CANR 44, 92;
DLB 346; WLIT 2
Eluard, Paul
See Grindel, Eugene
Eluard, Paul
See Grindel, Eugene

Elyot, Thomas 1490(?)-1546 .... **LC 11, 139**
See also DLB 136; RGEL 2

Elytis, Odysseus 1911-1996 .... **CLC 15, 49, 100; PC 21**
See Alepoudelis, Odysseus
See also CA 102; 151; CANR 94; CWW 2; DAM POET; DLB 329; EW 13; EWL 3; MTCW 1, 2; RGWL 2, 3

Emecheta, Buchi 1944- ... **BLC 1:2; CLC 14, 48, 128, 214**
See also AAYA 67; AFW; BW 2, 3; CA 81-84; CANR 27, 81, 126; CDWLB 3; CN 4, 5, 6, 7; CWRI 5; DA3; DAM MULT; DLB 117; EWL 3; FL 1:5; FW; MTCW 1, 2; MTFW 2005; NFS 12, 14; SATA 66; WLIT 2

Emerson, Mary Moody 1774-1863 .... **NCLC 66**

Emerson, Ralph Waldo 1803-1882 . **NCLC 1, 38, 98; PC 18; WLC 2**
See also AAYA 60; AMW; ANW; CDALB 1640-1865; DA; DA3; DAB; DAC; DAM MST, POET; DLB 1, 59, 73, 183, 223, 270; EXPP; LAIT 2; LMFS 1; NCFS 3; PFS 4, 17; RGAL 4; TUS; WP

Eminem 1972- .... **CLC 226**
See also CA 245

Eminescu, Mihail 1850-1889 .. **NCLC 33, 131**

Empedocles 5th cent. B.C.- .... **CMLC 50**
See also DLB 176

Empson, William 1906-1984 ... **CLC 3, 8, 19, 33, 34**
See also BRWS 2; CA 17-20R; 112; CANR 31, 61; CP 1, 2, 3; DLB 20; EWL 3; MTCW 1, 2; RGEL 2

Enchi, Fumiko (Ueda) 1905-1986 ..... **CLC 31**
See Enchi Fumiko
See also CA 129; 121; FW; MJW

Enchi Fumiko
See Enchi, Fumiko (Ueda)
See also DLB 182; EWL 3

Ende, Michael (Andreas Helmuth) 1929-1995 .... **CLC 31**
See also BYA 5; CA 118; 124; 149; CANR 36, 110; CLR 14, 138; DLB 75; MAICYA 1, 2; MAICYAS 1; SATA 61, 130; SATA-Brief 42; SATA-Obit 86

Endo, Shusaku 1923-1996 ..... **CLC 7, 14, 19, 54, 99; SSC 48; TCLC 152**
See Endo Shusaku
See also CA 29-32R; 153; CANR 21, 54, 131; DA3; DAM NOV; MTCW 1, 2; MTFW 2005; RGSF 2; RGWL 2, 3

Endo Shusaku
See Endo, Shusaku
See also CWW 2; DLB 182; EWL 3

Engel, Marian 1933-1985 .... **CLC 36; TCLC 137**
See also CA 25-28R; CANR 12; CN 2, 3; DLB 53; FW; INT CANR-12

Engelhardt, Frederick
See Hubbard, L. Ron

Engels, Friedrich 1820-1895 .. **NCLC 85, 114**
See also DLB 129; LATS 1:1

Enquist, Per Olov 1934- .... **CLC 257**
See also CA 109; 193; CANR 155; CWW 2; DLB 257; EWL 3

Enright, D(ennis) J(oseph) 1920-2002 .... **CLC 4, 8, 31; PC 93**
See also CA 1-4R; 211; CANR 1, 42, 83; CN 1, 2; CP 1, 2, 3, 4, 5, 6, 7; DLB 27; EWL 3; SATA 25; SATA-Obit 140

Ensler, Eve 1953- .... **CLC 212**
See also CA 172; CANR 126, 163; DFS 23

Enzensberger, Hans Magnus 1929- .... **CLC 43; PC 28**
See also CA 116; 119; CANR 103; CWW 2; EWL 3

Ephron, Nora 1941- .... **CLC 17, 31**
See also AAYA 35; AITN 2; CA 65-68; CANR 12, 39, 83, 161; DFS 22

Epicurus 341B.C.-270B.C. .... **CMLC 21**
See also DLB 176

Epinay, Louise d' 1726-1783 .... **LC 138**
See also DLB 313

Epsilon
See Betjeman, John

Epstein, Daniel Mark 1948- .... **CLC 7**
See also CA 49-52; CANR 2, 53, 90

Epstein, Jacob 1956- .... **CLC 19**
See also CA 114

Epstein, Jean 1897-1953 .... **TCLC 92**

Epstein, Joseph 1937- .... **CLC 39, 204**
See also AMWS 14; CA 112; 119; CANR 50, 65, 117, 164

Epstein, Leslie 1938- .... **CLC 27**
See also AMWS 12; CA 73-76, 215; CAAE 215; CAAS 12; CANR 23, 69, 162; DLB 299; RGHL

Equiano, Olaudah 1745(?)-1797 ..... **BLC 1:2; LC 16, 143**
See also AFAW 1, 2; CDWLB 3; DAM MULT; DLB 37, 50; WLIT 2

Erasmus, Desiderius 1469(?)-1536 ..... **LC 16, 93**
See also DLB 136; EW 2; LMFS 1; RGWL 2, 3; TWA

Erdman, Paul E. 1932-2007 .... **CLC 25**
See also AITN 1; CA 61-64; 259; CANR 13, 43, 84

Erdman, Paul Emil
See Erdman, Paul E.

Erdrich, Karen Louise
See Erdrich, Louise

Erdrich, Louise 1954- .... **CLC 39, 54, 120, 176; NNAL; PC 52**
See also AAYA 10, 47; AMWS 4; BEST 89:1; BPFB 1; CA 114; CANR 41, 62, 118, 138; CDALBS; CN 5, 6, 7; CP 6, 7; CPW; CWP; DA3; DAM MULT, NOV, POP; DLB 152, 175, 206; EWL 3; EXPP; FL 1:5; LAIT 5; LATS 1:2; MAL 5; MTCW 1, 2; MTFW 2005; NFS 5; PFS 14; RGAL 4; SATA 94, 141; SSFS 14, 22; TCWW 2

Erenburg, Ilya (Grigoryevich)
See Ehrenburg, Ilya (Grigoryevich)

Erickson, Stephen Michael
See Erickson, Steve

Erickson, Steve 1950- .... **CLC 64**
See also CA 129; CANR 60, 68, 136; MTFW 2005; SFW 4; SUFW 2

Erickson, Walter
See Fast, Howard

Ericson, Walter
See Fast, Howard

Eriksson, Buntel
See Bergman, Ingmar

Eriugena, John Scottus c. 810-877 .... **CMLC 65**
See also DLB 115

Ernaux, Annie 1940- .... **CLC 88, 184**
See also CA 147; CANR 93; MTFW 2005; NCFS 3, 5

Erskine, John 1879-1951 .... **TCLC 84**
See also CA 112; 159; DLB 9, 102; FANT

Erwin, Will
See Eisner, Will

Eschenbach, Wolfram von
See von Eschenbach, Wolfram
See also RGWL 3

Eseki, Bruno
See Mphahlele, Ezekiel

Esenin, S.A.
See Esenin, Sergei
See also EWL 3

Esenin, Sergei 1895-1925 .... **TCLC 4**
See Esenin, S.A.
See also CA 104; RGWL 2, 3

Esenin, Sergei Aleksandrovich
See Esenin, Sergei

Eshleman, Clayton 1935- .... **CLC 7**
See also CA 33-36R, 212; CAAE 212; CAAS 6; CANR 93; CP 1, 2, 3, 4, 5, 6, 7; DLB 5

Espada, Martin 1957- .... **PC 74**
See also CA 159; CANR 80; CP 7; EXPP; LLW; MAL 5; PFS 13, 16

Espriella, Don Manuel Alvarez
See Southey, Robert

Espriu, Salvador 1913-1985 .... **CLC 9**
See also CA 154; 115; DLB 134; EWL 3

Espronceda, Jose de 1808-1842 ..... **NCLC 39**

Esquivel, Laura 1950(?)- ... **CLC 141; HLCS 1**
See also AAYA 29; CA 143; CANR 68, 113, 161; DA3; DNFS 2; LAIT 3; LMFS 2; MTCW 2; MTFW 2005; NFS 5; WLIT 1

Esse, James
See Stephens, James

Esterbrook, Tom
See Hubbard, L. Ron

Esterhazy, Peter 1950- .... **CLC 251**
See also CA 140; CANR 137; CDWLB 4; CWW 2; DLB 232; EWL 3; RGWL 3

Estleman, Loren D. 1952- .... **CLC 48**
See also AAYA 27; CA 85-88; CANR 27, 74, 139, 177; CMW 4; CPW; DA3; DAM NOV, POP; DLB 226; INT CANR-27; MTCW 1, 2; MTFW 2005; TCWW 1, 2

Etherege, Sir George 1636-1692 . **DC 23; LC 78**
See also BRW 2; DAM DRAM; DLB 80; PAB; RGEL 2

Euclid 306B.C.-283B.C. .... **CMLC 25**

Eugenides, Jeffrey 1960- .... **CLC 81, 212**
See also AAYA 51; CA 144; CANR 120; MTFW 2005; NFS 24

Euripides c. 484B.C.-406B.C. .... **CMLC 23, 51; DC 4; WLCS**
See also AW 1; CDWLB 1; DA; DA3; DAB; DAC; DAM DRAM, MST; DFS 1, 4, 6, 25; DLB 176; LAIT 1; LMFS 1; RGWL 2, 3; WLIT 8

Eusebius c. 263-c. 339 .... **CMLC 103**

Evan, Evin
See Faust, Frederick (Schiller)

Evans, Caradoc 1878-1945 ... **SSC 43; TCLC 85**
See also DLB 162

Evans, Evan
See Faust, Frederick (Schiller)

Evans, Marian
See Eliot, George

Evans, Mary Ann
See Eliot, George
See also NFS 20

Evarts, Esther
See Benson, Sally

Evelyn, John 1620-1706 .... **LC 144**
See also BRW 2; RGEL 2

Everett, Percival 1956- .... **CLC 57**
See Everett, Percival L.
See also AMWS 18; BW 2; CA 129; CANR 94, 134, 179; CN 7; MTFW 2005

Everett, Percival L.
See Everett, Percival
See also CSW

Everson, R(onald) G(ilmour) 1903-1992 .... **CLC 27**
See also CA 17-20R; CP 1, 2, 3, 4; DLB 88

Everson, William (Oliver)
1912-1994 .... **CLC 1, 5, 14**
See Antoninus, Brother
See also BG 1:2; CA 9-12R; 145; CANR 20; CP 2, 3, 4, 5; DLB 5, 16, 212; MTCW 1

Evtushenko, Evgenii Aleksandrovich
See Yevtushenko, Yevgeny (Alexandrovich)
See also CWW 2; RGWL 2, 3

Ewart, Gavin (Buchanan)
1916-1995 .... **CLC 13, 46**
See also BRWS 7; CA 89-92; 150; CANR 17, 46; CP 1, 2, 3, 4, 5, 6; DLB 40; MTCW 1

Ewers, Hanns Heinz 1871-1943 ..... **TCLC 12**
See also CA 109; 149

Ewing, Frederick R.
See Sturgeon, Theodore (Hamilton)

Exley, Frederick (Earl) 1929-1992 .... **CLC 6, 11**
See also AITN 2; BPFB 1; CA 81-84; 138; CANR 117; DLB 143; DLBY 1981

Eynhardt, Guillermo
See Quiroga, Horacio (Sylvestre)

Ezekiel, Nissim (Moses) 1924-2004 .. **CLC 61**
See also CA 61-64; 223; CP 1, 2, 3, 4, 5, 6, 7; DLB 323; EWL 3

Ezekiel, Tish O'Dowd 1943- .... **CLC 34**
See also CA 129

Fadeev, Aleksandr Aleksandrovich
See Bulgya, Alexander Alexandrovich
See also DLB 272

Fadeev, Alexandr Alexandrovich
See Bulgya, Alexander Alexandrovich
See also EWL 3

Fadeyev, A.
See Bulgya, Alexander Alexandrovich

Fadeyev, Alexander TCLC 53
See Bulgya, Alexander Alexandrovich

Fagen, Donald 1948- .... **CLC 26**

Fainzil'berg, Il'ia Arnol'dovich
See Fainzilberg, Ilya Arnoldovich

Fainzilberg, Ilya Arnoldovich
1897-1937 .... **TCLC 21**
See Il'f, Il'ia
See also CA 120; 165; EWL 3

Fair, Ronald L. 1932- .... **CLC 18**
See also BW 1; CA 69-72; CANR 25; DLB 33

Fairbairn, Roger
See Carr, John Dickson

Fairbairns, Zoe (Ann) 1948- .... **CLC 32**
See also CA 103; CANR 21, 85; CN 4, 5, 6, 7

Fairfield, Flora
See Alcott, Louisa May

Fairman, Paul W. 1916-1977
See Queen, Ellery
See also CA 114; SFW 4

Falco, Gian
See Papini, Giovanni

Falconer, James
See Kirkup, James

Falconer, Kenneth
See Kornbluth, C(yril) M.

Falkland, Samuel
See Heijermans, Herman

Fallaci, Oriana 1930-2006 .... **CLC 11, 110**
See also CA 77-80; 253; CANR 15, 58, 134; FW; MTCW 1

Faludi, Susan 1959- .... **CLC 140**
See also CA 138; CANR 126; FW; MTFW 2; MTFW 2005; NCFS 3

Faludy, George 1913- .... **CLC 42**
See also CA 21-24R

Faludy, Gyoergy
See Faludy, George

Fanon, Frantz 1925-1961 ...... **BLC 1:2; CLC 74; TCLC 188**
See also BW 1; CA 116; 89-92; DAM MULT; DLB 296; LMFS 2; WLIT 2

Fanshawe, Ann 1625-1680 .... **LC 11**

Fante, John (Thomas) 1911-1983 .... **CLC 60; SSC 65**
See also AMWS 11; CA 69-72; 109; CANR 23, 104; DLB 130; DLBY 1983

Far, Sui Sin SSC 62
See Eaton, Edith Maude
See also SSFS 4

Farah, Nuruddin 1945- .. **BLC 1:2, 2:2; CLC 53, 137**
See also AFW; BW 2, 3; CA 106; CANR 81, 148; CDWLB 3; CN 4, 5, 6, 7; DAM MULT; DLB 125; EWL 3; WLIT 2

Fardusi
See Ferdowsi, Abu'l Qasem

Fargue, Leon-Paul 1876(?)-1947 .... **TCLC 11**
See also CA 109; CANR 107; DLB 258; EWL 3

Farigoule, Louis
See Romains, Jules

Farina, Richard 1936(?)-1966 .... **CLC 9**
See also CA 81-84; 25-28R

Farley, Walter (Lorimer)
1915-1989 .... **CLC 17**
See also AAYA 58; BYA 14; CA 17-20R; CANR 8, 29, 84; DLB 22; JRDA; MAICYA 1, 2; SATA 2, 43, 132; YAW

Farmer, Philip Jose 1918- .... **CLC 1, 19**
See also AAYA 28; BPFB 1; CA 1-4R; CANR 4, 35, 111; DLB 8; MTCW 1; SATA 93; SCFW 1, 2; SFW 4

Farquhar, George 1677-1707 .... **LC 21**
See also BRW 2; DAM DRAM; DLB 84; RGEL 2

Farrell, J(ames) G(ordon)
1935-1979 .... **CLC 6**
See also CA 73-76; 89-92; CANR 36; CN 1, 2; DLB 14, 271, 326; MTCW 1; RGEL 2; RHW; WLIT 4

Farrell, James T(homas) 1904-1979 . **CLC 1, 4, 8, 11, 66; SSC 28**
See also AMW; BPFB 1; CA 5-8R; 89-92; CANR 9, 61; CN 1, 2; DLB 4, 9, 86; DLBD 2; EWL 3; MAL 5; MTCW 1, 2; MTFW 2005; RGAL 4

Farrell, Warren (Thomas) 1943- ...... **CLC 70**
See also CA 146; CANR 120

Farren, Richard J.
See Betjeman, John

Farren, Richard M.
See Betjeman, John

Fassbinder, Rainer Werner
1946-1982 .... **CLC 20**
See also CA 93-96; 106; CANR 31

Fast, Howard 1914-2003 .... **CLC 23, 131**
See also AAYA 16; BPFB 1; CA 1-4R, 181; 214; CAAE 181; CAAS 18; CANR 1, 33, 54, 75, 98, 140; CMW 4; CN 1, 2, 3, 4, 5, 6, 7; CPW; DAM NOV; DLB 9; INT CANR-33; LATS 1:1; MAL 5; MTCW 2; MTFW 2005; RHW; SATA 7; SATA-Essay 107; TCWW 1, 2; YAW

Faulcon, Robert
See Holdstock, Robert

Faulkner, William (Cuthbert)
1897-1962 .... **CLC 1, 3, 6, 8, 9, 11, 14, 18, 28, 52, 68; SSC 1, 35, 42, 92, 97; TCLC 141; WLC 2**
See also AAYA 7; AMW; AMWR 1; BPFB 1; BYA 5, 15; CA 81-84; CANR 33; CDALB 1929-1941; DA; DA3; DAB; DAC; DAM MST, NOV; DLB 9, 11, 44, 102, 316, 330; DLBD 2; DLBY 1986, 1997; EWL 3; EXPN; EXPS; GL 2; LAIT

2; LATS 1:1; LMFS 2; MAL 5; MTCW 1, 2; MTFW 2005; NFS 4, 8, 13, 24; RGAL 4; RGSF 2; SSFS 2, 5, 6, 12; TUS

Fauset, Jessie Redmon
1882(?)-1961 ...... **BLC 1:2; CLC 19, 54; HR 1:2**
See also AFAW 2; BW 1; CA 109; CANR 83; DAM MULT; DLB 51; FW; LMFS 2; MAL 5; MBL

Faust, Frederick (Schiller)
1892-1944 .... **TCLC 49**
See Brand, Max; Dawson, Peter; Frederick, John
See also CA 108; 152; CANR 143; DAM POP; DLB 256; TUS

Faust, Irvin 1924- .... **CLC 8**
See also CA 33-36R; CANR 28, 67; CN 1, 2, 3, 4, 5, 6, 7; DLB 2, 28, 218, 278; DLBY 1980

Fawkes, Guy
See Benchley, Robert (Charles)

Fearing, Kenneth (Flexner)
1902-1961 .... **CLC 51**
See also CA 93-96; CANR 59; CMW 4; DLB 9; MAL 5; RGAL 4

Fecamps, Elise
See Creasey, John

Federman, Raymond 1928- .... **CLC 6, 47**
See also CA 17-20R, 208; CAAE 208; CAAS 8; CANR 10, 43, 83, 108; CN 3, 4, 5, 6; DLBY 1980

Federspiel, J.F. 1931-2007 .... **CLC 42**
See also CA 146; 257

Federspiel, Juerg F.
See Federspiel, J.F.

Federspiel, Jurg F.
See Federspiel, J.F.

Feiffer, Jules 1929- .... **CLC 2, 8, 64**
See also AAYA 3, 62; CA 17-20R; CAD; CANR 30, 59, 129, 161; CD 5, 6; DAM DRAM; DLB 7, 44; INT CANR-30; MTCW 1; SATA 8, 61, 111, 157

Feiffer, Jules Ralph
See Feiffer, Jules

Feige, Hermann Albert Otto Maximilian
See Traven, B.

Feinberg, David B. 1956-1994 .... **CLC 59**
See also CA 135; 147

Feinstein, Elaine 1930- .... **CLC 36**
See also CA 69-72; CAAS 1; CANR 31, 68, 121, 162; CN 3, 4, 5, 6, 7; CP 2, 3, 4, 5, 6, 7; CWP; DLB 14, 40; MTCW 1

Feke, Gilbert David CLC 65

Feldman, Irving (Mordecai) 1928- ..... **CLC 7**
See also CA 1-4R; CANR 1; CP 1, 2, 3, 4, 5, 6, 7; DLB 169; TCLE 1:1

Felix-Tchicaya, Gerald
See Tchicaya, Gerald Felix

Fellini, Federico 1920-1993 .... **CLC 16, 85**
See also CA 65-68; 143; CANR 33

Felltham, Owen 1602(?)-1668 .... **LC 92**
See also DLB 126, 151

Felsen, Henry Gregor 1916-1995 ..... **CLC 17**
See also CA 1-4R; 180; CANR 1; SAAS 2; SATA 1

Felski, Rita CLC 65

Fenelon, Francois de Pons de Salignac de la Mothe- 1651-1715 .... **LC 134**
See also DLB 268; EW 3; GFL Beginnings to 1789

Fenno, Jack
See Calisher, Hortense

Fenollosa, Ernest (Francisco)
1853-1908 .... **TCLC 91**

Fenton, James 1949- .... **CLC 32, 209**
See also CA 102; CANR 108, 160; CP 2, 3, 4, 5, 6, 7; DLB 40; PFS 11

Fenton, James Martin
See Fenton, James

Ferber, Edna 1887-1968 .... **CLC 18, 93**
See also AITN 1; CA 5-8R; 25-28R; CANR 68, 105; DLB 9, 28, 86, 266; MAL 5; MTCW 1, 2; MTFW 2005; RGAL 4; RHW; SATA 7; TCWW 1, 2

Ferdousi
See Ferdowsi, Abu'l Qasem

Ferdovsi
See Ferdowsi, Abu'l Qasem

Ferdowsi
See Ferdowsi, Abu'l Qasem

Ferdowsi, Abolghasem Mansour
See Ferdowsi, Abu'l Qasem

Ferdowsi, Abol-Qasem
See Ferdowsi, Abu'l Qasem

Ferdowsi, Abolqasem
See Ferdowsi, Abu'l Qasem

Ferdowsi, Abu'l Qasem
940-1020(?) .... **CMLC 43**
See Firdawsi, Abu al-Qasim
See also CA 276; RGWL 2, 3

Ferdowsi, A.M.
See Ferdowsi, Abu'l Qasem

Ferdowsi, Hakim Abolghasem
See Ferdowsi, Abu'l Qasem

Ferguson, Helen
See Kavan, Anna

Ferguson, Niall 1964- .... **CLC 134, 250**
See also CA 190; CANR 154

Ferguson, Niall Campbell
See Ferguson, Niall

Ferguson, Samuel 1810-1886 .... **NCLC 33**
See also DLB 32; RGEL 2

Fergusson, Robert 1750-1774 .... **LC 29**
See also DLB 109; RGEL 2

Ferling, Lawrence
See Ferlinghetti, Lawrence

Ferlinghetti, Lawrence 1919(?)- .... **CLC 2, 6, 10, 27, 111; PC 1**
See also AAYA 74; BG 1:2; CA 5-8R; CAD; CANR 3, 41, 73, 125, 172; CDALB 1941-1968; CP 1, 2, 3, 4, 5, 6, 7; DA3; DAM POET; DLB 5, 16; MAL 5; MTCW 1, 2; MTFW 2005; PFS 28; RGAL 4; WP

Ferlinghetti, Lawrence Monsanto
See Ferlinghetti, Lawrence

Fern, Fanny
See Parton, Sara Payson Willis

Fernandez, Vicente Garcia Huidobro
See Huidobro Fernandez, Vicente Garcia

Fernandez-Armesto, Felipe **CLC 70**
See Fernandez-Armesto, Felipe Fermin Ricardo
See also CANR 153

Fernandez-Armesto, Felipe Fermin Ricardo 1950-
See Fernandez-Armesto, Felipe
See also CA 142; CANR 93

Fernandez de Lizardi, Jose Joaquin
See Lizardi, Jose Joaquin Fernandez de

Ferre, Rosario 1938- ...... **CLC 139; HLCS 1; SSC 36, 106**
See also CA 131; CANR 55, 81, 134; CWW 2; DLB 145; EWL 3; HW 1, 2; LAWS 1; MTCW 2; MTFW 2005; WLIT 1

Ferrer, Gabriel (Francisco Victor) Miro
See Miro (Ferrer), Gabriel (Francisco Victor)

Ferrier, Susan (Edmonstone)
1782-1854 .... **NCLC 8**
See also DLB 116; RGEL 2

Ferrigno, Robert 1947- .... **CLC 65**
See also CA 140; CANR 125, 161

Ferron, Jacques 1921-1985 .... **CLC 94**
See also CA 117; 129; CCA 1; DAC; DLB 60; EWL 3

Feuchtwanger, Lion 1884-1958 .... **TCLC 3**
See also CA 104; 187; DLB 66; EWL 3; RGHL

Feuerbach, Ludwig 1804-1872 ..... **NCLC 139**
See also DLB 133

Feuillet, Octave 1821-1890 .... **NCLC 45**
See also DLB 192

Feydeau, Georges (Leon Jules Marie)
1862-1921 .... **TCLC 22**
See also CA 113; 152; CANR 84; DAM DRAM; DLB 192; EWL 3; GFL 1789 to the Present; RGWL 2, 3

Fichte, Johann Gottlieb
1762-1814 .... **NCLC 62**
See also DLB 90

Ficino, Marsilio 1433-1499 .... **LC 12, 152**
See also LMFS 1

Fiedeler, Hans
See Doeblin, Alfred

Fiedler, Leslie A(aron) 1917-2003 ..... **CLC 4, 13, 24**
See also AMWS 13; CA 9-12R; 212; CANR 7, 63; CN 1, 2, 3, 4, 5, 6; DLB 28, 67; EWL 3; MAL 5; MTCW 1, 2; RGAL 4; TUS

Field, Andrew 1938- .... **CLC 44**
See also CA 97-100; CANR 25

Field, Eugene 1850-1895 .... **NCLC 3**
See also DLB 23, 42, 140; DLBD 13; MAICYA 1, 2; RGAL 4; SATA 16

Field, Gans T.
See Wellman, Manly Wade

Field, Michael 1915-1971 .... **TCLC 43**
See also CA 29-32R

Fielding, Helen 1958- .... **CLC 146, 217**
See also AAYA 65; CA 172; CANR 127; DLB 231; MTFW 2005

Fielding, Henry 1707-1754 .... **LC 1, 46, 85, 151, 154; WLC 2**
See also BRW 3; BRWR 1; CDBLB 1660-1789; DA; DA3; DAB; DAC; DAM DRAM, MST, NOV; DLB 39, 84, 101; NFS 18; RGEL 2; TEA; WLIT 3

Fielding, Sarah 1710-1768 .... **LC 1, 44**
See also DLB 39; RGEL 2; TEA

Fields, W. C. 1880-1946 .... **TCLC 80**
See also DLB 44

Fierstein, Harvey (Forbes) 1954- ..... **CLC 33**
See also CA 123; 129; CAD; CD 5, 6; CPW; DA3; DAM DRAM, POP; DFS 6; DLB 266; GLL; MAL 5

Figes, Eva 1932- .... **CLC 31**
See also CA 53-56; CANR 4, 44, 83; CN 2, 3, 4, 5, 6, 7; DLB 14, 271; FW; RGHL

Filippo, Eduardo de
See de Filippo, Eduardo

Finch, Anne 1661-1720 ..... **LC 3, 137; PC 21**
See also BRWS 9; DLB 95

Finch, Robert (Duer Claydon)
1900-1995 .... **CLC 18**
See also CA 57-60; CANR 9, 24, 49; CP 1, 2, 3, 4, 5, 6; DLB 88

Findley, Timothy (Irving Frederick)
1930-2002 .... **CLC 27, 102**
See also CA 25-28R; 206; CANR 12, 42, 69, 109; CCA 1; CN 4, 5, 6, 7; DAC; DAM MST; DLB 53; FANT; RHW

Fink, William
See Mencken, H(enry) L(ouis)

Firbank, Louis 1942-
See Reed, Lou
See also CA 117

Firbank, (Arthur Annesley) Ronald
1886-1926 .... **TCLC 1**
See also BRWS 2; CA 104; 177; DLB 36; EWL 3; RGEL 2

Firdaosi
See Ferdowsi, Abu'l Qasem

Firdausi
See Ferdowsi, Abu'l Qasem

Firdavsi, Abulqosimi
See Ferdowsi, Abu'l Qasem

Firdavsii, Abulqosim
See Ferdowsi, Abu'l Qasem

Firdawsi, Abu al-Qasim
See Ferdowsi, Abu'l Qasem
See also WLIT 6

Firdosi
See Ferdowsi, Abu'l Qasem

Firdousi
See Ferdowsi, Abu'l Qasem

Firdousi, Abu'l-Qasim
See Ferdowsi, Abu'l Qasem

Firdovsi, A.
See Ferdowsi, Abu'l Qasem

Firdovsi, Abulgasim
See Ferdowsi, Abu'l Qasem

Firdusi
See Ferdowsi, Abu'l Qasem

Fish, Stanley
See Fish, Stanley Eugene

Fish, Stanley E.
See Fish, Stanley Eugene

Fish, Stanley Eugene 1938- .... **CLC 142**
See also CA 112; 132; CANR 90; DLB 67

Fisher, Dorothy (Frances) Canfield
1879-1958 .... **TCLC 87**
See also CA 114; 136; CANR 80; CLR 71; CWRI 5; DLB 9, 102, 284; MAICYA 1, 2; MAL 5; YABC 1

Fisher, M(ary) F(rances) K(ennedy)
1908-1992 .... **CLC 76, 87**
See also AMWS 17; CA 77-80; 138; CANR 44; MTCW 2

Fisher, Roy 1930- .... **CLC 25**
See also CA 81-84; CAAS 10; CANR 16; CP 1, 2, 3, 4, 5, 6, 7; DLB 40

Fisher, Rudolph 1897-1934 ...... **BLC 1:2; HR 1:2; SSC 25; TCLC 11**
See also BW 1, 3; CA 107; 124; CANR 80; DAM MULT; DLB 51, 102

Fisher, Vardis (Alvero) 1895-1968 .... **CLC 7; TCLC 140**
See also CA 5-8R; 25-28R; CANR 68; DLB 9, 206; MAL 5; RGAL 4; TCWW 1, 2

Fiske, Tarleton
See Bloch, Robert (Albert)

Fitch, Clarke
See Sinclair, Upton

Fitch, John IV
See Cormier, Robert

Fitzgerald, Captain Hugh
See Baum, L(yman) Frank

FitzGerald, Edward 1809-1883 ...... **NCLC 9, 153; PC 79**
See also BRW 4; DLB 32; RGEL 2

Fitzgerald, F(rancis) Scott (Key)
1896-1940 ... **SSC 6, 31, 75; TCLC 1, 6, 14, 28, 55, 157; WLC 2**
See also AAYA 24; AITN 1; AMW; AMWC 2; AMWR 1; BPFB 1; CA 110; 123; CDALB 1917-1929; DA; DA3; DAB; DAC; DAM MST, NOV; DLB 4, 9, 86, 219, 273; DLBD 1, 15, 16; DLBY 1981, 1996; EWL 3; EXPN; EXPS; LAIT 3; MAL 5; MTCW 1, 2; MTFW 2005; NFS 2, 19, 20; RGAL 4; RGSF 2; SSFS 4, 15, 21, 25; TUS

Fitzgerald, Penelope 1916-2000 . **CLC 19, 51, 61, 143**
See also BRWS 5; CA 85-88; 190; CAAS 10; CANR 56, 86, 131; CN 3, 4, 5, 6, 7; DLB 14, 194, 326; EWL 3; MTCW 2; MTFW 2005

Fitzgerald, Robert (Stuart)
1910-1985 .... **CLC 39**
See also CA 1-4R; 114; CANR 1; CP 1, 2, 3, 4; DLBY 1980; MAL 5

FitzGerald, Robert D(avid)
1902-1987 .... CLC 19
See also CA 17-20R; CP 1, 2, 3, 4; DLB
260; RGEL 2

Fitzgerald, Zelda (Sayre)
1900-1948 .... TCLC 52
See also AMWS 9; CA 117; 126; DLBY
1984

Flanagan, Thomas (James Bonner)
1923-2002 .... CLC 25, 52
See also CA 108; 206; CANR 55; CN 3, 4,
5, 6, 7; DLBY 1980; INT CA-108; MTCW
1; RHW; TCLE 1:1

Flaubert, Gustave 1821-1880 .... NCLC 2, 10,
19, 62, 66, 135, 179, 185; SSC 11, 60;
WLC 2
See also DA; DA3; DAB; DAC; DAM
MST, NOV; DLB 119, 301; EW 7; EXPS;
GFL 1789 to the Present; LAIT 2; LMFS
1; NFS 14; RGSF 2; RGWL 2, 3; SSFS
6; TWA

Flavius Josephus
See Josephus, Flavius

Flecker, Herman Elroy
See Flecker, (Herman) James Elroy

Flecker, (Herman) James Elroy
1884-1915 .... TCLC 43
See also CA 109; 150; DLB 10, 19; RGEL
2

Fleming, Ian 1908-1964 ... CLC 3, 30; TCLC
193
See also AAYA 26; BPFB 1; CA 5-8R;
CANR 59; CDBLB 1945-1960; CMW 4;
CPW; DA3; DAM POP; DLB 87, 201;
MSW; MTCW 1, 2; MTFW 2005; RGEL
2; SATA 9; TEA; YAW

Fleming, Ian Lancaster
See Fleming, Ian

Fleming, Thomas 1927- .... CLC 37
See also CA 5-8R; CANR 10, 102, 155;
INT CANR-10; SATA 8

Fleming, Thomas James
See Fleming, Thomas

Fletcher, John 1579-1625 . DC 6; LC 33, 151
See also BRW 2; CDBLB Before 1660;
DLB 58; RGEL 2; TEA

Fletcher, John Gould 1886-1950 .... TCLC 35
See also CA 107; 167; DLB 4, 45; LMFS
2; MAL 5; RGAL 4

Fleur, Paul
See Pohl, Frederik

Flieg, Helmut
See Heym, Stefan

Flooglebuckle, Al
See Spiegelman, Art

Flora, Fletcher 1914-1969
See Queen, Ellery
See also CA 1-4R; CANR 3, 85

Flying Officer X
See Bates, H(erbert) E(rnest)

Fo, Dario 1926- .... CLC 32, 109, 227; DC 10
See also CA 116; 128; CANR 68, 114, 134,
164; CWW 2; DA3; DAM DRAM; DFS
23; DLB 330; DLBY 1997; EWL 3;
MTCW 1, 2; MTFW 2005; WLIT 7

Foden, Giles 1967- .... CLC 231
See also CA 240; DLB 267; NFS 15

Fogarty, Jonathan Titulescu Esq.
See Farrell, James T(homas)

Follett, Ken 1949- .... CLC 18
See also AAYA 6, 50; BEST 89:4; BPFB 1;
CA 81-84; CANR 13, 33, 54, 102, 156;
CMW 4; CPW; DA3; DAM NOV, POP;
DLB 87; DLBY 1981; INT CANR-33;
MTCW 1

Follett, Kenneth Martin
See Follett, Ken

Fondane, Benjamin 1898-1944 ..... TCLC 159

Fontane, Theodor 1819-1898 . NCLC 26, 163
See also CDWLB 2; DLB 129; EW 6;
RGWL 2, 3; TWA

Fonte, Moderata 1555-1592 .... LC 118

Fontenelle, Bernard Le Bovier de
1657-1757 .... LC 140
See also DLB 268, 313; GFL Beginnings to
1789

Fontenot, Chester CLC 65

Fonvizin, Denis Ivanovich
1744(?)-1792 .... LC 81
See also DLB 150; RGWL 2, 3

Foote, Horton 1916- .... CLC 51, 91
See also CA 73-76; CAD; CANR 34, 51,
110; CD 5, 6; CSW; DA3; DAM DRAM;
DFS 20; DLB 26, 266; EWL 3; INT
CANR-34; MTFW 2005

Foote, Mary Hallock 1847-1938 .. TCLC 108
See also DLB 186, 188, 202, 221; TCWW
2

Foote, Samuel 1721-1777 .... LC 106
See also DLB 89; RGEL 2

Foote, Shelby 1916-2005 .... CLC 75, 224
See also AAYA 40; CA 5-8R; 240; CANR
3, 45, 74, 131; CN 1, 2, 3, 4, 5, 6, 7;
CPW; CSW; DA3; DAM NOV, POP;
DLB 2, 17; MAL 5; MTCW 2; MTFW
2005; RHW

Forbes, Cosmo
See Lewton, Val

Forbes, Esther 1891-1967 .... CLC 12
See also AAYA 17; BYA 2; CA 13-14; 25-
28R; CAP 1; CLR 27; DLB 22; JRDA;
MAICYA 1, 2; RHW; SATA 2, 100; YAW

Forche, Carolyn 1950- .. CLC 25, 83, 86; PC
10
See also CA 109; 117; CANR 50, 74, 138;
CP 4, 5, 6, 7; CWP; DA3; DAM POET;
DLB 5, 193; INT CA-117; MAL 5;
MTCW 2; MTFW 2005; PFS 18; RGAL
4

Forche, Carolyn Louise
See Forche, Carolyn

Ford, Elbur
See Hibbert, Eleanor Alice Burford

Ford, Ford Madox 1873-1939 ... TCLC 1, 15,
39, 57, 172
See Chaucer, Daniel
See also BRW 6; CA 104; 132; CANR 74;
CDBLB 1914-1945; DA3; DAM NOV;
DLB 34, 98, 162; EWL 3; MTCW 1, 2;
NFS 28; RGEL 2; TEA

Ford, Henry 1863-1947 .... TCLC 73
See also CA 115; 148

Ford, Jack
See Ford, John

Ford, John 1586-1639 .... DC 8; LC 68, 153
See also BRW 2; CDBLB Before 1660;
DA3; DAM DRAM; DFS 7; DLB 58;
IDTP; RGEL 2

Ford, John 1895-1973 .... CLC 16
See also AAYA 75; CA 187; 45-48

Ford, Richard 1944- .... CLC 46, 99, 205
See also AMWS 5; CA 69-72; CANR 11,
47, 86, 128, 164; CN 5, 6, 7; CSW; DLB
227; EWL 3; MAL 5; MTCW 2; MTFW
2005; NFS 25; RGAL 4; RGSF 2

Ford, Webster
See Masters, Edgar Lee

Foreman, Richard 1937- .... CLC 50
See also CA 65-68; CAD; CANR 32, 63,
143; CD 5, 6

Forester, C(ecil) S(cott) 1899-1966 . CLC 35;
TCLC 152
See also CA 73-76; 25-28R; CANR 83;
DLB 191; RGEL 2; RHW; SATA 13

Forez
See Mauriac, Francois (Charles)

Forman, James
See Forman, James D.

Forman, James D. 1932- .... CLC 21
See also AAYA 17; CA 9-12R; CANR 4,
19, 42; JRDA; MAICYA 1, 2; SATA 8,
70; YAW

Forman, James Douglas
See Forman, James D.

Forman, Milos 1932- .... CLC 164
See also AAYA 63; CA 109

Fornes, Maria Irene 1930- .... CLC 39, 61,
187; DC 10; HLCS 1
See also CA 25-28R; CAD; CANR 28, 81;
CD 5, 6; CWD; DFS 25; DLB 7, 341; HW
1, 2; INT CANR-28; LLW; MAL 5;
MTCW 1; RGAL 4

Forrest, Leon (Richard)
1937-1997 .... BLCS; CLC 4
See also AFAW 2; BW 2; CA 89-92; 162;
CAAS 7; CANR 25, 52, 87; CN 4, 5, 6;
DLB 33

Forster, E(dward) M(organ)
1879-1970 ...... CLC 1, 2, 3, 4, 9, 10, 13,
15, 22, 45, 77; SSC 27, 96; TCLC 125;
WLC 2
See also AAYA 2, 37; BRW 6; BRWR 2;
BYA 12; CA 13-14; 25-28R; CANR 45;
CAP 1; CDBLB 1914-1945; DA; DA3;
DAB; DAC; DAM MST, NOV; DLB 34,
98, 162, 178, 195; DLBD 10; EWL 3;
EXPN; LAIT 3; LMFS 1; MTCW 1, 2;
MTFW 2005; NCFS 1; NFS 3, 10, 11;
RGEL 2; RGSF 2; SATA 57; SUFW 1;
TEA; WLIT 4

Forster, John 1812-1876 .... NCLC 11
See also DLB 144, 184

Forster, Margaret 1938- .... CLC 149
See also CA 133; CANR 62, 115, 175; CN
4, 5, 6, 7; DLB 155, 271

Forsyth, Frederick 1938- .... CLC 2, 5, 36
See also BEST 89:4; CA 85-88; CANR 38,
62, 115, 137, 183; CMW 4; CN 3, 4, 5, 6,
7; CPW; DAM NOV, POP; DLB 87;
MTCW 1, 2; MTFW 2005

Forten, Charlotte L. 1837-1914 ..... BLC 1:2;
TCLC 16
See Grimke, Charlotte L(ottie) Forten
See also DLB 50, 239

Fortinbras
See Grieg, (Johan) Nordahl (Brun)

Foscolo, Ugo 1778-1827 .... NCLC 8, 97
See also EW 5; WLIT 7

Fosse, Bob 1927-1987
See Fosse, Robert L.
See also CA 110; 123

Fosse, Robert L. CLC 20
See Fosse, Bob

Foster, Hannah Webster
1758-1840 .... NCLC 99
See also DLB 37, 200; RGAL 4

Foster, Stephen Collins
1826-1864 .... NCLC 26
See also RGAL 4

Foucault, Michel 1926-1984 . CLC 31, 34, 69
See also CA 105; 113; CANR 34; DLB 242;
EW 13; EWL 3; GFL 1789 to the Present;
GLL 1; LMFS 2; MTCW 1, 2; TWA

Fouque, Friedrich (Heinrich Karl) de la
Motte 1777-1843 .... NCLC 2
See also DLB 90; RGWL 2, 3; SUFW 1

Fourier, Charles 1772-1837 .... NCLC 51

Fournier, Henri-Alban 1886-1914
See Alain-Fournier
See also CA 104; 179

Fournier, Pierre 1916-1997 .... CLC 11
See Gascar, Pierre
See also CA 89-92; CANR 16, 40

Fowles, John 1926-2005 .... **CLC 1, 2, 3, 4, 6, 9, 10, 15, 33, 87; SSC 33**
See also BPFB 1; BRWS 1; CA 5-8R; 245; CANR 25, 71, 103; CDBLB 1960 to Present; CN 1, 2, 3, 4, 5, 6, 7; DA3; DAB; DAC; DAM MST; DLB 14, 139, 207; EWL 3; HGG; MTCW 1, 2; MTFW 2005; NFS 21; RGEL 2; RHW; SATA 22; SATA-Obit 171; TEA; WLIT 4

Fowles, John Robert
See Fowles, John

Fox, Paula 1923- .... **CLC 2, 8, 121**
See also AAYA 3, 37; BYA 3, 8; CA 73-76; CANR 20, 36, 62, 105; CLR 1, 44, 96; DLB 52; JRDA; MAICYA 1, 2; MTCW 1; NFS 12; SATA 17, 60, 120, 167; WYA; YAW

Fox, William Price (Jr.) 1926- .... **CLC 22**
See also CA 17-20R; CAAS 19; CANR 11, 142; CSW; DLB 2; DLBY 1981

Foxe, John 1517(?)-1587 .... **LC 14**
See also DLB 132

Frame, Janet 1924-2004 ...... **CLC 2, 3, 6, 22, 66, 96, 237; SSC 29**
See also CA 1-4R; 224; CANR 2, 36, 76, 135; CN 1, 2, 3, 4, 5, 6, 7; CP 2, 3, 4; CWP; EWL 3; MTCW 1,2; RGEL 2; RGSF 2; SATA 119; TWA

France, Anatole TCLC 9
See Thibault, Jacques Anatole Francois
See also DLB 123, 330; EWL 3; GFL 1789 to the Present; RGWL 2, 3; SUFW 1

Francis, Claude CLC 50
See also CA 192

Francis, Dick 1920- .... **CLC 2, 22, 42, 102**
See Francis, Richard Stanley
See also AAYA 5, 21; BEST 89:3; BPFB 1; CA 5-8R; CANR 9, 42, 68, 100, 141, 179; CDBLB 1960 to Present; CMW 4; CN 7; DA3; DAM POP; DLB 87; INT CANR-9; MSW; MTCW 1, 2; MTFW 2005

Francis, Paula Marie
See Allen, Paula Gunn

Francis, Richard Stanley
See Francis, Dick
See also CN 2, 3, 4, 5, 6

Francis, Robert (Churchill)
1901-1987 .... **CLC 15; PC 34**
See also AMWS 9; CA 1-4R; 123; CANR 1; CP 1, 2, 3, 4; EXPP; PFS 12; TCLE 1:1

Francis, Lord Jeffrey
See Jeffrey, Francis
See also DLB 107

Frank, Anne(lies Marie)
1929-1945 .... **TCLC 17; WLC 2**
See also AAYA 12; BYA 1; CA 113; 133; CANR 68; CLR 101; DA; DA3; DAB; DAC; DAM MST; LAIT 4; MAICYA 2; MAICYAS 1; MTCW 1, 2; MTFW 2005; NCFS 2; RGHL; SATA 87; SATA-Brief 42; WYA; YAW

Frank, Bruno 1887-1945 .... **TCLC 81**
See also CA 189; DLB 118; EWL 3

Frank, Elizabeth 1945- .... **CLC 39**
See also CA 121; 126; CANR 78, 150; INT CA-126

Frankl, Viktor E(mil) 1905-1997 ...... **CLC 93**
See also CA 65-68; 161; RGHL

Franklin, Benjamin
See Hasek, Jaroslav (Matej Frantisek)

Franklin, Benjamin 1706-1790 .. **LC 25, 134; WLCS**
See also AMW; CDALB 1640-1865; DA; DA3; DAB; DAC; DAM MST; DLB 24, 43, 73, 183; LAIT 1; RGAL 4; TUS

Franklin, Madeleine
See L'Engle, Madeleine

Franklin, Madeleine L'Engle
See L'Engle, Madeleine

Franklin, Madeleine L'Engle Camp
See L'Engle, Madeleine

Franklin, (Stella Maria Sarah) Miles (Lampe) 1879-1954 .... **TCLC 7**
See also CA 104; 164; DLB 230; FW; MTCW 2; RGEL 2; TWA

Franzen, Jonathan 1959- .... **CLC 202**
See also AAYA 65; CA 129; CANR 105, 166

Fraser, Antonia 1932- .... **CLC 32, 107**
See also AAYA 57; CA 85-88; CANR 44, 65, 119, 164; CMW; DLB 276; MTCW 1, 2; MTFW 2005; SATA-Brief 32

Fraser, George MacDonald
1925-2008 .... **CLC 7**
See also AAYA 48; CA 45-48; 180; 268; CAAE 180; CANR 2, 48, 74; MTCW 2; RHW

Fraser, Sylvia 1935- .... **CLC 64**
See also CA 45-48; CANR 1, 16, 60; CCA 1

Frayn, Michael 1933- .... **CLC 3, 7, 31, 47, 176; DC 27**
See also AAYA 69; BRWC 2; BRWS 7; CA 5-8R; CANR 30, 69, 114, 133, 166; CBD; CD 5, 6; CN 1, 2, 3, 4, 5, 6, 7; DAM DRAM, NOV; DFS 22; DLB 13, 14, 194, 245; FANT; MTCW 1, 2; MTFW 2005; SFW 4

Fraze, Candida (Merrill) 1945- .... **CLC 50**
See also CA 126

Frazer, Andrew
See Marlowe, Stephen

Frazer, J(ames) G(eorge)
1854-1941 .... **TCLC 32**
See also BRWS 3; CA 118; NCFS 5

Frazer, Robert Caine
See Creasey, John

Frazer, Sir James George
See Frazer, J(ames) G(eorge)

Frazier, Charles 1950- .... **CLC 109, 224**
See also AAYA 34; CA 161; CANR 126, 170; CSW; DLB 292; MTFW 2005; NFS 25

Frazier, Charles R.
See Frazier, Charles

Frazier, Charles Robinson
See Frazier, Charles

Frazier, Ian 1951- .... **CLC 46**
See also CA 130; CANR 54, 93

Frederic, Harold 1856-1898 ... **NCLC 10, 175**
See also AMW; DLB 12, 23; DLBD 13; MAL 5; NFS 22; RGAL 4

Frederick, John
See Faust, Frederick (Schiller)
See also TCWW 2

Frederick the Great 1712-1786 .... **LC 14**

Fredro, Aleksander 1793-1876 .... **NCLC 8**

Freeling, Nicolas 1927-2003 .... **CLC 38**
See also CA 49-52; 218; CAAS 12; CANR 1, 17, 50, 84; CMW 4; CN 1, 2, 3, 4, 5, 6; DLB 87

Freeman, Douglas Southall
1886-1953 .... **TCLC 11**
See also CA 109; 195; DLB 17; DLBD 17

Freeman, Judith 1946- .... **CLC 55**
See also CA 148; CANR 120, 179; DLB 256

Freeman, Mary E(leanor) Wilkins
1852-1930 .... **SSC 1, 47, 113; TCLC 9**
See also CA 106; 177; DLB 12, 78, 221; EXPS; FW; HGG; MBL; RGAL 4; RGSF 2; SSFS 4, 8, 26; SUFW 1; TUS

Freeman, R(ichard) Austin
1862-1943 .... **TCLC 21**
See also CA 113; CANR 84; CMW 4; DLB 70

French, Albert 1943- .... **CLC 86**
See also BW 3; CA 167

French, Antonia
See Kureishi, Hanif

French, Marilyn 1929- .. **CLC 10, 18, 60, 177**
See also BPFB 1; CA 69-72; CANR 3, 31, 134, 163; CN 5, 6, 7; CPW; DAM DRAM, NOV, POP; FL 1:5; FW; INT CANR-31; MTCW 1, 2; MTFW 2005

French, Paul
See Asimov, Isaac

Freneau, Philip Morin 1752-1832 .. **NCLC 1, 111**
See also AMWS 2; DLB 37, 43; RGAL 4

Freud, Sigmund 1856-1939 .... **TCLC 52**
See also CA 115; 133; CANR 69; DLB 296; EW 8; EWL 3; LATS 1:1; MTCW 1, 2; MTFW 2005; NCFS 3; TWA

Freytag, Gustav 1816-1895 .... **NCLC 109**
See also DLB 129

Friedan, Betty 1921-2006 .... **CLC 74**
See also CA 65-68; 248; CANR 18, 45, 74; DLB 246; FW; MTCW 1, 2; MTFW 2005; NCFS 5

Friedan, Betty Naomi
See Friedan, Betty

Friedlander, Saul 1932- .... **CLC 90**
See also CA 117; 130; CANR 72; RGHL

Friedman, B(ernard) H(arper)
1926- .... **CLC 7**
See also CA 1-4R; CANR 3, 48

Friedman, Bruce Jay 1930- ...... **CLC 3, 5, 56**
See also CA 9-12R; CAD; CANR 25, 52, 101; CD 5, 6; CN 1, 2, 3, 4, 5, 6, 7; DLB 2, 28, 244; INT CANR-25; MAL 5; SSFS 18

Friel, Brian 1929- .. **CLC 5, 42, 59, 115, 253; DC 8; SSC 76**
See also BRWS 5; CA 21-24R; CANR 33, 69, 131; CBD; CD 5, 6; DFS 11; DLB 13, 319; EWL 3; MTCW 1; RGEL 2; TEA

Friis-Baastad, Babbis Ellinor
1921-1970 .... **CLC 12**
See also CA 17-20R; 134; SATA 7

Frisch, Max 1911-1991 ...... **CLC 3, 9, 14, 18, 32, 44; TCLC 121**
See also CA 85-88; 134; CANR 32, 74; CD-WLB 2; DAM DRAM, NOV; DFS 25; DLB 69, 124; EW 13; EWL 3; MTCW 1, 2; MTFW 2005; RGHL; RGWL 2, 3

Fromentin, Eugene (Samuel Auguste)
1820-1876 .... **NCLC 10, 125**
See also DLB 123; GFL 1789 to the Present

Frost, Frederick
See Faust, Frederick (Schiller)

Frost, Robert 1874-1963 . **CLC 1, 3, 4, 9, 10, 13, 15, 26, 34, 44; PC 1, 39, 71; WLC 2**
See also AAYA 21; AMW; AMWR 1; CA 89-92; CANR 33; CDALB 1917-1929; CLR 67; DA; DA3; DAB; DAC; DAM MST, POET; DLB 54, 284, 342; DLBD 7; EWL 3; EXPP; MAL 5; MTCW 1, 2; MTFW 2005; PAB; PFS 1, 2, 3, 4, 5, 6, 7, 10, 13; RGAL 4; SATA 14; TUS; WP; WYA

Frost, Robert Lee
See Frost, Robert

Froude, James Anthony
1818-1894 .... **NCLC 43**
See also DLB 18, 57, 144

Froy, Herald
See Waterhouse, Keith (Spencer)

Fry, Christopher 1907-2005 ... **CLC 2, 10, 14**
See also BRWS 3; CA 17-20R; 240; CAAS 23; CANR 9, 30, 74, 132; CBD; CD 5, 6; CP 1, 2, 3, 4, 5, 6, 7; DAM DRAM; DLB 13; EWL 3; MTCW 1, 2; MTFW 2005; RGEL 2; SATA 66; TEA

Frye, (Herman) Northrop
1912-1991 .... **CLC 24, 70; TCLC 165**
See also CA 5-8R; 133; CANR 8, 37; DLB
67, 68, 246; EWL 3; MTCW 1, 2; MTFW
2005; RGAL 4; TWA

Fuchs, Daniel 1909-1993 .... **CLC 8, 22**
See also CA 81-84; 142; CAAS 5; CANR
40; CN 1, 2, 3, 4, 5; DLB 9, 26, 28;
DLBY 1993; MAL 5

Fuchs, Daniel 1934- .... **CLC 34**
See also CA 37-40R; CANR 14, 48

Fuentes, Carlos 1928- .. **CLC 3, 8, 10, 13, 22,
41, 60, 113; HLC 1; SSC 24; WLC 2**
See also AAYA 4, 45; AITN 2; BPFB 1;
CA 69-72; CANR 10, 32, 68, 104, 138;
CDWLB 3; CWW 2; DA; DA3; DAB;
DAC; DAM MST, MULT, NOV; DLB
113; DNFS 2; EWL 3; HW 1, 2; LAIT 3;
LATS 1:2; LAW; LAWS 1; LMFS 2;
MTCW 1, 2; MTFW 2005; NFS 8; RGSF
2; RGWL 2, 3; TWA; WLIT 1

Fuentes, Gregorio Lopez y
See Lopez y Fuentes, Gregorio

Fuertes, Gloria 1918-1998 .... **PC 27**
See also CA 178, 180; DLB 108; HW 2;
SATA 115

Fugard, (Harold) Athol 1932- . **CLC 5, 9, 14,
25, 40, 80, 211; DC 3**
See also AAYA 17; AFW; CA 85-88; CANR
32, 54, 118; CD 5, 6; DAM DRAM; DFS
3, 6, 10, 24; DLB 225; DNFS 1, 2; EWL
3; LATS 1:2; MTCW 1; MTFW 2005;
RGEL 2; WLIT 2

Fugard, Sheila 1932- .... **CLC 48**
See also CA 125

Fujiwara no Teika 1162-1241 .... **CMLC 73**
See also DLB 203

Fukuyama, Francis 1952- .... **CLC 131**
See also CA 140; CANR 72, 125, 170

Fuller, Charles (H.), (Jr.) 1939- ..... **BLC 1:2;
CLC 25; DC 1**
See also BW 2; CA 108; 112; CAD; CANR
87; CD 5, 6; DAM DRAM, MULT; DFS
8; DLB 38, 266; EWL 3; INT CA-112;
MAL 5; MTCW 1

Fuller, Henry Blake 1857-1929 .... **TCLC 103**
See also CA 108; 177; DLB 12; RGAL 4

Fuller, John (Leopold) 1937- .... **CLC 62**
See also CA 21-24R; CANR 9, 44; CP 1, 2,
3, 4, 5, 6, 7; DLB 40

Fuller, Margaret
See Ossoli, Sarah Margaret (Fuller)
See also AMWS 2; DLB 183, 223, 239; FL
1:3

Fuller, Roy (Broadbent) 1912-1991 ... **CLC 4,
28**
See also BRWS 7; CA 5-8R; 135; CAAS
10; CANR 53, 83; CN 1, 2, 3, 4, 5; CP 1,
2, 3, 4, 5; CWRI 5; DLB 15, 20; EWL 3;
RGEL 2; SATA 87

Fuller, Sarah Margaret
See Ossoli, Sarah Margaret (Fuller)

Fuller, Sarah Margaret
See Ossoli, Sarah Margaret (Fuller)

Fuller, Thomas 1608-1661 .... **LC 111**
See also DLB 151

Fulton, Alice 1952- .... **CLC 52**
See also CA 116; CANR 57, 88; CP 5, 6, 7;
CWP; DLB 193; PFS 25

Furphy, Joseph 1843-1912 .... **TCLC 25**
See Collins, Tom
See also CA 163; DLB 230; EWL 3; RGEL
2

Furst, Alan 1941- .... **CLC 255**
See also CA 69-72; CANR 12, 34, 59, 102,
159; DLBY 01

Fuson, Robert H(enderson) 1927- .... **CLC 70**
See also CA 89-92; CANR 103

Fussell, Paul 1924- .... **CLC 74**
See also BEST 90:1; CA 17-20R; CANR 8,
21, 35, 69, 135; INT CANR-21; MTCW
1, 2; MTFW 2005

Futabatei, Shimei 1864-1909 .... **TCLC 44**
See Futabatei Shimei
See also CA 162; MJW

Futabatei Shimei
See Futabatei, Shimei
See also DLB 180; EWL 3

Futrelle, Jacques 1875-1912 .... **TCLC 19**
See also CA 113; 155; CMW 4

Gaboriau, Emile 1835-1873 .... **NCLC 14**
See also CMW 4; MSW

Gadda, Carlo Emilio 1893-1973 ...... **CLC 11;
TCLC 144**
See also CA 89-92; DLB 177; EWL 3;
WLIT 7

Gaddis, William 1922-1998 ... **CLC 1, 3, 6, 8,
10, 19, 43, 86**
See also AMWS 4; BPFB 1; CA 17-20R;
172; CANR 21, 48, 148; CN 1, 2, 3, 4, 5,
6; DLB 2, 278; EWL 3; MAL 5; MTCW
1, 2; MTFW 2005; RGAL 4

Gage, Walter
See Inge, William (Motter)

Gaiman, Neil 1960- .... **CLC 195**
See also AAYA 19, 42; CA 133; CANR 81,
129; CLR 109; DLB 261; HGG; MTFW
2005; SATA 85, 146; SFW 4; SUFW 2

Gaiman, Neil Richard
See Gaiman, Neil

Gaines, Ernest J. 1933- ..... **BLC 1:2; CLC 3,
11, 18, 86, 181; SSC 68**
See also AAYA 18; AFAW 1, 2; AITN 1;
BPFB 2; BW 2, 3; BYA 6; CA 9-12R;
CANR 6, 24, 42, 75, 126; CDALB 1968-
1988; CLR 62; CN 1, 2, 3, 4, 5, 6, 7;
CSW; DA3; DAM MULT; DLB 2, 33,
152; DLBY 1980; EWL 3; EXPN; LAIT
5; LATS 1:2; MAL 5; MTCW 1, 2;
MTFW 2005; NFS 5, 7, 16; RGAL 4;
RGSF 2; RHW; SATA 86; SSFS 5; YAW

Gaitskill, Mary 1954- .... **CLC 69**
See also CA 128; CANR 61, 152; DLB 244;
TCLE 1:1

Gaitskill, Mary Lawrence
See Gaitskill, Mary

Gaius Suetonius Tranquillus
See Suetonius

Galdos, Benito Perez
See Perez Galdos, Benito
See also EW 7

Gale, Zona 1874-1938 .... **DC 30; TCLC 7**
See also CA 105; 153; CANR 84; DAM
DRAM; DFS 17; DLB 9, 78, 228; RGAL
4

Galeano, Eduardo 1940- ... **CLC 72; HLCS 1**
See also CA 29-32R; CANR 13, 32, 100,
163; HW 1

Galeano, Eduardo Hughes
See Galeano, Eduardo

Galiano, Juan Valera y Alcala
See Valera y Alcala-Galiano, Juan

Galilei, Galileo 1564-1642 .... **LC 45**

Gallagher, Tess 1943- .... **CLC 18, 63; PC 9**
See also CA 106; CP 3, 4, 5, 6, 7; CWP;
DAM POET; DLB 120, 212, 244; PFS 16

Gallant, Mavis 1922- ..... **CLC 7, 18, 38, 172;
SSC 5, 78**
See also CA 69-72; CANR 29, 69, 117;
CCA 1; CN 1, 2, 3, 4, 5, 6, 7; DAC; DAM
MST; DLB 53; EWL 3; MTCW 1, 2;
MTFW 2005; RGEL 2; RGSF 2

Gallant, Roy A(rthur) 1924- .... **CLC 17**
See also CA 5-8R; CANR 4, 29, 54, 117;
CLR 30; MAICYA 1, 2; SATA 4, 68, 110

Gallico, Paul (William) 1897-1976 ..... **CLC 2**
See also AITN 1; CA 5-8R; 69-72; CANR
23; CN 1, 2; DLB 9, 171; FANT; MAI-
CYA 1, 2; SATA 13

Gallo, Max Louis 1932- .... **CLC 95**
See also CA 85-88

Gallois, Lucien
See Desnos, Robert

Gallup, Ralph
See Whitemore, Hugh (John)

Galsworthy, John 1867-1933 .... **SSC 22;
TCLC 1, 45; WLC 2**
See also BRW 6; CA 104; 141; CANR 75;
CDBLB 1890-1914; DA; DA3; DAB;
DAC; DAM DRAM, MST, NOV; DLB
10, 34, 98, 162, 330; DLBD 16; EWL 3;
MTCW 2; RGEL 2; SSFS 3; TEA

Galt, John 1779-1839 .... **NCLC 1, 110**
See also DLB 99, 116, 159; RGEL 2; RGSF
2

Galvin, James 1951- .... **CLC 38**
See also CA 108; CANR 26

Gamboa, Federico 1864-1939 .... **TCLC 36**
See also CA 167; HW 2; LAW

Gandhi, M. K.
See Gandhi, Mohandas Karamchand

Gandhi, Mahatma
See Gandhi, Mohandas Karamchand

Gandhi, Mohandas Karamchand
1869-1948 .... **TCLC 59**
See also CA 121; 132; DA3; DAM MULT;
DLB 323; MTCW 1, 2

Gann, Ernest Kellogg 1910-1991 ..... **CLC 23**
See also AITN 1; BPFB 2; CA 1-4R; 136;
CANR 1, 83; RHW

Gao Xingjian 1940- .... **CLC 167**
See Xingjian, Gao
See also MTFW 2005

Garber, Eric 1943(?)-
See Holleran, Andrew
See also CANR 89, 162

Garber, Esther
See Lee, Tanith

Garcia, Cristina 1958- .... **CLC 76**
See also AMWS 11; CA 141; CANR 73,
130, 172; CN 7; DLB 292; DNFS 1; EWL
3; HW 2; LLW; MTFW 2005

Garcia Lorca, Federico 1898-1936 ...... **DC 2;
HLC 2; PC 3; TCLC 1, 7, 49, 181,
197; WLC 2**
See Lorca, Federico Garcia
See also AAYA 46; CA 104; 131; CANR
81; DA; DA3; DAB; DAC; DAM DRAM,
MST, MULT, POET; DFS 4, 10; DLB
108; EWL 3; HW 1, 2; LATS 1:2; MTCW
1, 2; MTFW 2005; TWA

Garcia Marquez, Gabriel 1928- .... **CLC 2, 3,
8, 10, 15, 27, 47, 55, 68, 170, 254; HLC
1; SSC 8, 83; WLC 3**
See also AAYA 3, 33; BEST 89:1, 90:4;
BPFB 2; BYA 12, 16; CA 33-36R; CANR
10, 28, 50, 75, 82, 128; CDWLB 3; CPW;
CWW 2; DA; DA3; DAB; DAC; DAM
MST, MULT, NOV, POP; DLB 113, 330;
DNFS 1, 2; EWL 3; EXPN; EXPS; HW
1, 2; LAIT 2; LATS 1:2; LAW; LAWS 1;
LMFS 2; MTCW 1, 2; MTFW 2005;
NCFS 3; NFS 1, 5, 10; RGSF 2; RGWL
2, 3; SSFS 1, 6, 16, 21; TWA; WLIT 1

Garcia Marquez, Gabriel Jose
See Garcia Marquez, Gabriel

Garcilaso de la Vega, El Inca
1539-1616 .... **HLCS 1; LC 127**
See also DLB 318; LAW

Gard, Janice
See Latham, Jean Lee

Gard, Roger Martin du
See Martin du Gard, Roger

Gardam, Jane 1928- .... **CLC 43**
 See also CA 49-52; CANR 2, 18, 33, 54,
 106, 167; CLR 12; DLB 14, 161, 231;
 MAICYA 1, 2; MTCW 1; SAAS 9; SATA
 39, 76, 130; SATA-Brief 28; YAW
Gardam, Jane Mary
 See Gardam, Jane
Gardner, Herb(ert George)
 1934-2003 .... **CLC 44**
 See also CA 149; 220; CAD; CANR 119;
 CD 5, 6; DFS 18, 20
Gardner, John, Jr. 1933-1982 ... **CLC 2, 3, 5,**
 7, 8, 10, 18, 28, 34; SSC 7; TCLC 195
 See also AAYA 45; AITN 1; AMWS 6;
 BPFB 2; CA 65-68; 107; CANR 33, 73;
 CDALBS; CN 2, 3; CPW; DA3; DAM
 NOV, POP; DLB 2; DLBY 1982; EWL 3;
 FANT; LATS 1:2; MAL 5; MTCW 1, 2;
 MTFW 2005; NFS 3; RGAL 4; RGSF 2;
 SATA 40; SATA-Obit 31; SSFS 8
Gardner, John 1926-2007 .... **CLC 30**
 See also CA 103; 263; CANR 15, 69, 127,
 183; CMW 4; CPW; DAM POP; MTCW
 1
Gardner, John Edmund
 See Gardner, John
Gardner, Miriam
 See Bradley, Marion Zimmer
 See also GLL 1
Gardner, Noel
 See Kuttner, Henry
Gardons, S. S.
 See Snodgrass, W.D.
Garfield, Leon 1921-1996 .... **CLC 12**
 See also AAYA 8, 69; BYA 1, 3; CA 17-
 20R; 152; CANR 38, 41, 78; CLR 21;
 DLB 161; JRDA; MAICYA 1, 2; MAIC-
 YAS 1; SATA 1, 32, 76; SATA-Obit 90;
 TEA; WYA; YAW
Garland, (Hannibal) Hamlin
 1860-1940 .... **SSC 18, 117; TCLC 3**
 See also CA 104; DLB 12, 71, 78, 186;
 MAL 5; RGAL 4; RGSF 2; TCWW 1, 2
Garneau, (Hector de) Saint-Denys
 1912-1943 .... **TCLC 13**
 See also CA 111; DLB 88
Garner, Alan 1934- .... **CLC 17**
 See also AAYA 18; BYA 3, 5; CA 73-76,
 178; CAAE 178; CANR 15, 64, 134; CLR
 20, 130; CPW; DAB; DAM POP; DLB
 161, 261; FANT; MAICYA 1, 2; MTCW
 1, 2; MTFW 2005; SATA 18, 69; SATA-
 Essay 108; SUFW 1, 2; YAW
Garner, Hugh 1913-1979 .... **CLC 13**
 See Warwick, Jarvis
 See also CA 69-72; CANR 31; CCA 1; CN
 1, 2; DLB 68
Garnett, David 1892-1981 .... **CLC 3**
 See also CA 5-8R; 103; CANR 17, 79; CN
 1, 2; DLB 34; FANT; MTCW 2; RGEL 2;
 SFW 4; SUFW 1
Garnier, Robert c. 1545-1590 .... **LC 119**
 See also DLB 327; GFL Beginnings to 1789
Garrett, George 1929-2008 ... **CLC 3, 11, 51;**
 SSC 30
 See also AMWS 7; BPFB 2; CA 1-4R, 202;
 272; CAAE 202; CAAS 5; CANR 1, 42,
 67, 109; CN 1, 2, 3, 4, 5, 6, 7; CP 1, 2, 3,
 4, 5, 6, 7; CSW; DLB 2, 5, 130, 152;
 DLBY 1983
Garrett, George P.
 See Garrett, George
Garrett, George Palmer
 See Garrett, George
Garrett, George Palmer, Jr.
 See Garrett, George
Garrick, David 1717-1779 .... **LC 15, 156**
 See also DAM DRAM; DLB 84, 213;
 RGEL 2

Garrigue, Jean 1914-1972 .... **CLC 2, 8**
 See also CA 5-8R; 37-40R; CANR 20; CP
 1; MAL 5
Garrison, Frederick
 See Sinclair, Upton
Garrison, William Lloyd
 1805-1879 .... **NCLC 149**
 See also CDALB 1640-1865; DLB 1, 43,
 235
Garro, Elena 1920(?)-1998 .. **HLCS 1; TCLC**
 153
 See also CA 131; 169; CWW 2; DLB 145;
 EWL 3; HW 1; LAWS 1; WLIT 1
Garth, Will
 See Hamilton, Edmond; Kuttner, Henry
Garvey, Marcus (Moziah, Jr.)
 1887-1940 ..... **BLC 1:2; HR 1:2; TCLC**
 41
 See also BW 1; CA 120; 124; CANR 79;
 DAM MULT; DLB 345
Gary, Romain CLC 25
 See Kacew, Romain
 See also DLB 83, 299; RGHL
Gascar, Pierre CLC 11
 See Fournier, Pierre
 See also EWL 3; RGHL
Gascoigne, George 1539-1577 .... **LC 108**
 See also DLB 136; RGEL 2
Gascoyne, David (Emery)
 1916-2001 .... **CLC 45**
 See also CA 65-68; 200; CANR 10, 28, 54;
 CP 1, 2, 3, 4, 5, 6, 7; DLB 20; MTCW 1;
 RGEL 2
Gaskell, Elizabeth Cleghorn
 1810-1865 .... **NCLC 5, 70, 97, 137; SSC**
 25, 97
 See also BRW 5; CDBLB 1832-1890; DAB;
 DAM MST; DLB 21, 144, 159; RGEL 2;
 RGSF 2; TEA
Gass, William H. 1924- . **CLC 1, 2, 8, 11, 15,**
 39, 132; SSC 12
 See also AMWS 6; CA 17-20R; CANR 30,
 71, 100; CN 1, 2, 3, 4, 5, 6, 7; DLB 2,
 227; EWL 3; MAL 5; MTCW 1, 2;
 MTFW 2005; RGAL 4
Gassendi, Pierre 1592-1655 .... **LC 54**
 See also GFL Beginnings to 1789
Gasset, Jose Ortega y
 See Ortega y Gasset, Jose
Gates, Henry Louis, Jr. 1950- ... **BLCS; CLC**
 65
 See also BW 2, 3; CA 109; CANR 25, 53,
 75, 125; CSW; DA3; DAM MULT; DLB
 67; EWL 3; MAL 5; MTCW 2; MTFW
 2005; RGAL 4
Gatos, Stephanie
 See Katz, Steve
Gautier, Theophile 1811-1872 .. **NCLC 1, 59;**
 PC 18; SSC 20
 See also DAM POET; DLB 119; EW 6;
 GFL 1789 to the Present; RGWL 2, 3;
 SUFW; TWA
Gay, John 1685-1732 .... **LC 49**
 See also BRW 3; DAM DRAM; DLB 84,
 95; RGEL 2; WLIT 3
Gay, Oliver
 See Gogarty, Oliver St. John
Gay, Peter 1923- .... **CLC 158**
 See also CA 13-16R; CANR 18, 41, 77,
 147; INT CANR-18; RGHL
Gay, Peter Jack
 See Gay, Peter
Gaye, Marvin (Pentz, Jr.)
 1939-1984 .... **CLC 26**
 See also CA 195; 112
Gebler, Carlo 1954- .... **CLC 39**
 See also CA 119; 133; CANR 96; DLB 271

Gee, Maggie 1948- .... **CLC 57**
 See also CA 130; CANR 125; CN 4, 5, 6,
 7; DLB 207; MTFW 2005
Gee, Maurice 1931- .... **CLC 29**
 See also AAYA 42; CA 97-100; CANR 67,
 123; CLR 56; CN 2, 3, 4, 5, 6, 7; CWRI
 5; EWL 3; MAICYA 2; RGSF 2; SATA
 46, 101
Gee, Maurice Gough
 See Gee, Maurice
Geiogamah, Hanay 1945- .... **NNAL**
 See also CA 153; DAM MULT; DLB 175
Gelbart, Larry
 See Gelbart, Larry (Simon)
 See also CAD; CD 5, 6
Gelbart, Larry (Simon) 1928- .... **CLC 21, 61**
 See Gelbart, Larry
 See also CA 73-76; CANR 45, 94
Gelber, Jack 1932-2003 ...... **CLC 1, 6, 14, 79**
 See also CA 1-4R; 216; CAD; CANR 2;
 DLB 7, 228; MAL 5
Gellhorn, Martha (Ellis)
 1908-1998 .... **CLC 14, 60**
 See also CA 77-80; 164; CANR 44; CN 1,
 2, 3, 4, 5, 6 7; DLBY 1982, 1998
Genet, Jean 1910-1986 .. **CLC 1, 2, 5, 10, 14,**
 44, 46; DC 25; TCLC 128
 See also CA 13-16R; CANR 18; DA3;
 DAM DRAM; DFS 10; DLB 72, 321;
 DLBY 1986; EW 13; EWL 3; GFL 1789
 to the Present; GLL 1; LMFS 2; MTCW
 1, 2; MTFW 2005; RGWL 2, 3; TWA
Genlis, Stephanie-Felicite Ducrest
 1746-1830 .... **NCLC 166**
 See also DLB 313
Gent, Peter 1942- .... **CLC 29**
 See also AITN 1; CA 89-92; DLBY 1982
Gentile, Giovanni 1875-1944 .... **TCLC 96**
 See also CA 119
Geoffrey of Monmouth c.
 1100-1155 .... **CMLC 44**
 See also DLB 146; TEA
George, Jean
 See George, Jean Craighead
George, Jean Craighead 1919- .... **CLC 35**
 See also AAYA 8, 69; BYA 2, 4; CA 5-8R;
 CANR 25; CLR 1, 80, 136; DLB 52;
 JRDA; MAICYA 1, 2; SATA 2, 68, 124,
 170; WYA; YAW
George, Stefan (Anton) 1868-1933 . **TCLC 2,**
 14
 See also CA 104; 193; EW 8; EWL 3
Georges, Georges Martin
 See Simenon, Georges (Jacques Christian)
Gerald of Wales c. 1146-c. 1223 ... **CMLC 60**
Gerhardi, William Alexander
 See Gerhardie, William Alexander
Gerhardie, William Alexander
 1895-1977 .... **CLC 5**
 See also CA 25-28R; 73-76; CANR 18; CN
 1, 2; DLB 36; RGEL 2
Gerson, Jean 1363-1429 .... **LC 77**
 See also DLB 208
Gersonides 1288-1344 .... **CMLC 49**
 See also DLB 115
Gerstler, Amy 1956- .... **CLC 70**
 See also CA 146; CANR 99
Gertler, T. CLC 34
 See also CA 116; 121
Gertrude of Helfta c. 1256-c.
 1301 .... **CMLC 105**
Gertsen, Aleksandr Ivanovich
 See Herzen, Aleksandr Ivanovich
Ghalib NCLC 39, 78
 See Ghalib, Asadullah Khan
Ghalib, Asadullah Khan 1797-1869
 See Ghalib
 See also DAM POET; RGWL 2, 3

Ghelderode, Michel de 1898-1962 ..... **CLC 6, 11; DC 15; TCLC 187**
See also CA 85-88; CANR 40, 77; DAM DRAM; DLB 321; EW 11; EWL 3; TWA

Ghiselin, Brewster 1903-2001 .... **CLC 23**
See also CA 13-16R; CAAS 10; CANR 13; CP 1, 2, 3, 4, 5, 6, 7

Ghose, Aurabinda 1872-1950 .... **TCLC 63**
See Ghose, Aurobindo
See also CA 163

Ghose, Aurobindo
See Ghose, Aurabinda
See also EWL 3

Ghose, Zulfikar 1935- .... **CLC 42, 200**
See also CA 65-68; CANR 67; CN 1, 2, 3, 4, 5, 6, 7; CP 1, 2, 3, 4, 5, 6, 7; DLB 323; EWL 3

Ghosh, Amitav 1956- .... **CLC 44, 153**
See also CA 147; CANR 80, 158; CN 6, 7; DLB 323; WWE 1

Giacosa, Giuseppe 1847-1906 .... **TCLC 7**
See also CA 104

Gibb, Lee
See Waterhouse, Keith (Spencer)

Gibbon, Edward 1737-1794 .... **LC 97**
See also BRW 3; DLB 104, 336; RGEL 2

Gibbon, Lewis Grassic TCLC 4
See Mitchell, James Leslie
See also RGEL 2

Gibbons, Kaye 1960- .... **CLC 50, 88, 145**
See also AAYA 34; AMWS 10; CA 151; CANR 75, 127; CN 7; CSW; DA3; DAM POP; DLB 292; MTCW 2; MTFW 2005; NFS 3; RGAL 4; SATA 117

Gibran, Kahlil 1883-1931 ..... **PC 9; TCLC 1, 9, 205**
See also CA 104; 150; DA3; DAM POET, POP; DLB 346; EWL 3; MTCW 2; WLIT 6

Gibran, Khalil
See Gibran, Kahlil

Gibson, Mel 1956- .... **CLC 215**

Gibson, William 1914- .... **CLC 23**
See also CA 9-12R; CAD; CANR 9, 42, 75, 125; CD 5, 6; DA; DAB; DAC; DAM DRAM, MST; DFS 2; DLB 7; LAIT 2; MAL 5; MTCW 2; MTFW 2005; SATA 66; YAW

Gibson, William 1948- .... **CLC 39, 63, 186, 192; SSC 52**
See also AAYA 12, 59; AMWS 16; BPFB 2; CA 126; 133; CANR 52, 90, 106, 172; CN 6, 7; CPW; DA3; DAM POP; DLB 251; MTCW 2; MTFW 2005; SCFW 2; SFW 4; SSFS 26

Gibson, William Ford
See Gibson, William

Gide, Andre (Paul Guillaume) 1869-1951 ...... **SSC 13; TCLC 5, 12, 36, 177; WLC 3**
See also CA 104; 124; DA; DA3; DAB; DAC; DAM MST, NOV; DLB 65, 321, 330; EW 8; EWL 3; GFL 1789 to the Present; MTCW 1, 2; MTFW 2005; NFS 21; RGSF 2; RGWL 2, 3; TWA

Gifford, Barry 1946- .... **CLC 34**
See also CA 65-68; CANR 9, 30, 40, 90, 180

Gifford, Barry Colby
See Gifford, Barry

Gilbert, Frank
See De Voto, Bernard (Augustine)

Gilbert, W(illiam) S(chwenck) 1836-1911 .... **TCLC 3**
See also CA 104; 173; DAM DRAM, POET; DLB 344; RGEL 2; SATA 36

Gilbert of Poitiers c. 1085-1154 .... **CMLC 85**

Gilbreth, Frank B(unker), Jr. 1911-2001 .... **CLC 17**
See also CA 9-12R; SATA 2

Gilchrist, Ellen (Louise) 1935- .. **CLC 34, 48, 143; SSC 14, 63**
See also BPFB 2; CA 113; 116; CANR 41, 61, 104; CN 4, 5, 6, 7; CPW; CSW; DAM POP; DLB 130; EWL 3; EXPS; MTCW 1, 2; MTFW 2005; RGAL 4; RGSF 2; SSFS 9

Gildas fl. 6th cent. - .... **CMLC 99**

Giles, Molly 1942- .... **CLC 39**
See also CA 126; CANR 98

Gill, Eric TCLC 85
See Gill, (Arthur) Eric (Rowton Peter Joseph)

Gill, (Arthur) Eric (Rowton Peter Joseph) 1882-1940
See Gill, Eric
See also CA 120; DLB 98

Gill, Patrick
See Creasey, John

Gillette, Douglas CLC 70

Gilliam, Terry 1940- .... **CLC 21, 141**
See Monty Python
See also AAYA 19, 59; CA 108; 113; CANR 35; INT CA-113

Gilliam, Terry Vance
See Gilliam, Terry

Gillian, Jerry
See Gilliam, Terry

Gilliatt, Penelope (Ann Douglass) 1932-1993 .... **CLC 2, 10, 13, 53**
See also AITN 2; CA 13-16R; 141; CANR 49; CN 1, 2, 3, 4, 5; DLB 14

Gilligan, Carol 1936- .... **CLC 208**
See also CA 142; CANR 121; FW

Gilman, Charlotte (Anna) Perkins (Stetson) 1860-1935 ...... **SSC 13, 62; TCLC 9, 37, 117, 201**
See also AAYA 75; AMWS 11; BYA 11; CA 106; 150; DLB 221; EXPS; FL 1:5; FW; HGG; LAIT 2; MBL; MTCW 2; MTFW 2005; RGAL 4; RGSF 2; SFW 4; SSFS 1, 18

Gilmore, Mary (Jean Cameron) 1865-1962 .... **PC 87**
See also CA 114; DLB 260; RGEL 2; SATA 49

Gilmour, David 1946- .... **CLC 35**

Gilpin, William 1724-1804 .... **NCLC 30**

Gilray, J. D.
See Mencken, H(enry) L(ouis)

Gilroy, Frank D(aniel) 1925- .... **CLC 2**
See also CA 81-84; CAD; CANR 32, 64, 86; CD 5, 6; DFS 17; DLB 7

Gilstrap, John 1957(?)- .... **CLC 99**
See also AAYA 67; CA 160; CANR 101

Ginsberg, Allen 1926-1997 .... **CLC 1, 2, 3, 4, 6, 13, 36, 69, 109; PC 4, 47; TCLC 120; WLC 3**
See also AAYA 33; AITN 1; AMWC 1; AMWS 2; BG 1:2; CA 1-4R; 157; CANR 2, 41, 63, 95; CDALB 1941-1968; CP 1, 2, 3, 4, 5, 6; DA; DA3; DAB; DAC; DAM MST, POET; DLB 5, 16, 169, 237; EWL 3; GLL 1; LMFS 2; MAL 5; MTCW 1, 2; MTFW 2005; PAB; PFS 29; RGAL 4; TUS; WP

Ginzburg, Eugenia CLC 59
See Ginzburg, Evgeniia

Ginzburg, Evgeniia 1904-1977
See Ginzburg, Eugenia
See also DLB 302

Ginzburg, Natalia 1916-1991 .... **CLC 5, 11, 54, 70; SSC 65; TCLC 156**
See also CA 85-88; 135; CANR 33; DFS 14; DLB 177; EW 13; EWL 3; MTCW 1, 2; MTFW 2005; RGHL; RGWL 2, 3

Gioia, (Michael) Dana 1950- .... **CLC 251**
See also AMWS 15; CA 130; CANR 70, 88; CP 6, 7; DLB 120, 282; PFS 24

Giono, Jean 1895-1970 .... **CLC 4, 11; TCLC 124**
See also CA 45-48; 29-32R; CANR 2, 35; DLB 72, 321; EWL 3; GFL 1789 to the Present; MTCW 1; RGWL 2, 3

Giovanni, Nikki 1943- ... **BLC 1:2; CLC 2, 4, 19, 64, 117; PC 19; WLCS**
See also AAYA 22; AITN 1; BW 2, 3; CA 29-32R; CAAS 6; CANR 18, 41, 60, 91, 130, 175; CDALBS; CLR 6, 73; CP 2, 3, 4, 5, 6, 7; CSW; CWP; CWRI 5; DA; DA3; DAB; DAC; DAM MST, MULT, POET; DLB 5, 41; EWL 3; EXPP; INT CANR-18; MAICYA 1, 2; MAL 5; MTCW 1, 2; MTFW 2005; PFS 17, 28; RGAL 4; SATA 24, 107; TUS; YAW

Giovanni, Yolanda Cornelia
See Giovanni, Nikki

Giovanni, Yolande Cornelia
See Giovanni, Nikki

Giovanni, Yolande Cornelia, Jr.
See Giovanni, Nikki

Giovene, Andrea 1904-1998 .... **CLC 7**
See also CA 85-88

Gippius, Zinaida (Nikolaevna) 1869-1945
See Hippius, Zinaida (Nikolaevna)
See also CA 106; 212

Giraudoux, Jean(-Hippolyte) 1882-1944 .... **TCLC 2, 7**
See also CA 104; 196; DAM DRAM; DLB 65, 321; EW 9; EWL 3; GFL 1789 to the Present; RGWL 2, 3; TWA

Gironella, Jose Maria (Pous) 1917-2003 .... **CLC 11**
See also CA 101; 212; EWL 3; RGWL 2, 3

Gissing, George (Robert) 1857-1903 .... **SSC 37, 113; TCLC 3, 24, 47**
See also BRW 5; CA 105; 167; DLB 18, 135, 184; RGEL 2; TEA

Gitlin, Todd 1943- .... **CLC 201**
See also CA 29-32R; CANR 25, 50, 88, 179

Giurlani, Aldo
See Palazzeschi, Aldo

Gladkov, Fedor Vasil'evich
See Gladkov, Fyodor (Vasilyevich)
See also DLB 272

Gladkov, Fyodor (Vasilyevich) 1883-1958 .... **TCLC 27**
See Gladkov, Fedor Vasil'evich
See also CA 170; EWL 3

Glancy, Diane 1941- .... **CLC 210; NNAL**
See also CA 136; 225; CAAE 225; CAAS 24; CANR 87, 162; DLB 175

Glanville, Brian (Lester) 1931- .... **CLC 6**
See also CA 5-8R; CAAS 9; CANR 3, 70; CN 1, 2, 3, 4, 5, 6, 7; DLB 15, 139; SATA 42

Glasgow, Ellen (Anderson Gholson) 1873-1945 .... **SSC 34; TCLC 2, 7**
See also AMW; CA 104; 164; DLB 9, 12; MAL 5; MBL; MTCW 2; MTFW 2005; RGAL 4; RHW; SSFS 9; TUS

Glaspell, Susan 1882(?)-1948 ..... **DC 10; SSC 41; TCLC 55, 175**
See also AMWS 3; CA 110; 154; DFS 8, 18, 24; DLB 7, 9, 78, 228; MBL; RGAL 4; SSFS 3; TCWW 2; TUS; YABC 2

Glassco, John 1909-1981 .... **CLC 9**
See also CA 13-16R; 102; CANR 15; CN 1, 2; CP 1, 2, 3; DLB 68

Glasscock, Amnesia
See Steinbeck, John (Ernst)
Glasser, Ronald J. 1940(?)- .... **CLC 37**
See also CA 209
Glassman, Joyce
See Johnson, Joyce
Gleick, James (W.) 1954- .... **CLC 147**
See also CA 131; 137; CANR 97; INT CA-137
Glendinning, Victoria 1937- .... **CLC 50**
See also CA 120; 127; CANR 59, 89, 166; DLB 155
Glissant, Edouard (Mathieu)
1928- .... **CLC 10, 68**
See also CA 153; CANR 111; CWW 2; DAM MULT; EWL 3; RGWL 3
Gloag, Julian 1930- .... **CLC 40**
See also AITN 1; CA 65-68; CANR 10, 70; CN 1, 2, 3, 4, 5, 6
Glowacki, Aleksander
See Prus, Boleslaw
Gluck, Louise 1943- .... **CLC 7, 22, 44, 81, 160; PC 16**
See also AMWS 5; CA 33-36R; CANR 40, 69, 108, 133, 182; CP 1, 2, 3, 4, 5, 6, 7; CWP; DA3; DAM POET; DLB 5; MAL 5; MTCW 2; MTFW 2005; PFS 5, 15; RGAL 4; TCLE 1:1
Gluck, Louise Elisabeth
See Gluck, Louise
Glyn, Elinor 1864-1943 .... **TCLC 72**
See also DLB 153; RHW
Gobineau, Joseph-Arthur
1816-1882 .... **NCLC 17**
See also DLB 123; GFL 1789 to the Present
Godard, Jean-Luc 1930- .... **CLC 20**
See also CA 93-96
Godden, (Margaret) Rumer
1907-1998 .... **CLC 53**
See also AAYA 6; BPFB 2; BYA 2, 5; CA 5-8R; 172; CANR 4, 27, 36, 55, 80; CLR 20; CN 1, 2, 3, 4, 5, 6; CWRI 5; DLB 161; MAICYA 1, 2; RHW; SAAS 12; SATA 3, 36; SATA-Obit 109; TEA
Godoy Alcayaga, Lucila 1899-1957 .. **HLC 2; PC 32; TCLC 2**
See Mistral, Gabriela
See also BW 2; CA 104; 131; CANR 81; DAM MULT; DNFS; HW 1, 2; MTCW 1, 2; MTFW 2005
Godwin, Gail 1937- ...... **CLC 5, 8, 22, 31, 69, 125**
See also BPFB 2; CA 29-32R; CANR 15, 43, 69, 132; CN 3, 4, 5, 6, 7; CPW; CSW; DA3; DAM POP; DLB 6, 234; INT CANR-15; MAL 5; MTCW 1, 2; MTFW 2005
Godwin, Gail Kathleen
See Godwin, Gail
Godwin, William 1756-1836 .. **NCLC 14, 130**
See also CDBLB 1789-1832; CMW 4; DLB 39, 104, 142, 158, 163, 262, 336; GL 2; HGG; RGEL 2
Goebbels, Josef
See Goebbels, (Paul) Joseph
Goebbels, (Paul) Joseph
1897-1945 .... **TCLC 68**
See also CA 115; 148
Goebbels, Joseph Paul
See Goebbels, (Paul) Joseph
Goethe, Johann Wolfgang von
1749-1832 . **DC 20; NCLC 4, 22, 34, 90, 154; PC 5; SSC 38; WLC 3**
See also CDWLB 2; DA; DA3; DAB; DAC; DAM DRAM, MST, POET; DLB 94; EW 5; GL 2; LATS 1; LMFS 1:1; RGWL 2, 3; TWA

Gogarty, Oliver St. John
1878-1957 .... **TCLC 15**
See also CA 109; 150; DLB 15, 19; RGEL 2
Gogol, Nikolai (Vasilyevich)
1809-1852 .... **DC 1; NCLC 5, 15, 31, 162; SSC 4, 29, 52; WLC 3**
See also DA; DAB; DAC; DAM DRAM, MST; DFS 12; DLB 198; EW 6; EXPS; RGSF 2; RGWL 2, 3; SSFS 7; TWA
Goines, Donald 1937(?)-1974 .... **BLC 1:2; CLC 80**
See also AITN 1; BW 1, 3; CA 124; 114; CANR 82; CMW 4; DA3; DAM MULT, POP; DLB 33
Gold, Herbert 1924- ... **CLC 4, 7, 14, 42, 152**
See also CA 9-12R; CANR 17, 45, 125; CN 1, 2, 3, 4, 5, 6, 7; DLB 2; DLBY 1981; MAL 5
Goldbarth, Albert 1948- .... **CLC 5, 38**
See also AMWS 12; CA 53-56; CANR 6, 40; CP 3, 4, 5, 6, 7; DLB 120
Goldberg, Anatol 1910-1982 .... **CLC 34**
See also CA 131; 117
Goldemberg, Isaac 1945- .... **CLC 52**
See also CA 69-72; CAAS 12; CANR 11, 32; EWL 3; HW 1; WLIT 1
Golding, Arthur 1536-1606 .... **LC 101**
See also DLB 136
Golding, William 1911-1993 . **CLC 1, 2, 3, 8, 10, 17, 27, 58, 81; WLC 3**
See also AAYA 5, 44; BPFB 2; BRWR 1; BRWS 1; BYA 2; CA 5-8R; 141; CANR 13, 33, 54; CD 5; CDBLB 1945-1960; CLR 94, 130; CN 1, 2, 3, 4; DA; DA3; DAB; DAC; DAM MST, NOV; DLB 15, 100, 255, 326, 330; EWL 3; EXPN; HGG; LAIT 4; MTCW 1, 2; MTFW 2005; NFS 2; RGEL 2; RHW; SFW 4; TEA; WLIT 4; YAW
Golding, William Gerald
See Golding, William
Goldman, Emma 1869-1940 .... **TCLC 13**
See also CA 110; 150; DLB 221; FW; RGAL 4; TUS
Goldman, Francisco 1954- .... **CLC 76**
See also CA 162
Goldman, William 1931- .... **CLC 1, 48**
See also BPFB 2; CA 9-12R; CANR 29, 69, 106; CN 1, 2, 3, 4, 5, 6, 7; DLB 44; FANT; IDFW 3, 4
Goldman, William W.
See Goldman, William
Goldmann, Lucien 1913-1970 .... **CLC 24**
See also CA 25-28; CAP 2
Goldoni, Carlo 1707-1793 .... **LC 4, 152**
See also DAM DRAM; EW 4; RGWL 2, 3; WLIT 7
Goldsberry, Steven 1949- .... **CLC 34**
See also CA 131
Goldsmith, Oliver 1730(?)-1774 .... **DC 8; LC 2, 48, 122; PC 77; WLC 3**
See also BRW 3; CDBLB 1660-1789; DA; DAB; DAC; DAM DRAM, MST, NOV, POET; DFS 1; DLB 39, 89, 104, 109, 142, 336; IDTP; RGEL 2; SATA 26; TEA; WLIT 3
Goldsmith, Peter
See Priestley, J(ohn) B(oynton)
Goldstein, Rebecca 1950- .... **CLC 239**
See also CA 144; CANR 99, 165; TCLE 1:1
Goldstein, Rebecca Newberger
See Goldstein, Rebecca
Gombrowicz, Witold 1904-1969 .... **CLC 4, 7, 11, 49**
See also CA 19-20; 25-28R; CANR 105; CAP 2; CDWLB 4; DAM DRAM; DLB 215; EW 12; EWL 3; RGWL 2, 3; TWA

Gomez de Avellaneda, Gertrudis
1814-1873 .... **NCLC 111**
See also LAW
Gomez de la Serna, Ramon
1888-1963 .... **CLC 9**
See also CA 153; 116; CANR 79; EWL 3; HW 1, 2
Goncharov, Ivan Alexandrovich
1812-1891 .... **NCLC 1, 63**
See also DLB 238; EW 6; RGWL 2, 3
Goncourt, Edmond (Louis Antoine Huot) de
1822-1896 .... **NCLC 7**
See also DLB 123; EW 7; GFL 1789 to the Present; RGWL 2, 3
Goncourt, Jules (Alfred Huot) de
1830-1870 .... **NCLC 7**
See also DLB 123; EW 7; GFL 1789 to the Present; RGWL 2, 3
Gongora (y Argote), Luis de
1561-1627 .... **LC 72**
See also RGWL 2, 3
Gontier, Fernande 19(?)- .... **CLC 50**
Gonzalez Martinez, Enrique
See Gonzalez Martinez, Enrique
See also DLB 290
Gonzalez Martinez, Enrique
1871-1952 .... **TCLC 72**
See Gonzalez Martinez, Enrique
See also CA 166; CANR 81; EWL 3; HW 1, 2
Goodison, Lorna 1947- .... **BLC 2:2; PC 36**
See also CA 142; CANR 88; CP 5, 6, 7; CWP; DLB 157; EWL 3; PFS 25
Goodman, Allegra 1967- .... **CLC 241**
See also CA 204; CANR 162; DLB 244
Goodman, Paul 1911-1972 ..... **CLC 1, 2, 4, 7**
See also CA 19-20; 37-40R; CAD; CANR 34; CAP 2; CN 1; DLB 130, 246; MAL 5; MTCW 1; RGAL 4
Goodweather, Hartley
See King, Thomas
GoodWeather, Hartley
See King, Thomas
Googe, Barnabe 1540-1594 .... **LC 94**
See also DLB 132; RGEL 2
Gordimer, Nadine 1923- ...... **CLC 3, 5, 7, 10, 18, 33, 51, 70, 123, 160, 161, 263; SSC 17, 80; WLCS**
See also AAYA 39; AFW; BRWS 2; CA 5-8R; CANR 3, 28, 56, 88, 131; CN 1, 2, 3, 4, 5, 6, 7; DA; DA3; DAB; DAC; DAM MST, NOV; DLB 225, 326, 330; EWL 3; EXPS; INT CANR-28; LATS 1:2; MTCW 1, 2; MTFW 2005; NFS 4; RGEL 2; RGSF 2; SSFS 2, 14, 19; TWA; WLIT 2; YAW
Gordon, Adam Lindsay
1833-1870 .... **NCLC 21**
See also DLB 230
Gordon, Caroline 1895-1981 . **CLC 6, 13, 29, 83; SSC 15**
See also AMW; CA 11-12; 103; CANR 36; CAP 1; CN 1, 2; DLB 4, 9, 102; DLBD 17; DLBY 1981; EWL 3; MAL 5; MTCW 1, 2; MTFW 2005; RGAL 4; RGSF 2
Gordon, Charles William 1860-1937
See Connor, Ralph
See also CA 109
Gordon, Mary 1949- .. **CLC 13, 22, 128, 216; SSC 59**
See also AMWS 4; BPFB 2; CA 102; CANR 44, 92, 154, 179; CN 4, 5, 6, 7; DLB 6; DLBY 1981; FW; INT CA-102; MAL 5; MTCW 1
Gordon, Mary Catherine
See Gordon, Mary
Gordon, N. J.
See Bosman, Herman Charles

Gordon, Sol 1923- .... **CLC 26**
See also CA 53-56; CANR 4; SATA 11
Gordone, Charles 1925-1995 .... **BLC 2:2;
CLC 1, 4; DC 8**
See also BW 1, 3; CA 93-96, 180; 150;
CAAE 180; CAD; CANR 55; DAM
DRAM; DLB 7; INT CA-93-96; MTCW
1
Gore, Catherine 1800-1861 .... **NCLC 65**
See also DLB 116, 344; RGEL 2
Gorenko, Anna Andreevna
See Akhmatova, Anna
Gorky, Maxim SSC 28; TCLC 8; WLC 3
See Peshkov, Alexei Maximovich
See also DAB; DFS 9; DLB 295; EW 8;
EWL 3; TWA
Goryan, Sirak
See Saroyan, William
Gosse, Edmund (William)
1849-1928 .... **TCLC 28**
See also CA 117; DLB 57, 144, 184; RGEL
2
Gotlieb, Phyllis (Fay Bloom) 1926- .. **CLC 18**
See also CA 13-16R; CANR 7, 135; CN 7;
CP 1, 2, 3, 4; DLB 88, 251; SFW 4
Gottesman, S. D.
See Kornbluth, C(yril) M.; Pohl, Frederik
Gottfried von Strassburg fl. c.
1170-1215 .... **CMLC 10, 96**
See also CDWLB 2; DLB 138; EW 1;
RGWL 2, 3
Gotthelf, Jeremias 1797-1854 .... **NCLC 117**
See also DLB 133; RGWL 2, 3
Gottschalk, Laura Riding
See Jackson, Laura (Riding)
Gould, Lois 1932(?)-2002 .... **CLC 4, 10**
See also CA 77-80; 208; CANR 29; MTCW
1
Gould, Stephen Jay 1941-2002 .... **CLC 163**
See also AAYA 26; BEST 90:2; CA 77-80;
205; CANR 10, 27, 56, 75, 125; CPW;
INT CANR-27; MTCW 1, 2; MTFW 2005
Gourmont, Remy(-Marie-Charles) de
1858-1915 .... **TCLC 17**
See also CA 109; 150; GFL 1789 to the
Present; MTCW 2
Gournay, Marie le Jars de
See de Gournay, Marie le Jars
Govier, Katherine 1948- .... **CLC 51**
See also CA 101; CANR 18, 40, 128; CCA
1
Gower, John c. 1330-1408 .... **LC 76; PC 59**
See also BRW 1; DLB 146; RGEL 2
Goyen, (Charles) William
1915-1983 .... **CLC 5, 8, 14, 40**
See also AITN 2; CA 5-8R; 110; CANR 6,
71; CN 1, 2, 3; DLB 2, 218; DLBY 1983;
EWL 3; INT CANR-6; MAL 5
Goytisolo, Juan 1931- .... **CLC 5, 10, 23, 133;
HLC 1**
See also CA 85-88; CANR 32, 61, 131, 182;
CWW 2; DAM MULT; DLB 322; EWL
3; GLL 2; HW 1, 2; MTCW 1, 2; MTFW
2005
Gozzano, Guido 1883-1916 .... **PC 10**
See also CA 154; DLB 114; EWL 3
Gozzi, (Conte) Carlo 1720-1806 .... **NCLC 23**
Grabbe, Christian Dietrich
1801-1836 .... **NCLC 2**
See also DLB 133; RGWL 2, 3
Grace, Patricia Frances 1937- .... **CLC 56**
See also CA 176; CANR 118; CN 4, 5, 6,
7; EWL 3; RGSF 2
Gracian, Baltasar 1601-1658 .... **LC 15, 160**
Gracian y Morales, Baltasar
See Gracian, Baltasar

Gracq, Julien 1910-2007 ..... **CLC 11, 48, 259**
See also CA 122; 126; 267; CANR 141;
CWW 2; DLB 83; GFL 1789 to the
present
Grade, Chaim 1910-1982 .... **CLC 10**
See also CA 93-96; 107; DLB 333; EWL 3;
RGHL
Grade, Khayim
See Grade, Chaim
Graduate of Oxford, A
See Ruskin, John
Grafton, Garth
See Duncan, Sara Jeannette
Grafton, Sue 1940- .... **CLC 163**
See also AAYA 11, 49; BEST 90:3; CA 108;
CANR 31, 55, 111, 134; CMW 4; CPW;
CSW; DA3; DAM POP; DLB 226; FW;
MSW; MTFW 2005
Graham, John
See Phillips, David Graham
Graham, Jorie 1950- .... **CLC 48, 118; PC 59**
See also AAYA 67; CA 111; CANR 63, 118;
CP 4, 5, 6, 7; CWP; DLB 120; EWL 3;
MTFW 2005; PFS 10, 17; TCLE 1:1
Graham, R(obert) B(ontine) Cunninghame
See Cunninghame Graham, Robert
(Gallnigad) Bontine
See also DLB 98, 135, 174; RGEL 2; RGSF
2
Graham, Robert
See Haldeman, Joe
Graham, Tom
See Lewis, (Harry) Sinclair
Graham, W(illiam) S(ydney)
1918-1986 .... **CLC 29**
See also BRWS 7; CA 73-76; 118; CP 1, 2,
3, 4; DLB 20; RGEL 2
Graham, Winston (Mawdsley)
1910-2003 .... **CLC 23**
See also CA 49-52; 218; CANR 2, 22, 45,
66; CMW 4; CN 1, 2, 3, 4, 5, 6, 7; DLB
77; RHW
Grahame, Kenneth 1859-1932 ...... **TCLC 64,
136**
See also BYA 5; CA 108; 136; CANR 80;
CLR 5, 135; CWRI 5; DA3; DAB; DLB
34, 141, 178; FANT; MAICYA 1, 2;
MTCW 2; NFS 20; RGEL 2; SATA 100;
TEA; WCH; YABC 1
Granger, Darius John
See Marlowe, Stephen
Granin, Daniil 1918- .... **CLC 59**
See also DLB 302
Granovsky, Timofei Nikolaevich
1813-1855 .... **NCLC 75**
See also DLB 198
Grant, Skeeter
See Spiegelman, Art
Granville-Barker, Harley
1877-1946 .... **TCLC 2**
See Barker, Harley Granville
See also CA 104; 204; DAM DRAM;
RGEL 2
Granzotto, Gianni
See Granzotto, Giovanni Battista
Granzotto, Giovanni Battista
1914-1985 .... **CLC 70**
See also CA 166
Grasemann, Ruth Barbara
See Rendell, Ruth
Grass, Guenter
See Grass, Gunter
See also CWW 2; DLB 330; RGHL
Grass, Gunter 1927- .. **CLC 1, 2, 4, 6, 11, 15,
22, 32, 49, 88, 207; WLC 3**
See Grass, Guenter
See also BPFB 2; CA 13-16R; CANR 20,
75, 93, 133, 174; CDWLB 2; DA; DA3;
DAB; DAC; DAM MST, NOV; DLB 75,
124; EW 13; EWL 3; MTCW 1, 2; MTFW
2005; RGWL 2, 3; TWA

Grass, Gunter Wilhelm
See Grass, Gunter
Gratton, Thomas
See Hulme, T(homas) E(rnest)
Grau, Shirley Ann 1929- .... **CLC 4, 9, 146;
SSC 15**
See also CA 89-92; CANR 22, 69; CN 1, 2,
3, 4, 5, 6, 7; CSW; DLB 2, 218; INT CA-
89-92; CANR-22; MTCW 1
Gravel, Fern
See Hall, James Norman
Graver, Elizabeth 1964- .... **CLC 70**
See also CA 135; CANR 71, 129
Graves, Richard Perceval
1895-1985 .... **CLC 44**
See also CA 65-68; CANR 9, 26, 51
Graves, Robert 1895-1985 ... **CLC 1, 2, 6, 11,
39, 44, 45; PC 6**
See also BPFB 2; BRW 7; BYA 4; CA 5-8R;
117; CANR 5, 36; CDBLB 1914-1945;
CN 1, 2, 3; CP 1, 2, 3, 4; DA3; DAB;
DAC; DAM MST, POET; DLB 20, 100,
191; DLBD 18; DLBY 1985; EWL 3;
LATS 1:1; MTCW 1, 2; MTFW 2005;
NCFS 2; NFS 21; RGEL 2; RHW; SATA
45; TEA
Graves, Valerie
See Bradley, Marion Zimmer
Gray, Alasdair 1934- .... **CLC 41**
See also BRWS 9; CA 126; CANR 47, 69,
106, 140; CN 4, 5, 6, 7; DLB 194, 261,
319; HGG; INT CA-126; MTCW 1, 2;
MTFW 2005; RGSF 2; SUFW 2
Gray, Amlin 1946- .... **CLC 29**
See also CA 138
Gray, Francine du Plessix 1930- ..... **CLC 22,
153**
See also BEST 90:3; CA 61-64; CAAS 2;
CANR 11, 33, 75, 81; DAM NOV; INT
CANR-11; MTCW 1, 2; MTFW 2005
Gray, John (Henry) 1866-1934 ...... **TCLC 19**
See also CA 119; 162; RGEL 2
Gray, John Lee
See Jakes, John
Gray, Simon 1936-2008 .... **CLC 9, 14, 36**
See also AITN 1; CA 21-24R; 275; CAAS
3; CANR 32, 69; CBD; CD 5, 6; CN 1, 2,
3; DLB 13; EWL 3; MTCW 1; RGEL 2
Gray, Simon James Holliday
See Gray, Simon
Gray, Spalding 1941-2004 .... **CLC 49, 112;
DC 7**
See also AAYA 62; CA 128; 225; CAD;
CANR 74, 138; CD 5, 6; CPW; DAM
POP; MTCW 2; MTFW 2005
Gray, Thomas 1716-1771 ..... **LC 4, 40; PC 2,
80; WLC 3**
See also BRW 3; CDBLB 1660-1789; DA;
DA3; DAB; DAC; DAM MST; DLB 109;
EXPP; PAB; PFS 9; RGEL 2; TEA; WP
Grayson, David
See Baker, Ray Stannard
Grayson, Richard (A.) 1951- .... **CLC 38**
See also CA 85-88, 210; CAAE 210; CANR
14, 31, 57; DLB 234
Greeley, Andrew M. 1928- .... **CLC 28**
See also BPFB 2; CA 5-8R; CAAS 7;
CANR 7, 43, 69, 104, 136, 184; CMW 4;
CPW; DA3; DAM POP; MTCW 1, 2;
MTFW 2005
Green, Anna Katharine
1846-1935 .... **TCLC 63**
See also CA 112; 159; CMW 4; DLB 202,
221; MSW
Green, Brian
See Card, Orson Scott
Green, Hannah
See Greenberg, Joanne (Goldenberg)

Green, Hannah 1927(?)-1996 .... **CLC 3**
See also CA 73-76; CANR 59, 93; NFS 10

Green, Henry CLC 2, 13, 97
See Yorke, Henry Vincent
See also BRWS 2; CA 175; DLB 15; EWL
3; RGEL 2

Green, Julian CLC 3, 11, 77
See Green, Julien (Hartridge)
See also EWL 3; GFL 1789 to the Present;
MTCW 2

Green, Julien (Hartridge) 1900-1998
See Green, Julian
See also CA 21-24R; 169; CANR 33, 87;
CWW 2; DLB 4, 72; MTCW 1, 2; MTFW
2005

Green, Paul (Eliot) 1894-1981 .... **CLC 25**
See also AITN 1; CA 5-8R; 103; CAD;
CANR 3; DAM DRAM; DLB 7, 9, 249;
DLBY 1981; MAL 5; RGAL 4

Greenaway, Peter 1942- .... **CLC 159**
See also CA 127

Greenberg, Ivan 1908-1973
See Rahv, Philip
See also CA 85-88

Greenberg, Joanne (Goldenberg)
1932- .... **CLC 7, 30**
See also AAYA 12, 67; CA 5-8R; CANR
14, 32, 69; CN 6, 7; DLB 335; NFS 23;
SATA 25; YAW

Greenberg, Richard 1959(?)- .... **CLC 57**
See also CA 138; CAD; CD 5, 6; DFS 24

Greenblatt, Stephen J(ay) 1943- ...... **CLC 70**
See also CA 49-52; CANR 115

Greene, Bette 1934- .... **CLC 30**
See also AAYA 7, 69; BYA 3; CA 53-56;
CANR 4, 146; CLR 2; CWRI 5; JRDA;
LAIT 4; MAICYA 1, 2; NFS 10; SAAS
16; SATA 8, 102, 161; WYA; YAW

Greene, Gael CLC 8
See also CA 13-16R; CANR 10, 166

Greene, Graham 1904-1991 .. **CLC 1, 3, 6, 9,**
14, 18, 27, 37, 70, 72, 125; SSC 29;
WLC 3
See also AAYA 61; AITN 2; BPFB 2;
BRWR 2; BRWS 1; BYA 3; CA 13-16R;
133; CANR 35, 61, 131; CBD; CDBLB
1945-1960; CMW 4; CN 1, 2, 3, 4; DA;
DA3; DAB; DAC; DAM MST, NOV;
DLB 13, 15, 77, 100, 162, 201, 204;
DLBY 1991; EWL 3; MSW; MTCW 1, 2;
MTFW 2005; NFS 16; RGEL 2; SATA
20; SSFS 14; TEA; WLIT 4

Greene, Robert 1558-1592 .... **LC 41**
See also BRWS 8; DLB 62, 167; IDTP;
RGEL 2; TEA

Greer, Germaine 1939- .... **CLC 131**
See also AITN 1; CA 81-84; CANR 33, 70,
115, 133; FW; MTCW 1, 2; MTFW 2005

Greer, Richard
See Silverberg, Robert

Gregor, Arthur 1923- .... **CLC 9**
See also CA 25-28R; CAAS 10; CANR 11;
CP 1, 2, 3, 4, 5, 6, 7; SATA 36

Gregor, Lee
See Pohl, Frederik

Gregory, Lady Isabella Augusta (Persse)
1852-1932 .... **TCLC 1, 176**
See also BRW 6; CA 104; 184; DLB 10;
IDTP; RGEL 2

Gregory, J. Dennis
See Williams, John A(lfred)

Gregory of Nazianzus, St.
329-389 .... **CMLC 82**

Grekova, I. CLC 59
See Ventsel, Elena Sergeevna
See also CWW 2

Grendon, Stephen
See Derleth, August (William)

Grenville, Kate 1950- .... **CLC 61**
See also CA 118; CANR 53, 93, 156; CN
7; DLB 325

Grenville, Pelham
See Wodehouse, P(elham) G(renville)

Greve, Felix Paul (Berthold Friedrich)
1879-1948
See Grove, Frederick Philip
See also CA 104; 141, 175; CANR 79;
DAC; DAM MST

Greville, Fulke 1554-1628 .... **LC 79**
See also BRWS 11; DLB 62, 172; RGEL 2

Grey, Lady Jane 1537-1554 .... **LC 93**
See also DLB 132

Grey, Zane 1872-1939 .... **TCLC 6**
See also BPFB 2; CA 104; 132; DA3; DAM
POP; DLB 9, 212; MTCW 1, 2; MTFW
2005; RGAL 4; TCWW 1, 2; TUS

Griboedov, Aleksandr Sergeevich
1795(?)-1829 .... **NCLC 129**
See also DLB 205; RGWL 2, 3

Grieg, (Johan) Nordahl (Brun)
1902-1943 .... **TCLC 10**
See also CA 107; 189; EWL 3

Grieve, C(hristopher) M(urray)
1892-1978 .... **CLC 11, 19**
See MacDiarmid, Hugh; Pteleon
See also CA 5-8R; 85-88; CANR 33, 107;
DAM POET; MTCW 1; RGEL 2

Griffin, Gerald 1803-1840 .... **NCLC 7**
See also DLB 159; RGEL 2

Griffin, John Howard 1920-1980 ..... **CLC 68**
See also AITN 1; CA 1-4R; 101; CANR 2

Griffin, Peter 1942- .... **CLC 39**
See also CA 136

Griffith, David Lewelyn Wark
See Griffith, D.W.

Griffith, D.W. 1875(?)-1948 .... **TCLC 68**
See also AAYA 78; CA 119; 150; CANR 80

Griffith, Lawrence
See Griffith, D.W.

Griffiths, Trevor 1935- .... **CLC 13, 52**
See also CA 97-100; CANR 45; CBD; CD
5, 6; DLB 13, 245

Griggs, Sutton (Elbert)
1872-1930 .... **TCLC 77**
See also CA 123; 186; DLB 50

Grigson, Geoffrey (Edward Harvey)
1905-1985 .... **CLC 7, 39**
See also CA 25-28R; 118; CANR 20, 33;
CP 1, 2, 3, 4; DLB 27; MTCW 1, 2

Grile, Dod
See Bierce, Ambrose (Gwinett)

Grillparzer, Franz 1791-1872 .... **DC 14;**
NCLC 1, 102; SSC 37
See also CDWLB 2; DLB 133; EW 5;
RGWL 2, 3; TWA

Grimble, Reverend Charles James
See Eliot, T(homas) S(tearns)

Grimke, Angelina (Emily) Weld
1880-1958 .... **HR 1:2**
See Weld, Angelina (Emily) Grimke
See also BW 1; CA 124; DAM POET; DLB
50, 54

Grimke, Charlotte L(ottie) Forten
1837(?)-1914
See Forten, Charlotte L.
See also BW 1; CA 117; 124; DAM MULT,
POET

Grimm, Jacob Ludwig Karl
1785-1863 .... **NCLC 3, 77; SSC 36**
See Grimm Brothers
See also CLR 112; DLB 90; MAICYA 1, 2;
RGSF 2; RGWL 2, 3; SATA 22; WCH

Grimm, Wilhelm Karl 1786-1859 .. **NCLC 3,**
77; SSC 36
See Grimm Brothers
See also CDWLB 2; CLR 112; DLB 90;
MAICYA 1, 2; RGSF 2; RGWL 2, 3;
SATA 22; WCH

Grimm and Grim
See Grimm, Jacob Ludwig Karl; Grimm,
Wilhelm Karl

Grimm Brothers SSC 88
See Grimm, Jacob Ludwig Karl; Grimm,
Wilhelm Karl
See also CLR 112

Grimmelshausen, Hans Jakob Christoffel
von
See Grimmelshausen, Johann Jakob Christoffel von
See also RGWL 2, 3

Grimmelshausen, Johann Jakob Christoffel
von 1621-1676 .... **LC 6**
See Grimmelshausen, Hans Jakob Christof-
fel von
See also CDWLB 2; DLB 168

Grindel, Eugene 1895-1952 .... **PC 38; TCLC**
7, 41
See also CA 104; 193; EWL 3; GFL 1789
to the Present; LMFS 2; RGWL 2, 3

Grisham, John 1955- .... **CLC 84**
See also AAYA 14, 47; BPFB 2; CA 138;
CANR 47, 69, 114, 133; CMW 4; CN 6,
7; CPW; CSW; DA3; DAM POP; MSW;
MTCW 2; MTFW 2005

Grosseteste, Robert 1175(?)-1253 . **CMLC 62**
See also DLB 115

Grossman, David 1954- .... **CLC 67, 231**
See also CA 138; CANR 114, 175; CWW
2; DLB 299; EWL 3; RGHL; WLIT 6

Grossman, Vasilii Semenovich
See Grossman, Vasily (Semenovich)
See also DLB 272

Grossman, Vasily (Semenovich)
1905-1964 .... **CLC 41**
See Grossman, Vasilii Semenovich
See also CA 124; 130; MTCW 1; RGHL

Grove, Frederick Philip TCLC 4
See Greve, Felix Paul (Berthold Friedrich)
See also DLB 92; RGEL 2; TCWW 1, 2

Grubb
See Crumb, R.

Grumbach, Doris 1918- .... **CLC 13, 22, 64**
See also CA 5-8R; CAAS 2; CANR 9, 42,
70, 127; CN 6, 7; INT CANR-9; MTCW
2; MTFW 2005

Grundtvig, Nikolai Frederik Severin
1783-1872 .... **NCLC 1, 158**
See also DLB 300

Grunge
See Crumb, R.

Grunwald, Lisa 1959- .... **CLC 44**
See also CA 120; CANR 148

Gryphius, Andreas 1616-1664 .... **LC 89**
See also CDWLB 2; DLB 164; RGWL 2, 3

Guare, John 1938- .... **CLC 8, 14, 29, 67; DC**
20
See also CA 73-76; CAD; CANR 21, 69,
118; CD 5, 6; DAM DRAM; DFS 8, 13;
DLB 7, 249; EWL 3; MAL 5; MTCW 1,
2; RGAL 4

Guarini, Battista 1538-1612 .... **LC 102**
See also DLB 339

Gubar, Susan 1944- .... **CLC 145**
See also CA 108; CANR 45, 70, 139, 179;
FW; MTCW 1; RGAL 4

Gubar, Susan David
See Gubar, Susan

Gudjonsson, Halldor Kiljan 1902-1998
See Halldor Laxness
See also CA 103; 164

Guedes, Vincente
See Pessoa, Fernando
Guenter, Erich
See Eich, Gunter
Guest, Barbara 1920-2006 ... **CLC 34; PC 55**
See also BG 1:2; CA 25-28R; 248; CANR 11, 44, 84; CP 1, 2, 3, 4, 5, 6, 7; CWP; DLB 5, 193
Guest, Edgar A(lbert) 1881-1959 ... **TCLC 95**
See also CA 112; 168
Guest, Judith 1936- .... **CLC 8, 30**
See also AAYA 7, 66; CA 77-80; CANR 15, 75, 138; DA3; DAM NOV, POP; EXPN; INT CANR-15; LAIT 5; MTCW 1, 2; MTFW 2005; NFS 1
Guevara, Che CLC 87; HLC 1
See Guevara (Serna), Ernesto
Guevara (Serna), Ernesto
1928-1967 .... **CLC 87; HLC 1**
See Guevara, Che
See also CA 127; 111; CANR 56; DAM MULT; HW 1
Guicciardini, Francesco 1483-1540 ..... **LC 49**
Guido delle Colonne c. 1215-c.
1290 .... **CMLC 90**
Guild, Nicholas M. 1944- .... **CLC 33**
See also CA 93-96
Guillemin, Jacques
See Sartre, Jean-Paul
Guillen, Jorge 1893-1984 . **CLC 11; HLCS 1; PC 35**
See also CA 89-92; 112; DAM MULT, POET; DLB 108; EWL 3; HW 1; RGWL 2, 3
Guillen, Nicolas (Cristobal)
1902-1989 .... **BLC 1:2; CLC 48, 79; HLC 1; PC 23**
See also BW 2; CA 116; 125; 129; CANR 84; DAM MST, MULT, POET; DLB 283; EWL 3; HW 1; LAW; RGWL 2, 3; WP
Guillen y Alvarez, Jorge
See Guillen, Jorge
Guillevic, (Eugene) 1907-1997 .... **CLC 33**
See also CA 93-96; CWW 2
Guillois
See Desnos, Robert
Guillois, Valentin
See Desnos, Robert
Guimaraes Rosa, Joao 1908-1967 .... **HLCS 2**
See Rosa, Joao Guimaraes
See also CA 175; LAW; RGSF 2; RGWL 2, 3
Guiney, Louise Imogen
1861-1920 .... **TCLC 41**
See also CA 160; DLB 54; RGAL 4
Guinizelli, Guido c. 1230-1276 ...... **CMLC 49**
See Guinizzelli, Guido
Guinizzelli, Guido
See Guinizelli, Guido
See also WLIT 7
Guiraldes, Ricardo (Guillermo)
1886-1927 .... **TCLC 39**
See also CA 131; EWL 3; HW 1; LAW; MTCW 1
Gumilev, Nikolai (Stepanovich)
1886-1921 .... **TCLC 60**
See Gumilyov, Nikolay Stepanovich
See also CA 165; DLB 295
Gumilyov, Nikolay Stepanovich
See Gumilev, Nikolai (Stepanovich)
See also EWL 3
Gump, P. Q.
See Card, Orson Scott
Gump, P.Q.
See Card, Orson Scott

Gunesekera, Romesh 1954- .... **CLC 91**
See also BRWS 10; CA 159; CANR 140, 172; CN 6, 7; DLB 267, 323
Gunn, Bill CLC 5
See Gunn, William Harrison
See also DLB 38
Gunn, Thom(son William)
1929-2004 . **CLC 3, 6, 18, 32, 81; PC 26**
See also BRWS 4; CA 17-20R; 227; CANR 9, 33, 116; CDBLB 1960 to Present; CP 1, 2, 3, 4, 5, 6, 7; DAM POET; DLB 27; INT CANR-33; MTCW 1; PFS 9; RGEL 2
Gunn, William Harrison 1934(?)-1989
See Gunn, Bill
See also AITN 1; BW 1, 3; CA 13-16R; 128; CANR 12, 25, 76
Gunn Allen, Paula
See Allen, Paula Gunn
Gunnars, Kristjana 1948- .... **CLC 69**
See also CA 113; CCA 1; CP 6, 7; CWP; DLB 60
Gunter, Erich
See Eich, Gunter
Gurdjieff, G(eorgei) I(vanovich)
1877(?)-1949 .... **TCLC 71**
See also CA 157
Gurganus, Allan 1947- .... **CLC 70**
See also BEST 90:1; CA 135; CANR 114; CN 6, 7; CPW; CSW; DAM POP; GLL 1
Gurney, A. R.
See Gurney, A(lbert) R(amsdell), Jr.
See also DLB 266
Gurney, A(lbert) R(amsdell), Jr.
1930- .... **CLC 32, 50, 54**
See Gurney, A. R.
See also AMWS 5; CA 77-80; CAD; CANR 32, 64, 121; CD 5, 6; DAM DRAM; EWL 3
Gurney, Ivor (Bertie) 1890-1937 ... **TCLC 33**
See also BRW 6; CA 167; DLBY 2002; PAB; RGEL 2
Gurney, Peter
See Gurney, A(lbert) R(amsdell), Jr.
Guro, Elena (Genrikhovna)
1877-1913 .... **TCLC 56**
See also DLB 295
Gustafson, James M(oody) 1925- ... **CLC 100**
See also CA 25-28R; CANR 37
Gustafson, Ralph (Barker)
1909-1995 .... **CLC 36**
See also CA 21-24R; CANR 8, 45, 84; CP 1, 2, 3, 4, 5, 6; DLB 88; RGEL 2
Gut, Gom
See Simenon, Georges (Jacques Christian)
Guterson, David 1956- .... **CLC 91**
See also CA 132; CANR 73, 126; CN 7; DLB 292; MTCW 2; MTFW 2005; NFS 13
Guthrie, A(lfred) B(ertram), Jr.
1901-1991 .... **CLC 23**
See also CA 57-60; 134; CANR 24; CN 1, 2, 3; DLB 6, 212; MAL 5; SATA 62; SATA-Obit 67; TCWW 1, 2
Guthrie, Isobel
See Grieve, C(hristopher) M(urray)
Guthrie, Woodrow Wilson 1912-1967
See Guthrie, Woody
See also CA 113; 93-96
Guthrie, Woody CLC 35
See Guthrie, Woodrow Wilson
See also DLB 303; LAIT 3
Gutierrez Najera, Manuel
1859-1895 .... **HLCS 2; NCLC 133**
See also DLB 290; LAW

Guy, Rosa (Cuthbert) 1925- .... **CLC 26**
See also AAYA 4, 37; BW 2; CA 17-20R; CANR 14, 34, 83; CLR 13, 137; DLB 33; DNFS 1; JRDA; MAICYA 1, 2; SATA 14, 62, 122; YAW
Gwendolyn
See Bennett, (Enoch) Arnold
H. D. CLC 3, 8, 14, 31, 34, 73; PC 5
See Doolittle, Hilda
See also FL 1:5
H. de V.
See Buchan, John
Haavikko, Paavo Juhani 1931- .. **CLC 18, 34**
See also CA 106; CWW 2; EWL 3
Habbema, Koos
See Heijermans, Herman
Habermas, Juergen 1929- .... **CLC 104**
See also CA 109; CANR 85, 162; DLB 242
Habermas, Jurgen
See Habermas, Juergen
Hacker, Marilyn 1942- ...... **CLC 5, 9, 23, 72, 91; PC 47**
See also CA 77-80; CANR 68, 129; CP 3, 4, 5, 6, 7; CWP; DAM POET; DLB 120, 282; FW; GLL 2; MAL 5; PFS 19
Hadewijch of Antwerp fl. 1250- ... **CMLC 61**
See also RGWL 3
Hadrian 76-138 .... **CMLC 52**
Haeckel, Ernst Heinrich (Philipp August)
1834-1919 .... **TCLC 83**
See also CA 157
Hafiz c. 1326-1389(?) .... **CMLC 34**
See also RGWL 2, 3; WLIT 6
Hagedorn, Jessica T(arahata)
1949- .... **CLC 185**
See also CA 139; CANR 69; CWP; DLB 312; RGAL 4
Haggard, H(enry) Rider
1856-1925 .... **TCLC 11**
See also BRWS 3; BYA 4, 5; CA 108; 148; CANR 112; DLB 70, 156, 174, 178; FANT; LMFS 1; MTCW 2; RGEL 2; RHW; SATA 16; SCFW 1, 2; SFW 4; SUFW 1; WLIT 4
Hagiosy, L.
See Larbaud, Valery (Nicolas)
Hagiwara, Sakutaro 1886-1942 .... **PC 18; TCLC 60**
See Hagiwara Sakutaro
See also CA 154; RGWL 3
Hagiwara Sakutaro
See Hagiwara, Sakutaro
See also EWL 3
Haig, Fenil
See Ford, Ford Madox
Haig-Brown, Roderick (Langmere)
1908-1976 .... **CLC 21**
See also CA 5-8R; 69-72; CANR 4, 38, 83; CLR 31; CWRI 5; DLB 88; MAICYA 1, 2; SATA 12; TCWW 2
Haight, Rip
See Carpenter, John (Howard)
Haij, Vera
See Jansson, Tove (Marika)
Hailey, Arthur 1920-2004 .... **CLC 5**
See also AITN 2; BEST 90:3; BPFB 2; CA 1-4R; 233; CANR 2, 36, 75; CCA 1; CN 1, 2, 3, 4, 5, 6, 7; CPW; DAM NOV, POP; DLB 88; DLBY 1982; MTCW 1, 2; MTFW 2005
Hailey, Elizabeth Forsythe 1938- ..... **CLC 40**
See also CA 93-96, 188; CAAE 188; CAAS 1; CANR 15, 48; INT CANR-15
Haines, John (Meade) 1924- .... **CLC 58**
See also AMWS 12; CA 17-20R; CANR 13, 34; CP 1, 2, 3, 4, 5; CSW; DLB 5, 212; TCLE 1:1
Ha Jin
See Jin, Xuefei

Hakluyt, Richard 1552-1616 .... **LC 31**
  See also DLB 136; RGEL 2
Haldeman, Joe 1943- .... **CLC 61**
  See also AAYA 38; CA 53-56, 179; CAAE
  179; CAAS 25; CANR 6, 70, 72, 130,
  171; DLB 8; INT CANR-6; SCFW 2;
  SFW 4
Haldeman, Joe William
  See Haldeman, Joe
Hale, Janet Campbell 1947- .... **NNAL**
  See also CA 49-52; CANR 45, 75; DAM
  MULT; DLB 175; MTCW 2; MTFW 2005
Hale, Sarah Josepha (Buell)
  1788-1879 .... **NCLC 75**
  See also DLB 1, 42, 73, 243
Halevy, Elie 1870-1937 .... **TCLC 104**
Haley, Alex(ander Murray Palmer)
  1921-1992 ...... **BLC 1:2; CLC 8, 12, 76;
  TCLC 147**
  See also AAYA 26; BPFB 2; BW 2, 3; CA
  77-80; 136; CANR 61; CDALBS; CPW;
  CSW; DA; DA3; DAB; DAC; DAM MST,
  MULT, POP; DLB 38; LAIT 5; MTCW
  1, 2; NFS 9
Haliburton, Thomas Chandler
  1796-1865 .... **NCLC 15, 149**
  See also DLB 11, 99; RGEL 2; RGSF 2
Hall, Donald 1928- ... **CLC 1, 13, 37, 59, 151,
  240; PC 70**
  See also AAYA 63; CA 5-8R; CAAS 7;
  CANR 2, 44, 64, 106, 133; CP 1, 2, 3, 4,
  5, 6, 7; DAM POET; DLB 5, 342; MAL
  5; MTCW 2; MTFW 2005; RGAL 4;
  SATA 23, 97
Hall, Donald Andrew, Jr.
  See Hall, Donald
Hall, Frederic Sauser
  See Sauser-Hall, Frederic
Hall, James
  See Kuttner, Henry
Hall, James Norman 1887-1951 ..... **TCLC 23**
  See also CA 123; 173; LAIT 1; RHW 1;
  SATA 21
Hall, Joseph 1574-1656 .... **LC 91**
  See also DLB 121, 151; RGEL 2
Hall, Marguerite Radclyffe
  See Hall, Radclyffe
Hall, Radclyffe 1880-1943 .... **TCLC 12**
  See also BRWS 6; CA 110; 150; CANR 83;
  DLB 191; MTCW 2; MTFW 2005; RGEL
  2; RHW
Hall, Rodney 1935- .... **CLC 51**
  See also CA 109; CANR 69; CN 6, 7; CP
  1, 2, 3, 4, 5, 6, 7; DLB 289
Hallam, Arthur Henry
  1811-1833 .... **NCLC 110**
  See also DLB 32
Halldor Laxness CLC 25
  See Gudjonsson, Halldor Kiljan
  See also DLB 293; EW 12; EWL 3; RGWL
  2, 3
Halleck, Fitz-Greene 1790-1867 .... **NCLC 47**
  See also DLB 3, 250; RGAL 4
Halliday, Michael
  See Creasey, John
Halpern, Daniel 1945- .... **CLC 14**
  See also CA 33-36R; CANR 93, 174; CP 3,
  4, 5, 6, 7
Hamburger, Michael 1924-2007 ... **CLC 5, 14**
  See also CA 5-8R, 196; 261; CAAE 196;
  CAAS 4; CANR 2, 47; CP 1, 2, 3, 4, 5, 6,
  7; DLB 27
Hamburger, Michael Peter Leopold
  See Hamburger, Michael
Hamill, Pete 1935- .... **CLC 10, 261**
  See also CA 25-28R; CANR 18, 71, 127,
  180
Hamill, William Peter
  See Hamill, Pete

Hamilton, Alexander 1712-1756 .... **LC 150**
  See also DLB 31
Hamilton, Alexander
  1755(?)-1804 .... **NCLC 49**
  See also DLB 37
Hamilton, Clive
  See Lewis, C.S.
Hamilton, Edmond 1904-1977 .... **CLC 1**
  See also CA 1-4R; CANR 3, 84; DLB 8;
  SATA 118; SFW 4
Hamilton, Elizabeth 1758-1816 ... **NCLC 153**
  See also DLB 116, 158
Hamilton, Eugene (Jacob) Lee
  See Lee-Hamilton, Eugene (Jacob)
Hamilton, Franklin
  See Silverberg, Robert
Hamilton, Gail
  See Corcoran, Barbara (Asenath)
Hamilton, (Robert) Ian 1938-2001 . **CLC 191**
  See also CA 106; 203; DLB 40, 155
Hamilton, Jane 1957- .... **CLC 179**
  See also CA 147; CANR 85, 128; CN 7;
  MTFW 2005
Hamilton, Mollie
  See Kaye, M.M.
Hamilton, (Anthony Walter) Patrick
  1904-1962 .... **CLC 51**
  See also CA 176; 113; DLB 10, 191
Hamilton, Virginia 1936-2002 .... **CLC 26**
  See also AAYA 2, 21; BW 2, 3; BYA 1, 2,
  8; CA 25-28R; 206; CANR 20, 37, 73,
  126; CLR 1, 11, 40, 127; DAM MULT;
  DLB 33, 52; DLBY 2001; INT CANR-
  20; JRDA; LAIT 5; MAICYA 1, 2; MAI-
  CYAS 1; MTCW 1, 2; MTFW 2005;
  SATA 4, 56, 79, 123; SATA-Obit 132;
  WYA; YAW
Hammett, (Samuel) Dashiell
  1894-1961 ..... **CLC 3, 5, 10, 19, 47; SSC
  17; TCLC 187**
  See also AAYA 59; AITN 1; AMWS 4;
  BPFB 2; CA 81-84; CANR 42; CDALB
  1929-1941; CMW 4; DA3; DLB 226, 280;
  DLBD 6; DLBY 1996; EWL 3; LAIT 3;
  MAL 5; MSW; MTCW 1, 2; MTFW
  2005; NFS 21; RGAL 4; RGSF 2; TUS
Hammon, Jupiter 1720(?)-1800(?) . **BLC 1:2;
  NCLC 5; PC 16**
  See also DAM MULT, POET; DLB 31, 50
Hammond, Keith
  See Kuttner, Henry
Hamner, Earl (Henry), Jr. 1923- ...... **CLC 12**
  See also AITN 2; CA 73-76; DLB 6
Hampton, Christopher 1946- .... **CLC 4**
  See also CA 25-28R; CD 5, 6; DLB 13;
  MTCW 1
Hampton, Christopher James
  See Hampton, Christopher
Hamsun, Knut TCLC 2, 14, 49, 151, 203
  See Pedersen, Knut
  See also DLB 297, 330; EW 8; EWL 3;
  RGWL 2, 3
Handke, Peter 1942- .... **CLC 5, 8, 10, 15, 38,
  134; DC 17**
  See also CA 77-80; CANR 33, 75, 104, 133,
  180; CWW 2; DAM DRAM, NOV; DLB
  85, 124; EWL 3; MTCW 1, 2; MTFW
  2005; TWA
Handy, W(illiam) C(hristopher)
  1873-1958 .... **TCLC 97**
  See also BW 3; CA 121; 167
Hanley, James 1901-1985 ..... **CLC 3, 5, 8, 13**
  See also CA 73-76; 117; CANR 36; CBD;
  CN 1, 2, 3; DLB 191; EWL 3; MTCW 1;
  RGEL 2

Hannah, Barry 1942- .. **CLC 23, 38, 90; SSC
  94**
  See also BPFB 2; CA 108; 110; CANR 43,
  68, 113; CN 4, 5, 6, 7; CSW; DLB 6, 234;
  INT CA-110; MTCW 1; RGSF 2
Hannon, Ezra
  See Hunter, Evan
Hansberry, Lorraine (Vivian)
  1930-1965 ... **BLC 1:2, 2:2; CLC 17, 62;
  DC 2; TCLC 192**
  See also AAYA 25; AFAW 1, 2; AMWS 4;
  BW 1, 3; CA 109; 25-28R; CABS 3;
  CAD; CANR 58; CDALB 1941-1968;
  CWD; DA; DA3; DAB; DAC; DAM
  DRAM, MST, MULT; DFS 2; DLB 7, 38;
  EWL 3; FL 1:6; FW; LAIT 4; MAL 5;
  MTCW 1, 2; MTFW 2005; RGAL 4; TUS
Hansen, Joseph 1923-2004 .... **CLC 38**
  See Brock, Rose; Colton, James
  See also BPFB 2; CA 29-32R; 233; CAAS
  17; CANR 16, 44, 66, 125; CMW 4; DLB
  226; GLL 1; INT CANR-16
Hansen, Karen V. 1955- .... **CLC 65**
  See also CA 149; CANR 102
Hansen, Martin A(lfred)
  1909-1955 .... **TCLC 32**
  See also CA 167; DLB 214; EWL 3
Hanson, Kenneth O(stlin) 1922- ...... **CLC 13**
  See also CA 53-56; CANR 7; CP 1, 2, 3, 4,
  5
Hardwick, Elizabeth 1916-2007 .... **CLC 13**
  See also AMWS 3; CA 5-8R; 267; CANR
  3, 32, 70, 100, 139; CN 4, 5, 6; CSW;
  DA3; DAM NOV; DLB 6; MBL; MTCW
  1, 2; MTFW 2005; TCLE 1:1
Hardwick, Elizabeth Bruce
  See Hardwick, Elizabeth
Hardwick, Elizabeth Bruce
  See Hardwick, Elizabeth
Hardy, Thomas 1840-1928 . **PC 8, 92; SSC 2,
  60, 113; TCLC 4, 10, 18, 32, 48, 53, 72,
  143, 153; WLC 3**
  See also AAYA 69; BRW 6; BRWC 1, 2;
  BRWR 1; CA 104; 123; CDBLB 1890-
  1914; DA; DA3; DAB; DAC; DAM MST,
  NOV, POET; DLB 18, 19, 135, 284; EWL
  3; EXPN; EXPP; LAIT 2; MTCW 1, 2;
  MTFW 2005; NFS 3, 11, 15, 19; PFS 3,
  4, 18; RGEL 2; RGSF 2; TEA; WLIT 4
Hare, David 1947- .. **CLC 29, 58, 136; DC 26**
  See also BRWS 4; CA 97-100; CANR 39,
  91; CBD; CD 5, 6; DFS 4, 7, 16; DLB
  13, 310; MTCW 1; TEA
Harewood, John
  See Van Druten, John (William)
Harford, Henry
  See Hudson, W(illiam) H(enry)
Hargrave, Leonie
  See Disch, Thomas M.
**Hariri, Al- al-Qasim ibn 'Ali Abu
  Muhammad al-Basri**
  See al-Hariri, al-Qasim ibn 'Ali Abu Mu-
  hammad al-Basri
Harjo, Joy 1951- ..... **CLC 83; NNAL; PC 27**
  See also AMWS 12; CA 114; CANR 35,
  67, 91, 129; CP 6, 7; CWP; DAM MULT;
  DLB 120, 175, 342; EWL 3; MTCW 2;
  MTFW 2005; PFS 15; RGAL 4
Harlan, Louis R(udolph) 1922- .... **CLC 34**
  See also CA 21-24R; CANR 25, 55, 80
Harling, Robert 1951(?)- .... **CLC 53**
  See also CA 147
Harmon, William (Ruth) 1938- .... **CLC 38**
  See also CA 33-36R; CANR 14, 32, 35;
  SATA 65
Harper, F. E. W.
  See Harper, Frances Ellen Watkins
Harper, Frances E. W.
  See Harper, Frances Ellen Watkins

Harper, Frances E. Watkins
See Harper, Frances Ellen Watkins
Harper, Frances Ellen
See Harper, Frances Ellen Watkins
Harper, Frances Ellen Watkins
1825-1911 .. **BLC 1:2; PC 21; TCLC 14**
See also AFAW 1, 2; BW 1, 3; CA 111; 125;
CANR 79; DAM MULT, POET; DLB 50,
221; MBL; RGAL 4
Harper, Michael S(teven) 1938- ..... **BLC 2:2;**
CLC 7, 22
See also AFAW 2; BW 1; CA 33-36R, 224;
CAAE 224; CANR 24, 108; CP 2, 3, 4, 5,
6, 7; DLB 41; RGAL 4; TCLE 1:1
Harper, Mrs. F. E. W.
See Harper, Frances Ellen Watkins
Harpur, Charles 1813-1868 .... **NCLC 114**
See also DLB 230; RGEL 2
Harris, Christie
See Harris, Christie (Lucy) Irwin
Harris, Christie (Lucy) Irwin
1907-2002 .... **CLC 12**
See also CA 5-8R; CANR 6, 83; CLR 47;
DLB 88; JRDA; MAICYA 1, 2; SAAS 10;
SATA 6, 74; SATA-Essay 116
Harris, Frank 1856-1931 .... **TCLC 24**
See also CA 109; 150; CANR 80; DLB 156,
197; RGEL 2
Harris, George Washington
1814-1869 .... **NCLC 23, 165**
See also DLB 3, 11, 248; RGAL 4
Harris, Joel Chandler 1848-1908 ..... **SSC 19,**
103; TCLC 2
See also CA 104; 137; CANR 80; CLR 49,
128; DLB 11, 23, 42, 78, 91; LAIT 2;
MAICYA 1, 2; RGSF 2; SATA 100; WCH;
YABC 1
Harris, John (Wyndham Parkes Lucas)
Beynon 1903-1969
See Wyndham, John
See also CA 102; 89-92; CANR 84; SATA
118; SFW 4
Harris, MacDonald CLC 9
See Heiney, Donald (William)
Harris, Mark 1922-2007 .... **CLC 19**
See also CA 5-8R; 260; CAAS 3; CANR 2,
55, 83; CN 1, 2, 3, 4, 5, 6, 7; DLB 2;
DLBY 1980
Harris, Norman CLC 65
Harris, (Theodore) Wilson 1921- ... **BLC 2:2;**
CLC 25, 159
See also BRWS 5; BW 2, 3; CA 65-68;
CAAS 16; CANR 11, 27, 69, 114; CD-
WLB 3; CN 1, 2, 3, 4, 5, 6, 7; CP 1, 2, 3,
4, 5, 6, 7; DLB 117; EWL 3; MTCW 1;
RGEL 2
Harrison, Barbara Grizzuti
1934-2002 .... **CLC 144**
See also CA 77-80; 205; CANR 15, 48; INT
CANR-15
Harrison, Elizabeth (Allen) Cavanna
1909-2001
See Cavanna, Betty
See also CA 9-12R; 200; CANR 6, 27, 85,
104, 121; MAICYA 2; SATA 142; YAW
Harrison, Harry 1925- .... **CLC 42**
See also CA 1-4R; CANR 5, 21, 84; DLB
8; SATA 4; SCFW 4; SFW 4
Harrison, Harry Max
See Harrison, Harry
Harrison, James
See Harrison, Jim
Harrison, James Thomas
See Harrison, Jim
Harrison, Jim 1937- .... **CLC 6, 14, 33, 66,**
143; SSC 19
See also AMWS 8; CA 13-16R; CANR 8,
51, 79, 142; CN 5, 6; CP 1, 2, 3, 4, 5, 6;
DLBY 1982; INT CANR-8; RGAL 4;
TCWW 2; TUS

Harrison, Kathryn 1961- .... **CLC 70, 151**
See also CA 144; CANR 68, 122
Harrison, Tony 1937- .... **CLC 43, 129**
See also BRWS 5; CA 65-68; CANR 44,
98; CBD; CD 5, 6; CP 2, 3, 4, 5, 6, 7;
DLB 40, 245; MTCW 1; RGEL 2
Harriss, Will(ard Irvin) 1922- .... **CLC 34**
See also CA 111
Hart, Ellis
See Ellison, Harlan
Hart, Josephine 1942(?)- .... **CLC 70**
See also CA 138; CANR 70, 149; CPW;
DAM POP
Hart, Moss 1904-1961 .... **CLC 66**
See also CA 109; 89-92; CANR 84; DAM
DRAM; DFS 1; DLB 7, 266; RGAL 4
Harte, (Francis) Bret(t)
1836(?)-1902 ... **SSC 8, 59; TCLC 1, 25;**
WLC 3
See also AMWS 2; CA 104; 140; CANR
80; CDALB 1865-1917; DA; DA3; DAC;
DAM MST; DLB 12, 64, 74, 79, 186;
EXPS; LAIT 2; RGAL 4; RGSF 2; SATA
26; SSFS 3; TUS
Hartley, L(eslie) P(oles) 1895-1972 ... **CLC 2,**
22
See also BRWS 7; CA 45-48; 37-40R;
CANR 33; CN 1; DLB 15, 139; EWL 3;
HGG; MTCW 1, 2; MTFW 2005; RGEL
2; RGSF 2; SUFW 1
Hartman, Geoffrey H. 1929- .... **CLC 27**
See also CA 117; 125; CANR 79; DLB 67
Hartmann, Sadakichi 1869-1944 ... **TCLC 73**
See also CA 157; DLB 54
Hartmann von Aue c. 1170-c.
1210 .... **CMLC 15**
See also CDWLB 2; DLB 138; RGWL 2, 3
Hartog, Jan de
See de Hartog, Jan
Haruf, Kent 1943- .... **CLC 34**
See also AAYA 44; CA 149; CANR 91, 131
Harvey, Caroline
See Trollope, Joanna
Harvey, Gabriel 1550(?)-1631 .... **LC 88**
See also DLB 167, 213, 281
Harvey, Jack
See Rankin, Ian
Harwood, Ronald 1934- .... **CLC 32**
See also CA 1-4R; CANR 4, 55, 150; CBD;
CD 5, 6; DAM DRAM, MST; DLB 13
Hasegawa Tatsunosuke
See Futabatei, Shimei
Hasek, Jaroslav (Matej Frantisek)
1883-1923 .... **SSC 69; TCLC 4**
See also CA 104; 129; CDWLB 4; DLB
215; EW 9; EWL 3; MTCW 1, 2; RGSF
2; RGWL 2, 3
Hass, Robert 1941- ... **CLC 18, 39, 99; PC 16**
See also AMWS 6; CA 111; CANR 30, 50,
71; CP 3, 4, 5, 6, 7; DLB 105, 206; EWL
3; MAL 5; MTFW 2005; RGAL 4; SATA
94; TCLE 1:1
Hassler, Jon 1933-2008 .... **CLC 263**
See also CA 73-76; 270; CANR 21, 80, 161;
CN 6, 7; INT CANR-21; SATA 19; SATA-
Obit 191
Hassler, Jon Francis
See Hassler, Jon
Hastings, Hudson
See Kuttner, Henry
Hastings, Selina CLC 44
See also CA 257
Hastings, Selina Shirley
See Hastings, Selina
Hastings, Victor
See Disch, Thomas M.

Hathorne, John 1641-1717 .... **LC 38**
Hatteras, Amelia
See Mencken, H(enry) L(ouis)
Hatteras, Owen TCLC 18
See Mencken, H(enry) L(ouis); Nathan,
George Jean
Hauff, Wilhelm 1802-1827 .... **NCLC 185**
See also DLB 90; SUFW 1
Hauptmann, Gerhart (Johann Robert)
1862-1946 .... **SSC 37; TCLC 4**
See also CA 104; 153; CDWLB 2; DAM
DRAM; DLB 66, 118, 330; EW 8; EWL
3; RGSF 2; RGWL 2, 3; TWA
Havel, Vaclav 1936- ..... **CLC 25, 58, 65, 123;**
DC 6
See also CA 104; CANR 36, 63, 124, 175;
CDWLB 4; CWW 2; DA3; DAM DRAM;
DFS 10; DLB 232; EWL 3; LMFS 2;
MTCW 1, 2; MTFW 2005; RGWL 3
Haviaras, Stratis CLC 33
See Chaviaras, Strates
Hawes, Stephen 1475(?)-1529(?) .... **LC 17**
See also DLB 132; RGEL 2
Hawkes, John 1925-1998 .. **CLC 1, 2, 3, 4, 7,**
9, 14, 15, 27, 49
See also BPFB 2; CA 1-4R; 167; CANR 2,
47, 64; CN 1, 2, 3, 4, 5, 6; DLB 2, 7, 227;
DLBY 1980, 1998; EWL 3; MAL 5;
MTCW 1, 2; MTFW 2005; RGAL 4
Hawking, S. W.
See Hawking, Stephen W.
Hawking, Stephen W. 1942- ..... **CLC 63, 105**
See also AAYA 13; BEST 89:1; CA 126;
129; CANR 48, 115; CPW; DA3; MTCW
2; MTFW 2005
Hawking, Stephen William
See Hawking, Stephen W.
Hawkins, Anthony Hope
See Hope, Anthony
Hawthorne, Julian 1846-1934 .... **TCLC 25**
See also CA 165; HGG
Hawthorne, Nathaniel 1804-1864 ... **NCLC 2,**
10, 17, 23, 39, 79, 95, 158, 171, 191;
SSC 3, 29, 39, 89; WLC 3
See also AAYA 18; AMW; AMWC 1;
AMWR 1; BPFB 2; BYA 3; CDALB
1640-1865; CLR 103; DA; DA3; DAB;
DAC; DAM MST, NOV; DLB 1, 74, 183,
223, 269; EXPN; GL 2; HGG;
LAIT 1; NFS 1, 20; RGAL 4; RGSF 2;
SSFS 1, 7, 11, 15; SUFW 1; TUS; WCH;
YABC 2
Hawthorne, Sophia Peabody
1809-1871 .... **NCLC 150**
See also DLB 183, 239
Haxton, Josephine Ayres
See Douglas, Ellen
Hayaseca y Eizaguirre, Jorge
See Echegaray (y Eizaguirre), Jose (Maria
Waldo)
Hayashi, Fumiko 1904-1951 .... **TCLC 27**
See Hayashi Fumiko
See also CA 161
Hayashi Fumiko
See Hayashi, Fumiko
See also DLB 180; EWL 3
Haycraft, Anna 1932-2005
See Ellis, Alice Thomas
See also CA 122; 237; CANR 90, 141;
MTCW 2; MTFW 2005
Hayden, Robert E(arl) 1913-1980 . **BLC 1:2;**
CLC 5, 9, 14, 37; PC 6
See also AFAW 1, 2; AMWS 2; BW 1, 3;
CA 69-72; 97-100; CABS 2; CANR 24,
75, 82; CDALB 1941-1968; CP 1, 2, 3;
DA; DAC; DAM MST, MULT, POET;
DLB 5, 76; EWL 3; EXPP; MAL 5;
MTCW 1, 2; PFS 1; RGAL 4; SATA 19;
SATA-Obit 26; WP

Haydon, Benjamin Robert
    1786-1846 .... **NCLC 146**
    See also DLB 110
Hayek, F(riedrich) A(ugust von)
    1899-1992 .... **TCLC 109**
    See also CA 93-96; 137; CANR 20; MTCW
    1, 2
Hayford, J(oseph) E(phraim) Casely
    See Casely-Hayford, J(oseph) E(phraim)
Hayman, Ronald 1932- .... **CLC 44**
    See also CA 25-28R; CANR 18, 50, 88; CD
    5, 6; DLB 155
Hayne, Paul Hamilton 1830-1886 . **NCLC 94**
    See also DLB 3, 64, 79, 248; RGAL 4
Hays, Mary 1760-1843 .... **NCLC 114**
    See also DLB 142, 158; RGEL 2
Haywood, Eliza (Fowler)
    1693(?)-1756 .... **LC 1, 44**
    See also BRWS 12; DLB 39; RGEL 2
Hazlitt, William 1778-1830 ...... **NCLC 29, 82**
    See also BRW 4; DLB 110, 158; RGEL 2;
    TEA
Hazzard, Shirley 1931- .... **CLC 18, 218**
    See also CA 9-12R; CANR 4, 70, 127; CN
    1, 2, 3, 4, 5, 6, 7; DLB 289; DLBY 1982;
    MTCW 1
Head, Bessie 1937-1986 . **BLC 1:2, 2:2; CLC
    25, 67; SSC 52**
    See also AFW; BW 2, 3; CA 29-32R; 119;
    CANR 25, 82; CDWLB 3; CN 1, 2, 3, 4;
    DA3; DAM MULT; DLB 117, 225; EWL
    3; EXPS; FL 1:6; FW; MTCW 1, 2;
    MTFW 2005; RGSF 2; SSFS 5, 13; WLIT
    2; WWE 1
Headon, (Nicky) Topper 1956(?)- ..... **CLC 30**
Heaney, Seamus 1939- . **CLC 5, 7, 14, 25, 37,
    74, 91, 171, 225; PC 18; WLCS**
    See also AAYA 61; BRWR 1; BRWS 2; CA
    85-88; CANR 25, 48, 75, 91, 128, 184;
    CDBLB 1960 to Present; CP 1, 2, 3, 4, 5,
    6, 7; DA3; DAB; DAM POET; DLB 40,
    330; DLBY 1995; EWL 3; EXPP; MTCW
    1, 2; MTFW 2005; PAB; PFS 2, 5, 8, 17;
    RGEL 2; TEA; WLIT 4
Hearn, (Patricio) Lafcadio (Tessima Carlos)
    1850-1904 .... **TCLC 9**
    See also CA 105; 166; DLB 12, 78, 189;
    HGG; MAL 5; RGAL 4
Hearne, Samuel 1745-1792 .... **LC 95**
    See also DLB 99
Hearne, Vicki 1946-2001 .... **CLC 56**
    See also CA 139; 201
Hearon, Shelby 1931- .... **CLC 63**
    See also AITN 2; AMWS 8; CA 25-28R;
    CAAS 11; CANR 18, 48, 103, 146; CSW
Heat-Moon, William Least CLC 29
    See Trogdon, William (Lewis)
    See also AAYA 9
Hebbel, Friedrich 1813-1863 . **DC 21; NCLC
    43**
    See also CDWLB 2; DAM DRAM; DLB
    129; EW 6; RGWL 2, 3
Hebert, Anne 1916-2000 . **CLC 4, 13, 29, 246**
    See also CA 85-88; 187; CANR 69, 126;
    CCA 1; CWP; CWW 2; DA3; DAC;
    DAM POET; DLB 68; EWL 3; GFL
    1789 to the Present; MTCW 1, 2; MTFW
    2005; PFS 20
Hecht, Anthony (Evan) 1923-2004 .... **CLC 8,
    13, 19; PC 70**
    See also AMWS 10; CA 9-12R; 232; CANR
    6, 108; CP 1, 2, 3, 4, 5, 6, 7; DAM POET;
    DLB 5, 169; EWL 3; PFS 6; WP
Hecht, Ben 1894-1964 ..... **CLC 8; TCLC 101**
    See also CA 85-88; DFS 9; DLB 7, 9, 25,
    26, 28, 86; FANT; IDFW 3, 4; RGAL 4
Hedayat, Sadeq 1903-1951 .... **TCLC 21**
    See also CA 120; EWL 3; RGSF 2

Hegel, Georg Wilhelm Friedrich
    1770-1831 .... **NCLC 46, 151**
    See also DLB 90; TWA
Heidegger, Martin 1889-1976 .... **CLC 24**
    See also CA 81-84; 65-68; CANR 34; DLB
    296; MTCW 1, 2; MTFW 2005
Heidenstam, (Carl Gustaf) Verner von
    1859-1940 .... **TCLC 5**
    See also CA 104; DLB 330
Heidi Louise
    See Erdrich, Louise
Heifner, Jack 1946- .... **CLC 11**
    See also CA 105; CANR 47
Heijermans, Herman 1864-1924 .... **TCLC 24**
    See also CA 123; EWL 3
Heilbrun, Carolyn G(old)
    1926-2003 .... **CLC 25, 173**
    See Cross, Amanda
    See also CA 45-48; 220; CANR 1, 28, 58,
    94; FW
Hein, Christoph 1944- .... **CLC 154**
    See also CA 158; CANR 108; CDWLB 2;
    CWW 2; DLB 124
Heine, Heinrich 1797-1856 .... **NCLC 4, 54,
    147; PC 25**
    See also CDWLB 2; DLB 90; EW 5; RGWL
    2, 3; TWA
Heinemann, Larry 1944- .... **CLC 50**
    See also CA 110; CAAS 21; CANR 31, 81,
    156; DLBD 9; INT CANR-31
Heinemann, Larry Curtiss
    See Heinemann, Larry
Heiney, Donald (William) 1921-1993
    See Harris, MacDonald
    See also CA 1-4R; 142; CANR 3, 58; FANT
Heinlein, Robert A. 1907-1988 .. **CLC 1, 3, 8,
    14, 26, 55; SSC 55**
    See also AAYA 17; BPFB 2; BYA 4, 13;
    CA 1-4R; 125; CANR 1, 20, 53; CLR 75;
    CN 1, 2, 3, 4; CPW; DA3; DAM POP;
    DLB 8; EXPS; JRDA; LAIT 5; LMFS 2;
    MAICYA 1, 2; MTCW 1, 2; MTFW 2005;
    RGAL 4; SATA 9, 69; SATA-Obit 56;
    SCFW 1, 2; SFW 4; SSFS 7; YAW
Heldris of Cornwall fl. 13th cent.
    .... **CMLC 97**
Helforth, John
    See Doolittle, Hilda
Heliodorus fl. 3rd cent. - .... **CMLC 52**
    See also WLIT 8
Hellenhofferu, Vojtech Kapristian z
    See Hasek, Jaroslav (Matej Frantisek)
Heller, Joseph 1923-1999 . **CLC 1, 3, 5, 8, 11,
    36, 63; TCLC 131, 151; WLC 3**
    See also AAYA 24; AITN 1; AMWS 4;
    BPFB 2; BYA 1; CA 5-8R; 187; CABS 1;
    CANR 8, 42, 66, 126; CN 1, 2, 3, 4, 5, 6;
    CPW; DA; DA3; DAB; DAC; DAM MST,
    NOV, POP; DLB 2, 28, 227; DLBY 1980,
    2002; EWL 3; EXPN; INT CANR-8;
    LAIT 4; MAL 5; MTCW 1, 2; MTFW
    2005; NFS 1; RGAL 4; TUS; YAW
Hellman, Lillian 1905-1984 . **CLC 2, 4, 8, 14,
    18, 34, 44, 52; DC 1; TCLC 119**
    See also AAYA 47; AITN 1, 2; AMWS 1;
    CA 13-16R; 112; CAD; CANR 33; CWD;
    DA3; DAM DRAM; DFS 1, 3, 14; DLB
    7, 228; DLBY 1984; EWL 3; FL 1:6; FW;
    LAIT 3; MAL 5; MBL; MTCW 1, 2;
    MTFW 2005; RGAL 4; TUS
Helprin, Mark 1947- .... **CLC 7, 10, 22, 32**
    See also CA 81-84; CANR 47, 64, 124;
    CDALBS; CN 7; CPW; DA3; DAM NOV,
    POP; DLB 335; DLBY 1985; FANT;
    MAL 5; MTCW 1, 2; MTFW 2005; SSFS
    25; SUFW 2
Helvetius, Claude-Adrien 1715-1771 .. **LC 26**
    See also DLB 313

Helyar, Jane Penelope Josephine 1933-
    See Poole, Josephine
    See also CA 21-24R; CANR 10, 26; CWRI
    5; SATA 82, 138; SATA-Essay 138
Hemans, Felicia 1793-1835 ...... **NCLC 29, 71**
    See also DLB 96; RGEL 2
Hemingway, Ernest (Miller)
    1899-1961 .... **CLC 1, 3, 6, 8, 10, 13, 19,
    30, 34, 39, 41, 44, 50, 61, 80; SSC 1, 25,
    36, 40, 63, 117; TCLC 115, 203; WLC
    3**
    See also AAYA 19; AMW; AMWC 1;
    AMWR 1; BPFB 2; BYA 2, 3, 13, 15; CA
    77-80; CANR 34; CDALB 1917-1929;
    DA; DA3; DAB; DAC; DAM MST, NOV;
    DLB 4, 9, 102, 210, 308, 316, 330; DLBD
    1, 15, 16; DLBY 1981, 1987, 1996, 1998;
    EWL 3; EXPN; EXPS; LAIT 3, 4; LATS
    1:1; MAL 5; MTCW 1, 2; MTFW 2005;
    NFS 1, 5, 6, 14; RGAL 4; RGSF 2; SSFS
    17; TUS; WYA
Hempel, Amy 1951- .... **CLC 39**
    See also CA 118; 137; CANR 70, 166;
    DA3; DLB 218; EXPS; MTCW 2; MTFW
    2005; SSFS 2
Henderson, F. C.
    See Mencken, H(enry) L(ouis)
Henderson, Sylvia
    See Ashton-Warner, Sylvia (Constance)
Henderson, Zenna (Chlarson)
    1917-1983 .... **SSC 29**
    See also CA 1-4R; 133; CANR 1, 84; DLB
    8; SATA 5; SFW 4
Henkin, Joshua 1964- .... **CLC 119**
    See also CA 161
Henley, Beth CLC 23, 255; DC 6, 14
    See Henley, Elizabeth Becker
    See also AAYA 70; CABS 3; CAD; CD 5,
    6; CSW; CWD; DFS 2, 21; DLBY 1986;
    FW
Henley, Elizabeth Becker 1952-
    See Henley, Beth
    See also CA 107; CANR 32, 73, 140; DA3;
    DAM DRAM, MST; MTCW 1, 2; MTFW
    2005
Henley, William Ernest 1849-1903 .. **TCLC 8**
    See also CA 105; 234; DLB 19; RGEL 2
Hennissart, Martha 1929-
    See Lathen, Emma
    See also CA 85-88; CANR 64
Henry VIII 1491-1547 .... **LC 10**
    See also DLB 132
**Henry, O. SSC 5, 49, 117; TCLC 1, 19; WLC
    3**
    See Porter, William Sydney
    See also AAYA 41; AMWS 2; EXPS; MAL
    5; RGAL 4; RGSF 2; SSFS 2, 18; TCWW
    1, 2
Henry, Patrick 1736-1799 .... **LC 25**
    See also LAIT 1
Henryson, Robert 1430(?)-1506(?) ..... **LC 20,
    110; PC 65**
    See also BRWS 7; DLB 146; RGEL 2
Henschke, Alfred
    See Klabund
Henson, Lance 1944- .... **NNAL**
    See also CA 146; DLB 175
Hentoff, Nat(han Irving) 1925- .... **CLC 26**
    See also AAYA 4, 42; BYA 6; CA 1-4R;
    CAAS 6; CANR 5, 25, 77, 114; CLR 1,
    52; DLB 345; INT CANR-25; JRDA;
    MAICYA 1, 2; SATA 42, 69, 133; SATA-
    Brief 27; WYA; YAW
Heppenstall, (John) Rayner
    1911-1981 .... **CLC 10**
    See also CA 1-4R; 103; CANR 29; CN 1,
    2; CP 1, 2, 3; EWL 3
Heraclitus c. 540B.C.-c. 450B.C. ... **CMLC 22**
    See also DLB 176

Herbert, Frank 1920-1986 ... **CLC 12, 23, 35, 44, 85**
See also AAYA 21; BPFB 2; BYA 4, 14; CA 53-56; 118; CANR 5, 43; CDALBS; CPW; DAM POP; DLB 8; INT CANR-5; LAIT 5; MTCW 1, 2; MTFW 2005; NFS 17; SATA 9, 37; SATA-Obit 47; SCFW 1, 2; SFW 4; YAW

Herbert, George 1593-1633 . **LC 24, 121; PC 4**
See also BRW 2; BRWR 2; CDBLB Before 1660; DAB; DAM POET; DLB 126; EXPP; PFS 25; RGEL 2; TEA; WP

Herbert, Zbigniew 1924-1998 ..... **CLC 9, 43; PC 50; TCLC 168**
See also CA 89-92; 169; CANR 36, 74, 177; CDWLB 4; CWW 2; DAM POET; DLB 232; EWL 3; MTCW 1; PFS 22

Herbst, Josephine (Frey)
1897-1969 .... **CLC 34**
See also CA 5-8R; 25-28R; DLB 9

Herder, Johann Gottfried von
1744-1803 .... **NCLC 8, 186**
See also DLB 97; EW 4; TWA

Heredia, Jose Maria 1803-1839 .... **HLCS 2**
See also LAW

Hergesheimer, Joseph 1880-1954 ... **TCLC 11**
See also CA 109; 194; DLB 102, 9; RGAL 4

Herlihy, James Leo 1927-1993 .... **CLC 6**
See also CA 1-4R; 143; CAD; CANR 2; CN 1, 2, 3, 4, 5

Herman, William
See Bierce, Ambrose (Gwinett)

Hermogenes fl. c. 175- .... **CMLC 6**

Hernandez, Jose 1834-1886 .... **NCLC 17**
See also LAW; RGWL 2, 3; WLIT 1

Herodotus c. 484B.C.-c. 420B.C. .. **CMLC 17**
See also AW 1; CDWLB 1; DLB 176; RGWL 2, 3; TWA; WLIT 8

Herr, Michael 1940(?)- .... **CLC 231**
See also CA 89-92; CANR 68, 142; DLB 185; MTCW 1

Herrick, Robert 1591-1674 .. **LC 13, 145; PC 9**
See also BRW 2; BRWC 2; DA; DAB; DAC; DAM MST, POP; DLB 126; EXPP; PFS 13, 29; RGAL 4; RGEL 2; TEA; WP

Herring, Guilles
See Somerville, Edith Oenone

Herriot, James 1916-1995 .... **CLC 12**
See Wight, James Alfred
See also AAYA 1, 54; BPFB 2; CA 148; CANR 40; CLR 80; CPW; DAM POP; LAIT 3; MAICYA 2; MAICYAS 1; MTCW 2; SATA 86, 135; TEA; YAW

Herris, Violet
See Hunt, Violet

Herrmann, Dorothy 1941- .... **CLC 44**
See also CA 107

Herrmann, Taffy
See Herrmann, Dorothy

Hersey, John 1914-1993 .. **CLC 1, 2, 7, 9, 40, 81, 97**
See also AAYA 29; BPFB 2; CA 17-20R; 140; CANR 33; CDALBS; CN 1, 2, 3, 4, 5; CPW; DAM POP; DLB 6, 185, 278, 299; MAL 5; MTCW 1, 2; MTFW 2005; RGHL; SATA 25; SATA-Obit 76; TUS

Hervent, Maurice
See Grindel, Eugene

Herzen, Aleksandr Ivanovich
1812-1870 .... **NCLC 10, 61**
See Herzen, Alexander

Herzen, Alexander
See Herzen, Aleksandr Ivanovich
See also DLB 277

Herzl, Theodor 1860-1904 .... **TCLC 36**
See also CA 168

Herzog, Werner 1942- .... **CLC 16, 236**
See also CA 89-92

Hesiod fl. 8th cent. B.C.- .... **CMLC 5, 102**
See also AW 1; DLB 176; RGWL 2, 3; WLIT 8

Hesse, Hermann 1877-1962 ... **CLC 1, 2, 3, 6, 11, 17, 25, 69; SSC 9, 49; TCLC 148, 196; WLC 3**
See also AAYA 43; BPFB 2; CA 17-18; CAP 2; CDWLB 2; DA; DA3; DAB; DAC; DAM MST, NOV; DLB 66, 330; EW 9; EWL 3; EXPN; LAIT 1; MTCW 1, 2; MTFW 2005; NFS 6, 15, 24; RGWL 2, 3; SATA 50; TWA

Hewes, Cady
See De Voto, Bernard (Augustine)

Heyen, William 1940- .... **CLC 13, 18**
See also CA 33-36R; 220; CAAE 220; CAAS 9; CANR 98; CP 3, 4, 5, 6, 7; DLB 5; RGHL

Heyerdahl, Thor 1914-2002 .... **CLC 26**
See also CA 5-8R; 207; CANR 5, 22, 66, 73; LAIT 4; MTCW 1, 2; MTFW 2005; SATA 2, 52

Heym, Georg (Theodor Franz Arthur)
1887-1912 .... **TCLC 9**
See also CA 106; 181

Heym, Stefan 1913-2001 .... **CLC 41**
See also CA 9-12R; 203; CANR 4; CWW 2; DLB 69; EWL 3

Heyse, Paul (Johann Ludwig von)
1830-1914 .... **TCLC 8**
See also CA 104; 209; DLB 129, 330

Heyward, (Edwin) DuBose
1885-1940 .... **HR 1:2; TCLC 59**
See also CA 108; 157; DLB 7, 9, 45, 249; MAL 5; SATA 21

Heywood, John 1497(?)-1580(?) .... **LC 65**
See also DLB 136; RGEL 2

Heywood, Thomas 1573(?)-1641 . **DC 29; LC 111**
See also DAM DRAM; DLB 62; LMFS 1; RGEL 2; TEA

Hiaasen, Carl 1953- .... **CLC 238**
See also CA 105; CANR 22, 45, 65, 113, 133, 168; CMW 4; CPW; CSW; DA3; DLB 292; MTCW 2; MTFW 2005

Hibbert, Eleanor Alice Burford
1906-1993 .... **CLC 7**
See Holt, Victoria
See also BEST 90:4; CA 17-20R; 140; CANR 9, 28, 59; CMW 4; CPW; DAM POP; MTCW 1, 2; MTFW 2005; RHW; SATA 2; SATA-Obit 74

Hichens, Robert (Smythe)
1864-1950 .... **TCLC 64**
See also CA 162; DLB 153; HGG; RHW; SUFW

Higgins, Aidan 1927- .... **SSC 68**
See also CA 9-12R; CANR 70, 115, 148; CN 1, 2, 3, 4, 5, 6, 7; DLB 14

Higgins, George V(incent)
1939-1999 .... **CLC 4, 7, 10, 18**
See also BPFB 2; CA 77-80; 186; CAAS 5; CANR 17, 51, 89, 96; CMW 4; CN 2, 3, 4, 5, 6; DLB 2; DLBY 1981, 1998; INT CANR-17; MTCW 1

Higginson, Thomas Wentworth
1823-1911 .... **TCLC 36**
See also CA 162; DLB 1, 64, 243

Higgonet, Margaret CLC 65

Highet, Helen
See MacInnes, Helen (Clark)

Highsmith, Patricia 1921-1995 ...... **CLC 2, 4, 14, 42, 102**
See Morgan, Claire
See also AAYA 48; BRWS 5; CA 1-4R; 147; CANR 1, 20, 48, 62, 108; CMW 4; CN 1, 2, 3, 4, 5; CPW; DA3; DAM NOV, POP; DLB 306; MSW; MTCW 1, 2; MTFW 2005; NFS 27; SSFS 25

Highwater, Jamake (Mamake)
1942(?)-2001 .... **CLC 12**
See also AAYA 7, 69; BPFB 2; BYA 4; CA 65-68; 199; CAAS 7; CANR 10, 34, 84; CLR 17; CWRI 5; DLB 52; DLBY 1985; JRDA; MAICYA 1, 2; SATA 32, 69; SATA-Brief 30

Highway, Tomson 1951- ...... **CLC 92; NNAL**
See also CA 151; CANR 75; CCA 1; CD 5, 6; CN 7; DAC; DAM MULT; DFS 2; DLB 334; MTCW 2

Hijuelos, Oscar 1951- .... **CLC 65; HLC 1**
See also AAYA 25; AMWS 8; BEST 90:1; CA 123; CANR 50, 75, 125; CPW; DA3; DAM MULT, POP; DLB 145; HW 1, 2; LLW; MAL 5; MTCW 2; MTFW 2005; NFS 17; RGAL 4; WLIT 1

Hikmet, Nazim 1902-1963 .... **CLC 40**
See Nizami of Ganja
See also CA 141; 93-96; EWL 3; WLIT 6

Hildegard von Bingen 1098-1179 . **CMLC 20**
See also DLB 148

Hildesheimer, Wolfgang 1916-1991 .. **CLC 49**
See also CA 101; 135; DLB 69, 124; EWL 3; RGHL

Hill, Aaron 1685-1750 .... **LC 148**
See also DLB 84; RGEL 2

Hill, Geoffrey (William) 1932- ...... **CLC 5, 8, 18, 45, 251**
See also BRWS 5; CA 81-84; CANR 21, 89; CDBLB 1960 to Present; CP 1, 2, 3, 4, 5, 6, 7; DAM POET; DLB 40; EWL 3; MTCW 1; RGEL 2; RGHL

Hill, George Roy 1921-2002 .... **CLC 26**
See also CA 110; 122; 213

Hill, John
See Koontz, Dean R.

Hill, Susan 1942- .... **CLC 4, 113**
See also CA 33-36R; CANR 29, 69, 129, 172; CN 2, 3, 4, 5, 6, 7; DAB; DAM MST, NOV; DLB 14, 139; HGG; MTCW 1; RHW; SATA 183

Hill, Susan Elizabeth
See Hill, Susan

Hillard, Asa G. III CLC 70

Hillerman, Tony 1925-2008 ...... **CLC 62, 170**
See also AAYA 40; BEST 89:1; BPFB 2; CA 29-32R; CANR 21, 42, 65, 97, 134; CMW 4; CPW; DA3; DAM POP; DLB 206, 306; MAL 5; MSW; MTCW 2; MTFW 2005; RGAL 4; SATA 6; TCWW 2; YAW

Hillesum, Etty 1914-1943 .... **TCLC 49**
See also CA 137; RGHL

Hilliard, Noel (Harvey) 1929-1996 ... **CLC 15**
See also CA 9-12R; CANR 7, 69; CN 1, 2, 3, 4, 5, 6

Hillis, Rick 1956- .... **CLC 66**
See also CA 134

Hilton, James 1900-1954 .... **TCLC 21**
See also AAYA 76; CA 108; 169; DLB 34, 77; FANT; SATA 34

Hilton, Walter (?)-1396 .... **CMLC 58**
See also DLB 146; RGEL 2

Himes, Chester (Bomar)
1909-1984 .... **BLC 1:2; CLC 2, 4, 7, 18, 58, 108; TCLC 139**
See also AFAW 2; AMWS 16; BPFB 2; BW 2; CA 25-28R; 114; CANR 22, 89; CMW 4; CN 1, 2, 3; DAM MULT; DLB 2, 76, 143, 226; EWL 3; MAL 5; MSW; MTCW 1, 2; MTFW 2005; RGAL 4

Himmelfarb, Gertrude 1922- .... **CLC 202**
See also CA 49-52; CANR 28, 66, 102, 166

Hinde, Thomas CLC 6, 11
See Chitty, Thomas Willes
See also CN 1, 2, 3, 4, 5, 6; EWL 3

Hine, (William) Daryl 1936- .... **CLC 15**
See also CA 1-4R; CAAS 15; CANR 1, 20;
CP 1, 2, 3, 4, 5, 6, 7; DLB 60

Hinkson, Katharine Tynan
See Tynan, Katharine

Hinojosa, Rolando 1929- .... **HLC 1**
See Hinojosa-Smith, Rolando
See also CA 131; CAAS 16; CANR 62;
DAM MULT; DLB 82; HW 1, 2; LLW;
MTCW 2; MTFW 2005; RGAL 4

Hinton, S.E. 1950- .... **CLC 30, 111**
See also AAYA 2, 33; BPFB; BYA 2, 3;
CA 81-84; CANR 32, 62, 92, 133;
CDALBS; CLR 3, 23; CPW; DA; DA3;
DAB; DAC; DAM MST, NOV; JRDA;
LAIT 5; MAICYA 1, 2; MTCW 1, 2;
MTFW 2005; NFS 5, 9, 15, 16; SATA 19,
58, 115, 160; WYA; YAW

Hippius, Zinaida (Nikolaevna) **TCLC 9**
See Gippius, Zinaida (Nikolaevna)
See also DLB 295; EWL 3

Hiraoka, Kimitake 1925-1970
See Mishima, Yukio
See also CA 97-100; 29-32R; DA3; DAM
DRAM; GLL 1; MTCW 1, 2

Hirsch, E.D., Jr. 1928- .... **CLC 79**
See also CA 25-28R; CANR 27, 51, 146,
181; DLB 67; INT CANR-27; MTCW 1

Hirsch, Edward 1950- .... **CLC 31, 50**
See also CA 104; CANR 20, 42, 102, 167;
CP 6, 7; DLB 120; PFS 22

Hirsch, Eric Donald, Jr.
See Hirsch, E.D., Jr.

Hitchcock, Alfred (Joseph)
1899-1980 .... **CLC 16**
See also AAYA 22; CA 159; 97-100; SATA
27; SATA-Obit 24

Hitchens, Christopher 1949- .... **CLC 157**
See also CA 152; CANR 89, 155

Hitchens, Christopher Eric
See Hitchens, Christopher

Hitler, Adolf 1889-1945 .... **TCLC 53**
See also CA 117; 147

Hoagland, Edward (Morley) 1932- .. **CLC 28**
See also ANW; CA 1-4R; CANR 2, 31, 57,
107; CN 1, 2, 3, 4, 5, 6, 7; DLB 6; SATA
51; TCWW 2

Hoban, Russell 1925- .... **CLC 7, 25**
See also BPFB 2; CA 5-8R; CANR 23, 37,
66, 114, 138; CLR 3, 69, 139; CN 4, 5, 6,
7; CWRI 5; DAM NOV; DLB 52; FANT;
MAICYA 1, 2; MTCW 1, 2; MTFW 2005;
SATA 1, 40, 78, 136; SFW 4; SUFW 2;
TCLE 1:1

Hobbes, Thomas 1588-1679 .... **LC 36, 142**
See also DLB 151, 252, 281; RGEL 2

Hobbs, Perry
See Blackmur, R(ichard) P(almer)

Hobson, Laura Z(ametkin)
1900-1986 .... **CLC 7, 25**
See also BPFB 2; CA 17-20R; 118; CANR
55; CN 1, 2, 3, 4; DLB 28; SATA 52

Hoccleve, Thomas c. 1368-c. 1437 ...... **LC 75**
See also DLB 146; RGEL 2

Hoch, Edward D. 1930-2008
See Queen, Ellery
See also CA 29-32R; CANR 11, 27, 51, 97;
CMW 4; DLB 306; SFW 4

Hochhuth, Rolf 1931- .... **CLC 4, 11, 18**
See also CA 5-8R; CANR 33, 75, 136;
CWW 2; DAM DRAM; DLB 124; EWL
3; MTCW 1, 2; MTFW 2005; RGHL

Hochman, Sandra 1936- .... **CLC 3, 8**
See also CA 5-8R; CP 1, 2, 3, 4, 5; DLB 5

Hochwaelder, Fritz 1911-1986 .... **CLC 36**
See Hochwalder, Fritz
See also CA 29-32R; 120; CANR 42; DAM
DRAM; MTCW 1; RGWL 3

Hochwalder, Fritz
See Hochwaelder, Fritz
See also EWL 3; RGWL 2

Hocking, Mary (Eunice) 1921- .... **CLC 13**
See also CA 101; CANR 18, 40

Hodge, Merle 1944- .... **BLC 2:2**
See also EWL 3

Hodgins, Jack 1938- .... **CLC 23**
See also CA 93-96; CN 4, 5, 6, 7; DLB 60

Hodgson, William Hope
1877(?)-1918 .... **TCLC 13**
See also CA 111; 164; CMW 4; DLB 70,
153, 156, 178; HGG; MTCW 2; SFW 4;
SUFW 1

Hoeg, Peter 1957- .... **CLC 95, 156**
See also CA 151; CANR 75; CMW 4; DA3;
DLB 214; EWL 3; MTCW 2; MTFW
2005; NFS 17; RGWL 3; SSFS 18

Hoffman, Alice 1952- .... **CLC 51**
See also AAYA 37; AMWS 10; CA 77-80;
CANR 34, 66, 100, 138, 170; CN 4, 5, 6,
7; CPW; DAM NOV; DLB 292; MAL 5;
MTCW 1, 2; MTFW 2005; TCLE 1:1

Hoffman, Daniel (Gerard) 1923- . **CLC 6, 13,
23**
See also CA 1-4R; CANR 4, 142; CP 1, 2,
3, 4, 5, 6, 7; DLB 5; TCLE 1:1

Hoffman, Eva 1945- .... **CLC 182**
See also AMWS 16; CA 132; CANR 146

Hoffman, Stanley 1944- .... **CLC 5**
See also CA 77-80

Hoffman, William 1925- .... **CLC 141**
See also AMWS 18; CA 21-24R; CANR 9,
103; CSW; DLB 234; TCLE 1:1

Hoffman, William M.
See Hoffman, William M(oses)
See also CAD; CD 5, 6

Hoffman, William M(oses) 1939- ..... **CLC 40**
See Hoffman, William M.
See also CA 57-60; CANR 11, 71

Hoffmann, E(rnst) T(heodor) A(madeus)
1776-1822 ..... **NCLC 2, 183; SSC 13, 92**
See also CDWLB 2; CLR 133; DLB 90;
EW 5; GL 2; RGSF 2; RGWL 2, 3; SATA
27; SUFW 1; WCH

Hofmann, Gert 1931-1993 .... **CLC 54**
See also CA 128; CANR 145; EWL 3;
RGHL

Hofmannsthal, Hugo von 1874-1929 ... **DC 4;
TCLC 11**
See also CA 106; 153; CDWLB 2; DAM
DRAM; DFS 17; DLB 81, 118; EW 9;
EWL 3; RGWL 2, 3

Hogan, Linda 1947- ..... **CLC 73; NNAL; PC
35**
See also AMWS 4; ANW; BYA 12; CA 120,
226; CAAE 226; CANR 45, 73, 129;
CWP; DAM MULT; DLB 175; SATA
132; TCWW 2

Hogarth, Charles
See Creasey, John

Hogarth, Emmett
See Polonsky, Abraham (Lincoln)

Hogarth, William 1697-1764 .... **LC 112**
See also AAYA 56

Hogg, James 1770-1835 .... **NCLC 4, 109**
See also BRWS 10; DLB 93, 116, 159; GL
2; HGG; RGEL 2; SUFW 1

Holbach, Paul-Henri Thiry
1723-1789 .... **LC 14**
See also DLB 313

Holberg, Ludvig 1684-1754 .... **LC 6**
See also DLB 300; RGWL 2, 3

Holcroft, Thomas 1745-1809 .... **NCLC 85**
See also DLB 39, 89, 158; RGEL 2

Holden, Ursula 1921- .... **CLC 18**
See also CA 101; CAAS 8; CANR 22

Holderlin, (Johann Christian) Friedrich
1770-1843 .... **NCLC 16, 187; PC 4**
See also CDWLB 2; DLB 90; EW 5; RGWL
2, 3

Holding, James (Clark Carlisle, Jr.)
1907-1997
See Queen, Ellery
See also CA 25-28R; SATA 3

Holdstock, Robert 1948- .... **CLC 39**
See also CA 131; CANR 81; DLB 261;
FANT; HGG; SFW 4; SUFW 2

Holdstock, Robert P.
See Holdstock, Robert

Holinshed, Raphael fl. 1580- .... **LC 69**
See also DLB 167; RGEL 2

Holland, Isabelle (Christian)
1920-2002 .... **CLC 21**
See also AAYA 11, 64; CA 21-24R; 205;
CAAE 181; CANR 10, 25, 47; CLR 57;
CWRI 5; JRDA; LAIT 4; MAICYA 1, 2;
SATA 8, 70; SATA-Essay 103; SATA-Obit
132; WYA

Holland, Marcus
See Caldwell, (Janet Miriam) Taylor
(Holland)

Hollander, John 1929- .... **CLC 2, 5, 8, 14**
See also CA 1-4R; CANR 1, 52, 136; CP 1,
2, 3, 4, 5, 6, 7; DLB 5; MAL 5; SATA 13

Hollander, Paul
See Silverberg, Robert

Holleran, Andrew **CLC 38**
See Garber, Eric
See also CA 144; GLL 1

Holley, Marietta 1836(?)-1926 .... **TCLC 99**
See also CA 118; DLB 11; FL 1:3

Hollinghurst, Alan 1954- .... **CLC 55, 91**
See also BRWS 10; CA 114; CN 5, 6, 7;
DLB 207, 326; GLL 1

Hollis, Jim
See Summers, Hollis (Spurgeon, Jr.)

Holly, Buddy 1936-1959 .... **TCLC 65**
See also CA 213

Holmes, Gordon
See Shiel, M(atthew) P(hipps)

Holmes, John
See Souster, (Holmes) Raymond

Holmes, John Clellon 1926-1988 ...... **CLC 56**
See also BG 1:2; CA 9-12R; 125; CANR 4;
CN 1, 2, 3, 4; DLB 16, 237

Holmes, Oliver Wendell, Jr.
1841-1935 .... **TCLC 77**
See also CA 114; 186

Holmes, Oliver Wendell
1809-1894 .... **NCLC 14, 81; PC 71**
See also AMWS 1; CDALB 1640-1865;
DLB 1, 189, 235; EXPP; PFS 24; RGAL
4; SATA 34

Holmes, Raymond
See Souster, (Holmes) Raymond

Holt, Victoria
See Hibbert, Eleanor Alice Burford
See also BPFB 2

Holub, Miroslav 1923-1998 .... **CLC 4**
See also CA 21-24R; 169; CANR 10; CD-
WLB 4; CWW 2; DLB 232; EWL 3;
RGWL 3

Holz, Detlev
See Benjamin, Walter

Homer c. 8th cent. B.C.- .... **CMLC 1, 16, 61;
PC 23; WLCS**
See also AW 1; CDWLB 1; DA; DA3;
DAB; DAC; DAM MST, POET; DLB
176; EFS 1; LAIT 1; LMFS 1; RGWL 2,
3; TWA; WLIT 8; WP

Hong, Maxine Ting Ting
See Kingston, Maxine Hong

Hongo, Garrett Kaoru 1951- .... **PC 23**
See also CA 133; CAAS 22; CP 5, 6, 7; DLB 120, 312; EWL 3; EXPP; PFS 25; RGAL 4

Honig, Edwin 1919- .... **CLC 33**
See also CA 5-8R; CAAS 8; CANR 4, 45, 144; CP 1, 2, 3, 4, 5, 6, 7; DLB 5

Hood, Hugh (John Blagdon) 1928- . **CLC 15, 28; SSC 42**
See also CA 49-52; CAAS 17; CANR 1, 33, 87; CN 1, 2, 3, 4, 5, 6, 7; DLB 53; RGSF 2

Hood, Thomas 1799-1845 . **NCLC 16; PC 93**
See also BRW 4; DLB 96; RGEL 2

Hooker, (Peter) Jeremy 1941- .... **CLC 43**
See also CA 77-80; CANR 22; CP 2, 3, 4, 5, 6, 7; DLB 40

Hooker, Richard 1554-1600 .... **LC 95**
See also BRW 1; DLB 132; RGEL 2

Hooker, Thomas 1586-1647 .... **LC 137**
See also DLB 24

hooks, bell 1952(?)- .... **BLCS; CLC 94**
See also BW 2; CA 143; CANR 87, 126; DLB 246; MTCW 2; MTFW 2005; SATA 115, 170

Hooper, Johnson Jones 1815-1862 .... **NCLC 177**
See also DLB 3, 11, 248; RGAL 4

Hope, A(lec) D(erwent) 1907-2000 .... **CLC 3, 51; PC 56**
See also BRWS 7; CA 21-24R; 188; CANR 33, 74; CP 1, 2, 3, 4, 5; DLB 289; EWL 3; MTCW 1, 2; MTFW 2005; PFS 8; RGEL 2

Hope, Anthony 1863-1933 .... **TCLC 83**
See also CA 157; DLB 153, 156; RGEL 2; RHW

Hope, Brian
See Creasey, John

Hope, Christopher 1944- .... **CLC 52**
See also AFW; CA 106; CANR 47, 101, 177; CN 4, 5, 6, 7; DLB 225; SATA 62

Hope, Christopher David Tully
See Hope, Christopher

Hopkins, Gerard Manley 1844-1889 .... **NCLC 17, 189; PC 15; WLC 3**
See also BRW 5; BRWR 2; CDBLB 1890-1914; DA; DA3; DAB; DAC; DAM MST, POET; DLB 35, 57; EXPP; PAB; PFS 26; RGEL 2; TEA; WP

Hopkins, John (Richard) 1931-1998 .. **CLC 4**
See also CA 85-88; 169; CBD; CD 5, 6

Hopkins, Pauline Elizabeth 1859-1930 .... **BLC 1:2; TCLC 28**
See also AFAW 2; BW 2, 3; CA 141; CANR 82; DAM MULT; DLB 50

Hopkinson, Francis 1737-1791 .... **LC 25**
See also DLB 31; RGAL 4

Hopley-Woolrich, Cornell George 1903-1968
See Woolrich, Cornell
See also CA 13-14; CANR 58, 156; CAP 1; CMW 4; DLB 226; MTCW 2

Horace 65B.C.-8B.C. .... **CMLC 39; PC 46**
See also AW 2; CDWLB 1; DLB 211; RGWL 2, 3; WLIT 8

Horatio
See Proust, (Valentin-Louis-George-Eugene) Marcel

Horgan, Paul (George Vincent O'Shaughnessy) 1903-1995 .. **CLC 9, 53**
See also BPFB 2; CA 13-16R; 147; CANR 9, 35; CN 1, 2, 3, 4, 5; DAM NOV; DLB 102, 212; DLBY 1985; INT CANR-9; MTCW 1, 2; MTFW 2005; SATA 13; SATA-Obit 84; TCWW 1, 2

Horkheimer, Max 1895-1973 .... **TCLC 132**
See also CA 216; 41-44R; DLB 296

Horn, Peter
See Kuttner, Henry

Hornby, Nick 1957(?)- .... **CLC 243**
See also AAYA 74; CA 151; CANR 104, 151; CN 7; DLB 207

Horne, Frank (Smith) 1899-1974 ...... **HR 1:2**
See also BW 1; CA 125; 53-56; DLB 51; WP

Horne, Richard Henry Hengist 1802(?)-1884 .... **NCLC 127**
See also DLB 32; SATA 29

Hornem, Horace Esq.
See Byron, George Gordon (Noel)

Horne Tooke, John 1736-1812 ..... **NCLC 195**

Horney, Karen (Clementine Theodore Danielsen) 1885-1952 .... **TCLC 71**
See also CA 114; 165; DLB 246; FW

Hornung, E(rnest) W(illiam) 1866-1921 .... **TCLC 59**
See also CA 108; 160; CMW 4; DLB 70

Horovitz, Israel 1939- .... **CLC 56**
See also CA 33-36R; CAD; CANR 46, 59; CD 5, 6; DAM DRAM; DLB 7, 341; MAL 5

Horton, George Moses 1797(?)-1883(?) .... **NCLC 87**
See also DLB 50

Horvath, odon von 1901-1938
See von Horvath, Odon
See also EWL 3

Horvath, Oedoen von -1938
See von Horvath, Odon

Horwitz, Julius 1920-1986 .... **CLC 14**
See also CA 9-12R; 119; CANR 12

Horwitz, Ronald
See Harwood, Ronald

Hospital, Janette Turner 1942- .... **CLC 42, 145**
See also CA 108; CANR 48, 166; CN 5, 6, 7; DLB 325; DLBY 2002; RGSF 2

Hosseini, Khaled 1965- .... **CLC 254**
See also CA 225; SATA 156

Hostos, E. M. de
See Hostos (y Bonilla), Eugenio Maria de

Hostos, Eugenio M. de
See Hostos (y Bonilla), Eugenio Maria de

Hostos, Eugenio Maria
See Hostos (y Bonilla), Eugenio Maria de

Hostos (y Bonilla), Eugenio Maria de 1839-1903 .... **TCLC 24**
See also CA 123; 131; HW 1

Houdini
See Lovecraft, H. P.

Houellebecq, Michel 1958- .... **CLC 179**
See also CA 185; CANR 140; MTFW 2005

Hougan, Carolyn 1943-2007 .... **CLC 34**
See also CA 139; 257

Household, Geoffrey (Edward West) 1900-1988 .... **CLC 11**
See also CA 77-80; 126; CANR 58; CMW 4; CN 1, 2, 3, 4; DLB 87; SATA 14; SATA-Obit 59

Housman, A(lfred) E(dward) 1859-1936 .... **PC 2, 43; TCLC 1, 10; WLCS**
See also AAYA 66; BRW 6; CA 104; 125; DA; DA3; DAB; DAC; DAM MST, POET; DLB 19, 284; EWL 3; EXPP; MTCW 1, 2; MTFW 2005; PAB; PFS 4, 7; RGEL 2; TEA; WP

Housman, Laurence 1865-1959 .... **TCLC 7**
See also CA 106; 155; DLB 10; FANT; RGEL 2; SATA 25

Houston, Jeanne Wakatsuki 1934- .... **AAL**
See also AAYA 49; CA 103, 232; CAAE 232; CAAS 16; CANR 29, 123, 167; LAIT 4; SATA 78, 168; SATA-Essay 168

Hove, Chenjerai 1956- .... **BLC 2:2**
See also CP 7

Howard, Elizabeth Jane 1923- ..... **CLC 7, 29**
See also BRWS 11; CA 5-8R; CANR 8, 62, 146; CN 1, 2, 3, 4, 5, 6, 7

Howard, Maureen 1930- .... **CLC 5, 14, 46, 151**
See also CA 53-56; CANR 31, 75, 140; CN 4, 5, 6, 7; DLBY 1983; INT CANR-31; MTCW 1, 2; MTFW 2005

Howard, Richard 1929- .... **CLC 7, 10, 47**
See also AITN 1; CA 85-88; CANR 25, 80, 154; CP 1, 2, 3, 4, 5, 6, 7; DLB 5; INT CANR-25; MAL 5

Howard, Robert E 1906-1936 .... **TCLC 8**
See also BPFB 2; BYA 5; CA 105; 157; CANR 155; FANT; SUFW 1; TCWW 1, 2

Howard, Robert Ervin
See Howard, Robert E

Howard, Warren F.
See Pohl, Frederik

Howe, Fanny 1940- .... **CLC 47**
See also CA 117, 187; CAAE 187; CAAS 27; CANR 70, 116, 184; CP 6, 7; CWP; SATA-Brief 52

Howe, Fanny Quincy
See Howe, Fanny

Howe, Irving 1920-1993 .... **CLC 85**
See also AMWS 6; CA 9-12R; 141; CANR 21, 50; DLB 67; EWL 3; MAL 5; MTCW 1, 2; MTFW 2005

Howe, Julia Ward 1819-1910 . **PC 81; TCLC 21**
See also CA 117; 191; DLB 1, 189, 235; FW

Howe, Susan 1937- .... **CLC 72, 152; PC 54**
See also AMWS 4; CA 160; CP 5, 6, 7; CWP; DLB 120; FW; RGAL 4

Howe, Tina 1937- .... **CLC 48**
See also CA 109; CAD; CANR 125; CD 5, 6; CWD; DLB 341

Howell, James 1594(?)-1666 .... **LC 13**
See also DLB 151

Howells, W. D.
See Howells, William Dean

Howells, William D.
See Howells, William Dean

Howells, William Dean 1837-1920 ... **SSC 36; TCLC 7, 17, 41**
See also AMW; CA 104; 134; CDALB 1865-1917; DLB 12, 64, 74, 79, 189; LMFS 1; MAL 5; MTCW 2; RGAL 4; TUS

Howes, Barbara 1914-1996 .... **CLC 15**
See also CA 9-12R; 151; CAAS 3; CANR 53; CP 1, 2, 3, 4, 5, 6; SATA 5; TCLE 1:1

Hrabal, Bohumil 1914-1997 ...... **CLC 13, 67; TCLC 155**
See also CA 106; 156; CAAS 12; CANR 57; CWW 2; DLB 232; EWL 3; RGSF 2

Hrabanus Maurus 776(?)-856 .... **CMLC 78**
See also DLB 148

Hrotsvit of Gandersheim c. 935-c. 1000 .... **CMLC 29**
See also DLB 148

Hsi, Chu 1130-1200 .... **CMLC 42**

Hsun, Lu
See Lu Hsun

Hubbard, L. Ron 1911-1986 .... **CLC 43**
See also AAYA 64; CA 77-80; 118; CANR 52; CPW; DA3; DAM POP; FANT; MTCW 2; MTFW 2005; SFW 4

Hubbard, Lafayette Ronald
See Hubbard, L. Ron

Huch, Ricarda (Octavia) 1864-1947 .... **TCLC 13**
See also CA 111; 189; DLB 66; EWL 3

Huddle, David 1942- .... **CLC 49**
See also CA 57-60, 261; CAAS 20; CANR 89; DLB 130

Hudson, Jeffrey
    See Crichton, Michael
Hudson, W(illiam) H(enry)
    1841-1922 .... **TCLC 29**
    See also CA 115; 190; DLB 98, 153, 174;
    RGEL 2; SATA 35
Hueffer, Ford Madox
    See Ford, Ford Madox
Hughart, Barry 1934- .... **CLC 39**
    See also CA 137; FANT; SFW 4; SUFW 2
Hughes, Colin
    See Creasey, John
Hughes, David (John) 1930-2005 ..... **CLC 48**
    See also CA 116; 129; 238; CN 4, 5, 6, 7;
    DLB 14
Hughes, Edward James
    See Hughes, Ted
    See also DA3; DAM MST, POET
Hughes, (James Mercer) Langston
    1902-1967 .. **BLC 1:2; CLC 1, 5, 10, 15,**
    35, 44, 108; DC 3; HR 1:2; PC 1, 53;
    SSC 6, 90; WLC 3
    See also AAYA 12; AFAW 1, 2; AMWR 1;
    AMWS 1; BW 1, 3; CA 1-4R; 25-28R;
    CANR 1, 34, 82; CDALB 1929-1941;
    CLR 17; DA; DA3; DAB; DAC; DAM
    DRAM, MST, MULT, POET; DFS 6, 18;
    DLB 4, 7, 48, 51, 86, 228, 315; EWL 3;
    EXPP; EXPS; JRDA; LAIT 3; LMFS 2;
    MAICYA 1, 2; MAL 5; MTCW 1, 2;
    MTFW 2005; NFS 21; PAB; PFS 1, 3, 6,
    10, 15; RGAL 4; RGSF 2; SATA 4, 33;
    SSFS 4, 7; TUS; WCH; WP; YAW
Hughes, Richard (Arthur Warren)
    1900-1976 .... **CLC 1, 11; TCLC 204**
    See also CA 5-8R; 65-68; CANR 4; CN 1,
    2; DAM NOV; DLB 15, 161; EWL 3;
    MTCW 1; RGEL 2; SATA 8; SATA-Obit
    25
Hughes, Ted 1930-1998 . **CLC 2, 4, 9, 14, 37,**
    119; PC 7, 89
    See Hughes, Edward James
    See also BRWC 2; BRWR 2; BRWS 1; CA
    1-4R; 171; CANR 1, 33, 66, 108; CLR 3,
    131; CP 1, 2, 3, 4, 5, 6; DAB; DAC; DLB
    40, 161; EWL 3; EXPP; MAICYA 1, 2;
    MTCW 1, 2; MTFW 2005; PAB; PFS 4,
    19; RGEL 2; SATA 49; SATA-Brief 27;
    SATA-Obit 107; TEA; YAW
Hugo, Richard
    See Huch, Ricarda (Octavia)
Hugo, Richard F(ranklin)
    1923-1982 .... **CLC 6, 18, 32; PC 68**
    See also AMWS 6; CA 49-52; 108; CANR
    3; CP 1, 2, 3; DAM POET; DLB 5, 206;
    EWL 3; MAL 5; PFS 17; RGAL 4
Hugo, Victor (Marie) 1802-1885 .... **NCLC 3,**
    10, 21, 161, 189; PC 17; WLC 3
    See also AAYA 28; DA; DA3; DAB; DAC;
    DAM DRAM, MST, NOV, POET; DLB
    119, 192, 217; EFS 2; EW 6; EXPN; GFL
    1789 to the Present; LAIT 1, 2; NFS 5,
    20; RGWL 2, 3; SATA 47; TWA
Huidobro, Vicente
    See Huidobro Fernandez, Vicente Garcia
    See also DLB 283; EWL 3; LAW
Huidobro Fernandez, Vicente Garcia
    1893-1948 .... **TCLC 31**
    See Huidobro, Vicente
    See also CA 131; HW 1
Hulme, Keri 1947- .... **CLC 39, 130**
    See also CA 125; CANR 69; CN 4, 5, 6, 7;
    CP 6, 7; CWP; DLB 326; EWL 3; FW;
    INT CA-125; NFS 2
Hulme, T(homas) E(rnest)
    1883-1917 .... **TCLC 21**
    See also BRWS 6; CA 117; 203; DLB 19
Humboldt, Alexander von
    1769-1859 .... **NCLC 170**
    See also DLB 90

Humboldt, Wilhelm von
    1767-1835 .... **NCLC 134**
    See also DLB 90
Hume, David 1711-1776 .. **LC 7, 56, 156, 157**
    See also BRWS 3; DLB 104, 252, 336;
    LMFS 1; TEA
Humphrey, William 1924-1997 .... **CLC 45**
    See also AMWS 9; CA 77-80; 160; CANR
    68; CN 1, 2, 3, 4, 5, 6; CSW; DLB 6, 212,
    234, 278; TCWW 1, 2
Humphreys, Emyr Owen 1919- .... **CLC 47**
    See also CA 5-8R; CANR 3, 24; CN 1, 2,
    3, 4, 5, 6, 7; DLB 15
Humphreys, Josephine 1945- ..... **CLC 34, 57**
    See also CA 121; 127; CANR 97; CSW;
    DLB 292; INT CA-127
Huneker, James Gibbons
    1860-1921 .... **TCLC 65**
    See also CA 193; DLB 71; RGAL 4
Hungerford, Hesba Fay
    See Brinsmead, H(esba) F(ay)
Hungerford, Pixie
    See Brinsmead, H(esba) F(ay)
Hunt, E. Howard 1918-2007 .... **CLC 3**
    See also AITN 1; CA 45-48; 256; CANR 2,
    47, 103, 160; CMW 4
Hunt, Everette Howard, Jr.
    See Hunt, E. Howard
Hunt, Francesca
    See Holland, Isabelle (Christian)
Hunt, Howard
    See Hunt, E. Howard
Hunt, Kyle
    See Creasey, John
Hunt, (James Henry) Leigh
    1784-1859 .... **NCLC 1, 70; PC 73**
    See also DAM POET; DLB 96, 110, 144;
    RGEL 2; TEA
Hunt, Marsha 1946- .... **CLC 70**
    See also BW 2, 3; CA 143; CANR 79
Hunt, Violet 1866(?)-1942 .... **TCLC 53**
    See also CA 184; DLB 162, 197
Hunter, E. Waldo
    See Sturgeon, Theodore (Hamilton)
Hunter, Evan 1926-2005 .... **CLC 11, 31**
    See McBain, Ed
    See also AAYA 39; BPFB 2; CA 5-8R; 241;
    CANR 5, 38, 62, 97, 149; CMW 4; CN 1,
    2, 3, 4, 5, 6, 7; CPW; DAM POP; DLB
    306; DLBY 1982; INT CANR-5; MSW;
    MTCW 1; SATA 25; SATA-Obit 167;
    SFW 4
Hunter, Kristin
    See Lattany, Kristin (Elaine Eggleston)
    Hunter
    See also CN 1, 2, 3, 4, 5, 6
Hunter, Mary
    See Austin, Mary (Hunter)
Hunter, Mollie 1922- .... **CLC 21**
    See McIlwraith, Maureen Mollie Hunter
    See also AAYA 13, 71; BYA 6; CANR 37,
    78; CLR 25; DLB 161; JRDA; MAICYA
    1, 2; SAAS 7; SATA 54, 106, 139; SATA-
    Essay 139; WYA; YAW
Hunter, Robert (?)-1734 .... **LC 7**
Hurston, Zora Neale 1891-1960 ..... **BLC 1:2;**
    CLC 7, 30, 61; DC 12; HR 1:2; SSC 4,
    80; TCLC 121, 131; WLCS
    See also AAYA 15, 71; AFAW 1, 2; AMWS
    6; BW 1, 3; BYA 12; CA 85-88; CANR
    61; CDALBS; DA; DA3; DAC; DAM
    MST, MULT, NOV; DFS 6; DLB 51, 86;
    EWL 3; EXPN; EXPS; FL 1:6; FW; LAIT
    3; LATS 1:1; LMFS 2; MAL 5; MBL;
    MTCW 1, 2; MTFW 2005; NFS 3; RGAL
    4; RGSF 2; SSFS 1, 6, 11, 19, 21; TUS;
    YAW
Husserl, E. G.
    See Husserl, Edmund (Gustav Albrecht)

Husserl, Edmund (Gustav Albrecht)
    1859-1938 .... **TCLC 100**
    See also CA 116; 133; DLB 296
Huston, John (Marcellus)
    1906-1987 .... **CLC 20**
    See also CA 73-76; 123; CANR 34; DLB
    26
Hustvedt, Siri 1955- .... **CLC 76**
    See also CA 137; CANR 149
Hutcheson, Francis 1694-1746 .... **LC 157**
    See also DLB 252
Hutchinson, Lucy 1620-1675 .... **LC 149**
Hutten, Ulrich von 1488-1523 .... **LC 16**
    See also DLB 179
Huxley, Aldous (Leonard)
    1894-1963 .... **CLC 1, 3, 4, 5, 8, 11, 18,**
    35, 79; SSC 39; WLC 3
    See also AAYA 11; BPFB 2; BRW 7; CA
    85-88; CANR 44, 99; CDBLB 1914-1945;
    DA; DA3; DAB; DAC; DAM MST, NOV;
    DLB 36, 100, 162, 195, 255; EWL 3;
    EXPN; LAIT 5; LMFS 2; MTCW 1, 2;
    MTFW 2005; NFS 6; RGEL 2; SATA 63;
    SCFW 1, 2; SFW 4; TEA; YAW
Huxley, T(homas) H(enry)
    1825-1895 .... **NCLC 67**
    See also DLB 57; TEA
Huygens, Constantijn 1596-1687 .... **LC 114**
    See also RGWL 2, 3
Huysmans, Joris-Karl 1848-1907 ... **TCLC 7,**
    69, 212
    See also CA 104; 165; DLB 123; EW 7;
    GFL 1789 to the Present; LMFS 2; RGWL
    2, 3
Hwang, David Henry 1957- .... **CLC 55, 196;**
    DC 4, 23
    See also CA 127; 132; CAD; CANR 76,
    124; CD 5, 6; DA3; DAM DRAM; DFS
    11, 18; DLB 212, 228, 312; INT CA-132;
    MAL 5; MTCW 2; MTFW 2005; RGAL
    4
Hyde, Anthony 1946- .... **CLC 42**
    See Chase, Nicholas
    See also CA 136; CCA 1
Hyde, Margaret O. 1917- .... **CLC 21**
    See also CA 1-4R; CANR 1, 36, 137, 181;
    CLR 23; JRDA; MAICYA 1, 2; SAAS 8;
    SATA 1, 42, 76, 139
Hyde, Margaret Oldroyd
    See Hyde, Margaret O.
Hynes, James 1956(?)- .... **CLC 65**
    See also CA 164; CANR 105
Hypatia c. 370-415 .... **CMLC 35**
Ian, Janis 1951- .... **CLC 21**
    See also CA 105; 187
Ibanez, Vicente Blasco
    See Blasco Ibanez, Vicente
    See also DLB 322
Ibarbourou, Juana de
    1895(?)-1979 .... **HLCS 2**
    See also DLB 290; HW 1; LAW
Ibarguengoitia, Jorge 1928-1983 ..... **CLC 37;**
    TCLC 148
    See also CA 124; 113; EWL 3; HW 1
Ibn Arabi 1165-1240 .... **CMLC 105**
Ibn Battuta, Abu Abdalla
    1304-1368(?) .... **CMLC 57**
    See also WLIT 2
Ibn Hazm 994-1064 .... **CMLC 64**
Ibn Zaydun 1003-1070 .... **CMLC 89**
Ibsen, Henrik (Johan) 1828-1906 .. **DC 2, 30;**
    TCLC 2, 8, 16, 37, 52; WLC 3
    See also AAYA 46; CA 104; 141; DA; DA3;
    DAB; DAC; DAM DRAM, MST; DFS 1,
    6, 8, 10, 11, 15, 16, 25; EW 7; LAIT 2;
    LATS 1:1; MTFW 2005; RGWL 2, 3
Ibuse, Masuji 1898-1993 .... **CLC 22**
    See Ibuse Masuji
    See also CA 127; 141; MJW; RGWL 3

Ibuse Masuji
See Ibuse, Masuji
See also CWW 2; DLB 180; EWL 3

Ichikawa, Kon 1915-2008 .... **CLC 20**
See also CA 121; 269

Ichiyo, Higuchi 1872-1896 .... **NCLC 49**
See also MJW

Idle, Eric 1943- .... **CLC 21**
See Monty Python
See also CA 116; CANR 35, 91, 148

Idris, Yusuf 1927-1991 .... **SSC 74**
See also AFW; DLB 346; EWL 3; RGSF 2,
3; RGWL 3; WLIT 2

Ignatieff, Michael 1947- .... **CLC 236**
See also CA 144; CANR 88, 156; CN 6, 7;
DLB 267

Ignatieff, Michael Grant
See Ignatieff, Michael

Ignatow, David 1914-1997 .... **CLC 4, 7, 14,
40; PC 34**
See also CA 9-12R; 162; CAAS 3; CANR
31, 57, 96; CP 1, 2, 3, 4, 5, 6; DLB 5;
EWL 3; MAL 5

Ignotus
See Strachey, (Giles) Lytton

Ihimaera, Witi (Tame) 1944- .... **CLC 46**
See also CA 77-80; CANR 130; CN 2, 3, 4,
5, 6, 7; RGSF 2; SATA 148

Il'f, Il'ia
See Fainzilberg, Ilya Arnoldovich
See also DLB 272

Ilf, Ilya
See Fainzilberg, Ilya Arnoldovich

Illyes, Gyula 1902-1983 .... **PC 16**
See also CA 114; 109; CDWLB 4; DLB
215; EWL 3; RGWL 2, 3

Imalayen, Fatima-Zohra
See Djebar, Assia

Immermann, Karl (Lebrecht)
1796-1840 .... **NCLC 4, 49**
See also DLB 133

Ince, Thomas H. 1882-1924 .... **TCLC 89**
See also IDFW 3, 4

Inchbald, Elizabeth 1753-1821 ...... **NCLC 62**
See also DLB 39, 89; RGEL 2

Inclan, Ramon (Maria) del Valle
See Valle-Inclan, Ramon (Maria) del

Infante, G(uillermo) Cabrera
See Cabrera Infante, G.

Ingalls, Rachel 1940- .... **CLC 42**
See also CA 123; 127; CANR 154

Ingalls, Rachel Holmes
See Ingalls, Rachel

Ingamells, Reginald Charles
See Ingamells, Rex

Ingamells, Rex 1913-1955 .... **TCLC 35**
See also CA 167; DLB 260

Inge, William (Motter) 1913-1973 ..... **CLC 1,
8, 19**
See also CA 9-12R; CAD; CDALB 1941-
1968; DA3; DAM DRAM; DFS 1, 3, 5,
8; DLB 7, 249; EWL 3; MAL 5; MTCW
1, 2; MTFW 2005; RGAL 4; TUS

Ingelow, Jean 1820-1897 .... **NCLC 39, 107**
See also DLB 35, 163; FANT; SATA 33

Ingram, Willis J.
See Harris, Mark

Innaurato, Albert (F.) 1948(?)- ... **CLC 21, 60**
See also CA 115; 122; CAD; CANR 78;
CD 5, 6; INT CA-122

Innes, Michael
See Stewart, J(ohn) I(nnes) M(ackintosh)
See also DLB 276; MSW

Innis, Harold Adams 1894-1952 .... **TCLC 77**
See also CA 181; DLB 88

Insluis, Alanus de
See Alain de Lille

Iola
See Wells-Barnett, Ida B(ell)

Ionesco, Eugene 1912-1994 ... **CLC 1, 4, 6, 9,
11, 15, 41, 86; DC 12; WLC 3**
See also CA 9-12R; 144; CANR 55, 132;
CWW 2; DA; DA3; DAB; DAC; DAM
DRAM, MST; DFS 4, 9, 25; DLB 321;
EW 13; EWL 3; GFL 1789 to the Present;
LMFS 2; MTCW 1, 2; MTFW 2005;
RGWL 2, 3; SATA 7; SATA-Obit 79;
TWA

Iqbal, Muhammad 1877-1938 .... **TCLC 28**
See also CA 215; EWL 3

Ireland, Patrick
See O'Doherty, Brian

Irenaeus St. 130- .... **CMLC 42**

Irigaray, Luce 1930- .... **CLC 164**
See also CA 154; CANR 121; FW

Iron, Ralph
See Schreiner, Olive (Emilie Albertina)

Irving, John 1942- . **CLC 13, 23, 38, 112, 175**
See also AAYA 8, 62; AMWS 6; BEST
89:3; BPFB 2; CA 25-28R; CANR 28, 73,
112, 133; CN 3, 4, 5, 6, 7; CPW; DA3;
DAM NOV, POP; DLB 6, 278; DLBY
1982; EWL 3; MAL 5; MTCW 1, 2;
MTFW 2005; NFS 12, 14; RGAL 4; TUS

Irving, John Winslow
See Irving, John

Irving, Washington 1783-1859 . **NCLC 2, 19,
95; SSC 2, 37, 104; WLC 3**
See also AAYA 56; AMW; CDALB 1640-
1865; CLR 97; DA; DA3; DAB; DAC;
DAM MST; DLB 3, 11, 30, 59, 73, 74,
183, 186, 250, 254; EXPS; GL 2; LAIT
1; RGAL 4; RGSF 2; SSFS 1, 8, 16;
SUFW 1; TUS; WCH; YABC 2

Irwin, P. K.
See Page, P(atricia) K(athleen)

Isaacs, Jorge Ricardo 1837-1895 ... **NCLC 70**
See also LAW

Isaacs, Susan 1943- .... **CLC 32**
See also BEST 89:1; BPFB 2; CA 89-92;
CANR 20, 41, 65, 112, 134, 165; CPW;
DA3; DAM POP; INT CANR-20; MTCW
1, 2; MTFW 2005

Isherwood, Christopher 1904-1986 ... **CLC 1,
9, 11, 14, 44; SSC 56**
See also AMWS 14; BRW 7; CA 13-16R;
117; CANR 35, 97, 133; CN 1, 2, 3; DA3;
DAM DRAM, NOV; DLB 15, 195; DLBY
1986; EWL 3; IDTP; MTCW 1, 2; MTFW
2005; RGAL 4; RGEL 2; TUS; WLIT 4

Ishiguro, Kazuo 1954- . **CLC 27, 56, 59, 110,
219**
See also AAYA 58; BEST 90:2; BPFB 2;
BRWS 4; CA 120; CANR 49, 95, 133;
CN 5, 6, 7; DA3; DAM NOV; DLB 194,
326; EWL 3; MTCW 1, 2; MTFW 2005;
NFS 13; WLIT 4; WWE 1

Ishikawa, Hakuhin
See Ishikawa, Takuboku

Ishikawa, Takuboku 1886(?)-1912 ..... **PC 10;
TCLC 15**
See Ishikawa Takuboku
See also CA 113; 153; DAM POET

Isidore of Seville c. 560-636 .... **CMLC 101**

Iskander, Fazil (Abdulovich) 1929- .. **CLC 47**
See Iskander, Fazil' Abdulevich
See also CA 102; EWL 3

Iskander, Fazil' Abdulevich
See Iskander, Fazil (Abdulovich)
See also DLB 302

Isler, Alan (David) 1934- .... **CLC 91**
See also CA 156; CANR 105

Ivan IV 1530-1584 .... **LC 17**

Ivanov, V.I.
See Ivanov, Vyacheslav

Ivanov, Vyacheslav 1866-1949 .... **TCLC 33**
See also CA 122; EWL 3

Ivanov, Vyacheslav Ivanovich
See Ivanov, Vyacheslav

Ivask, Ivar Vidrik 1927-1992 .... **CLC 14**
See also CA 37-40R; 139; CANR 24

Ives, Morgan
See Bradley, Marion Zimmer
See also GLL 1

Izumi Shikibu c. 973-c. 1034 .... **CMLC 33**

J. R. S.
See Gogarty, Oliver St. John

Jabran, Kahlil
See Gibran, Kahlil

Jabran, Khalil
See Gibran, Kahlil

Jackson, Daniel
See Wingrove, David

Jackson, Helen Hunt 1830-1885 .... **NCLC 90**
See also DLB 42, 47, 186, 189; RGAL 4

Jackson, Jesse 1908-1983 .... **CLC 12**
See also BW 1; CA 25-28R; 109; CANR
27; CLR 28; CWRI 5; MAICYA 1, 2;
SATA 2, 29; SATA-Obit 48

Jackson, Laura (Riding) 1901-1991 .... **PC 44**
See Riding, Laura
See also CA 65-68; 135; CANR 28, 89;
DLB 48

Jackson, Sam
See Trumbo, Dalton

Jackson, Sara
See Wingrove, David

Jackson, Shirley 1919-1965 . **CLC 11, 60, 87;
SSC 9, 39; TCLC 187; WLC 3**
See also AAYA 9; AMWS 9; BPFB 2; CA
1-4R; 25-28R; CANR 4, 52; CDALB
1941-1968; DA; DA3; DAC; DAM MST;
DLB 6, 234; EXPS; HGG; LAIT 4; MAL
5; MTCW 2; MTFW 2005; RGAL 4;
RGSF 2; SATA 2; SSFS 1; SUFW 1, 2

Jacob, (Cyprien-)Max 1876-1944 .... **TCLC 6**
See also CA 104; 193; DLB 258; EWL 3;
GFL 1789 to the Present; GLL 2; RGWL
2, 3

Jacobs, Harriet A(nn)
1813(?)-1897 .... **NCLC 67, 162**
See also AFAW 1, 2; DLB 239; FL 1:3; FW;
LAIT 2; RGAL 4

Jacobs, Jim 1942- .... **CLC 12**
See also CA 97-100; INT CA-97-100

Jacobs, W(illiam) W(ymark)
1863-1943 .... **SSC 73; TCLC 22**
See also CA 121; 167; DLB 135; EXPS;
HGG; RGEL 2; RGSF 2; SSFS 2; SUFW
1

Jacobsen, Jens Peter 1847-1885 .... **NCLC 34**

Jacobsen, Josephine (Winder)
1908-2003 .... **CLC 48, 102; PC 62**
See also CA 33-36R; 218; CAAS 18; CANR
23, 48; CCA 1; CP 2, 3, 4, 5, 6, 7; DLB
244; PFS 23; TCLE 1:1

Jacobson, Dan 1929- ...... **CLC 4, 14; SSC 91**
See also AFW; CA 1-4R; CANR 2, 25, 66,
170; CN 1, 2, 3, 4, 5, 6, 7; DLB 14, 207,
225, 319; EWL 3; MTCW 1; RGSF 2

Jacopone da Todi 1236-1306 .... **CMLC 95**

Jacqueline
See Carpentier (y Valmont), Alejo

Jacques de Vitry c. 1160-1240 ...... **CMLC 63**
See also DLB 208

Jagger, Michael Philip
See Jagger, Mick

Jagger, Mick 1943- .... **CLC 17**
See also CA 239

Jahiz, al- c. 780-c. 869 .... **CMLC 25**
See also DLB 311

Jakes, John 1932- .... **CLC 29**
See also AAYA 32; BEST 89:4; BPFB 2;
CA 57-60, 214; CAAE 214; CANR 10,
43, 66, 111, 142, 171; CPW; CSW; DA3;
DAM NOV, POP; DLB 278; DLBY 1983;
FANT; INT CANR-10; MTCW 1, 2;
MTFW 2005; RHW; SATA 62; SFW 4;
TCWW 1, 2

Jakes, John William
See Jakes, John

James I 1394-1437 .... **LC 20**
See also RGEL 2

James, Andrew
See Kirkup, James

James, C(yril) L(ionel) R(obert)
1901-1989 .... **BLCS; CLC 33**
See also BW 2; CA 117; 125; 128; CANR
62; CN 1, 2, 3, 4; DLB 125; MTCW 1

James, Daniel (Lewis) 1911-1988
See Santiago, Danny
See also CA 174; 125

James, Dynely
See Mayne, William (James Carter)

James, Henry Sr. 1811-1882 .... **NCLC 53**

James, Henry 1843-1916 .... **SSC 8, 32, 47,
108; TCLC 2, 11, 24, 40, 47, 64, 171;
WLC 3**
See also AMW; AMWC 1; AMWR 1; BPFB
2; BRW 6; CA 104; 132; CDALB 1865-
1917; DA; DA3; DAB; DAC; DAM MST,
NOV; DLB 12, 71, 74, 189; DLBD 13;
EWL 3; EXPS; GL 2; HGG; LAIT 2;
MAL 5; MTCW 1, 2; MTFW 2005; NFS
12, 16, 19; RGAL 4; RGEL 2; RGSF 2;
SSFS 9; SUFW 1; TUS

James, M. R. SSC 93
See James, Montague (Rhodes)
See also DLB 156, 201

James, Mary
See Meaker, Marijane

James, Montague (Rhodes)
1862-1936 .... **SSC 16; TCLC 6**
See James, M. R.
See also CA 104; 203; HGG; RGEL 2;
RGSF 2; SUFW 1

James, P. D. CLC 18, 46, 122, 226
See White, Phyllis Dorothy James
See also BEST 90:2; BPFB 2; BRWS 4;
CDBLB 1960 to Present; CN 4, 5, 6; DLB
87, 276; DLBD 17; MSW

James, Philip
See Moorcock, Michael

James, Samuel
See Stephens, James

James, Seumas
See Stephens, James

James, Stephen
See Stephens, James

James, T.F.
See Fleming, Thomas

James, William 1842-1910 .... **TCLC 15, 32**
See also AMW; CA 109; 193; DLB 270,
284; MAL 5; NCFS 5; RGAL 4

Jameson, Anna 1794-1860 .... **NCLC 43**
See also DLB 99, 166

Jameson, Fredric 1934- .... **CLC 142**
See also CA 196; CANR 169; DLB 67;
LMFS 2

Jameson, Fredric R.
See Jameson, Fredric

James VI of Scotland 1566-1625 .... **LC 109**
See also DLB 151, 172

Jami, Nur al-Din 'Abd al-Rahman
1414-1492 .... **LC 9**

Jammes, Francis 1868-1938 .... **TCLC 75**
See also CA 198; EWL 3; GFL 1789 to the
Present

Jandl, Ernst 1925-2000 .... **CLC 34**
See also CA 200; EWL 3

Janowitz, Tama 1957- .... **CLC 43, 145**
See also CA 106; CANR 52, 89, 129; CN
5, 6, 7; CPW; DAM POP; DLB 292;
MTFW 2005

Jansson, Tove (Marika) 1914-2001 ... **SSC 96**
See also CA 17-20R; 196; CANR 38, 118;
CLR 2, 125; CWW 2; DLB 257; EWL 3;
MAICYA 1, 2; RGSF 2; SATA 3, 41

Japrisot, Sébastien 1931- .... **CLC 90**
See Rossi, Jean-Baptiste
See also CMW 4; NFS 18

Jarrell, Randall 1914-1965 .... **CLC 1, 2, 6, 9,
13, 49; PC 41; TCLC 177**
See also AMW; BYA 5; CA 5-8R; 25-28R;
CABS 2; CANR 6, 34; CDALB 1941-
1968; CLR 6, 111; CWRI 5; DAM POET;
DLB 48, 52; EWL 3; EXPP; MAICYA 1,
2; MAL 5; MTCW 1, 2; PAB; PFS 2;
RGAL 4; SATA 7

Jarry, Alfred 1873-1907 .... **SSC 20; TCLC 2,
14, 147**
See also CA 104; 153; DA3; DAM DRAM;
DFS 8; DLB 192, 258; EW 9; EWL 3;
GFL 1789 to the Present; RGWL 2, 3;
TWA

Jarvis, E.K.
See Ellison, Harlan; Silverberg, Robert

Jawien, Andrzej
See John Paul II, Pope

Jaynes, Roderick
See Coen, Ethan

Jeake, Samuel, Jr.
See Aiken, Conrad (Potter)

Jean Paul 1763-1825 .... **NCLC 7**

Jefferies, (John) Richard
1848-1887 .... **NCLC 47**
See also DLB 98, 141; RGEL 2; SATA 16;
SFW 4

Jeffers, John Robinson
See Jeffers, Robinson

Jeffers, Robinson 1887-1962 .... **CLC 2, 3, 11,
15, 54; PC 17; WLC 3**
See also AMWS 2; CA 85-88; CANR 35;
CDALB 1917-1929; DA; DAC; DAM
MST, POET; DLB 45, 212, 342; EWL 3;
MAL 5; MTCW 1, 2; MTFW 2005; PAB;
PFS 3, 4; RGAL 4

Jefferson, Janet
See Mencken, H(enry) L(ouis)

Jefferson, Thomas 1743-1826 . **NCLC 11, 103**
See also AAYA 54; ANW; CDALB 1640-
1865; DA3; DLB 31, 183; LAIT 1; RGAL
4

Jeffrey, Francis 1773-1850 .... **NCLC 33**
See Francis, Lord Jeffrey

Jelakowitch, Ivan
See Heijermans, Herman

Jelinek, Elfriede 1946- .... **CLC 169**
See also AAYA 68; CA 154; CANR 169;
DLB 85, 330; FW

Jellicoe, (Patricia) Ann 1927- .... **CLC 27**
See also CA 85-88; CBD; CD 5, 6; CWD;
CWRI 5; DLB 13, 233; FW

Jelloun, Tahar ben
See Ben Jelloun, Tahar

Jemyma
See Holley, Marietta

Jen, Gish AAL; CLC 70, 198, 260
See Jen, Lillian
See also AMWC 2; CN 7; DLB 312

Jen, Lillian 1955-
See Jen, Gish
See also CA 135; CANR 89, 130

Jenkins, (John) Robin 1912- .... **CLC 52**
See also CA 1-4R; CANR 1, 135; CN 1, 2,
3, 4, 5, 6, 7; DLB 14, 271

Jennings, Elizabeth (Joan)
1926-2001 .... **CLC 5, 14, 131**
See also BRWS 5; CA 61-64; 200; CAAS
5; CANR 8, 39, 66, 127; CP 1, 2, 3, 4, 5,
6, 7; CWP; DLB 27; EWL 3; MTCW 1;
SATA 66

Jennings, Waylon 1937-2002 .... **CLC 21**

Jensen, Johannes V(ilhelm)
1873-1950 .... **TCLC 41**
See also CA 170; DLB 214, 330; EWL 3;
RGWL 3

Jensen, Laura (Linnea) 1948- .... **CLC 37**
See also CA 103

Jerome, Saint 345-420 .... **CMLC 30**
See also RGWL 3

Jerome, Jerome K(lapka)
1859-1927 .... **TCLC 23**
See also CA 119; 177; DLB 10, 34, 135;
RGEL 2

Jerrold, Douglas William
1803-1857 .... **NCLC 2**
See also DLB 158, 159, 344; RGEL 2

Jewett, (Theodora) Sarah Orne
1849-1909 . **SSC 6, 44, 110; TCLC 1, 22**
See also AAYA 76; AMW; AMWC 2;
AMWR 2; CA 108; 127; CANR 71; DLB
12, 74, 221; EXPS; FL 1:3; FW; MAL 5;
MBL; NFS 15; RGAL 4; RGSF 2; SATA
15; SSFS 4

Jewsbury, Geraldine (Endsor)
1812-1880 .... **NCLC 22**
See also DLB 21

Jhabvala, Ruth Prawer 1927- . **CLC 4, 8, 29,
94, 138; SSC 91**
See also BRWS 5; CA 1-4R; CANR 2, 29,
51, 74, 91, 128; CN 1, 2, 3, 4, 5, 6, 7;
DAB; DAM NOV; DLB 139, 194, 323,
326; EWL 3; IDFW 3, 4; INT CANR-29;
MTCW 1, 2; MTFW 2005; RGSF 2;
RGWL 2; RHW; TEA

Jibran, Kahlil
See Gibran, Kahlil

Jibran, Khalil
See Gibran, Kahlil

Jiles, Paulette 1943- .... **CLC 13, 58**
See also CA 101; CANR 70, 124, 170; CP
5; CWP

Jimenez (Mantecon), Juan Ramon
1881-1958 .... **HLC 1; PC 7; TCLC 4,
183**
See also CA 104; 131; CANR 74; DAM
MULT, POET; DLB 134, 330; EW 9;
EWL 3; HW 1; MTCW 1, 2; MTFW
2005; RGWL 2, 3

Jimenez, Ramon
See Jimenez (Mantecon), Juan Ramon

Jimenez Mantecon, Juan
See Jimenez (Mantecon), Juan Ramon

Jin, Ba 1904-2005
See Pa Chin
See also CA 244; CWW 2; DLB 328

Jin, Ha
See Jin, Xuefei

Jin, Xuefei 1956- .... **CLC 109, 262**
See Ha Jin
See also CA 152; CANR 91, 130, 184; DLB
244, 292; MTFW 2005; NFS 25; SSFS 17

Jodelle, Etienne 1532-1573 .... **LC 119**
See also DLB 327; GFL Beginnings to 1789

Joel, Billy CLC 26
See Joel, William Martin

Joel, William Martin 1949-
See Joel, Billy
See also CA 108

John, St.
See John of Damascus, St.

John of Damascus, St. c.
675-749 .... **CMLC 27, 95**
John of Salisbury c. 1115-1180 ..... **CMLC 63**
John of the Cross, St. 1542-1591 .... **LC 18, 146**
See also RGWL 2, 3
John Paul II, Pope 1920-2005 .... **CLC 128**
See also CA 106; 133; 238
Johnson, B(ryan) S(tanley William)
1933-1973 .... **CLC 6, 9**
See also CA 9-12R; 53-56; CANR 9; CN 1; CP 1, 2; DLB 14, 40; EWL 3; RGEL 2
Johnson, Benjamin F., of Boone
See Riley, James Whitcomb
Johnson, Charles (Richard) 1948- . **BLC 1:2, 2:2; CLC 7, 51, 65, 163**
See also AFAW 2; AMWS 6; BW 2, 3; CA 116; CAAS 18; CANR 42, 66, 82, 129; CN 5, 6, 7; DAM MULT; DLB 33, 278; MAL 5; MTCW 2; MTFW 2005; RGAL 4; SSFS 16
Johnson, Charles S(purgeon)
1893-1956 .... **HR 1:3**
See also BW 1, 3; CA 125; CANR 82; DLB 51, 91
Johnson, Denis 1949- . **CLC 52, 160; SSC 56**
See also CA 117; 121; CANR 71, 99, 178; CN 4, 5, 6, 7; DLB 120
Johnson, Diane 1934- ...... **CLC 5, 13, 48, 244**
See also BPFB 2; CA 41-44R; CANR 17, 40, 62, 95, 155; CN 4, 5, 6, 7; DLBY 1980; INT CANR-17; MTCW 1
Johnson, E(mily) Pauline 1861-1913 . **NNAL**
See also CA 150; CCA 1; DAC; DAM MULT; DLB 92, 175; TCWW 2
Johnson, Eyvind (Olof Verner)
1900-1976 .... **CLC 14**
See also CA 73-76; 69-72; CANR 34, 101; DLB 259, 330; EW 12; EWL 3
Johnson, Fenton 1888-1958 .... **BLC 1:2**
See also BW 1; CA 118; 124; DAM MULT; DLB 45, 50
Johnson, Georgia Douglas (Camp)
1880-1966 .... **HR 1:3**
See also BW 1; CA 125; DLB 51, 249; WP
Johnson, Helene 1907-1995 .... **HR 1:3**
See also CA 181; DLB 51; WP
Johnson, J. R.
See James, C(yril) L(ionel) R(obert)
Johnson, James Weldon
1871-1938 .... **BLC 1:2; HR 1:3; PC 24; TCLC 3, 19, 175**
See also AAYA 73; AFAW 1, 2; BW 1, 3; CA 104; 125; CANR 82; CDALB 1917-1929; CLR 32; DA3; DAM MULT, POET; DLB 51; EWL 3; EXPP; LMFS 2; MAL 5; MTCW 1, 2; MTFW 2005; NFS 22; PFS 1; RGAL 4; SATA 31; TUS
Johnson, Joyce 1935- .... **CLC 58**
See also BG 1:3; CA 125; 129; CANR 102
Johnson, Judith (Emlyn) 1936- .... **CLC 7, 15**
See Sherwin, Judith Johnson
See also CA 25-28R; 153; CANR 34; CP 6, 7
Johnson, Lionel (Pigot)
1867-1902 .... **TCLC 19**
See also CA 117; 209; DLB 19; RGEL 2
Johnson, Marguerite Annie
See Angelou, Maya
Johnson, Mel
See Malzberg, Barry N(athaniel)
Johnson, Pamela Hansford
1912-1981 .... **CLC 1, 7, 27**
See also CA 1-4R; 104; CANR 2, 28; CN 1, 2, 3; DLB 15; MTCW 1, 2; MTFW 2005; RGEL 2
Johnson, Paul 1928- .... **CLC 147**
See also BEST 89:4; CA 17-20R; CANR 34, 62, 100, 155

Johnson, Paul Bede
See Johnson, Paul
Johnson, Robert CLC 70
Johnson, Robert 1911(?)-1938 .... **TCLC 69**
See also BW 3; CA 174
Johnson, Samuel 1709-1784 . **LC 15, 52, 128; PC 81; WLC 3**
See also BRW 3; BRWR 1; CDBLB 1660-1789; DA; DAB; DAC; DAM MST; DLB 39, 95, 104, 142, 213; LMFS 1; RGEL 2; TEA
Johnson, Stacie
See Myers, Walter Dean
Johnson, Uwe 1934-1984 .. **CLC 5, 10, 15, 40**
See also CA 1-4R; 112; CANR 1, 39; CD-WLB 2; DLB 75; EWL 3; MTCW 1; RGWL 2, 3
Johnston, Basil H. 1929- .... **NNAL**
See also CA 69-72; CANR 11, 28, 66; DAC; DAM MULT; DLB 60
Johnston, George (Benson) 1913- .... **CLC 51**
See also CA 1-4R; CANR 5, 20; CP 1, 2, 3, 4, 5, 6, 7; DLB 88
Johnston, Jennifer (Prudence)
1930- .... **CLC 7, 150, 228**
See also CA 85-88; CANR 92; CN 4, 5, 6, 7; DLB 14
Joinville, Jean de 1224(?)-1317 ..... **CMLC 38**
Jolley, Elizabeth 1923-2007 ..... **CLC 46, 256, 260; SSC 19**
See also CA 127; 257; CAAS 13; CANR 59; CN 4, 5, 6, 7; DLB 325; EWL 3; RGSF 2
Jolley, Monica Elizabeth
See Jolley, Elizabeth
Jones, Arthur Llewellyn 1863-1947
See Machen, Arthur
See also CA 104; 179; HGG
Jones, D(ouglas) G(ordon) 1929- ..... **CLC 10**
See also CA 29-32R; CANR 13, 90; CP 1, 2, 3, 4, 5, 6, 7; DLB 53
Jones, David (Michael) 1895-1974 .... **CLC 2, 4, 7, 13, 42**
See also BRW 6; BRWS 7; CA 9-12R; 53-56; CANR 28; CDBLB 1945-1960; CP 1, 2; DLB 20, 100; EWL 3; MTCW 1; PAB; RGEL 2
Jones, David Robert 1947-
See Bowie, David
See also CA 103; CANR 104
Jones, Diana Wynne 1934- .... **CLC 26**
See also AAYA 12; BYA 6, 7, 9, 11, 13, 16; CA 49-52; CANR 4, 26, 56, 120, 167; CLR 23, 120; DLB 161; FANT; JRDA; MAICYA 1, 2; MTFW 2005; SAAS 7; SATA 9, 70, 108, 160; SFW 4; SUFW 2; YAW
Jones, Edward P. 1950- .. **BLC 2:2; CLC 76, 223**
See also AAYA 71; BW 2, 3; CA 142; CANR 79, 134; CSW; MTFW 2005; NFS 26
Jones, Everett LeRoi
See Baraka, Amiri
Jones, Gayl 1949- ... **BLC 1:2; CLC 6, 9, 131**
See also AFAW 1, 2; BW 2, 3; CA 77-80; CANR 27, 66, 122; CN 4, 5, 6, 7; CSW; DA3; DAM MULT; DLB 33, 278; MAL 5; MTCW 1, 2; MTFW 2005; RGAL 4
Jones, James 1921-1977 ...... **CLC 1, 3, 10, 39**
See also AITN 1, 2; AMWS 11; BPFB 2; CA 1-4R; 69-72; CANR 6; CN 1, 2; DLB 2, 143; DLBD 17; DLBY 1998; EWL 3; MAL 5; MTCW 1; RGAL 4
Jones, John J.
See Lovecraft, H. P.
Jones, LeRoi CLC 1, 2, 3, 5, 10, 14
See Baraka, Amiri
See also CN 1, 2; CP 1, 2, 3; MTCW 2

Jones, Louis B. 1953- .... **CLC 65**
See also CA 141; CANR 73
Jones, Madison 1925- .... **CLC 4**
See also CA 13-16R; CAAS 11; CANR 7, 54, 83, 158; CN 1, 2, 3, 4, 5, 6, 7; CSW; DLB 152
Jones, Madison Percy, Jr.
See Jones, Madison
Jones, Mervyn 1922- .... **CLC 10, 52**
See also CA 45-48; CAAS 5; CANR 1, 91; CN 1, 2, 3, 4, 5, 6, 7; MTCW 1
Jones, Mick 1956(?)- .... **CLC 30**
Jones, Nettie (Pearl) 1941- .... **CLC 34**
See also BW 2; CA 137; CAAS 20; CANR 88
Jones, Peter 1802-1856 .... **NNAL**
Jones, Preston 1936-1979 .... **CLC 10**
See also CA 73-76; 89-92; DLB 7
Jones, Robert F(rancis) 1934-2003 .... **CLC 7**
See also CA 49-52; CANR 2, 61, 118
Jones, Rod 1953- .... **CLC 50**
See also CA 128
Jones, Terence Graham Parry
1942- .... **CLC 21**
See Jones, Terry; Monty Python
See also CA 112; 116; CANR 35, 93, 173; INT CA-116; SATA 127
Jones, Terry
See Jones, Terence Graham Parry
See also SATA 67; SATA-Brief 51
Jones, Thom (Douglas) 1945(?)- ..... **CLC 81; SSC 56**
See also CA 157; CANR 88; DLB 244; SSFS 23
Jong, Erica 1942- .... **CLC 4, 6, 8, 18, 83**
See also AITN 1; AMWS 5; BEST 90:2; BPFB 2; CA 73-76; CANR 26, 52, 75, 132, 166; CN 3, 4, 5, 6, 7; CP 2, 3, 4, 5, 6, 7; CPW; DA3; DAM NOV, POP; DLB 2, 5, 28, 152; FW; INT CANR-26; MAL 5; MTCW 1, 2; MTFW 2005
Jonson, Ben(jamin) 1572(?)-1637 . **DC 4; LC 6, 33, 110, 158; PC 17; WLC 3**
See also BRW 1; BRWC 1; BRWR 1; CD-BLB Before 1660; DA; DAB; DAC; DAM DRAM, MST, POET; DFS 4, 10; DLB 62, 121; LMFS 1; PFS 23; RGEL 2; TEA; WLIT 3
Jordan, June 1936-2002 .. **BLCS; CLC 5, 11, 23, 114, 230; PC 38**
See also AAYA 2, 66; AFAW 1, 2; BW 2, 3; CA 33-36R; 206; CANR 25, 70, 114, 154; CLR 10; CP 3, 4, 5, 6, 7; CWP; DAM MULT, POET; DLB 38; GLL 2; LAIT 5; MAICYA 1, 2; MTCW 1; SATA 4, 136; YAW
Jordan, June Meyer
See Jordan, June
Jordan, Neil 1950- .... **CLC 110**
See also CA 124; 130; CANR 54, 154; CN 4, 5, 6, 7; GLL 2; INT CA-130
Jordan, Neil Patrick
See Jordan, Neil
Jordan, Pat(rick M.) 1941- .... **CLC 37**
See also CA 33-36R; CANR 121
Jorgensen, Ivar
See Ellison, Harlan
Jorgenson, Ivar
See Silverberg, Robert
Joseph, George Ghevarughese CLC 70
Josephson, Mary
See O'Doherty, Brian
Josephus, Flavius c. 37-100 ..... **CMLC 13, 93**
See also AW 2; DLB 176; WLIT 8
Josiah Allen's Wife
See Holley, Marietta

Josipovici, Gabriel 1940- ...... **CLC 6, 43, 153**
See also CA 37-40R, 224; CAAE 224;
CAAS 8; CANR 47, 84; CN 3, 4, 5, 6, 7;
DLB 14, 319
Josipovici, Gabriel David
See Josipovici, Gabriel
Joubert, Joseph 1754-1824 .... **NCLC 9**
Jouve, Pierre Jean 1887-1976 .... **CLC 47**
See also CA 252; 65-68; DLB 258; EWL 3
Jovine, Francesco 1902-1950 .... **TCLC 79**
See also DLB 264; EWL 3
Joyaux, Julia
See Kristeva, Julia
Joyce, James (Augustine Aloysius)
1882-1941 .... **DC 16; PC 22; SSC 3, 26,**
44, 64; TCLC 3, 8, 16, 35, 52, 159;
WLC 3
See also AAYA 42; BRW 7; BRWC 1;
BRWR 1; BYA 11, 13; CA 104; 126; CD-
BLB 1914-1945; DA; DA3; DAB; DAC;
DAM MST, NOV, POET; DLB 10, 19,
36, 162, 247; EWL 3; EXPN; EXPS;
LAIT 3; LMFS 1, 2; MTCW 1, 2; MTFW
2005; NFS 7, 26; RGSF 2; SSFS 1, 19;
TEA; WLIT 4
Jozsef, Attila 1905-1937 .... **TCLC 22**
See also CA 116; 230; CDWLB 4; DLB
215; EWL 3
Juana Ines de la Cruz, Sor
1651(?)-1695 ... **HLCS 1; LC 5, 136; PC**
24
See also DLB 305; FW; LAW; RGWL 2, 3;
WLIT 1
Juana Inez de La Cruz, Sor
See Juana Ines de la Cruz, Sor
Juan Manuel, Don 1282-1348 .... **CMLC 88**
Judd, Cyril
See Kornbluth, C(yril) M.; Pohl, Frederik
Juenger, Ernst 1895-1998 .... **CLC 125**
See Junger, Ernst
See also CA 101; 167; CANR 21, 47, 106;
DLB 56
Julian of Norwich 1342(?)-1416(?) . **LC 6, 52**
See also BRWS 12; DLB 146; LMFS 1
Julius Caesar 100B.C.-44B.C.
See Caesar, Julius
See also CDWLB 1; DLB 211
Jung, Patricia B.
See Hope, Christopher
Junger, Ernst
See Juenger, Ernst
See also CDWLB 2; EWL 3; RGWL 2, 3
Junger, Sebastian 1962- .... **CLC 109**
See also AAYA 28; CA 165; CANR 130,
171; MTFW 2005
Juniper, Alex
See Hospital, Janette Turner
Junius
See Luxemburg, Rosa
Junzaburo, Nishiwaki
See Nishiwaki, Junzaburo
See also EWL 3
Just, Ward 1935- .... **CLC 4, 27**
See also CA 25-28R; CANR 32, 87; CN 6,
7; DLB 335; INT CANR-32
Just, Ward Swift
See Just, Ward
Justice, Donald 1925-2004 ... **CLC 6, 19, 102;**
PC 64
See also AMWS 7; CA 5-8R; 230; CANR
26, 54, 74, 121, 122, 169; CP 1, 2, 3, 4,
5, 6, 7; CSW; DAM POET; DLBY 1983;
EWL 3; INT CANR-26; MAL 5; MTCW
2; PFS 14; TCLE 1:1
Justice, Donald Rodney
See Justice, Donald
Juvenal c. 60-c. 130 .... **CMLC 8**
See also AW 2; CDWLB 1; DLB 211;
RGWL 2, 3; WLIT 8

Juvenis
See Bourne, Randolph S(illiman)
K., Alice
See Knapp, Caroline
Kabakov, Sasha CLC 59
Kabir 1398(?)-1448(?) .... **LC 109; PC 56**
See also RGWL 2, 3
Kacew, Romain 1914-1980
See Gary, Romain
See also CA 108; 102
Kadare, Ismail 1936- .... **CLC 52, 190**
See also CA 161; CANR 165; EWL 3;
RGWL 3
Kadohata, Cynthia 1956(?)- ..... **CLC 59, 122**
See also AAYA 71; CA 140; CANR 124;
CLR 121; SATA 155, 180
Kafka, Franz 1883-1924 ... **SSC 5, 29, 35, 60;**
TCLC 2, 6, 13, 29, 47, 53, 112, 179;
WLC 3
See also AAYA 31; BPFB 2; CA 105; 126;
CDWLB 2; DA; DA3; DAB; DAC; DAM
MST, NOV; DLB 81; EW 9; EWL 3;
EXPS; LATS 1:1; LMFS 2; MTCW 1, 2;
MTFW 2005; NFS 7; RGSF 2; RGWL 2,
3; SFW 4; SSFS 3, 7, 12; TWA
Kafu
See Nagai, Kafu
See also MJW
Kahanovitch, Pinchas
See Der Nister
Kahanovitsch, Pinkhes
See Der Nister
Kahanovitsh, Pinkhes
See Der Nister
Kahn, Roger 1927- .... **CLC 30**
See also CA 25-28R; CANR 44, 69, 152;
DLB 171; SATA 37
Kain, Saul
See Sassoon, Siegfried (Lorraine)
Kaiser, Georg 1878-1945 .... **TCLC 9**
See also CA 106; 190; CDWLB 2; DLB
124; EWL 3; LMFS 2; RGWL 2, 3
Kaledin, Sergei CLC 59
Kaletski, Alexander 1946- .... **CLC 39**
See also CA 118; 143
Kalidasa fl. c. 400-455 .... **CMLC 9; PC 22**
See also RGWL 2, 3
Kallman, Chester (Simon)
1921-1975 .... **CLC 2**
See also CA 45-48; 53-56; CANR 3; CP 1,
2
Kaminsky, Melvin CLC 12, 217
See Brooks, Mel
See also AAYA 13, 48; DLB 26
Kaminsky, Stuart M. 1934- .... **CLC 59**
See also CA 73-76; CANR 29, 53, 89, 161;
CMW 4
Kaminsky, Stuart Melvin
See Kaminsky, Stuart M.
Kamo no Chomei 1153(?)-1216 .... **CMLC 66**
See also DLB 203
Kamo no Nagaakira
See Kamo no Chomei
Kandinsky, Wassily 1866-1944 .... **TCLC 92**
See also AAYA 64; CA 118; 155
Kane, Francis
See Robbins, Harold
Kane, Henry 1918-
See Queen, Ellery
See also CA 156; CMW 4
Kane, Paul
See Simon, Paul
Kane, Sarah 1971-1999 .... **DC 31**
See also BRWS 8; CA 190; CD 5, 6; DLB
310
Kanin, Garson 1912-1999 .... **CLC 22**
See also AITN 1; CA 5-8R; 177; CAD;
CANR 7, 78; DLB 7; IDFW 3, 4

Kaniuk, Yoram 1930- .... **CLC 19**
See also CA 134; DLB 299; RGHL
Kant, Immanuel 1724-1804 ..... **NCLC 27, 67**
See also DLB 94
Kantor, MacKinlay 1904-1977 .... **CLC 7**
See also CA 61-64; 73-76; CANR 60, 63;
CN 1, 2; DLB 9, 102; MAL 5; MTCW 2;
RHW; TCWW 1, 2
Kanze Motokiyo
See Zeami
Kaplan, David Michael 1946- .... **CLC 50**
See also CA 187
Kaplan, James 1951- .... **CLC 59**
See also CA 135; CANR 121
Karadzic, Vuk Stefanovic
1787-1864 .... **NCLC 115**
See also CDWLB 4; DLB 147
Karageorge, Michael
See Anderson, Poul
Karamzin, Nikolai Mikhailovich
1766-1826 .... **NCLC 3, 173**
See also DLB 150; RGSF 2
Karapanou, Margarita 1946- .... **CLC 13**
See also CA 101
Karinthy, Frigyes 1887-1938 .... **TCLC 47**
See also CA 170; DLB 215; EWL 3
Karl, Frederick R(obert)
1927-2004 .... **CLC 34**
See also CA 5-8R; 226; CANR 3, 44, 143
Karr, Mary 1955- .... **CLC 188**
See also AMWS 11; CA 151; CANR 100;
MTFW 2005; NCFS 5
Kastel, Warren
See Silverberg, Robert
Kataev, Evgeny Petrovich 1903-1942
See Petrov, Evgeny
See also CA 120
Kataphusin
See Ruskin, John
Katz, Steve 1935- .... **CLC 47**
See also CA 25-28R; CAAS 14, 64; CANR
12; CN 4, 5, 6, 7; DLBY 1983
Kauffman, Janet 1945- .... **CLC 42**
See also CA 117; CANR 43, 84; DLB 218;
DLBY 1986
Kaufman, Bob (Garnell)
1925-1986 .... **CLC 49; PC 74**
See also BG 1:3; BW 1; CA 41-44R; 118;
CANR 22; CP 1; DLB 16, 41
Kaufman, George S. 1889-1961 ...... **CLC 38;**
DC 17
See also CA 108; 93-96; DAM DRAM;
DFS 1, 10; DLB 7; INT CA-108; MTCW
2; MTFW 2005; RGAL 4; TUS
Kaufman, Moises 1964- .... **DC 26**
See also CA 211; DFS 22; MTFW 2005
Kaufman, Sue CLC 3, 8
See Barondess, Sue K(aufman)
Kavafis, Konstantinos Petrou 1863-1933
See Cavafy, C(onstantine) P(eter)
See also CA 104
Kavan, Anna 1901-1968 .... **CLC 5, 13, 82**
See also BRWS 7; CA 5-8R; CANR 6, 57;
DLB 255; MTCW 1; RGEL 2; SFW 4
Kavanagh, Dan
See Barnes, Julian
Kavanagh, Julie 1952- .... **CLC 119**
See also CA 163
Kavanagh, Patrick (Joseph)
1904-1967 .... **CLC 22; PC 33**
See also BRWS 7; CA 123; 25-28R; DLB
15, 20; EWL 3; MTCW 1; RGEL 2
Kawabata, Yasunari 1899-1972 ..... **CLC 2, 5,**
9, 18, 107; SSC 17
See Kawabata Yasunari
See also CA 93-96; 33-36R; CANR 88;
DAM MULT; DLB 330; MJW; MTCW 2;
MTFW 2005; RGSF 2; RGWL 2, 3

Kawabata Yasunari
See Kawabata, Yasunari
See also DLB 180; EWL 3

Kaye, Mary Margaret
See Kaye, M.M.

Kaye, M.M. 1908-2004 .... **CLC 28**
See also CA 89-92; 223; CANR 24, 60, 102, 142; MTCW 1, 2; MTFW 2005; RHW; SATA 62; SATA-Obit 152

Kaye, Mollie
See Kaye, M.M.

Kaye-Smith, Sheila 1887-1956 .... **TCLC 20**
See also CA 118; 203; DLB 36

Kaymor, Patrice Maguilene
See Senghor, Leopold Sedar

Kazakov, Iurii Pavlovich
See Kazakov, Yuri Pavlovich
See also DLB 302

Kazakov, Yuri Pavlovich 1927-1982 . **SSC 43**
See Kazakov, Iurii Pavlovich; Kazakov, Yury
See also CA 5-8R; CANR 36; MTCW 1; RGSF 2

Kazakov, Yury
See Kazakov, Yuri Pavlovich
See also EWL 3

Kazan, Elia 1909-2003 .... **CLC 6, 16, 63**
See also CA 21-24R; 220; CANR 32, 78

Kazantzakis, Nikos 1883(?)-1957 .... **TCLC 2, 5, 33, 181**
See also BPFB 2; CA 105; 132; DA3; EW 9; EWL 3; MTCW 1, 2; MTFW 2005; RGWL 2, 3

Kazin, Alfred 1915-1998 ..... **CLC 34, 38, 119**
See also AMWS 8; CA 1-4R; CAAS 7; CANR 1, 45, 79; DLB 67; EWL 3

Keane, Mary Nesta (Skrine) 1904-1996
See Keane, Molly
See also CA 108; 114; 151; RHW

Keane, Molly CLC 31
See Keane, Mary Nesta (Skrine)
See also CN 5, 6; INT CA-114; TCLE 1:1

Keates, Jonathan 1946(?)- .... **CLC 34**
See also CA 163; CANR 126

Keaton, Buster 1895-1966 .... **CLC 20**
See also CA 194

Keats, John 1795-1821 ...... **NCLC 8, 73, 121; PC 1; WLC 3**
See also AAYA 58; BRW 4; BRWR 1; CD-BLB 1789-1832; DA; DA3; DAB; DAC; DAM MST, POET; DLB 96, 110; EXPP; LMFS 1; PAB; PFS 1, 2, 3, 9, 17; RGEL 2; TEA; WLIT 3; WP

Keble, John 1792-1866 .... **NCLC 87**
See also DLB 32, 55; RGEL 2

Keene, Donald 1922- .... **CLC 34**
See also CA 1-4R; CANR 5, 119

Keillor, Garrison 1942- ..... **CLC 40, 115, 222**
See also AAYA 2, 62; AMWS 16; BEST 89:3; BPFB 2; CA 111; 117; CANR 36, 59, 124, 180; CPW; DA3; DAM POP; DLBY 1987; EWL 3; MTCW 1, 2; MTFW 2005; SATA 58; TUS

Keith, Carlos
See Lewton, Val

Keith, Michael
See Hubbard, L. Ron

Kell, Joseph
See Burgess, Anthony

Keller, Gottfried 1819-1890 .... **NCLC 2; SSC 26, 107**
See also CDWLB 2; DLB 129; EW; RGSF 2; RGWL 2, 3

Keller, Nora Okja 1965- .... **CLC 109**
See also CA 187

Kellerman, Jonathan 1949- .... **CLC 44**
See also AAYA 35; BEST 90:1; CA 106; CANR 29, 51, 150, 183; CMW 4; CPW; DA3; DAM POP; INT CANR-29

Kelley, William Melvin 1937- .... **BLC 2:2; CLC 22**
See also BW 1; CA 77-80; CANR 27, 83; CN 1, 2, 3, 4, 5, 6, 7; DLB 33; EWL 3

Kellogg, Marjorie 1922-2005 .... **CLC 2**
See also CA 81-84; 246

Kellow, Kathleen
See Hibbert, Eleanor Alice Burford

Kelly, Lauren
See Oates, Joyce Carol

Kelly, M(ilton) T(errence) 1947- ...... **CLC 55**
See also CA 97-100; CAAS 22; CANR 19, 43, 84; CN 6

Kelly, Robert 1935- .... **SSC 50**
See also CA 17-20R; CAAS 19; CANR 47; CP 1, 2, 3, 4, 5, 6, 7; DLB 5, 130, 165

Kelman, James 1946- .... **CLC 58, 86**
See also BRWS 5; CA 148; CANR 85, 130; CN 5, 6, 7; DLB 194, 319, 326; RGSF 2; WLIT 4

Kemal, Yasar
See Kemal, Yashar
See also CWW 2; EWL 3; WLIT 6

Kemal, Yashar 1923(?)- .... **CLC 14, 29**
See also CA 89-92; CANR 44

Kemble, Fanny 1809-1893 .... **NCLC 18**
See also DLB 32

Kemelman, Harry 1908-1996 .... **CLC 2**
See also AITN 1; BPFB 2; CA 9-12R; 155; CANR 6, 71; CMW 4; DLB 28

Kempe, Margery 1373(?)-1440(?) ... **LC 6, 56**
See also BRWS 12; DLB 146; FL 1:1; RGEL 2

Kempis, Thomas a 1380-1471 .... **LC 11**

Kenan, Randall (G.) 1963- .... **BLC 2:2**
See also BW 2, 3; CA 142; CANR 86; CN 7; CSW; DLB 292; GLL 1

Kendall, Henry 1839-1882 .... **NCLC 12**
See also DLB 230

Keneally, Thomas 1935- .... **CLC 5, 8, 10, 14, 19, 27, 43, 117**
See also BRWS 4; CA 85-88; CANR 10, 50, 74, 130, 165; CN 1, 2, 3, 4, 5, 6, 7; CPW; DA3; DAM NOV; DLB 289, 299, 326; EWL 3; MTCW 1, 2; MTFW 2005; NFS 17; RGEL 2; RGHL; RHW

Keneally, Thomas Michael
See Keneally, Thomas

Kennedy, A. L. 1965- .... **CLC 188**
See also CA 168, 213; CAAE 213; CANR 108; CD 5, 6; CN 6, 7; DLB 271; RGSF 2

Kennedy, Adrienne (Lita) 1931- .... **BLC 1:2; CLC 66; DC 5**
See also AFAW 2; BW 2, 3; CA 103; CAAS 20; CABS 3; CANR 26, 53, 82; CD 5, 6; DAM MULT; DFS 9; DLB 38, 341; FW; MAL 5

Kennedy, Alison Louise
See Kennedy, A. L.

Kennedy, John Pendleton
1795-1870 .... **NCLC 2**
See also DLB 3, 248, 254; RGAL 4

Kennedy, Joseph Charles 1929-
See Kennedy, X. J.
See also CA 1-4R, 201; CAAE 201; CANR 4, 30, 40; CWRI 5; MAICYA 2; MAIC-YAS 1; SATA 14, 86, 130; SATA-Essay 130

Kennedy, William 1928- .. **CLC 6, 28, 34, 53, 239**
See also AAYA 1, 73; AMWS 7; BPFB 2; CA 85-88; CANR 14, 31, 76, 134; CN 4, 5, 6, 7; DA3; DAM NOV; DLB 143; DLBY 1985; EWL 3; INT CANR-31; MAL 5; MTCW 1, 2; MTFW 2005; SATA 57

Kennedy, X. J. CLC 8, 42; PC 93
See Kennedy, Joseph Charles
See also AMWS 15; CAAS 9; CLR 27; CP 1, 2, 3, 4, 5, 6, 7; DLB 5; SAAS 22

Kenny, Maurice (Francis) 1929- ..... **CLC 87; NNAL**
See also CA 144; CAAS 22; CANR 143; DAM MULT; DLB 175

Kent, Kelvin
See Kuttner, Henry

Kenton, Maxwell
See Southern, Terry

Kenyon, Jane 1947-1995 .... **PC 57**
See also AAYA 63; AMWS 7; CA 118; 148; CANR 44, 69, 172; CP 6, 7; CWP; DLB 120; PFS 9, 17; RGAL 4

Kenyon, Robert O.
See Kuttner, Henry

Kepler, Johannes 1571-1630 .... **LC 45**

Ker, Jill
See Conway, Jill K.

Kerkow, H. C.
See Lewton, Val

Kerouac, Jack 1922-1969
See Kerouac, Jean-Louis le Brisde
See also AITN 1; CA 5-8R; 25-28R; CANR 26, 54, 95, 184; DA; DA3; DAB; DAC; DAM MST, NOV, POET, POP; MTCW 1, 2; MTFW 2005

Kerouac, Jean-Louis le Brisde CLC 1, 2, 3, 5, 14, 29, 61; TCLC 117; WLC
See Kerouac, Jack
See also AAYA 25; AMWC 1; AMWS 3; BG 3; BPFB 2; CDALB 1941-1968; CP 1; CPW; DLB 2, 16, 237; DLBD 3; DLBY 1995; EWL 3; GLL 1; LATS 1:2; LMFS 2; MAL 5; NFS 8; RGAL 4; TUS; WP

Kerr, (Bridget) Jean (Collins)
1923(?)-2003 .... **CLC 22**
See also CA 5-8R; 212; CANR 7; INT CANR-7

Kerr, M. E.
See Meaker, Marijane

Kerr, Robert CLC 55

Kerrigan, (Thomas) Anthony 1918- .. **CLC 4, 6**
See also CA 49-52; CAAS 11; CANR 4

Kerry, Lois
See Duncan, Lois

Kesey, Ken 1935-2001 .... **CLC 1, 3, 6, 11, 46, 64, 184; WLC 3**
See also AAYA 25; BG 1:3; BPFB 2; CA 1-4R; 204; CANR 22, 38, 66, 124; CDALB 1968-1988; CN 1, 2, 3, 4, 5, 6, 7; CPW; DA; DA3; DAB; DAC; DAM MST, NOV, POP; DLB 2, 16, 206; EWL 3; EXPN; LAIT 4; MAL 5; MTCW 1, 2; MTFW 2005; NFS 2; RGAL 4; SATA 66; SATA-Obit 131; TUS; YAW

Kesselring, Joseph (Otto)
1902-1967 .... **CLC 45**
See also CA 150; DAM DRAM, MST; DFS 20

Kessler, Jascha (Frederick) 1929- ...... **CLC 4**
See also CA 17-20R; CANR 8, 48, 111; CP 1

Kettelkamp, Larry (Dale) 1933- .... **CLC 12**
See also CA 29-32R; CANR 16; SAAS 3; SATA 2

Key, Ellen (Karolina Sofia)
1849-1926 .... **TCLC 65**
See also DLB 259

Keyber, Conny
See Fielding, Henry

Keyes, Daniel 1927- .... **CLC 80**
   See also AAYA 23; BYA 11; CA 17-20R,
   181; CAAE 181; CANR 10, 26, 54, 74;
   DA; DA3; DAC; DAM MST, NOV;
   EXPN; LAIT 4; MTCW 2; MTFW 2005;
   NFS 2; SATA 37; SFW 4

Keynes, John Maynard
   1883-1946 .... **TCLC 64**
   See also CA 114; 162, 163; DLBD 10;
   MTCW 2; MTFW 2005

Khanshendel, Chiron
   See Rose, Wendy

Khayyam, Omar 1048-1131 ... **CMLC 11; PC
8**
   See Omar Khayyam
   See also DA3; DAM POET; WLIT 6

Kherdian, David 1931- .... **CLC 6, 9**
   See also AAYA 42; CA 21-24R, 192; CAAE
   192; CAAS 2; CANR 39, 78; CLR 24;
   JRDA; LAIT 3; MAICYA 1, 2; SATA 16,
   74; SATA-Essay 125

Khlebnikov, Velimir TCLC 20
   See Khlebnikov, Viktor Vladimirovich
   See also DLB 295; EW 10; EWL 3; RGWL
   2, 3

Khlebnikov, Viktor Vladimirovich 1885-1922
   See Khlebnikov, Velimir
   See also CA 117; 217

Khodasevich, V.F.
   See Khodasevich, Vladislav

Khodasevich, Vladislav
   1886-1939 .... **TCLC 15**
   See also CA 115; DLB 317; EWL 3

Khodasevich, Vladislav Felitsianovich
   See Khodasevich, Vladislav

Kielland, Alexander Lange
   1849-1906 .... **TCLC 5**
   See also CA 104

Kiely, Benedict 1919-2007 . **CLC 23, 43; SSC
58**
   See also CA 1-4R; 257; CANR 2, 84; CN
   1, 2, 3, 4, 5, 6, 7; DLB 15, 319; TCLE
   1:1

Kienzle, William X. 1928-2001 .... **CLC 25**
   See also CA 93-96; 203; CAAS 1; CANR
   9, 31, 59, 111; CMW 4; DA3; DAM POP;
   INT CANR-31; MSW; MTCW 1, 2;
   MTFW 2005

Kierkegaard, Soren 1813-1855 ..... **NCLC 34,
78, 125**
   See also DLB 300; EW 6; LMFS 2; RGWL
   3; TWA

Kieslowski, Krzysztof 1941-1996 .... **CLC 120**
   See also CA 147; 151

Killens, John Oliver 1916-1987 ...... **BLC 2:2;
CLC 10**
   See also BW 2; CA 77-80; 123; CAAS 2;
   CANR 26; CN 1, 2, 3, 4; DLB 33; EWL
   3

Killigrew, Anne 1660-1685 .... **LC 4, 73**
   See also DLB 131

Killigrew, Thomas 1612-1683 .... **LC 57**
   See also DLB 58; RGEL 2

Kim
   See Simenon, Georges (Jacques Christian)

Kincaid, Jamaica 1949- . **BLC 1:2, 2:2; CLC
43, 68, 137, 234; SSC 72**
   See also AAYA 13, 56; AFAW 2; AMWS 7;
   BRWS 7; BW 2, 3; CA 125; CANR 47,
   59, 95, 133; CDALBS; CDWLB 3; CLR
   63; CN 4, 5, 6, 7; DA3; DAM MULT,
   NOV; DLB 157, 227; DNFS 1; EWL 3;
   EXPS; FW; LATS 1:2; LMFS 2; MAL 5;
   MTCW 2; MTFW 2005; NCFS 1; NFS 3;
   SSFS 5, 7; TUS; WWE 1; YAW

King, Francis (Henry) 1923- .... **CLC 8, 53,
145**
   See also CA 1-4R; CANR 1, 33, 86; CN 1,
   2, 3, 4, 5, 6, 7; DAM NOV; DLB 15, 139;
   MTCW 1

King, Kennedy
   See Brown, George Douglas

King, Martin Luther, Jr.
   1929-1968 ... **BLC 1:2; CLC 83; WLCS**
   See also BW 2, 3; CA 25-28; CANR 27,
   44; CAP 2; DA; DA3; DAB; DAC; DAM
   MST, MULT; LAIT 5; LATS 1:2; MTCW
   1, 2; MTFW 2005; SATA 14

King, Stephen 1947- .... **CLC 12, 26, 37, 61,
113, 228, 244; SSC 17, 55**
   See also AAYA 1, 17; AMWS 5; BEST
   90:1; BPFB 2; CA 61-64; CANR 1, 30,
   52, 76, 119, 134, 168; CLR 124; CN 7;
   CPW; DA3; DAM NOV, POP; DLB 143;
   DLBY 1980; HGG; JRDA; LAIT 5;
   MTCW 1, 2; MTFW 2005; RGAL 4;
   SATA 9, 55, 161; SUFW 1, 2; WYAS 1;
   YAW

King, Stephen Edwin
   See King, Stephen

King, Steve
   See King, Stephen

King, Thomas 1943- .... **CLC 89, 171; NNAL**
   See also CA 144; CANR 95, 175; CCA 1;
   CN 6, 7; DAC; DAM MULT; DLB 175,
   334; SATA 96

King, Thomas Hunt
   See King, Thomas

Kingman, Lee CLC 17
   See Natti, (Mary) Lee
   See also CWRI 5; SAAS 3; SATA 1, 67

Kingsley, Charles 1819-1875 .... **NCLC 35**
   See also CLR 77; DLB 21, 32, 163, 178,
   190; FANT; MAICYA 2; MAICYAS 1;
   RGEL 2; WCH; YABC 2

Kingsley, Henry 1830-1876 .... **NCLC 107**
   See also DLB 21, 230; RGEL 2

Kingsley, Sidney 1906-1995 .... **CLC 44**
   See also CA 85-88; 147; CAD; DFS 14, 19;
   DLB 7; MAL 5; RGAL 4

Kingsolver, Barbara 1955- .... **CLC 55, 81,
130, 216**
   See also AAYA 15; AMWS 7; CA 129; 134;
   CANR 60, 96, 133, 179; CDALBS; CN
   7; CPW; CSW; DA3; DAM POP; DLB
   206; INT CA-134; LAIT 5; MTCW 2;
   MTFW 2005; NFS 5, 10, 12, 24; RGAL
   4; TCLE 1:1

Kingston, Maxine Hong 1940- .... **AAL; CLC
12, 19, 58, 121; WLCS**
   See also AAYA 8, 55; AMWS 5; BPFB 2;
   CA 69-72; CANR 13, 38, 74, 87, 128;
   CDALBS; CN 6, 7; DA3; DAM MULT,
   NOV; DLB 173, 212, 312; DLBY 1980;
   EWL 3; FL 1:6; FW; INT CANR-13;
   LAIT 5; MAL 5; MBL; MTCW 1, 2;
   MTFW 2005; NFS 6; RGAL 4; SATA 53;
   SSFS 3; TCWW 2

Kingston, Maxine Ting Ting Hong
   See Kingston, Maxine Hong

Kinnell, Galway 1927- ..... **CLC 1, 2, 3, 5, 13,
29, 129; PC 26**
   See also AMWS 3; CA 9-12R; CANR 10,
   34, 66, 116, 138, 175; CP 1, 2, 3, 4, 5, 6,
   7; DLB 5, 342; DLBY 1987; EWL 3; INT
   CANR-34; MAL 5; MTCW 1, 2; MTFW
   2005; PAB; PFS 9, 26; RGAL 4; TCLE
   1:1; WP

Kinsella, Thomas 1928- .... **CLC 4, 19, 138;
PC 69**
   See also BRWS 5; CA 17-20R; CANR 15,
   122; CP 1, 2, 3, 4, 5, 6, 7; DLB 27; EWL
   3; MTCW 1, 2; MTFW 2005; RGEL 2;
   TEA

Kinsella, W.P. 1935- .... **CLC 27, 43, 166**
   See also AAYA 7, 60; BPFB 2; CA 97-100,
   222; CAAE 222; CAAS 7; CANR 21, 35,
   66, 75, 129; CN 4, 5, 6, 7; CPW; DAC;
   DAM NOV, POP; FANT; INT CANR-21;
   LAIT 5; MTCW 1, 2; MTFW 2005; NFS
   15; RGSF 2

Kinsey, Alfred C(harles)
   1894-1956 .... **TCLC 91**
   See also CA 115; 170; MTCW 2

Kipling, (Joseph) Rudyard 1865-1936 . **PC 3,
91; SSC 5, 54, 110; TCLC 8, 17, 167;
WLC 3**
   See also AAYA 32; BRW 6; BRWC 1, 2;
   BYA 4; CA 105; 120; CANR 33; CDBLB
   1890-1914; CLR 39, 65; CWRI 5; DA;
   DA3; DAB; DAC; DAM MST, POET;
   DLB 19, 34, 141, 156, 330; EWL 3;
   EXPS; FANT; LAIT 3; LMFS 1; MAI-
   CYA 1, 2; MTCW 1, 2; MTFW 2005;
   NFS 21; PFS 22; RGEL 2; RGSF 2; SATA
   100; SFW 4; SSFS 8, 21, 22; SUFW 1;
   TEA; WCH; WLIT 4; YABC 2

Kircher, Athanasius 1602-1680 .... **LC 121**
   See also DLB 164

Kirk, Russell (Amos) 1918-1994 .. **TCLC 119**
   See also AITN 1; CA 1-4R; 145; CAAS 9;
   CANR 1, 20, 60; HGG; INT CANR-20;
   MTCW 1, 2

Kirkham, Dinah
   See Card, Orson Scott

Kirkland, Caroline M. 1801-1864 . **NCLC 85**
   See also DLB 3, 73, 74, 250, 254; DLBD
   13

Kirkup, James 1918- .... **CLC 1**
   See also CA 1-4R; CAAS 4; CANR 2; CP
   1, 2, 3, 4, 5, 6, 7; DLB 27; SATA 12

Kirkwood, James 1930(?)-1989 .... **CLC 9**
   See also AITN 2; CA 1-4R; 128; CANR 6,
   40; GLL 2

Kirsch, Sarah 1935- .... **CLC 176**
   See also CA 178; CWW 2; DLB 75; EWL
   3

Kirshner, Sidney
   See Kingsley, Sidney

Kis, Danilo 1935-1989 .... **CLC 57**
   See also CA 109; 118; 129; CANR 61; CD-
   WLB 4; DLB 181; EWL 3; MTCW 1;
   RGSF 2; RGWL 2, 3

Kissinger, Henry A(lfred) 1923- ..... **CLC 137**
   See also CA 1-4R; CANR 2, 33, 66, 109;
   MTCW 1

Kittel, Frederick August
   See Wilson, August

Kivi, Aleksis 1834-1872 .... **NCLC 30**

Kizer, Carolyn 1925- ..... **CLC 15, 39, 80; PC
66**
   See also CA 65-68; CAAS 5; CANR 24,
   70, 134; CP 1, 2, 3, 4, 5, 6, 7; CWP; DAM
   POET; DLB 5, 169; EWL 3; MAL 5;
   MTCW 2; MTFW 2005; PFS 18; TCLE
   1:1

Klabund 1890-1928 .... **TCLC 44**
   See also CA 162; DLB 66

Klappert, Peter 1942- .... **CLC 57**
   See also CA 33-36R; CSW; DLB 5

Klausner, Amos
   See Oz, Amos

Klein, A(braham) M(oses)
   1909-1972 .... **CLC 19**
   See also CA 101; 37-40R; CP 1; DAB;
   DAC; DAM MST; DLB 68; EWL 3;
   RGEL 2; RGHL

Klein, Joe
   See Klein, Joseph

Klein, Joseph 1946- .... **CLC 154**
   See also CA 85-88; CANR 55, 164

Klein, Norma 1938-1989 .... **CLC 30**
   See also AAYA 2, 35; BPFB 2; BYA 6, 7,
   8; CA 41-44R; 128; CANR 15, 37; CLR
   2, 19; INT CANR-15; JRDA; MAICYA
   1, 2; SAAS 1; SATA 7, 57; WYA; YAW

Klein, T.E.D. 1947- .... **CLC 34**
   See also CA 119; CANR 44, 75, 167; HGG

Klein, Theodore Eibon Donald
   See Klein, T.E.D.

Kleist, Heinrich von 1777-1811 .... **DC 29;**
NCLC 2, 37; SSC 22
See also CDWLB 2; DAM DRAM; DLB
90; EW 5; RGSF 2; RGWL 2, 3
Klima, Ivan 1931- .... **CLC 56, 172**
See also CA 25-28R; CANR 17, 50, 91;
CDWLB 4; CWW 2; DAM NOV; DLB
232; EWL 3; RGWL 3
Klimentev, Andrei Platonovich
See Klimentov, Andrei Platonovich
Klimentov, Andrei Platonovich
1899-1951 .... **SSC 42; TCLC 14**
See Platonov, Andrei Platonovich; Platonov,
Andrey Platonovich
See also CA 108; 232
Klinger, Friedrich Maximilian von
1752-1831 .... **NCLC 1**
See also DLB 94
Klingsor the Magician
See Hartmann, Sadakichi
Klopstock, Friedrich Gottlieb
1724-1803 .... **NCLC 11**
See also DLB 97; EW 4; RGWL 2, 3
Kluge, Alexander 1932- .... **SSC 61**
See also CA 81-84; CANR 163; DLB 75
Knapp, Caroline 1959-2002 .... **CLC 99**
See also CA 154; 207
Knebel, Fletcher 1911-1993 .... **CLC 14**
See also AITN 1; CA 1-4R; 140; CAAS 3;
CANR 1, 36; CN 1, 2, 3, 4, 5; SATA 36;
SATA-Obit 75
Knickerbocker, Diedrich
See Irving, Washington
Knight, Etheridge 1931-1991 .... **BLC 1:2;**
CLC 40; PC 14
See also BW 1, 3; CA 21-24R; 133; CANR
23, 82; CP 1, 2, 3, 4, 5; DAM POET; DLB
41; MTCW 2; MTFW 2005; RGAL 4;
TCLE 1:1
Knight, Sarah Kemble 1666-1727 .... **LC 7**
See also DLB 24, 200
Knister, Raymond 1899-1932 .... **TCLC 56**
See also CA 186; DLB 68; RGEL 2
Knowles, John 1926-2001 ... **CLC 1, 4, 10, 26**
See also AAYA 10, 72; AMWS 12; BPFB
2; BYA 3; CA 17-20R; 203; CANR 40,
74, 76, 132; CDALB 1968-1988; CLR 98;
CN 1, 2, 3, 4, 5, 6, 7; DA; DAC; DAM
MST, NOV; DLB 6; EXPN; MTCW 1, 2;
MTFW 2005; NFS 2; RGAL 4; SATA 8,
89; SATA-Obit 134; YAW
Knox, Calvin M.
See Silverberg, Robert
Knox, John c. 1505-1572 .... **LC 37**
See also DLB 132
Knye, Cassandra
See Disch, Thomas M.
Koch, C(hristopher) J(ohn) 1932- .... **CLC 42**
See also CA 127; CANR 84; CN 3, 4, 5, 6,
7; DLB 289
Koch, Christopher
See Koch, C(hristopher) J(ohn)
Koch, Kenneth 1925-2002 .... **CLC 5, 8, 44;**
PC 80
See also AMWS 15; CA 1-4R; 207; CAD;
CANR 6, 36, 57, 97, 131; CD 5, 6; CP 1,
2, 3, 4, 5, 6, 7; DAM POET; DLB 5; INT
CANR-36; MAL 5; MTCW 2; MTFW
2005; PFS 20; SATA 65; WP
Kochanowski, Jan 1530-1584 .... **LC 10**
See also RGWL 2, 3
Kock, Charles Paul de 1794-1871 . **NCLC 16**
Koda Rohan
See Koda Shigeyuki
Koda Rohan
See Koda Shigeyuki
Koda Shigeyuki 1867-1947 .... **TCLC 22**
See also CA 121; 183; DLB 180

Koestler, Arthur 1905-1983 ... **CLC 1, 3, 6, 8,**
15, 33
See also BRWS 1; CA 1-4R; 109; CANR 1,
33; CDBLB 1945-1960; CN 1, 2, 3;
DLBY 1983; EWL 3; MTCW 1, 2; MTFW
2005; NFS 19; RGEL 2
Kogawa, Joy Nozomi 1935- ..... **CLC 78, 129,**
262
See also AAYA 47; CA 101; CANR 19, 62,
126; CN 6, 7; CP 1; CWP; DAC; DAM
MST, MULT; DLB 334; FW; MTCW 2;
MTFW 2005; NFS 3; SATA 99
Kohout, Pavel 1928- .... **CLC 13**
See also CA 45-48; CANR 3
Koizumi, Yakumo
See Hearn, (Patricio) Lafcadio (Tessima
Carlos)
Kolmar, Gertrud 1894-1943 .... **TCLC 40**
See also CA 167; EWL 3; RGHL
Komunyakaa, Yusef 1947- . **BLC 2:2; BLCS;**
CLC 86, 94, 207; PC 51
See also AFAW 2; AMWS 13; CA 147;
CANR 83, 164; CP 6, 7; CSW; DLB 120;
EWL 3; PFS 5, 20; RGAL 4
Konigsberg, Alan Stewart
See Allen, Woody
Konrad, George
See Konrad, Gyorgy
Konrad, George
See Konrad, Gyorgy
Konrad, Gyorgy 1933- .... **CLC 4, 10, 73**
See also CA 85-88; CANR 97, 171; CD-
WLB 4; CWW 2; DLB 232; EWL 3
Konwicki, Tadeusz 1926- .... **CLC 8, 28, 54,**
117
See also CA 101; CAAS 9; CANR 39, 59;
CWW 2; DLB 232; EWL 3; IDFW 3;
MTCW 1
Koontz, Dean
See Koontz, Dean R.
Koontz, Dean R. 1945- .... **CLC 78, 206**
See also AAYA 9, 31; BEST 89:3, 90:2; CA
108; CANR 19, 36, 52, 95, 138, 176;
CMW 4; CPW; DA3; DAM NOV, POP;
DLB 292; HGG; MTCW 1; MTFW 2005;
SATA 92, 165; SFW 4; SUFW 2; YAW
Koontz, Dean Ray
See Koontz, Dean R.
Kopernik, Mikolaj
See Copernicus, Nicolaus
Kopit, Arthur (Lee) 1937- ...... **CLC 1, 18, 33**
See also AITN 1; CA 81-84; CABS 3;
CAD; CD 5, 6; DAM DRAM; DFS 7, 14,
24; DLB 7; MAL 5; MTCW 1; RGAL 4
Kopitar, Jernej (Bartholomaus)
1780-1844 .... **NCLC 117**
Kops, Bernard 1926- .... **CLC 4**
See also CA 5-8R; CANR 84, 159; CBD;
CN 1, 2, 3, 4, 5, 6, 7; CP 1, 2, 3, 4, 5, 6,
7; DLB 13; RGHL
Kornbluth, C(yril) M. 1923-1958 .... **TCLC 8**
See also CA 105; 160; DLB 8; SCFW 1, 2;
SFW 4
Korolenko, V.G.
See Korolenko, Vladimir G.
Korolenko, Vladimir
See Korolenko, Vladimir G.
Korolenko, Vladimir G.
1853-1921 .... **TCLC 22**
See also CA 121; DLB 277
Korolenko, Vladimir Galaktionovich
See Korolenko, Vladimir G.
Korzybski, Alfred (Habdank Skarbek)
1879-1950 .... **TCLC 61**
See also CA 123; 160

Kosinski, Jerzy 1933-1991 ..... **CLC 1, 2, 3, 6,**
10, 15, 53, 70
See also AMWS 7; BPFB 2; CA 17-20R;
134; CANR 9, 46; CN 1, 2, 3, 4; DA3;
DAM NOV; DLB 2, 299; EWL 3; HGG; MAL 5; MTCW 1, 2;
MTFW 2005; NFS 12; RGAL 4; RGHL;
TUS
Kostelanetz, Richard (Cory) 1940- .. **CLC 28**
See also CA 13-16R; CAAS 8; CANR 38,
77; CN 4, 5, 6; CP 2, 3, 4, 5, 6, 7
Kostrowitzki, Wilhelm Apollinaris de
1880-1918
See Apollinaire, Guillaume
See also CA 104
Kotlowitz, Robert 1924- .... **CLC 4**
See also CA 33-36R; CANR 36
Kotzebue, August (Friedrich Ferdinand) von
1761-1819 .... **NCLC 25**
See also DLB 94
Kotzwinkle, William 1938- ..... **CLC 5, 14, 35**
See also BPFB 2; CA 45-48; CANR 3, 44,
84, 129; CLR 6; CN 7; DLB 173; FANT;
MAICYA 1, 2; SATA 24, 70, 146; SFW
4; SUFW 2; YAW
Kowna, Stancy
See Szymborska, Wislawa
Kozol, Jonathan 1936- .... **CLC 17**
See also AAYA 46; CA 61-64; CANR 16,
45, 96, 178; MTFW 2005
Kozoll, Michael 1940(?)- .... **CLC 35**
Krakauer, Jon 1954- .... **CLC 248**
See also AAYA 24; AMWS 18; BYA 9; CA
153; CANR 131; MTFW 2005; SATA 108
Kramer, Kathryn 19(?)- .... **CLC 34**
Kramer, Larry 1935- .... **CLC 42; DC 8**
See also CA 124; 126; CANR 60, 132;
DAM POP; DLB 249; GLL 1
Krasicki, Ignacy 1735-1801 .... **NCLC 8**
Krasinski, Zygmunt 1812-1859 .... **NCLC 4**
See also RGWL 2, 3
Kraus, Karl 1874-1936 .... **TCLC 5**
See also CA 104; 216; DLB 118; EWL 3
Kreve (Mickevicius), Vincas
1882-1954 .... **TCLC 27**
See also CA 170; DLB 220; EWL 3
Kristeva, Julia 1941- .... **CLC 77, 140**
See also CA 154; CANR 99, 173; DLB 242;
EWL 3; FW; LMFS 2
Kristofferson, Kris 1936- .... **CLC 26**
See also CA 104
Krizanc, John 1956- .... **CLC 57**
See also CA 187
Krleza, Miroslav 1893-1981 .... **CLC 8, 114**
See also CA 97-100; 105; CANR 50; CD-
WLB 4; DLB 147; EW 11; RGWL 2, 3
Kroetsch, Robert (Paul) 1927- .... **CLC 5, 23,**
57, 132
See also CA 17-20R; CANR 8, 38; CCA 1;
CN 2, 3, 4, 5, 6, 7; CP 6, 7; DAC; DAM
POET; DLB 53; MTCW 1
Kroetz, Franz
See Kroetz, Franz Xaver
Kroetz, Franz Xaver 1946- .... **CLC 41**
See also CA 130; CANR 142; CWW 2;
EWL 3
Kroker, Arthur (W.) 1945- .... **CLC 77**
See also CA 161
Kroniuk, Lisa
See Berton, Pierre (Francis de Marigny)
Kropotkin, Peter (Aleksieevich)
1842-1921 .... **TCLC 36**
See Kropotkin, Petr Alekseevich
See also CA 119; 219
Kropotkin, Petr Alekseevich
See Kropotkin, Peter (Aleksieevich)
See also DLB 277
Krotkov, Yuri 1917-1981 .... **CLC 19**
See also CA 102

Krumb
See Crumb, R.

Krumgold, Joseph (Quincy)
1908-1980 .... **CLC 12**
See also BYA 1, 2; CA 9-12R; 101; CANR 7; MAICYA 1, 2; SATA 1, 48; SATA-Obit 23; YAW

Krumwitz
See Crumb, R.

Krutch, Joseph Wood 1893-1970 ..... **CLC 24**
See also ANW; CA 1-4R; 25-28R; CANR 4; DLB 63, 206, 275

Krutzch, Gus
See Eliot, T(homas) S(tearns)

Krylov, Ivan Andreevich
1768(?)-1844 .... **NCLC 1**
See also DLB 150

Kubin, Alfred (Leopold Isidor)
1877-1959 .... **TCLC 23**
See also CA 112; 149; CANR 104; DLB 81

Kubrick, Stanley 1928-1999 .... **CLC 16; TCLC 112**
See also AAYA 30; CA 81-84; 177; CANR 33; DLB 26

Kumin, Maxine 1925- .... **CLC 5, 13, 28, 164; PC 15**
See also AITN 2; AMWS 4; ANW; CA 1-4R, 271; CAAE 271; CAAS 8; CANR 1, 21, 69, 115, 140; CP 2, 3, 4, 5, 6, 7; CWP; DA3; DAM POET; DLB 5; EWL 3; EXPP; MTCW 1, 2; MTFW 2005; PAB; PFS 18; SATA 12

Kundera, Milan 1929- .. **CLC 4, 9, 19, 32, 68, 115, 135, 234; SSC 24**
See also AAYA 2, 62; BPFB 2; CA 85-88; CANR 19, 52, 74, 144; CDWLB 4; CWW 2; DA3; DAM NOV; DLB 232; EW 13; EWL 3; MTCW 1, 2; MTFW 2005; NFS 18, 27; RGSF 2; RGWL 3; SSFS 10

Kunene, Mazisi 1930-2006 .... **CLC 85**
See also BW 1, 3; CA 125; 252; CANR 81; CP 1, 6, 7; DLB 117

Kunene, Mazisi Raymond
See Kunene, Mazisi

Kunene, Mazisi Raymond Fakazi Mngoni
See Kunene, Mazisi

Kung, Hans CLC 130
See Kung, Hans

Kung, Hans 1928-
See Kung, Hans
See also CA 53-56; CANR 66, 134; MTCW 1, 2; MTFW 2005

Kunikida Doppo 1869(?)-1908
See Doppo, Kunikida
See also DLB 180; EWL 3

Kunitz, Stanley 1905-2006 ..... **CLC 6, 11, 14, 148; PC 19**
See also AMWS 3; CA 41-44R; 250; CANR 26, 57, 98; CP 1, 2, 3, 4, 5, 6, 7; DA3; DLB 48; INT CANR-26; MAL 5; MTCW 1, 2; MTFW 2005; PFS 11; RGAL 4

Kunitz, Stanley Jasspon
See Kunitz, Stanley

Kunze, Reiner 1933- .... **CLC 10**
See also CA 93-96; CWW 2; DLB 75; EWL 3

Kuprin, Aleksander Ivanovich
1870-1938 .... **TCLC 5**
See Kuprin, Aleksandr Ivanovich; Kuprin, Alexandr Ivanovich
See also CA 104; 182

Kuprin, Aleksandr Ivanovich
See Kuprin, Aleksander Ivanovich
See also DLB 295

Kuprin, Alexandr Ivanovich
See Kuprin, Aleksander Ivanovich
See also EWL 3

Kureishi, Hanif 1954- .. **CLC 64, 135; DC 26**
See also BRWS 11; CA 139; CANR 113; CBD; CD 5, 6; CN 6, 7; DLB 194, 245; GLL 2; IDFW 4; WLIT 4; WWE 1

Kurosawa, Akira 1910-1998 ..... **CLC 16, 119**
See also AAYA 11, 64; CA 101; 170; CANR 46; DAM MULT

Kushner, Tony 1956- .... **CLC 81, 203; DC 10**
See also AAYA 61; AMWS 9; CA 144; CAD; CANR 74, 130; CD 5, 6; DA3; DAM DRAM; DFS 5; DLB 228; EWL 3; GLL 1; LAIT 5; MAL 5; MTCW 2; MTFW 2005; RGAL 4; RGHL; SATA 160

Kuttner, Henry 1915-1958 .... **TCLC 10**
See also CA 107; 157; DLB 8; FANT; SCFW 1, 2; SFW 4

Kutty, Madhavi
See Das, Kamala

Kuzma, Greg 1944- .... **CLC 7**
See also CA 33-36R; CANR 70

Kuzmin, Mikhail (Alekseevich)
1872(?)-1936 .... **TCLC 40**
See also CA 170; DLB 295; EWL 3

Kyd, Thomas 1558-1594 ... **DC 3; LC 22, 125**
See also BRW 1; DAM DRAM; DFS 21; DLB 62; IDTP; LMFS 1; RGEL 2; TEA; WLIT 3

Kyprianos, Iossif
See Samarakis, Antonis

L. S.
See Stephen, Sir Leslie

Labe, Louise 1521-1566 .... **LC 120**
See also DLB 327

Labrunie, Gerard
See Nerval, Gerard de

La Bruyere, Jean de 1645-1696 .... **LC 17**
See also DLB 268; EW 3; GFL Beginnings to 1789

LaBute, Neil 1963- .... **CLC 225**
See also CA 240

Lacan, Jacques (Marie Emile)
1901-1981 .... **CLC 75**
See also CA 121; 104; DLB 296; EWL 3; TWA

Laclos, Pierre-Ambroise Francois
1741-1803 .... **NCLC 4, 87**
See also DLB 313; EW 4; GFL Beginnings to 1789; RGWL 2, 3

Lacolere, Francois
See Aragon, Louis

La Colere, Francois
See Aragon, Louis

La Deshabilleuse
See Simenon, Georges (Jacques Christian)

Lady Gregory
See Gregory, Lady Isabella Augusta (Persse)

Lady of Quality, A
See Bagnold, Enid

La Fayette, Marie-(Madelaine Pioche de la Vergne) 1634-1693 .... **LC 2, 144**
See Lafayette, Marie-Madeleine
See also GFL Beginnings to 1789; RGWL 2, 3

Lafayette, Marie-Madeleine
See La Fayette, Marie-(Madelaine Pioche de la Vergne)
See also DLB 268

Lafayette, Rene
See Hubbard, L. Ron

La Flesche, Francis 1857(?)-1932 ...... **NNAL**
See also CA 144; CANR 83; DLB 175

La Fontaine, Jean de 1621-1695 .... **LC 50**
See also DLB 268; EW 3; GFL Beginnings to 1789; MAICYA 1, 2; RGWL 2, 3; SATA 18

LaForet, Carmen 1921-2004 .... **CLC 219**
See also CA 246; CWW 2; DLB 322; EWL 3

LaForet Diaz, Carmen
See LaForet, Carmen

Laforgue, Jules 1860-1887 . **NCLC 5, 53; PC 14; SSC 20**
See also DLB 217; EW 7; GFL 1789 to the Present; RGWL 2, 3

Lagerkvist, Paer (Fabian)
1891-1974 ..... **CLC 7, 10, 13, 54; TCLC 144**
See Lagerkvist, Par
See also CA 85-88; 49-52; DA3; DAM DRAM, NOV; MTCW 1, 2; MTFW 2005; TWA

Lagerkvist, Par SSC 12
See Lagerkvist, Paer (Fabian)
See also DLB 259, 331; EW 10; EWL 3; RGSF 2; RGWL 2, 3

Lagerloef, Selma (Ottiliana Lovisa) TCLC 4, 36
See Lagerlof, Selma (Ottiliana Lovisa)
See also CA 108; MTCW 2

Lagerlof, Selma (Ottiliana Lovisa)
1858-1940
See Lagerloef, Selma (Ottiliana Lovisa)
See also CA 188; CLR 7; DLB 259, 331; RGWL 2, 3; SATA 15; SSFS 18

La Guma, Alex 1925-1985 .. **BLCS; CLC 19; TCLC 140**
See also AFW; BW 1, 3; CA 49-52; 118; CANR 25, 81; CDWLB 3; CN 1, 2, 3; CP 1; DAM NOV; DLB 117, 225; EWL 3; MTCW 1, 2; MTFW 2005; WLIT 2; WWE 1

Lahiri, Jhumpa 1967- .... **SSC 96**
See also AAYA 56; CA 193; CANR 134, 184; DLB 323; MTFW 2005; SSFS 19

Laidlaw, A. K.
See Grieve, C(hristopher) M(urray)

Lainez, Manuel Mujica
See Mujica Lainez, Manuel
See also HW 1

Laing, R(onald) D(avid) 1927-1989 . **CLC 95**
See also CA 107; 129; CANR 34; MTCW 1

Laishley, Alex
See Booth, Martin

Lamartine, Alphonse (Marie Louis Prat) de
1790-1869 .... **NCLC 11, 190; PC 16**
See also DAM POET; DLB 217; GFL 1789 to the Present; RGWL 2, 3

Lamb, Charles 1775-1834 ..... **NCLC 10, 113; SSC 112; WLC 3**
See also BRW 4; CDBLB 1789-1832; DA; DAB; DAC; DAM MST; DLB 93, 107, 163; RGEL 2; SATA 17; TEA

Lamb, Lady Caroline 1785-1828 ... **NCLC 38**
See also DLB 116

Lamb, Mary Ann 1764-1847 ...... **NCLC 125; SSC 112**
See also DLB 163; SATA 17

Lame Deer 1903(?)-1976 .... **NNAL**
See also CA 69-72

Lamming, George (William)
1927- . **BLC 1:2, 2:2; CLC 2, 4, 66, 144**
See also BW 2, 3; CA 85-88; CANR 26, 76; CDWLB 3; CN 1, 2, 3, 4, 5, 6, 7; CP 1; DAM MULT; DLB 125; EWL 3; MTCW 1, 2; MTFW 2005; NFS 15; RGEL 2

L'Amour, Louis 1908-1988 .... **CLC 25, 55**
See also AAYA 16; AITN 2; BEST 89:2; BPFB 2; CA 1-4R; 125; CANR 3, 25, 40; CPW; DA3; DAM NOV, POP; DLB 206; DLBY 1980; MTCW 1, 2; MTFW 2005; RGAL 4; TCWW 1, 2

Lampedusa, Giuseppe (Tomasi) di TCLC 13
See Tomasi di Lampedusa, Giuseppe
See also CA 164; EW 11; MTCW 2; MTFW 2005; RGWL 2, 3

Lampman, Archibald 1861-1899 .. **NCLC 25, 194**
See also DLB 92; RGEL 2; TWA

Lancaster, Bruce 1896-1963 .... **CLC 36**
See also CA 9-10; CANR 70; CAP 1; SATA 9

Lanchester, John 1962- .... **CLC 99**
See also CA 194; DLB 267

Landau, Mark Alexandrovich
See Aldanov, Mark (Alexandrovich)

Landau-Aldanov, Mark Alexandrovich
See Aldanov, Mark (Alexandrovich)

Landis, Jerry
See Simon, Paul

Landis, John 1950- .... **CLC 26**
See also CA 112; 122; CANR 128

Landolfi, Tommaso 1908-1979 .... **CLC 11, 49**
See also CA 127; 117; DLB 177; EWL 3

Landon, Letitia Elizabeth
1802-1838 .... **NCLC 15**
See also DLB 96

Landor, Walter Savage
1775-1864 .... **NCLC 14**
See also BRW 4; DLB 93, 107; RGEL 2

Landwirth, Heinz
See Lind, Jakov

Lane, Patrick 1939- .... **CLC 25**
See also CA 97-100; CANR 54; CP 3, 4, 5, 6, 7; DAM POET; DLB 53; INT CA-97-100

Lane, Rose Wilder 1887-1968 ...... **TCLC 177**
See also CA 102; CANR 63; SATA 29; SATA-Brief 28; TCWW 2

Lang, Andrew 1844-1912 .... **TCLC 16**
See also CA 114; 137; CANR 85; CLR 101; DLB 98, 141, 184; FANT; MAICYA 1, 2; RGEL 2; SATA 16; WCH

Lang, Fritz 1890-1976 .... **CLC 20, 103**
See also AAYA 65; CA 77-80; 69-72; CANR 30

Lange, John
See Crichton, Michael

Langer, Elinor 1939- .... **CLC 34**
See also CA 121

Langland, William 1332(?)-1400(?) .... **LC 19, 120**
See also BRW 1; DA; DAB; DAC; DAM MST, POET; DLB 146; RGEL 2; TEA; WLIT 3

Langstaff, Launcelot
See Irving, Washington

Lanier, Sidney 1842-1881 . **NCLC 6, 118; PC 50**
See also AMWS 1; DAM POET; DLB 64; DLBD 13; EXPP; MAICYA 1; PFS 14; RGAL 4; SATA 18

Lanyer, Aemilia 1569-1645 .... **LC 10, 30, 83; PC 60**
See also DLB 121

Lao-Tzu
See Lao Tzu

Lao Tzu c. 6th cent. B.C.-3rd cent.
B.C. .... **CMLC 7**

Lapine, James (Elliot) 1949- .... **CLC 39**
See also CA 123; 130; CANR 54, 128; DFS 25; DLB 341; INT CA-130

Larbaud, Valery (Nicolas)
1881-1957 .... **TCLC 9**
See also CA 106; 152; EWL 3; GFL 1789 to the Present

Larcom, Lucy 1824-1893 .... **NCLC 179**
See also AMWS 13; DLB 221, 243

Lardner, Ring
See Lardner, Ring(gold) W(ilmer)
See also BPFB 2; CDALB 1917-1929; DLB 11, 25, 86, 171; DLBD 16; MAL 5; RGAL 4; RGSF 2

Lardner, Ring W., Jr.
See Lardner, Ring(gold) W(ilmer)

Lardner, Ring(gold) W(ilmer)
1885-1933 .... **SSC 32; TCLC 2, 14**
See Lardner, Ring
See also AMW; CA 104; 131; MTCW 1, 2; MTFW 2005; TUS

Laredo, Betty
See Codrescu, Andrei

Larkin, Maia
See Wojciechowska, Maia (Teresa)

Larkin, Philip (Arthur) 1922-1985 ... **CLC 3, 5, 8, 9, 13, 18, 33, 39, 64; PC 21**
See also BRWS 1; CA 5-8R; 117; CANR 24, 62; CDBLB 1960 to Present; CP 1, 2, 3, 4; DA3; DAB; DAM MST, POET; DLB 27; EWL 3; MTCW 1, 2; MTFW 2005; PFS 3, 4, 12; RGEL 2

La Roche, Sophie von
1730-1807 .... **NCLC 121**
See also DLB 94

La Rochefoucauld, Francois
1613-1680 .... **LC 108**
See also DLB 268; EW 3; GFL Beginnings to 1789; RGWL 2, 3

Larra (y Sanchez de Castro), Mariano Jose de 1809-1837 .... **NCLC 17, 130**

Larsen, Eric 1941- .... **CLC 55**
See also CA 132

Larsen, Nella 1893(?)-1963 ... **BLC 1:2; CLC 37; HR 1:3; TCLC 200**
See also AFAW 1, 2; AMWS 18; BW 1; CA 125; CANR 83; DAM MULT; DLB 51; FW; LATS 1:1; LMFS 2

Larson, Charles R(aymond) 1938- ... **CLC 31**
See also CA 53-56; CANR 4, 121

Larson, Jonathan 1960-1996 .... **CLC 99**
See also AAYA 28; CA 156; DFS 23; MTFW 2005

La Sale, Antoine de c. 1386-1460(?) . **LC 104**
See also DLB 208

Las Casas, Bartolome de
1474-1566 .... **HLCS; LC 31**
See Casas, Bartolome de las
See also DLB 318; LAW

Lasch, Christopher 1932-1994 .... **CLC 102**
See also CA 73-76; 144; CANR 25, 118; DLB 246; MTCW 1, 2; MTFW 2005

Lasker-Schueler, Else 1869-1945 ... **TCLC 57**
See Lasker-Schuler, Else
See also CA 183; DLB 66, 124

Lasker-Schuler, Else
See Lasker-Schueler, Else
See also EWL 3

Laski, Harold J(oseph) 1893-1950 . **TCLC 79**
See also CA 188

Latham, Jean Lee 1902-1995 .... **CLC 12**
See also AITN 1; BYA 1; CA 5-8R; CANR 7, 84; CLR 50; MAICYA 1, 2; SATA 2, 68; YAW

Latham, Mavis
See Clark, Mavis Thorpe

Lathen, Emma **CLC 2**
See Hennissart, Martha; Latsis, Mary J(ane)
See also BPFB 2; CMW 4; DLB 306

Lathrop, Francis
See Leiber, Fritz (Reuter, Jr.)

Latsis, Mary J(ane) 1927-1997
See Lathen, Emma
See also CA 85-88; 162; CMW 4

Lattany, Kristin
See Lattany, Kristin (Elaine Eggleston) Hunter

Lattany, Kristin (Elaine Eggleston) Hunter
1931- .... **CLC 35**
See Hunter, Kristin
See also AITN 1; BW 1; BYA 3; CA 13-16R; CANR 13, 108; CLR 3; CN 7; DLB 33; INT CANR-13; MAICYA 1, 2; SAAS 10; SATA 12, 132; YAW

Lattimore, Richmond (Alexander)
1906-1984 .... **CLC 3**
See also CA 1-4R; 112; CANR 1; CP 1, 2, 3; MAL 5

Laughlin, James 1914-1997 .... **CLC 49**
See also CA 21-24R; 162; CAAS 22; CANR 9, 47; CP 1, 2, 3, 4, 5, 6; DLB 48; DLBY 1996, 1997

Laurence, Jean Margaret Wemyss
See Laurence, Margaret

Laurence, Margaret 1926-1987 ..... **CLC 3, 6, 13, 50, 62; SSC 7**
See also BYA 13; CA 5-8R; 121; CANR 33; CN 1, 2, 3, 4; DAC; DAM MST; DLB 53; EWL 3; FW; MTCW 1, 2; MTFW 2005; NFS 11; RGEL 2; RGSF 2; SATA-Obit 50; TCWW 2

Laurent, Antoine 1952- .... **CLC 50**

Lauscher, Hermann
See Hesse, Hermann

Lautreamont 1846-1870 .... **NCLC 12, 194; SSC 14**
See Lautreamont, Isidore Lucien Ducasse
See also GFL 1789 to the Present; RGWL 2, 3

Lautreamont, Isidore Lucien Ducasse
See Lautreamont
See also DLB 217

Lavater, Johann Kaspar
1741-1801 .... **NCLC 142**
See also DLB 97

Laverty, Donald
See Blish, James (Benjamin)

Lavin, Mary 1912-1996 . **CLC 4, 18, 99; SSC 4, 67**
See also CA 9-12R; 151; CANR 33; CN 1, 2, 3, 4, 5, 6; DLB 15, 319; FW; MTCW 1; RGEL 2; RGSF 2; SSFS 23

Lavond, Paul Dennis
See Kornbluth, C(yril) M.; Pohl, Frederik

Lawes, Henry 1596-1662 .... **LC 113**
See also DLB 126

Lawler, Ray
See Lawler, Raymond Evenor
See also DLB 289

Lawler, Raymond Evenor 1922- .... **CLC 58**
See Lawler, Ray
See also CA 103; CD 5, 6; RGEL 2

Lawrence, D(avid) H(erbert Richards)
1885-1930 .... **PC 54; SSC 4, 19, 73; TCLC 2, 9, 16, 33, 48, 61, 93; WLC 3**
See Chambers, Jessie
See also BPFB 2; BRW 7; BRWR 2; CA 104; 121; CANR 131; CDBLB 1914-1945; DA; DA3; DAB; DAC; DAM MST, NOV, POET; DLB 10, 19, 36, 98, 162, 195; EWL 3; EXPP; EXPS; LAIT 2, 3; MTCW 1, 2; MTFW 2005; NFS 18, 26; PFS 6; RGEL 2; RGSF 2; SSFS 2, 6; TEA; WLIT 4; WP

Lawrence, T(homas) E(dward)
1888-1935 .... **TCLC 18, 204**
See Dale, Colin
See also BRWS 2; CA 115; 167; DLB 195

Lawrence of Arabia
See Lawrence, T(homas) E(dward)

Lawson, Henry (Archibald Hertzberg)
1867-1922 .... **SSC 18; TCLC 27**
See also CA 120; 181; DLB 230; RGEL 2; RGSF 2

Lawton, Dennis
See Faust, Frederick (Schiller)

Layamon fl. c. 1200- .... **CMLC 10, 105**
See also DLB 146; RGEL 2

Laye, Camara 1928-1980 .. **BLC 1:2; CLC 4, 38**
See Camara Laye
See also AFW; BW 1; CA 85-88; 97-100; CANR 25; DAM MULT; MTCW 1, 2; WLIT 2

Layton, Irving 1912-2006 ..... **CLC 2, 15, 164**
    See also CA 1-4R; 247; CANR 2, 33, 43, 66, 129; CP 1, 2, 3, 4, 5, 6, 7; DAC; DAM MST, POET; DLB 88; EWL 3; MTCW 1, 2; PFS 12; RGEL 2
Layton, Irving Peter
    See Layton, Irving
Lazarus, Emma 1849-1887 ...... **NCLC 8, 109**
Lazarus, Felix
    See Cable, George Washington
Lazarus, Henry
    See Slavitt, David R.
Lea, Joan
    See Neufeld, John (Arthur)
Leacock, Stephen (Butler)
    1869-1944 .... **SSC 39; TCLC 2**
    See also CA 104; 141; CANR 80; DAC; DAM MST; DLB 92; EWL 3; MTCW 2; MTFW 2005; RGEL 2; RGSF 2
Lead, Jane Ward 1623-1704 .... **LC 72**
    See also DLB 131
Leapor, Mary 1722-1746 .... **LC 80; PC 85**
    See also DLB 109
Lear, Edward 1812-1888 ..... **NCLC 3; PC 65**
    See also AAYA 48; BRW 5; CLR 1, 75; DLB 32, 163, 166; MAICYA 1, 2; RGEL 2; SATA 18, 100; WCH; WP
Lear, Norman (Milton) 1922- .... **CLC 12**
    See also CA 73-76
Leautaud, Paul 1872-1956 .... **TCLC 83**
    See also CA 203; DLB 65; GFL 1789 to the Present
Leavis, F(rank) R(aymond)
    1895-1978 .... **CLC 24**
    See also BRW 7; CA 21-24R; 77-80; CANR 44; DLB 242; EWL 3; MTCW 1, 2; RGEL 2
Leavitt, David 1961- .... **CLC 34**
    See also CA 116; 122; CANR 50, 62, 101, 134, 177; CPW; DA3; DAM POP; DLB 130; GLL 1; INT CA-122; MAL 5; MTCW 2; MTFW 2005
Leblanc, Maurice (Marie Emile)
    1864-1941 .... **TCLC 49**
    See also CA 110; CMW 4
Lebowitz, Fran(ces Ann) 1951(?)- ... **CLC 11, 36**
    See also CA 81-84; CANR 14, 60, 70; INT CANR-14; MTCW 1
Lebrecht, Peter
    See Tieck, (Johann) Ludwig
le Carre, John
    See le Carre, John
le Carre, John 1931- .... **CLC 9, 15**
    See also AAYA 42; BEST 89:4; BPFB 2; BRWS 2; CA 5-8R; CANR 13, 33, 59, 107, 132, 172; CDBLB 1960 to Present; CMW 4; CN 1, 2, 3, 4, 5, 6, 7; CPW; DA3; DAM POP; DLB 87; EWL 3; MSW; MTCW 1, 2; MTFW 2005; RGEL 2; TEA
Le Clezio, J. M.G. 1940- .... **CLC 31, 155**
    See also CA 116; 128; CANR 147; CWW 2; DLB 83; EWL 3; GFL 1789 to the Present; RGSF 2
Le Clezio, Jean Marie Gustave
    See Le Clezio, J. M.G.
Leconte de Lisle, Charles-Marie-Rene
    1818-1894 .... **NCLC 29**
    See also DLB 217; EW 6; GFL 1789 to the Present
Le Coq, Monsieur
    See Simenon, Georges (Jacques Christian)
Leduc, Violette 1907-1972 .... **CLC 22**
    See also CA 13-14; 33-36R; CANR 69; CAP 1; EWL 3; GFL 1789 to the Present; GLL 1
Ledwidge, Francis 1887(?)-1917 .... **TCLC 23**
    See also CA 123; 203; DLB 20

Lee, Andrea 1953- .... **BLC 1:2; CLC 36**
    See also BW 1, 3; CA 125; CANR 82; DAM MULT
Lee, Andrew
    See Auchincloss, Louis
Lee, Chang-rae 1965- .... **CLC 91**
    See also CA 148; CANR 89; CN 7; DLB 312; LATS 1:2
Lee, Don L. CLC 2
    See Madhubuti, Haki R.
    See also CP 2, 3, 4, 5
Lee, George W(ashington)
    1894-1976 .... **BLC 1:2; CLC 52**
    See also BW 1; CA 125; CANR 83; DAM MULT; DLB 51
Lee, Harper 1926- ... **CLC 12, 60, 194; WLC 4**
    See also AAYA 13; AMWS 8; BPFB 2; BYA 3; CA 13-16R; CANR 51, 128; CDALB 1941-1968; CSW; DA; DA3; DAB; DAC; DAM MST, NOV; DLB 6; EXPN; LAIT 3; MAL 5; MTCW 1, 2; MTFW 2005; NFS 2; SATA 11; WYA; YAW
Lee, Helen Elaine 1959(?)- .... **CLC 86**
    See also CA 148
Lee, John CLC 70
Lee, Julian
    See Latham, Jean Lee
Lee, Larry
    See Lee, Lawrence
Lee, Laurie 1914-1997 .... **CLC 90**
    See also CA 77-80; 158; CANR 33, 73; CP 1, 2, 3, 4, 5, 6; CPW; DAB; DAM POP; DLB 27; MTCW 1; RGEL 2
Lee, Lawrence 1941-1990 .... **CLC 34**
    See also CA 131; CANR 43
Lee, Li-Young 1957- .... **CLC 164; PC 24**
    See also AMWS 15; CA 153; CANR 118; CP 6, 7; DLB 165, 312; LMFS 2; PFS 11, 15, 17
Lee, Manfred B. 1905-1971 .... **CLC 11**
    See Queen, Ellery
    See also CA 1-4R; 29-32R; CANR 2, 150; CMW 4; DLB 137
Lee, Manfred Bennington
    See Lee, Manfred B.
Lee, Nathaniel 1645(?)-1692 .... **LC 103**
    See also DLB 80; RGEL 2
Lee, Nelle Harper
    See Lee, Harper
Lee, Shelton Jackson
    See Lee, Spike
Lee, Sophia 1750-1824 .... **NCLC 191**
    See also DLB 39
Lee, Spike 1957(?)- .... **BLCS; CLC 105**
    See also AAYA 4, 29; BW 2, 3; CA 125; CANR 42, 164; DAM MULT
Lee, Stan 1922- .... **CLC 17**
    See also AAYA 5, 49; CA 108; 111; CANR 129; INT CA-111; MTFW 2005
Lee, Tanith 1947- .... **CLC 46**
    See also AAYA 15; CA 37-40R; CANR 53, 102, 145, 170; DLB 261; FANT; SATA 8, 88, 134, 185; SFW 4; SUFW 1, 2; YAW
Lee, Vernon SSC 33, 98; TCLC 5
    See Paget, Violet
    See also DLB 57, 153, 156, 174, 178; GLL 1; SUFW 1
Lee, William
    See Burroughs, William S.
    See also GLL 1
Lee, Willy
    See Burroughs, William S.
    See also GLL 1
Lee-Hamilton, Eugene (Jacob)
    1845-1907 .... **TCLC 22**
    See also CA 117; 234

Leet, Judith 1935- .... **CLC 11**
    See also CA 187
Le Fanu, Joseph Sheridan
    1814-1873 .... **NCLC 9, 58; SSC 14, 84**
    See also CMW 4; DA3; DAM POP; DLB 21, 70, 159, 178; GL 3; HGG; RGEL 2; RGSF 2; SUFW 1
Leffland, Ella 1931- .... **CLC 19**
    See also CA 29-32R; CANR 35, 78, 82; DLBY 1984; INT CANR-35; SATA 65; SSFS 24
Leger, Alexis
    See Leger, (Marie-Rene Auguste) Alexis Saint-Leger
Leger, (Marie-Rene Auguste) Alexis Saint-Leger 1887-1975 .. **CLC 4, 11, 46; PC 23**
    See Perse, Saint-John; Saint-John Perse
    See also CA 13-16R; 61-64; CANR 43; DAM POET; MTCW 1
Leger, Saintleger
    See Leger, (Marie-Rene Auguste) Alexis Saint-Leger
Le Guin, Ursula K. 1929- ...... **CLC 8, 13, 22, 45, 71, 136; SSC 12, 69**
    See also AAYA 9, 27; AITN 1; BPFB 2; BYA 5, 8, 11, 14; CA 21-24R; CANR 9, 32, 52, 74, 132; CDALB 1968-1988; CLR 3, 28, 91; CN 2, 3, 4, 5, 6, 7; CPW; DA3; DAB; DAC; DAM MST, POP; DLB 8, 52, 256, 275; EXPS; FANT; FW; INT CANR-32; JRDA; LAIT 5; MAICYA 1, 2; MAL 5; MTCW 1, 2; MTFW 2005; NFS 6, 9; SATA 4, 52, 99, 149, 194; SCFW 1, 2; SFW 4; SSFS 2; SUFW 1, 2; WYA; YAW
Lehmann, Rosamond (Nina)
    1901-1990 .... **CLC 5**
    See also CA 77-80; 131; CANR 8, 73; CN 1, 2, 3, 4; DLB 15; MTCW 2; RGEL 2; RHW
Leiber, Fritz (Reuter, Jr.)
    1910-1992 .... **CLC 25**
    See also AAYA 65; BPFB 2; CA 45-48; 139; CANR 2, 40, 86; CN 2, 3, 4, 5; DLB 8; FANT; HGG; MTCW 1, 2; MTFW 2005; SATA 45; SATA-Obit 73; SCFW 1, 2; SFW 4; SUFW 1, 2
Leibniz, Gottfried Wilhelm von
    1646-1716 .... **LC 35**
    See also DLB 168
Leino, Eino TCLC 24
    See Lonnbohm, Armas Eino Leopold
    See also EWL 3
Leiris, Michel (Julien) 1901-1990 ..... **CLC 61**
    See also CA 119; 128; 132; EWL 3; GFL 1789 to the Present
Leithauser, Brad 1953- .... **CLC 27**
    See also CA 107; CANR 27, 81, 171; CP 5, 6, 7; DLB 120, 282
le Jars de Gournay, Marie
    See de Gournay, Marie le Jars
Lelchuk, Alan 1938- .... **CLC 5**
    See also CA 45-48; CAAS 20; CANR 1, 70, 152; CN 3, 4, 5, 6, 7
Lem, Stanislaw 1921-2006 ..... **CLC 8, 15, 40, 149**
    See also AAYA 75; CA 105; 249; CAAS 1; CANR 32; CWW 2; MTCW 1; SCFW 1, 2; SFW 4
Lemann, Nancy (Elise) 1956- .... **CLC 39**
    See also CA 118; 136; CANR 121
Lemonnier, (Antoine Louis) Camille
    1844-1913 .... **TCLC 22**
    See also CA 121
Lenau, Nikolaus 1802-1850 .... **NCLC 16**
L'Engle, Madeleine 1918-2007 .... **CLC 12**
    See also AAYA 28; AITN 2; BPFB 2; BYA 2, 4, 5, 7; CA 1-4R; 264; CANR 3, 21, 39, 66, 107; CLR 1, 14, 57; CPW; CWRI

5; DA3; DAM POP; DLB 52; JRDA;
MAICYA 1, 2; MTCW 1, 2; MTFW 2005;
SAAS 15; SATA 1, 27, 75, 128; SATA-
Obit 186; SFW 4; WYA; YAW

L'Engle, Madeleine Camp Franklin
See L'Engle, Madeleine

Lengyel, Jozsef 1896-1975 .... **CLC 7**
See also CA 85-88; 57-60; CANR 71;
RGSF 2

Lenin 1870-1924
See Lenin, V. I.
See also CA 121; 168

Lenin, V. I. TCLC 67
See Lenin

Lennon, John (Ono) 1940-1980 .. **CLC 12, 35**
See also CA 102; SATA 114

Lennox, Charlotte Ramsay
1729(?)-1804 .... **NCLC 23, 134**
See also DLB 39; RGEL 2

Lentricchia, Frank, Jr.
See Lentricchia, Frank

Lentricchia, Frank 1940- .... **CLC 34**
See also CA 25-28R; CANR 19, 106, 148;
DLB 246

Lenz, Gunter CLC 65

Lenz, Jakob Michael Reinhold
1751-1792 .... **LC 100**
See also DLB 94; RGWL 2, 3

Lenz, Siegfried 1926- .... **CLC 27; SSC 33**
See also CA 89-92; CANR 80, 149; CWW
2; DLB 75; EWL 3; RGSF 2; RGWL 2, 3

Leon, David
See Jacob, (Cyprien-)Max

Leonard, Dutch
See Leonard, Elmore

Leonard, Elmore 1925- .... **CLC 28, 34, 71,
120, 222**
See also AAYA 22, 59; AITN 1; BEST 89:1,
90:4; BPFB 2; CA 81-84; CANR 12, 28,
53, 76, 96, 133, 176; CMW 4; CN 5, 6, 7;
CPW; DA3; DAM POP; DLB 173, 226;
INT CANR-28; MSW; MTCW 1, 2;
MTFW 2005; RGAL 4; SATA 163;
TCWW 1, 2

Leonard, Elmore John, Jr.
See Leonard, Elmore

Leonard, Hugh CLC 19
See Byrne, John Keyes
See also CBD; CD 5, 6; DFS 13, 24; DLB
13

Leonov, Leonid (Maximovich)
1899-1994 .... **CLC 92**
See Leonov, Leonid Maksimovich
See also CA 129; CANR 76; DAM NOV;
EWL 3; MTCW 1, 2; MTFW 2005

Leonov, Leonid Maksimovich
See Leonov, Leonid (Maximovich)
See also DLB 272

Leopardi, (Conte) Giacomo
1798-1837 .... **NCLC 22, 129; PC 37**
See also EW 5; RGWL 2, 3; WLIT 7; WP

Le Reveler
See Artaud, Antonin (Marie Joseph)

Lerman, Eleanor 1952- .... **CLC 9**
See also CA 85-88; CANR 69, 124, 184

Lerman, Rhoda 1936- .... **CLC 56**
See also CA 49-52; CANR 70

Lermontov, Mikhail Iur'evich
See Lermontov, Mikhail Yuryevich
See also DLB 205

Lermontov, Mikhail Yuryevich
1814-1841 .... **NCLC 5, 47, 126; PC 18**
See Lermontov, Mikhail Iur'evich
See also EW 6; RGWL 2, 3; TWA

Leroux, Gaston 1868-1927 .... **TCLC 25**
See also CA 108; 136; CANR 69; CMW 4;
MTFW 2005; NFS 20; SATA 65

Lesage, Alain-Rene 1668-1747 .... **LC 2, 28**
See also DLB 313; EW 3; GFL Beginnings
to 1789; RGWL 2, 3

Leskov, N(ikolai) S(emenovich) 1831-1895
See Leskov, Nikolai (Semenovich)

Leskov, Nikolai (Semyonovich)
1831-1895 ... **NCLC 25, 174; SSC 34, 96**
See Leskov, Nikolai Semenovich

Leskov, Nikolai Semenovich
See Leskov, Nikolai (Semyonovich)
See also DLB 238

Lesser, Milton
See Marlowe, Stephen

Lessing, Doris 1919- .. **CLC 1, 2, 3, 6, 10, 15,
22, 40, 94, 170, 254; SSC 6, 61; WLCS**
See also AAYA 57; AFW; BRWS 1; CA
9-12R; CAAS 14; CANR 33, 54, 76, 122,
179; CBD; CD 5, 6; CDBLB 1960 to
Present; CN 1, 2, 3, 4, 5, 6, 7; CWD; DA;
DA3; DAB; DAC; DAM MST, NOV;
DFS 20; DLB 15, 139; DLBY 1985; EWL
3; EXPS; FL 1:6; FW; LAIT 4; MTCW 1,
2; MTFW 2005; NFS 27; RGEL 2; RGSF
2; SFW 4; SSFS 1, 12, 20, 26; TEA;
WLIT 2, 4

Lessing, Doris May
See Lessing, Doris

Lessing, Gotthold Ephraim
1729-1781 .... **DC 26; LC 8, 124**
See also CDWLB 2; DLB 97; EW 4; RGWL
2, 3

Lester, Julius 1939- .... **BLC 2:2**
See also AAYA 12, 51; BW 2; BYA 3, 9,
11, 12; CA 17-20R; CANR 8, 23, 43, 129,
174; CLR 2, 41; JRDA; MAICYA 1, 2;
MAICYAS 1; MTFW 2005; SATA 12, 74,
112, 157; YAW

Lester, Richard 1932- .... **CLC 20**

Levenson, Jay CLC 70

Lever, Charles (James)
1806-1872 .... **NCLC 23**
See also DLB 21; RGEL 2

Leverson, Ada Esther
1862(?)-1933(?) .... **TCLC 18**
See Elaine
See also CA 117; 202; DLB 153; RGEL 2

Levertov, Denise 1923-1997 .. **CLC 1, 2, 3, 5,
8, 15, 28, 66; PC 11**
See also AMWS 3; CA 1-4R, 178; 163;
CAAE 178; CAAS 19; CANR 3, 29, 50,
108; CDALBS; CP 1, 2, 3, 4, 5, 6; CWP;
DAM POET; DLB 5, 165, 342; EWL 3;
EXPP; FW; INT CANR-29; MAL 5;
MTCW 1, 2; PAB; PFS 7, 17; RGAL 4;
RGHL; TUS; WP

Levi, Carlo 1902-1975 .... **TCLC 125**
See also CA 65-68; 53-56; CANR 10; EWL
3; RGWL 2, 3

Levi, Jonathan CLC 76
See also CA 197

Levi, Peter (Chad Tigar)
1931-2000 .... **CLC 41**
See also CA 5-8R; 187; CANR 34, 80; CP
1, 2, 3, 4, 5, 6, 7; DLB 40

Levi, Primo 1919-1987 ...... **CLC 37, 50; SSC
12; TCLC 109**
See also CA 13-16R; 122; CANR 12, 33,
61, 70, 132, 171; DLB 177, 299; EWL 3;
MTCW 1, 2; MTFW 2005; RGHL;
RGWL 2, 3; WLIT 7

Levin, Ira 1929-2007 .... **CLC 3, 6**
See also CA 21-24R; 266; CANR 17, 44,
74, 139; CMW 4; CN 1, 2, 3, 4, 5, 6, 7;
CPW; DA3; DAM POP; HGG; MTCW 1,
2; MTFW 2005; SATA 66; SATA-Obit
187; SFW 4

Levin, Ira Marvin
See Levin, Ira

Levin, Ira Marvin
See Levin, Ira

Levin, Meyer 1905-1981 .... **CLC 7**
See also AITN 1; CA 9-12R; 104; CANR
15; CN 1, 2, 3; DAM POP; DLB 9, 28;
DLBY 1981; MAL 5; RGHL; SATA 21;
SATA-Obit 27

Levine, Albert Norman
See Levine, Norman
See also CN 7

Levine, Norman 1923-2005 .... **CLC 54**
See Levine, Albert Norman
See also CA 73-76; 240; CAAS 23; CANR
14, 70; CN 1, 2, 3, 4, 5, 6; CP 1; DLB 88

Levine, Norman Albert
See Levine, Norman

Levine, Philip 1928- .. **CLC 2, 4, 5, 9, 14, 33,
118; PC 22**
See also AMWS 5; CA 9-12R; CANR 9,
37, 52, 116, 156; CP 1, 2, 3, 4, 5, 6, 7;
DAM POET; DLB 5; EWL 3; MAL 5;
PFS 8

Levinson, Deirdre 1931- .... **CLC 49**
See also CA 73-76; CANR 70

Levi-Strauss, Claude 1908- .... **CLC 38**
See also CA 1-4R; CANR 6, 32, 57; DLB
242; EWL 3; GFL 1789 to the Present;
MTCW 1, 2; TWA

Levitin, Sonia 1934- .... **CLC 17**
See also AAYA 13, 48; CA 29-32R; CANR
14, 32, 79, 182; CLR 53; JRDA; MAI-
CYA 1, 2; SAAS 2; SATA 4, 68, 119, 131,
192; SATA-Essay 131; YAW

Levon, O. U.
See Kesey, Ken

Levy, Amy 1861-1889 .... **NCLC 59, 203**
See also DLB 156, 240

Lewes, George Henry 1817-1878 ... **NCLC 25**
See also DLB 55, 144

Lewis, Alun 1915-1944 .... **SSC 40; TCLC 3**
See also BRW 7; CA 104; 188; DLB 20,
162; PAB; RGEL 2

Lewis, C. Day
See Day Lewis, C(ecil)
See also CN 1

Lewis, Cecil Day
See Day Lewis, C(ecil)

Lewis, Clive Staples
See Lewis, C.S.

Lewis, C.S. 1898-1963 ... **CLC 1, 3, 6, 14, 27,
124; WLC 4**
See also AAYA 3, 39; BPFB 2; BRWS 3;
BYA 15, 16; CA 81-84; CANR 33, 71,
132; CDBLB 1945-1960; CLR 3, 27, 109;
CWRI 5; DA; DA3; DAB; DAC; DAM
MST, NOV, POP; DLB 15, 100, 160, 255;
EWL 3; FANT; JRDA; LMFS 2; MAI-
CYA 1, 2; MTCW 1, 2; MTFW 2005;
NFS 24; RGEL 2; SATA 13, 100; SCFW
1, 2; SFW 4; SUFW 1; TEA; WCH;
WYA; YAW

Lewis, Janet 1899-1998 .... **CLC 41**
See Winters, Janet Lewis
See also CA 9-12R; 172; CANR 29, 63;
CAP 1; CN 1, 2, 3, 4, 5, 6; DLBY 1987;
RHW; TCWW 2

Lewis, Matthew Gregory
1775-1818 .... **NCLC 11, 62**
See also DLB 39, 158, 178; GL 3; HGG;
LMFS 1; RGEL 2; SUFW

Lewis, (Harry) Sinclair 1885-1951 . **TCLC 4,
13, 23, 39; WLC 4**
See also AMW; AMWC 1; BPFB 2; CA
104; 133; CANR 132; CDALB 1917-
1929; DA; DA3; DAB; DAC; DAM MST,
NOV; DLB 9, 102, 284, 331; DLBD 1;
EWL 3; LAIT 3; MAL 5; MTCW 1, 2;
MTFW 2005; NFS 15, 19, 22; RGAL 4;
TUS

Lewis, (Percy) Wyndham
1884(?)-1957 .. **SSC 34; TCLC 2, 9, 104**
See also AAYA 77; BRW 7; CA 104; 157;
DLB 15; EWL 3; FANT; MTCW 2;
MTFW 2005; RGEL 2

Lewisohn, Ludwig 1883-1955 .... **TCLC 19**
See also CA 107; 203; DLB 4, 9, 28, 102;
MAL 5

Lewton, Val 1904-1951 .... **TCLC 76**
See also CA 199; IDFW 3, 4

Leyner, Mark 1956- .... **CLC 92**
See also CA 110; CANR 28, 53; DA3; DLB
292; MTCW 2; MTFW 2005

Leyton, E.K.
See Campbell, Ramsey

Lezama Lima, Jose 1910-1976 .... **CLC 4, 10,**
101; HLCS 2
See also CA 77-80; CANR 71; DAM
MULT; DLB 113, 283; EWL 3; HW 1, 2;
LAW; RGWL 2, 3

L'Heureux, John (Clarke) 1934- ...... **CLC 52**
See also CA 13-16R; CANR 23, 45, 88; CP
1, 2, 3, 4; DLB 244

Li Ch'ing-chao 1081(?)-1141(?) .... **CMLC 71**

Liddell, C. H.
See Kuttner, Henry

Lie, Jonas (Lauritz Idemil)
1833-1908(?) .... **TCLC 5**
See also CA 115

Lieber, Joel 1937-1971 .... **CLC 6**
See also CA 73-76; 29-32R

Lieber, Stanley Martin
See Lee, Stan

Lieberman, Laurence (James)
1935- .... **CLC 4, 36**
See also CA 17-20R; CANR 8, 36, 89; CP
1, 2, 3, 4, 5, 6, 7

Lieh Tzu fl. 7th cent. B.C.-5th cent.
B.C. .... **CMLC 27**

Lieksman, Anders
See Haavikko, Paavo Juhani

Lifton, Robert Jay 1926- .... **CLC 67**
See also CA 17-20R; CANR 27, 78, 161;
INT CANR-27; SATA 66

Lightfoot, Gordon 1938- .... **CLC 26**
See also CA 109; 242

Lightfoot, Gordon Meredith
See Lightfoot, Gordon

Lightman, Alan P. 1948- .... **CLC 81**
See also CA 141; CANR 63, 105, 138, 178;
MTFW 2005

Lightman, Alan Paige
See Lightman, Alan P.

Ligotti, Thomas 1953- .... **CLC 44; SSC 16**
See also CA 123; CANR 49, 135; HGG;
SUFW 2

Ligotti, Thomas Robert
See Ligotti, Thomas

Li Ho 791-817 .... **PC 13**

Li Ju-chen c. 1763-c. 1830 .... **NCLC 137**

Liking, Werewere BLC 2:2
See Werewere Liking; Werewere Liking

Lilar, Francoise
See Mallet-Joris, Francoise

Liliencron, Detlev
See Liliencron, Detlev von

Liliencron, Detlev von 1844-1909 .. **TCLC 18**
See also CA 117

Liliencron, Friedrich Adolf Axel Detlev von
See Liliencron, Detlev von

Liliencron, Friedrich Detlev von
See Liliencron, Detlev von

Lille, Alain de
See Alain de Lille

Lillo, George 1691-1739 .... **LC 131**
See also DLB 84; RGEL 2

Lilly, William 1602-1681 .... **LC 27**

Lima, Jose Lezama
See Lezama Lima, Jose

Lima Barreto, Afonso Henrique de
1881-1922 .... **TCLC 23**
See Lima Barreto, Afonso Henriques de
See also CA 117; 181; LAW

Lima Barreto, Afonso Henriques de
See Lima Barreto, Afonso Henrique de
See also DLB 307

Limonov, Eduard
See Limonov, Edward
See also DLB 317

Limonov, Edward 1944- .... **CLC 67**
See Limonov, Eduard
See also CA 137

Lin, Frank
See Atherton, Gertrude (Franklin Horn)

Lin, Yutang 1895-1976 .... **TCLC 149**
See also CA 45-48; 65-68; CANR 2; RGAL
4

Lincoln, Abraham 1809-1865 .... **NCLC 18,**
201
See also LAIT 2

Lind, Jakov 1927-2007 ... **CLC 1, 2, 4, 27, 82**
See also CA 9-12R; 257; CAAS 4; CANR
7; DLB 299; EWL 3; RGHL

Lindbergh, Anne Morrow
1906-2001 .... **CLC 82**
See also BPFB 2; CA 17-20R; 193; CANR
16, 73; DAM NOV; MTCW 1, 2; MTFW
2005; SATA 33; SATA-Obit 125; TUS

Lindsay, David 1878(?)-1945 .... **TCLC 15**
See also CA 113; 187; DLB 255; FANT;
SFW 4; SUFW 1

Lindsay, (Nicholas) Vachel
1879-1931 .... **PC 23; TCLC 17; WLC 4**
See also AMWS 1; CA 114; 135; CANR
79; CDALB 1865-1917; DA; DA3; DAC;
DAM MST, POET; DLB 54; EWL 3;
EXPP; MAL 5; RGAL 4; SATA 40; WP

Linke-Poot
See Doeblin, Alfred

Linney, Romulus 1930- .... **CLC 51**
See also CA 1-4R; CAD; CANR 40, 44,
79; CD 5, 6; CSW; RGAL 4

Linton, Eliza Lynn 1822-1898 .... **NCLC 41**
See also DLB 18

Li Po 701-763 .... **CMLC 2, 86; PC 29**
See also PFS 20; WP

Lippard, George 1822-1854 .... **NCLC 198**
See also DLB 202

Lipsius, Justus 1547-1606 .... **LC 16**

Lipsyte, Robert 1938- .... **CLC 21**
See also AAYA 7, 45; CA 17-20R; CANR
8, 57, 146; CLR 23, 76; DA; DAC; DAM
MST, NOV; JRDA; LAIT 5; MAICYA 1,
2; SATA 5, 68, 113, 161; WYA; YAW

Lipsyte, Robert Michael
See Lipsyte, Robert

Lish, Gordon 1934- .... **CLC 45; SSC 18**
See also CA 113; 117; CANR 79, 151; DLB
130; INT CA-117

Lish, Gordon Jay
See Lish, Gordon

Lispector, Clarice 1925(?)-1977 .... **CLC 43;**
HLCS 2; SSC 34, 96
See also CA 139; 116; CANR 71; CDWLB
3; DLB 113, 307; DNFS 1; EWL 3; FW;
HW 2; LAW; RGSF 2; RGWL 2, 3; WLIT
1

Liszt, Franz 1811-1886 .... **NCLC 199**

Littell, Robert 1935(?)- .... **CLC 42**
See also CA 109; 112; CANR 64, 115, 162;
CMW 4

Little, Malcolm 1925-1965
See Malcolm X
See also BW 1, 3; CA 125; 111; CANR 82;
DA; DA3; DAB; DAC; DAM MST,
MULT; MTCW 1, 2; MTFW 2005

Littlewit, Humphrey Gent.
See Lovecraft, H. P.

Litwos
See Sienkiewicz, Henryk (Adam Alexander
Pius)

Liu, E. 1857-1909 .... **TCLC 15**
See also CA 115; 190; DLB 328

Lively, Penelope 1933- .... **CLC 32, 50**
See also BPFB 2; CA 41-44R; CANR 29,
67, 79, 131, 172; CLR 7; CN 5, 6, 7;
CWRI 5; DAM NOV; DLB 14, 161, 207,
326; FANT; JRDA; MAICYA 1, 2;
MTCW 1, 2; MTFW 2005; SATA 7, 60,
101, 164; TEA

Lively, Penelope Margaret
See Lively, Penelope

Livesay, Dorothy (Kathleen)
1909-1996 .... **CLC 4, 15, 79**
See also AITN 2; CA 25-28R; CAAS 8;
CANR 36, 67; CP 1, 2, 3, 4, 5; DAC;
DAM MST, POET; DLB 68; FW; MTCW
1; RGEL 2; TWA

Livius Andronicus c. 284B.C.-c.
204B.C. .... **CMLC 102**

Livy c. 59B.C.-c. 12 .... **CMLC 11**
See also AW 2; CDWLB 1; DLB 211;
RGWL 2, 3; WLIT 8

Lizardi, Jose Joaquin Fernandez de
1776-1827 .... **NCLC 30**
See also LAW

Llewellyn, Richard
See Llewellyn Lloyd, Richard Dafydd Viv-
ian
See also DLB 15

Llewellyn Lloyd, Richard Dafydd Vivian
1906-1983 .... **CLC 7, 80**
See Llewellyn, Richard
See also CA 53-56; 111; CANR 7, 71;
SATA 11; SATA-Obit 37

Llosa, Jorge Mario Pedro Vargas
See Vargas Llosa, Mario
See also RGWL 3

Llosa, Mario Vargas
See Vargas Llosa, Mario

Lloyd, Manda
See Mander, (Mary) Jane

Lloyd Webber, Andrew 1948-
See Webber, Andrew Lloyd
See also AAYA 1, 38; CA 116; 149; DAM
DRAM; SATA 56

Llull, Ramon c. 1235-c. 1316 .... **CMLC 12**

Lobb, Ebenezer
See Upward, Allen

Locke, Alain (Le Roy)
1886-1954 .... **BLCS; HR 1:3; TCLC 43**
See also AMWS 14; BW 1, 3; CA 106; 124;
CANR 79; DLB 51; LMFS 2; MAL 5;
RGAL 4

Locke, John 1632-1704 .... **LC 7, 35, 135**
See also DLB 31, 101, 213, 252; RGEL 2;
WLIT 3

Locke-Elliott, Sumner
See Elliott, Sumner Locke

Lockhart, John Gibson 1794-1854 .. **NCLC 6**
See also DLB 110, 116, 144

Lockridge, Ross (Franklin), Jr.
1914-1948 .... **TCLC 111**
See also CA 108; 145; CANR 79; DLB 143;
DLBY 1980; MAL 5; RGAL 4; RHW

Lockwood, Robert
See Johnson, Robert

Lodge, David 1935- .... **CLC 36, 141**
See also BEST 90:1; BRWS 4; CA 17-20R; CANR 19, 53, 92, 139; CN 1, 2, 3, 4, 5, 6, 7; CPW; DAM POP; DLB 14, 194; EWL 3; INT CANR-19; MTCW 1, 2; MTFW 2005

Lodge, Thomas 1558-1625 .... **LC 41**
See also DLB 172; RGEL 2

Loewinsohn, Ron(ald William)
1937- .... **CLC 52**
See also CA 25-28R; CANR 71; CP 1, 2, 3, 4

Logan, Jake
See Smith, Martin Cruz

Logan, John (Burton) 1923-1987 .... **CLC 5**
See also CA 77-80; 124; CANR 45; CP 1, 2, 3, 4; DLB 5

Lo Kuan-chung 1330(?)-1400(?) .... **LC 12**

Lomax, Pearl
See Cleage, Pearl

Lomax, Pearl Cleage
See Cleage, Pearl

Lombard, Nap
See Johnson, Pamela Hansford

Lombard, Peter 1100(?)-1160(?) ... **CMLC 72**

Lombino, Salvatore
See Hunter, Evan

London, Jack 1876-1916 .. **SSC 4, 49; TCLC 9, 15, 39; WLC 4**
See London, John Griffith
See also AAYA 13; AITN 2; AMW; BPFB 2; BYA 4, 13; CDALB 1865-1917; CLR 108; DLB 8, 12, 78, 212; EWL 3; EXPS; LAIT 3; MAL 5; NFS 8; RGAL 4; RGSF 2; SATA 18; SFW 4; SSFS 7; TCWW 1, 2; TUS; WYA; YAW

London, John Griffith 1876-1916
See London, Jack
See also AAYA 75; CA 110; 119; CANR 73; DA; DA3; DAB; DAC; DAM MST, NOV; JRDA; MAICYA 1, 2; MTCW 1, 2; MTFW 2005; NFS 19

Long, Emmett
See Leonard, Elmore

Longbaugh, Harry
See Goldman, William

Longfellow, Henry Wadsworth
1807-1882 .... **NCLC 2, 45, 101, 103; PC 30; WLCS**
See also AMW; AMWR 2; CDALB 1640-1865; CLR 99; DA; DA3; DAB; DAC; DAM MST, POET; DLB 1, 59, 235; EXPP; PAB; PFS 2, 7, 17; RGAL 4; SATA 19; TUS; WP

Longinus c. 1st cent. - .... **CMLC 27**
See also AW 2; DLB 176

Longley, Michael 1939- .... **CLC 29**
See also BRWS 8; CA 102; CP 1, 2, 3, 4, 5, 6, 7; DLB 40

Longstreet, Augustus Baldwin
1790-1870 .... **NCLC 159**
See also DLB 3, 11, 74, 248; RGAL 4

Longus fl. c. 2nd cent. - .... **CMLC 7**

Longway, A. Hugh
See Lang, Andrew

Lonnbohm, Armas Eino Leopold 1878-1926
See Leino, Eino
See also CA 123

Lonnrot, Elias 1802-1884 .... **NCLC 53**
See also EFS 1

Lonsdale, Roger CLC 65

Lopate, Phillip 1943- .... **CLC 29**
See also CA 97-100; CANR 88, 157; DLBY 1980; INT CA-97-100

Lopez, Barry (Holstun) 1945- .... **CLC 70**
See also AAYA 9, 63; ANW; CA 65-68; CANR 7, 23, 47, 68, 92; DLB 256, 275, 335; INT CANR-7, CANR-23; MTCW 1; RGAL 4; SATA 67

Lopez de Mendoza, Inigo
See Santillana, Inigo Lopez de Mendoza, Marques de

Lopez Portillo (y Pacheco), Jose
1920-2004 .... **CLC 46**
See also CA 129; 224; HW 1

Lopez y Fuentes, Gregorio
1897(?)-1966 .... **CLC 32**
See also CA 131; EWL 3; HW 1

Lorca, Federico Garcia TCLC 197
See Garcia Lorca, Federico
See also DFS 4; EW 11; PFS 20; RGWL 2, 3; WP

Lord, Audre
See Lorde, Audre
See also EWL 3

Lord, Bette Bao 1938- .... **AAL; CLC 23**
See also BEST 90:3; BPFB 2; CA 107; CANR 41, 79; INT CA-107; SATA 58

Lord Auch
See Bataille, Georges

Lord Brooke
See Greville, Fulke

Lord Byron
See Byron, George Gordon (Noel)

Lorde, Audre 1934-1992 .... **BLC 1:2, 2:2; CLC 18, 71; PC 12; TCLC 173**
See Domini, Rey; Lord, Audre
See also AFAW 1, 2; BW 1, 3; CA 25-28R; 142; CANR 16, 26, 46, 82; CP 2, 3, 4, 5; DA3; DAM MULT, POET; DLB 41; FW; MAL 5; MTCW 1, 2; MTFW 2005; PFS 16; RGAL 4

Lorde, Audre Geraldine
See Lorde, Audre

Lord Houghton
See Milnes, Richard Monckton

Lord Jeffrey
See Jeffrey, Francis

Loreaux, Nichol CLC 65

Lorenzini, Carlo 1826-1890
See Collodi, Carlo
See also MAICYA 1, 2; SATA 29, 100

Lorenzo, Heberto Padilla
See Padilla (Lorenzo), Heberto

Loris
See Hofmannsthal, Hugo von

Loti, Pierre TCLC 11
See Viaud, (Louis Marie) Julien
See also DLB 123; GFL 1789 to the Present

Lou, Henri
See Andreas-Salome, Lou

Louie, David Wong 1954- .... **CLC 70**
See also CA 139; CANR 120

Louis, Adrian C. NNAL
See also CA 223

Louis, Father M.
See Merton, Thomas (James)

Louise, Heidi
See Erdrich, Louise

Lovecraft, H. P. 1890-1937 .... **SSC 3, 52; TCLC 4, 22**
See also AAYA 14; BPFB 2; CA 104; 133; CANR 106; DA3; DAM POP; HGG; MTCW 1, 2; MTFW 2005; RGAL 4; SCFW 1, 2; SFW 4; SUFW

Lovecraft, Howard Phillips
See Lovecraft, H. P.

Lovelace, Earl 1935- .... **CLC 51**
See also BW 2; CA 77-80; CANR 41, 72, 114; CD 5, 6; CDWLB 3; CN 1, 2, 3, 4, 5, 6, 7; DLB 125; EWL 3; MTCW 1

Lovelace, Richard 1618-1658 ..... **LC 24, 158; PC 69**
See also BRW 2; DLB 131; EXPP; PAB; RGEL 2

Low, Penelope Margaret
See Lively, Penelope

Lowe, Pardee 1904- .... **AAL**

Lowell, Amy 1874-1925 ... **PC 13; TCLC 1, 8**
See also AAYA 57; AMW; CA 104; 151; DAM POET; DLB 54, 140; EWL 3; EXPP; LMFS 2; MAL 5; MBL; MTCW 2; MTFW 2005; RGAL 4; TUS

Lowell, James Russell 1819-1891 ... **NCLC 2, 90**
See also AMWS 1; CDALB 1640-1865; DLB 1, 11, 64, 79, 189, 235; RGAL 4

Lowell, Robert (Traill Spence, Jr.)
1917-1977 .... **CLC 1, 2, 3, 4, 5, 8, 9, 11, 15, 37, 124; PC 3; WLC 4**
See also AMW; AMWC 2; AMWR 2; CA 9-12R; 73-76; CABS 2; CAD; CANR 26, 60; CDALBS; CP 1, 2; DA; DA3; DAB; DAC; DAM MST, NOV; DLB 5, 169; EWL 3; MAL 5; MTCW 1, 2; MTFW 2005; PAB; PFS 6, 7; RGAL 4; WP

Lowenthal, Michael 1969- .... **CLC 119**
See also CA 150; CANR 115, 164

Lowenthal, Michael Francis
See Lowenthal, Michael

Lowndes, Marie Adelaide (Belloc)
1868-1947 .... **TCLC 12**
See also CA 107; CMW 4; DLB 70; RHW

Lowry, (Clarence) Malcolm
1909-1957 .... **SSC 31; TCLC 6, 40**
See also BPFB 2; BRWS 3; CA 105; 131; CANR 62, 105; CDBLB 1945-1960; DLB 15; EWL 3; MTCW 1, 2; MTFW 2005; RGEL 2

Lowry, Mina Gertrude 1882-1966
See Loy, Mina
See also CA 113

Lowry, Sam
See Soderbergh, Steven

Loxsmith, John
See Brunner, John (Kilian Houston)

Loy, Mina CLC 28; PC 16
See Lowry, Mina Gertrude
See also DAM POET; DLB 4, 54; PFS 20

Loyson-Bridet
See Schwob, Marcel (Mayer Andre)

Lucan 39-65 .... **CMLC 33**
See also AW 2; DLB 211; EFS 2; RGWL 2, 3

Lucas, Craig 1951- .... **CLC 64**
See also CA 137; CAD; CANR 71, 109, 142; CD 5, 6; GLL 2; MTFW 2005

Lucas, E(dward) V(errall)
1868-1938 .... **TCLC 73**
See also CA 176; DLB 98, 149, 153; SATA 20

Lucas, George 1944- .... **CLC 16, 252**
See also AAYA 1, 23; CA 77-80; CANR 30; SATA 56

Lucas, Hans
See Godard, Jean-Luc

Lucas, Victoria
See Plath, Sylvia

Lucian c. 125-c. 180 .... **CMLC 32**
See also AW 2; DLB 176; RGWL 2, 3

Lucilius c. 180B.C.-102B.C. .... **CMLC 82**
See also DLB 211

Lucretius c. 94B.C.-c. 49B.C. .... **CMLC 48**
See also AW 2; CDWLB 1; DLB 211; EFS 2; RGWL 2, 3; WLIT 8

Ludlam, Charles 1943-1987 .... **CLC 46, 50**
See also CA 85-88; 122; CAD; CANR 72, 86; DLB 266

Ludlum, Robert 1927-2001 .... **CLC 22, 43**
See also AAYA 10, 59; BEST 89:1, 90:3; BPFB 2; CA 33-36R; 195; CANR 25, 41, 68, 105, 131; CMW 4; CPW; DA3; DAM NOV, POP; DLBY 1982; MSW; MTCW 1, 2; MTFW 2005

Ludwig, Ken 1950- .... **CLC 60**
See also CA 195; CAD; CD 6

Ludwig, Otto 1813-1865 .... **NCLC 4**
See also DLB 129

Lugones, Leopoldo 1874-1938 .... **HLCS 2;
TCLC 15**
See also CA 116; 131; CANR 104; DLB
283; EWL 3; HW 1; LAW

Lu Hsun SSC 20; TCLC 3
See Shu-Jen, Chou
See also EWL 3

Lukacs, George CLC 24
See Lukacs, Gyorgy (Szegeny von)

Lukacs, Gyorgy (Szegeny von) 1885-1971
See Lukacs, George
See also CA 101; 29-32R; CANR 62; CD-
WLB 4; DLB 215, 242; EW 10; EWL 3;
MTCW 1, 2

Luke, Peter (Ambrose Cyprian)
1919-1995 .... **CLC 38**
See also CA 81-84; 147; CANR 72; CBD;
CD 5, 6; DLB 13

Lunar, Dennis
See Mungo, Raymond

Lurie, Alison 1926- ..... **CLC 4, 5, 18, 39, 175**
See also BPFB 2; CA 1-4R; CANR 2, 17,
50, 88; CN 1, 2, 3, 4, 5, 6, 7; DLB 2;
MAL 5; MTCW 1; NFS 24; SATA 46,
112; TCLE 1:1

Lustig, Arnost 1926- .... **CLC 56**
See also AAYA 3; CA 69-72; CANR 47,
102; CWW 2; DLB 232, 299; EWL 3;
RGHL; SATA 56

Luther, Martin 1483-1546 .... **LC 9, 37, 150**
See also CDWLB 2; DLB 179; EW 2;
RGWL 2, 3

Luxemburg, Rosa 1870(?)-1919 ..... **TCLC 63**
See also CA 118

Luzi, Mario (Egidio Vincenzo)
1914-2005 .... **CLC 13**
See also CA 61-64; 236; CANR 9, 70;
CWW 2; DLB 128; EWL 3

L'vov, Arkady CLC 59

Lydgate, John c. 1370-1450(?) .... **LC 81**
See also BRW 1; DLB 146; RGEL 2

Lyly, John 1554(?)-1606 .... **DC 7; LC 41**
See also BRW 1; DAM DRAM; DLB 62,
167; RGEL 2

L'Ymagier
See Gourmont, Remy(-Marie-Charles) de

Lynch, B. Suarez
See Borges, Jorge Luis

Lynch, David 1946- .... **CLC 66, 162**
See also AAYA 55; CA 124; 129; CANR
111

Lynch, David Keith
See Lynch, David

Lynch, James
See Andreyev, Leonid (Nikolaevich)

Lyndsay, Sir David 1485-1555 .... **LC 20**
See also RGEL 2

Lynn, Kenneth S(chuyler)
1923-2001 .... **CLC 50**
See also CA 1-4R; 196; CANR 3, 27, 65

Lynx
See West, Rebecca

Lyons, Marcus
See Blish, James (Benjamin)

Lyotard, Jean-Francois
1924-1998 .... **TCLC 103**
See also DLB 242; EWL 3

Lyre, Pinchbeck
See Sassoon, Siegfried (Lorraine)

Lytle, Andrew (Nelson) 1902-1995 ... **CLC 22**
See also CA 9-12R; 150; CANR 70; CN 1,
2, 3, 4, 5, 6; CSW; DLB 6; DLBY 1995;
RGAL 4; RHW

Lyttelton, George 1709-1773 .... **LC 10**
See also RGEL 2

Lytton of Knebworth, Baron
See Bulwer-Lytton, Edward (George Earle
Lytton)

Maalouf, Amin 1949- .... **CLC 248**
See also CA 212; DLB 346

Maas, Peter 1929-2001 .... **CLC 29**
See also CA 93-96; 201; INT CA-93-96;
MTCW 2; MTFW 2005

Mac A'Ghobhainn, Iain
See Smith, Iain Crichton

Macaulay, Catherine 1731-1791 .... **LC 64**
See also DLB 104, 336

Macaulay, (Emilie) Rose
1881(?)-1958 .... **TCLC 7, 44**
See also CA 104; DLB 36; EWL 3; RGEL
2; RHW

Macaulay, Thomas Babington
1800-1859 .... **NCLC 42**
See also BRW 4; CDBLB 1832-1890; DLB
32, 55; RGEL 2

MacBeth, George (Mann)
1932-1992 .... **CLC 2, 5, 9**
See also CA 25-28R; 136; CANR 61, 66;
CP 1, 2, 3, 4, 5; DLB 40; MTCW 1; PFS
8; SATA 4; SATA-Obit 70

MacCaig, Norman (Alexander)
1910-1996 .... **CLC 36**
See also BRWS 6; CA 9-12R; CANR 3, 34;
CP 1, 2, 3, 4, 5, 6; DAB; DAM POET;
DLB 27; EWL 3; RGEL 2

MacCarthy, Sir (Charles Otto) Desmond
1877-1952 .... **TCLC 36**
See also CA 167

**MacDiarmid, Hugh CLC 2, 4, 11, 19, 63; PC
9**
See Grieve, C(hristopher) M(urray)
See also BRWS 12; CDBLB 1945-1960;
CP 1, 2; DLB 20; EWL 3; RGEL 2

MacDonald, Anson
See Heinlein, Robert A.

Macdonald, Cynthia 1928- .... **CLC 13, 19**
See also CA 49-52; CANR 4, 44, 146; DLB
105

MacDonald, George 1824-1905 .... **TCLC 9,
113, 207**
See also AAYA 57; BYA 5; CA 106; 137;
CANR 80; CLR 67; DLB 18, 163, 178;
FANT; MAICYA 1, 2; RGEL 2; SATA 33,
100; SFW 4; SUFW; WCH

Macdonald, John
See Millar, Kenneth

MacDonald, John D. 1916-1986 .. **CLC 3, 27,
44**
See also BPFB 2; CA 1-4R; 121; CANR 1,
19, 60; CMW 4; CPW; DAM NOV, POP;
DLB 8, 306; DLBY 1986; MSW; MTCW
1, 2; MTFW 2005; SFW 4

Macdonald, John Ross
See Millar, Kenneth

Macdonald, Ross CLC 1, 2, 3, 14, 34, 41
See Millar, Kenneth
See also AMWS 4; BPFB 2; CN 1, 2, 3;
DLBD 6; MAL 5; MSW; RGAL 4

MacDougal, John
See Blish, James (Benjamin)

MacDowell, John
See Parks, Tim(othy Harold)

MacEwen, Gwendolyn (Margaret)
1941-1987 .... **CLC 13, 55**
See also CA 9-12R; 124; CANR 7, 22; CP
1, 2, 3, 4; DLB 53, 251; SATA 50; SATA-
Obit 55

MacGreevy, Thomas 1893-1967 .... **PC 82**
See also CA 262

Macha, Karel Hynek 1810-1846 .... **NCLC 46**

Machado (y Ruiz), Antonio
1875-1939 .... **TCLC 3**
See also CA 104; 174; DLB 108; EW 9;
EWL 3; HW 2; PFS 23; RGWL 2, 3

Machado de Assis, Joaquim Maria
1839-1908 . **BLC 1:2; HLCS 2; SSC 24;
TCLC 10**
See also CA 107; 153; CANR 91; DLB 307;
LAW; RGSF 2; RGWL 2, 3; TWA; WLIT
1

Machaut, Guillaume de c.
1300-1377 .... **CMLC 64**
See also DLB 208

Machen, Arthur SSC 20; TCLC 4
See Jones, Arthur Llewellyn
See also CA 179; DLB 156, 178; RGEL 2;
SUFW 1

Machiavelli, Niccolo 1469-1527 ... **DC 16; LC
8, 36, 140; WLCS**
See also AAYA 58; DA; DAB; DAC; DAM
MST; EW 2; LAIT 1; LMFS 1; NFS 9;
RGWL 2, 3; TWA; WLIT 7

MacInnes, Colin 1914-1976 .... **CLC 4, 23**
See also CA 69-72; 65-68; CANR 21; CN
1, 2; DLB 14; MTCW 1, 2; RGEL 2;
RHW

MacInnes, Helen (Clark)
1907-1985 .... **CLC 27, 39**
See also BPFB 2; CA 1-4R; 117; CANR 1,
28, 58; CMW 4; CN 1, 2; CPW; DAM
POP; DLB 87; MSW; MTCW 1, 2;
MTFW 2005; SATA 22; SATA-Obit 44

Mackay, Mary 1855-1924
See Corelli, Marie
See also CA 118; 177; FANT; RHW

Mackay, Shena 1944- .... **CLC 195**
See also CA 104; CANR 88, 139; DLB 231,
319; MTFW 2005

Mackenzie, Compton (Edward Montague)
1883-1972 .... **CLC 18; TCLC 116**
See also CA 21-22; 37-40R; CAP 2; CN 1;
DLB 34, 100; RGEL 2

Mackenzie, Henry 1745-1831 .... **NCLC 41**
See also DLB 39; RGEL 2

Mackey, Nathaniel 1947- .... **BLC 2:3; PC 49**
See also CA 153; CANR 114; CP 6, 7; DLB
169

Mackey, Nathaniel Ernest
See Mackey, Nathaniel

MacKinnon, Catharine A. 1946- .... **CLC 181**
See also CA 128; 132; CANR 73, 140; FW;
MTCW 2; MTFW 2005

Mackintosh, Elizabeth 1896(?)-1952
See Tey, Josephine
See also CA 110; CMW 4

Macklin, Charles 1699-1797 .... **LC 132**
See also DLB 89; RGEL 2

MacLaren, James
See Grieve, C(hristopher) M(urray)

MacLaverty, Bernard 1942- ..... **CLC 31, 243**
See also CA 116; 118; CANR 43, 88, 168;
CN 5, 6, 7; DLB 267; INT CA-118; RGSF
2

MacLean, Alistair (Stuart)
1922(?)-1987 .... **CLC 3, 13, 50, 63**
See also CA 57-60; 121; CANR 28, 61;
CMW 4; CP 2, 3, 4, 5, 6, 7; CPW; DAM
POP; DLB 276; MTCW 1; SATA 23;
SATA-Obit 50; TCWW 2

Maclean, Norman (Fitzroy)
1902-1990 .... **CLC 78; SSC 13**
See also AMWS 14; CA 102; 132; CANR
49; CPW; DAM POP; DLB 206; TCWW
2

MacLeish, Archibald 1892-1982 ... **CLC 3, 8,
14, 68; PC 47**
See also AMW; CA 9-12R; 106; CAD;
CANR 33, 63; CDALBS; CP 1, 2; DAM
POET; DFS 15; DLB 4, 7, 45; DLBY
1982; EWL 3; EXPP; MAL 5; MTCW 1,
2; MTFW 2005; PAB; PFS 5; RGAL 4;
TUS

MacLennan, (John) Hugh
1907-1990 .... **CLC 2, 14, 92**
See also CA 5-8R; 142; CANR 33; CN 1, 2, 3, 4; DAC; DAM MST; DLB 68; EWL 3; MTCW 1, 2; MTFW 2005; RGEL 2; TWA

MacLeod, Alistair 1936- .. **CLC 56, 165; SSC 90**
See also CA 123; CCA 1; DAC; DAM MST; DLB 60; MTCW 2; MTFW 2005; RGSF 2; TCLE 1:2

Macleod, Fiona
See Sharp, William
See also RGEL 2; SUFW

MacNeice, (Frederick) Louis
1907-1963 .... **CLC 1, 4, 10, 53; PC 61**
See also BRW 7; CA 85-88; CANR 61; DAB; DAM POET; DLB 10, 20; EWL 3; MTCW 1, 2; MTFW 2005; RGEL 2

MacNeill, Dand
See Fraser, George MacDonald

Macpherson, James 1736-1796 .... **LC 29**
See Ossian
See also BRWS 8; DLB 109, 336; RGEL 2

Macpherson, (Jean) Jay 1931- .... **CLC 14**
See also CA 5-8R; CANR 90; CP 1, 2, 3, 4, 6, 7; CWP; DLB 53

Macrobius fl. 430- .... **CMLC 48**

MacShane, Frank 1927-1999 .... **CLC 39**
See also CA 9-12R; 186; CANR 3, 33; DLB 111

Macumber, Mari
See Sandoz, Mari(e Susette)

Madach, Imre 1823-1864 .... **NCLC 19**

Madden, (Jerry) David 1933- .... **CLC 5, 15**
See also CA 1-4R; CAAS 3; CANR 4, 45; CN 3, 4, 5, 6, 7; CSW; DLB 6; MTCW 1

Maddern, Al(an)
See Ellison, Harlan

Madhubuti, Haki R. 1942- .... **BLC 1:2; CLC 6, 73; PC 5**
See Lee, Don L.
See also BW 2, 3; CA 73-76; CANR 24, 51, 73, 139; CP 6, 7; CSW; DAM MULT, POET; DLB 5, 41; DLBD 8; EWL 3; MAL 5; MTCW 2; MTFW 2005; RGAL 4

Madison, James 1751-1836 .... **NCLC 126**
See also DLB 37

Maepenn, Hugh
See Kuttner, Henry

Maepenn, K. H.
See Kuttner, Henry

Maeterlinck, Maurice 1862-1949 .... **DC 32; TCLC 3**
See also CA 104; 136; CANR 80; DAM DRAM; DLB 192, 331; EW 8; EWL 3; GFL 1789 to the Present; LMFS 2; RGWL 2, 3; SATA 66; TWA

Maginn, William 1794-1842 .... **NCLC 8**
See also DLB 110, 159

Mahapatra, Jayanta 1928- .... **CLC 33**
See also CA 73-76; CAAS 9; CANR 15, 33, 66, 87; CP 4, 5, 6, 7; DAM MULT; DLB 323

Mahfouz, Nagib
See Mahfouz, Naguib

Mahfouz, Naguib 1911(?)-2006 ..... **CLC 153; SSC 66**
See Mahfuz, Najib
See also AAYA 49; BEST 89:2; CA 128; 253; CANR 55, 101; DA3; DAM NOV; DLB 346; MTCW 1, 2; MTFW 2005; RGWL 2, 3; SSFS 9

Mahfouz, Naguib Abdel Aziz Al-Sabilgi
See Mahfouz, Naguib

Mahfouz, Najib
See Mahfouz, Naguib

Mahfuz, Najib **CLC 52, 55**
See Mahfouz, Naguib
See also AFW; CWW 2; DLB 331; DLBY 1988; EWL 3; RGSF 2; WLIT 6

Mahon, Derek 1941- .... **CLC 27; PC 60**
See also BRWS 6; CA 113; 128; CANR 88; CP 1, 2, 3, 4, 5, 6, 7; DLB 40; EWL 3

Maiakovskii, Vladimir
See Mayakovski, Vladimir (Vladimirovich)
See also IDTP; RGWL 2, 3

Mailer, Norman 1923-2007 ... **CLC 1, 2, 3, 4, 5, 8, 11, 14, 28, 39, 74, 111, 234**
See also AAYA 31; AITN 2; AMW; AMWC 2; AMWR 2; BPFB 2; CA 9-12R; 266; CABS 1; CANR 28, 74, 77, 130; CDALB 1968-1988; CN 1, 2, 3, 4, 5, 6, 7; CPW; DA; DA3; DAB; DAC; DAM MST, NOV, POP; DLB 2, 16, 28, 185, 278; DLBD 3; DLBY 1980, 1983; EWL 3; MAL 5; MTCW 1, 2; MTFW 2005; NFS 10; RGAL 4; TUS

Mailer, Norman Kingsley
See Mailer, Norman

Maillet, Antonine 1929- .... **CLC 54, 118**
See also CA 115; 120; CANR 46, 74, 77, 134; CCA 1; CWW 2; DAC; DLB 60; INT CA-120; MTCW 2; MTFW 2005

Maimonides, Moses 1135-1204 ..... **CMLC 76**
See also DLB 115

Mais, Roger 1905-1955 .... **TCLC 8**
See also BW 1, 3; CA 105; 124; CANR 82; CDWLB 3; DLB 125; EWL 3; MTCW 1; RGEL 2

Maistre, Joseph 1753-1821 .... **NCLC 37**
See also GFL 1789 to the Present

Maitland, Frederic William
1850-1906 .... **TCLC 65**

Maitland, Sara (Louise) 1950- .... **CLC 49**
See also BRWS 11; CA 69-72; CANR 13, 59; DLB 271; FW

Major, Clarence 1936- ...... **BLC 1:2; CLC 3, 19, 48**
See also AFAW 2; BW 2, 3; CA 21-24R; CAAS 6; CANR 13, 25, 53, 82; CN 3, 4, 5, 6, 7; CP 2, 3, 4, 5, 6, 7; CSW; DAM MULT; DLB 33; EWL 3; MAL 5; MSW

Major, Kevin (Gerald) 1949- .... **CLC 26**
See also AAYA 16; CA 97-100; CANR 21, 38, 112; CLR 11; DAC; DLB 60; INT CANR-21; JRDA; MAICYA 1, 2; MAIC-YAS 1; SATA 32, 82, 134; WYA; YAW

Maki, James
See Ozu, Yasujiro

Makin, Bathsua 1600-1675(?) .... **LC 137**

Makine, Andrei 1957-
See Makine, Andrei

Makine, Andrei 1957- .... **CLC 198**
See also CA 176; CANR 103, 162; MTFW 2005

Malabaila, Damiano
See Levi, Primo

Malamud, Bernard 1914-1986 .. **CLC 1, 2, 3, 5, 8, 9, 11, 18, 27, 44, 78, 85; SSC 15; TCLC 129, 184; WLC 4**
See also AAYA 16; AMWS 1; BPFB 2; BYA 15; CA 5-8R; 118; CABS 1; CANR 28, 62, 114; CDALB 1941-1968; CN 1, 2, 3, 4; CPW; DA; DA3; DAB; DAC; DAM MST, NOV, POP; DLB 2, 28, 152; DLBY 1980, 1986; EWL 3; EXPS; LAIT 4; LATS 1:1; MAL 5; MTCW 1, 2; MTFW 2005; NFS 27; RGAL 4; RGHL; RGSF 2; SSFS 8, 13, 16; TUS

Malan, Herman
See Bosman, Herman Charles; Bosman, Herman Charles

Malaparte, Curzio 1898-1957 .... **TCLC 52**
See also DLB 264

Malcolm, Dan
See Silverberg, Robert

Malcolm, Janet 1934- .... **CLC 201**
See also CA 123; CANR 89; NCFS 1

Malcolm X **BLC 1:2; CLC 82, 117; WLCS**
See Little, Malcolm
See also LAIT 5; NCFS 3

Malebranche, Nicolas 1638-1715 .... **LC 133**
See also GFL Beginnings to 1789

Malherbe, Francois de 1555-1628 .... **LC 5**
See also DLB 327; GFL Beginnings to 1789

Mallarme, Stephane 1842-1898 ...... **NCLC 4, 41; PC 4**
See also DAM POET; DLB 217; EW 7; GFL 1789 to the Present; LMFS 2; RGWL 2, 3; TWA

Mallet-Joris, Francoise 1930- .... **CLC 11**
See also CA 65-68; CANR 17; CWW 2; DLB 83; EWL 3; GFL 1789 to the Present

Malley, Ern
See McAuley, James Phillip

Mallon, Thomas 1951- .... **CLC 172**
See also CA 110; CANR 29, 57, 92

Mallowan, Agatha Christie
See Christie, Agatha (Mary Clarissa)

Maloff, Saul 1922- .... **CLC 5**
See also CA 33-36R

Malone, Louis
See MacNeice, (Frederick) Louis

Malone, Michael (Christopher)
1942- .... **CLC 43**
See also CA 77-80; CANR 14, 32, 57, 114

Malory, Sir Thomas 1410(?)-1471(?) . **LC 11, 88; WLCS**
See also BRW 1; BRWR 2; CDBLB Before 1660; DA; DAB; DAC; DAM MST; DLB 146; EFS 2; RGEL 2; SATA 59; SATA-Brief 33; TEA; WLIT 3

Malouf, David 1934- .... **CLC 28, 86, 245**
See also BRWS 12; CA 124; CANR 50, 76, 180; CN 3, 4, 5, 6, 7; CP 1, 3, 4, 5, 6, 7; DLB 289; EWL 3; MTCW 2; MTFW 2005; SSFS 24

Malouf, George Joseph David
See Malouf, David

Malraux, (Georges-)Andre
1901-1976 .... **CLC 1, 4, 9, 13, 15, 57; TCLC 209**
See also BPFB 2; CA 21-22; 69-72; CANR 34, 58; CAP 2; DA3; DAM NOV; DLB 72; EW 12; EWL 3; GFL 1789 to the Present; MTCW 1, 2; MTFW 2005; RGWL 2, 3; TWA

Malthus, Thomas Robert
1766-1834 .... **NCLC 145**
See also DLB 107, 158; RGEL 2

Malzberg, Barry N(athaniel) 1939- ... **CLC 7**
See also CA 61-64; CAAS 4; CANR 16; CMW 4; DLB 8; SFW 4

Mamet, David 1947- .. **CLC 9, 15, 34, 46, 91, 166; DC 4, 24**
See also AAYA 3, 60; AMWS 14; CA 81-84; CABS 3; CAD; CANR 15, 41, 67, 72, 129, 172; CD 5, 6; DA3; DAM DRAM; DFS 2, 3, 6, 12, 15; DLB 7; EWL 3; IDFW 4; MAL 5; MTCW 1, 2; MTFW 2005; RGAL 4

Mamet, David Alan
See Mamet, David

Mamoulian, Rouben (Zachary)
1897-1987 .... **CLC 16**
See also CA 25-28R; 124; CANR 85

Mandelshtam, Osip
See Mandelstam, Osip (Emilievich)
See also EW 10; EWL 3; RGWL 2, 3

Author Index

Mandelstam, Osip (Emilievich)
  1891(?)-1943(?) .... **PC 14; TCLC 2, 6**
  See Mandelshtam, Osip
  See also CA 104; 150; MTCW 2; TWA
Mander, (Mary) Jane 1877-1949 ... **TCLC 31**
  See also CA 162; RGEL 2
Mandeville, Bernard 1670-1733 .... **LC 82**
  See also DLB 101
Mandeville, Sir John fl. 1350- ...... **CMLC 19**
  See also DLB 146
Mandiargues, Andre Pieyre de CLC 41
  See Pieyre de Mandiargues, Andre
  See also DLB 83
Mandrake, Ethel Belle
  See Thurman, Wallace (Henry)
Mangan, James Clarence
  1803-1849 .... **NCLC 27**
  See also BRWS 13; RGEL 2
Maniere, J.-E.
  See Giraudoux, Jean(-Hippolyte)
Mankiewicz, Herman (Jacob)
  1897-1953 .... **TCLC 85**
  See also CA 120; 169; DLB 26; IDFW 3, 4
Manley, (Mary) Delariviere
  1672(?)-1724 .... **LC 1, 42**
  See also DLB 39, 80; RGEL 2
Mann, Abel
  See Creasey, John
Mann, Emily 1952- .... **DC 7**
  See also CA 130; CAD; CANR 55; CD 5,
  6; CWD; DLB 266
Mann, (Luiz) Heinrich 1871-1950 ... **TCLC 9**
  See also CA 106; 164, 181; DLB 66, 118;
  EW 8; EWL 3; RGWL 2, 3
Mann, (Paul) Thomas 1875-1955 . **SSC 5, 80,
  82; TCLC 2, 8, 14, 21, 35, 44, 60, 168;
  WLC 4**
  See also BPFB 2; CA 104; 128; CANR 133;
  CDWLB 2; DA; DA3; DAB; DAC; DAM
  MST, NOV; DLB 66, 331; EW 9; EWL 3;
  GLL 1; LATS 1:1; LMFS 1; MTCW 1, 2;
  MTFW 2005; NFS 17; RGSF 2; RGWL
  2, 3; SSFS 4, 9; TWA
Mannheim, Karl 1893-1947 .... **TCLC 65**
  See also CA 204
Manning, David
  See Faust, Frederick (Schiller)
Manning, Frederic 1882-1935 .... **TCLC 25**
  See also CA 124; 216; DLB 260
Manning, Olivia 1915-1980 .... **CLC 5, 19**
  See also CA 5-8R; 101; CANR 29; CN 1,
  2; EWL 3; FW; MTCW 1; RGEL 2
Mannyng, Robert c. 1264-c.
  1340 .... **CMLC 83**
  See also DLB 146
Mano, D. Keith 1942- .... **CLC 2, 10**
  See also CA 25-28R; CAAS 6; CANR 26,
  57; DLB 6
**Mansfield, Katherine SSC 9, 23, 38, 81;
  TCLC 2, 8, 39, 164; WLC 4**
  See Beauchamp, Kathleen Mansfield
  See also BPFB 2; BRW 7; DAB; DLB 162;
  EWL 3; EXPS; FW; GLL 1; RGEL 2;
  RGSF 2; SSFS 2, 8, 10, 11; WWE 1
Manso, Peter 1940- .... **CLC 39**
  See also CA 29-32R; CANR 44, 156
Mantecon, Juan Jimenez
  See Jimenez (Mantecon), Juan Ramon
Mantel, Hilary 1952- .... **CLC 144**
  See also CA 125; CANR 54, 101, 161; CN
  5, 6, 7; DLB 271; RHW
Mantel, Hilary Mary
  See Mantel, Hilary
Manton, Peter
  See Creasey, John
Man Without a Spleen, A
  See Chekhov, Anton (Pavlovich)

Manzano, Juan Franciso
  1797(?)-1854 .... **NCLC 155**
Manzoni, Alessandro 1785-1873 ... **NCLC 29,
  98**
  See also EW 5; RGWL 2, 3; TWA; WLIT 7
Map, Walter 1140-1209 .... **CMLC 32**
Mapu, Abraham (ben Jekutiel)
  1808-1867 .... **NCLC 18**
Mara, Sally
  See Queneau, Raymond
Maracle, Lee 1950- .... **NNAL**
  See also CA 149
Marat, Jean Paul 1743-1793 .... **LC 10**
Marcel, Gabriel Honore 1889-1973 . **CLC 15**
  See also CA 102; 45-48; EWL 3; MTCW 1,
  2
March, William TCLC 96
  See Campbell, William Edward March
  See also CA 216; DLB 9, 86, 316; MAL 5
Marchbanks, Samuel
  See Davies, Robertson
  See also CCA 1
Marchi, Giacomo
  See Bassani, Giorgio
Marcus Aurelius
  See Aurelius, Marcus
  See also AW 2
Marcuse, Herbert 1898-1979 .... **TCLC 207**
  See also CA 188; 89-92; DLB 242
Marguerite
  See de Navarre, Marguerite
Marguerite d'Angouleme
  See de Navarre, Marguerite
  See also GFL Beginnings to 1789
Marguerite de Navarre
  See de Navarre, Marguerite
  See also RGWL 2, 3
Margulies, Donald 1954- .... **CLC 76**
  See also AAYA 57; CA 200; CD 6; DFS 13;
  DLB 228
Marias, Javier 1951- .... **CLC 239**
  See also CA 167; CANR 109, 139; DLB
  322; HW 2; MTFW 2005
Marie de France c. 12th cent. - ..... **CMLC 8;
  PC 22**
  See also DLB 208; FW; RGWL 2, 3
Marie de l'Incarnation 1599-1672 ...... **LC 10**
Marier, Captain Victor
  See Griffith, D.W.
Mariner, Scott
  See Pohl, Frederik
Marinetti, Filippo Tommaso
  1876-1944 .... **TCLC 10**
  See also CA 107; DLB 114, 264; EW 9;
  EWL 3; WLIT 7
Marivaux, Pierre Carlet de Chamblain de
  1688-1763 .... **DC 7; LC 4, 123**
  See also DLB 314; GFL Beginnings to
  1789; RGWL 2, 3; TWA
Markandaya, Kamala CLC 8, 38
  See Taylor, Kamala
  See also BYA 13; CN 1, 2, 3, 4, 5, 6, 7;
  DLB 323; EWL 3
Markfield, Wallace (Arthur)
  1926-2002 .... **CLC 8**
  See also CA 69-72; 208; CAAS 3; CN 1, 2,
  3, 4, 5, 6, 7; DLB 2, 28; DLBY 2002
Markham, Edwin 1852-1940 .... **TCLC 47**
  See also CA 160; DLB 54, 186; MAL 5;
  RGAL 4
Markham, Robert
  See Amis, Kingsley
Marks, J.
  See Highwater, Jamake (Mamake)
Marks-Highwater, J.
  See Highwater, Jamake (Mamake)

Markson, David M. 1927- .... **CLC 67**
  See also AMWS 17; CA 49-52; CANR 1,
  91, 158; CN 5, 6
Markson, David Merrill
  See Markson, David M.
Marlatt, Daphne (Buckle) 1942- .... **CLC 168**
  See also CA 25-28R; CANR 17, 39; CN 6,
  7; CP 4, 5, 6, 7; CWP; DLB 60; FW
Marley, Bob CLC 17
  See Marley, Robert Nesta
Marley, Robert Nesta 1945-1981
  See Marley, Bob
  See also CA 107; 103
Marlowe, Christopher 1564-1593 . **DC 1; LC
  22, 47, 117; PC 57; WLC 4**
  See also BRW 1; BRWR 1; CDBLB Before
  1660; DA; DA3; DAB; DAC; DAM
  DRAM, MST; DFS 1, 5, 13, 21; DLB 62;
  EXPP; LMFS 1; PFS 22; RGEL 2; TEA;
  WLIT 3
Marlowe, Stephen 1928-2008 .... **CLC 70**
  See Queen, Ellery
  See also CA 13-16R; 269; CANR 6, 55;
  CMW 4; SFW 4
Marmion, Shakerley 1603-1639 .... **LC 89**
  See also DLB 58; RGEL 2
Marmontel, Jean-Francois 1723-1799 .. **LC 2**
  See also DLB 314
Maron, Monika 1941- .... **CLC 165**
  See also CA 201
Marot, Clement c. 1496-1544 .... **LC 133**
  See also DLB 327; GFL Beginnings to 1789
Marquand, John P(hillips)
  1893-1960 .... **CLC 2, 10**
  See also AMW; BPFB 2; CA 85-88; CANR
  73; CMW 4; DLB 9, 102; EWL 3; MAL
  5; MTCW 2; RGAL 4
Marques, Rene 1919-1979 .. **CLC 96; HLC 2**
  See also CA 97-100; 85-88; CANR 78;
  DAM MULT; DLB 305; EWL 3; HW 1,
  2; LAW; RGSF 2
Marquez, Gabriel Garcia
  See Garcia Marquez, Gabriel
Marquis, Don(ald Robert Perry)
  1878-1937 .... **TCLC 7**
  See also CA 104; 166; DLB 11, 25; MAL
  5; RGAL 4
Marquis de Sade
  See Sade, Donatien Alphonse Francois
Marric, J. J.
  See Creasey, John
  See also MSW
Marryat, Frederick 1792-1848 .... **NCLC 3**
  See also DLB 21, 163; RGEL 2; WCH
Marsden, James
  See Creasey, John
Marsh, Edward 1872-1953 .... **TCLC 99**
Marsh, (Edith) Ngaio 1895-1982 .. **CLC 7, 53**
  See also CA 9-12R; CANR 6, 58; CMW 4;
  CN 1, 2, 3; CPW; DAM POP; DLB 77;
  MSW; MTCW 1, 2; RGEL 2; TEA
Marshall, Allen
  See Westlake, Donald E.
Marshall, Garry 1934- .... **CLC 17**
  See also AAYA 3; CA 111; SATA 60
Marshall, Paule 1929- .... **BLC 1:3, 2:3; CLC
  27, 72, 253; SSC 3**
  See also AFAW 1, 2; AMWS 11; BPFB 2;
  BW 2, 3; CA 77-80; CANR 25, 73, 129;
  CN 1, 2, 3, 4, 5, 6, 7; DA3; DAM MULT;
  DLB 33, 157, 227; EWL 3; LATS 1:2;
  MAL 5; MTCW 1, 2; MTFW 2005;
  RGAL 4; SSFS 15
Marshallik
  See Zangwill, Israel
Marsilius of Inghen c.
  1340-1396 .... **CMLC 106**
Marsten, Richard
  See Hunter, Evan

Marston, John 1576-1634 .... **LC 33**
See also BRW 2; DAM DRAM; DLB 58, 172; RGEL 2

Martel, Yann 1963- .... **CLC 192**
See also AAYA 67; CA 146; CANR 114; DLB 326, 334; MTFW 2005; NFS 27

Martens, Adolphe-Adhemar
See Ghelderode, Michel de

Martha, Henry
See Harris, Mark

Marti, Jose PC 76
See Marti (y Perez), Jose (Julian)
See also DLB 290

Marti (y Perez), Jose (Julian)
1853-1895 .... **HLC 2; NCLC 63**
See Marti, Jose
See also DAM MULT; HW 2; LAW; RGWL 2, 3; WLIT 1

Martial c. 40-c. 104 .... **CMLC 35; PC 10**
See also AW 2; CDWLB 1; DLB 211; RGWL 2, 3

Martin, Ken
See Hubbard, L. Ron

Martin, Richard
See Creasey, John

Martin, Steve 1945- .... **CLC 30, 217**
See also AAYA 53; CA 97-100; CANR 30, 100, 140; DFS 19; MTCW 1; MTFW 2005

Martin, Valerie 1948- .... **CLC 89**
See also BEST 90:2; CA 85-88; CANR 49, 89, 165

Martin, Violet Florence 1862-1915 .. **SSC 56; TCLC 51**

Martin, Webber
See Silverberg, Robert

Martindale, Patrick Victor
See White, Patrick (Victor Martindale)

Martin du Gard, Roger
1881-1958 .... **TCLC 24**
See also CA 118; CANR 94; DLB 65, 331; EWL 3; GFL 1789 to the Present; RGWL 2, 3

Martineau, Harriet 1802-1876 ...... **NCLC 26, 137**
See also DLB 21, 55, 159, 163, 166, 190; FW; RGEL 2; YABC 2

Martines, Julia
See O'Faolain, Julia

Martinez, Enrique Gonzalez
See Gonzalez Martinez, Enrique

Martinez, Jacinto Benavente y
See Benavente (y Martinez), Jacinto

Martinez de la Rosa, Francisco de Paula
1787-1862 .... **NCLC 102**
See also TWA

Martinez Ruiz, Jose 1873-1967
See Azorin; Ruiz, Jose Martinez
See also CA 93-96; HW 1

Martinez Sierra, Gregorio
See Martinez Sierra, Maria

Martinez Sierra, Gregorio
1881-1947 .... **TCLC 6**
See also CA 115; EWL 3

Martinez Sierra, Maria 1874-1974 .. **TCLC 6**
See also CA 250; 115; EWL 3

Martinsen, Martin
See Follett, Ken

Martinson, Harry (Edmund)
1904-1978 .... **CLC 14**
See also CA 77-80; CANR 34, 130; DLB 259, 331; EWL 3

Martyn, Edward 1859-1923 .... **TCLC 131**
See also CA 179; DLB 10; RGEL 2

Marut, Ret
See Traven, B.

Marut, Robert
See Traven, B.

Marvell, Andrew 1621-1678 .... **LC 4, 43; PC 10, 86; WLC 4**
See also BRW 2; BRWR 2; CDBLB 1660-1789; DA; DAB; DAC; DAM MST, POET; DLB 131; EXPP; PFS 5; RGEL 2; TEA; WP

Marx, Karl (Heinrich)
1818-1883 .... **NCLC 17, 114**
See also DLB 129; LATS 1:1; TWA

Masaoka, Shiki -1902 .... **TCLC 18**
See Masaoka, Tsunenori
See also RGWL 3

Masaoka, Tsunenori 1867-1902
See Masaoka, Shiki
See also CA 117; 191; TWA

Masefield, John (Edward)
1878-1967 .... **CLC 11, 47; PC 78**
See also CA 19-20; 25-28R; CANR 33; CAP 2; CDBLB 1890-1914; DAM POET; DLB 10, 19, 153, 160; EWL 3; EXPP; FANT; MTCW 1, 2; PFS 5; RGEL 2; SATA 19

Maso, Carole 1955(?)- .... **CLC 44**
See also CA 170; CANR 148; CN 7; GLL 2; RGAL 4

Mason, Bobbie Ann 1940- ... **CLC 28, 43, 82, 154; SSC 4, 101**
See also AAYA 5, 42; AMWS 8; BPFB 2; CA 53-56; CANR 11, 31, 58, 83, 125, 169; CDALBS; CN 5, 6, 7; CSW; DA3; DLB 173; DLBY 1987; EWL 3; EXPS; INT CANR-31; MAL 5; MTCW 1, 2; MTFW 2005; NFS 4; RGAL 4; RGSF 2; SSFS 3, 8, 20; TCLE 1:2; YAW

Mason, Ernst
See Pohl, Frederik

Mason, Hunni B.
See Sternheim, (William Adolf) Carl

Mason, Lee W.
See Malzberg, Barry N(athaniel)

Mason, Nick 1945- .... **CLC 35**

Mason, Tally
See Derleth, August (William)

Mass, Anna CLC 59

Mass, William
See Gibson, William

Massinger, Philip 1583-1640 .... **LC 70**
See also BRWS 11; DLB 58; RGEL 2

Master Lao
See Lao Tzu

Masters, Edgar Lee 1868-1950 ...... **PC 1, 36; TCLC 2, 25; WLCS**
See also AMWS 1; CA 104; 133; CDALB 1865-1917; DA; DAC; DAM MST, POET; DLB 54; EWL 3; EXPP; MAL 5; MTCW 1, 2; MTFW 2005; RGAL 4; TUS; WP

Masters, Hilary 1928- .... **CLC 48**
See also CA 25-28R; 217; CAAE 217; CANR 13, 47, 97, 171; CN 6, 7; DLB 244

Masters, Hilary Thomas
See Masters, Hilary

Mastrosimone, William 1947- .... **CLC 36**
See also CA 186; CAD; CD 5, 6

Mathe, Albert
See Camus, Albert

Mather, Cotton 1663-1728 .... **LC 38**
See also AMWS 2; CDALB 1640-1865; DLB 24, 30, 140; RGAL 4; TUS

Mather, Increase 1639-1723 .... **LC 38**
See also DLB 24

Mathers, Marshall
See Eminem

Mathers, Marshall Bruce
See Eminem

Matheson, Richard 1926- .... **CLC 37**
See also AAYA 31; CA 97-100; CANR 88, 99; DLB 8, 44; HGG; INT CA-97-100; SCFW 1, 2; SFW 4; SUFW 2

Matheson, Richard Burton
See Matheson, Richard

Mathews, Harry 1930- .... **CLC 6, 52**
See also CA 21-24R; CAAS 6; CANR 18, 40, 98, 160; CN 5, 6, 7

Mathews, John Joseph 1894-1979 .. **CLC 84; NNAL**
See also CA 19-20; 142; CANR 45; CAP 2; DAM MULT; DLB 175; TCWW 1, 2

Mathias, Roland 1915-2007 .... **CLC 45**
See also CA 97-100; 263; CANR 19, 41; CP 1, 2, 3, 4, 5, 6, 7; DLB 27

Mathias, Roland Glyn
See Mathias, Roland

Matsuo Basho 1644(?)-1694 ...... **LC 62; PC 3**
See Basho, Matsuo
See also DAM POET; PFS 2, 7, 18

Mattheson, Rodney
See Creasey, John

Matthew of Vendome c. 1130-c. 1200 .... **CMLC 99**
See also DLB 208

Matthews, (James) Brander
1852-1929 .... **TCLC 95**
See also CA 181; DLB 71, 78; DLBD 13

Matthews, Greg 1949- .... **CLC 45**
See also CA 135

Matthews, William (Procter III)
1942-1997 .... **CLC 40**
See also AMWS 9; CA 29-32R; 162; CAAS 18; CANR 12, 57; CP 2, 3, 4, 5, 6; DLB 5

Matthias, John (Edward) 1941- .... **CLC 9**
See also CA 33-36R; CANR 56; CP 4, 5, 6, 7

Matthiessen, F(rancis) O(tto)
1902-1950 .... **TCLC 100**
See also CA 185; DLB 63; MAL 5

Matthiessen, Peter 1927- ... **CLC 5, 7, 11, 32, 64, 245**
See also AAYA 6, 40; AMWS 5; ANW; BEST 90:4; BPFB 2; CA 9-12R; CANR 21, 50, 73, 100, 138; CN 1, 2, 3, 4, 5, 6, 7; DA3; DAM NOV; DLB 6, 173, 275; MAL 5; MTCW 1, 2; MTFW 2005; SATA 27

Maturin, Charles Robert
1780(?)-1824 .... **NCLC 6, 169**
See also BRWS 8; DLB 178; GL 3; HGG; LMFS 1; RGEL 2; SUFW

Matute (Ausejo), Ana Maria 1925- .. **CLC 11**
See also CA 89-92; CANR 129; CWW 2; DLB 322; EWL 3; MTCW 1; RGSF 2

Maugham, W. S.
See Maugham, W(illiam) Somerset

Maugham, W(illiam) Somerset
1874-1965 .. **CLC 1, 11, 15, 67, 93; SSC 8, 94; TCLC 208; WLC 4**
See also AAYA 55; BPFB 2; BRW 6; CA 5-8R; 25-28R; CANR 40, 127; CDBLB 1914-1945; CMW 4; DA; DA3; DAB; DAC; DAM DRAM, MST, NOV; DFS 22; DLB 10, 36, 77, 100, 162, 195; EWL 3; LAIT 3; MTCW 1, 2; MTFW 2005; NFS 23; RGEL 2; RGSF 2; SATA 54; SSFS 17

Maugham, William Somerset
See Maugham, W(illiam) Somerset

Maupassant, (Henri Rene Albert) Guy de
1850-1893 . **NCLC 1, 42, 83; SSC 1, 64; WLC 4**
See also BYA 14; DA; DA3; DAB; DAC; DAM MST; DLB 123; EW 7; EXPS; GFL 1789 to the Present; LAIT 2; LMFS 1; RGSF 2; RGWL 2, 3; SSFS 4, 21; SUFW; TWA

Maupin, Armistead 1944- .... **CLC 95**
See also CA 125; 130; CANR 58, 101, 183; CPW; DA3; DAM POP; DLB 278; GLL 1; INT CA-130; MTCW 2; MTFW 2005

Maupin, Armistead Jones, Jr.
See Maupin, Armistead

Maurhut, Richard
See Traven, B.

Mauriac, Claude 1914-1996 .... **CLC 9**
See also CA 89-92; 152; CWW 2; DLB 83; EWL 3; GFL 1789 to the Present

Mauriac, Francois (Charles)
1885-1970 .... **CLC 4, 9, 56; SSC 24**
See also CA 25-28; CAP 2; DLB 65, 331; EW 10; EWL 3; GFL 1789 to the Present; MTCW 1, 2; MTFW 2005; RGWL 2, 3; TWA

Mavor, Osborne Henry 1888-1951
See Bridie, James
See also CA 104

Maxwell, Glyn 1962- .... **CLC 238**
See also CA 154; CANR 88, 183; CP 6, 7; PFS 23

Maxwell, William (Keepers, Jr.)
1908-2000 .... **CLC 19**
See also AMWS 8; CA 93-96; 189; CANR 54, 95; CN 1, 2, 3, 4, 5, 6, 7; DLB 218, 278; DLBY 1980; INT CA-93-96; MAL 5; SATA-Obit 128

May, Elaine 1932- .... **CLC 16**
See also CA 124; 142; CAD; CWD; DLB 44

Mayakovski, Vladimir (Vladimirovich)
1893-1930 .... **TCLC 4, 18**
See Maiakovskii, Vladimir; Mayakovsky, Vladimir
See also CA 104; 158; EWL 3; MTCW 2; MTFW 2005; SFW 4; TWA

Mayakovsky, Vladimir
See Mayakovski, Vladimir (Vladimirovich)
See also EW 11; WP

Mayhew, Henry 1812-1887 .... **NCLC 31**
See also DLB 18, 55, 190

Mayle, Peter 1939(?)- .... **CLC 89**
See also CA 139; CANR 64, 109, 168

Maynard, Joyce 1953- .... **CLC 23**
See also CA 111; 129; CANR 64, 169

Mayne, William (James Carter)
1928- .... **CLC 12**
See also AAYA 20; CA 9-12R; CANR 37, 80, 100; CLR 25, 123; FANT; JRDA; MAICYA 1, 2; MAICYAS 1; SAAS 11; SATA 6, 68, 122; SUFW 2; YAW

Mayo, Jim
See L'Amour, Louis

Maysles, Albert 1926- .... **CLC 16**
See also CA 29-32R

Maysles, David 1932-1987 .... **CLC 16**
See also CA 191

Mazer, Norma Fox 1931- .... **CLC 26**
See also AAYA 5, 36; BYA 1, 8; CA 69-72; CANR 12, 32, 66, 129; CLR 23; JRDA; MAICYA 1, 2; SAAS 1; SATA 24, 67, 105, 168; WYA; YAW

Mazzini, Guiseppe 1805-1872 .... **NCLC 34**

McAlmon, Robert (Menzies)
1895-1956 .... **TCLC 97**
See also CA 107; 168; DLB 4, 45; DLBD 15; GLL 1

McAuley, James Phillip 1917-1976 .. **CLC 45**
See also CA 97-100; CP 1, 2; DLB 260; RGEL 2

McBain, Ed
See Hunter, Evan
See also MSW

McBrien, William (Augustine)
1930- .... **CLC 44**
See also CA 107; CANR 90

McCabe, Patrick 1955- .... **CLC 133**
See also BRWS 9; CA 130; CANR 50, 90, 168; CN 6, 7; DLB 194

McCaffrey, Anne 1926- .... **CLC 17**
See also AAYA 6, 34; AITN 2; BEST 89:2; BPFB 2; BYA 5; CA 25-28R, 227; CAAE 227; CANR 15, 35, 55, 96, 169; CLR 49, 130; CPW; DA3; DAM NOV, POP; DLB 8; JRDA; MAICYA 1, 2; MTCW 1, 2; MTFW 2005; SAAS 11; SATA 8, 70, 116, 152; SATA-Essay 152; SFW 4; SUFW 2; WYA; YAW

McCaffrey, Anne Inez
See McCaffrey, Anne

McCall, Nathan 1955(?)- .... **CLC 86**
See also AAYA 59; BW 3; CA 146; CANR 88

McCann, Arthur
See Campbell, John W(ood, Jr.)

McCann, Edson
See Pohl, Frederik

McCarthy, Charles
See McCarthy, Cormac

McCarthy, Charles, Jr.
See McCarthy, Cormac

McCarthy, Cormac 1933- .... **CLC 4, 57, 101, 204**
See also AAYA 41; AMWS 8; BPFB 2; CA 13-16R; CANR 10, 42, 69, 101, 161, 171; CN 6, 7; CPW; CSW; DA3; DAM POP; DLB 6, 143, 256; EWL 3; LATS 1:2; MAL 5; MTCW 2; MTFW 2005; TCLE 1:2; TCWW 2

McCarthy, Mary (Therese)
1912-1989 .. **CLC 1, 3, 5, 14, 24, 39, 59; SSC 24**
See also AMW; BPFB 2; CA 5-8R; 129; CANR 16, 50, 64; CN 1, 2, 3, 4; DA3; DLB 2; DLBY 1981; EWL 3; FW; INT CANR-16; MAL 5; MBL; MTCW 1, 2; MTFW 2005; RGAL 4; TUS

McCartney, James Paul
See McCartney, Paul

McCartney, Paul 1942- .... **CLC 12, 35**
See also CA 146; CANR 111

McCauley, Stephen (D.) 1955- .... **CLC 50**
See also CA 141

McClaren, Peter CLC 70

McClure, Michael (Thomas) 1932- ... **CLC 6, 10**
See also BG 1:3; CA 21-24R; CAD; CANR 17, 46, 77, 131; CD 5, 6; CP 1, 2, 3, 4, 5, 6, 7; DLB 16; WP

McCorkle, Jill (Collins) 1958- .... **CLC 51**
See also CA 121; CANR 113; CSW; DLB 234; DLBY 1987; SSFS 24

McCourt, Frank 1930- .... **CLC 109**
See also AAYA 61; AMWS 12; CA 157; CANR 97, 138; MTFW 2005; NCFS 1

McCourt, James 1941- .... **CLC 5**
See also CA 57-60; CANR 98, 152

McCourt, Malachy 1931- .... **CLC 119**
See also SATA 126

McCoy, Edmund
See Gardner, John

McCoy, Horace (Stanley)
1897-1955 .... **TCLC 28**
See also AMWS 13; CA 108; 155; CMW 4; DLB 9

McCrae, John 1872-1918 .... **TCLC 12**
See also CA 109; DLB 92; PFS 5

McCreigh, James
See Pohl, Frederik

McCullers, (Lula) Carson (Smith)
1917-1967 .... **CLC 1, 4, 10, 12, 48, 100; SSC 9, 24, 99; TCLC 155; WLC 4**
See also AAYA 21; AMW; AMWC 2; BPFB 2; CA 5-8R; 25-28R; CABS 1, 3; CANR 18, 132; CDALB 1941-1968; DA; DA3; DAB; DAC; DAM MST, NOV; DFS 5, 18; DLB 2, 7, 173, 228; EWL 3; EXPS; FW; GLL 1; LAIT 3, 4; MAL 5; MBL; MTCW 1, 2; MTFW 2005; NFS 6, 13; RGAL 4; RGSF 2; SATA 27; SSFS 5; TUS; YAW

McCulloch, John Tyler
See Burroughs, Edgar Rice

McCullough, Colleen 1937- ...... **CLC 27, 107**
See also AAYA 36; BPFB 2; CA 81-84; CANR 17, 46, 67, 98, 139; CPW; DA3; DAM NOV, POP; MTCW 1, 2; MTFW 2005; RHW

McCunn, Ruthanne Lum 1946- .... **AAL**
See also CA 119; CANR 43, 96; DLB 312; LAIT 2; SATA 63

McDermott, Alice 1953- .... **CLC 90**
See also AMWS 18; CA 109; CANR 40, 90, 126, 181; CN 7; DLB 292; MTFW 2005; NFS 23

McElroy, Joseph 1930- .... **CLC 5, 47**
See also CA 17-20R; CANR 149; CN 3, 4, 5, 6, 7

McElroy, Joseph Prince
See McElroy, Joseph

McEwan, Ian 1948- ... **CLC 13, 66, 169; SSC 106**
See also BEST 90:4; BRWS 4; CA 61-64; CANR 14, 41, 69, 87, 132, 179; CN 3, 4, 5, 6, 7; DAM NOV; DLB 14, 194, 319, 326; HGG; MTCW 1, 2; MTFW 2005; RGSF 2; SUFW 2; TEA

McEwan, Ian Russell
See McEwan, Ian

McFadden, David 1940- .... **CLC 48**
See also CA 104; CP 1, 2, 3, 4, 5, 6, 7; DLB 60; INT CA-104

McFarland, Dennis 1950- .... **CLC 65**
See also CA 165; CANR 110, 179

McGahern, John 1934-2006 .... **CLC 5, 9, 48, 156; SSC 17**
See also CA 17-20R; 249; CANR 29, 68, 113; CN 1, 2, 3, 4, 5, 6, 7; DLB 14, 231, 319; MTCW 1

McGinley, Patrick (Anthony) 1937- . **CLC 41**
See also CA 120; 127; CANR 56; INT CA-127

McGinley, Phyllis 1905-1978 .... **CLC 14**
See also CA 9-12R; 77-80; CANR 19; CP 1, 2; CWRI 5; DLB 11, 48; MAL 5; PFS 9, 13; SATA 2, 44; SATA-Obit 24

McGinniss, Joe 1942- .... **CLC 32**
See also AITN 2; BEST 89:2; CA 25-28R; CANR 26, 70, 152; CPW; DLB 185; INT CANR-26

McGivern, Maureen Daly
See Daly, Maureen

McGivern, Maureen Patricia Daly
See Daly, Maureen

McGrath, Patrick 1950- .... **CLC 55**
See also CA 136; CANR 65, 148; CN 5, 6, 7; DLB 231; HGG; SUFW 2

McGrath, Thomas (Matthew)
1916-1990 .... **CLC 28, 59**
See also AMWS 10; CA 9-12R; 132; CANR 6, 33, 95; CP 1, 2, 3, 4, 5; DAM POET; MAL 5; MTCW 1; SATA 41; SATA-Obit 66

McGuane, Thomas 1939- ... **CLC 3, 7, 18, 45, 127**
See also AITN 2; BPFB 2; CA 49-52; CANR 5, 24, 49, 94, 164; CN 2, 3, 4, 5, 6, 7; DLB 2, 212; DLBY 1980; EWL 3; INT CANR-24; MAL 5; MTCW 1; MTFW 2005; TCWW 1, 2

McGuane, Thomas Francis III
See McGuane, Thomas

McGuckian, Medbh 1950- .... **CLC 48, 174;
PC 27**
  See also BRWS 5; CA 143; CP 4, 5, 6, 7;
  CWP; DAM POET; DLB 40
McHale, Tom 1942(?)-1982 .... **CLC 3, 5**
  See also AITN 1; CA 77-80; 106; CN 1, 2,
  3
McHugh, Heather 1948- .... **PC 61**
  See also CA 69-72; CANR 11, 28, 55, 92;
  CP 4, 5, 6, 7; CWP; PFS 24
McIlvanney, William 1936- .... **CLC 42**
  See also CA 25-28R; CANR 61; CMW 4;
  DLB 14, 207
McIlwraith, Maureen Mollie Hunter
  See Hunter, Mollie
  See also SATA 2
McInerney, Jay 1955- .... **CLC 34, 112**
  See also AAYA 18; BPFB 2; CA 116; 123;
  CANR 45, 68, 116, 176; CN 5, 6, 7; CPW;
  DA3; DAM POP; DLB 292; INT CA-123;
  MAL 5; MTCW 2; MTFW 2005
McIntyre, Vonda N. 1948- .... **CLC 18**
  See also CA 81-84; CANR 17, 34, 69;
  MTCW 1; SFW 4; YAW
McIntyre, Vonda Neel
  See McIntyre, Vonda N.
McKay, Claude **BLC 1:3; HR 1:3; PC 2;
  TCLC 7, 41; WLC 4**
  See McKay, Festus Claudius
  See also AFAW 1, 2; AMWS 10; DAB;
  DLB 4, 45, 51, 117; EWL 3; EXPP; GLL
  2; LAIT 3; LMFS 2; MAL 5; PAB; PFS
  4; RGAL 4; WP
McKay, Festus Claudius 1889-1948
  See McKay, Claude
  See also BW 1, 3; CA 104; 124; CANR 73;
  DA; DAC; DAM MST, MULT, NOV,
  POET; MTCW 1, 2; MTFW 2005; TUS
McKuen, Rod 1933- .... **CLC 1, 3**
  See also AITN 1; CA 41-44R; CANR 40;
  CP 1
McLoughlin, R. B.
  See Mencken, H(enry) L(ouis)
McLuhan, (Herbert) Marshall
  1911-1980 .... **CLC 37, 83**
  See also CA 9-12R; 102; CANR 12, 34, 61;
  DLB 88; INT CANR-12; MTCW 1, 2;
  MTFW 2005
McManus, Declan Patrick Aloysius
  See Costello, Elvis
McMillan, Terry 1951- .. **BLCS; CLC 50, 61,
  112**
  See also AAYA 21; AMWS 13; BPFB 2;
  BW 2, 3; CA 140; CANR 60, 104, 131;
  CN 7; CPW; DA3; DAM MULT, NOV,
  POP; MAL 5; MTCW 2; MTFW 2005;
  RGAL 4; YAW
McMurtry, Larry 1936- .... **CLC 2, 3, 7, 11,
  27, 44, 127, 250**
  See also AAYA 15; AITN 2; AMWS 5;
  BEST 89:2; BPFB 2; CA 5-8R; CANR
  19, 43, 64, 103, 170; CDALB 1968-1988;
  CN 2, 3, 4, 5, 6, 7; CPW; CSW; DA3;
  DAM NOV, POP; DLB 2, 143, 256;
  DLBY 1980, 1987; EWL 3; MAL 5;
  MTCW 1, 2; MTFW 2005; RGAL 4;
  TCWW 1, 2
McMurtry, Larry Jeff
  See McMurtry, Larry
McNally, Terrence 1939- ... **CLC 4, 7, 41, 91,
  252; DC 27**
  See also AAYA 62; AMWS 13; CA 45-48;
  CAD; CANR 2, 56, 116; CD 5, 6; DA3;
  DAM DRAM; DFS 16, 19; DLB 7, 249;
  EWL 3; GLL 1; MTCW 2; MTFW 2005
McNally, Thomas Michael
  See McNally, T.M.
McNally, T.M. 1961- .... **CLC 82**
  See also CA 246

McNamer, Deirdre 1950- .... **CLC 70**
  See also CA 188; CANR 163
McNeal, Tom **CLC 119**
  See also CA 252; SATA 194
McNeile, Herman Cyril 1888-1937
  See Sapper
  See also CA 184; CMW 4; DLB 77
McNickle, (William) D'Arcy
  1904-1977 .... **CLC 89; NNAL**
  See also CA 9-12R; 85-88; CANR 5, 45;
  DAM MULT; DLB 175, 212; RGAL 4;
  SATA-Obit 22; TCWW 1, 2
McPhee, John 1931- .... **CLC 36**
  See also AAYA 61; AMWS 3; ANW; BEST
  90:1; CA 65-68; CANR 20, 46, 64, 69,
  121, 165; CPW; DLB 185, 275; MTCW
  1, 2; MTFW 2005; TUS
McPhee, John Angus
  See McPhee, John
McPherson, James Alan, Jr.
  See McPherson, James Alan
McPherson, James Alan 1943- . **BLCS; CLC
  19, 77; SSC 95**
  See also BW 1, 3; CA 25-28R; 273; CAAE
  273; CAAS 17; CANR 24, 74, 140; CN
  3, 4, 5, 6; CSW; DLB 38, 244; EWL 3;
  MTCW 1, 2; MTFW 2005; RGAL 4;
  RGSF 2; SSFS 23
McPherson, William (Alexander)
  1933- .... **CLC 34**
  See also CA 69-72; CANR 28; INT
  CANR-28
McTaggart, J. McT. Ellis
  See McTaggart, John McTaggart Ellis
McTaggart, John McTaggart Ellis
  1866-1925 .... **TCLC 105**
  See also CA 120; DLB 262
Mda, Zakes 1948- .... **BLC 2:3; CLC 262**
  See also CA 205; CANR 151; CD 5, 6;
  DLB 225
Mda, Zanemvula
  See Mda, Zakes
Mda, Zanemvula Kizito Gatyeni
  See Mda, Zakes
Mead, George Herbert 1863-1931 . **TCLC 89**
  See also CA 212; DLB 270
Mead, Margaret 1901-1978 .... **CLC 37**
  See also AITN 1; CA 1-4R; 81-84; CANR
  4; DA3; FW; MTCW 1, 2; SATA-Obit 20
Meaker, M. J.
  See Meaker, Marijane
Meaker, Marijane 1927- .... **CLC 12, 35**
  See also AAYA 2, 23; BYA 1, 7, 8; CA 107;
  CANR 37, 63, 145, 180; CLR 29; GLL 2;
  INT CA-107; JRDA; MAICYA 1, 2; MAI-
  CYAS 1; MTCW 1; SAAS 1; SATA 20,
  61, 99, 160; SATA-Essay 111; WYA;
  YAW
Meaker, Marijane Agnes
  See Meaker, Marijane
Mechthild von Magdeburg c. 1207-c.
  1282 .... **CMLC 91**
  See also DLB 138
Medoff, Mark (Howard) 1940- .... **CLC 6, 23**
  See also AITN 1; CA 53-56; CAD; CANR
  5; CD 5, 6; DAM DRAM; DFS 4; DLB
  7; INT CANR-5
Medvedev, P. N.
  See Bakhtin, Mikhail Mikhailovich
Meged, Aharon
  See Megged, Aharon
Meged, Aron
  See Megged, Aharon
Megged, Aharon 1920- .... **CLC 9**
  See also CA 49-52; CAAS 13; CANR 1,
  140; EWL 3; RGHL
Mehta, Deepa 1950- .... **CLC 208**
Mehta, Gita 1943- .... **CLC 179**
  See also CA 225; CN 7; DNFS 2

Mehta, Ved 1934- .... **CLC 37**
  See also CA 1-4R; 212; CAAE 212; CANR
  2, 23, 69; DLB 323; MTCW 1; MTFW
  2005
Melanchthon, Philipp 1497-1560 .... **LC 90**
  See also DLB 179
Melanter
  See Blackmore, R(ichard) D(oddridge)
Meleager c. 140B.C.-c. 70B.C. ...... **CMLC 53**
Melies, Georges 1861-1938 .... **TCLC 81**
Melikow, Loris
  See Hofmannsthal, Hugo von
Melmoth, Sebastian
  See Wilde, Oscar
Melo Neto, Joao Cabral de
  See Cabral de Melo Neto, Joao
  See also CWW 2; EWL 3
Meltzer, Milton 1915- .... **CLC 26**
  See also AAYA 8, 45; BYA 2, 6; CA 13-
  16R; CANR 38, 92, 107; CLR 13; DLB
  61; JRDA; MAICYA 1, 2; SAAS 1; SATA
  1, 50, 80, 128; SATA-Essay 124; WYA;
  YAW
Melville, Herman 1819-1891 ..... **NCLC 3, 12,
  29, 45, 49, 91, 93, 123, 157, 181, 193;
  PC 82; SSC 1, 17, 46, 95; WLC 4**
  See also AAYA 25; AMW; AMWR 1;
  CDALB 1640-1865; DA; DA3; DAB;
  DAC; DAM MST, NOV; DLB 3, 74, 250,
  254; EXPN; EXPS; GL 3; LAIT 1, 2; NFS
  7, 9; RGAL 4; RGSF 2; SATA 59; SSFS
  3; TUS
Members, Mark
  See Powell, Anthony
Membreno, Alejandro **CLC 59**
Menand, Louis 1952- .... **CLC 208**
  See also CA 200
Menander c. 342B.C.-c. 293B.C. .... **CMLC 9,
  51, 101; DC 3**
  See also AW 1; CDWLB 1; DAM DRAM;
  DLB 176; LMFS 1; RGWL 2, 3
Menchu, Rigoberta 1959- .. **CLC 160; HLCS
  2**
  See also CA 175; CANR 135; DNFS 1;
  WLIT 1
Mencken, H(enry) L(ouis)
  1880-1956 .... **TCLC 13**
  See also AMW; CA 105; 125; CDALB
  1917-1929; DLB 11, 29, 63, 137, 222;
  EWL 3; MAL 5; MTCW 1, 2; MTFW
  2005; NCFS 4; RGAL 4; TUS
Mendelsohn, Jane 1965- .... **CLC 99**
  See also CA 154; CANR 94
Mendelssohn, Moses 1729-1786 .... **LC 142**
  See also DLB 97
Mendoza, Inigo Lopez de
  See Santillana, Inigo Lopez de Mendoza,
  Marques de
Menton, Francisco de
  See Chin, Frank (Chew, Jr.)
Mercer, David 1928-1980 .... **CLC 5**
  See also CA 9-12R; 102; CANR 23; CBD;
  DAM DRAM; DLB 13, 310; MTCW 1;
  RGEL 2
Merchant, Paul
  See Ellison, Harlan
Meredith, George 1828-1909 .. **PC 60; TCLC
  17, 43**
  See also CA 117; 153; CANR 80; CDBLB
  1832-1890; DAM POET; DLB 18, 35, 57,
  159; RGEL 2; TEA
Meredith, William 1919-2007 ...... **CLC 4, 13,
  22, 55; PC 28**
  See also CA 9-12R; 260; CAAS 14; CANR
  6, 40, 129; CP 1, 2, 3, 4, 5, 6, 7; DAM
  POET; DLB 5; MAL 5
Meredith, William Morris
  See Meredith, William

Merezhkovsky, Dmitrii Sergeevich
See Merezhkovsky, Dmitry Sergeyevich
See also DLB 295

Merezhkovsky, Dmitry Sergeevich
See Merezhkovsky, Dmitry Sergeyevich
See also EWL 3

Merezhkovsky, Dmitry Sergeyevich
1865-1941 .... TCLC 29
See Merezhkovsky, Dmitrii Sergeevich;
Merezhkovsky, Dmitry Sergeyevich
See also CA 169

Merimee, Prosper 1803-1870 ... NCLC 6, 65;
SSC 7, 77
See also DLB 119, 192; EW 6; EXPS; GFL
1789 to the Present; RGSF 2; RGWL 2,
3; SSFS 8; SUFW

Merkin, Daphne 1954- .... CLC 44
See also CA 123

Merleau-Ponty, Maurice
1908-1961 .... TCLC 156
See also CA 114; 89-92; DLB 296; GFL
1789 to the Present

Merlin, Arthur
See Blish, James (Benjamin)

Mernissi, Fatima 1940- .... CLC 171
See also CA 152; DLB 346; FW

Merrill, James 1926-1995 ...... CLC 2, 3, 6, 8,
13, 18, 34, 91; PC 28; TCLC 173
See also AMWS 3; CA 13-16R; 147; CANR
10, 49, 63, 108; CP 1, 2, 3, 4; DA3; DAM
POET; DLB 5, 165; DLBY 1985; EWL 3;
INT CANR-10; MAL 5; MTCW 1, 2;
MTFW 2005; PAB; PFS 23; RGAL 4

Merrill, James Ingram
See Merrill, James

Merriman, Alex
See Silverberg, Robert

Merriman, Brian 1747-1805 .... NCLC 70

Merritt, E. B.
See Waddington, Miriam

Merton, Thomas (James)
1915-1968 . CLC 1, 3, 11, 34, 83; PC 10
See also AAYA 61; AMWS 8; CA 5-8R;
25-28R; CANR 22, 53, 111, 131; DA3;
DLB 48; DLBY 1981; MAL 5; MTCW 1,
2; MTFW 2005

Merwin, W.S. 1927- ...... CLC 1, 2, 3, 5, 8, 13,
18, 45, 88; PC 45
See also AMWS 3; CA 13-16R; CANR 15,
51, 112, 140; CP 1, 2, 3, 4, 5, 6, 7; DA3;
DAM POET; DLB 5, 169, 342; EWL 3;
INT CANR-15; MAL 5; MTCW 1, 2;
MTFW 2005; PAB; PFS 5, 15; RGAL 4

Metastasio, Pietro 1698-1782 .... LC 115
See also RGWL 2, 3

Metcalf, John 1938- .... CLC 37; SSC 43
See also CA 113; CN 4, 5, 6, 7; DLB 60;
RGSF 2; TWA

Metcalf, Suzanne
See Baum, L(yman) Frank

Mew, Charlotte (Mary) 1870-1928 .. TCLC 8
See also CA 105; 189; DLB 19, 135; RGEL
2

Mewshaw, Michael 1943- .... CLC 9
See also CA 53-56; CANR 7, 47, 147;
DLBY 1980

Meyer, Conrad Ferdinand
1825-1898 .... NCLC 81; SSC 30
See also DLB 129; EW; RGWL 2, 3

Meyer, Gustav 1868-1932
See Meyrink, Gustav
See also CA 117; 190

Meyer, June
See Jordan, June

Meyer, Lynn
See Slavitt, David R.

Meyers, Jeffrey 1939- .... CLC 39
See also CA 73-76, 186; CAAE 186; CANR
54, 102, 159; DLB 111

Meynell, Alice (Christina Gertrude
Thompson) 1847-1922 .... TCLC 6
See also CA 104; 177; DLB 19, 98; RGEL
2

Meyrink, Gustav TCLC 21
See Meyer, Gustav
See also DLB 81; EWL 3

Mhlophe, Gcina 1960- .... BLC 2:3

Michaels, Leonard 1933-2003 ..... CLC 6, 25;
SSC 16
See also AMWS 16; CA 61-64; 216; CANR
21, 62, 119, 179; CN 3, 45, 6, 7; DLB
130; MTCW 1; TCLE 1:2

Michaux, Henri 1899-1984 .... CLC 8, 19
See also CA 85-88; 114; DLB 258; EWL 3;
GFL 1789 to the Present; RGWL 2, 3

Micheaux, Oscar (Devereaux)
1884-1951 .... TCLC 76
See also BW 3; CA 174; DLB 50; TCWW
2

Michelangelo 1475-1564 .... LC 12
See also AAYA 43

Michelet, Jules 1798-1874 .... NCLC 31
See also EW 5; GFL 1789 to the Present

Michels, Robert 1876-1936 .... TCLC 88
See also CA 212

Michener, James A. 1907(?)-1997 . CLC 1, 5,
11, 29, 60, 109
See also AAYA 27; AITN 1; BEST 90:1;
BPFB 2; CA 5-8R; 161; CANR 21, 45,
68; CN 1, 2, 3, 4, 5, 6; CPW; DA3; DAM
NOV, POP; DLB 6; MAL 5; MTCW 1, 2;
MTFW 2005; RHW; TCWW 1, 2

Mickiewicz, Adam 1798-1855 . NCLC 3, 101;
PC 38
See also EW 5; RGWL 2, 3

Middleton, (John) Christopher
1926- .... CLC 13
See also CA 13-16R; CANR 29, 54, 117;
CP 1, 2, 3, 4, 5, 6, 7; DLB 40

Middleton, Richard (Barham)
1882-1911 .... TCLC 56
See also CA 187; DLB 156; HGG

Middleton, Stanley 1919- .... CLC 7, 38
See also CA 25-28R; CAAS 23; CANR 21,
46, 81, 157; CN 1, 2, 3, 4, 5, 6, 7; DLB
14, 326

Middleton, Thomas 1580-1627 ...... DC 5; LC
33, 123
See also BRW 2; DAM DRAM, MST; DFS
18, 22; DLB 58; RGEL 2

Mieville, China 1972(?)- .... CLC 235
See also AAYA 52; CA 196; CANR 138;
MTFW 2005

Migueis, Jose Rodrigues 1901-1980 . CLC 10
See also DLB 287

Mikszath, Kalman 1847-1910 .... TCLC 31
See also CA 170

Miles, Jack CLC 100
See also CA 200

Miles, John Russiano
See Miles, Jack

Miles, Josephine (Louise)
1911-1985 .... CLC 1, 2, 14, 34, 39
See also CA 1-4R; 116; CANR 2, 55; CP 1,
2, 3, 4; DAM POET; DLB 48; MAL 5;
TCLE 1:2

Militant
See Sandburg, Carl (August)

Mill, Harriet (Hardy) Taylor
1807-1858 .... NCLC 102
See also FW

Mill, John Stuart 1806-1873 ... NCLC 11, 58,
179
See also CDBLB 1832-1890; DLB 55, 190,
262; FW 1; RGEL 2; TEA

Millar, Kenneth 1915-1983 .... CLC 14
See Macdonald, Ross
See also CA 9-12R; 110; CANR 16, 63,
107; CMW 4; CPW; DA3; DAM POP;
DLB 2, 226; DLBD 6; DLBY 1983;
MTCW 1, 2; MTFW 2005

Millay, E. Vincent
See Millay, Edna St. Vincent

Millay, Edna St. Vincent 1892-1950 ..... PC 6,
61; TCLC 4, 49, 169; WLCS
See Boyd, Nancy
See also AMW; CA 104; 130; CDALB
1917-1929; DA; DA3; DAB; DAC; DAM
MST, POET; DLB 45, 249; EWL 3;
EXPP; FL 1:6; MAL 5; MBL; MTCW 1,
2; MTFW 2005; PAB; PFS 3, 17; RGAL
4; TUS; WP

Miller, Arthur 1915-2005 ..... CLC 1, 2, 6, 10,
15, 26, 47, 78, 179; DC 1, 31; WLC 4
See also AAYA 15; AITN 1; AMW; AMWC
1; CA 1-4R; 236; CABS 3; CAD; CANR
2, 30, 54, 76, 132; CD 5, 6; CDALB
1941-1968; DA; DA3; DAB; DAC; DAM
DRAM, MST; DFS 1, 3, 8; DLB 7, 266;
EWL 3; LAIT 1, 4; LATS 1:2; MAL 5;
MTCW 1, 2; MTFW 2005; RGAL 4;
RGHL; TUS; WYAS 1

Miller, Henry (Valentine)
1891-1980 .... CLC 1, 2, 4, 9, 14, 43, 84;
TCLC 213; WLC 4
See also AMW; BPFB 2; CA 9-12R; 97-
100; CANR 33, 64; CDALB 1929-1941;
CN 1, 2; DA; DA3; DAB; DAC; DAM
MST, NOV; DLB 4, 9; DLBY 1980; EWL
3; MAL 5; MTCW 1, 2; MTFW 2005;
RGAL 4; TUS

Miller, Hugh 1802-1856 .... NCLC 143
See also DLB 190

Miller, Jason 1939(?)-2001 .... CLC 2
See also AITN 1; CA 73-76; 197; CAD;
CANR 130; DFS 12; DLB 7

Miller, Sue 1943- .... CLC 44
See also AMWS 12; BEST 90:3; CA 139;
CANR 59, 91, 128; DA3; DAM POP;
DLB 143

Miller, Walter M(ichael, Jr.)
1923-1996 .... CLC 4, 30
See also BPFB 2; CA 85-88; CANR 108;
DLB 8; SCFW 1, 2; SFW 4

Millett, Kate 1934- .... CLC 67
See also AITN 1; CA 73-76; CANR 32, 53,
76, 110; DA3; DLB 246; FW; GLL 1;
MTCW 1, 2; MTFW 2005

Millhauser, Steven 1943- ... CLC 21, 54, 109;
SSC 57
See also AAYA 76; CA 110; 111; CANR
63, 114, 133; CN 6, 7; DA3; DLB 2;
FANT; INT CA-111; MAL 5; MTCW 2;
MTFW 2005

Millhauser, Steven Lewis
See Millhauser, Steven

Millin, Sarah Gertrude 1889-1968 ... CLC 49
See also CA 102; 93-96; DLB 225; EWL 3

Milne, A. A. 1882-1956 .... TCLC 6, 88
See also BRWS 5; CA 104; 133; CLR 1,
26, 108; CMW 4; CWRI 5; DA3; DAB;
DAC; DAM MST; DLB 10, 77, 100, 160;
FANT; MAICYA 1, 2; MTCW 1, 2;
MTFW 2005; RGEL 2; SATA 100; WCH;
YABC 1

Milne, Alan Alexander
See Milne, A. A.

Milner, Ron(ald) 1938-2004 .. BLC 1:3; CLC
56
See also AITN 1; BW 1; CA 73-76; 230;
CAD; CANR 24, 81; CD 5, 6; DAM
MULT; DLB 38; MAL 5; MTCW 1

Milnes, Richard Monckton
1809-1885 .... NCLC 61
See also DLB 32, 184

Milosz, Czeslaw 1911-2004 .... **CLC 5, 11, 22, 31, 56, 82, 253; PC 8; WLCS**
See also AAYA 62; CA 81-84; 230; CANR 23, 51, 91, 126; CDWLB 4; CWW 2; DA3; DAM MST, POET; DLB 215, 331; EW 13; EWL 3; MTCW 1, 2; MTFW 2005; PFS 16, 29; RGHL; RGWL 2, 3

Milton, John 1608-1674 ..... **LC 9, 43, 92; PC 19, 29; WLC 4**
See also AAYA 65; BRW 2; BRWR 2; CD-BLB 1660-1789; DA; DA3; DAB; DAC; DAM MST, POET; DLB 131, 151, 281; EFS 1; EXPP; LAIT 1; PAB; PFS 3, 17; RGEL 2; TEA; WLIT 3; WP

Min, Anchee 1957- .... **CLC 86**
See also CA 146; CANR 94, 137; MTFW 2005

Minehaha, Cornelius
See Wedekind, Frank

Miner, Valerie 1947- .... **CLC 40**
See also CA 97-100; CANR 59, 177; FW; GLL 2

Minimo, Duca
See D'Annunzio, Gabriele

Minot, Susan (Anderson) 1956- ...... **CLC 44, 159**
See also AMWS 6; CA 134; CANR 118; CN 6, 7

Minus, Ed 1938- .... **CLC 39**
See also CA 185

Mirabai 1498(?)-1550(?) .... **LC 143; PC 48**
See also PFS 24

Miranda, Javier
See Bioy Casares, Adolfo
See also CWW 2

Mirbeau, Octave 1848-1917 .... **TCLC 55**
See also CA 216; DLB 123, 192; GFL 1789 to the Present

Mirikitani, Janice 1942- .... **AAL**
See also CA 211; DLB 312; RGAL 4

Mirk, John (?)-c. 1414 .... **LC 105**
See also DLB 146

Miro (Ferrer), Gabriel (Francisco Victor) 1879-1930 .... **TCLC 5**
See also CA 104; 185; DLB 322; EWL 3

Misharin, Alexandr CLC 59

Mishima, Yukio CLC 2, 4, 6, 9, 27; DC 1; SSC 4; TCLC 161; WLC 4
See Hiraoka, Kimitake
See also AAYA 50; BPFB 2; DLB 182; EWL 3; GLL 1; MJW; RGSF 2; RGWL 2, 3; SSFS 5, 12

Mistral, Frederic 1830-1914 .... **TCLC 51**
See also CA 122; 213; DLB 331; GFL 1789 to the Present

Mistral, Gabriela
See Godoy Alcayaga, Lucila
See also DLB 283, 331; DNFS 1; EWL 3; LAW; RGWL 2, 3; WP

Mistry, Rohinton 1952- ... **CLC 71, 196; SSC 73**
See also BRWS 10; CA 141; CANR 86, 114; CCA 1; CN 6, 7; DAC; DLB 334; SSFS 6

Mitchell, Clyde
See Ellison, Harlan; Silverberg, Robert

Mitchell, Emerson Blackhorse Barney 1945- .... **NNAL**
See also CA 45-48

Mitchell, James Leslie 1901-1935
See Gibbon, Lewis Grassic
See also CA 104; 188; DLB 15

Mitchell, Joni 1943- .... **CLC 12**
See also CA 112; CCA 1

Mitchell, Joseph (Quincy) 1908-1996 .... **CLC 98**
See also CA 77-80; 152; CANR 69; CN 1, 2, 3, 4, 5, 6; CSW; DLB 185; DLBY 1996

Mitchell, Margaret (Munnerlyn) 1900-1949 .... **TCLC 11, 170**
See also AAYA 23; BPFB 2; BYA 1; CA 109; 125; CANR 55, 94; CDALBS; DA3; DAM NOV, POP; DLB 9; LAIT 2; MAL 5; MTCW 1, 2; MTFW 2005; NFS 9; RGAL 4; RHW; TUS; WYAS 1; YAW

Mitchell, Peggy
See Mitchell, Margaret (Munnerlyn)

Mitchell, S(ilas) Weir 1829-1914 .... **TCLC 36**
See also CA 165; DLB 202; RGAL 4

Mitchell, W(illiam) O(rmond) 1914-1998 .... **CLC 25**
See also CA 77-80; 165; CANR 15, 43; CN 1, 2, 3, 4, 5, 6; DAC; DAM MST; DLB 88; TCLE 1:2

Mitchell, William (Lendrum) 1879-1936 .... **TCLC 81**
See also CA 213

Mitford, Mary Russell 1787-1855 ... **NCLC 4**
See also DLB 110, 116; RGEL 2

Mitford, Nancy 1904-1973 .... **CLC 44**
See also BRWS 10; CA 9-12R; CN 1; DLB 191; RGEL 2

Miyamoto, (Chujo) Yuriko 1899-1951 .... **TCLC 37**
See Miyamoto Yuriko
See also CA 170, 174

Miyamoto Yuriko
See Miyamoto, (Chujo) Yuriko
See also DLB 180

Miyazawa, Kenji 1896-1933 .... **TCLC 76**
See Miyazawa Kenji
See also CA 157; RGWL 3

Miyazawa Kenji
See Miyazawa, Kenji
See also EWL 3

Mizoguchi, Kenji 1898-1956 .... **TCLC 72**
See also CA 167

Mo, Timothy (Peter) 1950- .... **CLC 46, 134**
See also CA 117; CANR 128; CN 5, 6, 7; DLB 194; MTCW 1; WLIT 4; WWE 1

Modarressi, Taghi (M.) 1931-1997 ... **CLC 44**
See also CA 121; 134; INT CA-134

Modiano, Patrick (Jean) 1945- .... **CLC 18, 218**
See also CA 85-88; CANR 17, 40, 115; CWW 2; DLB 83, 299; EWL 3; RGHL

Mofolo, Thomas (Mokopu) 1875(?)-1948 .... **BLC 1:3; TCLC 22**
See also AFW; CA 121; 153; CANR 83; DAM MULT; DLB 225; EWL 3; MTCW 2; MTFW 2005; WLIT 2

Mohr, Nicholasa 1938- .... **CLC 12; HLC 2**
See also AAYA 8, 46; CA 49-52; CANR 1, 32, 64; CLR 22; DAM MULT; DLB 145; HW 1, 2; JRDA; LAIT 5; LLW; MAICYA 2; MAICYAS 1; RGAL 4; SAAS 8; SATA 8, 97; SATA-Essay 113; WYA; YAW

Moi, Toril 1953- .... **CLC 172**
See also CA 154; CANR 102; FW

Mojtabai, A(nn) G(race) 1938- ..... **CLC 5, 9, 15, 29**
See also CA 85-88; CANR 88

Moliere 1622-1673 ..... **DC 13; LC 10, 28, 64, 125, 127; WLC 4**
See also DA; DA3; DAB; DAC; DAM DRAM, MST; DFS 13, 18, 20; DLB 268; EW 3; GFL Beginnings to 1789; LATS 1:1; RGWL 2, 3; TWA

Molin, Charles
See Mayne, William (James Carter)

Molnar, Ferenc 1878-1952 .... **TCLC 20**
See also CA 109; 153; CANR 83; CDWLB 4; DAM DRAM; DLB 215; EWL 3; RGWL 2, 3

Momaday, N. Scott 1934- ...... **CLC 2, 19, 85, 95, 160; NNAL; PC 25; WLCS**
See also AAYA 11, 64; AMWS 4; ANW; BPFB 2; BYA 12; CA 25-28R; CANR 14, 34, 68, 134; CDALBS; CN 2, 3, 4, 5, 6, 7; CPW; DA; DA3; DAB; DAC; DAM MST, MULT, NOV, POP; DLB 143, 175, 256; EWL 3; EXPP; INT CANR-14; LAIT 4; LATS 1:2; MAL 5; MTCW 1, 2; MTFW 2005; NFS 10; PFS 2, 11; RGAL 4; SATA 48; SATA-Brief 30; TCWW 1, 2; WP; YAW

Monette, Paul 1945-1995 .... **CLC 82**
See also AMWS 10; CA 139; 147; CN 6; GLL 1

Monroe, Harriet 1860-1936 .... **TCLC 12**
See also CA 109; 204; DLB 54, 91

Monroe, Lyle
See Heinlein, Robert A.

Montagu, Elizabeth 1720-1800 .... **NCLC 7, 117**
See also FW

Montagu, Mary (Pierrepont) Wortley 1689-1762 .... **LC 9, 57; PC 16**
See also DLB 95, 101; FL 1:1; RGEL 2

Montagu, W. H.
See Coleridge, Samuel Taylor

Montague, John (Patrick) 1929- ..... **CLC 13, 46**
See also CA 9-12R; CANR 9, 69, 121; CP 1, 2, 3, 4, 5, 6, 7; DLB 40; EWL 3; MTCW 1; PFS 12; RGEL 2; TCLE 1:2

Montaigne, Michel (Eyquem) de 1533-1592 .... **LC 8, 105; WLC 4**
See also DA; DAB; DAC; DAM MST; DLB 327; EW 2; GFL Beginnings to 1789; LMFS 1; RGWL 2, 3; TWA

Montale, Eugenio 1896-1981 ... **CLC 7, 9, 18; PC 13**
See also CA 17-20R; 104; CANR 30; DLB 114, 331; EW 11; EWL 3; MTCW 1; PFS 22; RGWL 2, 3; TWA; WLIT 7

Montesquieu, Charles-Louis de Secondat 1689-1755 .... **LC 7, 69**
See also DLB 314; EW 3; GFL Beginnings to 1789; TWA

Montessori, Maria 1870-1952 ...... **TCLC 103**
See also CA 115; 147

Montgomery, (Robert) Bruce 1921(?)-1978
See Crispin, Edmund
See also CA 179; 104; CMW 4

Montgomery, L(ucy) M(aud) 1874-1942 .... **TCLC 51, 140**
See also AAYA 12; BYA 1; CA 108; 137; CLR 8, 91; DA3; DAC; DAM MST; DLB 92; DLBD 14; JRDA; MAICYA 1, 2; MTCW 2; MTFW 2005; RGEL 2; SATA 100; TWA; WCH; WYA; YABC 1

Montgomery, Marion, Jr. 1925- .... **CLC 7**
See also AITN 1; CA 1-4R; CANR 3, 48, 162; CSW; DLB 6

Montgomery, Marion H. 1925-
See Montgomery, Marion, Jr.

Montgomery, Max
See Davenport, Guy (Mattison, Jr.)

Montherlant, Henry (Milon) de 1896-1972 .... **CLC 8, 19**
See also CA 85-88; 37-40R; DAM DRAM; DLB 72, 321; EW 11; EWL 3; GFL 1789 to the Present; MTCW 1

Monty Python
See Chapman, Graham; Cleese, John (Marwood); Gilliam, Terry; Idle, Eric; Jones, Terence Graham Parry; Palin, Michael
See also AAYA 7

Moodie, Susanna (Strickland) 1803-1885 .... **NCLC 14, 113**
See also DLB 99

Moody, Hiram
See Moody, Rick

Moody, Hiram F. III
See Moody, Rick

Moody, Minerva
See Alcott, Louisa May

Moody, Rick 1961- .... **CLC 147**
See also CA 138; CANR 64, 112, 179;
MTFW 2005

Moody, William Vaughan
1869-1910 .... **TCLC 105**
See also CA 110; 178; DLB 7, 54; MAL 5;
RGAL 4

Mooney, Edward 1951-
See Mooney, Ted
See also CA 130

Mooney, Ted CLC 25
See Mooney, Edward

Moorcock, Michael 1939- ...... **CLC 5, 27, 58,**
236
See Bradbury, Edward P.
See also AAYA 26; CA 45-48; CAAS 5;
CANR 2, 17, 38, 64, 122; CN 5, 6, 7;
DLB 14, 231, 261, 319; FANT; MTCW 1,
2; MTFW 2005; SATA 93, 166; SCFW 1,
2; SFW 4; SUFW 1, 2

Moorcock, Michael John
See Moorcock, Michael

Moorcock, Michael John
See Moorcock, Michael

Moore, Al
See Moore, Alan

Moore, Alan 1953- .... **CLC 230**
See also AAYA 51; CA 204; CANR 138,
184; DLB 261; MTFW 2005; SFW 4

Moore, Brian 1921-1999 ... **CLC 1, 3, 5, 7, 8,**
19, 32, 90
See Bryan, Michael
See also BRWS 9; CA 1-4R; 174; CANR 1,
25, 42, 63; CCA 1; CN 1, 2, 3, 4, 5, 6;
DAB; DAC; DAM MST; DLB 251; EWL
3; FANT; MTCW 1, 2; MTFW 2005;
RGEL 2

Moore, Edward
See Muir, Edwin
See also RGEL 2

Moore, G. E. 1873-1958 .... **TCLC 89**
See also DLB 262

Moore, George Augustus
1852-1933 .... **SSC 19; TCLC 7**
See also BRW 6; CA 104; 177; DLB 10,
18, 57, 135; EWL 3; RGEL 2; RGSF 2

Moore, Lorrie CLC 39, 45, 68
See Moore, Marie Lorena
See also AMWS 10; CN 5, 6, 7; DLB 234;
SSFS 19

Moore, Marianne (Craig)
1887-1972 .... **CLC 1, 2, 4, 8, 10, 13, 19,**
47; PC 4, 49; WLCS
See also AMW; CA 1-4R; 33-36R; CANR
3, 61; CDALB 1929-1941; CP 1; DA;
DA3; DAB; DAC; DAM MST, POET;
DLB 45; DLBD 7; EWL 3; EXPP; FL 1:6;
MAL 5; MBL; MTCW 1, 2; MTFW 2005;
PAB; PFS 14, 17; RGAL 4; SATA 20;
TUS; WP

Moore, Marie Lorena 1957- .... **CLC 165**
See Moore, Lorrie
See also CA 116; CANR 39, 83, 139; DLB
234; MTFW 2005

Moore, Michael 1954- .... **CLC 218**
See also AAYA 53; CA 166; CANR 150

Moore, Thomas 1779-1852 .... **NCLC 6, 110**
See also DLB 96, 144; RGEL 2

Moorhouse, Frank 1938- .... **SSC 40**
See also CA 118; CANR 92; CN 3, 4, 5, 6,
7; DLB 289; RGSF 2

Mora, Pat 1942- .... **HLC 2**
See also AMWS 13; CA 129; CANR 57,
81, 112, 171; CLR 58; DAM MULT; DLB
209; HW 1, 2; LLW; MAICYA 2; MTFW
2005; SATA 92, 134, 186

Moraga, Cherrie 1952- ... **CLC 126, 250; DC**
22
See also CA 131; CANR 66, 154; DAM
MULT; DLB 82, 249; FW; GLL 1; HW 1,
2; LLW

Morand, Paul 1888-1976 .... **CLC 41; SSC 22**
See also CA 184; 69-72; DLB 65; EWL 3

Morante, Elsa 1918-1985 .... **CLC 8, 47**
See also CA 85-88; 117; CANR 35; DLB
177; EWL 3; MTCW 1, 2; MTFW 2005;
RGHL; RGWL 2, 3; WLIT 7

Moravia, Alberto CLC 2, 7, 11, 27, 46; SSC
26
See Pincherle, Alberto
See also DLB 177; EW 12; EWL 3; MTCW
2; RGSF 2; RGWL 2, 3; WLIT 7

Morck, Paul
See Rolvaag, O.E.

More, Hannah 1745-1833 ...... **NCLC 27, 141**
See also DLB 107, 109, 116, 158; RGEL 2

More, Henry 1614-1687 .... **LC 9**
See also DLB 126, 252

More, Sir Thomas 1478(?)-1535 ... **LC 10, 32,**
140
See also BRWC 1; BRWS 7; DLB 136, 281;
LMFS 1; RGEL 2; TEA

Moreas, Jean TCLC 18
See Papadiamantopoulos, Johannes
See also GFL 1789 to the Present

Moreton, Andrew Esq.
See Defoe, Daniel

Moreton, Lee
See Boucicault, Dion

Morgan, Berry 1919-2002 .... **CLC 6**
See also CA 49-52; 208; DLB 6

Morgan, Claire
See Highsmith, Patricia
See also GLL 1

Morgan, Edwin 1920- .... **CLC 31**
See also BRWS 9; CA 5-8R; CANR 3, 43,
90; CP 1, 2, 3, 4, 5, 6, 7; DLB 27

Morgan, Edwin George
See Morgan, Edwin

Morgan, (George) Frederick
1922-2004 .... **CLC 23**
See also CA 17-20R; 224; CANR 21, 144;
CP 2, 3, 4, 5, 6, 7

Morgan, Harriet
See Mencken, H(enry) L(ouis)

Morgan, Jane
See Cooper, James Fenimore

Morgan, Janet 1945- .... **CLC 39**
See also CA 65-68

Morgan, Lady 1776(?)-1859 .... **NCLC 29**
See also DLB 116, 158; RGEL 2

Morgan, Robin (Evonne) 1941- .... **CLC 2**
See also CA 69-72; CANR 29, 68; FW;
GLL 2; MTCW 1; SATA 80

Morgan, Scott
See Kuttner, Henry

Morgan, Seth 1949(?)-1990 .... **CLC 65**
See also CA 185

Morgenstern, Christian (Otto Josef
Wolfgang) 1871-1914 .... **TCLC 8**
See also CA 105; 191; EWL 3

Morgenstern, S.
See Goldman, William

Mori, Rintaro
See Mori Ogai
See also CA 110

Mori, Toshio 1910-1980 .... **AAL; SSC 83**
See also CA 116; 244; DLB 312; RGSF 2

Moricz, Zsigmond 1879-1942 .... **TCLC 33**
See also CA 165; DLB 215; EWL 3

Morike, Eduard (Friedrich)
1804-1875 .... **NCLC 10, 201**
See also DLB 133; RGWL 2, 3

Mori Ogai 1862-1922 .... **TCLC 14**
See Ogai
See also CA 164; DLB 180; EWL 3; RGWL
3; TWA

Moritz, Karl Philipp 1756-1793 .... **LC 2**
See also DLB 94

Morland, Peter Henry
See Faust, Frederick (Schiller)

Morley, Christopher (Darlington)
1890-1957 .... **TCLC 87**
See also CA 112; 213; DLB 9; MAL 5;
RGAL 4

Morren, Theophil
See Hofmannsthal, Hugo von

Morris, Bill 1952- .... **CLC 76**
See also CA 225

Morris, Julian
See West, Morris L(anglo)

Morris, Steveland Judkins (?)-
See Wonder, Stevie

Morris, William 1834-1896 . **NCLC 4; PC 55**
See also BRW 5; CDBLB 1832-1890; DLB
18, 35, 57, 156, 178, 184; FANT; RGEL
2; SFW 4; SUFW

Morris, Wright (Marion) 1910-1998 . **CLC 1,**
3, 7, 18, 37; TCLC 107
See also AMW; CA 9-12R; 167; CANR 21,
81; CN 1, 2, 3, 4, 5, 6; DLB 2, 206, 218;
DLBY 1981; EWL 3; MAL 5; MTCW 1,
2; MTFW 2005; RGAL 4; TCWW 1, 2

Morrison, Arthur 1863-1945 .... **SSC 40;**
TCLC 72
See also CA 120; 157; CMW 4; DLB 70,
135, 197; RGEL 2

Morrison, Chloe Anthony Wofford
See Morrison, Toni

Morrison, James Douglas 1943-1971
See Morrison, Jim
See also CA 73-76; CANR 40

Morrison, Jim CLC 17
See Morrison, James Douglas

Morrison, John Gordon 1904-1998 ... **SSC 93**
See also CA 103; CANR 92; DLB 260

Morrison, Toni 1931- . **BLC 1:3, 2:3; CLC 4,**
10, 22, 55, 81, 87, 173, 194; WLC 4
See also AAYA 1, 22, 61; AFAW 1, 2;
AMWC 1; AMWS 3; BPFB 2; BW 2, 3;
CA 29-32R; CANR 27, 42, 67, 113, 124;
CDALB 1968-1988; CLR 99; CN 3, 4, 5,
6, 7; CPW; DA; DA3; DAB; DAC; DAM
MST, MULT, NOV, POP; DLB 6, 33, 143,
331; DLBY 1981; EWL 3; EXPN; FL 1:6;
FW; GL 3; LAIT 2, 4; LATS 1:2; LMFS
2; MAL 5; MBL; MTCW 1, 2; MTFW
2005; NFS 1, 6, 8, 14; RGAL 4; RHW;
SATA 57, 144; SSFS 5; TCLE 1:2; TUS;
YAW

Morrison, Van 1945- .... **CLC 21**
See also CA 116; 168

Morrissy, Mary 1957- .... **CLC 99**
See also CA 205; DLB 267

Mortimer, John 1923- .... **CLC 28, 43**
See also CA 13-16R; CANR 21, 69, 109,
172; CBD; CD 5, 6; CDBLB 1960 to
Present; CMW 4; CN 5, 6, 7; CPW; DA3;
DAM DRAM, POP; DLB 13, 245, 271;
INT CANR-21; MSW; MTCW 1, 2;
MTFW 2005; RGEL 2

Mortimer, John Clifford
See Mortimer, John

Mortimer, Penelope (Ruth)
1918-1999 .... **CLC 5**
See also CA 57-60; 187; CANR 45, 88; CN
1, 2, 3, 4, 5, 6

Mortimer, Sir John
See Mortimer, John

Morton, Anthony
See Creasey, John

Morton, Thomas 1579(?)-1647(?) .... **LC 72**
See also DLB 24; RGEL 2

Mosca, Gaetano 1858-1941 .... **TCLC 75**

Moses, Daniel David 1952- .... **NNAL**
See also CA 186; CANR 160; DLB 334

Mosher, Howard Frank 1943- .... **CLC 62**
See also CA 139; CANR 65, 115, 181

Mosley, Nicholas 1923- .... **CLC 43, 70**
See also CA 69-72; CANR 41, 60, 108, 158;
CN 1, 2, 3, 4, 5, 6, 7; DLB 14, 207

Mosley, Walter 1952- .... **BLCS; CLC 97, 184**
See also AAYA 57; AMWS 13; BPFB 2;
BW 2; CA 142; CANR 57, 92, 136, 172;
CMW 4; CN 7; CPW; DA3; DAM MULT,
POP; DLB 306; MSW; MTCW 2; MTFW
2005

Moss, Howard 1922-1987 . **CLC 7, 14, 45, 50**
See also CA 1-4R; 123; CANR 1, 44; CP 1,
2, 3, 4; DAM POET; DLB 5

Mossgiel, Rab
See Burns, Robert

Motion, Andrew 1952- .... **CLC 47**
See also BRWS 7; CA 146; CANR 90, 142;
CP 4, 5, 6, 7; DLB 40; MTFW 2005

Motion, Andrew Peter
See Motion, Andrew

Motley, Willard (Francis)
1909-1965 .... **CLC 18**
See also AMWS 17; BW 1; CA 117; 106;
CANR 88; DLB 76, 143

Motoori, Norinaga 1730-1801 .... **NCLC 45**

Mott, Michael (Charles Alston)
1930- .... **CLC 15, 34**
See also CA 5-8R; CAAS 7; CANR 7, 29

Mountain Wolf Woman 1884-1960 . **CLC 92;**
NNAL
See also CA 144; CANR 90

Moure, Erin 1955- .... **CLC 88**
See also CA 113; CP 5, 6, 7; CWP; DLB
60

Mourning Dove 1885(?)-1936 .... **NNAL**
See also CA 144; CANR 90; DAM MULT;
DLB 175, 221

Mowat, Farley 1921- .... **CLC 26**
See also AAYA 1, 50; BYA 2; CA 1-4R;
CANR 4, 24, 42, 68, 108; CLR 20; CPW;
DAC; DAM MST; DLB 68; INT CANR-
24; JRDA; MAICYA 1, 2; MTCW 1, 2;
MTFW 2005; SATA 3, 55; YAW

Mowat, Farley McGill
See Mowat, Farley

Mowatt, Anna Cora 1819-1870 ..... **NCLC 74**
See also RGAL 4

Mo Yan CLC 257
See Moye, Guan

Moye, Guan 1956(?)-
See Mo Yan
See also CA 201

Moyers, Bill 1934- .... **CLC 74**
See also AITN 2; CA 61-64; CANR 31, 52,
148

Mphahlele, Es'kia
See Mphahlele, Ezekiel
See also AFW; CDWLB 3; CN 4, 5, 6; DLB
125, 225; RGSF 2; SSFS 11

Mphahlele, Ezekiel 1919-2008 .... **BLC 1:3;**
CLC 25, 133
See Mphahlele, Es'kia
See also BW 2, 3; CA 81-84; CANR 26,
76; CN 1, 2, 3; DA3; DAM MULT; EWL
3; MTCW 2; MTFW 2005; SATA 119

Mqhayi, S(amuel) E(dward) K(rune Loliwe)
1875-1945 .... **BLC 1:3; TCLC 25**
See also CA 153; CANR 87; DAM MULT

Mrozek, Slawomir 1930- .... **CLC 3, 13**
See also CA 13-16R; CAAS 10; CANR 29;
CDWLB 4; CWW 2; DLB 232; EWL 3;
MTCW 1

Mrs. Belloc-Lowndes
See Lowndes, Marie Adelaide (Belloc)

Mrs. Fairstar
See Horne, Richard Henry Hengist

M'Taggart, John M'Taggart Ellis
See McTaggart, John McTaggart Ellis

Mtwa, Percy (?)- .... **CLC 47**
See also CD 6

Mueller, Lisel 1924- .... **CLC 13, 51; PC 33**
See also CA 93-96; CP 6, 7; DLB 105; PFS
9, 13

Muggeridge, Malcolm (Thomas)
1903-1990 .... **TCLC 120**
See also AITN 1; CA 101; CANR 33, 63;
MTCW 1, 2

Muhammad 570-632 .... **WLCS**
See also DA; DAB; DAC; DAM MST;
DLB 311

Muir, Edwin 1887-1959 . **PC 49; TCLC 2, 87**
See Moore, Edward
See also BRWS 6; CA 104; 193; DLB 20,
100, 191; EWL 3; RGEL 2

Muir, John 1838-1914 .... **TCLC 28**
See also AMWS 9; ANW; CA 165; DLB
186, 275

Mujica Lainez, Manuel 1910-1984 ... **CLC 31**
See Lainez, Manuel Mujica
See also CA 81-84; 112; CANR 32; EWL
3; HW 1

Mukherjee, Bharati 1940- ..... **AAL; CLC 53,**
115, 235; SSC 38
See also AAYA 46; BEST 89:2; CA 107,
232; CAAE 232; CANR 45, 72, 128; CN
5, 6, 7; DAM NOV; DLB 60, 218, 323;
DNFS 1, 2; EWL 3; FW; MAL 5; MTCW
1, 2; MTFW 2005; RGAL 4; RGSF 2;
SSFS 7, 24; TUS; WWE 1

Muldoon, Paul 1951- .... **CLC 32, 72, 166**
See also BRWS 4; CA 113; 129; CANR 52,
91, 176; CP 2, 3, 4, 5, 6, 7; DAM POET;
DLB 40; INT CA-129; PFS 7, 22; TCLE
1:2

Mulisch, Harry (Kurt Victor)
1927- .... **CLC 42**
See also CA 9-12R; CANR 6, 26, 56, 110;
CWW 2; DLB 299; EWL 3

Mull, Martin 1943- .... **CLC 17**
See also CA 105

Muller, Wilhelm NCLC 73

Mulock, Dinah Maria
See Craik, Dinah Maria (Mulock)
See also RGEL 2

Multatuli 1820-1881 .... **NCLC 165**
See also RGWL 2, 3

Munday, Anthony 1560-1633 .... **LC 87**
See also DLB 62, 172; RGEL 2

Munford, Robert 1737(?)-1783 .... **LC 5**
See also DLB 31

Mungo, Raymond 1946- .... **CLC 72**
See also CA 49-52; CANR 2

Munro, Alice 1931- .... **CLC 6, 10, 19, 50, 95,**
222; SSC 3, 95; WLCS
See also AITN 2; BPFB 2; CA 33-36R;
CANR 33, 53, 75, 114, 177; CCA 1; CN
1, 2, 3, 4, 5, 6, 7; DA3; DAC; DAM MST,
NOV; DLB 53; EWL 3; MTCW 1, 2;
MTFW 2005; NFS 27; RGEL 2; RGSF 2;
SATA 29; SSFS 5, 13, 19; TCLE 1:2;
WWE 1

Munro, H(ector) H(ugh) 1870-1916
See Saki
See also AAYA 56; CA 104; 130; CANR
104; CDBLB 1890-1914; DA; DA3;
DAB; DAC; DAM MST, NOV; DLB 34,
162; EXPS; MTCW 1, 2; MTFW 2005;
RGEL 2; SSFS 15

Murakami, Haruki 1949- .... **CLC 150**
See Murakami Haruki
See also CA 165; CANR 102, 146; MJW;
RGWL 3; SFW 4; SSFS 23

Murakami Haruki
See Murakami, Haruki
See also CWW 2; DLB 182; EWL 3

Murasaki, Lady
See Murasaki Shikibu

Murasaki Shikibu 978(?)-1026(?) .. **CMLC 1,**
79
See also EFS 2; LATS 1:1; RGWL 2, 3

Murdoch, Iris 1919-1999 .. **CLC 1, 2, 3, 4, 6,**
8, 11, 15, 22, 31, 51; TCLC 171
See also BRWS 1; CA 13-16R; 179; CANR
8, 43, 68, 103, 142; CBD; CDBLB 1960
to Present; CN 1, 2, 3, 4, 5, 6; CWD;
DA3; DAB; DAC; DAM MST, NOV;
DLB 14, 194, 233, 326; EWL 3; INT
CANR-8; MTCW 1, 2; MTFW 2005; NFS
18; RGEL 2; TCLE 1:2; TEA; WLIT 4

Murfree, Mary Noailles 1850-1922 .. **SSC 22;**
TCLC 135
See also CA 122; 176; DLB 12, 74; RGAL
4

Murglie
See Murnau, F.W.

Murnau, Friedrich Wilhelm
See Murnau, F.W.

Murnau, F.W. 1888-1931 .... **TCLC 53**
See also CA 112

Murphy, Richard 1927- .... **CLC 41**
See also BRWS 5; CA 29-32R; CP 1, 2, 3,
4, 5, 6, 7; DLB 40; EWL 3

Murphy, Sylvia 1937- .... **CLC 34**
See also CA 121

Murphy, Thomas (Bernard) 1935- ... **CLC 51**
See Murphy, Tom
See also CA 101

Murphy, Tom
See Murphy, Thomas (Bernard)
See also DLB 310

Murray, Albert 1916- .... **BLC 2:3; CLC 73**
See also BW 2; CA 49-52; CANR 26, 52,
78, 160; CN 7; CSW; DLB 38; MTFW
2005

Murray, Albert L.
See Murray, Albert

Murray, James Augustus Henry
1837-1915 .... **TCLC 117**

Murray, Judith Sargent
1751-1820 .... **NCLC 63**
See also DLB 37, 200

Murray, Les(lie Allan) 1938- .... **CLC 40**
See also BRWS 7; CA 21-24R; CANR 11,
27, 56, 103; CP 1, 2, 3, 4, 5, 6, 7; DAM
POET; DLB 289; DLBY 2001; EWL 3;
RGEL 2

Murry, J. Middleton
See Murry, John Middleton

Murry, John Middleton
1889-1957 .... **TCLC 16**
See also CA 118; 217; DLB 149

Musgrave, Susan 1951- .... **CLC 13, 54**
See also CA 69-72; CANR 45, 84, 181;
CCA 1; CP 2, 3, 4, 5, 6, 7; CWP

Musil, Robert (Edler von)
1880-1942 .. **SSC 18; TCLC 12, 68, 213**
See also CA 109; CANR 55, 84; CDWLB
2; DLB 81, 124; EW 9; EWL 3; MTCW
2; RGSF 2; RGWL 2, 3

Muske, Carol CLC 90
See Muske-Dukes, Carol

Muske-Dukes, Carol 1945-
See Muske, Carol
See also CA 65-68, 203; CAAE 203; CANR
32, 70, 181; CWP; PFS 24

Musset, Alfred de 1810-1857 . **DC 27; NCLC 7, 150**
See also DLB 192, 217; EW 6; GFL 1789 to the Present; RGWL 2, 3; TWA

Musset, Louis Charles Alfred de
See Musset, Alfred de

Mussolini, Benito (Amilcare Andrea) 1883-1945 .... **TCLC 96**
See also CA 116

Mutanabbi, Al-
See al-Mutanabbi, Ahmad ibn al-Husayn Abu al-Tayyib al-Jufi al-Kindi
See also WLIT 6

My Brother's Brother
See Chekhov, Anton (Pavlovich)

Myers, L(eopold) H(amilton) 1881-1944 .... **TCLC 59**
See also CA 157; DLB 15; EWL 3; RGEL 2

Myers, Walter Dean 1937- ...... **BLC 1:3, 2:3; CLC 35**
See Myers, Walter M.
See also AAYA 4, 23; BW 2; BYA 6, 8, 11; CA 33-36R; CANR 20, 42, 67, 108, 184; CLR 4, 16, 35, 110; DAM MULT, NOV; DLB 33; INT CANR-20; JRDA; LAIT 5; MAICYA 1, 2; MAICYAS 1; MTCW 2; MTFW 2005; SAAS 2; SATA 41, 71, 109, 157, 193; SATA-Brief 27; WYA; YAW

Myers, Walter M.
See Myers, Walter Dean

Myles, Symon
See Follett, Ken

Nabokov, Vladimir (Vladimirovich) 1899-1977 .... **CLC 1, 2, 3, 6, 8, 11, 15, 23, 44, 46, 64; SSC 11, 86; TCLC 108, 189; WLC 4**
See also AAYA 45; AMW; AMWC 1; AMWR 1; BPFB 2; CA 5-8R; 69-72; CANR 20, 102; CDALB 1941-1968; CN 1, 2; CP 2; DA; DA3; DAB; DAC; DAM MST, NOV; DLB 2, 244, 278, 317; DLBD 3; DLBY 1980, 1991; EWL 3; EXPS; LATS 1:2; MAL 5; MTCW 1, 2; MTFW 2005; NCFS 4; NFS 9; RGAL 4; RGSF 2; SSFS 6, 15; TUS

Naevius c. 265B.C.-201B.C. .... **CMLC 37**
See also DLB 211

Nagai, Kafu 1879-1959 .... **TCLC 51**
See Kafu
See also CA 117; 276; DLB 180; EWL 3

Nagai, Sokichi
See Nagai, Kafu

Nagai Kafu
See Nagai, Kafu

Nagy, Laszlo 1925-1978 .... **CLC 7**
See also CA 129; 112

Naidu, Sarojini 1879-1949 .... **TCLC 80**
See also EWL 3; RGEL 2

Naipaul, Shiva 1945-1985 .... **CLC 32, 39; TCLC 153**
See also CA 110; 112; 116; CANR 33; CN 2, 3; DA3; DAM NOV; DLB 157; DLBY 1985; EWL 3; MTCW 1, 2; MTFW 2005

Naipaul, V.S. 1932- .. **CLC 4, 7, 9, 13, 18, 37, 105, 199; SSC 38**
See also BPFB 2; BRWS 1; CA 1-4R; CANR 1, 33, 51, 91, 126; CDBLB 1960 to Present; CDWLB 3; CN 1, 2, 3, 4, 5, 6, 7; DA3; DAB; DAC; DAM MST, NOV; DLB 125, 204, 207, 326, 331; DLBY 1985, 2001; EWL 3; LATS 1:2; MTCW 1, 2; MTFW 2005; RGEL 2; RGSF 2; TWA; WLIT 4; WWE 1

Nakos, Lilika 1903(?)-1989 .... **CLC 29**

Napoleon
See Yamamoto, Hisaye

Narayan, R.K. 1906-2001 ...... **CLC 7, 28, 47, 121, 211; SSC 25**
See also BPFB 2; CA 81-84; 196; CANR 33, 61, 112; CN 1, 2, 3, 4, 5, 6, 7; DA3; DAM NOV; DLB 323; DNFS 1; EWL 3; MTCW 1, 2; MTFW 2005; RGEL 2; RGSF 2; SATA 62; SSFS 5; WWE 1

Nash, (Frediric) Ogden 1902-1971 . **CLC 23; PC 21; TCLC 109**
See also CA 13-14; 29-32R; CANR 34, 61; CAP 1; CP 1; DAM POET; DLB 11; MAICYA 1, 2; MAL 5; MTCW 1, 2; RGAL 4; SATA 2, 46; WP

Nashe, Thomas 1567-1601(?) . **LC 41, 89; PC 82**
See also DLB 167; RGEL 2

Nathan, Daniel
See Dannay, Frederic

Nathan, George Jean 1882-1958 .... **TCLC 18**
See Hatteras, Owen
See also CA 114; 169; DLB 137; MAL 5

Natsume, Kinnosuke
See Natsume, Soseki

Natsume, Soseki 1867-1916 .... **TCLC 2, 10**
See Natsume Soseki; Soseki
See also CA 104; 195; RGWL 2, 3; TWA

Natsume Soseki
See Natsume, Soseki
See also DLB 180; EWL 3

Natti, (Mary) Lee 1919-
See Kingman, Lee
See also CA 5-8R; CANR 2

Navarre, Marguerite de
See de Navarre, Marguerite

Naylor, Gloria 1950- . **BLC 1:3; CLC 28, 52, 156, 261; WLCS**
See also AAYA 6, 39; AFAW 1, 2; AMWS 8; BW 2, 3; CA 107; CANR 27, 51, 74, 130; CN 4, 5, 6, 7; CPW; DA; DA3; DAC; DAM MST, MULT, NOV, POP; DLB 173; EWL 3; FW; MAL 5; MTCW 1, 2; MTFW 2005; NFS 4, 7; RGAL 4; TCLE 1:2; TUS

Neal, John 1793-1876 .... **NCLC 161**
See also DLB 1, 59, 243; FW; RGAL 4

Neff, Debra CLC 59

Neihardt, John Gneisenau 1881-1973 .... **CLC 32**
See also CA 13-14; CANR 65; CAP 1; DLB 9, 54, 256; LAIT 2; TCWW 1, 2

Nekrasov, Nikolai Alekseevich 1821-1878 .... **NCLC 11**
See also DLB 277

Nelligan, Emile 1879-1941 .... **TCLC 14**
See also CA 114; 204; DLB 92; EWL 3

Nelson, Willie 1933- .... **CLC 17**
See also CA 107; CANR 114, 178

Nemerov, Howard 1920-1991 .... **CLC 2, 6, 9, 36; PC 24; TCLC 124**
See also AMW; CA 1-4R; 134; CABS 2; CANR 1, 27, 53; CN 1, 2, 3; CP 1, 2, 3, 4, 5; DAM POET; DLB 5, 6; DLBY 1983; EWL 3; INT CANR-27; MAL 5; MTCW 1, 2; MTFW 2005; PFS 10, 14; RGAL 4

Nepos, Cornelius c. 99B.C.-c. 24B.C. .... **CMLC 89**
See also DLB 211

Neruda, Pablo 1904-1973 .. **CLC 1, 2, 5, 7, 9, 28, 62; HLC 2; PC 4, 64; WLC 4**
See also CA 19-20; 45-48; CANR 131; CAP 2; DA; DA3; DAB; DAC; DAM MST, MULT, POET; DLB 283, 331; DNFS 2; EWL 3; HW 1; LAW; MTCW 1, 2; MTFW 2005; PFS 11, 28; RGWL 2, 3; TWA; WLIT 1; WP

Nerval, Gerard de 1808-1855 ... **NCLC 1, 67; PC 13; SSC 18**
See also DLB 217; EW 6; GFL 1789 to the Present; RGSF 2; RGWL 2, 3

Nervo, (Jose) Amado (Ruiz de) 1870-1919 .... **HLCS 2; TCLC 11**
See also CA 109; 131; DLB 290; EWL 3; HW 1; LAW

Nesbit, Malcolm
See Chester, Alfred

Nessi, Pio Baroja y
See Baroja, Pio

Nestroy, Johann 1801-1862 .... **NCLC 42**
See also DLB 133; RGWL 2, 3

Netterville, Luke
See O'Grady, Standish (James)

Neufeld, John (Arthur) 1938- .... **CLC 17**
See also AAYA 11; CA 25-28R; CANR 11, 37, 56; CLR 52; MAICYA 1, 2; SAAS 3; SATA 6, 81, 131; SATA-Essay 131; YAW

Neumann, Alfred 1895-1952 .... **TCLC 100**
See also CA 183; DLB 56

Neumann, Ferenc
See Molnar, Ferenc

Neville, Emily Cheney 1919- .... **CLC 12**
See also BYA 2; CA 5-8R; CANR 3, 37, 85; JRDA; MAICYA 1, 2; SAAS 2; SATA 1; YAW

Newbound, Bernard Slade 1930-
See Slade, Bernard
See also CA 81-84; CANR 49; CD 5; DAM DRAM

Newby, P(ercy) H(oward) 1918-1997 .... **CLC 2, 13**
See also CA 5-8R; 161; CANR 32, 67; CN 1, 2, 3, 4, 5, 6; DAM NOV; DLB 15, 326; MTCW 1; RGEL 2

Newcastle
See Cavendish, Margaret Lucas

Newlove, Donald 1928- .... **CLC 6**
See also CA 29-32R; CANR 25

Newlove, John (Herbert) 1938- .... **CLC 14**
See also CA 21-24R; CANR 9, 25; CP 1, 2, 3, 4, 5, 6, 7

Newman, Charles 1938-2006 .... **CLC 2, 8**
See also CA 21-24R; 249; CANR 84; CN 3, 4, 5, 6

Newman, Charles Hamilton
See Newman, Charles

Newman, Edwin (Harold) 1919- ...... **CLC 14**
See also AITN 1; CA 69-72; CANR 5

Newman, John Henry 1801-1890 . **NCLC 38, 99**
See also BRWS 7; DLB 18, 32, 55; RGEL 2

Newton, (Sir) Isaac 1642-1727 ...... **LC 35, 53**
See also DLB 252

Newton, Suzanne 1936- .... **CLC 35**
See also BYA 7; CA 41-44R; CANR 14; JRDA; SATA 5, 77

New York Dept. of Ed. CLC 70

Nexo, Martin Andersen 1869-1954 .... **TCLC 43**
See also CA 202; DLB 214; EWL 3

Nezval, Vitezslav 1900-1958 .... **TCLC 44**
See also CA 123; CDWLB 4; DLB 215; EWL 3

Ng, Fae Myenne 1956- .... **CLC 81**
See also BYA 11; CA 146

Ngcobo, Lauretta 1931- .... **BLC 2:3**
See also CA 165

Ngema, Mbongeni 1955- .... **CLC 57**
See also BW 2; CA 143; CANR 84; CD 5, 6

Ngugi, James T. CLC 3, 7, 13, 182
See Ngugi wa Thiong'o
See also CN 1, 2

Ngugi, James Thiong'o
See Ngugi wa Thiong'o

Ngugi wa Thiong'o 1938- .... **BLC 1:3, 2:3; CLC 36, 182**
See Ngugi, James T.
See also AFW; BRWS 8; BW 2; CA 81-84; CANR 27, 58, 164; CD 3, 4, 5, 6, 7; CD-WLB 3; DAM MULT, NOV; DLB 125; DNFS 2; EWL 3; MTCW 1, 2; MTFW 2005; RGEL 2; WWE 1

Niatum, Duane 1938- .... **NNAL**
See also CA 41-44R; CANR 21, 45, 83; DLB 175

Nichol, B(arrie) P(hillip) 1944-1988 . **CLC 18**
See also CA 53-56; CP 1, 2, 3, 4; DLB 53; SATA 66

Nicholas of Autrecourt c.
1298-1369 .... **CMLC 108**

Nicholas of Cusa 1401-1464 .... **LC 80**
See also DLB 115

Nichols, John 1938- .... **CLC 38**
See also AMWS 13; CA 9-12R, 190; CAAE 190; CAAS 2; CANR 6, 70, 121; DLBY 1982; LATS 1:2; MTFW 2005; TCWW 1, 2

Nichols, Leigh
See Koontz, Dean R.

Nichols, Peter (Richard) 1927- .... **CLC 5, 36, 65**
See also CA 104; CANR 33, 86; CBD; CD 5, 6; DLB 13, 245; MTCW 1

Nicholson, Linda CLC 65

Ni Chuilleanain, Eilean 1942- .... **PC 34**
See also CA 126; CANR 53, 83; CP 5, 6, 7; CWP; DLB 40

Nicolas, F. R. E.
See Freeling, Nicolas

Niedecker, Lorine 1903-1970 ..... **CLC 10, 42; PC 42**
See also CA 25-28; CAP 2; DAM POET; DLB 48

Nietzsche, Friedrich (Wilhelm)
1844-1900 .... **TCLC 10, 18, 55**
See also CA 107; 121; CDWLB 2; DLB 129; EW 7; RGWL 2, 3; TWA

Nievo, Ippolito 1831-1861 .... **NCLC 22**

Nightingale, Anne Redmon 1943-
See Redmon, Anne
See also CA 103

Nightingale, Florence 1820-1910 ... **TCLC 85**
See also CA 188; DLB 166

Nijo Yoshimoto 1320-1388 .... **CMLC 49**
See also DLB 203

Nik. T. O.
See Annensky, Innokenty (Fyodorovich)

Nin, Anais 1903-1977 ..... **CLC 1, 4, 8, 11, 14, 60, 127; SSC 10**
See also AITN 2; AMWS 10; BPFB 2; CA 13-16R; 69-72; CANR 22, 53; CN 1, 2; DAM NOV, POP; DLB 2, 4, 152; EWL 3; GLL 2; MAL 5; MBL; MTCW 1, 2; MTFW 2005; RGAL 4; RGSF 2

Nisbet, Robert A(lexander)
1913-1996 .... **TCLC 117**
See also CA 25-28R; 153; CANR 17; INT CANR-17

Nishida, Kitaro 1870-1945 .... **TCLC 83**

Nishiwaki, Junzaburo 1894-1982 .... **PC 15**
See Junzaburo, Nishiwaki
See also CA 194; 107; MJW; RGWL 3

Nissenson, Hugh 1933- .... **CLC 4, 9**
See also CA 17-20R; CANR 27, 108, 151; CN 5, 6; DLB 28, 335

Nister, Der
See Der Nister
See also DLB 333; EWL 3

Niven, Larry 1938-
See Niven, Laurence VanCott
See also CA 21-24R, 207; CAAE 207; CAAS 12; CANR 14, 44, 66, 113, 155; CPW; DAM POP; MTCW 1, 2; SATA 95, 171; SFW 4

Niven, Laurence VanCott CLC 8
See Niven, Larry
See also AAYA 27; BPFB 2; BYA 10; DLB 8; SCFW 1, 2

Nixon, Agnes Eckhardt 1927- .... **CLC 21**
See also CA 110

Nizan, Paul 1905-1940 .... **TCLC 40**
See also CA 161; DLB 72; EWL 3; GFL 1789 to the Present

Nkosi, Lewis 1936- .... **BLC 1:3; CLC 45**
See also BW 1, 3; CA 65-68; CANR 27, 81; CBD; CD 5, 6; DAM MULT; DLB 157, 225; WWE 1

Nodier, (Jean) Charles (Emmanuel)
1780-1844 .... **NCLC 19**
See also DLB 119; GFL 1789 to the Present

Noguchi, Yone 1875-1947 .... **TCLC 80**

Nolan, Christopher 1965- .... **CLC 58**
See also CA 111; CANR 88

Noon, Jeff 1957- .... **CLC 91**
See also CA 148; CANR 83; DLB 267; SFW 4

Norden, Charles
See Durrell, Lawrence (George)

Nordhoff, Charles Bernard
1887-1947 .... **TCLC 23**
See also CA 108; 211; DLB 9; LAIT 1; RHW 1; SATA 23

Norfolk, Lawrence 1963- .... **CLC 76**
See also CA 144; CANR 85; CN 6, 7; DLB 267

Norman, Marsha (Williams) 1947- . **CLC 28, 186; DC 8**
See also CA 105; CABS 3; CAD; CANR 41, 131; CD 5, 6; CSW; CWD; DAM DRAM; DFS 2; DLB 266; DLBY 1984; FW; MAL 5

Normyx
See Douglas, (George) Norman

Norris, (Benjamin) Frank(lin, Jr.)
1870-1902 . **SSC 28; TCLC 24, 155, 211**
See also AAYA 57; AMW; AMWC 2; BPFB 2; CA 110; 160; CDALB 1865-1917; DLB 12, 71, 186; LMFS 2; MAL 5; NFS 12; RGAL 4; TCWW 1, 2; TUS

Norris, Kathleen 1947- .... **CLC 248**
See also CA 160; CANR 113

Norris, Leslie 1921-2006 .... **CLC 14**
See also CA 11-12; 251; CANR 14, 117; CAP 1; CP 1, 2, 3, 4, 5, 6, 7; DLB 27, 256

North, Andrew
See Norton, Andre

North, Anthony
See Koontz, Dean R.

North, Captain George
See Stevenson, Robert Louis (Balfour)

North, Captain George
See Stevenson, Robert Louis (Balfour)

North, Milou
See Erdrich, Louise

Northrup, B. A.
See Hubbard, L. Ron

North Staffs
See Hulme, T(homas) E(rnest)

Northup, Solomon 1808-1863 ...... **NCLC 105**

Norton, Alice Mary
See Norton, Andre
See also MAICYA 1; SATA 1, 43

Norton, Andre 1912-2005 .... **CLC 12**
See Norton, Alice Mary
See also AAYA 14; BPFB 2; BYA 4, 10, 12; CA 1-4R; 237; CANR 2, 31, 68, 108, 149; CLR 50; DLB 8, 52; JRDA; MAICYA 2; MTCW 1; SATA 91; SUFW 1, 2; YAW

Norton, Caroline 1808-1877 .. **NCLC 47, 205**
See also DLB 21, 159, 199

Norway, Nevil Shute 1899-1960
See Shute, Nevil
See also CA 102; 93-96; CANR 85; MTCW 2

Norwid, Cyprian Kamil
1821-1883 .... **NCLC 17**
See also RGWL 3

Nosille, Nabrah
See Ellison, Harlan

Nossack, Hans Erich 1901-1977 .... **CLC 6**
See also CA 93-96; 85-88; CANR 156; DLB 69; EWL 3

Nostradamus 1503-1566 .... **LC 27**

Nosu, Chuji
See Ozu, Yasujiro

Notenburg, Eleanora (Genrikhovna) von
See Guro, Elena (Genrikhovna)

Nova, Craig 1945- .... **CLC 7, 31**
See also CA 45-48; CANR 2, 53, 127

Novak, Joseph
See Kosinski, Jerzy

Novalis 1772-1801 .... **NCLC 13, 178**
See also CDWLB 2; DLB 90; EW 5; RGWL 2, 3

Novick, Peter 1934- .... **CLC 164**
See also CA 188

Novis, Emile
See Weil, Simone (Adolphine)

Nowlan, Alden (Albert) 1933-1983 ... **CLC 15**
See also CA 9-12R; CANR 5; CP 1, 2, 3; DAC; DAM MST; DLB 53; PFS 12

Noyes, Alfred 1880-1958 ...... **PC 27; TCLC 7**
See also CA 104; 188; DLB 20; EXPP; FANT; PFS 4; RGEL 2

Nugent, Richard Bruce
1906(?)-1987 .... **HR 1:3**
See also BW 1; CA 125; DLB 51; GLL 2

Nunez, Elizabeth 1944- .... **BLC 2:3**
See also CA 223

Nunn, Kem CLC 34
See also CA 159

Nussbaum, Martha Craven 1947- .. **CLC 203**
See also CA 134; CANR 102, 176

Nwapa, Flora (Nwanzuruaha)
1931-1993 .... **BLCS; CLC 133**
See also BW 2; CA 143; CANR 83; CD-WLB 3; CWRI 5; DLB 125; EWL 3; WLIT 2

Nye, Robert 1939- .... **CLC 13, 42**
See also BRWS 10; CA 33-36R; CANR 29, 67, 107; CN 1, 2, 3, 4, 5, 6, 7; CP 1, 2, 3, 4, 5, 6, 7; CWRI 5; DAM NOV; DLB 14, 271; FANT; HGG; MTCW 1; RHW; SATA 6

Nyro, Laura 1947-1997 .... **CLC 17**
See also CA 194

Oates, Joyce Carol 1938- .. **CLC 1, 2, 3, 6, 9, 11, 15, 19, 33, 52, 108, 134, 228; SSC 6, 70; WLC 4**
See also AAYA 15, 52; AITN 1; AMWS 2; BEST 89:2; BPFB 2; BYA 11; CA 5-8R; CANR 25, 45, 74, 113, 129, 165; CDALB 1968-1988; CN 1, 2, 3, 4, 5, 6, 7; CP 5, 6, 7; CPW; CWP; DA; DA3; DAB; DAC; DAM MST, NOV, POP; DLB 2, 5, 130; DLBY 1981; EWL 3; EXPS; FL 1:6; FW; GL 3; HGG; INT CANR-25; LAIT 4; MAL 5; MBL; MTCW 1, 2; MTFW 2005; NFS 8, 24; RGAL 4; RGSF 2; SATA 159; SSFS 1, 8, 17; SUFW 2; TUS

O'Brian, E.G.
See Clarke, Arthur C.

O'Brian, Patrick 1914-2000 .... **CLC 152**
See also AAYA 55; BRWS 12; CA 144; 187; CANR 74; CPW; MTCW 2; MTFW 2005; RHW

O'Brien, Darcy 1939-1998 .... **CLC 11**
See also CA 21-24R; 167; CANR 8, 59

O'Brien, Edna 1932- ..... **CLC 3, 5, 8, 13, 36, 65, 116, 237; SSC 10, 77**
See also BRWS 5; CA 1-4R; CANR 6, 41, 65, 102, 169; CDBLB 1960 to Present; CN 1, 2, 3, 4, 5, 6, 7; DA3; DAM NOV; DLB 14, 231, 319; EWL 3; FW; MTCW 1, 2; MTFW 2005; RGSF 2; WLIT 4

O'Brien, E.G.
See Clarke, Arthur C.

O'Brien, Fitz-James 1828-1862 ..... **NCLC 21**
See also DLB 74; RGAL 4; SUFW

O'Brien, Flann **CLC 1, 4, 5, 7, 10, 47**
See O Nuallain, Brian
See also BRWS 2; DLB 231; EWL 3; RGEL 2

O'Brien, Richard 1942- .... **CLC 17**
See also CA 124

O'Brien, Tim 1946- .... **CLC 7, 19, 40, 103, 211; SSC 74**
See also AAYA 16; AMWS 5; CA 85-88; CANR 40, 58, 133; CDALBS; CN 5, 6, 7; CPW; DA3; DAM POP; DLB 152; DLBD 9; DLBY 1980; LATS 1:2; MAL 5; MTCW 2; MTFW 2005; RGAL 4; SSFS 5, 15; TCLE 1:2

Obstfelder, Sigbjoern 1866-1900 .... **TCLC 23**
See also CA 123

O'Casey, Sean 1880-1964 .... **CLC 1, 5, 9, 11, 15, 88; DC 12; WLCS**
See also BRW 7; CA 89-92; CANR 62; CBD; CDBLB 1914-1945; DA3; DAB; DAC; DAM DRAM, MST; DFS 19; DLB 10; EWL 3; MTCW 1, 2; MTFW 2005; RGEL 2; TEA; WLIT 4

O'Cathasaigh, Sean
See O'Casey, Sean

Occom, Samson 1723-1792 .... **LC 60; NNAL**
See also DLB 175

Occomy, Marita (Odette) Bonner 1899(?)-1971
See Bonner, Marita
See also BW 2; CA 142; DFS 13; DLB 51, 228

Ochs, Phil(ip David) 1940-1976 .... **CLC 17**
See also CA 185; 65-68

O'Connor, Edwin (Greene) 1918-1968 .... **CLC 14**
See also CA 93-96; 25-28R; MAL 5

O'Connor, (Mary) Flannery 1925-1964 .... **CLC 1, 2, 3, 6, 10, 13, 15, 21, 66, 104; SSC 1, 23, 61, 82, 111; TCLC 132; WLC 4**
See also AAYA 7; AMW; AMWR 2; BPFB 3; BYA 16; CA 1-4R; CANR 3, 41; CDALB 1941-1968; DA; DA3; DAB; DAC; DAM MST, NOV; DLB 2, 152; DLBD 12; DLBY 1980; EWL 3; EXPS; LAIT 5; MAL 5; MBL; MTCW 1, 2; MTFW 2005; NFS 3, 21; RGAL 4; RGSF 2; SSFS 2, 7, 10, 19; TUS

O'Connor, Frank 1903-1966 ... **CLC 23; SSC 5, 109**
See O'Donovan, Michael Francis
See also DLB 162; EWL 3; RGSF 2; SSFS 5

O'Dell, Scott 1898-1989 .... **CLC 30**
See also AAYA 3, 44; BPFB 3; BYA 1, 2, 3, 5; CA 61-64; 129; CANR 12, 30, 112; CLR 1, 16, 126; DLB 52; JRDA; MAICYA 1, 2; SATA 12, 60, 134; WYA; YAW

Odets, Clifford 1906-1963 ..... **CLC 2, 28, 98; DC 6**
See also AMWS 2; CA 85-88; CAD; CANR 62; DAM DRAM; DFS 3, 17, 20; DLB 7, 26, 341; EWL 3; MAL 5; MTCW 1, 2; MTFW 2005; RGAL 4; TUS

O'Doherty, Brian 1928- .... **CLC 76**
See also CA 105; CANR 108

O'Donnell, K. M.
See Malzberg, Barry N(athaniel)

O'Donnell, Lawrence
See Kuttner, Henry

O'Donovan, Michael Francis 1903-1966 .... **CLC 14**
See O'Connor, Frank
See also CA 93-96; CANR 84

Oe, Kenzaburo 1935- .. **CLC 10, 36, 86, 187; SSC 20**
See Oe Kenzaburo
See also CA 97-100; CANR 36, 50, 74, 126; DA3; DAM NOV; DLB 182, 331; DLBY 1994; LATS 1:2; MJW; MTCW 1, 2; MTFW 2005; RGSF 2; RGWL 2, 3

Oe Kenzaburo
See Oe, Kenzaburo
See also CWW 2; EWL 3

O'Faolain, Julia 1932- .... **CLC 6, 19, 47, 108**
See also CA 81-84; CAAS 2; CANR 12, 61; CN 2, 3, 4, 5, 6, 7; DLB 14, 231, 319; FW; MTCW 1; RHW

O'Faolain, Sean 1900-1991 ...... **CLC 1, 7, 14, 32, 70; SSC 13; TCLC 143**
See also CA 61-64; 134; CANR 12, 66; CN 1, 2, 3, 4; DLB 15, 162; MTCW 1, 2; MTFW 2005; RGEL 2; RGSF 2

O'Flaherty, Liam 1896-1984 .... **CLC 5, 34; SSC 6, 116**
See also CA 101; 113; CANR 35; CN 1, 2, 3; DLB 36, 162; DLBY 1984; MTCW 1, 2; MTFW 2005; RGEL 2; RGSF 2; SSFS 5, 20

Ogai
See Mori Ogai
See also MJW

Ogilvy, Gavin
See Barrie, J(ames) M(atthew)

O'Grady, Standish (James) 1846-1928 .... **TCLC 5**
See also CA 104; 157

O'Grady, Timothy 1951- .... **CLC 59**
See also CA 138

O'Hara, Frank 1926-1966 .... **CLC 2, 5, 13, 78; PC 45**
See also CA 9-12R; 25-28R; CANR 33; DA3; DAM POET; DLB 5, 16, 193; EWL 3; MAL 5; MTCW 1, 2; MTFW 2005; PFS 8, 12; RGAL 4; WP

O'Hara, John (Henry) 1905-1970 . **CLC 1, 2, 3, 6, 11, 42; SSC 15**
See also AMW; BPFB 3; CA 5-8R; 25-28R; CANR 31, 60; CDALB 1929-1941; DAM NOV; DLB 9, 86, 324; DLBD 2; EWL 3; MAL 5; MTCW 1, 2; MTFW 2005; NFS 11; RGAL 4; RGSF 2

O'Hehir, Diana 1929- .... **CLC 41**
See also CA 245; CANR 177

O'Hehir, Diana F.
See O'Hehir, Diana

Ohiyesa
See Eastman, Charles A(lexander)

Okada, John 1923-1971 .... **AAL**
See also BYA 14; CA 212; DLB 312; NFS 25

Okigbo, Christopher 1930-1967 ..... **BLC 1:3; CLC 25, 84; PC 7; TCLC 171**
See also AFW; BW 1, 3; CA 77-80; CANR 74; CDWLB 3; DAM MULT, POET; DLB 125; EWL 3; MTCW 1, 2; MTFW 2005; RGEL 2

Okigbo, Christopher Ifenayichukwu
See Okigbo, Christopher

Okri, Ben 1959- .... **BLC 2:3; CLC 87, 223**
See also AFW; BRWS 5; BW 2, 3; CA 130; 138; CANR 65, 128; CN 5, 6, 7; DLB 157, 231, 319, 326; EWL 3; INT CA-138; MTCW 2; MTFW 2005; RGSF 2; SSFS 20; WLIT 2; WWE 1

Olds, Sharon 1942- .. **CLC 32, 39, 85; PC 22**
See also AMWS 10; CA 101; CANR 18, 41, 66, 98, 135; CP 5, 6, 7; CPW; CWP; DAM POET; DLB 120; MAL 5; MTCW 2; MTFW 2005; PFS 17

Oldstyle, Jonathan
See Irving, Washington

Olesha, Iurii
See Olesha, Yuri (Karlovich)
See also RGWL 2

Olesha, Iurii Karlovich
See Olesha, Yuri (Karlovich)
See also DLB 272

Olesha, Yuri (Karlovich) 1899-1960 . **CLC 8; SSC 69; TCLC 136**
See Olesha, Iurii; Olesha, Iurii Karlovich; Olesha, Yury Karlovich
See also CA 85-88; EW 11; RGWL 3

Olesha, Yury Karlovich
See Olesha, Yuri (Karlovich)
See also EWL 3

Oliphant, Mrs.
See Oliphant, Margaret (Oliphant Wilson)
See also SUFW

Oliphant, Laurence 1829(?)-1888 .. **NCLC 47**
See also DLB 18, 166

Oliphant, Margaret (Oliphant Wilson) 1828-1897 .... **NCLC 11, 61; SSC 25**
See Oliphant, Mrs.
See also BRWS 10; DLB 18, 159, 190; HGG; RGEL 2; RGSF 2

Oliver, Mary 1935- ... **CLC 19, 34, 98; PC 75**
See also AMWS 7; CA 21-24R; CANR 9, 43, 84, 92, 138; CP 4, 5, 6, 7; CWP; DLB 5, 193, 342; EWL 3; MTFW 2005; PFS 15

Olivier, Laurence (Kerr) 1907-1989 . **CLC 20**
See also CA 111; 150; 129

Olsen, Tillie 1912-2007 .... **CLC 4, 13, 114; SSC 11, 103**
See also AAYA 51; AMWS 13; BYA 11; CA 1-4R; 256; CANR 1, 43, 74, 132; CDALBS; CN 2, 3, 4, 5, 6, 7; DA; DA3; DAB; DAC; DAM MST; DLB 28, 206; DLBY 1980; EWL 3; EXPS; FW; MAL 5; MTCW 1, 2; MTFW 2005; RGAL 4; RGSF 2; SSFS 1; TCLE 1:2; TCWW 2; TUS

Olson, Charles (John) 1910-1970 .. **CLC 1, 2, 5, 6, 9, 11, 29; PC 19**
See also AMWS 2; CA 13-16; 25-28R; CABS 2; CANR 35, 61; CAP 1; CP 1; DAM POET; DLB 5, 16, 193; EWL 3; MAL 5; MTCW 1, 2; RGAL 4; WP

Olson, Merle Theodore
See Olson, Toby

Olson, Toby 1937- .... **CLC 28**
See also CA 65-68; CAAS 11; CANR 9, 31, 84, 175; CP 3, 4, 5, 6, 7

Olyesha, Yuri
See Olesha, Yuri (Karlovich)

Olympiodorus of Thebes c. 375-c. 430 .... **CMLC 59**

Omar Khayyam
See Khayyam, Omar
See also RGWL 2, 3

Ondaatje, Michael 1943- ..... **CLC 14, 29, 51, 76, 180, 258; PC 28**
See also AAYA 66; CA 77-80; CANR 42, 74, 109, 133, 172; CN 5, 6, 7; CP 1, 2, 3, 4, 5, 6, 7; DA3; DAB; DAC; DAM MST;

DLB 60, 323, 326; EWL 3; LATS 1:2;
LMFS 2; MTCW 2; MTFW 2005; NFS
23; PFS 8, 19; TCLE 1:2; TWA; WWE 1

Ondaatje, Philip Michael
See Ondaatje, Michael

Oneal, Elizabeth 1934-
See Oneal, Zibby
See also CA 106; CANR 28, 84; MAICYA
1, 2; SATA 30, 82; YAW

Oneal, Zibby CLC 30
See Oneal, Elizabeth
See also AAYA 5, 41; BYA 13; CLR 13;
JRDA; WYA

O'Neill, Eugene (Gladstone)
1888-1953 ... **DC 20; TCLC 1, 6, 27, 49;
WLC 4**
See also AAYA 54; AITN 1; AMW; AMWC
1; CA 110; 132; CAD; CANR 131;
CDALB 1929-1941; DA; DA3; DAB;
DAC; DAM DRAM, MST; DFS 2, 4, 5,
6, 9, 11, 12, 16, 20; DLB 7, 331; EWL 3;
LAIT 3; LMFS 2; MAL 5; MTCW 1, 2;
MTFW 2005; RGAL 4; TUS

Onetti, Juan Carlos 1909-1994 ... **CLC 7, 10;
HLCS 2; SSC 23; TCLC 131**
See also CA 85-88; 145; CANR 32, 63; CD-
WLB 3; CWW 2; DAM MULT, NOV;
DLB 113; EWL 3; HW 1, 2; LAW;
MTCW 1, 2; MTFW 2005; RGSF 2

O Nuallain, Brian 1911-1966
See O'Brien, Flann
See also CA 21-22; 25-28R; CAP 2; DLB
231; FANT; TEA

Ophuls, Max
See Ophuls, Max

Ophuls, Max 1902-1957 .... **TCLC 79**
See also CA 113

Opie, Amelia 1769-1853 .... **NCLC 65**
See also DLB 116, 159; RGEL 2

Oppen, George 1908-1984 ..... **CLC 7, 13, 34;
PC 35; TCLC 107**
See also CA 13-16R; 113; CANR 8, 82; CP
1, 2, 3; DLB 5, 165

Oppenheim, E(dward) Phillips
1866-1946 .... **TCLC 45**
See also CA 111; 202; CMW 4; DLB 70

Oppenheimer, Max
See Ophuls, Max

Opuls, Max
See Ophuls, Max

Orage, A(lfred) R(ichard)
1873-1934 .... **TCLC 157**
See also CA 122

Origen c. 185-c. 254 .... **CMLC 19**

Orlovitz, Gil 1918-1973 .... **CLC 22**
See also CA 77-80; 45-48; CN 1; CP 1, 2;
DLB 2, 5

Orosius c. 385-c. 420 .... **CMLC 100**

O'Rourke, Patrick Jake
See O'Rourke, P.J.

O'Rourke, P.J. 1947- .... **CLC 209**
See also CA 77-80; CANR 13, 41, 67, 111,
155; CPW; DAM POP; DLB 185

Orris
See Ingelow, Jean

Ortega y Gasset, Jose 1883-1955 ...... **HLC 2;
TCLC 9**
See also CA 106; 130; DAM MULT; EW 9;
EWL 3; HW 1, 2; MTCW 1, 2; MTFW
2005

Ortese, Anna Maria 1914-1998 .... **CLC 89**
See also DLB 177; EWL 3

Ortiz, Simon
See Ortiz, Simon J.

Ortiz, Simon J. 1941- . **CLC 45, 208; NNAL;
PC 17**
See also AMWS 4; CA 134; CANR 69, 118,
164; CP 3, 4, 5, 6, 7; DAM MULT, POET;
DLB 120, 175, 256, 342; EXPP; MAL 5;
PFS 4, 16; RGAL 4; SSFS 22; TCWW 2

Ortiz, Simon Joseph
See Ortiz, Simon J.

Orton, Joe CLC 4, 13, 43; DC 3; TCLC 157
See Orton, John Kingsley
See also BRWS 5; CBD; CDBLB 1960 to
Present; DFS 3, 6; DLB 13, 310; GLL 1;
RGEL 2; TEA; WLIT 4

Orton, John Kingsley 1933-1967
See Orton, Joe
See also CA 85-88; CANR 35, 66; DAM
DRAM; MTCW 1, 2; MTFW 2005

**Orwell, George SSC 68; TCLC 2, 6, 15, 31,
51, 128, 129; WLC 4**
See Blair, Eric (Arthur)
See also BPFB 3; BRW 7; BYA 5; CDBLB
1945-1960; CLR 68; DAB; DLB 15, 98,
195, 255; EWL 3; EXPN; LAIT 4, 5;
LATS 1:1; NFS 3, 7; RGEL 2; SCFW 1,
2; SFW 4; SSFS 4; TEA; WLIT 4; YAW

Osborne, David
See Silverberg, Robert

Osborne, Dorothy 1627-1695 .... **LC 141**

Osborne, George
See Silverberg, Robert

Osborne, John 1929-1994 .... **CLC 1, 2, 5, 11,
45; TCLC 153; WLC 4**
See also BRWS 1; CA 13-16R; 147; CANR
21, 56; CBD; CDBLB 1945-1960; DA;
DAB; DAC; DAM DRAM, MST; DFS 4,
19, 24; DLB 13; EWL 3; MTCW 1, 2;
MTFW 2005; RGEL 2

Osborne, Lawrence 1958- .... **CLC 50**
See also CA 189; CANR 152

Osbourne, Lloyd 1868-1947 .... **TCLC 93**

Osgood, Frances Sargent
1811-1850 .... **NCLC 141**
See also DLB 250

Oshima, Nagisa 1932- .... **CLC 20**
See also CA 116; 121; CANR 78

Oskison, John Milton
1874-1947 .... **NNAL; TCLC 35**
See also CA 144; CANR 84; DAM MULT;
DLB 175

Ossian c. 3rd cent. - .... **CMLC 28**
See Macpherson, James

Ossoli, Sarah Margaret (Fuller)
1810-1850 .... **NCLC 5, 50**
See Fuller, Margaret
See also CDALB 1640-1865; DLB 1, 59,
73; FW; LMFS 1; SATA 25

Ostriker, Alicia 1937- .... **CLC 132**
See also CA 25-28R; CAAS 24; CANR 10,
30, 62, 99, 167; CWP; DLB 120; EXPP;
PFS 19, 26

Ostriker, Alicia Suskin
See Ostriker, Alicia

Ostrovsky, Aleksandr Nikolaevich
See Ostrovsky, Alexander
See also DLB 277

Ostrovsky, Alexander 1823-1886 .. **NCLC 30,
57**
See Ostrovsky, Aleksandr Nikolaevich

Osundare, Niyi 1947- .... **BLC 2:3**
See also AFW; BW 3; CA 176; CDWLB 3;
CP 7; DLB 157

Otero, Blas de 1916-1979 .... **CLC 11**
See also CA 89-92; DLB 134; EWL 3

O'Trigger, Sir Lucius
See Horne, Richard Henry Hengist

Otto, Rudolf 1869-1937 .... **TCLC 85**

Otto, Whitney 1955- .... **CLC 70**
See also CA 140; CANR 120

Otway, Thomas 1652-1685 ... **DC 24; LC 106**
See also DAM DRAM; DLB 80; RGEL 2

Ouida TCLC 43
See De La Ramee, Marie Louise
See also DLB 18, 156; RGEL 2

Ouologuem, Yambo 1940- .... **CLC 146**
See also CA 111; 176

Ousmane, Sembene 1923-2007 .... **BLC 1:3,
2:3; CLC 66**
See also AFW; BW 1, 3; CA 117; 125; 261;
CANR 81; CWW 2; EWL 3; MTCW 1;
WLIT 2

Ovid 43B.C.-17 .... **CMLC 7, 108; PC 2**
See also AW 2; CDWLB 1; DA3; DAM
POET; DLB 211; PFS 22; RGWL 2, 3;
WLIT 8; WP

Owen, Hugh
See Faust, Frederick (Schiller)

Owen, Wilfred (Edward Salter)
1893-1918 ... **PC 19; TCLC 5, 27; WLC
4**
See also BRW 6; CA 104; 141; CDBLB
1914-1945; DA; DAB; DAC; DAM MST,
POET; DLB 20; EWL 3; EXPP; MTCW
2; MTFW 2005; PFS 10; RGEL 2; WLIT
4

Owens, Louis (Dean) 1948-2002 .... **NNAL**
See also CA 137, 179; 207; CAAE 179;
CAAS 24; CANR 71

Owens, Rochelle 1936- .... **CLC 8**
See also CA 17-20R; CAAS 2; CAD;
CANR 39; CD 5, 6; CP 1, 2, 3, 4, 5, 6, 7;
CWD; CWP

Oz, Amos 1939- ...... **CLC 5, 8, 11, 27, 33, 54;
SSC 66**
See also CA 53-56; CANR 27, 47, 65, 113,
138, 175; CWW 2; DAM NOV; EWL 3;
MTCW 1, 2; MTFW 2005; RGHL; RGSF
2; RGWL 3; WLIT 6

Ozick, Cynthia 1928- . **CLC 3, 7, 28, 62, 155,
262; SSC 15, 60**
See also AMWS 5; BEST 90:1; CA 17-20R;
CANR 23, 58, 116, 160; CN 3, 4, 5, 6, 7;
CPW; DA3; DAM NOV, POP; DLB 28,
152, 299; DLBY 1982; EWL 3; EXPS;
INT CANR-23; MAL 5; MTCW 1, 2;
MTFW 2005; RGAL 4; RGHL; RGSF 2;
SSFS 3, 12, 22

Ozu, Yasujiro 1903-1963 .... **CLC 16**
See also CA 112

Pabst, G. W. 1885-1967 .... **TCLC 127**

Pacheco, C.
See Pessoa, Fernando

Pacheco, Jose Emilio 1939- .... **HLC 2**
See also CA 111; 131; CANR 65; CWW 2;
DAM MULT; DLB 290; EWL 3; HW 1,
2; RGSF 2

Pa Chin CLC 18
See Jin, Ba
See also EWL 3

Pack, Robert 1929- .... **CLC 13**
See also CA 1-4R; CANR 3, 44, 82; CP 1,
2, 3, 4, 5, 6, 7; DLB 5; SATA 118

Packer, Vin
See Meaker, Marijane

Padgett, Lewis
See Kuttner, Henry

Padilla (Lorenzo), Heberto
1932-2000 .... **CLC 38**
See also AITN 1; CA 123; 131; 189; CWW
2; EWL 3; HW 1

Page, James Patrick 1944-
See Page, Jimmy
See also CA 204

Page, Jimmy 1944- .... **CLC 12**
See Page, James Patrick

Page, Louise 1955- .... **CLC 40**
See also CA 140; CANR 76; CBD; CD 5,
6; CWD; DLB 233

Page, P(atricia) K(athleen) 1916- ...... **CLC 7, 18; PC 12**
See Cape, Judith
See also CA 53-56; CANR 4, 22, 65; CP 1, 2, 3, 4, 5, 6, 7; DAC; DAM MST; DLB 68; MTCW 1; RGEL 2

Page, Stanton
See Fuller, Henry Blake

Page, Thomas Nelson 1853-1922 .... **SSC 23**
See also CA 118; 177; DLB 12, 78; DLBD 13; RGAL 4

Pagels, Elaine
See Pagels, Elaine Hiesey

Pagels, Elaine Hiesey 1943- .... **CLC 104**
See also CA 45-48; CANR 2, 24, 51, 151; FW; NCFS 4

Paget, Violet 1856-1935
See Lee, Vernon
See also CA 104; 166; GLL 1; HGG

Paget-Lowe, Henry
See Lovecraft, H. P.

Paglia, Camille 1947- .... **CLC 68**
See also CA 140; CANR 72, 139; CPW; FW; GLL 2; MTCW 2; MTFW 2005

Pagnol, Marcel (Paul)
1895-1974 .... **TCLC 208**
See also CA 128; 49-52; DLB 321; EWL 3; GFL 1789 to the Present; MTCW 1; RGWL 2, 3

Paige, Richard
See Koontz, Dean R.

Paine, Thomas 1737-1809 .... **NCLC 62**
See also AMWS 1; CDALB 1640-1865; DLB 31, 43, 73, 158; LAIT 1; RGAL 4; RGEL 2; TUS

Pakenham, Antonia
See Fraser, Antonia

Palamas, Costis
See Palamas, Kostes

Palamas, Kostes 1859-1943 .... **TCLC 5**
See Palamas, Kostis
See also CA 105; 190; RGWL 2, 3

Palamas, Kostis
See Palamas, Kostes
See also EWL 3

Palazzeschi, Aldo 1885-1974 .... **CLC 11**
See also CA 89-92; 53-56; DLB 114, 264; EWL 3

Pales Matos, Luis 1898-1959 .... **HLCS 2**
See Pales Matos, Luis
See also DLB 290; HW 1; LAW

Paley, Grace 1922-2007 ... **CLC 4, 6, 37, 140; SSC 8**
See also AMWS 6; CA 25-28R; 263; CANR 13, 46, 74, 118; CN 2, 3, 4, 5, 6, 7; CPW; DA3; DAM POP; DLB 28, 218; EWL 3; EXPS; FW; INT CANR-13; MAL 5; MBL; MTCW 1, 2; MTFW 2005; RGAL 4; RGSF 2; SSFS 3, 20

Paley, Grace Goodside
See Paley, Grace

Palin, Michael 1943- .... **CLC 21**
See Monty Python
See also CA 107; CANR 35, 109, 179; SATA 67

Palin, Michael Edward
See Palin, Michael

Palliser, Charles 1947- .... **CLC 65**
See also CA 136; CANR 76; CN 5, 6, 7

Palma, Ricardo 1833-1919 .... **TCLC 29**
See also CA 168; LAW

Pamuk, Orhan 1952- .... **CLC 185**
See also CA 142; CANR 75, 127, 172; CWW 2; NFS 27; WLIT 6

Pancake, Breece Dexter 1952-1979
See Pancake, Breece D'J
See also CA 123; 109

Pancake, Breece D'J **CLC 29; SSC 61**
See Pancake, Breece Dexter
See also DLB 130

Panchenko, Nikolai **CLC 59**

Pankhurst, Emmeline (Goulden)
1858-1928 .... **TCLC 100**
See also CA 116; FW

Panko, Rudy
See Gogol, Nikolai (Vasilyevich)

Papadiamantis, Alexandros
1851-1911 .... **TCLC 29**
See also CA 168; EWL 3

Papadiamantopoulos, Johannes 1856-1910
See Moreas, Jean
See also CA 117; 242

Papini, Giovanni 1881-1956 .... **TCLC 22**
See also CA 121; 180; DLB 264

Paracelsus 1493-1541 .... **LC 14**
See also DLB 179

Parasol, Peter
See Stevens, Wallace

Pardo Bazan, Emilia 1851-1921 .... **SSC 30; TCLC 189**
See also EWL 3; FW; RGSF 2; RGWL 2, 3

Paredes, Americo 1915-1999 .... **PC 83**
See also CA 37-40R; 179; DLB 209; EXPP; HW 1

Pareto, Vilfredo 1848-1923 .... **TCLC 69**
See also CA 175

Paretsky, Sara 1947- .... **CLC 135**
See also AAYA 30; BEST 90:3; CA 125; 129; CANR 59, 95, 184; CMW 4; CPW; DA3; DAM POP; DLB 306; INT CA-129; MSW; RGAL 4

Paretsky, Sara N.
See Paretsky, Sara

Parfenie, Maria
See Codrescu, Andrei

Parini, Jay (Lee) 1948- .... **CLC 54, 133**
See also CA 97-100, 229; CAAE 229; CAAS 16; CANR 32, 87

Park, Jordan
See Kornbluth, C(yril) M.; Pohl, Frederik

Park, Robert E(zra) 1864-1944 ..... **TCLC 73**
See also CA 122; 165

Parker, Bert
See Ellison, Harlan

Parker, Dorothy (Rothschild)
1893-1967 . **CLC 15, 68; PC 28; SSC 2, 101; TCLC 143**
See also AMWS 9; CA 19-20; 25-28R; CAP 2; DA3; DAM POET; DLB 11, 45, 86; EXPP; FW; MAL 5; MBL; MTCW 1, 2; MTFW 2005; PFS 18; RGAL 4; RGSF 2; TUS

Parker, Robert B. 1932- .... **CLC 27**
See also AAYA 28; BEST 89:4; BPFB 3; CA 49-52; CANR 1, 26, 52, 89, 128, 165; CMW 4; CPW; DAM NOV, POP; DLB 306; INT CANR-26; MSW; MTCW 1; MTFW 2005

Parker, Robert Brown
See Parker, Robert B.

Parker, Theodore 1810-1860 .... **NCLC 186**
See also DLB 1, 235

Parkin, Frank 1940- .... **CLC 43**
See also CA 147

Parkman, Francis, Jr. 1823-1893 .. **NCLC 12**
See also AMWS 2; DLB 1, 30, 183, 186, 235; RGAL 4

Parks, Gordon 1912-2006 . **BLC 1:3; CLC 1, 16**
See also AAYA 36; AITN 2; BW 2, 3; CA 41-44R; 249; CANR 26, 66, 145; DA3; DAM MULT; DLB 33; MTCW 2; MTFW 2005; SATA 8, 108; SATA-Obit 175

Parks, Suzan-Lori 1964(?)- ..... **BLC 2:3; DC 23**
See also AAYA 55; CA 201; CAD; CD 5, 6; CWD; DFS 22; DLB 341; RGAL 4

Parks, Tim(othy Harold) 1954- ..... **CLC 147**
See also CA 126; 131; CANR 77, 144; CN 7; DLB 231; INT CA-131

Parmenides c. 515B.C.-c.
450B.C. .... **CMLC 22**
See also DLB 176

Parnell, Thomas 1679-1718 .... **LC 3**
See also DLB 95; RGEL 2

Parr, Catherine c. 1513(?)-1548 .... **LC 86**
See also DLB 136

Parra, Nicanor 1914- ... **CLC 2, 102; HLC 2; PC 39**
See also CA 85-88; CANR 32; CWW 2; DAM MULT; DLB 283; EWL 3; HW 1; LAW; MTCW 1

Parra Sanojo, Ana Teresa de la
1890-1936 .... **HLCS 2**
See de la Parra, (Ana) Teresa (Sonojo)
See also LAW

Parrish, Mary Frances
See Fisher, M(ary) F(rances) K(ennedy)

Parshchikov, Aleksei 1954- .... **CLC 59**
See Parshchikov, Aleksei Maksimovich

Parshchikov, Aleksei Maksimovich
See Parshchikov, Aleksei
See also DLB 285

Parson, Professor
See Coleridge, Samuel Taylor

Parson Lot
See Kingsley, Charles

Parton, Sara Payson Willis
1811-1872 .... **NCLC 86**
See also DLB 43, 74, 239

Partridge, Anthony
See Oppenheim, E(dward) Phillips

Pascal, Blaise 1623-1662 .... **LC 35**
See also DLB 268; EW 3; GFL Beginnings to 1789; RGWL 2, 3; TWA

Pascoli, Giovanni 1855-1912 .... **TCLC 45**
See also CA 170; EW 7; EWL 3

Pasolini, Pier Paolo 1922-1975 .. **CLC 20, 37, 106; PC 17**
See also CA 93-96; 61-64; CANR 63; DLB 128, 177; EWL 3; MTCW 1; RGWL 2, 3

Pasquini
See Silone, Ignazio

Pastan, Linda (Olenik) 1932- .... **CLC 27**
See also CA 61-64; CANR 18, 40, 61, 113; CP 3, 4, 5, 6, 7; CSW; CWP; DAM POET; DLB 5; PFS 8, 25

Pasternak, Boris 1890-1960 ... **CLC 7, 10, 18, 63; PC 6; SSC 31; TCLC 188; WLC 4**
See also BPFB 3; CA 127; 116; DA; DA3; DAB; DAC; DAM MST, NOV, POET; DLB 302, 331; EW 10; MTCW 1, 2; MTFW 2005; NFS 26; RGSF 2; RGWL 2, 3; TWA; WP

Patchen, Kenneth 1911-1972 .... **CLC 1, 2, 18**
See also BG 1:3; CA 1-4R; 33-36R; CANR 3, 35; CN 1; CP 1; DAM POET; DLB 16, 48; EWL 3; MAL 5; MTCW 1; RGAL 4

Patchett, Ann 1963- .... **CLC 244**
See also AAYA 69; AMWS 12; CA 139; CANR 64, 110, 167; MTFW 2005

Pater, Walter (Horatio) 1839-1894 . **NCLC 7, 90, 159**
See also BRW 5; CDBLB 1832-1890; DLB 57, 156; RGEL 2; TEA

Paterson, A(ndrew) B(arton)
1864-1941 .... **TCLC 32**
See also CA 155; DLB 230; RGEL 2; SATA 97

Paterson, Banjo
See Paterson, A(ndrew) B(arton)

Paterson, Katherine 1932- .... **CLC 12, 30**
See also AAYA 1, 31; BYA 1, 2, 7; CA 21-
24R; CANR 28, 59, 111, 173; CLR 7, 50,
127; CWRI 5; DLB 52; JRDA; LAIT 4;
MAICYA 1, 2; MAICYAS 1; MTCW 1;
SATA 13, 53, 92, 133; WYA; YAW

Paterson, Katherine Womeldorf
See Paterson, Katherine

Patmore, Coventry Kersey Dighton
1823-1896 .... **NCLC 9; PC 59**
See also DLB 35, 98; RGEL 2; TEA

Paton, Alan 1903-1988 ..... **CLC 4, 10, 25, 55,**
106; TCLC 165; WLC 4
See also AAYA 26; AFW; BPFB 3; BRWS
2; BYA 1; CA 13-16; 125; CANR 22;
CAP 1; CN 1, 2, 3, 4; DA; DA3; DAB;
DAC; DAM MST, NOV; DLB 225;
DLBD 17; EWL 3; EXPN; LAIT 4;
MTCW 1, 2; MTFW 2005; NFS 3, 12;
RGEL 2; SATA 11; SATA-Obit 56; TWA;
WLIT 2; WWE 1

Paton Walsh, Gillian
See Paton Walsh, Jill
See also AAYA 47; BYA 1, 8

Paton Walsh, Jill 1937- .... **CLC 35**
See also Paton Walsh, Gillian; Walsh, Jill Paton
See also AAYA 11; CA 262; CAAE 262;
CANR 38, 83, 158; CLR 2, 65; DLB 161;
JRDA; MAICYA 1, 2; SAAS 3; SATA 4,
72, 109, 190; SATA-Essay 190; YAW

Patsauq, Markoosie 1942- .... **NNAL**
See also CA 101; CLR 23; CWRI 5; DAM
MULT

Patterson, (Horace) Orlando (Lloyd)
1940- .... **BLCS**
See also BW 1; CA 65-68; CANR 27, 84;
CN 1, 2, 3, 4, 5, 6

Patton, George S(mith), Jr.
1885-1945 .... **TCLC 79**
See also CA 189

Paulding, James Kirke 1778-1860 ... **NCLC 2**
See also DLB 3, 59, 74, 250; RGAL 4

Paulin, Thomas Neilson
See Paulin, Tom

Paulin, Tom 1949- .... **CLC 37, 177**
See also CA 123; 128; CANR 98; CP 3, 4,
5, 6, 7; DLB 40

Pausanias c. 1st cent. - .... **CMLC 36**

Paustovsky, Konstantin (Georgievich)
1892-1968 .... **CLC 40**
See also CA 93-96; 25-28R; DLB 272;
EWL 3

Pavese, Cesare 1908-1950 .... **PC 13; SSC 19;**
TCLC 3
See also CA 104; 169; DLB 128, 177; EW
12; EWL 3; PFS 20; RGSF 2; RGWL 2,
3; TWA; WLIT 7

Pavic, Milorad 1929- .... **CLC 60**
See also CA 136; CDWLB 4; CWW 2; DLB
181; EWL 3; RGWL 3

Pavlov, Ivan Petrovich 1849-1936 . **TCLC 91**
See also CA 118; 180

Pavlova, Karolina Karlovna
1807-1893 .... **NCLC 138**
See also DLB 205

Payne, Alan
See Jakes, John

Payne, Rachel Ann
See Jakes, John

Paz, Gil
See Lugones, Leopoldo

Paz, Octavio 1914-1998 . **CLC 3, 4, 6, 10, 19,**
51, 65, 119; HLC 2; PC 1, 48; TCLC
211; WLC 4
See also AAYA 50; CA 73-76; 165; CANR
32, 65, 104; CWW 2; DA; DA3; DAB;
DAC; DAM MST, MULT, POET; DLB
290, 331; DLBY 1990, 1998; DNFS 1;

EWL 3; HW 1, 2; LAW; LAWS 1; MTCW
1, 2; MTFW 2005; PFS 18; RGWL 2, 3;
SSFS 13; TWA; WLIT 1

p'Bitek, Okot 1931-1982 . **BLC 1:3; CLC 96;**
TCLC 149
See also AFW; BW 2, 3; CA 124; 107;
CANR 82; CP 1, 2, 3; DAM MULT; DLB
125; EWL 3; MTCW 1, 2; MTFW 2005;
RGEL 2; WLIT 2

Peabody, Elizabeth Palmer
1804-1894 .... **NCLC 169**
See also DLB 1, 223

Peacham, Henry 1578-1644(?) .... **LC 119**
See also DLB 151

Peacock, Molly 1947- .... **CLC 60**
See also CA 103, 262; CAAE 262; CAAS
21; CANR 52, 84; CP 5, 6, 7; CWP; DLB
120, 282

Peacock, Thomas Love
1785-1866 .... **NCLC 22; PC 87**
See also BRW 4; DLB 96, 116; RGEL 2;
RGSF 2

Peake, Mervyn 1911-1968 .... **CLC 7, 54**
See also CA 5-8R; 25-28R; CANR 3; DLB
15, 160, 255; FANT; MTCW 1; RGEL 2;
SATA 23; SFW 4

Pearce, Philippa 1920-2006
See Christie, Philippa
See also CA 5-8R; 255; CANR 4, 109;
CWRI 5; FANT; MAICYA 2; SATA-Obit
179

Pearl, Eric
See Elman, Richard (Martin)

Pearson, Jean Mary
See Gardam, Jane

Pearson, T. R. 1956- .... **CLC 39**
See also CA 120; 130; CANR 97, 147;
CSW; INT CA-130

Pearson, Thomas Reid
See Pearson, T. R.

Peck, Dale 1967- .... **CLC 81**
See also CA 146; CANR 72, 127, 180; GLL
2

Peck, John (Frederick) 1941- .... **CLC 3**
See also CA 49-52; CANR 3, 100; CP 4, 5,
6, 7

Peck, Richard 1934- .... **CLC 21**
See also AAYA 1, 24; BYA 1, 6, 8, 11; CA
85-88; CANR 19, 38, 129, 178; CLR 15;
INT CANR-19; JRDA; MAICYA 1, 2;
SAAS 2; SATA 18, 55, 97, 110, 158, 190;
SATA-Essay 110; WYA; YAW

Peck, Richard Wayne
See Peck, Richard

Peck, Robert Newton 1928- .... **CLC 17**
See also AAYA 3, 43; BYA 1, 6; CA 81-84,
182; CAAE 182; CANR 31, 63, 127; CLR
45; DA; DAC; DAM MST; JRDA; LAIT
3; MAICYA 1, 2; SAAS 1; SATA 21, 62,
111, 156; SATA-Essay 108; WYA; YAW

Peckinpah, David Samuel
See Peckinpah, Sam

Peckinpah, Sam 1925-1984 .... **CLC 20**
See also CA 109; 114; CANR 82

Pedersen, Knut 1859-1952
See Hamsun, Knut
See also CA 104; 119; CANR 63; MTCW
1, 2

Peele, George 1556-1596 .... **DC 27; LC 115**
See also BRW 1; DLB 62, 167; RGEL 2

Peeslake, Gaffer
See Durrell, Lawrence (George)

Peguy, Charles (Pierre)
1873-1914 .... **TCLC 10**
See also CA 107; 193; DLB 258; EWL 3;
GFL 1789 to the Present

Peirce, Charles Sanders
1839-1914 .... **TCLC 81**
See also CA 194; DLB 270

Pelecanos, George P. 1957- .... **CLC 236**
See also CA 138; CANR 122, 165; DLB
306

Pelevin, Victor 1962- .... **CLC 238**
See Pelevin, Viktor Olegovich
See also CA 154; CANR 88, 159

Pelevin, Viktor Olegovich
See Pelevin, Victor
See also DLB 285

Pellicer, Carlos 1897(?)-1977 .... **HLCS 2**
See also CA 153; 69-72; DLB 290; EWL 3;
HW 1

Pena, Ramon del Valle y
See Valle-Inclan, Ramon (Maria) del

Pendennis, Arthur Esquir
See Thackeray, William Makepeace

Penn, Arthur
See Matthews, (James) Brander

Penn, William 1644-1718 .... **LC 25**
See also DLB 24

PEPECE
See Prado (Calvo), Pedro

Pepys, Samuel 1633-1703 ... **LC 11, 58; WLC**
4
See also BRW 2; CDBLB 1660-1789; DA;
DA3; DAB; DAC; DAM MST; DLB 101,
213; NCFS 4; RGEL 2; TEA; WLIT 3

Percy, Thomas 1729-1811 .... **NCLC 95**
See also DLB 104

Percy, Walker 1916-1990 .... **CLC 2, 3, 6, 8,**
14, 18, 47, 65
See also AMWS 3; BPFB 3; CA 1-4R; 131;
CANR 1, 23, 64; CN 1, 2, 3, 4; CPW;
CSW; DA3; DAM NOV, POP; DLB 2;
DLBY 1980, 1990; EWL 3; MAL 5;
MTCW 1, 2; MTFW 2005; RGAL 4; TUS

Percy, William Alexander
1885-1942 .... **TCLC 84**
See also CA 163; MTCW 2

Perec, Georges 1936-1982 .... **CLC 56, 116**
See also CA 141; DLB 83, 299; EWL 3;
GFL 1789 to the Present; RGHL; RGWL
3

Pereda (y Sanchez de Porrua), Jose Maria
de 1833-1906 .... **TCLC 16**
See also CA 117

Pereda y Porrua, Jose Maria de
See Pereda (y Sanchez de Porrua), Jose
Maria de

Peregoy, George Weems
See Mencken, H(enry) L(ouis)

Perelman, S(idney) J(oseph)
1904-1979 .. **CLC 3, 5, 9, 15, 23, 44, 49;**
SSC 32
See also AITN 1, 2; BPFB 3; CA 73-76;
89-92; CANR 18; DAM DRAM; DLB 11,
44; MTCW 1, 2; MTFW 2005; RGAL 4

Peret, Benjamin 1899-1959 .... **PC 33; TCLC**
20
See also CA 117; 186; GFL 1789 to the
Present

Peretz, Isaac Leib
See Peretz, Isaac Loeb
See also CA 201; DLB 333

Peretz, Isaac Loeb 1851(?)-1915 ...... **SSC 26;**
TCLC 16
See Peretz, Isaac Leib
See also CA 109

Peretz, Yitzhok Leibush
See Peretz, Isaac Loeb

Perez Galdos, Benito 1843-1920 ..... **HLCS 2;**
TCLC 27
See Galdos, Benito Perez
See also CA 125; 153; EWL 3; HW 1;
RGWL 2, 3

Peri Rossi, Cristina 1941- .. **CLC 156; HLCS**
2
See also CA 131; CANR 59, 81; CWW 2;
DLB 145, 290; EWL 3; HW 1, 2

Perlata
See Peret, Benjamin
Perloff, Marjorie G(abrielle)
1931- .... **CLC 137**
See also CA 57-60; CANR 7, 22, 49, 104
Perrault, Charles 1628-1703 .... **LC 2, 56**
See also BYA 4; CLR 79, 134; DLB 268;
GFL Beginnings to 1789; MAICYA 1, 2;
RGWL 2, 3; SATA 25; WCH
Perry, Anne 1938- .... **CLC 126**
See also CA 101; CANR 22, 50, 84, 150,
177; CMW 4; CN 6, 7; CPW; DLB 276
Perry, Brighton
See Sherwood, Robert E(mmet)
Perse, St.-John
See Leger, (Marie-Rene Auguste) Alexis
Saint-Leger
Perse, Saint-John
See Leger, (Marie-Rene Auguste) Alexis
Saint-Leger
See also DLB 258, 331; RGWL 3
Persius 34-62 .... **CMLC 74**
See also AW 2; DLB 211; RGWL 2, 3
Perutz, Leo(pold) 1882-1957 .... **TCLC 60**
See also CA 147; DLB 81
Peseenz, Tulio F.
See Lopez y Fuentes, Gregorio
Pesetsky, Bette 1932- .... **CLC 28**
See also CA 133; DLB 130
Peshkov, Alexei Maximovich 1868-1936
See Gorky, Maxim
See also CA 105; 141; CANR 83; DA;
DAC; DAM DRAM, MST, NOV; MTCW
2; MTFW 2005
Pessoa, Fernando 1888-1935 .... **HLC 2; PC
20; TCLC 27**
See also CA 125; 183; CANR 182; DAM
MULT; DLB 287; EW 10; EWL 3; RGWL
2, 3; WP
Pessoa, Fernando Antonio Nogueira
See Pessoa, Fernando
Peterkin, Julia Mood 1880-1961 ...... **CLC 31**
See also CA 102; DLB 9
Peters, Joan K(aren) 1945- .... **CLC 39**
See also CA 158; CANR 109
Peters, Robert L(ouis) 1924- .... **CLC 7**
See also CA 13-16R; CAAS 8; CP 1, 5, 6,
7; DLB 105
Petofi, Sandor 1823-1849 .... **NCLC 21**
See also RGWL 2, 3
Petrakis, Harry Mark 1923- .... **CLC 3**
See also CA 9-12R; CANR 4, 30, 85, 155;
CN 1, 2, 3, 4, 5, 6, 7
Petrarch 1304-1374 .... **CMLC 20; PC 8**
See also DA3; DAM POET; EW 2; LMFS
1; RGWL 2, 3; WLIT 7
Petronius c. 20-66 .... **CMLC 34**
See also AW 2; CDWLB 1; DLB 211;
RGWL 2, 3; WLIT 8
Petrov, Evgeny .... **TCLC 21**
See Kataev, Evgeny Petrovich
Petry, Ann (Lane) 1908-1997 .. **CLC 1, 7, 18;
TCLC 112**
See also AFAW 1, 2; BPFB 3; BW 1, 3;
BYA 2; CA 5-8R; 157; CAAS 6; CANR
4, 46; CLR 12; CN 1, 2, 3, 4, 5, 6; DLB
76; EWL 3; JRDA; LAIT 1; MAICYA 1,
2; MAICYAS 1; MTCW 1; RGAL 4;
SATA 5; SATA-Obit 94; TUS
Petursson, Halligrimur 1614-1674 .... **LC 8**
Peychinovich
See Vazov, Ivan (Minchov)
Phaedrus c. 15B.C.-c. 50 .... **CMLC 25**
See also DLB 211
Phelps (Ward), Elizabeth Stuart
See Phelps, Elizabeth Stuart
See also FW

Phelps, Elizabeth Stuart
1844-1911 .... **TCLC 113**
See Phelps (Ward), Elizabeth Stuart
See also CA 242; DLB 74
Pheradausi
See Ferdowsi, Abu'l Qasem
Philippe de Remi c. 1247-1296 ... **CMLC 102**
Philips, Katherine 1632-1664 ..... **LC 30, 145;
PC 40**
See also DLB 131; RGEL 2
Philipson, Ilene J. 1950- .... **CLC 65**
See also CA 219
Philipson, Morris H. 1926- .... **CLC 53**
See also CA 1-4R; CANR 4
Phillips, Caryl 1958- .... **BLCS; CLC 96, 224**
See also BRWS 5; BW 2; CA 141; CANR
63, 104, 140; CBD; CD 5, 6; CN 5, 6, 7;
DA3; DAM MULT; DLB 157; EWL 3;
MTCW 2; MTFW 2005; WLIT 4; WWE
1
Phillips, David Graham
1867-1911 .... **TCLC 44**
See also CA 108; 176; DLB 9, 12, 303;
RGAL 4
Phillips, Jack
See Sandburg, Carl (August)
Phillips, Jayne Anne 1952- .... **CLC 15, 33,
139; SSC 16**
See also AAYA 57; BPFB 3; CA 101;
CANR 24, 50, 96; CN 4, 5, 6, 7; CSW;
DLBY 1980; INT CANR-24; MTCW 1,
2; MTFW 2005; RGAL 4; RGSF 2; SSFS
4
Phillips, Richard
See Dick, Philip K.
Phillips, Robert (Schaeffer) 1938- .... **CLC 28**
See also CA 17-20R; CAAS 13; CANR 8;
DLB 105
Phillips, Ward
See Lovecraft, H. P.
Philo c. 20B.C.-c. 50 .... **CMLC 100**
See also DLB 176
Philostratus, Flavius c. 179-c.
244 .... **CMLC 62**
Phiradausi
See Ferdowsi, Abu'l Qasem
Piccolo, Lucio 1901-1969 .... **CLC 13**
See also CA 97-100; DLB 114; EWL 3
Pickthall, Marjorie L(owry) C(hristie)
1883-1922 .... **TCLC 21**
See also CA 107; DLB 92
Pico della Mirandola, Giovanni
1463-1494 .... **LC 15**
See also LMFS 1
Piercy, Marge 1936- .... **CLC 3, 6, 14, 18, 27,
62, 128; PC 29**
See also BPFB 3; CA 21-24R, 187; CAAE
187; CAAS 1; CANR 13, 43, 66, 111; CN
3, 4, 5, 6, 7; CP 1, 2, 3, 4, 5, 6, 7; CWP;
DLB 120, 227; EXPP; FW; MAL 5;
MTCW 1, 2; MTFW 2005; PFS 9, 22;
SFW 4
Piers, Robert
See Anthony, Piers
Pieyre de Mandiargues, Andre 1909-1991
See Mandiargues, Andre Pieyre de
See also CA 103; 136; CANR 22, 82; EWL
3; GFL 1789 to the Present
Pilnyak, Boris 1894-1938 . **SSC 48; TCLC 23**
See Vogau, Boris Andreyevich
See also EWL 3
Pinchback, Eugene
See Toomer, Jean
Pincherle, Alberto 1907-1990 ...... **CLC 11, 18**
See Moravia, Alberto
See also CA 25-28R; 132; CANR 33, 63,
142; DAM NOV; MTCW 1; MTFW 2005
Pinckney, Darryl 1953- .... **CLC 76**
See also BW 2, 3; CA 143; CANR 79

Pindar 518(?)B.C.-438(?)B.C. .... **CMLC 12;
PC 19**
See also AW 1; CDWLB 1; DLB 176;
RGWL 2
Pineda, Cecile 1942- .... **CLC 39**
See also CA 118; DLB 209
Pinero, Arthur Wing 1855-1934 .... **TCLC 32**
See also CA 110; 153; DAM DRAM; DLB
10, 344; RGEL 2
Pinero, Miguel (Antonio Gomez)
1946-1988 .... **CLC 4, 55**
See also CA 61-64; 125; CAD; CANR 29,
90; DLB 266; HW 1; LLW
Pinget, Robert 1919-1997 .... **CLC 7, 13, 37**
See also CA 85-88; 160; CWW 2; DLB 83;
EWL 3; GFL 1789 to the Present
Pink Floyd
See Barrett, (Roger) Syd; Gilmour, David;
Mason, Nick; Waters, Roger; Wright, Rick
Pinkney, Edward 1802-1828 .... **NCLC 31**
See also DLB 248
Pinkwater, D. Manus
See Pinkwater, Daniel Manus
Pinkwater, Daniel
See Pinkwater, Daniel Manus
Pinkwater, Daniel M.
See Pinkwater, Daniel Manus
Pinkwater, Daniel Manus 1941- .... **CLC 35**
See also AAYA 1, 46; BYA 9; CA 29-32R;
CANR 12, 38, 89, 143; CLR 4; CSW;
FANT; JRDA; MAICYA 1, 2; SAAS 3;
SATA 8, 46, 76, 114, 158; SFW 4; YAW
Pinkwater, Manus
See Pinkwater, Daniel Manus
Pinsky, Robert 1940- .... **CLC 9, 19, 38, 94,
121, 216; PC 27**
See also AMWS 6; CA 29-32R; CAAS 4;
CANR 58, 97, 138, 177; CP 3, 4, 5, 6, 7;
DA3; DAM POET; DLBY 1982, 1998;
MAL 5; MTCW 2; MTFW 2005; PFS 18;
RGAL 4; TCLE 1:2
Pinta, Harold
See Pinter, Harold
Pinter, Harold 1930- .. **CLC 1, 3, 6, 9, 11, 15,
27, 58, 73, 199; DC 15; WLC 4**
See also BRWR 1; BRWS 1; CA 5-8R;
CANR 33, 65, 112, 145; CBD; CD 5, 6;
CDBLB 1960 to Present; CP 1; DA; DA3;
DAB; DAC; DAM DRAM, MST; DFS 3,
5, 7, 14, 25; DLB 13, 310, 331; EWL 3;
IDFW 3, 4; LMFS 2; MTCW 1, 2; MTFW
2005; RGEL 2; RGHL; TEA
Piozzi, Hester Lynch (Thrale)
1741-1821 .... **NCLC 57**
See also DLB 104, 142
Pirandello, Luigi 1867-1936 .. **DC 5; SSC 22;
TCLC 4, 29, 172; WLC 4**
See also CA 104; 153; CANR 103; DA;
DA3; DAB; DAC; DAM DRAM, MST;
DFS 4, 9; DLB 264, 331; EW 8; EWL 3;
MTCW 2; MTFW 2005; RGSF 2; RGWL
2, 3; WLIT 7
Pirdousi
See Ferdowsi, Abu'l Qasem
Pirdousi, Abul-Qasim
See Ferdowsi, Abu'l Qasem
Pirsig, Robert M(aynard) 1928- ... **CLC 4, 6,
73**
See also CA 53-56; CANR 42, 74; CPW 1;
DA3; DAM POP; MTCW 1, 2; MTFW
2005; SATA 39
Pisan, Christine de
See Christine de Pizan
Pisarev, Dmitrii Ivanovich
See Pisarev, Dmitry Ivanovich
See also DLB 277
Pisarev, Dmitry Ivanovich
1840-1868 .... **NCLC 25**
See also Pisarev, Dmitrii Ivanovich

Pix, Mary (Griffith) 1666-1709 ..... **LC 8, 149**
See also DLB 80

Pixerecourt, (Rene Charles) Guilbert de
1773-1844 .... **NCLC 39**
See also DLB 192; GFL 1789 to the Present

Plaatje, Sol(omon) T(shekisho)
1878-1932 .... **BLCS; TCLC 73**
See also BW 2, 3; CA 141; CANR 79; DLB
125, 225

Plaidy, Jean
See Hibbert, Eleanor Alice Burford

Planche, James Robinson
1796-1880 .... **NCLC 42**
See also RGEL 2

Plant, Robert 1948- .... **CLC 12**

Plante, David 1940- .... **CLC 7, 23, 38**
See also CA 37-40R; CANR 12, 36, 58, 82,
152; CN 2, 3, 4, 5, 6, 7; DAM NOV;
DLBY 1983; INT CANR-12; MTCW 1

Plante, David Robert
See Plante, David

Plath, Sylvia 1932-1963 ..... **CLC 1, 2, 3, 5, 9,
11, 14, 17, 50, 51, 62, 111; PC 1, 37;
WLC 4**
See also AAYA 13; AMWR 2; AMWS 1;
BPFB 3; CA 19-20; CANR 34, 101; CAP
2; CDALB 1941-1968; DA; DA3; DAB;
DAC; DAM MST, POET; DLB 5, 6, 152;
EWL 3; EXPN; EXPP; FL 1:6; FW; LAIT
4; MAL 5; MBL; MTCW 1, 2; MTFW
2005; NFS 1; PAB; PFS 1, 15, 28; RGAL
4; SATA 96; TUS; WP; YAW

Plato c. 428B.C.-347B.C. .... **CMLC 8, 75, 98;
WLCS**
See also AW 1; CDWLB 1; DA; DA3;
DAB; DAC; DAM MST; DLB 176; LAIT
1; LATS 1:1; RGWL 2, 3; WLIT 8

Platonov, Andrei
See Klimentov, Andrei Platonovich

Platonov, Andrei Platonovich
See Klimentov, Andrei Platonovich
See also DLB 272

Platonov, Andrey Platonovich
See Klimentov, Andrei Platonovich
See also EWL 3

Platt, Kin 1911- .... **CLC 26**
See also AAYA 11; CA 17-20R; CANR 11;
JRDA; SAAS 17; SATA 21, 86; WYA

Plautus c. 254B.C.-c. 184B.C. .... **CMLC 24,
92; DC 6**
See also AW 1; CDWLB 1; DLB 211;
RGWL 2, 3; WLIT 8

Plick et Plock
See Simenon, Georges (Jacques Christian)

Plieksans, Janis
See Rainis, Janis

Plimpton, George 1927-2003 .... **CLC 36**
See also AITN 1; AMWS 16; CA 21-24R;
224; CANR 32, 70, 103, 133; DLB 185,
241; MTCW 1, 2; MTFW 2005; SATA
10; SATA-Obit 150

Pliny the Elder c. 23-79 .... **CMLC 23**
See also DLB 211

Pliny the Younger c. 61-c. 112 ...... **CMLC 62**
See also AW 2; DLB 211

Plomer, William Charles Franklin
1903-1973 .... **CLC 4, 8**
See also AFW; BRWS 11; CA 21-22; CANR
34; CAP 2; CN 1; CP 1, 2; DLB 20, 162,
191, 225; EWL 3; MTCW 1; RGEL 2;
RGSF 2; SATA 24

Plotinus 204-270 .... **CMLC 46**
See also CDWLB 1; DLB 176

Plowman, Piers
See Kavanagh, Patrick (Joseph)

Plum, J.
See Wodehouse, P(elham) G(renville)

Plumly, Stanley (Ross) 1939- .... **CLC 33**
See also CA 108; 110; CANR 97; CP 3, 4,
5, 6, 7; DLB 5, 193; INT CA-110

Plumpe, Friedrich Wilhelm
See Murnau, F.W.

Plutarch c. 46-c. 120 .... **CMLC 60**
See also AW 2; CDWLB 1; DLB 176;
RGWL 2, 3; TWA; WLIT 8

Po Chu-i 772-846 .... **CMLC 24**

Podhoretz, Norman 1930- .... **CLC 189**
See also AMWS 8; CA 9-12R; CANR 7,
78, 135, 179

Poe, Edgar Allan 1809-1849 ..... **NCLC 1, 16,
55, 78, 94, 97, 117; PC 1, 54; SSC 1,
22, 34, 35, 54, 88, 111; WLC 4**
See also AAYA 14; AMW; AMWC 1;
AMWR 2; BPFB 3; BYA 5, 11; CDALB
1640-1865; CMW 4; DA; DA3; DAB;
DAC; DAM MST, POET; DLB 3, 59, 73,
74, 248, 254; EXPP; EXPS; GL 3; HGG;
LAIT 2; LATS 1:1; LMFS 1; MSW; PAB;
PFS 1, 3, 9; RGAL 4; RGSF 2; SATA 23;
SCFW 1, 2; SFW 4; SSFS 2, 4, 7, 8, 16,
26; SUFW; TUS; WP; WYA

Poet of Titchfield Street, The
See Pound, Ezra (Weston Loomis)

Poggio Bracciolini, Gian Francesco
1380-1459 .... **LC 125**

Pohl, Frederik 1919- .... **CLC 18; SSC 25**
See also AAYA 24; CA 61-64, 188; CAAE
188; CAAS 1; CANR 11, 37, 81, 140; CN
1, 2, 3, 4, 5, 6; DLB 8; INT CANR-11;
MTCW 1, 2; MTFW 2005; SATA 24;
SCFW 1, 2; SFW 4

Poirier, Louis
See Gracq, Julien

Poitier, Sidney 1927- .... **CLC 26**
See also AAYA 60; BW 1; CA 117; CANR
94

Pokagon, Simon 1830-1899 .... **NNAL**
See also DAM MULT

Polanski, Roman 1933- .... **CLC 16, 178**
See also CA 77-80

Poliakoff, Stephen 1952- .... **CLC 38**
See also CA 106; CANR 116; CBD; CD 5,
6; DLB 13

Police, The
See Copeland, Stewart (Armstrong); Summers, Andy

Polidori, John William
1795-1821 .... **NCLC 51; SSC 97**
See also DLB 116; HGG

Poliziano, Angelo 1454-1494 .... **LC 120**
See also WLIT 7

Pollitt, Katha 1949- .... **CLC 28, 122**
See also CA 120; 122; CANR 66, 108, 164;
MTCW 1, 2; MTFW 2005

Pollock, (Mary) Sharon 1936- .... **CLC 50**
See also CA 141; CANR 132; CD 5; CWD;
DAC; DAM DRAM, MST; DFS 3; DLB
60; FW

Pollock, Sharon 1936- .... **DC 20**
See also CD 6

Polo, Marco 1254-1324 .... **CMLC 15**
See also WLIT 7

Polonsky, Abraham (Lincoln)
1910-1999 .... **CLC 92**
See also CA 104; 187; DLB 26; INT CA-
104

Polybius c. 200B.C.-c. 118B.C. ...... **CMLC 17**
See also AW 1; DLB 176; RGWL 2, 3

Pomerance, Bernard 1940- .... **CLC 13**
See also CA 101; CAD; CANR 49, 134;
CD 5, 6; DAM DRAM; DFS 9; LAIT 2

Ponge, Francis 1899-1988 .... **CLC 6, 18**
See also CA 85-88; 126; CANR 40, 86;
DAM POET; DLBY 2002; EWL 3; GFL
1789 to the Present; RGWL 2, 3

Poniatowska, Elena 1932- . **CLC 140; HLC 2**
See also CA 101; CANR 32, 66, 107, 156;
CDWLB 3; CWW 2; DAM MULT; DLB
113; EWL 3; HW 1, 2; LAWS 1; WLIT 1

Pontoppidan, Henrik 1857-1943 .... **TCLC 29**
See also CA 170; DLB 300, 331

Ponty, Maurice Merleau
See Merleau-Ponty, Maurice

Poole, Josephine CLC 17
See Helyar, Jane Penelope Josephine
See also SAAS 2; SATA 5

Popa, Vasko 1922-1991 . **CLC 19; TCLC 167**
See also CA 112; 148; CDWLB 4; DLB
181; EWL 3; RGWL 2, 3

Pope, Alexander 1688-1744 ...... **LC 3, 58, 60,
64; PC 26; WLC 5**
See also BRW 3; BRWC 1; BRWR 1; CD-
BLB 1660-1789; DA; DA3; DAB; DAC;
DAM MST, POET; DLB 95, 101, 213;
EXPP; PAB; PFS 12; RGEL 2; WLIT 3;
WP

Popov, Evgenii Anatol'evich
See Popov, Yevgeny
See also DLB 285

Popov, Yevgeny CLC 59
See Popov, Evgenii Anatol'evich

Poquelin, Jean-Baptiste
See Moliere

Porete, Marguerite (?)-1310 .... **CMLC 73**
See also DLB 208

Porphyry c. 233-c. 305 .... **CMLC 71**

Porter, Connie (Rose) 1959(?)- .... **CLC 70**
See also AAYA 65; BW 2, 3; CA 142;
CANR 90, 109; SATA 81, 129

Porter, Gene(va Grace) Stratton TCLC 21
See Stratton-Porter, Gene(va Grace)
See also BPFB 3; CA 112; CWRI 5; RHW

Porter, Katherine Anne 1890-1980 ... **CLC 1,
3, 7, 10, 13, 15, 27, 101; SSC 4, 31, 43,
108**
See also AAYA 42; AITN 2; AMW; BPFB
3; CA 1-4R; 101; CANR 1, 65; CDALBS;
CN 1, 2; DA; DA3; DAB; DAC; DAM
MST, NOV; DLB 4, 9, 102; DLBD 12;
DLBY 1980; EWL 3; EXPS; LAIT 3;
MAL 5; MBL; MTCW 1, 2; MTFW 2005;
NFS 14; RGAL 4; RGSF 2; SATA 39;
SATA-Obit 23; SSFS 1, 8, 11, 16, 23;
TCWW 2; TUS

Porter, Peter (Neville Frederick)
1929- .... **CLC 5, 13, 33**
See also CA 85-88; CP 1, 2, 3, 4, 5, 6, 7;
DLB 40, 289; WWE 1

Porter, William Sydney 1862-1910
See Henry, O.
See also CA 104; 131; CDALB 1865-1917;
DA; DA3; DAB; DAC; DAM MST; DLB
12, 78, 79; MTCW 1, 2; MTFW 2005;
TUS; YABC 2

Portillo (y Pacheco), Jose Lopez
See Lopez Portillo (y Pacheco), Jose

Portillo Trambley, Estela 1927-1998 .. **HLC 2**
See Trambley, Estela Portillo
See also CANR 32; DAM MULT; DLB
209; HW 1

Posey, Alexander (Lawrence)
1873-1908 .... **NNAL**
See also CA 144; CANR 80; DAM MULT;
DLB 175

Posse, Abel CLC 70
See also CA 252

Post, Melville Davisson
1869-1930 .... **TCLC 39**
See also CA 110; 202; CMW 4

Postman, Neil 1931(?)-2003 .... **CLC 244**
See also CA 102; 221

Potok, Chaim 1929-2002 ... **CLC 2, 7, 14, 26, 112**
See also AAYA 15, 50; AITN 1, 2; BPFB 3; BYA 1; CA 17-20R; 208; CANR 19, 35, 64, 98; CLR 92; CN 4, 5, 6; DA3; DAM NOV; DLB 28, 152; EXPN; INT CANR-19; LAIT 4; MTCW 1, 2; MTFW 2005; NFS 4; RGHL; SATA 33, 106; SATA-Obit 134; TUS; YAW

Potok, Herbert Harold -2002
See Potok, Chaim

Potok, Herman Harold
See Potok, Chaim

Potter, Dennis (Christopher George)
1935-1994 .... **CLC 58, 86, 123**
See also BRWS 10; CA 107; 145; CANR 33, 61; CBD; DLB 233; MTCW 1

Pound, Ezra (Weston Loomis)
1885-1972 .. **CLC 1, 2, 3, 4, 5, 7, 10, 13, 18, 34, 48, 50, 112; PC 4; WLC 5**
See also AAYA 47; AMW; AMWR 1; CA 5-8R; 37-40R; CANR 40; CDALB 1917-1929; CP 1; DA; DA3; DAB; DAC; DAM MST, POET; DLB 4, 45, 63; DLBD 15; EFS 2; EWL 3; EXPP; LMFS 2; MAL 5; MTCW 1, 2; MTFW 2005; PAB; PFS 2, 8, 16; RGAL 4; TUS; WP

Povod, Reinaldo 1959-1994 .... **CLC 44**
See also CA 136; 146; CANR 83

Powell, Adam Clayton, Jr.
1908-1972 .... **BLC 1:3; CLC 89**
See also BW 1, 3; CA 102; 33-36R; CANR 86; DAM MULT; DLB 345

Powell, Anthony 1905-2000 ... **CLC 1, 3, 7, 9, 10, 31**
See also BRW 7; CA 1-4R; 189; CANR 1, 32, 62, 107; CDBLB 1945-1960; CN 1, 2, 3, 4, 5, 6; DLB 15; EWL 3; MTCW 1, 2; MTFW 2005; RGEL 2; TEA

Powell, Dawn 1896(?)-1965 .... **CLC 66**
See also CA 5-8R; CANR 121; DLBY 1997

Powell, Padgett 1952- .... **CLC 34**
See also CA 126; CANR 63, 101; CSW; DLB 234; DLBY 01; SSFS 25

Powell, (Oval) Talmage 1920-2000
See Queen, Ellery
See also CA 5-8R; CANR 2, 80

Power, Susan 1961- .... **CLC 91**
See also BYA 14; CA 160; CANR 135; NFS 11

Powers, J(ames) F(arl) 1917-1999 ..... **CLC 1, 4, 8, 57; SSC 4**
See also CA 1-4R; 181; CANR 2, 61; CN 1, 2, 3, 4, 5, 6; DLB 130; MTCW 1; RGAL 4; RGSF 2

Powers, John J(ames) 1945-
See Powers, John R.
See also CA 69-72

Powers, John R. CLC 66
See Powers, John J(ames)

Powers, Richard 1957- .... **CLC 93**
See also AMWS 9; BPFB 3; CA 148; CANR 80, 180; CN 6, 7; MTFW 2005; TCLE 1:2

Powers, Richard S.
See Powers, Richard

Pownall, David 1938- .... **CLC 10**
See also CA 89-92, 180; CAAS 18; CANR 49, 101; CBD; CD 5, 6; CN 4, 5, 6, 7; DLB 14

Powys, John Cowper 1872-1963 ... **CLC 7, 9, 15, 46, 125**
See also CA 85-88; CANR 106; DLB 15, 255; EWL 3; FANT; MTCW 1, 2; MTFW 2005; RGEL 2; SUFW

Powys, T(heodore) F(rancis)
1875-1953 .... **TCLC 9**
See also BRWS 8; CA 106; 189; DLB 36, 162; EWL 3; FANT; RGEL 2; SUFW

Pozzo, Modesta
See Fonte, Moderata

Prado (Calvo), Pedro 1886-1952 ... **TCLC 75**
See also CA 131; DLB 283; HW 1; LAW

Prager, Emily 1952- .... **CLC 56**
See also CA 204

Pratchett, Terence David John
See Pratchett, Terry

Pratchett, Terry 1948- .... **CLC 197**
See also AAYA 19, 54; BPFB 3; CA 143; CANR 87, 126, 170; CLR 64; CN 6, 7; CPW; CWRI 5; FANT; MTFW 2005; SATA 82, 139, 185; SFW 4; SUFW 2

Pratolini, Vasco 1913-1991 .... **TCLC 124**
See also CA 211; DLB 177; EWL 3; RGWL 2, 3

Pratt, E(dwin) J(ohn) 1883(?)-1964 . **CLC 19**
See also CA 141; 93-96; CANR 77; DAC; DAM POET; DLB 92; EWL 3; RGEL 2; TWA

Premchand TCLC 21
See Srivastava, Dhanpat Rai
See also EWL 3

Prescott, William Hickling
1796-1859 .... **NCLC 163**
See also DLB 1, 30, 59, 235

Preseren, France 1800-1849 .... **NCLC 127**
See also CDWLB 4; DLB 147

Preussler, Otfried 1923- .... **CLC 17**
See also CA 77-80; SATA 24

Prevert, Jacques (Henri Marie)
1900-1977 .... **CLC 15**
See also CA 77-80; 69-72; CANR 29, 61; DLB 258; EWL 3; GFL 1789 to the Present; IDFW 3, 4; MTCW 1; RGWL 2, 3; SATA-Obit 30

Prevost, (Antoine Francois)
1697-1763 .... **LC 1**
See also DLB 314; EW 4; GFL Beginnings to 1789; RGWL 2, 3

Price, Edward Reynolds
See Price, Reynolds

Price, Reynolds 1933- .. **CLC 3, 6, 13, 43, 50, 63, 212; SSC 22**
See also AMWS 6; CA 1-4R; CANR 1, 37, 57, 87, 128, 177; CN 1, 2, 3, 4, 5, 6, 7; CSW; DAM NOV; DLB 2, 218, 278; EWL 3; INT CANR-37; MAL 5; MTFW 2005; NFS 18

Price, Richard 1949- .... **CLC 6, 12**
See also CA 49-52; CANR 3, 147; CN 7; DLBY 1981

Prichard, Katharine Susannah
1883-1969 .... **CLC 46**
See also CA 11-12; CANR 33; CAP 1; DLB 260; MTCW 1; RGEL 2; RGSF 2; SATA 66

Priestley, J(ohn) B(oynton)
1894-1984 .... **CLC 2, 5, 9, 34**
See also BRW 7; CA 9-12R; 113; CANR 33; CDBLB 1914-1945; CN 1, 2, 3; DA3; DAM DRAM, NOV; DLB 10, 34, 77, 100, 139; DLBY 1984; EWL 3; MTCW 1, 2; MTFW 2005; RGEL 2; SFW 4

Prince 1958- .... **CLC 35**
See also CA 213

Prince, F(rank) T(empleton)
1912-2003 .... **CLC 22**
See also CA 101; 219; CANR 43, 79; CP 1, 2, 3, 4, 5, 6, 7; DLB 20

Prince Kropotkin
See Kropotkin, Peter (Alekseievich)

Prior, Matthew 1664-1721 .... **LC 4**
See also DLB 95; RGEL 2

Prishvin, Mikhail 1873-1954 .... **TCLC 75**
See Prishvin, Mikhail Mikhailovich

Prishvin, Mikhail Mikhailovich
See Prishvin, Mikhail
See also DLB 272; EWL 3

Pritchard, William H(arrison)
1932- .... **CLC 34**
See also CA 65-68; CANR 23, 95; DLB 111

Pritchett, V(ictor) S(awdon)
1900-1997 ... **CLC 5, 13, 15, 41; SSC 14**
See also BPFB 3; BRWS 3; CA 61-64; 157; CANR 31, 63; CN 1, 2, 3, 4, 5, 6; DA3; DAM NOV; DLB 15, 139; EWL 3; MTCW 1, 2; MTFW 2005; RGEL 2; RGSF 2; TEA

Private 19022
See Manning, Frederic

Probst, Mark 1925- .... **CLC 59**
See also CA 130

Procaccino, Michael
See Cristofer, Michael

Proclus c. 412-c. 485 .... **CMLC 81**

Prokosch, Frederic 1908-1989 ...... **CLC 4, 48**
See also CA 73-76; 128; CANR 82; CN 1, 2, 3, 4; CP 1, 2, 3, 4; DLB 48; MTCW 2

Propertius, Sextus c. 50B.C.-c. 16B.C. .... **CMLC 32**
See also AW 2; CDWLB 1; DLB 211; RGWL 2, 3; WLIT 8

Prophet, The
See Dreiser, Theodore

Prose, Francine 1947- .... **CLC 45, 231**
See also AMWS 16; CA 109; 112; CANR 46, 95, 132, 175; DLB 234; MTFW 2005; SATA 101, 149

Protagoras c. 490B.C.-420B.C. ...... **CMLC 85**
See also DLB 176

Proudhon
See Cunha, Euclides (Rodrigues Pimenta) da

Proulx, Annie
See Proulx, E. Annie

Proulx, E. Annie 1935- ...... **CLC 81, 158, 250**
See also AMWS 7; BPFB 3; CA 145; CANR 65, 110; CN 6, 7; CPW 1; DA3; DAM POP; DLB 335; MAL 5; MTCW 2; MTFW 2005; SSFS 18, 23

Proulx, Edna Annie
See Proulx, E. Annie

Proust, (Valentin-Louis-George-Eugene)
Marcel 1871-1922 ..... **SSC 75; TCLC 7, 13, 33; WLC 5**
See also AAYA 58; BPFB 3; CA 104; 120; CANR 110; DA; DA3; DAB; DAC; DAM MST, NOV; DLB 65; EW 8; EWL 3; GFL 1789 to the Present; MTCW 1, 2; MTFW 2005; RGWL 2, 3; TWA

Prowler, Harley
See Masters, Edgar Lee

Prudentius, Aurelius Clemens 348-c. 405 .... **CMLC 78**
See also EW 1; RGWL 2, 3

Prudhomme, Rene Francois Armand
1839-1907
See Sully Prudhomme, Rene-Francois-Armand
See also CA 170

Prus, Boleslaw 1845-1912 .... **TCLC 48**
See also RGWL 2, 3

Prynne, William 1600-1669 .... **LC 148**

Prynne, Xavier
See Hardwick, Elizabeth

Pryor, Aaron Richard
See Pryor, Richard

Pryor, Richard 1940-2005 .... **CLC 26**
See also CA 122; 152; 246

Pryor, Richard Franklin Lenox Thomas
See Pryor, Richard

Przybyszewski, Stanislaw
1868-1927 .... **TCLC 36**
See also CA 160; DLB 66; EWL 3

Pseudo-Dionysius the Areopagite fl. c. 5th cent. - .... **CMLC 89**
See also DLB 115

Pteleon
See Grieve, C(hristopher) M(urray)
See also DAM POET

Puckett, Lute
See Masters, Edgar Lee

Puig, Manuel 1932-1990 .... **CLC 3, 5, 10, 28, 65, 133; HLC 2**
See also BPFB 3; CA 45-48; CANR 2, 32, 63; CDWLB 3; DA3; DAM MULT; DLB 113; DNFS 1; EWL 3; GLL 1; HW 1, 2; LAW; MTCW 1, 2; MTFW 2005; RGWL 2, 3; TWA; WLIT 1

Pulitzer, Joseph 1847-1911 .... **TCLC 76**
See also CA 114; DLB 23

Pullman, Philip 1946- .... **CLC 245**
See also AAYA 15, 41; BRWS 13; BYA 8, 13; CA 127; CANR 50, 77, 105, 134; CLR 20, 62, 84; JRDA; MAICYA 1, 2; MAICYAS 1; MTFW 2005; SAAS 17; SATA 65, 103, 150; SUFW 2; WYAS 1; YAW

Purchas, Samuel 1577(?)-1626 .... **LC 70**
See also DLB 151

Purdy, A(lfred) W(ellington)
1918-2000 .... **CLC 3, 6, 14, 50**
See also CA 81-84; 189; CAAS 17; CANR 42, 66; CP 1, 2, 3, 4, 5, 6, 7; DAC; DAM MST, POET; DLB 88; PFS 5; RGEL 2

Purdy, James (Amos) 1923- .... **CLC 2, 4, 10, 28, 52**
See also AMWS 7; CA 33-36R; CAAS 1; CANR 19, 51, 132; CN 1, 2, 3, 4, 5, 6, 7; DLB 2, 218; EWL 3; INT CANR-19; MAL 5; MTCW 1; RGAL 4

Pure, Simon
See Swinnerton, Frank Arthur

Pushkin, Aleksandr Sergeevich
See Pushkin, Alexander (Sergeyevich)
See also DLB 205

Pushkin, Alexander (Sergeyevich)
1799-1837 .... **NCLC 3, 27, 83; PC 10; SSC 27, 55, 99; WLC 5**
See Pushkin, Aleksandr Sergeevich
See also DA; DA3; DAB; DAC; DAM DRAM, MST, POET; EW 5; EXPS; PFS 28; RGSF 2; RGWL 2, 3; SATA 61; SSFS 9; TWA

P'u Sung-ling 1640-1715 .... **LC 49; SSC 31**

Putnam, Arthur Lee
See Alger, Horatio, Jr.

Puttenham, George 1529(?)-1590 ...... **LC 116**
See also DLB 281

Puzo, Mario 1920-1999 .... **CLC 1, 2, 6, 36, 107**
See also BPFB 3; CA 65-68; 185; CANR 4, 42, 65, 99, 131; CN 1, 2, 3, 4, 5, 6; CPW; DA3; DAM NOV, POP; DLB 6; MTCW 1, 2; MTFW 2005; NFS 16; RGAL 4

Pygge, Edward
See Barnes, Julian

Pyle, Ernest Taylor 1900-1945
See Pyle, Ernie
See also CA 115; 160

Pyle, Ernie **TCLC 75**
See Pyle, Ernest Taylor
See also DLB 29; MTCW 2

Pyle, Howard 1853-1911 .... **TCLC 81**
See also AAYA 57; BYA 2, 4; CA 109; 137; CLR 22, 117; DLB 42, 188; DLBD 13; LAIT 1; MAICYA 1, 2; SATA 16, 100; WCH; YAW

Pym, Barbara (Mary Crampton)
1913-1980 .... **CLC 13, 19, 37, 111**
See also BPFB 3; BRWS 2; CA 13-14; 97-100; CANR 13, 34; CAP 1; DLB 14, 207; DLBY 1987; EWL 3; MTCW 1, 2; MTFW 2005; RGEL 2; TEA

Pynchon, Thomas 1937- .. **CLC 2, 3, 6, 9, 11, 18, 33, 62, 72, 123, 192, 213; SSC 14, 84; WLC 5**
See also AMWS 2; BEST 90:2; BPFB 3; CA 17-20R; CANR 22, 46, 73, 142; CN 1, 2, 3, 4, 5, 6, 7; CPW 1; DA; DA3; DAB; DAC; DAM MST, NOV, POP; DLB 2, 173; EWL 3; MAL 5; MTCW 1, 2; MTFW 2005; NFS 23; RGAL 4; SFW 4; TCLE 1:2; TUS

Pythagoras c. 582B.C.-c. 507B.C. . **CMLC 22**
See also DLB 176

Q
See Quiller-Couch, Sir Arthur (Thomas)

Qian, Chongzhu
See Ch'ien, Chung-shu

Qian, Sima 145B.C.-c. 89B.C. .... **CMLC 72**

Qian Zhongshu
See Ch'ien, Chung-shu
See also CWW 2; DLB 328

Qroll
See Dagerman, Stig (Halvard)

Quarles, Francis 1592-1644 .... **LC 117**
See also DLB 126; RGEL 2

Quarrington, Paul 1953- .... **CLC 65**
See also CA 129; CANR 62, 95

Quarrington, Paul Lewis
See Quarrington, Paul

Quasimodo, Salvatore 1901-1968 .... **CLC 10; PC 47**
See also CA 13-16; 25-28R; CAP 1; DLB 114, 332; EW 12; EWL 3; MTCW 1; RGWL 2, 3

Quatermass, Martin
See Carpenter, John (Howard)

Quay, Stephen 1947- .... **CLC 95**
See also CA 189

Quay, Timothy 1947- .... **CLC 95**
See also CA 189

Queen, Ellery **CLC 3, 11**
See Dannay, Frederic; Davidson, Avram (James); Deming, Richard; Fairman, Paul W.; Flora, Fletcher; Hoch, Edward D.; Holding, James (Clark Carlisle, Jr.); Kane, Henry; Lee, Manfred B.; Marlowe, Stephen; Powell, (Oval) Talmage; Sheldon, Walter J(ames); Sturgeon, Theodore (Hamilton); Tracy, Don(ald Fiske); Vance, Jack
See also BPFB 3; CMW 4; MSW; RGAL 4

Queneau, Raymond 1903-1976 ..... **CLC 2, 5, 10, 42**
See also CA 77-80; 69-72; CANR 32; DLB 72, 258; EW 12; EWL 3; GFL 1789 to the Present; MTCW 1, 2; RGWL 2, 3

Quevedo, Francisco de 1580-1645 ...... **LC 23, 160**

Quiller-Couch, Sir Arthur (Thomas)
1863-1944 .... **TCLC 53**
See also CA 118; 166; DLB 135, 153, 190; HGG; RGEL 2; SUFW 1

Quin, Ann 1936-1973 .... **CLC 6**
See also CA 9-12R; 45-48; CANR 148; CN 1; DLB 14, 231

Quin, Ann Marie
See Quin, Ann

Quincey, Thomas de
See De Quincey, Thomas

Quindlen, Anna 1953- .... **CLC 191**
See also AAYA 35; AMWS 17; CA 138; CANR 73, 126; DA3; DLB 292; MTCW 2; MTFW 2005

Quinn, Martin
See Smith, Martin Cruz

Quinn, Peter 1947- .... **CLC 91**
See also CA 197; CANR 147

Quinn, Peter A.
See Quinn, Peter

Quinn, Simon
See Smith, Martin Cruz

Quintana, Leroy V. 1944- ...... **HLC 2; PC 36**
See also CA 131; CANR 65, 139; DAM MULT; DLB 82; HW 1, 2

Quintilian c. 40-c. 100 .... **CMLC 77**
See also AW 2; DLB 211; RGWL 2, 3

Quintillian 0035-0100 .... **CMLC 77**

Quiroga, Horacio (Sylvestre)
1878-1937 ... **HLC 2; SSC 89; TCLC 20**
See also CA 117; 131; DAM MULT; EWL 3; HW 1; LAW; MTCW 1; RGSF 2; WLIT 1

Quoirez, Françoise 1935-2004 .... **CLC 9**
See Sagan, Françoise
See also CA 49-52; 231; CANR 6, 39, 73; MTCW 1, 2; MTFW 2005; TWA

Raabe, Wilhelm (Karl) 1831-1910 . **TCLC 45**
See also CA 167; DLB 129

Rabe, David (William) 1940- .. **CLC 4, 8, 33, 200; DC 16**
See also CA 85-88; CABS 3; CAD; CANR 59, 129; CD 5, 6; DAM DRAM; DFS 3, 8, 13; DLB 7, 228; EWL 3; MAL 5

Rabelais, Francois 1494-1553 .... **LC 5, 60; WLC 5**
See also DA; DAB; DAC; DAM MST; DLB 327; EW 2; GFL Beginnings to 1789; LMFS 1; RGWL 2, 3; TWA

Rabi'a al-'Adawiyya c. 717-c. 801 .... **CMLC 83**
See also DLB 311

Rabinovitch, Sholem 1859-1916
See Sholom Aleichem
See also CA 104

Rabinyan, Dorit 1972- .... **CLC 119**
See also CA 170; CANR 147

Rachilde
See Vallette, Marguerite Eymery; Vallette, Marguerite Eymery
See also EWL 3

Racine, Jean 1639-1699 .. **DC 32; LC 28, 113**
See also DA3; DAB; DAM MST; DLB 268; EW 3; GFL Beginnings to 1789; LMFS 1; RGWL 2, 3; TWA

Radcliffe, Ann (Ward) 1764-1823 ... **NCLC 6, 55, 106**
See also DLB 39, 178; GL 3; HGG; LMFS 1; RGEL 2; SUFW; WLIT 3

Radclyffe-Hall, Marguerite
See Hall, Radclyffe

Radiguet, Raymond 1903-1923 ...... **TCLC 29**
See also CA 162; DLB 65; EWL 3; GFL 1789 to the Present; RGWL 2, 3

Radishchev, Aleksandr Nikolaevich
1749-1802 .... **NCLC 190**
See also DLB 150

Radishchev, Alexander
See Radishchev, Aleksandr Nikolaevich

Radnoti, Miklos 1909-1944 .... **TCLC 16**
See also CA 118; 212; CDWLB 4; DLB 215; EWL 3; RGHL; RGWL 2, 3

Rado, James 1939- .... **CLC 17**
See also CA 105

Radvanyi, Netty 1900-1983
See Seghers, Anna
See also CA 85-88; 110; CANR 82

Rae, Ben
See Griffiths, Trevor

Raeburn, John (Hay) 1941- .... **CLC 34**
See also CA 57-60

Ragni, Gerome 1942-1991 .... **CLC 17**
See also CA 105; 134

Rahv, Philip **CLC 24**
See Greenberg, Ivan
See also DLB 137; MAL 5

Raimund, Ferdinand Jakob
1790-1836 .... **NCLC 69**
See also DLB 90

Raine, Craig 1944- .... **CLC 32, 103**
See also BRWS 13; CA 108; CANR 29, 51, 103, 171; CP 3, 4, 5, 6, 7; DLB 40; PFS 7

Raine, Craig Anthony
See Raine, Craig

Raine, Kathleen (Jessie) 1908-2003 .. **CLC 7, 45**
See also CA 85-88; 218; CANR 46, 109; CP 1, 2, 3, 4, 5, 6, 7; DLB 20; EWL 3; MTCW 1; RGEL 2

Rainis, Janis 1865-1929 .... **TCLC 29**
See also CA 170; CDWLB 4; DLB 220; EWL 3

Rakosi, Carl CLC 47
See Rawley, Callman
See also CA 228; CAAS 5; CP 1, 2, 3, 4, 5, 6, 7; DLB 193

Ralegh, Sir Walter
See Raleigh, Sir Walter
See also BRW 1; RGEL 2; WP

Raleigh, Richard
See Lovecraft, H. P.

Raleigh, Sir Walter 1554(?)-1618 .... **LC 31, 39; PC 31**
See Ralegh, Sir Walter
See also CDBLB Before 1660; DLB 172; EXPP; PFS 14; TEA

Rallentando, H. P.
See Sayers, Dorothy L(eigh)

Ramal, Walter
See de la Mare, Walter (John)

Ramana Maharshi 1879-1950 .... **TCLC 84**

Ramoacn y Cajal, Santiago 1852-1934 .... **TCLC 93**

Ramon, Juan
See Jimenez (Mantecon), Juan Ramon

Ramos, Graciliano 1892-1953 .... **TCLC 32**
See also CA 167; DLB 307; EWL 3; HW 2; LAW; WLIT 1

Rampersad, Arnold 1941- .... **CLC 44**
See also BW 2, 3; CA 127; 133; CANR 81; DLB 111; INT CA-133

Rampling, Anne
See Rice, Anne
See also GLL 2

Ramsay, Allan 1686(?)-1758 .... **LC 29**
See also DLB 95; RGEL 2

Ramsay, Jay
See Campbell, Ramsey

Ramuz, Charles-Ferdinand 1878-1947 .... **TCLC 33**
See also CA 165; EWL 3

Rand, Ayn 1905-1982 **CLC 3, 30, 44, 79; SSC 116; WLC 5**
See also AAYA 10; AMWS 4; BPFB 3; BYA 12; CA 13-16R; 105; CANR 27, 73; CDALBS; CN 1, 2, 3; CPW; DA; DA3; DAC; DAM MST, NOV, POP; DLB 227, 279; MTCW 1, 2; MTFW 2005; NFS 10, 16; RGAL 4; SFW 4; TUS; YAW

Randall, Dudley (Felker) 1914-2000 .... **BLC 1:3; CLC 1, 135; PC 86**
See also BW 1, 3; CA 25-28R; 189; CANR 23, 82; CP 1, 2, 3, 4, 5; DAM MULT; DLB 41; PFS 5

Randall, Robert
See Silverberg, Robert

Ranger, Ken
See Creasey, John

Rank, Otto 1884-1939 .... **TCLC 115**

Rankin, Ian 1960- .... **CLC 257**
See also BRWS 10; CA 148; CANR 81, 137, 171; DLB 267; MTFW 2005

Rankin, Ian James
See Rankin, Ian

Ransom, John Crowe 1888-1974 .. **CLC 2, 4, 5, 11, 24; PC 61**
See also AMW; CA 5-8R; 49-52; CANR 6, 34; CDALBS; CP 1, 2; DA3; DAM POET; DLB 45, 63; EWL 3; EXPP; MAL 5; MTCW 1, 2; MTFW 2005; RGAL 4; TUS

Rao, Raja 1908-2006 . **CLC 25, 56, 255; SSC 99**
See also CA 73-76; 252; CANR 51; CN 1, 2, 3, 4, 5, 6; DAM NOV; DLB 323; EWL 3; MTCW 1, 2; MTFW 2005; RGEL 2; RGSF 2

Raphael, Frederic (Michael) 1931- ... **CLC 2, 14**
See also CA 1-4R; CANR 1, 86; CN 1, 2, 3, 4, 5, 6, 7; DLB 14, 319; TCLE 1:2

Raphael, Lev 1954- .... **CLC 232**
See also CA 134; CANR 72, 145; GLL 1

Ratcliffe, James P.
See Mencken, H(enry) L(ouis)

Rathbone, Julian 1935-2008 .... **CLC 41**
See also CA 101; 269; CANR 34, 73, 152

Rathbone, Julian Christopher
See Rathbone, Julian

Rattigan, Terence (Mervyn) 1911-1977 .... **CLC 7; DC 18**
See also BRWS 7; CA 85-88; 73-76; CBD; CDBLB 1945-1960; DAM DRAM; DFS 8; DLB 13; IDFW 3, 4; MTCW 1, 2; MTFW 2005; RGEL 2

Ratushinskaya, Irina 1954- .... **CLC 54**
See also CA 129; CANR 68; CWW 2

Raven, Simon (Arthur Noel) 1927-2001 .... **CLC 14**
See also CA 81-84; 197; CANR 86; CN 1, 2, 3, 4, 5, 6; DLB 271

Ravenna, Michael
See Welty, Eudora

Rawley, Callman 1903-2004
See Rakosi, Carl
See also CA 21-24R; 228; CANR 12, 32, 91

Rawlings, Marjorie Kinnan 1896-1953 .... **TCLC 4**
See also AAYA 20; AMWS 10; ANW; BPFB 3; BYA 3; CA 104; 137; CANR 74; CLR 63; DLB 9, 22, 102; DLBD 17; JRDA; MAICYA 1, 2; MAL 5; MTCW 2; MTFW 2005; RGAL 4; SATA 100; WCH; YABC 1; YAW

Ray, Satyajit 1921-1992 .... **CLC 16, 76**
See also CA 114; 137; DAM MULT

Read, Herbert Edward 1893-1968 ..... **CLC 4**
See also BRW 6; CA 85-88; 25-28R; DLB 20, 149; EWL 3; PAB; RGEL 2

Read, Piers Paul 1941- .... **CLC 4, 10, 25**
See also CA 21-24R; CANR 38, 86, 150; CN 2, 3, 4, 5, 6, 7; DLB 14; SATA 21

Reade, Charles 1814-1884 .... **NCLC 2, 74**
See also DLB 21; RGEL 2

Reade, Hamish
See Gray, Simon

Reading, Peter 1946- .... **CLC 47**
See also BRWS 8; CA 103; CANR 46, 96; CP 5, 6, 7; DLB 40

Reaney, James 1926-2008 .... **CLC 13**
See also CA 41-44R; CAAS 15; CANR 42; CD 5, 6; CP 1, 2, 3, 4, 5, 6, 7; DAC; DAM MST; DLB 68; RGEL 2; SATA 43

Reaney, James Crerar
See Reaney, James

Rebreanu, Liviu 1885-1944 .... **TCLC 28**
See also CA 165; DLB 220; EWL 3

Rechy, John 1934- ..... **CLC 1, 7, 14, 18, 107; HLC 2**
See also CA 5-8R; 195; CAAE 195; CAAS 4; CANR 6, 32, 64, 152; CN 1, 2, 3, 4, 5, 6, 7; DAM MULT; DLB 122, 278; DLBY 1982; HW 1, 2; INT CANR-6; LLW; MAL 5; RGAL 4

Rechy, John Francisco
See Rechy, John

Redcam, Tom 1870-1933 .... **TCLC 25**

Reddin, Keith 1956- .... **CLC 67**
See also CAD; CD 6

Redgrove, Peter (William) 1932-2003 .... **CLC 6, 41**
See also BRWS 6; CA 1-4R; 217; CANR 3, 39, 77; CP 1, 2, 3, 4, 5, 6, 7; DLB 40; TCLE 1:2

Redmon, Anne CLC 22
See Nightingale, Anne Redmon
See also DLBY 1986

Reed, Eliot
See Ambler, Eric

Reed, Ishmael 1938- . **BLC 1:3; CLC 2, 3, 5, 6, 13, 32, 60, 174; PC 68**
See also AFAW 1, 2; AMWS 10; BPFB 3; BW 2, 3; CA 21-24R; CANR 25, 48, 74, 128; CN 1, 2, 3, 4, 5, 6, 7; CP 1, 2, 3, 4, 5, 6, 7; CSW; DA3; DAM MULT; DLB 2, 5, 33, 169, 227; DLBD 8; EWL 3; LMFS 2; MAL 5; MSW; MTCW 1, 2; MTFW 2005; PFS 6; RGAL 4; TCWW 2

Reed, John (Silas) 1887-1920 .... **TCLC 9**
See also CA 106; 195; MAL 5; TUS

Reed, Lou CLC 21
See Firbank, Louis

Reese, Lizette Woodworth 1856-1935 .... **PC 29; TCLC 181**
See also CA 180; DLB 54

Reeve, Clara 1729-1807 .... **NCLC 19**
See also DLB 39; RGEL 2

Reich, Wilhelm 1897-1957 .... **TCLC 57**
See also CA 199

Reid, Christopher (John) 1949- .... **CLC 33**
See also CA 140; CANR 89; CP 4, 5, 6, 7; DLB 40; EWL 3

Reid, Desmond
See Moorcock, Michael

Reid Banks, Lynne 1929-
See Banks, Lynne Reid
See also AAYA 49; CA 1-4R; CANR 6, 22, 38, 87; CLR 24, 86; CN 1, 2, 3, 7; JRDA; MAICYA 1, 2; SATA 22, 75, 111, 165; YAW

Reilly, William K.
See Creasey, John

Reiner, Max
See Caldwell, (Janet Miriam) Taylor (Holland)

Reis, Ricardo
See Pessoa, Fernando

Reizenstein, Elmer Leopold
See Rice, Elmer (Leopold)
See also EWL 3

Remarque, Erich Maria 1898-1970 . **CLC 21**
See also AAYA 27; BPFB 3; CA 77-80; 29-32R; CDWLB 2; DA; DA3; DAB; DAC; DAM MST, NOV; DLB 56; EWL 3; EXPN; LAIT 3; MTCW 1, 2; MTFW 2005; NFS 4; RGHL; RGWL 2, 3

Remington, Frederic S(ackrider) 1861-1909 .... **TCLC 89**
See also CA 108; 169; DLB 12, 186, 188; SATA 41; TCWW 2

Remizov, A.
See Remizov, Aleksei (Mikhailovich)

Remizov, A. M.
See Remizov, Aleksei (Mikhailovich)

Remizov, Aleksei (Mikhailovich) 1877-1957 .... **TCLC 27**
See Remizov, Alexey Mikhailovich
See also CA 125; 133; DLB 295

Remizov, Alexey Mikhailovich
See Remizov, Aleksei (Mikhailovich)
See also EWL 3

Renan, Joseph Ernest 1823-1892 . NCLC 26, 145
See also GFL 1789 to the Present

Renard, Jules(-Pierre) 1864-1910 .. TCLC 17
See also CA 117; 202; GFL 1789 to the Present

Renart, Jean fl. 13th cent. - .... CMLC 83

Renault, Mary CLC 3, 11, 17
See Challans, Mary
See also BPFB 3; BYA 2; CN 1, 2, 3; DLBY 1983; EWL 3; GLL 1; LAIT 1; RGEL 2; RHW

Rendell, Ruth 1930- .... CLC 28, 48
See Vine, Barbara
See also BPFB 3; BRWS 9; CA 109; CANR 32, 52, 74, 127, 162; CN 5, 6, 7; CPW; DAM POP; DLB 87, 276; INT CANR-32; MSW; MTCW 1, 2; MTFW 2005

Rendell, Ruth Barbara
See Rendell, Ruth

Renoir, Jean 1894-1979 .... CLC 20
See also CA 129; 85-88

Rensie, Willis
See Eisner, Will

Resnais, Alain 1922- .... CLC 16

Revard, Carter 1931- .... NNAL
See also CA 144; CANR 81, 153; PFS 5

Reverdy, Pierre 1889-1960 .... CLC 53
See also CA 97-100; 89-92; DLB 258; EWL 3; GFL 1789 to the Present

Rexroth, Kenneth 1905-1982 .... CLC 1, 2, 6, 11, 22, 49, 112; PC 20
See also BG 1:3; CA 5-8R; 107; CANR 14, 34, 63; CDALB 1941-1968; CP 1, 2, 3; DAM POET; DLB 16, 48, 165, 212; DLBY 1982; EWL 3; INT CANR-14; MAL 5; MTCW 1, 2; MTFW 2005; RGAL 4

Reyes, Alfonso 1889-1959 .... HLCS 2; TCLC 33
See also CA 131; EWL 3; HW 1; LAW

Reyes y Basoalto, Ricardo Eliecer Neftali
See Neruda, Pablo

Reymont, Wladyslaw (Stanislaw) 1868(?)-1925 .... TCLC 5
See also CA 104; DLB 332; EWL 3

Reynolds, John Hamilton 1794-1852 .... NCLC 146
See also DLB 96

Reynolds, Jonathan 1942- .... CLC 6, 38
See also CA 65-68; CANR 28, 176

Reynolds, Joshua 1723-1792 .... LC 15
See also DLB 104

Reynolds, Michael S(hane) 1937-2000 .... CLC 44
See also CA 65-68; 189; CANR 9, 89, 97

Reznikoff, Charles 1894-1976 .... CLC 9
See also AMWS 14; CA 33-36; 61-64; CAP 2; CP 1, 2; DLB 28, 45; RGHL; WP

Rezzori, Gregor von
See Rezzori d'Arezzo, Gregor von

Rezzori d'Arezzo, Gregor von 1914-1998 .... CLC 25
See also CA 122; 136; 167

Rhine, Richard
See Silverstein, Alvin; Silverstein, Virginia B(arbara Opshelor)

Rhodes, Eugene Manlove 1869-1934 .... TCLC 53
See also CA 198; DLB 256; TCWW 1, 2

R'hoone, Lord
See Balzac, Honore de

Rhys, Jean 1890-1979 .... CLC 2, 4, 6, 14, 19, 51, 124; SSC 21, 76
See also BRWS 2; CA 25-28R; 85-88; CANR 35, 62; CDBLB 1945-1960; CD-WLB 3; CN 1, 2; DA3; DAM NOV; DLB

36, 117, 162; DNFS 2; EWL 3; LATS 1:1; MTCW 1, 2; MTFW 2005; NFS 19; RGEL 2; RGSF 2; RHW; TEA; WWE 1

Ribeiro, Darcy 1922-1997 .... CLC 34
See also CA 33-36R; 156; EWL 3

Ribeiro, Joao Ubaldo (Osorio Pimentel) 1941- .... CLC 10, 67
See also CA 81-84; CWW 2; EWL 3

Ribman, Ronald (Burt) 1932- .... CLC 7
See also CA 21-24R; CAD; CANR 46, 80; CD 5, 6

Ricci, Nino 1959- .... CLC 70
See also CA 137; CANR 130; CCA 1

Ricci, Nino Pio
See Ricci, Nino

Rice, Anne 1941- .... CLC 41, 128
See Rampling, Anne
See also AAYA 9, 53; AMWS 7; BEST 89:2; BPFB 3; CA 65-68; CANR 12, 36, 53, 74, 100, 133; CN 6, 7; CPW; CSW; DA3; DAM POP; DLB 292; GL 3; GLL 2; HGG; MTCW 2; MTFW 2005; SUFW 2; YAW

Rice, Elmer (Leopold) 1892-1967 ...... CLC 7, 49
See Reizenstein, Elmer Leopold
See also CA 21-22; 25-28R; CAP 2; DAM DRAM; DFS 12; DLB 4, 7; IDTP; MAL 5; MTCW 1, 2; RGAL 4

Rice, Tim(othy Miles Bindon) 1944- .... CLC 21
See also CA 103; CANR 46; DFS 7

Rich, Adrienne 1929- ..... CLC 3, 6, 7, 11, 18, 36, 73, 76, 125; PC 5
See also AAYA 69; AMWR 2; AMWS 1; CA 9-12R; CANR 20, 53, 74, 128; CDALBS; CP 1, 2, 3, 4, 5, 6, 7; CSW; CWP; DA3; DAM POET; DLB 5, 67; EWL 3; EXPP; FL 1:6; FW; MAL 5; MBL; MTCW 1, 2; MTFW 2005; PAB; PFS 15, 29; RGAL 4; RGHL; WP

Rich, Barbara
See Graves, Robert

Rich, Robert
See Trumbo, Dalton

Richard, Keith CLC 17
See Richards, Keith

Richards, David Adams 1950- .... CLC 59
See also CA 93-96; CANR 60, 110, 156; CN 7; DAC; DLB 53; TCLE 1:2

Richards, I(vor) A(rmstrong) 1893-1979 .... CLC 14, 24
See also BRWS 2; CA 41-44R; 89-92; CANR 34, 74; CP 1, 2; DLB 27; EWL 3; MTCW 2; RGEL 2

Richards, Keith 1943-
See Richard, Keith
See also CA 107; CANR 77

Richardson, Anne
See Roiphe, Anne

Richardson, Dorothy Miller 1873-1957 .... TCLC 3, 203
See also BRWS 13; CA 104; 192; DLB 36; EWL 3; FW; RGEL 2

Richardson (Robertson), Ethel Florence Lindesay 1870-1946
See Richardson, Henry Handel
See also CA 105; 190; DLB 230; RHW

Richardson, Henry Handel TCLC 4
See Richardson (Robertson), Ethel Florence Lindesay
See also DLB 197; EWL 3; RGEL 2; RGSF 2

Richardson, John 1796-1852 .... NCLC 55
See also CCA 1; DAC; DLB 99

Richardson, Samuel 1689-1761 ...... LC 1, 44, 138; WLC 5
See also BRW 3; CDBLB 1660-1789; DA; DAB; DAC; DAM MST, NOV; DLB 39; RGEL 2; TEA; WLIT 3

Richardson, Willis 1889-1977 .... HR 1:3
See also BW 1; CA 124; DLB 51; SATA 60

Richler, Mordecai 1931-2001 .... CLC 3, 5, 9, 13, 18, 46, 70, 185
See also AITN 1; CA 65-68; 201; CANR 31, 62, 111; CCA 1; CLR 17; CN 1, 2, 3, 4, 5, 7; CWRI 5; DAC; DAM MST, NOV; DLB 53; EWL 3; MAICYA 1, 2; MTCW 1, 2; MTFW 2005; RGEL 2; RGHL; SATA 44, 98; SATA-Brief 27; TWA

Richter, Conrad (Michael) 1890-1968 .... CLC 30
See also AAYA 21; AMWS 18; BYA 2; CA 5-8R; 25-28R; CANR 23; DLB 9, 212; LAIT 1; MAL 5; MTCW 1, 2; MTFW 2005; RGAL 4; SATA 3; TCWW 1, 2; TUS; YAW

Ricostranza, Tom
See Ellis, Trey

Riddell, Charlotte 1832-1906 .... TCLC 40
See Riddell, Mrs. J. H.
See also CA 165; DLB 156

Riddell, Mrs. J. H.
See Riddell, Charlotte
See also HGG; SUFW

Ridge, John Rollin 1827-1867 ...... NCLC 82; NNAL
See also CA 144; DAM MULT; DLB 175

Ridgeway, Jason
See Marlowe, Stephen

Ridgway, Keith 1965- .... CLC 119
See also CA 172; CANR 144

Riding, Laura CLC 3, 7
See Jackson, Laura (Riding)
See also CP 1, 2, 3, 4, 5; RGAL 4

Riefenstahl, Berta Helene Amalia 1902-2003
See Riefenstahl, Leni
See also CA 108; 220

Riefenstahl, Leni CLC 16, 190
See Riefenstahl, Berta Helene Amalia

Riffe, Ernest
See Bergman, Ingmar

Riffe, Ernest Ingmar
See Bergman, Ingmar

Riggs, (Rolla) Lynn 1899-1954 .... NNAL; TCLC 56
See also CA 144; DAM MULT; DLB 175

Riis, Jacob A(ugust) 1849-1914 ..... TCLC 80
See also CA 113; 168; DLB 23

Riley, James Whitcomb 1849-1916 .... PC 48; TCLC 51
See also CA 118; 137; DAM POET; MAICYA 1, 2; RGAL 4; SATA 17

Riley, Tex
See Creasey, John

Rilke, Rainer Maria 1875-1926 .... PC 2; TCLC 1, 6, 19, 195
See also CA 104; 132; CANR 62, 99; CD-WLB 2; DA3; DAM POET; DLB 81; EW 9; EWL 3; MTCW 1, 2; MTFW 2005; PFS 19, 27; RGWL 2, 3; TWA; WP

Rimbaud, (Jean Nicolas) Arthur 1854-1891 ... NCLC 4, 35, 82; PC 3, 57; WLC 5
See also DA; DA3; DAB; DAC; DAM MST, POET; DLB 217; EW 7; GFL 1789 to the Present; LMFS 2; PFS 28; RGWL 2, 3; TWA; WP

Rinehart, Mary Roberts 1876-1958 .... TCLC 52
See also BPFB 3; CA 108; 166; RGAL 4; RHW

Ringmaster, The
See Mencken, H(enry) L(ouis)

Ringwood, Gwen(dolyn Margaret) Pharis
1910-1984 .... **CLC 48**
See also CA 148; 112; DLB 88

Rio, Michel 1945(?)- .... **CLC 43**
See also CA 201

Rios, Alberto 1952- .... **PC 57**
See also AAYA 66; AMWS 4; CA 113;
CANR 34, 79, 137; CP 6, 7; DLB 122;
HW 2; MTFW 2005; PFS 11

Ritsos, Giannes
See Ritsos, Yannis

Ritsos, Yannis 1909-1990 .... **CLC 6, 13, 31**
See also CA 77-80; 133; CANR 39, 61; EW
12; EWL 3; MTCW 1; RGWL 2, 3

Ritter, Erika 1948(?)- .... **CLC 52**
See also CD 5, 6; CWD

Rivera, Jose Eustasio 1889-1928 ... **TCLC 35**
See also CA 162; EWL 3; HW 1, 2; LAW

Rivera, Tomas 1935-1984 .... **HLCS 2**
See also CA 49-52; CANR 32; DLB 82;
HW 1; LLW; RGAL 4; SSFS 15; TCWW
2; WLIT 1

Rivers, Conrad Kent 1933-1968 .... **CLC 1**
See also BW 1; CA 85-88; DLB 41

Rivers, Elfrida
See Bradley, Marion Zimmer
See also GLL 1

Riverside, John
See Heinlein, Robert A.

Rizal, Jose 1861-1896 .... **NCLC 27**

Roa Bastos, Augusto 1917-2005 ...... **CLC 45;
HLC 2**
See also CA 131; 238; CWW 2; DAM
MULT; DLB 113; EWL 3; HW 1; LAW;
RGSF 2; WLIT 1

Roa Bastos, Augusto Jose Antonio
See Roa Bastos, Augusto

Robbe-Grillet, Alain 1922-2008 ..... **CLC 1, 2,
4, 6, 8, 10, 14, 43, 128**
See also BPFB 3; CA 9-12R; 269; CANR
33, 65, 115; CWW 2; DLB 83; EW 13;
EWL 3; GFL 1789 to the Present; IDFW
3, 4; MTCW 1, 2; MTFW 2005; RGWL
2, 3; SSFS 15

Robbins, Harold 1916-1997 .... **CLC 5**
See also BPFB 3; CA 73-76; 162; CANR
26, 54, 112, 156; DA3; DAM NOV;
MTCW 1, 2

Robbins, Thomas Eugene 1936-
See Robbins, Tom
See also CA 81-84; CANR 29, 59, 95, 139;
CN 7; CPW; CSW; DA3; DAM NOV,
POP; MTCW 1, 2; MTFW 2005

Robbins, Tom **CLC 9, 32, 64**
See Robbins, Thomas Eugene
See also AAYA 32; AMWS 10; BEST 90:3;
BPFB 3; CN 3, 4, 5, 6, 7; DLBY 1980

Robbins, Trina 1938- .... **CLC 21**
See also AAYA 61; CA 128; CANR 152

Robert de Boron fl. 12th cent. - .... **CMLC 94**

Roberts, Charles G(eorge) D(ouglas)
1860-1943 .... **SSC 91; TCLC 8**
See also CA 105; 188; CLR 33; CWRI 5;
DLB 92; RGEL 2; RGSF 2; SATA 88;
SATA-Brief 29

Roberts, Elizabeth Madox
1886-1941 .... **TCLC 68**
See also CA 111; 166; CLR 100; CWRI 5;
DLB 9, 54, 102; RGAL 4; RHW; SATA
33; SATA-Brief 27; TCWW 2; WCH

Roberts, Kate 1891-1985 .... **CLC 15**
See also CA 107; 116; DLB 319

Roberts, Keith (John Kingston)
1935-2000 .... **CLC 14**
See also BRWS 10; CA 25-28R; CANR 46;
DLB 261; SFW 4

Roberts, Kenneth (Lewis)
1885-1957 .... **TCLC 23**
See also CA 109; 199; DLB 9; MAL 5;
RGAL 4; RHW

Roberts, Michele 1949- .... **CLC 48, 178**
See also CA 115; CANR 58, 120, 164; CN
6, 7; DLB 231; FW

Roberts, Michele Brigitte
See Roberts, Michele

Robertson, Ellis
See Ellison, Harlan; Silverberg, Robert

Robertson, Thomas William
1829-1871 .... **NCLC 35**
See Robertson, Tom
See also DAM DRAM; DLB 344

Robertson, Tom
See Robertson, Thomas William
See also RGEL 2

Robeson, Kenneth
See Dent, Lester

Robinson, Edwin Arlington
1869-1935 .... **PC 1, 35; TCLC 5, 101**
See also AAYA 72; AMW; CA 104; 133;
CDALB 1865-1917; DA; DAC; DAM
MST, POET; DLB 54; EWL 3; EXPP;
MAL 5; MTCW 1, 2; MTFW 2005; PAB;
PFS 4; RGAL 4; WP

Robinson, Henry Crabb
1775-1867 .... **NCLC 15**
See also DLB 107

Robinson, Jill 1936- .... **CLC 10**
See also CA 102; CANR 120; INT CA-102

Robinson, Kim Stanley 1952- ... **CLC 34, 248**
See also AAYA 26; CA 126; CANR 113,
139, 173; CN 6, 7; MTFW 2005; SATA
109; SCFW 2; SFW 4

Robinson, Lloyd
See Silverberg, Robert

Robinson, Marilynne 1944- ...... **CLC 25, 180**
See also AAYA 69; CA 116; CANR 80, 140;
CN 4, 5, 6, 7; DLB 206; MTFW 2005;
NFS 24

Robinson, Mary 1758-1800 .... **NCLC 142**
See also BRWS 13; DLB 158; FW

Robinson, Smokey **CLC 21**
See Robinson, William, Jr.

Robinson, William, Jr. 1940-
See Robinson, Smokey
See also CA 116

Robison, Mary 1949- .... **CLC 42, 98**
See also CA 113; 116; CANR 87; CN 4, 5,
6, 7; DLB 130; INT CA-116; RGSF 2

Roches, Catherine des 1542-1587 ...... **LC 117**
See also DLB 327

Rochester
See Wilmot, John
See also RGEL 2

Rod, Edouard 1857-1910 .... **TCLC 52**

Roddenberry, Eugene Wesley 1921-1991
See Roddenberry, Gene
See also CA 110; 135; CANR 37; SATA 45;
SATA-Obit 69

Roddenberry, Gene **CLC 17**
See Roddenberry, Eugene Wesley
See also AAYA 5; SATA-Obit 69

Rodgers, Mary 1931- .... **CLC 12**
See also BYA 5; CA 49-52; CANR 8, 55,
90; CLR 20; CWRI 5; INT CANR-8;
JRDA; MAICYA 1, 2; SATA 8, 130

Rodgers, W(illiam) R(obert)
1909-1969 .... **CLC 7**
See also CA 85-88; DLB 20; RGEL 2

Rodman, Eric
See Silverberg, Robert

Rodman, Howard 1920(?)-1985 .... **CLC 65**
See also CA 118

Rodman, Maia
See Wojciechowska, Maia (Teresa)

Rodo, Jose Enrique 1871(?)-1917 .... **HLCS 2**
See also CA 178; EWL 3; HW 2; LAW

Rodolph, Utto
See Ouologuem, Yambo

Rodriguez, Claudio 1934-1999 .... **CLC 10**
See also CA 188; DLB 134

Rodriguez, Richard 1944- .... **CLC 155; HLC
2**
See also AMWS 14; CA 110; CANR 66,
116; DAM MULT; DLB 82, 256; HW 1,
2; LAIT 5; LLW; MTFW 2005; NCFS 3;
WLIT 1

Roethke, Theodore 1908-1963 ... **CLC 1, 3, 8,
11, 19, 46, 101; PC 15**
See also AMW; CA 81-84; CABS 2;
CDALB 1941-1968; DA3; DAM POET;
DLB 5, 206; EWL 3; EXPP; MAL 5;
MTCW 1, 2; PAB; PFS 3; RGAL 4; WP

Roethke, Theodore Huebner
See Roethke, Theodore

Rogers, Carl R(ansom)
1902-1987 .... **TCLC 125**
See also CA 1-4R; 121; CANR 1, 18;
MTCW 1

Rogers, Samuel 1763-1855 .... **NCLC 69**
See also DLB 93; RGEL 2

Rogers, Thomas 1927-2007 .... **CLC 57**
See also CA 89-92; 259; CANR 163; INT
CA-89-92

Rogers, Thomas Hunton
See Rogers, Thomas

Rogers, Will(iam Penn Adair)
1879-1935 .... **NNAL; TCLC 8, 71**
See also CA 105; 144; DA3; DAM MULT;
DLB 11; MTCW 2

Rogin, Gilbert 1929- .... **CLC 18**
See also CA 65-68; CANR 15

Rohan, Koda
See Koda Shigeyuki

Rohlfs, Anna Katharine Green
See Green, Anna Katharine

Rohmer, Eric **CLC 16**
See Scherer, Jean-Marie Maurice

Rohmer, Sax **TCLC 28**
See Ward, Arthur Henry Sarsfield
See also DLB 70; MSW; SUFW

Roiphe, Anne 1935- .... **CLC 3, 9**
See also CA 89-92; CANR 45, 73, 138, 170;
DLBY 1980; INT CA-89-92

Roiphe, Anne Richardson
See Roiphe, Anne

Rojas, Fernando de 1475-1541 ... **HLCS 1, 2;
LC 23**
See also DLB 286; RGWL 2, 3

Rojas, Gonzalo 1917- .... **HLCS 2**
See also CA 178; HW 2; LAWS 1

Rolaag, Ole Edvart
See Rolvaag, O.E.

Roland (de la Platiere), Marie-Jeanne
1754-1793 .... **LC 98**
See also DLB 314

**Rolfe, Frederick (William Serafino Austin
Lewis Mary)** 1860-1913 .... **TCLC 12**
See Al Siddik
See also CA 107; 210; DLB 34, 156; RGEL
2

Rolland, Romain 1866-1944 .... **TCLC 23**
See also CA 118; 197; DLB 65, 284, 332;
EWL 3; GFL 1789 to the Present; RGWL
2, 3

Rolle, Richard c. 1300-c. 1349 ...... **CMLC 21**
See also DLB 146; LMFS 1; RGEL 2

Rolvaag, O.E.
See Rolvaag, O.E.

Rolvaag, O.E.
See Rolvaag, O.E.

Rolvaag, O.E. 1876-1931 .... **TCLC 17, 207**
    See also AAYA 75; CA 117; 171; DLB 9,
    212; MAL 5; NFS 5; RGAL 4; TCWW 1,
    2
Romain Arnaud, Saint
    See Aragon, Louis
Romains, Jules 1885-1972 .... **CLC 7**
    See also CA 85-88; CANR 34; DLB 65,
    321; EWL 3; GFL 1789 to the Present;
    MTCW 1
Romero, Jose Ruben 1890-1952 .... **TCLC 14**
    See also CA 114; 131; EWL 3; HW 1; LAW
Ronsard, Pierre de 1524-1585 . **LC 6, 54; PC
    11**
    See also DLB 327; EW 2; GFL Beginnings
    to 1789; RGWL 2, 3; TWA
Rooke, Leon 1934- .... **CLC 25, 34**
    See also CA 25-28R; CANR 23, 53; CCA
    1; CPW; DAM POP
Roosevelt, Franklin Delano
    1882-1945 .... **TCLC 93**
    See also CA 116; 173; LAIT 3
Roosevelt, Theodore 1858-1919 ..... **TCLC 69**
    See also CA 115; 170; DLB 47, 186, 275
Roper, Margaret c. 1505-1544 .... **LC 147**
Roper, William 1498-1578 .... **LC 10**
Roquelaure, A. N.
    See Rice, Anne
Rosa, Joao Guimaraes 1908-1967 ... **CLC 23;
    HLCS 1**
    See Guimaraes Rosa, Joao
    See also CA 89-92; DLB 113, 307; EWL 3;
    WLIT 1
Rose, Wendy 1948- . **CLC 85; NNAL; PC 13**
    See also CA 53-56; CANR 5, 51; CWP;
    DAM MULT; DLB 175; PFS 13; RGAL
    4; SATA 12
Rosen, R.D. 1949- .... **CLC 39**
    See also CA 77-80; CANR 62, 120, 175;
    CMW 4; INT CANR-30
Rosen, Richard
    See Rosen, R.D.
Rosen, Richard Dean
    See Rosen, R.D.
Rosenberg, Isaac 1890-1918 .... **TCLC 12**
    See also BRW 6; CA 107; 188; DLB 20,
    216; EWL 3; PAB; RGEL 2
Rosenblatt, Joe CLC 15
    See Rosenblatt, Joseph
    See also CP 3, 4, 5, 6, 7
Rosenblatt, Joseph 1933-
    See Rosenblatt, Joe
    See also CA 89-92; CP 1, 2; INT CA-89-92
Rosenfeld, Samuel
    See Tzara, Tristan
Rosenstock, Sami
    See Tzara, Tristan
Rosenstock, Samuel
    See Tzara, Tristan
Rosenthal, M(acha) L(ouis)
    1917-1996 .... **CLC 28**
    See also CA 1-4R; 152; CAAS 6; CANR 4,
    51; CP 1, 2, 3, 4, 5, 6; DLB 5; SATA 59
Ross, Barnaby
    See Dannay, Frederic; Lee, Manfred B.
Ross, Bernard L.
    See Follett, Ken
Ross, J. H.
    See Lawrence, T(homas) E(dward)
Ross, John Hume
    See Lawrence, T(homas) E(dward)
Ross, Martin 1862-1915
    See Martin, Violet Florence
    See also DLB 135; GLL 2; RGEL 2; RGSF
    2

Ross, (James) Sinclair 1908-1996 ... **CLC 13;
    SSC 24**
    See also CA 73-76; CANR 81; CN 1, 2, 3,
    4, 5, 6; DAC; DAM MST; DLB 88;
    RGEL 2; RGSF 2; TCWW 1, 2
Rossetti, Christina 1830-1894 ... **NCLC 2, 50,
    66, 186; PC 7; WLC 5**
    See also AAYA 51; BRW 5; BYA 4; CLR
    115; DA; DA3; DAB; DAC; DAM MST,
    POET; DLB 35, 163, 240; EXPP; FL 1:3;
    LATS 1:1; MAICYA 1, 2; PFS 10, 14, 27;
    RGEL 2; SATA 20; TEA; WCH
Rossetti, Christina Georgina
    See Rossetti, Christina
Rossetti, Dante Gabriel 1828-1882 . **NCLC 4,
    77; PC 44; WLC 5**
    See also AAYA 51; BRW 5; CDBLB 1832-
    1890; DA; DAB; DAC; DAM MST,
    POET; DLB 35; EXPP; RGEL 2; TEA
Rossi, Cristina Peri
    See Peri Rossi, Cristina
Rossi, Jean-Baptiste 1931-2003
    See Japrisot, Sebastien
    See also CA 201; 215
Rossner, Judith 1935-2005 .... **CLC 6, 9, 29**
    See also AITN 2; BEST 90:3; BPFB 3; CA
    17-20R; 242; CANR 18, 51, 73; CN 4, 5,
    6, 7; DLB 6; INT CANR-18; MAL 5;
    MTCW 1, 2; MTFW 2005
Rossner, Judith Perelman
    See Rossner, Judith
Rostand, Edmond (Eugene Alexis)
    1868-1918 .... **DC 10; TCLC 6, 37**
    See also CA 104; 126; DA; DA3; DAB;
    DAC; DAM DRAM, MST; DFS 1; DLB
    192; LAIT 1; MTCW 1; RGWL 2, 3;
    TWA
Roth, Henry 1906-1995 ..... **CLC 2, 6, 11, 104**
    See also AMWS 9; CA 11-12; 149; CANR
    38, 63; CAP 1; CN 1, 2, 3, 4, 5, 6; DA3;
    DLB 28; EWL 3; MAL 5; MTCW 1, 2;
    MTFW 2005; RGAL 4
Roth, (Moses) Joseph 1894-1939 ... **TCLC 33**
    See also CA 160; DLB 85; EWL 3; RGWL
    2, 3
Roth, Philip 1933- ... **CLC 1, 2, 3, 4, 6, 9, 15,
    22, 31, 47, 66, 86, 119, 201; SSC 26,
    102; WLC 5**
    See also AAYA 67; AMWR 2; AMWS 3;
    BEST 90:3; BPFB 3; CA 1-4R; CANR 1,
    22, 36, 55, 89, 132, 170; CDALB 1968-
    1988; CN 3, 4, 5, 6, 7; CPW 1; DA; DA3;
    DAB; DAC; DAM MST, NOV, POP;
    DLB 2, 28, 173; DLBY 1982; EWL 3;
    MAL 5; MTCW 1, 2; MTFW 2005; NFS
    25; RGAL 4; RGHL; RGSF 2; SSFS 12,
    18; TUS
Roth, Philip Milton
    See Roth, Philip
Rothenberg, Jerome 1931- .... **CLC 6, 57**
    See also CA 45-48; CANR 1, 106; CP 1, 2,
    3, 4, 5, 6, 7; DLB 5, 193
Rotter, Pat CLC 65
Roumain, Jacques (Jean Baptiste)
    1907-1944 .... **BLC 1:3; TCLC 19**
    See also BW 1; CA 117; 125; DAM MULT;
    EWL 3
Rourke, Constance Mayfield
    1885-1941 .... **TCLC 12**
    See also CA 107; 200; MAL 5; YABC 1
Rousseau, Jean-Baptiste 1671-1741 ...... **LC 9**
Rousseau, Jean-Jacques 1712-1778 .... **LC 14,
    36, 122; WLC 5**
    See also DA; DA3; DAB; DAC; DAM
    MST; DLB 314; EW 4; GFL Beginnings
    to 1789; LMFS 1; RGWL 2, 3; TWA
Roussel, Raymond 1877-1933 .... **TCLC 20**
    See also CA 117; 201; EWL 3; GFL 1789
    to the Present

Rovit, Earl (Herbert) 1927- .... **CLC 7**
    See also CA 5-8R; CANR 12
Rowe, Elizabeth Singer 1674-1737 ..... **LC 44**
    See also DLB 39, 95
Rowe, Nicholas 1674-1718 .... **LC 8**
    See also DLB 84; RGEL 2
Rowlandson, Mary 1637(?)-1678 .... **LC 66**
    See also DLB 24, 200; RGAL 4
Rowley, Ames Dorrance
    See Lovecraft, H. P.
Rowley, William 1585(?)-1626 ... **LC 100, 123**
    See also DFS 22; DLB 58; RGEL 2
Rowling, J.K. 1965- .... **CLC 137, 217**
    See also AAYA 34; BYA 11, 13, 14; CA
    173; CANR 128, 157; CLR 66, 80, 112;
    MAICYA 1; MTFW 2005; SATA 109,
    174; SUFW 2
Rowling, Joanne Kathleen
    See Rowling, J.K.
Rowson, Susanna Haswell
    1762(?)-1824 .... **NCLC 5, 69, 182**
    See also AMWS 15; DLB 37, 200; RGAL 4
Roy, Arundhati 1960(?)- .... **CLC 109, 210**
    See also CA 163; CANR 90, 126; CN 7;
    DLB 323, 326; DLBY 1997; EWL 3;
    LATS 1:2; MTFW 2005; NFS 22; WWE
    1
Roy, Gabrielle 1909-1983 .... **CLC 10, 14**
    See also CA 53-56; 110; CANR 5, 61; CCA
    1; DAB; DAC; DAM MST; DLB 68;
    EWL 3; MTCW 1; RGWL 2, 3; SATA
    104; TCLE 1:2
Royko, Mike 1932-1997 .... **CLC 109**
    See also CA 89-92; 157; CANR 26, 111;
    CPW
Rozanov, Vasilii Vasil'evich
    See Rozanov, Vassili
    See also DLB 295
Rozanov, Vasily Vasilyevich
    See Rozanov, Vassili
    See also EWL 3
Rozanov, Vassili 1856-1919 .... **TCLC 104**
    See Rozanov, Vasilii Vasil'evich; Rozanov,
    Vasily Vasilyevich
Rozewicz, Tadeusz 1921- ...... **CLC 9, 23, 139**
    See also CA 108; CANR 36, 66; CWW 2;
    DA3; DAM POET; DLB 232; EWL 3;
    MTCW 1, 2; MTFW 2005; RGHL;
    RGWL 3
Ruark, Gibbons 1941- .... **CLC 3**
    See also CA 33-36R; CAAS 23; CANR 14,
    31, 57; DLB 120
Rubens, Bernice (Ruth) 1923-2004 . **CLC 19,
    31**
    See also CA 25-28R; 232; CANR 33, 65,
    128; CN 1, 2, 3, 4, 5, 6, 7; DLB 14, 207,
    326; MTCW 1
Rubin, Harold
    See Robbins, Harold
Rudkin, (James) David 1936- .... **CLC 14**
    See also CA 89-92; CBD; CD 5, 6; DLB 13
Rudnik, Raphael 1933- .... **CLC 7**
    See also CA 29-32R
Ruffian, M.
    See Hasek, Jaroslav (Matej Frantisek)
Ruiz, Jose Martinez CLC 11
    See Martinez Ruiz, Jose
Ruiz, Juan c. 1283-c. 1350 .... **CMLC 66**
Rukeyser, Muriel 1913-1980 . **CLC 6, 10, 15,
    27; PC 12**
    See also AMWS 6; CA 5-8R; 93-96; CANR
    26, 60; CP 1, 2, 3; DA3; DAM POET;
    DLB 48; EWL 3; FW; GLL 2; MAL 5;
    MTCW 1, 2; PFS 10, 29; RGAL 4; SATA-
    Obit 22
Rule, Jane 1931-2007 .... **CLC 27, 265**
    See also CA 25-28R; 266; CAAS 18; CANR
    12, 87; CN 4, 5, 6, 7; DLB 60; FW

Rule, Jane Vance
See Rule, Jane

Rulfo, Juan 1918-1986 .. **CLC 8, 80; HLC 2; SSC 25**
See also CA 85-88; 118; CANR 26; CD-WLB 3; DAM MULT; DLB 113; EWL 3; HW 1, 2; LAW; MTCW 1, 2; RGSF 2; RGWL 2, 3; WLIT 1

Rumi, Jalal al-Din 1207-1273 ...... **CMLC 20; PC 45**
See also AAYA 64; RGWL 2, 3; WLIT 6; WP

Runeberg, Johan 1804-1877 .... **NCLC 41**

Runyon, (Alfred) Damon
1884(?)-1946 .... **TCLC 10**
See also CA 107; 165; DLB 11, 86, 171; MAL 5; MTCW 2; RGAL 4

Rush, Norman 1933- .... **CLC 44**
See also CA 121; 126; CANR 130; INT CA-126

Rushdie, Salman 1947- .... **CLC 23, 31, 55, 100, 191; SSC 83; WLCS**
See also AAYA 65; BEST 89:3; BPFB 3; BRWS 4; CA 108; 111; CANR 33, 56, 108, 133; CLR 125; CN 4, 5, 6, 7; CPW 1; DA3; DAB; DAC; DAM MST, NOV, POP; DLB 194, 323, 326; EWL 3; FANT; INT CA-111; LATS 1:2; LMFS 2; MTCW 1, 2; MTFW 2005; NFS 22, 23; RGEL 2; RGSF 2; TEA; WLIT 4

Rushforth, Peter 1945-2005 .... **CLC 19**
See also CA 101; 243

Rushforth, Peter Scott
See Rushforth, Peter

Ruskin, John 1819-1900 .... **TCLC 63**
See also BRW 5; BYA 5; CA 114; 129; CD-BLB 1832-1890; DLB 55, 163, 190; RGEL 2; SATA 24; TEA; WCH

Russ, Joanna 1937- .... **CLC 15**
See also BPFB 3; CA 25-28; CANR 11, 31, 65; CN 4, 5, 6, 7; DLB 8; FW; GLL 1; MTCW 1; SCFW 1, 2; SFW 4

Russ, Richard Patrick
See O'Brian, Patrick

Russell, George William 1867-1935
See A.E.; Baker, Jean H.
See also BRWS 8; CA 104; 153; CDBLB 1890-1914; DAM POET; EWL 3; RGEL 2

Russell, Jeffrey Burton 1934- .... **CLC 70**
See also CA 25-28R; CANR 11, 28, 52, 179

Russell, (Henry) Ken(neth Alfred)
1927- .... **CLC 16**
See also CA 105

Russell, William Martin 1947-
See Russell, Willy
See also CA 164; CANR 107

Russell, Willy CLC 60
See Russell, William Martin
See also CBD; CD 5, 6; DLB 233

Russo, Richard 1949- .... **CLC 181**
See also AMWS 12; CA 127; 133; CANR 87, 114; NFS 25

Rutebeuf fl. c. 1249-1277 .... **CMLC 104**
See also DLB 208

Rutherford, Mark TCLC 25
See White, William Hale
See also DLB 18; RGEL 2

Ruysbroeck, Jan van 1293-1381 ... **CMLC 85**

Ruyslinck, Ward CLC 14
See Belser, Reimond Karel Maria de

Ryan, Cornelius (John) 1920-1974 ..... **CLC 7**
See also CA 69-72; 53-56; CANR 38

Ryan, Michael 1946- .... **CLC 65**
See also CA 49-52; CANR 109; DLBY 1982

Ryan, Tim
See Dent, Lester

Rybakov, Anatoli (Naumovich)
1911-1998 .... **CLC 23, 53**
See Rybakov, Anatolii (Naumovich)
See also CA 126; 135; 172; SATA 79; SATA-Obit 108

Rybakov, Anatolii (Naumovich)
See Rybakov, Anatoli (Naumovich)
See also DLB 302; RGHL

Ryder, Jonathan
See Ludlum, Robert

Ryga, George 1932-1987 .... **CLC 14**
See also CA 101; 124; CANR 43, 90; CCA 1; DAC; DAM MST; DLB 60

Rymer, Thomas 1643(?)-1713 .... **LC 132**
See also DLB 101, 336

S. H.
See Hartmann, Sadakichi

S. S.
See Sassoon, Siegfried (Lorraine)

Sa'adawi, al- Nawal
See El Saadawi, Nawal
See also AFW; EWL 3

Saadawi, Nawal El
See El Saadawi, Nawal

Saadiah Gaon 882-942 .... **CMLC 97**

Saba, Umberto 1883-1957 .... **TCLC 33**
See also CA 144; CANR 79; DLB 114; EWL 3; RGWL 2, 3

Sabatini, Rafael 1875-1950 .... **TCLC 47**
See also BPFB 3; CA 162; RHW

Sabato, Ernesto 1911- ... **CLC 10, 23; HLC 2**
See also CA 97-100; CANR 32, 65; CD-WLB 3; CWW 2; DAM MULT; DLB 145; EWL 3; HW 1, 2; LAW; MTCW 1, 2; MTFW 2005

Sa-Carneiro, Mario de 1890-1916 . **TCLC 83**
See also DLB 287; EWL 3

Sacastru, Martin
See Bioy Casares, Adolfo
See also CWW 2

Sacher-Masoch, Leopold von
1836(?)-1895 .... **NCLC 31**

Sachs, Hans 1494-1576 .... **LC 95**
See also CDWLB 2; DLB 179; RGWL 2, 3

Sachs, Marilyn 1927- .... **CLC 35**
See also AAYA 2; BYA 6; CA 17-20R; CANR 13, 47, 150; CLR 2; JRDA; MAI-CYA 1, 2; SAAS 2; SATA 3, 68, 164; SATA-Essay 110; WYA; YAW

Sachs, Marilyn Stickle
See Sachs, Marilyn

Sachs, Nelly 1891-1970 .. **CLC 14, 98; PC 78**
See also CA 17-18; 25-28R; CANR 87; CAP 2; DLB 332; EWL 3; MTCW 2; MTFW 2005; PFS 20; RGHL; RGWL 2, 3

Sackler, Howard (Oliver)
1929-1982 .... **CLC 14**
See also CA 61-64; 108; CAD; CANR 30; DFS 15; DLB 7

Sacks, Oliver 1933- .... **CLC 67, 202**
See also CA 53-56; CANR 28, 50, 76, 146; CPW; DA3; INT CANR-28; MTCW 1, 2; MTFW 2005

Sacks, Oliver Wolf
See Sacks, Oliver

Sackville, Thomas 1536-1608 .... **LC 98**
See also DAM DRAM; DLB 62, 132; RGEL 2

Sadakichi
See Hartmann, Sadakichi

Sa'dawi, Nawal al-
See El Saadawi, Nawal
See also CWW 2

Sade, Donatien Alphonse Francois
1740-1814 .... **NCLC 3, 47**
See also DLB 314; EW 4; GFL Beginnings to 1789; RGWL 2, 3

Sade, Marquis de
See Sade, Donatien Alphonse Francois

Sadoff, Ira 1945- .... **CLC 9**
See also CA 53-56; CANR 5, 21, 109; DLB 120

Saetone
See Camus, Albert

Safire, William 1929- .... **CLC 10**
See also CA 17-20R; CANR 31, 54, 91, 148

Sagan, Carl 1934-1996 .... **CLC 30, 112**
See also AAYA 2, 62; CA 25-28R; 155; CANR 11, 36, 74; CPW; DA3; MTCW 1, 2; MTFW 2005; SATA 58; SATA-Obit 94

Sagan, Francoise CLC 3, 6, 9, 17, 36
See Quoirez, Francoise
See also CWW 2; DLB 83; EWL 3; GFL 1789 to the Present; MTCW 2

Sahgal, Nayantara (Pandit) 1927- .... **CLC 41**
See also CA 9-12R; CANR 11, 88; CN 1, 2, 3, 4, 5, 6, 7; DLB 323

Said, Edward W. 1935-2003 .... **CLC 123**
See also CA 21-24R; 220; CANR 45, 74, 107, 131; DLB 67, 346; MTCW 2; MTFW 2005

Saikaku, Ihara 1642-1693 .... **LC 141**
See also RGWL 3

Saikaku Ihara
See Saikaku, Ihara

Saint, H(arry) F. 1941- .... **CLC 50**
See also CA 127

St. Aubin de Teran, Lisa 1953-
See Teran, Lisa St. Aubin de
See also CA 118; 126; CN 6, 7; INT CA-126

Saint Birgitta of Sweden c.
1303-1373 .... **CMLC 24**

Sainte-Beuve, Charles Augustin
1804-1869 .... **NCLC 5**
See also DLB 217; EW 6; GFL 1789 to the Present

Saint-Exupery, Antoine de
1900-1944 .... **TCLC 2, 56, 169; WLC**
See also AAYA 63; BPFB 3; BYA 3; CA 108; 132; CLR 10; DA3; DAM NOV; DLB 72; EW 12; EWL 3; GFL 1789 to the Present; LAIT 3; MAICYA 1, 2; MTCW 1, 2; MTFW 2005; RGWL 2, 3; SATA 20; TWA

Saint-Exupery, Antoine Jean Baptiste Marie Roger de
See Saint-Exupery, Antoine de

St. John, David
See Hunt, E. Howard

St. John, J. Hector
See Crevecoeur, Michel Guillaume Jean de

Saint-John Perse
See Leger, (Marie-Rene Auguste) Alexis Saint-Leger
See also EW 10; EWL 3; GFL 1789 to the Present; RGWL 2

Saintsbury, George (Edward Bateman)
1845-1933 .... **TCLC 31**
See also CA 160; DLB 57, 149

Sait Faik TCLC 23
See Abasiyanik, Sait Faik

Saki SSC 12, 115; TCLC 3; WLC 5
See Munro, H(ector) H(ugh)
See also BRWS 6; BYA 11; LAIT 2; RGEL 2; SSFS 1; SUFW

Sala, George Augustus 1828-1895 . **NCLC 46**

Saladin 1138-1193 .... **CMLC 38**

Salama, Hannu 1936- .... **CLC 18**
See also CA 244; EWL 3

Salamanca, J(ack) R(ichard) 1922- .. **CLC 4, 15**
See also CA 25-28R; 193; CAAE 193

Salas, Floyd Francis 1931- .... **HLC 2**
See also CA 119; CAAS 27; CANR 44, 75, 93; DAM MULT; DLB 82; HW 1, 2; MTCW 2; MTFW 2005

Sale, J. Kirkpatrick
See Sale, Kirkpatrick

Sale, John Kirkpatrick
See Sale, Kirkpatrick

Sale, Kirkpatrick 1937- .... **CLC 68**
See also CA 13-16R; CANR 10, 147

Salinas, Luis Omar 1937- ... **CLC 90; HLC 2**
See also AMWS 13; CA 131; CANR 81, 153; DAM MULT; DLB 82; HW 1, 2

Salinas (y Serrano), Pedro
1891(?)-1951 .... **TCLC 17, 212**
See also CA 117; DLB 134; EWL 3

Salinger, J.D. 1919- . **CLC 1, 3, 8, 12, 55, 56, 138, 243; SSC 2, 28, 65; WLC 5**
See also AAYA 2, 36; AMW; AMWC 1; BPFB 3; CA 5-8R; CANR 39, 129; CDALB 1941-1968; CLR 18; CN 1, 2, 3, 4, 5, 6, 7; CPW 1; DA; DA3; DAB; DAC; DAM MST, NOV, POP; DLB 2, 102, 173; EWL 3; EXPN; LAIT 4; MAICYA 1, 2; MAL 5; MTCW 1, 2; MTFW 2005; NFS 1; RGAL 4; RGSF 2; SATA 67; SSFS 17; TUS; WYA; YAW

Salisbury, John
See Caute, (John) David

Sallust c. 86B.C.-35B.C. .... **CMLC 68**
See also AW 2; CDWLB 1; DLB 211; RGWL 2, 3

Salter, James 1925- .. **CLC 7, 52, 59; SSC 58**
See also AMWS 9; CA 73-76; CANR 107, 160; DLB 130; SSFS 25

Saltus, Edgar (Everton) 1855-1921 . **TCLC 8**
See also CA 105; DLB 202; RGAL 4

Saltykov, Mikhail Evgrafovich
1826-1889 .... **NCLC 16**
See also DLB 238:

Saltykov-Shchedrin, N.
See Saltykov, Mikhail Evgrafovich

Samarakis, Andonis
See Samarakis, Antonis
See also EWL 3

Samarakis, Antonis 1919-2003 .... **CLC 5**
See Samarakis, Andonis
See also CA 25-28R; 224; CAAS 16; CANR 36

Sanchez, Florencio 1875-1910 .... **TCLC 37**
See also CA 153; DLB 305; EWL 3; HW 1; LAW

Sanchez, Luis Rafael 1936- .... **CLC 23**
See also CA 128; DLB 305; EWL 3; HW 1; WLIT 1

Sanchez, Sonia 1934- . **BLC 1:3, 2:3; CLC 5, 116, 215; PC 9**
See also BW 2, 3; CA 33-36R; CANR 24, 49, 74, 115; CLR 18; CP 2, 3, 4, 5, 6, 7; CSW; CWP; DA3; DAM MULT; DLB 41; DLBD 8; EWL 3; MAICYA 1, 2; MAL 5; MTCW 1, 2; MTFW 2005; PFS 26; SATA 22, 136; WP

Sancho, Ignatius 1729-1780 .... **LC 84**

Sand, George 1804-1876 .... **DC 29; NCLC 2, 42, 57, 174; WLC 5**
See also DA; DA3; DAB; DAC; DAM MST, NOV; DLB 119, 192; EW 6; FL 1:3; FW; GFL 1789 to the Present; RGWL 2, 3; TWA

Sandburg, Carl (August) 1878-1967 . **CLC 1, 4, 10, 15, 35; PC 2, 41; WLC 5**
See also AAYA 24; AMW; BYA 1, 3; CA 5-8R; 25-28R; CANR 35; CDALB 1865-1917; CLR 67; DA; DA3; DAB; DAC; DAM MST, POET; DLB 17, 54, 284; EWL 3; EXPP; LAIT 2; MAICYA 1, 2; MAL 5; MTCW 1, 2; MTFW 2005; PAB; PFS 3, 6, 12; RGAL 4; SATA 8; TUS; WCH; WP; WYA

Sandburg, Charles
See Sandburg, Carl (August)

Sandburg, Charles A.
See Sandburg, Carl (August)

Sanders, (James) Ed(ward) 1939- .... **CLC 53**
See Sanders, Edward
See also BG 1:3; CA 13-16R; CAAS 21; CANR 13, 44, 78; CP 1, 2, 3, 4, 5, 6, 7; DAM POET; DLB 16, 244

Sanders, Edward
See Sanders, (James) Ed(ward)
See also DLB 244

Sanders, Lawrence 1920-1998 .... **CLC 41**
See also BEST 89:4; BPFB 3; CA 81-84; 165; CANR 33, 62; CMW 4; CPW; DA3; DAM POP; MTCW 1

Sanders, Noah
See Blount, Roy, Jr.

Sanders, Winston P.
See Anderson, Poul

Sandoz, Mari(e Susette) 1900-1966 .. **CLC 28**
See also CA 1-4R; 25-28R; CANR 17, 64; DLB 9, 212; LAIT 2; MTCW 1, 2; SATA 5; TCWW 1, 2

Sandys, George 1578-1644 .... **LC 80**
See also DLB 24, 121

Saner, Reg(inald Anthony) 1931- ...... **CLC 9**
See also CA 65-68; CP 3, 4, 5, 6, 7

Sankara 788-820 .... **CMLC 32**

Sannazaro, Jacopo 1456(?)-1530 .... **LC 8**
See also RGWL 2, 3; WLIT 7

Sansom, William 1912-1976 . **CLC 2, 6; SSC 21**
See also CA 5-8R; 65-68; CANR 42; CN 1, 2; DAM NOV; DLB 139; EWL 3; MTCW 1; RGEL 2; RGSF 2

Santayana, George 1863-1952 .... **TCLC 40**
See also AMW; CA 115; 194; DLB 54, 71, 246, 270; DLBD 13; EWL 3; MAL 5; RGAL 4; TUS

Santiago, Danny CLC 33
See James, Daniel (Lewis)
See also DLB 122

Santillana, Inigo Lopez de Mendoza, Marques de 1398-1458 .... **LC 111**
See also DLB 286

Santmyer, Helen Hooven
1895-1986 .... **CLC 33; TCLC 133**
See also CA 1-4R; 118; CANR 15, 33; DLBY 1984; MTCW 1; RHW

Santoka, Taneda 1882-1940 .... **TCLC 72**

Santos, Bienvenido N(uqui)
1911-1996 ... **AAL; CLC 22; TCLC 156**
See also CA 101; 151; CANR 19, 46; CP 1; DAM MULT; DLB 312; EWL; RGAL 4; SSFS 19

Sapir, Edward 1884-1939 .... **TCLC 108**
See also CA 211; DLB 92

Sapper TCLC 44
See McNeile, Herman Cyril

Sapphire 1950- .... **CLC 99**
See also CA 262

Sapphire, Brenda
See Sapphire

Sappho fl. 6th cent. B.C.- ... **CMLC 3, 67; PC 5**
See also CDWLB 1; DA3; DAM POET; DLB 176; FL 1:1; PFS 20; RGWL 2, 3; WLIT 8; WP

Saramago, Jose 1922- ..... **CLC 119; HLCS 1**
See also CA 153; CANR 96, 164; CWW 2; DLB 287, 332; EWL 3; LATS 1:2; NFS 27; SSFS 23

Sarduy, Severo 1937-1993 .... **CLC 6, 97; HLCS 2; TCLC 167**
See also CA 89-92; 142; CANR 58, 81; CWW 2; DLB 113; EWL 3; HW 1, 2; LAW

Sargeson, Frank 1903-1982 ..... **CLC 31; SSC 99**
See also CA 25-28R; 106; CANR 38, 79; CN 1, 2, 3; EWL 3; GLL 2; RGEL 2; RGSF 2; SSFS 20

Sarmiento, Domingo Faustino
1811-1888 .... **HLCS 2; NCLC 123**
See also LAW; WLIT 1

Sarmiento, Felix Ruben Garcia
See Dario, Ruben

Saro-Wiwa, Ken(ule Beeson)
1941-1995 .... **CLC 114; TCLC 200**
See also BW 2; CA 142; 150; CANR 60; DLB 157

Saroyan, William 1908-1981 ... **CLC 1, 8, 10, 29, 34, 56; DC 28; SSC 21; TCLC 137; WLC 5**
See also AAYA 66; CA 5-8R; 103; CAD; CANR 30; CDALBS; CN 1, 2; DA; DA3; DAB; DAC; DAM DRAM, MST, NOV; DFS 17; DLB 7, 9, 86; DLBY 1981; EWL 3; LAIT 4; MAL 5; MTCW 1, 2; MTFW 2005; RGAL 4; RGSF 2; SATA 23; SATA-Obit 24; SSFS 14; TUS

Sarraute, Nathalie 1900-1999 .... **CLC 1, 2, 4, 8, 10, 31, 80; TCLC 145**
See also BPFB 3; CA 9-12R; 187; CANR 23, 66, 134; CWW 2; DLB 83, 321; EW 12; EWL 3; GFL 1789 to the Present; MTCW 1, 2; MTFW 2005; RGWL 2, 3

Sarton, May 1912-1995 ... **CLC 4, 14, 49, 91; PC 39; TCLC 120**
See also AMWS 8; CA 1-4R; 149; CANR 1, 34, 55, 116; CN 1, 2, 3, 4, 5, 6; CP 1, 2, 3, 4, 5, 6; DAM POET; DLB 48; DLBY 1981; EWL 3; FW; INT CANR-34; MAL 5; MTCW 1, 2; MTFW 2005; RGAL 4; SATA 36; SATA-Obit 86; TUS

Sartre, Jean-Paul 1905-1980 . **CLC 1, 4, 7, 9, 13, 18, 24, 44, 50, 52; DC 3; SSC 32; WLC 5**
See also AAYA 62; CA 9-12R; 97-100; CANR 21; DA; DA3; DAB; DAC; DAM DRAM, MST, NOV; DFS 5; DLB 72, 296, 321, 332; EW 12; EWL 3; GFL 1789 to the Present; LMFS 2; MTCW 1, 2; MTFW 2005; NFS 21; RGHL; RGSF 2; RGWL 2, 3; SSFS 9; TWA

Sassoon, Siegfried (Lorraine)
1886-1967 .... **CLC 36, 130; PC 12**
See also BRW 6; CA 104; 25-28R; CANR 36; DAB; DAM MST, NOV, POET; DLB 20, 191; DLBD 18; EWL 3; MTCW 1, 2; MTFW 2005; PAB; PFS 28; RGEL 2; TEA

Satterfield, Charles
See Pohl, Frederik

Satyremont
See Peret, Benjamin

Saul, John III
See Saul, John

Saul, John 1942- .... **CLC 46**
See also AAYA 10, 62; BEST 90:4; CA 81-84; CANR 16, 40, 81, 176; CPW; DAM NOV, POP; HGG; SATA 98

Saul, John W.
See Saul, John

Saul, John W. III
See Saul, John

Saul, John Woodruff III
See Saul, John

Saunders, Caleb
See Heinlein, Robert A.

Saura (Atares), Carlos 1932-1998 .... **CLC 20**
See also CA 114; 131; CANR 79; HW 1

Sauser, Frederic Louis
See Sauser-Hall, Frederic

Sauser-Hall, Frederic 1887-1961 ...... **CLC 18**
See Cendrars, Blaise
See also CA 102; 93-96; CANR 36, 62;
MTCW 1

Saussure, Ferdinand de
1857-1913 .... **TCLC 49**
See also DLB 242

Savage, Catharine
See Brosman, Catharine Savage

Savage, Richard 1697(?)-1743 .... **LC 96**
See also DLB 95; RGEL 2

Savage, Thomas 1915-2003 .... **CLC 40**
See also CA 126; 132; 218; CAAS 15; CN
6, 7; INT CA-132; SATA-Obit 147;
TCWW 2

Savan, Glenn 1953-2003 .... **CLC 50**
See also CA 225

Savonarola, Girolamo 1452-1498 ...... **LC 152**
See also LMFS 1

Sax, Robert
See Johnson, Robert

Saxo Grammaticus c. 1150-c.
1222 .... **CMLC 58**

Saxton, Robert
See Johnson, Robert

Sayers, Dorothy L(eigh) 1893-1957 . **SSC 71;**
TCLC 2, 15
See also BPFB 3; BRWS 3; CA 104; 119;
CANR 60; CDBLB 1914-1945; CMW 4;
DAM POP; DLB 10, 36, 77, 100; MSW;
MTCW 1, 2; MTFW 2005; RGEL 2;
SSFS 12; TEA

Sayers, Valerie 1952- .... **CLC 50, 122**
See also CA 134; CANR 61; CSW

Sayles, John (Thomas) 1950- .... **CLC 7, 10,**
14, 198
See also CA 57-60; CANR 41, 84; DLB 44

Scamander, Newt
See Rowling, J.K.

Scammell, Michael 1935- .... **CLC 34**
See also CA 156

Scannel, John Vernon
See Scannell, Vernon

Scannell, Vernon 1922-2007 .... **CLC 49**
See also CA 5-8R; 266; CANR 8, 24, 57,
143; CN 1, 2; CP 1, 2, 3, 4, 5, 6, 7; CWRI
5; DLB 27; SATA 59; SATA-Obit 188

Scarlett, Susan
See Streatfeild, Noel

Scarron 1847-1910
See Mikszath, Kalman

Scarron, Paul 1610-1660 .... **LC 116**
See also GFL Beginnings to 1789; RGWL
2, 3

Schaeffer, Susan Fromberg 1941- ..... **CLC 6,**
11, 22
See also CA 49-52; CANR 18, 65, 160; CN
4, 5, 6, 7; DLB 28, 299; MTCW 1, 2;
MTFW 2005; SATA 22

Schama, Simon 1945- .... **CLC 150**
See also BEST 89:4; CA 105; CANR 39,
91, 168

Schama, Simon Michael
See Schama, Simon

Schary, Jill
See Robinson, Jill

Schell, Jonathan 1943- .... **CLC 35**
See also CA 73-76; CANR 12, 117

Schelling, Friedrich Wilhelm Joseph von
1775-1854 .... **NCLC 30**
See also DLB 90

Scherer, Jean-Marie Maurice 1920-
See Rohmer, Eric
See also CA 110

Schevill, James (Erwin) 1920- .... **CLC 7**
See also CA 5-8R; CAAS 12; CAD; CD 5,
6; CP 1, 2, 3, 4, 5

Schiller, Friedrich von 1759-1805 ...... **DC 12;**
NCLC 39, 69, 166
See also CDWLB 2; DAM DRAM; DLB
94; EW 5; RGWL 2, 3; TWA

Schisgal, Murray (Joseph) 1926- .... **CLC 6**
See also CA 21-24R; CAD; CANR 48, 86;
CD 5, 6; MAL 5

Schlee, Ann 1934- .... **CLC 35**
See also CA 101; CANR 29, 88; SATA 44;
SATA-Brief 36

Schlegel, August Wilhelm von
1767-1845 .... **NCLC 15, 142**
See also DLB 94; RGWL 2, 3

Schlegel, Friedrich 1772-1829 .... **NCLC 45**
See also DLB 90; EW 5; RGWL 2, 3; TWA

Schlegel, Johann Elias (von)
1719(?)-1749 .... **LC 5**

Schleiermacher, Friedrich
1768-1834 .... **NCLC 107**
See also DLB 90

Schlesinger, Arthur M., Jr.
1917-2007 .... **CLC 84**
See Schlesinger, Arthur Meier
See also AITN 1; CA 1-4R; 257; CANR 1,
28, 58, 105; DLB 17; INT CANR-28;
MTCW 1, 2; SATA 61; SATA-Obit 181

Schlink, Bernhard 1944- .... **CLC 174**
See also CA 163; CANR 116, 175; RGHL

Schmidt, Arno (Otto) 1914-1979 ...... **CLC 56**
See also CA 128; 109; DLB 69; EWL 3

Schmitz, Aron Hector 1861-1928
See Svevo, Italo
See also CA 104; 122; MTCW 1

Schnackenberg, Gjertrud 1953- ...... **CLC 40;**
PC 45
See also AMWS 15; CA 116; CANR 100;
CP 5, 6, 7; CWP; DLB 120, 282; PFS 13,
25

Schnackenberg, Gjertrud Cecelia
See Schnackenberg, Gjertrud

Schneider, Leonard Alfred 1925-1966
See Bruce, Lenny
See also CA 89-92

Schnitzler, Arthur 1862-1931 ..... **DC 17; SSC**
15, 61; TCLC 4
See also CA 104; CDWLB 2; DLB 81, 118;
EW 8; EWL 3; RGSF 2; RGWL 2, 3

Schoenberg, Arnold Franz Walter
1874-1951 .... **TCLC 75**
See also CA 109; 188

Schonberg, Arnold
See Schoenberg, Arnold Franz Walter

Schopenhauer, Arthur 1788-1860 . **NCLC 51,**
157
See also DLB 90; EW 5

Schor, Sandra (M.) 1932(?)-1990 ..... **CLC 65**
See also CA 132

Schorer, Mark 1908-1977 .... **CLC 9**
See also CA 5-8R; 73-76; CANR 7; CN 1,
2; DLB 103

Schrader, Paul (Joseph) 1946- . **CLC 26, 212**
See also CA 37-40R; CANR 41; DLB 44

Schreber, Daniel 1842-1911 .... **TCLC 123**

Schreiner, Olive (Emilie Albertina)
1855-1920 .... **TCLC 9**
See also AFW; BRWS 2; CA 105; 154;
DLB 18, 156, 190, 225; EWL 3; FW;
RGEL 2; TWA; WLIT 2; WWE 1

Schulberg, Budd 1914- .... **CLC 7, 48**
See also AMWS 18; BPFB 3; CA 25-28R;
CANR 19, 87, 178; CN 1, 2, 3, 4, 5, 6, 7;
DLB 6, 26, 28; DLBY 1981, 2001; MAL
5

Schulberg, Budd Wilson
See Schulberg, Budd

Schulman, Arnold
See Trumbo, Dalton

Schulz, Bruno 1892-1942 .. **SSC 13; TCLC 5,**
51
See also CA 115; 123; CANR 86; CDWLB
4; DLB 215; EWL 3; MTCW 2; MTFW
2005; RGSF 2; RGWL 2, 3

Schulz, Charles M. 1922-2000 .... **CLC 12**
See also AAYA 39; CA 9-12R; 187; CANR
6, 132; INT CANR-6; MTFW 2005;
SATA 10; SATA-Obit 118

Schulz, Charles Monroe
See Schulz, Charles M.

Schumacher, E(rnst) F(riedrich)
1911-1977 .... **CLC 80**
See also CA 81-84; 73-76; CANR 34, 85

Schumann, Robert 1810-1856 ...... **NCLC 143**

Schuyler, George Samuel 1895-1977 . **HR 1:3**
See also BW 2; CA 81-84; 73-76; CANR
42; DLB 29, 51

Schuyler, James Marcus 1923-1991 .. **CLC 5,**
23; PC 88
See also CA 101; 134; CP 1, 2, 3, 4, 5;
DAM POET; DLB 5, 169; EWL 3; INT
CA-101; MAL 5; WP

Schwartz, Delmore (David)
1913-1966 . **CLC 2, 4, 10, 45, 87; PC 8;**
SSC 105
See also AMWS 2; CA 17-18; 25-28R;
CANR 35; CAP 2; DLB 28, 48; EWL 3;
MAL 5; MTCW 1, 2; MTFW 2005; PAB;
RGAL 4; TUS

Schwartz, Ernst
See Ozu, Yasujiro

Schwartz, John Burnham 1965- .... **CLC 59**
See also CA 132; CANR 116

Schwartz, Lynne Sharon 1939- .... **CLC 31**
See also CA 103; CANR 44, 89, 160; DLB
218; MTCW 2; MTFW 2005

Schwartz, Muriel A.
See Eliot, T(homas) S(tearns)

Schwarz-Bart, Andre 1928-2006 .... **CLC 2, 4**
See also CA 89-92; 253; CANR 109; DLB
299; RGHL

Schwarz-Bart, Simone 1938- . **BLCS; CLC 7**
See also BW 2; CA 97-100; CANR 117;
EWL 3

Schwerner, Armand 1927-1999 .... **PC 42**
See also CA 9-12R; 179; CANR 50, 85; CP
2, 3, 4, 5, 6; DLB 165

Schwitters, Kurt (Hermann Edward Karl
Julius) 1887-1948 .... **TCLC 95**
See also CA 158

Schwob, Marcel (Mayer Andre)
1867-1905 .... **TCLC 20**
See also CA 117; 168; DLB 123; GFL 1789
to the Present

Sciascia, Leonardo 1921-1989 .. **CLC 8, 9, 41**
See also CA 85-88; 130; CANR 35; DLB
177; EWL 3; MTCW 1; RGWL 2, 3

Scoppettone, Sandra 1936- .... **CLC 26**
See Early, Jack
See also AAYA 11, 65; BYA 8; CA 5-8R;
CANR 41, 73, 157; GLL 1; MAICYA 2;
MAICYAS 1; SATA 9, 92; WYA; YAW

Scorsese, Martin 1942- .... **CLC 20, 89, 207**
See also AAYA 38; CA 110; 114; CANR
46, 85

Scotland, Jay
See Jakes, John

Scott, Duncan Campbell
1862-1947 .... **TCLC 6**
See also CA 104; 153; DAC; DLB 92;
RGEL 2

Scott, Evelyn 1893-1963 .... **CLC 43**
See also CA 104; 112; CANR 64; DLB 9,
48; RHW

Scott, F(rancis) R(eginald)
1899-1985 .... **CLC 22**
See also CA 101; 114; CANR 87; CP 1, 2,
3, 4; DLB 88; INT CA-101; RGEL 2

Scott, Frank
See Scott, F(rancis) R(eginald)
Scott, Joan CLC 65
Scott, Joanna 1960- .... **CLC 50**
See also AMWS 17; CA 126; CANR 53, 92, 168
Scott, Joanna Jeanne
See Scott, Joanna
Scott, Paul (Mark) 1920-1978 ...... **CLC 9, 60**
See also BRWS 1; CA 81-84; 77-80; CANR 33; CN 1, 2; DLB 14, 207, 326; EWL 3; MTCW 1; RGEL 2; RHW; WWE 1
Scott, Ridley 1937- .... **CLC 183**
See also AAYA 13, 43
Scott, Sarah 1723-1795 .... **LC 44**
See also DLB 39
Scott, Sir Walter 1771-1832 .... **NCLC 15, 69, 110; PC 13; SSC 32; WLC 5**
See also AAYA 22; BRW 4; BYA 2; CD-BLB 1789-1832; DA; DAB; DAC; DAM MST, NOV, POET; DLB 93, 107, 116, 144, 159; GL 3; HGG; LAIT 1; RGEL 2; RGSF 2; SSFS 10; SUFW 1; TEA; WLIT 3; YABC 2
Scribe, (Augustin) Eugene 1791-1861 . **DC 5; NCLC 16**
See also DAM DRAM; DLB 192; GFL 1789 to the Present; RGWL 2, 3
Scrum, R.
See Crumb, R.
Scudery, Georges de 1601-1667 .... **LC 75**
See also GFL Beginnings to 1789
Scudery, Madeleine de 1607-1701 . **LC 2, 58**
See also DLB 268; GFL Beginnings to 1789
Scum
See Crumb, R.
Scumbag, Little Bobby
See Crumb, R.
Seabrook, John
See Hubbard, L. Ron
Seacole, Mary Jane Grant
1805-1881 .... **NCLC 147**
See also DLB 166
Sealy, I(rwin) Allan 1951- .... **CLC 55**
See also CA 136; CN 6, 7
Search, Alexander
See Pessoa, Fernando
Sebald, W(infried) G(eorg)
1944-2001 .... **CLC 194**
See also BRWS 8; CA 159; 202; CANR 98; MTFW 2005; RGHL
Sebastian, Lee
See Silverberg, Robert
Sebastian Owl
See Thompson, Hunter S.
Sebestyen, Igen
See Sebestyen, Ouida
Sebestyen, Ouida 1924- .... **CLC 30**
See also AAYA 8; BYA 7; CA 107; CANR 40, 114; CLR 17; JRDA; MAICYA 1, 2; SAAS 10; SATA 39, 140; WYA; YAW
Sebold, Alice 1963(?)- .... **CLC 193**
See also AAYA 56; CA 203; CANR 181; MTFW 2005
Second Duke of Buckingham
See Villiers, George
Secundus, H. Scriblerus
See Fielding, Henry
Sedges, John
See Buck, Pearl S(ydenstricker)
Sedgwick, Catharine Maria
1789-1867 .... **NCLC 19, 98**
See also DLB 1, 74, 183, 239, 243, 254; FL 1:3; RGAL 4
Sedulius Scottus 9th cent. -c. 874 .. **CMLC 86**
Seebohm, Victoria
See Glendinning, Victoria

Seelye, John (Douglas) 1931- .... **CLC 7**
See also CA 97-100; CANR 70; INT CA-97-100; TCWW 1, 2
Seferiades, Giorgos Stylianou 1900-1971
See Seferis, George
See also CA 5-8R; 33-36R; CANR 5, 36; MTCW 1
Seferis, George CLC 5, 11; PC 66; TCLC 213
See Seferiades, Giorgos Stylianou
See also DLB 332; EW 12; EWL 3; RGWL 2, 3
Segal, Erich (Wolf) 1937- .... **CLC 3, 10**
See also BEST 89:1; BPFB 3; CA 25-28R; CANR 20, 36, 65, 113; CPW; DAM POP; DLBY 1986; INT CANR-20; MTCW 1
Seger, Bob 1945- .... **CLC 35**
Seghers, Anna CLC 7
See Radvanyi, Netty
See also CDWLB 2; DLB 69; EWL 3
Seidel, Frederick 1936- .... **CLC 18**
See also CA 13-16R; CANR 8, 99, 180; CP 1, 2, 3, 4, 5, 6, 7; DLBY 1984
Seidel, Frederick Lewis
See Seidel, Frederick
Seifert, Jaroslav 1901-1986 . **CLC 34, 44, 93; PC 47**
See also CA 127; CDWLB 4; DLB 215, 332; EWL 3; MTCW 1, 2
Sei Shonagon c. 966-1017(?) ..... **CMLC 6, 89**
Sejour, Victor 1817-1874 .... **DC 10**
See also DLB 50
Sejour Marcou et Ferrand, Juan Victor
See Sejour, Victor
Selby, Hubert, Jr. 1928-2004 ..... **CLC 1, 2, 4, 8; SSC 20**
See also CA 13-16R; 226; CANR 33, 85; CN 1, 2, 3, 4, 5, 6, 7; DLB 2, 227; MAL 5
Selzer, Richard 1928- .... **CLC 74**
See also CA 65-68; CANR 14, 106
Sembene, Ousmane
See Ousmane, Sembene
Senancour, Etienne Pivert de
1770-1846 .... **NCLC 16**
See also DLB 119; GFL 1789 to the Present
Sender, Ramon (Jose) 1902-1982 ...... **CLC 8; HLC 2; TCLC 136**
See also CA 5-8R; 105; CANR 8; DAM MULT; DLB 322; EWL 3; HW 1; MTCW 1; RGWL 2, 3
Seneca, Lucius Annaeus c. 1B.C.-c. 65 .... **CMLC 6, 107; DC 5**
See also AW 2; CDWLB 1; DAM DRAM; DLB 211; RGWL 2, 3; TWA; WLIT 8
Senghor, Leopold Sedar
1906-2001 .. **BLC 1:3; CLC 54, 130; PC 25**
See also AFW; BW 2; CA 116; 125; 203; CANR 47, 74, 134; CWW 2; DAM MULT, POET; DNFS 2; EWL 3; GFL 1789 to the Present; MTCW 1, 2; MTFW 2005; TWA
Senior, Olive (Marjorie) 1941- .... **SSC 78**
See also BW 3; CA 154; CANR 86, 126; CN 6; CP 6, 7; CWP; DLB 157; EWL 3; RGSF 2
Senna, Danzy 1970- .... **CLC 119**
See also CA 169; CANR 130, 184
Serling, (Edward) Rod(man)
1924-1975 .... **CLC 30**
See also AAYA 14; AITN 1; CA 162; 57-60; DLB 26; SFW 4
Serna, Ramon Gomez de la
See Gomez de la Serna, Ramon
Serpieres
See Guillevic, (Eugene)

Service, Robert
See Service, Robert W(illiam)
See also BYA 4; DAB; DLB 92
Service, Robert W(illiam)
1874(?)-1958 ... **PC 70; TCLC 15; WLC 5**
See Service, Robert
See also CA 115; 140; CANR 84; DA; DAC; DAM MST, POET; PFS 10; RGEL 2; SATA 20
Seth, Vikram 1952- .... **CLC 43, 90**
See also BRWS 10; CA 121; 127; CANR 50, 74, 131; CN 6, 7; CP 5, 6, 7; DA3; DAM MULT; DLB 120, 271, 282, 323; EWL 3; INT CA-127; MTCW 2; MTFW 2005; WWE 1
Seton, Cynthia Propper 1926-1982 .. **CLC 27**
See also CA 5-8R; 108; CANR 7
Seton, Ernest (Evan) Thompson
1860-1946 .... **TCLC 31**
See also ANW; BYA 3; CA 109; 204; CLR 59; DLB 92; DLBD 13; JRDA; SATA 18
Seton-Thompson, Ernest
See Seton, Ernest (Evan) Thompson
Settle, Mary Lee 1918-2005 .... **CLC 19, 61**
See also BPFB 3; CA 89-92; 243; CAAS 1; CANR 44, 87, 126, 182; CN 6, 7; CSW; DLB 6; INT CA-89-92
Seuphor, Michel
See Arp, Jean
Sevigne, Marie (de Rabutin-Chantal)
1626-1696 .... **LC 11, 144**
See Sevigne, Marie de Rabutin Chantal
See also GFL Beginnings to 1789; TWA
Sevigne, Marie de Rabutin Chantal
See Sevigne, Marie (de Rabutin-Chantal)
See also DLB 268
Sewall, Samuel 1652-1730 .... **LC 38**
See also DLB 24; RGAL 4
Sexton, Anne (Harvey) 1928-1974 ..... **CLC 2, 4, 6, 8, 10, 15, 53, 123; PC 2, 79; WLC 5**
See also AMWS 2; CA 1-4R; 53-56; CABS 2; CANR 3, 36; CDALB 1941-1968; CP 1, 2; DA; DA3; DAB; DAC; DAM MST, POET; DLB 5, 169; EWL 3; EXPP; FL 1:6; FW; MAL 5; MBL; MTCW 1, 2; MTFW 2005; PAB; PFS 4, 14; RGAL 4; RGHL; SATA 10; TUS
Shaara, Jeff 1952- .... **CLC 119**
See also AAYA 70; CA 163; CANR 109, 172; CN 7; MTFW 2005
Shaara, Michael 1929-1988 .... **CLC 15**
See also AAYA 71; AITN 1; BPFB 3; CA 102; 125; CANR 52, 85; DAM POP; DLBY 1983; MTFW 2005; NFS 26
Shackleton, C.C.
See Aldiss, Brian W.
Shacochis, Bob CLC 39
See Shacochis, Robert G.
Shacochis, Robert G. 1951-
See Shacochis, Bob
See also CA 119; 124; CANR 100; INT CA-124
Shadwell, Thomas 1641(?)-1692 .... **LC 114**
See also DLB 80; IDTP; RGEL 2
Shaffer, Anthony 1926-2001 .... **CLC 19**
See also CA 110; 116; 200; CBD; CD 5, 6; DAM DRAM; DFS 13; DLB 13
Shaffer, Anthony Joshua
See Shaffer, Anthony
Shaffer, Peter 1926- ... **CLC 5, 14, 18, 37, 60; DC 7**
See also BRWS 1; CA 25-28R; CANR 25, 47, 74, 118; CBD; CD 5, 6; CDBLB 1960 to Present; DA3; DAB; DAM DRAM, MST; DFS 5, 13; DLB 13, 233; EWL 3; MTCW 1, 2; MTFW 2005; RGEL 2; TEA

Shakespeare, William 1564-1616 . **PC 84, 89; WLC 5**
See also AAYA 35; BRW 1; CDBLB Before 1660; DA; DA3; DAB; DAC; DAM DRAM, MST, POET; DFS 20, 21; DLB 62, 172, 263; EXPP; LAIT 1; LATS 1:1; LMFS 1; PAB; PFS 1, 2, 3, 4, 5, 8, 9; RGEL 2; TEA; WLIT 3; WP; WS; WYA

Shakey, Bernard
See Young, Neil

Shalamov, Varlam (Tikhonovich)
1907-1982 .... **CLC 18**
See also CA 129; 105; DLB 302; RGSF 2

Shamloo, Ahmad
See Shamlu, Ahmad

Shamlou, Ahmad
See Shamlu, Ahmad

Shamlu, Ahmad 1925-2000 .... **CLC 10**
See also CA 216; CWW 2

Shammas, Anton 1951- .... **CLC 55**
See also CA 199; DLB 346

Shandling, Arline
See Berriault, Gina

Shange, Ntozake 1948- .. **BLC 1:3, 2:3; CLC 8, 25, 38, 74, 126; DC 3**
See also AAYA 9, 66; AFAW 1, 2; BW 2; CA 85-88; CABS 3; CAD; CANR 27, 48, 74, 131; CD 5, 6; CP 5, 6, 7; CWD; CWP; DA3; DAM DRAM, MULT; DFS 2, 11; DLB 38, 249; FW; LAIT 4, 5; MAL 5; MTCW 1, 2; MTFW 2005; NFS 11; RGAL 4; SATA 157; YAW

Shanley, John Patrick 1950- .... **CLC 75**
See also AAYA 74; AMWS 14; CA 128; 133; CAD; CANR 83, 154; CD 5, 6; DFS 23

Shapcott, Thomas W(illiam) 1935- .. **CLC 38**
See also CA 69-72; CANR 49, 83, 103; CP 1, 2, 3, 4, 5, 6, 7; DLB 289

Shapiro, Jane 1942- .... **CLC 76**
See also CA 196

Shapiro, Karl 1913-2000 ... **CLC 4, 8, 15, 53; PC 25**
See also AMWS 2; CA 1-4R; 188; CAAS 6; CANR 1, 36, 66; CP 1, 2, 3, 4, 5, 6; DLB 48; EWL 3; EXPP; MAL 5; MTCW 1, 2; MTFW 2005; PFS 3; RGAL 4

Sharp, William 1855-1905 .... **TCLC 39**
See Macleod, Fiona
See also CA 160; DLB 156; RGEL 2

Sharpe, Thomas Ridley 1928-
See Sharpe, Tom
See also CA 114; 122; CANR 85; INT CA-122

Sharpe, Tom CLC 36
See Sharpe, Thomas Ridley
See also CN 4, 5, 6, 7; DLB 14, 231

Shatrov, Mikhail CLC 59

Shaw, Bernard
See Shaw, George Bernard
See also DLB 10, 57, 190

Shaw, G. Bernard
See Shaw, George Bernard

Shaw, George Bernard 1856-1950 ..... **DC 23; TCLC 3, 9, 21, 45, 205; WLC 5**
See Shaw, Bernard
See also AAYA 61; BRW 6; BRWC 1; BRWR 2; CA 104; 128; CDBLB 1914-1945; DA; DA3; DAB; DAC; DAM DRAM, MST; DFS 1, 3, 6, 11, 19, 22; DLB 332; EWL 3; LAIT 3; LATS 1:1; MTCW 1, 2; MTFW 2005; RGEL 2; TEA; WLIT 4

Shaw, Henry Wheeler 1818-1885 .. **NCLC 15**
See also DLB 11; RGAL 4

Shaw, Irwin 1913-1984 .... **CLC 7, 23, 34**
See also AITN 1; BPFB 3; CA 13-16R; 112; CANR 21; CDALB 1941-1968; CN 1, 2, 3; CPW; DAM DRAM, POP; DLB 6, 102; DLBY 1984; MAL 5; MTCW 1, 21; MTFW 2005

Shaw, Robert (Archibald)
1927-1978 .... **CLC 5**
See also AITN 1; CA 1-4R; 81-84; CANR 4; CN 1, 2; DLB 13, 14

Shaw, T. E.
See Lawrence, T(homas) E(dward)

Shawn, Wallace 1943- .... **CLC 41**
See also CA 112; CAD; CD 5, 6; DLB 266

Shaykh, al- Hanan
See al-Shaykh, Hanan

Shchedrin, N.
See Saltykov, Mikhail Evgrafovich

Shea, Lisa 1953- .... **CLC 86**
See also CA 147

Sheed, Wilfrid 1930- .... **CLC 2, 4, 10, 53**
See also CA 65-68; CANR 30, 66, 181; CN 1, 2, 3, 4, 5, 6, 7; DLB 6; MAL 5; MTCW 1, 2; MTFW 2005

Sheed, Wilfrid John Joseph
See Sheed, Wilfrid

Sheehy, Gail 1937- .... **CLC 171**
See also CA 49-52; CANR 1, 33, 55, 92; CPW; MTCW 1

Sheldon, Alice Hastings Bradley
1915(?)-1987
See Tiptree, James, Jr.
See also CA 108; 122; CANR 34; INT CA-108; MTCW 1

Sheldon, John
See Bloch, Robert (Albert)

Sheldon, Walter J(ames) 1917-1996
See Queen, Ellery
See also AITN 1; CA 25-28R; CANR 10

Shelley, Mary Wollstonecraft (Godwin)
1797-1851 .... **NCLC 14, 59, 103, 170; SSC 92; WLC 5**
See also AAYA 20; BPFB 3; BRW 3; BRWC 2; BRWS 3; BYA 5; CDBLB 1789-1832; CLR 133; DA; DA3; DAB; DAC; DAM MST, NOV; DLB 110, 116, 159, 178; EXPN; FL 1:3; GL 3; HGG; LAIT 1; LMFS 1, 2; NFS 1; RGEL 2; SATA 29; SCFW 1, 2; SFW 4; TEA; WLIT 3

Shelley, Percy Bysshe 1792-1822 .. **NCLC 18, 93, 143, 175; PC 14, 67; WLC 5**
See also AAYA 61; BRW 4; BRWR 1; CDBLB 1789-1832; DA; DA3; DAB; DAC; DAM MST, POET; DLB 96, 110, 158; EXPP; LMFS 1; PAB; PFS 2, 27; RGEL 2; TEA; WLIT 3; WP

Shepard, James R.
See Shepard, Jim

Shepard, Jim 1956- .... **CLC 36**
See also AAYA 73; CA 137; CANR 59, 104, 160; SATA 90, 164

Shepard, Lucius 1947- .... **CLC 34**
See also CA 128; 141; CANR 81, 124, 178; HGG; SCFW 2; SFW 4; SUFW 2

Shepard, Sam 1943- .... **CLC 4, 6, 17, 34, 41, 44, 169; DC 5**
See also AAYA 1, 58; AMWS 3; CA 69-72; CABS 3; CAD; CANR 22, 120, 140; CD 5, 6; DA3; DAM DRAM; DFS 3, 6, 7, 14; DLB 7, 212, 341; EWL 3; IDFW 3, 4; MAL 5; MTCW 1, 2; MTFW 2005; RGAL 4

Shepherd, Jean (Parker)
1921-1999 .... **TCLC 177**
See also AAYA 69; AITN 2; CA 77-80; 187

Shepherd, Michael
See Ludlum, Robert

Sherburne, Zoa (Lillian Morin)
1912-1995 .... **CLC 30**
See also AAYA 13; CA 1-4R; 176; CANR 3, 37; MAICYA 1, 2; SAAS 18; SATA 3; YAW

Sheridan, Frances 1724-1766 .... **LC 7**
See also DLB 39, 84

Sheridan, Richard Brinsley
1751-1816 . **DC 1; NCLC 5, 91; WLC 5**
See also BRW 3; CDBLB 1660-1789; DA; DAB; DAC; DAM DRAM, MST; DFS 15; DLB 89; WLIT 3

Sherman, Jonathan Marc 1968- .... **CLC 55**
See also CA 230

Sherman, Martin 1941(?)- .... **CLC 19**
See also CA 116; 123; CAD; CANR 86; CD 5, 6; DFS 20; DLB 228; GLL 1; IDTP; RGHL

Sherwin, Judith Johnson
See Johnson, Judith (Emlyn)
See also CANR 85; CP 2, 3, 4, 5; CWP

Sherwood, Frances 1940- .... **CLC 81**
See also CA 146, 220; CAAE 220; CANR 158

Sherwood, Robert E(mmet)
1896-1955 .... **TCLC 3**
See also CA 104; 153; CANR 86; DAM DRAM; DFS 11, 15, 17; DLB 7, 26, 249; IDFW 3, 4; MAL 5; RGAL 4

Shestov, Lev 1866-1938 .... **TCLC 56**

Shevchenko, Taras 1814-1861 .... **NCLC 54**

Shiel, M(atthew) P(hipps)
1865-1947 .... **TCLC 8**
See Holmes, Gordon
See also CA 106; 160; DLB 153; HGG; MTCW 2; MTFW 2005; SCFW 1, 2; SFW 4; SUFW

Shields, Carol 1935-2003 .. **CLC 91, 113, 193**
See also AMWS 7; CA 81-84; 218; CANR 51, 74, 98, 133; CCA 1; CN 6, 7; CPW; DA3; DAC; DLB 334; MTCW 2; MTFW 2005; NFS 23

Shields, David 1956- .... **CLC 97**
See also CA 124; CANR 48, 99, 112, 157

Shields, David Jonathan
See Shields, David

Shiga, Naoya 1883-1971 .... **CLC 33; SSC 23; TCLC 172**
See Shiga Naoya
See also CA 101; 33-36R; MJW; RGWL 3

Shiga Naoya
See Shiga, Naoya
See also DLB 180; EWL 3; RGWL 3

Shilts, Randy 1951-1994 .... **CLC 85**
See also AAYA 19; CA 115; 127; 144; CANR 45; DA3; GLL 1; INT CA-127; MTCW 2; MTFW 2005

Shimazaki, Haruki 1872-1943
See Shimazaki Toson
See also CA 105; 134; CANR 84; RGWL 3

Shimazaki Toson TCLC 5
See Shimazaki, Haruki
See also DLB 180; EWL 3

Shirley, James 1596-1666 .... **DC 25; LC 96**
See also DLB 58; RGEL 2

Shirley Hastings, Selina
See Hastings, Selina

Sholokhov, Mikhail (Aleksandrovich)
1905-1984 .... **CLC 7, 15**
See also CA 101; 112; DLB 272, 332; EWL 3; MTCW 1, 2; MTFW 2005; RGWL 2, 3; SATA-Obit 36

Sholom Aleichem 1859-1916 .... **SSC 33; TCLC 1, 35**
See Rabinovitch, Sholem
See also DLB 333; TWA

Shone, Patric
See Hanley, James

Showalter, Elaine 1941- .... **CLC 169**
See also CA 57-60; CANR 58, 106; DLB 67; FW; GLL 2

Shreve, Susan
See Shreve, Susan Richards

Shreve, Susan Richards 1939- .... **CLC 23**
See also CA 49-52; CAAS 5; CANR 5, 38, 69, 100, 159; MAICYA 1, 2; SATA 46, 95, 152; SATA-Brief 41

Shue, Larry 1946-1985 .... **CLC 52**
See also CA 145; 117; DAM DRAM; DFS 7

Shu-Jen, Chou 1881-1936
See Lu Hsun
See also CA 104

Shulman, Alix Kates 1932- .... **CLC 2, 10**
See also CA 29-32R; CANR 43; FW; SATA 7

Shuster, Joe 1914-1992 .... **CLC 21**
See also AAYA 50

Shute, Nevil **CLC 30**
See Norway, Nevil Shute
See also BPFB 3; DLB 255; NFS 9; RHW; SFW 4

Shuttle, Penelope (Diane) 1947- .... **CLC 7**
See also CA 93-96; CANR 39, 84, 92, 108; CP 3, 4, 5, 6, 7; CWP; DLB 14, 40

Shvarts, Elena 1948- .... **PC 50**
See also CA 147

Sidhwa, Bapsi 1939-
See Sidhwa, Bapsy (N.)
See also CN 6, 7; DLB 323

Sidhwa, Bapsy (N.) 1938- .... **CLC 168**
See Sidhwa, Bapsi
See also CA 108; CANR 25, 57; FW

Sidney, Mary 1561-1621 .... **LC 19, 39**
See Sidney Herbert, Mary

Sidney, Sir Philip 1554-1586 .... **LC 19, 39, 131; PC 32**
See also BRW 1; BRWR 2; CDBLB Before 1660; DA; DA3; DAB; DAC; DAM MST, POET; DLB 167; EXPP; PAB; RGEL 2; TEA; WP

Sidney Herbert, Mary
See Sidney, Mary
See also DLB 167

Siegel, Jerome 1914-1996 .... **CLC 21**
See Siegel, Jerry
See also CA 116; 169; 151

Siegel, Jerry
See Siegel, Jerome
See also AAYA 50

Sienkiewicz, Henryk (Adam Alexander Pius) 1846-1916 .... **TCLC 3**
See also CA 104; 134; CANR 84; DLB 332; EWL 3; RGSF 2; RGWL 2, 3

Sierra, Gregorio Martinez
See Martinez Sierra, Gregorio

Sierra, Maria de la O'LeJarraga Martinez
See Martinez Sierra, Maria

Sigal, Clancy 1926- .... **CLC 7**
See also CA 1-4R; CANR 85, 184; CN 1, 2, 3, 4, 5, 6, 7

Siger of Brabant 1240(?)-1284(?) . **CMLC 69**
See also DLB 115

Sigourney, Lydia H.
See Sigourney, Lydia Howard (Huntley)
See also DLB 73, 183

Sigourney, Lydia Howard (Huntley) 1791-1865 .... **NCLC 21, 87**
See Sigourney, Lydia H.; Sigourney, Lydia Huntley
See also DLB 1

Sigourney, Lydia Huntley
See Sigourney, Lydia Howard (Huntley)
See also DLB 42, 239, 243

Siguenza y Gongora, Carlos de 1645-1700 .... **HLCS 2; LC 8**
See also LAW

Sigurjonsson, Johann
See Sigurjonsson, Johann

Sigurjonsson, Johann 1880-1919 ... **TCLC 27**
See also CA 170; DLB 293; EWL 3

Sikelianos, Angelos 1884-1951 .... **PC 29; TCLC 39**
See also EWL 3; RGWL 2, 3

Silkin, Jon 1930-1997 .... **CLC 2, 6, 43**
See also CA 5-8R; CAAS 5; CANR 89; CP 1, 2, 3, 4, 5, 6; DLB 27

Silko, Leslie 1948- ...... **CLC 23, 74, 114, 211; NNAL; SSC 37, 66; WLCS**
See also AAYA 14; AMWS 4; ANW; BYA 12; CA 115; 122; CANR 45, 65, 118; CN 4, 5, 6, 7; CP 4, 5, 6, 7; CPW 1; CWP; DA; DA3; DAC; DAM MST, MULT, POP; DLB 143, 175, 256, 275; EWL 3; EXPP; EXPS; LAIT 4; MAL 5; MTCW 2; MTFW 2005; NFS 4; PFS 9, 16; RGAL 4; RGSF 2; SSFS 4, 8, 10, 11; TCWW 1, 2

Sillanpaa, Frans Eemil 1888-1964 ... **CLC 19**
See also CA 129; 93-96; DLB 332; EWL 3; MTCW 1

Sillitoe, Alan 1928- .. **CLC 1, 3, 6, 10, 19, 57, 148**
See also AITN 1; BRWS 5; CA 9-12R, 191; CAAE 191; CAAS 2; CANR 8, 26, 55, 139; CDBLB 1960 to Present; CN 1, 2, 3, 4, 5, 6; CP 1, 2, 3, 4, 5; DLB 14, 139; EWL 3; MTCW 1, 2; MTFW 2005; RGEL 2; RGSF 2; SATA 61

Silone, Ignazio 1900-1978 .... **CLC 4**
See also CA 25-28; 81-84; CANR 34; CAP 2; DLB 264; EW 12; EWL 3; MTCW 1; RGSF 2; RGWL 2, 3

Silone, Ignazione
See Silone, Ignazio

Silver, Joan Micklin 1935- .... **CLC 20**
See also CA 114; 121; INT CA-121

Silver, Nicholas
See Faust, Frederick (Schiller)

Silverberg, Robert 1935- .... **CLC 7, 140**
See also AAYA 24; BPFB 3; BYA 7, 9; CA 1-4R, 186; CAAE 186; CAAS 3; CANR 1, 20, 36, 85, 140, 175; CLR 59; CN 6, 7; CPW; DAM POP; DLB 8; INT CANR-20; MAICYA 1, 2; MTCW 1, 2; MTFW 2005; SATA 13, 91; SATA-Essay 104; SCFW 1, 2; SFW 4; SUFW 2

Silverstein, Alvin 1933- .... **CLC 17**
See also CA 49-52; CANR 2; CLR 25; JRDA; MAICYA 1, 2; SATA 8, 69, 124

Silverstein, Shel 1932-1999 .... **PC 49**
See also AAYA 40; BW 3; CA 107; 179; CANR 47, 74, 81; CLR 5, 96; CWRI 5; JRDA; MAICYA 1, 2; MTCW 2; MTFW 2005; SATA 33, 92; SATA-Brief 27; SATA-Obit 116

Silverstein, Virginia B(arbara Opshelor) 1937- .... **CLC 17**
See also CA 49-52; CANR 2; CLR 25; JRDA; MAICYA 1, 2; SATA 8, 69, 124

Sim, Georges
See Simenon, Georges (Jacques Christian)

Simak, Clifford D(onald) 1904-1988 . **CLC 1, 55**
See also CA 1-4R; 125; CANR 1, 35; DLB 8; MTCW 1; SATA-Obit 56; SCFW 1, 2; SFW 4

Simenon, Georges (Jacques Christian) 1903-1989 .... **CLC 1, 2, 3, 8, 18, 47**
See also BPFB 3; CA 85-88; 129; CANR 35; CMW 4; DA3; DAM POP; DLB 72; DLBY 1989; EW 12; EWL 3; GFL 1789 to the Present; MSW; MTCW 1, 2; MTFW 2005; RGWL 2, 3

Simic, Charles 1938- .... **CLC 6, 9, 22, 49, 68, 130, 256; PC 69**
See also AAYA 78; AMWS 8; CA 29-32R; CAAS 4; CANR 12, 33, 52, 61, 96, 140; CP 2, 3, 4, 5, 6, 7; DA3; DAM POET; DLB 105; MAL 5; MTCW 2; MTFW 2005; PFS 7; RGAL 4; WP

Simmel, Georg 1858-1918 .... **TCLC 64**
See also CA 157; DLB 296

Simmons, Charles (Paul) 1924- .... **CLC 57**
See also CA 89-92; INT CA-89-92

Simmons, Dan 1948- .... **CLC 44**
See also AAYA 16, 54; CA 138; CANR 53, 81, 126, 174; CPW; DAM POP; HGG; SUFW 2

Simmons, James (Stewart Alexander) 1933- .... **CLC 43**
See also CA 105; CAAS 21; CP 1, 2, 3, 4, 5, 6, 7; DLB 40

Simmons, Richard
See Simmons, Dan

Simms, William Gilmore 1806-1870 .... **NCLC 3**
See also DLB 3, 30, 59, 73, 248, 254; RGAL 4

Simon, Carly 1945- .... **CLC 26**
See also CA 105

Simon, Claude 1913-2005 ... **CLC 4, 9, 15, 39**
See also CA 89-92; 241; CANR 33, 117; CWW 2; DAM NOV; DLB 83, 332; EW 13; EWL 3; GFL 1789 to the Present; MTCW 1

Simon, Claude Eugene Henri
See Simon, Claude

Simon, Claude Henri Eugene
See Simon, Claude

Simon, Marvin Neil
See Simon, Neil

Simon, Myles
See Follett, Ken

Simon, Neil 1927- .... **CLC 6, 11, 31, 39, 70, 233; DC 14**
See also AAYA 32; AITN 1; AMWS 4; CA 21-24R; CAD; CANR 26, 54, 87, 126; CD 5, 6; DA3; DAM DRAM; DFS 2, 6, 12, 18,, 24; DLB 7, 266; LAIT 4; MAL 5; MTCW 1, 2; MTFW 2005; RGAL 4; TUS

Simon, Paul 1941(?)- .... **CLC 17**
See also CA 116; 153; CANR 152

Simon, Paul Frederick
See Simon, Paul

Simonon, Paul 1956(?)- .... **CLC 30**

Simonson, Rick **CLC 70**

Simpson, Harriette
See Arnow, Harriette (Louisa) Simpson

Simpson, Louis 1923- ... **CLC 4, 7, 9, 32, 149**
See also AMWS 9; CA 1-4R; CAAS 4; CANR 1, 61, 140; CP 1, 2, 3, 4, 5, 6, 7; DAM POET; DLB 5; MAL 5; MTCW 1, 2; MTFW 2005; PFS 7, 11, 14; RGAL 4

Simpson, Mona 1957- .... **CLC 44, 146**
See also CA 122; 135; CANR 68, 103; CN 6, 7; EWL 3

Simpson, Mona Elizabeth
See Simpson, Mona

Simpson, N(orman) F(rederick) 1919- .... **CLC 29**
See also CA 13-16R; CBD; DLB 13; RGEL 2

Sinclair, Andrew (Annandale) 1935- . **CLC 2, 14**
See also CA 9-12R; CAAS 5; CANR 14, 38, 91; CN 1, 2, 3, 4, 5, 6, 7; DLB 14; FANT; MTCW 1

Sinclair, Emil
See Hesse, Hermann

Sinclair, Iain 1943- .... **CLC 76**
See also CA 132; CANR 81, 157; CP 5, 6, 7; HGG

Sinclair, Iain MacGregor
  See Sinclair, Iain
Sinclair, Irene
  See Griffith, D.W.
Sinclair, Julian
  See Sinclair, May
Sinclair, Mary Amelia St. Clair (?)-
  See Sinclair, May
Sinclair, May 1865-1946 .... TCLC 3, 11
  See also CA 104; 166; DLB 36, 135; EWL
  3; HGG; RGEL 2; RHW; SUFW
Sinclair, Roy
  See Griffith, D.W.
Sinclair, Upton 1878-1968 ...... CLC 1, 11, 15,
  63; TCLC 160; WLC 5
  See also AAYA 63; AMWS 5; BPFB 3;
  BYA 2; CA 5-8R; 25-28R; CANR 7;
  CDALB 1929-1941; DA; DA3; DAB;
  DAC; DAM MST, NOV; DLB 9; EWL 3;
  INT CANR-7; LAIT 3; MAL 5; MTCW
  1, 2; MTFW 2005; NFS 6; RGAL 4;
  SATA 9; TUS; YAW
Sinclair, Upton Beall
  See Sinclair, Upton
Singe, (Edmund) J(ohn) M(illington)
  1871-1909 .... WLC
Singer, Isaac
  See Singer, Isaac Bashevis
Singer, Isaac Bashevis 1904-1991 .. CLC 1, 3,
  6, 9, 11, 15, 23, 38, 69, 111; SSC 3, 53,
  80; WLC 5
  See also AAYA 32; AITN 1, 2; AMW;
  AMWR 2; BPFB 3; BYA 1, 4; CA 1-4R;
  134; CANR 1, 39, 106; CDALB 1941-
  1968; CLR 1; CN 1, 2, 3, 4; CWRI 5;
  DA; DA3; DAB; DAC; DAM MST, NOV;
  DLB 6, 28, 52, 278, 332, 333; DLBY
  1991; EWL 3; EXPS; HGG; JRDA; LAIT
  3; MAICYA 1, 2; MAL 5; MTCW 1, 2;
  MTFW 2005; RGAL 4; RGHL; RGSF 2;
  SATA 3, 27; SATA-Obit 68; SSFS 2, 12,
  16; TUS; TWA
Singer, Israel Joshua 1893-1944 .... TCLC 33
  See also CA 169; DLB 333; EWL 3
Singh, Khushwant 1915- .... CLC 11
  See also CA 9-12R; CAAS 9; CANR 6, 84;
  CN 1, 2, 3, 4, 5, 6, 7; DLB 323; EWL 3;
  RGEL 2
Singleton, Ann
  See Benedict, Ruth
Singleton, John 1968(?)- .... CLC 156
  See also AAYA 50; BW 2, 3; CA 138;
  CANR 67, 82; DAM MULT
Siniavskii, Andrei
  See Sinyavsky, Andrei (Donatevich)
  See also CWW 2
Sinjohn, John
  See Galsworthy, John
Sinyavsky, Andrei (Donatevich)
  1925-1997 .... CLC 8
  See Siniavskii, Andrei; Sinyavsky, Andrey
  Donatovich; Tertz, Abram
  See also CA 85-88; 159
Sinyavsky, Andrey Donatovich
  See Sinyavsky, Andrei (Donatevich)
  See also EWL 3
Sirin, V.
  See Nabokov, Vladimir (Vladimirovich)
Sissman, L(ouis) E(dward)
  1928-1976 .... CLC 9, 18
  See also CA 21-24R; 65-68; CANR 13; CP
  2; DLB 5
Sisson, C(harles) H(ubert)
  1914-2003 .... CLC 8
  See also BRWS 11; CA 1-4R; 220; CAAS
  3; CANR 3, 48, 84; CP 1, 2, 3, 4, 5, 6, 7;
  DLB 27
Sitting Bull 1831(?)-1890 .... NNAL
  See also DA3; DAM MULT

Sitwell, Dame Edith 1887-1964 ..... CLC 2, 9,
  67; PC 3
  See also BRW 7; CA 9-12R; CANR 35;
  CDBLB 1945-1960; DAM POET; DLB
  20; EWL 3; MTCW 1, 2; MTFW 2005;
  RGEL 2; TEA
Siwaarmill, H. P.
  See Sharp, William
Sjoewall, Maj 1935- .... CLC 7
  See Sjowall, Maj
  See also CA 65-68; CANR 73
Sjowall, Maj
  See Sjoewall, Maj
  See also BPFB 3; CMW 4; MSW
Skelton, John 1460(?)-1529 ..... LC 71; PC 25
  See also BRW 1; DLB 136; RGEL 2
Skelton, Robin 1925-1997 .... CLC 13
  See Zuk, Georges
  See also AITN 2; CA 5-8R; 160; CAAS 5;
  CANR 28, 89; CCA 1; CP 1, 2, 3, 4, 5, 6;
  DLB 27, 53
Skolimowski, Jerzy 1938- .... CLC 20
  See also CA 128
Skram, Amalie (Bertha)
  1847-1905 .... TCLC 25
  See also CA 165
Skvorecky, Josef 1924- . CLC 15, 39, 69, 152
  See also CA 61-64; CAAS 1; CANR 10,
  34, 63, 108; CDWLB 4; CWW 2; DA3;
  DAC; DAM NOV; DLB 232; EWL 3;
  MTCW 1, 2; MTFW 2005
Slade, Bernard 1930- .... CLC 11, 46
  See Newbound, Bernard Slade
  See also CAAS 9; CCA 1; CD 6; DLB 53
Slaughter, Carolyn 1946- .... CLC 56
  See also CA 85-88; CANR 85, 169; CN 5,
  6, 7
Slaughter, Frank G(ill) 1908-2001 ... CLC 29
  See also AITN 2; CA 5-8R; 197; CANR 5,
  85; INT CANR-5; RHW
Slavitt, David R. 1935- .... CLC 5, 14
  See also CA 21-24R; CAAS 3; CANR 41,
  83, 166; CN 1, 2; CP 1, 2, 3, 4, 5, 6, 7;
  DLB 5, 6
Slavitt, David Rytman
  See Slavitt, David R.
Slesinger, Tess 1905-1945 .... TCLC 10
  See also CA 107; 199; DLB 102
Slessor, Kenneth 1901-1971 .... CLC 14
  See also CA 102; 89-92; DLB 260; RGEL
  2
Slowacki, Juliusz 1809-1849 .... NCLC 15
  See also RGWL 3
Smart, Christopher 1722-1771 .... LC 3, 134;
  PC 13
  See also DAM POET; DLB 109; RGEL 2
Smart, Elizabeth 1913-1986 .... CLC 54
  See also CA 81-84; 118; CN 4; DLB 88
Smiley, Jane 1949- ...... CLC 53, 76, 144, 236
  See also AAYA 66; AMWS 6; BPFB 3; CA
  104; CANR 30, 50, 74, 96, 158; CN 6, 7;
  CPW 1; DA3; DAM POP; DLB 227, 234;
  EWL 3; INT CANR-30; MAL 5; MTFW
  2005; SSFS 19
Smiley, Jane Graves
  See Smiley, Jane
Smith, A(rthur) J(ames) M(arshall)
  1902-1980 .... CLC 15
  See also CA 1-4R; 102; CANR 4; CP 1, 2,
  3; DAC; DLB 88; RGEL 2
Smith, Adam 1723(?)-1790 .... LC 36
  See also DLB 104, 252, 336; RGEL 2
Smith, Alexander 1829-1867 .... NCLC 59
  See also DLB 32, 55
Smith, Anna Deavere 1950- ...... CLC 86, 241
  See also CA 133; CANR 103; CD 5, 6; DFS
  2, 22; DLB 341

Smith, Betty (Wehner) 1904-1972 .... CLC 19
  See also AAYA 72; BPFB 3; BYA 3; CA
  5-8R; 33-36R; DLBY 1982; LAIT 3;
  RGAL 4; SATA 6
Smith, Charlotte (Turner)
  1749-1806 .... NCLC 23, 115
  See also DLB 39, 109; RGEL 2; TEA
Smith, Clark Ashton 1893-1961 .... CLC 43
  See also AAYA 76; CA 143; CANR 81;
  FANT; HGG; MTCW 2; SCFW 1, 2; SFW
  4; SUFW
Smith, Dave CLC 22, 42
  See Smith, David (Jeddie)
  See also CAAS 7; CP 3, 4, 5, 6, 7; DLB 5
Smith, David (Jeddie) 1942-
  See Smith, Dave
  See also CA 49-52; CANR 1, 59, 120;
  CSW; DAM POET
Smith, Iain Crichton 1928-1998 .... CLC 64
  See also BRWS 9; CA 21-24R; 171; CN 1,
  2, 3, 4, 5, 6; CP 1, 2, 3, 4, 5, 6; DLB 40,
  139, 319; RGSF 2
Smith, John 1580(?)-1631 .... LC 9
  See also DLB 24, 30; TUS
Smith, Johnston
  See Crane, Stephen (Townley)
Smith, Joseph, Jr. 1805-1844 .... NCLC 53
Smith, Kevin 1970- .... CLC 223
  See also AAYA 37; CA 166; CANR 131
Smith, Lee 1944- .... CLC 25, 73, 258
  See also CA 114; 119; CANR 46, 118, 173;
  CN 7; CSW; DLB 143; DLBY 1983;
  EWL 3; INT CA-119; RGAL 4
Smith, Martin
  See Smith, Martin Cruz
Smith, Martin Cruz 1942- .. CLC 25; NNAL
  See Smith, Martin Cruz
  See also BEST 89:4; BPFB 3; CA 85-88;
  CANR 6, 23, 43, 65, 119, 184; CMW 4;
  CPW; DAM MULT, POP; HGG; INT
  CANR-23; MTCW 2; MTFW 2005;
  RGAL 4
Smith, Patti 1946- .... CLC 12
  See also CA 93-96; CANR 63, 168
Smith, Pauline (Urmson)
  1882-1959 .... TCLC 25
  See also DLB 225; EWL 3
Smith, Rosamond
  See Oates, Joyce Carol
Smith, Seba 1792-1868 .... NCLC 187
  See also DLB 1, 11, 243
Smith, Sheila Kaye
  See Kaye-Smith, Sheila
Smith, Stevie 1902-1971 .... CLC 3, 8, 25, 44;
  PC 12
  See also BRWS 2; CA 17-18; 29-32R;
  CANR 35; CAP 2; CP 1; DAM POET;
  DLB 20; EWL 3; MTCW 1, 2; PAB; PFS
  3; RGEL 2; TEA
Smith, Wilbur 1933- .... CLC 33
  See also CA 13-16R; CANR 7, 46, 66, 134,
  180; CPW; MTCW 1, 2; MTFW 2005
Smith, Wilbur Addison
  See Smith, Wilbur
Smith, William Jay 1918- .... CLC 6
  See also AMWS 13; CA 5-8R; CANR 44,
  106; CP 1, 2, 3, 4, 5, 6, 7; CSW; CWRI
  5; DLB 5; MAICYA 1, 2; SAAS 22;
  SATA 2, 68, 154; SATA-Essay 154; TCLE
  1:2
Smith, Woodrow Wilson
  See Kuttner, Henry
Smith, Zadie 1975- .... CLC 158
  See also AAYA 50; CA 193; MTFW 2005
Smolenskin, Peretz 1842-1885 .... NCLC 30
Smollett, Tobias (George) 1721-1771 ... LC 2,
  46
  See also BRW 3; CDBLB 1660-1789; DLB
  39, 104; RGEL 2; TEA

Snodgrass, W.D. 1926- .... **CLC 2, 6, 10, 18, 68; PC 74**
See also AMWS 6; CA 1-4R; CANR 6, 36, 65, 85; CP 1, 2, 3, 4, 5, 6, 7; DAM POET; DLB 5; MAL 5; MTCW 1, 2; MTFW 2005; PFS 29; RGAL 4; TCLE 1:2

Snorri Sturluson 1179-1241 .... **CMLC 56**
See also RGWL 2, 3

Snow, C(harles) P(ercy) 1905-1980 ... **CLC 1, 4, 6, 9, 13, 19**
See also BRW 7; CA 5-8R; 101; CANR 28; CDBLB 1945-1960; CN 1, 2; DAM NOV; DLB 15, 77; DLBD 17; EWL 3; MTCW 1, 2; MTFW 2005; RGEL 2; TEA

Snow, Frances Compton
See Adams, Henry (Brooks)

Snyder, Gary 1930- . **CLC 1, 2, 5, 9, 32, 120; PC 21**
See also AAYA 72; AMWS 8; ANW; BG 1:3; CA 17-20R; CANR 30, 60, 125; CP 1, 2, 3, 4, 5, 6, 7; DA3; DAM POET; DLB 5, 16, 165, 212, 237, 275, 342; EWL 3; MAL 5; MTCW 2; MTFW 2005; PFS 9, 19; RGAL 4; WP

Snyder, Zilpha Keatley 1927- .... **CLC 17**
See also AAYA 15; BYA 1; CA 9-12R, 252; CAAE 252; CANR 38; CLR 31, 121; JRDA; MAICYA 1, 2; SAAS 2; SATA 1, 28, 75, 110, 163; SATA-Essay 112, 163; YAW

Soares, Bernardo
See Pessoa, Fernando

Sobh, A.
See Shamlu, Ahmad

Sobh, Alef
See Shamlu, Ahmad

Sobol, Joshua 1939- .... **CLC 60**
See Sobol, Yehoshua
See also CA 200; RGHL

Sobol, Yehoshua 1939-
See Sobol, Joshua
See also CWW 2

Socrates 470B.C.-399B.C. .... **CMLC 27**

Soderberg, Hjalmar 1869-1941 ...... **TCLC 39**
See also DLB 259; EWL 3; RGSF 2

Soderbergh, Steven 1963- .... **CLC 154**
See also AAYA 43; CA 243

Soderbergh, Steven Andrew
See Soderbergh, Steven

Sodergran, Edith (Irene) 1892-1923
See Soedergran, Edith (Irene)
See also CA 202; DLB 259; EW 11; EWL 3; RGWL 2, 3

Soedergran, Edith (Irene)
1892-1923 .... **TCLC 31**
See Sodergran, Edith (Irene)

Softly, Edgar
See Lovecraft, H. P.

Softly, Edward
See Lovecraft, H. P.

Sokolov, Alexander V(sevolodovich) 1943-
See Sokolov, Sasha
See also CA 73-76

Sokolov, Raymond 1941- .... **CLC 7**
See also CA 85-88

Sokolov, Sasha **CLC 59**
See Sokolov, Alexander V(sevolodovich)
See also CWW 2; DLB 285; EWL 3; RGWL 2, 3

Solo, Jay
See Ellison, Harlan

Sologub, Fyodor **TCLC 9**
See Teternikov, Fyodor Kuzmich
See also EWL 3

Solomons, Ikey Esquir
See Thackeray, William Makepeace

Solomos, Dionysios 1798-1857 .... **NCLC 15**

Solwoska, Mara
See French, Marilyn

Solzhenitsyn, Aleksandr 1918-2008 ... **CLC 1, 2, 4, 7, 9, 10, 18, 26, 34, 78, 134, 235; SSC 32, 105; WLC 5**
See Solzhenitsyn, Aleksandr Isayevich
See also AAYA 49; AITN 1; BPFB 3; CA 69-72; CANR 40, 65, 116; DA; DA3; DAB; DAC; DAM MST, NOV; DLB 302, 332; EW 13; EXPS; LAIT 4; MTCW 1, 2; MTFW 2005; NFS 6; RGSF 2; RGWL 2, 3; SSFS 9; TWA

Solzhenitsyn, Aleksandr I.
See Solzhenitsyn, Aleksandr

Solzhenitsyn, Aleksandr Isayevich
See Solzhenitsyn, Aleksandr
See also CWW 2; EWL 3

Somers, Jane
See Lessing, Doris

Somerville, Edith Oenone
1858-1949 .... **SSC 56; TCLC 51**
See also CA 196; DLB 135; RGEL 2; RGSF 2

Somerville & Ross
See Martin, Violet Florence; Somerville, Edith Oenone

Sommer, Scott 1951- .... **CLC 25**
See also CA 106

Sommers, Christina Hoff 1950- ...... **CLC 197**
See also CA 153; CANR 95

Sondheim, Stephen 1930- .. **CLC 30, 39, 147; DC 22**
See also AAYA 11, 66; CA 103; CANR 47, 67, 125; DAM DRAM; DFS 25; LAIT 4

Sondheim, Stephen Joshua
See Sondheim, Stephen

Sone, Monica 1919- .... **AAL**
See also DLB 312

Song, Cathy 1955- .... **AAL; PC 21**
See also CA 154; CANR 118; CWP; DLB 169, 312; EXPP; FW; PFS 5

Sontag, Susan 1933-2004 ... **CLC 1, 2, 10, 13, 31, 105, 195**
See also AMWS 3; CA 17-20R; 234; CANR 25, 51, 74, 97, 184; CN 1, 2, 3, 4, 5, 6, 7; CPW; DA3; DAM POP; DLB 2, 67; EWL 3; MAL 5; MBL; MTCW 1, 2; MTFW 2005; RGAL 4; RHW; SSFS 10

Sophocles 496(?)B.C.-406(?)B.C. .... **CMLC 2, 47, 51, 86; DC 1; WLCS**
See also AW 1; CDWLB 1; DA; DA3; DAB; DAC; DAM DRAM, MST; DFS 1, 4, 8, 24; DLB 176; LAIT 1; LATS 1:1; LMFS 1; RGWL 2, 3; TWA; WLIT 8

Sordello 1189-1269 .... **CMLC 15**

Sorel, Georges 1847-1922 .... **TCLC 91**
See also CA 118; 188

Sorel, Julia
See Drexler, Rosalyn

Sorokin, Vladimir **CLC 59**
See Sorokin, Vladimir Georgievich
See also CA 258

Sorokin, Vladimir Georgievich
See Sorokin, Vladimir
See also DLB 285

Sorrentino, Gilbert 1929-2006 .... **CLC 3, 7, 14, 22, 40, 247**
See also CA 77-80; 250; CANR 14, 33, 115, 157; CN 3, 4, 5, 6, 7; CP 1, 2, 3, 4, 5, 6, 7; DLB 5, 173; DLBY 1980; INT CANR-14

Soseki
See Natsume, Soseki
See also MJW

Soto, Gary 1952- ... **CLC 32, 80; HLC 2; PC 28**
See also AAYA 10, 37; BYA 11; CA 119; 125; CANR 50, 74, 107, 157; CLR 38; CP 4, 5, 6, 7; DAM MULT; DLB 82; EWL 3; EXPP; HW 1, 2; INT CA-125;

JRDA; LLW; MAICYA 2; MAICYAS 1; MAL 5; MTCW 2; MTFW 2005; PFS 7; RGAL 4; SATA 80, 120, 174; WYA; YAW

Soupault, Philippe 1897-1990 .... **CLC 68**
See also CA 116; 147; 131; EWL 3; GFL 1789 to the Present; LMFS 2

Souster, (Holmes) Raymond 1921- .... **CLC 5, 14**
See also CA 13-16R; CAAS 14; CANR 13, 29, 53; CP 1, 2, 3, 4, 5, 6, 7; DA3; DAC; DAM POET; DLB 88; RGEL 2; SATA 63

Southern, Terry 1924(?)-1995 .... **CLC 7**
See also AMWS 11; BPFB 3; CA 1-4R; 150; CANR 1, 55, 107; CN 1, 2, 3, 4, 5, 6; DLB 2; IDFW 3, 4

Southerne, Thomas 1660-1746 .... **LC 99**
See also DLB 80; RGEL 2

Southey, Robert 1774-1843 .... **NCLC 8, 97**
See also BRW 4; DLB 93, 107, 142; RGEL 2; SATA 54

Southwell, Robert 1561(?)-1595 .... **LC 108**
See also DLB 167; RGEL 2; TEA

Southworth, Emma Dorothy Eliza Nevitte
1819-1899 .... **NCLC 26**
See also DLB 239

Souza, Ernest
See Scott, Evelyn

Soyinka, Wole 1934- .. **BLC 1:3, 2:3; CLC 3, 5, 14, 36, 44, 179; DC 2; WLC 5**
See also AFW; BW 2, 3; CA 13-16R; CANR 27, 39, 82, 136; CD 5, 6; CDWLB 3; CN 6, 7; CP 1, 2, 3, 4, 5, 6 ,7; DA; DA3; DAB; DAC; DAM DRAM, MST, MULT; DFS 10; DLB 125, 332; EWL 3; MTCW 1, 2; MTFW 2005; PFS 27; RGEL 2; TWA; WLIT 2; WWE 1

Spackman, W(illiam) M(ode)
1905-1990 .... **CLC 46**
See also CA 81-84; 132

Spacks, Barry (Bernard) 1931- .... **CLC 14**
See also CA 154; CANR 33, 109; CP 3, 4, 5, 6, 7; DLB 105

Spanidou, Irini 1946- .... **CLC 44**
See also CA 185; CANR 179

Spark, Muriel 1918-2006 .... **CLC 2, 3, 5, 8, 13, 18, 40, 94, 242; SSC 10, 115**
See also BRWS 1; CA 5-8R; 251; CANR 12, 36, 76, 89, 131; CDBLB 1945-1960; CN 1, 2, 3, 4, 5, 6, 7; CP 1, 2, 3, 4, 5, 6, 7; DA3; DAB; DAC; DAM MST, NOV; DLB 15, 139; EWL 3; FW; INT CANR-12; LAIT 4; MTCW 1, 2; MTFW 2005; NFS 22; RGEL 2; TEA; WLIT 4; YAW

Spark, Muriel Sarah
See Spark, Muriel

Spaulding, Douglas
See Bradbury, Ray

Spaulding, Leonard
See Bradbury, Ray

Speght, Rachel 1597-c. 1630 .... **LC 97**
See also DLB 126

Spence, J. A. D.
See Eliot, T(homas) S(tearns)

Spencer, Anne 1882-1975 ...... **HR 1:3; PC 77**
See also BW 2; CA 161; DLB 51, 54

Spencer, Elizabeth 1921- .... **CLC 22; SSC 57**
See also CA 13-16R; CANR 32, 65, 87; CN 1, 2, 3, 4, 5, 6, 7; CSW; DLB 6, 218; EWL 3; MTCW 1; RGAL 4; SATA 14

Spencer, Leonard G.
See Silverberg, Robert

Spencer, Scott 1945- .... **CLC 30**
See also CA 113; CANR 51, 148; DLBY 1986

Spender, Stephen 1909-1995 ..... **CLC 1, 2, 5, 10, 41, 91; PC 71**
See also BRWS 2; CA 9-12R; 149; CANR 31, 54; CDBLB 1945-1960; CP 1, 2, 3, 4, 5, 6; DA3; DAM POET; DLB 20; EWL 3; MTCW 1, 2; MTFW 2005; PAB; PFS 23; RGEL 2; TEA

Spengler, Oswald (Arnold Gottfried)
1880-1936 .... **TCLC 25**
See also CA 118; 189

Spenser, Edmund 1552(?)-1599 ...... **LC 5, 39,
117; PC 8, 42; WLC 5**
See also AAYA 60; BRW 1; CDBLB Before
1660; DA; DA3; DAB; DAC; DAM MST,
POET; DLB 167; EFS 2; EXPP; PAB;
RGEL 2; TEA; WLIT 3; WP

Spicer, Jack 1925-1965 .... **CLC 8, 18, 72**
See also BG 1:3; CA 85-88; DAM POET;
DLB 5, 16, 193; GLL 1; WP

Spiegelman, Art 1948- .... **CLC 76, 178**
See also AAYA 10, 46; CA 125; CANR 41,
55, 74, 124; DLB 299; MTCW 2; MTFW
2005; RGHL; SATA 109, 158; YAW

Spielberg, Peter 1929- .... **CLC 6**
See also CA 5-8R; CANR 4, 48; DLBY
1981

Spielberg, Steven 1947- .... **CLC 20, 188**
See also AAYA 8, 24; CA 77-80; CANR
32; SATA 32

Spillane, Frank Morrison
See Spillane, Mickey
See also BPFB 3; CMW 4; DLB 226; MSW

Spillane, Mickey 1918-2006 .. **CLC 3, 13, 241**
See Spillane, Frank Morrison
See also CA 25-28R; 252; CANR 28, 63,
125; DA3; MTCW 1, 2; MTFW 2005;
SATA 66; SATA-Obit 176

Spinoza, Benedictus de 1632-1677 .. **LC 9, 58**

Spinrad, Norman (Richard) 1940- ... **CLC 46**
See also BPFB 3; CA 37-40R, 233; CAAE
233; CAAS 19; CANR 20, 91; DLB 8;
INT CANR-20; SFW 4

Spitteler, Carl 1845-1924 .... **TCLC 12**
See also CA 109; DLB 129, 332; EWL 3

Spitteler, Karl Friedrich Georg
See Spitteler, Carl

Spivack, Kathleen (Romola Drucker)
1938- .... **CLC 6**
See also CA 49-52

Spivak, Gayatri Chakravorty
1942- .... **CLC 233**
See also CA 110; 154; CANR 91; FW;
LMFS 2

Spofford, Harriet (Elizabeth) Prescott
1835-1921 .... **SSC 87**
See also CA 201; DLB 74, 221

Spoto, Donald 1941- .... **CLC 39**
See also CA 65-68; CANR 11, 57, 93, 173

Springsteen, Bruce 1949- .... **CLC 17**
See also CA 111

Springsteen, Bruce F.
See Springsteen, Bruce

Spurling, Hilary 1940- .... **CLC 34**
See also CA 104; CANR 25, 52, 94, 157

Spurling, Susan Hilary
See Spurling, Hilary

Spyker, John Howland
See Elman, Richard (Martin)

Squared, A.
See Abbott, Edwin A.

Squires, (James) Radcliffe
1917-1993 .... **CLC 51**
See also CA 1-4R; 140; CANR 6, 21; CP 1,
2, 3, 4, 5

Srivastava, Dhanpat Rai 1880(?)-1936
See Premchand
See also CA 118; 197

Ssu-ma Ch'ien c. 145B.C.-c.
86B.C. .... **CMLC 96**

Ssu-ma T'an (?)-c. 110B.C. .... **CMLC 96**

Stacy, Donald
See Pohl, Frederik

Stael
See Stael-Holstein, Anne Louise Germaine
Necker
See also EW 5; RGWL 2, 3

Stael, Germaine de
See Stael-Holstein, Anne Louise Germaine
Necker
See also DLB 119, 192; FL 1:3; FW; GFL
1789 to the Present; TWA

**Stael-Holstein, Anne Louise Germaine
Necker** 1766-1817 .... **NCLC 3, 91**
See Stael; Stael, Germaine de

Stafford, Jean 1915-1979 .. **CLC 4, 7, 19, 68;
SSC 26, 86**
See also CA 1-4R; 85-88; CANR 3, 65; CN
1, 2; DLB 2, 173; MAL 5; MTCW 1, 2;
MTFW 2005; RGAL 4; RGSF 2; SATA-
Obit 22; SSFS 21; TCWW 1, 2; TUS

Stafford, William (Edgar)
1914-1993 .... **CLC 4, 7, 29; PC 71**
See also AMWS 11; CA 5-8R; 142; CAAS
3; CANR 5, 22; CP 1, 2, 3, 4, 5; DAM
POET; DLB 5, 206; EXPP; INT CANR-
22; MAL 5; PFS 2, 8, 16; RGAL 4; WP

Stagnelius, Eric Johan 1793-1823 . **NCLC 61**

Staines, Trevor
See Brunner, John (Kilian Houston)

Stairs, Gordon
See Austin, Mary (Hunter)

Stalin, Joseph 1879-1953 .... **TCLC 92**

Stampa, Gaspara c. 1524-1554 .. **LC 114; PC
43**
See also RGWL 2, 3; WLIT 7

Stampflinger, K.A.
See Benjamin, Walter

Stancykowna
See Szymborska, Wislawa

Standing Bear, Luther
1868(?)-1939(?) .... **NNAL**
See also CA 113; 144; DAM MULT

Stanislavsky, Constantin
1863(?)-1938 .... **TCLC 167**
See also CA 118

Stanislavsky, Konstantin
See Stanislavsky, Constantin

Stanislavsky, Konstantin Sergeievich
See Stanislavsky, Constantin

Stanislavsky, Konstantin Sergeivich
See Stanislavsky, Constantin

Stanislavsky, Konstantin Sergeyevich
See Stanislavsky, Constantin

Stannard, Martin 1947- .... **CLC 44**
See also CA 142; DLB 155

Stanton, Elizabeth Cady
1815-1902 .... **TCLC 73**
See also CA 171; DLB 79; FL 1:3; FW

Stanton, Maura 1946- .... **CLC 9**
See also CA 89-92; CANR 15, 123; DLB
120

Stanton, Schuyler
See Baum, L(yman) Frank

Stapledon, (William) Olaf
1886-1950 .... **TCLC 22**
See also CA 111; 162; DLB 15, 255; SCFW
1, 2; SFW 4

Starbuck, George (Edwin)
1931-1996 .... **CLC 53**
See also CA 21-24R; 153; CANR 23; CP 1,
2, 3, 4, 5, 6; DAM POET

Stark, Richard
See Westlake, Donald E.

Statius c. 45-c. 96 .... **CMLC 91**
See also AW 2; DLB 211

Staunton, Schuyler
See Baum, L(yman) Frank

Stead, Christina (Ellen) 1902-1983 ... **CLC 2,
5, 8, 32, 80**
See also BRWS 4; CA 13-16R; 109; CANR
33, 40; CN 1, 2, 3; DLB 260; EWL 3;
FW; MTCW 1, 2; MTFW 2005; NFS 27;
RGEL 2; RGSF 2; WWE 1

Stead, William Thomas
1849-1912 .... **TCLC 48**
See also BRWS 13; CA 167

Stebnitsky, M.
See Leskov, Nikolai (Semyonovich)

Steele, Richard 1672-1729 .... **LC 18, 156**
See also BRW 3; CDBLB 1660-1789; DLB
84, 101; RGEL 2; WLIT 3

Steele, Timothy (Reid) 1948- .... **CLC 45**
See also CA 93-96; CANR 16, 50, 92; CP
5, 6, 7; DLB 120, 282

Steffens, (Joseph) Lincoln
1866-1936 .... **TCLC 20**
See also CA 117; 198; DLB 303; MAL 5

Stegner, Wallace (Earle) 1909-1993 .. **CLC 9,
49, 81; SSC 27**
See also AITN 1; AMWS 4; ANW; BEST
90:3; BPFB 3; CA 1-4R; 141; CAAS 9;
CANR 1, 21, 46; CN 1, 2, 3, 4, 5; DAM
NOV; DLB 9, 206, 275; DLBY 1993;
EWL 3; MAL 5; MTCW 1, 2; MTFW
2005; RGAL 4; TCWW 1, 2; TUS

Stein, Gertrude 1874-1946 .... **DC 19; PC 18;
SSC 42, 105; TCLC 1, 6, 28, 48; WLC
5**
See also AAYA 64; AMW; AMWC 2; CA
104; 132; CANR 108; CDALB 1917-
1929; DA; DA3; DAB; DAC; DAM MST,
NOV, POET; DLB 4, 54, 86, 228; DLBD
15; EWL 3; EXPS; FL 1:6; GLL 1; MAL
5; MBL; MTCW 1, 2; MTFW 2005;
NCFS 4; NFS 27; RGAL 4; RGSF 2;
SSFS 5; TUS; WP

Steinbeck, John (Ernst) 1902-1968 ... **CLC 1,
5, 9, 13, 21, 34, 45, 75, 124; SSC 11, 37,
77; TCLC 135; WLC 5**
See also AAYA 12; AMW; BPFB 3; BYA 2,
3, 13; CA 1-4R; 25-28R; CANR 1, 35;
CDALB 1929-1941; DA; DA3; DAB;
DAC; DAM DRAM, MST, NOV; DLB 7,
9, 212, 275, 309, 332; DLBD 2; EWL 3;
EXPS; LAIT 3; MAL 5; MTCW 1, 2;
MTFW 2005; NFS 1, 5, 7, 17, 19, 28;
RGAL 4; RGSF 2; RHW; SATA 9; SSFS
3, 6, 22; TCWW 1, 2; TUS; WYA; YAW

Steinem, Gloria 1934- .... **CLC 63**
See also CA 53-56; CANR 28, 51, 139;
DLB 246; FL 1:1; FW; MTCW 1, 2;
MTFW 2005

Steiner, George 1929- .... **CLC 24, 221**
See also CA 73-76; CANR 31, 67, 108;
DAM NOV; DLB 67, 299; EWL 3;
MTCW 1, 2; MTFW 2005; RGHL; SATA
62

Steiner, K. Leslie
See Delany, Samuel R., Jr.

Steiner, Rudolf 1861-1925 .... **TCLC 13**
See also CA 107

Stendhal 1783-1842 .... **NCLC 23, 46, 178;
SSC 27; WLC 5**
See also DA; DA3; DAB; DAC; DAM
MST, NOV; DLB 119; EW 5; GFL 1789
to the Present; RGWL 2, 3; TWA

Stephen, Adeline Virginia
See Woolf, (Adeline) Virginia

Stephen, Sir Leslie 1832-1904 .... **TCLC 23**
See also BRW 5; CA 123; DLB 57, 144,
190

Stephen, Sir Leslie
See Stephen, Sir Leslie

Stephen, Virginia
See Woolf, (Adeline) Virginia

Stephens, James 1882(?)-1950 .... **SSC 50;
TCLC 4**
See also CA 104; 192; DLB 19, 153, 162;
EWL 3; FANT; RGEL 2; SUFW

Stephens, Reed
See Donaldson, Stephen R.

Stephenson, Neal 1959- .... CLC 220
See also AAYA 38; CA 122; CANR 88, 138;
CN 7; MTFW 2005; SFW 4
Steptoe, Lydia
See Barnes, Djuna
See also GLL 1
Sterchi, Beat 1949- .... CLC 65
See also CA 203
Sterling, Brett
See Bradbury, Ray; Hamilton, Edmond
Sterling, Bruce 1954- .... CLC 72
See also AAYA 78; CA 119; CANR 44, 135,
184; CN 7; MTFW 2005; SCFW 2; SFW
4
Sterling, George 1869-1926 .... TCLC 20
See also CA 117; 165; DLB 54
Stern, Gerald 1925- .... CLC 40, 100
See also AMWS 9; CA 81-84; CANR 28,
94; CP 3, 4, 5, 6, 7; DLB 105; PFS 26;
RGAL 4
Stern, Richard (Gustave) 1928- ... CLC 4, 39
See also CA 1-4R; CANR 1, 25, 52, 120;
CN 1, 2, 3, 4, 5, 6, 7; DLB 218; DLBY
1987; INT CANR-25
Sternberg, Josef von 1894-1969 .... CLC 20
See also CA 81-84
Sterne, Laurence 1713-1768 .. LC 2, 48, 156;
WLC 5
See also BRW 3; BRWC 1; CDBLB 1660-
1789; DA; DAB; DAC; DAM MST, NOV;
DLB 39; RGEL 2; TEA
Sternheim, (William Adolf) Carl
1878-1942 .... TCLC 8
See also CA 105; 193; DLB 56, 118; EWL
3; IDTP; RGWL 2, 3
Stevens, Margaret Dean
See Aldrich, Bess Streeter
Stevens, Mark 1951- .... CLC 34
See also CA 122
Stevens, Wallace 1879-1955 . PC 6; TCLC 3,
12, 45; WLC 5
See also AMW; AMWR 1; CA 104; 124;
CANR 181; CDALB 1929-1941; DA;
DA3; DAB; DAC; DAM MST, POET;
DLB 54, 342; EWL 3; EXPP; MAL 5;
MTCW 1, 2; PAB; PFS 13, 16; RGAL 4;
TUS; WP
Stevenson, Anne (Katharine) 1933- .. CLC 7,
33
See also BRWS 6; CA 17-20R; CAAS 9;
CANR 9, 33, 123; CP 3, 4, 5, 6, 7; CWP;
DLB 40; MTCW 1; RHW
Stevenson, Robert Louis (Balfour)
1850-1894 ...... NCLC 5, 14, 63, 193; PC
84; SSC 11, 51; WLC 5
See also AAYA 24; BPFB 3; BRW 5;
BRWC 1; BRWR 1; BYA 1, 2, 4, 13; CD-
BLB 1890-1914; CLR 10, 11, 107; DA;
DA3; DAB; DAC; DAM MST, NOV;
DLB 18, 57, 141, 156, 174; DLBD 13;
GL 3; HGG; JRDA; LAIT 1, 3; MAICYA
1, 2; NFS 11, 20; RGEL 2; RGSF 2;
SATA 100; SUFW; TEA; WCH; WLIT 4;
WYA; YABC 2; YAW
Stewart, J(ohn) I(nnes) M(ackintosh)
1906-1994 .... CLC 7, 14, 32
See Innes, Michael
See also CA 85-88; 147; CAAS 3; CANR
47; CMW 4; CN 1, 2, 3, 4, 5; MTCW 1,
2
Stewart, Mary (Florence Elinor)
1916- .... CLC 7, 35, 117
See also AAYA 29, 73; BPFB 3; CA 1-4R;
CANR 1, 59, 130; CMW 4; CPW; DAB;
FANT; RHW; SATA 12; YAW
Stewart, Mary Rainbow
See Stewart, Mary (Florence Elinor)
Stifle, June
See Campbell, Maria

Stifter, Adalbert 1805-1868 ... NCLC 41, 198;
SSC 28
See also CDWLB 2; DLB 133; RGSF 2;
RGWL 2, 3
Still, James 1906-2001 .... CLC 49
See also CA 65-68; 195; CAAS 17; CANR
10, 26; CSW; DLB 9; DLBY 01; SATA
29; SATA-Obit 127
Sting 1951-
See Sumner, Gordon Matthew
See also CA 167
Stirling, Arthur
See Sinclair, Upton
Stitt, Milan 1941- .... CLC 29
See also CA 69-72
Stockton, Francis Richard 1834-1902
See Stockton, Frank R.
See also AAYA 68; CA 108; 137; MAICYA
1, 2; SATA 44; SFW 4
Stockton, Frank R. TCLC 47
See Stockton, Francis Richard
See also BYA 4, 13; DLB 42, 74; DLBD
13; EXPS; SATA-Brief 32; SSFS 3;
SUFW; WCH
Stoddard, Charles
See Kuttner, Henry
Stoker, Abraham 1847-1912
See Stoker, Bram
See also CA 105; 150; DA; DA3; DAC;
DAM MST, NOV; HGG; MTFW 2005;
SATA 29
Stoker, Bram SSC 62; TCLC 8, 144; WLC 6
See Stoker, Abraham
See also CA 23; BPFB 3; BRWS 3; BYA
5; CDBLB 1890-1914; DAB; DLB 304;
GL 3; LATS 1:1; NFS 18; RGEL 2;
SUFW; TEA; WLIT 4
Stolz, Mary 1920-2006 .... CLC 12
See also AAYA 8, 73; AITN 1; CA 5-8R;
255; CANR 13, 41, 112; JRDA; MAICYA
1, 2; SAAS 3; SATA 10, 71, 133; SATA-
Obit 180; YAW
Stolz, Mary Slattery
See Stolz, Mary
Stone, Irving 1903-1989 .... CLC 7
See also AITN 1; BPFB 3; CA 1-4R; 129;
CAAS 3; CANR 1, 23; CN 1, 2, 3, 4;
CPW; DA3; DAM POP; INT CANR-23;
MTCW 1, 2; MTFW 2005; RHW; SATA
3; SATA-Obit 64
Stone, Oliver 1946- .... CLC 73
See also AAYA 15, 64; CA 110; CANR 55,
125
Stone, Oliver William
See Stone, Oliver
Stone, Robert 1937- .... CLC 5, 23, 42, 175
See also AMWS 5; BPFB 3; CA 85-88;
CANR 23, 66, 95, 173; CN 4, 5, 6, 7;
DLB 152; EWL 3; INT CANR-23; MAL
5; MTCW 1; MTFW 2005
Stone, Robert Anthony
See Stone, Robert
Stone, Ruth 1915- .... PC 53
See also CA 45-48; CANR 2, 91; CP 5, 6,
7; CSW; DLB 105; PFS 19
Stone, Zachary
See Follett, Ken
Stoppard, Tom 1937- ... CLC 1, 3, 4, 5, 8, 15,
29, 34, 63, 91; DC 6, 30; WLC 6
See also AAYA 63; BRWC 1; BRWR 2;
BRWS 1; CA 81-84; CANR 39, 67, 125;
CBD; CD 5, 6; CDBLB 1960 to Present;
DA; DA3; DAB; DAC; DAM DRAM,
MST, POP; DFS 2, 5, 8, 11, 13, 16; DLB 13,
233; DLBY 1985; EWL 3; LATS 1:2;
MTCW 1, 2; MTFW 2005; RGEL 2;
TEA; WLIT 4

Storey, David (Malcolm) 1933- . CLC 2, 4, 5,
8
See also BRWS 1; CA 81-84; CANR 36;
CBD; CD 5, 6; CN 1, 2, 3, 4, 5, 6; DAM
DRAM; DLB 13, 14, 207, 245, 326; EWL
3; MTCW 1; RGEL 2
Storm, Hyemeyohsts 1935- ... CLC 3; NNAL
See also CA 81-84; CANR 45; DAM MULT
Storm, (Hans) Theodor (Woldsen)
1817-1888 ... NCLC 1, 195; SSC 27, 106
See also CDWLB 2; DLB 129; EW; RGSF
2; RGWL 2, 3
Storni, Alfonsina 1892-1938 . HLC 2; PC 33;
TCLC 5
See also CA 104; 131; DAM MULT; DLB
283; HW 1; LAW
Stoughton, William 1631-1701 .... LC 38
See also DLB 24
Stout, Rex (Todhunter) 1886-1975 ..... CLC 3
See also AITN 2; BPFB 3; CA 61-64;
CANR 71; CMW 4; CN 2; DLB 306;
MSW; RGAL 4
Stow, (Julian) Randolph 1935- ... CLC 23, 48
See also CA 13-16R; CANR 33; CN 1, 2,
3, 4, 5, 6; CP 1, 2, 3, 4; DLB 260;
MTCW 1; RGEL 2
Stowe, Harriet (Elizabeth) Beecher
1811-1896 .... NCLC 3, 50, 133, 195;
WLC 6
See also AAYA 53; AMWS 1; CDALB
1865-1917; CLR 131; DA; DA3; DAB;
DAC; DAM MST, NOV; DLB 1, 12, 42,
74, 189, 239, 243; EXPN; FL 1:3; JRDA;
LAIT 2; MAICYA 1, 2; NFS 6; RGAL 4;
TUS; YABC 1
Strabo c. 64B.C.-c. 25 .... CMLC 37
See also DLB 176
Strachey, (Giles) Lytton
1880-1932 .... TCLC 12
See also BRWS 2; CA 110; 178; DLB 149;
DLBD 10; EWL 3; MTCW 2; NCFS 4
Stramm, August 1874-1915 .... PC 50
See also CA 195; EWL 3
Strand, Mark 1934- .. CLC 6, 18, 41, 71; PC
63
See also AMWS 4; CA 21-24R; CANR 40,
65, 100; CP 1, 2, 3, 4, 5, 6, 7; DAM
POET; DLB 5; EWL 3; MAL 5; PAB;
PFS 9, 18; RGAL 4; SATA 41; TCLE 1:2
Stratton-Porter, Gene(va Grace) 1863-1924
See Porter, Gene(va Grace) Stratton
See also ANW; CA 137; CLR 87; DLB 221;
DLBD 14; MAICYA 1, 2; SATA 15
Straub, Peter 1943- .... CLC 28, 107
See also BEST 89:1; BPFB 3; CA 85-88;
CANR 28, 65, 109; CPW; DAM POP;
DLBY 1984; HGG; MTCW 1, 2; MTFW
2005; SUFW 2
Straub, Peter Francis
See Straub, Peter
Strauss, Botho 1944- .... CLC 22
See also CA 157; CWW 2; DLB 124
Strauss, Leo 1899-1973 .... TCLC 141
See also CA 101; 45-48; CANR 122
Streatfeild, Mary Noel
See Streatfeild, Noel
Streatfeild, Noel 1897(?)-1986 .... CLC 21
See also CA 81-84; 120; CANR 31; CLR
17, 83; CWRI 5; DLB 160; MAICYA 1,
2; SATA 20; SATA-Obit 48
Stribling, T(homas) S(igismund)
1881-1965 .... CLC 23
See also CA 189; 107; CMW 4; DLB 9;
RGAL 4
Strindberg, (Johan) August
1849-1912 ... DC 18; TCLC 1, 8, 21, 47;
WLC 6
See also CA 104; 135; DA; DA3; DAB;
DAC; DAM DRAM, MST; DFS 4, 9;

DLB 259; EW 7; EWL 3; IDTP; LMFS
2; MTCW 2; MTFW 2005; RGWL 2, 3;
TWA
Stringer, Arthur 1874-1950 .... **TCLC 37**
See also CA 161; DLB 92
Stringer, David
See Roberts, Keith (John Kingston)
Stroheim, Erich von 1885-1957 ..... **TCLC 71**
Strugatskii, Arkadii (Natanovich)
1925-1991 .... **CLC 27**
See Strugatsky, Arkadii Natanovich
See also CA 106; 135; SFW 4
Strugatskii, Boris (Natanovich)
1933- .... **CLC 27**
See Strugatsky, Boris (Natanovich)
See also CA 106; SFW 4
Strugatsky, Arkadii Natanovich
See Strugatskii, Arkadii (Natanovich)
See also DLB 302
Strugatsky, Boris (Natanovich)
See Strugatskii, Boris (Natanovich)
See also DLB 302
Strummer, Joe 1952-2002 .... **CLC 30**
Strunk, William, Jr. 1869-1946 ...... **TCLC 92**
See also CA 118; 164; NCFS 5
Stryk, Lucien 1924- .... **PC 27**
See also CA 13-16R; CANR 10, 28, 55,
110; CP 1, 2, 3, 4, 5, 6, 7
Stuart, Don A.
See Campbell, John W(ood, Jr.)
Stuart, Ian
See MacLean, Alistair (Stuart)
Stuart, Jesse (Hilton) 1906-1984 ... **CLC 1, 8,
11, 14, 34; SSC 31**
See also CA 5-8R; 112; CANR 31; CN 1,
2, 3; DLB 9, 48, 102; DLBY 1984; SATA
2; SATA-Obit 36
Stubblefield, Sally
See Trumbo, Dalton
Sturgeon, Theodore (Hamilton)
1918-1985 .... **CLC 22, 39**
See Queen, Ellery
See also AAYA 51; BPFB 3; BYA 9, 10;
CA 81-84; 116; CANR 32, 103; DLB 8;
DLBY 1985; HGG; MTCW 1, 2; MTFW
2005; SCFW; SFW 4; SUFW
Sturges, Preston 1898-1959 .... **TCLC 48**
See also CA 114; 149; DLB 26
Styron, William 1925-2006 .. **CLC 1, 3, 5, 11,
15, 60, 232, 244; SSC 25**
See also AMW; AMWC 2; BEST 90:4;
BPFB 3; CA 5-8R; 255; CANR 6, 33, 74,
126; CDALB 1968-1988; CN 1, 2, 3, 4,
5, 6, 7; CPW; CSW; DA3; DAM NOV,
POP; DLB 2, 143, 299; DLBY 1980;
EWL 3; INT CANR-6; LAIT 2; MAL 5;
MTCW 1, 2; MTFW 2005; NCFS 1; NFS
22; RGAL 4; RGHL; RHW; TUS
Styron, William Clark
See Styron, William
Su, Chien 1884-1918
See Su Man-shu
See also CA 123
Suarez Lynch, B.
See Bioy Casares, Adolfo; Borges, Jorge
Luis
Suassuna, Ariano Vilar 1927- .... **HLCS 1**
See also CA 178; DLB 307; HW 2; LAW
Suckert, Kurt Erich
See Malaparte, Curzio
Suckling, Sir John 1609-1642 . **LC 75; PC 30**
See also BRW 2; DAM POET; DLB 58,
126; EXPP; PAB; RGEL 2
Suckow, Ruth 1892-1960 .... **SSC 18**
See also CA 193; 113; DLB 9, 102; RGAL
4; TCWW 2
Sudermann, Hermann 1857-1928 .. **TCLC 15**
See also CA 107; 201; DLB 118

Sue, Eugene 1804-1857 .... **NCLC 1**
See also DLB 119
Sueskind, Patrick 1949- .... **CLC 44, 182**
See Suskind, Patrick
Suetonius c. 70-c. 130 .... **CMLC 60**
See also AW 2; DLB 211; RGWL 2, 3;
WLIT 8
Sukenick, Ronald 1932-2004 ..... **CLC 3, 4, 6,
48**
See also CA 25-28R; 209; 229; CAAE 209;
CAAS 8; CANR 32, 89; CN 3, 4, 5, 6, 7;
DLB 173; DLBY 1981
Suknaski, Andrew 1942- .... **CLC 19**
See also CA 101; CP 3, 4, 5, 6, 7; DLB 53
Sullivan, Vernon
See Vian, Boris
Sully Prudhomme, Rene-Francois-Armand
1839-1907 .... **TCLC 31**
See Prudhomme, Rene Francois Armand
See also DLB 332; GFL 1789 to the Present
Su Man-shu .... **TCLC 24**
See Su, Chien
See also EWL 3
Sumarokov, Aleksandr Petrovich
1717-1777 .... **LC 104**
See also DLB 150
Summerforest, Ivy B.
See Kirkup, James
Summers, Andrew James
See Summers, Andy
Summers, Andy 1942- .... **CLC 26**
See also CA 255
Summers, Hollis (Spurgeon, Jr.)
1916- .... **CLC 10**
See also CA 5-8R; CANR 3; CN 1, 2, 3;
CP 1, 2, 3, 4; DLB 6; TCLE 1:2
**Summers, (Alphonsus Joseph-Mary
Augustus) Montague**
1880-1948 .... **TCLC 16**
See also CA 118; 163
Sumner, Gordon Matthew .... **CLC 26**
See Police, The; Sting
Sun Tzu c. 400B.C.-c. 320B.C. ...... **CMLC 56**
Surrey, Henry Howard 1517-1574 ... **LC 121;
PC 59**
See also BRW 1; RGEL 2
Surtees, Robert Smith 1805-1864 .. **NCLC 14**
See also DLB 21; RGEL 2
Susann, Jacqueline 1921-1974 .... **CLC 3**
See also AITN 1; BPFB 3; CA 65-68; 53-
56; MTCW 1, 2
Su Shi
See Su Shih
See also RGWL 2, 3
Su Shih 1036-1101 .... **CMLC 15**
See Su Shi
Suskind, Patrick .... **CLC 182**
See Sueskind, Patrick
See also BPFB 3; CA 145; CWW 2
Suso, Heinrich c. 1295-1366 .... **CMLC 87**
Sutcliff, Rosemary 1920-1992 .... **CLC 26**
See also AAYA 10; BYA 1, 4; CA 5-8R;
139; CANR 37; CLR 1, 37, 138; CPW;
DAB; DAC; DAM MST, POP; JRDA;
LATS 1:1; MAICYA 1, 2; MAICYAS 1;
RHW; SATA 6, 44, 78; SATA-Obit 73;
WYA; YAW
Sutherland, Efua (Theodora Morgue)
1924-1996 .... **BLC 2:3**
See also AFW; BW 1; CA 105; CWD; DLB
117; EWL 3; IDTP; SATA 25
Sutro, Alfred 1863-1933 .... **TCLC 6**
See also CA 105; 185; DLB 10; RGEL 2
Sutton, Henry
See Slavitt, David R.
Suzuki, D. T.
See Suzuki, Daisetz Teitaro
Suzuki, Daisetz T.
See Suzuki, Daisetz Teitaro

Suzuki, Daisetz Teitaro
1870-1966 .... **TCLC 109**
See also CA 121; 111; MTCW 1, 2; MTFW
2005
Suzuki, Teitaro
See Suzuki, Daisetz Teitaro
Svevo, Italo .... **SSC 25; TCLC 2, 35**
See Schmitz, Aron Hector
See also DLB 264; EW 8; EWL 3; RGWL
2, 3; WLIT 7
Swados, Elizabeth 1951- .... **CLC 12**
See also CA 97-100; CANR 49, 163; INT
CA-97-100
Swados, Elizabeth A.
See Swados, Elizabeth
Swados, Harvey 1920-1972 .... **CLC 5**
See also CA 5-8R; 37-40R; CANR 6; CN
1; DLB 2, 335; MAL 5
Swados, Liz
See Swados, Elizabeth
Swan, Gladys 1934- .... **CLC 69**
See also CA 101; CANR 17, 39; TCLE 1:2
Swanson, Logan
See Matheson, Richard
Swarthout, Glendon (Fred)
1918-1992 .... **CLC 35**
See also AAYA 55; CA 1-4R; 139; CANR
1, 47; CN 1, 2, 3, 4, 5; LAIT 5; SATA 26;
TCWW 1, 2; YAW
Swedenborg, Emanuel 1688-1772 ..... **LC 105**
Sweet, Sarah C.
See Jewett, (Theodora) Sarah Orne
Swenson, May 1919-1989 ...... **CLC 4, 14, 61,
106; PC 14**
See also AMWS 4; CA 5-8R; 130; CANR
36, 61, 131; CP 1, 2, 3, 4; DA; DAB;
DAC; DAM MST, POET; DLB 5; EXPP;
GLL 2; MAL 5; MTCW 1, 2; MTFW
2005; PFS 16; SATA 15; WP
Swift, Augustus
See Lovecraft, H. P.
Swift, Graham 1949- .... **CLC 41, 88, 233**
See also BRWC 2; BRWS 5; CA 117; 122;
CANR 46, 71, 128, 181; CN 4, 5, 6, 7;
DLB 194, 326; MTCW 2; MTFW 2005;
NFS 18; RGSF 2
Swift, Jonathan 1667-1745 ..... **LC 1, 42, 101;
PC 9; WLC 6**
See also AAYA 41; BRW 3; BRWC 1;
BRWR 1; BYA 5, 14; CDBLB 1660-1789;
CLR 53; DA; DA3; DAB; DAC; DAM
MST, NOV, POET; DLB 39, 95, 101;
EXPN; LAIT 1; NFS 6; PFS 27; RGEL 2;
SATA 19; TEA; WCH; WLIT 3
Swinburne, Algernon Charles
1837-1909 ... **PC 24; TCLC 8, 36; WLC
6**
See also BRW 5; CA 105; 140; CDBLB
1832-1890; DA; DA3; DAB; DAC; DAM
MST, POET; DLB 35, 57; PAB; RGEL 2;
TEA
Swinfen, Ann .... **CLC 34**
See also CA 202
Swinnerton, Frank (Arthur)
1884-1982 .... **CLC 31**
See also CA 202; 108; CN 1, 2, 3; DLB 34
Swinnerton, Frank Arthur
1884-1982 .... **CLC 31**
See also CA 108; DLB 34
Swithen, John
See King, Stephen
Sylvia
See Ashton-Warner, Sylvia (Constance)
Symmes, Robert Edward
See Duncan, Robert
Symonds, John Addington
1840-1893 .... **NCLC 34**
See also DLB 57, 144

Symons, Arthur 1865-1945 .... **TCLC 11**
    See also CA 107; 189; DLB 19, 57, 149;
    RGEL 2
Symons, Julian (Gustave)
    1912-1994 .... **CLC 2, 14, 32**
    See also CA 49-52; 147; CAAS 3; CANR
    3, 33, 59; CMW 4; CN 1, 2, 3, 4, 5; CP 1,
    3, 4; DLB 87, 155; DLBY 1992; MSW;
    MTCW 1
Synge, (Edmund) J(ohn) M(illington)
    1871-1909 .... **DC 2; TCLC 6, 37**
    See also BRW 6; BRWR 1; CA 104; 141;
    CDBLB 1890-1914; DAM DRAM; DFS
    18; DLB 10, 19; EWL 3; RGEL 2; TEA;
    WLIT 4
Syruc, J.
    See Milosz, Czeslaw
Szirtes, George 1948- .... **CLC 46; PC 51**
    See also CA 109; CANR 27, 61, 117; CP 4,
    5, 6, 7
Szymborska, Wislawa 1923- ... **CLC 99, 190;**
    PC 44
    See also AAYA 76; CA 154; CANR 91, 133,
    181; CDWLB 4; CWP; CWW 2; DA3;
    DLB 232, 332; DLBY 1996; EWL 3;
    MTCW 2; MTFW 2005; PFS 15, 27;
    RGHL; RGWL 3
T. O., Nik
    See Annensky, Innokenty (Fyodorovich)
Tabori, George 1914-2007 .... **CLC 19**
    See also CA 49-52; 262; CANR 4, 69;
    CBD; CD 5, 6; DLB 245; RGHL
Tacitus c. 55-c. 117 .... **CMLC 56**
    See also AW 2; CDWLB 1; DLB 211;
    RGWL 2, 3; WLIT 8
Tadjo, Veronique 1955- .... **BLC 2:3**
    See also EWL 3
Tagore, Rabindranath 1861-1941 .... **PC 8;**
    SSC 48; TCLC 3, 53
    See also CA 104; 120; DA3; DAM DRAM,
    POET; DLB 323, 332; EWL 3; MTCW 1,
    2; MTFW 2005; PFS 18; RGEL 2; RGSF
    2; RGWL 2, 3; TWA
Taine, Hippolyte Adolphe
    1828-1893 .... **NCLC 15**
    See also EW 7; GFL 1789 to the Present
Talayesva, Don C. 1890-(?) .... **NNAL**
Talese, Gay 1932- .... **CLC 37, 232**
    See also AITN 1; AMWS 17; CA 1-4R;
    CANR 9, 58, 137, 177; DLB 185; INT
    CANR-9; MTCW 1, 2; MTFW 2005
Tallent, Elizabeth 1954- .... **CLC 45**
    See also CA 117; CANR 72; DLB 130
Tallmountain, Mary 1918-1997 .... **NNAL**
    See also CA 146; 161; DLB 193
Tally, Ted 1952- .... **CLC 42**
    See also CA 120; 124; CAD; CANR 125;
    CD 5, 6; INT CA-124
Talvik, Heiti 1904-1947 .... **TCLC 87**
    See also EWL 3
Tamayo y Baus, Manuel
    1829-1898 .... **NCLC 1**
Tammsaare, A(nton) H(ansen)
    1878-1940 .... **TCLC 27**
    See also CA 164; CDWLB 4; DLB 220;
    EWL 3
Tam'si, Tchicaya U
    See Tchicaya, Gerald Felix
Tan, Amy 1952- ..... **AAL; CLC 59, 120, 151,**
    257
    See also AAYA 9, 48; AMWS 10; BEST
    89:3; BPFB 3; CA 136; CANR 54, 105,
    132; CDALBS; CN 6, 7; CPW 1; DA3;
    DAM MULT, NOV, POP; DLB 173, 312;
    EXPN; FL 1:6; FW; LAIT 3, 5; MAL 5;
    MTCW 2; MTFW 2005; NFS 1, 13, 16;
    RGAL 4; SATA 75; SSFS 9; YAW
Tandem, Carl Felix
    See Spitteler, Carl

Tandem, Felix
    See Spitteler, Carl
Tanizaki, Jun'ichiro 1886-1965 ... **CLC 8, 14,**
    28; SSC 21
    See also Tanizaki Jun'ichiro
    See also CA 93-96; 25-28R; MJW; MTCW
    2; MTFW 2005; RGSF 2; RGWL 2
Tanizaki Jun'ichiro
    See Tanizaki, Jun'ichiro
    See also DLB 180; EWL 3
Tannen, Deborah 1945- .... **CLC 206**
    See also CA 118; CANR 95
Tannen, Deborah Frances
    See Tannen, Deborah
Tanner, William
    See Amis, Kingsley
Tante, Dilly
    See Kunitz, Stanley
Tao Lao
    See Storni, Alfonsina
Tapahonso, Luci 1953- .... **NNAL; PC 65**
    See also CA 145; CANR 72, 127; DLB 175
Tarantino, Quentin (Jerome)
    1963- .... **CLC 125, 230**
    See also AAYA 58; CA 171; CANR 125
Tarassoff, Lev
    See Troyat, Henri
Tarbell, Ida M(inerva) 1857-1944 . **TCLC 40**
    See also CA 122; 181; DLB 47
Tardieu d'Esclavelles,
    Louise-Florence-Petronille
    See Epinay, Louise d'
Tarkington, (Newton) Booth
    1869-1946 .... **TCLC 9**
    See also BPFB 3; BYA 3; CA 110; 143;
    CWRI 5; DLB 9, 102; MAL 5; MTCW 2;
    RGAL 4; SATA 17
Tarkovskii, Andrei Arsen'evich
    See Tarkovsky, Andrei (Arsenyevich)
Tarkovsky, Andrei (Arsenyevich)
    1932-1986 .... **CLC 75**
    See also CA 127
Tartt, Donna 1964(?)- .... **CLC 76**
    See also AAYA 56; CA 142; CANR 135;
    MTFW 2005
Tasso, Torquato 1544-1595 .... **LC 5, 94**
    See also EFS 2; EW 2; RGWL 2, 3; WLIT
    7
Tate, (John Orley) Allen 1899-1979 .. **CLC 2,**
    4, 6, 9, 11, 14, 24; PC 50
    See also AMW; CA 5-8R; 85-88; CANR
    32, 108; CN 1, 2; CP 1, 2; DLB 4, 45, 63;
    DLBD 17; EWL 3; MAL 5; MTCW 1, 2;
    MTFW 2005; RGAL 4; RHW
Tate, Ellalice
    See Hibbert, Eleanor Alice Burford
Tate, James (Vincent) 1943- ..... **CLC 2, 6, 25**
    See also CA 21-24R; CANR 29, 57, 114;
    CP 1, 2, 3, 4, 5, 6, 7; DLB 5, 169; EWL
    3; PFS 10, 15; RGAL 4; WP
Tate, Nahum 1652(?)-1715 .... **LC 109**
    See also DLB 80; RGEL 2
Tauler, Johannes c. 1300-1361 ...... **CMLC 37**
    See also DLB 179; LMFS 1
Tavel, Ronald 1940- .... **CLC 6**
    See also CA 21-24R; CAD; CANR 33; CD
    5, 6
Taviani, Paolo 1931- .... **CLC 70**
    See also CA 153
Taylor, Bayard 1825-1878 .... **NCLC 89**
    See also DLB 3, 189, 250, 254; RGAL 4
Taylor, C(ecil) P(hilip) 1929-1981 .... **CLC 27**
    See also CA 25-28R; 105; CANR 47; CBD
Taylor, Edward 1642(?)-1729 . **LC 11; PC 63**
    See also AMW; DA; DAB; DAC; DAM
    MST, POET; DLB 24; EXPP; RGAL 4;
    TUS
Taylor, Eleanor Ross 1920- .... **CLC 5**
    See also CA 81-84; CANR 70

Taylor, Elizabeth 1912-1975 .... **CLC 2, 4, 29;**
    SSC 100
    See also CA 13-16R; CANR 9, 70; CN 1,
    2; DLB 139; MTCW 1; RGEL 2; SATA
    13
Taylor, Frederick Winslow
    1856-1915 .... **TCLC 76**
    See also CA 188
Taylor, Henry 1942- .... **CLC 44**
    See also CA 33-36R; CAAS 7; CANR 31,
    178; CP 6, 7; DLB 5; PFS 10
Taylor, Henry Splawn
    See Taylor, Henry
Taylor, Kamala 1924-2004
    See Markandaya, Kamala
    See also CA 77-80; 227; MTFW 2005; NFS
    13
Taylor, Mildred D. 1943- .... **CLC 21**
    See also AAYA 10, 47; BW 1; BYA 3, 8;
    CA 85-88; CANR 25, 115, 136; CLR 9,
    59, 90; CSW; DLB 52; JRDA; LAIT 3;
    MAICYA 1, 2; MTFW 2005; SAAS 5;
    SATA 135; WYA; YAW
Taylor, Peter (Hillsman) 1917-1994 .. **CLC 1,**
    4, 18, 37, 44, 50, 71; SSC 10, 84
    See also AMWS 5; BPFB 3; CA 13-16R;
    147; CANR 9, 50; CN 1, 2, 3, 4, 5; CSW;
    DLB 218, 278; DLBY 1981, 1994; EWL
    3; EXPS; INT CANR-9; MAL 5; MTCW
    1, 2; MTFW 2005; RGSF 2; SSFS 9; TUS
Taylor, Robert Lewis 1912-1998 .... **CLC 14**
    See also CA 1-4R; 170; CANR 3, 64; CN
    1, 2; SATA 10; TCWW 1, 2
Tchekhov, Anton
    See Chekhov, Anton (Pavlovich)
Tchicaya, Gerald Felix 1931-1988 .. **CLC 101**
    See Tchicaya U Tam'si
    See also CA 129; 125; CANR 81
Tchicaya U Tam'si
    See Tchicaya, Gerald Felix
    See also EWL 3
Teasdale, Sara 1884-1933 .... **PC 31; TCLC 4**
    See also CA 104; 163; DLB 45; GLL 1;
    PFS 14; RGAL 4; SATA 32; TUS
Tecumseh 1768-1813 .... **NNAL**
    See also DAM MULT
Tegner, Esaias 1782-1846 .... **NCLC 2**
Teilhard de Chardin, (Marie Joseph) Pierre
    1881-1955 .... **TCLC 9**
    See also CA 105; 210; GFL 1789 to the
    Present
Temple, Ann
    See Mortimer, Penelope (Ruth)
Tennant, Emma 1937- .... **CLC 13, 52**
    See also BRWS 9; CA 65-68; CAAS 9;
    CANR 10, 38, 59, 88, 177; CN 3, 4, 5, 6,
    7; DLB 14; EWL 3; SFW 4
Tenneshaw, S.M.
    See Silverberg, Robert
Tenney, Tabitha Gilman
    1762-1837 .... **NCLC 122**
    See also DLB 37, 200
Tennyson, Alfred 1809-1892 ... **NCLC 30, 65,**
    115, 202; PC 6; WLC 6
    See also AAYA 50; BRW 4; CDBLB 1832-
    1890; DA; DA3; DAB; DAC; DAM MST,
    POET; DLB 32; EXPP; PAB; PFS 1, 2, 4,
    11, 15, 19; RGEL 2; TEA; WLIT 4; WP
Teran, Lisa St. Aubin de CLC 36
    See St. Aubin de Teran, Lisa
Terence c. 184B.C.-c. 159B.C. ...... **CMLC 14;**
    DC 7
    See also AW 1; CDWLB 1; DLB 211;
    RGWL 2, 3; TWA; WLIT 8
Teresa de Jesus, St. 1515-1582 .... **LC 18, 149**
Teresa of Avila, St.
    See Teresa de Jesus, St.
Terkel, Louis CLC 38
    See Terkel, Studs
    See also AAYA 32; AITN 1; MTCW 2; TUS

Terkel, Studs 1912-2008
See Terkel, Louis
See also CA 57-60; CANR 18, 45, 67, 132; DA3; MTCW 1, 2; MTFW 2005

Terry, C. V.
See Slaughter, Frank G(ill)

Terry, Megan 1932- .... **CLC 19; DC 13**
See also CA 77-80; CABS 3; CAD; CANR 43; CD 5, 6; CWD; DFS 18; DLB 7, 249; GLL 2

Tertullian c. 155-c. 245 .... **CMLC 29**

Tertz, Abram
See Sinyavsky, Andrei (Donatevich)
See also RGSF 2

Tesich, Steve 1943(?)-1996 .... **CLC 40, 69**
See also CA 105; 152; CAD; DLBY 1983

Tesla, Nikola 1856-1943 .... **TCLC 88**

Teternikov, Fyodor Kuzmich 1863-1927
See Sologub, Fyodor
See also CA 104

Tevis, Walter 1928-1984 .... **CLC 42**
See also CA 113; SFW 4

Tey, Josephine TCLC 14
See Mackintosh, Elizabeth
See also DLB 77; MSW

Thackeray, William Makepeace
1811-1863 ...... **NCLC 5, 14, 22, 43, 169; WLC 6**
See also BRW 5; BRWC 2; CDBLB 1832-1890; DA; DA3; DAB; DAC; DAM MST, NOV; DLB 21, 55, 159, 163; NFS 13; RGEL 2; SATA 23; TEA; WLIT 3

Thakura, Ravindranatha
See Tagore, Rabindranath

Thames, C. H.
See Marlowe, Stephen

Tharoor, Shashi 1956- .... **CLC 70**
See also CA 141; CANR 91; CN 6, 7

Thelwall, John 1764-1834 .... **NCLC 162**
See also DLB 93, 158

Thelwell, Michael Miles 1939- .... **CLC 22**
See also BW 2; CA 101

Theobald, Lewis, Jr.
See Lovecraft, H. P.

Theocritus c. 310B.C.- .... **CMLC 45**
See also AW 1; DLB 176; RGWL 2, 3

Theodorescu, Ion N. 1880-1967
See Arghezi, Tudor
See also CA 116

Theriault, Yves 1915-1983 .... **CLC 79**
See also CA 102; CANR 150; CCA 1; DAC; DAM MST; DLB 88; EWL 3

Theroux, Alexander 1939- .... **CLC 2, 25**
See also CA 85-88; CANR 20, 63; CN 4, 5, 6, 7

Theroux, Alexander Louis
See Theroux, Alexander

Theroux, Paul 1941- .... **CLC 5, 8, 11, 15, 28, 46, 159**
See also AAYA 28; AMWS 8; BEST 89:4; BPFB 3; CA 33-36R; CANR 20, 45, 74, 133, 179; CDALBS; CN 1, 2, 3, 4, 5, 6, 7; CP 1; CPW 1; DA3; DAM POP; DLB 2, 218; EWL 3; HGG; MAL 5; MTCW 1, 2; MTFW 2005; RGAL 4; SATA 44, 109; TUS

Theroux, Paul Edward
See Theroux, Paul

Thesen, Sharon 1946- .... **CLC 56**
See also CA 163; CANR 125; CP 5, 6, 7; CWP

Thespis fl. 6th cent. B.C.- .... **CMLC 51**
See also LMFS 1

Thevenin, Denis
See Duhamel, Georges

Thibault, Jacques Anatole Francois
1844-1924
See France, Anatole
See also CA 106; 127; DA3; DAM NOV; MTCW 1, 2; TWA

Thiele, Colin 1920-2006 .... **CLC 17**
See also CA 29-32R; CANR 12, 28, 53, 105; CLR 27; CP 1, 2; DLB 289; MAICYA 1, 2; SAAS 2; SATA 14, 72, 125; YAW

Thiong'o, Ngugi Wa
See Ngugi wa Thiong'o

Thistlethwaite, Bel
See Wetherald, Agnes Ethelwyn

Thomas, Audrey (Callahan) 1935- .... **CLC 7, 13, 37, 107; SSC 20**
See also AITN 2; CA 21-24R; 237; CAAE 237; CAAS 19; CANR 36, 58; CN 2, 3, 4, 5, 6, 7; DLB 60; MTCW 1; RGSF 2

Thomas, Augustus 1857-1934 .... **TCLC 97**
See also MAL 5

Thomas, D.M. 1935- ..... **CLC 13, 22, 31, 132**
See also BPFB 3; BRWS 4; CA 61-64; CAAS 11; CANR 17, 45, 75; CDBLB 1960 to Present; CN 4, 5, 6, 7; CP 1, 2, 3, 4, 5, 6, 7; DA3; DLB 40, 207, 299; HGG; INT CANR-17; MTCW 1, 2; MTFW 2005; RGHL; SFW 4

Thomas, Dylan (Marlais) 1914-1953 .... **PC 2, 52; SSC 3, 44; TCLC 1, 8, 45, 105; WLC 6**
See also AAYA 45; BRWS 1; CA 104; 120; CANR 65; CDBLB 1945-1960; DA; DA3; DAB; DAC; DAM DRAM, MST, POET; DLB 13, 20, 139; EWL 3; EXPP; LAIT 3; MTCW 1, 2; MTFW 2005; PAB; PFS 1, 3, 8; RGEL 2; RGSF 2; SATA 60; TEA; WLIT 4; WP

Thomas, (Philip) Edward 1878-1917 . **PC 53; TCLC 10**
See also BRW 6; BRWS 3; CA 106; 153; DAM POET; DLB 19, 98, 156, 216; EWL 3; PAB; RGEL 2

Thomas, J.F.
See Fleming, Thomas

Thomas, Joyce Carol 1938- .... **CLC 35**
See also AAYA 12, 54; BW 2, 3; CA 113; 116; CANR 48, 114, 135; CLR 19; DLB 33; INT CA-116; JRDA; MAICYA 1, 2; MTCW 1, 2; MTFW 2005; SAAS 7; SATA 40, 78, 123, 137; SATA-Essay 137; WYA; YAW

Thomas, Lewis 1913-1993 .... **CLC 35**
See also ANW; CA 85-88; 143; CANR 38, 60; DLB 275; MTCW 1, 2

Thomas, M. Carey 1857-1935 .... **TCLC 89**
See also FW

Thomas, Paul
See Mann, (Paul) Thomas

Thomas, Piri 1928- .... **CLC 17; HLCS 2**
See also CA 73-76; HW 1; LLW

Thomas, R(onald) S(tuart)
1913-2000 .... **CLC 6, 13, 48**
See also BRWS 12; CA 89-92; 189; CAAS 4; CANR 30; CDBLB 1960 to Present; CP 1, 2, 3, 4, 5, 6, 7; DAB; DAM POET; DLB 27; EWL 3; MTCW 1; RGEL 2

Thomas, Ross (Elmore) 1926-1995 .. **CLC 39**
See also CA 33-36R; 150; CANR 22, 63; CMW 4

Thompson, Francis (Joseph)
1859-1907 .... **TCLC 4**
See also BRW 5; CA 104; 189; CDBLB 1890-1914; DLB 19; RGEL 2; TEA

Thompson, Francis Clegg
See Mencken, H(enry) L(ouis)

Thompson, Hunter S. 1937(?)-2005 .. **CLC 9, 17, 40, 104, 229**
See also AAYA 45; BEST 89:1; BPFB 3; CA 17-20R; 236; CANR 23, 46, 74, 77, 111, 133; CPW; CSW; DA3; DAM POP; DLB 185; MTCW 1, 2; MTFW 2005; TUS

Thompson, James Myers
See Thompson, Jim

Thompson, Jim 1906-1977 .... **CLC 69**
See also BPFB 3; CA 140; CMW 4; CPW; DLB 226; MSW

Thompson, Judith (Clare Francesca)
1954- .... **CLC 39**
See also CA 143; CD 5, 6; CWD; DFS 22; DLB 334

Thomson, James 1700-1748 .... **LC 16, 29, 40**
See also BRWS 3; DAM POET; DLB 95; RGEL 2

Thomson, James 1834-1882 .... **NCLC 18**
See also DAM POET; DLB 35; RGEL 2

Thoreau, Henry David 1817-1862 .. **NCLC 7, 21, 61, 138; PC 30; WLC 6**
See also AAYA 42; AMW; ANW; BYA 3; CDALB 1640-1865; DA; DA3; DAB; DAC; DAM MST; DLB 1, 183, 223, 270, 298; LAIT 2; LMFS 1; NCFS 3; RGAL 4; TUS

Thorndike, E. L.
See Thorndike, Edward L(ee)

Thorndike, Edward L(ee)
1874-1949 .... **TCLC 107**
See also CA 121

Thornton, Hall
See Silverberg, Robert

Thorpe, Adam 1956- .... **CLC 176**
See also CA 129; CANR 92, 160; DLB 231

Thorpe, Thomas Bangs
1815-1878 .... **NCLC 183**
See also DLB 3, 11, 248; RGAL 4

Thubron, Colin 1939- .... **CLC 163**
See also CA 25-28R; CANR 12, 29, 59, 95, 171; CN 5, 6, 7; DLB 204, 231

Thubron, Colin Gerald Dryden
See Thubron, Colin

Thucydides c. 455B.C.-c. 395B.C. . **CMLC 17**
See also AW 1; DLB 176; RGWL 2, 3; WLIT 8

Thumboo, Edwin Nadason 1933- .... **PC 30**
See also CA 194; CP 1

Thurber, James (Grover)
1894-1961 .. **CLC 5, 11, 25, 125; SSC 1, 47**
See also AAYA 56; AMWS 1; BPFB 3; BYA 5; CA 73-76; CANR 17, 39; CDALB 1929-1941; CWRI 5; DA; DA3; DAB; DAC; DAM DRAM, MST, NOV; DLB 4, 11, 22, 102; EWL 3; EXPS; FANT; LAIT 3; MAICYA 1, 2; MAL 5; MTCW 1, 2; MTFW 2005; RGAL 4; RGSF 2; SATA 13; SSFS 1, 10, 19; SUFW; TUS

Thurman, Wallace (Henry)
1902-1934 .. **BLC 1:3; HR 1:3; TCLC 6**
See also BW 1, 3; CA 104; 124; CANR 81; DAM MULT; DLB 51

Tibullus c. 54B.C.-c. 18B.C. .... **CMLC 36**
See also AW 2; DLB 211; RGWL 2, 3; WLIT 8

Ticheburn, Cheviot
See Ainsworth, William Harrison

Tieck, (Johann) Ludwig
1773-1853 ..... **NCLC 5, 46; SSC 31, 100**
See also CDWLB 2; DLB 90; EW 5; IDTP; RGSF 2; RGWL 2, 3; SUFW

Tiger, Derry
See Ellison, Harlan

Tilghman, Christopher 1946- .... **CLC 65**
See also CA 159; CANR 135, 151; CSW; DLB 244

Tillich, Paul (Johannes)
1886-1965 .... **CLC 131**
See also CA 5-8R; 25-28R; CANR 33;
MTCW 1, 2

Tillinghast, Richard (Williford)
1940- .... **CLC 29**
See also CA 29-32R; CAAS 23; CANR 26,
51, 96; CP 2, 3, 4, 5, 6, 7; CSW

Tillman, Lynne (?)- .... CLC 231
See also CA 173; CANR 144, 172

Timrod, Henry 1828-1867 .... **NCLC 25**
See also DLB 3, 248; RGAL 4

Tindall, Gillian (Elizabeth) 1938- ...... **CLC 7**
See also CA 21-24R; CANR 11, 65, 107;
CN 1, 2, 3, 4, 5, 6, 7

Tiptree, James, Jr. CLC 48, 50
See Sheldon, Alice Hastings Bradley
See also DLB 8; SCFW 1, 2; SFW 4

Tirone Smith, Mary-Ann 1944- .... **CLC 39**
See also CA 118; 136; CANR 113; SATA
143

Tirso de Molina 1580(?)-1648 .... **DC 13;**
HLCS 2; LC 73
See also RGWL 2, 3

Titmarsh, Michael Angelo
See Thackeray, William Makepeace

Tocqueville, Alexis (Charles Henri Maurice
Clerel Comte) de 1805-1859 .. **NCLC 7,**
63
See also EW 6; GFL 1789 to the Present;
TWA

Toer, Pramoedya Ananta
1925-2006 .... **CLC 186**
See also CA 197; 251; CANR 170; RGWL
3

Toffler, Alvin 1928- .... **CLC 168**
See also CA 13-16R; CANR 15, 46, 67,
183; CPW; DAM POP; MTCW 1, 2

Toibin, Colm 1955- .... **CLC 162**
See also CA 142; CANR 81, 149; CN 7;
DLB 271

Tolkien, John Ronald Reuel
See Tolkien, J.R.R

Tolkien, J.R.R 1892-1973 ...... **CLC 1, 2, 3, 8,**
12, 38; TCLC 137; WLC 6
See also AAYA 10; AITN 1; BPFB 3;
BRWC 2; BRWS 2; CA 17-18; 45-48;
CANR 36, 134; CAP 2; CDBLB 1914-
1945; CLR 56; CN 1; CPW 1; CWRI 5;
DA; DA3; DAB; DAC; DAM MST, NOV,
POP; DLB 15, 160, 255; EFS 2; EWL 3;
FANT; JRDA; LAIT 1; LATS 1:2; LMFS
2; MAICYA 1, 2; MTCW 1, 2; MTFW
2005; NFS 8, 26; RGEL 2; SATA 2, 32,
100; SATA-Obit 24; SFW 4; SUFW; TEA;
WCH; WYA; YAW

Toller, Ernst 1893-1939 .... **TCLC 10**
See also CA 107; 186; DLB 124; EWL 3;
RGWL 2, 3

Tolson, M. B.
See Tolson, Melvin B(eaunorus)

Tolson, Melvin B(eaunorus)
1898(?)-1966 .... **BLC 1:3; CLC 36, 105;**
PC 88
See also AFAW 1, 2; BW 1, 3; CA 124; 89-
92; CANR 80; DAM MULT, POET; DLB
48, 76; MAL 5; RGAL 4

Tolstoi, Aleksei Nikolaevich
See Tolstoy, Alexey Nikolaevich

Tolstoi, Lev
See Tolstoy, Leo (Nikolaevich)
See also RGSF 2; RGWL 2, 3

Tolstoy, Aleksei Nikolaevich
See Tolstoy, Alexey Nikolaevich
See also DLB 272

Tolstoy, Alexey Nikolaevich
1882-1945 .... **TCLC 18**
See Tolstoy, Aleksei Nikolaevich
See also CA 107; 158; EWL 3; SFW 4

Tolstoy, Leo (Nikolaevich)
1828-1910 . **SSC 9, 30, 45, 54; TCLC 4,**
11, 17, 28, 44, 79, 173; WLC 6
See Tolstoi, Lev
See also AAYA 56; CA 104; 123; DA; DA3;
DAB; DAC; DAM MST, NOV; DLB 238;
EFS 2; EW 7; EXPS; IDTP; LAIT 2;
LATS 1:1; LMFS 1; NFS 10, 28; SATA
26; SSFS 5; TWA

Tolstoy, Count Leo
See Tolstoy, Leo (Nikolaevich)

Tomalin, Claire 1933- .... **CLC 166**
See also CA 89-92; CANR 52, 88, 165;
DLB 155

Tomasi di Lampedusa, Giuseppe 1896-1957
See Lampedusa, Giuseppe (Tomasi) di
See also CA 111; DLB 177; EWL 3; WLIT
7

Tomlin, Lily 1939(?)-
See Tomlin, Mary Jean
See also CA 117

Tomlin, Mary Jean CLC 17
See Tomlin, Lily

Tomline, F. Latour
See Gilbert, W(illiam) S(chwenck)

Tomlinson, (Alfred) Charles 1927- .... **CLC 2,**
4, 6, 13, 45; PC 17
See also CA 5-8R; CANR 33; CP 1, 2, 3, 4,
5, 6, 7; DAM POET; DLB 40; TCLE 1:2

Tomlinson, H(enry) M(ajor)
1873-1958 .... **TCLC 71**
See also CA 118; 161; DLB 36, 100, 195

Tonna, Charlotte Elizabeth
1790-1846 .... **NCLC 135**
See also DLB 163

Tonson, Jacob fl. 1655(?)-1736 .... **LC 86**
See also DLB 170

Toole, John Kennedy 1937-1969 ..... **CLC 19,**
64
See also BPFB 3; CA 104; DLBY 1981;
MTCW 2; MTFW 2005

Toomer, Eugene
See Toomer, Jean

Toomer, Eugene Pinchback
See Toomer, Jean

Toomer, Jean 1894-1967 ... **BLC 1:3; CLC 1,**
4, 13, 22; HR 1:3; PC 7; SSC 1, 45;
TCLC 172; WLCS
See also AFAW 1, 2; AMWS 3, 9; BW 1;
CA 85-88; CDALB 1917-1929; DA3;
DAM MULT; DLB 45, 51; EWL 3; EXPP;
EXPS; LMFS 2; MAL 5; MTCW 1, 2;
MTFW 2005; NFS 11; RGAL 4; RGSF 2;
SSFS 5

Toomer, Nathan Jean
See Toomer, Jean

Toomer, Nathan Pinchback
See Toomer, Jean

Torley, Luke
See Blish, James (Benjamin)

Tornimparte, Alessandra
See Ginzburg, Natalia

Torre, Raoul della
See Mencken, H(enry) L(ouis)

Torrence, Ridgely 1874-1950 .... **TCLC 97**
See also DLB 54, 249; MAL 5

Torrey, E. Fuller 1937- .... **CLC 34**
See also CA 119; CANR 71, 158

Torrey, Edwin Fuller
See Torrey, E. Fuller

Torsvan, Ben Traven
See Traven, B.

Torsvan, Benno Traven
See Traven, B.

Torsvan, Berick Traven
See Traven, B.

Torsvan, Berwick Traven
See Traven, B.

Torsvan, Bruno Traven
See Traven, B.

Torsvan, Traven
See Traven, B.

Tourneur, Cyril 1575(?)-1626 .... **LC 66**
See also BRW 2; DAM DRAM; DLB 58;
RGEL 2

Tournier, Michel 1924- .... **CLC 6, 23, 36, 95,**
249; SSC 88
See also CA 49-52; CANR 3, 36, 74, 149;
CWW 2; DLB 83; EWL 3; GFL 1789 to
the Present; MTCW 1, 2; SATA 23

Tournier, Michel Edouard
See Tournier, Michel

Tournimparte, Alessandra
See Ginzburg, Natalia

Towers, Ivar
See Kornbluth, C(yril) M.

Towne, Robert (Burton) 1936(?)- ..... **CLC 87**
See also CA 108; DLB 44; IDFW 3, 4

Townsend, Sue CLC 61
See Townsend, Susan Lilian
See also AAYA 28; CA 119; 127; CANR
65, 107; CBD; CD 5, 6; CPW; CWD;
DAB; DAC; DAM MST; DLB 271; INT
CA-127; SATA 55, 93; SATA-Brief 48;
YAW

Townsend, Susan Lilian 1946-
See Townsend, Sue

Townshend, Pete
See Townshend, Peter (Dennis Blandford)

Townshend, Peter (Dennis Blandford)
1945- .... **CLC 17, 42**
See also CA 107

Tozzi, Federigo 1883-1920 .... **TCLC 31**
See also CA 160; CANR 110; DLB 264;
EWL 3; WLIT 7

Tracy, Don(ald Fiske) 1905-1970(?)
See Queen, Ellery
See also CA 1-4R; 176; CANR 2

Trafford, F. G.
See Riddell, Charlotte

Traherne, Thomas 1637(?)-1674 .. **LC 99; PC**
70
See also BRW 2; BRWS 11; DLB 131;
PAB; RGEL 2

Traill, Catharine Parr 1802-1899 .. **NCLC 31**
See also DLB 99

Trakl, Georg 1887-1914 .... **PC 20; TCLC 5**
See also CA 104; 165; EW 10; EWL 3;
LMFS 2; MTCW 2; RGWL 2, 3

Trambley, Estela Portillo TCLC 163
See Portillo Trambley, Estela
See also CA 77-80; RGAL 4

Tranquilli, Secondino
See Silone, Ignazio

Transtroemer, Tomas Gosta
See Transtromer, Tomas

Transtromer, Tomas (Gosta)
See Transtromer, Tomas
See also CWW 2

Transtromer, Tomas 1931- .... **CLC 52, 65**
See also CA 117; 129; CAAS 17; CANR
115, 172; DAM POET; DLB 257; EWL
3; PFS 21

Transtromer, Tomas Goesta
See Transtromer, Tomas

Transtromer, Tomas Gosta
See Transtromer, Tomas

Transtromer, Tomas Gosta
See Transtromer, Tomas

Traven, B. 1882(?)-1969 .... **CLC 8, 11**
See also CA 19-20; 25-28R; CAP 2; DLB
9, 56; EWL 3; MTCW 1; RGAL 4

Trediakovsky, Vasilii Kirillovich
1703-1769 .... **LC 68**
See also DLB 150

Treitel, Jonathan 1959- .... **CLC 70**
See also CA 210; DLB 267

Trelawny, Edward John
1792-1881 .... **NCLC 85**
See also DLB 110, 116, 144

Tremain, Rose 1943- .... **CLC 42**
See also CA 97-100; CANR 44, 95; CN 4,
5, 6, 7; DLB 14, 271; RGSF 2; RHW

Tremblay, Michel 1942- .... **CLC 29, 102, 225**
See also CA 116; 128; CCA 1; CWW 2;
DAC; DAM MST; DLB 60; EWL 3; GLL
1; MTCW 1, 2; MTFW 2005

Trevanian CLC 29
See Whitaker, Rod

Trevisa, John c. 1342-c. 1402 .... **LC 139**
See also BRWS 9; DLB 146

Trevor, Glen
See Hilton, James

Trevor, William 1928- ... **CLC 1, 2, 3, 4, 5, 6,
7; SSC 21, 58**
See also BRWS 4; CA 9-12R; CANR 4, 37,
55, 76, 102, 139; CBD; CD 5, 6; DAM
NOV; DLB 14, 139; EWL 3; INT CANR-
37; LATS 1:2; MTCW 1, 2; MTFW 2005;
RGEL 2; RGSF 2; SSFS 10; TCLE 1:2;
TEA

Trifonov, Iurii (Valentinovich)
See Trifonov, Yuri (Valentinovich)
See also DLB 302; RGWL 2, 3

Trifonov, Yuri (Valentinovich)
1925-1981 .... **CLC 45**
See Trifonov, Iurii (Valentinovich); Trifonov, Yury Valentinovich
See also CA 126; 103; MTCW 1

Trifonov, Yury Valentinovich
See Trifonov, Yuri (Valentinovich)
See also EWL 3

Trilling, Diana (Rubin) 1905-1996 . **CLC 129**
See also CA 5-8R; 154; CANR 10, 46; INT
CANR-10; MTCW 1, 2

Trilling, Lionel 1905-1975 ..... **CLC 9, 11, 24;
SSC 75**
See also AMWS 3; CA 9-12R; 61-64;
CANR 10, 105; CN 1, 2; DLB 28, 63;
EWL 3; INT CANR-10; MAL 5; MTCW
1, 2; RGAL 4; TUS

Trimball, W. H.
See Mencken, H(enry) L(ouis)

Tristan
See Gomez de la Serna, Ramon

Tristram
See Housman, A(lfred) E(dward)

Trogdon, William (Lewis) 1939-
See Heat-Moon, William Least
See also AAYA 66; CA 115; 119; CANR
47, 89; CPW; INT CA-119

Trollope, Anthony 1815-1882 .... **NCLC 6, 33,
101; SSC 28; WLC 6**
See also BRW 5; CDBLB 1832-1890; DA;
DA3; DAB; DAC; DAM MST, NOV;
DLB 21, 57, 159; RGEL 2; RGSF 2;
SATA 22

Trollope, Frances 1779-1863 .... **NCLC 30**
See also DLB 21, 166

Trollope, Joanna 1943- .... **CLC 186**
See also CA 101; CANR 58, 95, 149; CN
7; CPW; DLB 207; RHW

Trotsky, Leon 1879-1940 .... **TCLC 22**
See also CA 118; 167

Trotter (Cockburn), Catharine
1679-1749 .... **LC 8**
See also DLB 84, 252

Trotter, Wilfred 1872-1939 .... **TCLC 97**

Troupe, Quincy 1943- .... **BLC 2:3**
See also BW 2; CA 113; 124; CANR 43,
90, 126; DLB 41

Trout, Kilgore
See Farmer, Philip Jose

Trow, George William Swift
See Trow, George W.S.

Trow, George W.S. 1943-2006 .... **CLC 52**
See also CA 126; 255; CANR 91

Troyat, Henri 1911-2007 .... **CLC 23**
See also CA 45-48; 258; CANR 2, 33, 67,
117; GFL 1789 to the Present; MTCW 1

Trudeau, Garry B. CLC 12
See Trudeau, G.B.
See also AAYA 10; AITN 2

Trudeau, G.B. 1948-
See Trudeau, Garry B.
See also AAYA 60; CA 81-84; CANR 31;
SATA 35, 168

Truffaut, Francois 1932-1984 ... **CLC 20, 101**
See also CA 81-84; 113; CANR 34

Trumbo, Dalton 1905-1976 .... **CLC 19**
See also CA 21-24R; 69-72; CANR 10; CN
1, 2; DLB 26; IDFW 3, 4; YAW

Trumbull, John 1750-1831 .... **NCLC 30**
See also DLB 31; RGAL 4

Trundlett, Helen B.
See Eliot, T(homas) S(tearns)

Truth, Sojourner 1797(?)-1883 ...... **NCLC 94**
See also DLB 239; FW; LAIT 2

Tryon, Thomas 1926-1991 .... **CLC 3, 11**
See also AITN 1; BPFB 3; CA 29-32R; 135;
CANR 32, 77; CPW; DA3; DAM POP;
HGG; MTCW 1

Tryon, Tom
See Tryon, Thomas

Ts'ao Hsueh-ch'in 1715(?)-1763 .... **LC 1**

Tsurayuki Ed. fl. 10th cent. - .... **PC 73**

Tsushima, Shuji 1909-1948
See Dazai Osamu
See also CA 107

Tsvetaeva (Efron), Marina (Ivanovna)
1892-1941 .... **PC 14; TCLC 7, 35**
See also CA 104; 128; CANR 73; DLB 295;
EW 11; MTCW 1, 2; PFS 29; RGWL 2, 3

Tuck, Lily 1938- .... **CLC 70**
See also AAYA 74; CA 139; CANR 90

Tuckerman, Frederick Goddard
1821-1873 .... **PC 85**
See also DLB 243; RGAL 4

Tu Fu 712-770 .... **PC 9**
See Du Fu
See also DAM MULT; TWA; WP

Tulsidas, Gosvami 1532(?)-1623 .... **LC 158**
See also RGWL 2, 3

Tunis, John R(oberts) 1889-1975 ..... **CLC 12**
See also BYA 1; CA 61-64; CANR 62; DLB
22, 171; JRDA; MAICYA 1, 2; SATA 37;
SATA-Brief 30; YAW

Tuohy, Frank CLC 37
See Tuohy, John Francis
See also CN 1, 2, 3, 4, 5, 6, 7; DLB 14,
139

Tuohy, John Francis 1925-
See Tuohy, Frank
See also CA 5-8R; 178; CANR 3, 47

Turco, Lewis (Putnam) 1934- ..... **CLC 11, 63**
See also CA 13-16R; CAAS 22; CANR 24,
51; CP 1, 2, 3, 4, 5, 6, 7; DLBY 1984;
TCLE 1:2

Turgenev, Ivan (Sergeevich)
1818-1883 ..... **DC 7; NCLC 21, 37, 122;
SSC 7, 57; WLC 6**
See also AAYA 58; DA; DAB; DAC; DAM
MST, NOV; DFS 6; DLB 238, 284; EW
6; LATS 1:1; NFS 16; RGSF 2; RGWL 2,
3; TWA

Turgot, Anne-Robert-Jacques
1727-1781 .... **LC 26**
See also DLB 314

Turner, Frederick 1943- .... **CLC 48**
See also CA 73-76; 227; CAAE 227; CAAS
10; CANR 12, 30, 56; DLB 40, 282

Turton, James
See Crace, Jim

Tutu, Desmond M(pilo) 1931- .... **BLC 1:3;
CLC 80**
See also BW 1, 3; CA 125; CANR 67, 81;
DAM MULT

Tutuola, Amos 1920-1997 .... **BLC 1:3, 2:3;
CLC 5, 14, 29; TCLC 188**
See also AAYA 76; AFW; BW 2, 3; CA
9-12R; 159; CANR 27, 66; CDWLB 3;
CN 1, 2, 3, 4, 5, 6; DA3; DAM MULT;
DLB 125; DNFS 2; EWL 3; MTCW 1, 2;
MTFW 2005; RGEL 2; WLIT 2

**Twain, Mark SSC 6, 26, 34, 87; TCLC 6, 12,
19, 36, 48, 59, 161, 185; WLC 6**
See Clemens, Samuel Langhorne
See also AAYA 20; AMW; AMWC 1; BPFB
3; BYA 2, 3, 11, 14; CLR 58, 60, 66; DLB
11, 343; EXPN; EXPS; FANT; LAIT 2;
MAL 5; NCFS 4; NFS 1, 6; RGAL 4;
RGSF 2; SFW 4; SSFS 1, 7, 16, 21;
SUFW; TUS; WCH; WYA; YAW

Tyler, Anne 1941- . **CLC 7, 11, 18, 28, 44, 59,
103, 205, 265**
See also AAYA 18, 60; AMWS 4; BEST
89:1; BPFB 3; BYA 12; CA 9-12R; CANR
11, 33, 53, 109, 132, 168; CDALBS; CN
1, 2, 3, 4, 5, 6, 7; CPW; CSW; DAM
NOV, POP; DLB 6, 143; DLBY 1982;
EWL 3; EXPN; LATS 1:2; MAL 5; MBL;
MTCW 1, 2; MTFW 2005; NFS 2, 7, 10;
RGAL 4; SATA 7, 90, 173; SSFS 17;
TCLE 1:2; TUS; YAW

Tyler, Royall 1757-1826 .... **NCLC 3**
See also DLB 37; RGAL 4

Tynan, Katharine 1861-1931 .... **TCLC 3**
See also CA 104; 167; DLB 153, 240; FW

Tyndale, William c. 1484-1536 .... **LC 103**
See also DLB 132

Tyutchev, Fyodor 1803-1873 .... **NCLC 34**

Tzara, Tristan 1896-1963 .... **CLC 47; PC 27;
TCLC 168**
See also CA 153; 89-92; DAM POET; EWL
3; MTCW 2

Uc de Saint Circ c. 1190B.C.-13th cent.
B.C. .... **CMLC 102**

Uchida, Yoshiko 1921-1992 .... **AAL**
See also AAYA 16; BYA 2, 3; CA 13-16R;
139; CANR 6, 22, 47, 61; CDALBS; CLR
6, 56; CWRI 5; DLB 312; JRDA; MAI-
CYA 1, 2; MTCW 1, 2; MTFW 2005;
NFS 26; SAAS 1; SATA 1, 53; SATA-Obit
72

Udall, Nicholas 1504-1556 .... **LC 84**
See also DLB 62; RGEL 2

Ueda Akinari 1734-1809 .... **NCLC 131**

Uhry, Alfred 1936- .... **CLC 55; DC 28**
See also CA 127; 133; CAD; CANR 112;
CD 5, 6; CSW; DA3; DAM DRAM, POP;
DFS 11, 15; INT CA-133; MTFW 2005

Ulf, Haerved
See Strindberg, (Johan) August

Ulf, Harved
See Strindberg, (Johan) August

Ulibarri, Sabine R(eyes)
1919-2003 .... **CLC 83; HLCS 2**
See also CA 131; 214; CANR 81; DAM
MULT; DLB 82; HW 1, 2; RGSF 2

Unamuno (y Jugo), Miguel de
1864-1936 .. **HLC 2; SSC 11, 69; TCLC
2, 9, 148**
See also CA 104; 131; CANR 81; DAM
MULT, NOV; DLB 108, 322; EW 8; EWL
3; HW 1, 2; MTCW 1, 2; MTFW 2005;
RGSF 2; RGWL 2, 3; SSFS 20; TWA

Uncle Shelby
See Silverstein, Shel

Undercliffe, Errol
See Campbell, Ramsey

Underwood, Miles
See Glassco, John

Undset, Sigrid 1882-1949 .... **TCLC 3, 197; WLC 6**
See also AAYA 77; CA 104; 129; DA; DA3; DAB; DAC; DAM MST, NOV; DLB 293, 332; EW 9; EWL 3; FW; MTCW 1, 2; MTFW 2005; RGWL 2, 3

Ungaretti, Giuseppe 1888-1970 ... **CLC 7, 11, 15; PC 57; TCLC 200**
See also CA 19-20; 25-28R; CAP 2; DLB 114; EW 10; EWL 3; PFS 20; RGWL 2, 3; WLIT 7

Unger, Douglas 1952- .... **CLC 34**
See also CA 130; CANR 94, 155

Unsworth, Barry 1930- .... **CLC 76, 127**
See also BRWS 7; CA 25-28R; CANR 30, 54, 125, 171; CN 6, 7; DLB 194, 326

Unsworth, Barry Forster
See Unsworth, Barry

Updike, John 1932- . **CLC 1, 2, 3, 5, 7, 9, 13, 15, 23, 34, 43, 70, 139, 214; PC 90; SSC 13, 27, 103; WLC 6**
See also AAYA 36; AMW; AMWC 1; AMWR 1; BPFB 3; BYA 12; CA 1-4R; CABS 1; CANR 4, 33, 51, 94, 133; CDALB 1968-1988; CN 1, 2, 3, 4, 5, 6, 7; CP 1, 2, 3, 4, 5, 6, 7; CPW 1; DA; DA3; DAB; DAC; DAM MST, NOV, POET, POP; DLB 2, 5, 143, 218, 227; DLBD 3; DLBY 1980, 1982, 1997; EWL 3; EXPP; HGG; MAL 5; MTCW 1, 2; MTFW 2005; NFS 12, 24; RGAL 4; RGSF 2; SSFS 3, 19; TUS

Updike, John Hoyer
See Updike, John

Upshaw, Margaret Mitchell
See Mitchell, Margaret (Munnerlyn)

Upton, Mark
See Sanders, Lawrence

Upward, Allen 1863-1926 .... **TCLC 85**
See also CA 117; 187; DLB 36

Urdang, Constance (Henriette)
1922-1996 .... **CLC 47**
See also CA 21-24R; CANR 9, 24; CP 1, 2, 3, 4, 5, 6; CWP

Urfe, Honore d' 1567(?)-1625 .... **LC 132**
See also DLB 268; GFL Beginnings to 1789; RGWL 2, 3

Uriel, Henry
See Faust, Frederick (Schiller)

Uris, Leon 1924-2003 .... **CLC 7, 32**
See also AITN 1, 2; BEST 89:2; BPFB 3; CA 1-4R; 217; CANR 1, 40, 65, 123; CN 1, 2, 3, 4, 5, 6; CPW 1; DA3; DAM NOV, POP; MTCW 1, 2; MTFW 2005; RGHL; SATA 49; SATA-Obit 146

Urista (Heredia), Alberto (Baltazar)
1947- .... **HLCS 1**
See Alurista
See also CA 182; CANR 2, 32; HW 1

Urmuz
See Codrescu, Andrei

Urquhart, Guy
See McAlmon, Robert (Menzies)

Urquhart, Jane 1949- .... **CLC 90, 242**
See also CA 113; CANR 32, 68, 116, 157; CCA 1; DAC; DLB 334

Usigli, Rodolfo 1905-1979 .... **HLCS 1**
See also CA 131; DLB 305; EWL 3; HW 1; LAW

Usk, Thomas (?)-1388 .... **CMLC 76**
See also DLB 146

Ustinov, Peter (Alexander)
1921-2004 .... **CLC 1**
See also AITN 1; CA 13-16R; 225; CANR 25, 51; CBD; CD 5, 6; DLB 13; MTCW 2

U Tam'si, Gerald Felix Tchicaya
See Tchicaya, Gerald Felix

U Tam'si, Tchicaya
See Tchicaya, Gerald Felix

Vachss, Andrew 1942- .... **CLC 106**
See also CA 118, 214; CAAE 214; CANR 44, 95, 153; CMW 4

Vachss, Andrew H.
See Vachss, Andrew

Vachss, Andrew Henry
See Vachss, Andrew

Vaculik, Ludvik 1926- .... **CLC 7**
See also CA 53-56; CANR 72; CWW 2; DLB 232; EWL 3

Vaihinger, Hans 1852-1933 .... **TCLC 71**
See also CA 116; 166

Valdez, Luis (Miguel) 1940- ..... **CLC 84; DC 10; HLC 2**
See also CA 101; CAD; CANR 32, 81; CD 5, 6; DAM MULT; DFS 5; DLB 122; EWL 3; HW 1; LAIT 4; LLW

Valenzuela, Luisa 1938- .... **CLC 31, 104; HLCS 2; SSC 14, 82**
See also CA 101; CANR 32, 65, 123; CD-WLB 3; CWW 2; DAM MULT; DLB 113; EWL 3; FW; HW 1, 2; LAW; RGSF 2; RGWL 3

Valera y Alcala-Galiano, Juan
1824-1905 .... **TCLC 10**
See also CA 106

Valerius Maximus CMLC 64
See also DLB 211

Valery, (Ambroise) Paul (Toussaint Jules)
1871-1945 .... **PC 9; TCLC 4, 15**
See also CA 104; 122; DA3; DAM POET; DLB 258; EW 8; EWL 3; GFL 1789 to the Present; MTCW 1, 2; MTFW 2005; RGWL 2, 3; TWA

Valle-Inclan, Ramon (Maria) del
1866-1936 .... **HLC 2; TCLC 5**
See del Valle-Inclan, Ramon (Maria)
See also CA 106; 153; CANR 80; DAM MULT; DLB 134; EW 8; EWL 3; HW 2; RGSF 2; RGWL 2, 3

Vallejo, Antonio Buero
See Buero Vallejo, Antonio

Vallejo, Cesar (Abraham)
1892-1938 .... **HLC 2; TCLC 3, 56**
See also CA 105; 153; DAM MULT; DLB 290; EWL 3; HW 1; LAW; PFS 26; RGWL 2, 3

Valles, Jules 1832-1885 .... **NCLC 71**
See also DLB 123; GFL 1789 to the Present

Vallette, Marguerite Eymery
1860-1953 .... **TCLC 67**
See Rachilde
See also CA 182; DLB 123, 192

Valle Y Pena, Ramon del
See Valle-Inclan, Ramon (Maria) del

Van Ash, Cay 1918-1994 .... **CLC 34**
See also CA 220

Vanbrugh, Sir John 1664-1726 .... **LC 21**
See also BRW 2; DAM DRAM; DLB 80; IDTP; RGEL 2

Van Campen, Karl
See Campbell, John W(ood, Jr.)

Vance, Gerald
See Silverberg, Robert

Vance, Jack 1916-
See Queen, Ellery; Vance, John Holbrook
See also CA 29-32R; CANR 17, 65, 154; CMW 4; MTCW 1

Vance, John Holbrook CLC 35
See Vance, Jack
See also DLB 8; FANT; SCFW 1, 2; SFW 4; SUFW 1, 2

Van Den Bogarde, Derek Jules Gaspard Ulric Niven 1921-1999 .... **CLC 14**
See Bogarde, Dirk
See also CA 77-80; 179

Vandenburgh, Jane CLC 59
See also CA 168

Vanderhaeghe, Guy 1951- .... **CLC 41**
See also BPFB 3; CA 113; CANR 72, 145; CN 7; DLB 334

van der Post, Laurens (Jan)
1906-1996 .... **CLC 5**
See also AFW; CA 5-8R; 155; CANR 35; CN 1, 2, 3, 4, 5, 6; DLB 204; RGEL 2

van de Wetering, Janwillem
1931-2008 .... **CLC 47**
See also CA 49-52; 274; CANR 4, 62, 90; CMW 4

Van Dine, S. S. TCLC 23
See Wright, Willard Huntington
See also DLB 306; MSW

Van Doren, Carl (Clinton)
1885-1950 .... **TCLC 18**
See also CA 111; 168

Van Doren, Mark 1894-1972 .... **CLC 6, 10**
See also CA 1-4R; 37-40R; CANR 3; CN 1; CP 1; DLB 45, 284, 335; MAL 5; MTCW 1, 2; RGAL 4

Van Druten, John (William)
1901-1957 .... **TCLC 2**
See also CA 104; 161; DLB 10; MAL 5; RGAL 4

Van Duyn, Mona 1921-2004 .... **CLC 3, 7, 63, 116**
See also CA 9-12R; 234; CANR 7, 38, 60, 116; CP 1, 2, 3, 4, 5, 6, 7; CWP; DAM POET; DLB 5; MAL 5; MTFW 2005; PFS 20

Van Dyne, Edith
See Baum, L(yman) Frank

van Herk, Aritha 1954- .... **CLC 249**
See also CA 101; CANR 94; DLB 334

van Itallie, Jean-Claude 1936- .... **CLC 3**
See also CA 45-48; CAAS 2; CAD; CANR 1, 48; CD 5, 6; DLB 7

Van Loot, Cornelius Obenchain
See Roberts, Kenneth (Lewis)

van Ostaijen, Paul 1896-1928 .... **TCLC 33**
See also CA 163

Van Peebles, Melvin 1932- .... **CLC 2, 20**
See also BW 2, 3; CA 85-88; CANR 27, 67, 82; DAM MULT

van Schendel, Arthur(-Francois-Emile)
1874-1946 .... **TCLC 56**
See also EWL 3

Vansittart, Peter 1920-2008 .... **CLC 42**
See also CA 1-4R; CANR 3, 49, 90; CN 4, 5, 6, 7; RHW

Van Vechten, Carl 1880-1964 ... **CLC 33; HR 1:3**
See also AMWS 2; CA 183; 89-92; DLB 4, 9, 51; RGAL 4

van Vogt, A(lfred) E(lton) 1912-2000 . **CLC 1**
See also BPFB 3; BYA 13, 14; CA 21-24R; 190; CANR 28; DLB 8, 251; SATA 14; SATA-Obit 124; SCFW 1, 2; SFW 4

Vara, Madeleine
See Jackson, Laura (Riding)

Varda, Agnes 1928- .... **CLC 16**
See also CA 116; 122

Vargas Llosa, Jorge Mario Pedro
See Vargas Llosa, Mario

Vargas Llosa, Mario 1936- .. **CLC 3, 6, 9, 10, 15, 31, 42, 85, 181; HLC 2**
See Llosa, Jorge Mario Pedro Vargas
See also BPFB 3; CA 73-76; CANR 18, 32, 42, 67, 116, 140, 173; CDWLB 3; CWW 2; DA; DA3; DAB; DAC; DAM MST, MULT, NOV; DLB 145; DNFS 2; EWL

3; HW 1, 2; LAIT 5; LATS 1:2; LAW; LAWS 1; MTCW 1, 2; MTFW 2005; RGWL 2; SSFS 14; TWA; WLIT 1

Varnhagen von Ense, Rahel 1771-1833 .... **NCLC 130**
See also DLB 90

Vasari, Giorgio 1511-1574 .... **LC 114**

Vasilikos, Vasiles
See Vassilikos, Vassilis

Vasiliu, George
See Bacovia, George

Vasiliu, Gheorghe
See Bacovia, George
See also CA 123; 189

Vassa, Gustavus
See Equiano, Olaudah

Vassilikos, Vassilis 1933- .... **CLC 4, 8**
See also CA 81-84; CANR 75, 149; EWL 3

Vaughan, Henry 1621-1695 .... **LC 27; PC 81**
See also BRW 2; DLB 131; PAB; RGEL 2

Vaughn, Stephanie CLC 62

Vazov, Ivan (Minchov) 1850-1921 . **TCLC 25**
See also CA 121; 167; CDWLB 4; DLB 147

Veblen, Thorstein B(unde) 1857-1929 .... **TCLC 31**
See also AMWS 1; CA 115; 165; DLB 246; MAL 5

Vega, Lope de 1562-1635 ... **HLCS 2; LC 23, 119**
See also EW 2; RGWL 2, 3

Veldeke, Heinrich von c. 1145-c. 1190 .... **CMLC 85**

Vendler, Helen (Hennessy) 1933- ... **CLC 138**
See also CA 41-44R; CANR 25, 72, 136; MTCW 1, 2; MTFW 2005

Venison, Alfred
See Pound, Ezra (Weston Loomis)

Ventsel, Elena Sergeevna 1907-2002
See Grekova, I.
See also CA 154

Verdi, Marie de
See Mencken, H(enry) L(ouis)

Verdu, Matilde
See Cela, Camilo Jose

Verga, Giovanni (Carmelo) 1840-1922 .... **SSC 21, 87; TCLC 3**
See also CA 104; 123; CANR 101; EW 7; EWL 3; RGSF 2; RGWL 2, 3; WLIT 7

Vergil 70B.C.-19B.C. .. **CMLC 9, 40, 101; PC 12; WLCS**
See Virgil
See also AW 2; DA; DA3; DAB; DAC; DAM MST, POET; EFS 1; LMFS 1

Vergil, Polydore c. 1470-1555 .... **LC 108**
See also DLB 132

Verhaeren, Emile (Adolphe Gustave) 1855-1916 .... **TCLC 12**
See also CA 109; EWL 3; GFL 1789 to the Present

Verlaine, Paul (Marie) 1844-1896 .. **NCLC 2, 51; PC 2, 32**
See also DAM POET; DLB 217; EW 7; GFL 1789 to the Present; LMFS 2; RGWL 2, 3; TWA

Verne, Jules (Gabriel) 1828-1905 ... **TCLC 6, 52**
See also AAYA 16; BYA 4; CA 110; 131; CLR 88; DA3; DLB 123; GFL 1789 to the Present; JRDA; LAIT 2; LMFS 2; MAICYA 1, 2; MTFW 2005; RGWL 2, 3; SATA 21; SCFW 1, 2; SFW 4; TWA; WCH

Verus, Marcus Annius
See Aurelius, Marcus

Very, Jones 1813-1880 .... **NCLC 9; PC 86**
See also DLB 1, 243; RGAL 4

Vesaas, Tarjei 1897-1970 .... **CLC 48**
See also CA 190; 29-32R; DLB 297; EW 11; EWL 3; RGWL 3

Vialis, Gaston
See Simenon, Georges (Jacques Christian)

Vian, Boris 1920-1959(?) .... **TCLC 9**
See also CA 106; 164; CANR 111; DLB 72, 321; EWL 3; GFL 1789 to the Present; MTCW 2; RGWL 2, 3

Viaud, (Louis Marie) Julien 1850-1923
See Loti, Pierre
See also CA 107

Vicar, Henry
See Felsen, Henry Gregor

Vicente, Gil 1465-c. 1536 .... **LC 99**
See also DLB 318; IDTP; RGWL 2, 3

Vicker, Angus
See Felsen, Henry Gregor

Vico, Giambattista LC 138
See Vico, Giovanni Battista
See also WLIT 7

Vico, Giovanni Battista 1668-1744
See Vico, Giambattista
See also EW 3

Vidal, Eugene Luther Gore
See Vidal, Gore

Vidal, Gore 1925- ...... **CLC 2, 4, 6, 8, 10, 22, 33, 72, 142**
See also AAYA 64; AITN 1; AMWS 4; BEST 90:2; BPFB 3; CA 5-8R; CAD; CANR 13, 45, 65, 100, 132, 167; CD 5, 6; CDALBS; CN 1, 2, 3, 4, 5, 6, 7; CPW; DA3; DAM NOV, POP; DFS 2; DLB 6, 152; EWL 3; GLL 1; INT CANR-13; MAL 5; MTCW 1, 2; MTFW 2005; RGAL 4; RHW; TUS

Viereck, Peter 1916-2006 .... **CLC 4; PC 27**
See also CA 1-4R; 250; CANR 1, 47; CP 1, 2, 3, 4, 5, 6, 7; DLB 5; MAL 5; PFS 9, 14

Viereck, Peter Robert Edwin
See Viereck, Peter

Vigny, Alfred (Victor) de 1797-1863 .... **NCLC 7, 102; PC 26**
See also DAM POET; DLB 119, 192, 217; EW 5; GFL 1789 to the Present; RGWL 2, 3

Vilakazi, Benedict Wallet 1906-1947 .... **TCLC 37**
See also CA 168

Vile, Curt
See Moore, Alan

Villa, Jose Garcia 1914-1997 ... **AAL; PC 22; TCLC 176**
See also CA 25-28R; CANR 12, 118; CP 1, 2, 3, 4; DLB 312; EWL 3; EXPP

Villard, Oswald Garrison 1872-1949 .... **TCLC 160**
See also CA 113; 162; DLB 25, 91

Villarreal, Jose Antonio 1924- .... **HLC 2**
See also CA 133; CANR 93; DAM MULT; DLB 82; HW 1; LAIT 4; RGAL 4

Villaurrutia, Xavier 1903-1950 ...... **TCLC 80**
See also CA 192; EWL 3; HW 1; LAW

Villaverde, Cirilo 1812-1894 .... **NCLC 121**
See also LAW

Villehardouin, Geoffroi de 1150(?)-1218(?) .... **CMLC 38**

Villiers, George 1628-1687 .... **LC 107**
See also DLB 80; RGEL 2

Villiers de l'Isle Adam, Jean Marie Mathias Philippe Auguste 1838-1889 ... **NCLC 3; SSC 14**
See also DLB 123, 192; GFL 1789 to the Present; RGSF 2

Villon, Francois 1431-1463(?) . **LC 62; PC 13**
See also DLB 208; EW 2; RGWL 2, 3; TWA

Vine, Barbara CLC 50
See Rendell, Ruth
See also BEST 90:4

Vinge, Joan (Carol) D(ennison) 1948- .... **CLC 30; SSC 24**
See also AAYA 32; BPFB 3; CA 93-96; CANR 72; SATA 36, 113; SFW 4; YAW

Viola, Herman J(oseph) 1938- .... **CLC 70**
See also CA 61-64; CANR 8, 23, 48, 91; SATA 126

Violis, G.
See Simenon, Georges (Jacques Christian)

Viramontes, Helena Maria 1954- .... **HLCS 2**
See also CA 159; CANR 182; DLB 122; HW 2; LLW

Virgil
See Vergil
See also CDWLB 1; DLB 211; LAIT 1; RGWL 2, 3; WLIT 8; WP

Visconti, Luchino 1906-1976 .... **CLC 16**
See also CA 81-84; 65-68; CANR 39

Vitry, Jacques de
See Jacques de Vitry

Vittorini, Elio 1908-1966 .... **CLC 6, 9, 14**
See also CA 133; 25-28R; DLB 264; EW 12; EWL 3; RGWL 2, 3

Vivekananda, Swami 1863-1902 .... **TCLC 88**

Vizenor, Gerald Robert 1934- .... **CLC 103, 263; NNAL**
See also CA 13-16R; 205; CAAE 205; CAAS 22; CANR 5, 21, 44, 67; DAM MULT; DLB 175, 227; MTCW 2; MTFW 2005; TCWW 2

Vizinczey, Stephen 1933- .... **CLC 40**
See also CA 128; CCA 1; INT CA-128

Vliet, R(ussell) G(ordon) 1929-1984 .... **CLC 22**
See also CA 37-40R; 112; CANR 18; CP 2, 3

Vogau, Boris Andreyevich 1894-1938
See Pilnyak, Boris
See also CA 123; 218

Vogel, Paula A. 1951- .... **CLC 76; DC 19**
See also CA 108; CAD; CANR 119, 140; CD 5, 6; CWD; DFS 14; DLB 341; MTFW 2005; RGAL 4

Voigt, Cynthia 1942- .... **CLC 30**
See also AAYA 3, 30; BYA 1, 3, 6, 7, 8; CA 106; CANR 18, 37, 40, 94, 145; CLR 13, 48; INT CANR-18; JRDA; LAIT 5; MAICYA 1, 2; MAICYAS 1; MTFW 2005; SATA 48, 79, 116, 160; SATA-Brief 33; WYA; YAW

Voigt, Ellen Bryant 1943- .... **CLC 54**
See also CA 69-72; CANR 11, 29, 55, 115, 171; CP 5, 6, 7; CSW; CWP; DLB 120; PFS 23

Voinovich, Vladimir 1932- .. **CLC 10, 49, 147**
See also CA 81-84; CAAS 12; CANR 33, 67, 150; CWW 2; DLB 302; MTCW 1

Voinovich, Vladimir Nikolaevich
See Voinovich, Vladimir

Vollmann, William T. 1959- ...... **CLC 89, 227**
See also AMWS 17; CA 134; CANR 67, 116; CN 7; CPW; DA3; DAM NOV, POP; MTCW 2; MTFW 2005

Voloshinov, V. N.
See Bakhtin, Mikhail Mikhailovich

Voltaire 1694-1778 .. **LC 14, 79, 110; SSC 12, 112; WLC 6**
See also BYA 13; DA; DA3; DAB; DAC; DAM DRAM, MST; DLB 314; EW 4; GFL Beginnings to 1789; LATS 1:1; LMFS 1; NFS 7; RGWL 2, 3; TWA

von Aschendrof, Baron Ignatz
See Ford, Ford Madox

von Chamisso, Adelbert
See Chamisso, Adelbert von

von Daeniken, Erich 1935- .... **CLC 30**
See also AITN 1; CA 37-40R; CANR 17, 44

von Daniken, Erich
See von Daeniken, Erich

von Eschenbach, Wolfram c. 1170-c. 1220 .... **CMLC 5**
See Eschenbach, Wolfram von
See also CDWLB 2; DLB 138; EW 1; RGWL 2

von Hartmann, Eduard 1842-1906 .... **TCLC 96**

von Hayek, Friedrich August
See Hayek, F(riedrich) A(ugust von)

von Heidenstam, (Carl Gustaf) Verner
See Heidenstam, (Carl Gustaf) Verner von

von Heyse, Paul (Johann Ludwig)
See Heyse, Paul (Johann Ludwig von)

von Hofmannsthal, Hugo
See Hofmannsthal, Hugo von

von Horvath, Odon
See von Horvath, Odon

von Horvath, Odon
See von Horvath, Odon

von Horvath, Odon 1901-1938 .... **TCLC 45**
See von Horvath, Oedoen
See also CA 118; 194; DLB 85, 124; RGWL 2, 3

von Horvath, Oedoen
See von Horvath, Odon
See also CA 184

von Kleist, Heinrich
See Kleist, Heinrich von

Vonnegut, Kurt, Jr.
See Vonnegut, Kurt

Vonnegut, Kurt 1922-2007 .... **CLC 1, 2, 3, 4, 5, 8, 12, 22, 40, 60, 111, 212, 254; SSC 8; WLC 6**
See also AAYA 6, 44; AITN 1; AMWS 2; BEST 90:4; BPFB 3; BYA 3, 14; CA 1-4R; 259; CANR 1, 25, 49, 75, 92; CDALB 1968-1988; CN 1, 2, 3, 4, 5, 6, 7; CPW 1; DA; DA3; DAB; DAC; DAM MST, NOV, POP; DLB 2, 8, 152; DLBD 3; DLBY 1980; EWL 3; EXPN; EXPS; LAIT 4; LMFS 2; MAL 5; MTCW 1, 2; MTFW 2005; NFS 3, 28; RGAL 4; SCFW; SFW 4; SSFS 5; TUS; YAW

Von Rachen, Kurt
See Hubbard, L. Ron

von Sternberg, Josef
See Sternberg, Josef von

Vorster, Gordon 1924- .... **CLC 34**
See also CA 133

Vosce, Trudie
See Ozick, Cynthia

Voznesensky, Andrei (Andreievich) 1933- .... **CLC 1, 15, 57**
See Voznesensky, Andrey
See also CA 89-92; CANR 37; CWW 2; DAM POET; MTCW 1

Voznesensky, Andrey
See Voznesensky, Andrei (Andreievich)
See also EWL 3

Wace, Robert c. 1100-c. 1175 .... **CMLC 55**
See also DLB 146

Waddington, Miriam 1917-2004 .... **CLC 28**
See also CA 21-24R; 225; CANR 12, 30; CCA 1; CP 1, 2, 3, 4, 5, 6, 7; DLB 68

Wagman, Fredrica 1937- .... **CLC 7**
See also CA 97-100; CANR 166; INT CA-97-100

Wagner, Linda W.
See Wagner-Martin, Linda (C.)

Wagner, Linda Welshimer
See Wagner-Martin, Linda (C.)

Wagner, Richard 1813-1883 ..... **NCLC 9, 119**
See also DLB 129; EW 6

Wagner-Martin, Linda (C.) 1936- .... **CLC 50**
See also CA 159; CANR 135

Wagoner, David (Russell) 1926- .... **CLC 3, 5, 15; PC 33**
See also AMWS 9; CA 1-4R; CAAS 3; CANR 2, 71; CN 1, 2, 3, 4, 5, 6, 7; CP 1, 2, 3, 4, 5, 6, 7; DLB 5, 256; SATA 14; TCWW 1, 2

Wah, Fred(erick James) 1939- .... **CLC 44**
See also CA 107; 141; CP 1, 6, 7; DLB 60

Wahloo, Per 1926-1975 .... **CLC 7**
See also BPFB 3; CA 61-64; CANR 73; CMW 4; MSW

Wahloo, Peter
See Wahloo, Per

Wain, John (Barrington) 1925-1994 . **CLC 2, 11, 15, 46**
See also CA 5-8R; 145; CAAS 4; CANR 23, 54; CDBLB 1960 to Present; CN 1, 2, 3, 4, 5; CP 1, 2, 3, 4, 5; DLB 15, 27, 139, 155; EWL 3; MTCW 1, 2; MTFW 2005

Wajda, Andrzej 1926- .... **CLC 16, 219**
See also CA 102

Wakefield, Dan 1932- .... **CLC 7**
See also CA 21-24R, 211; CAAE 211; CAAS 7; CN 4, 5, 6, 7

Wakefield, Herbert Russell 1888-1965 .... **TCLC 120**
See also CA 5-8R; CANR 77; HGG; SUFW

Wakoski, Diane 1937- ...... **CLC 2, 4, 7, 9, 11, 40; PC 15**
See also CA 13-16R, 216; CAAE 216; CAAS 1; CANR 9, 60, 106; CP 1, 2, 3, 4, 5, 6, 7; CWP; DAM POET; DLB 5; INT CANR-9; MAL 5; MTCW 2; MTFW 2005

Wakoski-Sherbell, Diane
See Wakoski, Diane

Walcott, Derek 1930- . **BLC 1:3, 2:3; CLC 2, 4, 9, 14, 25, 42, 67, 76, 160; DC 7; PC 46**
See also BW 2; CA 89-92; CANR 26, 47, 75, 80, 130; CBD; CD 5, 6; CDWLB 3; CP 1, 2, 3, 4, 5, 6, 7; DA3; DAB; DAC; DAM MST, MULT, POET; DLB 117, 332; DLBY 1981; DNFS 1; EFS 1; EWL 3; LMFS 2; MTCW 1, 2; MTFW 2005; PFS 6; RGEL 2; TWA; WWE 1

Waldman, Anne (Lesley) 1945- .... **CLC 7**
See also BG 1:3; CA 37-40R; CAAS 17; CANR 34, 69, 116; CP 1, 2, 3, 4, 5, 6, 7; CWP; DLB 16

Waldo, E. Hunter
See Sturgeon, Theodore (Hamilton)

Waldo, Edward Hamilton
See Sturgeon, Theodore (Hamilton)

Walker, Alice 1944- .... **BLC 1:3, 2:3; CLC 5, 6, 9, 19, 27, 46, 58, 103, 167; PC 30; SSC 5; WLCS**
See also AAYA 3, 33; AFAW 1, 2; AMWS 3; BEST 89:4; BPFB 3; BW 2, 3; CA 37-40R; CANR 9, 27, 49, 66, 82, 131; CDALB 1968-1988; CN 4, 5, 6, 7; CPW; CSW; DA; DA3; DAB; DAC; DAM MST, MULT, NOV, POET, POP; DLB 6, 33, 143; EWL 3; EXPN; EXPS; FL 1:6; FW; INT CANR-27; LAIT 3; MAL 5; MBL; MTCW 1, 2; MTFW 2005; NFS 5; RGAL 4; RGSF 2; SATA 31; SSFS 2, 11; TUS; YAW

Walker, Alice Malsenior
See Walker, Alice

Walker, David Harry 1911-1992 ...... **CLC 14**
See also CA 1-4R; 137; CANR 1; CN 1, 2; CWRI 5; SATA 8; SATA-Obit 71

Walker, Edward Joseph 1934-2004
See Walker, Ted
See also CA 21-24R; 226; CANR 12, 28, 53

Walker, George F(rederick) 1947- .. **CLC 44, 61**
See also CA 103; CANR 21, 43, 59; CD 5, 6; DAB; DAC; DAM MST; DLB 60

Walker, Joseph A. 1935-2003 .... **CLC 19**
See also BW 1, 3; CA 89-92; CAD; CANR 26, 143; CD 5, 6; DAM DRAM, MST; DFS 12; DLB 38

Walker, Margaret 1915-1998 .... **BLC 1:3; CLC 1, 6; PC 20; TCLC 129**
See also AFAW 1, 2; BW 2, 3; CA 73-76; 172; CANR 26, 54, 76, 136; CN 1, 2, 3, 4, 5, 6; CP 1, 2, 3, 4, 5, 6; CSW; DAM MULT; DLB 76, 152; EXPP; FW; MAL 5; MTCW 1, 2; MTFW 2005; RGAL 4; RHW

Walker, Ted CLC 13
See Walker, Edward Joseph
See also CP 1, 2, 3, 4, 5, 6, 7; DLB 40

Wallace, David Foster 1962-2008 .... **CLC 50, 114; SSC 68**
See also AAYA 50; AMWS 10; CA 132; CANR 59, 133; CN 7; DA3; MTCW 2; MTFW 2005

Wallace, Dexter
See Masters, Edgar Lee

Wallace, (Richard Horatio) Edgar 1875-1932 .... **TCLC 57**
See also CA 115; 218; CMW 4; DLB 70; MSW; RGEL 2

Wallace, Irving 1916-1990 .... **CLC 7, 13**
See also AITN 1; BPFB 3; CA 1-4R; 132; CAAS 1; CANR 1, 27; CPW; DAM NOV, POP; INT CANR-27; MTCW 1, 2

Wallant, Edward Lewis 1926-1962 ... **CLC 5, 10**
See also CA 1-4R; CANR 22; DLB 2, 28, 143, 299; EWL 3; MAL 5; MTCW 1, 2; RGAL 4; RGHL

Wallas, Graham 1858-1932 .... **TCLC 91**

Waller, Edmund 1606-1687 .... **LC 86; PC 72**
See also BRW 2; DAM POET; DLB 126; PAB; RGEL 2

Walley, Byron
See Card, Orson Scott

Walpole, Horace 1717-1797 ..... **LC 2, 49, 152**
See also BRW 3; DLB 39, 104, 213; GL 3; HGG; LMFS 1; RGEL 2; SUFW 1; TEA

Walpole, Hugh (Seymour) 1884-1941 .... **TCLC 5**
See also CA 104; 165; DLB 34; HGG; MTCW 2; RGEL 2; RHW

Walrond, Eric (Derwent) 1898-1966 . **HR 1:3**
See also BW 1; CA 125; DLB 51

Walser, Martin 1927- .... **CLC 27, 183**
See also CA 57-60; CANR 8, 46, 145; CWW 2; DLB 75, 124; EWL 3

Walser, Robert 1878-1956 ..... **SSC 20; TCLC 18**
See also CA 118; 165; CANR 100; DLB 66; EWL 3

Walsh, Gillian Paton
See Paton Walsh, Jill

Walsh, Jill Paton CLC 35
See Paton Walsh, Jill
See also CLR 2, 65, 128; WYA

Walter, Villiam Christian
See Andersen, Hans Christian

Walters, Anna L(ee) 1946- .... **NNAL**
See also CA 73-76

Walther von der Vogelweide c. 1170-1228 .... **CMLC 56**

Walton, Izaak 1593-1683 .... **LC 72**
See also BRW 2; CDBLB Before 1660; DLB 151, 213; RGEL 2

Walzer, Michael (Laban) 1935- ...... **CLC 238**
See also CA 37-40R; CANR 15, 48, 127

Wambaugh, Joseph, Jr. 1937- ...... **CLC 3, 18**
See also AITN 1; BEST 89:3; BPFB 3; CA 33-36R; CANR 42, 65, 115, 167; CMW 4; CPW 1; DA3; DAM NOV, POP; DLB 6; DLBY 1983; MSW; MTCW 1, 2

Wambaugh, Joseph Aloysius
See Wambaugh, Joseph, Jr.

Wang Wei 699(?)-761(?) . **CMLC 100; PC 18**
See also TWA

Warburton, William 1698-1779 .... **LC 97**
See also DLB 104

Ward, Arthur Henry Sarsfield 1883-1959
See Rohmer, Sax
See also CA 108; 173; CMW 4; HGG

Ward, Douglas Turner 1930- .... **CLC 19**
See also BW 1; CA 81-84; CAD; CANR 27; CD 5, 6; DLB 7, 38

Ward, E. D.
See Lucas, E(dward) V(errall)

Ward, Mrs. Humphry 1851-1920
See Ward, Mary Augusta
See also RGEL 2

Ward, Mary Augusta 1851-1920 ... **TCLC 55**
See Ward, Mrs. Humphry
See also DLB 18

Ward, Nathaniel 1578(?)-1652 .... **LC 114**
See also DLB 24

Ward, Peter
See Faust, Frederick (Schiller)

Warhol, Andy 1928(?)-1987 .... **CLC 20**
See also AAYA 12; BEST 89:4; CA 89-92; 121; CANR 34

Warner, Francis (Robert Le Plastrier)
1937- .... **CLC 14**
See also CA 53-56; CANR 11; CP 1, 2, 3, 4

Warner, Marina 1946- .... **CLC 59, 231**
See also CA 65-68; CANR 21, 55, 118; CN 5, 6, 7; DLB 194; MTFW 2005

Warner, Rex (Ernest) 1905-1986 ...... **CLC 45**
See also CA 89-92; 119; CN 1, 2, 3, 4; CP 1, 2, 3, 4; DLB 15; RGEL 2; RHW

Warner, Susan (Bogert)
1819-1885 .... **NCLC 31, 146**
See also AMWS 18; DLB 3, 42, 239, 250, 254

Warner, Sylvia (Constance) Ashton
See Ashton-Warner, Sylvia (Constance)

Warner, Sylvia Townsend
1893-1978 .. **CLC 7, 19; SSC 23; TCLC 131**
See also BRWS 7; CA 61-64; 77-80; CANR 16, 60, 104; CN 1, 2; DLB 34, 139; EWL 3; FANT; FW; MTCW 1, 2; RGEL 2; RGSF 2; RHW

Warren, Mercy Otis 1728-1814 ..... **NCLC 13**
See also DLB 31, 200; RGAL 4; TUS

Warren, Robert Penn 1905-1989 .. **CLC 1, 4, 6, 8, 10, 13, 18, 39, 53, 59; PC 37; SSC 4, 58; WLC 6**
See also AITN 1; AMW; AMWC 2; BPFB 3; BYA 1; CA 13-16R; 129; CANR 10, 47; CDALB 1968-1988; CN 1, 2, 3, 4; CP 1, 2, 3, 4; DA; DA3; DAB; DAC; DAM MST, NOV, POET; DLB 2, 48, 152, 320; DLBY 1980, 1989; EWL 3; INT CANR-10; MAL 5; MTCW 1, 2; MTFW 2005; NFS 13; RGAL 4; RGSF 2; RHW; SATA 46; SATA-Obit 63; SSFS 8; TUS

Warrigal, Jack
See Furphy, Joseph

Warshofsky, Isaac
See Singer, Isaac Bashevis

Warton, Joseph 1722-1800 ... **LC 128; NCLC 118**
See also DLB 104, 109; RGEL 2

Warton, Thomas 1728-1790 .... **LC 15, 82**
See also DAM POET; DLB 104, 109, 336; RGEL 2

Waruk, Kona
See Harris, (Theodore) Wilson

Warung, Price TCLC 45
See Astley, William
See also DLB 230; RGEL 2

Warwick, Jarvis
See Garner, Hugh
See also CCA 1

Washington, Alex
See Harris, Mark

Washington, Booker T(aliaferro)
1856-1915 .... **BLC 1:3; TCLC 10**
See also BW 1; CA 114; 125; DA3; DAM MULT; DLB 345; LAIT 2; RGAL 4; SATA 28

Washington, George 1732-1799 .... **LC 25**
See also DLB 31

Wassermann, (Karl) Jakob
1873-1934 .... **TCLC 6**
See also CA 104; 163; DLB 66; EWL 3

Wasserstein, Wendy 1950-2006 . **CLC 32, 59, 90, 183; DC 4**
See also AAYA 73; AMWS 15; CA 121; 129; 247; CABS 3; CAD; CANR 53, 75, 128; CD 5, 6; CWD; DA3; DAM DRAM; DFS 5, 17; DLB 228; EWL 3; FW; INT CA-129; MAL 5; MTCW 2; MTFW 2005; SATA 94; SATA-Obit 174

Waterhouse, Keith (Spencer) 1929- . **CLC 47**
See also BRWS 13; CA 5-8R; CANR 38, 67, 109; CBD; CD 6; CN 1, 2, 3, 4, 5, 6, 7; DLB 13, 15; MTCW 1, 2; MTFW 2005

Waters, Frank (Joseph) 1902-1995 .. **CLC 88**
See also CA 5-8R; 149; CAAS 13; CANR 3, 18, 63, 121; DLB 212; DLBY 1986; RGAL 4; TCWW 1, 2

Waters, Mary C. CLC 70

Waters, Roger 1944- .... **CLC 35**

Watkins, Frances Ellen
See Harper, Frances Ellen Watkins

Watkins, Gerrold
See Malzberg, Barry N(athaniel)

Watkins, Gloria Jean
See hooks, bell

Watkins, Paul 1964- .... **CLC 55**
See also CA 132; CANR 62, 98

Watkins, Vernon Phillips
1906-1967 .... **CLC 43**
See also CA 9-10; 25-28R; CAP 1; DLB 20; EWL 3; RGEL 2

Watson, Irving S.
See Mencken, H(enry) L(ouis)

Watson, John H.
See Farmer, Philip Jose

Watson, Richard F.
See Silverberg, Robert

Watts, Ephraim
See Horne, Richard Henry Hengist

Watts, Isaac 1674-1748 .... **LC 98**
See also DLB 95; RGEL 2; SATA 52

Waugh, Auberon (Alexander)
1939-2001 .... **CLC 7**
See also CA 45-48; 192; CANR 6, 22, 92; CN 1, 2, 3; DLB 14, 194

Waugh, Evelyn 1903-1966 ... **CLC 1, 3, 8, 13, 19, 27, 44, 107; SSC 41; WLC 6**
See also AAYA 78; BPFB 3; BRW 7; CA 85-88; 25-28R; CANR 22; CDBLB 1914-1945; DA; DA3; DAB; DAC; DAM MST, NOV, POP; DLB 15, 162, 195; EWL 3; MTCW 1, 2; MTFW 2005; NFS 13, 17; RGEL 2; RGSF 2; TEA; WLIT 4

Waugh, Evelyn Arthur St. John
See Waugh, Evelyn

Waugh, Harriet 1944- .... **CLC 6**
See also CA 85-88; CANR 22

Ways, C.R.
See Blount, Roy, Jr.

Waystaff, Simon
See Swift, Jonathan

Webb, Beatrice (Martha Potter)
1858-1943 .... **TCLC 22**
See also CA 117; 162; DLB 190; FW

Webb, Charles (Richard) 1939- .... **CLC 7**
See also CA 25-28R; CANR 114

Webb, Frank J. NCLC 143
See also DLB 50

Webb, James, Jr.
See Webb, James

Webb, James 1946- .... **CLC 22**
See also CA 81-84; CANR 156

Webb, James H.
See Webb, James

Webb, James Henry
See Webb, James

Webb, Mary Gladys (Meredith)
1881-1927 .... **TCLC 24**
See also CA 182; 123; DLB 34; FW; RGEL 2

Webb, Mrs. Sidney
See Webb, Beatrice (Martha Potter)

Webb, Phyllis 1927- .... **CLC 18**
See also CA 104; CANR 23; CCA 1; CP 1, 2, 3, 4, 5, 6, 7; CWP; DLB 53

Webb, Sidney (James) 1859-1947 .. **TCLC 22**
See also CA 117; 163; DLB 190

Webber, Andrew Lloyd CLC 21
See Lloyd Webber, Andrew
See also DFS 7

Weber, Lenora Mattingly
1895-1971 .... **CLC 12**
See also CA 19-20; 29-32R; CAP 1; SATA 2; SATA-Obit 26

Weber, Max 1864-1920 .... **TCLC 69**
See also CA 109; 189; DLB 296

Webster, John 1580(?)-1634(?) ...... **DC 2; LC 33, 84, 124; WLC 6**
See also BRW 2; CDBLB Before 1660; DA; DAB; DAC; DAM DRAM, MST; DFS 17, 19; DLB 58; IDTP; RGEL 2; WLIT 3

Webster, Noah 1758-1843 .... **NCLC 30**
See also DLB 1, 37, 42, 43, 73, 243

Wedekind, Benjamin Franklin
See Wedekind, Frank

Wedekind, Frank 1864-1918 .... **TCLC 7**
See also CA 104; 153; CANR 121, 122; CDWLB 2; DAM DRAM; DLB 118; EW 8; EWL 3; LMFS 2; RGWL 2, 3

Wehr, Demaris CLC 65

Weidman, Jerome 1913-1998 .... **CLC 7**
See also AITN 2; CA 1-4R; 171; CAD; CANR 1; CD 1, 2, 3, 4, 5; DLB 28

Weil, Simone (Adolphine)
1909-1943 .... **TCLC 23**
See also CA 117; 159; EW 12; EWL 3; FW; GFL 1789 to the Present; MTCW 2

Weininger, Otto 1880-1903 .... **TCLC 84**

Weinstein, Nathan
See West, Nathanael

Weinstein, Nathan von Wallenstein
See West, Nathanael

Weir, Peter (Lindsay) 1944- .... **CLC 20**
See also CA 113; 123

Weiss, Peter (Ulrich) 1916-1982 .. **CLC 3, 15, 51; TCLC 152**
See also CA 45-48; 106; CANR 3; DAM DRAM; DFS 3; DLB 69, 124; EWL 3; RGHL; RGWL 2, 3

Weiss, Theodore (Russell)
1916-2003 .... **CLC 3, 8, 14**
See also CA 9-12R; 189; 216; CAAE 189; CAAS 2; CANR 46, 94; CP 1, 2, 3, 4, 5, 6, 7; DLB 5; TCLE 1:2

Welch, (Maurice) Denton
1915-1948 .... **TCLC 22**
See also BRWS 8, 9; CA 121; 148; RGEL
2

Welch, James (Phillip) 1940-2003 ..... **CLC 6,
14, 52, 249; NNAL; PC 62**
See also CA 85-88; 219; CANR 42, 66, 107;
CN 5, 6, 7; CP 2, 3, 4, 5, 6, 7; CPW;
DAM MULT, POP; DLB 175, 256; LATS
1:1; NFS 23; RGAL 4; TCWW 1, 2

Weldon, Fay 1931- . **CLC 6, 9, 11, 19, 36, 59,
122**
See also BRWS 4; CA 21-24R; CANR 16,
46, 63, 97, 137; CDBLB 1960 to Present;
CN 3, 4, 5, 6, 7; CPW; DAM POP; DLB
14, 194, 319; EWL 3; FW; HGG; INT
CANR-16; MTCW 1, 2; MTFW 2005;
RGEL 2; RGSF 2

Wellek, Rene 1903-1995 .... **CLC 28**
See also CA 5-8R; 150; CAAS 7; CANR 8;
DLB 63; EWL 3; INT CANR-8

Weller, Michael 1942- .... **CLC 10, 53**
See also CA 85-88; CAD; CD 5, 6

Weller, Paul 1958- .... **CLC 26**

Wellershoff, Dieter 1925- .... **CLC 46**
See also CA 89-92; CANR 16, 37

Welles, (George) Orson 1915-1985 .. **CLC 20,
80**
See also AAYA 40; CA 93-96; 117

Wellman, John McDowell 1945-
See Wellman, Mac
See also CA 166; CD 5

Wellman, Mac CLC 65
See Wellman, John McDowell; Wellman,
John McDowell
See also CAD; CD 6; RGAL 4

Wellman, Manly Wade 1903-1986 ... **CLC 49**
See also CA 1-4R; 118; CANR 6, 16, 44;
FANT; SATA 6; SATA-Obit 47; SFW 4;
SUFW

Wells, Carolyn 1869(?)-1942 .... **TCLC 35**
See also CA 113; 185; CMW 4; DLB 11

Wells, H(erbert) G(eorge) 1866-1946 . **SSC 6,
70; TCLC 6, 12, 19, 133; WLC 6**
See also AAYA 18; BPFB 3; BRW 6; CA
110; 121; CDBLB 1914-1945; CLR 64,
133; DA; DA3; DAB; DAC; DAM MST,
NOV; DLB 34, 70, 156, 178; EWL 3;
EXPS; HGG; LAIT 3; MTCW
1, 2; MTFW 2005; NFS 17, 20; RGEL 2;
RGSF 2; SATA 20; SCFW 1, 2; SFW 4;
SSFS 3; SUFW; TEA; WCH; WLIT 4;
YAW

Wells, Rosemary 1943- .... **CLC 12**
See also AAYA 13; BYA 7, 8; CA 85-88;
CANR 48, 120, 179; CLR 16, 69; CWRI
5; MAICYA 1, 2; SAAS 1; SATA 18, 69,
114, 156; YAW

Wells-Barnett, Ida B(ell)
1862-1931 .... **TCLC 125**
See also CA 182; DLB 23, 221

Welsh, Irvine 1958- .... **CLC 144**
See also CA 173; CANR 146; CN 7; DLB
271

Welty, Eudora 1909-2001 .... **CLC 1, 2, 5, 14,
22, 33, 105, 220; SSC 1, 27, 51, 111;
WLC 6**
See also AAYA 48; AMW; AMWR 1; BPFB
3; CA 9-12R; 199; CABS 1; CANR 32,
65, 128; CDALB 1941-1968; CN 1, 2, 3,
4, 5, 6, 7; CSW; DA; DA3; DAB; DAC;
DAM MST, NOV; DLB 2, 102, 143;
DLBD 12; DLBY 1987, 2001; EWL 3;
EXPS; HGG; LAIT 3; MAL 5; MBL;
MTCW 1, 2; MTFW 2005; NFS 13, 15;
RGAL 4; RGSF 2; RHW; SSFS 2, 10, 26;
TUS

Welty, Eudora Alice
See Welty, Eudora

Wen I-to 1899-1946 .... **TCLC 28**
See also EWL 3

Wentworth, Robert
See Hamilton, Edmond

Werfel, Franz (Viktor) 1890-1945 ... **TCLC 8**
See also CA 104; 161; DLB 81, 124; EWL
3; RGWL 2, 3

Wergeland, Henrik Arnold
1808-1845 .... **NCLC 5**

Werner, Friedrich Ludwig Zacharias
1768-1823 .... **NCLC 189**
See also DLB 94

Werner, Zacharias
See Werner, Friedrich Ludwig Zacharias

Wersba, Barbara 1932- .... **CLC 30**
See also AAYA 2, 30; BYA 6, 12, 13; CA
29-32R, 182; CAAE 182; CANR 16, 38;
CLR 3, 78; DLB 52; JRDA; MAICYA 1,
2; SAAS 2; SATA 1, 58; SATA-Essay 103;
WYA; YAW

Wertmueller, Lina 1928- .... **CLC 16**
See also CA 97-100; CANR 39, 78

Wescott, Glenway 1901-1987 .. **CLC 13; SSC
35**
See also CA 13-16R; 121; CANR 23, 70;
CN 1, 2, 3, 4; DLB 4, 9, 102; MAL 5;
RGAL 4

Wesker, Arnold 1932- .... **CLC 3, 5, 42**
See also CA 1-4R; CAAS 7; CANR 1, 33;
CBD; CD 5, 6; CDBLB 1960 to Present;
DAB; DAM DRAM; DLB 13, 310, 319;
EWL 3; MTCW 1; RGEL 2; TEA

Wesley, Charles 1707-1788 .... **LC 128**
See also DLB 95; RGEL 2

Wesley, John 1703-1791 .... **LC 88**
See also DLB 104

Wesley, Richard (Errol) 1945- .... **CLC 7**
See also BW 1; CA 57-60; CAD; CANR
27; CD 5, 6; DLB 38

Wessel, Johan Herman 1742-1785 .... **LC 7**
See also DLB 300

West, Anthony (Panther)
1914-1987 .... **CLC 50**
See also CA 45-48; 124; CANR 3, 19; CN
1, 2, 3, 4; DLB 15

West, C. P.
See Wodehouse, P(elham) G(renville)

West, Cornel 1953- .... **BLCS; CLC 134**
See also CA 144; CANR 91, 159; DLB 246

West, Cornel Ronald
See West, Cornel

West, Delno C(loyde), Jr. 1936- .... **CLC 70**
See also CA 57-60

West, Dorothy 1907-1998 ...... **HR 1:3; TCLC
108**
See also AMWS 18; BW 2; CA 143; 169;
DLB 76

West, (Mary) Jessamyn 1902-1984 ... **CLC 7,
17**
See also CA 9-12R; 112; CANR 27; CN 1,
2, 3; DLB 6; DLBY 1984; MTCW 1, 2;
RGAL 4; RHW; SATA-Obit 37; TCWW
2; TUS; YAW

West, Morris L(anglo) 1916-1999 ..... **CLC 6,
33**
See also BPFB 3; CA 5-8R; 187; CANR
24, 49, 64; CN 1, 2, 3, 4, 5, 6; CPW; DLB
289; MTCW 1, 2; MTFW 2005

West, Nathanael 1903-1940 ...... **SSC 16, 116;
TCLC 1, 14, 44**
See also AAYA 77; AMW; AMWR 2; BPFB
3; CA 104; 125; CDALB 1929-1941;
DA3; DLB 4, 9, 28; EWL 3; MAL 5;
MTCW 1, 2; MTFW 2005; NFS 16;
RGAL 4; TUS

West, Owen
See Koontz, Dean R.

West, Paul 1930- .... **CLC 7, 14, 96, 226**
See also CA 13-16R; CAAS 7; CANR 22,
53, 76, 89, 136; CN 1, 2, 3, 4, 5, 6, 7;
DLB 14; INT CANR-22; MTCW 2;
MTFW 2005

West, Rebecca 1892-1983 ... **CLC 7, 9, 31, 50**
See also BPFB 3; BRWS 3; CA 5-8R; 109;
CANR 19; CN 1, 2, 3; DLB 36; DLBY
1983; EWL 3; FW; MTCW 1, 2; MTFW
2005; NCFS 4; RGEL 2; TEA

Westall, Robert (Atkinson)
1929-1993 .... **CLC 17**
See also AAYA 12; BYA 2, 6, 7, 8, 9, 15;
CA 69-72; 141; CANR 18, 68; CLR 13;
FANT; JRDA; MAICYA 1, 2; MAICYAS
1; SAAS 2; SATA 23, 69; SATA-Obit 75;
WYA; YAW

Westermarck, Edward 1862-1939 . **TCLC 87**

Westlake, Donald E. 1933- .... **CLC 7, 33**
See also BPFB 3; CA 17-20R; CAAS 13;
CANR 16, 44, 65, 94, 137; CMW 4;
CPW; DAM POP; INT CANR-16; MSW;
MTCW 2; MTFW 2005

Westlake, Donald Edwin
See Westlake, Donald E.

Westmacott, Mary
See Christie, Agatha (Mary Clarissa)

Weston, Allen
See Norton, Andre

Wetcheek, J. L.
See Feuchtwanger, Lion

Wetering, Janwillem van de
See van de Wetering, Janwillem

Wetherald, Agnes Ethelwyn
1857-1940 .... **TCLC 81**
See also CA 202; DLB 99

Wetherell, Elizabeth
See Warner, Susan (Bogert)

Whale, James 1889-1957 .... **TCLC 63**
See also AAYA 75

Whalen, Philip (Glenn) 1923-2002 .... **CLC 6,
29**
See also BG 1:3; CA 9-12R; 209; CANR 5,
39; CP 1, 2, 3, 4, 5, 6, 7; DLB 16; WP

Wharton, Edith (Newbold Jones)
1862-1937 ... **SSC 6, 84; TCLC 3, 9, 27,
53, 129, 149; WLC 6**
See also AAYA 25; AMW; AMWC 2;
AMWR 1; BPFB 3; CA 104; 132; CDALB
1865-1917; CLR 136; DA; DA3; DAB;
DAC; DAM MST, NOV; DLB 4, 9, 12,
78, 189; DLBD 13; EWL 3; EXPS; FL
1:6; GL 3; HGG; LAIT 2, 3; LATS 1:1;
MAL 5; MBL; MTCW 1, 2; MTFW 2005;
NFS 5, 11, 15, 20; RGAL 4; RGSF 2;
RHW; SSFS 6, 7; SUFW; TUS

Wharton, James
See Mencken, H(enry) L(ouis)

Wharton, William 1925-2008 ..... **CLC 18, 37**
See also CA 93-96; CN 4, 5, 6, 7; DLBY
1980; INT CA-93-96

Wheatley (Peters), Phillis
1753(?)-1784 .... **BLC 1:3; LC 3, 50; PC
3; WLC 6**
See also AFAW 1, 2; CDALB 1640-1865;
DA; DA3; DAC; DAM MST, MULT,
POET; DLB 31, 50; EXPP; FL 1:1; PFS
13, 29; RGAL 4

Wheelock, John Hall 1886-1978 .... **CLC 14**
See also CA 13-16R; 77-80; CANR 14; CP
1, 2; DLB 45; MAL 5

Whim-Wham
See Curnow, (Thomas) Allen (Monro)

Whisp, Kennilworthy
See Rowling, J.K.

Whitaker, Rod 1931-2005
See Trevanian
See also CA 29-32R; 246; CANR 45, 153;
CMW 4

White, Babington
 See Braddon, Mary Elizabeth
White, E. B. 1899-1985 .... **CLC 10, 34, 39**
 See also AAYA 62; AITN 2; AMWS 1; CA
 13-16R; 116; CANR 16, 37; CDALBS;
 CLR 1, 21, 107; CPW; DA3; DAM POP;
 DLB 11, 22; EWL 3; FANT; MAICYA 1,
 2; MAL 5; MTCW 1, 2; MTFW 2005;
 NCFS 5; RGAL 4; SATA 2, 29, 100;
 SATA-Obit 44; TUS
White, Edmund 1940- .... **CLC 27, 110**
 See also AAYA 7; CA 45-48; CANR 3, 19,
 36, 62, 107, 133, 172; CN 5, 6, 7; DA3;
 DAM POP; DLB 227; MTCW 1, 2;
 MTFW 2005
White, Edmund Valentine III
 See White, Edmund
White, Elwyn Brooks
 See White, E. B.
White, Hayden V. 1928- .... **CLC 148**
 See also CA 128; CANR 135; DLB 246
White, Patrick (Victor Martindale)
 1912-1990 ...... **CLC 3, 4, 5, 7, 9, 18, 65,
 69; SSC 39; TCLC 176**
 See also BRWS 1; CA 81-84; 132; CANR
 43; CN 1, 2, 3, 4; DLB 260, 332; EWL 3;
 MTCW 1; RGEL 2; RGSF 2; RHW;
 TWA; WWE 1
White, Phyllis Dorothy James 1920-
 See James, P. D.
 See also CA 21-24R; CANR 17, 43, 65,
 112; CMW 4; CN 7; CPW; DA3; DAM
 POP; MTCW 1, 2; MTFW 2005; TEA
White, T(erence) H(anbury)
 1906-1964 .... **CLC 30**
 See also AAYA 22; BPFB 3; BYA 4, 5; CA
 73-76; CANR 37; CLR 139; DLB 160;
 FANT; JRDA; LAIT 1; MAICYA 1, 2;
 RGEL 2; SATA 12; SUFW 1; YAW
White, Terence de Vere 1912-1994 ... **CLC 49**
 See also CA 49-52; 145; CANR 3
White, Walter
 See White, Walter F(rancis)
White, Walter F(rancis)
 1893-1955 ..... **BLC 1:3; HR 1:3; TCLC
 15**
 See also BW 1; CA 115; 124; DAM MULT;
 DLB 51
White, William Hale 1831-1913
 See Rutherford, Mark
 See also CA 121; 189
Whitehead, Alfred North
 1861-1947 .... **TCLC 97**
 See also CA 117; 165; DLB 100, 262
Whitehead, Colson 1969- ...... **BLC 2:3; CLC
 232**
 See also CA 202; CANR 162
Whitehead, E(dward) A(nthony)
 1933- .... **CLC 5**
 See Whitehead, Ted
 See also CA 65-68; CANR 58, 118; CBD;
 CD 5; DLB 310
Whitehead, Ted
 See Whitehead, E(dward) A(nthony)
 See also CD 6
Whiteman, Roberta J. Hill 1947- ...... **NNAL**
 See also CA 146
Whitemore, Hugh (John) 1936- .... **CLC 37**
 See also CA 132; CANR 77; CBD; CD 5,
 6; INT CA-132
Whitman, Sarah Helen (Power)
 1803-1878 .... **NCLC 19**
 See also DLB 1, 243
Whitman, Walt(er) 1819-1892 .. **NCLC 4, 31,
 81, 205; PC 3, 91; WLC 6**
 See also AAYA 42; AMW; AMWR 1;
 CDALB 1640-1865; DA; DA3; DAB;
 DAC; DAM MST, POET; DLB 3, 64,
 224, 250; EXPP; LAIT 2; LMFS 1; PAB;
 PFS 2, 3, 13, 22; RGAL 4; SATA 20;
 TUS; WP; WYAS 1

Whitney, Isabella fl. 1565-fl. 1575 ..... **LC 130**
 See also DLB 136
Whitney, Phyllis A. 1903-2008 .... **CLC 42**
 See also AAYA 36; AITN 2; BEST 90:3;
 CA 1-4R; 269; CANR 3, 25, 38, 60; CLR
 59; CMW 4; CPW; DA3; DAM POP;
 JRDA; MAICYA 1, 2; MTCW 2; RHW;
 SATA 1, 30; SATA-Obit 189; YAW
Whitney, Phyllis Ayame
 See Whitney, Phyllis A.
Whitney, Phyllis Ayame
 See Whitney, Phyllis A.
Whittemore, (Edward) Reed, Jr.
 1919- .... **CLC 4**
 See also CA 9-12R, 219; CAAE 219; CAAS
 8; CANR 4, 119; CP 1, 2, 3, 4, 5, 6, 7;
 DLB 5; MAL 5
Whittier, John Greenleaf
 1807-1892 .... **NCLC 8, 59; PC 93**
 See also AMWS 1; DLB 1, 243; RGAL 4
Whittlebot, Hernia
 See Coward, Noel (Peirce)
Wicker, Thomas Grey
 See Wicker, Tom
Wicker, Tom 1926- .... **CLC 7**
 See also CA 65-68; CANR 21, 46, 141, 179
Wicomb, Zoe 1948- .... **BLC 2:3**
 See also CA 127; CANR 106, 167; DLB
 225
Wideman, John Edgar 1941- .. **BLC 1:3, 2:3;
 CLC 5, 34, 36, 67, 122; SSC 62**
 See also AFAW 1, 2; AMWS 10; BPFB 4;
 BW 2, 3; CA 85-88; CANR 14, 42, 67,
 109, 140; CN 4, 5, 6, 7; DAM MULT;
 DLB 33, 143; MAL 5; MTCW 2; MTFW
 2005; RGAL 4; RGSF 2; SSFS 6, 12, 24;
 TCLE 1:2
Wiebe, Rudy 1934- . **CLC 6, 11, 14, 138, 263**
 See also CA 37-40R; CANR 42, 67, 123;
 CN 1, 2, 3, 4, 5, 6, 7; DAC; DAM MST;
 DLB 60; RHW; SATA 156
Wiebe, Rudy Henry
 See Wiebe, Rudy
Wieland, Christoph Martin
 1733-1813 .... **NCLC 17, 177**
 See also DLB 97; EW 4; LMFS 1; RGWL
 2, 3
Wiene, Robert 1881-1938 .... **TCLC 56**
Wieners, John 1934- .... **CLC 7**
 See also BG 1:3; CA 13-16R; CP 1, 2, 3, 4,
 5, 6, 7; DLB 16; WP
Wiesel, Elie 1928- ...... **CLC 3, 5, 11, 37, 165;
 WLCS**
 See also AAYA 7, 54; AITN 1; CA 5-8R;
 CAAS 4; CANR 8, 40, 65, 125; CDALBS;
 CWW 2; DA; DA3; DAB; DAC; DAM
 MST, NOV; DLB 83, 299; DLBY 1987;
 EWL 3; INT CANR-8; LAIT 4; MTCW
 1, 2; MTFW 2005; NCFS 4; NFS 4;
 RGHL; RGWL 3; SATA 56; YAW
Wiesel, Eliezer
 See Wiesel, Elie
Wiggins, Marianne 1947- .... **CLC 57**
 See also AAYA 70; BEST 89:3; CA 130;
 CANR 60, 139, 180; CN 7; DLB 335
Wigglesworth, Michael 1631-1705 .... **LC 106**
 See also DLB 24; RGAL 4
Wiggs, Susan CLC 70
 See also CA 201; CANR 173
Wight, James Alfred 1916-1995
 See Herriot, James
 See also CA 77-80; SATA 55; SATA-Brief
 44
Wilbur, Richard 1921- .. **CLC 3, 6, 9, 14, 53,
 110; PC 51**
 See also AAYA 72; AMWS 3; CA 1-4R;
 CABS 2; CANR 2, 29, 76, 93, 139;
 CDALBS; CP 1, 2, 3, 4, 5, 6, 7; DA;
 DAB; DAC; DAM MST, POET; DLB 5,

169; EWL 3; EXPP; INT CANR-29;
 MAL 5; MTCW 1, 2; MTFW 2005; PAB;
 PFS 11, 12, 16, 29; RGAL 4; SATA 9,
 108; WP
Wilbur, Richard Purdy
 See Wilbur, Richard
Wild, Peter 1940- .... **CLC 14**
 See also CA 37-40R; CP 1, 2, 3, 4, 5, 6, 7;
 DLB 5
Wilde, Oscar 1854(?)-1900 ... **DC 17; SSC 11,
 77; TCLC 1, 8, 23, 41, 175; WLC 6**
 See also AAYA 49; BRW 5; BRWC 1, 2;
 BRWR 2; BYA 15; CA 104; 119; CANR
 112; CDBLB 1890-1914; CLR 114; DA;
 DA3; DAB; DAC; DAM DRAM, MST,
 NOV; DFS 4, 8, 9, 21; DLB 10, 19, 34,
 57, 141, 156, 190, 344; EXPS; FANT; GL
 3; LATS 1:1; NFS 20; RGEL 2; RGSF 2;
 SATA 24; SSFS 7; SUFW; TEA; WCH;
 WLIT 4
Wilde, Oscar Fingal O'Flahertie Willis
 See Wilde, Oscar
Wilder, Billy CLC 20
 See Wilder, Samuel
 See also AAYA 66; DLB 26
Wilder, Samuel 1906-2002
 See Wilder, Billy
 See also CA 89-92; 205
Wilder, Stephen
 See Marlowe, Stephen
Wilder, Thornton (Niven)
 1897-1975 .. **CLC 1, 5, 6, 10, 15, 35, 82;
 DC 1, 24; WLC 6**
 See also AAYA 29; AITN 2; AMW; CA 13-
 16R; 61-64; CAD; CANR 40, 132;
 CDALBS; CN 1, 2; DA; DA3; DAB;
 DAC; DAM DRAM, MST, NOV; DFS 1,
 4, 16; DLB 4, 7, 9, 228; DLBY 1997;
 EWL 3; LAIT 3; MAL 5; MTCW 1, 2;
 MTFW 2005; NFS 24; RGAL 4; RHW;
 WYAS 1
Wilding, Michael 1942- ...... **CLC 73; SSC 50**
 See also CA 104; CANR 24, 49, 106; CN
 4, 5, 6, 7; DLB 325; RGSF 2
Wiley, Richard 1944- .... **CLC 44**
 See also CA 121; 129; CANR 71
Wilhelm, Kate CLC 7
 See Wilhelm, Katie
 See also AAYA 20; BYA 16; CAAS 5; DLB
 8; INT CANR-17; SCFW 2
Wilhelm, Katie 1928-
 See Wilhelm, Kate
 See also CA 37-40R; CANR 17, 36, 60, 94;
 MTCW 1; SFW 4
Wilkins, Mary
 See Freeman, Mary E(leanor) Wilkins
Willard, Nancy 1936- .... **CLC 7, 37**
 See also BYA 5; CA 89-92; CANR 10, 39,
 68, 107, 152, 183; CLR 5; CP 2, 3, 4, 5;
 CWP; CWRI 5; DLB 5, 52; FANT; MAI-
 CYA 1, 2; MTCW 1; SATA 37, 71, 127,
 191; SATA-Brief 30; SUFW 2; TCLE 1:2
William of Malmesbury c. 1090B.C.-c.
 1140B.C. .... **CMLC 57**
William of Moerbeke c. 1215-c.
 1286 .... **CMLC 91**
William of Ockham 1290-1349 ..... **CMLC 32**
Williams, Ben Ames 1889-1953 ..... **TCLC 89**
 See also CA 183; DLB 102
Williams, Charles
 See Collier, James Lincoln
Williams, Charles (Walter Stansby)
 1886-1945 .... **TCLC 1, 11**
 See also BRWS 9; CA 104; 163; DLB 100,
 153, 255; FANT; RGEL 2; SUFW 1
Williams, C.K. 1936- .... **CLC 33, 56, 148**
 See also CA 37-40R; CAAS 26; CANR 57,
 106; CP 1, 2, 3, 4, 5, 6, 7; DAM POET;
 DLB 5; MAL 5

Williams, Ella Gwendolen Rees
See Rhys, Jean
Williams, (George) Emlyn
1905-1987 .... **CLC 15**
See also CA 104; 123; CANR 36; DAM
DRAM; DLB 10, 77; IDTP; MTCW 1
Williams, Hank 1923-1953 .... **TCLC 81**
See Williams, Hiram King
Williams, Helen Maria
1761-1827 .... **NCLC 135**
See also DLB 158
Williams, Hiram Hank
See Williams, Hank
Williams, Hiram King
See Williams, Hank
See also CA 188
Williams, Hugo (Mordaunt) 1942- ... **CLC 42**
See also CA 17-20R; CANR 45, 119; CP 1,
2, 3, 4, 5, 6, 7; DLB 40
Williams, J. Walker
See Wodehouse, P(elham) G(renville)
Williams, John A(lfred) 1925- .... **BLC 1:3;
CLC 5, 13**
See also AFAW 2; BW 2, 3; CA 53-56, 195;
CAAE 195; CAAS 3; CANR 6, 26, 51,
118; CN 1, 2, 3, 4, 5, 6, 7; CSW; DAM
MULT; DLB 2, 33; EWL 3; INT CANR-6;
MAL 5; RGAL 4; SFW 4
Williams, Jonathan 1929-2008 .... **CLC 13**
See also CA 9-12R; 270; CAAS 12; CANR
8, 108; CP 1, 2, 3, 4, 5, 6, 7; DLB 5
Williams, Jonathan Chamberlain
See Williams, Jonathan
Williams, Joy 1944- .... **CLC 31**
See also CA 41-44R; CANR 22, 48, 97,
168; DLB 335; SSFS 25
Williams, Norman 1952- .... **CLC 39**
See also CA 118
Williams, Roger 1603(?)-1683 .... **LC 129**
See also DLB 24
Williams, Sherley Anne
1944-1999 .... **BLC 1:3; CLC 89**
See also AFAW 2; BW 2, 3; CA 73-76; 185;
CANR 25, 82; DAM MULT; POET; DLB
41; INT CANR-25; SATA 78; SATA-Obit
116
Williams, Shirley
See Williams, Sherley Anne
Williams, Tennessee 1911-1983 . **CLC 1, 2, 5,
7, 8, 11, 15, 19, 30, 39, 45, 71, 111; DC
4; SSC 81; WLC 6**
See also AAYA 31; AITN 1, 2; AMW;
AMWC 1; CA 5-8R; 108; CABS 3; CAD;
CANR 31, 132, 174; CDALB 1941-1968;
CN 1, 2, 3; DA; DA3; DAB; DAC; DAM
DRAM, MST; DFS 17; DLB 7, 341;
DLBD 4; DLBY 1983; EWL 3; GLL 1;
LAIT 4; LATS 1:2; MAL 5; MTCW 1, 2;
MTFW 2005; RGAL 4; TUS
Williams, Thomas (Alonzo)
1926-1990 .... **CLC 14**
See also CA 1-4R; 132; CANR 2
Williams, Thomas Lanier
See Williams, Tennessee
Williams, William C.
See Williams, William Carlos
Williams, William Carlos
1883-1963 .... **CLC 1, 2, 5, 9, 13, 22, 42,
67; PC 7; SSC 31; WLC 6**
See also AAYA 46; AMW; AMWR 1; CA
89-92; CANR 34; CDALB 1917-1929;
DA; DA3; DAB; DAC; DAM MST,
POET; DLB 4, 16, 54, 86; EWL 3; EXPP;
MAL 5; MTCW 1, 2; MTFW 2005; NCFS
4; PAB; PFS 1, 6, 11; RGAL 4; RGSF 2;
TUS; WP

Williamson, David (Keith) 1942- ..... **CLC 56**
See also CA 103; CANR 41; CD 5, 6; DLB
289
Williamson, Jack **CLC 29**
See Williamson, John Stewart
See also CAAS 8; DLB 8; SCFW 1, 2
Williamson, John Stewart 1908-2006
See Williamson, Jack
See also AAYA 76; CA 17-20R; 255; CANR
23, 70, 153; SFW 4
Willie, Frederick
See Lovecraft, H. P.
Willingham, Calder (Baynard, Jr.)
1922-1995 .... **CLC 5, 51**
See also CA 5-8R; 147; CANR 3; CN 1, 2,
3, 4, 5; CSW; DLB 2, 44; IDFW 3, 4;
MTCW 1
Willis, Charles
See Clarke, Arthur C.
Willis, Nathaniel Parker
1806-1867 .... **NCLC 194**
See also DLB 3, 59, 73, 74, 183, 250;
DLBD 13; RGAL 4
Willy
See Colette, (Sidonie-Gabrielle)
Willy, Colette
See Colette, (Sidonie-Gabrielle)
See also GLL 1
Wilmot, John 1647-1680 .... **LC 75; PC 66**
See Rochester
See also BRW 2; DLB 131; PAB
Wilson, A.N. 1950- .... **CLC 33**
See also BRWS 6; CA 112; 122; CANR
156; CN 4, 5, 6, 7; DLB 14, 155, 194;
MTCW 2
Wilson, Andrew Norman
See Wilson, A.N.
Wilson, Angus (Frank Johnstone)
1913-1991 . **CLC 2, 3, 5, 25, 34; SSC 21**
See also BRWS 1; CA 5-8R; 134; CANR
21; CN 1, 2, 3, 4; DLB 15, 139, 155;
EWL 3; MTCW 1, 2; MTFW 2005; RGEL
2; RGSF 2
Wilson, August 1945-2005 .... **BLC 1:3, 2:3;
CLC 39, 50, 63, 118, 222; DC 2, 31;
WLCS**
See also AAYA 16; AFAW 2; AMWS 8; BW
2, 3; CA 115; 122; 244; CAD; CANR 42,
54, 76, 128; CD 5, 6; DA; DA3; DAB;
DAC; DAM DRAM, MST, MULT; DFS
3, 7, 15, 17, 24; DLB 228; EWL 3; LAIT
4; LATS 1:2; MAL 5; MTCW 1, 2;
MTFW 2005; RGAL 4
Wilson, Brian 1942- .... **CLC 12**
Wilson, Colin (Henry) 1931- .... **CLC 3, 14**
See also CA 1-4R; CAAS 5; CANR 1, 22,
33, 77; CMW 4; CN 1, 2, 3, 4, 5, 6; DLB
14, 194; HGG; MTCW 1; SFW 4
Wilson, Dirk
See Pohl, Frederik
Wilson, Edmund 1895-1972 .. **CLC 1, 2, 3, 8,
24**
See also AMW; CA 1-4R; 37-40R; CANR
1, 46, 110; CN 1; DLB 63; EWL 3; MAL
5; MTCW 1, 2; MTFW 2005; RGAL 4;
TUS
Wilson, Ethel Davis (Bryant)
1888(?)-1980 .... **CLC 13**
See also CA 102; CN 1, 2; DAC; DAM
POET; DLB 68; MTCW 1; RGEL 2
Wilson, Harriet
See Wilson, Harriet E. Adams
See also DLB 239
Wilson, Harriet E.
See Wilson, Harriet E. Adams
See also DLB 243

Wilson, Harriet E. Adams
1827(?)-1863(?) ...... **BLC 1:3; NCLC 78**
See Wilson, Harriet; Wilson, Harriet E.
See also DAM MULT; DLB 50
Wilson, John 1785-1854 .... **NCLC 5**
See also DLB 110
Wilson, John (Anthony) Burgess
See Burgess, Anthony
Wilson, Katharina **CLC 65**
Wilson, Lanford 1937- .. **CLC 7, 14, 36, 197;
DC 19**
See also CA 17-20R; CABS 3; CAD; CANR
45, 96; CD 5, 6; DAM DRAM; DFS 4, 9,
12, 16, 20; DLB 7, 341; EWL 3; MAL 5;
TUS
Wilson, Robert M. 1941- .... **CLC 7, 9**
See also CA 49-52; CAD; CANR 2, 41; CD
5, 6; MTCW 1
Wilson, Robert McLiam 1964- .... **CLC 59**
See also CA 132; DLB 267
Wilson, Sloan 1920-2003 .... **CLC 32**
See also CA 1-4R; 216; CANR 1, 44; CN
1, 2, 3, 4, 5, 6
Wilson, Snoo 1948- .... **CLC 33**
See also CA 69-72; CBD; CD 5, 6
Wilson, William S(mith) 1932- .... **CLC 49**
See also CA 81-84
Wilson, (Thomas) Woodrow
1856-1924 .... **TCLC 79**
See also CA 166; DLB 47
Winchester, Simon 1944- .... **CLC 257**
See also AAYA 66; CA 107; CANR 90, 130
Winchilsea, Anne (Kingsmill) Finch
1661-1720
See Finch, Anne
See also RGEL 2
Winckelmann, Johann Joachim
1717-1768 .... **LC 129**
See also DLB 97
Windham, Basil
See Wodehouse, P(elham) G(renville)
Wingrove, David 1954- .... **CLC 68**
See also CA 133; SFW 4
Winnemucca, Sarah 1844-1891 .... **NCLC 79;
NNAL**
See also DAM MULT; DLB 175; RGAL 4
Winstanley, Gerrard 1609-1676 .... **LC 52**
Wintergreen, Jane
See Duncan, Sara Jeannette
Winters, Arthur Yvor
See Winters, Yvor
Winters, Janet Lewis **CLC 41**
See Lewis, Janet
See also DLBY 1987
Winters, Yvor 1900-1968 .. **CLC 4, 8, 32; PC
82**
See also AMWS 2; CA 11-12; 25-28R; CAP
1; DLB 48; EWL 3; MAL 5; MTCW 1;
RGAL 4
Winterson, Jeanette 1959- .... **CLC 64, 158**
See also BRWS 4; CA 136; CANR 58, 116,
181; CN 5, 6, 7; CPW; DA3; DAM POP;
DLB 207, 261; FANT; FW; GLL 1;
MTCW 2; MTFW 2005; RHW; SATA 190
Winthrop, John 1588-1649 .... **LC 31, 107**
See also DLB 24, 30
Winton, Tim 1960- .... **CLC 251**
See also AAYA 34; CA 152; CANR 118;
CN 6, 7; DLB 325; SATA 98
Wirth, Louis 1897-1952 .... **TCLC 92**
See also CA 210
Wiseman, Frederick 1930- .... **CLC 20**
See also CA 159
Wister, Owen 1860-1938 ..... **SSC 100; TCLC
21**
See also BPFB 3; CA 108; 162; DLB 9, 78,
186; RGAL 4; SATA 62; TCWW 1, 2
Wither, George 1588-1667 .... **LC 96**
See also DLB 121; RGEL 2

Witkacy
See Witkiewicz, Stanislaw Ignacy
Witkiewicz, Stanislaw Ignacy
1885-1939 .... **TCLC 8**
See also CA 105; 162; CDWLB 4; DLB
215; EW 10; EWL 3; RGWL 2, 3; SFW 4
Wittgenstein, Ludwig (Josef Johann)
1889-1951 .... **TCLC 59**
See also CA 113; 164; DLB 262; MTCW 2
Wittig, Monique 1935-2003 .... **CLC 22**
See also CA 116; 135; 212; CANR 143;
CWW 2; DLB 83; EWL 3; FW; GLL 1
Wittlin, Jozef 1896-1976 .... **CLC 25**
See also CA 49-52; 65-68; CANR 3; EWL
3
Wodehouse, P(elham) G(renville)
1881-1975 .. **CLC 1, 2, 5, 10, 22; SSC 2,**
115; TCLC 108
See also AAYA 65; AITN 2; BRWS 3; CA
45-48; 57-60; CANR 3, 33; CDBLB
1914-1945; CN 1, 2; CPW 1; DA3; DAB;
DAC; DAM NOV; DLB 34, 162; EWL 3;
MTCW 1, 2; MTFW 2005; RGEL 2;
RGSF 2; SATA 22; SSFS 10
Woiwode, L.
See Woiwode, Larry (Alfred)
Woiwode, Larry (Alfred) 1941- ... **CLC 6, 10**
See also CA 73-76; CANR 16, 94; CN 3, 4,
5, 6, 7; DLB 6; INT CANR-16
Wojciechowska, Maia (Teresa)
1927-2002 .... **CLC 26**
See also AAYA 8, 46; BYA 3; CA 9-12R;
183; 209; CAAE 183; CANR 4, 41; CLR
1; JRDA; MAICYA 1, 2; SAAS 1; SATA
1, 28, 83; SATA-Essay 104; SATA-Obit
134; YAW
Wojtyla, Karol (Josef)
See John Paul II, Pope
Wojtyla, Karol (Jozef)
See John Paul II, Pope
Wolf, Christa 1929- ...... **CLC 14, 29, 58, 150,**
261
See also CA 85-88; CANR 45, 123; CD-
WLB 2; CWW 2; DLB 75; EWL 3; FW;
MTCW 1; RGWL 2, 3; SSFS 14
Wolf, Naomi 1962- .... **CLC 157**
See also CA 141; CANR 110; FW; MTFW
2005
Wolfe, Gene 1931- .... **CLC 25**
See also AAYA 35; CA 57-60; CAAS 9;
CANR 6, 32, 60, 152; CPW; DAM POP;
DLB 8; FANT; MTCW 2; MTFW 2005;
SATA 118, 165; SCFW 2; SFW 4; SUFW
2
Wolfe, Gene Rodman
See Wolfe, Gene
Wolfe, George C. 1954- .... **BLCS; CLC 49**
See also CA 149; CAD; CD 5, 6
Wolfe, Thomas (Clayton)
1900-1938 .... **SSC 33, 113; TCLC 4, 13,**
29, 61; WLC 6
See also AMW; BPFB 3; CA 104; 132;
CANR 102; CDALB 1929-1941; DA;
DA3; DAB; DAC; DAM MST, NOV;
DLB 9, 102, 229; DLBD 2, 16; DLBY
1985, 1997; EWL 3; MAL 5; MTCW 1,
2; NFS 18; RGAL 4; SSFS 18; TUS
Wolfe, Thomas Kennerly, Jr.
1931- .... **CLC 147**
See Wolfe, Tom
See also CA 13-16R; CANR 9, 33, 70, 104;
DA3; DAM POP; DLB 185; EWL 3; INT
CANR-9; MTCW 1, 2; MTFW 2005; TUS
Wolfe, Tom CLC 1, 2, 9, 15, 35, 51
See Wolfe, Thomas Kennerly, Jr.
See also AAYA 8, 67; AITN 2; AMWS 3;
BEST 89:1; BPFB 3; CN 5, 6, 7; CPW;
CSW; DLB 152; LAIT 5; RGAL 4
Wolff, Geoffrey 1937- .... **CLC 41**
See also CA 29-32R; CANR 29, 43, 78, 154

Wolff, Geoffrey Ansell
See Wolff, Geoffrey
Wolff, Sonia
See Levitin, Sonia
Wolff, Tobias 1945- .... **CLC 39, 64, 172; SSC**
63
See also AAYA 16; AMWS 7; BEST 90:2;
BYA 12; CA 114; 117; CAAS 22; CANR
54, 76, 96; CN 5, 6, 7; CSW; DA3; DLB
130; EWL 3; INT CA-117; MTCW 2;
MTFW 2005; RGAL 4; RGSF 2; SSFS 4,
11
Wolitzer, Hilma 1930- .... **CLC 17**
See also CA 65-68; CANR 18, 40, 172; INT
CANR-18; SATA 31; YAW
Wollstonecraft, Mary 1759-1797 .... **LC 5, 50,**
90, 147
See also BRWS 3; CDBLB 1789-1832;
DLB 39, 104, 158, 252; FL 1:1; FW;
LAIT 1; RGEL 2; TEA; WLIT 3
Wonder, Stevie 1950- .... **CLC 12**
See also CA 111
Wong, Jade Snow 1922-2006 .... **CLC 17**
See also CA 109; 249; CANR 91; SATA
112; SATA-Obit 175
Wood, Ellen Price
See Wood, Mrs. Henry
Wood, Mrs. Henry 1814-1887 ...... **NCLC 178**
See also CMW 4; DLB 18; SUFW
Wood, James 1965- .... **CLC 238**
See also CA 235
Woodberry, George Edward
1855-1930 .... **TCLC 73**
See also CA 165; DLB 71, 103
Woodcott, Keith
See Brunner, John (Kilian Houston)
Woodruff, Robert W.
See Mencken, H(enry) L(ouis)
Woodward, Bob 1943- .... **CLC 240**
See also CA 69-72; CANR 31, 67, 107, 176;
MTCW 1
Woodward, Robert Upshur
See Woodward, Bob
Woolf, (Adeline) Virginia 1882-1941 .. **SSC 7,**
79; TCLC 1, 5, 20, 43, 56, 101, 123,
128; WLC 6
See also AAYA 44; BPFB 3; BRW 7;
BRWC 2; BRWR 1; CA 104; 130; CANR
64, 132; CDBLB 1914-1945; DA; DA3;
DAB; DAC; DAM MST, NOV; DLB 36,
100, 162; DLBD 10; EWL 3; EXPS; FL
1:6; FW; LAIT 3; LATS 1:1; LMFS 2;
MTCW 1, 2; MTFW 2005; NCFS 2; NFS
8, 12, 28; RGEL 2; RGSF 2; SSFS 4, 12;
TEA; WLIT 4
Woollcott, Alexander (Humphreys)
1887-1943 .... **TCLC 5**
See also CA 105; 161; DLB 29
Woolman, John 1720-1772 .... **LC 155**
See also DLB 31
Woolrich, Cornell CLC 77
See Hopley-Woolrich, Cornell George
See also MSW
Woolson, Constance Fenimore
1840-1894 .... **NCLC 82; SSC 90**
See also DLB 12, 74, 189, 221; RGAL 4
Wordsworth, Dorothy 1771-1855 . **NCLC 25,**
138
See also DLB 107
Wordsworth, William 1770-1850 .. **NCLC 12,**
38, 111, 166; PC 4, 67; WLC 6
See also AAYA 70; BRW 4; BRWC 1; CD-
BLB 1789-1832; DA; DA3; DAB; DAC;
DAM MST, POET; DLB 93, 107; EXPP;
LATS 1:1; LMFS 1; PAB; PFS 2; RGEL
2; TEA; WLIT 3; WP
Wotton, Sir Henry 1568-1639 .... **LC 68**
See also DLB 121; RGEL 2

Wouk, Herman 1915- .... **CLC 1, 9, 38**
See also BPFB 2, 3; CA 5-8R; CANR 6,
33, 67, 146; CDALBS; CN 1, 2, 3, 4, 5,
6; CPW; DA3; DAM NOV, POP; DLBY
1982; INT CANR-6; LAIT 4; MAL 5;
MTCW 1, 2; MTFW 2005; NFS 7; TUS
Wright, Charles 1935- ... **CLC 6, 13, 28, 119,**
146
See also AMWS 5; CA 29-32R; CAAS 7;
CANR 23, 36, 62, 88, 135, 180; CP 3, 4,
5, 6, 7; DLB 165; DLBY 1982; EWL 3;
MTCW 1, 2; MTFW 2005; PFS 10
Wright, Charles Penzel, Jr.
See Wright, Charles
Wright, Charles Stevenson
1932-2008 .... **BLC 1:3; CLC 49**
See also BW 1; CA 9-12R; CANR 26; CN
1, 2, 3, 4, 5, 6, 7; DAM MULT, POET;
DLB 33
Wright, Frances 1795-1852 .... **NCLC 74**
See also DLB 73
Wright, Frank Lloyd 1867-1959 .... **TCLC 95**
See also AAYA 33; CA 174
Wright, Harold Bell 1872-1944 .... **TCLC 183**
See also BPFB 3; CA 110; DLB 9; TCWW
2
Wright, Jack R.
See Harris, Mark
Wright, James (Arlington)
1927-1980 .... **CLC 3, 5, 10, 28; PC 36**
See also AITN 2; AMWS 3; CA 49-52; 97-
100; CANR 4, 34, 64; CDALBS; CP 1, 2;
DAM POET; DLB 5, 169, 342; EWL 3;
EXPP; MAL 5; MTCW 1, 2; MTFW
2005; PFS 7, 8; RGAL 4; TUS; WP
Wright, Judith 1915-2000 ... **CLC 11, 53; PC**
14
See also CA 13-16R; 188; CANR 31, 76,
93; CP 1, 2, 3, 4, 5, 6, 7; CWP; DLB 260;
EWL 3; MTCW 1, 2; MTFW 2005; PFS
8; RGEL 2; SATA 14; SATA-Obit 121
Wright, L(aurali) R. 1939- .... **CLC 44**
See also CA 138; CMW 4
Wright, Richard (Nathaniel)
1908-1960 .... **BLC 1:3; CLC 1, 3, 4, 9,**
14, 21, 48, 74; SSC 2, 109; TCLC 136,
180; WLC 6
See also AAYA 5, 42; AFAW 1, 2; AMW;
BPFB 3; BW 1; BYA 2; CA 108; CANR
64; CDALB 1929-1941; DA; DA3; DAB;
DAC; DAM MST, MULT, NOV; DLB 76,
102; DLBD 2; EWL 3; EXPN; LAIT 3,
4; MAL 5; MTCW 1, 2; MTFW 2005;
NCFS 1; NFS 1, 7; RGAL 4; RGSF 2;
SSFS 3, 9, 15, 20; TUS; YAW
Wright, Richard B. 1937- .... **CLC 6**
See also CA 85-88; CANR 120; DLB 53
Wright, Richard Bruce
See Wright, Richard B.
Wright, Rick 1945- .... **CLC 35**
Wright, Rowland
See Wells, Carolyn
Wright, Stephen 1946- .... **CLC 33**
See also CA 237
Wright, Willard Huntington 1888-1939
See Van Dine, S. S.
See also CA 115; 189; CMW 4; DLBD 16
Wright, William 1930- .... **CLC 44**
See also CA 53-56; CANR 7, 23, 154
Wroth, Lady Mary 1587-1653(?) .... **LC 30,**
139; PC 38
See also DLB 121
Wu Ch'eng-en 1500(?)-1582(?) .... **LC 7**
Wu Ching-tzu 1701-1754 .... **LC 2**
Wulfstan c. 10th cent. -1023 .... **CMLC 59**
Wurlitzer, Rudolph 1938(?)- ... **CLC 2, 4, 15**
See also CA 85-88; CN 4, 5, 6, 7; DLB 173

Wyatt, Sir Thomas c. 1503-1542 . **LC 70; PC 27**
See also BRW 1; DLB 132; EXPP; PFS 25; RGEL 2; TEA

Wycherley, William 1640-1716 .... **LC 8, 21, 102, 136**
See also BRW 2; CDBLB 1660-1789; DAM DRAM; DLB 80; RGEL 2

Wyclif, John c. 1330-1384 .... **CMLC 70**
See also DLB 146

Wylie, Elinor (Morton Hoyt) 1885-1928 .... **PC 23; TCLC 8**
See also AMWS 1; CA 105; 162; DLB 9, 45; EXPP; MAL 5; RGAL 4

Wylie, Philip (Gordon) 1902-1971 ... **CLC 43**
See also CA 21-22; 33-36R; CAP 2; CN 1; DLB 9; SFW 4

Wyndham, John **CLC 19**
See Harris, John (Wyndham Parkes Lucas) Beynon
See also BRWS 13; DLB 255; SCFW 1, 2

Wyss, Johann David Von 1743-1818 .... **NCLC 10**
See also CLR 92; JRDA; MAICYA 1, 2; SATA 29; SATA-Brief 27

Xenophon c. 430B.C.-c. 354B.C. ... **CMLC 17**
See also AW 1; DLB 176; RGWL 2, 3; WLIT 8

Xingjian, Gao 1940-
See Gao Xingjian
See also CA 193; DFS 21; DLB 330; RGWL 3

Yakamochi 718-785 .... **CMLC 45; PC 48**

Yakumo Koizumi
See Hearn, (Patricio) Lafcadio (Tessima Carlos)

Yamada, Mitsuye (May) 1923- .... **PC 44**
See also CA 77-80

Yamamoto, Hisaye 1921- .... **AAL; SSC 34**
See also CA 214; DAM MULT; DLB 312; LAIT 4; SSFS 14

Yamauchi, Wakako 1924- .... **AAL**
See also CA 214; DLB 312

Yanez, Jose Donoso
See Donoso (Yanez), Jose

Yanovsky, Basile S.
See Yanovsky, V(assily) S(emenovich)

Yanovsky, V(assily) S(emenovich) 1906-1989 .... **CLC 2, 18**
See also CA 97-100; 129

Yates, Richard 1926-1992 .... **CLC 7, 8, 23**
See also AMWS 11; CA 5-8R; 139; CANR 10, 43; CN 1, 2, 3, 4, 5; DLB 2, 234; DLBY 1981, 1992; INT CANR-10; SSFS 24

Yau, John 1950- .... **PC 61**
See also CA 154; CANR 89; CP 4, 5, 6, 7; DLB 234, 312; PFS 26

Yearsley, Ann 1753-1806 .... **NCLC 174**
See also DLB 109

Yeats, W. B.
See Yeats, William Butler

Yeats, William Butler 1865-1939 . **PC 20, 51; TCLC 1, 11, 18, 31, 93, 116; WLC 6**
See also AAYA 48; BRW 6; BRWR 1; CA 104; 127; CANR 45; CDBLB 1890-1914; DA; DA3; DAB; DAC; DAM DRAM, MST, POET; DLB 10, 19, 98, 156, 332; EWL 3; EXPP; MTCW 1, 2; MTFW 2005; NCFS 3; PAB; PFS 1, 2, 5, 7, 13, 15; RGEL 2; TEA; WLIT 4; WP

Yehoshua, A.B. 1936- .... **CLC 13, 31, 243**
See also CA 33-36R; CANR 43, 90, 145; CWW 2; EWL 3; RGHL; RGSF 2; RGWL 3; WLIT 6

Yehoshua, Abraham B.
See Yehoshua, A.B.

Yellow Bird
See Ridge, John Rollin

Yep, Laurence 1948- .... **CLC 35**
See also AAYA 5, 31; BYA 7; CA 49-52; CANR 1, 46, 92, 161; CLR 3, 17, 54, 132; DLB 52, 312; FANT; JRDA; MAICYA 1, 2; MAICYAS 1; SATA 7, 69, 123, 176; WYA; YAW

Yep, Laurence Michael
See Yep, Laurence

Yerby, Frank G(arvin) 1916-1991 . **BLC 1:3; CLC 1, 7, 22**
See also BPFB 3; BW 1, 3; CA 9-12R; 136; CANR 16, 52; CN 1, 2, 3, 4, 5; DAM MULT; DLB 76; INT CANR-16; MTCW 1; RGAL 4; RHW

Yesenin, Sergei Aleksandrovich
See Esenin, Sergei

Yevtushenko, Yevgeny (Alexandrovich) 1933- ...... **CLC 1, 3, 13, 26, 51, 126; PC 40**
See Evtushenko, Evgenii Aleksandrovich
See also CA 81-84; CANR 33, 54; DAM POET; EWL 3; MTCW 1; PFS 29; RGHL

Yezierska, Anzia 1885(?)-1970 .... **CLC 46; TCLC 205**
See also CA 126; 89-92; DLB 28, 221; FW; MTCW 1; RGAL 4; SSFS 15

Yglesias, Helen 1915-2008 .... **CLC 7, 22**
See also CA 37-40R; 272; CAAS 20; CANR 15, 65, 95; CN 4, 5, 6, 7; INT CANR-15; MTCW 1

Yokomitsu, Riichi 1898-1947 .... **TCLC 47**
See also CA 170; EWL 3

Yolen, Jane 1939- .... **CLC 256**
See also AAYA 4, 22; BPFB 3; BYA 9, 10, 11, 14, 16; CA 13-16R; CANR 11, 29, 56, 91, 126; CLR 4, 44; CWRI 5; DLB 52; FANT; INT CANR-29; JRDA; MAICYA 1, 2; MTFW 2005; SAAS 1; SATA 4, 40, 75, 112, 158, 194; SATA-Essay 111; SFW 4; SUFW 2; WYA; YAW

Yonge, Charlotte (Mary) 1823-1901 .... **TCLC 48**
See also CA 109; 163; DLB 18, 163; RGEL 2; SATA 17; WCH

York, Jeremy
See Creasey, John

York, Simon
See Heinlein, Robert A.

Yorke, Henry Vincent 1905-1974 ..... **CLC 13**
See Green, Henry
See also CA 85-88; 49-52

Yosano, Akiko 1878-1942 ... **PC 11; TCLC 59**
See also CA 161; EWL 3; RGWL 3

Yoshimoto, Banana **CLC 84**
See Yoshimoto, Mahoko
See also AAYA 50; NFS 7

Yoshimoto, Mahoko 1964-
See Yoshimoto, Banana
See also CA 144; CANR 98, 160; SSFS 16

Young, Al(bert James) 1939- .... **BLC 1:3; CLC 19**
See also BW 2, 3; CA 29-32R; CANR 26, 65, 109; CN 2, 3, 4, 5, 6, 7; CP 1, 2, 3, 4, 5, 6, 7; DAM MULT; DLB 33

Young, Andrew (John) 1885-1971 ...... **CLC 5**
See also CA 5-8R; CANR 7, 29; CP 1; RGEL 2

Young, Collier
See Bloch, Robert (Albert)

Young, Edward 1683-1765 .... **LC 3, 40**
See also DLB 95; RGEL 2

Young, Marguerite (Vivian) 1909-1995 .... **CLC 82**
See also CA 13-16; 150; CAP 1; CN 1, 2, 3, 4, 5, 6

Young, Neil 1945- .... **CLC 17**
See also CA 110; CCA 1

Young Bear, Ray A. 1950- ... **CLC 94; NNAL**
See also CA 146; DAM MULT; DLB 175; MAL 5

Yourcenar, Marguerite 1903-1987 ... **CLC 19, 38, 50, 87; TCLC 193**
See also BPFB 3; CA 69-72; CANR 23, 60, 93; DAM NOV; DLB 72; DLBY 1988; EW 12; EWL 3; GFL 1789 to the Present; GLL 1; MTCW 1, 2; MTFW 2005; RGWL 2, 3

Yuan, Chu 340(?)B.C.-278(?)B.C. . **CMLC 36**

Yurick, Sol 1925- .... **CLC 6**
See also CA 13-16R; CANR 25; CN 1, 2, 3, 4, 5, 6, 7; MAL 5

Zabolotsky, Nikolai Alekseevich 1903-1958 .... **TCLC 52**
See Zabolotsky, Nikolay Alekseevich
See also CA 116; 164

Zabolotsky, Nikolay Alekseevich
See Zabolotsky, Nikolai Alekseevich
See also EWL 3

Zagajewski, Adam 1945- .... **PC 27**
See also CA 186; DLB 232; EWL 3; PFS 25

Zalygin, Sergei -2000 .... **CLC 59**

Zalygin, Sergei (Pavlovich) 1913-2000 .... **CLC 59**
See also DLB 302

Zamiatin, Evgenii
See Zamyatin, Evgeny Ivanovich
See also RGSF 2; RGWL 2, 3

Zamiatin, Evgenii Ivanovich
See Zamyatin, Evgeny Ivanovich
See also DLB 272

Zamiatin, Yevgenii
See Zamyatin, Evgeny Ivanovich

Zamora, Bernice (B. Ortiz) 1938- .. **CLC 89; HLC 2**
See also CA 151; CANR 80; DAM MULT; DLB 82; HW 1, 2

Zamyatin, Evgeny Ivanovich 1884-1937 .... **SSC 89; TCLC 8, 37**
See Zamiatin, Evgenii; Zamiatin, Evgenii Ivanovich; Zamyatin, Yevgeny Ivanovich
See also CA 105; 166; SFW 4

Zamyatin, Yevgeny Ivanovich
See Zamyatin, Evgeny Ivanovich
See also EW 10; EWL 3

Zangwill, Israel 1864-1926 ... **SSC 44; TCLC 16**
See also CA 109; 167; CMW 4; DLB 10, 135, 197; RGEL 2

Zanzotto, Andrea 1921- .... **PC 65**
See also CA 208; CWW 2; DLB 128; EWL 3

Zappa, Francis Vincent, Jr. 1940-1993
See Zappa, Frank
See also CA 108; 143; CANR 57

Zappa, Frank **CLC 17**
See Zappa, Francis Vincent, Jr.

Zaturenska, Marya 1902-1982 ..... **CLC 6, 11**
See also CA 13-16R; 105; CANR 22; CP 1, 2, 3

Zayas y Sotomayor, Maria de 1590-c. 1661 .... **LC 102; SSC 94**
See also RGSF 2

Zeami 1363-1443 .... **DC 7; LC 86**
See also DLB 203; RGWL 2, 3

Zelazny, Roger 1937-1995 .... **CLC 21**
See also AAYA 7, 68; BPFB 3; CA 21-24R; 148; CANR 26, 60; CN 6; DLB 8; FANT; MTCW 1, 2; MTFW 2005; SATA 57; SATA-Brief 39; SCFW 1, 2; SFW 4; SUFW 1, 2

Zephaniah, Benjamin 1958- .... **BLC 2:3**
See also CA 147; CANR 103, 156, 177; CP 5, 6, 7; SATA 86, 140, 189

Zhang Ailing
See Chang, Eileen

Zhdanov, Andrei Alexandrovich
  1896-1948 .... **TCLC 18**
  See also CA 117; 167
Zhukovsky, Vasilii Andreevich
  See Zhukovsky, Vasily (Andreevich)
  See also DLB 205
Zhukovsky, Vasily (Andreevich)
  1783-1852 .... **NCLC 35**
  See Zhukovsky, Vasilii Andreevich
Ziegenhagen, Eric CLC 55
Zimmer, Jill Schary
  See Robinson, Jill
Zimmerman, Robert
  See Dylan, Bob
Zindel, Paul 1936-2003 ...... **CLC 6, 26; DC 5**
  See also AAYA 2, 37; BYA 2, 3, 8, 11, 14;
  CA 73-76; 213; CAD; CANR 31, 65, 108;
  CD 5, 6; CDALBS; CLR 3, 45, 85; DA;
  DA3; DAB; DAC; DAM DRAM, MST,
  NOV; DFS 12; DLB 7, 52; JRDA; LAIT
  5; MAICYA 1, 2; MTCW 1, 2; MTFW
  2005; NFS 14; SATA 16, 58, 102; SATA-
  Obit 142; WYA; YAW
Zinger, Yisroel-Yehoyshue
  See Singer, Israel Joshua
Zinger, Yitskhok
  See Singer, Isaac Bashevis

Zinn, Howard 1922- .... **CLC 199**
  See also CA 1-4R; CANR 2, 33, 90, 159
Zinov'Ev, A.A.
  See Zinoviev, Alexander
Zinov'ev, Aleksandr
  See Zinoviev, Alexander
  See also DLB 302
Zinoviev, Alexander 1922-2006 .... **CLC 19**
  See Zinov'ev, Aleksandr
  See also CA 116; 133; 250; CAAS 10
Zinoviev, Alexander Aleksandrovich
  See Zinoviev, Alexander
Zizek, Slavoj 1949- .... **CLC 188**
  See also CA 201; CANR 171; MTFW 2005
Zobel, Joseph 1915-2006 .... **BLC 2:3**
Zoilus
  See Lovecraft, H. P.
Zola, Emile (Edouard Charles Antoine)
  1840-1902 ...... **SSC 109; TCLC 1, 6, 21,**
  41; WLC 6
  See also CA 104; 138; DA; DA3; DAB;
  DAC; DAM MST, NOV; DLB 123; EW
  7; GFL 1789 to the Present; IDTP; LMFS
  1, 2; RGWL 2; TWA
Zoline, Pamela 1941- .... **CLC 62**
  See also CA 161; SFW 4

Zoroaster 628(?)B.C.-551(?)B.C. ... **CMLC 40**
Zorrilla y Moral, Jose 1817-1893 .... **NCLC 6**
Zoshchenko, Mikhail 1895-1958 ...... **SSC 15;**
  TCLC 15
  See also CA 115; 160; EWL 3; RGSF 2;
  RGWL 3
Zoshchenko, Mikhail Mikhailovich
  See Zoshchenko, Mikhail
Zuckmayer, Carl 1896-1977 .... **CLC 18;**
  TCLC 191
  See also CA 69-72; DLB 56, 124; EWL 3;
  RGWL 2, 3
Zuk, Georges
  See Skelton, Robin
  See also CCA 1
Zukofsky, Louis 1904-1978 ... **CLC 1, 2, 4, 7,**
  11, 18; PC 11
  See also AMWS 3; CA 9-12R; 77-80;
  CANR 39; CP 1, 2; DAM POET; DLB 5,
  165; EWL 3; MAL 5; MTCW 1; RGAL 4
Zweig, Arnold 1887-1968 .... **TCLC 199**
  See also CA 189; 115; DLB 66; EWL 3
Zweig, Paul 1935-1984 .... **CLC 34, 42**
  See also CA 85-88; 113
Zweig, Stefan 1881-1942 .... **TCLC 17**
  See also CA 112; 170; DLB 81, 118; EWL
  3; RGHL
Zwingli, Huldreich 1484-1531 .... **LC 37**
  See also DLB 179

PC Cumulative Nationality Index

AMERICAN

Ai 72
Aiken, Conrad (Potter) 26
Alexie, Sherman 53
Ammons, A(rchie) R(andolph) 16
Angelou, Maya 32
Ashbery, John (Lawrence) 26
Auden, W(ystan) H(ugh) 1, 92
Baca, Jimmy Santiago 41
Baraka, Amiri 4
Benét, Stephen Vincent 64
Berry, Wendell (Erdman) 28
Berryman, John 64
Bishop, Elizabeth 3, 34
Bly, Robert (Elwood) 39
Bogan, Louise 12
Bradstreet, Anne 10
Braithwaite, William 52
Brodsky, Joseph 9
Brooks, Gwendolyn (Elizabeth) 7
Brown, Sterling Allen 55
Bryant, William Cullen 20
Bukowski, Charles 18
Cage, John 58
Carruth, Hayden 10
Carver, Raymond 54
Cervantes, Lorna Dee 35
Chin, Marilyn (Mei Ling) 40
Ciardi, John 69
Cisneros, Sandra 52
Clampitt, Amy 19
Clifton, (Thelma) Lucille 17
Collins, Billy 68
Corso, (Nunzio) Gregory 33
Crane, (Harold) Hart 3
Creeley, Robert 73
Cullen, Countée 20
Cummings, E(dward) E(stlin) 5
Cunningham, J(ames) V(incent) 92
Dickey, James (Lafayette) 40
Dickinson, Emily (Elizabeth) 1
Doolittle, Hilda 5
Doty, Mark 53
Dove, Rita (Frances) 6
Dunbar, Paul Laurence 5
Duncan, Robert (Edward) 2, 75
Dylan, Bob 37
Eberhart, Richard 76
Eliot, T(homas) S(tearns) 5, 31
Emerson, Ralph Waldo 18
Erdrich, Louise 52
Espada, Martín 74
Ferlinghetti, Lawrence (Monsanto) 1
Forché, Carolyn (Louise) 10
Francis, Robert (Churchill) 34
Frost, Robert (Lee) 1, 39, 71

Gallagher, Tess 9
Ginsberg, Allen 4, 47
Giovanni, Nikki 19
Glück, Louise (Elisabeth) 16
Graham, Jorie 59
Guest, Barbara 55
Hacker, Marilyn 47
Hall, Donald 70
Hammon, Jupiter 16
Harjo, Joy 27
Harper, Frances Ellen Watkins 21
Hass, Robert 16
Hayden, Robert E(arl) 6
H. D. 5
Hecht, Anthony 70
Hogan, Linda 35
Holmes, Oliver Wendell 71
Hongo, Garrett Kaoru 23
Howe, Susan 54
Hughes, (James) Langston 1, 53
Hugo, Richard 68
Ignatow, David 34
Jackson, Laura (Riding) 44
Jacobsen, Josephine 62
Jarrell, Randall 41
Jeffers, (John) Robinson 17
Johnson, James Weldon 24
Jordan, June 38
Justice, Donald 64
Kaufman, Bob 74
Kennedy, X. J. 93
Kenyon, Jane 57
Kinnell, Galway 26
Kizer, Carolyn 66
Knight, Etheridge 14
Komunyakaa, Yusef 51
Kumin, Maxine (Winokur) 15
Kunitz, Stanley (Jasspon) 19
Lanier, Sidney 50
Levertov, Denise 11
Levine, Philip 22
Lindsay, (Nicholas) Vachel 23
Longfellow, Henry Wadsworth 30
Lorde, Audre (Geraldine) 12
Lowell, Amy 13
Lowell, Robert (Traill Spence Jr.) 3
Loy, Mina 16
MacLeish, Archibald 47
Mackey, Nathaniel 49
Madhubuti, Haki R. 5
Masters, Edgar Lee 1, 36
McHugh, Heather 61
Meredith, William (Morris) 28
Merrill, James (Ingram) 28
Merton, Thomas 10
Merwin, W. S. 45

Millay, Edna St. Vincent 6, 61
Momaday, N(avarre) Scott 25
Moore, Marianne (Craig) 4, 49
Mueller, Lisel 33
Nash, (Fredric) Ogden 21
Nemerov, Howard (Stanley) 24
Niedecker, Lorine 42
O'Hara, Frank 45
Olds, Sharon 22
Oliver, Mary 75
Olson, Charles (John) 19
Oppen, George 35
Ortiz, Simon J(oseph) 17
Parker, Dorothy (Rothschild) 28
Piercy, Marge 29
Pinsky, Robert 27
Plath, Sylvia 1, 37
Poe, Edgar Allan 1, 54
Pound, Ezra (Weston Loomis) 4
Quintana, Leroy V. 36
Randall, Dudley 86
Ransom, John Crowe 61
Reed, Ishmael 68
Reese, Lizette Woodworth 29
Rexroth, Kenneth 20
Rich, Adrienne (Cecile) 5
Riley, James Whitcomb 48
Ríos, Alberto 57
Robinson, Edwin Arlington 1, 35
Roethke, Theodore (Huebner) 15
Rose, Wendy 13
Rukeyser, Muriel 12
Sanchez, Sonia 9
Sandburg, Carl (August) 2, 41
Sarton, (Eleanor) May 39
Schwartz, Delmore (David) 8
Schnackenberg, Gjertrud 45
Schuyler, James 88
Schwerner, Armand 42
Sexton, Anne (Harvey) 2
Shapiro, Karl (Jay) 25
Silverstein, Shel 49
Simic, Charles 69
Snodgrass, W. D. 74
Snyder, Gary (Sherman) 21
Song, Cathy 21
Soto, Gary 28
Spencer, Anne 77
Spicer, Jack 78
Stafford, William 71
Stein, Gertrude 18
Stevens, Wallace 6
Stone, Ruth 53
Strand, Mark 63
Stryk, Lucien 27
Swenson, May 14

Tapahonso, Luci **65**
Tate, Allen **50**
Taylor, Edward **63**
Teasdale, Sara **31**
Thoreau, Henry David **30**
Tolson, Melvin B. **88**
Toomer, Jean **7**
Tuckerman, Frederick Goddard **85**
Updike, John **90**
Urista, Alberto H. **34**
Very, Jones **86**
Viereck, Peter (Robert Edwin) **27**
Wagoner, David (Russell) **33**
Wakoski, Diane **15**
Walker, Alice (Malsenior) **30**
Walker, Margaret (Abigail) **20**
Warren, Robert Penn **37**
Welch, James **62**
Wheatley (Peters), Phillis **3**
Whitman, Walt(er) **3, 91**
Whittier, John Greenleaf **93**
Wilbur, Richard **51**
Williams, William Carlos **7**
Wright, James (Arlington) **36**
Wylie, Elinor (Morton Hoyt) **23**
Yamada, Mitsuye **44**
Yau, John **61**
Zukofsky, Louis **11**

ARGENTINIAN

Borges, Jorge Luis **22, 32**
Storni, Alfonsina **33**

AUSTRALIAN

Gilmore, Mary **87**
Hope, A. D. **56**
Wright, Judith (Arundell) **14**

AUSTRIAN

Trakl, Georg **20**

BARBADIAN

Brathwaite, Edward Kamau **56**

CANADIAN

Atwood, Margaret (Eleanor) **8**
Birney, (Alfred) Earle **52**
Bissett, Bill **14**
Carman, (William) Bliss **34**
Carson, Anne **64**
Ondaatje, (Philip) Michael **28**
Page, P(atricia) K(athleen) **12**
Service, Robert **70**

CHILEAN

Godoy Alcayaga, Lucila **32**
Neruda, Pablo **4, 64**
Parra, Nicanor **39**

CHINESE

Li Ho **13**
Li Po **29**
Tu Fu **9**
Wang Wei **18**

CUBAN

Guillén, Nicolás (Cristobal) **23**
Martí, José **76**

CZECH

Seifert, Jaroslav **47**

ENGLISH

Arnold, Matthew **5**
Auden, W(ystan) H(ugh) **1**
Barker, George **77**
Barker, Jane **91**
Barrett Browning, Elizabeth **6, 62**
Behn, Aphra **13, 88**
Belloc, (Joseph) Hilaire (Pierre Sebastien Rene Swanton) **24**
Betjeman, John **75**
Blake, William **12, 63**
Blunden, Edmund **66**
Bradstreet, Anne **10**
Bridges, Robert (Seymour) **28**
Brontë, Emily (Jane) **8**
Brooke, Rupert (Chawner) **24**
Browning, Robert **2, 61**
Byron, George Gordon (Noel) **16**
Campion, Thomas **87**
Carroll, Lewis **18, 74**
Carew, Thomas **29**
Chaucer, Geoffrey **19, 58**
Chesterton, G(ilbert) K(eith) **28**
Clare, John **23**
Coleridge, Samuel Taylor **11, 39, 67**
Collins, William **72**
Cowley, Abraham **90**
Cowper, William **40**
Crashaw, Richard **84**
Davie, Donald (Alfred) **29**
Day Lewis, C(ecil) **11**
de La Mare, Walter **77**
Donne, John **1, 43**
Dryden, John **25**
Duck, Stephen **89**
Eliot, George **20**
Eliot, T(homas) S(tearns) **5, 31, 90**
Enright, D. J. **93**
Finch, Anne **21**
Gower, John **59**
Graves, Robert (von Ranke) **6**
Gray, Thomas **2**
Gunn, Thom(son William) **26**
Hardy, Thomas **8, 92**
Herbert, George **4**
Herrick, Robert **9**
Hood, Thomas **93**
Hopkins, Gerard Manley **15**
Housman, A(lfred) E(dward) **2, 43**
Howard, Henry (Earl of Surrey) **59**
Hughes, Ted **7, 89**
Hunt, Leigh **73**
Jonson, Ben(jamin) **17**
Keats, John **1**
Kipling, (Joseph) Rudyard **3, 91**
Lanyer, Aemilia **60**
Larkin, Philip (Arthur) **21**
Lawrence, D(avid) (H)erbert **54**
Leapor, Mary **85**
Lear, Edward **65**
Levertov, Denise **11**
Lovelace, Richard **69**
Loy, Mina **16**
Marlowe, Christopher **57**
Marvell, Andrew **10, 86**
Masefield, John **78**
Meredith, George **60**
Milton, John **19, 29**
Montagu, Mary (Pierrepont) Wortley **16**
Morris, William **55**
Noyes, Alfred **27**
Owen, Wilfred (Edward Salter) **19**
Page, P(atricia) K(athleen) **12**

Patmore, Coventry **59**
Peacock, Thomas Love **87**
Philips, Katherine **40**
Pope, Alexander **26**
Raleigh, Walter **31**
Rossetti, Christina (Georgina) **7**
Rossetti, Dante Gabriel **44**
Sassoon, Siegfried (Lorraine) **12**
Shelley, Percy Bysshe **14, 67**
Sidney, Philip **32**
Sitwell, Edith **3**
Skelton, John **25**
Smart, Christopher **13**
Smith, Stevie **12**
Spender, Stephen **71**
Spenser, Edmund **8, 42**
Suckling, John **30**
Swift, Jonathan **9**
Swinburne, Algernon Charles **24**
Tennyson, Alfred **6**
Thomas, (Philip) Edward **53**
Tomlinson, (Alfred) Charles **17**
Traherne, Thomas **70**
Waller, Edmund **72**
Wilmot, John (Earl of Rochester) **66**
Wordsworth, William **4, 67**
Wroth, Mary **38**
Wyatt, Thomas **27**

FILIPINO

Villa, José García **22**

FRENCH

Apollinaire, Guillaume **7**
Baudelaire, Charles **1**
Bonnefoy, Yves **58**
Breton, André **15**
Char, René **56**
Christine de Pizan **68**
Éluard, Paul **38**
Gautier, Théophile **18**
Hugo, Victor (Marie) **17**
Laforgue, Jules **14**
Lamartine, Alphonse (Marie Louis Prat) de **16**
Leger, (Marie-Rene Auguste) Alexis Saint-Leger **23**
Mallarmé, Stéphane **4**
Marie de France **22**
Merton, Thomas **10**
Nerval, Gérard de **13**
Péret, Benjamin **33**
Rimbaud, (Jean Nicolas) Arthur **3, 57**
Ronsard, Pierre de **11**
Tzara, Tristan **27**
Valéry, (Ambroise) Paul (Toussaint Jules) **9**
Verlaine, Paul (Marie) **2, 32**
Vigny, Alfred (Victor) de **26**
Villon, François **13**

GERMAN

Benn, Gottfried **35**
Bukowski, Charles **18**
Enzensberger, Hans Magnus **28**
Goethe, Johann Wolfgang von **5**
Heine, Heinrich **25**
Hölderlin, (Johann Christian) Friedrich **4**
Mueller, Lisel **33**
Rilke, Rainer Maria **2**
Sachs, Nelly **78**
Stramm, August **50**

GREEK

Cavafy, C(onstantine) P(eter) **36**
Elytis, Odysseus **21**
Homer **23**
Pindar **19**
Sappho **5**
Seferis, George **66**
Sikelianos, Angelos **29**

HUNGARIAN

Illyés, Gyula **16**
Szirtes, George **51**

INDIAN

Das, Kamala **43**
Kabir **56**
Kalidasa **22**
Mirabai **48**
Tagore, Rabindranath **8**

IRISH

Boland, Eavan **58**
Day Lewis, C(ecil) **11**
Goldsmith, Oliver **77**
Heaney, Seamus (Justin) **18**
Joyce, James (Augustine Aloysius) **22**
Kavanagh, Patrick (Joseph) **33**
Kinsella, Thomas **69**
MacNeice, Louis **61**
Mahon, Derek **60**
McGuckian, Medbh **27**
Ní Chuilleanáin, Eiléan **34**
Swift, Jonathan **9**
Yeats, William Butler **20, 51**

ISRAELI

Amichai, Yehuda **38**

ITALIAN

Ariosto, Ludovico **42**
Carducci, Giosue **46**
Dante **21**
Gozzano, Guido **10**
Leopardi, Giacomo **37**
Martial **10**
Montale, Eugenio **13**
Pasolini, Pier Paolo **17**
Pavese, Cesare **13**
Petrarch **8**
Quasimodo, Salvatore **47**
Stampa, Gaspara **43**
Ungaretti, Giuseppe **57**
Zanzotto, Andrea **65**

JAMAICAN

Goodison, Lorna **36**

JAPANESE

Hagiwara, Sakutaro **18**
Ishikawa, Takuboku **10**
Matsuo Basho **3**
Nishiwaki, Junzaburō **15**
Yosano Akiko **11**

LEBANESE

Gibran, Kahlil **9**

MARTINICAN

Césaire, Aimé (Fernand) **25**

MEXICAN

Juana Inés de la Cruz **24**
Paz, Octavio **1, 48**
Urista, Alberto H. **34**

NEW ZEALAND

Curnow, (Thomas) Allen (Monro) **48**

NICARAGUAN

Alegria, Claribel **26**
Cardenal, Ernesto **22**
Darío, Rubén **15**

NIGERIAN

Okigbo, Christopher (Ifenayichukwu) **7**

PALESTINIAN

Darwish, Mahmoud **86**

PERSIAN

Khayyam, Omar **8**
Rumi, Jalâl al-Din **45**

POLISH

Herbert, Zbigniew **50**
Mickiewicz, Adam **38**
Milosz, Czeslaw **8**
Szymborska, Wisława **44**
Zagajewski, Adam **27**

PORTUGUESE

Camões, Luís de **31**
Pessoa, Fernando (António Nogueira) **20**

PUERTO RICAN

Cruz, Victor Hernández **37**

ROMAN

Horace **46**
Martial **10**
Ovid **2**
Vergil **12**

ROMANIAN

Cassian, Nina **17**
Celan, Paul **10**
Tzara, Tristan **27**

RUSSIAN

Akhmadulina, Bella **43**
Akhmatova, Anna **2, 55**
Bely, Andrey **11**
Blok, Alexander (Alexandrovich) **21**
Brodsky, Joseph **9**
Lermontov, Mikhail Yuryevich **18**
Mandelstam, Osip (Emilievich) **14**
Pasternak, Boris (Leonidovich) **6**
Pushkin, Alexander (Sergeyevich) **10**
Shvarts, Elena **50**
Tsvetaeva (Efron), Marina (Ivanovna) **14**
Yevtushenko, Yevgeny (Alexandrovich) **40**

SALVADORAN

Alegria, Claribel **26**
Dalton, Roque **36**

SCOTTISH

Burns, Robert **6**
Dunbar, William **67**
Henryson, Robert **65**
Muir, Edwin **49**
Scott, Walter **13**
Spark, Muriel **72**
Stevenson, Robert Louis **84**

SENEGALESE

Senghor, Léopold Sédar **25**

SINGAPORAN

Thumboo, Edwin Nadason **30**

SOUTH AFRICAN

Brutus, Dennis **24**

SPANISH

Castro, Rosalia de **41**
Cernuda, Luis **62**
Fuertes, Gloria **27**
García Lorca, Federico **3**
Guillén, Jorge **35**
Jiménez (Mantecón), Juan Ramón **7**

ST. LUCIAN

Walcott, Derek **46**

SWEDISH

Ekeloef, (Bengt) Gunnar **23**

SYRIAN

Gibran, Kahlil **9**

WELSH

Abse, Dannie **41**
Dafydd ap Gwilym **56**
Thomas, Dylan (Marlais) **2, 52**

Nationality Index

PC-93 Title Index

"Abraham Davenport" (Whittier) **93**:239, 251, 275

"Abram Morrison" (Whittier) **93**:238-39, 252

"Abyss" (Kennedy) **93**:145

"Address to The Steam-Washing Company" (Hood) **93**:116

"Agape" (Enright) **93**:29

"Akiko San" (Enright) **93**:20, 33-34

"Ambition" (Kennedy) **93**:150-51

Among the Hills, and Other Poems (Whittier) **93**:175-76, 230, 238-39, 267, 345, 349

"Amplifier" (Enright) **93**:4

"Amy Wentworth" (Whittier) **93**:175, 247-48, 250, 266-67

"Anniversary Poem" (Whittier) **93**:315

"Ant Trap" (Kennedy) **93**:139

"Arab Music" (Enright) **93**:32

"Arisen at Last" (Whittier) **93**:211

"Ars Poetica" (Kennedy) **93**:138, 145

"Art for the Sake of Something Very Misty Indeed" (Enright) **93**:4

"Artificer" (Kennedy) **93**:139

"The Assistant Draper's Petition" (Hood) **93**:43, 83

"Astrea at the Capital" (Whittier) **93**:207

"At Colonus" (Kennedy) **93**:143

"At Last" (Whittier) **93**:169, 275

At Sundown (Whittier) **93**:345

"At the Last Rites for Two Hotrodders" (Kennedy) **93**:131

"At the Stoplight by the Paupers' Graves" (Kennedy) **93**:141

"At Washington" (Whittier) **93**:207

"Autumn" (Hood) **93**:42, 62, 65-66, 78, 117

"B Negative" (Kennedy) **93**:138

"Bad Baby" (Enright) **93**:34

"Baie des Anges, Nice" (Enright) **93**:16

"The Ballad of Sally Brown and Ben the Carpenter" (Hood) **93**:44, 51-52, 62, 72, 122

Ballads of New England (Whittier) **93**:349

"The Bandit" (Hood) **93**:114

"Barbara Frietchie" (Whittier) **93**:167, 174, 184, 232, 239, 247, 280, 348

"Barclay of Ury" (Whittier) **93**:221, 245

"The Barefoot Boy" (Whittier) **93**:172, 232-33, 239, 252, 266-67

"The Battle Autumn of 1862" (Whittier) **93**:185, 213

"Bianca's Dream" (Hood) **93**:80

"Birchbrook Hill" (Whittier) **93**:239, 251

"Birth Report" (Kennedy) **93**:140

"The Black Fox" (Whittier) **93**:243

"A Black Job" (Hood) **93**:99-100

"Black Velvet Art" (Kennedy) **93**:151

"Blue Umbrellas" (Enright) **93**:11

"Board of Selection" (Enright) **93**:33

"Bobsled" (Kennedy) **93**:135

"The Branded Hand" (Whittier) **93**:210, 317

Brats (Kennedy) **93**:133-35

Bread Rather than Blossoms (Enright) **93**:4, 6

Breaking and Entering (Kennedy) **93**:130, 142-43, 148, 152

"The Brewing of Soma" (Whittier) **93**:169, 239, 345

"The Bridal of Pennacook" (Whittier) **93**:171, 224

"The Bridge of Sighs" (Hood) **93**:44, 61, 69, 81, 87-88, 102, 105, 118-19, 123-24

"Broken Fingernails" (Enright) **93**:18, 35

"The Brothers" (Whittier) **93**:193

"The Brown Dwarf of Rügen" (Whittier) **93**:249

"Brown of Ossawatomie" (Whittier) **93**:280-81

Bulsh (Kennedy) **93**:142-43, 148

"Burial of Barber" (Whittier) **93**:211

"The Burning of the Books" (Enright) **93**:21

"Burns" (Whittier) **93**:259

"Busy Body under a Cherry Tree" (Enright) **93**:6

"Byron. Written after a perusal of his works" (Whittier) **93**:195

"Carrier Bag" (Enright) **93**:34

"Cassandra Southwick" (Whittier) **93**:198, 244-45

"Categories" (Kennedy) **93**:149

Celebrations after the Death of John Brennan (Kennedy) **93**:143

"Central Heat" (Kennedy) **93**:147

"The Changeling" (Whittier) **93**:176, 250

"Changing the Subject" (Enright) **93**:7

"The Chapel of the Hermits" (Whittier) **93**:170, 172, 222

The Chapel of the Hermits, and Other Poems (Whittier) **93**:266

"The Chicken's Foot" (Enright) **93**:10

Child-Life: A Collection of Poems (Whittier) **93**:216

"Children Killed in War" (Enright) **93**:35

"The Christian Slave" (Whittier) **93**:239, 312, 314-17

"Christmas Abrupted" (Kennedy) **93**:151

"City Churchyard" (Kennedy) **93**:150

"The Clear Vision" (Whittier) **93**:349

"Clerical Oppressors" (Whittier) **93**:207, 314, 336-37

"Close Call" (Kennedy) **93**:153

"Cobbler Keezar's Vision" (Whittier) **93**:175, 252

Collected Poems 1987 (Enright) **93**:18-30

"Come to Sunny S" (Enright) **93**:21

"The Comic Annual" (Hood) **93**:46

"Comic Melodies" (Hood) **93**:46

"The Confessions of a Bachelor" (Whittier) **93**:200

"Conformity" (Kennedy) **93**:145

"Consumer's Report" (Kennedy) **93**:130

"The Countess" (Whittier) **93**:175, 247, 267

"Covering the Massacre" (Kennedy) **93**:153

"Creation Morning" (Kennedy) **93**:142, 149

"The Crisis" (Whittier) **93**:209

Cross Ties (Kennedy) **93**:143-44, 147-50, 152

"Cross Ties" (Kennedy) **93**:138-41, 143, 147, 149

"Cultural Freedom" (Enright) **93**:21

"The Curse of the Charter-Breakers" (Whittier) **93**:336

"The Cypress Tree of Ceylon" (Whittier) **93**:222, 239

"Daniel Neall" (Whittier) **93**:314

Dark Horses: New Poems (Kennedy) **93**:133, 146, 150-52

"A Day in an Undisciplined Garden" (Enright) **93**:9

"The Days Gone By" (Whittier) **93**:201

"The Dead Feast of the Kol-Folk" (Whittier) **93**:221

"The Dead Ship of Harpswell" (Whittier) **93**:176

"The Death of Professor Backwards" (Kennedy) **93**:130

"The Death-Bed" (Hood) **93**:62, 81, 121-22

"Death's Ramble" (Hood) **93**:44, 52, 80

"Deir El Bahari: Queen Hatsheput's Temple" (Enright) **93**:32

"The Deity" (Whittier) **93**:194

"The Demon Ship" (Hood) **93**:44, 52, 73, 80

"The Departure of Summer" (Hood) **93**:66, 117

"The Desert-Born" (Hood) **93**:105

Did Adam Name the Vinegarroon? (Kennedy) **93**:146

"Dirty English Potatoes" (Kennedy) **93**:149

"Disarmament" (Whittier) **93**:189

"Displaced Person Looks at a Cage-Bird" (Enright) **93**:15, 18

"Doctor Doctor" (Enright) **93**:20-21

"The Double-Headed Snake of Newbury" (Whittier) **93**:173, 227, 239, 251, 346

"The Doves and the Crows" (Hood) **93**:99-100

"Down in Dallas" (Kennedy) **93**:138

Drat These Brats (Kennedy) **93**:134

The Dream of Eugene Aram (Hood) **93**:46, 60, 62, 64, 81, 83, 89, 118

"Dreaming in the Shanghai Restaurant" (Enright) **93**:21

"Drivers of Diaper-Service Trucks Are Sad" (Kennedy) **93**:143

"A Drop of Gin" (Hood) **93**:84, 101-2

"The Drunkard to His Bottle" (Whittier) **93**:200

"Edible Aid" (Enright) **93**:18

"The Egyptian Cat" (Enright) **93**:32

Elefantina's Dream (Kennedy) **93**:135

"Elliott" (Whittier) **93**:167

"The Elm Tree" (Hood) **93**:44, 83, 99-100, 105, 117

Elympics (Kennedy) **93**:135

"The Emerald Isle" (Whittier) **93**:194

Emily Dickinson in Southern California (Kennedy) **93**:143

"Emily Dickinson in Southern California" (Kennedy) **93**:143

"End of a Hot Day" (Enright) **93**:11-12

"Entrance Visa" (Enright) **93**:8, 18

"Envoi" (Kennedy) **93**:149

"Epigrams" (Kennedy) **93**:150

"Epigraph for a Banned Book" (Kennedy) **93**:145

"Epiphany" (Kennedy) **93**:150

"Epitaph Proposed for the Headstone of S. R. Quiett" (Kennedy) **93**:152-53

The Epping Hunt (Hood) **93**:44, 46, 61, 89
"The Eternal Goodness" (Whittier) **93**:344
Eugene Aram (Hood)
   See *The Dream of Eugene Aram*
"Eva" (Whittier) **93**:337
"Even So" (Enright) **93**:33
"An Ew Erra" (Enright) **93**:36
"Exile?" (Enright) **93**:15
"The Exiles" (Whittier) **93**:198, 243-44
"The Exile's Departure" (Whittier) **93**:193, 260
"Expostulation" (Whittier) **93**:314-15
"An Extract from 'A New England Legend'"
   (Whittier) **93**:221
"Faces from a Bestiary" (Kennedy) **93**:148
"Fair Ines" (Hood) **93**:58, 79, 117
"Fair Quakeress" (Whittier) **93**:262
"The Fairies" (Enright) **93**:4
"The Faithful" (Enright) **93**:26
"Faithless Nelly Gray" (Hood) **93**:44, 47, 72, 121
"Faithless Sally Brown" (Hood)
   See *"The Ballad of Sally Brown and Ben the Carpenter"*
"Fall Song" (Kennedy) **93**:145
"The Farewell" (Whittier) **93**:183, 343
"Farewell Life" (Hood) **93**:81
"Fat Cats in Egypt" (Kennedy) **93**:153
A Faust Book (Enright) **93**:22, 27-28, 36
"Ein feste Burg ist unser Gott" (Whittier) **93**:213, 343, 347
"First Confession" (Kennedy) **93**:141, 147-48
"First Death" (Enright) **93**:11-13, 32
"The Fishermen" (Whittier) **93**:172
"Five-and-Dime, Late Thirties" (Kennedy) **93**:152
"Flagellant's Song" (Kennedy) **93**:144
"Flowers in Winter" (Whittier) **93**:172
"For Children, If They'll Take 'Em" (Kennedy) **93**:147
French Leave: Translations (Kennedy) **93**:145-47, 150
Fresh Brats (Kennedy) **93**:134
"Friendly Epistle to Mrs. Fry" (Hood) **93**:116
"From Little Acorns" (Enright) **93**:36
"From Perugia" (Whittier) **93**:269
"The Frost Spirit" (Whittier) **93**:270
"The Fruit Gift" (Whittier) **93**:230, 239
"Funeral Tree of the Sokokis" (Whittier) **93**:172
"The Gallows" (Whittier) **93**:356-57, 359
"The Garrison of Cape Ann" (Whittier) **93**:247, 270, 344, 347
"Godspeed" (Whittier) **93**:218
"Golgotha" (Kennedy) **93**:132, 142
"GP" (Enright) **93**:32
"Grasshopper" (Kennedy) **93**:146
"Great Chain of Being" (Kennedy) **93**:144
"A Greeting" (Whittier) **93**:338
Growing Into Love (Kennedy) **93**:138-43, 148, 152
"Growing Into Love" (Kennedy) **93**:138
"Hail, Star of Science!" (Whittier) **93**:196
Hangover Mass (Kennedy) **93**:147-48
"Hangover Mass" (Kennedy) **93**:148
"Happy New Year" (Enright) **93**:5, 19
"Hare" (Kennedy) **93**:146
"The Haschish" (Whittier) **93**:319, 344
The Haunted House (Hood) **93**:44, 62, 81, 85-86, 105, 107, 117, 119
"Haverhill" (Whittier) **93**:223
"Hearthside Story" (Kennedy) **93**:138
"The Henchman" (Whittier) **93**:229, 235, 239, 249
"Hero and Leander" (Hood) **93**:67-68, 74-77, 117
"High-mindedness of an English Poet" (Enright) **93**:23
"The Hive at Gettysburg" (Whittier) **93**:275
"Hohenlinden" (Hood) **93**:72
Home Ballads and Poems (Whittier) **93**:167, 266, 346-47, 350
"The Homestead" (Whittier) **93**:238-39
"Hoods Own" (Hood) **93**:89

"Hospital Journal" (Enright) **93**:32
"House Down" (Enright) **93**:5
"How Many Devils Can Dance on the Point" (Enright) **93**:21, 35
"How Right They Were, The Chinese Poets" (Enright) **93**:9, 18, 35
"How the Women Went from Dover" (Whittier) **93**:225, 247-48, 250
"Howard at Atlanta" (Whittier) **93**:316, 318
"The Human Sacrifice" (Whittier) **93**:356-57, 359
"The Hunters of Men" (Whittier) **93**:207, 243, 343
"The Huskers" (Whittier) **93**:172
"Hymn for the Celebration of Emancipation at Newburyport" (Whittier) **93**:213
"I love thee" (Hood) **93**:78
"I Remember, I Remember" (Hood) **93**:62, 79, 103, 117
"I Was a Middle-Aged Corrupter of Youth" (Enright) **93**:33
"Ichabod" (Whittier) **93**:177, 185, 210, 235, 239, 264-68, 280-81, 335, 344
"If You Got a Notion" (Kennedy) **93**:144
"In a Prominent Bar in Secaucus One Day" (Kennedy) **93**:129, 138, 148, 153
"In Memoriam" (Enright) **93**:33
"In School-Days" (Whittier) **93**:238-39, 252-53
In War Time, and Other Poems (Whittier) **93**:181, 347-48
"Inscriptions After Fact" (Kennedy) **93**:142
"Insects" (Enright) **93**:9
Instant Chronicles (Enright) **93**:22-23, 33
"Intermission with Peanuts" (Kennedy) **93**:137
"Invitations to the Dance" (Kennedy) **93**:150-51
"Invocation" (Kennedy) **93**:152, 158
"The Irish Schoolmaster" (Hood) **93**:52, 72
"Isabella" (Hood) **93**:67
"The Issue" (Whittier) **93**:321
"It Is Poetry" (Enright) **93**:25
"Italy" (Whittier) **93**:269
"J. G. Whittier to the 'Rustic Bard'" (Whittier) **93**:200
"J. T. on his Travels" (Enright) **93**:33
"Jack Hall" (Hood) **93**:52
"John Brown's Kiss" (Whittier) **93**:281
"The Jubilee Singers" (Whittier) **93**:318
"Kallundborg Church" (Whittier) **93**:176, 249
"The Kansas Emigrants" (Whittier) **93**:211
"Kathleen" (Whittier) **93**:172, 223, 239, 245, 267
"The Khan's Devil" (Whittier) **93**:222
"King Solomon and the Ants" (Whittier) **93**:222
"King Volmer and Elsie" (Whittier) **93**:167, 221, 249
"The King's Missive" (Whittier) **93**:174, 177, 198, 247
The King's Missive, and Other Poems (Whittier) **93**:177
"The Korean Emergency" (Kennedy) **93**:142
"Kossuth" (Whittier) **93**:266
"A Kyoto Garden" (Enright) **93**:5
"Ladies Looking for Lice" (Kennedy) **93**:137, 148
"The Lady's Dream" (Hood) **93**:87, 102
"Lafayette" (Whittier) **93**:193
"Lamia" (Hood) **93**:65, 79
"Last Child" (Kennedy) **93**:140, 143, 149
"The Last Man" (Hood) **93**:52-53, 72-73, 81, 117-19
"Last Poem" (Kennedy) **93**:147
"The Last Walk in Autumn" (Whittier) **93**:231, 239, 263
"The Laughing Hyena by Hokusai" (Enright) **93**:8, 32
"Laus Deo" (Whittier) **93**:186, 213, 239, 304, 348
"The Lay of the Labourer" (Hood) **93**:87, 102, 105, 119
"Laying Down the Law" (Hood) **93**:100
Lays of My Home, and Other Poems (Whittier) **93**:266

"Leave of Absence" (Kennedy) **93**:137-38
"The Legend of St. Mark" (Whittier) **93**:221
Legends of New England in Prose and Verse (Whittier) **93**:170, 193, 243, 260
"Letter from a Missionary of the Methodist Episcopal Church, South, in Kansas, to a Distinguished Politician" (Whittier) **93**:211, 239, 265-66, 344
"Life and Letters" (Enright) **93**:17
"Lines Addressed to Miss Roberts on Her Departure for India" (Hood) **93**:54
"Lines on a Fly-Leaf" (Whittier) **93**:176
"Lines on the Portrait of a Celebrated Publisher" (Whittier) **93**:239, 314, 319
"Lines Suggested by Reading a State Paper" (Whittier) **93**:266
"Lines to a Lady on Her Departure for India" (Hood) **93**:54
"Lines, Written on Being Told There Was Too Much of Levity in My Later Writings" (Whittier) **93**:200
"Lines, Written on Reading Several Pamphlets Published by Clergymen Against the Abolition of the Gallows" (Whittier)
   See *"The Gallows"*
"Little Elegy" (Kennedy) **93**:129, 138
"Loneliness" (Whittier) **93**:195
The Lords of Misrule: Poems, 1992-2001 (Kennedy) **93**:150, 152
"The Lost Occasion" (Whittier) **93**:177
"Lucknow" (Whittier)
   See *"The Pipes of Lucknow"*
"Lycus the Centaur" (Hood) **93**:42, 55, 57-58, 64, 67-68, 74, 76-77, 79, 117
"Mabel Martin, a Harvest Idyll" (Whittier) **93**:227, 239
"The Man in the Manmade Moon" (Kennedy) **93**:138
"La Marais du Cygne" (Whittier) **93**:212
"Marguerite" (Whittier) **93**:267
"The Martyr" (Whittier) **93**:192
"Mary Garvin" (Whittier) **93**:170, 172, 267
"Mary's Ghost" (Hood) **93**:52
"Massachusetts to Virginia" (Whittier) **93**:209, 239, 264, 315
"Maud Muller" (Whittier) **93**:167, 170, 172-73, 233, 239, 250, 266-67, 344
"Mean Gnome Day" (Kennedy) **93**:141
"The Meeting" (Whittier) **93**:198
"Meeting the Minister for Culture" (Enright) **93**:21
"Melancholy Ode" (Hood)
   See *"Ode to Melancholy"*
"Memories" (Whittier) **93**:197
"Mermaid of Margate" (Hood) **93**:44, 52
"Metropolitan Water Bawd" (Enright) **93**:36
"Micah" (Whittier) **93**:195
"The Midnight Scene" (Whittier) **93**:193
The Minimus Poems (Kennedy) **93**:151-52
"Miriam" (Whittier) **93**:176, 188, 222
"Misgiving at Dusk" (Enright) **93**:35
Miss Kilmansegg and Her Precious Leg: A Golden Legend (Hood) **93**:61-62, 81, 83, 102, 104-5, 115, 118-19
Missing Link (Kennedy) **93**:147-48
"Mithridates at Chios" (Whittier) **93**:314
Mogg Megone (Whittier) **93**:171, 221
Moll Pitcher and the Minstrel Girl (Whittier) **93**:170, 221
"Moloch in State Street" (Whittier) **93**:211
"Monadnock from Wachusett" (Whittier) **93**:239
"Monkey" (Enright) **93**:14
"Montezuma" (Whittier) **93**:198
"Montgomery's Return" (Whittier) **93**:193
"The Monuments of Hiroshima" (Enright) **93**:14, 19
"Moral Reflections on the Cross of St. Paul's" (Hood) **93**:122
"Moral Songs" (Hood) **93**:72
"More Memories of Underdevelopment" (Enright) **93**:27

"Mortal Landscape" (Kennedy) **93**:147
"Mountain Pictures" (Whittier) **93**:231
"Mr. Withering's Cure" (Hood) **93**:99
"My Namesake" (Whittier) **93**:239, 261
"My Playmate" (Whittier) **93**:235, 252-53, 267, 347
"My Psalm" (Whittier) **93**:347
"My Soul and I" (Whittier) **93**:270, 272
"My Triumph" (Whittier) **93**:349
"Nelly Gray" (Hood)
    See "Faithless Nelly Gray"
"New England" (Whittier) **93**:260
"The New Wife and the Old" (Whittier) **93**:223, 244
"The New Year" (Whittier) **93**:206, 314, 317
"New Year's Address" (Whittier) **93**:193, 199
"News from China" (Hood) **93**:99
"Night steals upon the world" (Whittier) **93**:201
"The Nineteen-thirties" (Kennedy) **93**:140
"No Neutral Stone" (Kennedy) **93**:149
"The Noodle-Vendor's Flute" (Enright) **93**:9, 20
"Nothing in Heaven Functions As It Ought" (Kennedy) **93**:131, 142
"Nude Descending a Staircase" (Kennedy) **93**:136, 147, 150
Nude Descending a Staircase: Poems, Songs, A Ballad (Kennedy) **93**:128, 133, 136-38, 141-42, 148, 152
"O lady, leave thy silken thread" (Hood) **93**:78
"Ocean" (Whittier) **93**:195
"Ode to Autumn" (Hood)
    See "Autumn"
"Ode to Dr. Kitchener" (Hood) **93**:42, 47
"Ode to George Colman the Younger" (Hood) **93**:48
"Ode to Melancholy" (Hood) **93**:44, 62, 65-67, 78, 117
"Ode to Miss Kelly on Her Opening the Strand Theater" (Hood) **93**:64
"Ode to Mr. Graham" (Hood) **93**:48
"Ode to Rae Wilson" (Hood) **93**:118
"Ode to the Moon" (Hood) **93**:66
Odes and Addresses to Great People (Hood) **93**:41-43, 46-51, 54, 64, 72, 114, 116, 118
"The Odor of Verbena" (Whittier) **93**:274
"Official Piety" (Whittier) **93**:239
"The Old Burying Ground" (Whittier) **93**:239
Old Men and Comets (Enright) **93**:31-32
"The Old South" (Whittier) **93**:198
"Omnibus" (Hood) **93**:99
"On a Prayer-Book" (Whittier) **93**:239
One Winter Night in August and Other Nonsense Jingles (Kennedy) **93**:129-30, 133
"One-Night Homecoming" (Kennedy) **93**:140
"Oriental Maxims" (Whittier) **93**:187
"Oriental Politics" (Enright) **93**:15
"Origin of the Haiku" (Enright) **93**:27
"O'Riley's Late-Bloomed Little Son" (Kennedy) **93**:139
"Our Countrymen in Chains" (Whittier) **93**:239
"Our Master" (Whittier) **93**:235, 239
"The Outlaw" (Whittier) **93**:201
"Overheard in the Louvre" (Kennedy) **93**:138
"The Over-Heart" (Whittier) **93**:188
"The Pageant" (Whittier) **93**:349
"The Palatine" (Whittier) **93**:247-48
"The Panorama" (Whittier) **93**:239, 316-23, 326, 328-30, 343
The Panorama, and Other Poems (Whittier) **93**:266
Paradise Illustrated (Enright) **93**:22, 27-28, 36
"A Parental Ode to My Son, Aged Three Years and Five Months" (Hood) **93**:122
"The Pastoral Letter" (Whittier) **93**:314, 337
"The Pauper's Christmas Carol" (Hood) **93**:47, 85, 101-2, 118
"The Pawnee Brave" (Whittier) **93**:198
"The Peaceful Island" (Enright) **93**:15, 17
"Pennsylvania Letter" (Whittier) **93**:314

"The Pennsylvania Pilgrim" (Whittier) **93**:176, 225-26, 238-39, 253
"Perplexities" (Kennedy) **93**:153
The Phantom Ice Cream Man: More Nonsense Verse (Kennedy) **93**:130, 133
"The Pied Piper of Akashi" (Enright) **93**:18
"Pierrot's Soliloquy" (Kennedy) **93**:145
"Pileup" (Kennedy) **93**:150
"Pillar of Glory" (Whittier) **93**:196
"The Pipes of Lucknow" (Whittier) **93**:175, 268-69
"The Playmate" (Whittier) **93**:267
"The Plea of the Midsummer Fairies" (Hood) **93**:42, 56-57, 59, 62, 67, 74, 77, 80, 117
The Plea of the Midsummer Fairies, Hero and Leander, Lycus the Centaur, and Other Poems (Hood) **93**:46, 55, 65, 74, 77, 79-81, 89, 117
Poems Written during the Progress of the Abolition Question in the United States, Between the Years 1830 and 1838 (Whittier) **93**:318, 336-39
"The Poet in Retirement" (Enright) **93**:7
The Poetical Works of John Greenleaf Whittier (Whittier) **93**:266, 318
"Poets" (Kennedy) **93**:139
"The Poet's Portion" (Hood) **93**:62, 66-67, 79
"A Polished Performance" (Enright) **93**:13, 25
"Political Meeting" (Enright) **93**:21, 35
"Pompey's Ghost" (Hood) **93**:99
"Pont Mirabeau" (Kennedy) **93**:145-46, 150
"The Popular Cupid" (Hood) **93**:52
"Pottery Class" (Kennedy) **93**:139
"Prayer" (Enright) **93**:29, 36
"The Preacher" (Whittier) **93**:176, 188-89, 251
"The Prelude" (Whittier) **93**:239, 267, 275, 345, 349
"The Pressed Gentian" (Whittier) **93**:275
"Prime Minister" (Enright) **93**:21
"Processional" (Enright) **93**:34
"The Proclamation" (Whittier) **93**:213, 348
"Proem" (Whittier) **93**:198, 239, 347
"The Prophecy of Samuel Sewall" (Whittier) **93**:173, 227, 229, 239, 251-52, 271, 346
"Protest" (Kennedy) **93**:143
"Psalm 72: Man Declared a Treasure" (Enright) **93**:6
"Psalm for Supersunday" (Enright) **93**:24, 29, 34
"Purchas His Pilgrimes" (Enright) **93**:4
"The Purpose of Time Is to Prevent Everything from Happening at Once" (Kennedy) **93**:152
"The Quaker Alumni" (Whittier) **93**:198
"Queen Mab" (Hood) **93**:45
"Questions of Life" (Whittier) **93**:170, 172, 267
"Rabbi Ismael" (Whittier) **93**:221
"Randolph of Roanoke" (Whittier) **93**:263
"R-and-R Centre" (Enright) **93**:33
"Reading Trip" (Kennedy) **93**:139
"The Reformer" (Whittier) **93**:167
"Religious Phase" (Enright) **93**:28
"Remembrance Sunday" (Enright) **93**:28
"The Rendition" (Whittier) **93**:167, 210-11
"A Retrospective Review" (Hood) **93**:58, 79
"Rice Coming Into Town" (Enright) **93**:13
"Ritner" (Whittier) **93**:206
"Rondeau" (Kennedy) **93**:137
"Ruth" (Hood) **93**:58, 66, 78, 117-18
"A Sabbath Scene" (Whittier) **93**:210, 333-36, 339, 344
"Sacrifice" (Whittier)
    See "The Human Sacrifice"
Sad Ires and Others (Enright) **93**:27-28
"Sailors with the Clap" (Kennedy) **93**:152
"Sally Brown" (Hood)
    See "The Ballad of Sally Brown and Ben the Carpenter"
"Salute Sweet Deceptions" (Kennedy) **93**:152-53
"Satori" (Kennedy) **93**:138
"Saying No" (Enright) **93**:8

"School-Days" (Whittier) **93**:267
"A Sea Dream" (Whittier) **93**:197, 252
"The Sea of Death" (Hood) **93**:58, 66, 117, 119
"Sentimentalist's Song, or Answers for Everything" (Kennedy) **93**:144
"September Twelfth, 2001" (Kennedy) **93**:154
"Sex Manual" (Kennedy) **93**:131
"The Shadow and the Light" (Whittier) **93**:347
"Shah Akbar" (Whittier) **93**:176
"The Shipbuilders" (Whittier) **93**:172
"The Shoemakers" (Whittier) **93**:172
"The Short Life of Kazuo Yamamoto" (Enright) **93**:5, 18
"The Shorter View" (Kennedy) **93**:139-40, 149
"A Sign" (Enright) **93**:25
"Silence" (Hood) **93**:78, 117, 119
"Since Then" (Enright) **93**:32
"The Singer" (Whittier) **93**:215
"The Sirens" (Kennedy) **93**:147, 149
"The Sisters" (Whittier) **93**:248-49
"Skipper Ireson's Ride" (Whittier) **93**:167, 173-74, 228-29, 234-36, 239-40, 245, 266, 281, 346
"The Slaves of Martinique" (Whittier) **93**:317
"The Slave-Ships" (Whittier) **93**:312-15
"Snapshots" (Kennedy) **93**:140
Snow-Bound: A Winter Idyl (Whittier) **93**:167, 170, 173, 176, 194, 215, 225, 235-40, 253-54, 257, 267-71, 273-75, 281, 285-87, 289, 293, 298, 304-10, 341, 348, 350
"Solitary Confinement" (Kennedy) **93**:131, 137-38
Some Men Are Brothers (Enright) **93**:4, 9, 13
"Song for Music" (Hood) **93**:62, 78
"A Song for the Time" (Whittier) **93**:321
"Song: Great Chain of Being" (Kennedy) **93**:143
"A Song Inscribed to the Fremont Clubs" (Whittier) **93**:212
"Song of Indian Women" (Whittier) **93**:171
"Song of Slaves in the Desert" (Whittier) **93**:265, 268, 343
"Song of the Negro Boatmen" (Whittier) **93**:315, 318
"The Song of the Shirt" (Hood) **93**:44, 47, 60-62, 69, 81-82, 84-85, 87, 101-5, 108, 116, 118-19
"A Song of the Time" (Whittier) **93**:212
"The Song of Vermonters" (Whittier) **93**:243
"Song to the Tune of 'Somebody Stole My Gal'" (Kennedy) **93**:138, 144, 148
Songs of Labor, and Other Poems (Whittier) **93**:170, 172, 266, 277
Songs of Three Centuries (Whittier) **93**:216
"Sonnet for Hélène" (Kennedy) **93**:145
"Sonnet: To Fancy" (Hood)
    See "To Fancy"
"Sonnet Written in Keats's 'Endymion'" (Hood) **93**:67
"The Soul of a Schoolboy" (Enright) **93**:24
"A Spiritual Manifestation" (Whittier) **93**:252
"Stanzas" (Hood) **93**:121-22
"Stanzas for the Times" (Whittier) **93**:206, 315
"Staring into a River Till Moved by It" (Kennedy) **93**:151
"The Stars are with the Voyager" (Hood) **93**:78
"The Stations of King's Cross" (Enright) **93**:28
"Stop That Clowning at Once If Not Sooner" (Enright) **93**:14
"Street Moths" (Kennedy) **93**:153
"Suggestions by Steam" (Hood) **93**:102
"A Summer Pilgrimage" (Whittier) **93**:239-40
"A Summons" (Whittier) **93**:206, 314-15
"Sun" (Kennedy) **93**:147
"Sunset on the Bearcamp" (Whittier) **93**:193
The Supernaturalism of New England (Whittier) **93**:267, 277
"Superstition" (Whittier) **93**:193
"The Sweep's Complaint" (Hood) **93**:100
"The Switzer's Song" (Whittier) **93**:198
"The Sycamores" (Whittier) **93**:252
"Take Back the Bowl!" (Whittier) **93**:260

Title Index

"Tea Ceremony" (Enright) **93**:19-20

"Telling the Bees" (Whittier) **93**:166-67, 173, 234-36, 239-40, 247, 250, 265-70, 344, 347

"The Tent on the Beach" (Whittier) **93**:167, 170, 172, 176, 232, 238-39, 262, 339

The Tent on the Beach, and Other Poems (Whittier) **93**:224, 346

The Terrible Shears: Scenes from a Twenties Childhood (Enright) **93**:16-17, 22-23, 28-29, 33

"Texas" (Whittier) **93**:208

"Then and Now" (Kennedy) **93**:153

Three Tenors, One Vehicle (Kennedy) **93**:144-45

"Thy Will Be Done" (Whittier) **93**:181, 213

"Tim Turpin" (Hood) **93**:52

"Times" (Whittier)

    See *"Stanzas for the Times"*

"The Times" (Whittier) **93**:201

To a Child Embracing his Mother (Hood) **93**:62

"To a Cold Beauty" (Hood) **93**:48

"To a Critic" (Hood) **93**:80

"To a Southern Statesman" (Whittier) **93**:209

"To a War Poet" (Enright) **93**:33

"To an Alexandrian Poet" (Enright) **93**:7

"To Delaware" (Whittier) **93**:208

"To Dorothy on Her Exclusion from the *Guinness Book of World Records* " (Kennedy) **93**:129

"To Fancy" (Hood) **93**:65, 78, 117

"To Faneuil Hall" (Whittier) **93**:208

"To Hope" (Hood) **93**:62, 65

"To John C. Fremont" (Whittier) **93**:213

"To Massachusetts" (Whittier) **93**:209

"To My Old Schoolmaster" (Whittier) **93**:172, 252, 266-68

"To My Sister" (Whittier) **93**:266-67, 306

"To Nahant" (Whittier) **93**:193

"To Old Cavafy from a New Country" (Enright) **93**:34

"To Oliver Wendell Holmes" (Whittier) **93**:275, 345

"To Ronge" (Whittier) **93**:166

"To Silence" (Hood) **93**:59

"To the Memory of Chatterton, Who Died Aged 17" (Whittier) **93**:193

"To the Memory of David Sands" (Whittier) **93**:194

"To the Merrimack" (Whittier) **93**:201

"To the Thirty-Ninth Congress" (Whittier) **93**:213

"To William H. Seward" (Whittier) **93**:212

"Toussaint L'Ouverture" (Whittier) **93**:312, 316-18, 343

"The Training" (Whittier) **93**:269

"Transparency" (Kennedy) **93**:141

"Trinitas" (Whittier) **93**:239

"The Truce of Piscataqua" (Whittier) **93**:172, 267

"Trust" (Whittier) **93**:239

"Twelve Dead, Hundreds Homeless" (Kennedy) **93**:150

"Two Apparitions" (Kennedy) **93**:141

"Two Bad Things in Infant School" (Enright) **93**:24

"The Two Peacocks of Bedfont" (Hood) **93**:42, 58, 66, 77, 117

"The Two Swans" (Hood) **93**:62, 66-67

"Two Views of Rhyme and Meter" (Kennedy) **93**:149

"Ultimate Motel" (Kennedy) **93**:144

"Uncle Ool's Song against the Ill-Paid Life of Poetry" (Kennedy) **93**:144

"Unknown to Mr. Colburn" (Hood) **93**:91, 105

"Unlawful Assembly" (Enright) **93**:21

"The Vanishers" (Whittier) **93**:270-72

Voices of Freedom (Whittier) **93**:182, 318

"The Waiting" (Whittier) **93**:239

"Warm Protest" (Enright) **93**:34

"The Watchers" (Whittier) **93**:314, 317

"A Water Glass of Whisky" (Kennedy) **93**:138

"The Water Lady" (Hood) **93**:66

"A Waterloo Ballad" (Hood) **93**:116

"West Somerville, Mass." (Kennedy) **93**:132, 139

"What Became of What-Was-His Name?" (Enright) **93**:21

"What the Voice Said" (Whittier) **93**:166

"When, like the cloud before the sun" (Whittier) **93**:200

"Where Are the Snows of Yesteryear" (Kennedy) **93**:137

"Where Charity Begins" (Enright) **93**:6

Whims and Oddities (Hood) **93**:42, 45, 51-55, 72-74, 80, 89, 117

Whimsicalities: A Periodic Gathering (Hood) **93**:47, 82-83, 89, 99

Winter Idyl (Whittier)

    See *Snow-Bound: A Winter Idyl*

Winter Thunder (Kennedy) **93**:150-51

"Winter Thunder" (Kennedy) **93**:151

"The Wish of To-day" (Whittier) **93**:169

"The Witch of Wenham" (Whittier) **93**:173, 226, 239, 247-48

"The Witch's Daughter" (Whittier) **93**:166-67, 173, 239, 267

"Woman in Rain" (Kennedy) **93**:150

"The Woodpile Skull" (Kennedy) **93**:150-51

"A Word for the Hour" (Whittier) **93**:212, 348

"A Word from Hart Crane's Ghost" (Kennedy) **93**:147

"Words Without Songs" (Enright) **93**:15

"The Workhouse Clock" (Hood) **93**:87, 99, 102, 119

"The Wounded Soldier" (Whittier) **93**:193

"The Wreck of Rivermouth" (Whittier) **93**:176, 242, 247, 249

"Written Off" (Enright) **93**:7

"The Yankee Girl" (Whittier) **93**:291